FIREFLY

5-Language VISUAL Dictionary

ENGLISH • FRENCH • SPANISH
ITALIAN • GERMAN

IGOR JOURIST

FIREFLY BOOKS

A FIREFLY BOOK

Published by Firefly Books Ltd. 2016

First printing

Publisher Cataloging-in-Publication Data (U.S.)

Names: Jourist, Igor, 1969-, author.
Title: Firefly 5 language visual dictionary : English, French, German, Italian, Spanish / Igor Jourist.
Description: Richmond Hill, Ontario, Canada : Firefly Books, 2016. | Includes index. | Summary: "This dictionary covers all 5 of the languages (English, French, German, Italian, Spanish) with well researched terminology and over 4,000 images" -- Provided by publisher.
Identifiers: ISBN 978-1-77085-768-1 (hardcover)
Subjects: LCSH: Picture dictionaries, Polyglot. | Dictionaries, Polyglot.
Classification: LCC P361.J687 |DDC 413 – dc23

Library and Archives Canada Cataloguing in Publication

Jourist, Igor, author
Firefly 5 language visual dictionary : English, French,
German, Italian, Spanish / Igor Jourist ; Nancy Foran, general editor.
Includes index.
Text in English, French, German, Italian, and Spanish.
ISBN 978-1-77085-768-1 (hardback)
1. Dictionaries, Polyglot. 2. Picture dictionaries, Polyglot.
I. Foran, Nancy, editor II. Title.
P361.J68 2016 413'.17 C2016-903738-X

Published in the United States by
Firefly Books (U.S.) Inc.
P.O. Box 1338, Ellicott Station
Buffalo, New York 14205

Published in Canada by
Firefly Books Ltd.
50 Staples Avenue, Unit 1
Richmond Hill, Ontario L4B 0A7

Illustrations, terminology and production: Jourist Verlags GmbH, Hamburg

jourist

Cover design: Jacqueline Hope Raynor

Printed in China

LIST OF CHAPTERS

CONTENTS

HOW TO USE THE DICTIONARY

Subtheme
The 14 themes are divided into more specific subjects, which group related objects together.

Indicator
These lines link the vocabulary with the specific part of the illustration that is being identified.

Topic
Some subthemes are divided into topics, which are more specific and more closely related groupings.

Subtopic
Subtopics are the smallest, most specific and most closely related groupings.

HOUSEHOLD FURNISHINGS
Furniture

Sofas
Different styles of upholstered seats with arms and a back, long enough to accommodate more than one person.

sectional sofa
A sofa separated into sections that can be moved to change the configuration.

backrest
The raised portion behind the seat of a chair or sofa, on which one may lean backwards.

seat cushion
A stuffed pad placed on top of a chair to provide comfortable support for sitting.

leg
A support attached to the bottom of a piece of furniture to stabilize or raise it.

arm
The raised portion at the side of a chair or sofa, providing a place for one to rest their arms.

ottoman
A small piece of furniture, usually upholstered and without back or arms, often used as stool or footstool.

loveseat
A sofa designed to hold only two people.

chaise longe
An elongated cushioned seat that is designed to allow one to stretch out in a half-lying, half-sitting position.

bench
A piece of furniture that is not fully upholstered, designed to seat two or more people.

208 HOUSING

Object illustration

A detailed illustration of the object being defined; for some illustrations, several parts are identified and defined.

HOUSEHOLD FURNISHINGS
Furniture

Storage furniture

Furniture that is designed to hold objects, such as clothing or kitchenware, for easy accessibility.

liquor cabinet
A glass-fronted cabinet with shelves on which bottles of liquor and drinking glasses are stored and displayed.

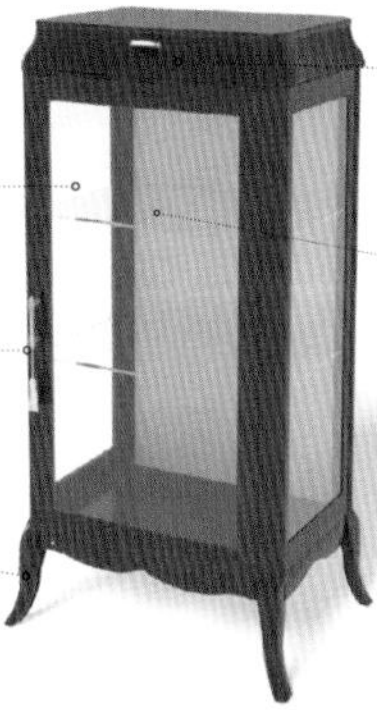

door
A hinged barrier that is swung open to gain access to the piece's inside compartment.

pull
A piece of solid or flexible material attached to an object that can be grasped and pulled, such as on a door.

leg
A support attached to the bottom of a piece of furniture; it is used to stabilize the piece or raise it.

drawer
A box-shaped compartment used for storage.

shelf
A flat, elongated surface built into a piece of furniture on which objects are stored.

chest of drawers
A piece of furniture made up of a number of drawers set into a box-like frame, typically used to store clothing.

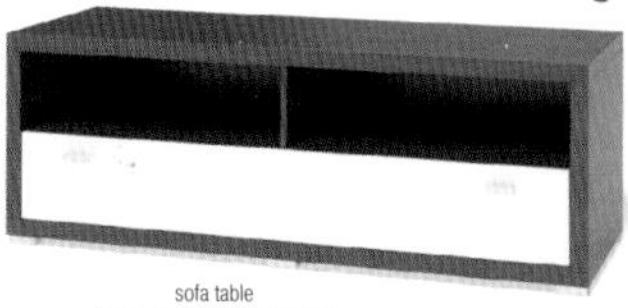

sofa table
A long, low table that is usually placed against the exposed back of a sofa.

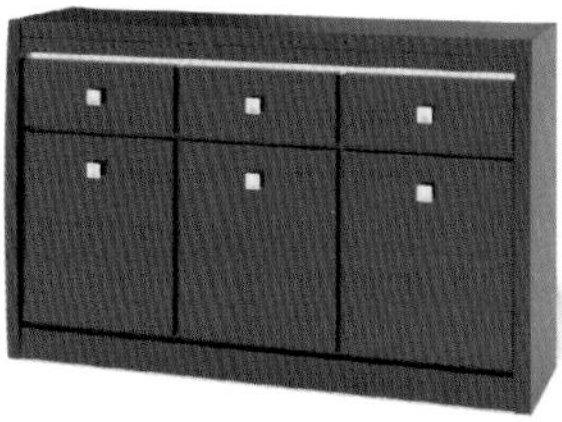

sideboard
A piece of furniture that is typically placed against the wall of a dining or living room, used to hold refreshments.

display cabinet
A glass-fronted cabinet with shelves, typically used to showcase objects.

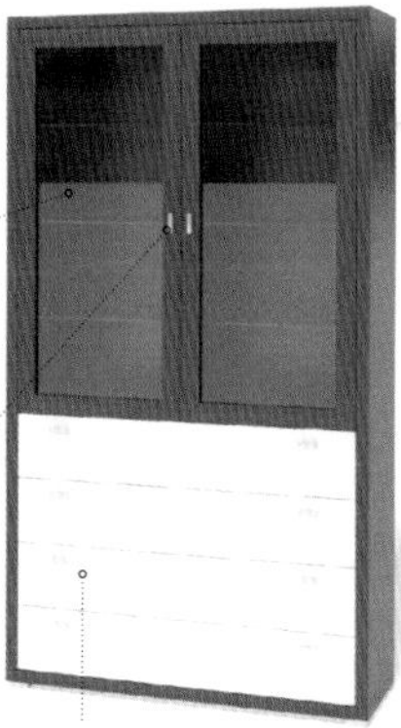

glass door
A hinged barrier with a glass insert. It is swung open to gain access to the inside compartment.

pull
A piece of solid or flexible material attached to an object that can be grasped and pulled, such as on a door.

drawer
A box-shaped compartment used for storage.

HOUSING 209

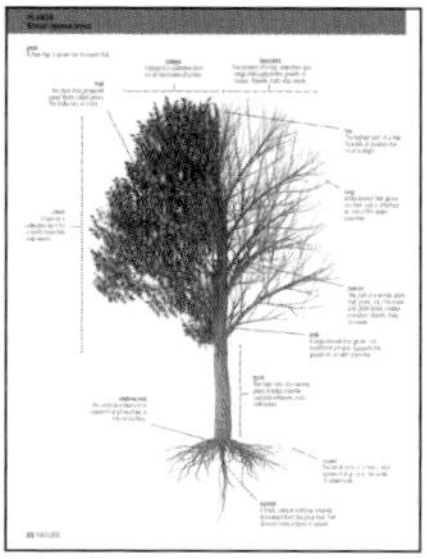

Special views

For objects with a more complex anatomy, such as the tree above, a special view shows multiple layers, providing a deeper understanding of the object and its associated vocabulary.

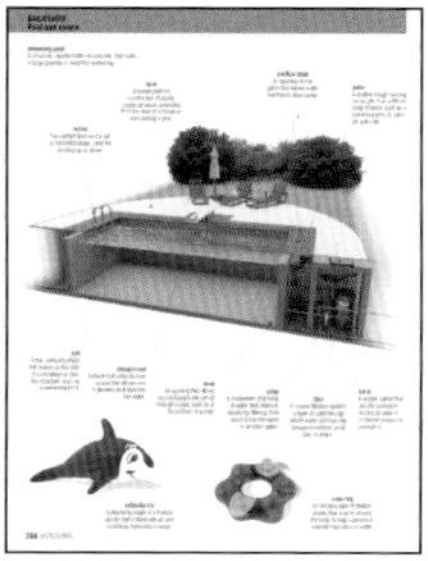

Cross section

Detailed cross sections show an object's internal components and workings.

Theme

There are 14 themes, covering every important aspect of the modern world.

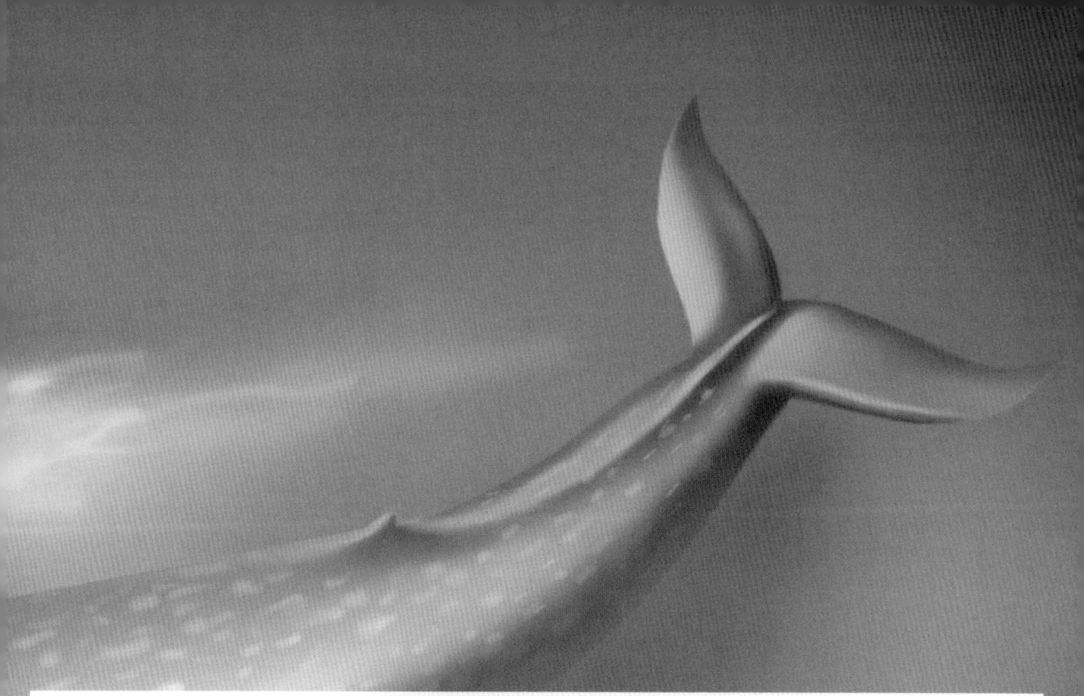

NATURE

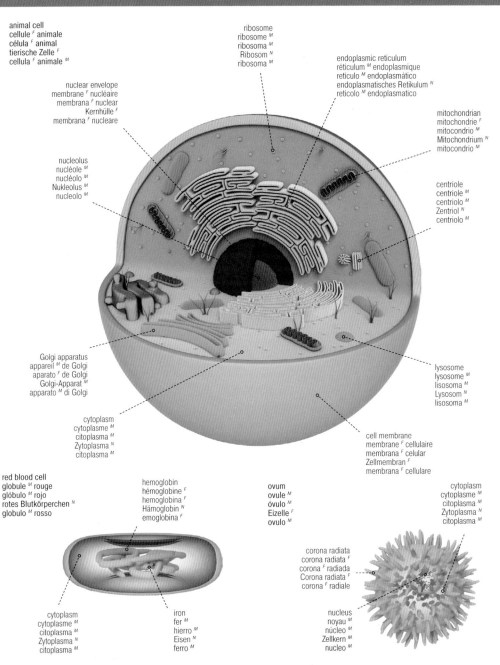

animal cell
cellule [F] animale
célula [F] animal
tierische Zelle [F]
cellula [F] animale [M]

ribosome
ribosome [M]
ribosoma [M]
Ribosom [N]
ribosoma [M]

endoplasmic reticulum
réticulum [M] endoplasmique
retículo [M] endoplasmático
endoplasmatisches Retikulum [N]
reticolo [M] endoplasmatico

nuclear envelope
membrane [F] nucléaire
membrana [F] nuclear
Kernhülle [F]
membrana [F] nucleare

mitochondrian
mitochondrie [F]
mitocondrio [M]
Mitochondrium [N]
mitocondrio [M]

nucleolus
nucléole [M]
nucléolo [M]
Nukleolus [M]
nucleolo [M]

centriole
centriole [M]
centriolo [M]
Zentriol [N]
centriolo [M]

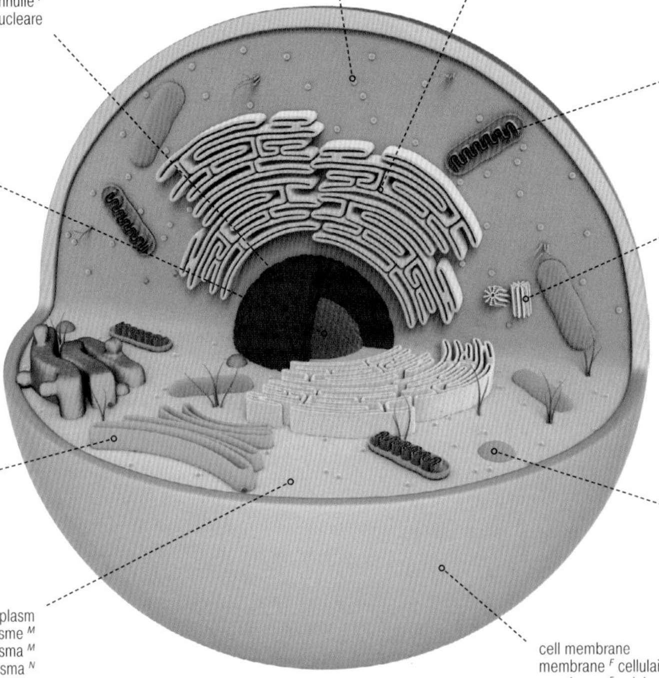

Golgi apparatus
appareil [M] de Golgi
aparato [F] de Golgi
Golgi-Apparat [M]
apparato [M] di Golgi

lysosome
lysosome [M]
lisosoma [M]
Lysosom [N]
lisosoma [M]

cytoplasm
cytoplasme [M]
citoplasma [M]
Zytoplasma [N]
citoplasma [M]

cell membrane
membrane [F] cellulaire
membrana [F] celular
Zellmembran [F]
membrana [F] cellulare

red blood cell
globule [M] rouge
glóbulo [M] rojo
rotes Blutkörperchen [N]
globulo [M] rosso

hemoglobin
hémoglobine [F]
hemoglobina [F]
Hämoglobin [N]
emoglobina [F]

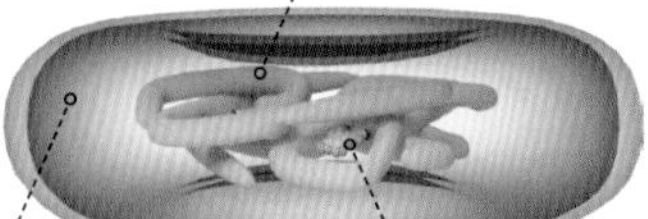

cytoplasm
cytoplasme [M]
citoplasma [M]
Zytoplasma [N]
citoplasma [M]

iron
fer [M]
hierro [M]
Eisen [N]
ferro [M]

ovum
ovule [M]
óvulo [M]
Eizelle [F]
ovulo [M]

cytoplasm
cytoplasme [M]
citoplasma [M]
Zytoplasma [N]
citoplasma [M]

corona radiata
corona radiata [F]
corona [F] radiada
Corona radiata [F]
corona [F] radiale

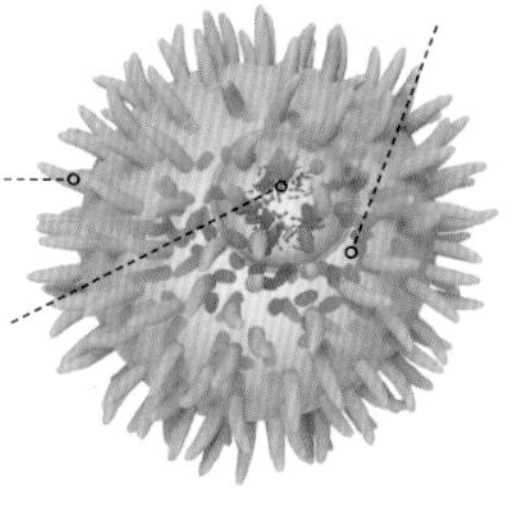

nucleus
noyau [M]
núcleo [M]
Zellkern [M]
nucleo [M]

Arabian horse
cheval M arabe
caballo M árabe
Pferd N
cavallo M arabo

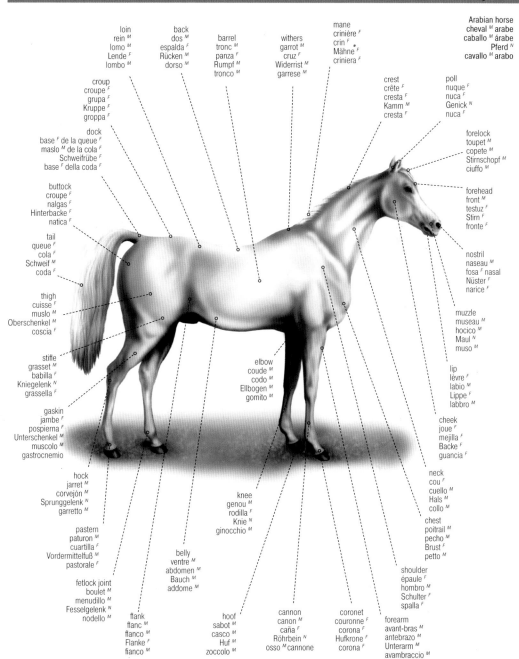

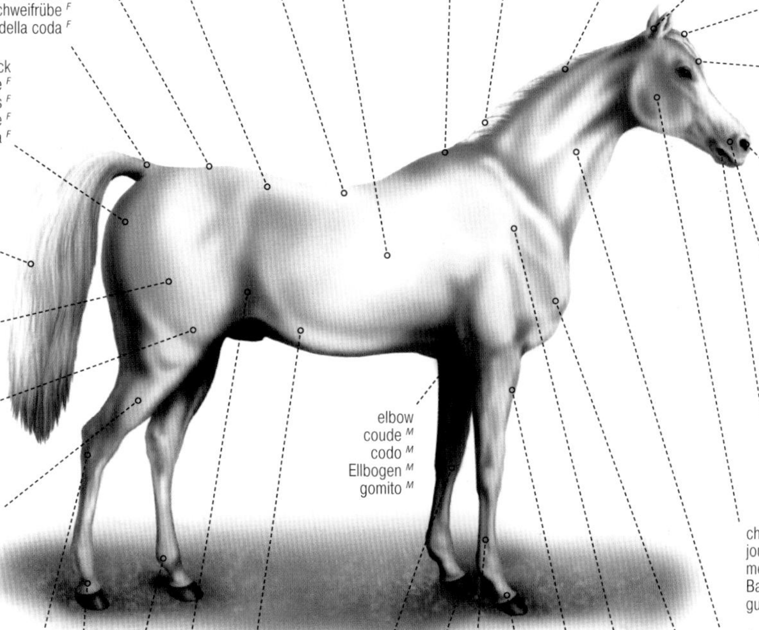
loin
rein M
lomo M
Lende F
lombo M
back
dos M
espalda F
Rücken M
dorso M
barrel
tronc M
panza F
Rumpf M
tronco M
withers
garrot M
cruz F
Widerrist M
garrese M
mane
crinière F
crin F
Mähne F
criniera F
crest
crête F
cresta F
Kamm M
cresta F
poll
nuque F
nuca F
Genick N
nuca F
croup
croupe F
grupa F
Kruppe F
groppa F
dock
base F de la queue F
maslo M de la cola F
Schweifrübe F
base F della coda F
forelock
toupet M
copete M
Stirnschopf M
ciuffo M
buttock
croupe F
nalgas F
Hinterbacke F
natica F
forehead
front M
testuz F
Stirn F
fronte F
tail
queue F
cola F
Schweif M
coda F
nostril
naseau M
fosa F nasal
Nüster F
narice F
thigh
cuisse F
muslo M
Oberschenkel M
coscia F
muzzle
museau M
hocico M
Maul N
muso M
stifle
grasset M
babilla F
Kniegelenk N
grassella F
elbow
coude M
codo M
Ellbogen M
gomito M
lip
lèvre F
labio M
Lippe F
labbro M
gaskin
jambe F
pospierna F
Unterschenkel M
muscolo M
gastrocnemio
cheek
joue F
mejilla F
Backe F
guancia F
hock
jarret M
corvejón M
Sprunggelenk N
garretto M
neck
cou F
cuello M
Hals M
collo M
knee
genou M
rodilla F
Knie N
ginocchio M
chest
poitrail M
pecho M
Brust F
petto M
pastern
paturon M
cuartilla F
Vordermittelfuß M
pastorale F
belly
ventre M
abdomen M
Bauch M
addome M
shoulder
épaule F
hombro M
Schulter F
spalla F
fetlock joint
boulet M
menudillo M
Fesselgelenk N
nodello M
flank
flanc M
flanco M
Flanke F
fianco M
hoof
sabot M
casco M
Huf M
zoccolo M
cannon
canon M
caña F
Röhrbein N
osso M cannone
coronet
couronne F
corona F
Hufkrone F
corona F
forearm
avant-bras M
antebrazo M
Unterarm M
avambraccio M

white-tailed deer
cerf M de Virginie
venado M de cola F blanca
Weißwedelhirsch M
cervo M dalla coda F bianca

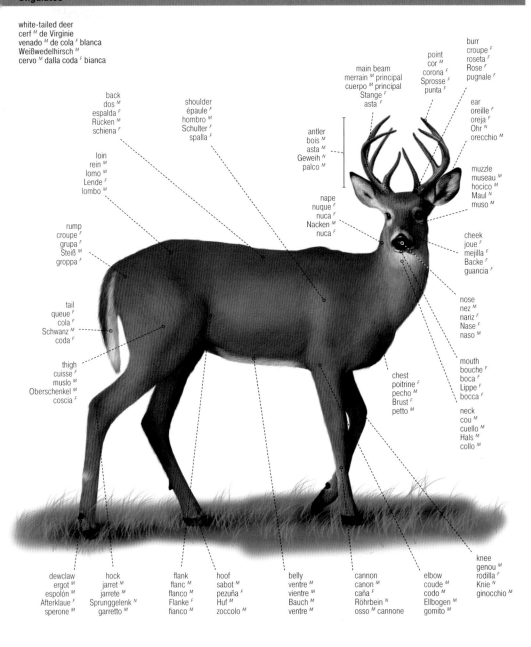

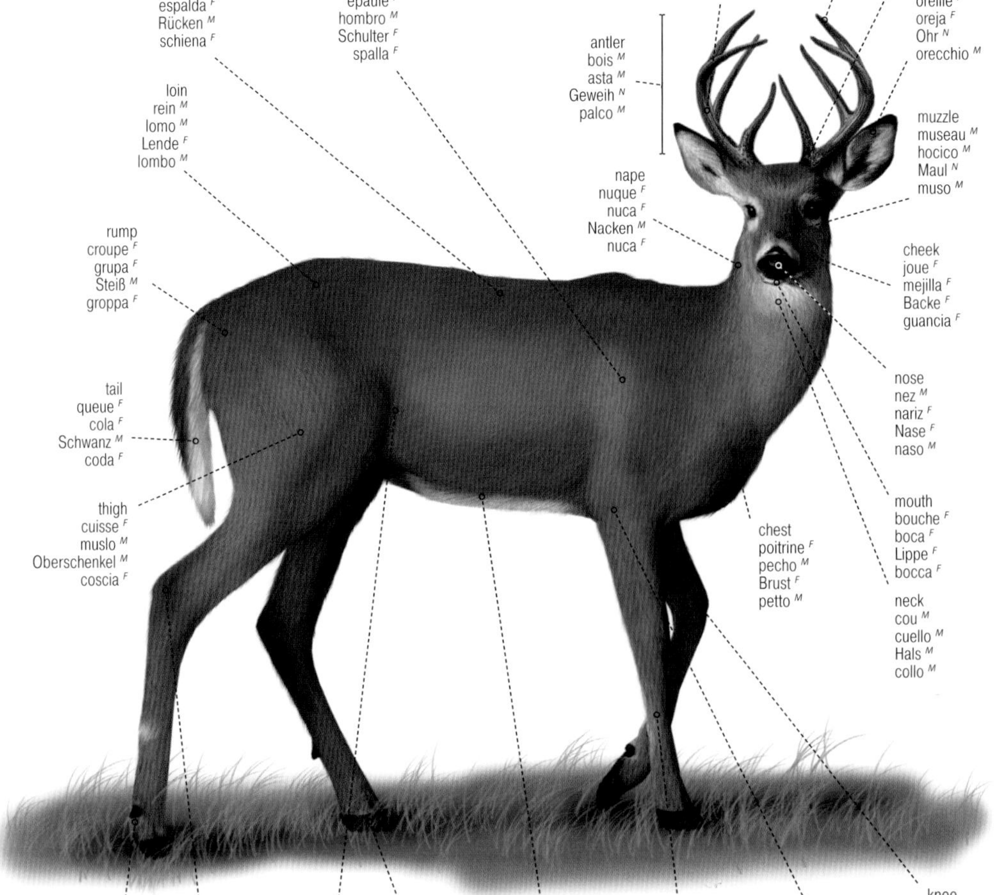
main beam
merrain M principal
cuerpo M principal
Stange F
asta F
point
cor M
corona F
Sprosse F
punta F
burr
croupe F
roseta F
Rose F
pugnale F
back
dos M
espalda F
Rücken M
schiena F
shoulder
épaule F
hombro M
Schulter F
spalla F
ear
oreille F
oreja F
Ohr N
orecchio M
antler
bois M
asta M
Geweih N
palco M
loin
rein M
lomo M
Lende F
lombo M
muzzle
museau M
hocico M
Maul N
muso M
nape
nuque F
nuca F
Nacken M
nuca F
rump
croupe F
grupa F
Steiß M
groppa F
cheek
joue F
mejilla F
Backe F
guancia F
nose
nez M
nariz F
Nase F
naso M
tail
queue F
cola F
Schwanz M
coda F
mouth
bouche F
boca F
Lippe F
bocca F
thigh
cuisse F
muslo M
Oberschenkel M
coscia F
chest
poitrine F
pecho M
Brust F
petto M
neck
cou M
cuello M
Hals M
collo M
knee
genou M
rodilla F
Knie N
ginocchio M
dewclaw
ergot M
espolón M
Afterklaue F
sperone M
hock
jarret M
jarrete M
Sprunggelenk N
garretto M
flank
flanc M
flanco M
Flanke F
fianco M
hoof
sabot M
pezuña F
Huf M
zoccolo M
belly
ventre M
vientre M
Bauch M
ventre M
cannon
canon M
caña F
Röhrbein N
osso M cannone
elbow
coude M
codo M
Ellbogen M
gomito M

antelope
antilope [F]
antílope [M]
Antilope [F]
antilope [F]

alpine ibex
bouquetin [M]
cabra [F] salvaje de los Alpes
Alpensteinbock [M]
stambecco [M] alpino

reindeer
caribou [M]
reno [M]
Rentier [N]
renna [F]

elk
wapiti [M]
alce [M]
Wapiti [M]
wapiti [M]

gazelle
gazelle [F]
gacela [F]
Gazelle [F]
gazzella [F]

moose
orignal [M]
alce [M] americano
Elch [M]
alce [F]

musk ox
bœuf ^{M} musqué
buey ^{M} almizclero
Moschusochse ^{M}
bue ^{M} muschiato

buffalo
bison ^{M} d'Amérique ^{F}
búfalo ^{M}
Büffel ^{M}
bufalo ^{M}

bison
bison ^{M}
bisonte ^{M}
Bison ^{M}
bisonte ^{M}

tapir
tapir ^{M}
tapir ^{M} / danta ^{F}
Tapir ^{M}
tapiro ^{M}

goat
chèvre ^F^
cabra ^F^
Ziege ^F^
capra ^F^

bighorn sheep
mouflon ^M^ d'Amérique ^F^
muflón ^M^
Dickhornschaf ^N^
pecora ^F^ delle Montagne ^F^
Rocciose

cashmere goat
chèvre ^F^ cachemire
cabra ^F^ de cachemira
Kaschmirziege ^F^
capra ^F^ cashmere

western roe deer
chevreuil ^M^
corzo ^M^
Europäisches Reh ^N^
capriolo ^M^

mule
mulet ^M^
mula ^F^
Maultier ^N^
mulo ^M^

rhinoceros
rhinocéros *M*
rinoceronte *M*
Nashorn *N*
rinoceronte *M*

hippopotamus
hippopotame *M*
hipopótamo *M*
Flusspferd *N*
ippopotamo *M*

giraffe
girafe *F*
jirafa *F*
Giraffe *F*
giraffa *F*

Asian elephant
éléphant *M* d'Asie *F*
elefante *M* asiático
Asiatischer Elefant *M*
elefante *M* asiatico

dromedary camel
dromadaire [M]
dromedario [M]
Dromedar [N]
dromedario [M]

Bactrian camel
chameau [M] de Bactriane [F]
camello [M] bactriano
Trampeltier [N]
cammello [M] della Battriana [F]

llama
lama [M]
llama [F]
Lama [N]
lama [M]

zebra
zèbre [M]
cebra [F]
Zebra [N]
zebra [F]

cow
vache [F]
vaca [F]
Rind [N]
mucca [F]

donkey
âne [M]
burro [M]
Esel [M]
asino [M]

wild boar
sanglier [M]
jabalí [M]
Wildschwein [N]
cinghiale [M]

pig
cochon [M]
cerdo [M]
Schwein [N]
maiale [M]

sheep
mouton [M]
oveja [F]
Schaf [N]
pecora [F]

polar bear
ours ^{M} polaire
oso ^{M} polar
Eisbär ^{M}
orso ^{M} polare

black bear
ours ^{M} noir
oso ^{M} negro americano
Schwarzbär ^{M}
orso ^{M} nero ^{M}

giant panda
panda ^{M} géant
oso ^{M} panda
Großer Panda ^{M}
panda ^{M}

grizzly bear
grizzli ^{M}
oso ^{M} pardo
Grizzlybär ^{M}
orso ^{M} grigio

cougar
puma [M]
puma [M]
Puma [M]
puma [M]

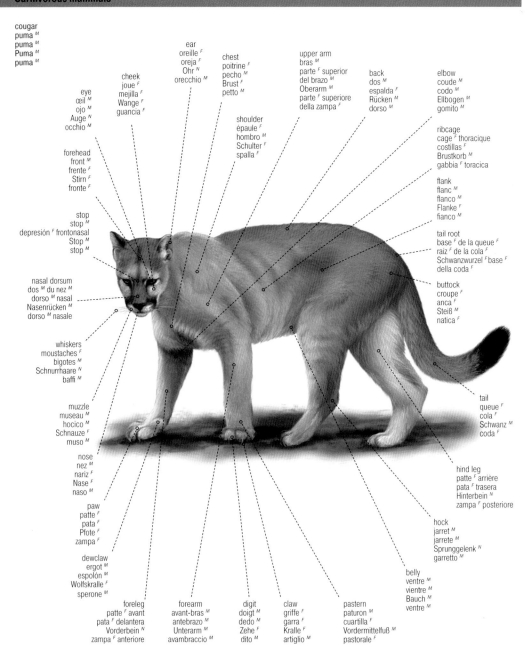

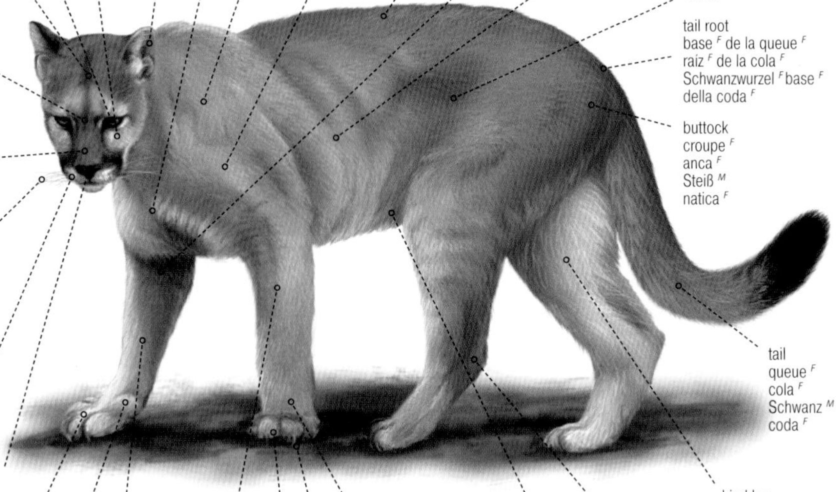
ear
oreille [F]
oreja [F]
Ohr [N]
orecchio [M]
chest
poitrine [F]
pecho [M]
Brust [F]
petto [M]
upper arm
bras [M]
parte [F] superior del brazo [M]
Oberarm [M]
parte [F] superiore della zampa [F]
back
dos [M]
espalda [F]
Rücken [M]
dorso [M]
elbow
coude [M]
codo [M]
Ellbogen [M]
gomito [M]
cheek
joue [F]
mejilla [F]
Wange [F]
guancia [F]
eye
œil [M]
ojo [M]
Auge [N]
occhio [M]
shoulder
épaule [F]
hombro [M]
Schulter [F]
spalla [F]
ribcage
cage [F] thoracique
costillas [F]
Brustkorb [M]
gabbia [F] toracica
forehead
front [M]
frente [F]
Stirn [F]
fronte [F]
flank
flanc [M]
flanco [M]
Flanke [F]
fianco [M]
stop
stop [M]
depresión [F] frontonasal
Stop [M]
stop [M]
tail root
base [F] de la queue [F]
raíz [F] de la cola [F]
Schwanzwurzel [F] base [F] della coda [F]
nasal dorsum
dos [M] du nez [M]
dorso [M] nasal
Nasenrücken [M]
dorso [M] nasale
buttock
croupe [F]
anca [F]
Steiß [M]
natica [F]
whiskers
moustaches [F]
bigotes [M]
Schnurrhaare [N]
baffi [M]
tail
queue [F]
cola [F]
Schwanz [M]
coda [F]
muzzle
museau [M]
hocico [M]
Schnauze [F]
muso [M]
nose
nez [M]
nariz [F]
Nase [F]
naso [M]
hind leg
patte [F] arrière
pata [F] trasera
Hinterbein [N]
zampa [F] posteriore
paw
patte [F]
pata [F]
Pfote [F]
zampa [F]
hock
jarret [M]
jarrete [M]
Sprunggelenk [N]
garretto [M]
dewclaw
ergot [M]
espolón [M]
Wolfskralle [F]
sperone [M]
belly
ventre [M]
vientre [M]
Bauch [M]
ventre [M]
foreleg
patte [F] avant
pata [F] delantera
Vorderbein [N]
zampa [F] anteriore
forearm
avant-bras [M]
antebrazo [M]
Unterarm [M]
avambraccio [M]
digit
doigt [M]
dedo [M]
Zehe [F]
dito [M]
claw
griffe [F]
garra [F]
Kralle [F]
artiglio [M]
pastern
paturon [M]
cuartilla [F]
Vordermittelfuß [M]
pastorale [F]

wolf
loup [M]
lobo [M]
Wolf [M]
lupo [M]

cheetah
guépard [M]
guepardo [M]
Gepard [M]
ghepardo [M]

lion
lion [M]
león [M]
Löwe [M]
leone [M]

jackal
chacal [M]
chacal [M]
Schakal [M]
sciacallo [M]

lynx
lynx [M]
lince [M]
Luchs [M]
lince [F]

striped hyena
hyène ^{F} rayée
hiena ^{F} rayada
Streifenhyäne ^{F}
iena ^{F} striata

spotted hyena
hyène ^{F} tachetée
hiena ^{F} manchada
Tüpfelhyäne ^{F}
iena ^{F} maculata

snow leopard
léopard ^{M} des neiges ^{F}
leopardo ^{M} de las nieves ^{F}
Schneeleopard ^{M}
leopardo ^{M} delle nevi ^{F}

tiger
tigre ^{M}
tigre ^{M}
Tiger ^{M}
tigre ^{F}

jaguar
jaguar ^{M}
jaguar ^{M}
Jaguar ^{M}
giaguaro ^{M}

badger
blaireau [M]
tejón [M]
Dachs [M]
tasso [M]

otter
loutre [F]
nutria [F] europea
Otter [M]
lontra [F]

stoat
hermine [F]
armiño [M]
Hermelin [N]
ermellino [M]

polecat
mouffette [F] tachetée
turón [M]
Iltis [M]
puzzola [F]

skunk
mouffette [F]
mofeta [F] / zorrillo [M]
Stinktier [N]
moffetta [F]

racoon
raton laveur [M]
mapache [M]
Waschbär [M]
procione [M]

jungle cat
chaus ^{M}
gato ^{M} salvaje
Rohrkatze ^{F}
gatto ^{M} della giungla ^{F}

marten
martre ^{F}
marta ^{F} europea
Marder ^{M}
martora ^{F}

wolverine
carcajou ^{M}
glotón ^{M}
Vielfraß ^{M}
ghiottone ^{M}

wildcat
chat ^{M} sauvage
gato ^{M} montés
Wildkatze ^{F}
gatto ^{M} selvatico

red fox
renard ^{M} roux
zorro ^{M} rojo
Rotfuchs ^{M}
volpe ^{F} rossa

gray seal
phoque ^{M} gris
foca ^{F}
Kegelrobbe ^{F}
foca ^{F} grigia

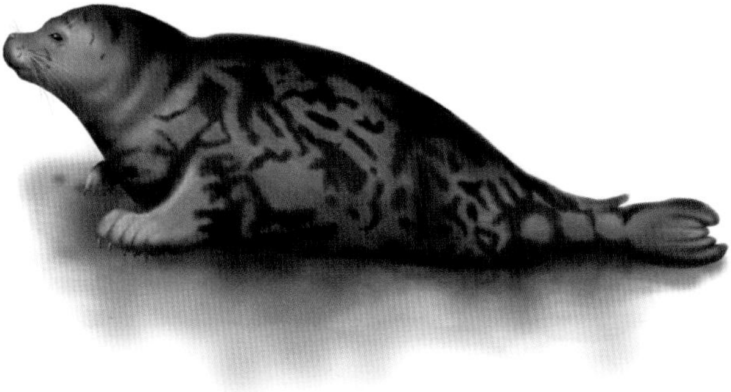

fur seal
otarie ^{F} à fourrure ^{F}
foca ^{M} peletera
Seebär ^{M}
otaria ^{F} orsina

walrus
morse ^{M}
morsa ^{F}
Walross ^{N}
tricheco ^{M}

sea lion
otarie ^{F}
león ^{M} marino
Seelöwe ^{M}
leone ^{M} marino

rottweiler
rottweiler [M]
rottweiler [M]
Rottweiler [M]
rottweiler [M]

bulldog
bulldog [M]
buldog [M]
Bulldogge [F]
bulldog [M]

Siberian husky
husky [M] sibérien
husky [M] siberiano
Siberian Husky [M]
husky [M] siberiano

collie
colley [M]
collie [M]
Collie [M]
collie [M]

dachshund
teckel [M]
perro [M] salchicha [F]
Dackel [M]
bassotto [M]

poodle
caniche [M]
caniche [M]
Pudel [M]
barboncino [M]

German shepherd
berger [M] allemand
pastor [M] alemán
Deutscher Schäferhund [M]
pastore [M] tedesco

golden retriever
golden [M] retriever
golden retriever [M]
Golden Retriever [M]
golden retriever [M]

dalmatian
dalmatien [M]
dálmata [M]
Dalmatiner [M]
dalmata [M]

Chihuahua
chihuahua [M]
Chihuahua [M]
Chihuahua [M]
chihuahua [M]

Labrador retriever
labrador ^{M}
labrador ^{M}
Labrador-Retriever ^{M}
labrador ^{M}

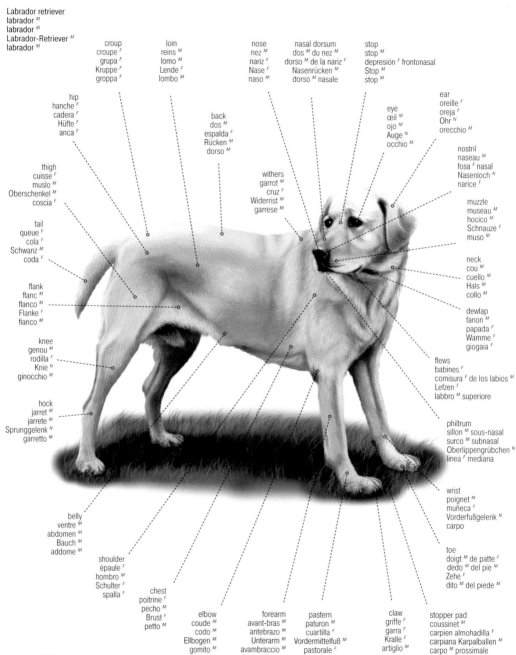

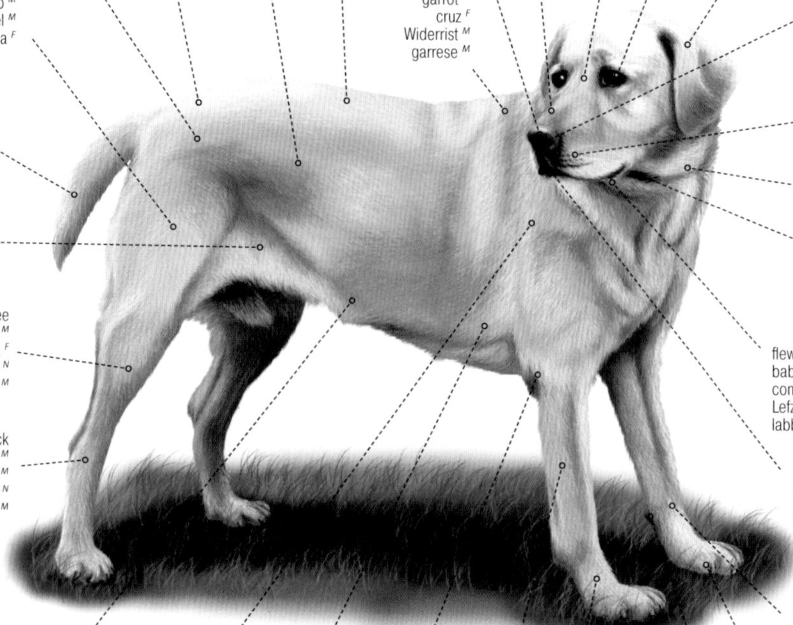
croup
croupe ^{F}
grupa ^{F}
Kruppe ^{F}
groppa ^{F}
loin
reins ^{M}
lomo ^{M}
Lende ^{F}
lombo ^{M}
nose
nez ^{M}
nariz ^{F}
Nase ^{F}
naso ^{M}
nasal dorsum
dos ^{M} du nez ^{M}
dorso ^{M} de la nariz ^{F}
Nasenrücken ^{M}
dorso ^{M} nasale
stop
stop ^{M}
depresión ^{F} frontonasal
Stop ^{M}
stop ^{M}
hip
hanche ^{F}
cadera ^{F}
Hüfte ^{F}
anca ^{F}
back
dos ^{M}
espalda ^{F}
Rücken ^{M}
dorso ^{M}
eye
œil ^{M}
ojo ^{M}
Auge ^{N}
occhio ^{M}
ear
oreille ^{F}
oreja ^{F}
Ohr ^{N}
orecchio ^{M}
nostril
naseau ^{M}
fosa ^{F} nasal
Nasenloch ^{N}
narice ^{F}
thigh
cuisse ^{F}
muslo ^{M}
Oberschenkel ^{M}
coscia ^{F}
withers
garrot ^{M}
cruz ^{F}
Widerrist ^{M}
garrese ^{M}
muzzle
museau ^{M}
hocico ^{M}
Schnauze ^{F}
muso ^{M}
tail
queue ^{F}
cola ^{F}
Schwanz ^{M}
coda ^{F}
neck
cou ^{M}
cuello ^{M}
Hals ^{M}
collo ^{M}
flank
flanc ^{M}
flanco ^{M}
Flanke ^{F}
fianco ^{M}
dewlap
fanon ^{M}
papada ^{F}
Wamme ^{F}
giogaia ^{F}
knee
genou ^{M}
rodilla ^{F}
Knie ^{N}
ginocchio ^{M}
flews
babines ^{F}
comisura ^{F} de los labios ^{M}
Lefzen ^{F}
labbro ^{M} superiore
hock
jarret ^{M}
jarrete ^{M}
Sprunggelenk ^{N}
garretto ^{M}
philtrum
sillon ^{M} sous-nasal
surco ^{M} subnasal
Oberlippengrübchen ^{N}
linea ^{F} mediana
wrist
poignet ^{M}
muñeca ^{F}
Vorderfußgelenk ^{N}
carpo
belly
ventre ^{M}
abdomen ^{M}
Bauch ^{M}
addome ^{M}
toe
doigt ^{M} de patte ^{F}
dedo ^{M} del pie ^{M}
Zehe ^{F}
dito ^{M} del piede ^{M}
shoulder
épaule ^{F}
hombro ^{M}
Schulter ^{F}
spalla ^{F}
chest
poitrine ^{F}
pecho ^{M}
Brust ^{F}
petto ^{M}
elbow
coude ^{M}
codo ^{M}
Ellbogen ^{M}
gomito ^{M}
forearm
avant-bras ^{M}
antebrazo ^{M}
Unterarm ^{M}
avambraccio ^{M}
pastern
paturon ^{M}
cuartilla ^{F}
Vordermittelfuß ^{M}
pastorale ^{F}
claw
griffe ^{F}
garra ^{F}
Kralle ^{F}
artiglio ^{M}
stopper pad
coussinet ^{M}
carpien almohadilla ^{F}
carpiana Karpalballen ^{M}
carpo ^{M} prossimale

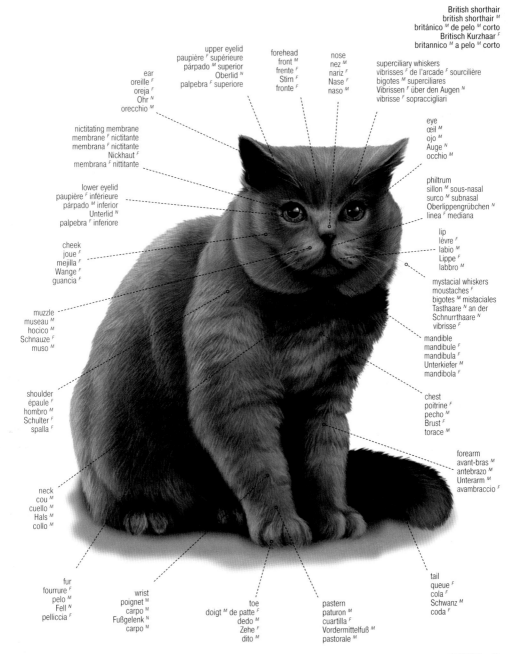

British shorthair
british shorthair M
británico M de pelo M corto
Britisch Kurzhaar F
britannico M a pelo M corto

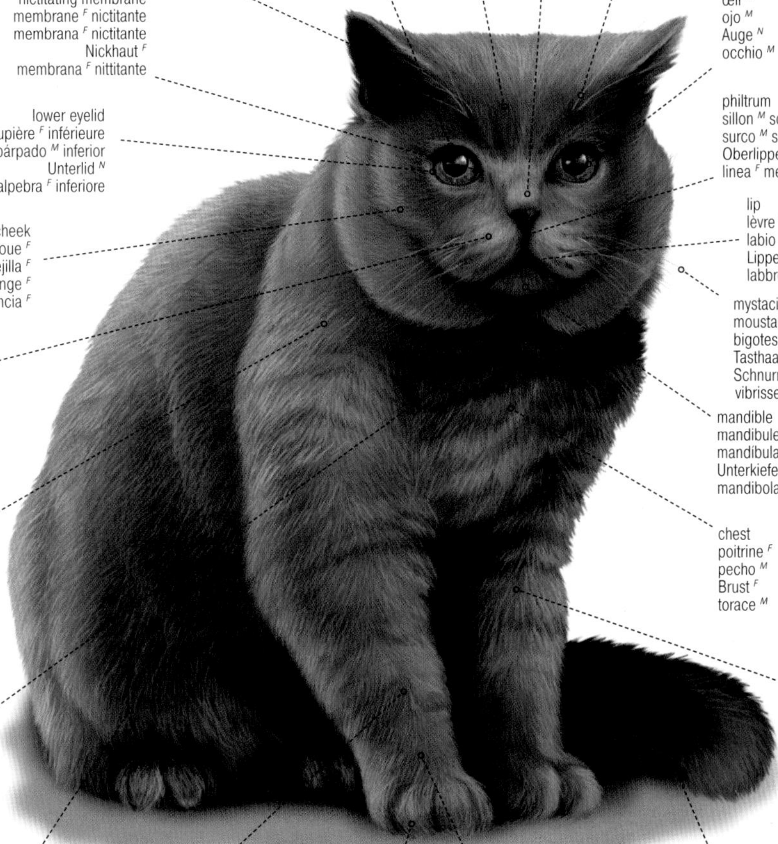
upper eyelid
paupière F supérieure
párpado M superior
Oberlid N
palpebra F superiore
forehead
front M
frente F
Stirn F
fronte F
nose
nez M
nariz F
Nase F
naso M
superciliary whiskers
vibrisses F de l'arcade F sourcilière
bigotes M superciliares
Vibrissen F über den Augen N
vibrisse F sopraccigliari
ear
oreille F
oreja F
Ohr N
orecchio M
eye
œil M
ojo M
Auge N
occhio M
nictitating membrane
membrane F nictitante
membrana F nictitante
Nickhaut F
membrana F nittitante
philtrum
sillon M sous-nasal
surco M subnasal
Oberlippengrübchen N
linea F mediana
lower eyelid
paupière F inférieure
párpado M inferior
Unterlid N
palpebra F inferiore
lip
lèvre F
labio M
Lippe F
labbro M
cheek
joue F
mejilla F
Wange F
guancia F
mystacial whiskers
moustaches F
bigotes M mistaciales
Tasthaare N an der
Schnurrthaare N
vibrisse F
muzzle
museau M
hocico M
Schnauze F
muso M
mandible
mandibule F
mandíbula F
Unterkiefer M
mandibola F
shoulder
épaule F
hombro M
Schulter F
spalla F
chest
poitrine F
pecho M
Brust F
torace M
forearm
avant-bras M
antebrazo M
Unterarm M
avambraccio F
neck
cou M
cuello M
Hals M
collo M
tail
queue F
cola F
Schwanz M
coda F
fur
fourrure F
pelo M
Fell N
pelliccia F
wrist
poignet M
carpo M
Fußgelenk N
carpo M
toe
doigt M de patte F
dedo M
Zehe F
dito M
pastern
paturon M
cuartilla F
Vordermittelfuß M
pastorale M

Norwegian forest cat
chat [M] norvégien
gato [M] del bosque [M] de Noruega [F]
Norwegische Waldkatze [F]
gatto [M] delle foreste [F] norvegesi

Russian blue
chat [M] bleu russe
azul ruso [M]
Russisch Blau [F]
gatto [M] blu [M] di Russia [F]

Maine coon
maine coon [M]
gato [M] maine coon
Maine-Coon-Katze [F]
Maine [M] Coon

Persian cat
chat [M] persan
persa [M]
Perserkatze [F]
Persiano [M]

Siamese cat
chat [M] siamois
siamés [M]
Siamkatze [F]
Siamese [M]

rabbit
lapin [M]
conejo [M]
Kaninchen [N]
coniglio [M]

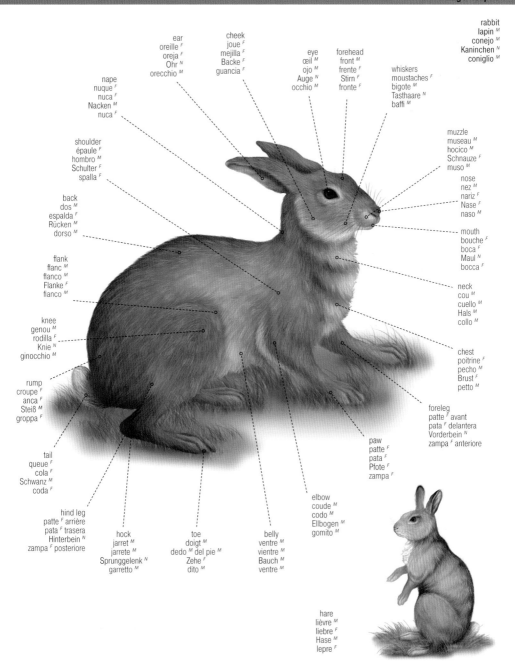

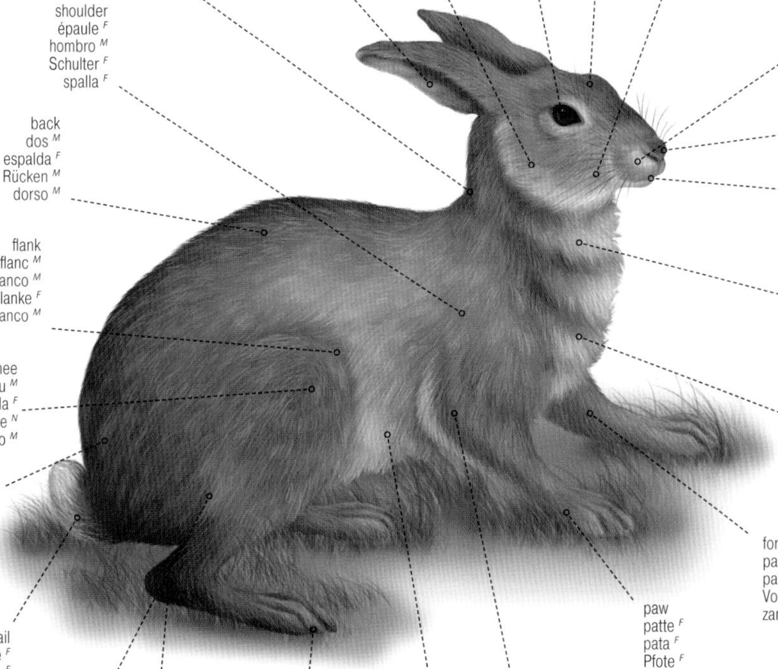
ear
oreille [F]
oreja [F]
Ohr [N]
orecchio [M]
cheek
joue [F]
mejilla [F]
Backe [F]
guancia [F]
eye
œil [M]
ojo [M]
Auge [N]
occhio [M]
forehead
front [M]
frente [F]
Stirn [F]
fronte [F]
whiskers
moustaches [F]
bigote [M]
Tasthaare [N]
baffi [M]
nape
nuque [F]
nuca [F]
Nacken [M]
nuca [F]
shoulder
épaule [F]
hombro [M]
Schulter [F]
spalla [F]
muzzle
museau [M]
hocico [M]
Schnauze [F]
muso [M]
nose
nez [M]
nariz [F]
Nase [F]
naso [M]
back
dos [M]
espalda [F]
Rücken [M]
dorso [M]
mouth
bouche [F]
boca [F]
Maul [N]
bocca [F]
flank
flanc [M]
flanco [M]
Flanke [F]
fianco [M]
neck
cou [M]
cuello [M]
Hals [M]
collo [M]
knee
genou [M]
rodilla [F]
Knie [N]
ginocchio [M]
chest
poitrine [F]
pecho [M]
Brust [F]
petto [M]
rump
croupe [F]
anca [F]
Steiß [M]
groppa [F]
foreleg
patte [F] avant
pata [F] delantera
Vorderbein [N]
zampa [F] anteriore
paw
patte [F]
pata [F]
Pfote [F]
zampa [F]
tail
queue [F]
cola [F]
Schwanz [M]
coda [F]
elbow
coude [M]
codo [M]
Ellbogen [M]
gomito [M]
hind leg
patte [F] arrière
pata [F] trasera
Hinterbein [N]
zampa [F] posteriore
hock
jarret [M]
jarrete [M]
Sprunggelenk [N]
garretto [M]
toe
doigt [M]
dedo [M] del pie [M]
Zehe [F]
dito [M]
belly
ventre [M]
vientre [M]
Bauch [M]
ventre [M]

hare
lièvre [M]
liebre [F]
Hase [M]
lepre [F]

koala
koala [M]
koala [M]
Koala [M]
koala [M]

ear
oreille [F]
oreja [F]
Ohr [N]
orecchio [M]

head
tête [F]
cabeza [F]
Kopf [M]
testa [F]

cheek
joue [F]
mejilla [F]
Backe [F]
guancia [F]

eye
œil [M]
ojo [M]
Auge [N]
occhio [M]

mouth
bouche [F]
boca [F]
Mund [M]
bocca [F]

nose
nez [M]
nariz [F]
Nase [F]
naso [M]

forelimb
membre [M] antérieur
extremidad [F] anterior
Vordergliedmaße [F]
arto [M] anteriore

chest
poitrine [F]
pecho [M]
Brust [F]
petto [M]

hind limb
membre [M] postérieur
extremidad [F] posterior
Hintergliedmaße [F]
arto [M] posteriore

opposable digit
doigt [M] opposable
dedo [M] oponible
opponierbare Finger [M]
dito [M] opponibile

digit
doigt [M]
dedo [M]
Greiffinger [M]
dito [M]

hind paw
patte [F] arrière
pata [F] posterior
Hinterpfote [F]
zampa [F] posteriore

forepaw
patte [F] avant
pata [F] delantera
Vorderpfote [F]
zampa [F] anteriore [M]

claw
griffe [F]
garra [F]
Kralle [F]
artiglio [M]

kangaroo
kangourou [M]
canguro [M]
Känguru [N]
canguro [M]

opossum
opossum [M]
zarigüeya [F]
Opossum [N]
opossum [M]

house mouse
souris [F] commune
ratón [M] común
Hausmaus [F]
topo [M] comune

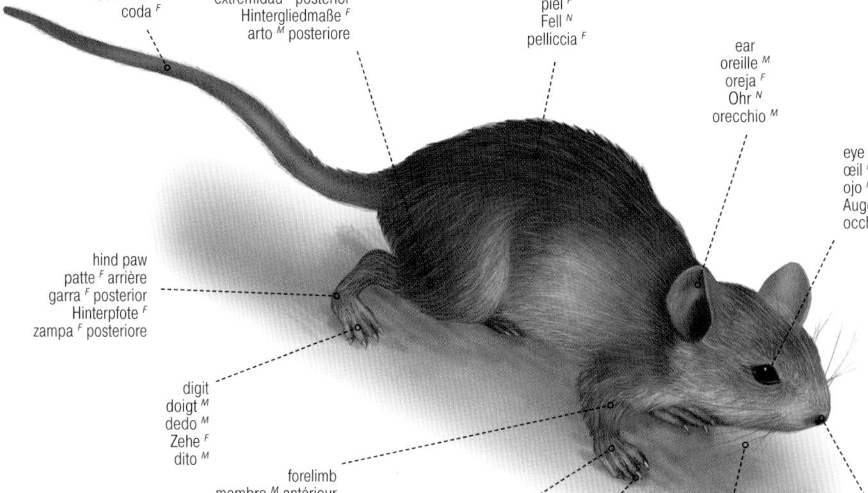
tail
queue [F]
cola [F]
Schwanz [M]
coda [F]
hind limb
membre [M] postérieur
extremidad [F] posterior
Hintergliedmaße [F]
arto [M] posteriore
fur
fourrure [F]
piel [F]
Fell [N]
pelliccia [F]
ear
oreille [M]
oreja [F]
Ohr [N]
orecchio [M]
eye
œil [M]
ojo [M]
Auge [N]
occhio [M]
hind paw
patte [F] arrière
garra [F] posterior
Hinterpfote [F]
zampa [F] posteriore
digit
doigt [M]
dedo [M]
Zehe [F]
dito [M]
forelimb
membre [M] antérieur
extremidad [F] anterior
Vordergliedmaße [F]
arto [M] anteriore
forepaw
patte [F] avant
zarpa [F]
Vorderpfote [F]
zampa [F] anteriore
claw
griffe [F]
garra [F]
Kralle [F]
artiglio [F]
whiskers
vibrisses [F]
bigotes [M]
Schnurrhaare [F]
baffi [M]
nose
nez [M]
nariz [F]
Nase [F]
naso [M]

field vole
campagnol [M] agreste
topillo [M] agreste
Feldmaus [F]
topo [M] di campagna [F]

brown rat
rat [M] brun
rata [F] parda
Wanderratte [F]
ratto [M] marrone

porcupine
porc-épic [M]
puercoespín [M]
Stachelschwein [N]
porcospino [M]

red-rumped agouti
agouti [M] doré
agutí [M] brasileño
Goldaguti [N]
aguti [M] rossiccio

beaver
castor [M]
castor [M]
Biber [M]
castoro [M]

muskrat
rat [M] musqué
rata [F] almizclera
Bisamratte [F]
topo [M] muschiato

chinchilla
chinchilla [M]
chinchilla [F]
Chinchilla [N]
cincillà [M]

gray squirrel
écureuil [M] gris
ardilla [F] gris
Grauhörnchen [N]
scoiattolo [M] grigio

marmot
marmotte [F] commune
marmota [F]
Murmeltier [N]
marmotta [F]

guinea pig
cochon [M] d'Inde [F]
conejillo [M] de Indias [F] / cobayo [M]
Meerschweinchen [N]
porcellino [M] d'India [F]

hamster
hamster [M]
hámster [M]
Hamster [M]
criceto [M]

jerboa
gerboise [F]
jerbo [M]
Springmaus [F]
gerboa [M]

chipmunk
tamia [M] rayé
ardilla [F] rayada
Streifenhörnchen [N]
tamia [M]

Monotremes

platypus
ornithorynque [M]
ornitorrinco [M]
Schnabeltier [N]
ornitorinco [M]

humpback whale
baleine [F] à bosse [F]
ballena [F] jorobada
Buckelwal [M]
megattera [F]

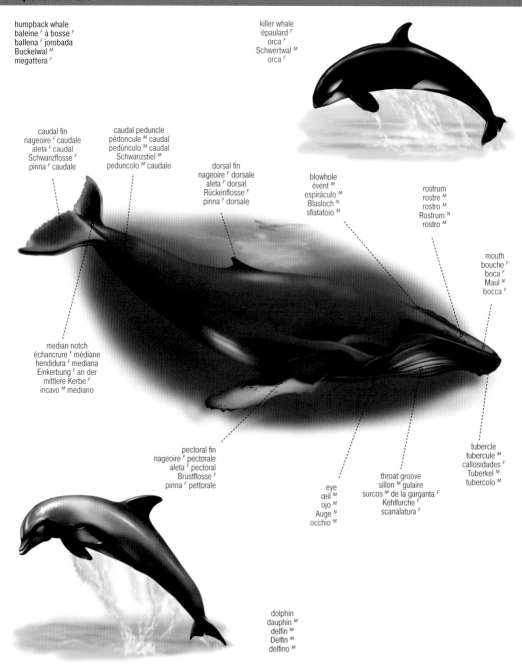

killer whale
épaulard [F]
orca [F]
Schwertwal [M]
orca [F]

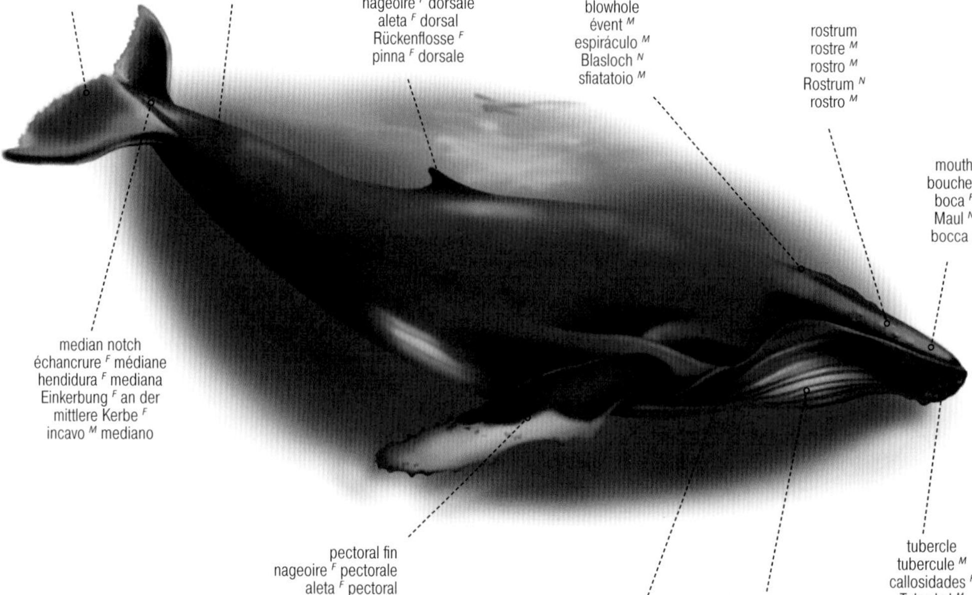
caudal fin
nageoire [F] caudale
aleta [F] caudal
Schwanzflosse [F]
pinna [F] caudale
caudal peduncle
pédoncule [M] caudal
pedúnculo [M] caudal
Schwanzstiel [M]
peduncolo [M] caudale
dorsal fin
nageoire [F] dorsale
aleta [F] dorsal
Rückenflosse [F]
pinna [F] dorsale
blowhole
évent [M]
espiráculo [M]
Blasloch [N]
sfiatatoio [M]
rostrum
rostre [M]
rostro [M]
Rostrum [N]
rostro [M]
mouth
bouche [F]
boca [F]
Maul [N]
bocca [F]
median notch
échancrure [F] médiane
hendidura [F] mediana
Einkerbung [F] an der
mittlere Kerbe [F]
incavo [M] mediano
pectoral fin
nageoire [F] pectorale
aleta [F] pectoral
Brustflosse [F]
pinna [F] pettorale
eye
œil [M]
ojo [M]
Auge [N]
occhio [M]
throat groove
sillon [M] gulaire
surcos [M] de la garganta [F]
Kehlfurche [F]
scanalatura [F]
tubercle
tubercule [M]
callosidades [F]
Tuberkel [M]
tubercolo [M]

dolphin
dauphin [M]
delfín [M]
Delfin [M]
delfino [M]

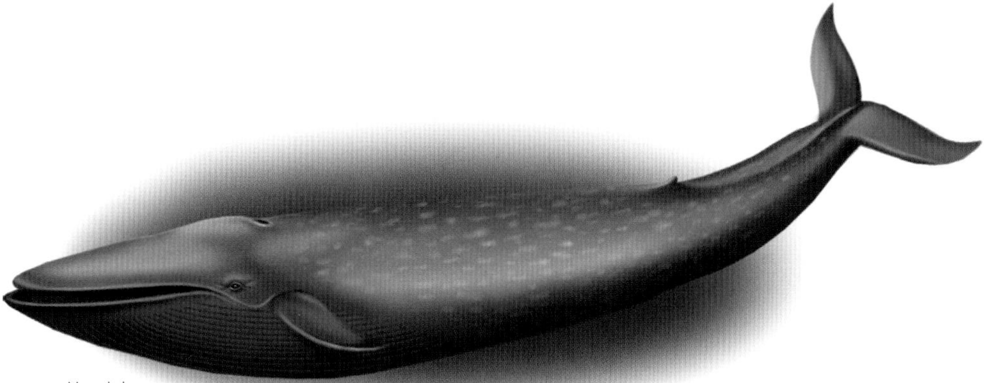

blue whale
rorqual [M] bleu
ballena [F] azul
Blauwal [M]
balenottera [F] azzurra

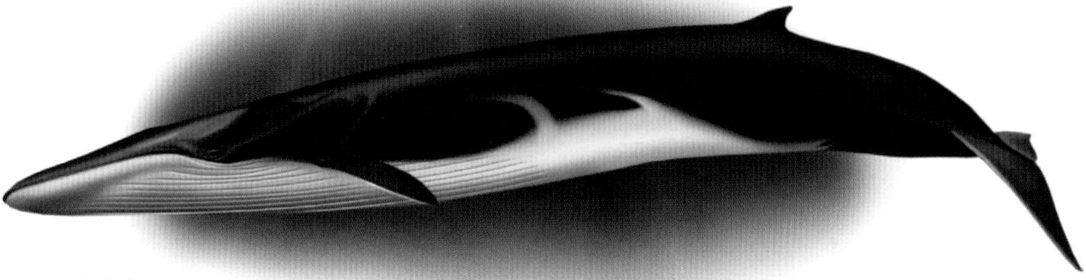

fin whale
rorqual [M] commun
rorcual [M] común
Finnwal [M]
balenottera [F] comune

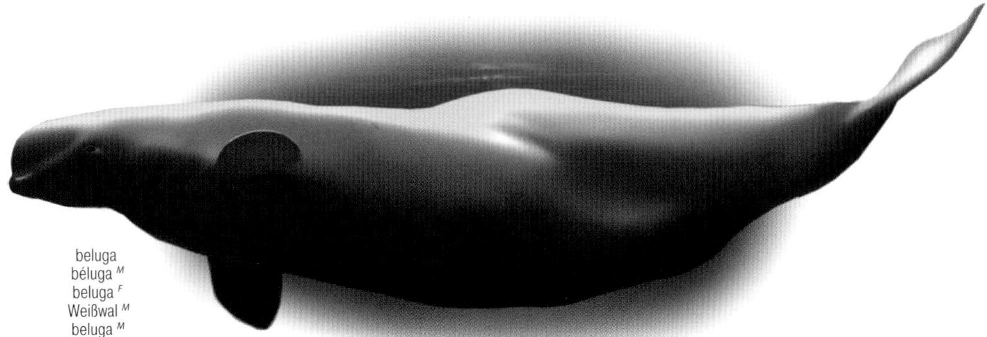

beluga
béluga [M]
beluga [F]
Weißwal [M]
beluga [M]

Galápagos tortoise
tortue [F] géante des Galapagos [M]
tortuga [F] de las galápagos
Galápagos-Schildkröte [F]
tartaruga [F] delle Galapagos [F]

vertebral scute
plaque [F] vertébrale
escudo [M] vertebral
Wirbelschild [M]
scudo [M] vertebrale
carapace
carapace [F]
caparazón [M]
Rückenschild [M]
carapace [M]
costal scute
plaque [F] costale
escudo [M] costal
Rippenschild [M]
scuto [M] costale
neck
cou [M]
cuello [M]
Hals [M]
collo [M]
eye
œil [M]
ojo [M]
Auge [N]
occhio [M]
marginal scute
plaque [F] marginale
escudo [M] marginal
Randschild [M]
scuto [M] marginale
horny beak
bec corné [M]
pico [M] calloso
Hornschnabel [M]
becco [M] corneo
pygal plate
plaque [F] pygale
escudo [M] precentral
Schwanzschild [M]
placca [F] pigale
mouth
bouche [F]
boca [F]
Maul [N]
bocca [F]
leg
patte [F]
pierna [F]
Bein [N]
zampa [F]
scale
écaille [F]
escama [F]
Schuppe [F]
squama [F]
plastron
plastron [M]
plastrón [M]
Bauchpanzer [M]
petto [M]
claw
griffe [F]
garra [F]
Kralle [F]
artiglio [M]

Blanding's turtle
tortue [F] mouchetée
tortuga [F] Blandingii
amerikanische Sumpfschildkröte [F]
tartaruga [F] del Blanding

green sea turtle
tortue [F] verte
tortuga [F] marina verde
Grüne Meeresschildkröte [F]
tartaruga [F] marina verde

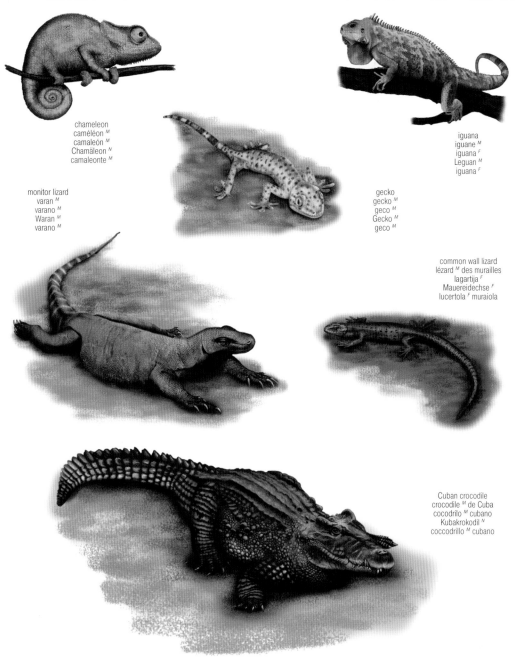

chameleon
caméléon ^{M}
camaleón ^{M}
Chamäleon ^{N}
camaleonte ^{M}

iguana
iguane ^{M}
iguana ^{F}
Leguan ^{M}
iguana ^{F}

gecko
gecko ^{M}
geco ^{M}
Gecko ^{M}
geco ^{M}

monitor lizard
varan ^{M}
varano ^{M}
Waran ^{M}
varano ^{M}

common wall lizard
lézard ^{M} des murailles
lagartija ^{F}
Mauereidechse ^{F}
lucertola ^{F} muraiola

Cuban crocodile
crocodile ^{M} de Cuba
cocodrilo ^{M} cubano
Kubakrokodil ^{N}
coccodrillo ^{M} cubano

caiman
caïman ^{M}
caimán ^{M}
Kaiman ^{M}
caimano ^{M}

alligator
alligator ^{M}
caimán ^{M} americano
Mississippi-Alligator ^{M}
alligatore ^{M}

Nile crocodile
crocodile ^{M} du Nil ^{M}
cocodrilo ^{M} del Nilo ^{M}
Nilkrokodil ^{N}
coccodrillo ^{M} del Nilo ^{M}

Snakes

Serpents [M] | Serpientes [F] | Schlangen [F] | Serpenti [M]

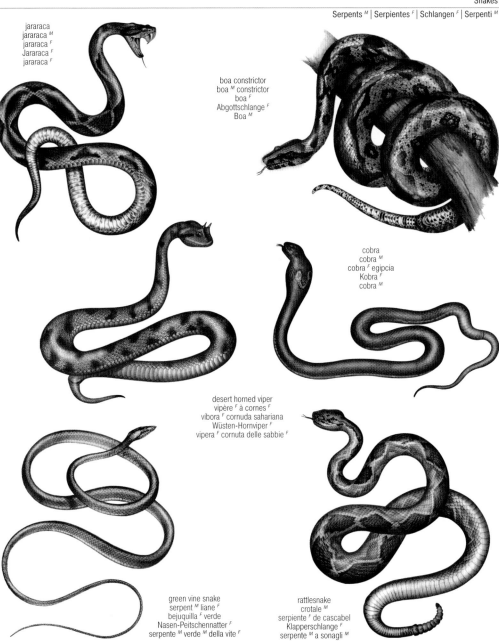

jararaca
jararaca [M]
jararaca [F]
Jararaca [F]
jararaca [F]

boa constrictor
boa [M] constrictor
boa [F]
Abgottschlange [F]
Boa [M]

desert horned viper
vipère [F] à cornes [F]
víbora [F] cornuda sahariana
Wüsten-Hornviper [F]
vipera [F] cornuta delle sabbie [F]

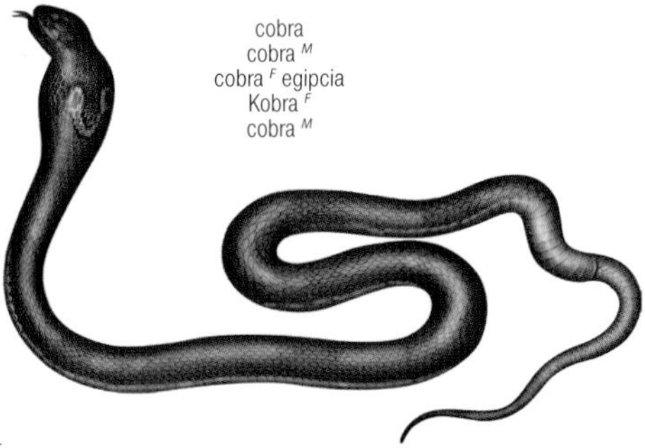

cobra
cobra [M]
cobra [F] egipcia
Kobra [F]
cobra [M]

green vine snake
serpent [M] liane [F]
bejuquilla [F] verde
Nasen-Peitschennatter [F]
serpente [M] verde [M] della vite [F]

rattlesnake
crotale [M]
serpiente [F] de cascabel
Klapperschlange [F]
serpente [M] a sonagli [M]

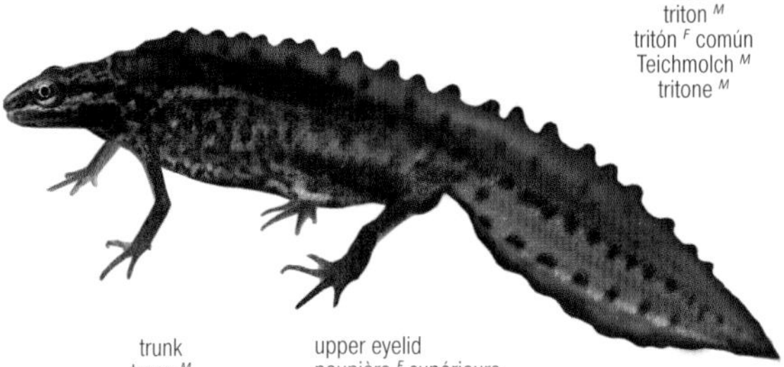
newt
triton [M]
tritón [F] común
Teichmolch [M]
tritone [M]

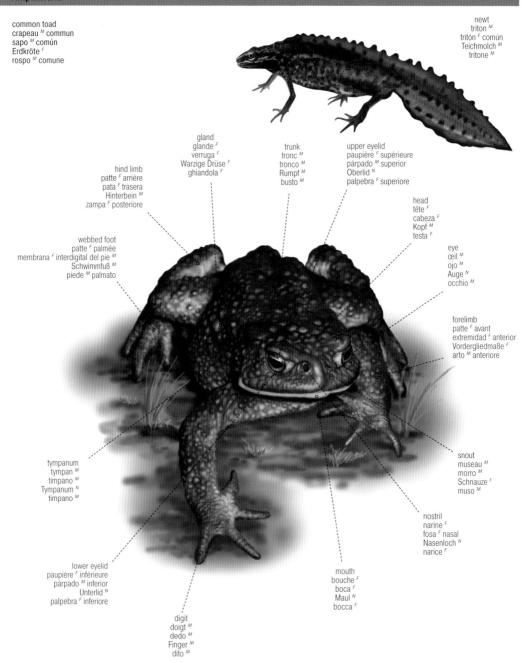

common toad
crapeau [M] commun
sapo [M] común
Erdkröte [F]
rospo [M] comune
gland
glande [F]
verruga [F]
Warzige Drüse [F]
ghiandola [F]
trunk
tronc [M]
tronco [M]
Rumpf [M]
busto [M]
upper eyelid
paupière [F] supérieure
párpado [M] superior
Oberlid [N]
palpebra [F] superiore
hind limb
patte [F] arrière
pata [F] trasera
Hinterbein [M]
zampa [F] posteriore
head
tête [F]
cabeza [F]
Kopf [M]
testa [F]
webbed foot
patte [F] palmée
membrana [F] interdigital del pie [M]
Schwimmfuß [M]
piede [M] palmato
eye
œil [M]
ojo [M]
Auge [N]
occhio [M]
forelimb
patte [F] avant
extremidad [F] anterior
Vordergliedmaße [F]
arto [M] anteriore
tympanum
tympan [M]
tímpano [M]
Tympanum [N]
timpano [M]
snout
museau [M]
morro [M]
Schnauze [F]
muso [M]
nostril
narine [F]
fosa [F] nasal
Nasenloch [N]
narice [F]
lower eyelid
paupière [F] inférieure
párpado [M] inferior
Unterlid [N]
palpebra [F] inferiore
mouth
bouche [F]
boca [F]
Maul [N]
bocca [F]
digit
doigt [M]
dedo [M]
Finger [M]
dito [M]

cane toad
crapaud [M] géant
sapo [M] de caña [F]
Agakröte [F]
rospo [M] delle canne [F]

salamander
salamandre [F]
salamandra [F]
Salamander [M]
salamandra [F]

common frog
grenouille [F] rousse
rana [F] común
Grasfrosch [M]
rana [F] rossa

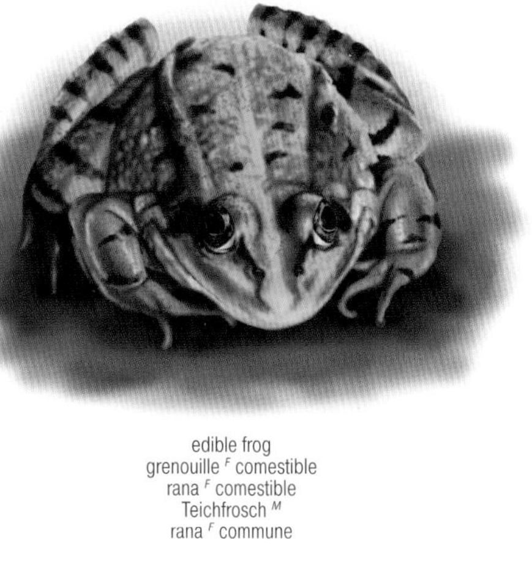

edible frog
grenouille [F] comestible
rana [F] comestible
Teichfrosch [M]
rana [F] commune

tree frog
rainette [F]
rana [F] de cristal [M]
Glasfrosch [M]
rane [F] di vetro [M]

bat
chauve-souris [F]
murciélago [M]
Fledermaus [F]
pipistrello [M]

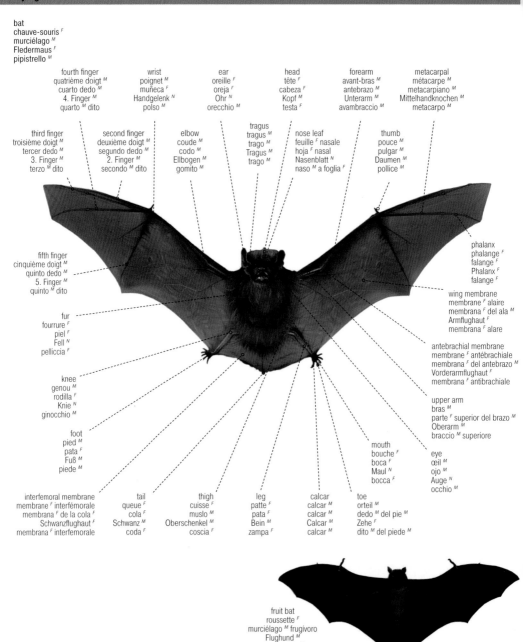

fourth finger
quatrième doigt [M]
cuarto dedo [M]
4. Finger [M]
quarto [M] dito

wrist
poignet [M]
muñeca [F]
Handgelenk [N]
polso [M]

ear
oreille [F]
oreja [F]
Ohr [N]
orecchio [M]

head
tête [F]
cabeza [F]
Kopf [M]
testa [F]

forearm
avant-bras [M]
antebrazo [M]
Unterarm [M]
avambraccio [M]

metacarpal
métacarpe [M]
metacarpiano [M]
Mittelhandknochen [M]
metacarpo [M]

third finger
troisième doigt [M]
tercer dedo [M]
3. Finger [M]
terzo [M] dito

second finger
deuxième doigt [M]
segundo dedo [M]
2. Finger [M]
secondo [M] dito

elbow
coude [M]
codo [M]
Ellbogen [M]
gomito [M]

tragus
tragus [M]
trago [M]
Tragus [M]
trago [M]

nose leaf
feuille [F] nasale
hoja [F] nasal
Nasenblatt [N]
naso [M] a foglia [F]

thumb
pouce [M]
pulgar [M]
Daumen [M]
pollice [M]

phalanx
phalange [F]
falange [F]
Phalanx [F]
falange [F]

fifth finger
cinquième doigt [M]
quinto dedo [M]
5. Finger [M]
quinto [M] dito

wing membrane
membrane [F] alaire
membrana [F] del ala [M]
Armflughaut [F]
membrana [F] alare

fur
fourrure [F]
piel [F]
Fell [N]
pelliccia [F]

antebrachial membrane
membrane [F] antébrachiale
membrana [F] del antebrazo [M]
Vorderarmflughaut [F]
membrana [F] antibrachiale

knee
genou [M]
rodilla [F]
Knie [N]
ginocchio [M]

upper arm
bras [M]
parte [F] superior del brazo [M]
Oberarm [M]
braccio [M] superiore

foot
pied [M]
pata [F]
Fuß [M]
piede [M]

mouth
bouche [F]
boca [F]
Maul [N]
bocca [F]

eye
œil [M]
ojo [M]
Auge [N]
occhio [M]

interfemoral membrane
membrane [F] interfémorale
membrana [F] de la cola [F]
Schwanzflughaut [F]
membrana [F] interfemorale

tail
queue [F]
cola [F]
Schwanz [M]
coda [F]

thigh
cuisse [F]
muslo [M]
Oberschenkel [M]
coscia [F]

leg
patte [F]
pata [F]
Bein [M]
zampa [F]

calcar
calcar [M]
calcar [M]
Calcar [M]
calcar [M]

toe
orteil [M]
dedo [M] del pie [M]
Zehe [F]
dito [M] del piede [M]

fruit bat
roussette [F]
murciélago [M] frugívoro
Flughund [M]
pteropodide [M]

mole
taupe F
topo M
Maulwurf M
talpa F

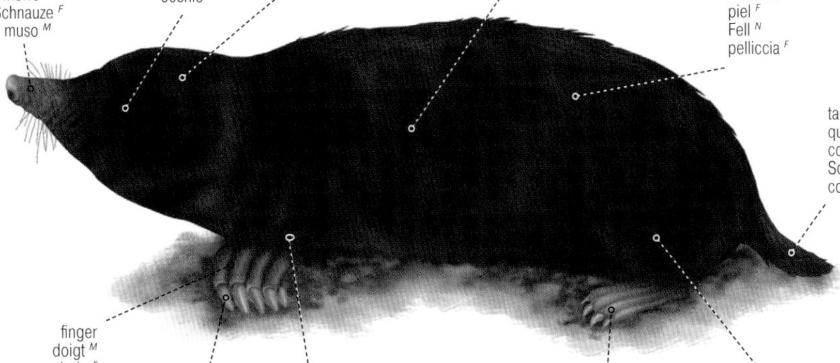
snout
museau M
morro M
Schnauze F
muso M
eye
œil M
ojo M
Auge N
occhio M
head
tête F
cabeza F
Kopf M
testa F
body
corps M
cuerpo M
Körper M
corpo M
fur
fourrure F
piel F
Fell N
pelliccia F
tail
queue F
cola F
Schwanz M
coda F
finger
doigt M
dedo F
Finger M
dito M
claw
griffe F
garra F
Kralle F
artiglio M
forelimb
patte F avant
extremidad F anterior
Vordergliedmaße F
arto M anteriore
toe
doigt M de patte F
dedo M del pie M
Zehe F
dito M del piede M
hind limb
patte F arrière
extremidad F posterior
Hintergliedmaße F
arto M posteriore

hedgehog
hérisson M
erizo M
Igel M
riccio M

pangolin
pangolin M
pangolín M
Schuppentier N
pangolino M

giant anteater
tamanoir M
oso M hormiguero
Großer Ameisenbär M
formichiere M gigante

armadillo
tatou M
armadillo M
Gürteltier N
armadillo M

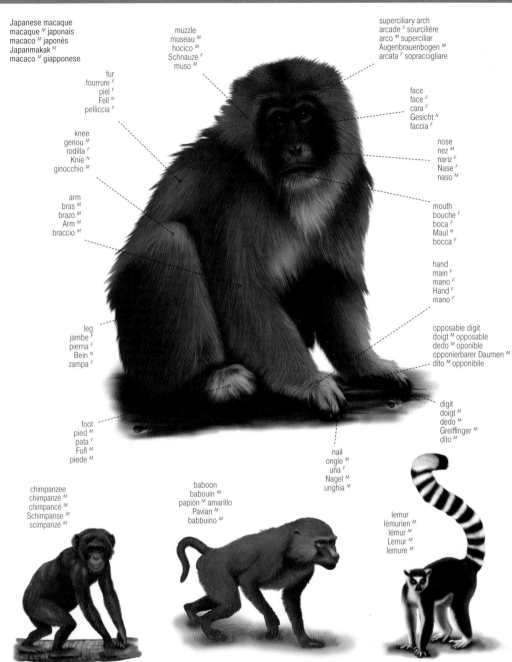

Japanese macaque
macaque [M] japonais
macaco [M] japonés
Japanmakak [M]
macaco [M] giapponese
muzzle
museau [M]
hocico [M]
Schnauze [F]
muso [M]
superciliary arch
arcade [F] sourcilière
arco [M] superciliar
Augenbrauenbogen [M]
arcata [F] sopraccigliare
fur
fourrure [F]
piel [F]
Fell [N]
pelliccia [F]
face
face [F]
cara [F]
Gesicht [N]
faccia [F]
knee
genou [M]
rodilla [F]
Knie [N]
ginocchio [M]
nose
nez [M]
nariz [F]
Nase [F]
naso [M]
arm
bras [M]
brazo [M]
Arm [M]
braccio [M]
mouth
bouche [F]
boca [F]
Maul [N]
bocca [F]
hand
main [F]
mano [F]
Hand [F]
mano [F]
leg
jambe [F]
pierna [F]
Bein [N]
zampa [F]
opposable digit
doigt [M] opposable
dedo [M] oponible
opponierbarer Daumen [M]
dito [M] opponibile
foot
pied [M]
pata [F]
Fuß [M]
piede [M]
digit
doigt [M]
dedo [M]
Greiffinger [M]
dito [M]
nail
ongle [M]
uña [F]
Nagel [M]
unghia [M]

chimpanzee
chimpanzé [M]
chimpancé [M]
Schimpanse [M]
scimpanzé [M]

baboon
babouin [M]
papión [M] amarillo
Pavian [M]
babbuino [M]

lemur
lémurien [M]
lémur [M]
Lemur [M]
lemure [M]

orangutan
orang-outan [M]
orangután [M]
Orang-Utan [M]
orangotango [M]

lion tamarin
tamarin-lion [M]
mono [M] tití
Löwenäffchen [N]
scimmia [F] leonina

red howler monkey
singe [M] hurleur [M] roux
mono [M] aullador rojo
Roter Brüllaffe [M]
aluatta [F] rossa

slow loris
loris [M]
loris [M] perezosos
Plumplori [M]
loris [M] lento

mandrill
mandrill [M]
mandril [M]
Mandrill [M]
mandrillo [M]

gorilla
gorille [M]
gorila [M]
Gorilla [M]
gorilla [M]

lobster
homard [M]
bogavante [M]
Hummer [M]
aragosta [F]

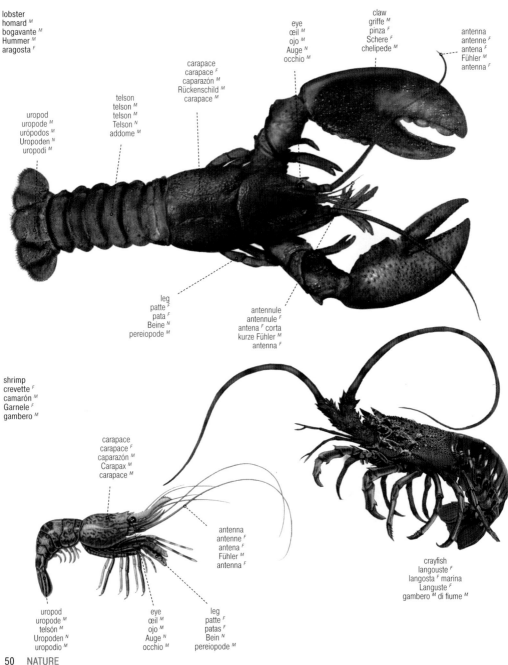

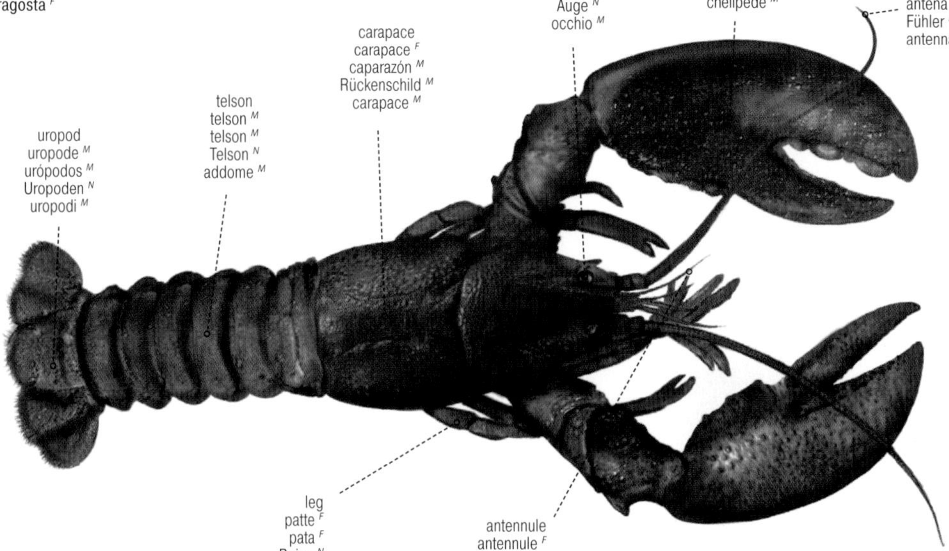
eye
œil [M]
ojo [M]
Auge [N]
occhio [M]
claw
griffe [M]
pinza [F]
Schere [F]
chelipede [M]
antenna
antenne [F]
antena [F]
Fühler [M]
antenna [F]
carapace
carapace [F]
caparazón [M]
Rückenschild [M]
carapace [M]
telson
telson [M]
telson [M]
Telson [N]
addome [M]
uropod
uropode [M]
urópodos [M]
Uropoden [N]
uropodi [M]
leg
patte [F]
pata [F]
Beine [N]
pereiopode [M]
antennule
antennule [F]
antena [F] corta
kurze Fühler [M]
antenna [F]

shrimp
crevette [F]
camarón [M]
Garnele [F]
gambero [M]

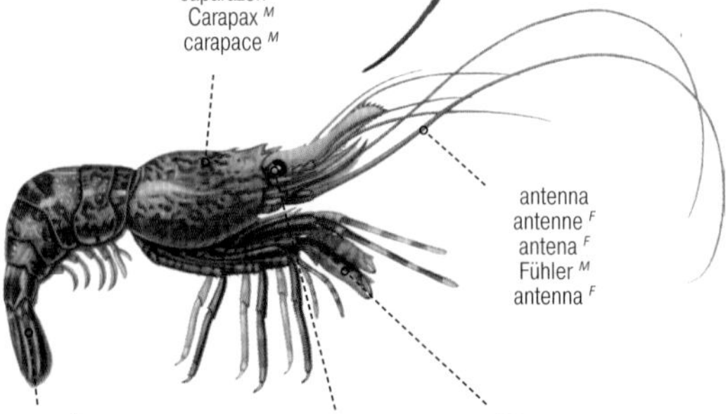
carapace
carapace [F]
caparazón [M]
Carapax [M]
carapace [M]
antenna
antenne [F]
antena [F]
Fühler [M]
antenna [F]
uropod
uropode [M]
telsón [M]
Uropoden [N]
uropodio [M]
eye
œil [M]
ojo [M]
Auge [N]
occhio [M]
leg
patte [F]
patas [F]
Bein [N]
pereiopode [M]

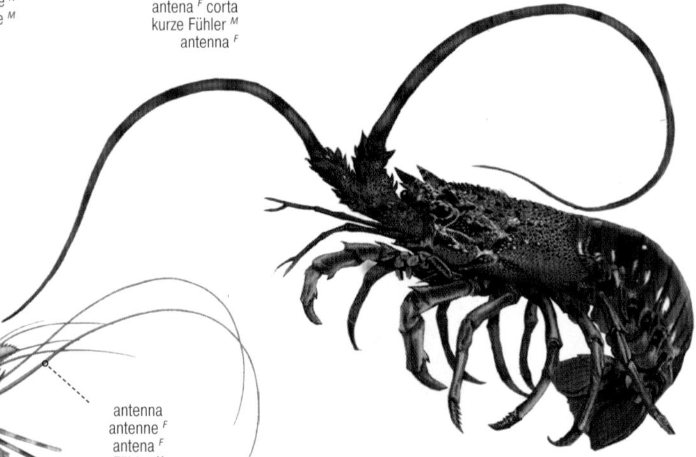

crayfish
langouste [F]
langosta [F] marina
Languste [F]
gambero [M] di fiume [M]

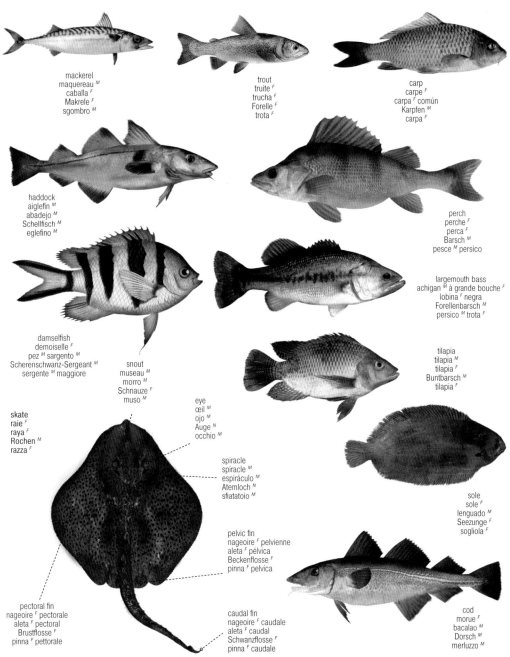

mackerel
maquereau [M]
caballa [F]
Makrele [F]
sgombro [M]

trout
truite [F]
trucha [F]
Forelle [F]
trota [F]

carp
carpe [F]
carpa [F] común
Karpfen [M]
carpa [F]

haddock
aiglefin [M]
abadejo [M]
Schellfisch [M]
eglefino [M]

perch
perche [F]
perca [F]
Barsch [M]
pesce [M] persico

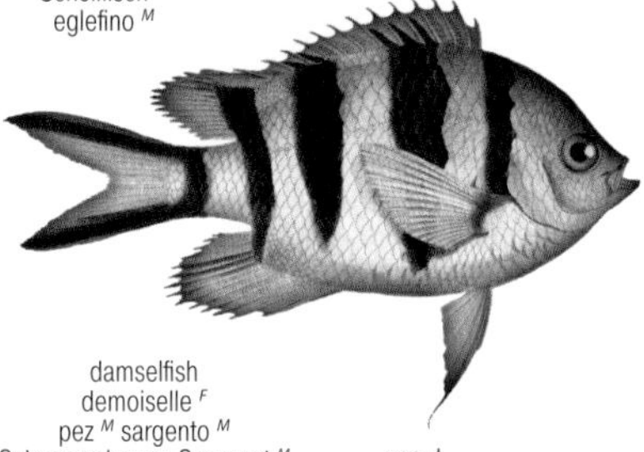

damselfish
demoiselle [F]
pez [M] sargento [M]
Scherenschwanz-Sergeant [M]
sergente [M] maggiore

largemouth bass
achigan [M] à grande bouche [F]
lobina [F] negra
Forellenbarsch [M]
persico [M] trota [F]

tilapia
tilapia [M]
tilapia [F]
Buntbarsch [M]
tilapia [F]

skate
raie [F]
raya [F]
Rochen [M]
razza [F]

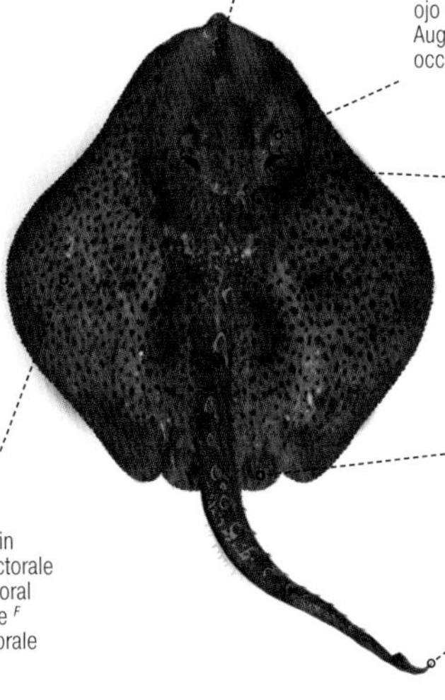

snout
museau [M]
morro [M]
Schnauze [F]
muso [M]

eye
œil [M]
ojo [M]
Auge [N]
occhio [M]

spiracle
spiracle [M]
espiráculo [M]
Atemloch [N]
sfiatatoio [M]

pelvic fin
nageoire [F] pelvienne
aleta [F] pélvica
Beckenflosse [F]
pinna [F] pelvica

pectoral fin
nageoire [F] pectorale
aleta [F] pectoral
Brustflosse [F]
pinna [F] pettorale

caudal fin
nageoire [F] caudale
aleta [F] caudal
Schwanzflosse [F]
pinna [F] caudale

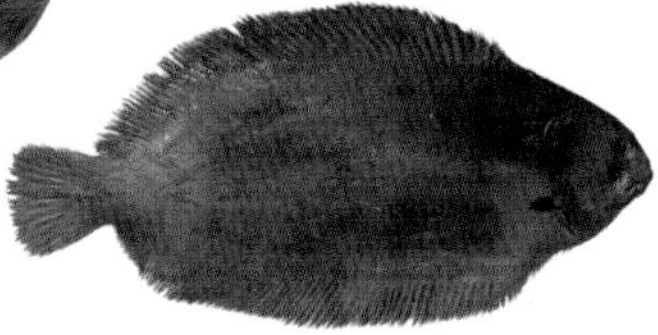

sole
sole [F]
lenguado [M]
Seezunge [F]
sogliola [F]

cod
morue [F]
bacalao [M]
Dorsch [M]
merluzzo [M]

blue shark
requin [M] bleu
tiburón [M] azul
Blauhai [M]
squalo [M] blu

salmon
saumon [M]
salmón [M]
Lachs [M]
salmone [M]

pike
brochet [M]
lucio [M]
Hecht [M]
luccio [M]

channel catfish
barbue [F] de rivière [F]
pez gato [M] americano
getüpfelter Gabelwels [M]
pesce [M] gatto [M] maculato

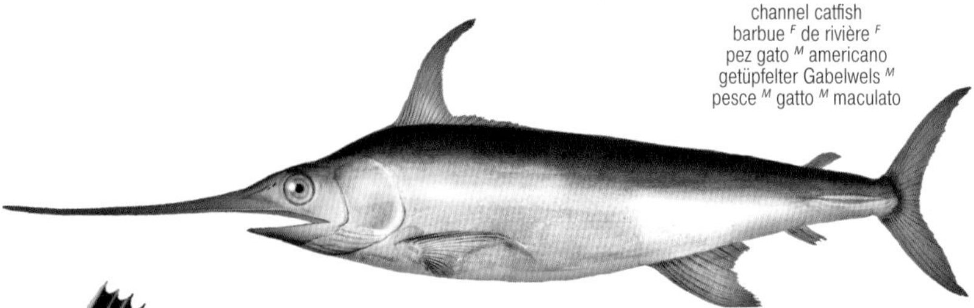

swordfish
espadon [M]
pez [M] espada [F]
Schwertfisch [M]
pesce [M] spada [F]

tuna
thon [M]
atún [M]
Thunfisch [M]
tonno [M]

sturgeon
esturgeon [M]
esturión [M]
Stör [M]
storione [M]

octopus
pieuvre [F]
pulpo [M]
Oktopus [M]
polpo [M]

mantle
manteau [M]
manto [M]
Mantel [M]
mantello [M]

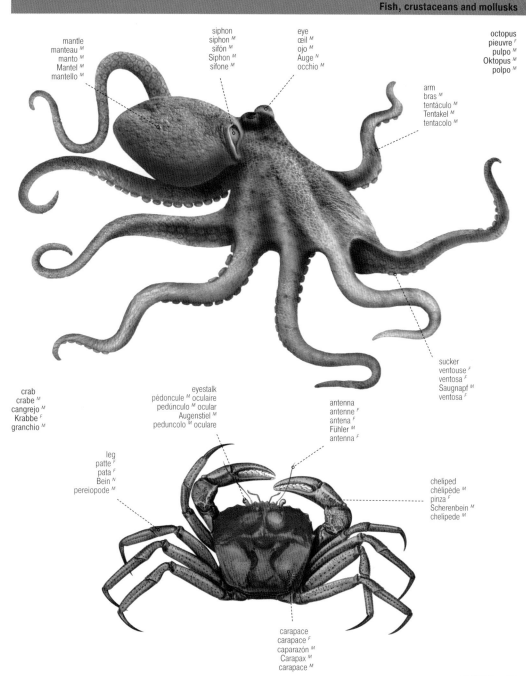

siphon
siphon [M]
sifón [M]
Siphon [M]
sifone [M]

eye
œil [M]
ojo [M]
Auge [N]
occhio [M]

arm
bras [M]
tentáculo [M]
Tentakel [M]
tentacolo [M]

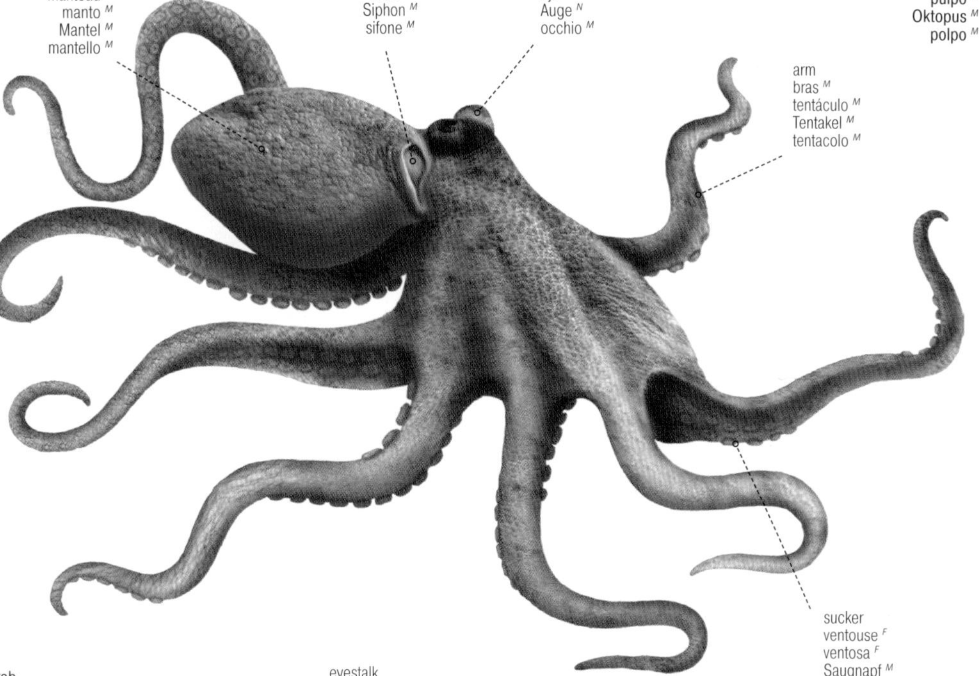

sucker
ventouse [F]
ventosa [F]
Saugnapf [M]
ventosa [F]

crab
crabe [M]
cangrejo [M]
Krabbe [F]
granchio [M]

eyestalk
pédoncule [M] oculaire
pedúnculo [M] ocular
Augenstiel [M]
peduncolo [M] oculare

antenna
antenne [F]
antena [F]
Fühler [M]
antenna [F]

leg
patte [F]
pata [F]
Bein [N]
pereiopode [M]

cheliped
chélipède [M]
pinza [F]
Scherenbein [M]
chelipede [M]

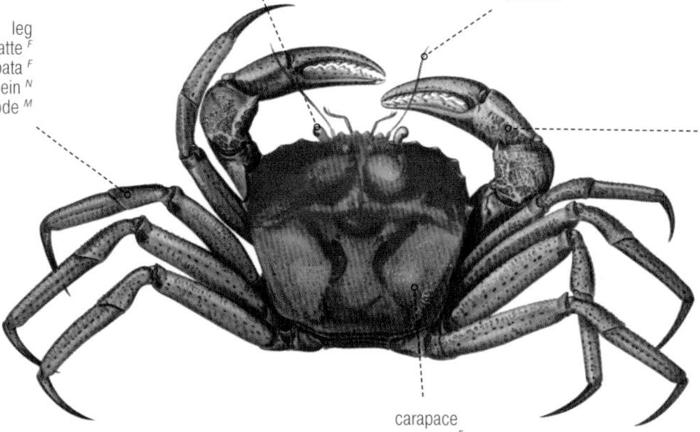

carapace
carapace [F]
caparazón [M]
Carapax [M]
carapace [M]

Eurasian jay
geai M des chênes M
arrendajo M
Eichelhäher M
ghiandaia F eurasiatica

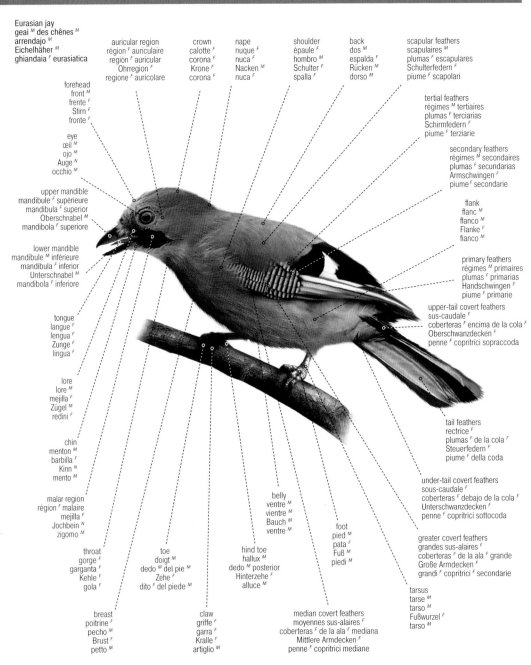

auricular region
région F auriculaire
región F auricular
Ohrregion F
regione F auricolare
crown
calotte F
corona F
Krone F
corona F
nape
nuque F
nuca F
Nacken M
nuca F
shoulder
épaule F
hombro M
Schulter F
spalla F
back
dos M
espalda F
Rücken M
dorso M
scapular feathers
scapulaires M
plumas F escapulares
Schulterfedern F
piume F scapolari
forehead
front M
frente F
Stirn F
fronte F
tertial feathers
régimes M tertiaires
plumas F terciarias
Schirmfedern F
piume F terziarie
eye
œil M
ojo M
Auge N
occhio M
secondary feathers
régimes M secondaires
plumas F secundarias
Armschwingen F
piume F secondarie
upper mandible
mandibule F supérieure
mandíbula F superior
Oberschnabel M
mandibola F superiore
flank
flanc M
flanco M
Flanke F
fianco M
lower mandible
mandibule M inférieure
mandíbula F inferior
Unterschnabel M
mandibola F inferiore
primary feathers
régimes M primaires
plumas F primarias
Handschwingen F
piume F primarie
upper-tail covert feathers
sus-caudale F
coberteras F encima de la cola F
Oberschwanzdecken F
penne F copritrici sopraccoda
tongue
langue F
lengua F
Zunge F
lingua F
lore
lore M
mejilla F
Zügel M
redini F
tail feathers
rectrice F
plumas F de la cola F
Steuerfedern F
piume F della coda
chin
menton M
barbilla F
Kinn N
mento M
under-tail covert feathers
sous-caudale F
coberteras F debajo de la cola F
Unterschwanzdecken F
penne F copritrici sottocoda
malar region
région F malaire
mejilla F
Jochbein N
zigomo M
belly
ventre M
vientre M
Bauch M
ventre M
foot
pied M
pata F
Fuß M
piedi M
greater covert feathers
grandes sus-alaires F
coberteras F de la ala F grande
Große Armdecken F
grandi F copritrici F secondarie
throat
gorge F
garganta F
Kehle F
gola F
toe
doigt M
dedo M del pie M
Zehe F
dito F del piede M
hind toe
hallux M
dedo M posterior
Hinterzehe F
alluce M
tarsus
tarse M
tarso M
Fußwurzel F
tarso M
breast
poitrine F
pecho M
Brust F
petto M
claw
griffe F
garra F
Kralle F
artiglio M
median covert feathers
moyennes sus-alaires F
coberteras F de la ala F mediana
Mittlere Armdecken F
penne F copritrici mediane

Eurasian siskin
tarin [M] des aulnes [M]
lúgano [M]
Erlenzeisig [M]
lucherino [M]

bullfinch
bouvreuil [M] pivoine
camachuelo [M]
Gimpel [M]
ciuffolotto [M]

common swift
martinet [M] noir
vencejo [M] común
Mauersegler [M]
rondone [M]

greater titmouse
mésange [F] charbonnière
herrerillo [M] común
Kohlmeise [F]
cincia [F]

pigeon
pigeon [M]
paloma [F]
Taube [F]
piccione [M]

blue jay
geai [M] bleu
urraca [F] azul
Blauhäher [M]
ghiandaia [F] azzurra

red-backed shrike
pie-grièche [F] écorcheur
alcaudón [M] dorsirrojo
Neuntöter [M]
avèrla [F] piccola

woodpecker
pic [M]
pájaro [M] carpintero
Specht [M]
picchio [M]

hummingbird
colibri [M]
colibri [M]
Kolibri [M]
colibrí [M]

black-capped chickadee
mésange [F] à tête [F] noire
carbonero [M] cabecinegro
Schwarzkopfmeise [F]
capinera [F]

kingfisher
martin-pêcheur [M]
martín pescador [M]
Eisvogel [M]
martin [M] pescatore

cockatiel
calopsitte [F] élégante
cacatúa [F] ninfa [F]
Nymphensittich [M]
calopsitta [F]

barn swallow
hirondelle [F] rustique
golondrina [F] común
Rauchschwalbe [F]
rondine [F]

American goldfinch
chardonneret [M] jaune
jilguero [M] americano
Goldzeisig [M]
lucherino [M] americano

cardinal
cardinal [M]
cardenal [M]
Rotkardinal [M]
cardinale [M]

American robin
merle [M] d'Amérique [F]
mirlo [M] americano
Wanderdrossel [F]
pettirosso [M] americano

American crow
corneille [F] d'Amérique [F]
cuervo [M] americano
Amerikanische Krähe [F]
cornacchia [F] americana

nightingale
rossignol [M]
ruiseñor [M]
Nachtigall [F]
usignolo [M]

thrush
grive [F] vraie
tordo [M]
Drossel [F]
turdide [M]

starling
étourneau [M] sansonnet
estornino [M]
Star [M]
storno [M]

sparrow
moineau [M]
gorrión [M]
Sperling [M]
passero [M]

owl
hibou [M]
búho [M]
Eule [F]
gufo [M]

partridge
perdrix [F]
perdiz [F]
Rebhuhn [N]
pernice [F]

gyrfalcon
faucon [M] gerfaut
halcón [M] gerifalte
Gerfalke [M]
girfalco [M]

stork
cigogne [F]
cigüeña [F]
Storch [M]
cicogna [F]

condor
condor ^{M}
cóndor ^{M}
Kondor ^{M}
condor ^{M}

ruffed grouse
gélinotte ^{F} huppée
perdiz ^{F} martineta copetona
Kragenhuhn ^{N}
tetraone ^{M} dal collare

bald eagle
pygargue ^{M} à tête ^{F} blanche
águila ^{F} calva
Weißkopfseeadler ^{M}
aquila ^{F} calva

rooster
coq ^{M}
gallo ^{M}
Hahn ^{M}
gallo ^{M}

ostrich
autruche ^{F}
avestruz ^{F}
Strauß ^{M}
struzzo ^{M}

peacock
paon ^{M}
pavo ^{M} real
Pfau ^{M}
pavone ^{M}

sharp-tailed grouse
tétras ^{M} à queue ^{F} fine
gallo ^{M} de las praderas ^{F} rabudo
Schweifhuhn ^{N}
pernice ^{F} codaguzza

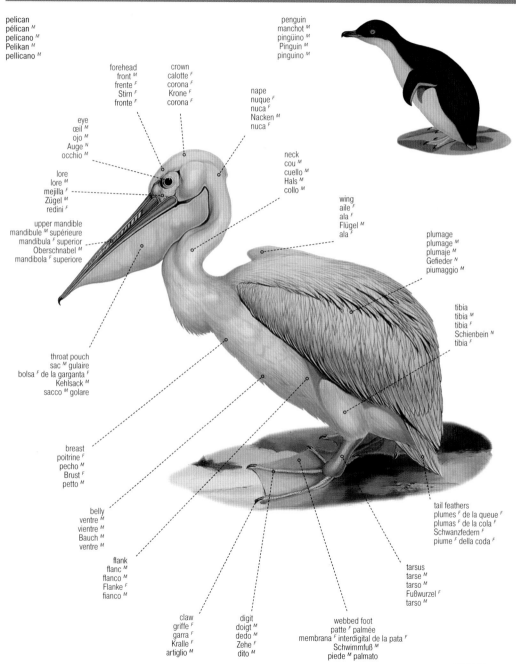

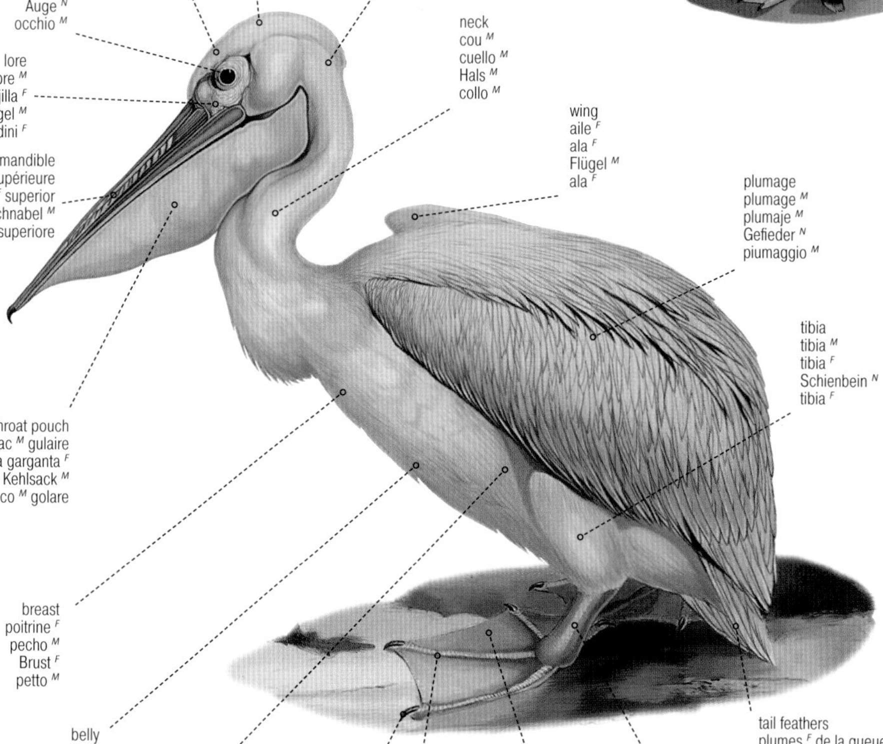
pelican
pélican M
pelícano M
Pelikan M
pellicano M
forehead
front M
frente F
Stirn F
fronte F
crown
calotte F
corona F
Krone F
corona F
nape
nuque F
nuca F
Nacken M
nuca F
eye
œil M
ojo M
Auge N
occhio M
lore
lore M
mejilla F
Zügel M
redini F
neck
cou M
cuello M
Hals M
collo M
wing
aile F
ala F
Flügel M
ala F
upper mandible
mandibule M supérieure
mandíbula F superior
Oberschnabel M
mandibola F superiore
plumage
plumage M
plumaje M
Gefieder N
piumaggio M
tibia
tibia M
tibia F
Schienbein N
tibia F
throat pouch
sac M gulaire
bolsa F de la garganta F
Kehlsack M
sacco M golare
breast
poitrine F
pecho M
Brust F
petto M
belly
ventre M
vientre M
Bauch M
ventre M
tail feathers
plumes F de la queue F
plumas F de la cola F
Schwanzfedern F
piume F della coda F
flank
flanc M
flanco M
Flanke F
fianco M
tarsus
tarse M
tarso M
Fußwurzel F
tarso M
claw
griffe F
garra F
Kralle F
artiglio M
digit
doigt M
dedo M
Zehe F
dito M
webbed foot
patte F palmée
membrana F interdigital de la pata F
Schwimmfuß M
piede M palmato

penguin
manchot M
pingüino M
Pinguin M
pinguino M

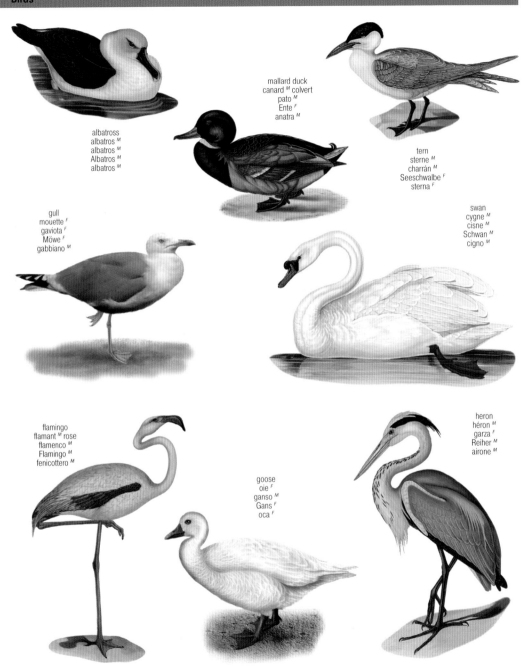

albatross
albatros [M]
albatros [M]
Albatros [M]
albatros [M]

mallard duck
canard [M] colvert
pato [M]
Ente [F]
anatra [M]

tern
sterne [M]
charrán [M]
Seeschwalbe [F]
sterna [F]

gull
mouette [F]
gaviota [F]
Möwe [F]
gabbiano [M]

swan
cygne [M]
cisne [M]
Schwan [M]
cigno [M]

flamingo
flamant [M] rose
flamenco [M]
Flamingo [M]
fenicottero [M]

goose
oie [F]
ganso [M]
Gans [F]
oca [F]

heron
héron [M]
garza [F]
Reiher [M]
airone [M]

Arachnids

Arachnides [M] | Arácnidos [M] | Spinnentiere [N] | Aracnidi [M]

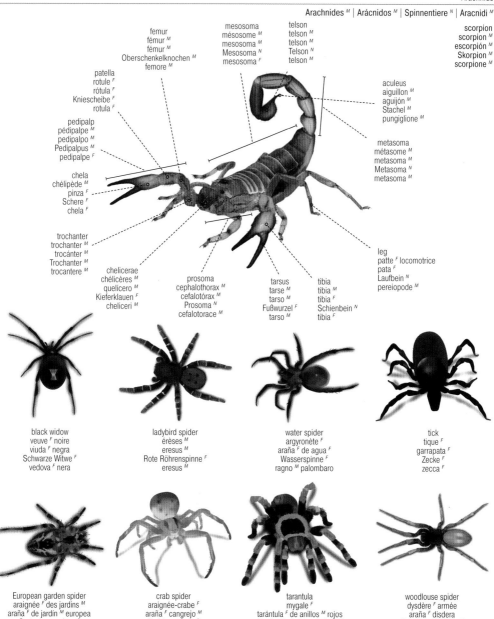

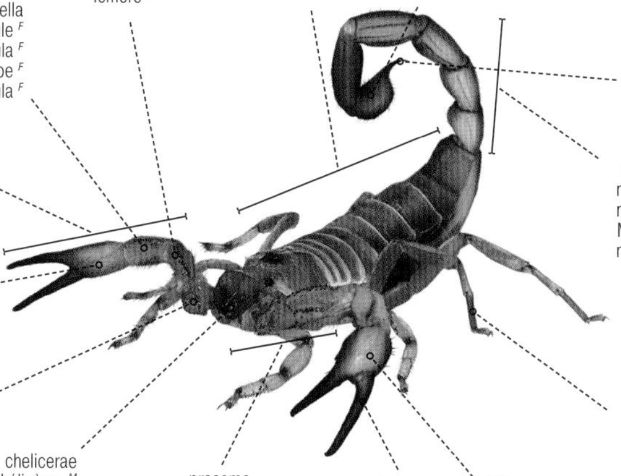
scorpion
scorpion [M]
escorpión [M]
Skorpion [M]
scorpione [M]
femur
fémur [M]
fémur [M]
Oberschenkelknochen [M]
femore [M]
mesosoma
mésosome [M]
mesosoma [M]
Mesosoma [N]
mesosoma [F]
telson
telson [M]
telson [M]
Telson [N]
telson [M]
patella
rotule [F]
rótula [F]
Kniescheibe [F]
rotula [F]
aculeus
aiguillon [M]
aguijón [M]
Stachel [M]
pungiglione [M]
pedipalp
pédipalpe [M]
pedipalpo [M]
Pedipalpus [M]
pedipalpe [F]
metasoma
métasome [M]
metasoma [M]
Metasoma [N]
metasoma [M]
chela
chélipède [M]
pinza [F]
Schere [F]
chela [F]
trochanter
trochanter [M]
trocánter [M]
Trochanter [M]
trocantere [M]
leg
patte [F] locomotrice
pata [F]
Laufbein [N]
pereiopode [M]
chelicerae
chélicères [M]
quelícero [M]
Kieferklauen [F]
cheliceri [M]
prosoma
cephalothorax [M]
cefalotórax [M]
Prosoma [N]
cefalotorace [M]
tarsus
tarse [M]
tarso [M]
Fußwurzel [F]
tarso [M]
tibia
tibia [M]
tibia [F]
Schienbein [N]
tibia [F]

black widow
veuve [F] noire
viuda [F] negra
Schwarze Witwe [F]
vedova [F] nera

ladybird spider
érèses [M]
eresus [M]
Rote Röhrenspinne [F]
eresus [M]

water spider
argyronète [F]
araña [F] de agua [F]
Wasserspinne [F]
ragno [M] palombaro

tick
tique [F]
garrapata [F]
Zecke [F]
zecca [F]

European garden spider
araignée [F] des jardins [M]
araña [F] de jardín [M] europea
Gartenkreuzspinne [F]
ragno [M] crociato

crab spider
araignée-crabe [F]
araña [F] cangrejo [M]
Krabbenspinne [F]
ragno-granchio [M]

tarantula
mygale [F]
tarántula [F] de anillos [M] rojos
Mexikanische Vogelspinne [F]
tarantola [F]

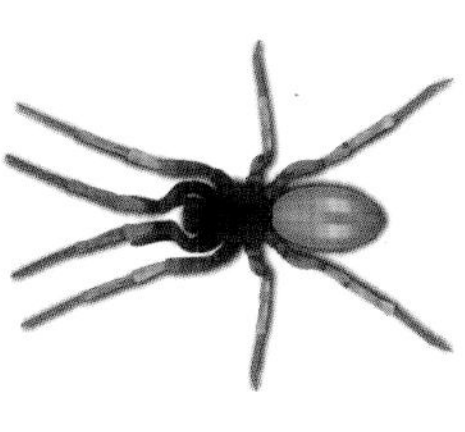

woodlouse spider
dysdère [F] armée
araña [F] disdera
Sechsaugenspinne [F]
Dysdera [F] crocata

Beetles

Coléoptères ^{M} | Escarabajos ^{M} | Käfer ^{M} | Scarabei ^{M}

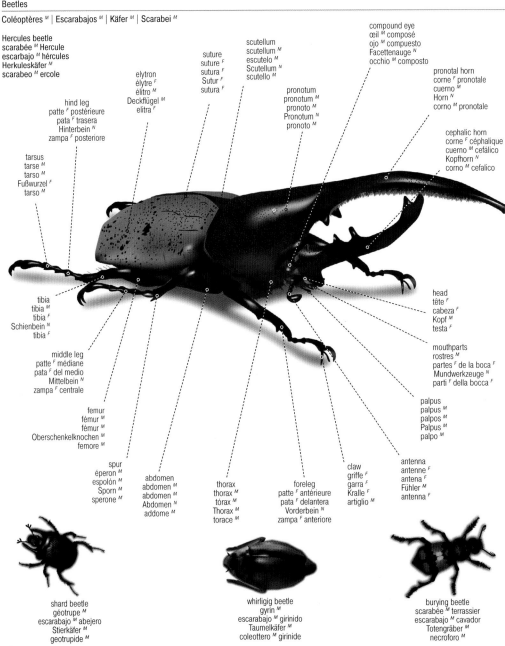

Hercules beetle
scarabée ^{M} Hercule
escarbajo ^{M} hércules
Herkuleskäfer ^{M}
scarabeo ^{M} ercole

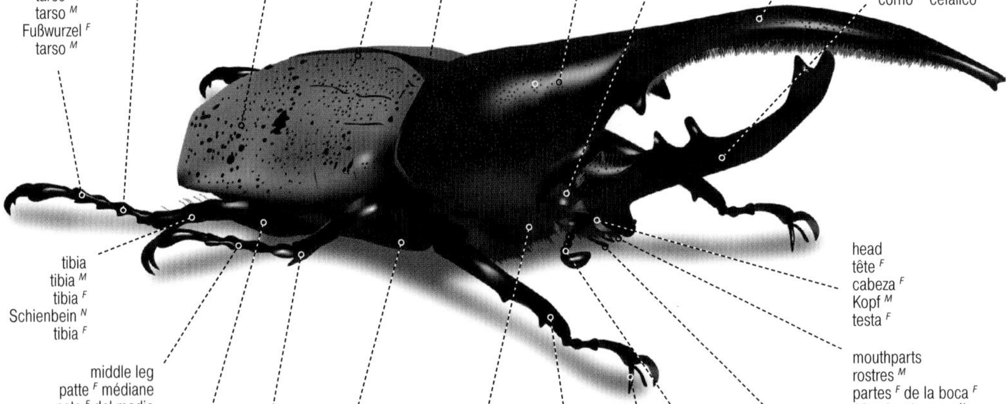
compound eye
œil ^{M} composé
ojo ^{M} compuesto
Facettenauge ^{N}
occhio ^{M} composto
scutellum
scutellum ^{M}
escutelo ^{M}
Scutellum ^{N}
scutello ^{M}
suture
suture ^{F}
sutura ^{F}
Sutur ^{F}
sutura ^{F}
elytron
élytre ^{F}
élitro ^{M}
Deckflügel ^{M}
elitra ^{F}
hind leg
patte ^{F} postérieure
pata ^{F} trasera
Hinterbein ^{N}
zampa ^{F} posteriore
tarsus
tarse ^{M}
tarso ^{M}
Fußwurzel ^{F}
tarso ^{M}
pronotum
pronotum ^{M}
pronoto ^{M}
Pronotum ^{N}
pronoto ^{M}
pronotal horn
corne ^{F} pronotale
cuerno ^{M}
Horn ^{N}
corno ^{M} pronotale
cephalic horn
corne ^{F} céphalique
cuerno ^{M} cefálico
Kopfhorn ^{N}
corno ^{M} cefalico
tibia
tibia ^{M}
tibia ^{F}
Schienbein ^{N}
tibia ^{F}
head
tête ^{F}
cabeza ^{F}
Kopf ^{M}
testa ^{F}
mouthparts
rostres ^{M}
partes ^{F} de la boca ^{F}
Mundwerkzeuge ^{N}
parti ^{F} della bocca ^{F}
middle leg
patte ^{F} médiane
pata ^{F} del medio
Mittelbein ^{N}
zampa ^{F} centrale
palpus
palpus ^{M}
palpos ^{M}
Palpus ^{M}
palpo ^{M}
femur
fémur ^{M}
fémur ^{M}
Oberschenkelknochen ^{M}
femore ^{M}
spur
éperon ^{M}
espolón ^{M}
Sporn ^{M}
sperone ^{M}
abdomen
abdomen ^{M}
abdomen ^{M}
Abdomen ^{N}
addome ^{M}
thorax
thorax ^{M}
tórax ^{M}
Thorax ^{M}
torace ^{M}
foreleg
patte ^{F} antérieure
pata ^{F} delantera
Vorderbein ^{N}
zampa ^{F} anteriore
claw
griffe ^{F}
garra ^{F}
Kralle ^{F}
artiglio ^{M}
antenna
antenne ^{F}
antena ^{F}
Fühler ^{M}
antenna ^{F}

shard beetle
géotrupe ^{M}
escarabajo ^{M} abejero
Stierkäfer ^{M}
geotrupide ^{M}

whirligig beetle
gyrin ^{M}
escarabajo ^{M} girínido
Taumelkäfer ^{M}
coleottero ^{M} girinide

burying beetle
scarabée ^{M} terrassier
escarabajo ^{M} cavador
Totengräber ^{M}
necroforo ^{M}

Carabus problematicus (Lat.)
carabe [M] problématique
Carabus problematicus
Blauvioletter Waldlaufkäfer [M]
carabus [M] problematicus

furniture beetle
anobie [M] ponctué
carcoma [F]
Gemeiner Nagekäfter [M]
tarlo [M] del legno [M]

Sagra buqueti (Lat.)
sagre de buquet [M]
Sagra buqueti
Froschkäfer [M]
sagra [F] buqueti

black vine weevil
otiorhynque [M] de la vigne [F]
gorgojo [M] negro de la vid [F]
Gefurchter Dickmaulrüssler [M]
oziorrinco [M] della vite [F]

cockchafer
hanneton [M] commun
escarabajo [M] sanjuanero
Maikäfer [M]
maggiolino [M]

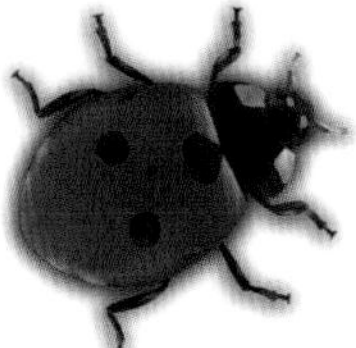

ladybug
coccinelle [F]
mariquita [F]
Marienkäfer [M]
coccinella [F]

thick-legged flower beetle
œdémère [M] noble
Oedemera nobilis
Grüner Scheinbockkäfer [M]
edemera [F] nobile

rhinoceros beetle
scarabée-rhinocéros [M]
escarabajo [M] rinoceronte [M] europeo
Nashornkäfer [M]
blatta [F] rinoceronte [F] europea

stag beetle
lucane [M] cerf-volant [M]
ciervo [M] volante
Hirschkäfer [M]
cervo [M] volante

Colorado potato beetle
doryphore [M] de la pomme [F] de terre [F]
escarabajo [M] de la patata [F]
Kartoffelkäfer [M]
dorifora [F] della patata

rose chafer
hanneton [M] des roses
Cetonia aurata
Goldglänzender Rosenkäfer [M]
cetonia [F] aurata

goliath beetle
goliath [M]
escarabajo [M] Goliat
Goliathkäfer [M]
scarafaggio [M] Goliath

larch ladybug
aphidecta obliterata [F]
Aphidecta obliterata
Nadelbaum-Marienkäfer [M]
Aphidecta [F] obliterata

dung beetle
stercoraire [M]
escarabajo [M] pelotero
Heiliger Pillendreher [M]
scarabeo [M] stercorario

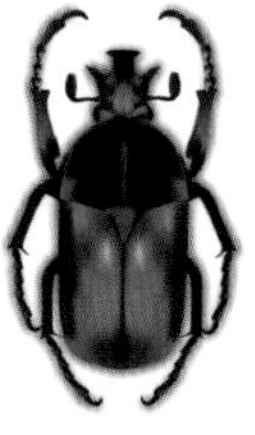

flower beetle
cétoine [M]
escarabajo [M] de las flores [F]
Grüner Blumenkäfer [M]
cetoniino [M]

golden scarab beetle
scarabée [M] doré
escarabajo [M] dorado
Goldkäfer [M]
chrysina resplendens [F]

Butterflies and moths

Papillons M diurnes et nocturnes | Mariposas F y polillas F | Schmetterlinge M und Falter M | Farfalle F e falene F

swallowtail caterpillar
chenille F de papillon M porte-queue
gusano M de mariposa F macaón M
Schwalbenschwanz-Raupe F
bruco M di macaone M

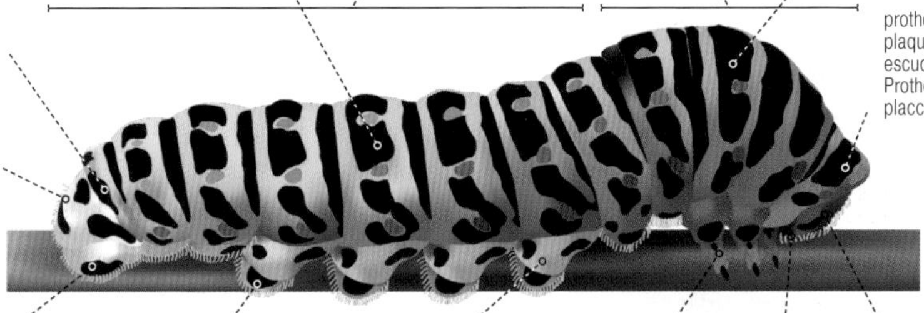

abdominal segment
segment M abdominal
segmento M abdominal
Bauchsegment N
segmento M addominale
abdomen
abdomen M
abdomen M
Bauch M
addome M
thorax
thorax M
tórax M
Thorax M
torace M
thoracic segment
segment M thoracique
segmento M torácico
Thoraxsegment N
segmento M toracico
subdorsal line
ligne F subdorsale
línea F subdorsal
Subdorsallinie F
linea F subdorsale
prothoracic shield
plaque F prothoracique
escudo M protorácico
Prothoraxschild M
placca F protoracica
anal plate
plaque F anale
placa F anal
Analschild M
placca F anale
anal proleg
fausse patte F anale
propata F anal
Nachschieber M
regione F anale
crochet
crochet M
patas F
Häkchen N
uncino M
proleg
fausse patte F
propatas F
Bauchbein N
pseudozampa F
true leg
vraie patte F
pata F verdadera
Bein N
zampa F
mandible
mandibule F
mandíbula F
Mandibel F
mandibola F
head
tête F
cabeza F
Kopf M
testa F

swallowtail chrysalis
chrysalide F de papillon M porte-queue
crisálida F de mariposa F macaón M
Schwalbenschwanz-Puppe F
crisalide F di macaone M

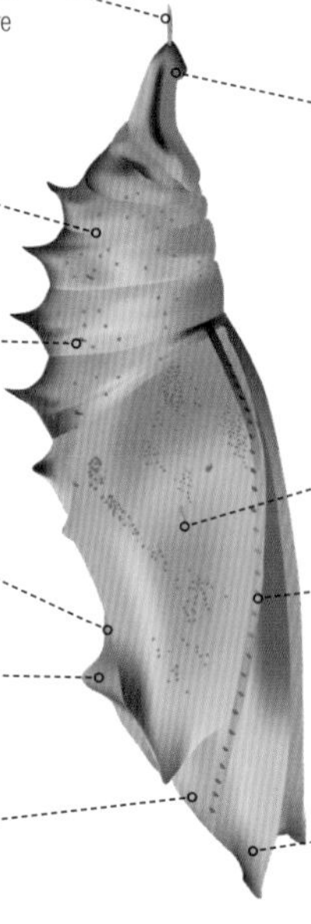

cremastral hook
crochet M du crémaster M
gancho M cremáster M
Häkchen N am Cremaster M
uncino M posteriore
cremaster
crémaster M
cremáster M
Cremaster M
cremastere M
abdomen
abdomen M
abdomen M
Bauch M
addome M
spiracle
stigmate M
espiráculo M
Atemloch N
sfiatatoio M
wing
aile F
ala F
Flügel M
ala F
metathorax
métathorax M
metatórax M
Hinterbrust F
metatorace M
antenna
antenne F
antena F
Fühler M
antenna F
mesothorax
mesothorax M
mesotórax M
Mittelbrust F
mesotorace M
prothorax
prothorax M
protórax M
Vorderbrust F
protorace M
head
tête F
cabeza F
Kopf M
testa F

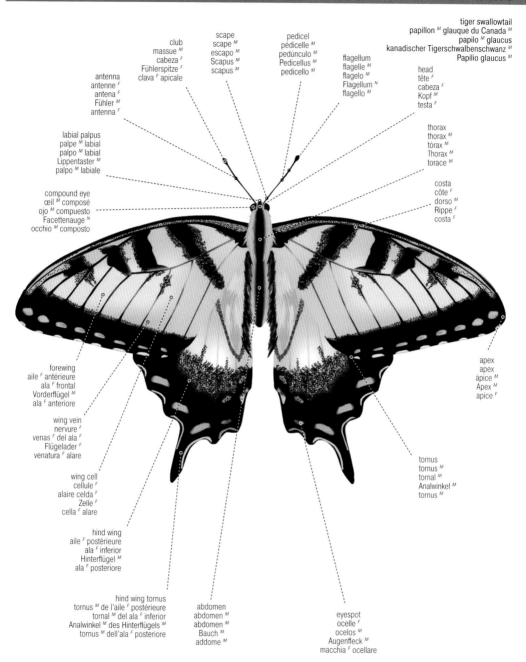

tiger swallowtail
papillon [M] glauque du Canada [M]
papilo [M] glaucus
kanadischer Tigerschwalbenschwanz [M]
Papilio glaucus [M]
club
massue [M]
cabeza [F]
Fühlerspitze [F]
clava [F] apicale
scape
scape [M]
escapo [M]
Scapus [M]
scapus [M]
pedicel
pédicelle [M]
pedúnculo [M]
Pedicellus [M]
pedicello [M]
flagellum
flagelle [M]
flagelo [M]
Flagellum [N]
flagello [M]
antenna
antenne [F]
antena [F]
Fühler [M]
antenna [F]
head
tête [F]
cabeza [F]
Kopf [M]
testa [F]
labial palpus
palpe [M] labial
palpo [M] labial
Lippentaster [M]
palpo [M] labiale
thorax
thorax [M]
tórax [M]
Thorax [M]
torace [M]
compound eye
œil [M] composé
ojo [M] compuesto
Facettenauge [N]
occhio [M] composto
costa
côte [F]
dorso [M]
Rippe [F]
costa [F]
forewing
aile [F] antérieure
ala [F] frontal
Vorderflügel [M]
ala [F] anteriore
apex
apex
ápice [M]
Apex [M]
apice [F]
wing vein
nervure [F]
venas [F] del ala [F]
Flügelader [F]
venatura [F] alare
tornus
tornus [M]
tornal [M]
Analwinkel [M]
tornus [M]
wing cell
cellule [F]
alaire celda [F]
Zelle [F]
cella [F] alare
hind wing
aile [F] postérieure
ala [F] inferior
Hinterflügel [M]
ala [F] posteriore
hind wing tornus
tornus [M] de l'aile [F] postérieure
tornal [M] del ala [F] inferior
Analwinkel [M] des Hinterflügels [M]
tornus [M] dell'ala [F] posteriore
abdomen
abdomen [M]
abdomen [M]
Bauch [M]
addome [M]
eyespot
ocelle [F]
ocelos [M]
Augenfleck [M]
macchia [F] ocellare

Adonis blue
azuré [M] bleu céleste
mariposa [F] niña [M] celeste
Himmelblauer Bläuling [M]
adone [M] blu

clothes moth
mite [F]
polilla [F]
Kleidermotte [F]
tarma [F]

lappet moth
papillon [M] à épaulettes [F]
procesionaria [F] del pino [M]
Kiefernspinner [M]
bombice [M] del pino [M]

cabbage white
piéride [F] du chou [M]
blanquita de la col [F]
Kleiner Kohlweißling [M]
cavolaia [F] minore

silkmoth
bombyx [M] du mûrier [M]
gusano [M] de seda [F]
Seidenspinner [M]
bombice [M] del gelso [M]

monarch butterfly
monarque [M]
mariposa [F] monarca
Monarchfalter [M]
monarca [F]

buff-tip
bucéphale [F]
mariposa [F] pájaro [M] luna [F]
Mondvogel [M]
phalera buchefala [F]

scarce swallowtail
flambé [M]
podalirio [M]
Segelfalter [M]
podalirio [M]

brimstone
citron [M]
popilla [F] limonera
Zitronenfalter [M]
cedronella [F]

Apollo
Apollon ^{M}
apolo ^{F}
Apollo ^{M}
Apollo ^{M}

luna moth
papillon ^{M} lune
Actias luna
Luna-Motte ^{F}
farfalla ^{F} luna ^{F}

black-veined white
piéride ^{F} de l'aubépine ^{F}
blanca ^{F} del majuelo ^{M}
Baumweißling ^{M}
Pieride ^{M} del biancospino ^{M}

blue morpho
morpho ^{M} bleu
mariposa ^{F} morpho azul
Blauer Morphofalter ^{M}
morpho ^{M} blu

Brahmin moth
brahmaea wallichii ^{M}
Brahmaea wallichii
Brahmaea wallichii
brahmaea wallichii ^{F}

divana diva
divana diva ^{F}
divana ^{F}
Divana diva
Divana ^{F} diva

purple emperor
grand Mars changeant ^{M}
Apatura iris ^{F}
Großer Schillerfalter ^{M}
farfalla ^{F} iride

Hercules moth
coscinocera ^{F} hercules
mariposa ^{F} hércules
Herkulesspinner ^{M}
falena ^{F} Ercole ^{M}

spear-marked black moth
géomètre ^{M} noir du bouleau ^{M}
Rheumaptera hastata
Großer Speerspanner ^{M}
rheumaptera ^{F} hastata

Wasps and wasp-like insects

Guêpes F et insectes M similaires | Avispas F e insectos M parecidos | Wespen F und Hautflügler M | Vespe F e insetti M simili

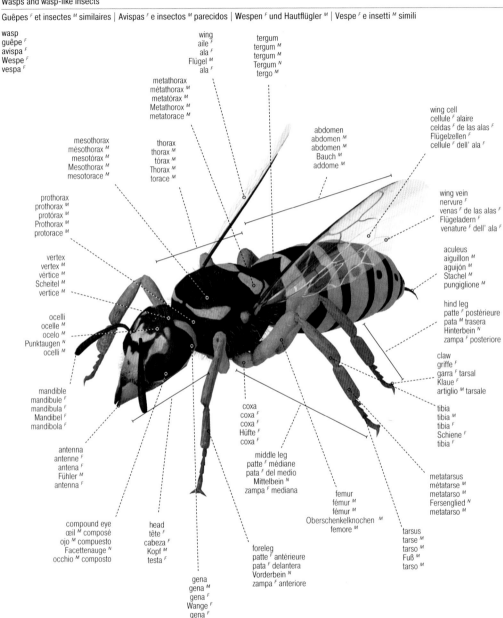

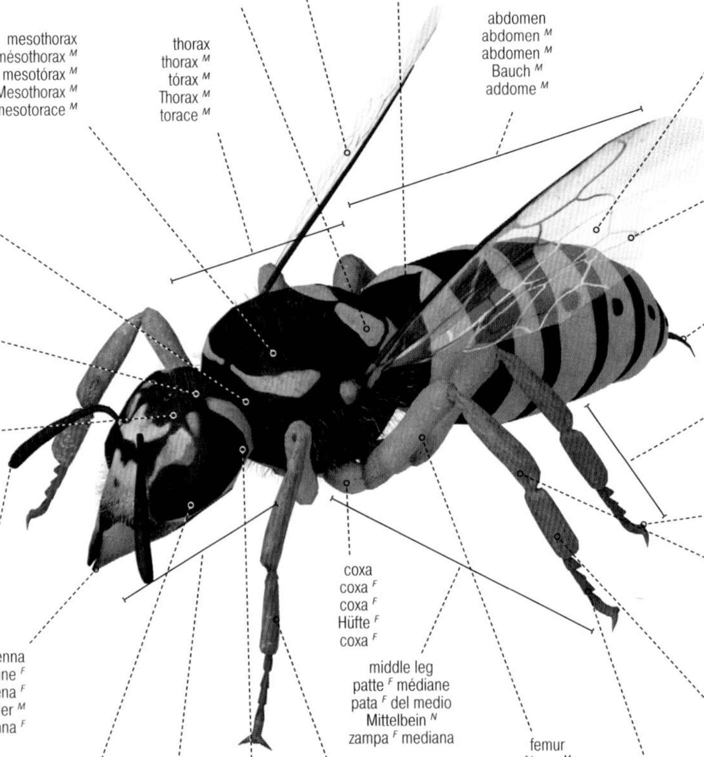
wasp
guêpe F
avispa F
Wespe F
vespa F
wing
aile F
ala F
Flügel M
ala F
tergum
tergum M
tergum M
Tergum N
tergo M
metathorax
métathorax M
metatórax M
Metathorax M
metatorace M
wing cell
cellule F alaire
celdas F de las alas F
Flügelzellen F
cellule F dell' ala F
abdomen
abdomen M
abdomen M
Bauch M
addome M
mesothorax
mésothorax M
mesotórax M
Mesothorax M
mesotorace M
thorax
thorax M
tórax M
Thorax M
torace M
wing vein
nervure F
venas F de las alas F
Flügeladern F
venature F dell' ala F
prothorax
prothorax M
protórax M
Prothorax M
protorace M
aculeus
aiguillon M
aguijón M
Stachel M
pungiglione M
vertex
vertex M
vértice M
Scheitel M
vertice M
hind leg
patte F postérieure
pata M trasera
Hinterbein N
zampa F posteriore
ocelli
ocelle M
ocelo M
Punktaugen N
ocelli M
claw
griffe F
garra F tarsal
Klaue F
artiglio M tarsale
mandible
mandibule F
mandíbula F
Mandibel F
mandibola F
tibia
tibia M
tibia F
Schiene F
tibia F
coxa
coxa F
coxa F
Hüfte F
coxa F
antenna
antenne F
antena F
Fühler M
antenna F
middle leg
patte F médiane
pata F del medio
Mittelbein N
zampa F mediana
metatarsus
métatarse M
metatarso M
Fersenglied N
metatarso M
femur
fémur M
fémur M
Oberschenkelknochen M
femore M
compound eye
œil M composé
ojo M compuesto
Facettenauge N
occhio M composto
head
tête F
cabeza F
Kopf M
testa F
tarsus
tarse M
tarso M
Fuß M
tarso M
foreleg
patte F antérieure
pata F delantera
Vorderbein N
zampa F anteriore
gena
gena M
gena F
Wange F
gena F

ant
fourmi ^{F}
hormiga ^{F}
Ameise ^{F}
formica ^{F}

buff-tailed bumblebee
bourdon ^{M} terrestre
abejorro ^{M} común
Dunkle Erdhummel ^{F}
bombo ^{M} terrestre

hornet
frelon ^{M}
avispón ^{M}
Hornisse ^{F}
calabrone ^{M}

red wood ant
fourmi ^{F} rousse
hormiga ^{F} roja de la madera ^{F}
Rote Waldameise ^{F}
formica ^{F} rossa

honey bee
abeille ^{F} domestique
abeja ^{F} europea
Honigbiene ^{F}
ape ^{F} europea

mud dauber
guêpe ^{F} maçonneuse
avispa ^{F} alfarera
Sceliphron ^{F}
vespa ^{F} fango ^{M}

True flies

Diptères ^{M} | Moscas ^{F} verdaderas | Zweiflügler ^{M} | Ditteri ^{M}

horsefly
taon ^{M}
tábano ^{M}
Bremse ^{F}
tafano ^{M}

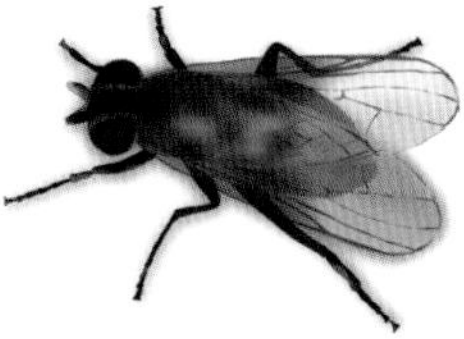

common housefly
mouche ^{F} domestique
mosca ^{F}
Stubenfliege ^{F}
mosca ^{F} comune

flesh fly
mouche ^{F} à viande ^{F}
moscarda ^{F} de la carne ^{F}
Fleischfliege ^{F}
mosca ^{F} carnaria

little housefly
petite mouche ^{F} domestique
mosca ^{F} doméstica
Kleine Stubenfliege ^{F}
piccola mosca ^{F} domestica

blackfly
simulie ^{F}
mosca ^{F} negra
Kriebelmücke ^{F}
simulide ^{M}

blowfly
calliphore ^{F}
califórido ^{M}
Schmeißfliege ^{F}
calliforide ^{F}

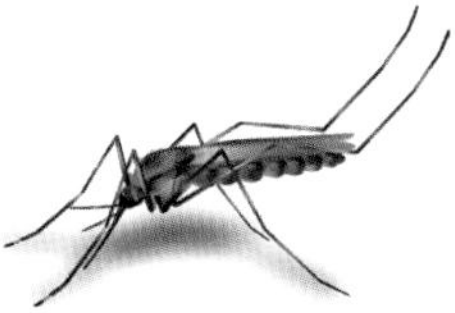

mosquito
maringouin ^{M}
mosquito ^{M}
Stechmücke ^{F}
zanzara ^{F}

tsetse fly
mouche ^{F} tsé-tsé
mosca ^{F} tse-tse
Tsetsefliege ^{F}
mosca ^{F} tse-tse

Neoptera

Néoptères M | Neópteros M | Neuflügler M | Neotteri M

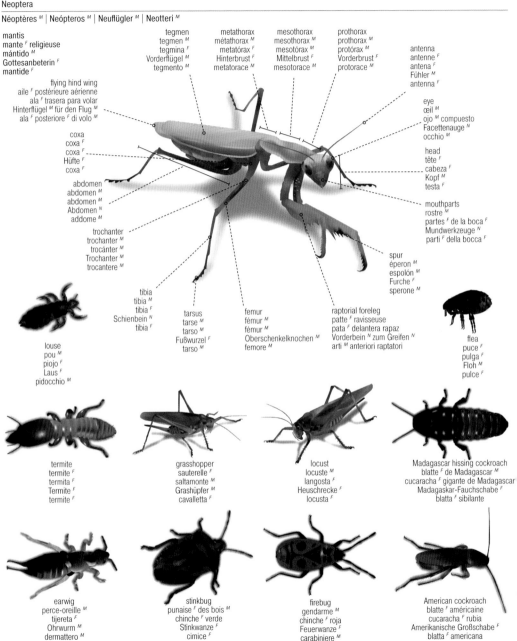

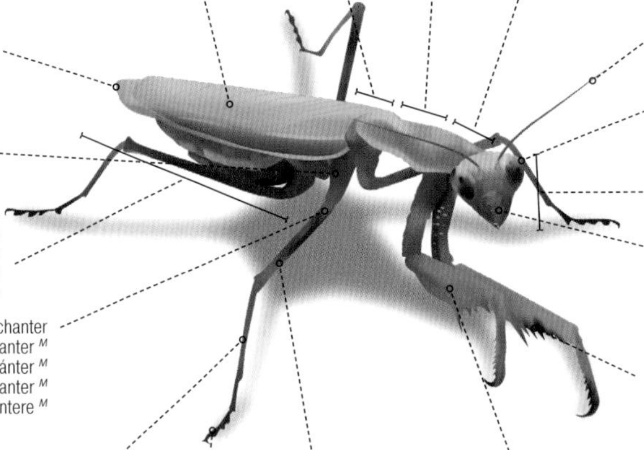
mantis
mante F religieuse
mántido M
Gottesanbeterin F
mantide F

tegmen
tegmen M
tegmina F
Vorderflügel M
tegmento M

metathorax
métathorax M
metatórax F
Hinterbrust F
metatorace M

mesothorax
mesothorax M
mesotórax M
Mittelbrust F
mesotorace M

prothorax
prothorax M
protórax M
Vorderbrust F
protorace M

antenna
antenne F
antena F
Fühler M
antenna F

flying hind wing
aile F postérieure aérienne
ala F trasera para volar
Hinterflügel M für den Flug M
ala F posteriore F di volo M

eye
œil M
ojo M compuesto
Facettenauge N
occhio M

coxa
coxa F
coxa F
Hüfte F
coxa F

head
tête F
cabeza F
Kopf M
testa F

abdomen
abdomen M
abdomen M
Abdomen N
addome M

mouthparts
rostre M
partes F de la boca F
Mundwerkzeuge N
parti F della bocca F

trochanter
trochanter M
trocánter M
Trochanter M
trocantere M

spur
éperon M
espolón M
Furche F
sperone M

tibia
tibia M
tibia F
Schienbein N
tibia F

tarsus
tarse M
tarso M
Fußwurzel F
tarso M

femur
fémur M
fémur M
Oberschenkelknochen M
femore M

raptorial foreleg
patte F ravisseuse
pata F delantera rapaz
Vorderbein N zum Greifen N
arti M anteriori raptatori

louse
pou M
piojo F
Laus F
pidocchio M

flea
puce F
pulga F
Floh M
pulce F

termite
termite F
termita F
Termite F
termite F

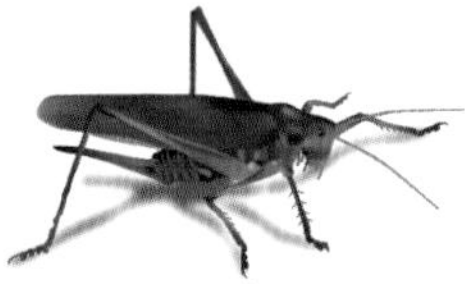

grasshopper
sauterelle F
saltamonte M
Grashüpfer M
cavalletta F

locust
locuste M
langosta F
Heuschrecke F
locusta F

Madagascar hissing cockroach
blatte F de Madagascar M
cucaracha F gigante de Madagascar
Madagaskar-Fauchschabe F
blatta F sibilante

earwig
perce-oreille M
tijereta F
Ohrwurm M
dermattero M

stinkbug
punaise F des bois M
chinche F verde
Stinkwanze F
cimice F

firebug
gendarme M
chinche F roja
Feuerwanze F
carabiniere M

American cockroach
blatte F américaine
cucaracha F rubia
Amerikanische Großschabe F
blatta F americana

Odonata

Odonates [M] | Odonatos [M] | Libellen [F] | Odonati [M]

dragonfly
libellule [F]
libélula [F]
Libelle [F]
libellula [F]

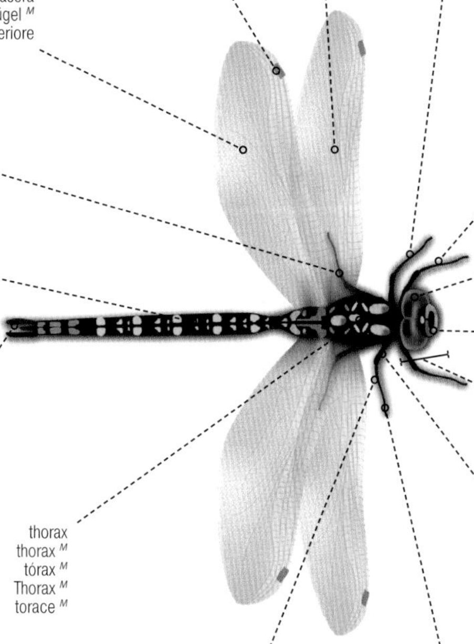
stigma
stigma M
pterostigma M
Flügelmal N
stigma M
forewing
aile F antérieure
ala F delantera
Vorderflügel M
ala F anteriore
middle leg
patte F médiane
pata F del medio
Mittelbein N
zampa F centrale
hind wing
aile F postérieure
ala F trasera
Hinterflügel M
ala F posteriore
foreleg
patte F avant
pata F delantera
Vorderbein N
zampa F anteriore
hind leg
patte F arrière
pata F trasera
Hinterbein N
zampa F posteriore
eye
œil M
ojo M compuesto
Facettenauge N
occhio M
abdomen
abdomen M
abdomen M segmentado
Segmentiertes Abdomen N
addome M
frons
front M
frente F
Stirn F
fronte F
terminal appendages
appendices M anaux
apéndice M abdominal
Hinterleibsanhänge M
appendici F terminali
head
tête F
cabeza F
Kopf M
testa F
thorax
thorax M
tórax M
Thorax M
torace M
femur
fémur M
fémur M
Schenkel M
femore M
tibia
tibia M
tibia F
Beinschiene F
tibia F
tarsus
tarse M
tarso M
Fuß M
tarso M

Worms and worm-like insects

Vers [M] et insectes [M] similaires | Gusanos [M] e insectos [M] similares | Würmer [M] und Tausendfüßler [M] | Vermi [M] e insetti [M] simili

millipede
diplopode [M]
milpiés [M]
Tausendfüßler [M]
millepiedi [M]

earthworm
ver de terre [M]
lombríz [F] de tierra [F]
Regenwurm [M]
lombrico [M]

plant cell
célula ^{F} vegetal
cellule ^{F} végétale
Pflanzenzelle ^{F}
cellula ^{F} vegetale

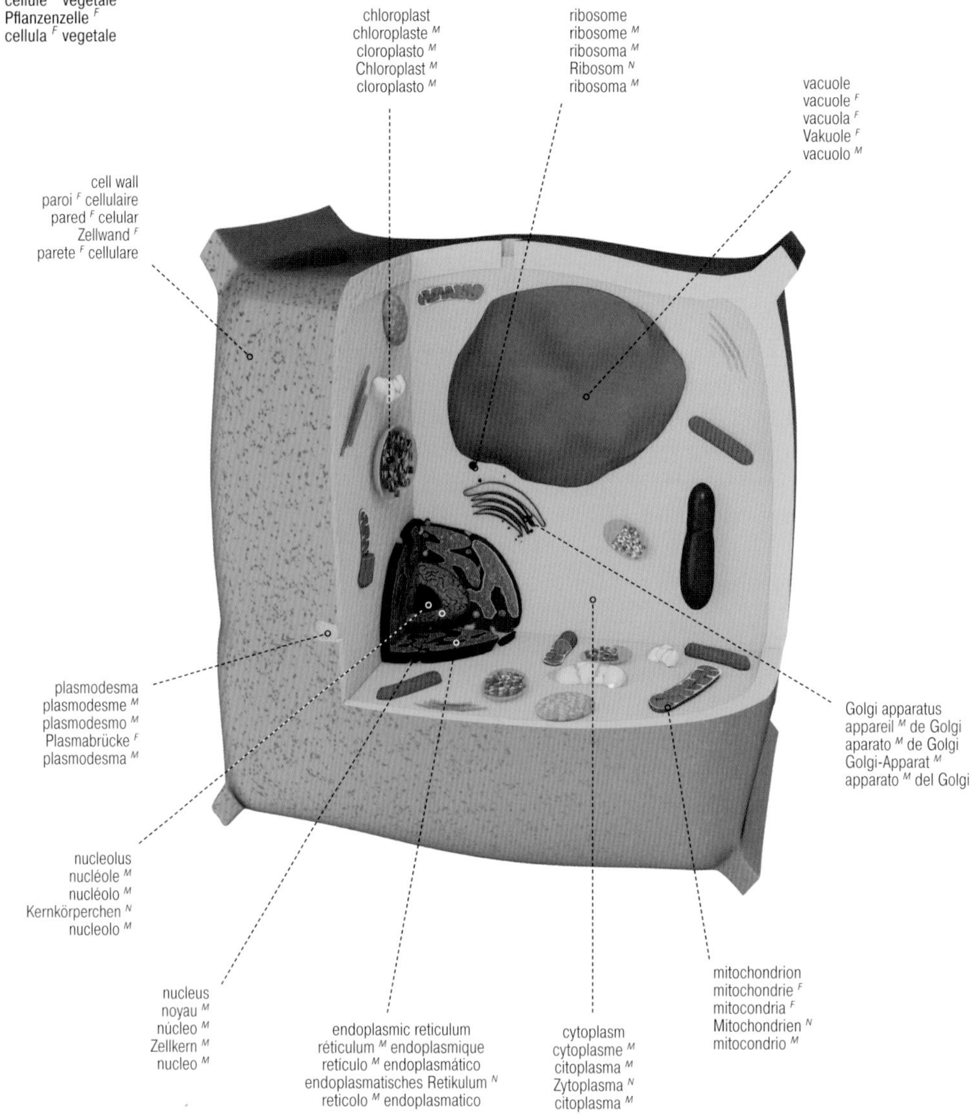
chloroplast
chloroplaste M
cloroplasto M
Chloroplast M
cloroplasto M
ribosome
ribosome M
ribosoma M
Ribosom N
ribosoma M
vacuole
vacuole F
vacuola F
Vakuole F
vacuolo M
cell wall
paroi F cellulaire
pared F celular
Zellwand F
parete F cellulare
plasmodesma
plasmodesme M
plasmodesmo M
Plasmabrücke F
plasmodesma M
Golgi apparatus
appareil M de Golgi
aparato M de Golgi
Golgi-Apparat M
apparato M del Golgi
nucleolus
nucléole M
nucléolo M
Kernkörperchen N
nucleolo M
mitochondrion
mitochondrie F
mitocondria F
Mitochondrien N
mitocondrio M
nucleus
noyau M
núcleo M
Zellkern M
nucleo M
endoplasmic reticulum
réticulum M endoplasmique
retículo M endoplasmático
endoplasmatisches Retikulum N
reticolo M endoplasmatico
cytoplasm
cytoplasme M
citoplasma M
Zytoplasma N
citoplasma M

coffee
caféier M
café M
Kaffee M
caffè M

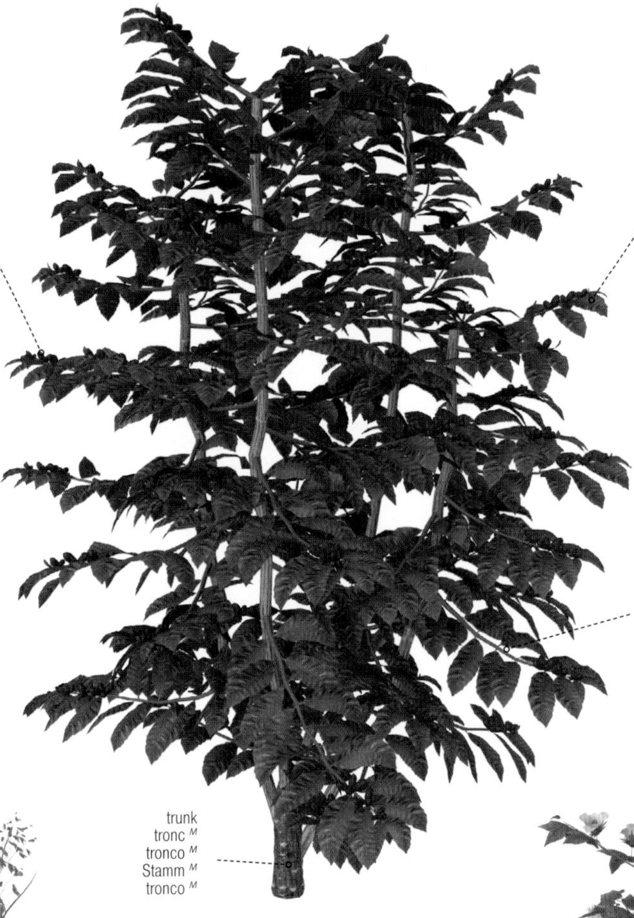
coffee bean
grain M de café M
grano M de café M
Kaffeebohne F
chicco M di caffé M
leaf
feuille F
hoja F
Blatt N
foglia F
branch
branche F
rama F
Ast M
ramo M
trunk
tronc M
tronco M
Stamm M
tronco M

oat
avoine M
avena F
Hafer M
avena F

lavender
lavande F
lavanda F
Lavendel M
lavanda F

cotton
coton M
algodón M
Baumwolle F
cotone M

grape
raisin M
uva F
Weintraube F
vite F

vine shoot
sarment M
retoño M de la vit F
Weinranke F
sarmento M
fruit
tige F
fruta F
Frucht F
frutto M
leaf
feuille F
hoja F
Blatt N
foglia F
trunk
tronc M
tronco M
Stamm M
tronco M
support
tuteur M
soporte M
Spalierstange F
supporto M

sunflower
tournesol M
girasol M
Sonnenblume F
girasole M

tea
théier M
té M
Tee M
té M

soybean
soja M
soja F
Sojabohne F
soia F

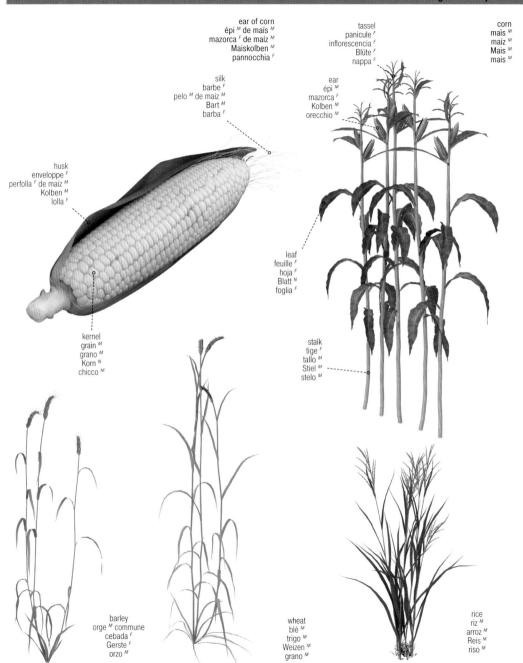

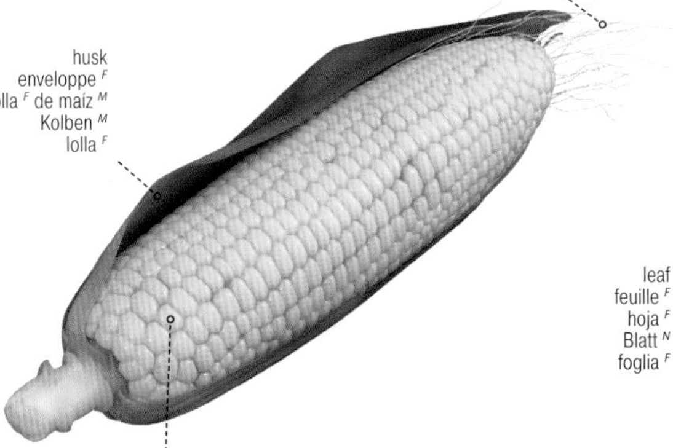
ear of corn
épi [M] de maïs [M]
mazorca [F] de maíz [M]
Maiskolben [M]
pannocchia [F]
silk
barbe [F]
pelo [M] de maíz [M]
Bart [M]
barba [F]
husk
enveloppe [F]
perfolla [F] de maíz [M]
Kolben [M]
lolla [F]
kernel
grain [M]
grano [M]
Korn [N]
chicco [M]

tassel
panicule [F]
inflorescencia [F]
Blüte [F]
nappa [F]
ear
épi [M]
mazorca [F]
Kolben [M]
orecchio [M]
leaf
feuille [F]
hoja [F]
Blatt [N]
foglia [F]
stalk
tige [F]
tallo [M]
Stiel [M]
stelo [M]

corn
maïs [M]
maíz [M]
Mais [M]
mais [M]

barley
orge [M] commune
cebada [F]
Gerste [F]
orzo [M]

wheat
blé [M]
trigo [M]
Weizen [M]
grano [M]

rice
riz [M]
arroz [M]
Reis [M]
riso [M]

geranium
géranium [M]
geranio [M]
Geranie [F]
geranio [M]
flower
fleur [F]
flor [M]
Blüte [F]
fiore [M]
petal
pétale [M]
pétalo [M]
Blütenblatt [N]
petalo [M]
flower bud
bourgeon [M] à fleurs [F]
capullo [M] de flor [F]
Knospe [F]
bocciolo [M]
stalk
tige [F]
tallo [M]
Stiel [M]
stelo [M]
leaf
feuille [F]
hoja [F]
Blatt [N]
foglia [F]

marigold
souci [M]
caléndula [F]
Ringelblume [F]
calendula [F]

calla lily
arum [M] d'Éthiopie [F]
cala [F]
Zimmercalla [F]
calla [F]

hydrangea
hortensia [M]
hortensia [F]
Hortensie [F]
ortensia [F]

Fruits and vegetables

Fruits ^{M} et légumes ^{M} | Frutas ^{F} y vegetales ^{M} | Obst ^{N} und Gemüse ^{N} | Frutta ^{F} e verdura ^{F}

strawberry
fraisier ^{M}
fresa ^{F}
Erdbeere ^{F}
fragola ^{F}

flower
fleur F
flor F
Blüte F
fiore M
leaf
feuille F
hoja F
Blatt N
foglia F
unripe berry
fraise F non mûre
baya F verde
Unreife Beere F
bacca F acerba
stem
tige F
tallo M
Stiel M
fusto M
berry
fraise F
baya F
Beere F
bacca F

broccoli
brocoli ^{M}
brócoli ^{M}
Brokkoli ^{M}
broccoli ^{M}

cauliflower
chou-fleur ^{M}
coliflor ^{F}
Blumenkohl ^{M}
cavolfiore ^{M}

lettuce
laitue ^{F}
lechuga ^{F}
Kopfsalat ^{M}
lattuga ^{F}

carrot
carotte [F]
zanahoria [F]
Karotte [F]
carota [F]

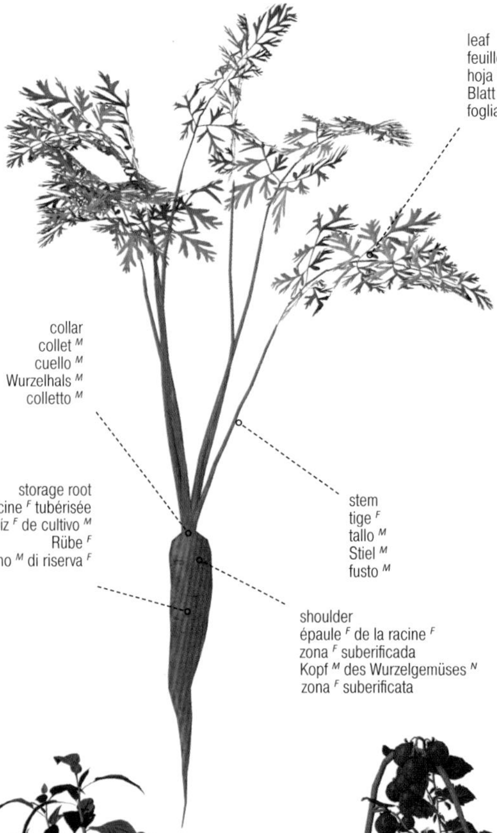
leaf
feuille [F]
hoja [F]
Blatt [N]
foglia [F]
collar
collet [M]
cuello [M]
Wurzelhals [M]
colletto [M]
stem
tige [F]
tallo [M]
Stiel [M]
fusto [M]
storage root
racine [F] tubérisée
raiz [F] de cultivo [M]
Rübe [F]
organo [M] di riserva [F]
shoulder
épaule [F] de la racine [F]
zona [F] suberificada
Kopf [M] des Wurzelgemüses [N]
zona [F] suberificata

pea
pois [M]
guisantes [M]
Erbse [F]
pisello [M]

chili
piment [M] fort
chile [M]
Chilipfeffer [M]
peperoncino [M]

tomato
tomate [F]
tomate [M]
Tomate [F]
pomodoro [M]

eggplant
aubergine [F]
berenjena [F]
Aubergine [F]
melanzana [F]

squash
courge [F]
calabacita [M]
Kürbis [M]
zucca [F]

zucchini
zucchini [M]
calabacín [M]
Zucchini [F]
zucchina [F]

watermelon
melon [M] d'eau [F]
sandía [F]
Wassermelone [F]
anguria [F]

cantaloupe
cantaloup [M]
melón [M]
Cantaloupe-Melone [F]
melone [M] di Cantalupo

onion
oignon [M]
cebolla [F]
Zwiebel [F]
cipolla [F]

cucumber
concombre [M]
pepino [M]
Gurke [F]
cetriolo [M]

pear
poirier M
pera F
Birne F
pera F

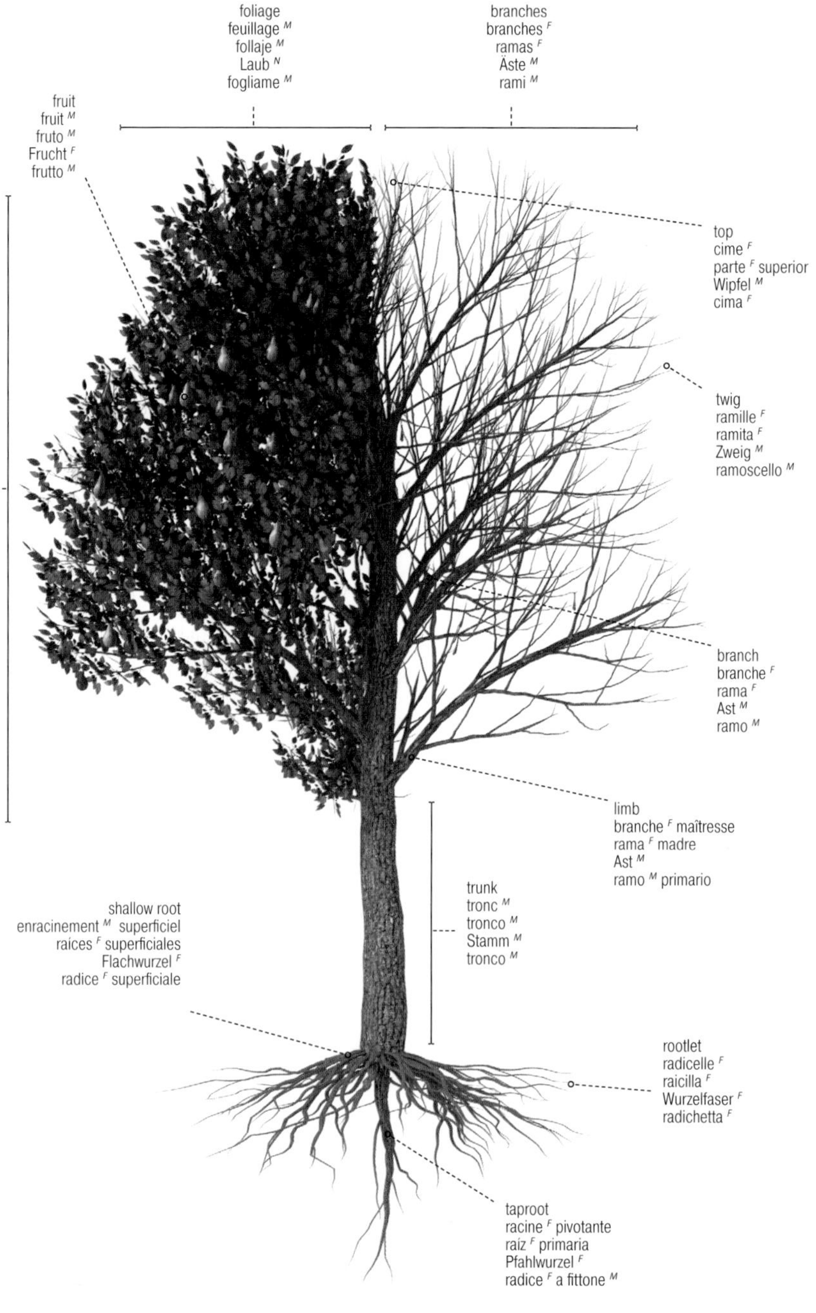
foliage
feuillage M
follaje M
Laub N
fogliame M
branches
branches F
ramas F
Äste M
rami M
fruit
fruit M
fruto M
Frucht F
frutto M
top
cime F
parte F superior
Wipfel M
cima F
twig
ramille F
ramita F
Zweig M
ramoscello M
crown
houppier M
copa F
Krone F
chioma F
branch
branche F
rama F
Ast M
ramo M
limb
branche F maîtresse
rama F madre
Ast M
ramo M primario
trunk
tronc M
tronco M
Stamm M
tronco M
shallow root
enracinement M superficiel
raíces F superficiales
Flachwurzel F
radice F superficiale
rootlet
radicelle F
raicilla F
Wurzelfaser F
radichetta F
taproot
racine F pivotante
raíz F primaria
Pfahlwurzel F
radice F a fittone M

American sycamore
platane ^{M} occidental
plátano ^{M} occidental
Amerikanische Platane ^{F}
platano ^{M} occidentale

English oak
chêne ^{M} pédonculé
roble ^{M} común
Deutsche Eiche ^{F}
farnia ^{F}

apple
pommier ^{M}
manzano ^{M}
Apfel ^{M}
melo ^{M}

holly
houx ^{M}
acebo ^{M}
Stechpalme ^{F}
agrifoglio ^{M}

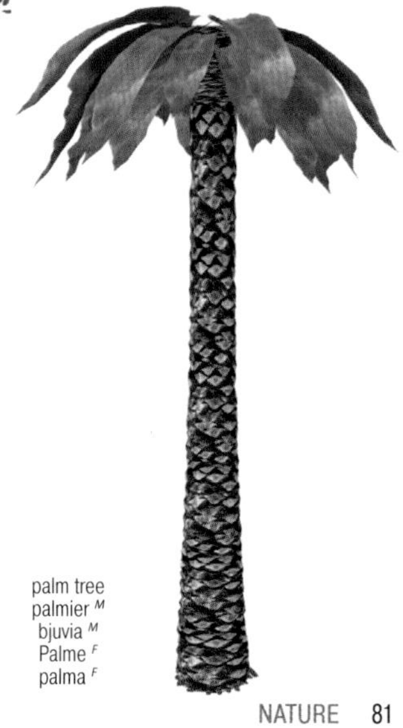

palm tree
palmier ^{M}
bjuvia ^{M}
Palme ^{F}
palma ^{F}

European aspen
tremble [M]
álamo [M] temblón
Espe [F]
pioppio [M] tremulo

red oak
chêne [M] rouge
roble [M] rojo
Roteiche [F]
quercia [F] rossa

ash
frêne [M]
fresno [M] norteño
Esche [F]
frassino [M]

sugar maple
érable [M] à sucre [M]
arce [M] azucarero
Zucker-Ahorn [M]
acero [M] zuccherino

rubber tree
hévéa [M]
árbol [M] de caucho [M]
Gummibaum [M]
albero [M] della gomma [F]

olive
olivier [M]
olivo [M]
Olive [F]
ulivo [M]

large-leaf linden
tilleul [M] à grandes feuilles [F]
tilo [M] de hoja [F] ancha
Breitblättrige Linde [F]
tiglio [M] dalle foglie [F] larghe

black alder
aulne [M] noir
aliso [M] negro
Schwarzerle [F]
ontano [M]

hawthorn
aubépine [F]
espino [M] blanco
Hagedorn [M]
biancospino [M]

ginkgo tree
ginkgo [M]
gingko [M]
Ginkgobaum [M]
ginko [M]

American beech
hêtre ^{M} à grandes feuilles ^{F}
haya ^{F} americana
Amerikanische Buche ^{F}
faggio ^{M} americano

chestnut
châtaigner ^{M}
castaño ^{M}
Kastanie ^{F}
castagno ^{M}

silver birch
bouleau ^{M} blanc d'Europe ^{F}
abedul ^{M} común
Weißbirke ^{F}
betulla ^{F} argentata

hornbeam
charme ^{M}
carpe ^{M}
Hainbuche ^{F}
carpino ^{M} bianco

juniper
genévrier [M]
enebro [M] común
Wacholder [M]
ginepro [M]

western red cedar
thuya [M] géant
tuya [F] gigante
Riesenlebensbaum [M]
cedro [M] gigante

Caucasian fir
sapin [M] de Nordmann
abeto [M] del Cáucaso
Nordmanntanne [F]
abete [M] del Caucaso [M]

English yew
if [M] commun
tejo [M] común
Europäische Eibe [F]
tasso [M]

Colorado blue spruce
épinette [F] du Colorado [M]
pícea [F] azul de Colorado
Blaufichte [F]
abete [M] del Colorado [M]

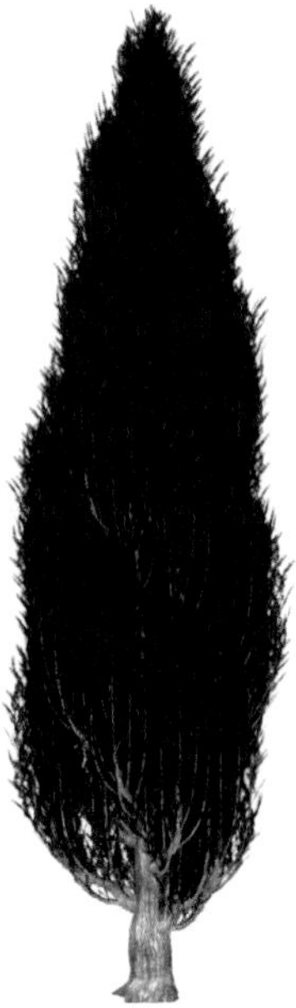

Italian cypress
cyprès [M] d'Italie [F]
ciprés [M] mediterráneo
Italienische Zypresse [F]
cipresso [M] mediterraneo

red pine
pin [M] rouge
pino [M] rojo
Amerikanische Rot-Kiefer [F]
pino [M] rosso

Norway spruce
épinette [F] de Norvège [F]
pícea [F] común
Gemeine Fichte [F]
abete [M] rosso

white pine
pin [M] blanc
pino [M] blanco
Weymouth-Kiefer [F]
pino [M] bianco

rhododendron
rhododendron [M]
rododendro [M] común
Rhododendron [M]
rododendro [M]
flower
fleur [F]
flor [F]
Blüte [F]
fiore [M]
leaf
feuille [F]
hoja [F]
Blatt [N]
foglia [F]
branch
branche [F]
rama [F]
Ast [M]
ramo [M]
trunk
tronc [M]
tronco [M]
Stamm [M]
tronco [M]

golden bamboo
bambou [M] doré
bambú [M] dorado
Goldrohrbambus [M]
bambù [M] dorato

magnolia
magnolia [M]
magnolia [F]
Magnolie [F]
magnolia [F]

structure of a flower
structure [F] d'une fleur [F]
estructura [F] de una flor [F]
Aufbau [M] der Blume [F]
struttura [F] di un fiore [M]

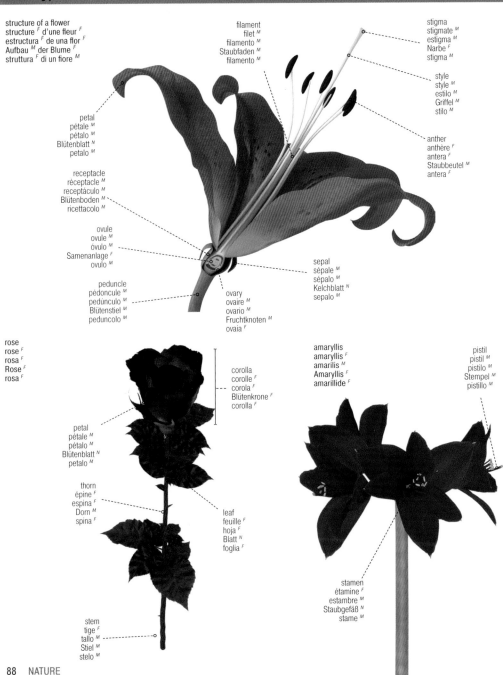

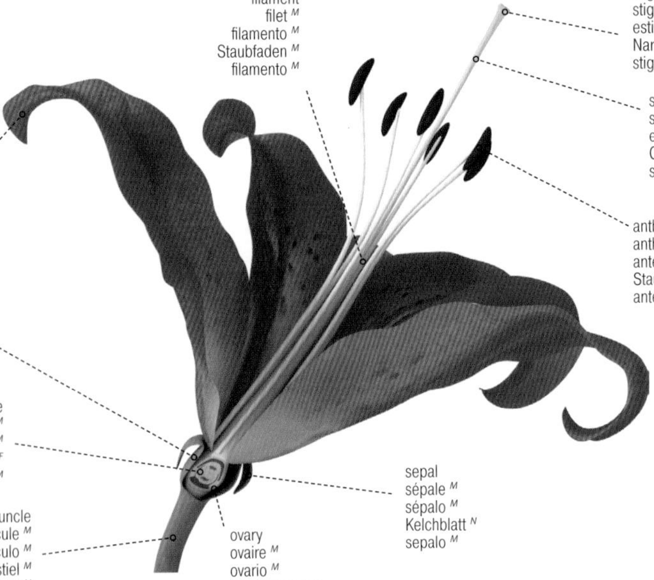
filament
filet [M]
filamento [M]
Staubfaden [M]
filamento [M]
stigma
stigmate [M]
estigma [M]
Narbe [F]
stigma [M]
style
style [M]
estilo [M]
Griffel [M]
stilo [M]
petal
pétale [M]
pétalo [M]
Blütenblatt [N]
petalo [M]
anther
anthère [F]
antera [F]
Staubbeutel [M]
antera [F]
receptacle
réceptacle [M]
receptáculo [M]
Blütenboden [M]
ricettacolo [M]
ovule
ovule [M]
óvulo [M]
Samenanlage [F]
ovulo [M]
sepal
sépale [M]
sépalo [M]
Kelchblatt [N]
sepalo [M]
peduncle
pédoncule [M]
pedúnculo [M]
Blütenstiel [M]
peduncolo [M]
ovary
ovaire [M]
ovario [M]
Fruchtknoten [M]
ovaia [F]

rose
rose [F]
rosa [F]
Rose [F]
rosa [F]

corolla
corolle [F]
corola [F]
Blütenkrone [F]
corolla [F]
petal
pétale [M]
pétalo [M]
Blütenblatt [N]
petalo [M]
thorn
épine [F]
espina [F]
Dorn [M]
spina [F]
leaf
feuille [F]
hoja [F]
Blatt [N]
foglia [F]
stem
tige [F]
tallo [M]
Stiel [M]
stelo [M]

amaryllis
amaryllis [F]
amarilis [M]
Amaryllis [F]
amarillide [F]

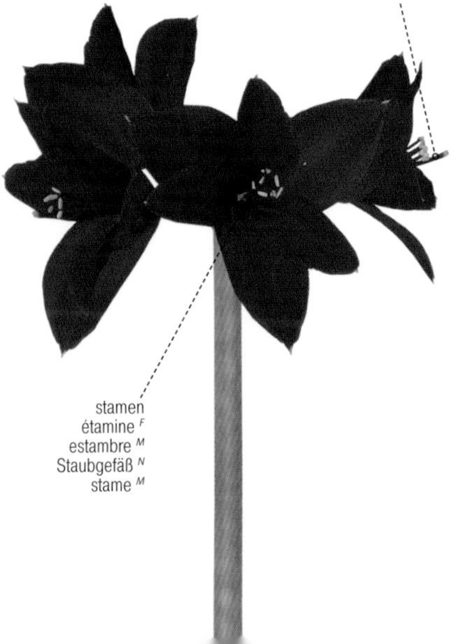
pistil
pistil [M]
pistilo [M]
Stempel [M]
pistillo [M]
stamen
étamine [F]
estambre [M]
Staubgefäß [N]
stame [M]

hyacinth
jacinthe [F]
jacinto [M]
Hyazinthe [F]
giacinto [M]

daisy
marguerite [F]
margarita [F]
Margerite [F]
margherita [F]

carnation
œillet [M] des fleuristes [M]
clavel [M]
Nelke [F]
garofano [M]

iris
iris [M]
lirio [M] holandés
Iris [F]
iris [M]

bird of paradise
oiseau [M] de paradis [M]
ave [F] del paraíso [M]
Paradiesvogelblume [F]
strelizia [F]

Asiatic lily
lys [M] asiatique
lirio [M]
Lilie [F]
giglio [M]

crocus
crocus [M]
crocus [M]
Krokus [M]
croco [M]

bromeliad
bromélia [M]
estrella [F] escarlata
Bromelie [F]
bromelia [F]

peony
pivoine [F]
peonía [F]
Pfingstrose [F]
peonia [F]

PLANTS
Flowering plants

gerbera daisy
gerbera [M] de Jameson [M]
margarita [F] africana
Spinnengerbera [F]
gerbera [F]

orchid
orchidée [F]
orquídea [F]
Orchidee [F]
orchidea [F]

gladiolus
glaïeul [M]
gladiolo [M]
Gladiole [F]
gladiolo [M]

tulip
tulipe [F]
tulipán [M]
Tulpe [F]
tulipano [M]

Houseplants

dragon tree
dragonnier [M]
dracaena [F] de puntas [F] rojas
Drachenbaum [M]
dracena [F]

leaf
feuille [F]
hoja [F]
Blatt [N]
foglia [F]

trunk
tronc [M]
tronco [M]
Stamm [M]
tronco [M]

soil
terreau [M]
tierra [F]
Erde [F]
terreno [M]

pot
pot [M]
tiesto [M] / maceta [F]
Blumentopf [M]
vaso [M]

cactus
cactus [M]
cactus [M] de barril [M]
Kaktus [M]
cactus [M]

sago palm
sagoutier [M]
palmera [F] sagú
Sagopalme [F]
palma sago [M]

weeping fig
figuier M pleureur
Laurel M de la India F
Birkenfeige F
ficus M benjamina

ivy
lierre M
hiedra F
Efeu M
edera F

croton
croton M
crotón M
Kroton M
croton M

fern
fougère F
helecho M común
Farn M
felce F

fan palm
talipot M de l'Inde F
palma F de abanico M
Fächerpalme F
palma F

Aquatic plants

lotus
lotus M
loto M
Lotosblume F
loto M

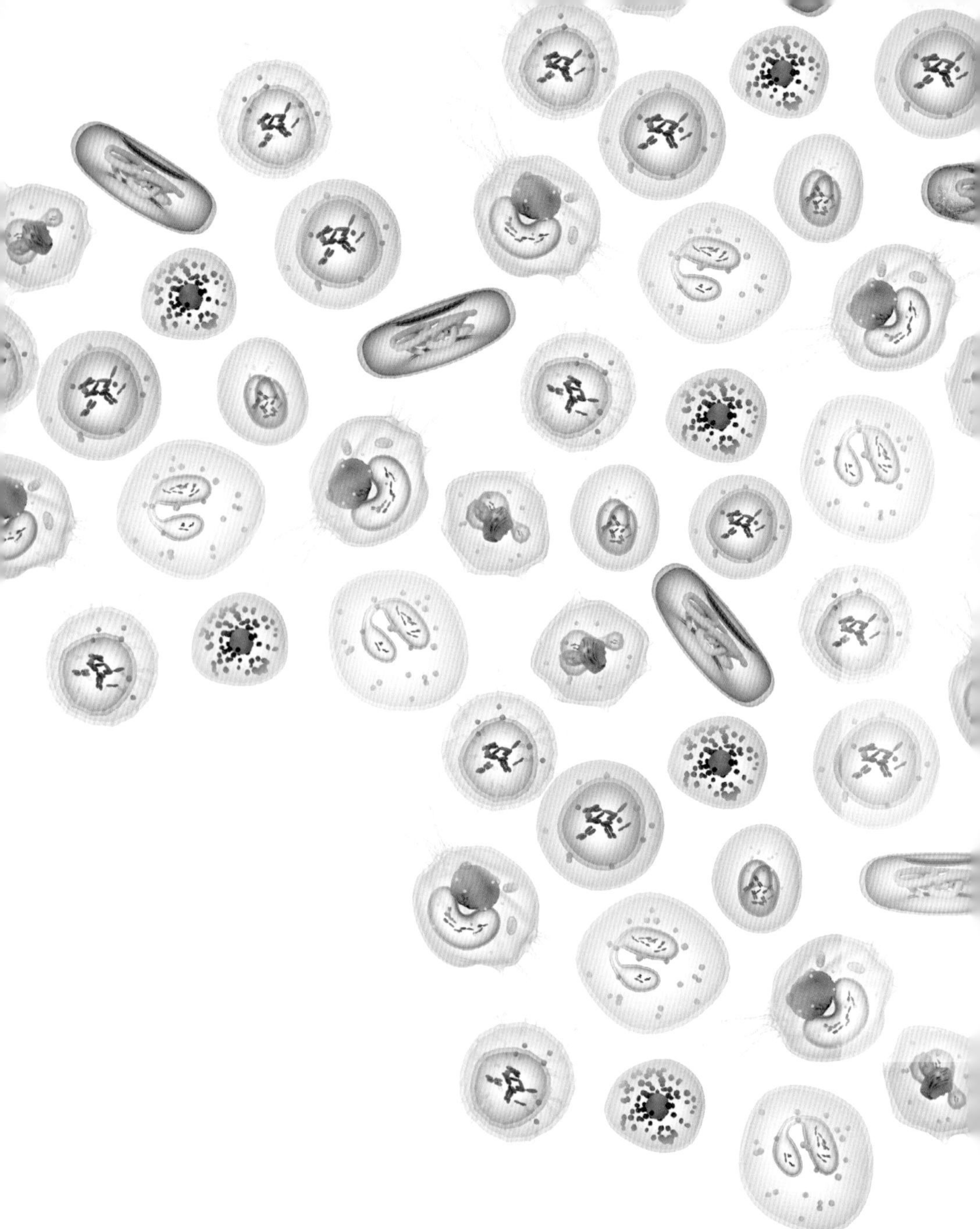

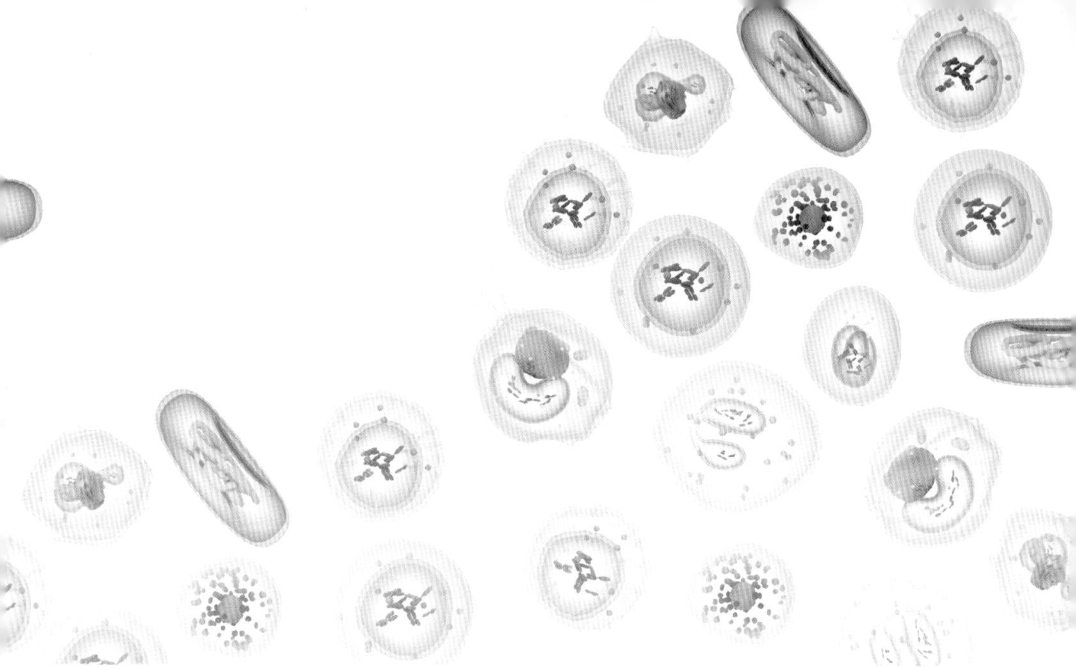

HUMAN BEING

anterior view of female body
vue [F] antérieure du corps [M] féminin
vista [F] anterior del cuerpo [M] femenino
Vorderansicht [F] eines weiblichen Körpers [M]
vista [F] anteriore di un corpo [M] femminile

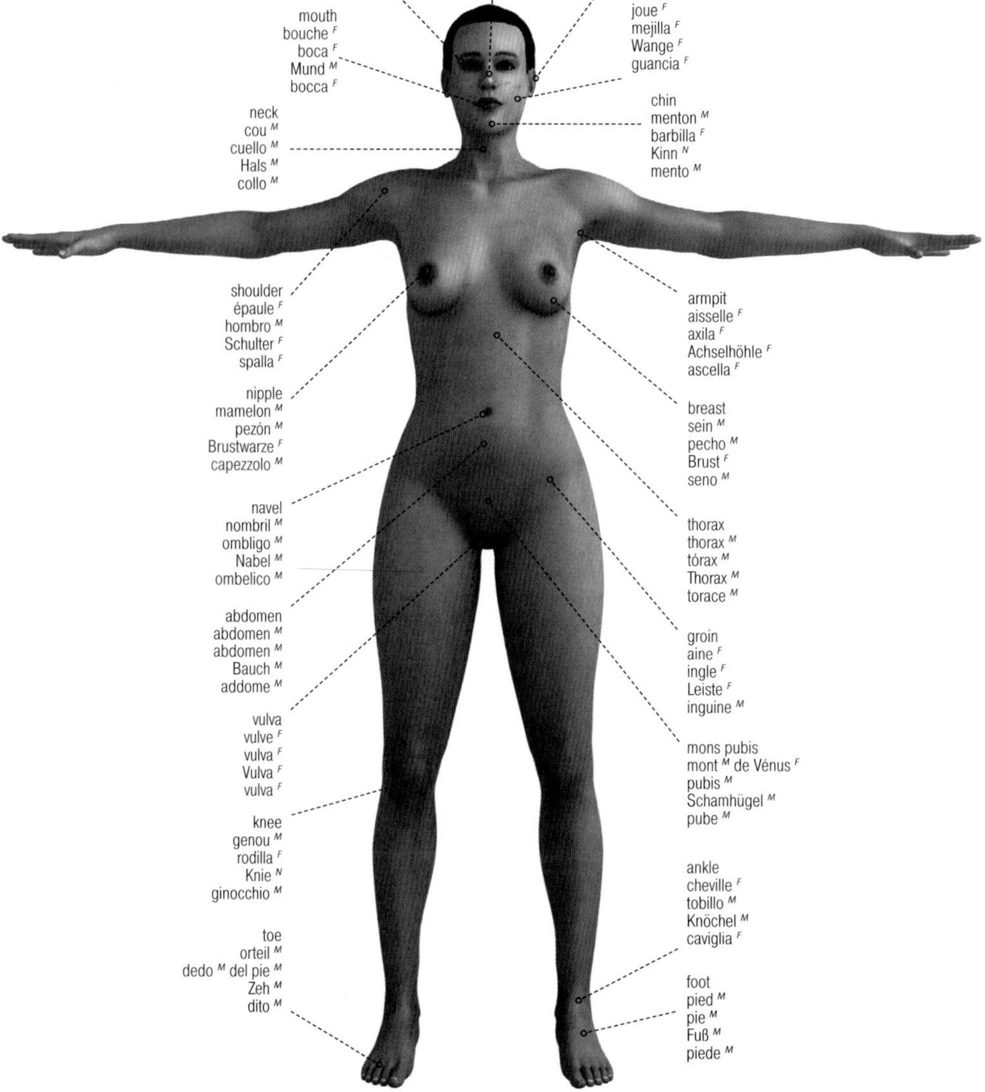
nose
nez [M]
nariz [F]
Nase [F]
naso [M]
eye
œil [M]
ojo [M]
Auge [N]
occhio [M]
ear
oreille [F]
oído [M]
Ohr [N]
orecchio [M]
cheek
joue [F]
mejilla [F]
Wange [F]
guancia [F]
mouth
bouche [F]
boca [F]
Mund [M]
bocca [F]
chin
menton [M]
barbilla [F]
Kinn [N]
mento [M]
neck
cou [M]
cuello [M]
Hals [M]
collo [M]
shoulder
épaule [F]
hombro [M]
Schulter [F]
spalla [F]
armpit
aisselle [F]
axila [F]
Achselhöhle [F]
ascella [F]
nipple
mamelon [M]
pezón [M]
Brustwarze [F]
capezzolo [M]
breast
sein [M]
pecho [M]
Brust [F]
seno [M]
navel
nombril [M]
ombligo [M]
Nabel [M]
ombelico [M]
thorax
thorax [M]
tórax [M]
Thorax [M]
torace [M]
abdomen
abdomen [M]
abdomen [M]
Bauch [M]
addome [M]
groin
aine [F]
ingle [F]
Leiste [F]
inguine [M]
vulva
vulve [F]
vulva [F]
Vulva [F]
vulva [F]
mons pubis
mont [M] de Vénus [F]
pubis [M]
Schamhügel [M]
pube [M]
knee
genou [M]
rodilla [F]
Knie [N]
ginocchio [M]
ankle
cheville [F]
tobillo [M]
Knöchel [M]
caviglia [F]
toe
orteil [M]
dedo [M] del pie [M]
Zeh [M]
dito [M]
foot
pied [M]
pie [M]
Fuß [M]
piede [M]

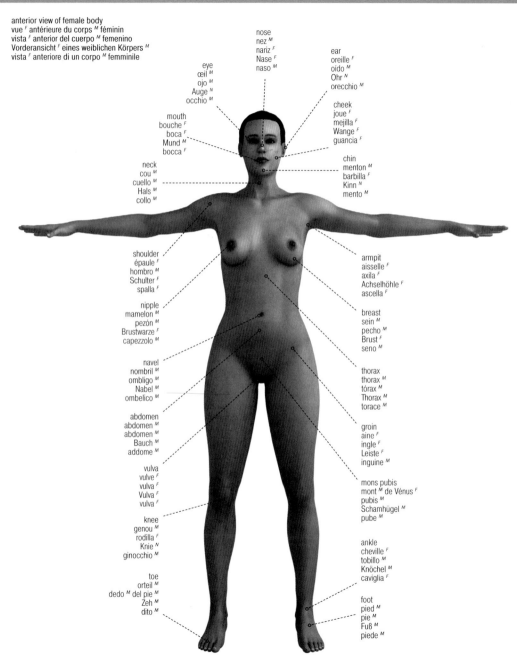

posterior view of female body
vue F postérieure du corps M féminin
vista F posterior del cuerpo M femenino
Hinteransicht F eines weiblichen Körpers M
vista F posteriore di un corpo M femminile

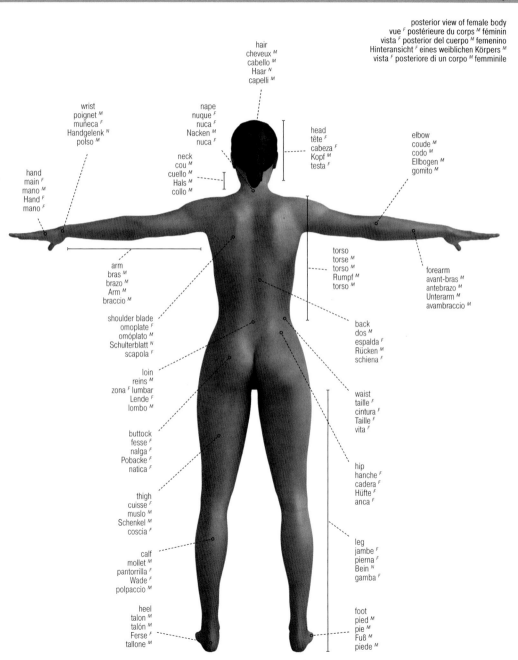

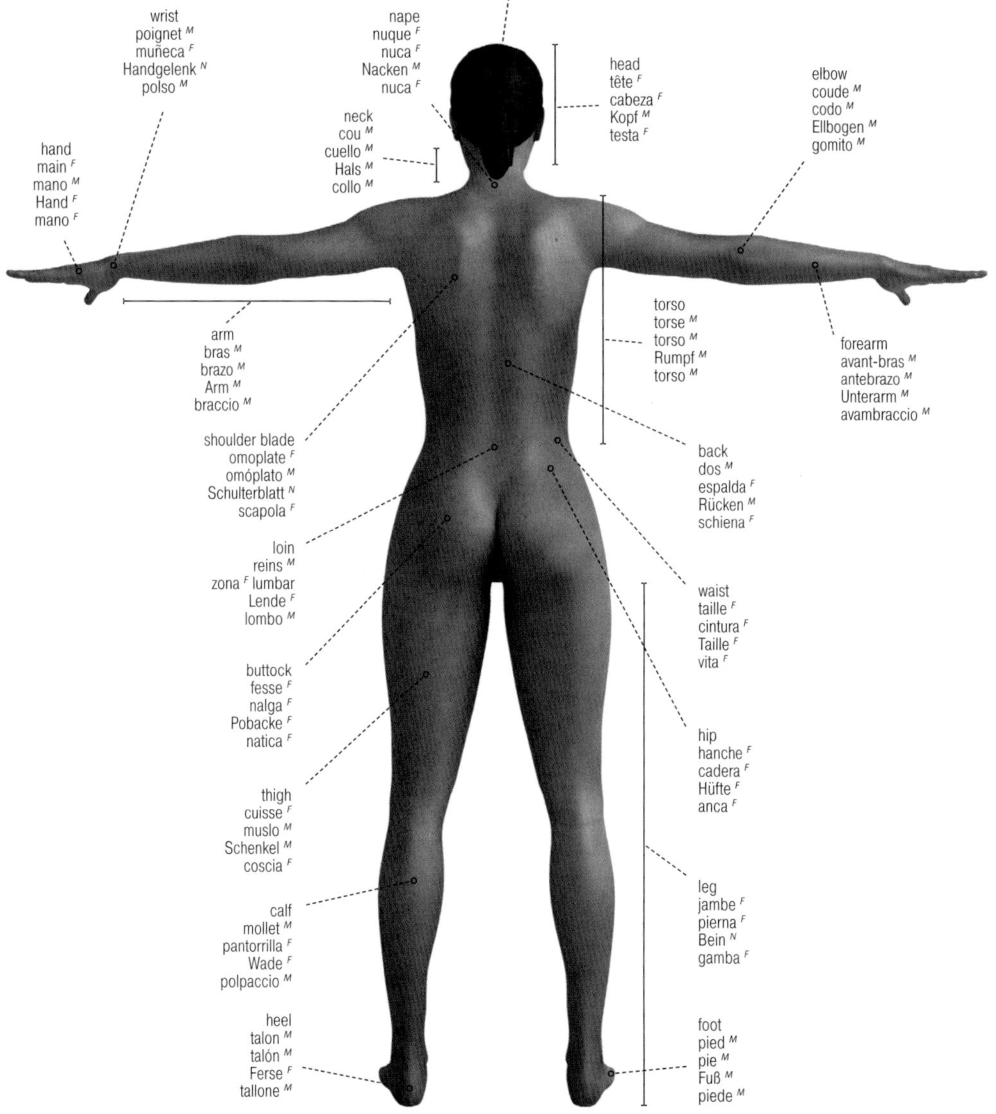
hair
cheveux M
cabello M
Haar N
capelli M
wrist
poignet M
muñeca F
Handgelenk N
polso M
nape
nuque F
nuca F
Nacken M
nuca F
head
tête F
cabeza F
Kopf M
testa F
elbow
coude M
codo M
Ellbogen M
gomito M
hand
main F
mano M
Hand F
mano F
neck
cou M
cuello M
Hals M
collo M
torso
torse M
torso M
Rumpf M
torso M
arm
bras M
brazo M
Arm M
braccio M
forearm
avant-bras M
antebrazo M
Unterarm M
avambraccio M
shoulder blade
omoplate F
omóplato M
Schulterblatt N
scapola F
back
dos M
espalda F
Rücken M
schiena F
loin
reins M
zona F lumbar
Lende F
lombo M
waist
taille F
cintura F
Taille F
vita F
buttock
fesse F
nalga F
Pobacke F
natica F
hip
hanche F
cadera F
Hüfte F
anca F
thigh
cuisse F
muslo M
Schenkel M
coscia F
leg
jambe F
pierna F
Bein N
gamba F
calf
mollet M
pantorrilla F
Wade F
polpaccio M
heel
talon M
talón M
Ferse F
tallone M
foot
pied M
pie M
Fuß M
piede M

anterior view of male body
vue [F] antérieure du corps [M] masculin
vista [F] anterior del cuerpo [M] masculino
Vorderansicht [F] eines männlichen Körpers [M]
vista [F] anteriore di un corpo [M] maschile

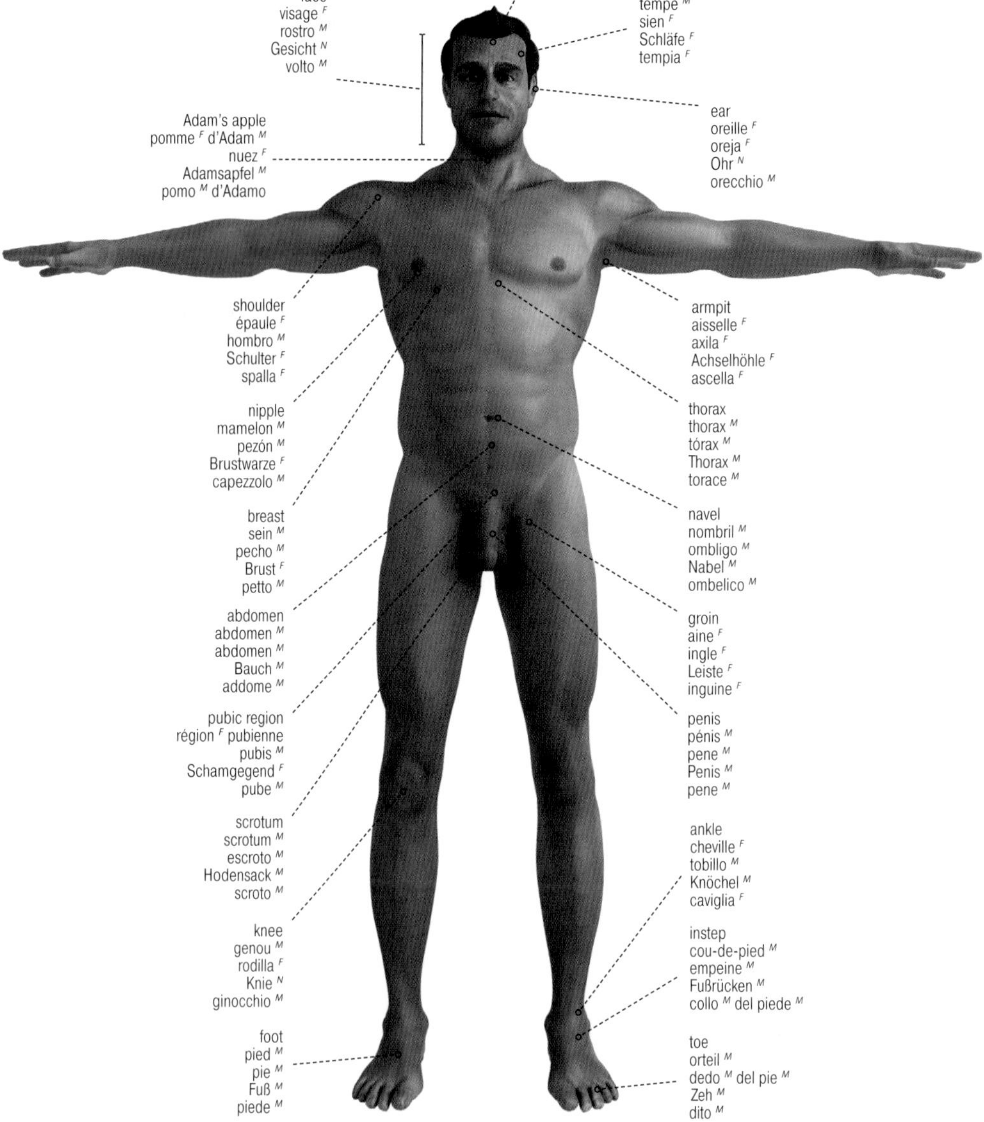
forehead
front [M]
frente [F]
Stirn [F]
fronte [F]
face
visage [F]
rostro [M]
Gesicht [N]
volto [M]
Adam's apple
pomme [F] d'Adam [M]
nuez [F]
Adamsapfel [M]
pomo [M] d'Adamo
shoulder
épaule [F]
hombro [M]
Schulter [F]
spalla [F]
nipple
mamelon [M]
pezón [M]
Brustwarze [F]
capezzolo [M]
breast
sein [M]
pecho [M]
Brust [F]
petto [M]
abdomen
abdomen [M]
abdomen [M]
Bauch [M]
addome [M]
pubic region
région [F] pubienne
pubis [M]
Schamgegend [F]
pube [M]
scrotum
scrotum [M]
escroto [M]
Hodensack [M]
scroto [M]
knee
genou [M]
rodilla [F]
Knie [N]
ginocchio [M]
foot
pied [M]
pie [M]
Fuß [M]
piede [M]
temple
tempe [M]
sien [F]
Schläfe [F]
tempia [F]
ear
oreille [F]
oreja [F]
Ohr [N]
orecchio [M]
armpit
aisselle [F]
axila [F]
Achselhöhle [F]
ascella [F]
thorax
thorax [M]
tórax [M]
Thorax [M]
torace [M]
navel
nombril [M]
ombligo [M]
Nabel [M]
ombelico [M]
groin
aine [F]
ingle [F]
Leiste [F]
inguine [F]
penis
pénis [M]
pene [M]
Penis [M]
pene [M]
ankle
cheville [F]
tobillo [M]
Knöchel [M]
caviglia [F]
instep
cou-de-pied [M]
empeine [M]
Fußrücken [M]
collo [M] del piede [M]
toe
orteil [M]
dedo [M] del pie [M]
Zeh [M]
dito [M]

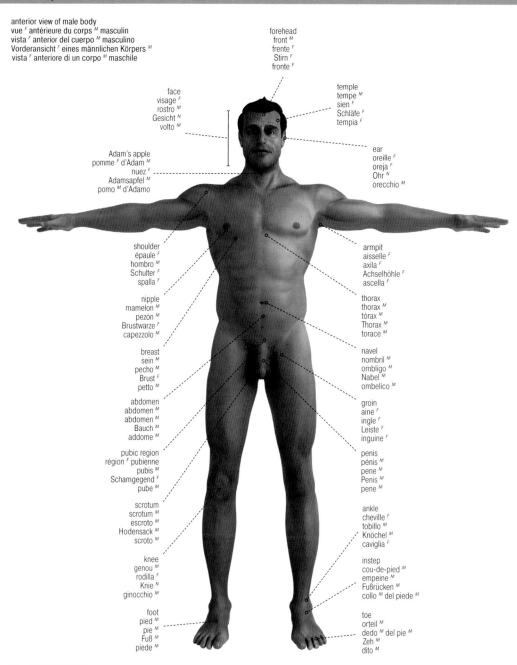

posterior view of male body
vue [F] postérieure du corps [M] masculin
vista [F] posterior del cuerpo [M] masculino
Hinteransicht [F] eines männlichen Körpers [M]
vista [F] posteriore di un corpo [M] maschile

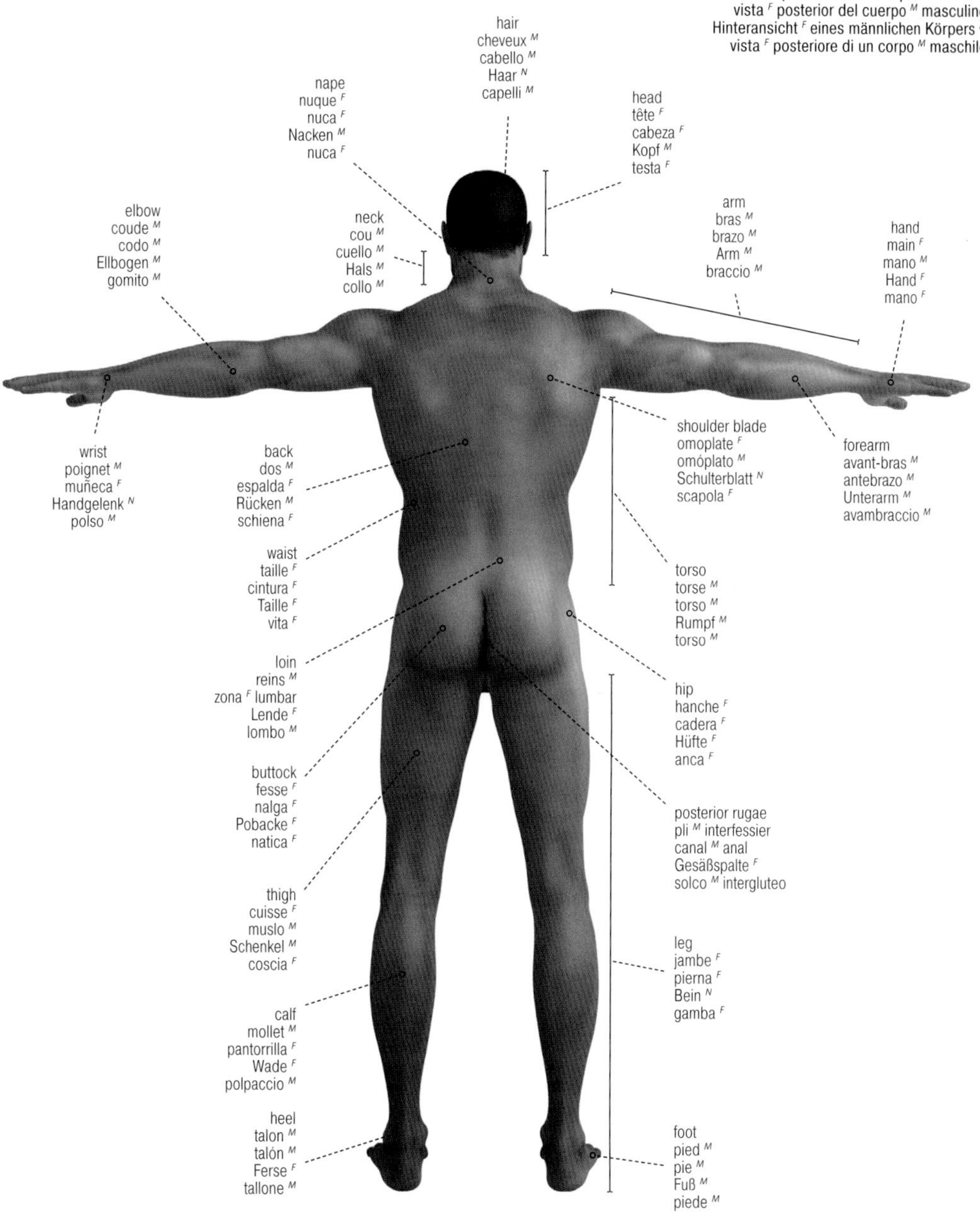
hair
cheveux M
cabello M
Haar N
capelli M
nape
nuque F
nuca F
Nacken M
nuca F
head
tête F
cabeza F
Kopf M
testa F
elbow
coude M
codo M
Ellbogen M
gomito M
neck
cou M
cuello M
Hals M
collo M
arm
bras M
brazo M
Arm M
braccio M
hand
main F
mano M
Hand F
mano F
wrist
poignet M
muñeca F
Handgelenk N
polso M
back
dos M
espalda F
Rücken M
schiena F
shoulder blade
omoplate F
omóplato M
Schulterblatt N
scapola F
forearm
avant-bras M
antebrazo M
Unterarm M
avambraccio M
waist
taille F
cintura F
Taille F
vita F
torso
torse M
torso M
Rumpf M
torso M
loin
reins M
zona F lumbar
Lende F
lombo M
hip
hanche F
cadera F
Hüfte F
anca F
buttock
fesse F
nalga F
Pobacke F
natica F
posterior rugae
pli M interfessier
canal M anal
Gesäßspalte F
solco M intergluteo
thigh
cuisse F
muslo M
Schenkel M
coscia F
leg
jambe F
pierna F
Bein N
gamba F
calf
mollet M
pantorrilla F
Wade F
polpaccio M
heel
talon M
talón M
Ferse F
tallone M
foot
pied M
pie M
Fuß M
piede M

anterior view of main muscles
vue ^{F} antérieure des muscles ^{M} principaux
vista ^{F} anterior de los músculos ^{M} principales
Vorderansicht ^{F} der Muskulatur ^{F}
vista ^{F} anteriore dei muscoli ^{M} principali

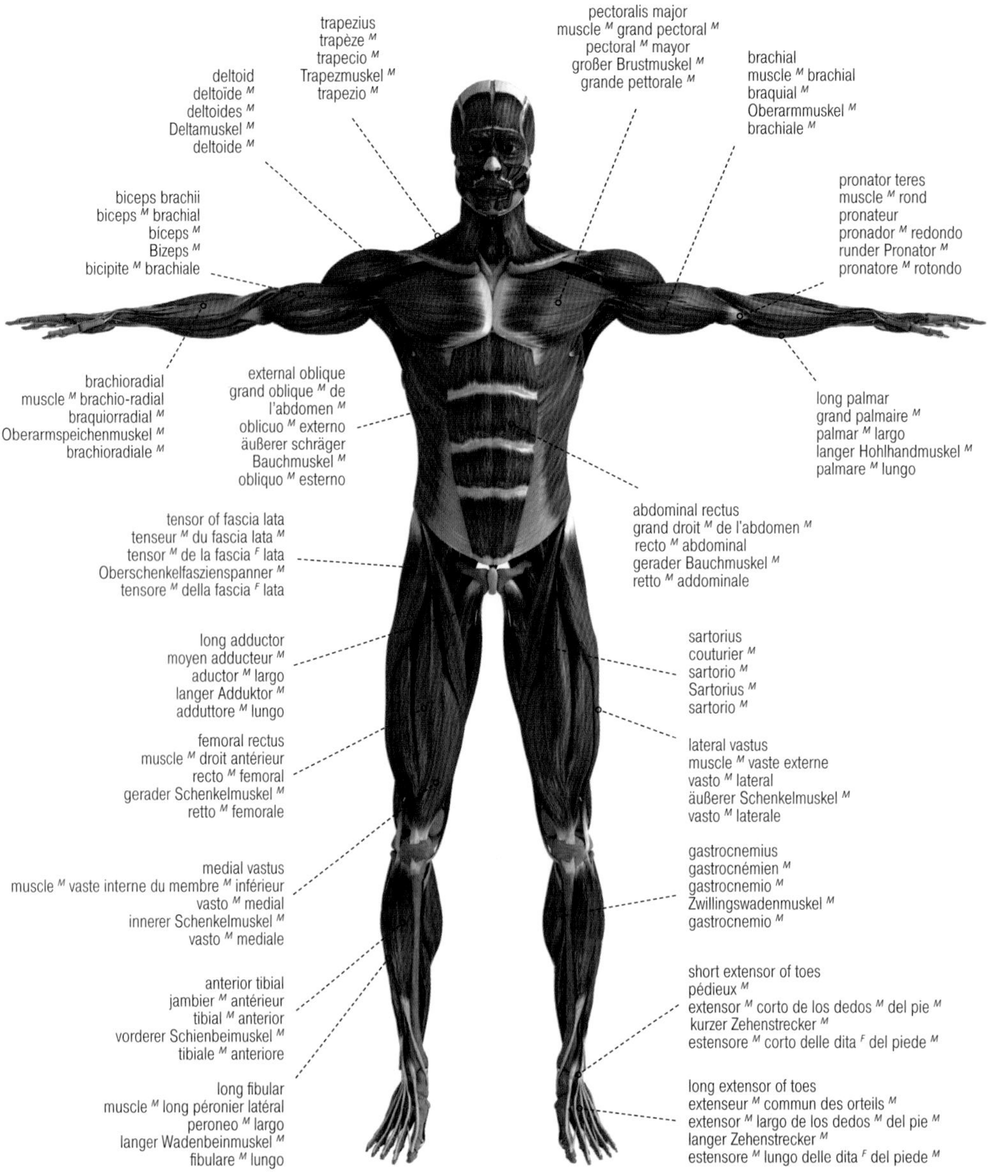
trapezius
trapèze ^{M}
trapecio ^{M}
Trapezmuskel ^{M}
trapezio ^{M}
pectoralis major
muscle ^{M} grand pectoral ^{M}
pectoral ^{M} mayor
großer Brustmuskel ^{M}
grande pettorale ^{M}
deltoid
deltoïde ^{M}
deltoides ^{M}
Deltamuskel ^{M}
deltoide ^{M}
brachial
muscle ^{M} brachial
braquial ^{M}
Oberarmmuskel ^{M}
brachiale ^{M}
biceps brachii
biceps ^{M} brachial
bíceps ^{M}
Bizeps ^{M}
bicipite ^{M} brachiale
pronator teres
muscle ^{M} rond pronateur
pronador ^{M} redondo
runder Pronator ^{M}
pronatore ^{M} rotondo
brachioradial
muscle ^{M} brachio-radial
braquiorradial ^{M}
Oberarmspeichenmuskel ^{M}
brachioradiale ^{M}
external oblique
grand oblique ^{M} de l'abdomen ^{M}
oblicuo ^{M} externo
äußerer schräger Bauchmuskel ^{M}
obliquo ^{M} esterno
long palmar
grand palmaire ^{M}
palmar ^{M} largo
langer Hohlhandmuskel ^{M}
palmare ^{M} lungo
abdominal rectus
grand droit ^{M} de l'abdomen ^{M}
recto ^{M} abdominal
gerader Bauchmuskel ^{M}
retto ^{M} addominale
tensor of fascia lata
tenseur ^{M} du fascia lata ^{M}
tensor ^{M} de la fascia ^{F} lata
Oberschenkelfaszienspanner ^{M}
tensore ^{M} della fascia ^{F} lata
long adductor
moyen adducteur ^{M}
aductor ^{M} largo
langer Adduktor ^{M}
adduttore ^{M} lungo
sartorius
couturier ^{M}
sartorio ^{M}
Sartorius ^{M}
sartorio ^{M}
femoral rectus
muscle ^{M} droit antérieur
recto ^{M} femoral
gerader Schenkelmuskel ^{M}
retto ^{M} femorale
lateral vastus
muscle ^{M} vaste externe
vasto ^{M} lateral
äußerer Schenkelmuskel ^{M}
vasto ^{M} laterale
medial vastus
muscle ^{M} vaste interne du membre ^{M} inférieur
vasto ^{M} medial
innerer Schenkelmuskel ^{M}
vasto ^{M} mediale
gastrocnemius
gastrocnémien ^{M}
gastrocnemio ^{M}
Zwillingswadenmuskel ^{M}
gastrocnemio ^{M}
anterior tibial
jambier ^{M} antérieur
tibial ^{M} anterior
vorderer Schienbeinmuskel ^{M}
tibiale ^{M} anteriore
short extensor of toes
pédieux ^{M}
extensor ^{M} corto de los dedos ^{M} del pie ^{M}
kurzer Zehenstrecker ^{M}
estensore ^{M} corto delle dita ^{F} del piede ^{M}
long fibular
muscle ^{M} long péronier latéral
peroneo ^{M} largo
langer Wadenbeinmuskel ^{M}
fibulare ^{M} lungo
long extensor of toes
extenseur ^{M} commun des orteils ^{M}
extensor ^{M} largo de los dedos ^{M} del pie ^{M}
langer Zehenstrecker ^{M}
estensore ^{M} lungo delle dita ^{F} del piede ^{M}

posterior view of main muscles
vue ^{F} postérieure des muscles ^{M} principaux
vista ^{F} posterior de los músculos ^{M} principales
Hinteransicht ^{F} der Muskulatur ^{F}
vista ^{F} posteriore dei muscoli ^{M} principali

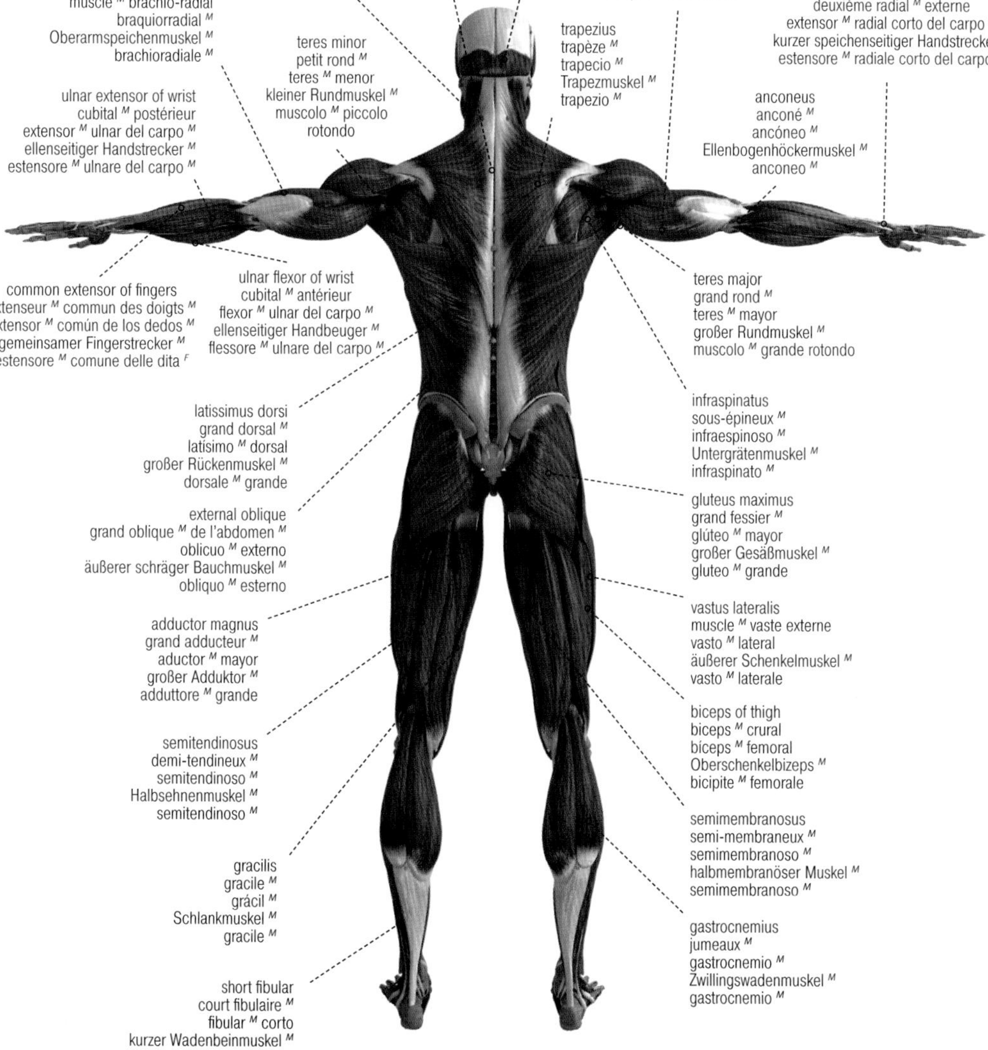

semispinalis capitis
muscle ^{M} grand complexus ^{M}
semiespinoso ^{M} de la cabeza ^{F}
Halbdornmuskel ^{M}
semispinale ^{M} della testa ^{F}

occipitalis
os ^{M} occipital
occipital ^{M}
Hinterhauptmuskel ^{M}
occipitale ^{M}

splenius of head
splénius ^{M} de la tête ^{F}
esplenio ^{M} de la cabeza ^{F}
Riemenmuskel ^{M}
splenio ^{M} della testa ^{F}

triceps of arm
triceps ^{M} brachial
tríceps ^{M} del brazo ^{M}
Armtrizeps ^{M}
tricipite ^{M} del braccio ^{M}

brachioradial
muscle ^{M} brachio-radial
braquiorradial ^{M}
Oberarmspeichenmuskel ^{M}
brachioradiale ^{M}

teres minor
petit rond ^{M}
teres ^{M} menor
kleiner Rundmuskel ^{M}
muscolo ^{M} piccolo rotondo

trapezius
trapèze ^{M}
trapecio ^{M}
Trapezmuskel ^{M}
trapezio ^{M}

short radial extensor of wrist
deuxième radial ^{M} externe
extensor ^{M} radial corto del carpo ^{M}
kurzer speichenseitiger Handstrecker ^{M}
estensore ^{M} radiale corto del carpo ^{M}

ulnar extensor of wrist
cubital ^{M} postérieur
extensor ^{M} ulnar del carpo ^{M}
ellenseitiger Handstrecker ^{M}
estensore ^{M} ulnare del carpo ^{M}

anconeus
anconé ^{M}
ancóneo ^{M}
Ellenbogenhöckermuskel ^{M}
anconeo ^{M}

common extensor of fingers
extenseur ^{M} commun des doigts ^{M}
extensor ^{M} común de los dedos ^{M}
gemeinsamer Fingerstrecker ^{M}
estensore ^{M} comune delle dita ^{F}

ulnar flexor of wrist
cubital ^{M} antérieur
flexor ^{M} ulnar del carpo ^{M}
ellenseitiger Handbeuger ^{M}
flessore ^{M} ulnare del carpo ^{M}

teres major
grand rond ^{M}
teres ^{M} mayor
großer Rundmuskel ^{M}
muscolo ^{M} grande rotondo

latissimus dorsi
grand dorsal ^{M}
latísimo ^{M} dorsal
großer Rückenmuskel ^{M}
dorsale ^{M} grande

infraspinatus
sous-épineux ^{M}
infraespinoso ^{M}
Untergrätenmuskel ^{M}
infraspinato ^{M}

external oblique
grand oblique ^{M} de l'abdomen ^{M}
oblicuo ^{M} externo
äußerer schräger Bauchmuskel ^{M}
obliquo ^{M} esterno

gluteus maximus
grand fessier ^{M}
glúteo ^{M} mayor
großer Gesäßmuskel ^{M}
gluteo ^{M} grande

adductor magnus
grand adducteur ^{M}
aductor ^{M} mayor
großer Adduktor ^{M}
adduttore ^{M} grande

vastus lateralis
muscle ^{M} vaste externe
vasto ^{M} lateral
äußerer Schenkelmuskel ^{M}
vasto ^{M} laterale

semitendinosus
demi-tendineux ^{M}
semitendinoso ^{M}
Halbsehnenmuskel ^{M}
semitendinoso ^{M}

biceps of thigh
biceps ^{M} crural
bíceps ^{M} femoral
Oberschenkelbizeps ^{M}
bicipite ^{M} femorale

gracilis
gracile ^{M}
grácil ^{M}
Schlankmuskel ^{M}
gracile ^{M}

semimembranosus
semi-membraneux ^{M}
semimembranoso ^{M}
halbmembranöser Muskel ^{M}
semimembranoso ^{M}

short fibular
court fibulaire ^{M}
fibular ^{M} corto
kurzer Wadenbeinmuskel ^{M}
peroneo ^{M} corto

gastrocnemius
jumeaux ^{M}
gastrocnemio ^{M}
Zwillingswadenmuskel ^{M}
gastrocnemio ^{M}

facial muscles
muscles M du visage M
músculos M faciales
Gesichtsmuskeln M
muscoli M facciali

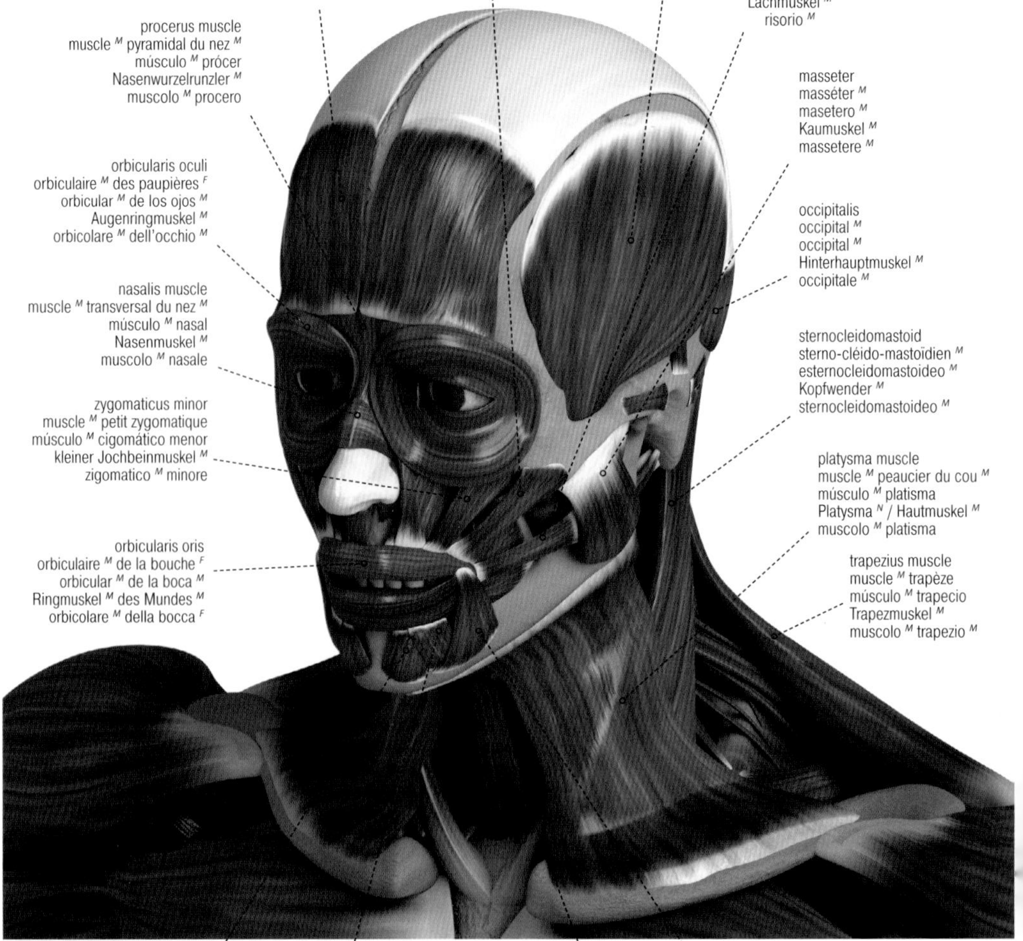
frontalis
frontal M
frontal M
Stirnmuskel M
frontale M
zygomaticus major muscle
muscle M grand zygomatique
músculo M cigomático mayor
großer Jochbeinmuskel M
muscolo M zigomatico maggiore
temporal muscle
muscle M temporal
músculo M temporal
Schläfenmuskel M
temporale M
risorius
muscle M risorius
músculo M risorio
Lachmuskel M
risorio M
procerus muscle
muscle M pyramidal du nez M
músculo M prócer
Nasenwurzelrunzler M
muscolo M procero
masseter
masséter M
masetero M
Kaumuskel M
massetere M
orbicularis oculi
orbiculaire M des paupières F
orbicular M de los ojos M
Augenringmuskel M
orbicolare M dell'occhio M
occipitalis
occipital M
occipital M
Hinterhauptmuskel M
occipitale M
nasalis muscle
muscle M transversal du nez M
músculo M nasal
Nasenmuskel M
muscolo M nasale
sternocleidomastoid
sterno-cléido-mastoïdien M
esternocleidomastoideo M
Kopfwender M
sternocleidomastoideo M
zygomaticus minor
muscle M petit zygomatique
músculo M cigomático menor
kleiner Jochbeinmuskel M
zigomatico M minore
platysma muscle
muscle M peaucier du cou M
músculo M platisma
Platysma N / Hautmuskel M
muscolo M platisma
orbicularis oris
orbiculaire M de la bouche F
orbicular M de la boca M
Ringmuskel M des Mundes M
orbicolare M della bocca F
trapezius muscle
muscle M trapèze
músculo M trapecio
Trapezmuskel M
muscolo M trapezio M
mentalis
muscle M de la houppe F du menton M
músculo M mentoniano
Kinnmuskel M
mentale M
depressor labii inferioris muscle
muscle M abaisseur de la lèvre F inférieure
músculo M depresor del labio M inferior
Niederzieher M der Unterlippe F
muscolo M depressore del labbro M inferiore
sternothyroid muscle
muscle M sternothyroïdien
esternotiroideo M
Brustbein-Schildknorpel-Muskel M
muscolo M sternotiroideo
depressor anguli oris muscle
muscle M abaisseur de l'angle M de la bouche F
músculo M depresor del ángulo M de la boca F
Mundwinkelniederzieher M
muscolo M depressore dell'angolo M della bocca F

skin section
section F de peau F
sección F de la piel F
Hautschnitt M
sezione F della cute F

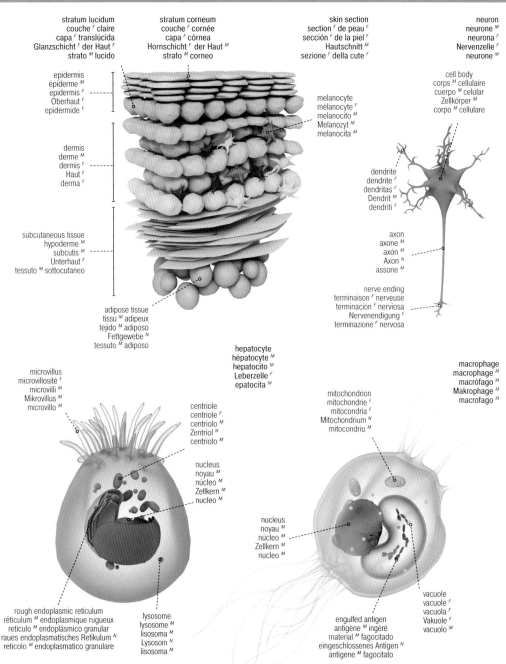

stratum lucidum
couche F claire
capa F translúcida
Glanzschicht F der Haut F
strato M lucido
stratum corneum
couche F cornée
capa F córnea
Hornschicht F der Haut M
strato M corneo
epidermis
épiderme M
epidermis F
Oberhaut F
epidermide F
melanocyte
mélanocyte F
melanocito M
Melanozyt M
melanocita M
dermis
derme M
dermis F
Haut F
derma F
subcutaneous tissue
hypoderme M
subcutis M
Unterhaut F
tessuto M sottocutaneo
adipose tissue
tissu M adipeux
tejido M adiposo
Fettgewebe N
tessuto M adiposo

neuron
neurone M
neurona F
Nervenzelle F
neurone M

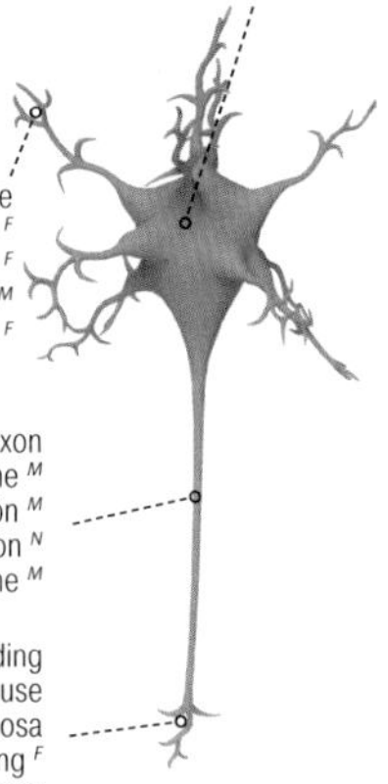
cell body
corps M cellulaire
cuerpo M celular
Zellkörper M
corpo M cellulare
dendrite
dendrite F
dendritas F
Dendrit M
dendriti F
axon
axone M
axón M
Axon N
assone M
nerve ending
terminaison F nerveuse
terminación F nerviosa
Nervenendigung F
terminazione F nervosa

hepatocyte
hépatocyte M
hepatocito M
Leberzelle F
epatocita M

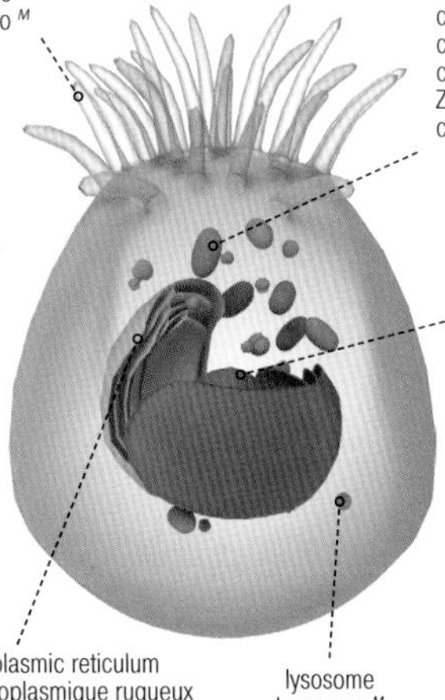
microvillus
microvillosité F
microvilli M
Mikrovillus M
microvillo M
centriole
centriole F
centriolo M
Zentriol N
centriolo M
nucleus
noyau M
núcleo M
Zellkern M
nucleo M
rough endoplasmic reticulum
réticulum M endoplasmique rugueux
retículo M endoplásmico granular
raues endoplasmatisches Retikulum N
reticolo M endoplasmatico granulare
lysosome
lysosome M
lisosoma M
Lysosom N
lisosoma M

macrophage
macrophage M
macrófago M
Makrophage M
macrofago M

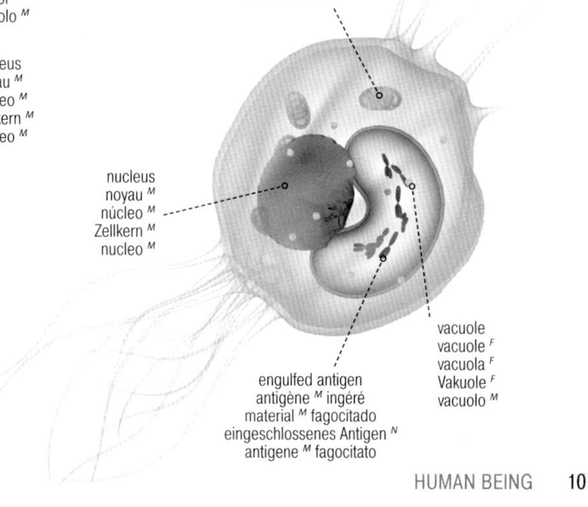
mitochondrion
mitochondrie F
mitocondria F
Mitochondrium N
mitocondrio M
nucleus
noyau M
núcleo M
Zellkern M
nucleo M
vacuole
vacuole F
vacuola F
Vakuole F
vacuolo M
engulfed antigen
antigène M ingéré
material M fagocitado
eingeschlossenes Antigen N
antigene M fagocitato

anterior view of skeleton
vue [F] antérieure du squelette [M]
vista [F] anterior del esqueleto [M]
Vorderansicht [F] des Skeletts [N]
vista [F] anteriore dello scheletro [M]

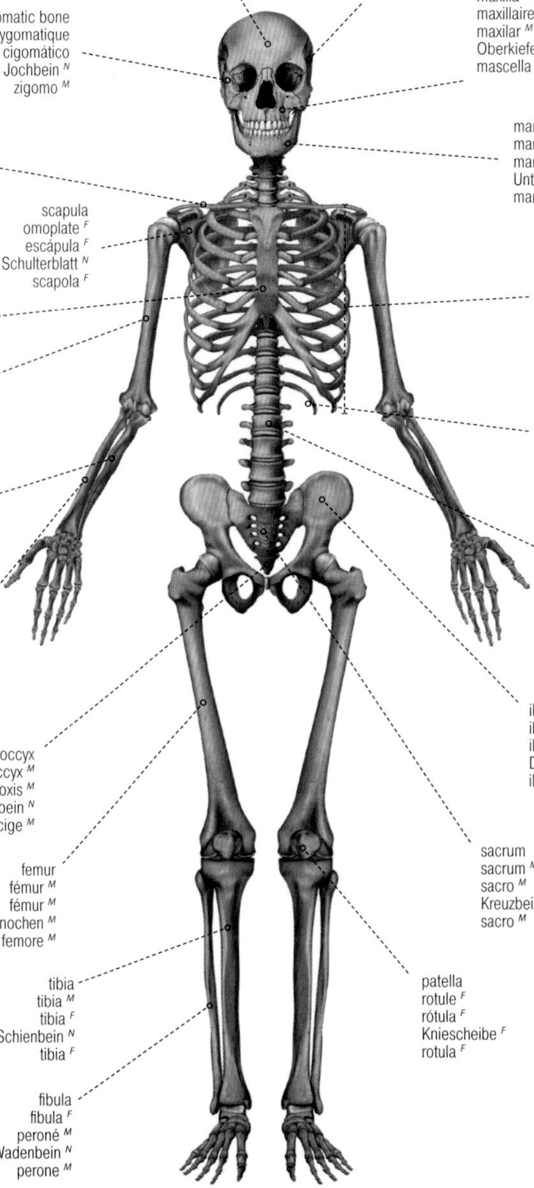
frontal bone
os [M] frontal
hueso [M] frontal
Stirnbein [N]
osso [M] frontale
temporal bone
os [M] temporal
hueso [M] temporal
Schläfenbein [N]
osso [M] temporale
maxilla
maxillaire [M]
maxilar [M]
Oberkiefer [M]
mascella [F]
zygomatic bone
os [M] zygomatique
hueso [M] cigomático
Jochbein [N]
zigomo [M]
clavicle
clavicule [F]
clavícula [F]
Schlüsselbein [N]
clavicola [F]
mandible
mandibule [F]
mandíbula [F]
Unterkiefer [M]
mandibola [F]
scapula
omoplate [F]
escápula [F]
Schulterblatt [N]
scapola [F]
ribs
côtes [F]
costillas [F]
Rippen [F]
costole [F]
sternum
sternum [M]
esternón [M]
Sternum [N]
sterno [M]
humerus
humérus [M]
húmero [M]
Oberarmknochen [M]
omero [M]
floating rib
côte [F] flottante
costilla [F] flotante
freie Rippe [F]
costola [F] fluttuante
ulna
cubitus [M]
cúbito [M]
Elle [F]
ulna [F]
spinal column
colonne [F] vertébrale
columna [F] vertebral
Wirbelsäule [F]
colonna [F] vertebrale
radius
radius [M]
radio [M]
Speiche [F]
radio [M]
ilium
ilion [M]
ilion [M]
Darmbein [N]
ilio [M]
coccyx
coccyx [M]
coxis [M]
Steißbein [N]
coccige [M]
sacrum
sacrum [M]
sacro [M]
Kreuzbein [N]
sacro [M]
femur
fémur [M]
fémur [M]
Oberschenkelknochen [M]
femore [M]
patella
rotule [F]
rótula [F]
Kniescheibe [F]
rotula [F]
tibia
tibia [M]
tibia [F]
Schienbein [N]
tibia [F]
fibula
fibula [F]
peroné [M]
Wadenbein [N]
perone [M]

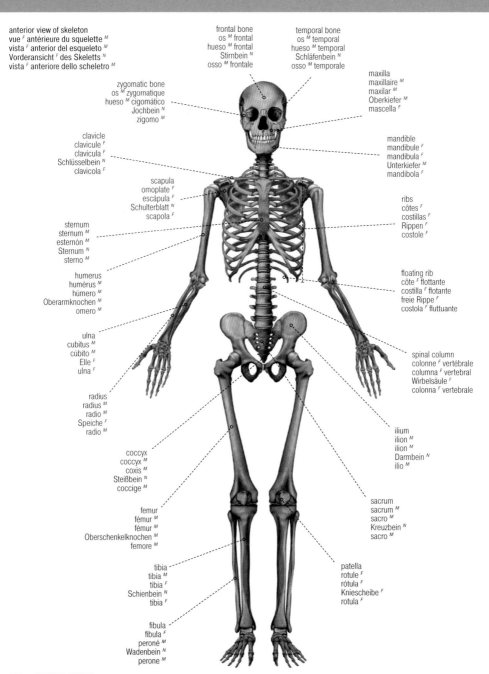

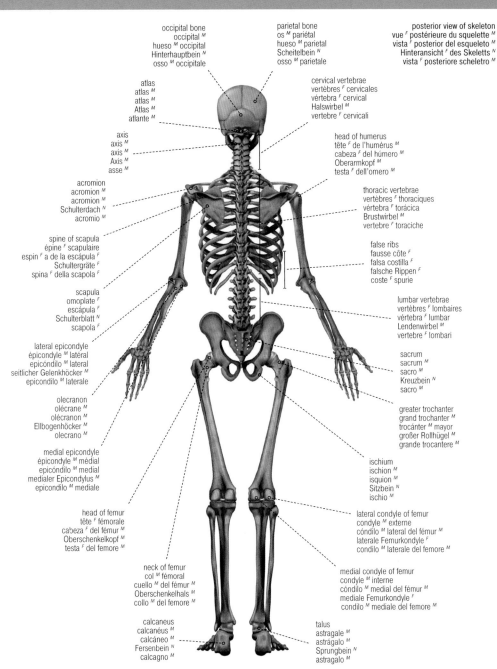

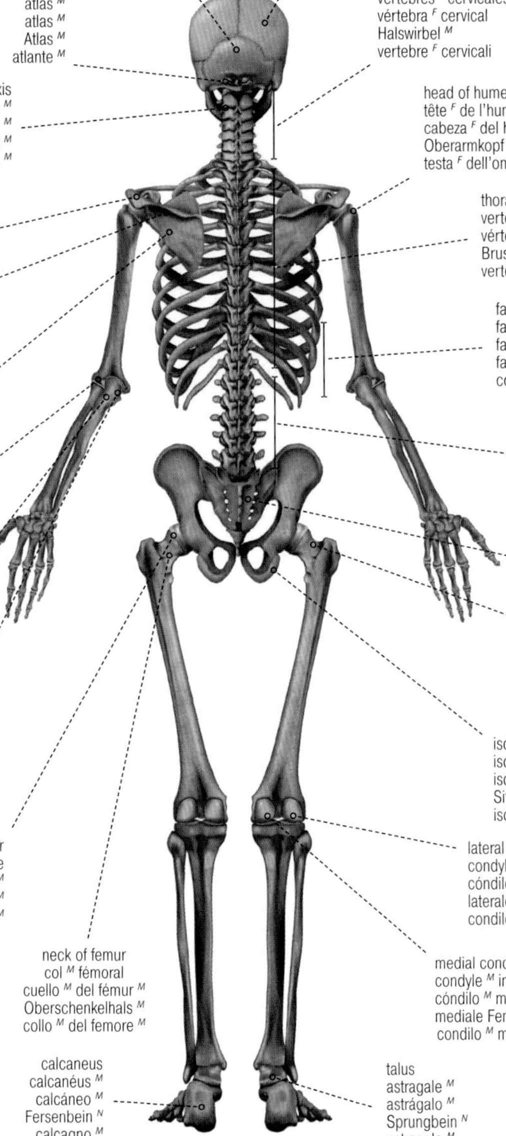
posterior view of skeleton
vue [F] postérieure du squelette [M]
vista [F] posterior del esqueleto [M]
Hinteransicht [F] des Skeletts [N]
vista [F] posteriore scheletro [M]
occipital bone
occipital [M]
hueso [M] occipital
Hinterhauptbein [N]
osso [M] occipitale
parietal bone
os [M] pariétal
hueso [M] parietal
Scheitelbein [N]
osso [M] parietale
atlas
atlas [M]
atlas [M]
Atlas [M]
atlante [M]
cervical vertebrae
vertèbres [F] cervicales
vértebra [F] cervical
Halswirbel [M]
vertebre [F] cervicali
axis
axis [M]
axis [M]
Axis [M]
asse [M]
head of humerus
tête [F] de l'humérus [M]
cabeza [F] del húmero [M]
Oberarmkopf [M]
testa [F] dell'omero [M]
acromion
acromion [M]
acromion [M]
Schulterdach [N]
acromio [M]
thoracic vertebrae
vertèbres [F] thoraciques
vértebra [F] torácica
Brustwirbel [M]
vertebre [F] toraciche
spine of scapula
épine [F] scapulaire
espin [F] a de la escápula [F]
Schultergräte [F]
spina [F] della scapola [F]
false ribs
fausse côte [F]
falsa costilla [F]
falsche Rippen [F]
coste [F] spurie
scapula
omoplate [F]
escápula [F]
Schulterblatt [N]
scapola [F]
lumbar vertebrae
vertèbres [F] lombaires
vértebra [F] lumbar
Lendenwirbel [M]
vertebre [F] lombari
lateral epicondyle
épicondyle [M] latéral
epicóndilo [M] lateral
seitlicher Gelenkhöcker [M]
epicondilo [M] laterale
sacrum
sacrum [M]
sacro [M]
Kreuzbein [N]
sacro [M]
olecranon
olécrane [M]
olécranon [M]
Ellbogenhöcker [M]
olecrano [M]
greater trochanter
grand trochanter [M]
trocánter [M] mayor
großer Rollhügel [M]
grande trocantere [M]
medial epicondyle
épicondyle [M] médial
epicóndilo [M] medial
medialer Epicondylus [M]
epicondilo [M] mediale
ischium
ischion [M]
isquion [M]
Sitzbein [N]
ischio [M]
head of femur
tête [F] fémorale
cabeza [F] del fémur [M]
Oberschenkelkopf [M]
testa [F] del femore [M]
lateral condyle of femur
condyle [M] externe
cóndilo [M] lateral del fémur [M]
laterale Femurkondyle [F]
condilo [M] laterale del femore [M]
neck of femur
col [M] fémoral
cuello [M] del fémur [M]
Oberschenkelhals [M]
collo [M] del femore [M]
medial condyle of femur
condyle [M] interne
cóndilo [M] medial del fémur [M]
mediale Femurkondyle [F]
condilo [M] mediale del femore [M]
calcaneus
calcanéus [M]
calcáneo [M]
Fersenbein [N]
calcagno [M]
talus
astragale [M]
astrágalo [M]
Sprungbein [N]
astragalo [M]

shoulder bones
os [M] de l'épaule [F]
huesos [M] del hombro [M]
Schulter [F]
ossa [F] della spalla [F]

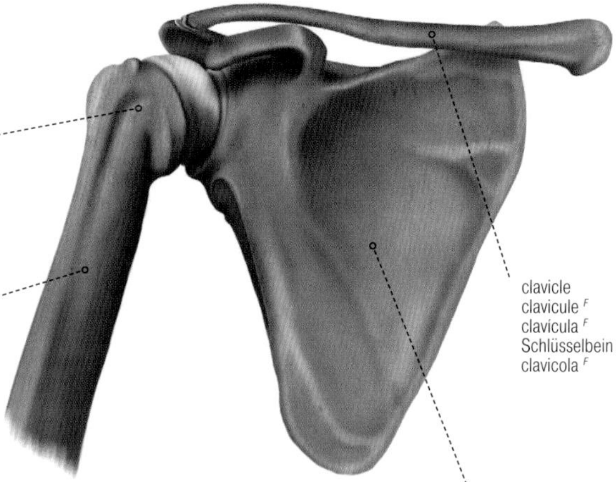
head of humerus
tête [F] de l'humérus [M]
cabeza [F] del húmero [M]
Oberarmkopf [M]
testa [F] dell'omero [M]
humerus
humérus [M]
húmero [M]
Oberarmknochen [M]
omero [M]
clavicle
clavicule [F]
clavícula [F]
Schlüsselbein [N]
clavicola [F]
scapula
omoplate [F]
escápula [F]
Schulterblatt [N]
scapola [F]

foot bones
os [M] du pied [M]
huesos [M] del pie [M]
Fußknochen [M]
ossa [M] del piede [M]

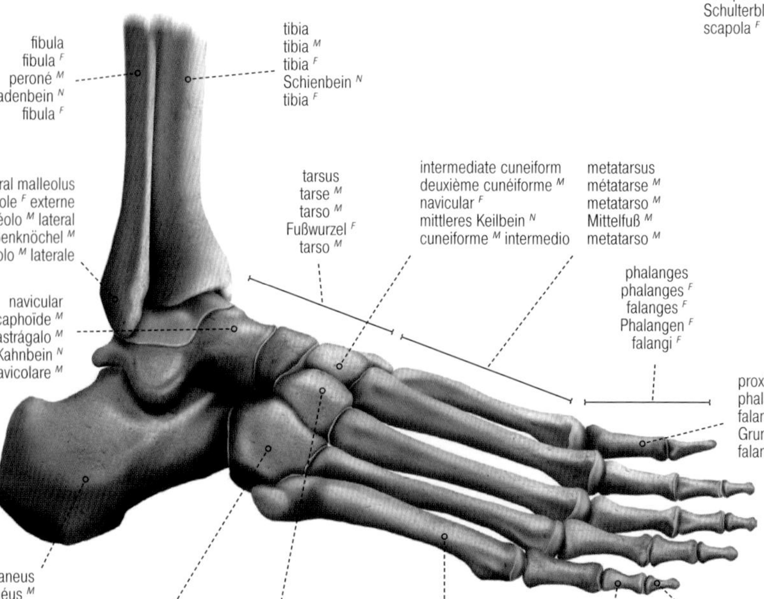
fibula
fibula [F]
peroné [M]
Wadenbein [N]
fibula [F]
tibia
tibia [M]
tibia [F]
Schienbein [N]
tibia [F]
lateral malleolus
malléole [F] externe
maléolo [M] lateral
Außenknöchel [M]
malleolo [M] laterale
tarsus
tarse [M]
tarso [M]
Fußwurzel [F]
tarso [M]
intermediate cuneiform
deuxième cunéiforme [M]
navicular [F]
mittleres Keilbein [N]
cuneiforme [M] intermedio
metatarsus
métatarse [M]
metatarso [M]
Mittelfuß [M]
metatarso [M]
navicular
scaphoïde [M]
astrágalo [M]
Kahnbein [N]
navicolare [M]
phalanges
phalanges [F]
falanges [F]
Phalangen [F]
falangi [F]
proximal phalanx
phalange [F] proximale
falange [F] proximal
Grundglied [N]
falange [F] prossimale
calcaneus
calcanéus [M]
calcáneo [M]
Fersenbein [N]
calcagno [M]
cuboid
cuboïde [M]
cuboides [M]
Würfelbein [N]
cuboide [M]
lateral cuneiform
troisième cunéiforme [M]
hueso [M] cuneiforme lateral
äußeres Keilbein [N]
cuneiforme [M] laterale
metatarsal
métatarsien [M]
metatarsal [M]
Mittelfußknochen [M]
metatarsale [M]
middle phalanx
phalangine [F]
falange [F] media
Mittelglied [N]
falange [F] media
distal phalanx
phalange [F] distale
falange [F] distal
Endglied [N]
falange [F] distale

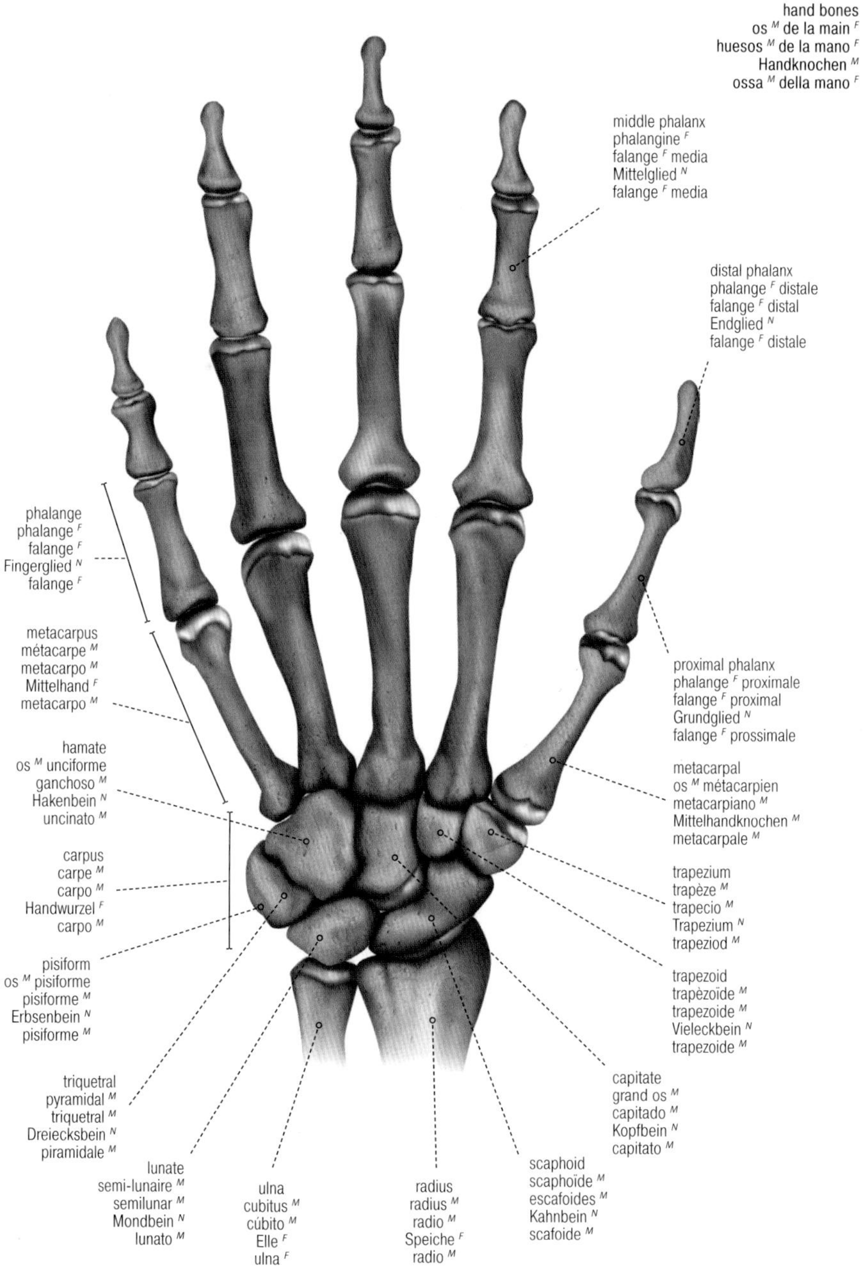
hand bones
os M de la main F
huesos M de la mano F
Handknochen M
ossa M della mano F
middle phalanx
phalangine F
falange F media
Mittelglied N
falange F media
distal phalanx
phalange F distale
falange F distal
Endglied N
falange F distale
phalange
phalange F
falange F
Fingerglied N
falange F
metacarpus
métacarpe M
metacarpo M
Mittelhand F
metacarpo M
proximal phalanx
phalange F proximale
falange F proximal
Grundglied N
falange F prossimale
hamate
os M unciforme
ganchoso M
Hakenbein N
uncinato M
metacarpal
os M métacarpien
metacarpiano M
Mittelhandknochen M
metacarpale M
carpus
carpe M
carpo M
Handwurzel F
carpo M
trapezium
trapèze M
trapecio M
Trapezium N
trapeziod M
pisiform
os M pisiforme
pisiforme M
Erbsenbein N
pisiforme M
trapezoid
trapèzoïde M
trapezoide M
Vieleckbein N
trapezoide M
triquetral
pyramidal M
triquetral M
Dreiecksbein N
piramidale M
capitate
grand os M
capitado M
Kopfbein N
capitato M
lunate
semi-lunaire M
semilunar M
Mondbein N
lunato M
ulna
cubitus M
cúbito M
Elle F
ulna F
radius
radius M
radio M
Speiche F
radio M
scaphoid
scaphoïde M
escafoides M
Kahnbein N
scafoide M

knee
genou [M]
rodilla [F]
Knie [N]
ginocchio [M]

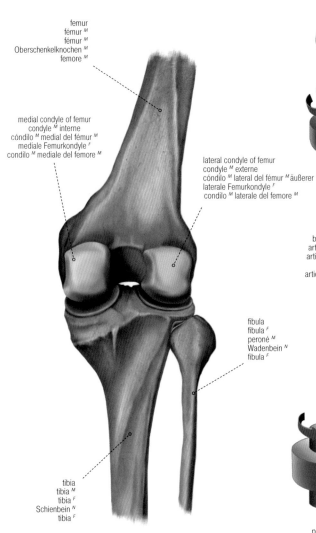

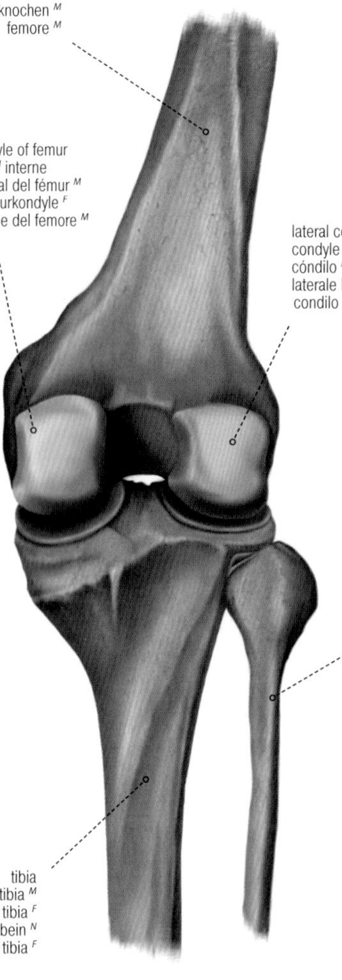
femur
fémur [M]
fémur [M]
Oberschenkelknochen [M]
femore [M]
medial condyle of femur
condyle [M] interne
cóndilo [M] medial del fémur [M]
mediale Femurkondyle [F]
condilo [M] mediale del femore [M]
lateral condyle of femur
condyle [M] externe
cóndilo [M] lateral del fémur [M] äußerer
laterale Femurkondyle [F]
condilo [M] laterale del femore [M]
fibula
fibula [F]
peroné [M]
Wadenbein [N]
fibula [F]
tibia
tibia [M]
tibia [F]
Schienbein [N]
tibia [F]

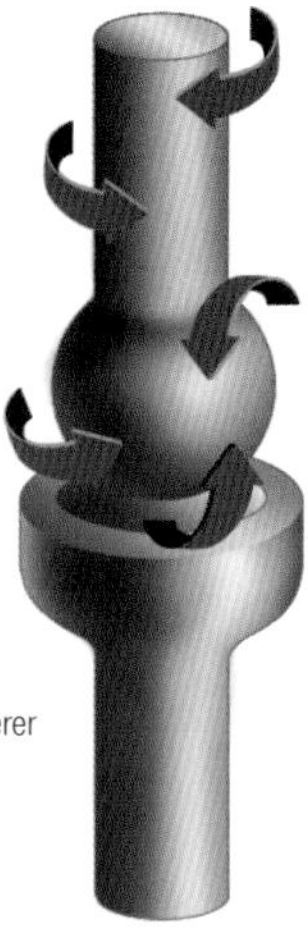

ball-and-socket joint
articulation [F] sphéroïde
articulación [F] esferoidea
Kugelgelenk [N]
articolazione [F] sferoidale

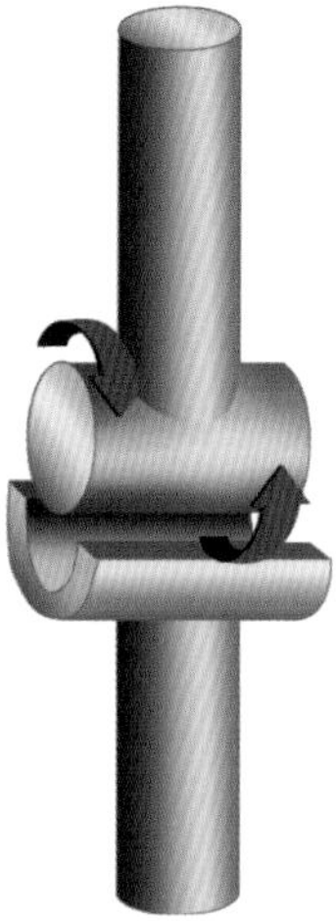

hinge joint
articulation [F] à charnière [F]
articulación [F] en bisagra [F]
Scharniergelenk [N]
articolazione [F] a cerniera [F]

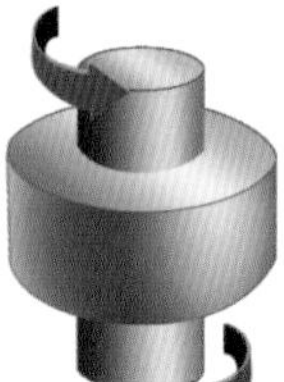

pivot joint
articulation [F] pivot [M]
articulación [F] pivotante
Zapfengelenk [N]
articolazione [F] pivot [M]

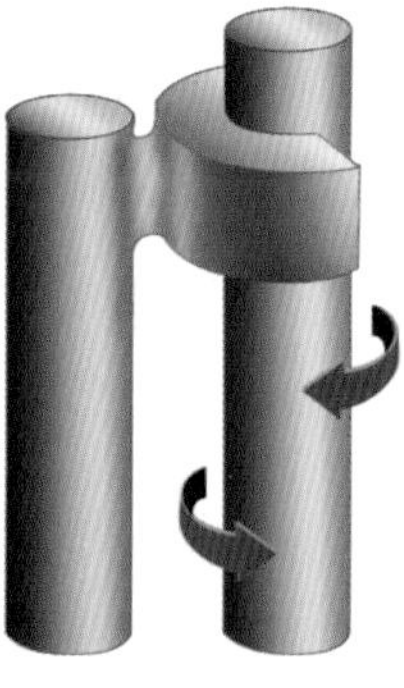

elbow
coude ^{M}
codo ^{M}
Ellbogen ^{M}
gomito ^{M}

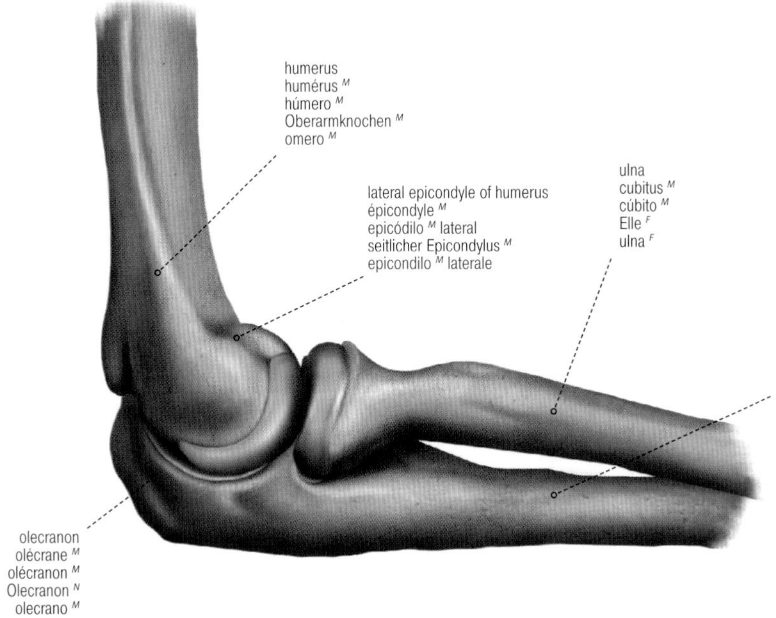
humerus
humérus ^{M}
húmero ^{M}
Oberarmknochen ^{M}
omero ^{M}
lateral epicondyle of humerus
épicondyle ^{M}
epicódilo ^{M} lateral
seitlicher Epicondylus ^{M}
epicondilo ^{M} laterale
ulna
cubitus ^{M}
cúbito ^{M}
Elle ^{F}
ulna ^{F}
radius
radius ^{M}
radio ^{M}
Speiche ^{F}
radio ^{M}
olecranon
olécrane ^{M}
olécranon ^{M}
Olecranon ^{N}
olecrano ^{M}

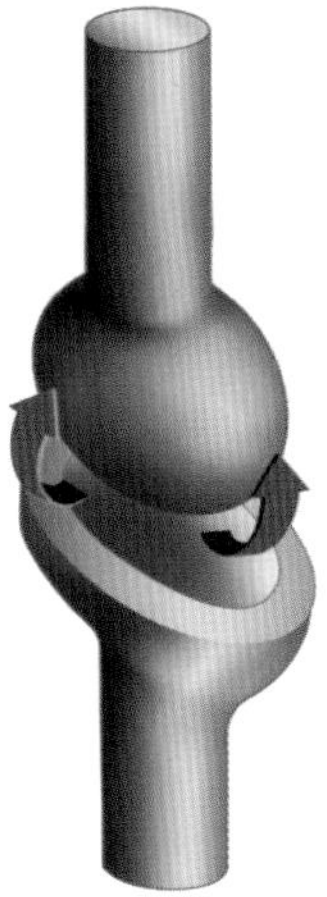

condyloid joint
articulation ^{F} ellipsoïdale
articulación ^{F} elipsoidea
Ellipsoidgelenk ^{N}
articolazione ^{F} condiloidea

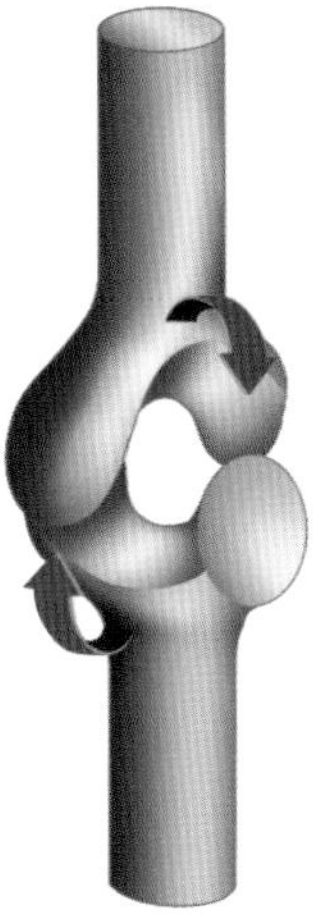

saddle joint
articulation ^{F} en selle ^{F}
articulación ^{F} en silla ^{F} de montar
Sattelgelenk ^{N}
articolazione ^{F} a sella ^{F}

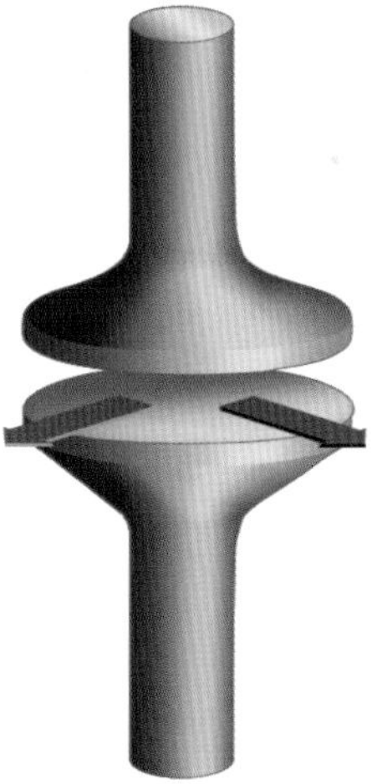

gliding joint
articulation ^{F} arthrodiale
articulación ^{F} deslizante
Arthrodialgelenk ^{N}
articolazione ^{F} piana

spinal column
colonne [F] vertébrale
columna [F] vertebral
Wirbelsäule [F]
colonna [F] vertebrale

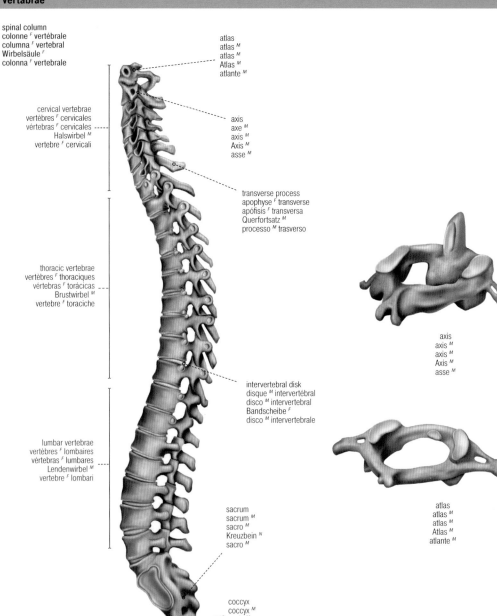

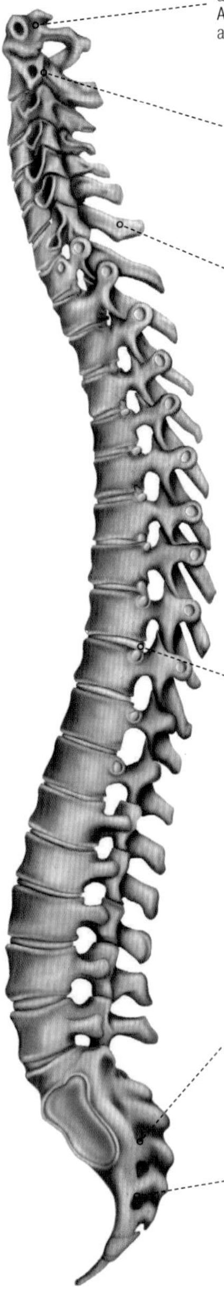
atlas
atlas [M]
atlas [M]
Atlas [M]
atlante [M]
cervical vertebrae
vertèbres [F] cervicales
vértebras [F] cervicales
Halswirbel [M]
vertebre [F] cervicali
axis
axe [M]
axis [M]
Axis [M]
asse [M]
transverse process
apophyse [F] transverse
apófisis [F] transversa
Querfortsatz [M]
processo [M] trasverso
thoracic vertebrae
vertèbres [F] thoraciques
vértebras [F] torácicas
Brustwirbel [M]
vertebre [F] toraciche
intervertebral disk
disque [M] intervertébral
disco [M] intervertebral
Bandscheibe [F]
disco [M] intervertebrale
lumbar vertebrae
vertèbres [F] lombaires
vértebras [F] lumbares
Lendenwirbel [M]
vertebre [F] lombari
sacrum
sacrum [M]
sacro [M]
Kreuzbein [N]
sacro [M]
coccyx
coccyx [M]
coxis [M]
Steißbein [N]
coccige [M]

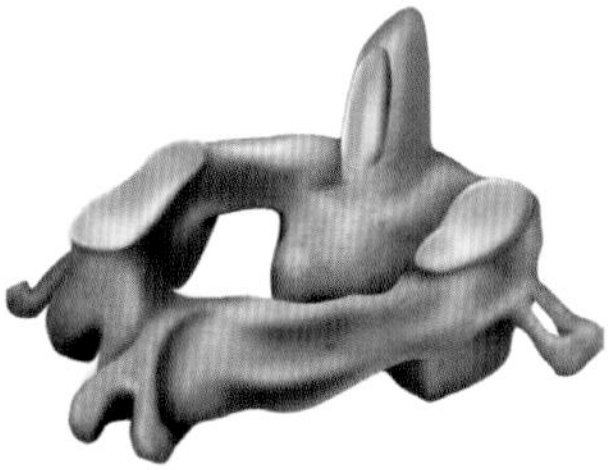

axis
axis [M]
axis [M]
Axis [M]
asse [M]

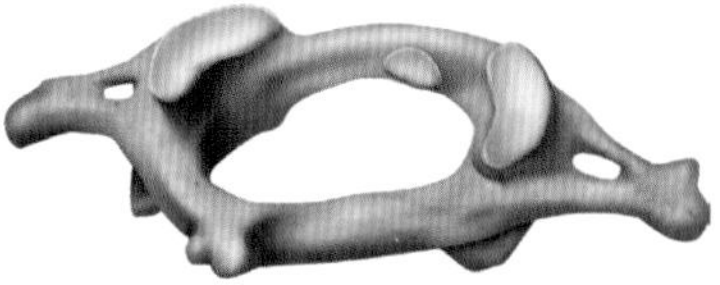

atlas
atlas [M]
atlas [M]
Atlas [M]
atlante [M]

sacrum
sacrum [M]
sacro [M]
Kreuzbein [N]
sacro [M]

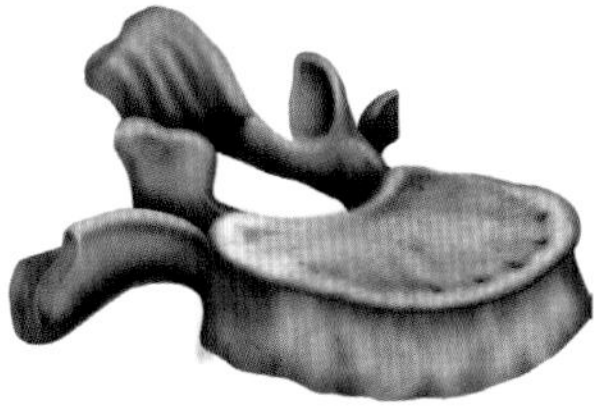

lumbar vertebra
vertèbre [F] lombaire
vértebras [F] lumbares
Lendenwirbel [M]
vertebra [F] lombare

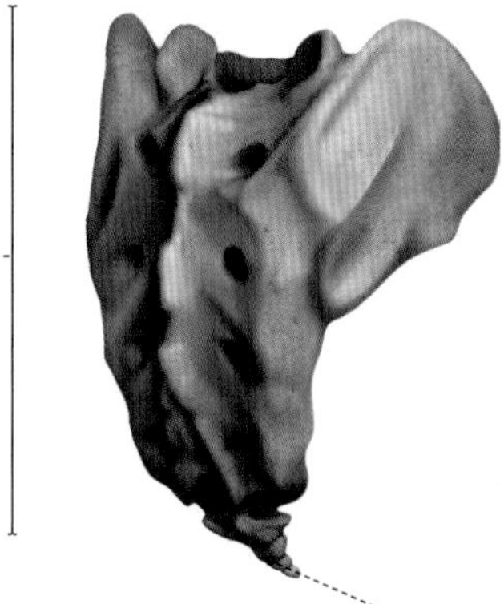
sacrum
sacrum [M]
sacro [M]
Kreuzbein [N]
sacro [M]
coccyx
coccyx [M]
coxis [M]
Steißbein [N]
coccige [M]

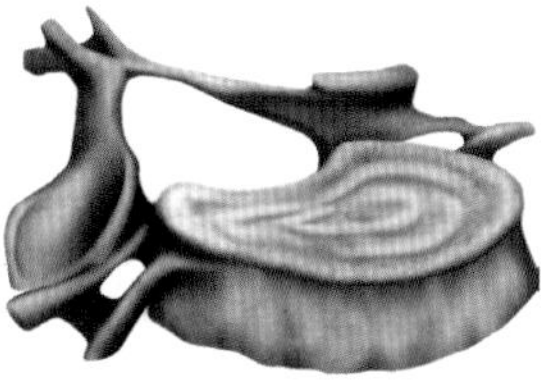

cervical vertebra
vertèbre [F] cervicale
vértebras [F] cervicales
Halswirbel [M]
vertebra [F] cervicale

thoracic vertebra
vertèbre [F] thoracique
vértebra [F] torácica
Brustwirbel [M]
vertebra [F] toracica

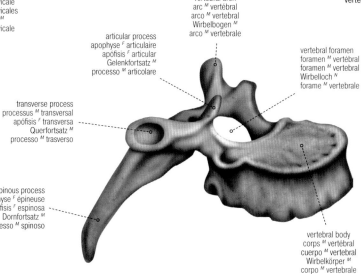

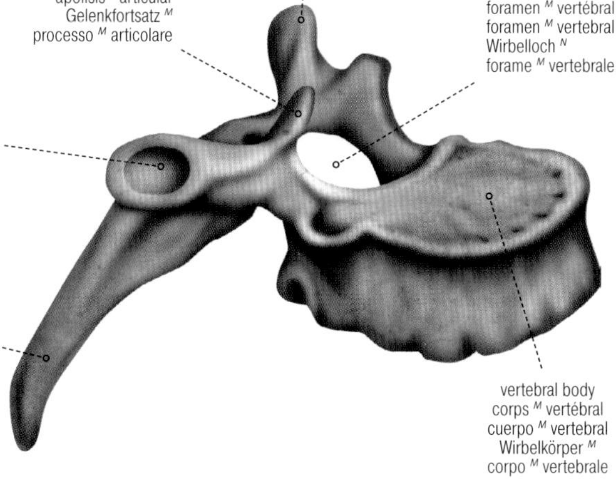
vertebral arch
arc [M] vertébral
arco [M] vertebral
Wirbelbogen [M]
arco [M] vertebrale
articular process
apophyse [F] articulaire
apófisis [F] articular
Gelenkfortsatz [M]
processo [M] articolare
vertebral foramen
foramen [M] vertébral
foramen [M] vertebral
Wirbelloch [N]
forame [M] vertebrale
transverse process
processus [M] transversal
apófisis [F] transversa
Querfortsatz [M]
processo [M] trasverso
spinous process
apophyse [F] épineuse
apófisis [F] espinosa
Dornfortsatz [M]
processo [M] spinoso
vertebral body
corps [M] vertébral
cuerpo [M] vertebral
Wirbelkörper [M]
corpo [M] vertebrale

adult's skull
crâne [M] d'un adulte [M]
cráneo [M] de un adulto [M]
Schädel [M] eines Erwachsenen [M]
cranio [M] di un adulto [M]

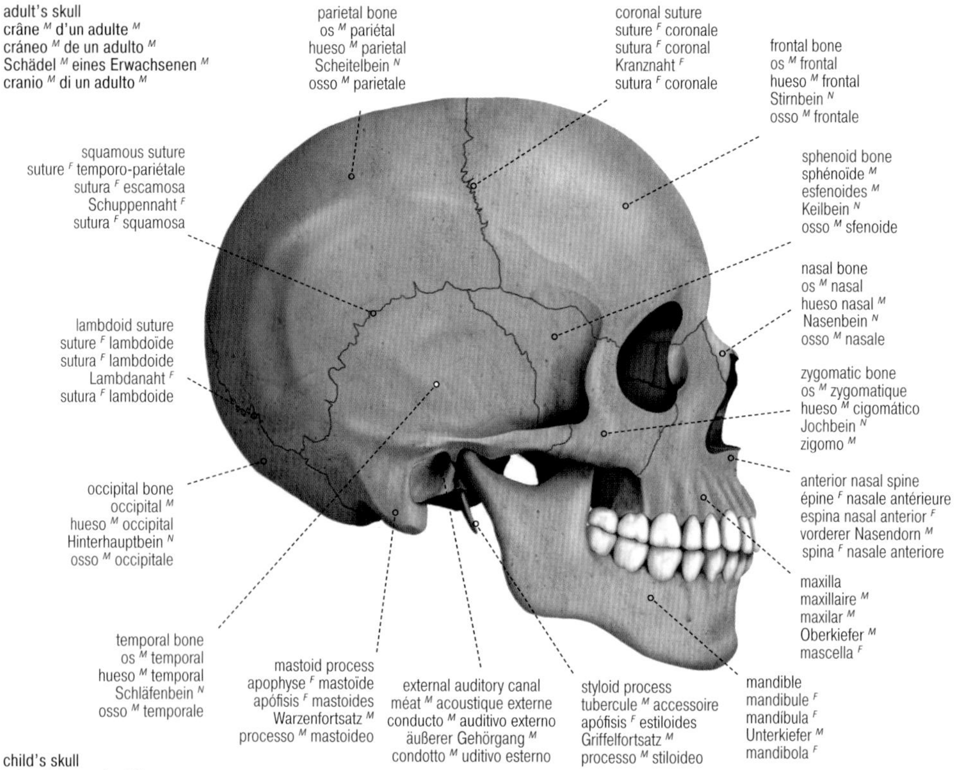
parietal bone
os [M] pariétal
hueso [M] parietal
Scheitelbein [N]
osso [M] parietale
coronal suture
suture [F] coronale
sutura [F] coronal
Kranznaht [F]
sutura [F] coronale
frontal bone
os [M] frontal
hueso [M] frontal
Stirnbein [N]
osso [M] frontale
squamous suture
suture [F] temporo-pariétale
sutura [F] escamosa
Schuppennaht [F]
sutura [F] squamosa
sphenoid bone
sphénoïde [M]
esfenoides [M]
Keilbein [N]
osso [M] sfenoide
nasal bone
os [M] nasal
hueso nasal [M]
Nasenbein [N]
osso [M] nasale
lambdoid suture
suture [F] lambdoïde
sutura [F] lambdoide
Lambdanaht [F]
sutura [F] lambdoide
zygomatic bone
os [M] zygomatique
hueso [M] cigomático
Jochbein [N]
zigomo [M]
anterior nasal spine
épine [F] nasale antérieure
espina nasal anterior [F]
vorderer Nasendorn [M]
spina [F] nasale anteriore
occipital bone
occipital [M]
hueso [M] occipital
Hinterhauptbein [N]
osso [M] occipitale
maxilla
maxillaire [M]
maxilar [M]
Oberkiefer [M]
mascella [F]
temporal bone
os [M] temporal
hueso [M] temporal
Schläfenbein [N]
osso [M] temporale
mastoid process
apophyse [F] mastoïde
apófisis [F] mastoides
Warzenfortsatz [M]
processo [M] mastoideo
external auditory canal
méat [M] acoustique externe
conducto [M] auditivo externo
äußerer Gehörgang [M]
condotto [M] uditivo esterno
styloid process
tubercule [M] accessoire
apófisis [F] estiloides
Griffelfortsatz [M]
processo [M] stiloideo
mandible
mandibule [F]
mandíbula [F]
Unterkiefer [M]
mandibola [F]

child's skull
crâne [M] d'un enfant [M]
cráneo [M] de un niño [M]
Schädel [M] eines Kindes [N]
cranio [M] di un bambino [M]

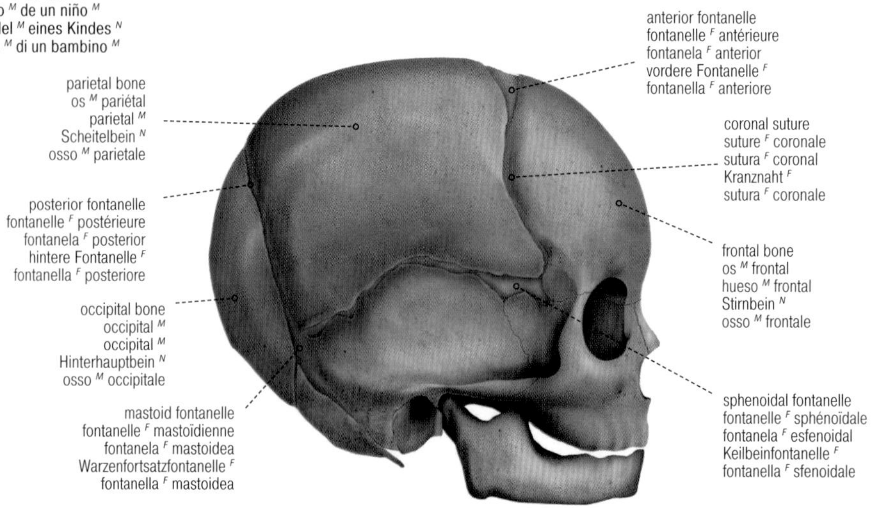
anterior fontanelle
fontanelle [F] antérieure
fontanela [F] anterior
vordere Fontanelle [F]
fontanella [F] anteriore
parietal bone
os [M] pariétal
parietal [M]
Scheitelbein [N]
osso [M] parietale
coronal suture
suture [F] coronale
sutura [F] coronal
Kranznaht [F]
sutura [F] coronale
posterior fontanelle
fontanelle [F] postérieure
fontanela [F] posterior
hintere Fontanelle [F]
fontanella [F] posteriore
frontal bone
os [M] frontal
hueso [M] frontal
Stirnbein [N]
osso [M] frontale
occipital bone
occipital [M]
occipital [M]
Hinterhauptbein [N]
osso [M] occipitale
mastoid fontanelle
fontanelle [F] mastoïdienne
fontanela [F] mastoidea
Warzenfortsatzfontanelle [F]
fontanella [F] mastoidea
sphenoidal fontanelle
fontanelle [F] sphénoïdale
fontanela [F] esfenoidal
Keilbeinfontanelle [F]
fontanella [F] sfenoidale

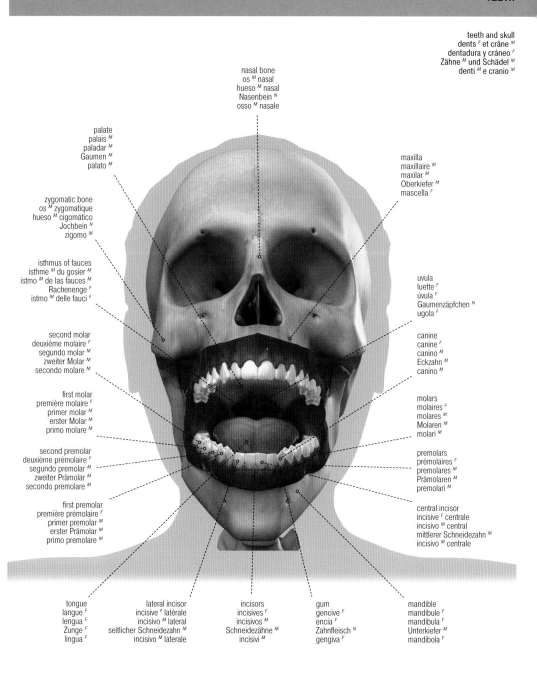

teeth and skull
dents [F] et crâne [M]
dentadura y cráneo [F]
Zähne [M] und Schädel [M]
denti [M] e cranio [M]

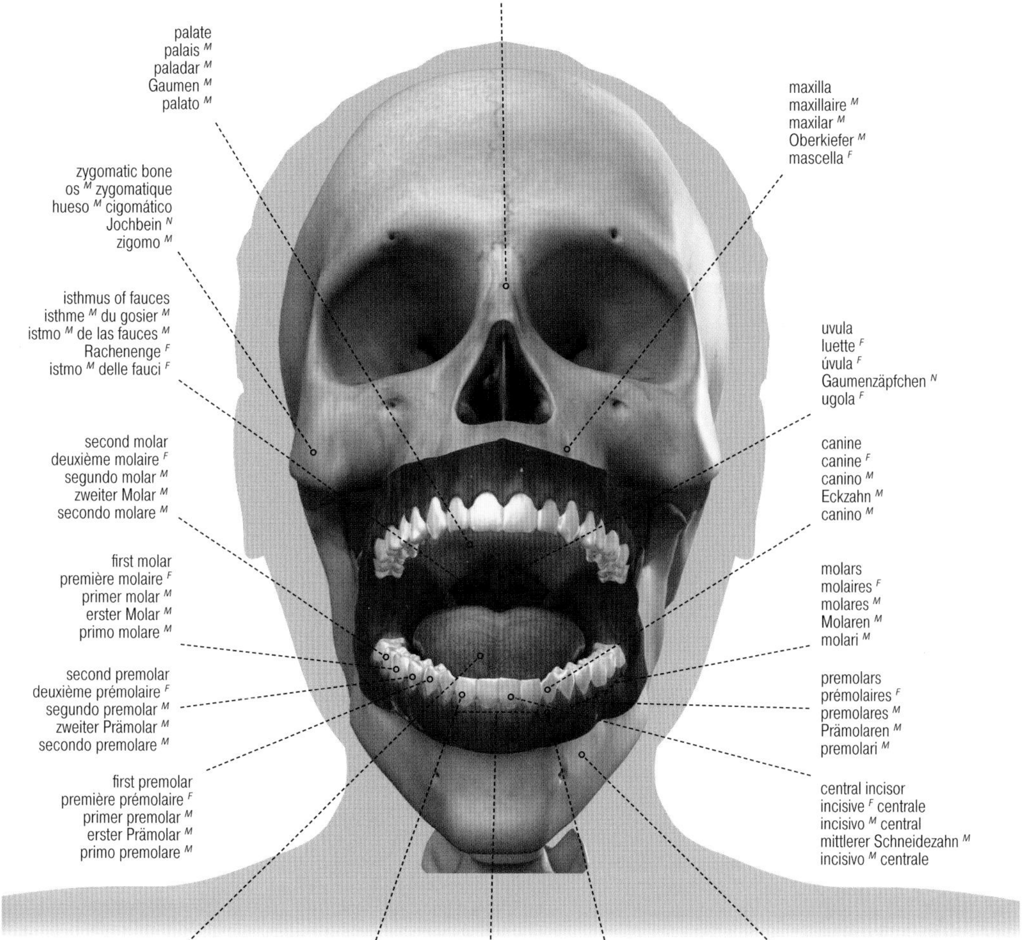
nasal bone
os [M] nasal
hueso [M] nasal
Nasenbein [N]
osso [M] nasale
palate
palais [M]
paladar [M]
Gaumen [M]
palato [M]
maxilla
maxillaire [M]
maxilar [M]
Oberkiefer [M]
mascella [F]
zygomatic bone
os [M] zygomatique
hueso [M] cigomático
Jochbein [N]
zigomo [M]
isthmus of fauces
isthme [M] du gosier [M]
istmo [M] de las fauces [M]
Rachenenge [F]
istmo [M] delle fauci [F]
uvula
luette [F]
úvula [F]
Gaumenzäpfchen [N]
ugola [F]
second molar
deuxième molaire [F]
segundo molar [M]
zweiter Molar [M]
secondo molare [M]
canine
canine [F]
canino [M]
Eckzahn [M]
canino [M]
first molar
première molaire [F]
primer molar [M]
erster Molar [M]
primo molare [M]
molars
molaires [F]
molares [M]
Molaren [M]
molari [M]
second premolar
deuxième prémolaire [F]
segundo premolar [M]
zweiter Prämolar [M]
secondo premolare [M]
premolars
prémolaires [F]
premolares [M]
Prämolaren [M]
premolari [M]
first premolar
première prémolaire [F]
primer premolar [M]
erster Prämolar [M]
primo premolare [M]
central incisor
incisive [F] centrale
incisivo [M] central
mittlerer Schneidezahn [M]
incisivo [M] centrale
tongue
langue [F]
lengua [F]
Zunge [F]
lingua [F]
lateral incisor
incisive [F] latérale
incisivo [M] lateral
seitlicher Schneidezahn [M]
incisivo [M] laterale
incisors
incisives [F]
incisivos [M]
Schneidezähne [M]
incisivi [M]
gum
gencive [F]
encía [F]
Zahnfleisch [N]
gengiva [F]
mandible
mandibule [F]
mandíbula [F]
Unterkiefer [M]
mandibola [F]

cross section of molar
coupe F transversale d'une molaire F
sección F transversal de un molar F
Querschnitt M eines Molars M
sezione F trasversale di un molare M

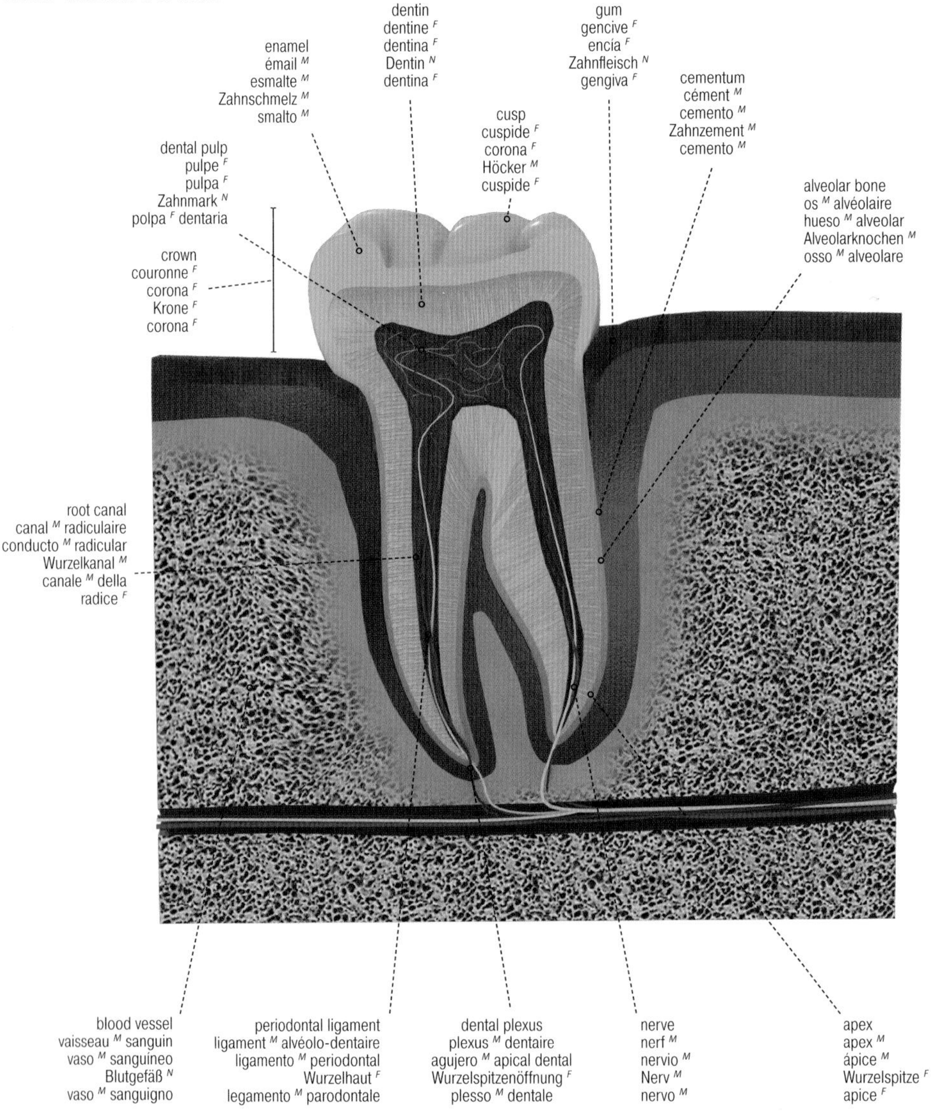
dentin
dentine F
dentina F
Dentin N
dentina F
gum
gencive F
encía F
Zahnfleisch N
gengiva F
enamel
émail M
esmalte M
Zahnschmelz M
smalto M
cementum
cément M
cemento M
Zahnzement M
cemento M
cusp
cuspide F
corona F
Höcker M
cuspide F
dental pulp
pulpe F
pulpa F
Zahnmark N
polpa F dentaria
alveolar bone
os M alvéolaire
hueso M alveolar
Alveolarknochen M
osso M alveolare
crown
couronne F
corona F
Krone F
corona F
root canal
canal M radiculaire
conducto M radicular
Wurzelkanal M
canale M della radice F
blood vessel
vaisseau M sanguin
vaso M sanguíneo
Blutgefäß N
vaso M sanguigno
periodontal ligament
ligament M alvéolo-dentaire
ligamento M periodontal
Wurzelhaut F
legamento M parodontale
dental plexus
plexus M dentaire
agujero M apical dental
Wurzelspitzenöffnung F
plesso M dentale
nerve
nerf M
nervio M
Nerv M
nervo M
apex
apex M
ápice M
Wurzelspitze F
apice F

respiratory organs
organes [M] respiratoire
órganos [M] respiratorios
Atmungsorgane [N]
apparato [M] respiratorio

lungs
poumons [M]
pulmones [M]
Lungen [F]
polmoni [M]

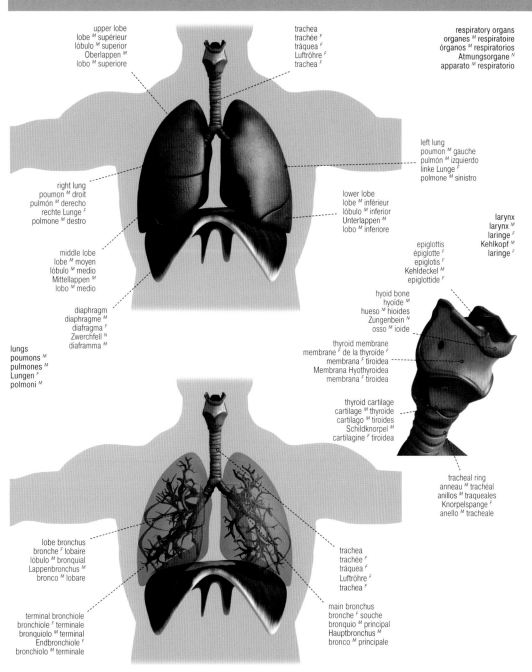

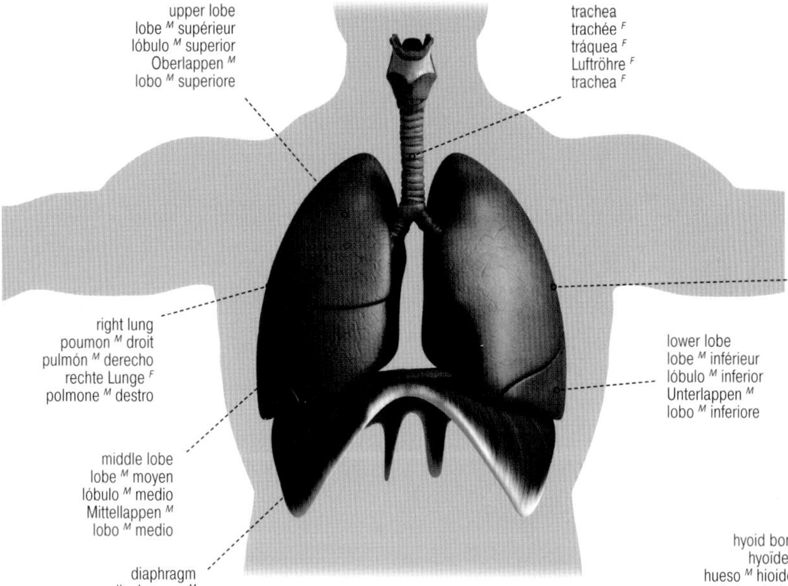
upper lobe
lobe [M] supérieur
lóbulo [M] superior
Oberlappen [M]
lobo [M] superiore
trachea
trachée [F]
tráquea [F]
Luftröhre [F]
trachea [F]
left lung
poumon [M] gauche
pulmón [M] izquierdo
linke Lunge [F]
polmone [M] sinistro
right lung
poumon [M] droit
pulmón [M] derecho
rechte Lunge [F]
polmone [M] destro
lower lobe
lobe [M] inférieur
lóbulo [M] inferior
Unterlappen [M]
lobo [M] inferiore
middle lobe
lobe [M] moyen
lóbulo [M] medio
Mittellappen [M]
lobo [M] medio
diaphragm
diaphragme [M]
diafragma [F]
Zwerchfell [N]
diaframma [M]

larynx
larynx [M]
laringe [F]
Kehlkopf [M]
laringe [F]

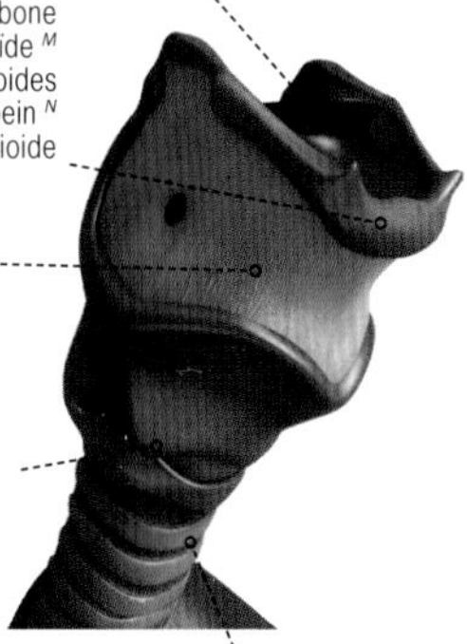
epiglottis
épiglotte [F]
epiglotis [F]
Kehldeckel [M]
epiglottide [F]
hyoid bone
hyoïde [M]
hueso [M] hioides
Zungenbein [N]
osso [M] ioide
thyroid membrane
membrane [F] de la thyroïde [F]
membrana [F] tiroidea
Membrana Hyothyroidea
membrana [F] tiroidea
thyroid cartilage
cartilage [M] thyroïde
cartílago [M] tiroides
Schildknorpel [M]
cartilagine [F] tiroidea
tracheal ring
anneau [M] trachéal
anillos [M] traqueales
Knorpelspange [F]
anello [M] tracheale

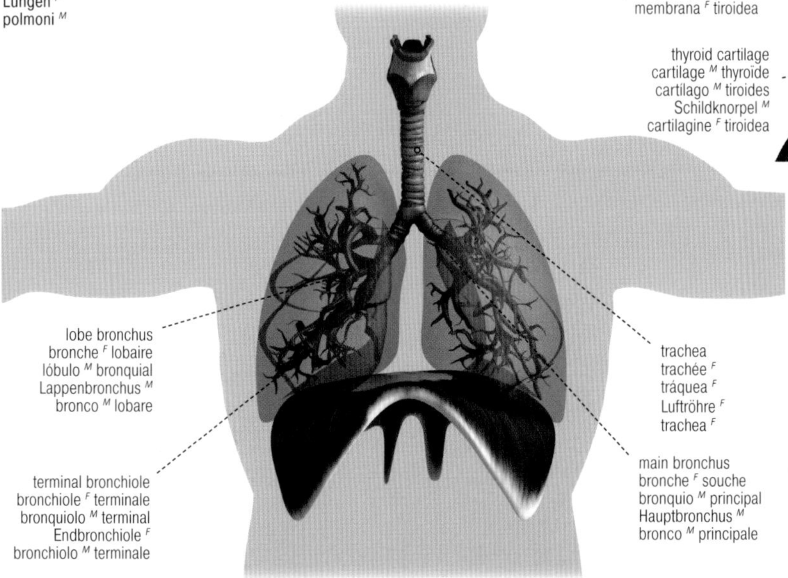
lobe bronchus
bronche [F] lobaire
lóbulo [M] bronquial
Lappenbronchus [M]
bronco [M] lobare
trachea
trachée [F]
tráquea [F]
Luftröhre [F]
trachea [F]
terminal bronchiole
bronchiole [F] terminale
bronquiolo [M] terminal
Endbronchiole [F]
bronchiolo [M] terminale
main bronchus
bronche [F] souche
bronquio [M] principal
Hauptbronchus [M]
bronco [M] principale

principal arteries
artères F principales
arterias F principales
Hauptarterien F
arterie F principali

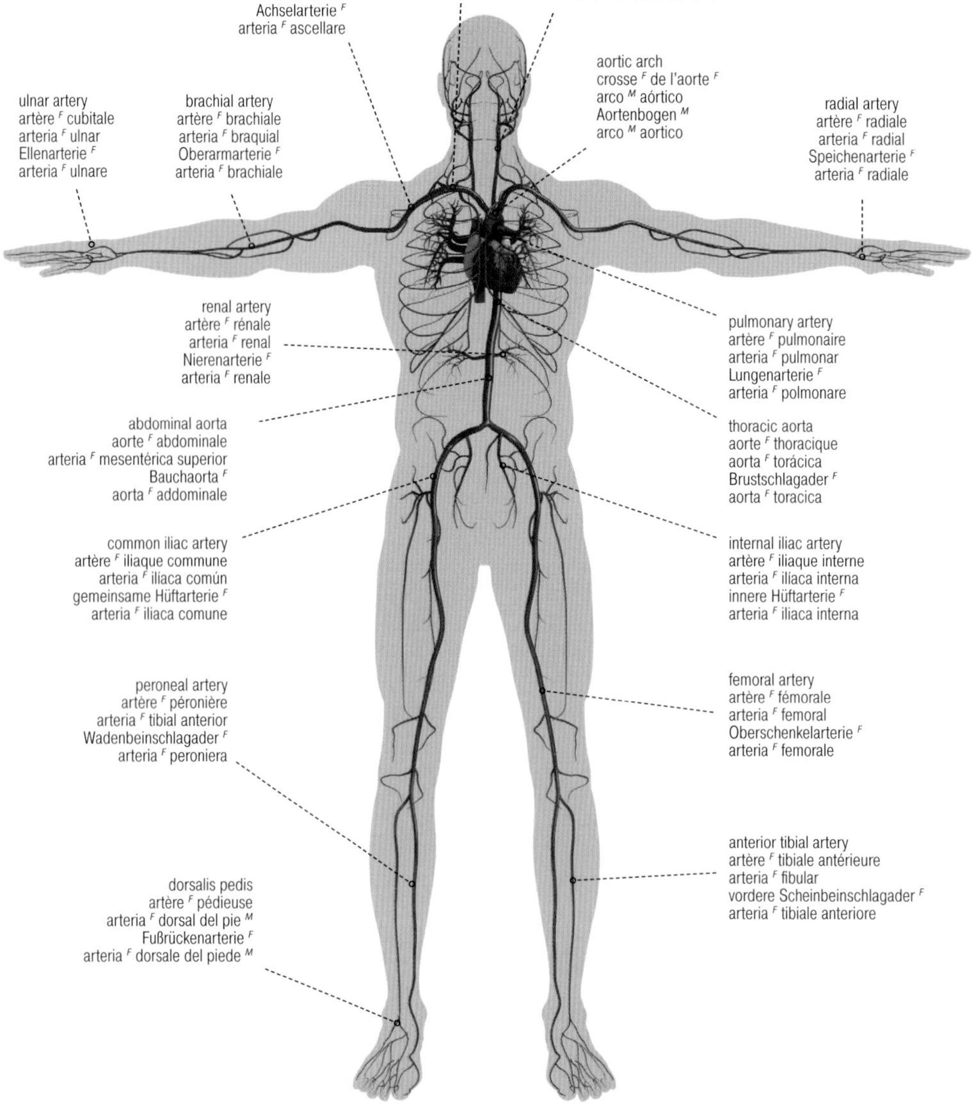
subclavian artery
artère F subclavière
arteria F subclavia
Schlüsselbeinarterie F
arteria F succlavia
common carotid artery
artère F carotide commune
arteria F carótida común
gemeinsame Kopfschlagader F
arteria F carotide comune
axillary artery
artère F axillaire
arteria F axilar
Achselarterie F
arteria F ascellare
aortic arch
crosse F de l'aorte F
arco M aórtico
Aortenbogen M
arco M aortico
ulnar artery
artère F cubitale
arteria F ulnar
Ellenarterie F
arteria F ulnare
brachial artery
artère F brachiale
arteria F braquial
Oberarmarterie F
arteria F brachiale
radial artery
artère F radiale
arteria F radial
Speichenarterie F
arteria F radiale
renal artery
artère F rénale
arteria F renal
Nierenarterie F
arteria F renale
pulmonary artery
artère F pulmonaire
arteria F pulmonar
Lungenarterie F
arteria F polmonare
abdominal aorta
aorte F abdominale
arteria F mesentérica superior
Bauchaorta F
aorta F addominale
thoracic aorta
aorte F thoracique
aorta F torácica
Brustschlagader F
aorta F toracica
common iliac artery
artère F iliaque commune
arteria F ilíaca común
gemeinsame Hüftarterie F
arteria F iliaca comune
internal iliac artery
artère F iliaque interne
arteria F ilíaca interna
innere Hüftarterie F
arteria F iliaca interna
peroneal artery
artère F péronière
arteria F tibial anterior
Wadenbeinschlagader F
arteria F peroniera
femoral artery
artère F fémorale
arteria F femoral
Oberschenkelarterie F
arteria F femorale
anterior tibial artery
artère F tibiale antérieure
arteria F fibular
vordere Scheinbeinschlagader F
arteria F tibiale anteriore
dorsalis pedis
artère F pédieuse
arteria F dorsal del pie M
Fußrückenarterie F
arteria F dorsale del piede M

principal veins
veines F principales
venas F principales
Hauptvenen F
vene F principali

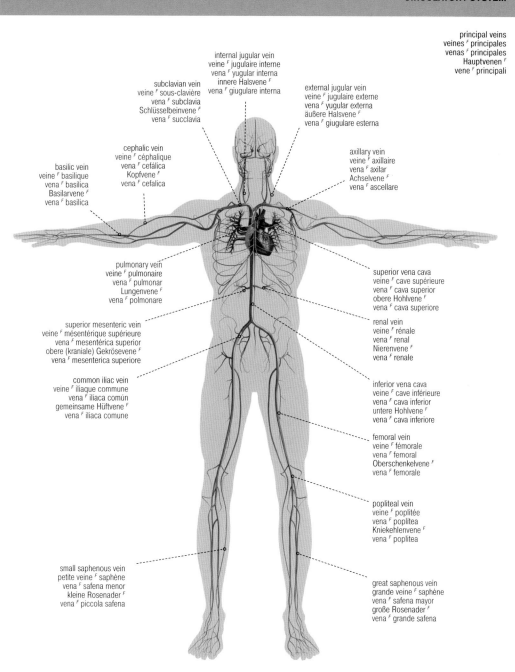

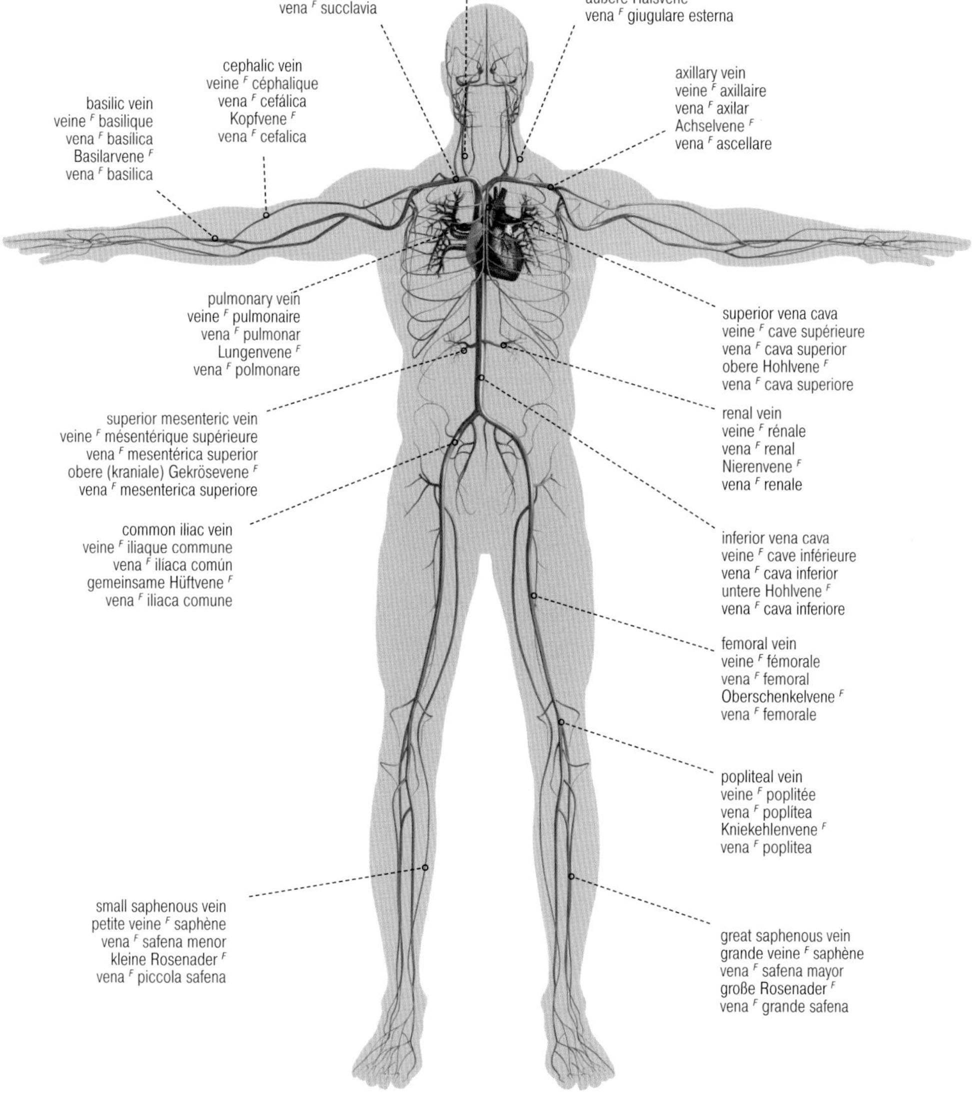

internal jugular vein
veine F jugulaire interne
vena F yugular interna
innere Halsvene F
vena F giugulare interna
subclavian vein
veine F sous-clavière
vena F subclavia
Schlüsselbeinvene F
vena F succlavia
external jugular vein
veine F jugulaire externe
vena F yugular externa
äußere Halsvene F
vena F giugulare esterna
cephalic vein
veine F céphalique
vena F cefálica
Kopfvene F
vena F cefalica
basilic vein
veine F basilique
vena F basílica
Basilarvene F
vena F basilica
axillary vein
veine F axillaire
vena F axilar
Achselvene F
vena F ascellare
pulmonary vein
veine F pulmonaire
vena F pulmonar
Lungenvene F
vena F polmonare
superior vena cava
veine F cave supérieure
vena F cava superior
obere Hohlvene F
vena F cava superiore
superior mesenteric vein
veine F mésentérique supérieure
vena F mesentérica superior
obere (kraniale) Gekrösevene F
vena F mesenterica superiore
renal vein
veine F rénale
vena F renal
Nierenvene F
vena F renale
common iliac vein
veine F iliaque commune
vena F ilíaca común
gemeinsame Hüftvene F
vena F iliaca comune
inferior vena cava
veine F cave inférieure
vena F cava inferior
untere Hohlvene F
vena F cava inferiore
femoral vein
veine F fémorale
vena F femoral
Oberschenkelvene F
vena F femorale
popliteal vein
veine F poplitée
vena F poplítea
Kniekehlenvene F
vena F poplitea
small saphenous vein
petite veine F saphène
vena F safena menor
kleine Rosenader F
vena F piccola safena
great saphenous vein
grande veine F saphène
vena F safena mayor
große Rosenader F
vena F grande safena

heart
cœur M
corazón M
Herz N
cuore M

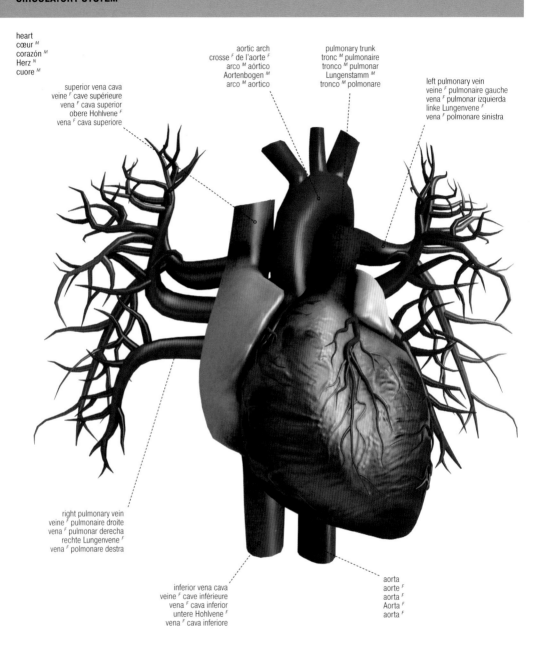

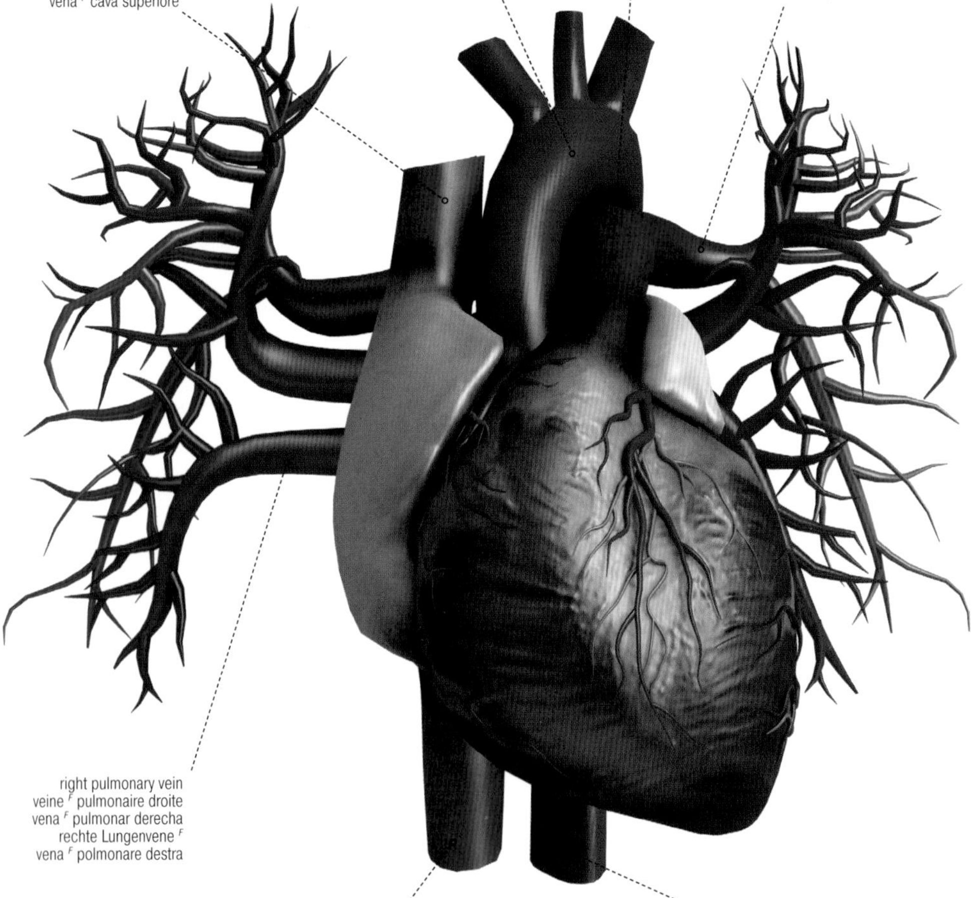
aortic arch
crosse F de l'aorte F
arco M aórtico
Aortenbogen M
arco M aortico
pulmonary trunk
tronc M pulmonaire
tronco M pulmonar
Lungenstamm M
tronco M polmonare
superior vena cava
veine F cave supérieure
vena F cava superior
obere Hohlvene F
vena F cava superiore
left pulmonary vein
veine F pulmonaire gauche
vena F pulmonar izquierda
linke Lungenvene F
vena F polmonare sinistra
right pulmonary vein
veine F pulmonaire droite
vena F pulmonar derecha
rechte Lungenvene F
vena F polmonare destra
inferior vena cava
veine F cave inférieure
vena F cava inferior
untere Hohlvene F
vena F cava inferiore
aorta
aorte F
aorta F
Aorta F
aorta F

cross section of heart
coupe F transversale du cœur M
sección F transversal de corazón M
Herz N im Querschnitt M
sezione F del cuore M

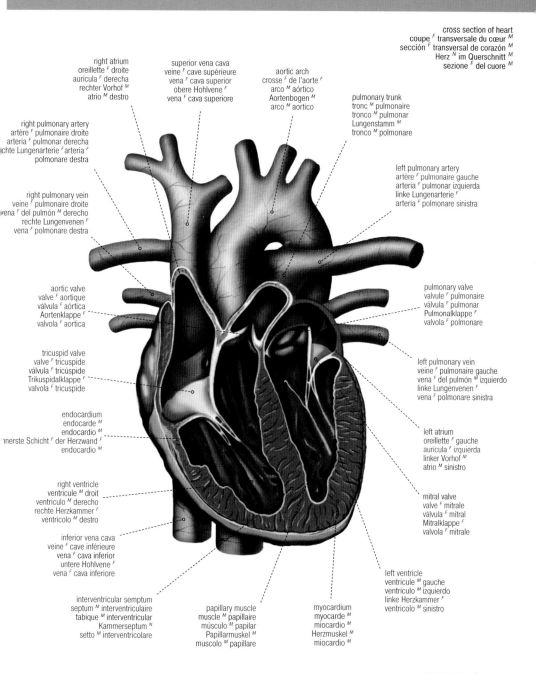

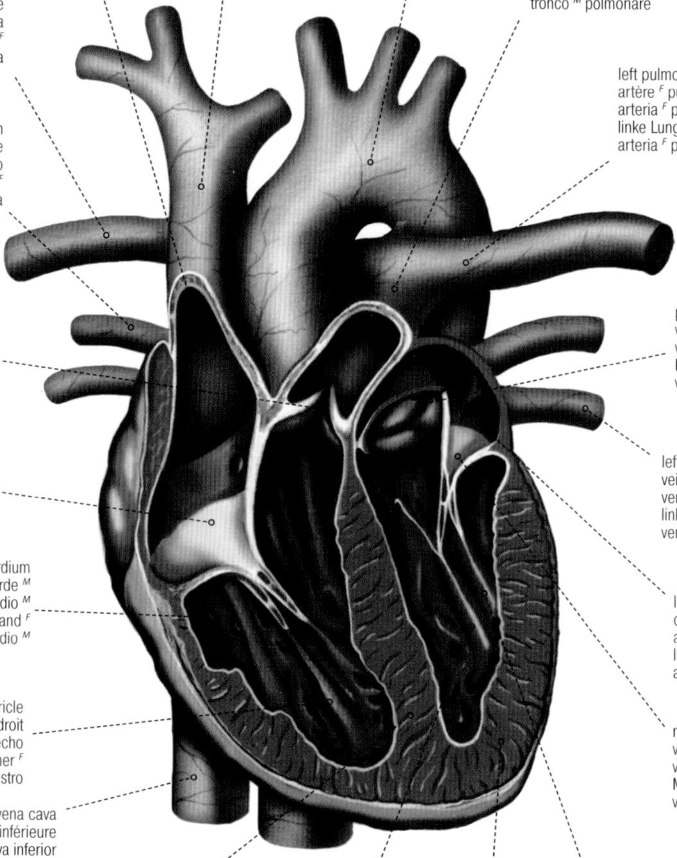
right atrium
oreillette F droite
aurícula F derecha
rechter Vorhof M
atrio M destro
superior vena cava
veine F cave supérieure
vena F cava superior
obere Hohlvene F
vena F cava superiore
aortic arch
crosse F de l'aorte F
arco M aórtico
Aortenbogen M
arco M aortico
pulmonary trunk
tronc M pulmonaire
tronco M pulmonar
Lungenstamm M
tronco M polmonare
right pulmonary artery
artère F pulmonaire droite
arteria F pulmonar derecha
chte Lungenarterie F arteria F
polmonare destra
left pulmonary artery
artère F pulmonaire gauche
arteria F pulmonar izquierda
linke Lungenarterie F
arteria F polmonare sinistra
right pulmonary vein
veine F pulmonaire droite
vena F del pulmón M derecho
rechte Lungenvenen F
vena F polmonare destra
aortic valve
valve F aortique
válvula F aórtica
Aortenklappe F
valvola F aortica
pulmonary valve
valvule F pulmonaire
válvula F pulmonar
Pulmonalklappe F
valvola F polmonare
tricuspid valve
valve F tricuspide
válvula F tricúspide
Trikuspidalklappe F
valvola F tricuspide
left pulmonary vein
veine F pulmonaire gauche
vena F del pulmón M izquierdo
linke Lungenvenen F
vena F polmonare sinistra
endocardium
endocarde M
endocardio M
nnerste Schicht F der Herzwand F
endocardio M
left atrium
oreillette F gauche
aurícula F izquierda
linker Vorhof M
atrio M sinistro
right ventricle
ventricule M droit
ventrículo M derecho
rechte Herzkammer F
ventricolo M destro
mitral valve
valve F mitrale
válvula F mitral
Mitralklappe F
valvola F mitrale
inferior vena cava
veine F cave inférieure
vena F cava inferior
untere Hohlvene F
vena F cava inferiore
left ventricle
ventricule M gauche
ventrículo M izquierdo
linke Herzkammer F
ventricolo M sinistro
interventricular semptum
septum M interventriculaire
tabique M interventricular
Kammerseptum N
setto M interventricolare
papillary muscle
muscle M papillaire
músculo M papilar
Papillarmuskel M
muscolo M papillare
myocardium
myocarde M
miocardio M
Herzmuskel M
miocardio M

anterior view of brain
vue [F] antérieure du cerveau [M]
vista [F] anterior del cerebro [M]
Vorderansicht [F] des Gehirns [N]
vista [F] anteriore del cervello [M]

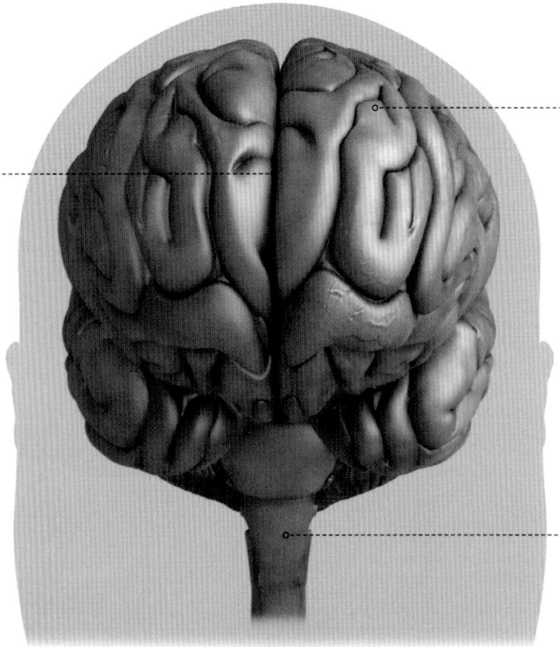
longitudinal fissure
scissure [F] interhémisphérique
fisura [F] longitudinal
Hirnlängsfurche [F]
fessura [F] longitudinale
cerebral cortex
cortex [M] cérébral
corteza [F] cerebral
Hirnrinde [F]
corteccia [F] cerebrale
medulla oblongata
bulbe [M] rachidien
médula oblongada [F]
verlängertes Rückenmark [N]
midollo [M] allungato

posterior view of brain
vue [F] postérieure du cerveau [M]
vista [F] posterior del cerebro [M]
Rückansicht [F] des Gehirns [N]
vista [F] posteriore del cervello [M]

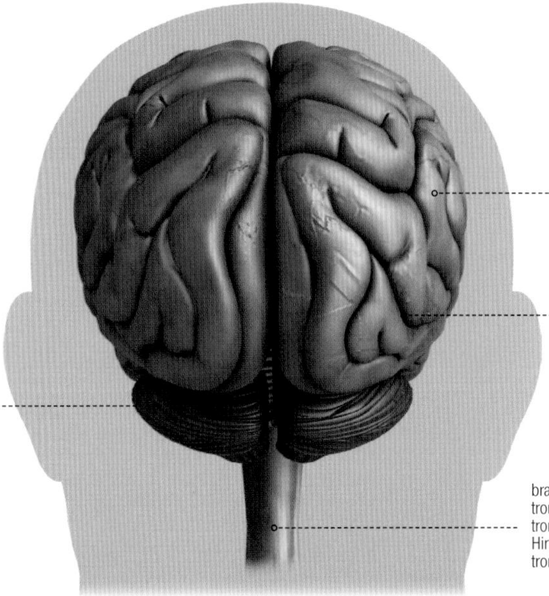
gyrus
gyrus [F]
giro [M]
Gyrus [M]
giro [M]
sulcus
sillon [M]
surco [M]
Sulkus [M]
solco [M]
cerebellum
cervelet [M]
cerebelo [M]
Kleinhirn [N]
cervelletto [M]
brain stem
tronc [M] cérébral
tronco [M] del encéfalo [M]
Hirnstamm [M]
tronco [M] encefalico

cross section of brain
coupe [F] transversale du cerveau [M]
vista [F] transversal del cerebro [M]
Querschnitt [M] des Gehirns [N]
sezione [F] trasversale del cervello [M]

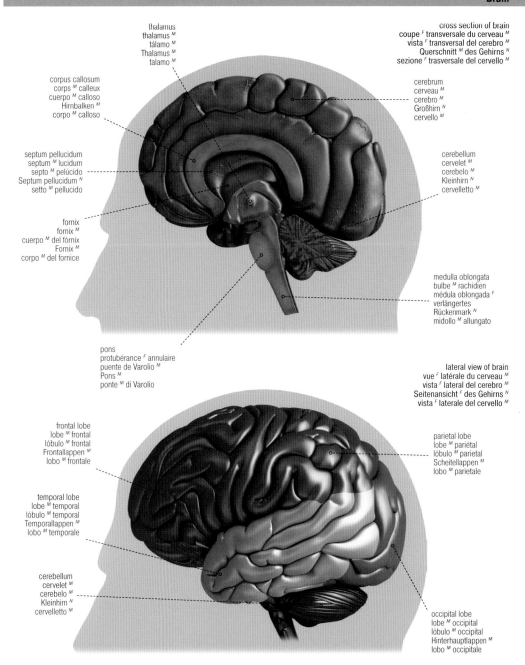

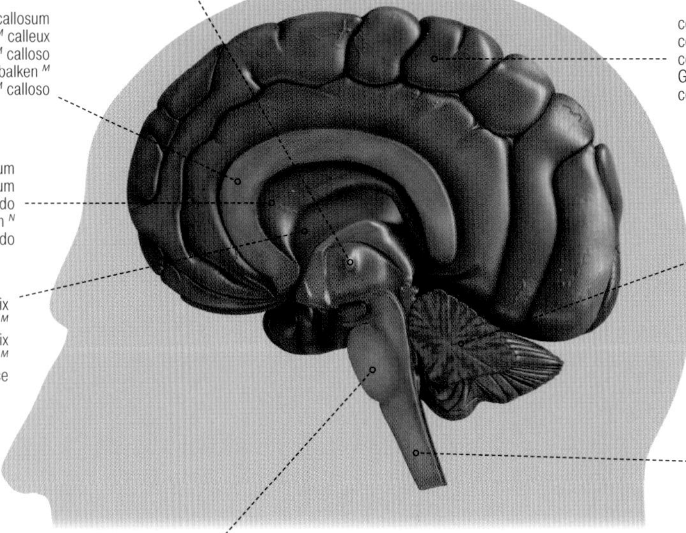
thalamus
thalamus [M]
tálamo [M]
Thalamus [M]
talamo [M]
corpus callosum
corps [M] calleux
cuerpo [M] calloso
Hirnbalken [M]
corpo [M] calloso
cerebrum
cerveau [M]
cerebro [M]
Großhirn [N]
cervello [M]
septum pellucidum
septum [M] lucidum
septo [M] pelúcido
Septum pellucidum [N]
setto [M] pellucido
cerebellum
cervelet [M]
cerebelo [M]
Kleinhirn [N]
cervelletto [M]
fornix
fornix [M]
cuerpo [M] del fórnix
Fornix [M]
corpo [M] del fornice
medulla oblongata
bulbe [M] rachidien
médula oblongada [F]
verlängertes
Rückenmark [N]
midollo [M] allungato
pons
protubérance [F] annulaire
puente de Varolio [M]
Pons [M]
ponte [M] di Varolio

lateral view of brain
vue [F] latérale du cerveau [M]
vista [F] lateral del cerebro [M]
Seitenansicht [F] des Gehirns [N]
vista [F] laterale del cervello [M]

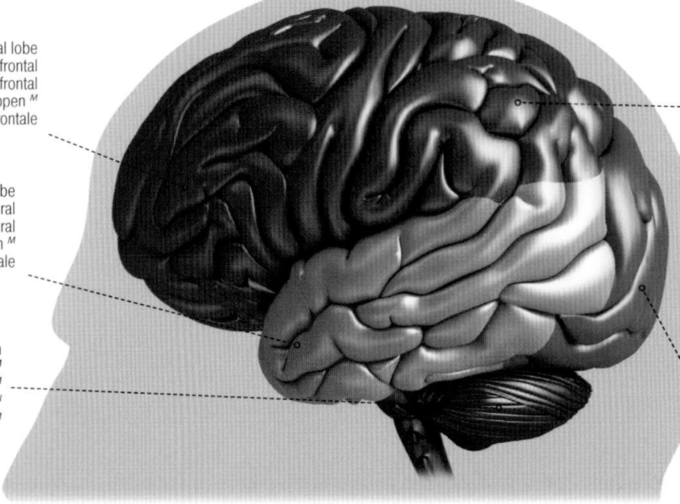
frontal lobe
lobe [M] frontal
lóbulo [M] frontal
Frontallappen [M]
lobo [M] frontale
parietal lobe
lobe [M] pariétal
lóbulo [M] parietal
Scheitellappen [M]
lobo [M] parietale
temporal lobe
lobe [M] temporal
lóbulo [M] temporal
Temporallappen [M]
lobo [M] temporale
cerebellum
cervelet [M]
cerebelo [M]
Kleinhirn [N]
cervelletto [M]
occipital lobe
lobe [M] occipital
lóbulo [M] occipital
Hinterhauptlappen [M]
lobo [M] occipitale

main structure of nervous system
structure [F] principale du système [M] nerveux
estructura [F] principal del sistema [M] nervioso
Hauptstruktur [F] des Nervensystems [N]
struttura [F] del sistema [F] nervoso

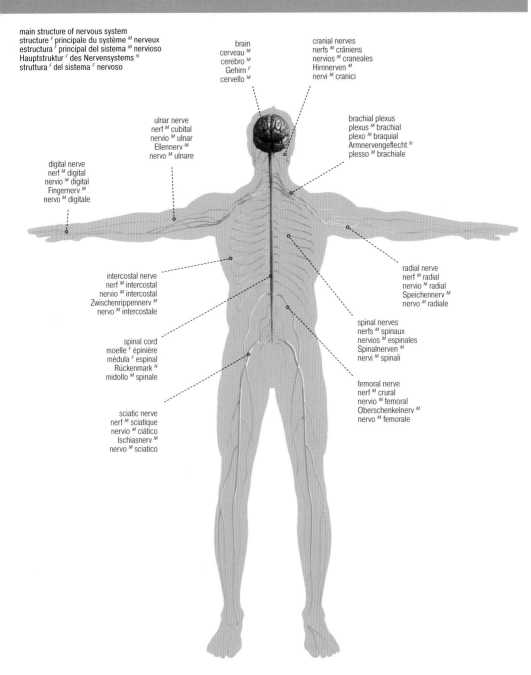

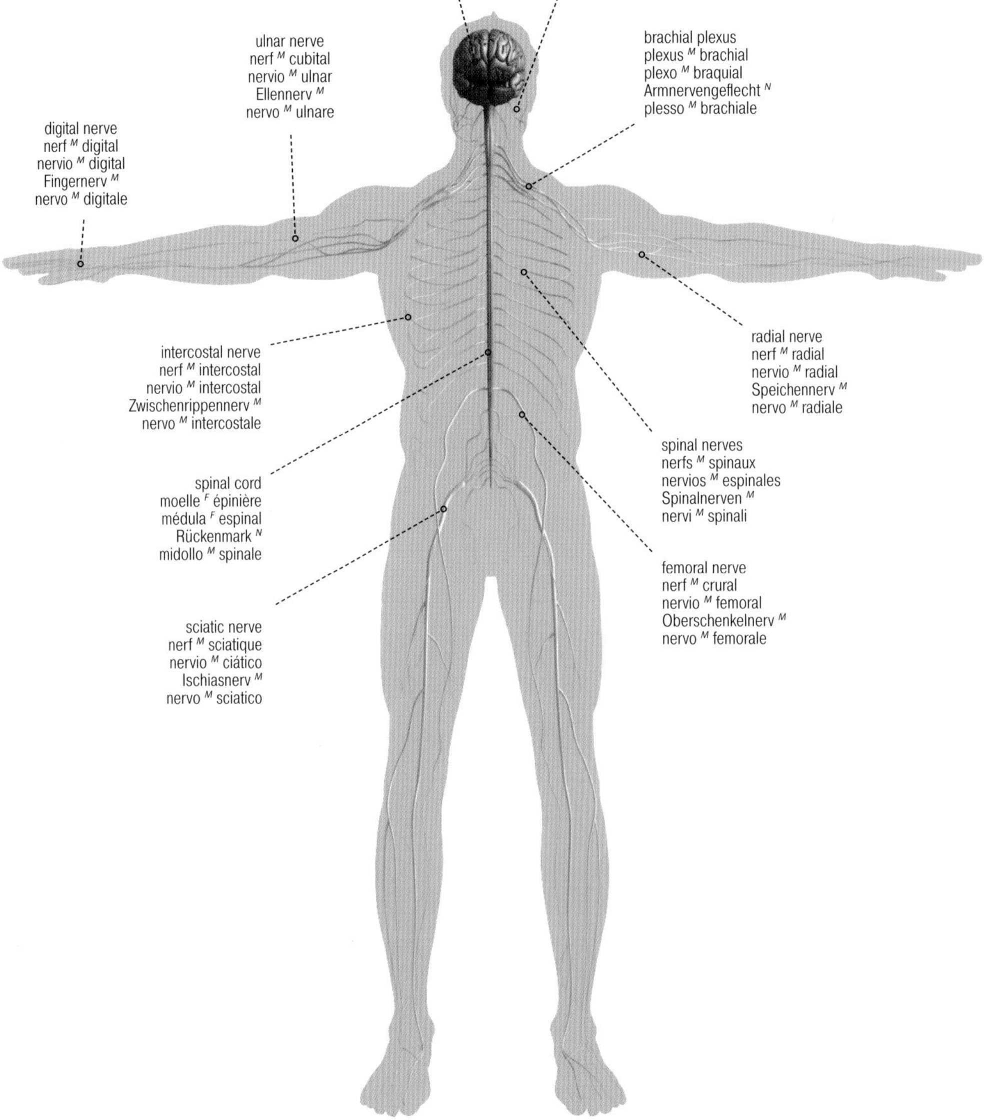
brain
cerveau [M]
cerebro [M]
Gehirn [F]
cervello [M]
cranial nerves
nerfs [M] crâniens
nervios [M] craneales
Hirnnerven [M]
nervi [M] cranici
ulnar nerve
nerf [M] cubital
nervio [M] ulnar
Ellennerv [M]
nervo [M] ulnare
brachial plexus
plexus [M] brachial
plexo [M] braquial
Armnervengeflecht [N]
plesso [M] brachiale
digital nerve
nerf [M] digital
nervio [M] digital
Fingernerv [M]
nervo [M] digitale
radial nerve
nerf [M] radial
nervio [M] radial
Speichennerv [M]
nervo [M] radiale
intercostal nerve
nerf [M] intercostal
nervio [M] intercostal
Zwischenrippennerv [M]
nervo [M] intercostale
spinal nerves
nerfs [M] spinaux
nervios [M] espinales
Spinalnerven [M]
nervi [M] spinali
spinal cord
moelle [F] épinière
médula [F] espinal
Rückenmark [N]
midollo [M] spinale
femoral nerve
nerf [M] crural
nervio [M] femoral
Oberschenkelnerv [M]
nervo [M] femorale
sciatic nerve
nerf [M] sciatique
nervio [M] ciático
Ischiasnerv [M]
nervo [M] sciatico

lymphatic organs
organes M lymphatiques
órganos M linfáticos
Lymphorgane N
sistema M linfatico

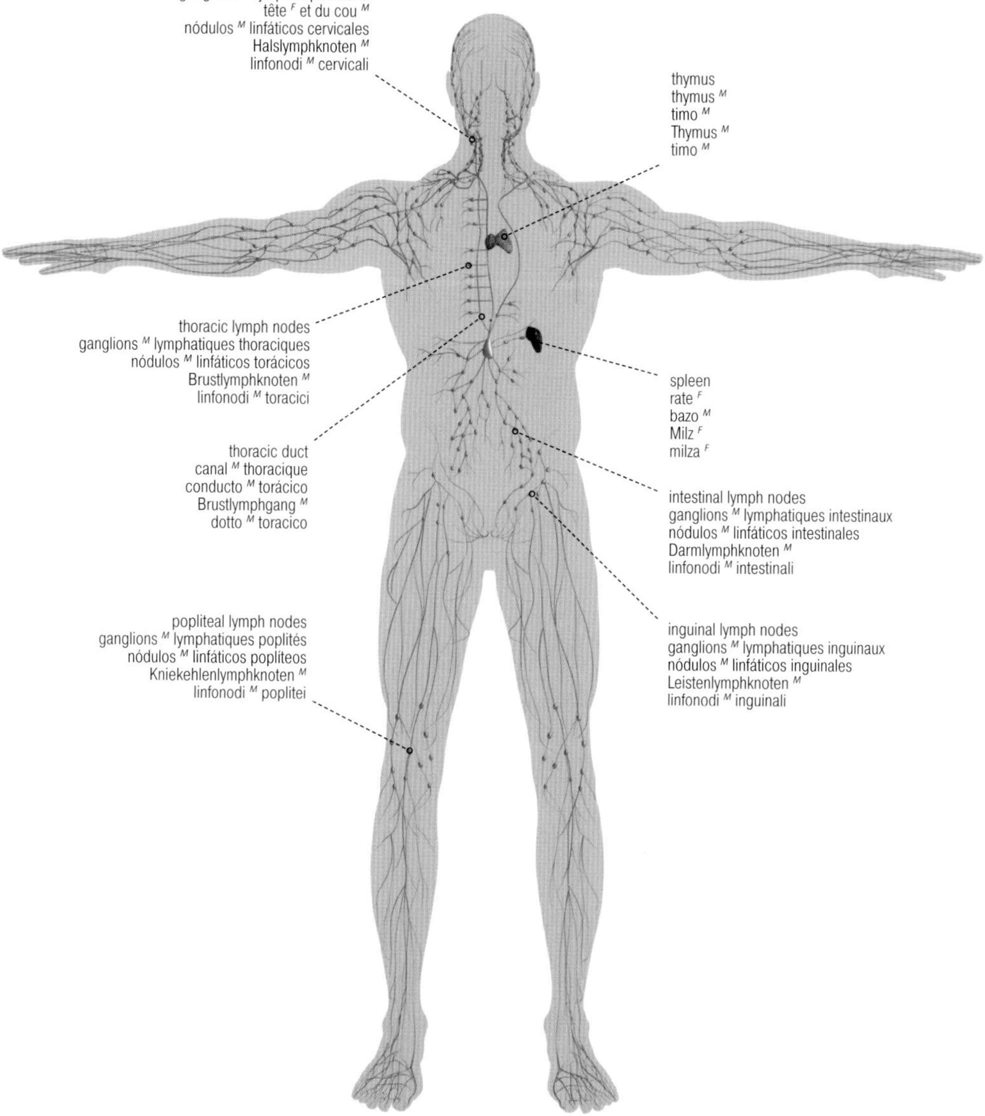
cervical lymph nodes
ganglions M lymphatiques de la tête F et du cou M
nódulos M linfáticos cervicales
Halslymphknoten M
linfonodi M cervicali
thymus
thymus M
timo M
Thymus M
timo M
thoracic lymph nodes
ganglions M lymphatiques thoraciques
nódulos M linfáticos torácicos
Brustlymphknoten M
linfonodi M toracici
spleen
rate F
bazo M
Milz F
milza F
thoracic duct
canal M thoracique
conducto M torácico
Brustlymphgang M
dotto M toracico
intestinal lymph nodes
ganglions M lymphatiques intestinaux
nódulos M linfáticos intestinales
Darmlymphknoten M
linfonodi M intestinali
popliteal lymph nodes
ganglions M lymphatiques poplités
nódulos M linfáticos poplíteos
Kniekehlenlymphknoten M
linfonodi M poplitei
inguinal lymph nodes
ganglions M lymphatiques inguinaux
nódulos M linfáticos inguinales
Leistenlymphknoten M
linfonodi M inguinali

breast
sein [M]
pecho [M]
Brust [F]
seno [M]

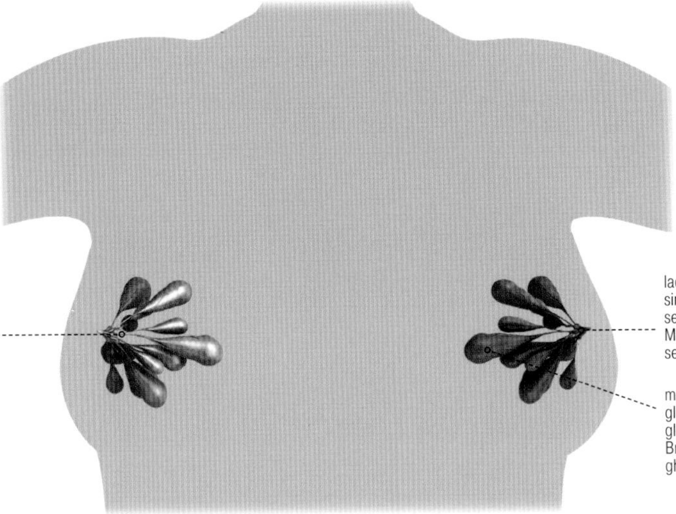
lactiferous duct
canal [M] galactophore
conducto [M] lactífero
Milchgang [M]
dotto [M] galattoforo
lactiferous sinus
sinus [M] galactophore
seno [M] lactífero
Milchsäckchen [N]
seno [M] galattoforo
mammary gland
glande [F] mammaire
glándula [F] mamaria
Brustdrüse [F]
ghiandola [F] mammaria

female reproductive organs
organes [M] reproducteurs féminins
órganos [M] reproductores femeninos
weibliche Fortpflanzungsorgane [N]
organi [M] riproduttivi femminili

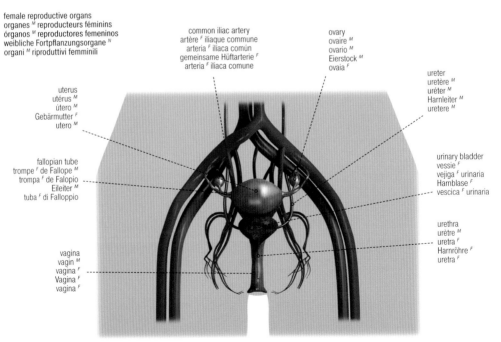

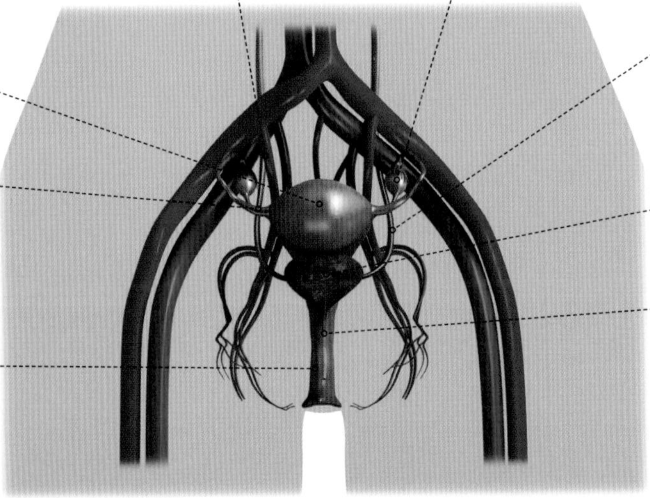
common iliac artery
artère [F] iliaque commune
arteria [F] iliaca común
gemeinsame Hüftarterie [F]
arteria [F] iliaca comune
ovary
ovaire [M]
ovario [M]
Eierstock [M]
ovaia [F]
ureter
uretère [M]
uréter [M]
Harnleiter [M]
uretere [M]
uterus
utérus [M]
útero [M]
Gebärmutter [F]
utero [M]
fallopian tube
trompe [F] de Fallope [M]
trompa [F] de Falopio
Eileiter [M]
tuba [F] di Falloppio
urinary bladder
vessie [F]
vejiga [F] urinaria
Harnblase [F]
vescica [F] urinaria
urethra
urètre [M]
uretra [F]
Harnröhre [F]
uretra [F]
vagina
vagin [M]
vagina [F]
Vagina [F]
vagina [F]

male reproductive organs
organes ^{M} reproducteurs masculins
órganos ^{M} reproductores masculinos
männliche Fortpflanzungsorgane ^{N}
sistema ^{M} riproduttivo maschile

urinary bladder
vessie ^{F}
vejiga ^{F} urinaria
Harnblase ^{F}
vescica ^{F} urinaria

penis
pénis ^{M}
pene ^{M}
Penis ^{M}
pene ^{M}

testicle
testicule ^{M}
testículo ^{M}
Hoden ^{M}
testicolo ^{M}

glans penis
gland ^{M}
glande ^{M}
Peniseichel ^{F}
glande ^{M} del pene ^{M}

prostate
prostate ^{F}
próstata ^{F}
Prostata ^{F}
prostata ^{F}

vas deferens
canal ^{M} déférent
conducto ^{M} espermático
Samenleiter ^{M}
dotto ^{M} deferente

bulbocavernous muscle
muscle ^{M} bulbocaverneux
músculo ^{M} bulbocavernoso
Musculus bulbospongiosus ^{M}
muscolo ^{M} bulbocavernoso

epididymis
épididyme ^{M}
epidídimo ^{M}
Nebenhoden ^{M}
epididimo ^{M}

URINARY SYSTEM

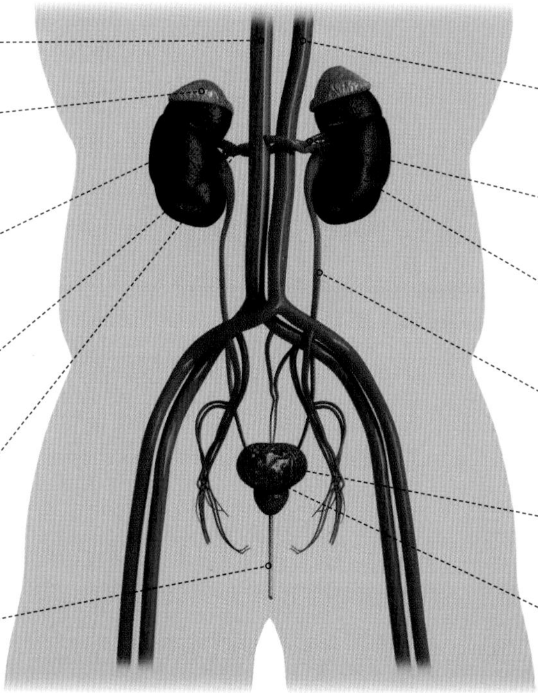
urinary organs
organes ^{M} urinaires
órganos ^{M} urinarios
Harnweg ^{M}
apparato ^{M} urinario

inferior vena cava
veine ^{F} cave inférieure
vena ^{F} cava inferior
untere Hohlvene ^{F}
vena ^{F} cava inferiore

adrenal gland
glande ^{F} surrénale
glándula ^{F} suprarrenal
Nebenniere ^{F}
ghiandola ^{F} surrenale

right kidney
rein ^{M} droit
riñón ^{M} derecho
rechte Niere ^{F}
rene ^{M} destro

renal hilum
hile ^{M}
hilio ^{M} renal
Nierenpforte ^{F}
ilo ^{M} renale

renal vein
veine ^{F} rénale
vena ^{F} renal
Nierenvene ^{F}
vena ^{F} renale

urethra
urètre ^{M}
uretra ^{F}
Harnröhre ^{F}
uretra ^{F}

abdominal aorta
aorte ^{F} abdominale
aorta ^{F} abdominal
Bauchaorta ^{F}
aorta ^{F} addominale

renal artery
artère ^{F} rénale
arteria ^{F} renal
Nierenarterie ^{F}
arteria ^{F} renale

left kidney
rein ^{M} gauche
riñón ^{M} izquierdo
linke Niere ^{F}
rene ^{M} sinistro

ureter
uretère ^{M}
uréter ^{M}
Harnleiter ^{M}
uretere ^{M}

detrusor urinae
détrusor ^{M}
músculo ^{M} detrusor
Detrusormuskel ^{M}
muscolo ^{M} detrusore

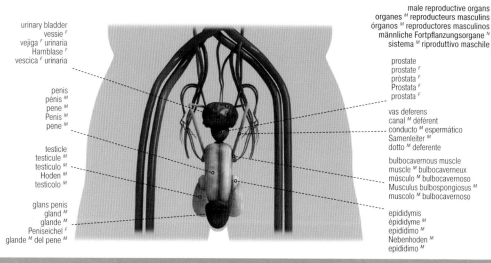

urinary bladder
vessie ^{F}
vejiga ^{F} urinaria
Harnblase ^{F}
vescica ^{F} urinaria

anterior view of digestive system
vue [F] antérieure de l'appareil [M] digestif
vista [F] anterior del sistema [M] digestivo
Vorderansicht [F] des Verdauungssystems [N]
apparato [M] digerente vista [F] anteriore

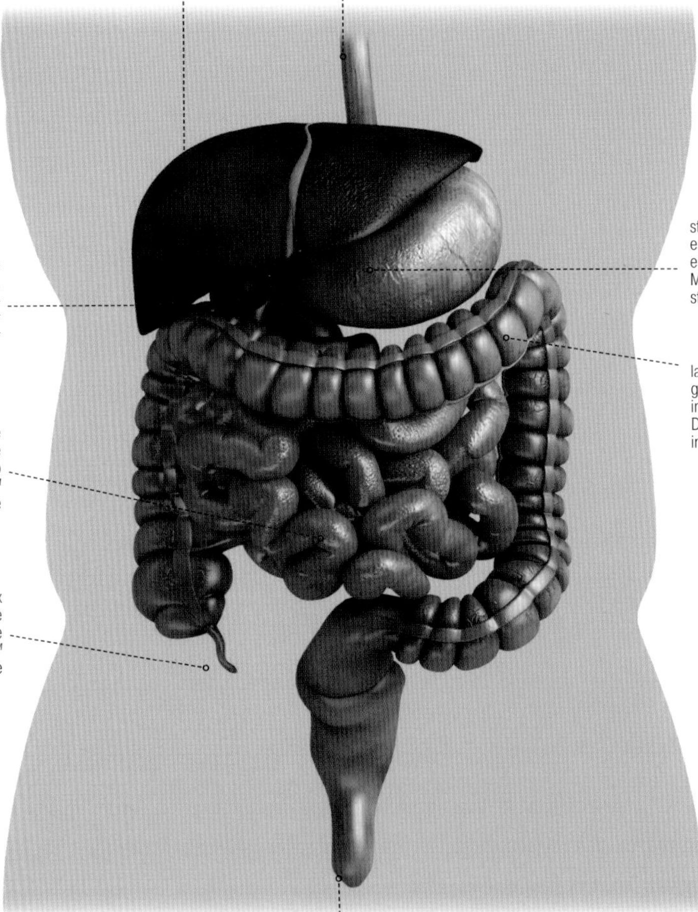

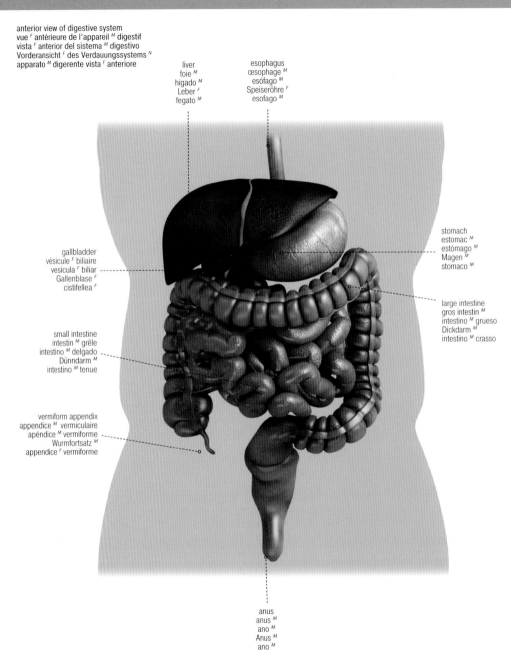

liver
foie [M]
hígado [M]
Leber [F]
fegato [M]

esophagus
œsophage [M]
esófago [M]
Speiseröhre [F]
esofago [M]

stomach
estomac [M]
estómago [M]
Magen [M]
stomaco [M]

gallbladder
vésicule [F] biliaire
vesícula [F] biliar
Gallenblase [F]
cistifellea [F]

large intestine
gros intestin [M]
intestino [M] grueso
Dickdarm [M]
intestino [M] crasso

small intestine
intestin [M] grêle
intestino [M] delgado
Dünndarm [M]
intestino [M] tenue

vermiform appendix
appendice [M] vermiculaire
apéndice [M] vermiforme
Wurmfortsatz [M]
appendice [F] vermiforme

anus
anus [M]
ano [M]
Anus [M]
ano [M]

posterior view of digestive system
vue ^F postérieure de l'appareil ^M digestif
vista ^F posterior del sistema ^M digestivo
Hinteransicht ^F des Verdauungssystems ^N
apparato ^M digerente vista ^F posteriore

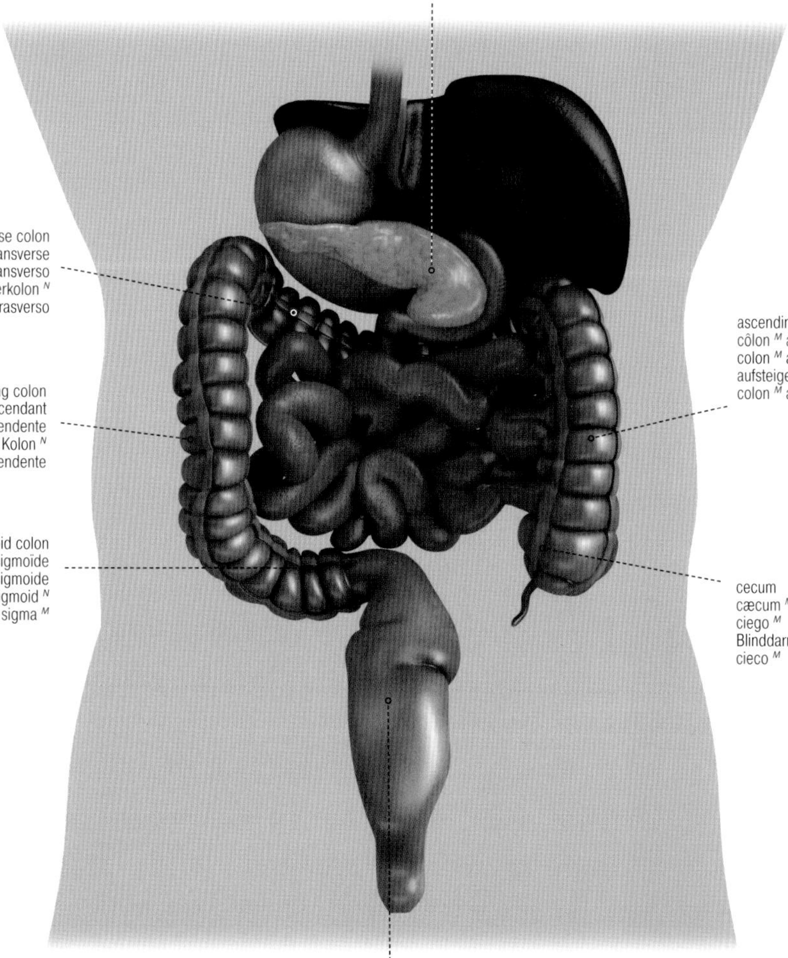
pancreas
pancréas M
páncreas M
Bauchspeicheldrüse F
pancreas M
transverse colon
côlon M transverse
colon M transverso
Querkolon N
colon M trasverso
ascending colon
côlon M ascendant
colon M ascendente
aufsteigendes Kolon N
colon M ascendente
descending colon
côlon M descendant
colon M descendente
absteigendes Kolon N
colon M discendente
sigmoid colon
côlon M sigmoïde
colon M sigmoide
Sigmoid N
sigma M
cecum
cæcum M
ciego M
Blinddarm M
cieco M
rectum
rectum M
recto M
Rektum N
retto M

female endocrine system
système ᴹ endocrinien féminin
sistema ᴹ endocrino femenino
weibliches Hormonsystem ᴺ
sistema ᴹ endocrino femminile

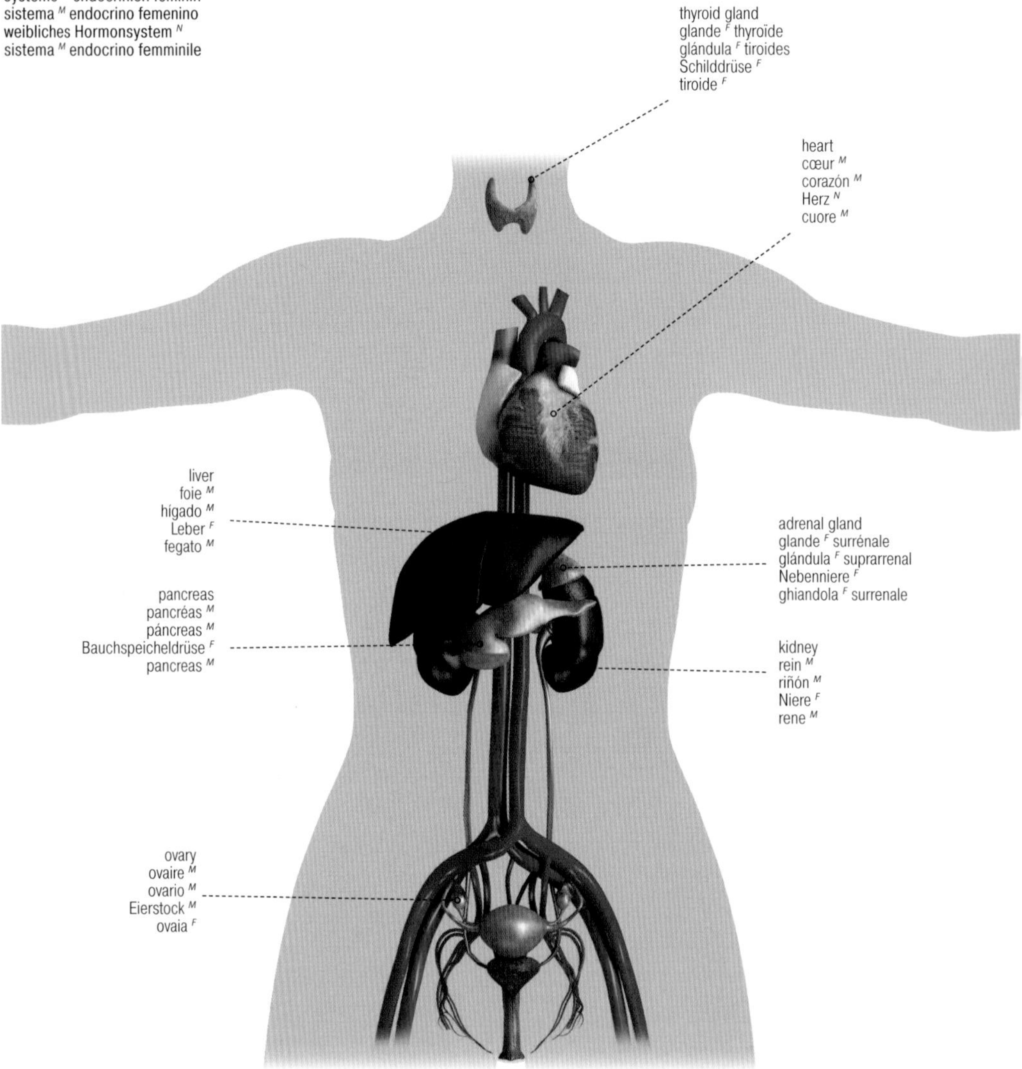
thyroid gland
glande F thyroïde
glándula F tiroides
Schilddrüse F
tiroide F
heart
cœur M
corazón M
Herz N
cuore M
liver
foie M
hígado M
Leber F
fegato M
adrenal gland
glande F surrénale
glándula F suprarrenal
Nebenniere F
ghiandola F surrenale
pancreas
pancréas M
páncreas M
Bauchspeicheldrüse F
pancreas M
kidney
rein M
riñón M
Niere F
rene M
ovary
ovaire M
ovario M
Eierstock M
ovaia F

hand
main [F]
mano [F]
Hand [F]
mano [F]

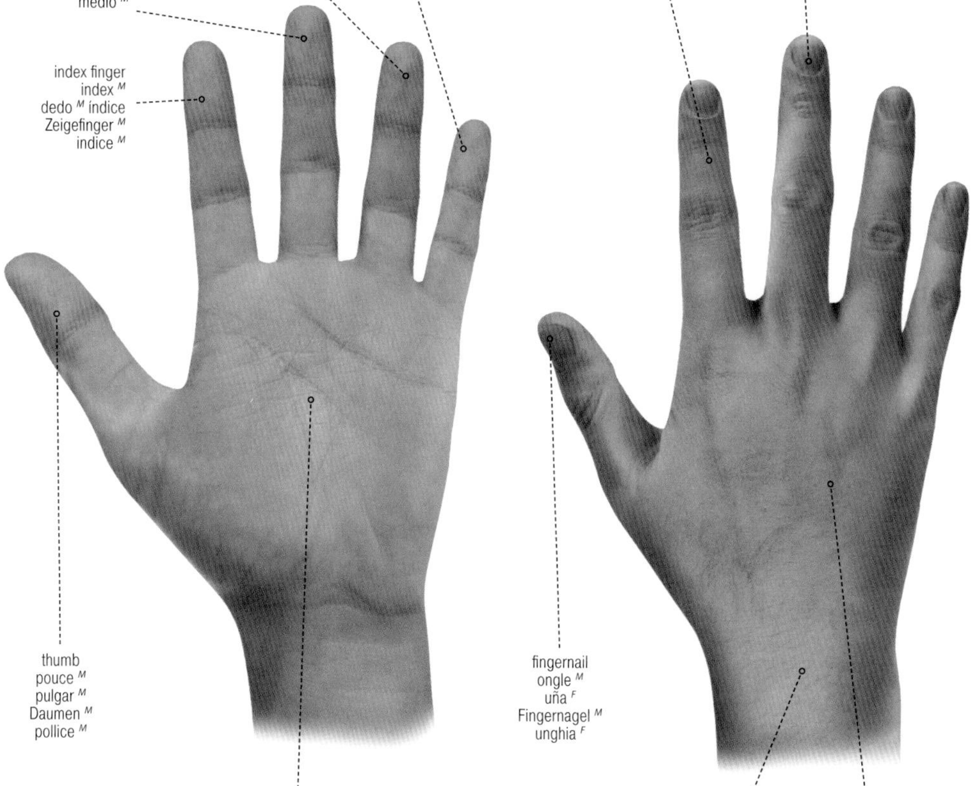

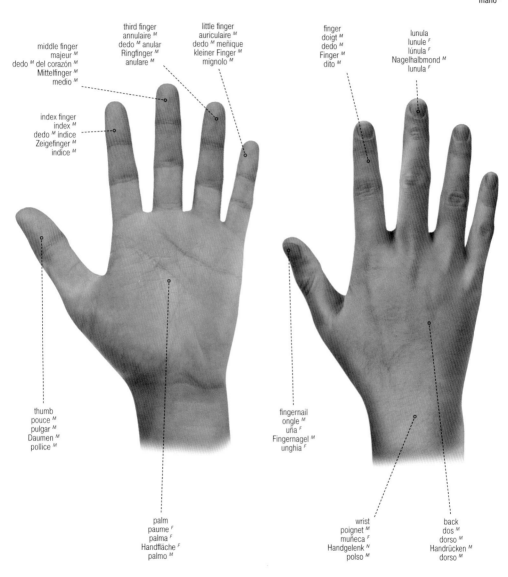

middle finger
majeur [M]
dedo [M] del corazón [M]
Mittelfinger [M]
medio [M]
third finger
annulaire [M]
dedo [M] anular
Ringfinger [M]
anulare [M]
little finger
auriculaire [M]
dedo [M] meñique
kleiner Finger [M]
mignolo [M]
index finger
index [M]
dedo [M] índice
Zeigefinger [M]
indice [M]
thumb
pouce [M]
pulgar [M]
Daumen [M]
pollice [M]
palm
paume [F]
palma [F]
Handfläche [F]
palmo [M]
finger
doigt [M]
dedo [M]
Finger [M]
dito [M]
lunula
lunule [F]
lúnula [F]
Nagelhalbmond [M]
lunula [F]
fingernail
ongle [M]
uña [F]
Fingernagel [M]
unghia [F]
wrist
poignet [M]
muñeca [F]
Handgelenk [N]
polso [M]
back
dos [M]
dorso [M]
Handrücken [M]
dorso [M]

ear
oreille F
oído M
Ohr N
orecchio M

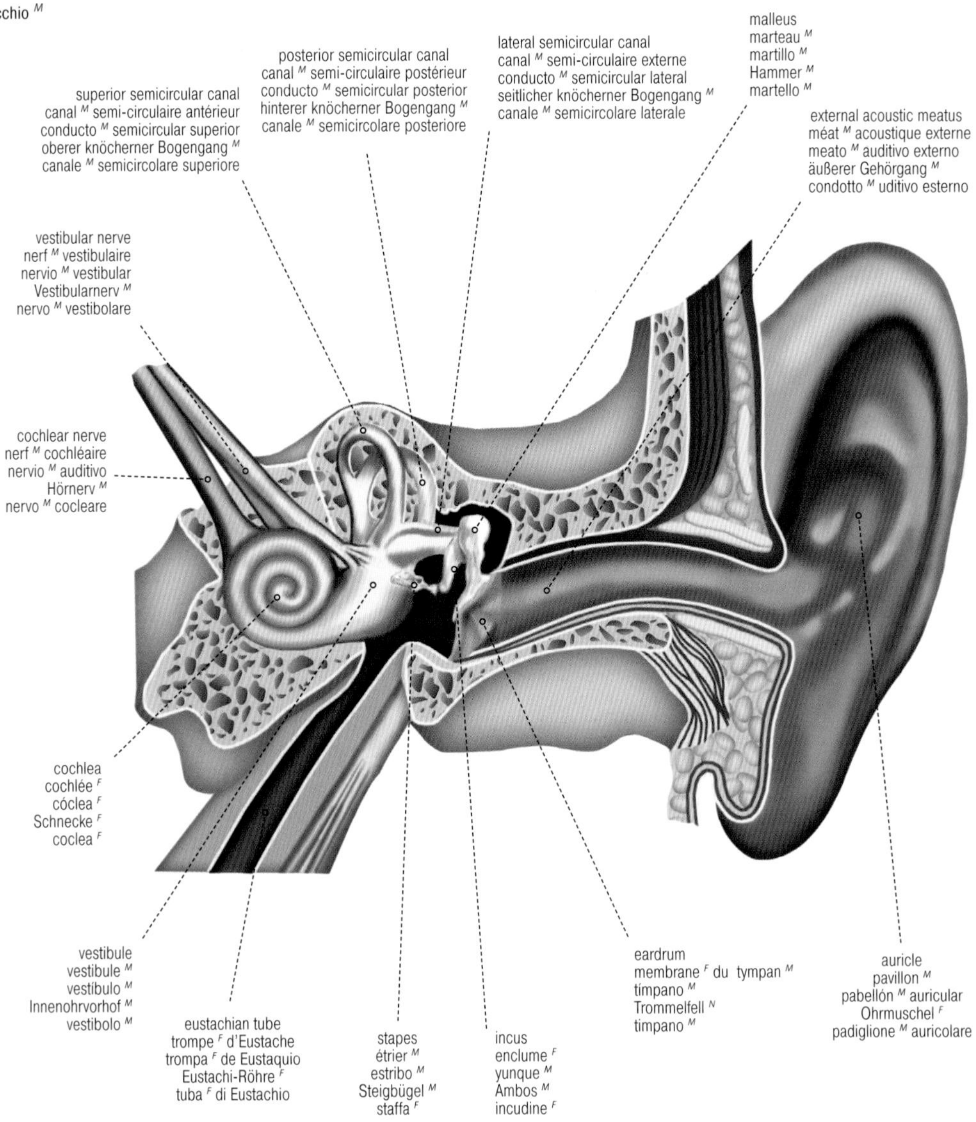
superior semicircular canal
canal M semi-circulaire antérieur
conducto M semicircular superior
oberer knöcherner Bogengang M
canale M semicircolare superiore
posterior semicircular canal
canal M semi-circulaire postérieur
conducto M semicircular posterior
hinterer knöcherner Bogengang M
canale M semicircolare posteriore
lateral semicircular canal
canal M semi-circulaire externe
conducto M semicircular lateral
seitlicher knöcherner Bogengang M
canale M semicircolare laterale
malleus
marteau M
martillo M
Hammer M
martello M
external acoustic meatus
méat M acoustique externe
meato M auditivo externo
äußerer Gehörgang M
condotto M uditivo esterno
vestibular nerve
nerf M vestibulaire
nervio M vestibular
Vestibularnerv M
nervo M vestibolare
cochlear nerve
nerf M cochléaire
nervio M auditivo
Hörnerv M
nervo M cocleare
cochlea
cochlée F
cóclea F
Schnecke F
coclea F
vestibule
vestibule M
vestíbulo M
Innenohrvorhof M
vestibolo M
eustachian tube
trompe F d'Eustache
trompa F de Eustaquio
Eustachi-Röhre F
tuba F di Eustachio
stapes
étrier M
estribo M
Steigbügel M
staffa F
incus
enclume F
yunque M
Ambos M
incudine F
eardrum
membrane F du tympan M
tímpano M
Trommelfell N
timpano M
auricle
pavillon M
pabellón M auricular
Ohrmuschel F
padiglione M auricolare

eye
œil M
ojo M
Auge N
occhio M

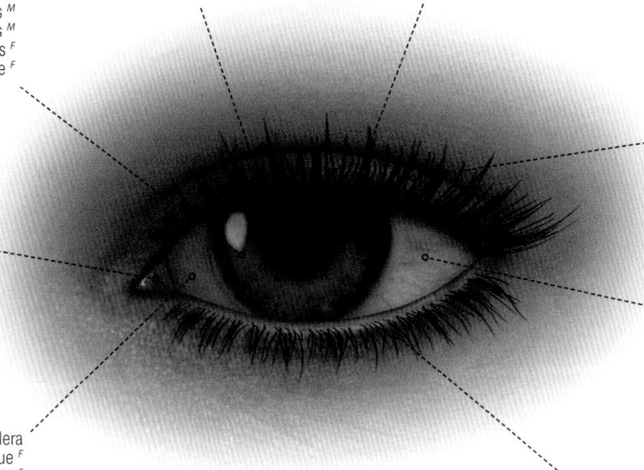
pupil
pupille F
pupila F
Pupille F
pupilla F
eyelash
cil M
pestaña F
Wimper F
ciglia F
iris
iris M
iris M
Iris F
iride F
upper eyelid
paupière F supérieure
párpado M superior
Oberlid N
palpebra F superiore
lachrymal carunkel
caroncule F lacrymale
carúncula F lacrimal
Tränenkarunkel F
caruncola F lacrimale
conjunctiva
conjonctive F
conjuntiva F
Bindehaut F
congiuntiva F
sclera
sclérotique F
esclerótica F
Lederhaut F
sclera F
lower eyelid
paupière F inférieure
párpado M inferior
Unterlid N
palpebra F inferiore

eyeball
globe M oculaire
globo M ocular
Augapfel M
bulbo M oculare

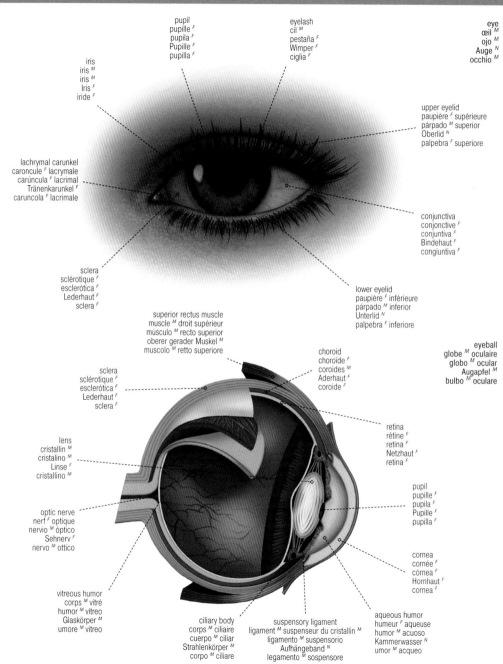

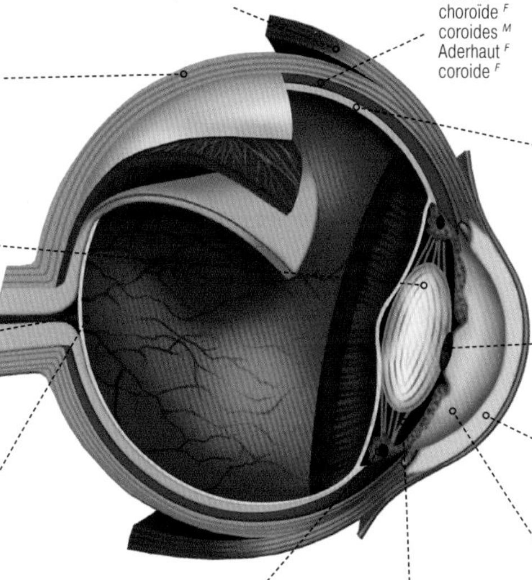
superior rectus muscle
muscle M droit supérieur
músculo M recto superior
oberer gerader Muskel M
muscolo M retto superiore
choroid
choroïde F
coroides M
Aderhaut F
coroide F
sclera
sclérotique F
esclerótica F
Lederhaut F
sclera F
retina
rétine F
retina F
Netzhaut F
retina F
lens
cristallin M
cristalino M
Linse F
cristallino M
pupil
pupille F
pupila F
Pupille F
pupilla F
optic nerve
nerf F optique
nervio M óptico
Sehnerv F
nervo M ottico
cornea
cornée F
córnea F
Hornhaut F
cornea F
vitreous humor
corps M vitré
humor M vítreo
Glaskörper M
umore M vitreo
ciliary body
corps M ciliaire
cuerpo M ciliar
Strahlenkörper M
corpo M ciliare
suspensory ligament
ligament M suspenseur du cristallin M
ligamento M suspensorio
Aufhängeband N
legamento M sospensore
aqueous humor
humeur F aqueuse
humor M acuoso
Kammerwasser N
umor M acqueo

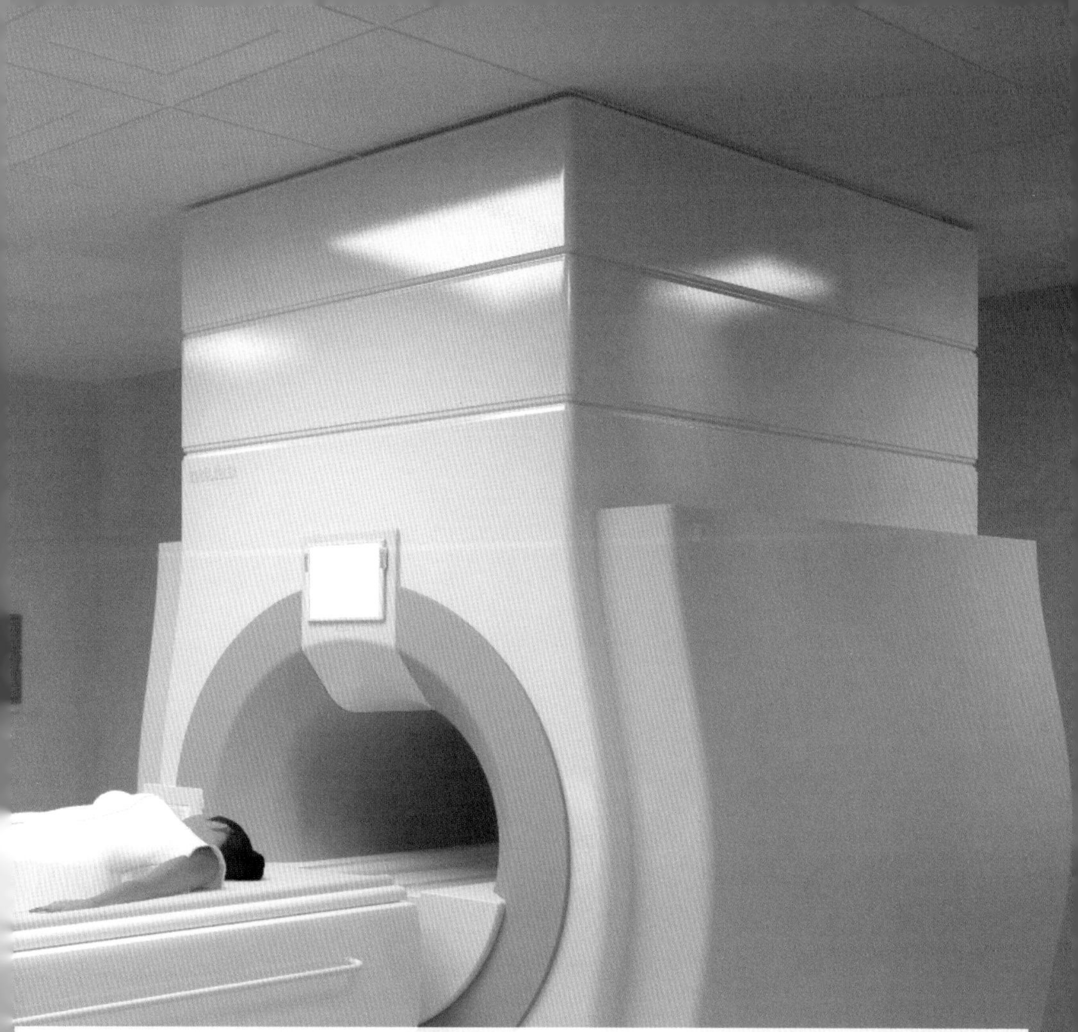

HEALTH AND MEDICINE

angiography room
salle [F] d'angiographie [F]
sala [F] de angiografía [F]
Angiografieraum [M]
camera [F] angiografica

mattress
matelas [M]
colchón [M]
Matratze [F]
materasso [M]

video monitor
moniteur [M] vidéo [F]
monitor [M] de vídeo [M]
Videomonitor [M]
monitor [M] video [M]

radiologist
radiologiste [M]
radiólogo [M]
Radiologe [M]
radiologo [M]

camera housing
boîtier [M] de caméra [M]
recinto [M] de la cámara [F]
Kameragehäuse [N]
alloggiamento [M] per videocamera [F]

image intensifier
intensificateur [M] d'image [F]
intensificador de imagen [M]
Bildverstärker [M]
intensificatore [M] d'immagine [F]

C-arm crawler carriage
bras [M] articulé pour bras [M] en C
carro [M] móvil de brazo [M] en C
C-Bogen-Schlitten [M]
carrello [M] mobile con braccio [M] a C

angiography machine
appareil [M] d'angiographie [F]
angiógrafo [M]
Angiografie-Apparat [M]
macchina [F] angiografica

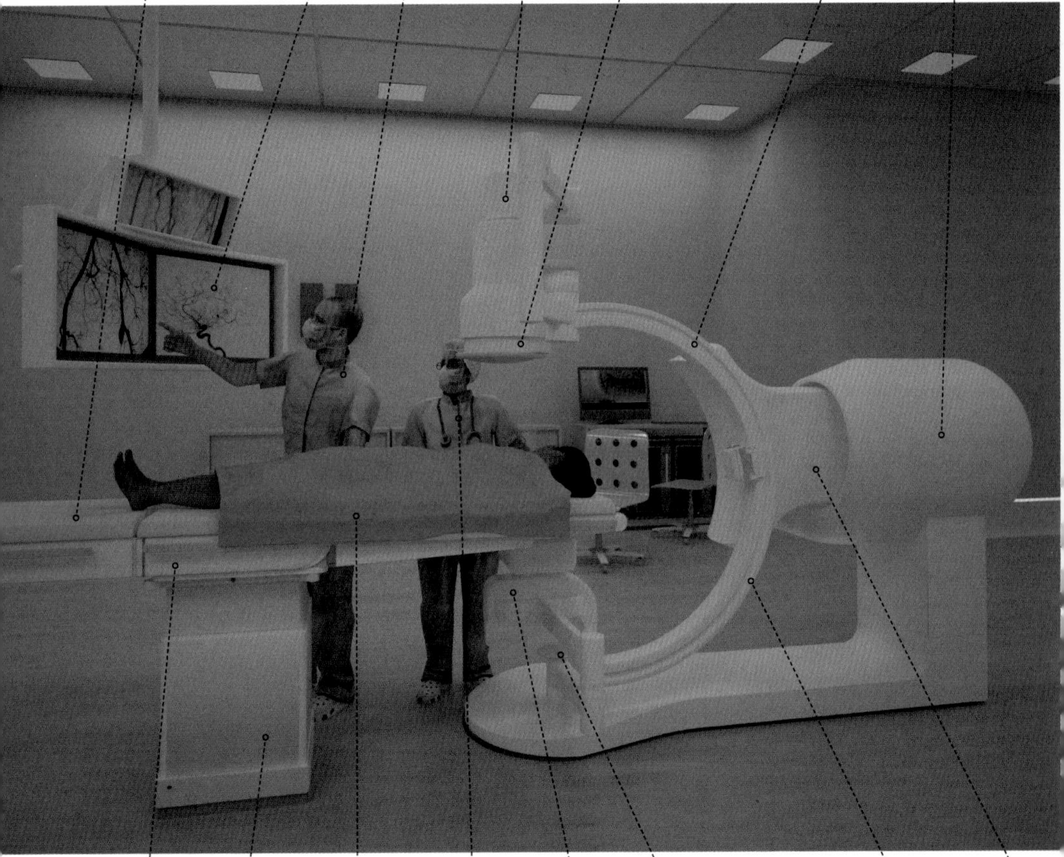

height-adjustable pedestal
socle [M] à hauteur [F] réglable
base [F] de altura [F] ajustable
höhenverstellbares Fußteil [N]
piedistallo [M] regolabile in altezza [F]

scrub nurse
infirmière [F] en service [M] interne
enfermera [F] de quirófano [M]
Operationsschwester [F]
infermiera [F] di sala [F] operatoria

X-ray tube
tube [M] à rayons X [M]
tubo de rayos [M] X
Röntgenrohr [N]
tubo [M] radiogeno

non-movable C-arm track
guide [M] pour bras [M] en C non amovible
carril [M] fijo de brazo [M] en C
nichtbewegliche C-Bogen-Spurstange [F]
percorso [M] esterno del braccio [M] a C fisso

patient support table
table [F] de support [M] pour patient [M]
camilla [F] para el paciente [F]
Patientenlagerungstisch [M]
tavolo [M] di supporto [M] per il paziente [M]

surgical drape
champs [M] opératoires
gas [F] a quirúrgica
Operationsabdecktuch [N]
telo [M] chirurgico

collimator housing
boîtier [M] du collimateur [M]
recinto [M] de colimador [M]
Kollimatorgehäuse [N]
supporto [M] collimatore

support arm
bras [M] de support [M]
brazo [M] auxiliar
Tragarm [M]
braccio [M] di supporto [M]

MRI (magnetic resonance imaging) room
salle [F] d'imagerie par résonance magnétique (IRM) [F]
sala [F] de resonancia [F] magnética
MRT-Raum [M]
sala [F] di risonanza [F] magnetica

file cabinet
classeur [M]
archivo [M]
Aktenschrank [M]
schedario [M]

technician's room
salle [F] du technicien [M]
sala [F] de operadores
Kontrollraum [M]
stanza [F] dell'operatore [M]

screened glass
écran [M] de verre [M]
pantalla [F] de cristal [M]
Glasschutz [M]
schermo [M] di vetro [M]

display device
dispositif [M] d'affichage [M]
pantalla [F]
Anzeige [F]
dispositivo [M] di visualizzazione [F]

MRI scanner
appareil [M] d'IRM [M]
escáner [M] de IRM
Kernspinntomograph [M]
scanner [M] di risonanza [F] magnetica

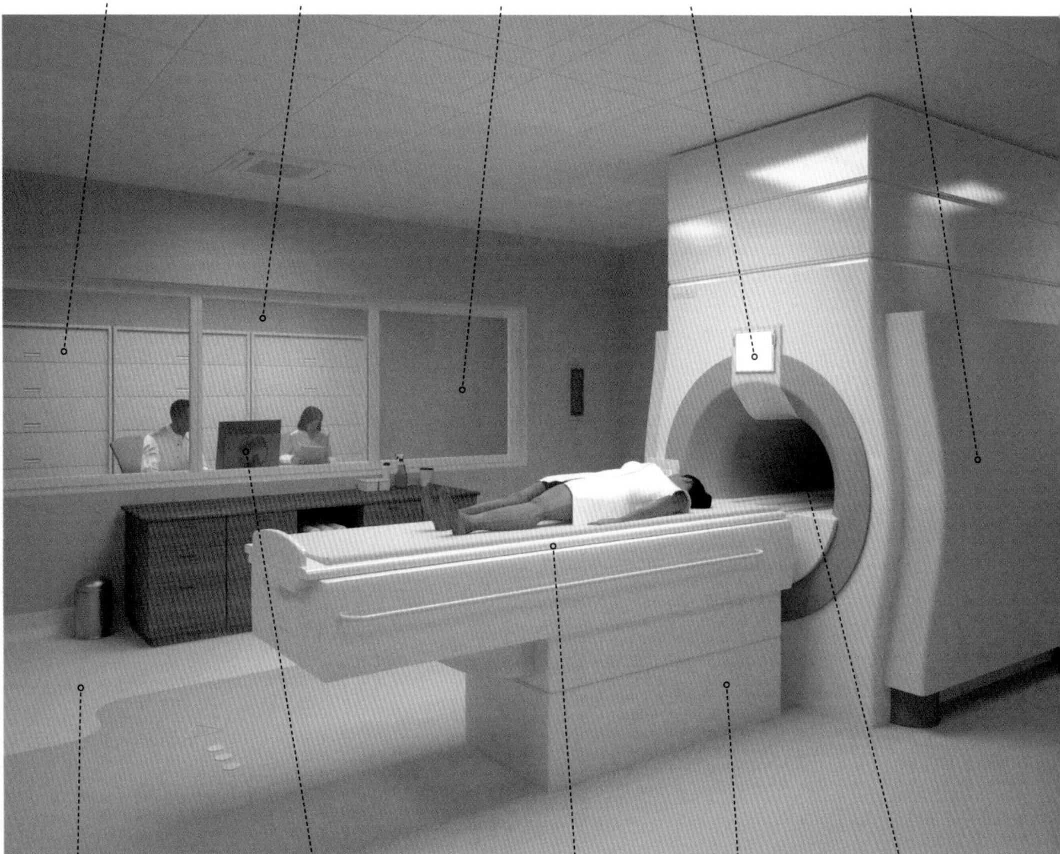

procedure room
salle [F] d'invention [F]
sala [F] del escáner [M]
Tomografieraum [M]
stanza [F] dell'esame [M]

computer with image-capturing hardware
ordinateur [M] avec système [M] d'acquisition [F] d'images [F]
PC [M] con sistema [F] de captura [F] de imágenes [F]
PC [M] mit Bilderfassungshardware [F]
PC [M] con hardware [M] di acquisizione [F] di immagini [F]

motorized table
table [F] motorisée
mesa [F] motorizada
motorbetriebener Tisch [M]
lettino [M] motorizzato

pedestal
base [F] de l'appareil [M]
base [F]
Fußteil [N]
piedistallo [M]

scanning tube
tube [M] de balayage [M]
tubo [M] de escáner [M]
Tomografieröhre [F]
tubo [M] di scansione [F]

operating room
salle [F] d'opération [F]
sala [F] de operaciones [F]
Operationsraum [M]
sala [F] operatoria

ceiling light
plafonnier [M]
luces [F]
Deckenleuchte [F]
plafoniera [F]

video monitor
moniteur [M] vidéo [M]
monitor [M] de vídeo [M]
Videomonitor [M]
monitor [M]

scrub nurse
infirmière [F] en service [M] interne
enfermera [F] de quirófano [M]
OP-Schwester [F]
infermiera [F] di sala [F] operatoria

surgical mask
masque [M] chirurgical
mascarilla [F] de operaciones [F]
Operationsmaske [F]
mascherina [F] chirurgica

anesthesiologist
anesthésiste [M]
anestesista [M]
Anästhesist [M]
anestesista [M]

multi-movement pendant
suspension [F] multimouvements
brazo [M] multimovimiento
mehrfach bewegliche Aufhängung [F]
supporto [M] a soffitto [M] con meccanismo [M] girevole

operating light
éclairage [M] opératoire
luz [F] principal
Operationslampe [F]
lampada [F] scialitica

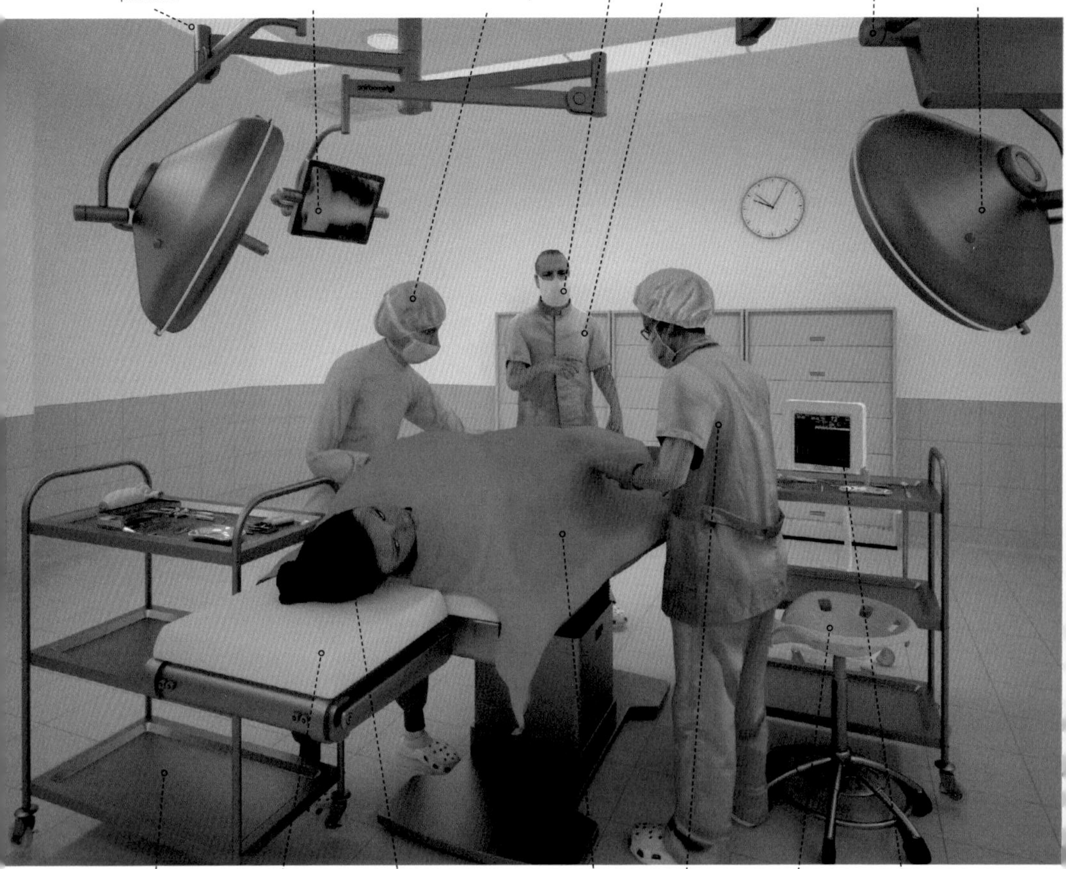

instrument cart
chariot [M] à instruments [M]
carrito [M] de instrumental [M]
Instrumentenwagen [M]
carrello [M] portastrumenti` [M]

operating table
table [F] d'opération [F]
mesa [F] de operaciones [F]
OP-Tisch [M]
tavolo [M] operatorio

patient
patient [M]
paciente [M]
Patient [M]
paziente [M]

surgical drape
champs [M] opératoires
sábana [F] quirúrgica [F]
Operationstuch [N]
telo [M] chirurgico

surgeon
chirurgien [M]
cirujano [M]
Chirurg [M]
chirurgo [M]

adjustable stool
tabouret [M] ajustable
taburete [M] ajustable
verstellbarer Chirurgenstuhl [M]
sgabello [M] regolabileght

patient monitor
moniteur [M] du patient [M]
monitor [M] del paciente
Patientenmonitor [M]
monitor [M] del paziente [M]

hospital room
chambre [F] d'hôpital [M]
habitación [F] de hospital [M]
Krankenhauszimmer [N]
stanza [F] d'ospedale [M]

nurse call button
bouton [M] d'appel [M] de l'infirmière [F]
botón [M] para llamar a la enfermera [F]
Krankenschwester-Ruftaste [F]
pulsante [M] di chiamata [F] infermiera [F]

privacy screen
écran [M] d'intimité [F]
biombo [M]
Paravent [M/N]
pannello [M] divisorio [M]

over-bed light
lumière [F] de lit [M]
lámpara [F]
Bettleuchte [F]
luce [F] da letto [M]

IV (intravenous) stand
tige [F] porte-sérum [M]
soporte [M] para bolsa [F] intravenosa
Infusionsständer [M]
asta [F] da flebo [F]

medical utility table
guéridon [M]
mesa [F] para instrumental [M] médico
Instrumententisch [M]
tavolo [M] per uso [M] medico

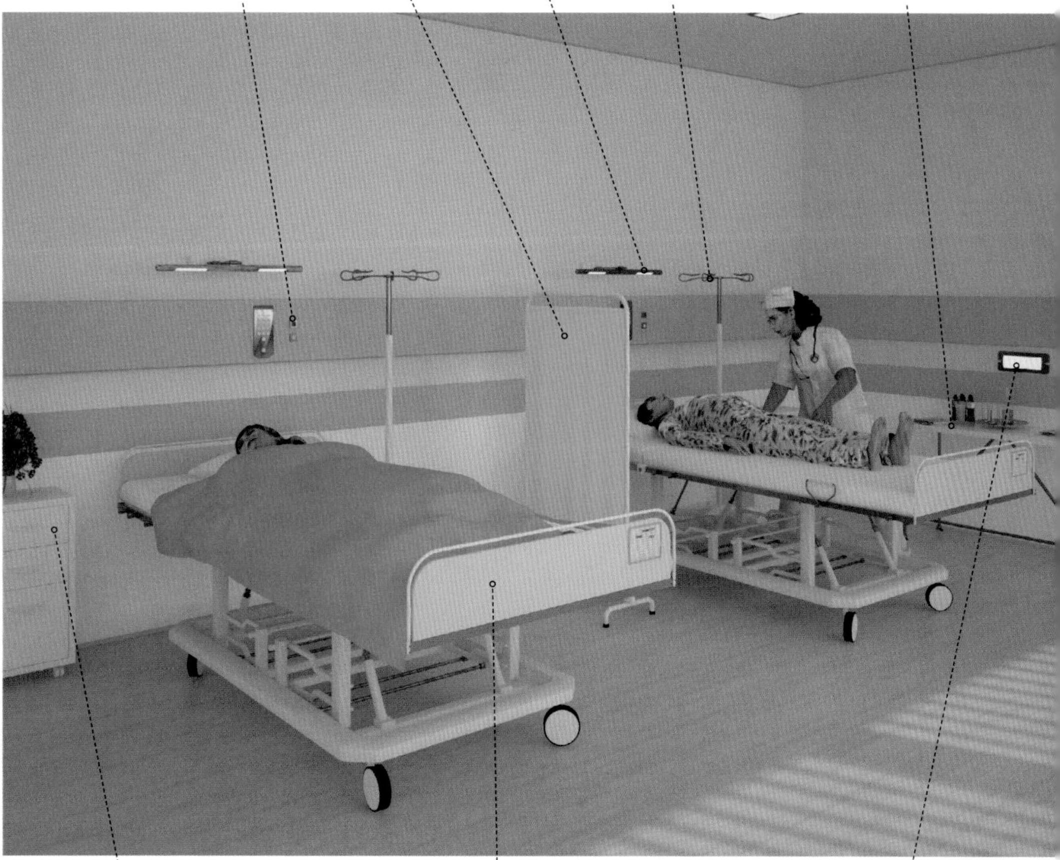

bedside table
table [F] de chevet [M]
mesa [F] auxiliar
Nachttisch [M]
comodino [M]

adjustable hospital bed
lit [M] d'hôpital [M] réglable
cama [F] regulable de hospital [M]
verstellbares Krankenbett [N]
letto [M] d'ospedale [M] regolabile

wall light
lumière [F] murale
luz [F] de pared [F]
Wandleuchte [F] luce [F]
da parete [F]

intensive care unit
unité [F] de soins [M] intensifs
unidad [F] de cuidados [M] intensivos
Intensivstation [F]
unità [M] di terapia [F] intensiva

numeric fields
champs [M] numériques
campos [M] de parámetro [M]
numerische Parameterfelder [N]
campi [M] numerici

waveform fields
champs [M] d'ondes [F]
campos [M] de onda [F]
Wellenformfelder [F]
campi [M] d'onda [F]

patient monitor
moniteur [M] du patient [M]
monitor [M] del paciente [M]
Patientenmonitor [M]
monitor [M] del paziente [M]

patient connection panel
panneau [M] de connexion [F] au patient [M]
panel [M] de conexión [F] con el paciente [M]
Patientenanschlussleiste [F]
pannello [M] di collegamento [M] al paziente [M]

cart
chariot [M]
carrito [M]
Wagen [M]
carrello [M]

bedside table
table [F] de chevet [M]
mesa [F] auxiliar
Nachttisch [M]
comodino [M]

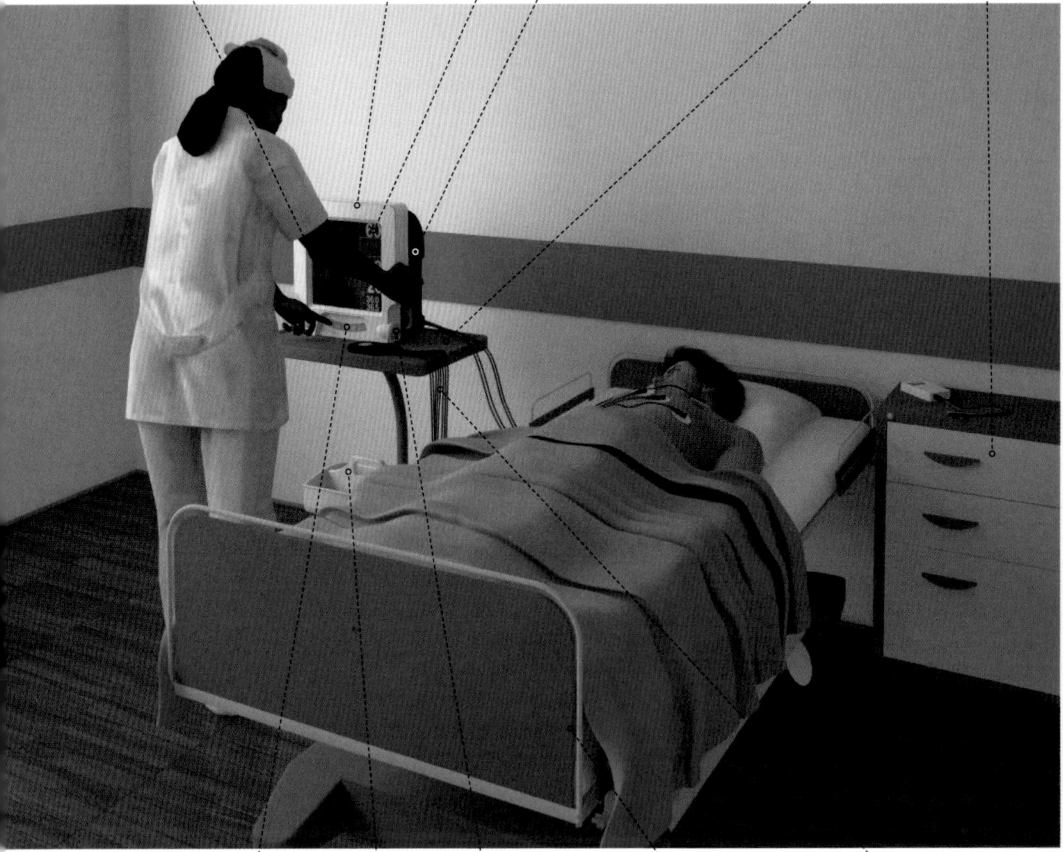

function buttons
boutons [M] de fonctions [M]
botones [M] de funciones [F]
Funktionstasten [F]
tasti [M] funzione [F]

utility basket
panier [M] tout usage [M]
cesta [F] de instrumental [M]
Allzweckkorb [M]
cestino [M] degli strumenti [M]

trim knob
bouton [M] de réglage [M]
perilla [F] de ajuste [M]
Drehknopf [M]
manopola [F] di regolazione [F]

adjustable hospital bed
lit [M] d'hôpital [M] réglable
cama [F] regulable de hospital [M]
verstellbares Krankenhausbett [N]
letto [M] di ospedale [M] regolabile

cables
câbles [M]
cables [M]
Kabel [N]
cavi [M]

physical therapy room
salle F de physiothérapie F
unidad F de medicina F deportiva y rehabilitación F
Physiotherapieraum M
centro M di riabilitazione F

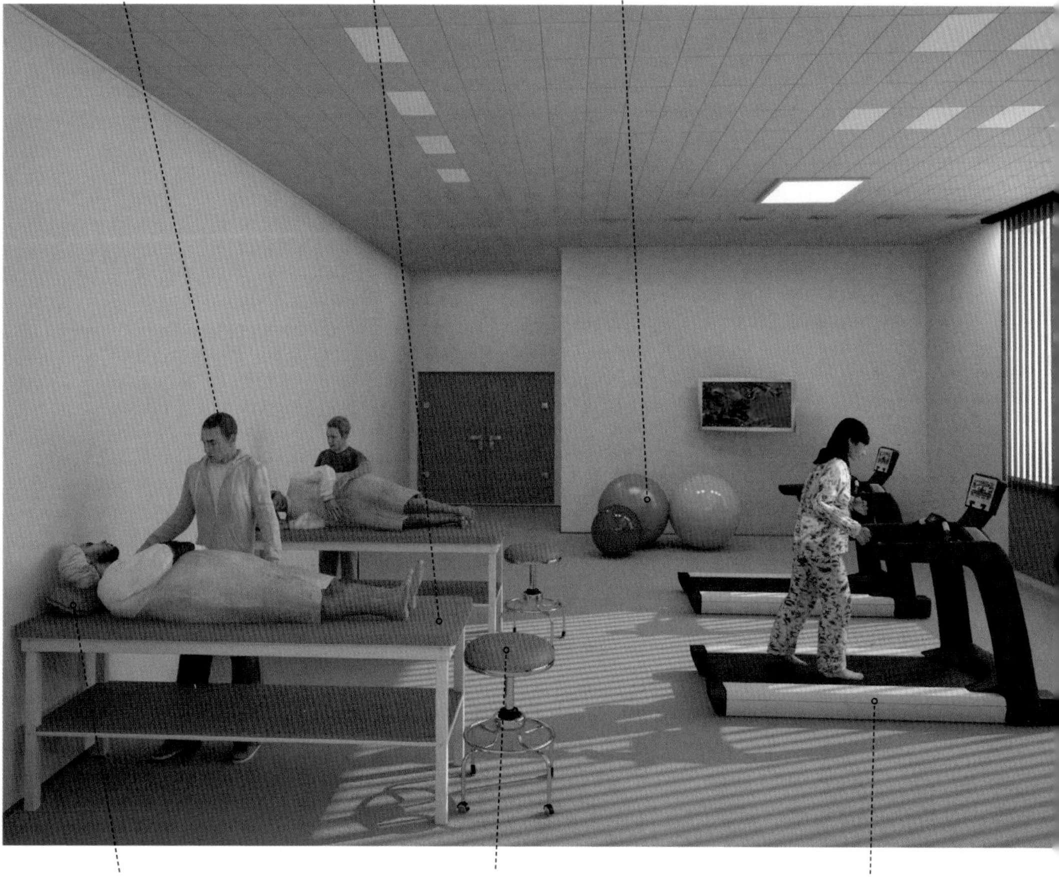
physical therapist
physiothérapeute M
fisioterapeuta M
Physiotherapeut M
fisioterapista M
treatment table
table F de traitement M
camilla F de tratamiento M
Behandlungstisch M
lettino M per trattamento M
fitness ball
ballon M d'exercice M
pelota F de ejercicio M
Fitnessball M
palla F da ginnastica M
bolster
traversin M
almohada F
Nackenstütze F
cuscino M
adjustable stool
tabouret M ajustable
taburete M ajustable
verstellbarer Hocker M
sgabello M regolabile
treadmill
tapis M roulant
cinta F para caminar
Laufband N
tapis M roulant

gynecological examination room
salle [F] d'examen [M] gynécologique
sala [F] de examen [M] ginecológico
gynäkologischer Untersuchungsraum [M]
ambulatorio [M] ginecologico

doctor's writing pad
bloc-notes [M] du médecin [M]
bloc [M] del médico [M]
Arztschreibblock [M]
cartella [F] del medico [M]

ceiling-mounted monitor
moniteur [M] suspendu au plafond [M]
monitor [M] anclado al techo [M]
Deckenmonitor [M]
monitor [M] da soffitto [M]

examination chair
fauteuil [M] d'examen [M]
silla [F] de exploración [F]
Untersuchungsstuhl [M]
poltrona [F] da visita [F]

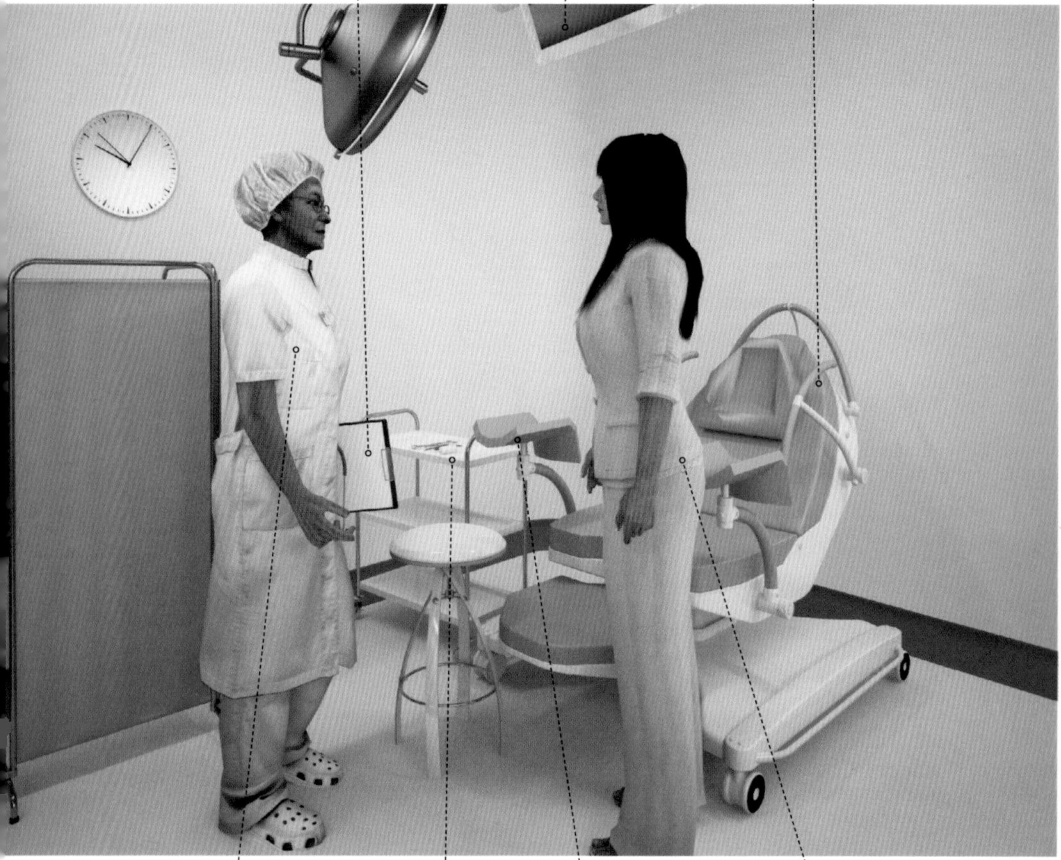

gynecologist
gynécologue [M]
ginecóloga [F]
Gynäkologin [F]
ginecologo [M]

instrument cart
chariot [M] d'instruments [M]
carrito [M] de instrumental [M]
Instrumentenwagen [M]
carrello [M] portastrumenti [M]

leg support
appui-jambes [M]
soporte [M] para piernas [F]
Beinstütze [F]
supporto [M] delle gambe [F]

patient
patiente [F]
paciente [M]
Patientin [F]
paziente [F]

anesthesia monitor
moniteur ^{M} d'anesthésie ^{F}
monitor ^{M} de anestesia ^{F}
Anästhesiemonitor ^{M}
monitor ^{M} da anestesia ^{F}

neonatal intensive care unit
unité ^{F} de soins ^{M} intensifs néonataux
unidad ^{F} de cuidados ^{M} intensivos para neonatos
Neugeborenen ^{N} Intensivstation ^{F}
unità ^{F} di terapia ^{F} intensiva neonatale

incubator
incubateur ^{M}
incubadora ^{F}
Brutkasten ^{M}
incubatrice ^{F}

mattress
matelas ^{M}
colchón ^{M}
Matratze ^{F}
materasso ^{M}

canopy
habitacle ^{M}
cubierta ^{F}
Oberteil ^{N}
baldacchino ^{M}

newborn
nouveau-né ^{M}
niño ^{M} recién nacido
Neugeborenes ^{N}
neonato ^{M}

mattress tray
socle ^{M} pour matelas ^{M}
base ^{F} del colchón ^{M}
Matratzenablage ^{F}
base ^{F} per materasso ^{M}

porthole
hublot ^{M}
acceso ^{M} para las manos ^{M}
bullaugenähnliche Öffnung ^{F}
oblò ^{M}

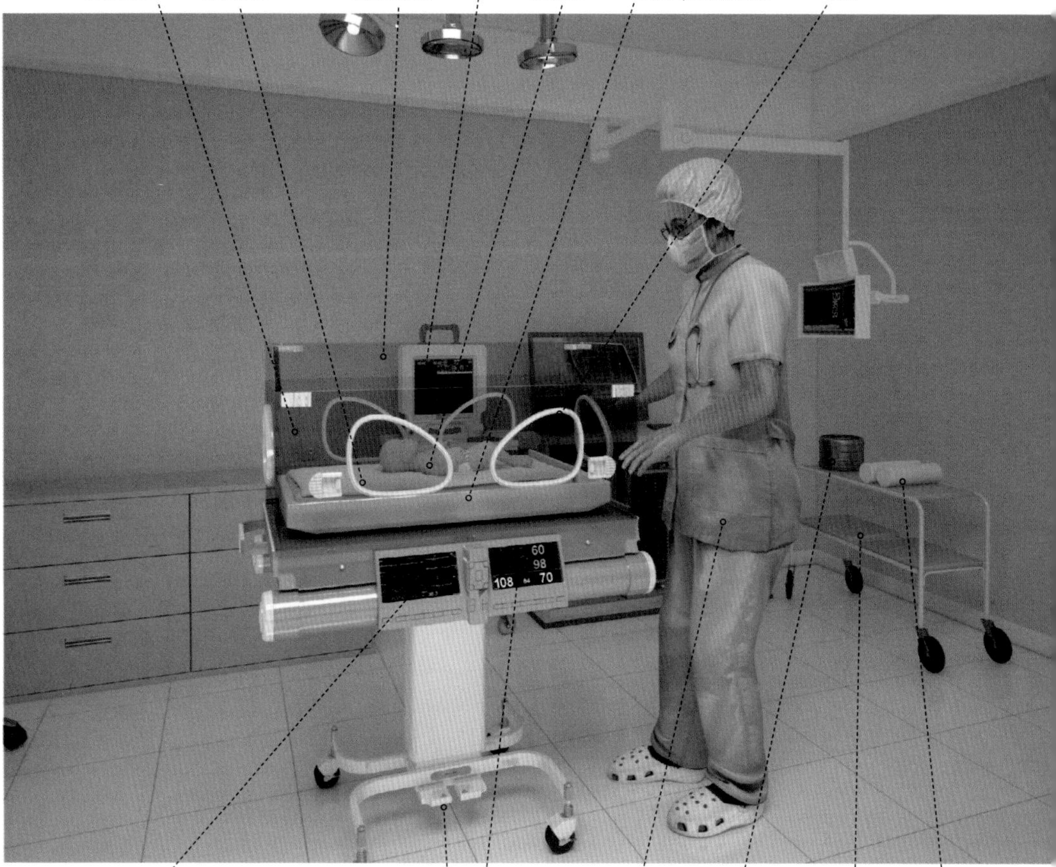

display panel
panneau ^{M} d'affichage ^{F}
pantalla ^{F}
Anzeigetafel ^{F}
monitor ^{M}

height-adjustment foot pedals
pédales ^{F} pour réglage ^{M} de la hauteur ^{F}
pedales ^{M} de ajuste ^{M} vertical
Fußschalter ^{M} für vertikale Höhenverstellung ^{F}
pedali ^{M} per la regolazione ^{F} dell'altezza ^{F}

neonatologist
néonatologiste ^{M}
neonatóloga ^{F}
Neonatologin ^{F}
neonatologo ^{M}

dressing container
récipient ^{M} à pansements ^{M}
tambor ^{M} de esterilización ^{F}
Verbandtrommel ^{F}
cestello ^{M} per medicazioni ^{F}

underpad
protège-drap ^{M}
empapador ^{M}
Unterlage ^{F}
cuscino ^{M} anti-incontinenza

control and information panel
panneau ^{M} de contrôle ^{M} et d'information ^{F}
panel ^{M} de controle ^{M} información ^{F}
Bedien- und Informationsfeld ^{N}
pannello ^{M} di controllo ^{M} e informazioni ^{F}

two-tier medical utility cart
guéridon ^{M} médical à deux niveaux ^{M}
carrito de instrumental con dos niveles ^{M}
zweistufiger medizinischer Gerätewagen ^{M}
carrello ^{M} medico a due livelli ^{M}

dental room
cabinet [M] dentaire
sala [F] dental
zahnärztlicher Raum [M]
studio [M] dentistico

emesis basin
bassin [M] réniforme
batea [F]
Nierenschale [F]
bacinella [F] reniforme

dental chair
fauteuil [M] dentaire
sillón [M] de dentista [M]
Zahnarztstuhl [M]
poltrona [F] odontoiatrica

operating light
lampe [F] d'opération [F]
lámpara [F] operatoria
OP-Leuchte [F]
lampada [F] operatoria

delivery system
système [M] d'adminstration [F] de soins [M]
bandeja [F] de utensilios [M]
Liefersystem [N]
sistema [F] di erogazione [F]

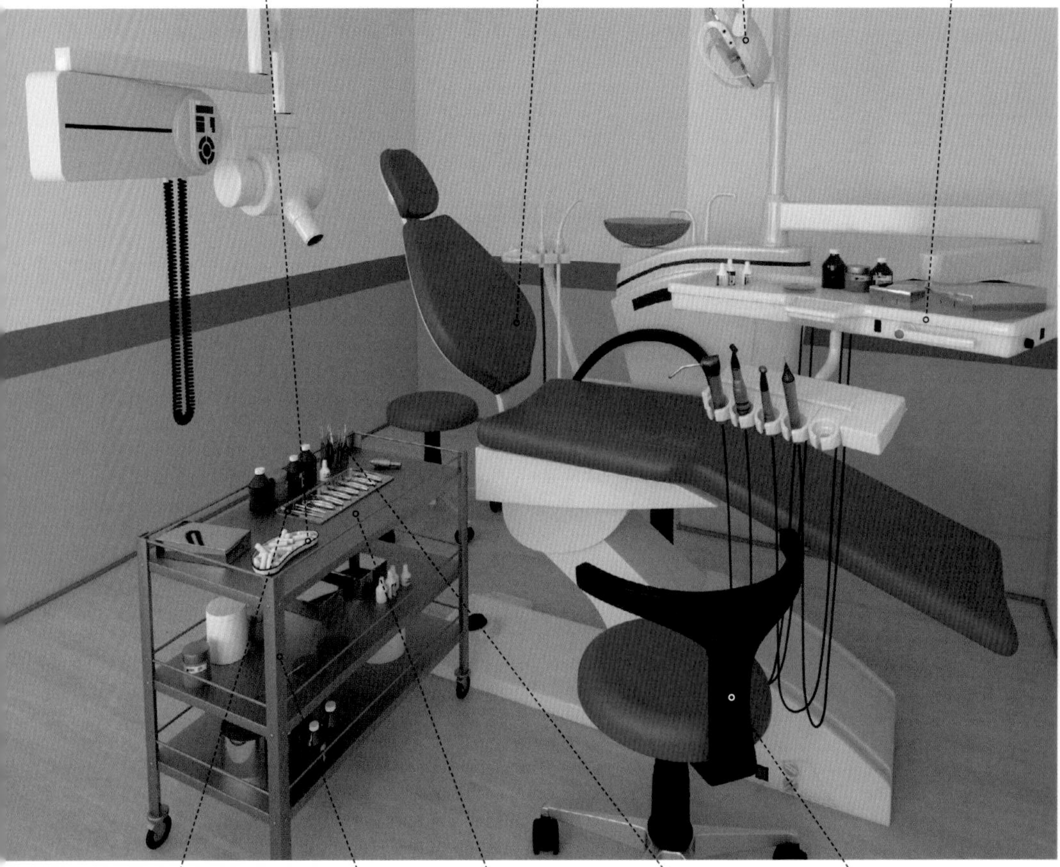

dental mirror
miroir [M] buccal
espejo [M] bucal
Mundspiegel [M]
specchietto [M] orale

Mayo instrument stand
plateau [M] à instruments [M] Mayo
mesa [F] instrumental de Mayo
Mayo-Instrumentenständer [M]
tavolo [M] di Mayo

work tray
plateau [M] de travail [M]
bandeja [F] de trabajo [M]
Arbeitstablett [N]
vassoio [M] ausiliario

dental tweezers
pinces [F] dentaires
pinzas [F] dentales
Zahnpinzette [F]
pinzette [F] dentali

adjustable stool
tabouret [M] ajustable
taburete [M] ajustable
verstellbarer Stuhl [M]
sgabello [M] regolabile

psychotherapy room
salle [F] de psychothérapie [F]
sala [F] de psicoterapia [F]
Psychotherapieraum [M]
studio [M] di psicoterapia [F]

therapy couch
canapé [M] de thérapie [F]
sillón [M] de terapia [F]
Therapieliege [F]
lettino [M] da terapia [F]

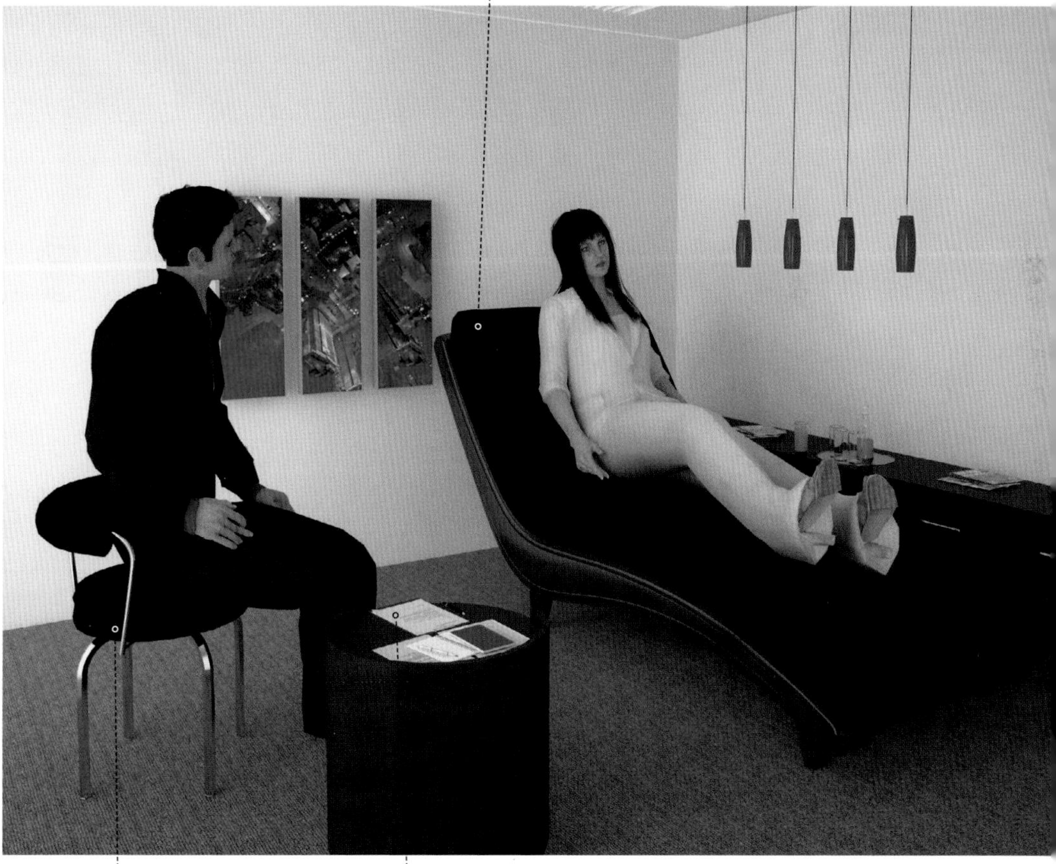

therapist's chair
fauteuil [M] du thérapeute [M]
silla [F] para el terapeuta [F]
Therapeutenstuhl [M]
sedia [F] del terapista [M]

therapist's notes
notes [F] du thérapeute [M]
apuntes [M] del terapeuta [F]
Therapeutennotizen [F]
taccuino [M] del terapista [M]

infant warmer
incubateur [M]
calentador para infantes [M]
Säuglingswärmer [M]
culla [F] termica

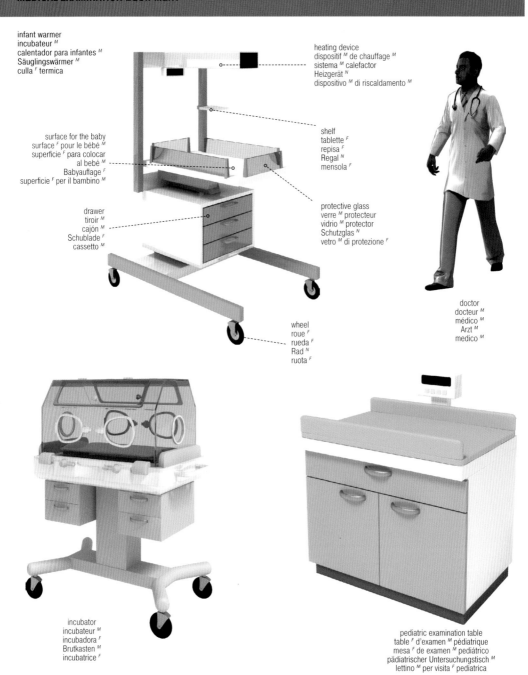

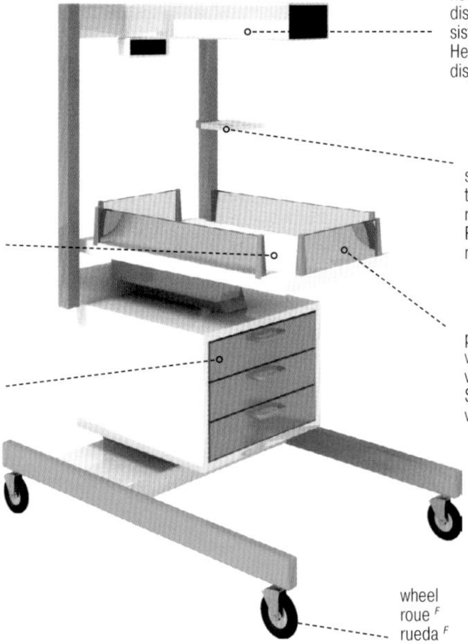

heating device
dispositif [M] de chauffage [M]
sistema [M] calefactor
Heizgerät [N]
dispositivo [M] di riscaldamento [M]

shelf
tablette [F]
repisa [F]
Regal [N]
mensola [F]

surface for the baby
surface [F] pour le bébé [M]
superficie [F] para colocar al bebé [M]
Babyauflage [F]
superficie [F] per il bambino [M]

protective glass
verre [M] protecteur
vidrio [M] protector
Schutzglas [N]
vetro [M] di protezione [F]

drawer
tiroir [M]
cajón [M]
Schublade [F]
cassetto [M]

wheel
roue [F]
rueda [F]
Rad [N]
ruota [F]

doctor
docteur [M]
médico [M]
Arzt [M]
medico [M]

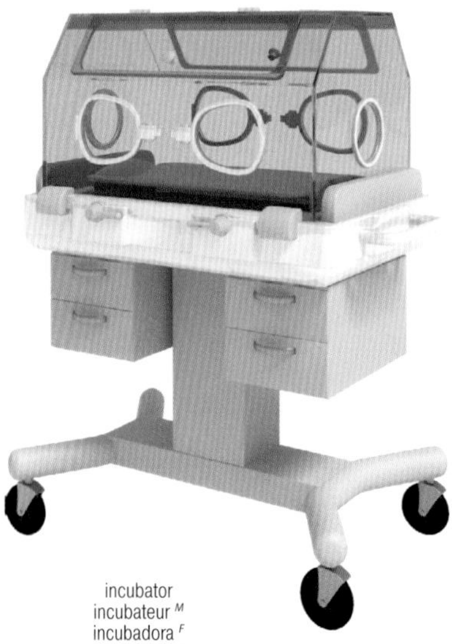

incubator
incubateur [M]
incubadora [F]
Brutkasten [M]
incubatrice [F]

pediatric examination table
table [F] d'examen [M] pédiatrique
mesa [F] de examen [M] pediátrico
pädiatrischer Untersuchungstisch [M]
lettino [M] per visita [F] pediatrica

manual defibrillator
défibrillateur [M] manuel
desfibrilador [M]
manueller Defibrillator [M]
defibrillatore [M]

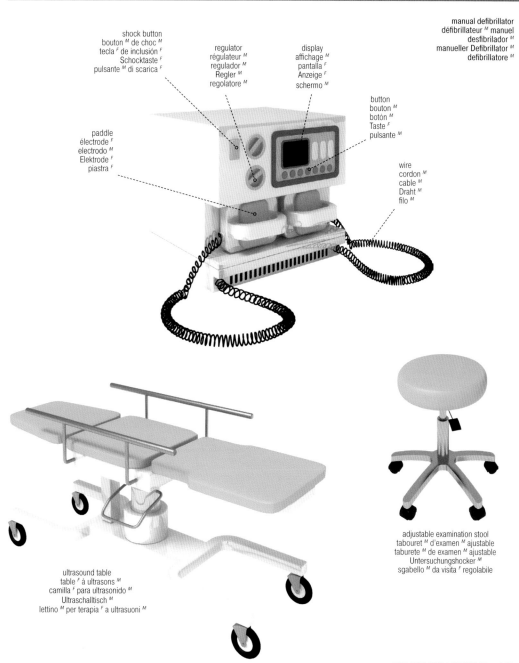

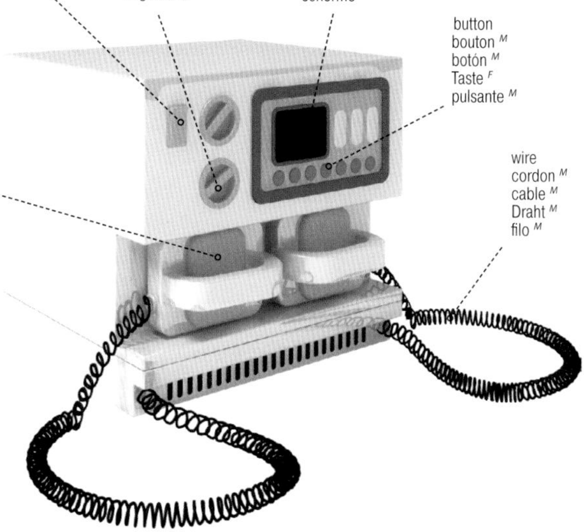
shock button
bouton [M] de choc [M]
tecla [F] de inclusión [F]
Schocktaste [F]
pulsante [M] di scarica [F]
regulator
régulateur [M]
regulador [M]
Regler [M]
regolatore [M]
display
affichage [M]
pantalla [F]
Anzeige [F]
schermo [M]
button
bouton [M]
botón [M]
Taste [F]
pulsante [M]
paddle
électrode [F]
electrodo [M]
Elektrode [F]
piastra [F]
wire
cordon [M]
cable [M]
Draht [M]
filo [M]

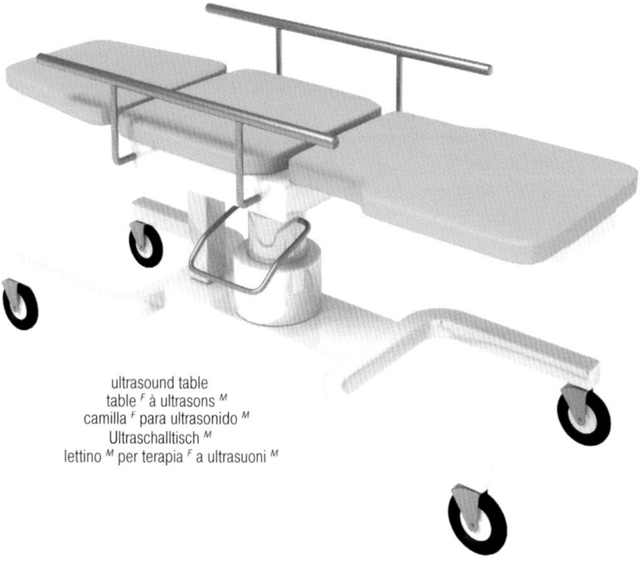

ultrasound table
table [F] à ultrasons [M]
camilla [F] para ultrasonido [M]
Ultraschalltisch [M]
lettino [M] per terapia [F] a ultrasuoni [M]

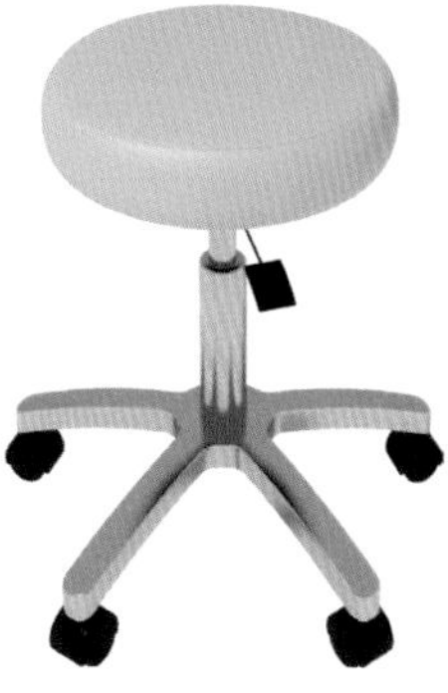

adjustable examination stool
tabouret [M] d'examen [M] ajustable
taburete [M] de examen [M] ajustable
Untersuchungshocker [M]
sgabello [M] da visita [F] regolabile

electric hospital bed
lit [M] d'hôpital [M] électrique
cama [F] eléctrica
elektrisches Krankenhausbett [N]
lettino [M] da degerza [F] elettrico

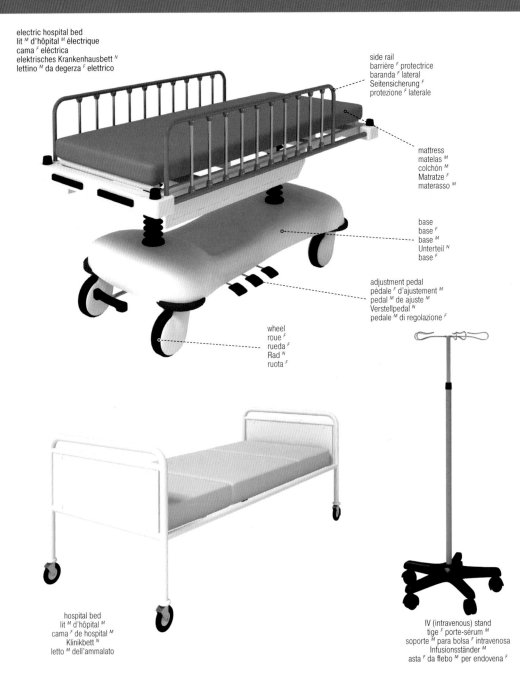

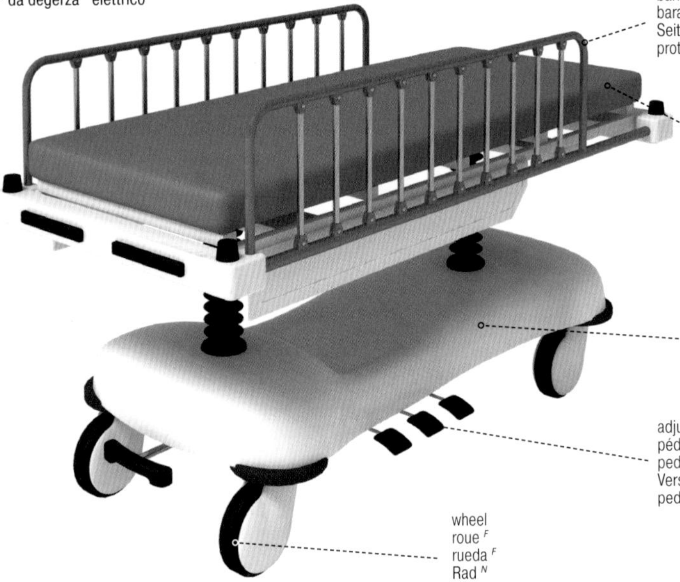
side rail
barrière [F] protectrice
baranda [F] lateral
Seitensicherung [F]
protezione [F] laterale
mattress
matelas [M]
colchón [M]
Matratze [F]
materasso [M]
base
base [F]
base [M]
Unterteil [N]
base [F]
adjustment pedal
pédale [F] d'ajustement [M]
pedal [M] de ajuste [M]
Verstellpedal [N]
pedale [M] di regolazione [F]
wheel
roue [F]
rueda [F]
Rad [N]
ruota [F]

hospital bed
lit [M] d'hôpital [M]
cama [F] de hospital [M]
Klinikbett [N]
letto [M] dell'ammalato

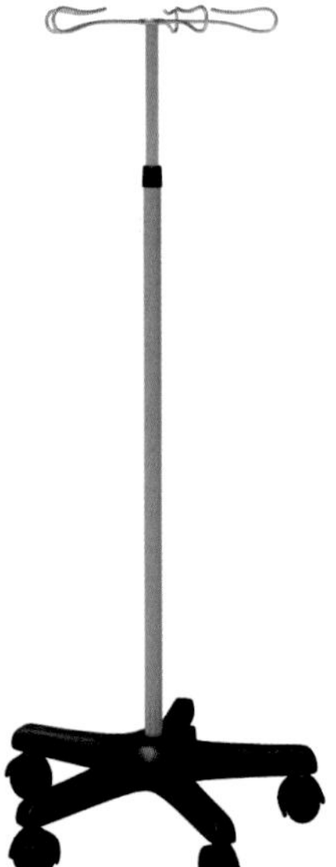

IV (intravenous) stand
tige [F] porte-sérum [M]
soporte [M] para bolsa [F] intravenosa
Infusionsständer [M]
asta [F] da flebo [M] per endovena [F]

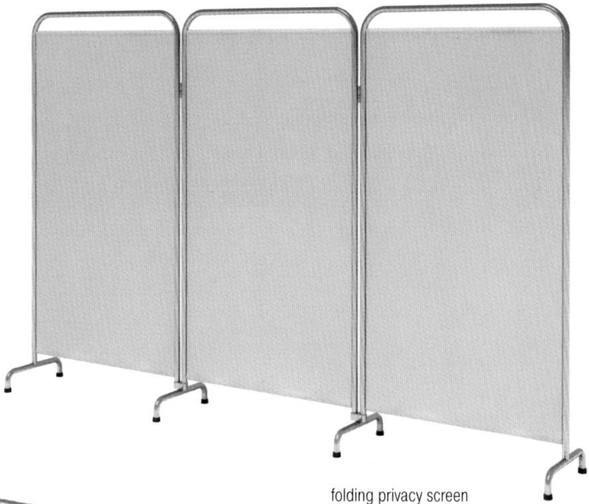

folding privacy screen
écran [M] d'intimité [F] pliant
biombo [M] plegable
faltbarer Paravent [M]
pannello [M] divisorio [M] pieghevole

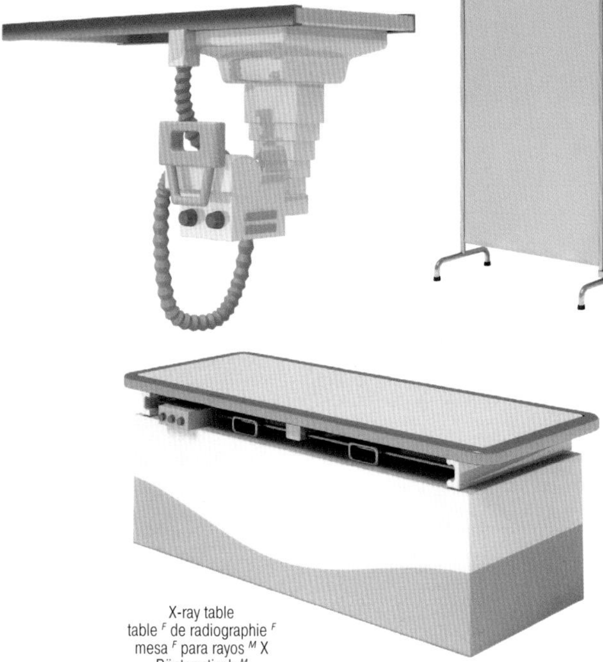

X-ray table
table [F] de radiographie [F]
mesa [F] para rayos [M] X
Röntgentisch [M]
tavolo [M] per radiografia [F]

X-ray viewer
négatoscope [M]
visor de rayos [M] X
Röntgenbildbetrachter [M]
negatoscopio [M]

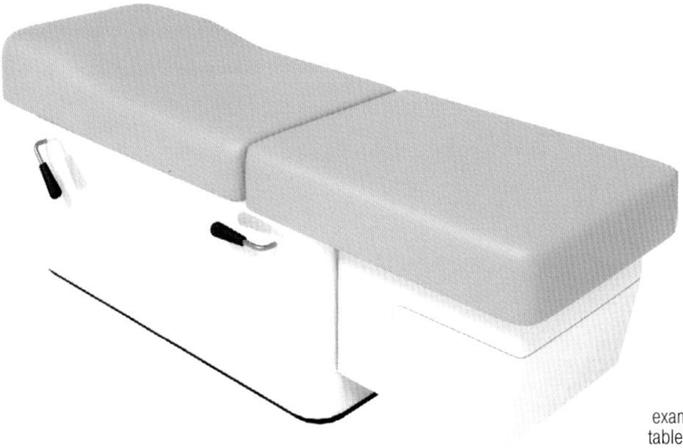

examination table
table [F] d'examen [M]
camilla [F] de exploración [F]
Untersuchungstisch [M]
lettino [M] per visita [F] medica

MEDICAL EXAMINATION EQUIPMENT

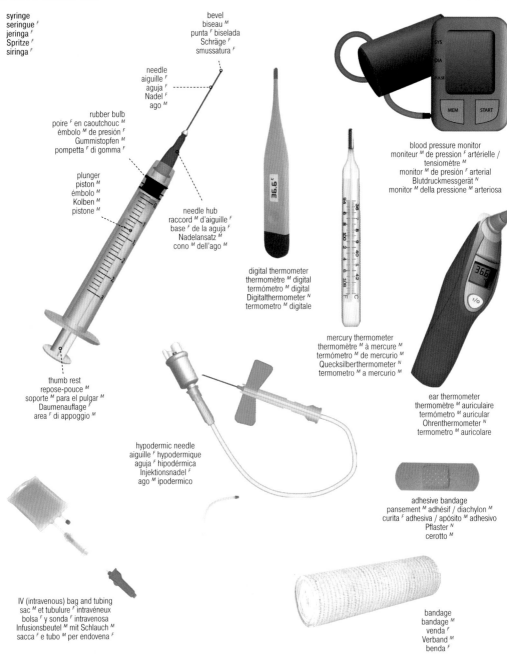

syringe
seringue F
jeringa F
Spritze F
siringa F

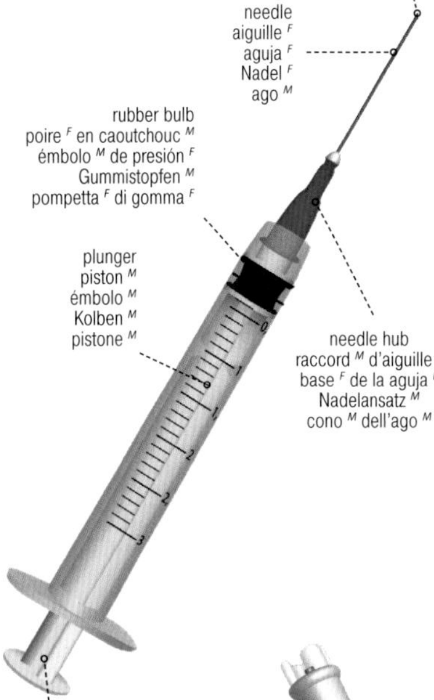
bevel
biseau M
punta F biselada
Schräge F
smussatura F
needle
aiguille F
aguja F
Nadel F
ago M
rubber bulb
poire F en caoutchouc M
émbolo M de presión F
Gummistopfen M
pompetta F di gomma F
plunger
piston M
émbolo M
Kolben M
pistone M
needle hub
raccord M d'aiguille F
base F de la aguja F
Nadelansatz M
cono M dell'ago M
thumb rest
repose-pouce M
soporte M para el pulgar M
Daumenauflage F
area F di appoggio M

36.6°C

digital thermometer
thermomètre M digital
termómetro M digital
Digitalthermometer N
termometro M digitale

mercury thermometer
thermomètre M à mercure M
termómetro M de mercurio M
Quecksilberthermometer N
termometro M a mercurio M

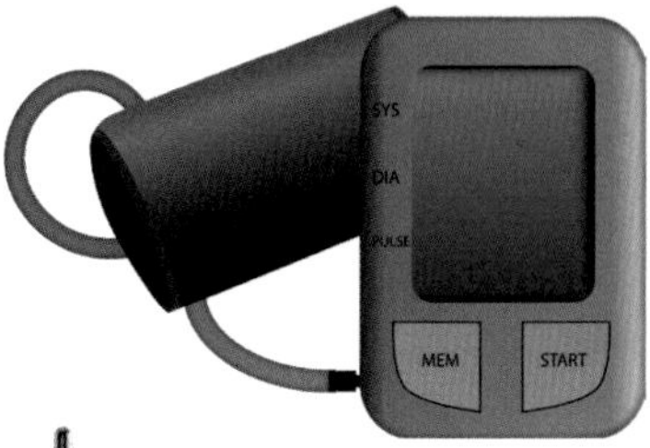
SYS
DIA
PULSE
MEM
START

blood pressure monitor
moniteur M de pression F artérielle / tensiomètre M
monitor M de presión F arterial
Blutdruckmessgerät N
monitor M della pressione M arteriosa

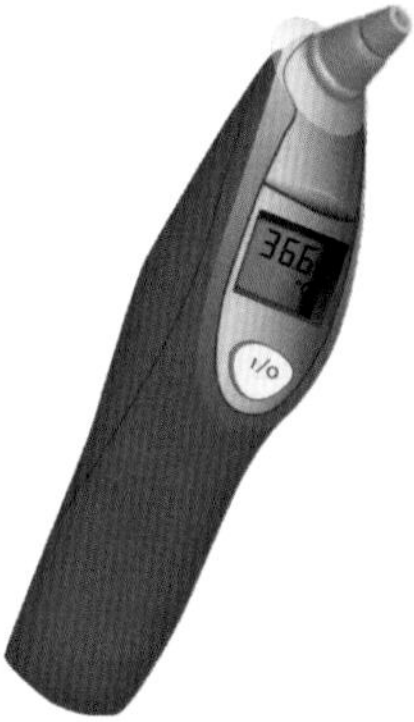
I/O

ear thermometer
thermomètre M auriculaire
termómetro M auricular
Ohrenthermometer N
termometro M auricolare

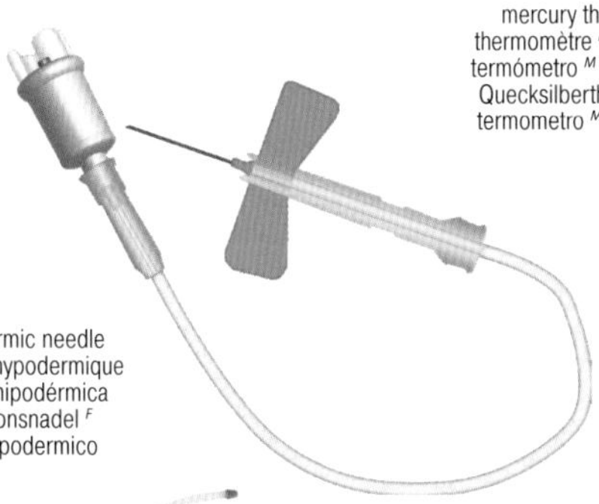

hypodermic needle
aiguille F hypodermique
aguja F hipodérmica
Injektionsnadel F
ago M ipodermico

IV (intravenous) bag and tubing
sac M et tubulure F intraveineux
bolsa F y sonda F intravenosa
Infusionsbeutel M mit Schlauch M
sacca F e tubo M per endovena F

adhesive bandage
pansement M adhésif / diachylon M
curita F adhesiva / apósito M adhesivo
Pflaster N
cerotto M

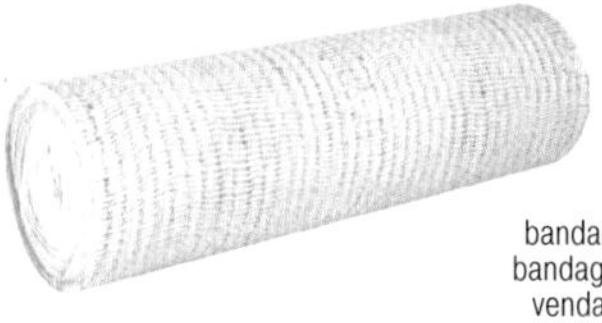

bandage
bandage M
venda F
Verband M
benda F

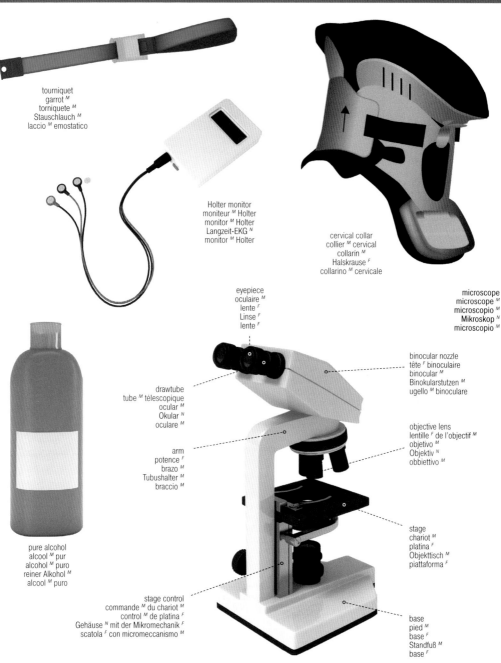

tourniquet
garrot ᴹ
torniquete ᴹ
Stauschlauch ᴹ
laccio ᴹ emostatico

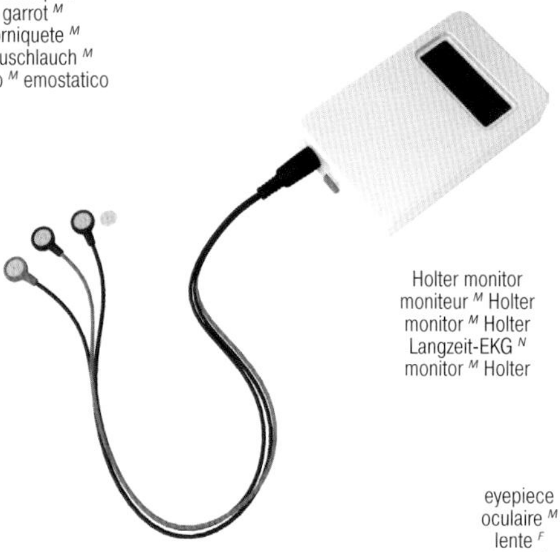

Holter monitor
moniteur ᴹ Holter
monitor ᴹ Holter
Langzeit-EKG ᴺ
monitor ᴹ Holter

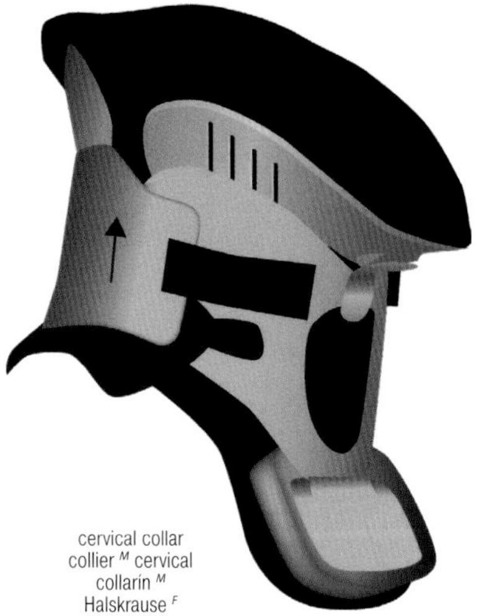

cervical collar
collier ᴹ cervical
collarín ᴹ
Halskrause ᶠ
collarino ᴹ cervicale

pure alcohol
alcool ᴹ pur
alcohol ᴹ puro
reiner Alkohol ᴹ
alcool ᴹ puro

microscope
microscope ᴹ
microscopio ᴹ
Mikroskop ᴺ
microscopio ᴹ

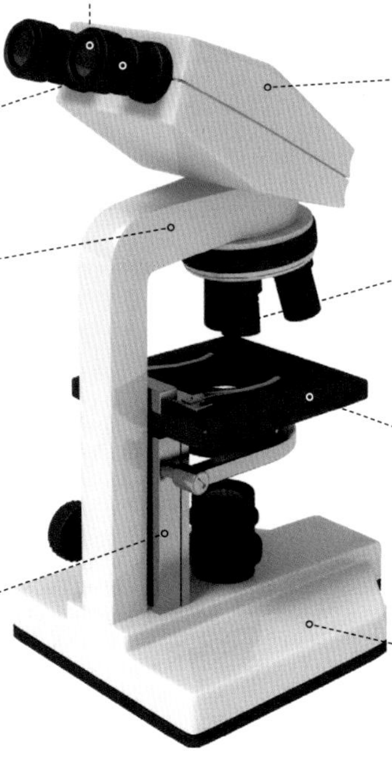
eyepiece
oculaire ᴹ
lente ᶠ
Linse ᶠ
lente ᶠ
binocular nozzle
tête ᶠ binoculaire
binocular ᴹ
Binokularstutzen ᴹ
ugello ᴹ binoculare
drawtube
tube ᴹ télescopique
ocular ᴹ
Okular ᴺ
oculare ᴹ
objective lens
lentille ᶠ de l'objectif ᴹ
objetivo ᴹ
Objektiv ᴺ
obbiettivo ᴹ
arm
potence ᶠ
brazo ᴹ
Tubushalter ᴹ
braccio ᴹ
stage
chariot ᴹ
platina ᶠ
Objekttisch ᴹ
piattaforma ᶠ
stage control
commande ᴹ du chariot ᴹ
control ᴹ de platina ᶠ
Gehäuse ᴺ mit der Mikromechanik ᶠ
scatola ᶠ con micromeccanismo ᴹ
base
pied ᴹ
base ᶠ
Standfuß ᴹ
base ᶠ

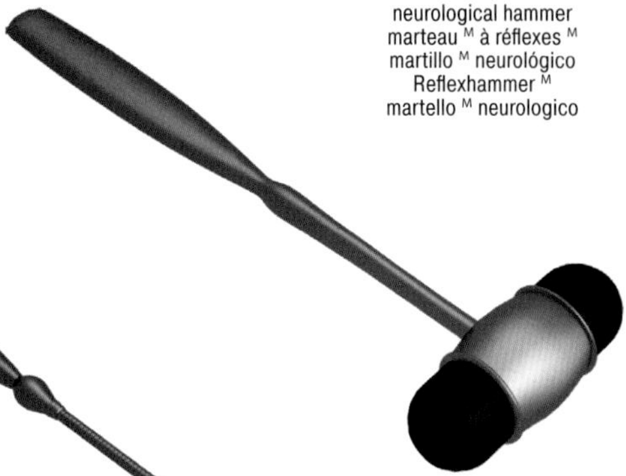

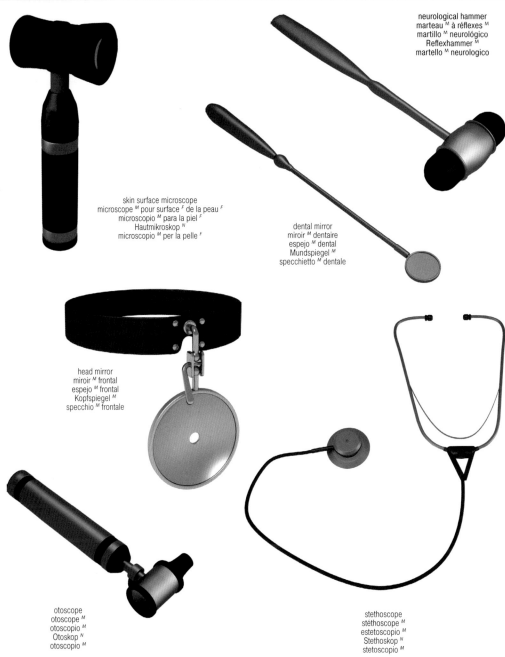

neurological hammer
marteau M à réflexes M
martillo M neurológico
Reflexhammer M
martello M neurologico

skin surface microscope
microscope M pour surface F de la peau F
microscopio M para la piel F
Hautmikroskop N
microscopio M per la pelle F

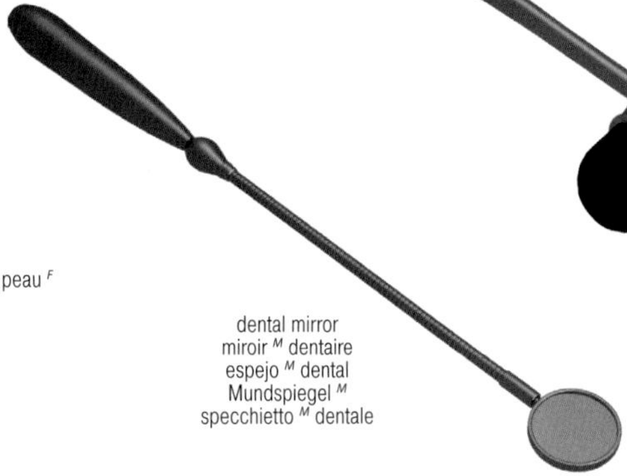

dental mirror
miroir M dentaire
espejo M dental
Mundspiegel M
specchietto M dentale

head mirror
miroir M frontal
espejo M frontal
Kopfspiegel M
specchio M frontale

otoscope
otoscope M
otoscopio M
Otoskop N
otoscopio M

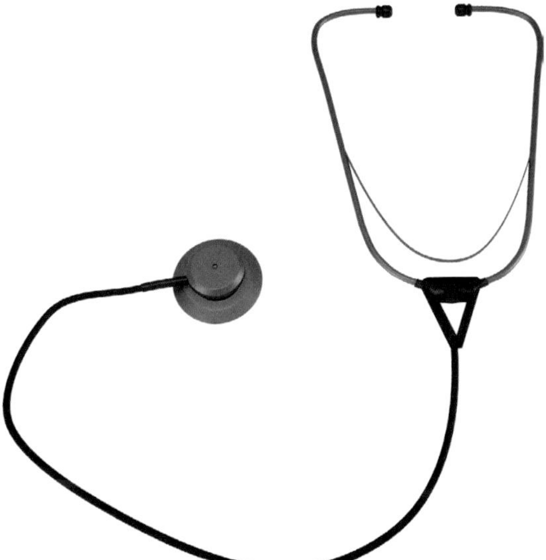

stethoscope
stéthoscope M
estetoscopio M
Stethoskop N
stetoscopio M

suppository
suppositoire M
supositorio M
Zäpfchen N
supposta F

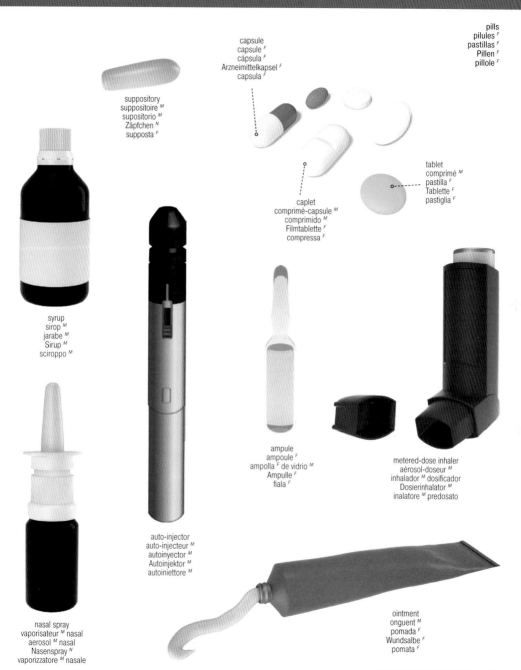

pills
pilules F
pastillas F
Pillen F
pillole F

capsule
capsule F
cápsula F
Arzneimittelkapsel F
capsula F

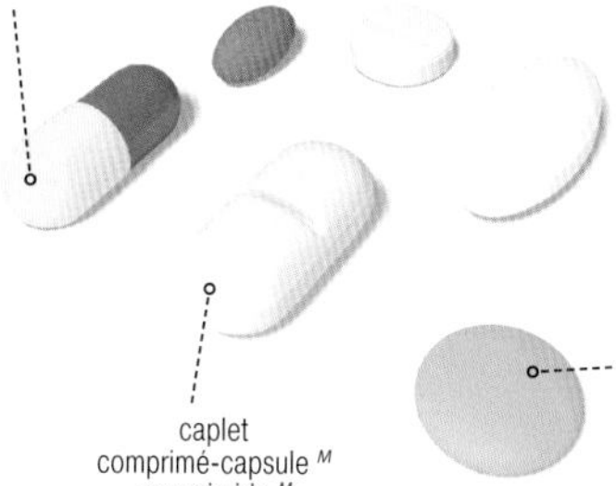

caplet
comprimé-capsule M
comprimido M
Filmtablette F
compressa F

tablet
comprimé M
pastilla F
Tablette F
pastiglia F

syrup
sirop M
jarabe M
Sirup M
sciroppo M

auto-injector
auto-injecteur M
autoinyector M
Autoinjektor M
autoiniettore M

ampule
ampoule F
ampolla F de vidrio M
Ampulle F
fiala F

metered-dose inhaler
aérosol-doseur M
inhalador M dosificador
Dosierinhalator M
inalatore M predosato

nasal spray
vaporisateur M nasal
aerosol M nasal
Nasenspray N
vaporizzatore M nasale

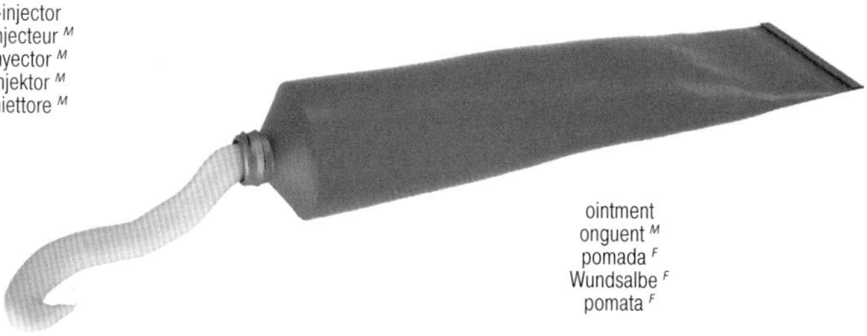

ointment
onguent M
pomada F
Wundsalbe F
pomata F

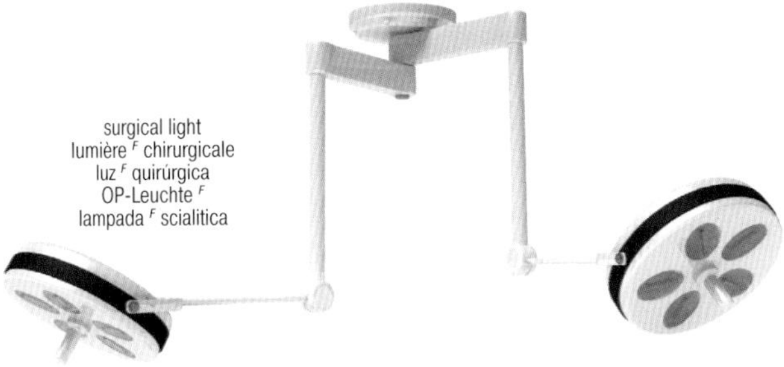

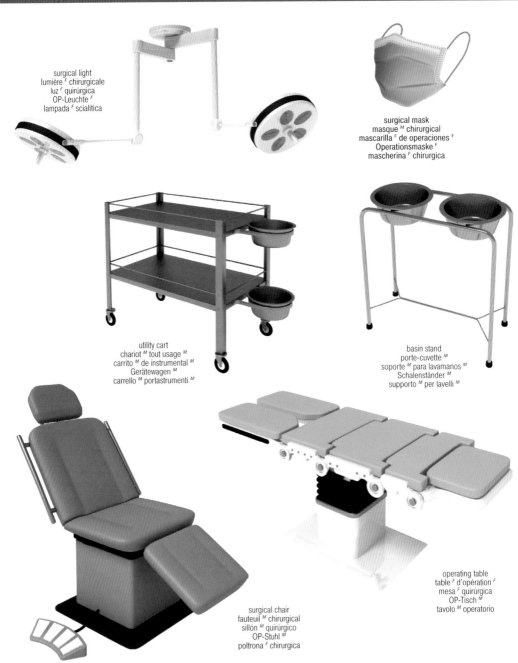

surgical light
lumière [F] chirurgicale
luz [F] quirúrgica
OP-Leuchte [F]
lampada [F] scialitica

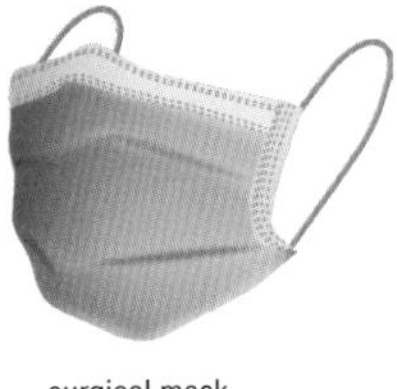

surgical mask
masque [M] chirurgical
mascarilla [F] de operaciones [F]
Operationsmaske [F]
mascherina [F] chirurgica

utility cart
chariot [M] tout usage [M]
carrito [M] de instrumental [M]
Gerätewagen [M]
carrello [M] portastrumenti [M]

basin stand
porte-cuvette [M]
soporte [M] para lavamanos [M]
Schalenständer [M]
supporto [M] per lavelli [M]

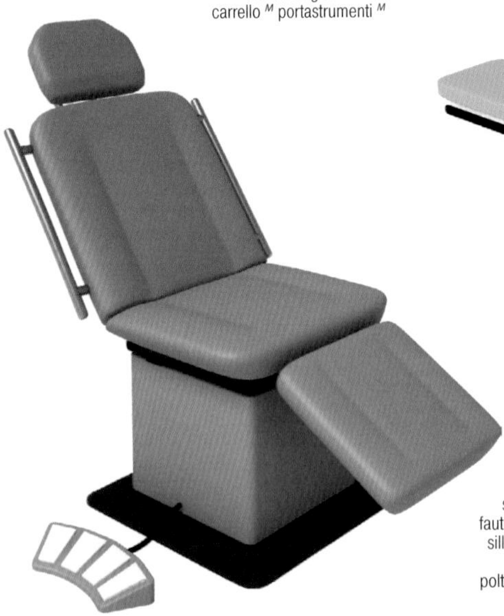

surgical chair
fauteuil [M] chirurgical
sillón [M] quirúrgico
OP-Stuhl [M]
poltrona [F] chirurgica

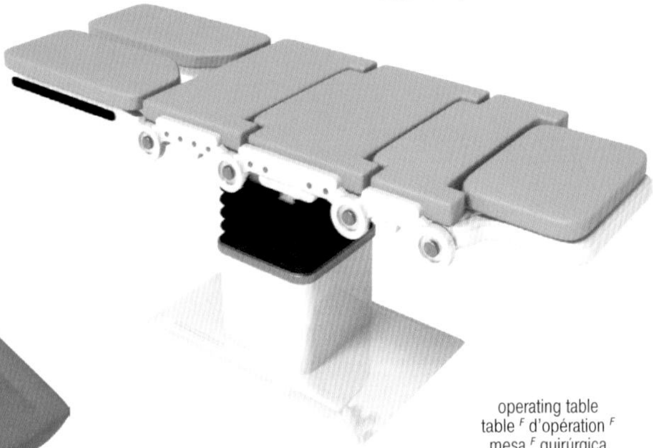

operating table
table [F] d'opération [F]
mesa [F] quirúrgica
OP-Tisch [M]
tavolo [M] operatorio

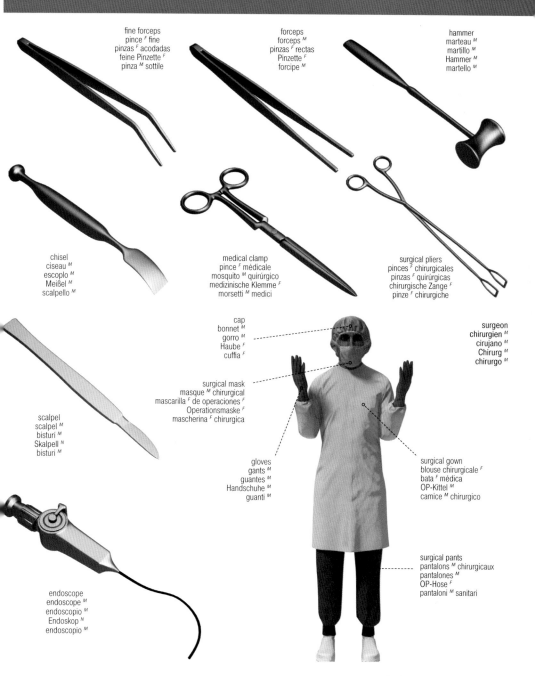

fine forceps
pince F fine
pinzas F acodadas
feine Pinzette F
pinza M sottile

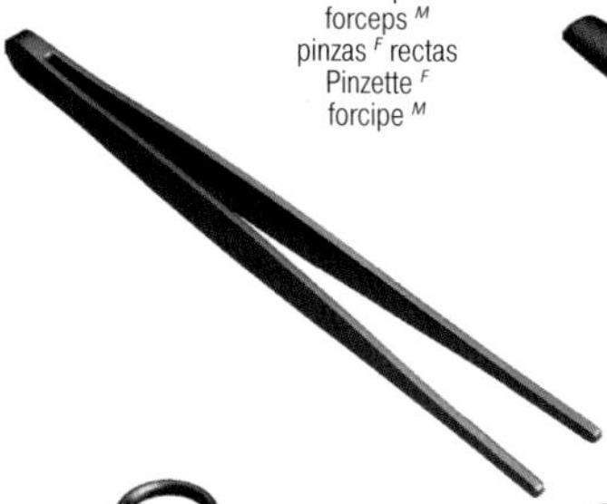

forceps
forceps M
pinzas F rectas
Pinzette F
forcipe M

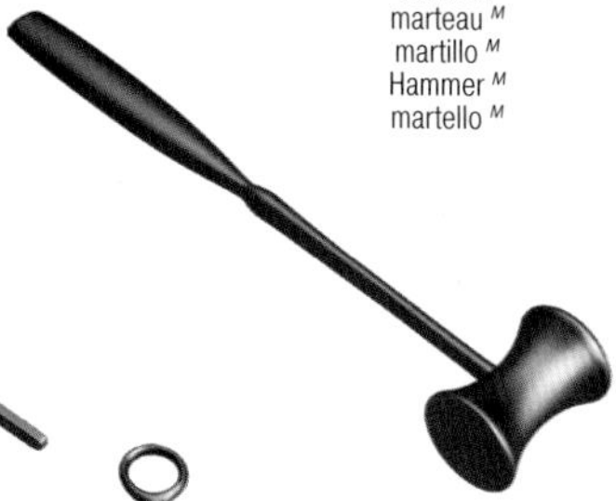

hammer
marteau M
martillo M
Hammer M
martello M

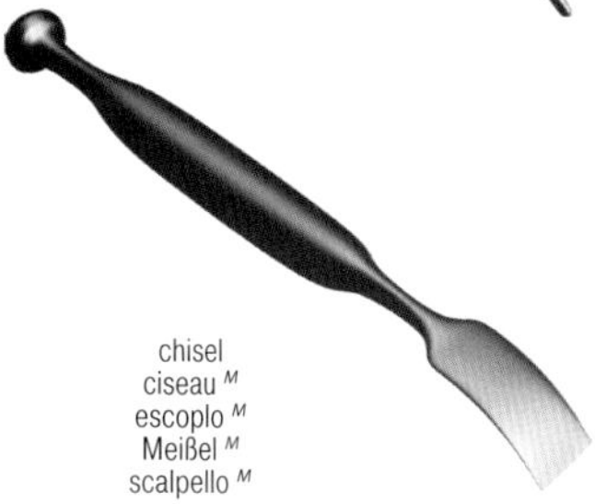

chisel
ciseau M
escoplo M
Meißel M
scalpello M

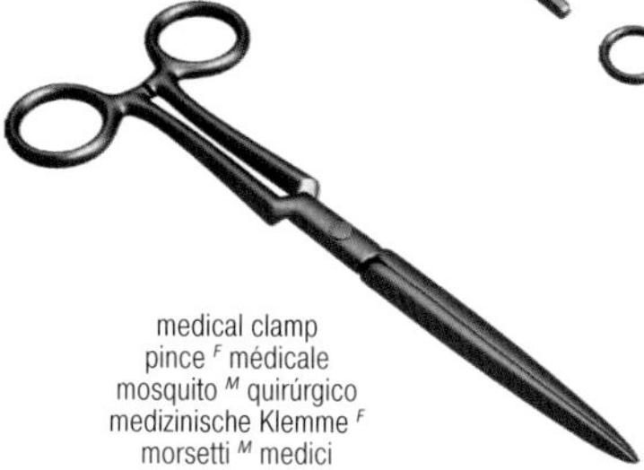

medical clamp
pince F médicale
mosquito M quirúrgico
medizinische Klemme F
morsetti M medici

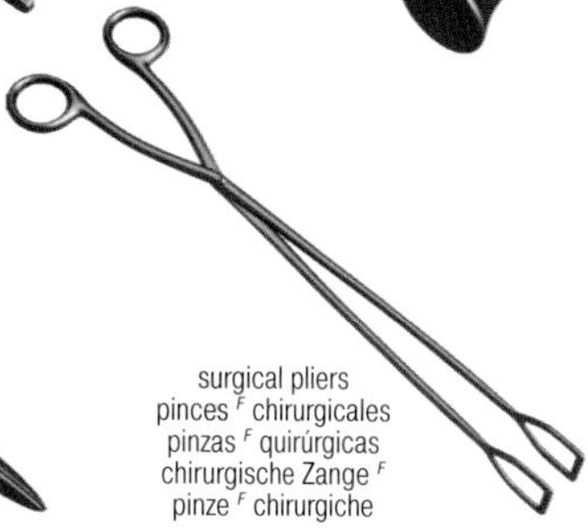

surgical pliers
pinces F chirurgicales
pinzas F quirúrgicas
chirurgische Zange F
pinze F chirurgiche

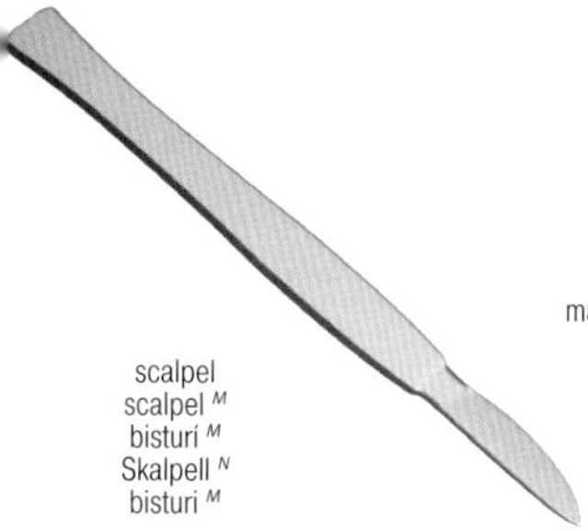

scalpel
scalpel M
bisturí M
Skalpell N
bisturi M

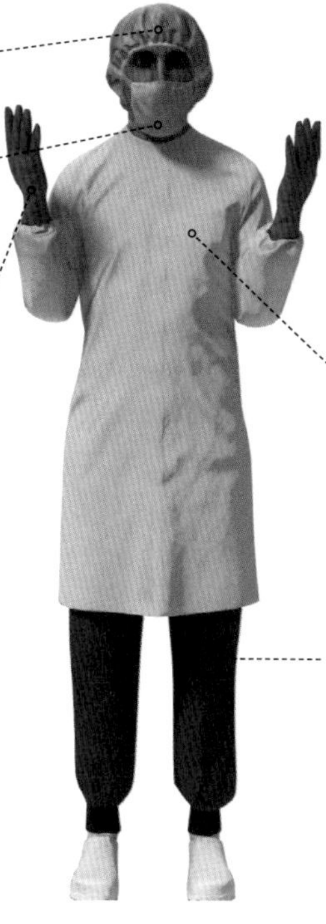

surgeon
chirurgien M
cirujano M
Chirurg M
chirurgo M

cap
bonnet M
gorro M
Haube F
cuffia F

surgical mask
masque M chirurgical
mascarilla F de operaciones F
Operationsmaske F
mascherina F chirurgica

gloves
gants M
guantes M
Handschuhe M
guanti M

surgical gown
blouse chirurgicale F
bata F médica
OP-Kittel M
camice M chirurgico

surgical pants
pantalons M chirurgicaux
pantalones M
OP-Hose F
pantaloni M sanitari

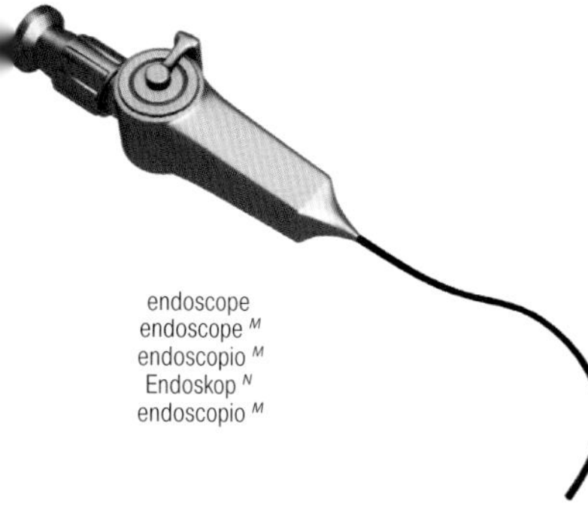

endoscope
endoscope M
endoscopio M
Endoskop N
endoscopio M

four-wheel walker
déambulateur ^{M}
andadera ^{F}
vierrädriger Rollator ^{M}
deambulatore ^{M}

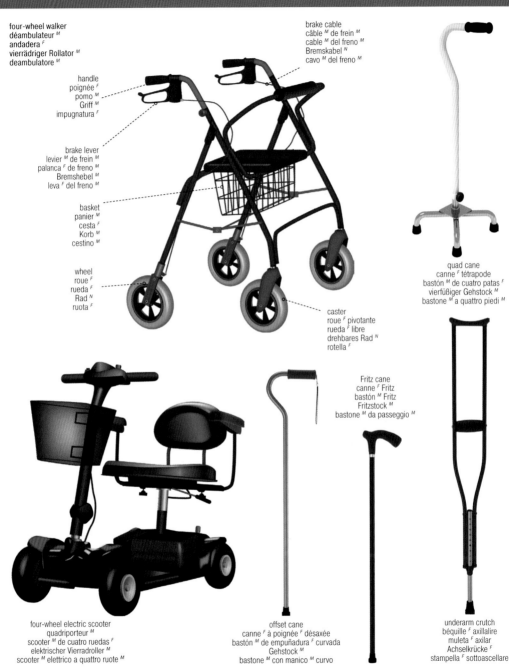

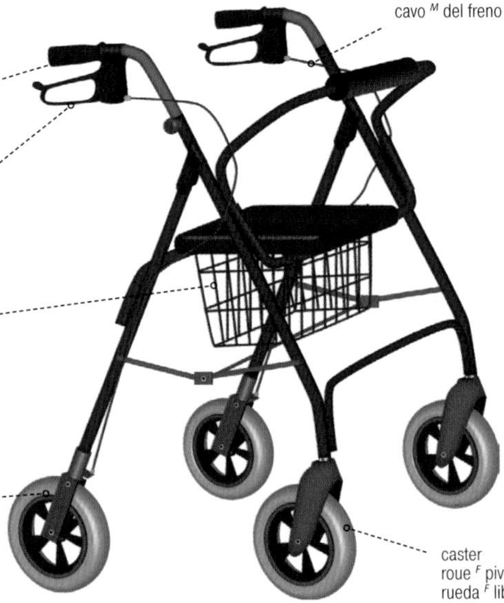

handle
poignée ^{F}
pomo ^{M}
Griff ^{M}
impugnatura ^{F}

brake cable
câble ^{M} de frein ^{M}
cable ^{M} del freno ^{M}
Bremskabel ^{N}
cavo ^{M} del freno ^{M}

brake lever
levier ^{M} de frein ^{M}
palanca ^{F} de freno ^{M}
Bremshebel ^{M}
leva ^{F} del freno ^{M}

basket
panier ^{M}
cesta ^{F}
Korb ^{M}
cestino ^{M}

wheel
roue ^{F}
rueda ^{F}
Rad ^{N}
ruota ^{F}

caster
roue ^{F} pivotante
rueda ^{F} libre
drehbares Rad ^{N}
rotella ^{F}

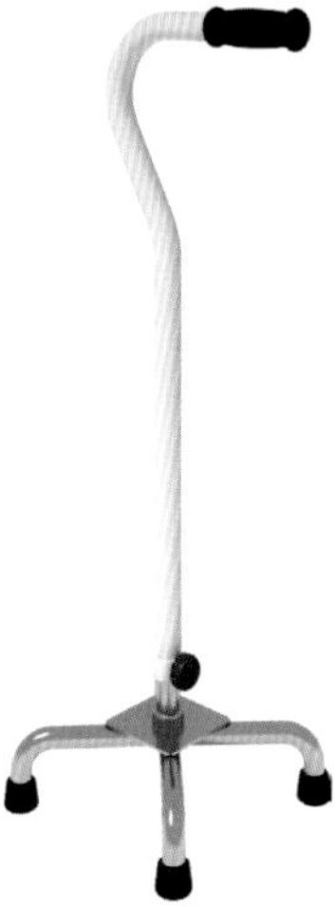

quad cane
canne ^{F} tétrapode
bastón ^{M} de cuatro patas ^{F}
vierfüßiger Gehstock ^{M}
bastone ^{M} a quattro piedi ^{M}

four-wheel electric scooter
quadriporteur ^{M}
scooter ^{M} de cuatro ruedas ^{F}
elektrischer Vierradroller ^{M}
scooter ^{M} elettrico a quattro ruote ^{M}

offset cane
canne ^{F} à poignée ^{F} désaxée
bastón ^{M} de empuñadura ^{F} curvada
Gehstock ^{M}
bastone ^{M} con manico ^{M} curvo

Fritz cane
canne ^{F} Fritz
bastón ^{M} Fritz
Fritzstock ^{M}
bastone ^{M} da passeggio ^{M}

underarm crutch
béquille ^{F} axillaire
muleta ^{F} axilar
Achselkrücke ^{F}
stampella ^{F} sottoascellare

forearm crutch
béquille F d'avant-bras M
muleta F de antebrazo M
Unterarmgehstütze F
mpella F avambraccio M canadese

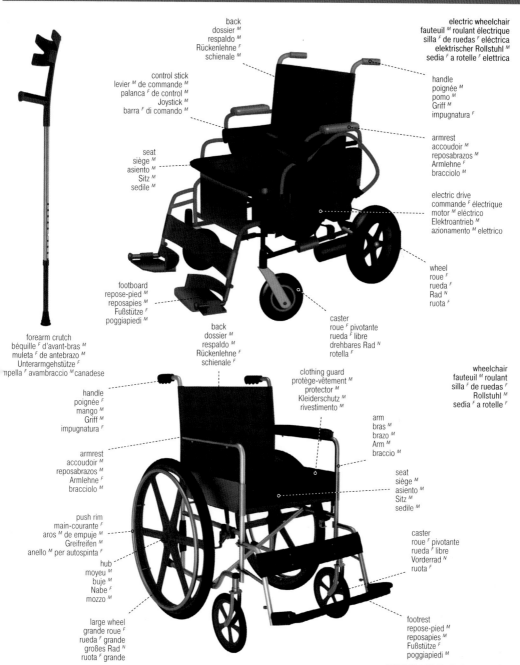

electric wheelchair
fauteuil M roulant électrique
silla F de ruedas F eléctrica
elektrischer Rollstuhl M
sedia F a rotelle F elettrica

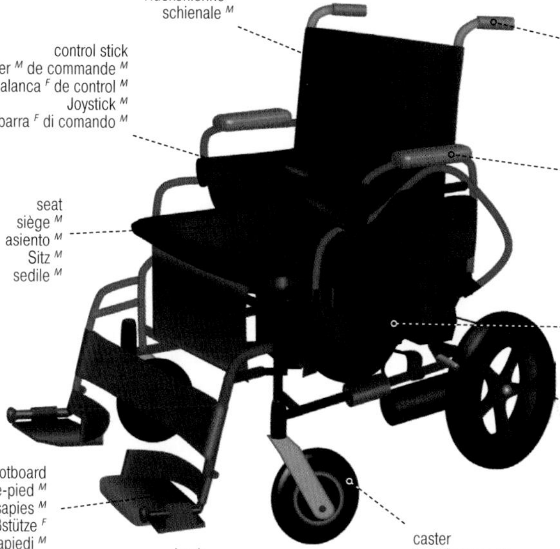
back
dossier M
respaldo M
Rückenlehne F
schienale M
control stick
levier M de commande M
palanca F de control M
Joystick M
barra F di comando M
seat
siège M
asiento M
Sitz M
sedile M
footboard
repose-pied M
reposapies M
Fußstütze F
poggiapiedi M
handle
poignée M
pomo M
Griff M
impugnatura F
armrest
accoudoir M
reposabrazos M
Armlehne F
bracciolo M
electric drive
commande F électrique
motor M eléctrico
Elektroantrieb M
azionamento M elettrico
wheel
roue F
rueda F
Rad N
ruota F
caster
roue F pivotante
rueda F libre
drehbares Rad N
rotella F

wheelchair
fauteuil M roulant
silla F de ruedas F
Rollstuhl M
sedia F a rotelle F

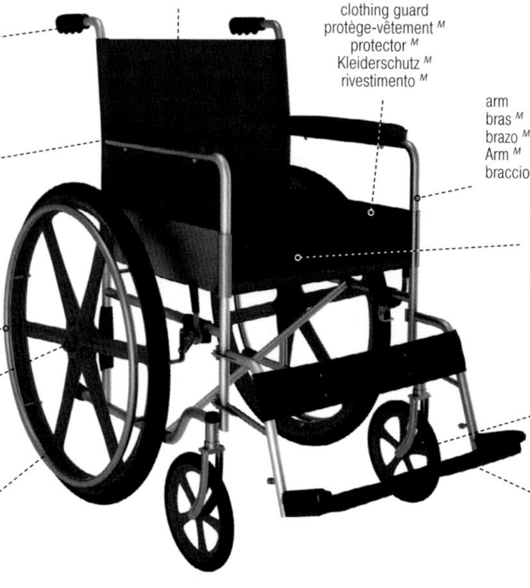
back
dossier M
respaldo M
Rückenlehne F
schienale F
handle
poignée F
mango M
Griff M
impugnatura F
armrest
accoudoir M
reposabrazos M
Armlehne F
bracciolo M
push rim
main-courante F
aros M de empuje M
Greifreifen M
anello M per autospinta F
hub
moyeu M
buje M
Nabe F
mozzo M
large wheel
grande roue F
rueda F grande
großes Rad N
ruota F grande
clothing guard
protège-vêtement M
protector M
Kleiderschutz M
rivestimento M
arm
bras M
brazo M
Arm M
braccio M
seat
siège M
asiento M
Sitz M
sedile M
caster
roue F pivotante
rueda F libre
Vorderrad N
ruota F
footrest
repose-pied M
reposapies M
Fußstütze F
poggiapiedi M

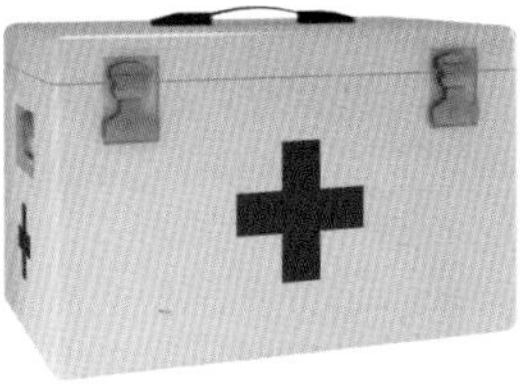

first aid kit
trousse [F] de premiers soins [M]
kit [M] de primeros auxilios [M]
Erste-Hilfe-Kit [N]
kit [M] di pronto soccorso [M]

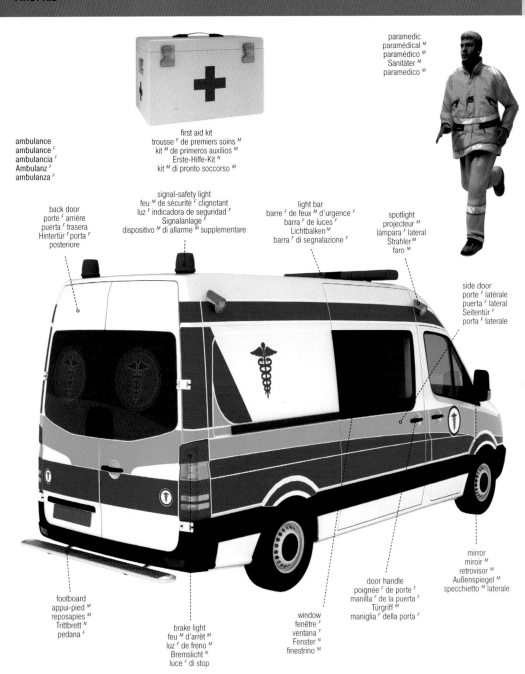

paramedic
paramédical [M]
paramédico [M]
Sanitäter [M]
paramedico [M]

ambulance
ambulance [F]
ambulancia [F]
Ambulanz [F]
ambulanza [F]

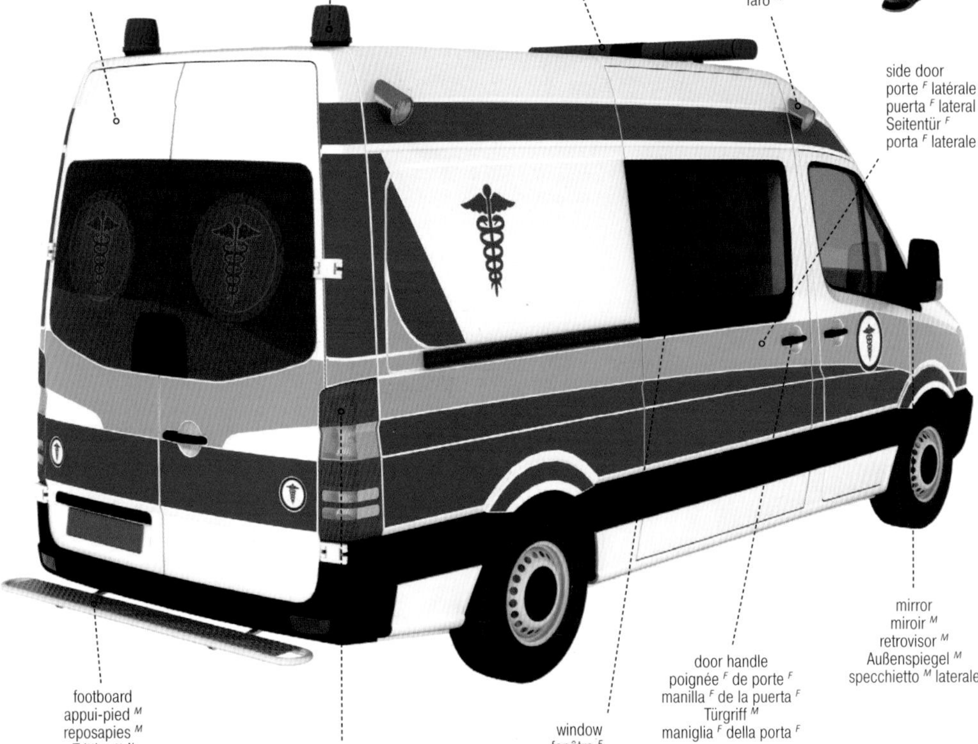
back door
porte [F] arrière
puerta [F] trasera
Hintertür [F] porta [F]
posteriore
signal-safety light
feu [M] de sécurité [F] clignotant
luz [F] indicadora de seguridad [F]
Signalanlage [F]
dispositivo [M] di allarme [M] supplementare
light bar
barre [F] de feux [M] d'urgence [F]
barra [F] de luces [F]
Lichtbalken [M]
barra [F] di segnalazione [F]
spotlight
projecteur [M]
lámpara [F] lateral
Strahler [M]
faro [M]
side door
porte [F] latérale
puerta [F] lateral
Seitentür [F]
porta [F] laterale
mirror
miroir [M]
retrovisor [M]
Außenspiegel [M]
specchietto [M] laterale
door handle
poignée [F] de porte [F]
manilla [F] de la puerta [F]
Türgriff [M]
maniglia [F] della porta [F]
window
fenêtre [F]
ventana [F]
Fenster [N]
finestrino [M]
brake light
feu [M] d'arrêt [M]
luz [F] de freno [M]
Bremslicht [N]
luce [F] di stop
footboard
appui-pied [M]
reposapies [M]
Trittbrett [N]
pedana [F]

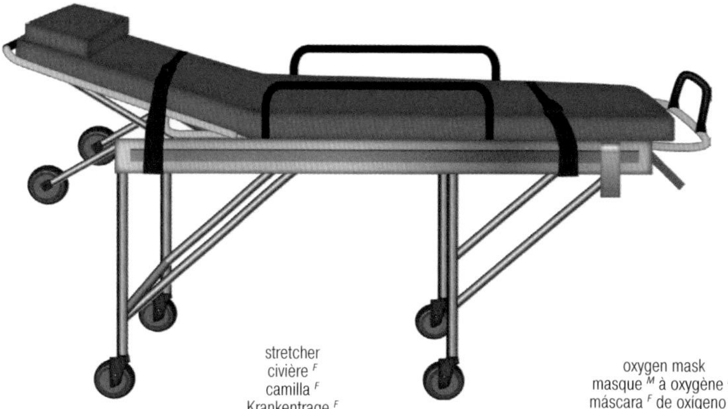

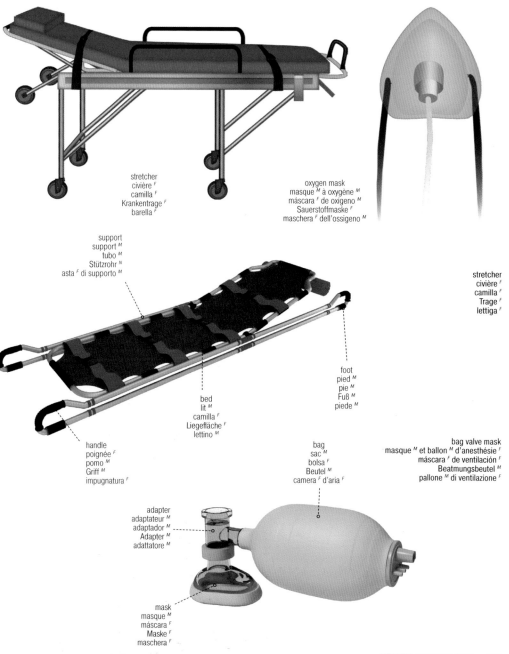

stretcher
civière F
camilla F
Krankentrage F
barella F

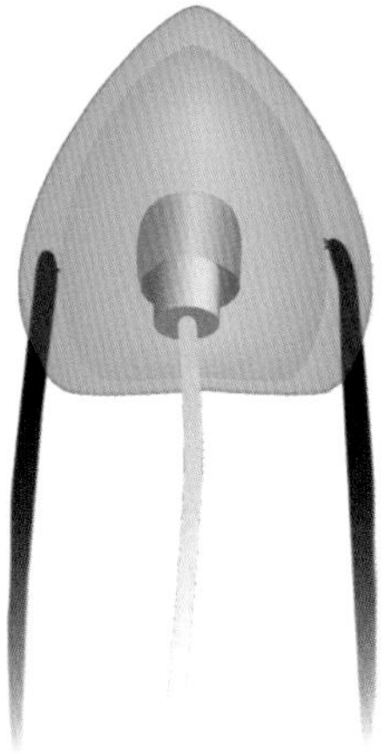

oxygen mask
masque M à oxygène M
máscara F de oxigeno M
Sauerstoffmaske F
maschera F dell'ossigeno M

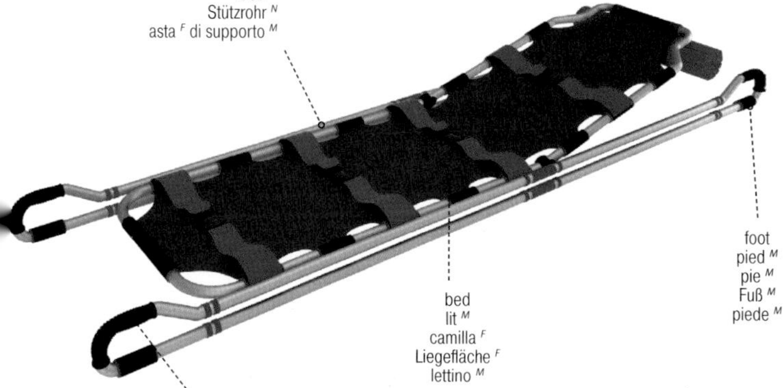

stretcher
civière F
camilla F
Trage F
lettiga F
support
support M
tubo M
Stützrohr N
asta F di supporto M
foot
pied M
pie M
Fuß M
piede M
bed
lit M
camilla F
Liegefläche F
lettino M
handle
poignée F
pomo M
Griff M
impugnatura F

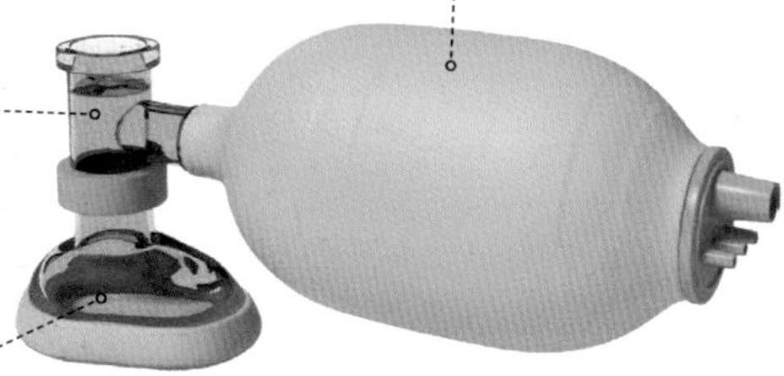

bag valve mask
masque M et ballon M d'anesthésie F
máscara F de ventilación F
Beatmungsbeutel M
pallone M di ventilazione F
bag
sac M
bolsa F
Beutel M
camera F d'aria F
adapter
adaptateur M
adaptador M
Adapter M
adattatore M
mask
masque M
máscara F
Maske F
maschera F

HOUSING

ground floor of house
rez-de-chaussée ^{M} de la maison ^{F}
planta ^{F} baja de una casa ^{F}
Erdgeschoss ^{N}
primo piano ^{M}

refrigerator
réfrigérateur ^{M}
nevera ^{F}
Kühlschrank ^{M}
frigorifero ^{M}

kitchen
cuisine ^{F}
cocina ^{F}
Küche ^{F}
cucina ^{F}

cabinets
armoires ^{F}
estantes ^{M}
Schränke ^{M}
pensile ^{M}

powder room
salle ^{F} de toilette ^{F}
baño ^{M} de invitados ^{M}
Gästebadezimmer ^{N}
bagno ^{M} per gli ospiti ^{M}

stairs
escalier ^{M}
escaleras ^{F}
Treppe ^{F}
scale ^{F}

breakfast bar
comptoir-repas ^{M}
mesa ^{F} de desayuno ^{M}
Frühstücksbar ^{F}
banco ^{M} da colazione ^{F}

bar stool
tabouret ^{M} de bar
taburetes ^{M}
Barhocker ^{M}
sgabelli ^{M}

dining room
salle ^{F} à manger
comedor ^{M}
Esszimmer ^{N}
sala ^{F} da pranzo ^{M}

mailbox
boîte ^{F} aux lettres ^{F}
buzón ^{M}
Briefkasten ^{M}
cassetta ^{F} della posta ^{F}

dining table
table ^{F} de salle ^{F} à manger
mesa ^{F} de comedor ^{M}
Esstisch ^{M}
tavolo ^{M} da pranzo ^{M}

picture
photographie ^{F}
cuadro ^{M}
Bild ^{N}
quadro ^{M}

dining chair
chaise ^{F} de salle ^{F} à manger
sillas ^{F} de comedor ^{M}
Esszimmerstuhl ^{M}
sedie ^{F} del tavolo ^{M} da pranzo ^{M}

front door
porte ^{F} d'entrée ^{F}
puerta ^{F} principal
Haustür ^{F}
porta ^{F} d'ingresso ^{M}

front steps
marches ^{F} à l'entrée ^{F}
escalones ^{M} de la entrada ^{F}
Eingangsstufen ^{F}
scale ^{F} d'ingresso ^{M}

doorbell
sonnette ^{F} de porte ^{F}
timbre ^{M}
Türklingel ^{F}
campanello ^{M}

patio
terrasse ^{F}
terraza ^{F}
Terasse ^{F}
patio ^{M}

patio umbrella
parasol ^{M}
sombrilla para terraza ^{F}
Terassenschirm ^{M}
ombrellone ^{M} da giardino ^{M}

fence
clôture ^{F}
valla ^{F}
Zaun ^{M}
recinzione ^{F}

flower bed
plate-bande
parterres
Blumenbeet
fioriere

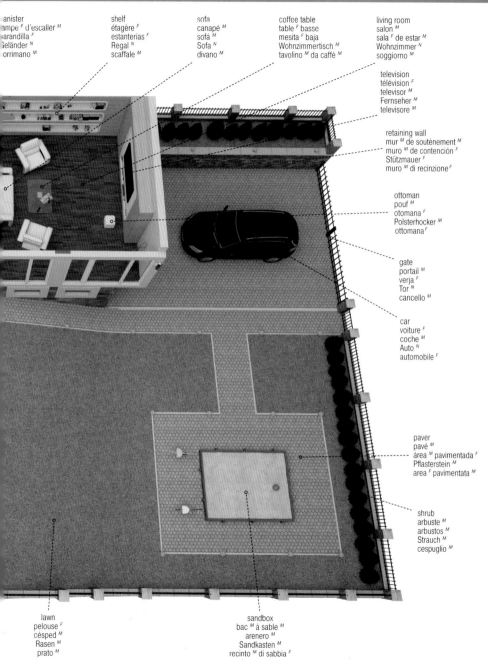

anister
ampe F d'escalier M
arandilla F
eländer N
orrimano M
shelf
étagère F
estanterías F
Regal N
scaffale M
sofa
canapé M
sofá M
Sofa N
divano M
coffee table
table F basse
mesita F baja
Wohnzimmertisch M
tavolino M da caffè M
living room
salon M
sala F de estar M
Wohnzimmer N
soggiorno M
television
télévision F
televisor M
Fernseher M
televisore M
retaining wall
mur M de soutènement M
muro M de contención F
Stützmauer F
muro M di recinzione F
ottoman
pouf M
otomana F
Polsterhocker M
ottomana F
gate
portail M
verja F
Tor N
cancello M
car
voiture F
coche M
Auto N
automobile F
paver
pavé M
área M pavimentada F
Pflasterstein M
area F pavimentata M
shrub
arbuste M
arbustos M
Strauch M
cespuglio M
lawn
pelouse F
césped M
Rasen M
prato M
sandbox
bac M à sable M
arenero M
Sandkasten M
recinto M di sabbia F

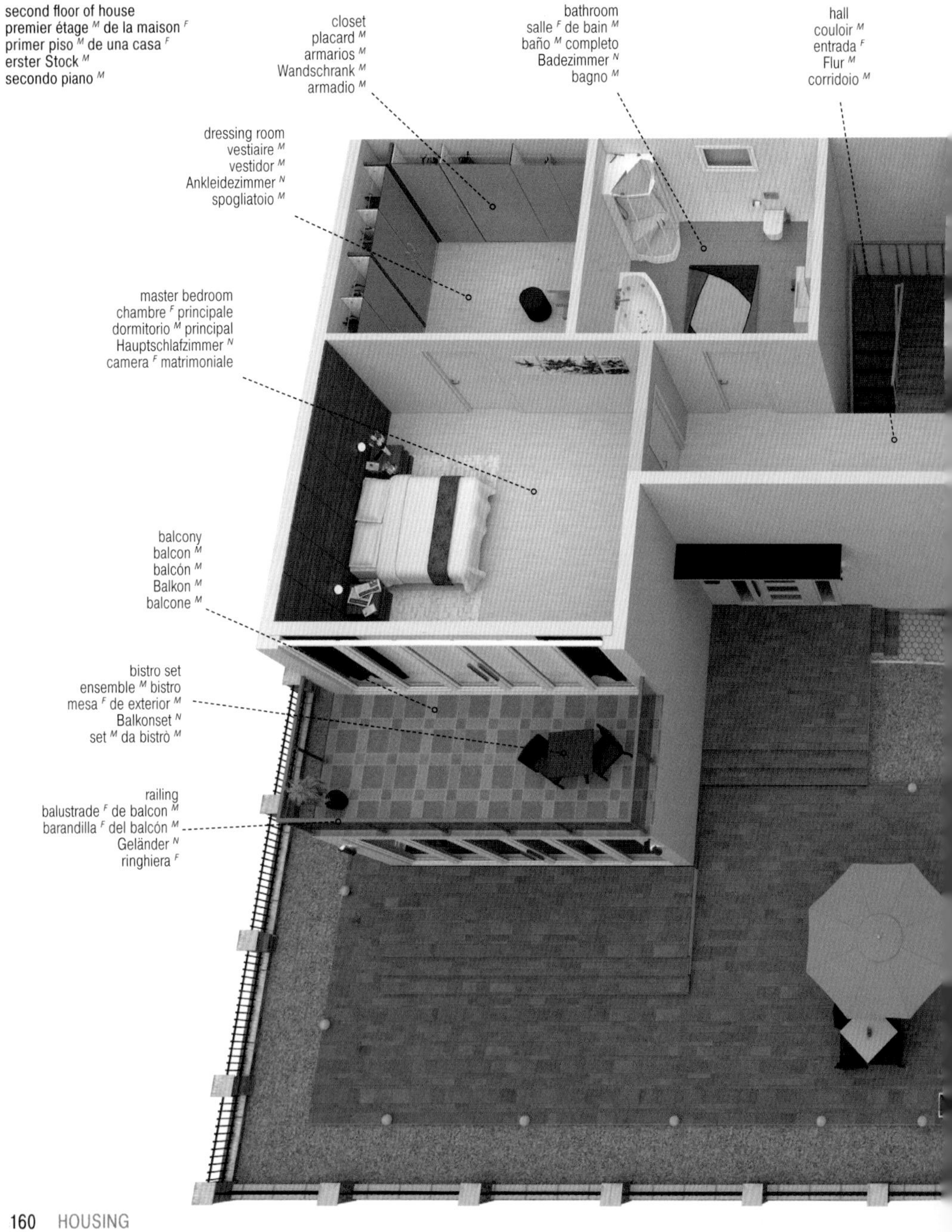
second floor of house
premier étage M de la maison F
primer piso M de una casa F
erster Stock M
secondo piano M
closet
placard M
armarios M
Wandschrank M
armadio M
bathroom
salle F de bain M
baño M completo
Badezimmer N
bagno M
hall
couloir M
entrada F
Flur M
corridoio M
dressing room
vestiaire M
vestidor M
Ankleidezimmer N
spogliatoio M
master bedroom
chambre F principale
dormitorio M principal
Hauptschlafzimmer N
camera F matrimoniale
balcony
balcon M
balcón M
Balkon M
balcone M
bistro set
ensemble M bistro
mesa F de exterior M
Balkonset N
set M da bistrò M
railing
balustrade F de balcon M
barandilla F del balcón M
Geländer N
ringhiera F

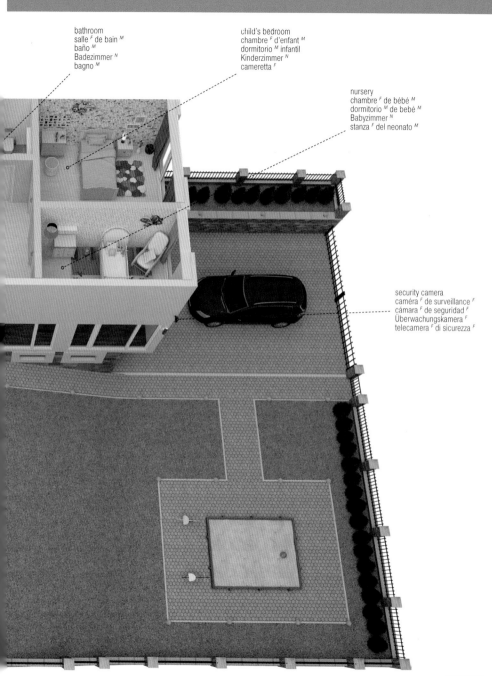

bathroom
salle F de bain M
baño M
Badezimmer N
bagno M
child's bedroom
chambre F d'enfant M
dormitorio M infantil
Kinderzimmer N
cameretta F
nursery
chambre F de bébé M
dormitorio M de bebé M
Babyzimmer N
stanza F del neonato M
security camera
caméra F de surveillance F
cámara F de seguridad F
Überwachungskamera F
telecamera F di sicurezza F

exterior of house
extérieur M de la maison F
exterior M del hogar M
Außenansicht F des Hauses N
esterno M della casa F

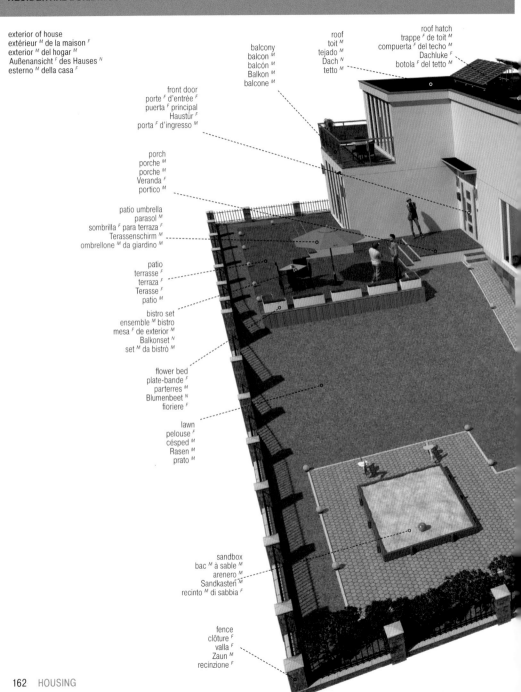

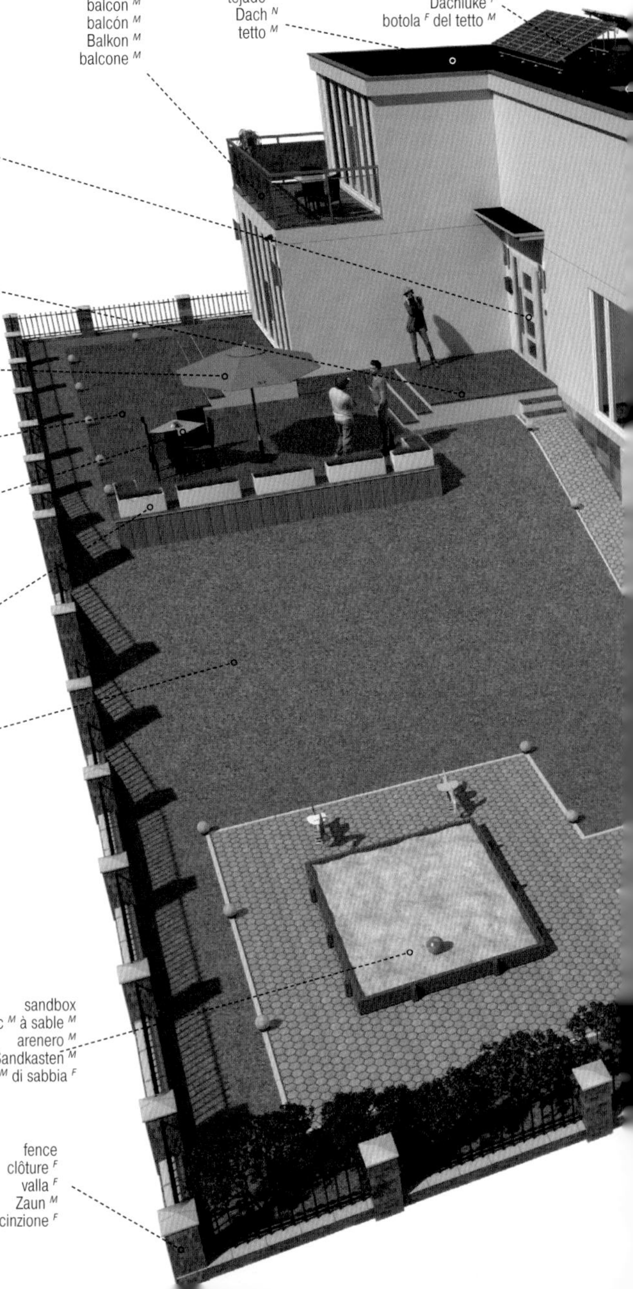
roof hatch
trappe F de toit M
compuerta F del techo M
Dachluke F
botola F del tetto M
roof
toit M
tejado M
Dach N
tetto M
balcony
balcon M
balcón M
Balkon M
balcone M
front door
porte F d'entrée F
puerta F principal
Haustür F
porta F d'ingresso M
porch
porche M
porche M
Veranda F
portico M
patio umbrella
parasol M
sombrilla F para terraza F
Terassenschirm M
ombrellone M da giardino M
patio
terrasse F
terraza F
Terasse F
patio M
bistro set
ensemble M bistro
mesa F de exterior M
Balkonset N
set M da bistrò M
flower bed
plate-bande F
parterres M
Blumenbeet N
fioriere F
lawn
pelouse F
césped M
Rasen M
prato M
sandbox
bac M à sable M
arenero M
Sandkasten M
recinto M di sabbia F
fence
clôture F
valla F
Zaun M
recinzione F

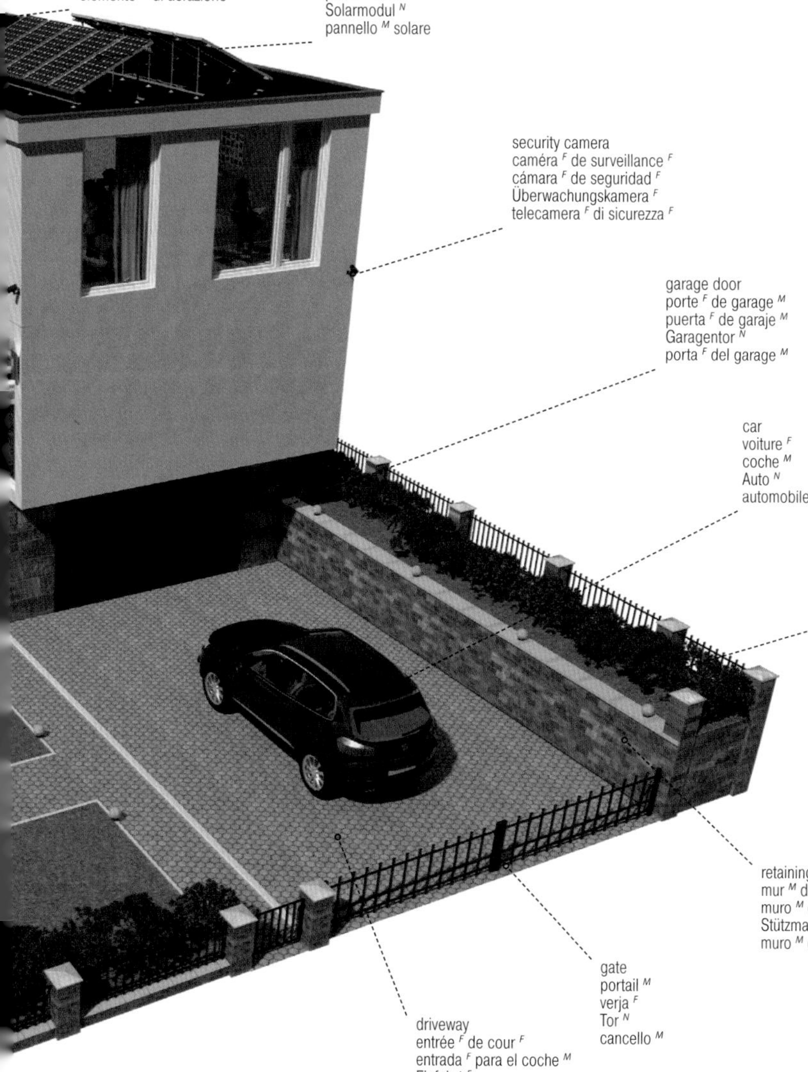

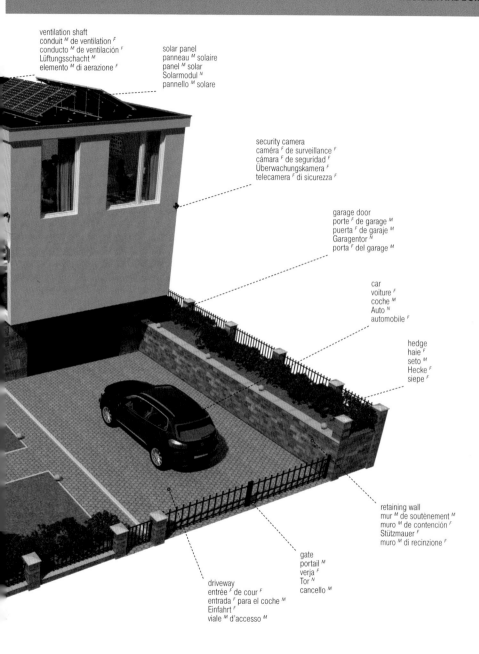

ventilation shaft
conduit M de ventilation F
conducto M de ventilación F
Lüftungsschacht M
elemento M di aerazione F
solar panel
panneau M solaire
panel M solar
Solarmodul N
pannello M solare
security camera
caméra F de surveillance F
cámara F de seguridad F
Überwachungskamera F
telecamera F di sicurezza F
garage door
porte F de garage M
puerta F de garaje M
Garagentor N
porta F del garage M
car
voiture F
coche M
Auto N
automobile F
hedge
haie F
seto M
Hecke F
siepe F
retaining wall
mur M de soutènement M
muro M de contención F
Stützmauer F
muro M di recinzione F
gate
portail M
verja F
Tor N
cancello M
driveway
entrée F de cour F
entrada F para el coche M
Einfahrt F
viale M d'accesso M

apartment building
immeuble [M] d'appartements [M]
bloque [M] de apartamentos [M]
Wohnblock [M]
condominio [M]

facade
façade [F]
fachada [F]
Fassade [F]
facciata [F] principale

penthouse
appartement-terrasse [M]
penthouse [M]
Penthouse [N]
attico [M]

balcony door
porte [F] de balcon [M]
puerta [F] del balcón [M]
Balkontür [F]
portafinestra [F] del balcone [M]

balcony
balcon [M]
balcón [M]
Balkon [M]
balcone [M]

balcony railing
balustrade [F] de balcon [M]
barandilla [F] del balcón [M]
Balkongeländer [N]
ringhiera [F] del balcone [M]

resident
résident [M]
residente [M]
Bewohner [M]
condomino [M]

window
fenêtre [F]
ventana [F]
Fenster [N]
finestra [F]

intercom
interphone [M]
intercomunicador [M]
Sprechanlage [F]
citofono [M]

main entrance
entrée [F] principale
entrada [F] principal
Haupteingang [M]
ingresso [M] principale

satellite dish
antenne F parabolique
antena F parabólica
Satellitenschüssel F
parabola F satellitare
antenna
antenne F
antena F
Antenne F
antenna F
patio umbrella
parasol M
sombrilla para terraza F
Terrassenschirm M
ombrellone M da terrazzo M
patio
terrasse F
terraza F
Terrasse F
terrazzo M

living room
salon [M]
sala [F] de estar
Wohnzimmer [N]
soggiorno [M]

book
livre [M]
libro [M]
Buch [N]
librio [M]

fruit bowl
bol [M] à fruits [M]
frutero [M]
Obstschale [F]
fruttiera [F]

bookshelf
étagère [F] de bibliothèque [F]
librero [M]
Bücherregal [N]
libreria [F]

sofa
canapé [M]
sofá [M]
Couch [F]
divano [M]

magazine
magazine [M]
revista [F]
Zeitschrift [F]
rivista [F]

coffee table
table [F] basse
mesita [F] baja
Wohnzimmertisch [M]
tavolino [M] da caffè [M]

remote control
télécommande [F]
control [M] remoto
Fernbedienung [F]
telecomando [M]

DVD
DVD [M]
DVD [M]
DVD [F]
DVD [M]

DVD player
lecteur [M] DVD [M]
reproductor [M] de DVD [M]
DVD-Player [M]
lettore [M] DVD [M]

television
télévision [F]
televisor [M]
Fernseher [M]
televisore [M]

shelf
étagère [F]
estante [M]
Regal [N]
mensola [F]

cushion
coussin [M]
cojín [M]
Kissen [N]
cuscino [M]

armchair
fauteuil [M]
sillón [M]
Sessel [M]
poltrona [F]

ottoman
pouf [M]
otomana [F]
Polsterhocker [M]
ottomana [F]

potted plant
plante [F] en pot [M]
planta [F] de interior [M]
Topfpflanze [F]
pianta [F] in vaso [M]

master bedroom
chambre F principale
dormitorio M principal
Hauptschlafzimmer N
camera F matrimoniale
curtain
rideau M
cortina F
Vorhang M
tenda F
light fixture
luminaire M
lámpara F
Leuchtkörper M
lampada F
photograph
photographie F
foto F
Foto N
fotografia F
nightstand
table F de nuit F
mesa F de noche F
Nachttisch M
comodino M
rug
tapis M
alfombra F
Teppich M
tappeto M
book
livre M
libro M
Buch N
libro M
bed
lit M
cama F
Bett N
letto M

pillow
oreiller [M]
almohada [F]
Kissen [N]
cuscino [M]

light switch
interrupteur [M] d'éclairage [M]
interruptor [M] de luz [F]
Lichtschalter [M]
interruttore [M]

closet door
porte [F] de placard [M]
puerta [F] de armario [M]
Tür [F]
porta [F]

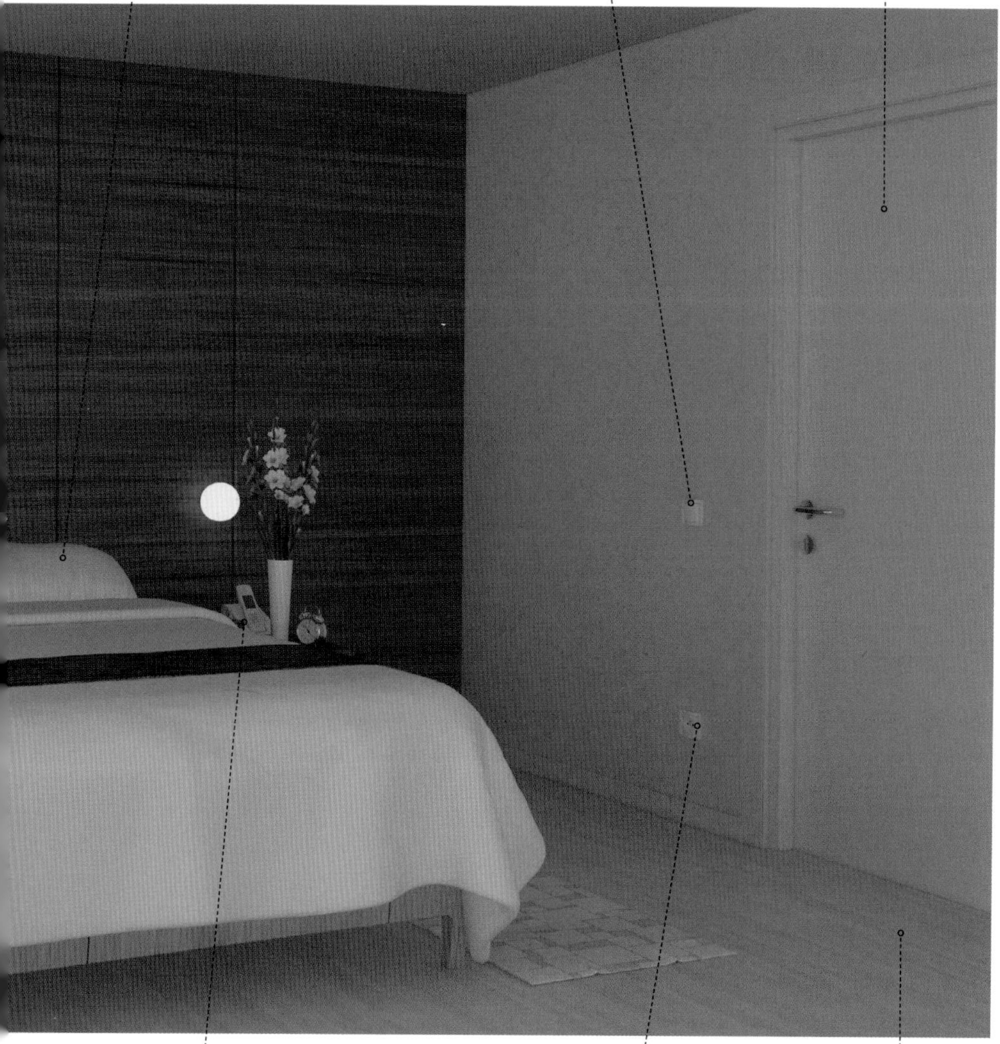

telephone
téléphone [M]
teléfono [M]
Telefon [N]
telefono [M]

electrical outlet
prise électrique [F]
enchufe [M]
Steckdose [F]
presa [F] di corrente [F]

hardwood floor
plancher [M] de bois [M] franc
suelo [M] de madera [F]
Hartholzboden [M]
parquet [M]

bathroom
salle [F] de bain [M]
sala [F] de baño [M]
Badezimmer [N]
bagno [M]

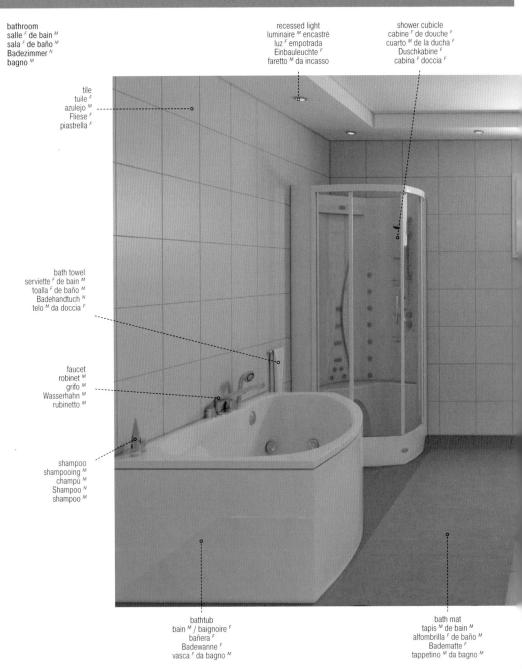

recessed light
luminaire [M] encastré
luz [F] empotrada
Einbauleuchte [F]
faretto [M] da incasso
shower cubicle
cabine [F] de douche [F]
cuarto [M] de la ducha [F]
Duschkabine [F]
cabina [F] doccia [F]
tile
tuile [F]
azulejo [M]
Fliese [F]
piastrella [F]
bath towel
serviette [F] de bain [M]
toalla [F] de baño [M]
Badehandtuch [N]
telo [M] da doccia [F]
faucet
robinet [M]
grifo [M]
Wasserhahn [M]
rubinetto [M]
shampoo
shampooing [M]
champú [M]
Shampoo [N]
shampoo [M]
bathtub
bain [M] / baignoire [F]
bañera [F]
Badewanne [F]
vasca [F] da bagno [M]
bath mat
tapis [M] de bain [M]
alfombrilla [F] de baño [M]
Badematte [F]
tappetino [M] da bagno [M]

window
fenêtre F
ventana F
Fenster N
finestra F
toilet
toilette F
inodoro M
Toilette F
gabinetto M
mirror
miroir M
espejo M
Spiegel M
specchio M
fan
ventilateur M
extractor M
Dunstabzug M
aspiratore M
medicine cabinet
armoire F à pharmacie F
botiquín M
Medizinschrank M
armadietto M dei medicinali M
soap dish
porte-savon M
jabonera F
Seifenschale F
portasapone M
faucet
robinet M
grifo M
Wasserhahn M
rubinetto M
toothbrush
brosse F à dents F
cepillo M de dientes M
Zahnbürste F
spazzolino M
toothbrush holder
porte-brosses M à dents F
vaso M para cepillo M de dientes M
Zahnbürstenhalter M
portaspazzolini M
lotion
lotion F
crema F
Lotion F
sapone M liquido
sink
lavabo M
lavabo M
Waschbecken N
lavandino M
hand towel
essuie-main M
toalla F de mano M
Handtuch N
asciugamano M
floor
plancher M
suelo M
Fußboden M
pavimento M
toilet paper
papier M hygiénique
papel M higiénico
Toilettenpapier N
carta F igienica
toilet brush
brosse F pour cuvettes F
cepillo M para limpiar el inodoro M
Toilettenbürste F
scopino M
wastebasket
poubelle F
papelera F
Abfalleimer M
cestino M
vanity
meuble-lavabo M
mueble M de baño M
Beckenunterschrank M
toletta F

girl's room
chambre [F] de fille [F]
dormitorio [M] de niña [F]
Mädchenzimmer [N]
cameretta [F]

wall decal
décalque [M] mural
vinilo [M] decorativo
Wandaufkleber [M]
adesivo [M] da parete [F]

clock
horloge [F]
reloj [M]
Wanduhr [F]
orologio [M]

photograph
photographie [F]
fotografía [F]
Foto [N]
fotografia [F]

chest of drawers
commode [F]
cajonera [F]
Kommode [F]
cassettiera [F]

pillow
oreiller [M]
almohada [F]
Kissen [N]
cuscino [M]

sheets
draps [M]
sábanas [F]
Bettlaken [N]
lenzuola [F]

bed
lit [M]
cama [F]
Bett [N]
letto [M]

wallpaper
papier M peint
papel M tapiz M
Tapete F
carta F da parati M

picture
illustration F
cuadro M
Bild N
quadro M

lamp
lampe F
lámpara F
Lampe F
lampada F

toy
jouet M
juguete M
Spielzeug N
giocattolo M

nightstand
table F de nuit F
mesita F de noche F
Nachttisch M
comodino M

hardwood floor
plancher M de bois M franc
suelo M de madera F
Hartholzboden M
parquet M

throw rug
carpette F
alfombra F
Teppich M
tappeto M

nursery
chambre F de bébé M
dormitorio M del bebé M
Kinderzimmer N
stanza F del neonato M

baby lotion
lotion F pour bébés M
loción M infantil
Babylotion F
lozione F per bimbi M
shelf
étagère F
estante M
Regal N
mensola F
changing table
table F à changer
mesa F para cambiar al bebé M
Wickeltisch M
fasciatoio M
toy
jouet M
juguete M
Spielzeug N
giocattolo M

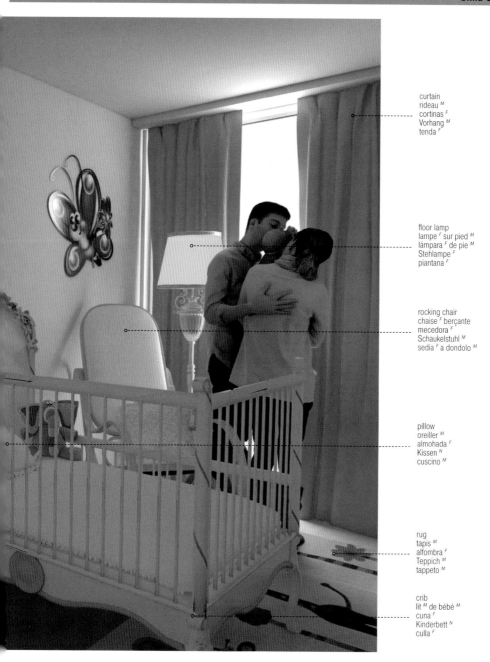

curtain
rideau [M]
cortinas [F]
Vorhang [M]
tenda [F]
floor lamp
lampe [F] sur pied [M]
lámpara [F] de pie [M]
Stehlampe [F]
piantana [F]
rocking chair
chaise [F] berçante
mecedora [F]
Schaukelstuhl [M]
sedia [F] a dondolo [M]
pillow
oreiller [M]
almohada [F]
Kissen [N]
cuscino [M]
rug
tapis [M]
alfombra [F]
Teppich [M]
tappeto [M]
crib
lit [M] de bébé [M]
cuna [F]
Kinderbett [N]
culla [F]

Children's furniture

Meubles [M] pour enfants [M] | Muebles [M] infantiles | Kindermobiliar [N] | Mobili [M] per bambini [M]

changing table
table [F] à langer
mesa [F] para cambiar al bebé [M]
Wickeltisch [M]
fasciatoio [M]

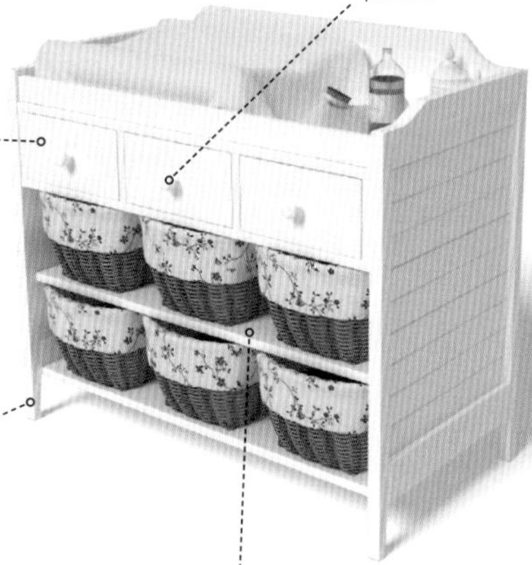

knob
bouton [M]
tirador [M]
Griff [M]
pomello [M]

drawer
tiroir [M]
cajón [M]
Schublade [F]
cassetto [M]

leg
pied [M]
pata [F]
Bein [N]
gamba [F]

shelf
étagère [F]
estante [M]
Regal [N]
mensola [F]

armoire
armoire [F]
armario [M]
Kleiderschrank [M]
armadio [M]

high chair
chaise [F] haute
sillita [F] alta
Hochstuhl [M]
seggiolone [M]

back
dossier [M]
respaldo [M]
Lehne [F]
schienale [M]

tray
plateau [M]
bandeja [F]
Tablett [N]
vassoio [M]

seat
siège [M]
asiento [M]
Sitz [M]
sedile [M]

footrest
repose-pied [M]
reposapiés [M]
Fußstütze [F]
poggiapiedi [M]

leg
pied [M]
pata [F]
Stuhlbein [N]
gamba [F]

desk and chair
bureau [M] et chaise [F]
mesa [F] y silla [F]
Schreibtisch mit Stuhl [M]
scrivania [F] e sedia [F]

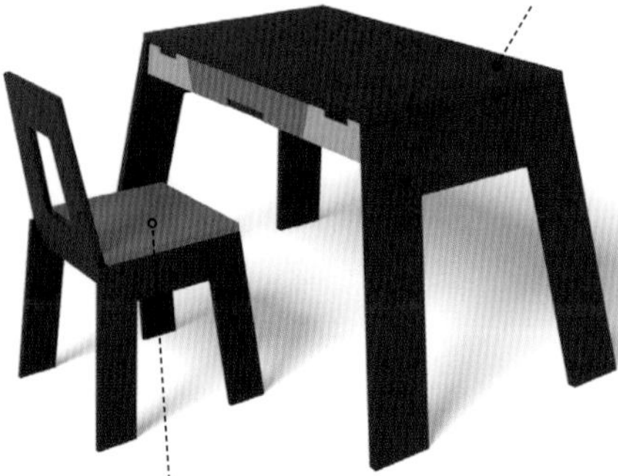

desk
bureau [M]
escritorio [M]
Schreibtisch [M]
scrivania [F]

chair
chaise [F]
silla [F]
Stuhl [M]
sedia [F]

bunk bed
lit [M] superposé
literas [F]
Hochbett [N]
letto [M] a castello [M]

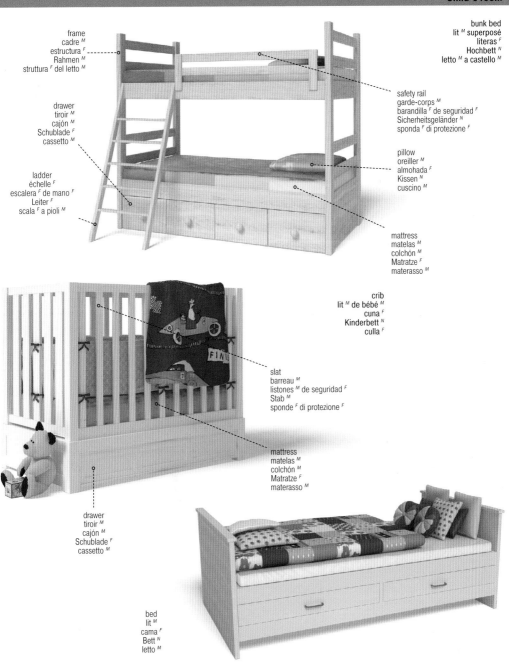

frame
cadre [M]
estructura [F]
Rahmen [M]
struttura [F] del letto [M]

drawer
tiroir [M]
cajón [M]
Schublade [F]
cassetto [M]

ladder
échelle [F]
escalera [F] de mano [F]
Leiter [F]
scala [F] a pioli [M]

safety rail
garde-corps [M]
barandilla [F] de seguridad [F]
Sicherheitsgeländer [N]
sponda [F] di protezione [F]

pillow
oreiller [M]
almohada [F]
Kissen [N]
cuscino [M]

mattress
matelas [M]
colchón [M]
Matratze [F]
materasso [M]

crib
lit [M] de bébé [M]
cuna [F]
Kinderbett [N]
culla [F]

FINIS

slat
barreau [M]
listones [M] de seguridad [F]
Stab [M]
sponde [F] di protezione [F]

mattress
matelas [M]
colchón [M]
Matratze [F]
materasso [M]

drawer
tiroir [M]
cajón [M]
Schublade [F]
cassetto [M]

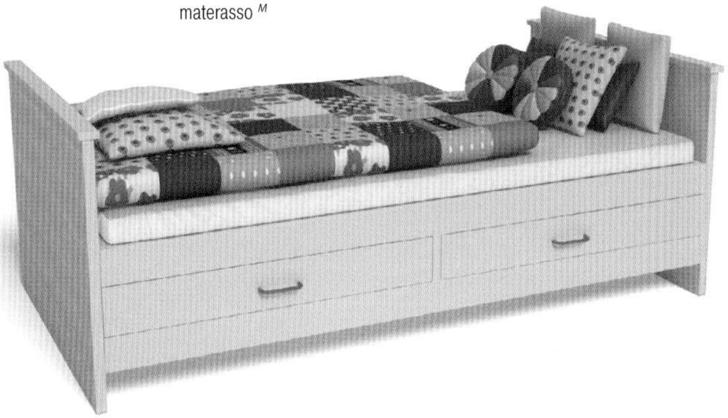

bed
lit [M]
cama [F]
Bett [N]
letto [M]

kitchen
cuisine F
Electrodomésticos M de cocina F
Küche F
cucina F

picture
photographie F
foto F
Bild N
quadro M
clock
horloge F
reloj M
Wanduhr F
orologio M
refrigerator
réfrigérateur M
nevera F
Kühlschrank M
frigorifero M
microwave
micro-ondes M
microondas M
Mikrowelle F
forno M a microonde F
breakfast bar
comptoir-repas M
barra americana F
Frühstücksbar F
banco M per la colazione F
bar stool
tabouret M de bar M
taburete M
Barhocker M
sgabello M
oven
four M
horno M
Ofen M
forno M
coffee machine
machine F à espresso M
cafetera F
Kaffeemaschine F
macchina F del caffè M
wine fridge
réfrigérateur M à vin M
frigorífico M para vino M
Weinschrank M
cantinetta-frigo F

range hood
hotte [F] de cuisine [F]
campana [F]
Abzugshaube [F]
cappa [F] aspirante
wine glass
verre [M] à vin [M]
copa [F] de vino [M]
Weinglas [N]
calice [M]
canister
pot [M] à ingrédient [M]
bote [M]
Behälter [M]
barattolo [M]
cup
tasse [F]
taza [F]
Tasse [F]
tazza [F]
faucet
robinet [M]
grifo [M]
Wasserhahn [M]
rubinetto [M]
cabinet
armoire [F]
alacenas [F]
Schrank [M]
pensile [M]
cooktop
plaque [F] de cuisson [F]
tapa [F] de cocina [F]
Herdplatte [F]
piano [M] cottura [F]
countertop
plan [M] de travail [M]
encimera [F]
Arbeitsplatte [F]
piano [M] di lavoro [M]
dishwasher
lave-vaisselle [M]
lavavajillas [M]
Geschirrspüler [M]
lavastoviglie [F]
sink
évier [M]
fregadero [M]
Spülbecken [N]
lavandino [M]
tiled floor
carrelage [M]
suelo [M] de baldosas [M]
Fliesenboden [M]
pavimento [M] piastrellato

Large appliances

Gros électroménagers [M] | Electrodomésticos [M] de cocina [F] | Großgeräte [N] | Elettrodomestici [M] grandi

refrigerator
réfrigérateur [M]
nevera [F]
Kühlschrank [M]
frigorifero [M]
shelf
étagère [F]
estante [M]
Regal [N]
ripiano [M]
egg tray
plateau [M] à œufs [M]
bandeja [F] de huevos [M]
Eierablage [F]
ripiano [M] porta uova [F]
refrigerator compartment door
porte [F] du compartiment [M] réfrigérateur [M]
puerta [F] de la nevera [F]
Kühlschranktür [F]
sportello [M] del frigorifero [M]
handle
poignée [F]
asa [F]
Griff [M]
maniglia [F]
freezer compartment
compartiment [M] congélateur [M]
congelador [M]
Gefrierfach [N]
congelatore [M]
drawer
tiroir [M]
cajón [M]
Schublade [F]
cassetto [M]
crisper
bac [M] à légumes [M]
cajón [M] de las verduras [F] de la nevera [F]
Gemüsefach [N]
cassetto [M] verdura [F]
freezer compartment door
porte [F] du compartiment [M] congélateur [M]
puerta [F] del congelador [M]
Gefrierfachtür [F]
sportello [M] del freezer [M]

side-by-side refrigerator and freezer
réfrigérateur-congélateur [M] côte à côte
nevera [F] de doble puerta [F]
Doppeltürkühlschrank [M]
frigorifero [M] a doppia porta [F]

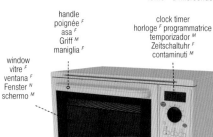

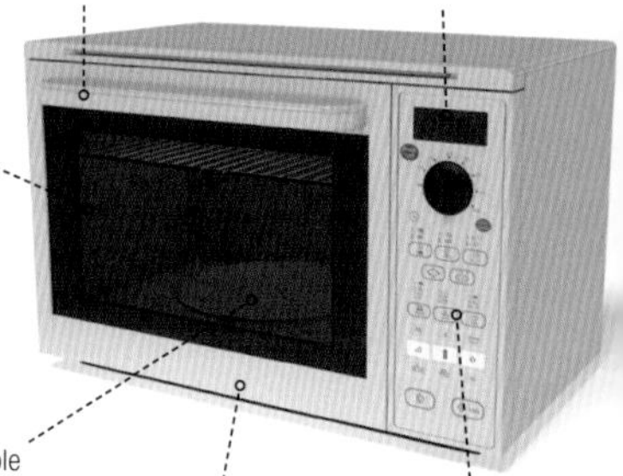
microwave
micro-ondes [M]
microondas [M]
Mikrowelle [F]
forno [M] a microonde [F]
handle
poignée [F]
asa [F]
Griff [M]
maniglia [F]
clock timer
horloge [F] programmatrice
temporizador [M]
Zeitschaltuhr [F]
contaminuti [M]
window
vitre [F]
ventana [F]
Fenster [N]
schermo [M]
turntable
plateau [M] tournant
bandeja [F] giratoria
Drehscheibe [F]
piatto [M] rotante
door
porte [F]
puerta [F]
Tür [F]
sportello [M]
control panel
panneau [M] de commande [F]
panel [M] de control [M]
Bedienfeld [N]
pannello [M] di controllo [M]

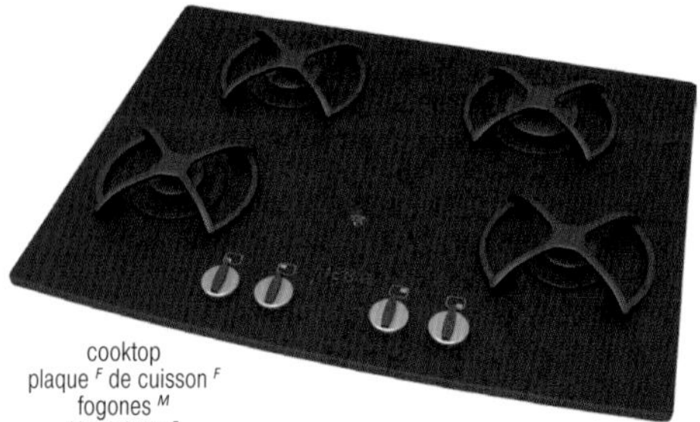
cooktop
plaque [F] de cuisson [F]
fogones [M]
Herdplatte [F]
piano [M] cottura [F]

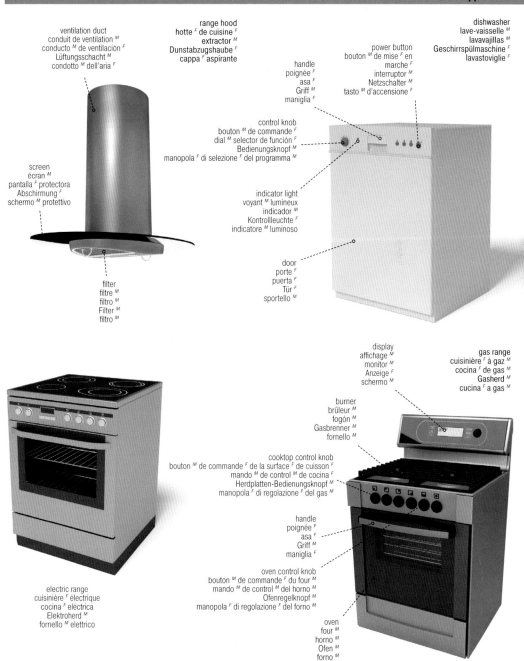

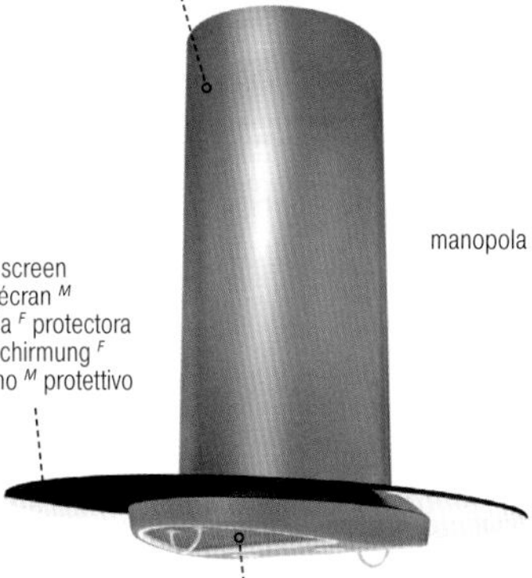
range hood
hotte F de cuisine F
extractor M
Dunstabzugshaube F
cappa F aspirante
ventilation duct
conduit de ventilation M
conducto M de ventilación F
Lüftungsschacht M
condotto M dell'aria F
screen
écran M
pantalla F protectora
Abschirmung F
schermo M protettivo
filter
filtre M
filtro M
Filter M
filtro M

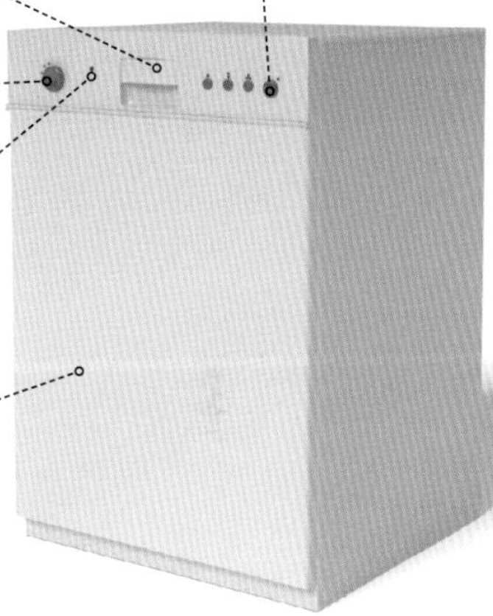
dishwasher
lave-vaisselle M
lavavajillas M
Geschirrspülmaschine F
lavastoviglie F
power button
bouton M de mise F en marche F
interruptor M
Netzschalter M
tasto M d'accensione F
handle
poignée F
asa F
Griff M
maniglia F
control knob
bouton M de commande F
dial M selector de función F
Bedienungsknopf M
manopola F di selezione F del programma M
indicator light
voyant M lumineux
indicador M
Kontrollleuchte F
indicatore M luminoso
door
porte F
puerta F
Tür F
sportello M

electric range
cuisinière F électrique
cocina F eléctrica
Elektroherd M
fornello M elettrico

gas range
cuisinière F à gaz M
cocina F de gas M
Gasherd M
cucina F a gas M
display
affichage M
monitor M
Anzeige F
schermo M
burner
brûleur M
fogón M
Gasbrenner M
fornello M
cooktop control knob
bouton M de commande F de la surface F de cuisson F
mando M de control M de cocina F
Herdplatten-Bedienungsknopf M
manopola F di regolazione F del gas M
handle
poignée F
asa F
Griff M
maniglia F
oven control knob
bouton M de commande F du four M
mando M de control M del horno M
Ofenregelknopf M
manopola F di regolazione F del forno M
oven
four M
horno M
Ofen M
forno M

Small appliances

Petits appareils [M] | Electrodomésticos [M] pequeños | Haushaltsgeräte [N] | Elettrodomestici [M] piccoli

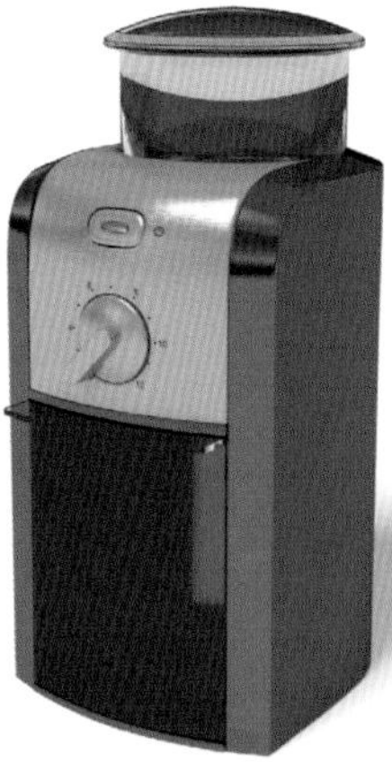

coffee grinder
moulin [M] à café [M]
molinillo [M] de café [M]
Kaffeemühle [F]
macina [F] caffè [M]

espresso machine
machine [F] à espresso [M]
cafetera [F] espresso [F]
Espressomaschine [F]
macchina [F] per il caffè [M] espresso

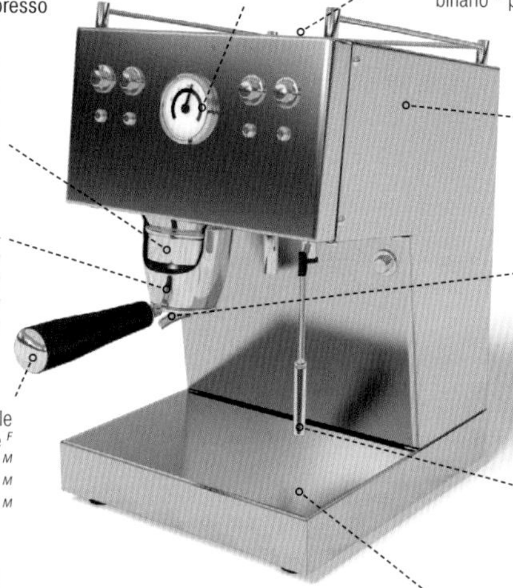

pressure gauge
manomètre [M]
medidor [M] de presión [F]
Druckanzeige [F]
manometro [M]

cup-warming tray
plateau [M] chauffant pour tasses [F]
bandeja [F] calienta tazas [F]
Tassenwärmer [M]
binario [M] per tazzina [F]

group head
tête [F] supérieure
cabezal [M]
Brühkopf [M]
testa [F] d'infusione [F]

water tank
réservoir [M] d'eau [F]
depósito [M] de agua [F]
Wasserbehälter [M]
serbatoio [M] dell'acqua [F]

filter holder
porte-filtre [M]
cesto [M] del filtro [M]
Filterhalter [M]
portafiltri [M]

spout
bec [M] verseur
pico [M]
Ausguss [M]
beccuccio [M]

handle
poignée [F]
mango [M]
Griff [M]
manopola [F] portafiltri [M]

steam nozzle
buse [F] à vapeur [F]
boquilla [F] de vapor [M]
Dampfdüse [F]
beccuccio [M] del vapore [M]

drip tray
plateau [M] perforé
bandeja [F] de goteo [M]
Abtropfschale [F]
vassoio [M] raccogligocce

automatic drip coffeemaker
cafetière [F] à filtre [M] électrique
cafetera [F] de goteo [M]
Filterkaffeemaschine [F]
macchina [F] da caffè [F] a filtro [M]

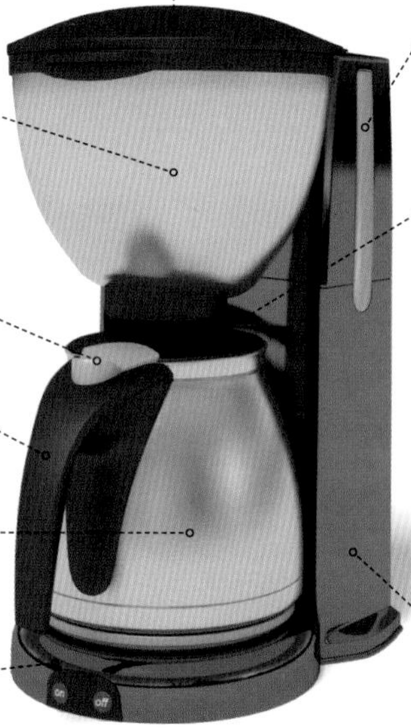

lid
couvercle [M]
tapa [F] del filtro [M]
Deckel [M]
coperchio [M] del filtro [M]

water-level indicator
indicateur [M] de niveau [M] d'eau [F]
indicador [M] del nivel [M] de agua [F]
Wassermengenanzeige [F]
indicatore [M] del livello [M] dell'acqua [F]

basket
panier [M]
cesto [M] del filtro [M]
Filterkorb [M]
scomparto [M] del filtro [M]

pot lid
couvercle [M]
tapa [F] de la cafetera [F]
Kannendeckel [M]
coperchio [M] del bollitore [M]

lid-release button
bouton [M] d'ouverture [F] du couvercle [M]
botón [M] para abrir la tapa [F]
Deckelöffner [M]
tasto [M] di apertura [F] del coperchio [M]

handle
poignée [F]
mango [M]
Griff [M]
impugnatura [F]

pot
verseuse [F] à café [M]
cafetera [F]
Kanne [F]
bollitore [M]

warming plate
plaque [F] chauffante
placa [F] calentadora
Wärmplatte [F]
piastra [F] riscaldante

water reservoir
réservoir [M] d'eau [F]
depósito [M] de agua [F]
Wasserbehälter [M]
serbatoio [M] dell'acqua [F]

blender
mélangeur [M]
batidora [F]
Mixer [M]
frullatore [M]

juicer
centrifugeuse F
extractor M **de jugos** M
Entsafter M
estrattore M **di succo** M

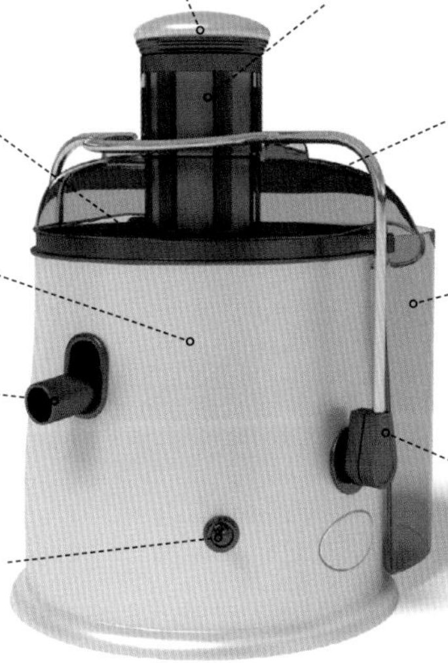

pusher
poussoir M
empujador M
Stopfer M
pressino M per alimenti M

feed tube
tube M d'alimentation F
tubo M de alimentación F
Einfüllrohr N
tubo M di alimentazione F

filter
filtre M
filtro M
Filter M
filtro M

lid
couvercle M
tapa F
Deckel M
coperchio M

motor housing
boîtier M du moteur M
compartimento M del motor M
Motorgehäuse N
alloggiamento M motore M

pulp container
réservoir M à pulpe F
depósito M de pulpa F
Fruchtfleischbehälter M
contenitore M raccoglipolpa

spout
bec M verseur
pico M
Ausguss M
beccuccio M

safety latch
verrou M de sécurité F
gancho M de seguridad F
Sicherheitsverriegelung F
braccio M bloccante di sicurezza F

power button
bouton M de mise F en marche F
interruptor M
Netzschalter M
tasto M d'accensione F

immersion blender
mélangeur M à main F
batidora F de mano M
Pürierstab M
frullatore M ad immersione F

electric kettle
bouilloire F **électrique**
tetera F **eléctrica**
Wasserkocher M
bollitore M **elettrico**

electric citrus juicer
presse-agrumes M **électrique**
exprimidor M **de cítricos** M
elektrische Zitruspresse F
spremiagrumi M **elettrico**

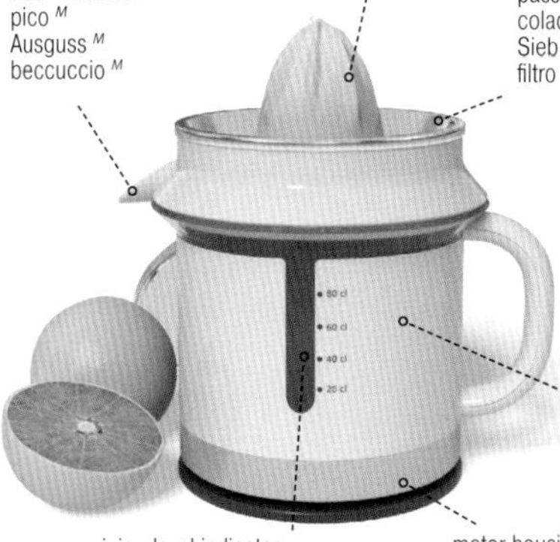

reamer
cône M
exprimidor M
Kegel M
spremiagrumi M

spout
bec M verseur
pico M
Ausguss M
beccuccio M

strainer
passoire F
colador M
Sieb N
filtro M

bowl
bol M
jarra F
Schüssel F
brocca F

juice-level indicator
indicateur M de niveau M de jus M
indicador M de nivel M de zumo
Saftmengenanzeige F
indicatore M del livello M del succo M

motor housing
boîtier M du moteur M
compartimento M del motor M
Motorgehäuse N
alloggiamento M motore M

spout
bec M verseur
pico M
Ausguss M
beccuccio M

lid
couvercle M
tapa F
Deckel M
coperchio M

lid-release button
bouton M d'ouverture F du couvercle M
botón M para abrir la tapa F
Deckelöffner M
tasto M di apertura F del coperchio M

power switch
interrupteur M d'alimentation F
interruptor M
Netzschalter M
tasto M d'accensione F

handle
poignée F
asa F
Griff M
impugnatura F

base
socle M
soporte M
Unterteil N
base F

indicator light
voyant M lumineux
luz F indicadora
Leuchtanzeige F
spia F di corrente F

toaster oven
four [M] grille-pain [M]
horno [M] tostador
Toasterofen [M]
fornetto [M] elettrico

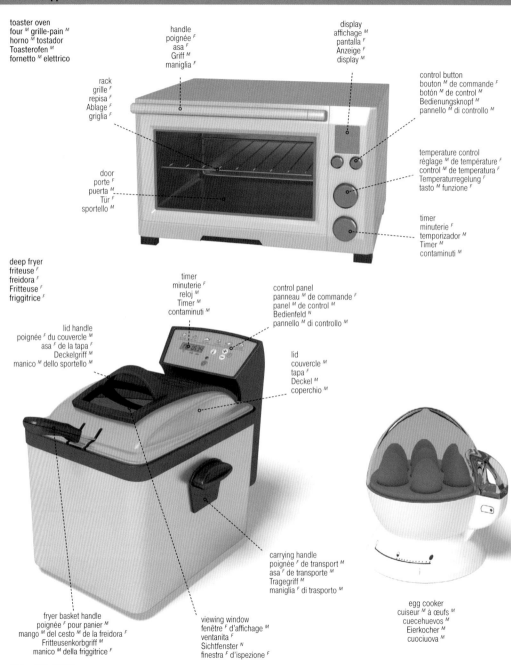

handle
poignée [F]
asa [F]
Griff [M]
maniglia [F]
display
affichage [M]
pantalla [F]
Anzeige [F]
display [M]
rack
grille [F]
repisa [F]
Ablage [F]
griglia [F]
control button
bouton [M] de commande [F]
botón [M] de control [M]
Bedienungsknopf [M]
pannello [M] di controllo [M]
temperature control
réglage [M] de température [F]
control [M] de temperatura [F]
Temperaturregelung [F]
tasto [M] funzione [F]
door
porte [F]
puerta [M]
Tür [F]
sportello [M]
timer
minuterie [F]
temporizador [M]
Timer [M]
contaminuti [M]

deep fryer
friteuse [F]
freidora [F]
Fritteuse [F]
friggitrice [F]

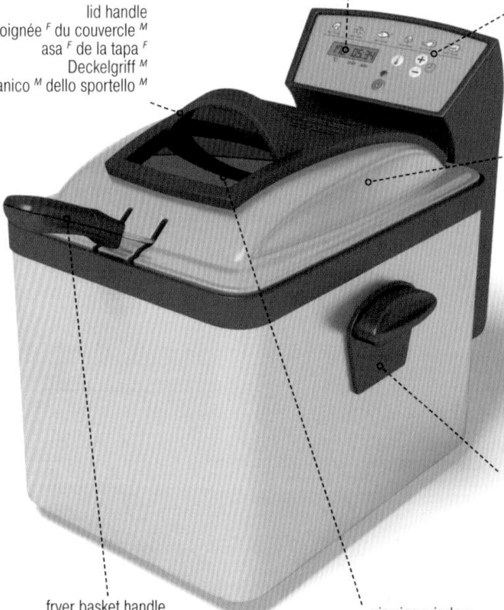

timer
minuterie [F]
reloj [M]
Timer [M]
contaminuti [M]
control panel
panneau [M] de commande [F]
panel [M] de control [M]
Bedienfeld [N]
pannello [M] di controllo [M]
lid handle
poignée [F] du couvercle [M]
asa [F] de la tapa [F]
Deckelgriff [M]
manico [M] dello sportello [M]
lid
couvercle [M]
tapa [F]
Deckel [M]
coperchio [M]
carrying handle
poignée [F] de transport [M]
asa [F] de transporte [M]
Tragegriff [M]
maniglia [F] di trasporto [M]
fryer basket handle
poignée [F] pour panier [M]
mango [M] del cesto [M] de la freidora [F]
Fritteusenkorbgriff [M]
manico [M] della friggitrice [F]
viewing window
fenêtre [F] d'affichage [M]
ventanita [F]
Sichtfenster [N]
finestra [F] d'ispezione [F]

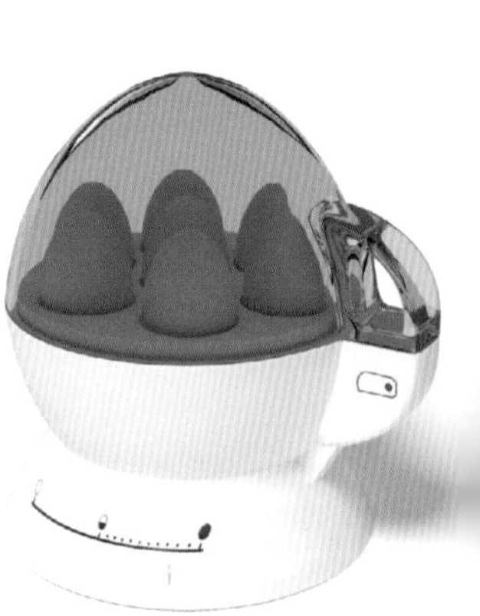

egg cooker
cuiseur [M] à œufs [M]
cuecehuevos [M]
Eierkocher [M]
cuociuova [M]

toaster
grille-pain [M]
tostadora [F]
Toaster [M]
tostapane [M]

slot
fente [F]
ranura [F]
Schlitz [M]
bocca [F] di caricamento [M]

control buttons
touches [F] de fonction [F]
botones [M] de control [M]
Bedienungsknöpfe [M]
pulsanti [M] di funzione [F]

crumb tray
ramasse-miettes [M]
bandeja [F] recogemigas
Krümelablage [F]
raccoglibriciole [M]

lever
levier [M]
palanca [F]
Hebel [M]
leva [F]

browning control
commande [F] de brunissement [M]
control [M] de potencia [F]
Bräunungsregler [M]
manopola [F] di regolazione [F] del grado [M] di tostatura [F]

table grill
barbecue [M] de table [F]
parrilla [F] de mesa [F]
Tischgrill [M]
grill [M] da tavolo [M]

waffle iron
gaufrier [M]
gofrera [F]
Waffeleisen [N]
macchina [M] per waffle [M]

bread maker
machine [F] à pain [M]
máquina [F] de pan [M]
Brotbackautomat [M]
macchina [F] per il pane [M]

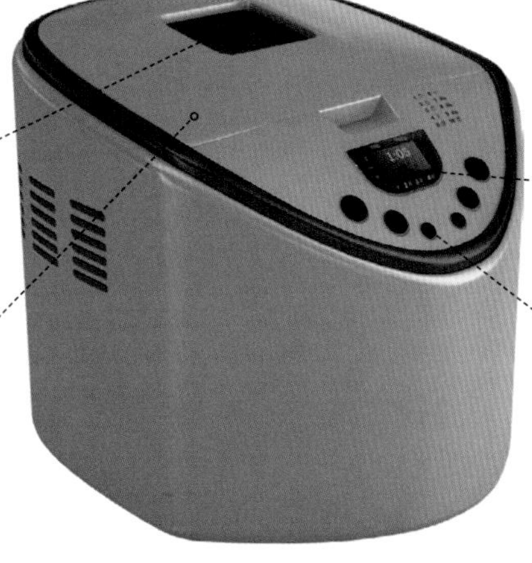

window
hublot [M]
ventana [F]
Sichtfenster [N]
finestra [F] di controllo [M]

liquid-crystal display (LCD)
affichage [M] à cristaux [M] liquides (ACL)
pantalla [F] de cristal [M] liquido
LCD [N]
display [M] a cristalli [M] liquidi (LCD)

lid
couvercle [M]
tapa [F]
Deckel [M]
coperchio [M]

control buttons
touches [F] de fonction [F]
botones [M] de control [M]
Bedienungsknöpfe [M]
pulsanti [M] di funzione [F]

food processor
robot [M] de cuisine [F]
robot [M] de cocina [F]
Küchenmaschine [F]
robot [M] da cucina [F]

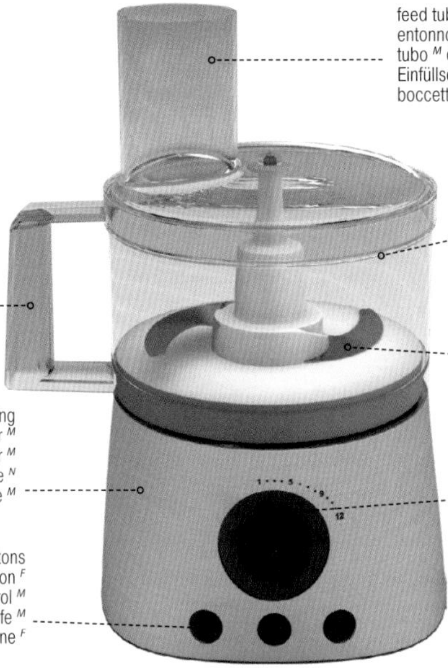

feed tube
entonnoir [M]
tubo [M] de entrada [F]
Einfüllschacht [M]
boccetta [F]

bowl
bol [M]
tazón [M]
Schüssel [F]
ciotola [F]

handle
poignée [F]
mango [M]
Griff [M]
impugnatura [F]

blade
lame [F]
cuchilla [F]
Klinge [F]
lama [F]

motor housing
bloc-moteur [M]
compartimento [M] del motor [M]
Motorengehäuse [N]
alloggiamento [M] del motore [M]

control pad
touche [F] de commande [F]
panel [M] de control [M]
Schaltregler [M]
pulsantiera [F] di comando [M]

control buttons
touches de fonction [F]
botones [M] de control [M]
Bedienungsknöpfe [M]
pulsanti [M] di funzione [F]

dehydrator
déshydrateur [M]
deshidratadora [F]
Dörrautomat [M]
disidratatore [M]

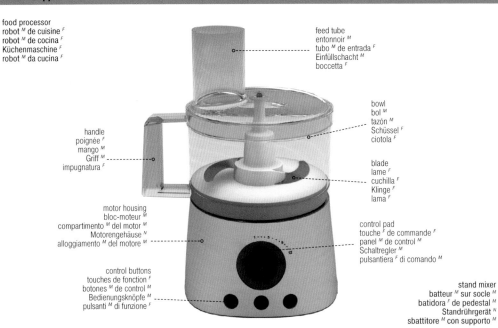

stand mixer
batteur [M] sur socle [M]
batidora [F] de pedestal [M]
Standrührgerät [N]
sbattitore [M] con supporto [M]

tilt-back head
tête [F] basculante
cabeza [F] móvil
hochklappbares Kopfteil [N]
testa [F] ribaltabile

beater
fouet [M]
varilla [F] de batir
Rührbesen [M]
frusta [F]

mixing bowl
bol [M]
tazón [M] de mezclar
Rührschüssel [F]
ciotola [F]

electric meat grinder
hache-viande [M] électrique
triturador [M] de carne [F] eléctrico
elektrischer Fleischwolf [M]
tritacarne [M] elettrico

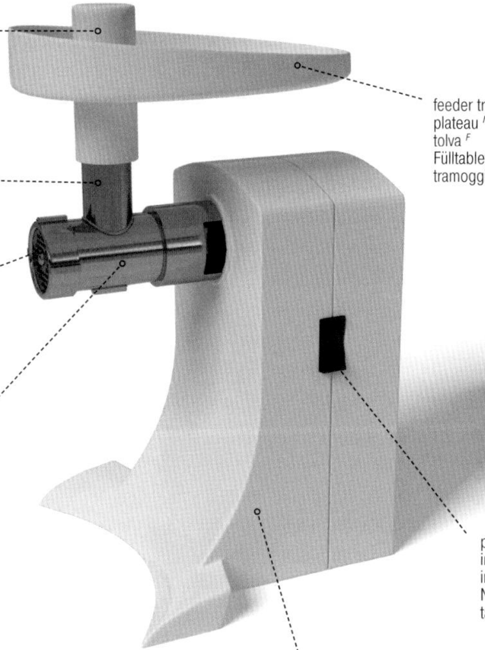

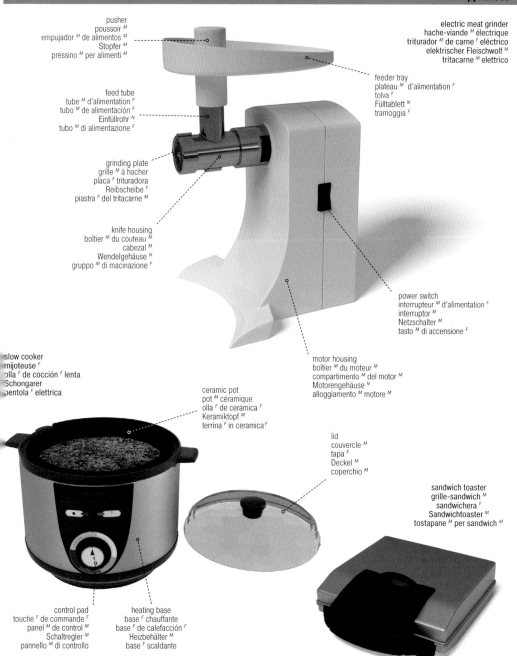

pusher
poussoir [M]
empujador [M] de alimentos [M]
Stopfer [M]
pressino [M] per alimenti [M]

feeder tray
plateau [M] d'alimentation [F]
tolva [F]
Fülltablett [N]
tramoggia [F]

feed tube
tube [M] d'alimentation [F]
tubo [M] de alimentación [F]
Einfüllrohr [N]
tubo [M] di alimentazione [F]

grinding plate
grille [M] à hacher
placa [F] trituradora
Reibscheibe [F]
piastra [F] del tritacarne [M]

knife housing
boîtier [M] du couteau [M]
cabezal [M]
Wendelgehäuse [N]
gruppo [M] di macinazione [F]

power switch
interrupteur [M] d'alimentation [F]
interruptor [M]
Netzschalter [M]
tasto [M] di accensione [F]

motor housing
boîtier [M] du moteur [M]
compartimento [M] del motor [M]
Motorengehäuse [N]
alloggiamento [M] motore [M]

slow cooker
mijoteuse [F]
olla [F] de cocción [F] lenta
Schongarer
pentola [F] elettrica

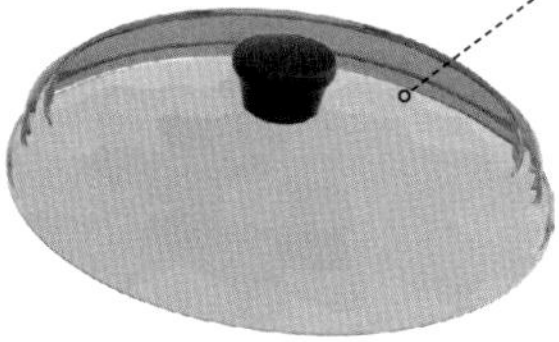

ceramic pot
pot [M] céramique
olla [F] de cerámica [F]
Keramiktopf [M]
terrina [F] in ceramica [F]

lid
couvercle [M]
tapa [F]
Deckel [M]
coperchio [M]

control pad
touche [F] de commande [F]
panel [M] de control [M]
Schaltregler [M]
pannello [M] di controllo

heating base
base [F] chauffante
base [F] de calefacción [F]
Heizbehälter [M]
base [F] scaldante

sandwich toaster
grille-sandwich [M]
sandwichera [F]
Sandwichtoaster [M]
tostapane [M] per sandwich [M]

table setting
couvert [M] de table [F]
disposición [F] de la mesa [F]
Tischgedeck [N]
allestimento [M] della tavola [F]

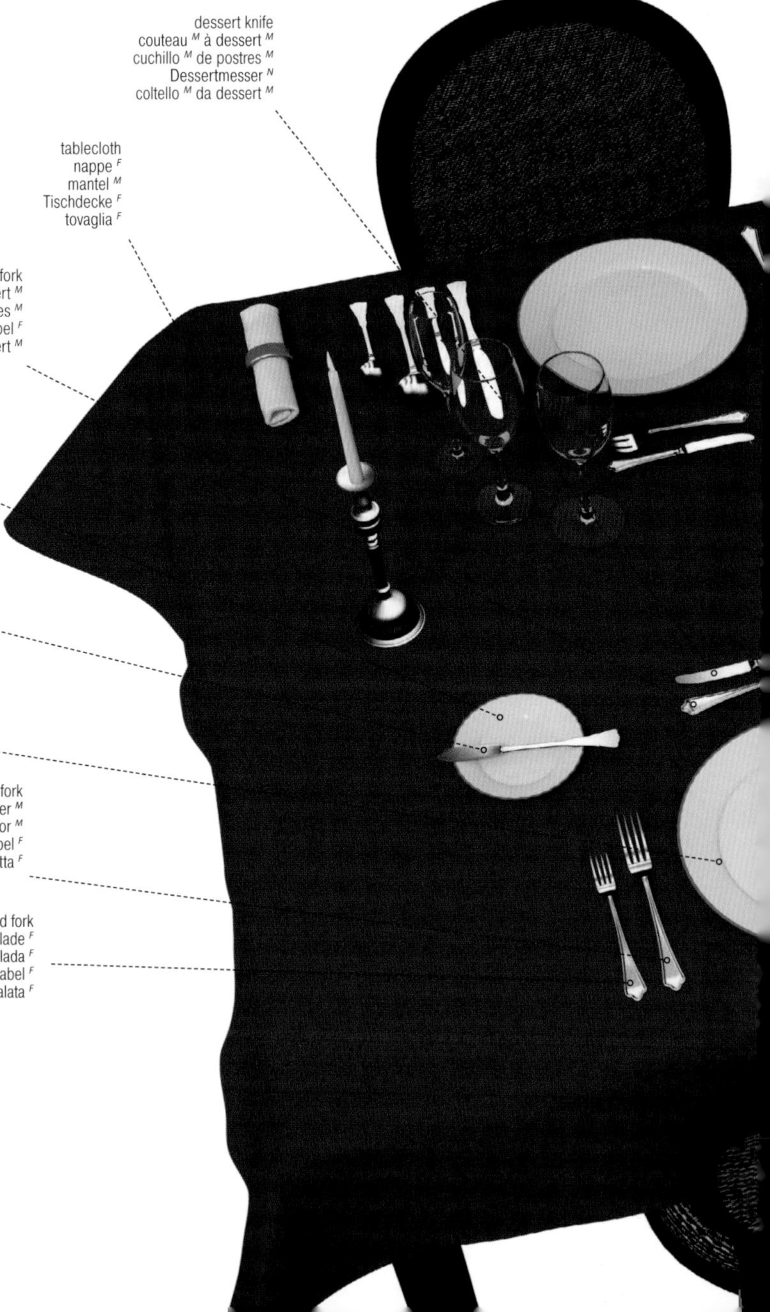

dessert knife
couteau [M] à dessert [M]
cuchillo [M] de postres [M]
Dessertmesser [N]
coltello [M] da dessert [M]

tablecloth
nappe [F]
mantel [M]
Tischdecke [F]
tovaglia [F]

dessert fork
fourchette [F] à dessert [M]
tenedor [M] de postres [M]
Dessertgabel [F]
forchetta [F] da dessert [M]

bread-and-butter plate
assiette [F] à pain [M]
plato [M] auxiliar
Brot und Butterteller [M]
piattino [M] da pane [M]

butter knife
couteau [M] à beurre [M]
cuchillo [M] para untar
Buttermesser [N]
coltello [M] per il burro [M]

dinner plate
assiette [F] à dîner [M]
plato [M]
Essteller [M]
piatto [M]

dinner fork
fourchette [F] à dîner [M]
tenedor [M]
Speisegabel [F]
forchetta [F]

salad fork
fourchette [F] à salade [F]
tenedor [M] de ensalada [F]
Salatgabel [F]
forchetta [F] per insalata [F]

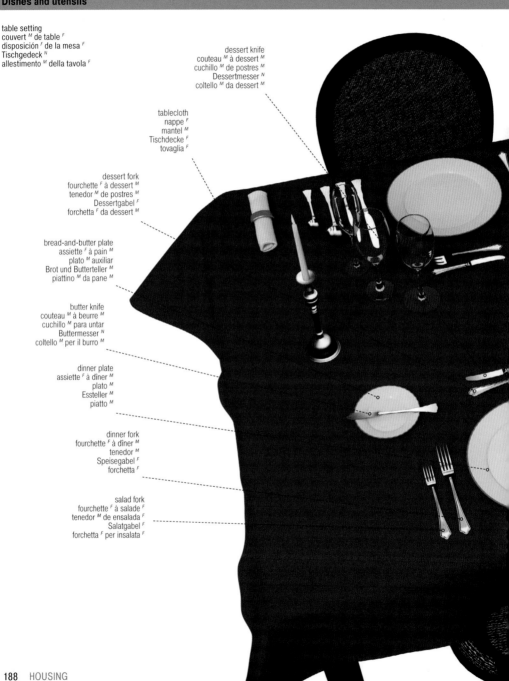

red wine glass
verre [M] à vin [M] rouge
copa [F] de vino [M] tinto
Rotweinglas [N]
calice [M] da vino [M] rosso
candle
bougie [F]
vela [F]
Kerze [F]
candela [F]
candlestick
chandelier [M]
candelero [M]
Kerzenhalter [M]
candeliere [M]
white wine glass
verre [M] à vin [M] blanc
copa [F] de vino [M] blanco
Weißweinglas [N]
calice [M] da vino [M] bianco
ice bucket
seau [M] à glace [F]
cubitera [F]
Eiskübel [M]
secchiello [M] per il ghiaccio [M]
champagne flute
coupe [F] de champagne [M]
copa [F] alta de champán [M]
Sektglas [N]
calice [F] da champagne [M]
napkin
serviette [F]
servilleta [F]
Serviette [F]
tovagliolo [M]
teaspoon
cuillère [F] à thé [M]/à café [M]
cucharilla [F]
Teelöffel [M]
cucchiaino [M]
soupspoon
cuillère [F] à soupe [F]
cuchara [F]
Esslöffel [M]
cucchiaio [M] da tavola [F]
fish knife
couteau [M] à poisson [M]
cuchillo [M] de aperitivo [M]
Fischmesser [N]
coltello [M] da antipasto [M]
dinner knife
couteau [M] de table [F]
cuchillo [M]
Speisemesser [N]
coltello [M]

Cutlery

Coutellerie ^{F} | Cubertería ^{F} | Besteck ^{N} | Posate ^{F}

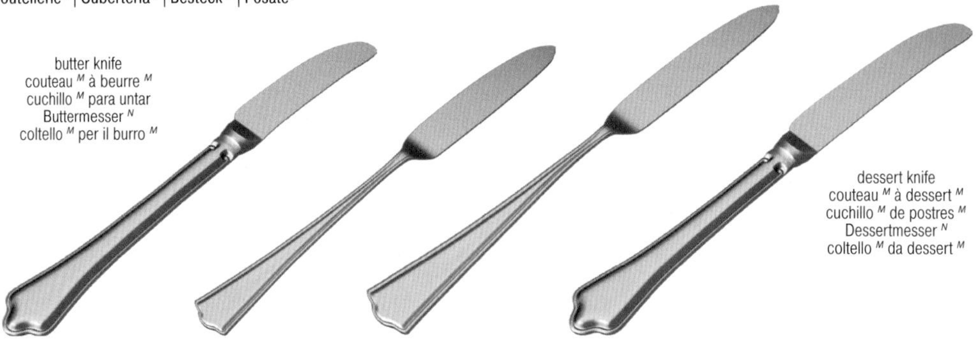

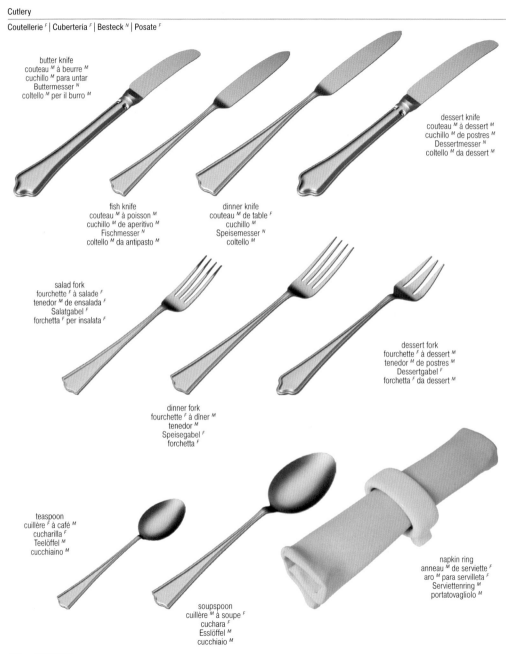

butter knife
couteau ^{M} à beurre ^{M}
cuchillo ^{M} para untar
Buttermesser ^{N}
coltello ^{M} per il burro ^{M}

fish knife
couteau ^{M} à poisson ^{M}
cuchillo ^{M} de aperitivo ^{M}
Fischmesser ^{N}
coltello ^{M} da antipasto ^{M}

dinner knife
couteau ^{M} de table ^{F}
cuchillo ^{M}
Speisemesser ^{N}
coltello ^{M}

dessert knife
couteau ^{M} à dessert ^{M}
cuchillo ^{M} de postres ^{M}
Dessertmesser ^{N}
coltello ^{M} da dessert ^{M}

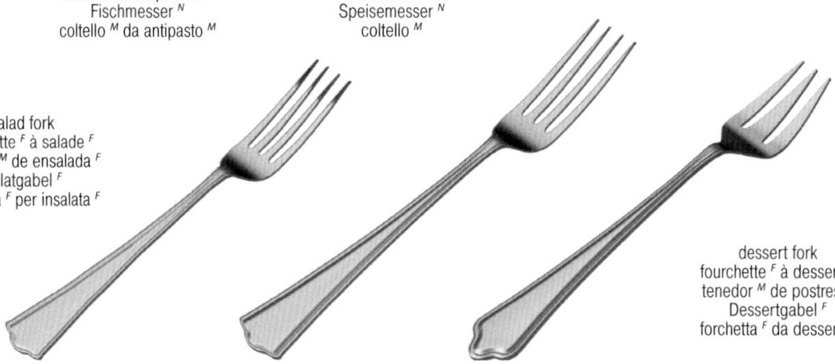

salad fork
fourchette ^{F} à salade ^{F}
tenedor ^{M} de ensalada ^{F}
Salatgabel ^{F}
forchetta ^{F} per insalata ^{F}

dinner fork
fourchette ^{F} à dîner ^{M}
tenedor ^{M}
Speisegabel ^{F}
forchetta ^{F}

dessert fork
fourchette ^{F} à dessert ^{M}
tenedor ^{M} de postres ^{M}
Dessertgabel ^{F}
forchetta ^{F} da dessert ^{M}

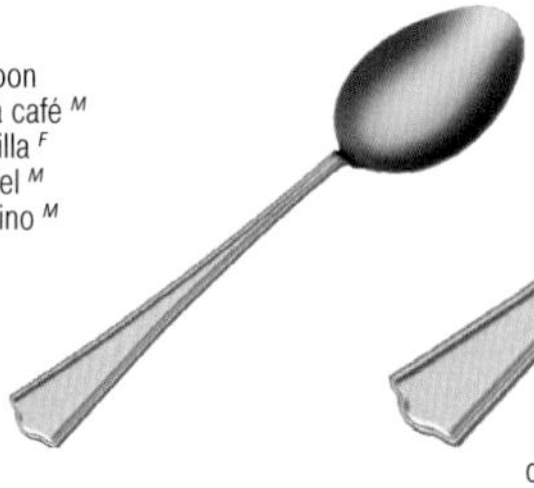

teaspoon
cuillère ^{F} à café ^{M}
cucharilla ^{F}
Teelöffel ^{M}
cucchiaino ^{M}

soupspoon
cuillère ^{M} à soupe ^{F}
cuchara ^{F}
Esslöffel ^{M}
cucchiaio ^{M}

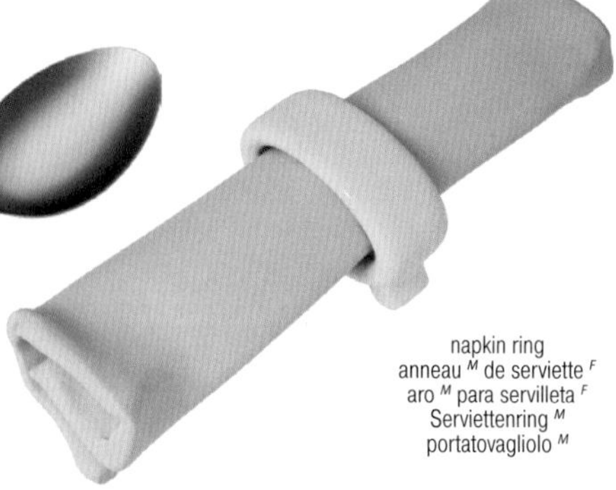

napkin ring
anneau ^{M} de serviette ^{F}
aro ^{M} para servilleta ^{F}
Serviettenring ^{M}
portatovagliolo ^{M}

Kitchen knives

Couteaux ^{M} de cuisine ^{F} | Cuchillos ^{M} de cocina ^{F} | Küchenmesser ^{N} | Coltelli ^{M} da cucina ^{F}

whetstone
pierre ^{F} à aiguiser
piedra ^{F} de afilar
Wetzstein ^{M}
cote ^{F}

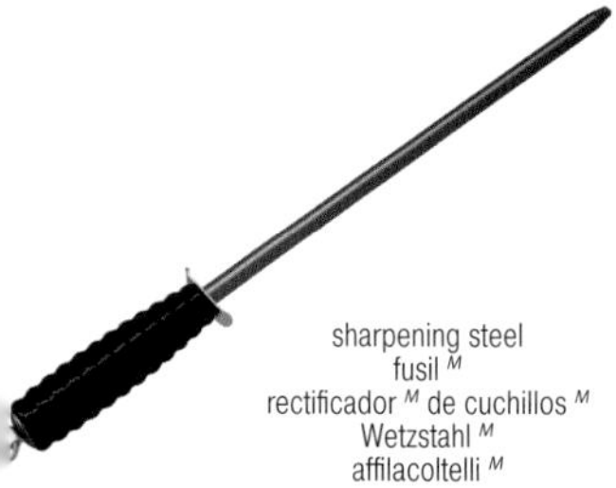

sharpening steel
fusil ^{M}
rectificador ^{M} de cuchillos ^{M}
Wetzstahl ^{M}
affilacoltelli ^{M}

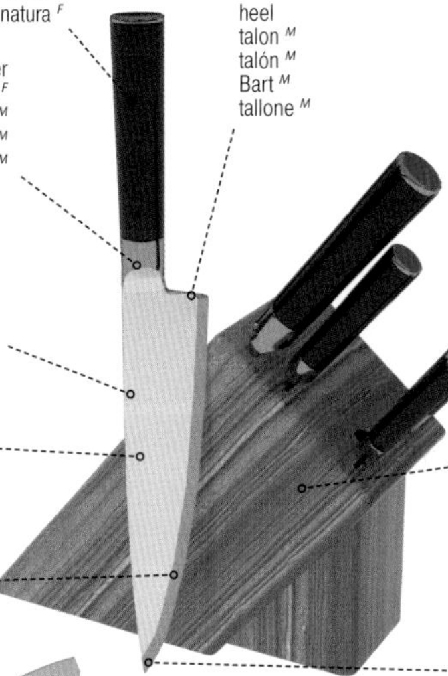

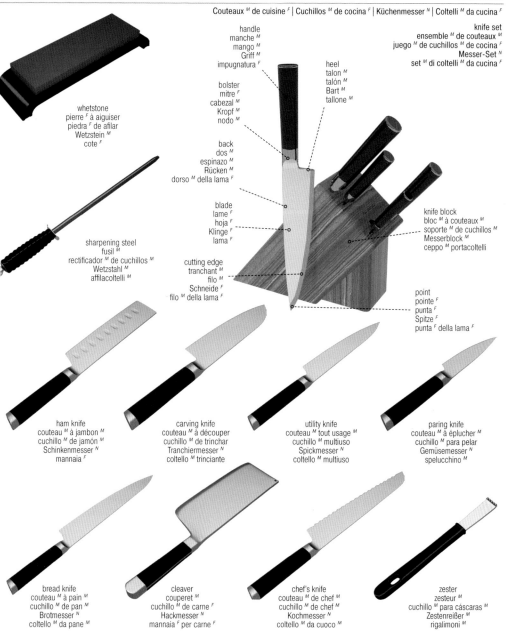

handle
manche ^{M}
mango ^{M}
Griff ^{M}
impugnatura ^{F}

heel
talon ^{M}
talón ^{M}
Bart ^{M}
tallone ^{M}

knife set
ensemble ^{M} de couteaux ^{M}
juego ^{M} de cuchillos ^{M} de cocina ^{F}
Messer-Set ^{N}
set ^{M} di coltelli ^{M} da cucina ^{F}

bolster
mitre ^{F}
cabezal ^{M}
Kropf ^{M}
nodo ^{M}

back
dos ^{M}
espinazo ^{M}
Rücken ^{M}
dorso ^{M} della lama ^{F}

blade
lame ^{F}
hoja ^{F}
Klinge ^{F}
lama ^{F}

knife block
bloc ^{M} à couteaux ^{M}
soporte ^{M} de cuchillos ^{M}
Messerblock ^{M}
ceppo ^{M} portacoltelli

cutting edge
tranchant ^{M}
filo ^{M}
Schneide ^{F}
filo ^{M} della lama ^{F}

point
pointe ^{F}
punta ^{F}
Spitze ^{F}
punta ^{F} della lama ^{F}

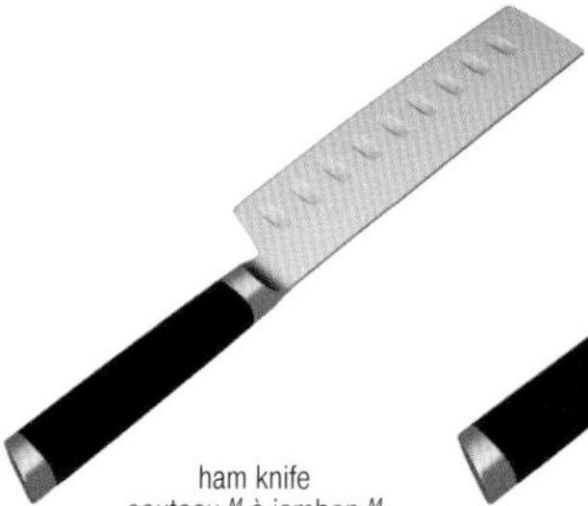

ham knife
couteau ^{M} à jambon ^{M}
cuchillo ^{M} de jamón ^{M}
Schinkenmesser ^{N}
mannaia ^{F}

carving knife
couteau ^{M} à découper
cuchillo ^{M} de trinchar
Tranchiermesser ^{N}
coltello ^{M} trinciante

utility knife
couteau ^{M} tout usage ^{M}
cuchillo ^{M} multiuso
Spickmesser ^{N}
coltello ^{M} multiuso

paring knife
couteau ^{M} à éplucher ^{M}
cuchillo ^{M} para pelar
Gemüsemesser ^{N}
spelucchino ^{M}

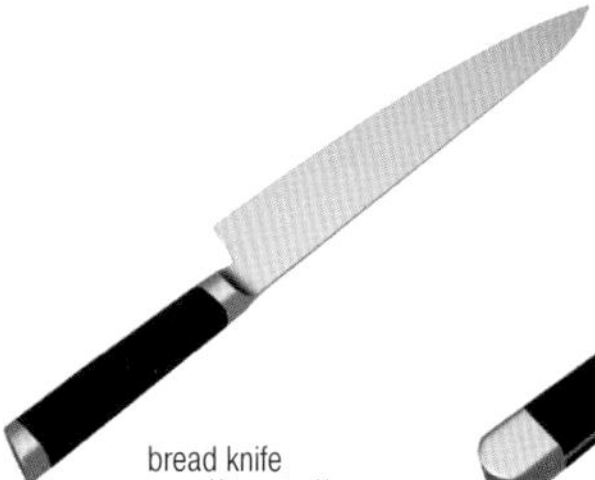

bread knife
couteau ^{M} à pain ^{M}
cuchillo ^{M} de pan ^{M}
Brotmesser ^{N}
coltello ^{M} da pane ^{M}

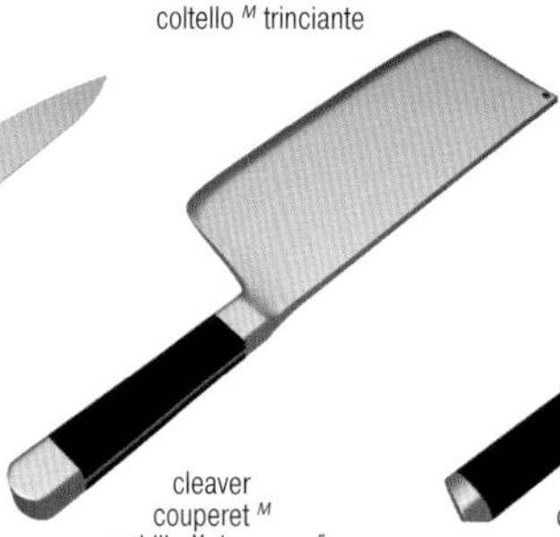

cleaver
couperet ^{M}
cuchillo ^{M} de carne ^{F}
Hackmesser ^{N}
mannaia ^{F} per carne ^{F}

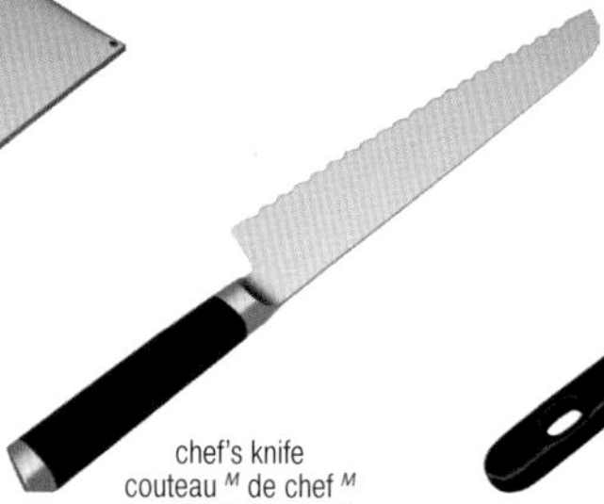

chef's knife
couteau ^{M} de chef ^{M}
cuchillo ^{M} de chef ^{M}
Kochmesser ^{N}
coltello ^{M} da cuoco ^{M}

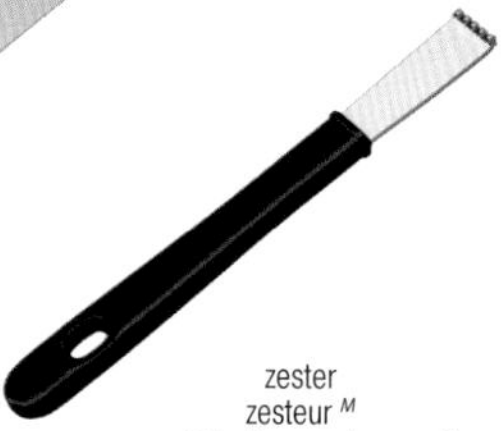

zester
zesteur ^{M}
cuchillo ^{M} para cáscaras ^{M}
Zestenreißer ^{M}
rigalimoni ^{M}

Tableware

Vaisselle [F] | Vajilla [F] | Essgeschirr [N] | Stoviglie [F]

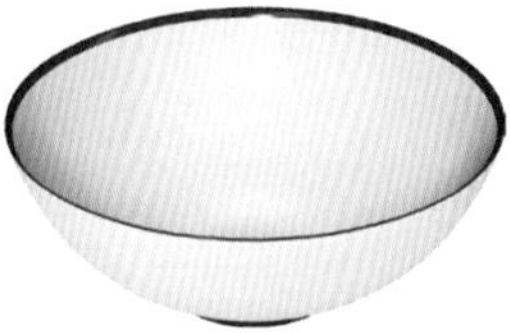

cereal bowl
bol [M] à céréales [F]
tazón [M] para cereales [M]
Müslischale [F]
ciotola [F] per cereali

rice bowl
bol [M] à riz [M]
tazón [M] de arróz [M]
Reisschale [F]
ciotola [F] da riso [M]

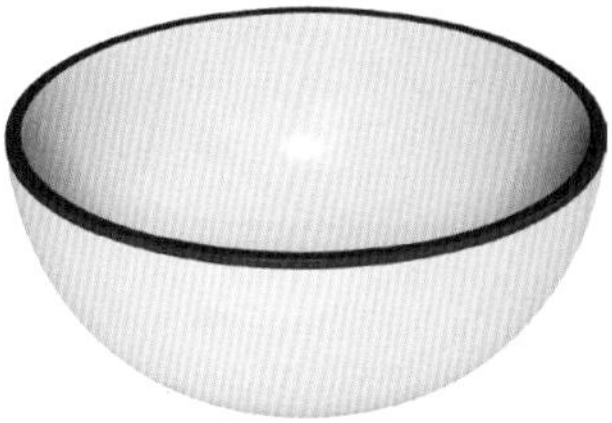

soup bowl
bol [M] à soupe [F]
bol [M] de sopa [F]
Suppenschale [F]
scodella [F] per zuppa [F]

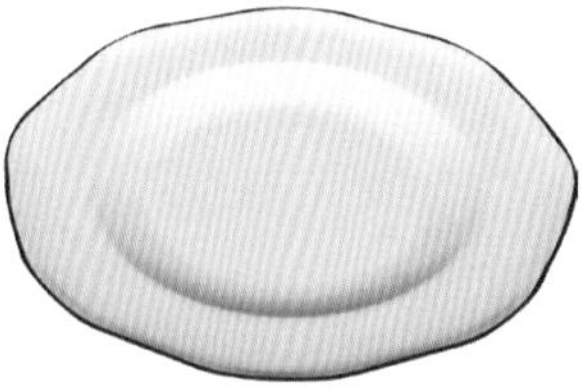

rimmed plate
assiette [F]
plato [M] con borde [M]
Teller mit Rand [M]
piatto [M] con bordo

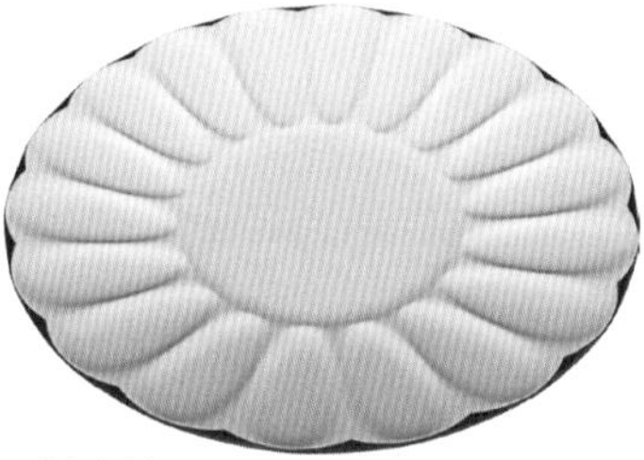

fluted plate
assiette [F] cannelée
plato [M] con relieve [M]
geriffelter Teller [M]
piatto [M] con rilievi [M]

vase
vase [F]
jarrón [M]
Vase [F]
vaso [M]

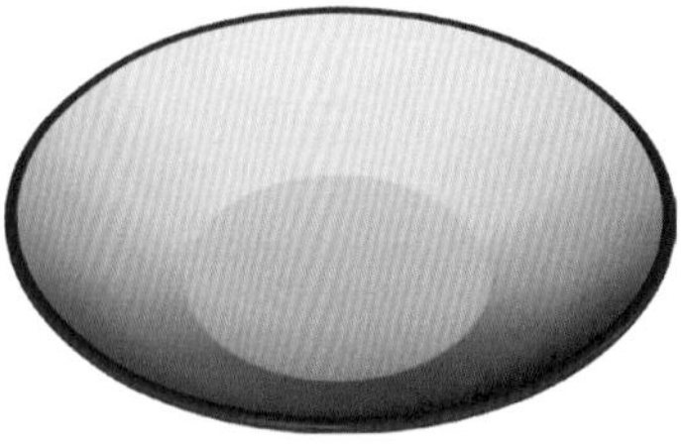

deep plate
assiette [F] creuse
plato [M] hondo
tiefer Teller [M]
piatto [M] fondo

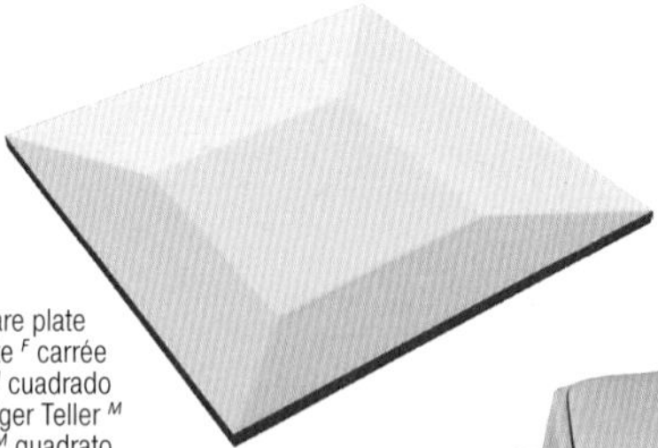

square plate
assiette [F] carrée
plato [M] cuadrado
viereckiger Teller [M]
piatto [M] quadrato

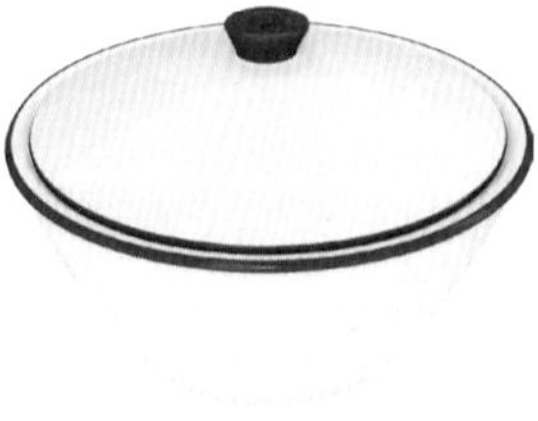

vegetable bowl
bol [M] à légumes [M]
bol [M] con tapa [F]
Gemüseschüssel [F]
coppa [F] con coperchio [M]

mug
tasse [F]
taza [F]
Henkelbecher [M]
tazza [F]

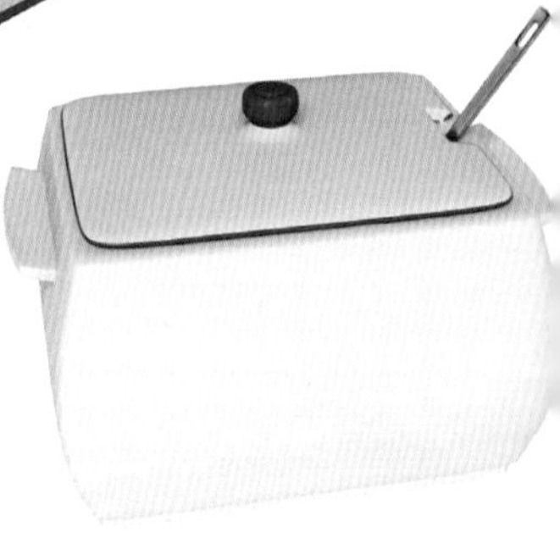

square tureen
soupière [F] carrée
sopera [F] cuadrada
viereckige Schüssel [F]
zuppiera [F] quadrata

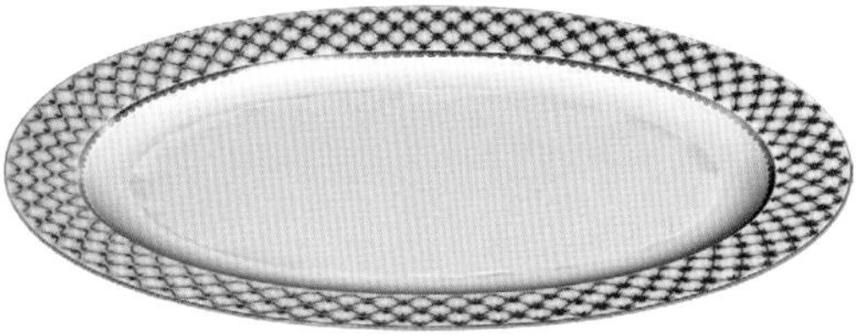

platter
plat [M]
plato [M] de servir
Servierplatte [F]
vassoio [M] da portata [F]

dinner plate
assiette [F] à dîner [M]
plato [M] llano
Speiseteller [M]
piatto [M] da portata [F]

dessert plate
assiette [F] à dessert [M]
plato [M] de postres [M]
Dessertteller [M]
piatto [M] da dessert [M]

spoon rest
repose-cuillère [M]
portacucharas [M]
Löffelablage [F]
poggiamestolo [M]

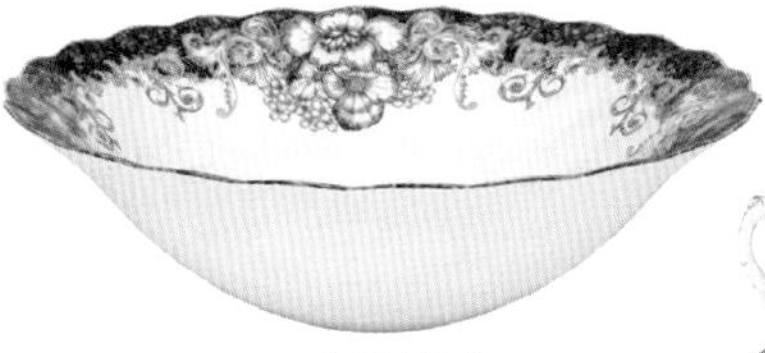

dessert bowl
coupe [F] à dessert [M]
tazón [M] de postres [M]
Dessertschale [F]
insalatiera [F]

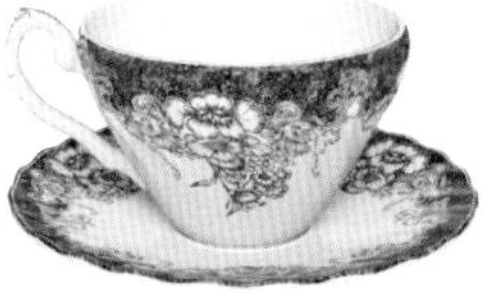

cup and saucer
tasse [F] et soucoupe [F]
taza [F] y plato [M]
Tasse [F] mit Untertasse [F]
tazza [F] da tè [M] e piattino [M]

soup tureen
soupière [F]
fuente [F]
Suppentopf [M]
zuppiera [F]

teapot
théière [F]
tetera [F]
Teekanne [F]
teiera [F]

creamer
pot [M] à lait
jarra [F] de leche [F]
Milchkännchen [N]
brocca [F] per il latte [M]

sugar bowl
sucrier [M]
azucarero [M]
Zuckerdose [F]
zuccheriera [F]

Kitchen utensils

Ustensiles [M] de cuisine [F] | Utensilios [M] de cocina [F] | Küchenutensilien [N] | Utensili [M] da cucina [F]

cube slicer
trancheur [M] de cubes [M]
cortador [M] en cubitos [M]
Würfelschneider [M]
griglia [F] tagliapasta

electronic kitchen scale
balance [F] de cuisine [F] électronique
balanza [F] digital de cocina [F]
digitale Küchenwaage [F]
bilancia [F] elettronica da cucina [F]
bowl
bol [M]
bandeja [F]
Schüssel [F]
bacinella [F]
platform
plate-forme [F]
plataforma [F]
Plattform [F]
piatto [M]
display
affichage [M]
pantalla [F]
Anzeige [F]
display [M]

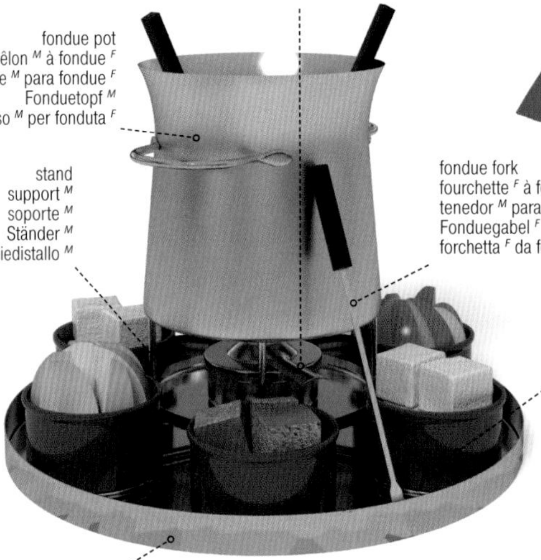
fondue set
service [M] à fondue [F]
fondue [F]
Fondueset [N]
set [M] per fonduta [F]
burner
réchaud [M]
quemador [M]
Brenner [M]
fornello [M]
fondue pot
poêlon [M] à fondue [F]
recipiente [M] para fondue [F]
Fonduetopf [M]
vaso [M] per fonduta [F]
stand
support [M]
soporte [M]
Ständer [M]
piedistallo [M]
fondue fork
fourchette [F] à fondue [F]
tenedor [M] para fondue [F]
Fonduegabel [F]
forchetta [F] da fonduta [F]
bowl
bol [M]
tazón [M]
Schüssel [F]
ciotola [F]
tray
plateau [M]
bandeja [F]
Tablett [N]
vassoio [M]

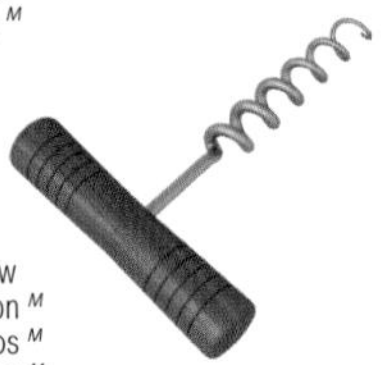
corkscrew
tire-bouchon [M]
sacacorchos [M]
Korkenzieher [M]
cavatappi [M]

manual coffee grinder
moulin [M] à café [M] manuel
molinillo [M] de café [M]
Handkaffeemühle [F]
macinacaffè [M] manuale

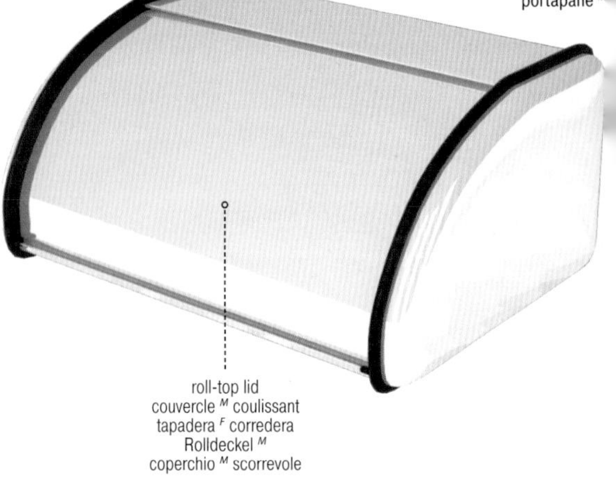
bread box
boîte [F] à pain [M]
panera [F]
Brotkasten [M]
portapane [M]
roll-top lid
couvercle [M] coulissant
tapadera [F] corredera
Rolldeckel [M]
coperchio [M] scorrevole

pastry blender
mélangeur [M] à pâtisserie [F]
amasadora [F]
Teigmischer [M]
miscelatore [M] da pasticceria [F] manuale

citrus juicer
presse-agrumes [M]
exprimidor [M] de cítricos [M]
Zitruspresse [F]
spremiagrumi [M]

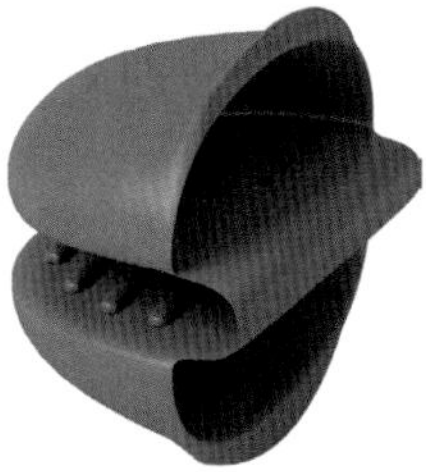

pot grabber
poignée [F] de four [M]
agarrador [M]
Topfgreifer [M]
presina [F]

100
125
75
50
°C
175
25
0
225
250

meat thermometer
thermomètre [M] à viande [F]
termómetro [M] de cocina [F]
Fleischthermometer [N]
termometro [M] da cucina [F]

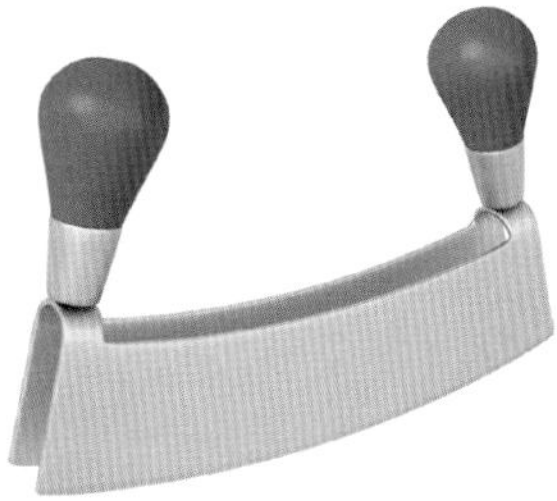

mezzaluna
hachoir [M] berceuse [F]
medialuna [F]
Wiegemesser [N]
mezzaluna [F]

peeler
éplucheur [M]
pelador [M]
Schäler [M]
pelapatate [M]

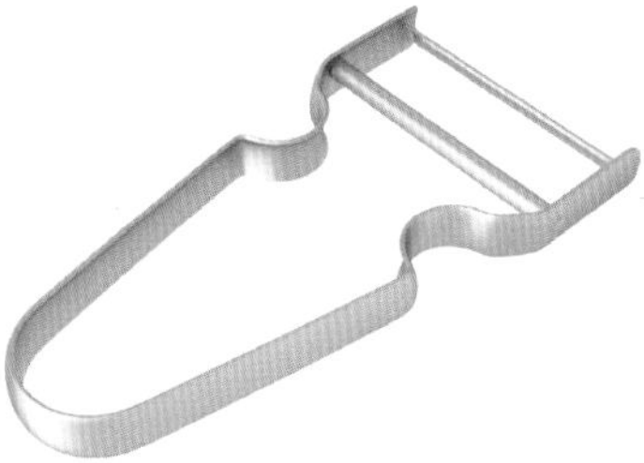

apple corer and slicer
coupe-pommes [M]
cortador [M] de manzanas [F]
Apfelteiler [M]
affettamela [M] con snocciolatore [M]

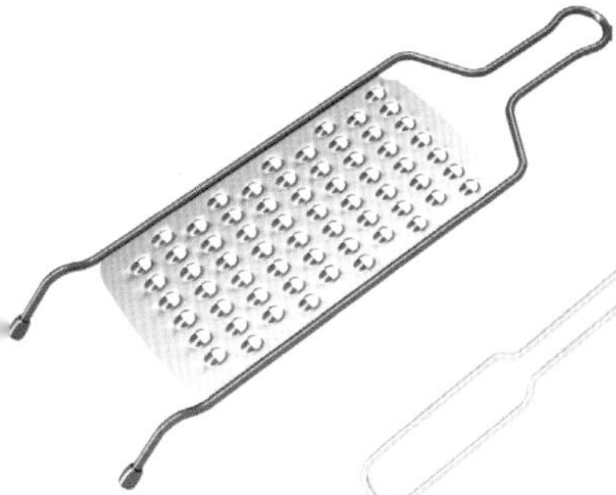

grater
râpe [F]
rallador [M]
Reibe [F]
grattugia [F]

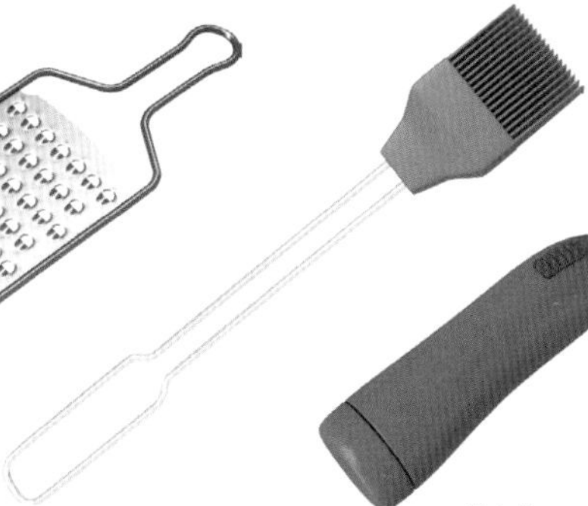

pastry brush
pinceau [F] à pâtisserie
brocha [F] de repostería [F]
Teigpinsel [M]
pennello [M] da cucina [F]

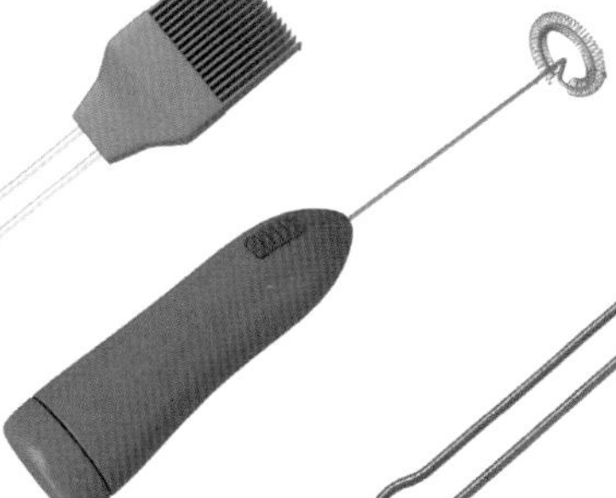

milk frother
mousseur [M] à lait [M]
batidor [M] de leche [F]
Milchschäumer [M]
montalatte [M]

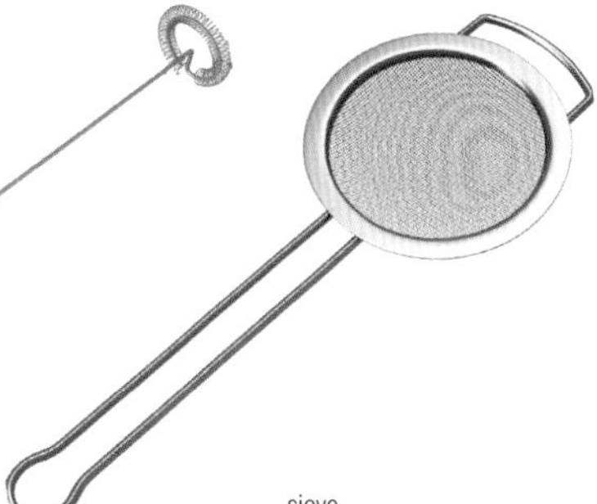

sieve
tamis [M]
colador [M]
Sieb [N]
passino [M]

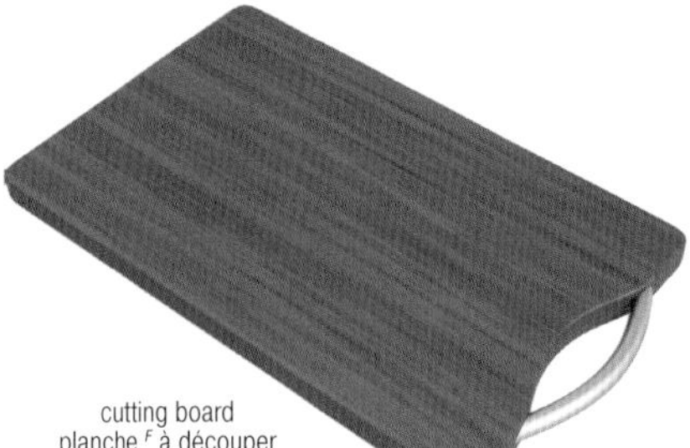

cutting board
planche F à découper
tabla de cortar F
Schneidebrett N
tagliere M

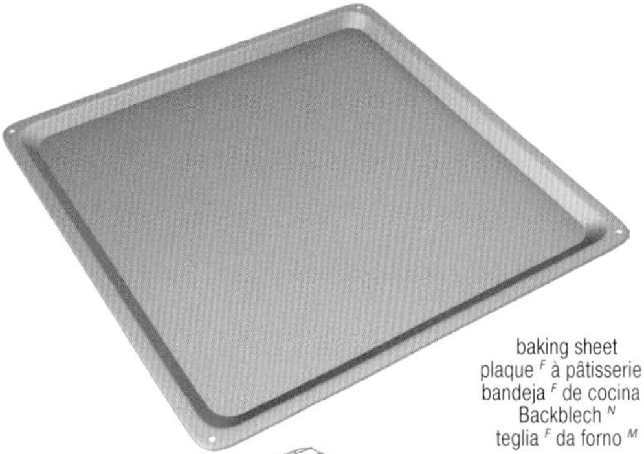

baking sheet
plaque F à pâtisserie F
bandeja F de cocina F
Backblech N
teglia F da forno M

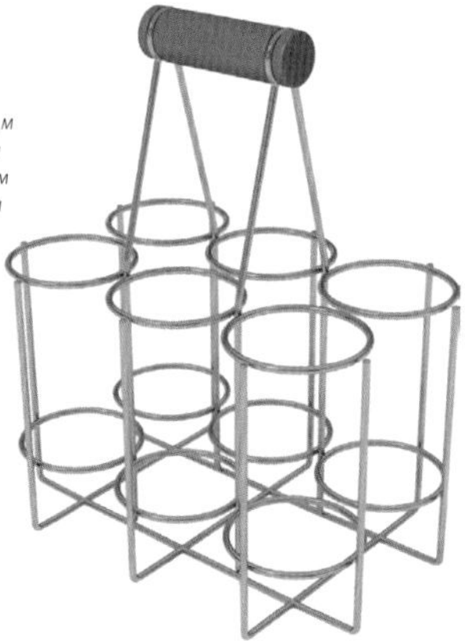

bottle carrier
porte-bouteilles M
portabotellas M
Flaschenträger M
portabottiglie M

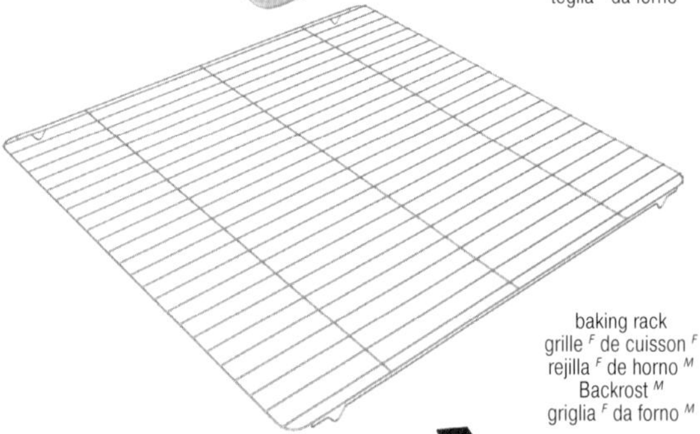

baking rack
grille F de cuisson F
rejilla F de horno M
Backrost M
griglia F da forno M

measuring spoon
cuillère F à mesurer
cuchara F de medir
Messlöffel M
misurini M a cucchiaio M

measuring cup
tasse F à mesurer
taza F de medir
Messbecher M
misurini M a tazza F

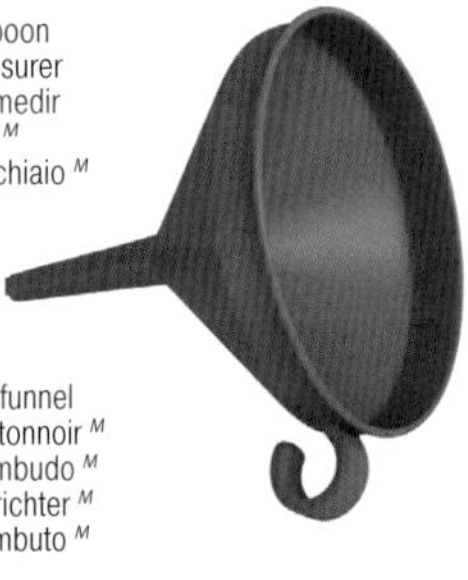

funnel
entonnoir M
embudo M
Trichter M
imbuto M

sifter
tamis M
cedazo M
Sieb N
setaccio M

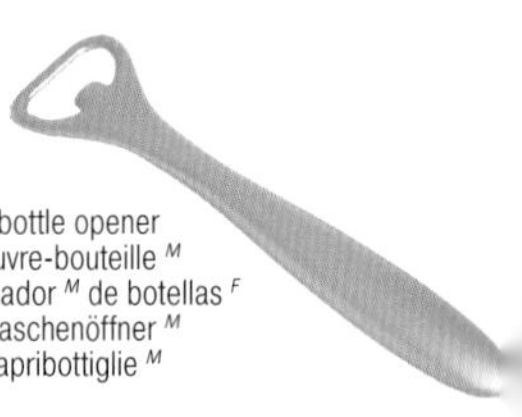

bottle opener
ouvre-bouteille M
destapador M de botellas F
Flaschenöffner M
apribottiglie M

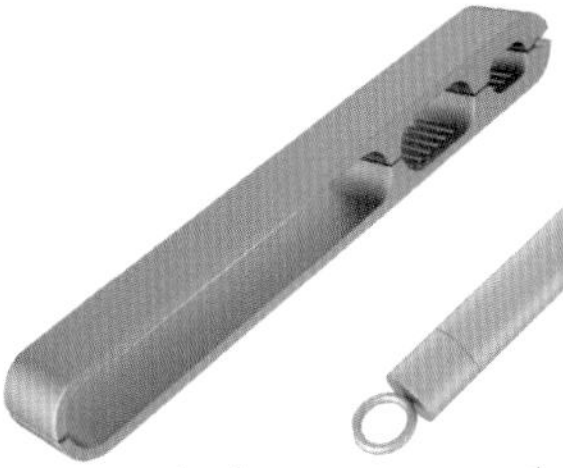

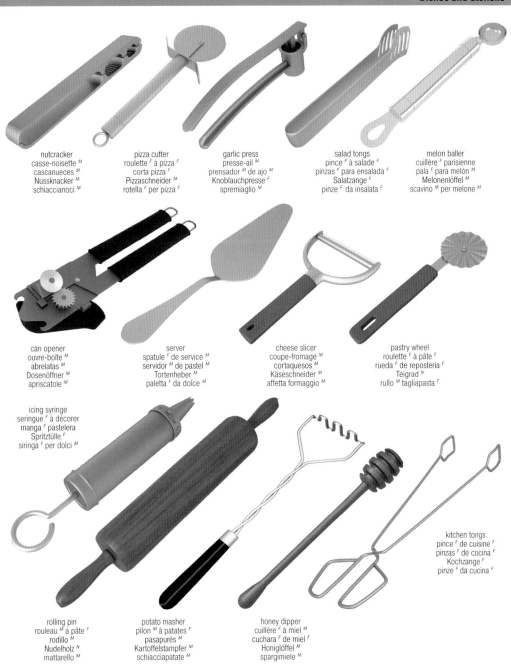

nutcracker
casse-noisette [M]
cascanueces [M]
Nussknacker [M]
schiaccianoci [M]

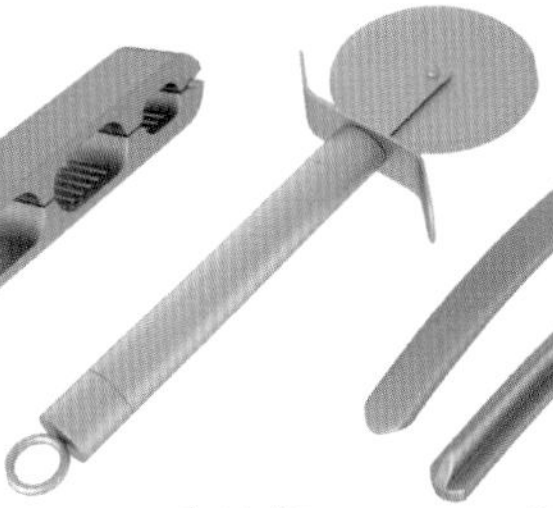

pizza cutter
roulette [F] à pizza [F]
corta pizza [F]
Pizzaschneider [M]
rotella [F] per pizza [F]

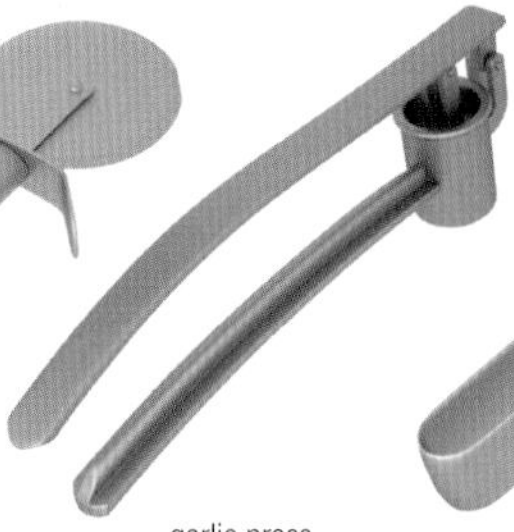

garlic press
presse-ail [M]
prensador [M] de ajo [M]
Knoblauchpresse [F]
spremiaglio [M]

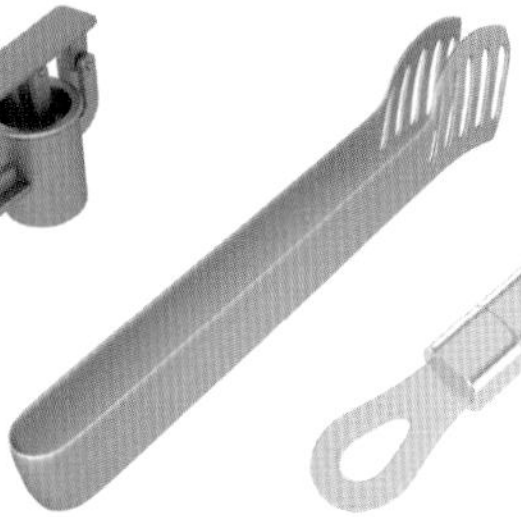

salad tongs
pince [F] à salade [F]
pinzas [F] para ensalada [F]
Salatzange [F]
pinze [F] da insalata [F]

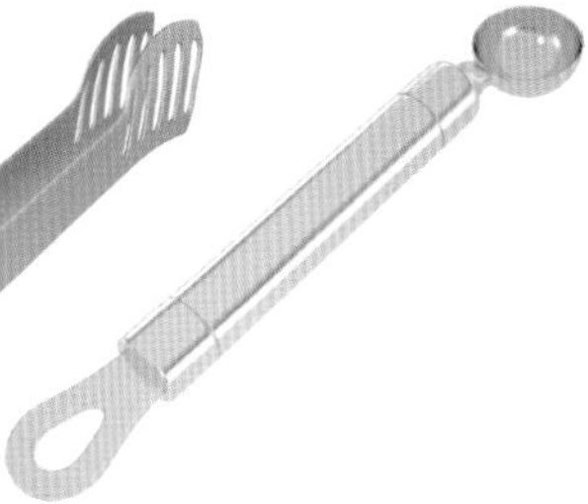

melon baller
cuillère [F] parisienne
pala [F] para melón [M]
Melonenlöffel [M]
scavino [M] per melone [M]

can opener
ouvre-boîte [M]
abrelatas [M]
Dosenöffner [M]
apriscatole [M]

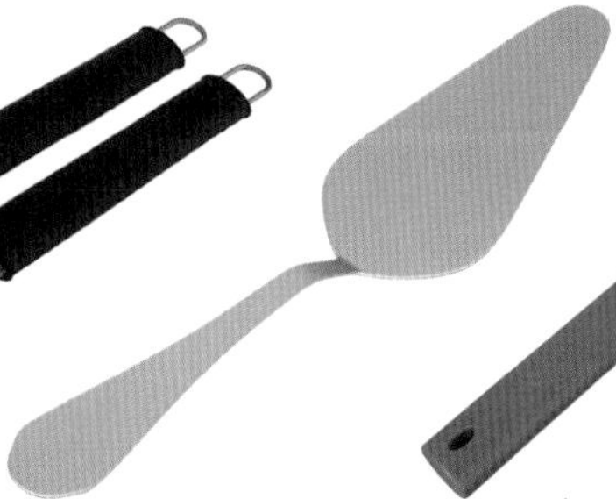

server
spatule [F] de service [M]
servidor [M] de pastel [M]
Tortenheber [M]
paletta [F] da dolce [M]

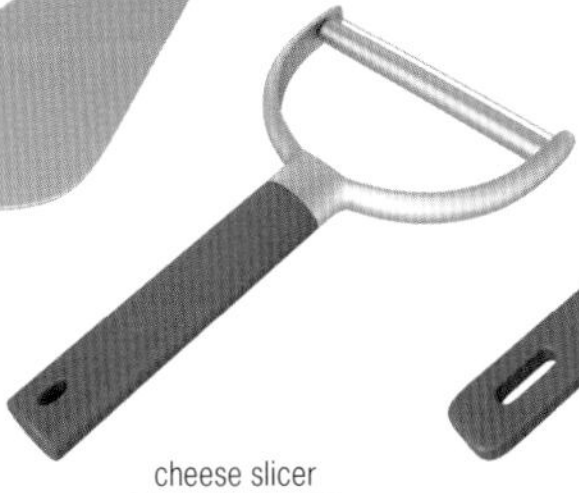

cheese slicer
coupe-fromage [M]
cortaquesos [M]
Käseschneider [M]
affetta formaggio [M]

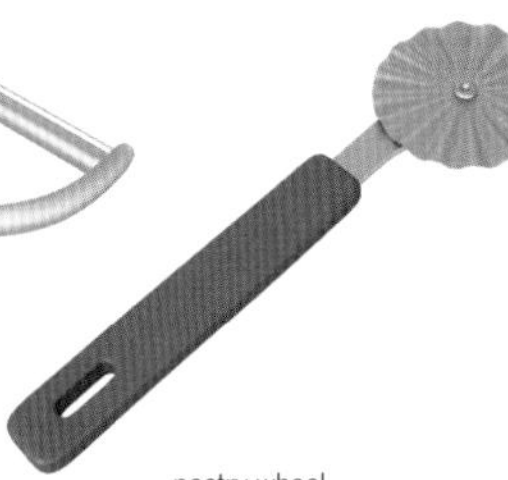

pastry wheel
roulette [F] à pâte [F]
rueda [F] de repostería [F]
Teigrad [N]
rullo [M] tagliapasta [F]

icing syringe
seringue [F] à décorer
manga [F] pastelera
Spritztülle [F]
siringa [F] per dolci [M]

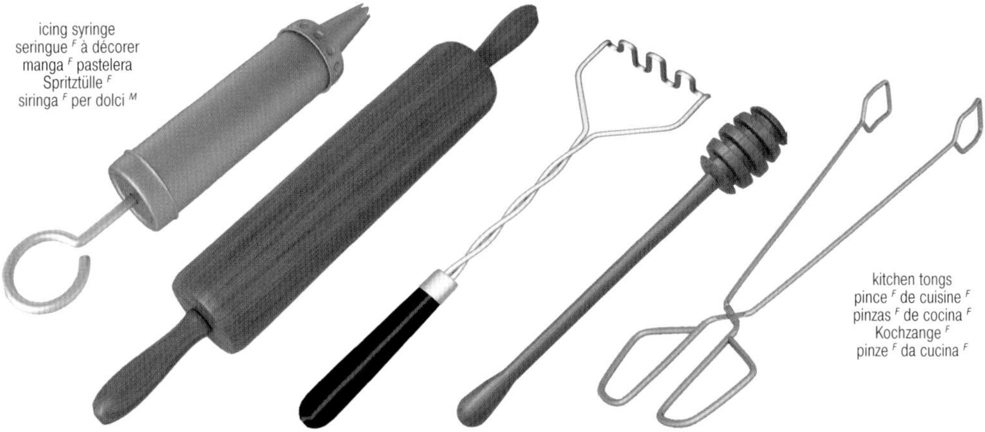

rolling pin
rouleau [M] à pâte [F]
rodillo [M]
Nudelholz [N]
mattarello [M]

potato masher
pilon [M] à patates [F]
pasapurés [M]
Kartoffelstampfer [M]
schiacciapatate [M]

honey dipper
cuillère [F] à miel [M]
cuchara [F] de miel [F]
Honiglöffel [M]
spargimiele [M]

kitchen tongs
pince [F] de cuisine [F]
pinzas [F] de cocina [F]
Kochzange [F]
pinze [F] da cucina [F]

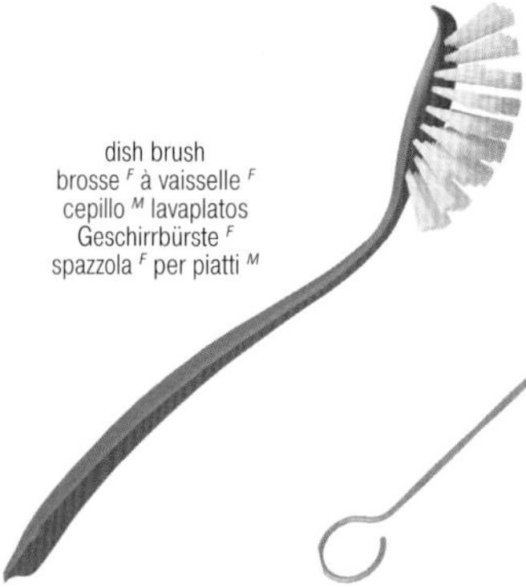

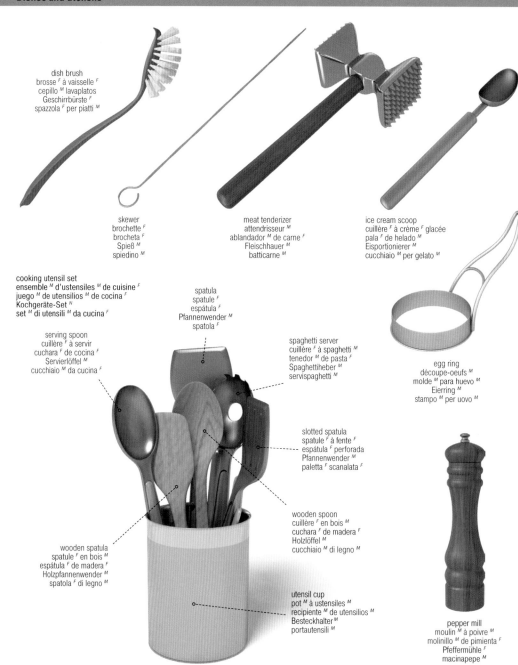

dish brush
brosse[F] à vaisselle[F]
cepillo[M] lavaplatos
Geschirrbürste[F]
spazzola[F] per piatti[M]

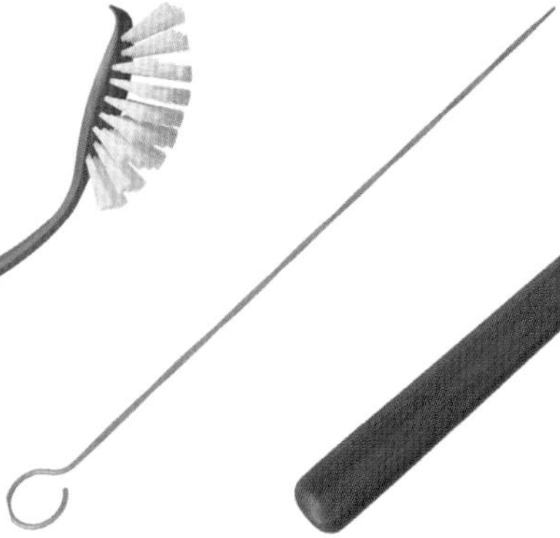

skewer
brochette[F]
brocheta[F]
Spieß[M]
spiedino[M]

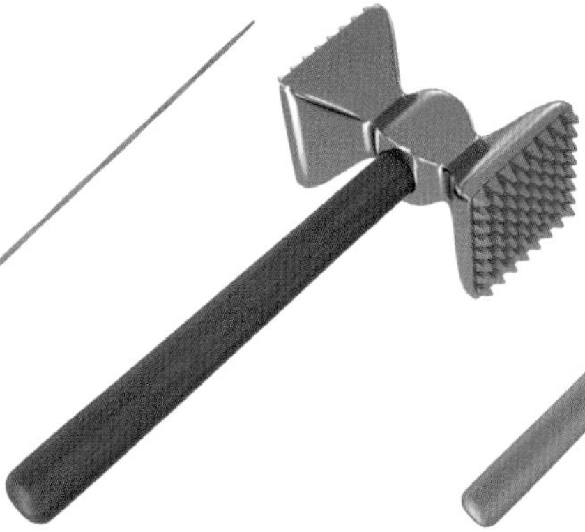

meat tenderizer
attendrisseur[M]
ablandador[M] de carne[F]
Fleischhauer[M]
batticarne[M]

ice cream scoop
cuillère[F] à crème[F] glacée
pala[F] de helado[M]
Eisportionierer[M]
cucchiaio[M] per gelato[M]

cooking utensil set
ensemble[M] d'ustensiles[M] de cuisine[F]
juego[M] de utensilios[M] de cocina[F]
Kochgeräte-Set[N]
set[M] di utensili[M] da cucina[F]

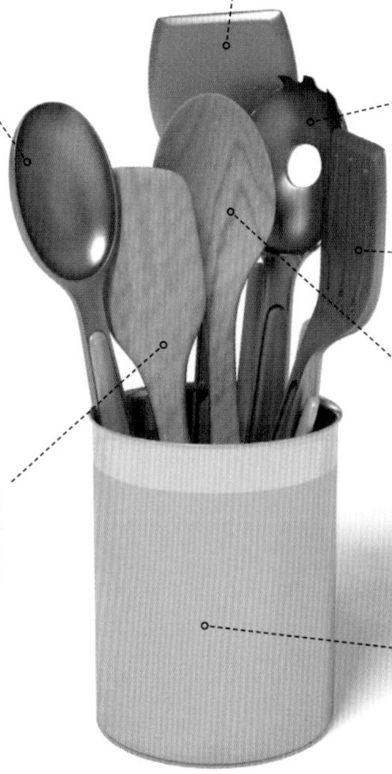

spatula
spatule[F]
espátula[F]
Pfannenwender[M]
spatola[F]

serving spoon
cuillère[F] à servir
cuchara[F] de cocina[F]
Servierlöffel[M]
cucchiaio[M] da cucina[F]

spaghetti server
cuillère[F] à spaghetti[M]
tenedor[M] de pasta[F]
Spaghettiheber[M]
servispaghetti[M]

slotted spatula
spatule[F] à fente[F]
espátula[F] perforada
Pfannenwender[M]
paletta[F] scanalata[F]

wooden spoon
cuillère[F] en bois[M]
cuchara[F] de madera[F]
Holzlöffel[M]
cucchiaio[M] di legno[M]

wooden spatula
spatule[F] en bois[M]
espátula[F] de madera[F]
Holzpfannenwender[M]
spatola[F] di legno[M]

utensil cup
pot[M] à ustensiles[M]
recipiente[M] de utensilios[M]
Besteckhalter[M]
portautensili[M]

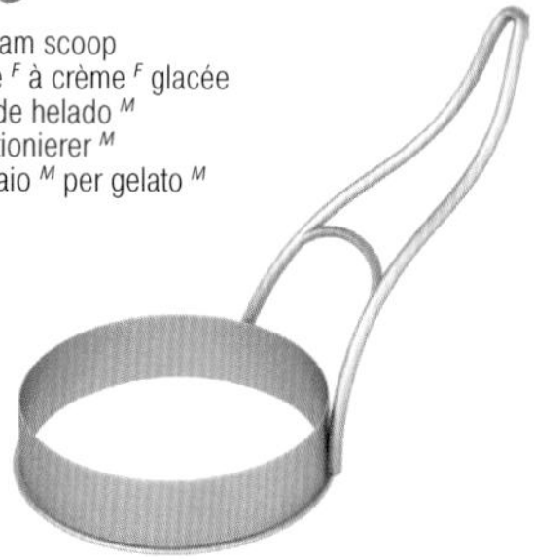

egg ring
découpe-oeufs[M]
molde[M] para huevo[M]
Eierring[M]
stampo[M] per uovo[M]

pepper mill
moulin[M] à poivre[M]
molinillo[M] de pimienta[F]
Pfeffermühle[F]
macinapepe[M]

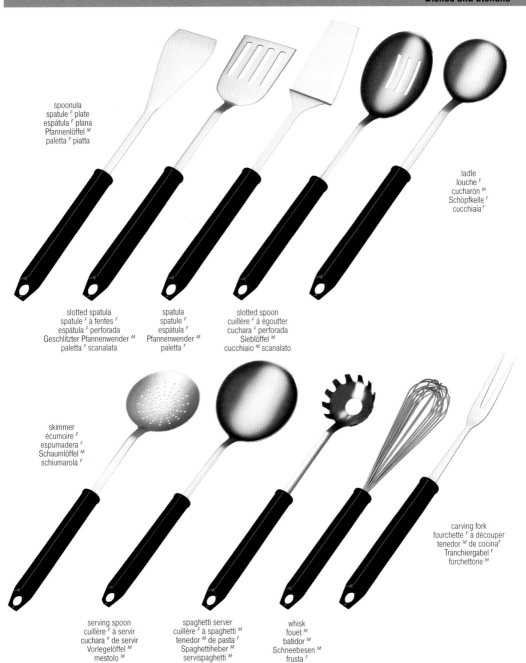

spoonula
spatule ^{F} plate
espátula ^{F} plana
Pfannenlöffel ^{M}
paletta ^{F} piatta

ladle
louche ^{F}
cucharón ^{M}
Schöpfkelle ^{F}
cucchiaia ^{F}

slotted spatula
spatule ^{F} à fentes ^{F}
espátula ^{F} perforada
Geschlitzter Pfannenwender ^{M}
paletta ^{F} scanalata

spatula
spatule ^{F}
espátula ^{F}
Pfannenwender ^{M}
paletta ^{F}

slotted spoon
cuillère ^{F} à égoutter
cuchara ^{F} perforada
Sieblöffel ^{M}
cucchiaio ^{M} scanalato

skimmer
écumoire ^{F}
espumadera ^{F}
Schaumlöffel ^{M}
schiumarola ^{F}

carving fork
fourchette ^{F} à découper
tenedor ^{M} de cocina ^{F}
Tranchiergabel ^{F}
forchettone ^{M}

serving spoon
cuillère ^{F} à servir
cuchara ^{F} de servir
Vorlegelöffel ^{M}
mestolo ^{M}

spaghetti server
cuillère ^{F} à spaghetti ^{M}
tenedor ^{M} de pasta ^{F}
Spaghettiheber ^{M}
servispaghetti ^{M}

whisk
fouet ^{M}
batidor ^{M}
Schneebesen ^{M}
frusta ^{F}

coffee carafe
carafe [F] de café [M]
jarra [F] de café [M]
Kaffeekanne [F]
brocca [F] per il caffè [M]

measuring cup
tasse [F] à mesurer
taza [F] de medir
Messebecher [M]
caraffa [F] graduata

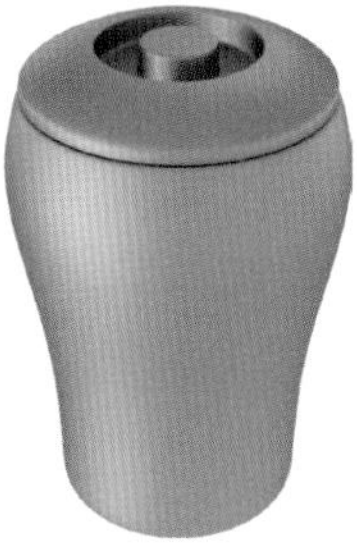

ice bucket
seau [M] à glace [F]
cubitera [F]
Eiskübel [M]
secchiello [M] per il ghiaccio [M]

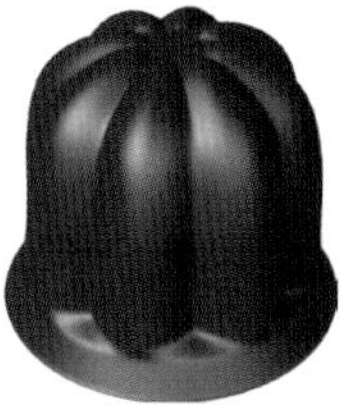

mold
moule [M]
molde [M] para pasteles [M]
Backform [F]
stampo [M] per dolci [M]

mortar and pestle
mortier [M] et pilon [M]
mortero [M] y pilón [M]
Mörser und Stößel [M]
mortaio [M] e pestello [M]

plastic storage container
contenant [M] de plastique [M]
recipiente [M] de plástico [M]
Plastikaufbewahrbehälter [M]
contenitore [M] di plastica [F]

mixing bowl
bol [M] à mélanger
bol [M] mezclador
Rührschüssel [F]
ciotola [F] per impasto [M]

saucepan
casserole [F]
cacerola [F]
Stielkasserolle [F]
tegame [M]

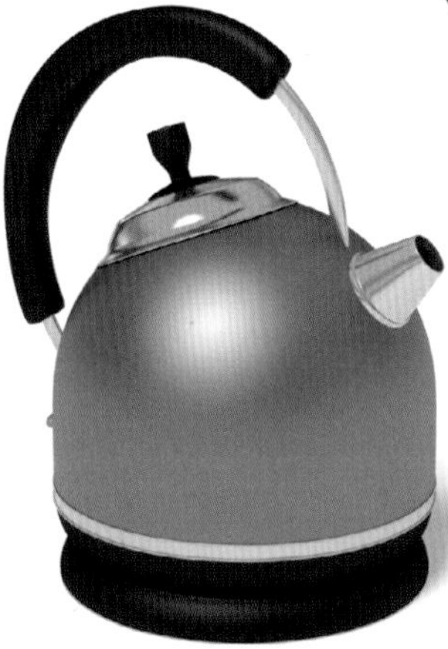

kettle
bouilloire [F]
pava [F]
Teekessel [M]
bollitore [M] per tè [M]

pie dish
moule [M] à tarte [F]
molde [M] para tartas [F]
Pie-Backform [F]
tortiera [F]

double boiler
bain-marie [M]
cacerola [F] para baño [M] María [F]
Wasserbadtopf [M]
pentola [F] per bagnomaria

wok
wok [M]
wok [M]
Wok [M]
wok [M]

skillet
poêle [F]
sartén [F]
Bratpfanne [F]
padella [F]

frying pan
poêle [M] à frire
sartén [F]
Bratpfanne [F]
padella [F] per friggere

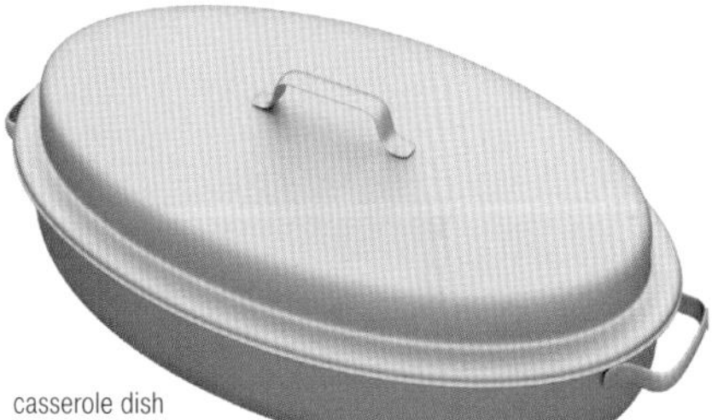

casserole dish
cocotte [F]
cacerola [F] ovalada
Auflaufform [F]
casseruola [F] ovale

stock pot
marmite [F]
olla [F] sopera [F]
Suppentopf [M]
pentola [F] per stufato [M]

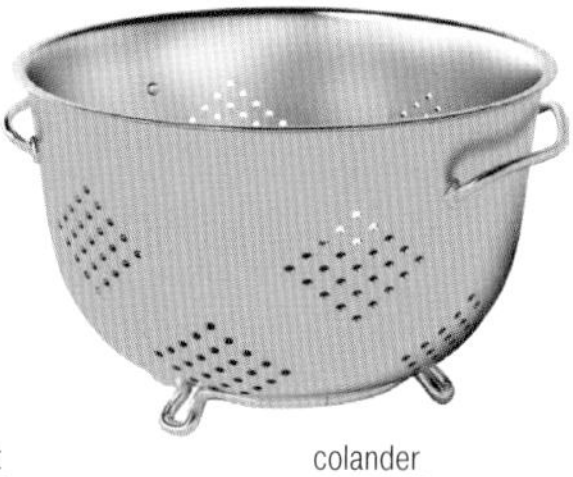

colander
passoire [M]
colador [M]
Sieb [N]
scolapasta [M]

salad spinner
essoreuse [F] à salade [F]
centrifugador [M] de ensalada [F]
Salatschleuder [F]
centrifuga [F] per insalata [F]

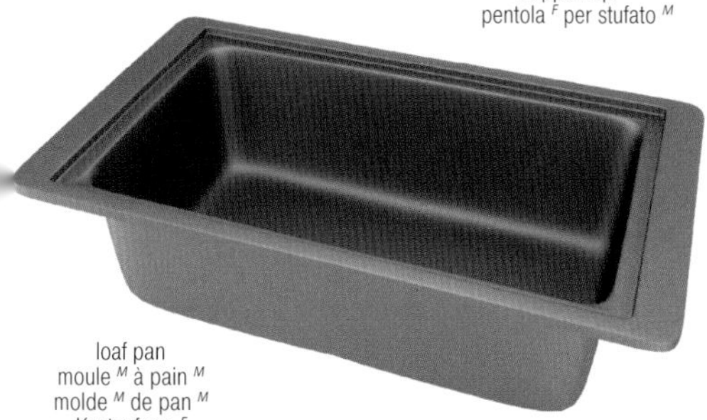

loaf pan
moule [M] à pain [M]
molde [M] de pan [M]
Kastenform [F]
stampo [M] per pane [M]

roasting pan
rôtissoire [F]
bandeja [F] para asados [M]
Brätform [F]
casseruola [F]

Glassware

Verrerie [F] | Cristalería [F] | Glasware [F] | Oggetti [M] di vetro [M]

water glass
verre [M] à eau [F]
vaso [M] de agua [F]
Wasserglas [N]
bicchiere [M] da acqua [F]

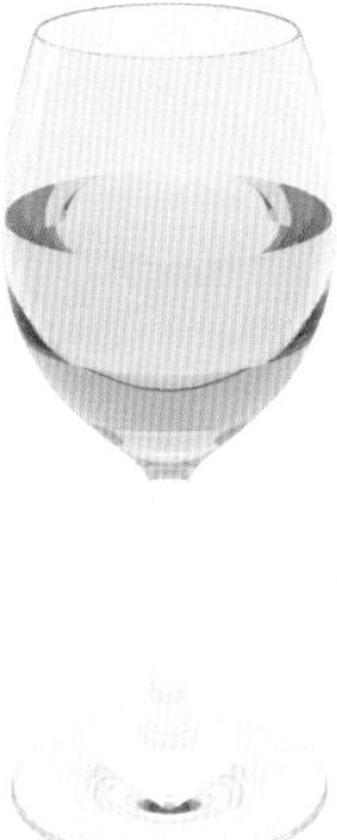

white wine glass
verre [M] à vin [M] blanc
copa [F] de vino [M] blanco
Weißweinglas [N]
calice [M] da vino [M] bianco

champagne flute
flûte [F] à champagne [M]
copa [F] alta de champán [M]
Sektglas [N]
calice [M] da champagne [M]

Alsace glass
verre [M] à vin [M] d'Alsace [F]
copa [F] de vino [M] del Alsacia [F]
Elsassglas [N]
calice [M] da vino [M] del Reno [M]

decanter
carafe [F]
decantador [M]
Karaffe [F]
decanter [M]

cocktail glass
verre [M] à cocktail [M]
copa [F] de cóctel [M]
Cocktailglas [N]
bicchiere [M] da cocktail [M]

champagne glass
verre [M] à champagne [M]
copa [F] baja de champán [M]
Sektschale [F]
coppa [F] di champagne [M]

sherry glass
verre [M] à sherry [M]
copa [F] de jerez [M]
Sherryglas [N]
bicchiere [M] da porto [M]

red wine glass
verre [M] à vin [M] rouge
copa [F] de vino [M] tinto
Rotweinglas [N]
calice [M] da vino [M] rosso

burgundy glass
verre [M] à bourgogne [M]
copa [F] de Borgoña [F]
Burgunderglas [N]
calice [M] da burgundy [M]

port glass
verre [M] à porto [M]
copa [F] de oporto [M]
Portglas [F]
bicchiere [M] da bordeaux [M]

brandy snifter
verre [M] à cognac [M]
copa [F] de coñac [M]
Weinbrandschwenker [M]
snifter [M] da brandy [M]

liqueur glass
verre [M] à liqueur [F]
copa [F] de licor [M]
Likörglass [N]
bicchiere [M] da liquore [M]

beer mug
chope [F] à bière [F]
jarra [F] de cerveza [F]
Bierkrug [M]
boccale [M] da birra [F]

beer glass
verre [M] à bière [F]
vaso [M] de cerveza [F]
Bierglas [N]
bicchiere [M] da birra [F]

old-fashioned glass
verre [M] à whisky [M]
vaso [M] de whisky [M]
Whiskyglas [N]
bicchiere [M] da whiskey [M]

Tables

Tables ^{M} | Mesas ^{F} | Tische ^{M} | Tavoli ^{M}

console table
console ^{F}
consola ^{F}
Konsolentisch ^{M}
consolle ^{F}

nightstand
table ^{F} de nuit ^{F}
mesilla ^{F} de noche ^{F}
Nachttisch ^{M}
comodino ^{M}

dining table
table ^{F} de salle ^{F} à manger
mesa ^{F} de comedor ^{M}
Esstisch ^{M}
tavolo ^{M} da pranzo ^{M}

writing desk
secrétaire ^{M}
escritorio ^{M}
Schreibtisch ^{M}
scrittoio ^{M}

telephone table
table [F] de téléphone [M]
mesita [F] de teléfono [M]
Telefontisch [M]
tavolino [M] per il telefono [M]

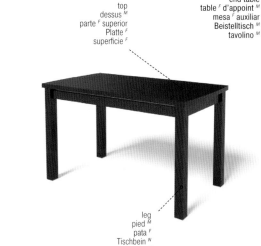

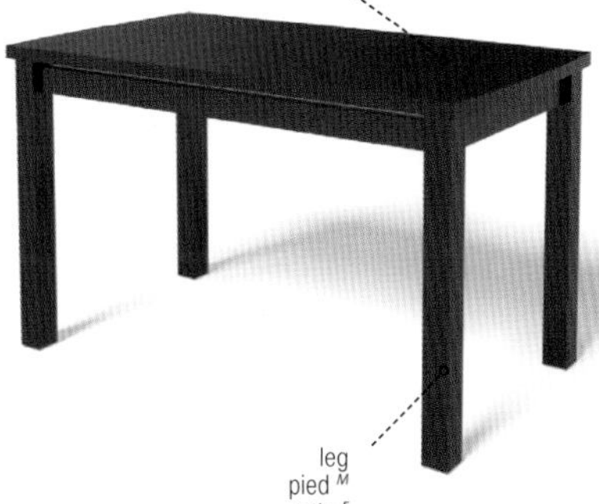
top
dessus [M]
parte [F] superior
Platte [F]
superficie [F]
leg
pied [M]
pata [F]
Tischbein [N]
gamba [F]

end table
table [F] d'appoint [M]
mesa [F] auxiliar
Beistelltisch [M]
tavolino [M]

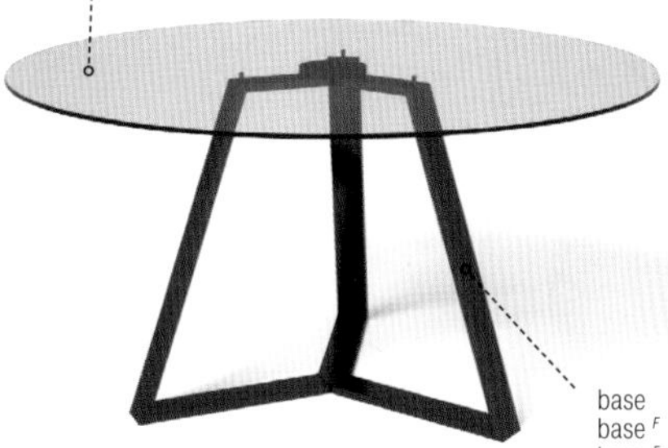
tempered glass
verre [M] trempé
vidrio [M] templado
Hartglas [N]
superficie [F] in vetro [M]
temperato
base
base [F]
base [F]
Unterteil [N]
base [F]

patio table
table [F] de jardin [M]
mesa [F] de terraza [F]
Terassentisch [M]
tavolo [M] da patio [M]

vanity
coiffeuse [F]
tocador [M]
Schminktisch [M]
toilette [F]

coffee table
table [F] basse
mesita [F] baja
Wohnzimmertisch [M]
tavolino [M] da caffè [M]

Chairs

Chaises [F] | Sillas [F] | Stühle [M] | Sedie [F]

bergère
bergère [F]
poltrona [F]
Bergère [F]
poltrona [F] bergère

leather armchair
fauteuil [M] en cuir [M]
sillón [M] de cuero [M]
Ledersessel [M]
poltrona [F] in pelle [F]

back
dossier [M]
respaldo [M]
Rückenlehne [F]
schienale [M]

arm
bras [M]
brazo [M]
Armlehne [F]
bracciolo [M]

seat
siège [M]
asiento [M]
Sitz [M]
seduta [F]

leg
pied [M]
pata [F]
Standbein [N]
gamba [F]

armchair
fauteuil [M]
sillón [M]
Lehnstuhl [M]
poltroncina [F]

stool
tabouret [M]
taburete [M]
Hocker [M]
sgabello [M]

Voltaire chair
Voltaire [M]
silla [F] francesa
Voltaire-Sessel [M]
poltrona [F] in stile [M] Luigi XV

easy chair
fauteuil [M]
butaca [F]
Lehnsessel [M]
poltrona [F]

cushioned armchair
fauteuil [M] rembourré [M]
sillón [M] acolchado
gepolsterter Sessel [M]
sedia [F] imbottita

kitchen chair
chaise [F] de cuisine [F]
silla [F] de cocina [F]
Küchenstuhl [M]
sedia [F] cantilever

folding chair
chaise [F] pliante
silla [F] plegable
Klappstuhl [M]
sedia [F] pieghevole

stacking chair
chaise [F] empilable
silla [F] apilable
Stapelstuhl [M]
sedia [F] impilabile

bar stool
tabouret [M] de bar [M]
taburete [M] de bar [M]
Barhocker [M]
sgabello [M] da bar [M]

rocking chair
chaise [F] berçante
mecedora [F]
Schaukelstuhl [M]
sedia [F] a dondolo [M]

dining chair
chaise [F] de salle [F] à manger
mesa [F] de comedor [M]
Esszimmerstuhl [M]
sedia [F] del tavolo [M] da pranzo [M]

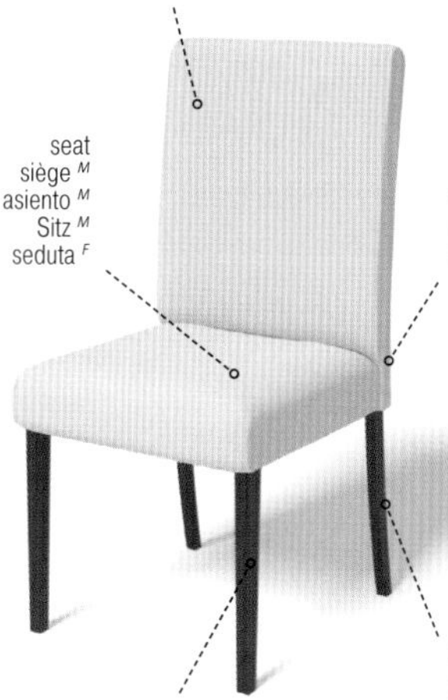

back
dossier [M]
respaldo [M]
Rückenlehne [F]
schienale [M]

seat
siège [M]
asiento [M]
Sitz [M]
seduta [F]

upholstery
rembourrage [M]
tapizado [M]
Polster [N]
fodera [F]

front leg
pied [M] avant pata [F]
delantera
Vorderbein [N]
gamba [F] anteriore

back leg
pied [M] arrière pata [F]
trasera
Hinterbein [N]
gamba [F] posteriore

director's chair
fauteuil [M] de metteur [M] en scène [F]
silla [F] de director [M]
Regiestuhl [M]
sedia [F] da regista [M]

Sofas

Canapés [M] | Sofás [M] | Sofas [N] | Divani [M]

sectional sofa
canapé [M] modulaire
sofá [M] seccional
Anbausofa [N]
divano [M] componibile

backrest
dossier [M]
respaldo [M]
Rückenlehne [F]
schienale [M]
seat cushion
coussin [M]
asiento [M] acolchado
Sitzpolster [N]
cuscino [M] per seduta [F]
leg
pied [M]
pata [F]
Standbein [N]
gamba [F]
arm
bras [M]
brazo [M]
Armlehne [F]
bracciolo [M]

loveseat
causeuse [F]
sofá [M] estrecho
Zweisitzer [M]
divano [M] a due posti [M]

ottoman
tabouret [M]
otomana [F]
Ottomane [F]
ottomana [F]

bench
banc [M]
banco [M] acolchado
Banksofa [N]
panca [F] divano [M]

chaise longue
chaise [F] longue
chaiselongue [F]
Chaiselounge [F]
chaise [F] longue

Storage furniture

Meubles [M] de rangement [M] | Muebles [M] para almacenaje [M] | Schränke [M] und Regale [N] | Mobili [M] contenitori

liquor cabinet
bar [M]
mueble [M] bar
Schrank [M] für Spirituosen [F]
mobile [M] bar [M]

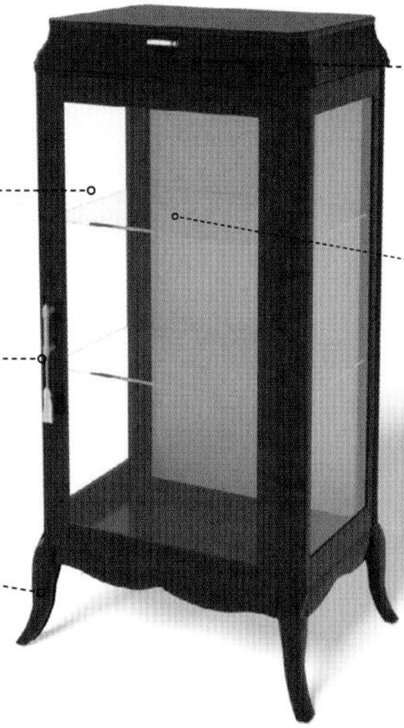

door
porte [F]
puerta [F]
Tür [F]
sportello [M]

pull
poignée [F]
tirador [M]
Griff [M]
maniglia [F]

leg
pied [M]
pata [F]
Standbein [N]
gamba [F]

drawer
tiroir [M]
cajón [M]
Schublade [F]
cassetto [M]

shelf
étagère [F]
estante [M]
Regal [N]
mensola [F]

chest of drawers
commode [F]
cajonera [F]
Kommode [F]
cassettone [M]

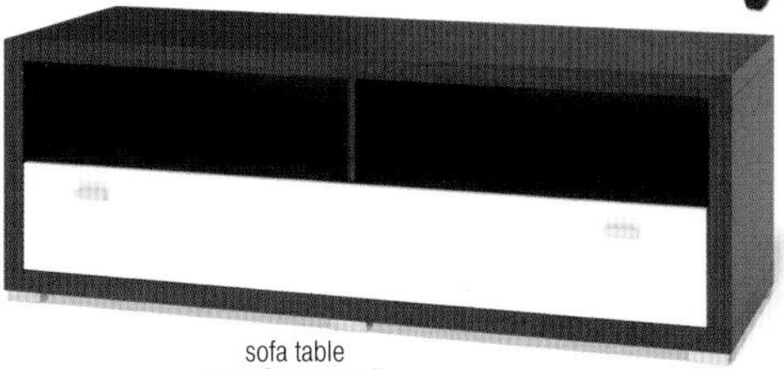

sofa table
table [F] de salon [M]
mesa [F] de sofá [M]
Sofatisch [M]
tavolino [M] da soggiorno [M]

display cabinet
armoire [F] vitrée
vitrina [F]
Schauvitrine [F]
vetrina [F]

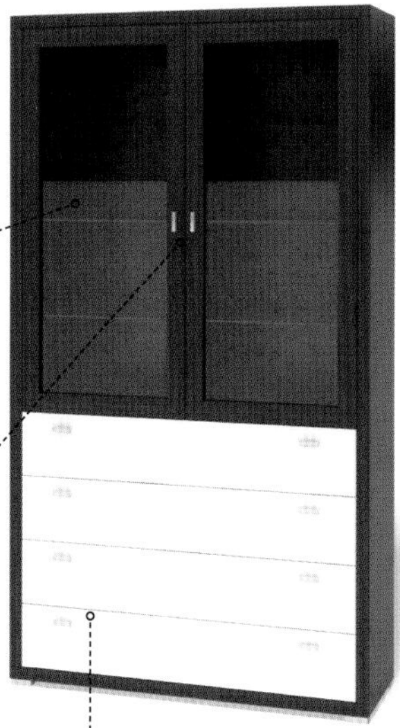

glass door
porte [F] en verre [M]
puerta [F] de cristal [M]
Glastür [F]
vetrinetta [F]

pull
poignée [F]
tirador [M]
Griff [M]
maniglia [F]

drawer
tiroir [M]
cajón [M]
Schublade [F]
cassetto [M]

sideboard
buffet [M]
aparador [M]
Sideboard [N]
credenza [F]

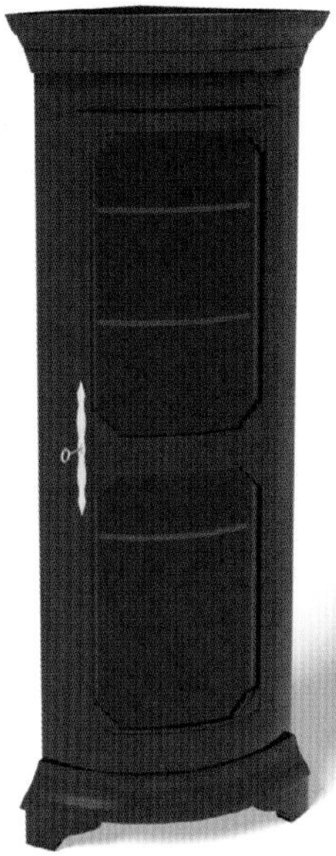

corner cabinet
armoire [F] de coin [M]
rinconera [F]
Eckschrank [M]
mobile [M] ad angolo [M]

wall unit
unité [F] murale
mueble [M] de pared [F]
Schrankwand [F]
parete [F] attrezzata

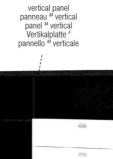

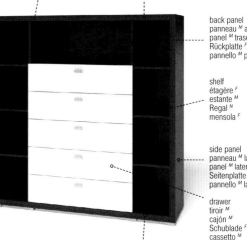

vertical panel
panneau [M] vertical
panel [M] vertical
Vertikalplatte [F]
pannello [M] verticale
top panel
panneau [M] supérieur
panel [M] superior
obere Platte [F]
pannello [M] superiore
back panel
panneau [M] arrière
panel [M] trasero
Rückplatte [F]
pannello [M] posteriore
shelf
étagère [F]
estante [M]
Regal [N]
mensola [F]
side panel
panneau [M] latéral
panel [M] lateral
Seitenplatte [F]
pannello [M] laterale
drawer
tiroir [M]
cajón [M]
Schublade [F]
cassetto [M]
bottom panel
panneau [M] inférieur
panel [M] inferior
untere Platte [F]
pannello [M] inferiore

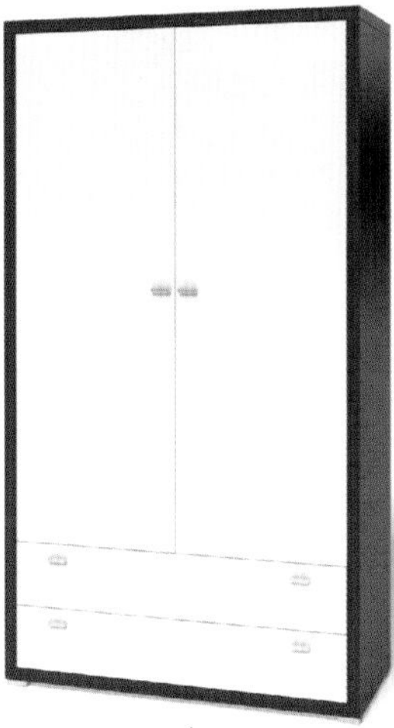

armoire
armoire [F]
armario [M] ropero
Kleiderschrank [M]
armadio [M]

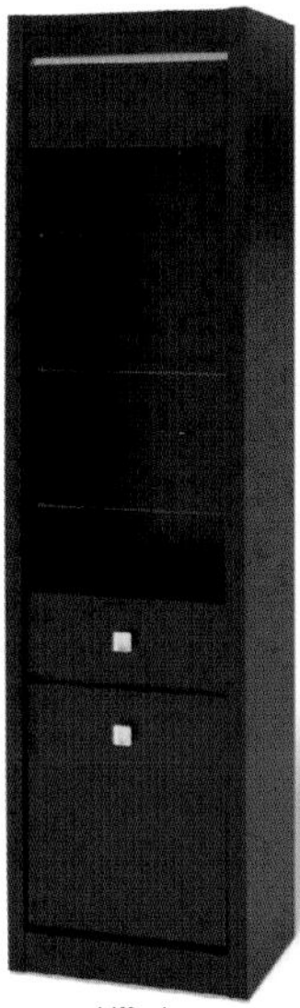

chiffonier
chiffonnier [M]
chifonier [M]
Chiffonier [N]
stipo [M] a cassettini [M]

bookcase
bibliothèque [F]
librero [M]
Bücherregal [N]
libreria [F]

Domestic appliances

Appareils électroménagers M | Electrodomésticos M | Haushaltsgeräte N | Elettrodomestici M

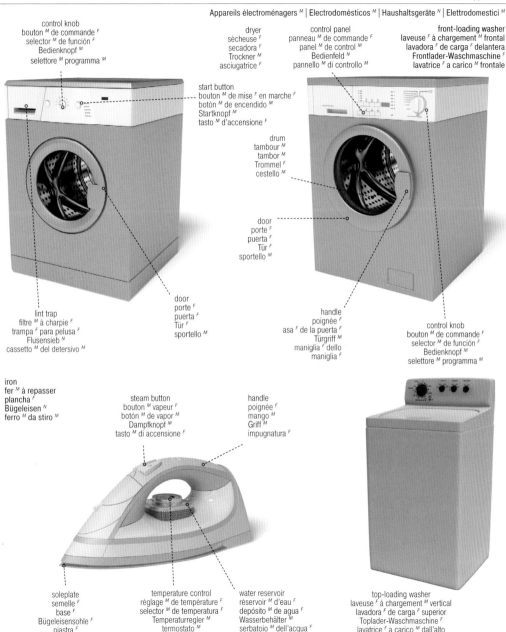

dryer
sècheuse F
secadora F
Trockner M
asciugatrice F

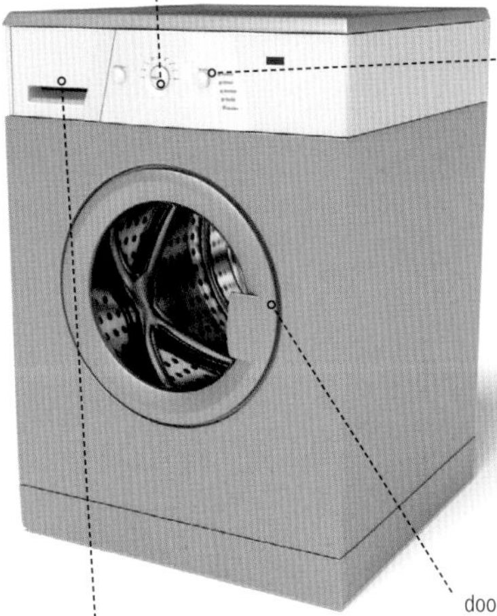
control knob
bouton M de commande F
selector M de función F
Bedienknopf M
selettore M programma M
start button
bouton M de mise F en marche F
botón M de encendido M
Startknopf M
tasto M d'accensione F
lint trap
filtre M à charpie F
trampa F para pelusa F
Flusensieb N
cassetto M del detersivo M
door
porte F
puerta F
Tür F
sportello M

front-loading washer
laveuse F à chargement M frontal
lavadora F de carga F delantera
Frontlader-Waschmaschine F
lavatrice F a carico M frontale

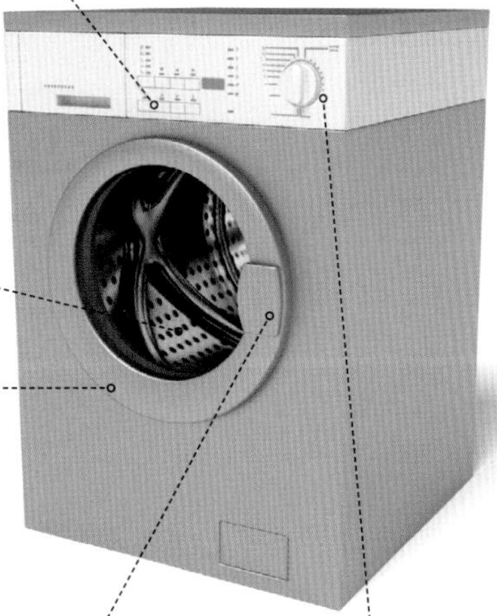
control panel
panneau M de commande F
panel M de control M
Bedienfeld N
pannello M di controllo M
drum
tambour M
tambor M
Trommel F
cestello M
door
porte F
puerta F
Tür F
sportello M
handle
poignée F
asa F de la puerta F
Türgriff M
maniglia F dello
maniglia F
control knob
bouton M de commande F
selector M de función F
Bedienknopf M
selettore M programma M

iron
fer M à repasser
plancha F
Bügeleisen N
ferro M da stiro M

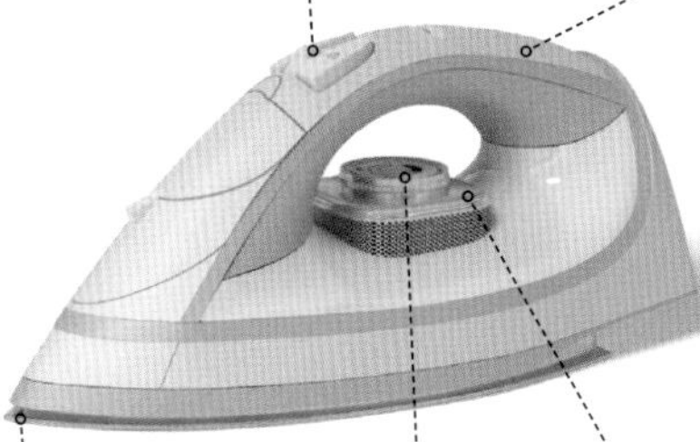
steam button
bouton M vapeur F
botón M de vapor M
Dampfknopf M
tasto M di accensione F
handle
poignée F
mango M
Griff M
impugnatura F
soleplate
semelle F
base F
Bügeleisensohle F
piastra F
temperature control
réglage M de température F
selector M de temperatura F
Temperaturregler M
termostato M
water reservoir
réservoir M d'eau F
depósito M de agua F
Wasserbehälter M
serbatoio M dell'acqua F

top-loading washer
laveuse F à chargement M vertical
lavadora F de carga F superior
Toplader-Waschmaschine F
lavatrice F a carico M dall'alto

ceiling fan
ventilateur ^{M} de plafond ^{M}
ventilador ^{M} de techo ^{M}
Deckenventilator ^{M}
ventilatore ^{M} da soffitto ^{M}

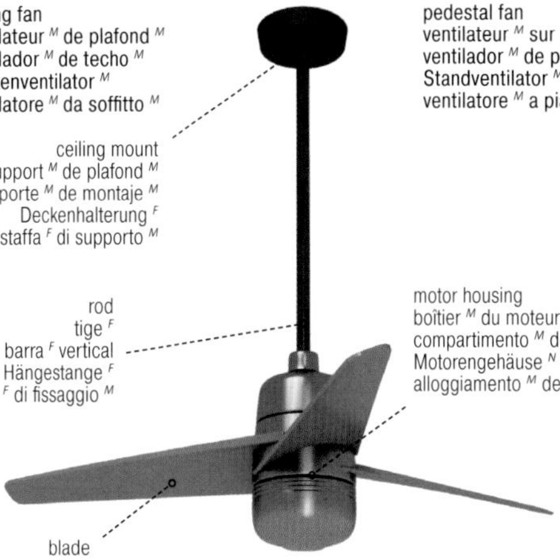

ceiling mount
support ^{M} de plafond ^{M}
soporte ^{M} de montaje ^{M}
Deckenhalterung ^{F}
staffa ^{F} di supporto ^{M}

rod
tige ^{F}
barra ^{F} vertical
Hängestange ^{F}
asta ^{F} di fissaggio ^{M}

motor housing
boîtier ^{M} du moteur ^{M}
compartimento ^{M} del motor ^{M}
Motorengehäuse ^{N}
alloggiamento ^{M} del motore ^{M}

blade
pale ^{F}
aspa ^{M}
Flügel ^{M}
pala ^{F}

pedestal fan
ventilateur ^{M} sur pied ^{M}
ventilador ^{M} de pie ^{M}
Standventilator ^{M}
ventilatore ^{M} a piantana ^{F}

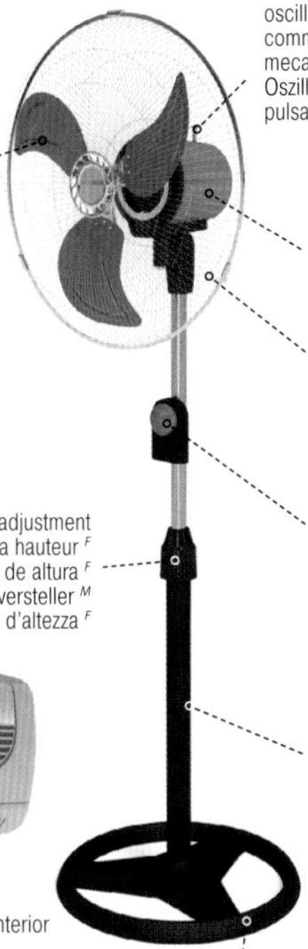

oscillation control
commande ^{F} d'oscillation ^{F}
mecanismo ^{M} de oscilación ^{F}
Oszillationsschalter ^{M}
pulsante ^{M} per oscillazione ^{F}

blade
lame ^{F}
aspa ^{F}
Flügel ^{F}
pala ^{F}

motor housing
boîtier ^{M} du moteur ^{M}
compartimento ^{M} del motor ^{M}
Motorengehäuse ^{N}
alloggiamento ^{M} del motore ^{M}

safety guard
grille ^{F} de protection ^{F}
protector ^{M} de seguridad ^{F}
Schutzgitter ^{N}
griglia ^{F} di protezione ^{F}

height adjustment
réglage ^{M} de la hauteur ^{F}
ajuste ^{M} de altura ^{F}
Höhenversteller ^{M}
regolatore ^{M} d'altezza ^{F}

speed control
commande ^{F} de vitesse ^{F}
control ^{M} de velocidad ^{F}
Geschwindigkeitsregler ^{M}
regolatore ^{M} di velocità ^{F}

stand
pied ^{M}
soporte ^{M}
Stand ^{M}
supporto ^{M}

base
base ^{F}
base ^{F}
Fußteil ^{N}
base ^{F}

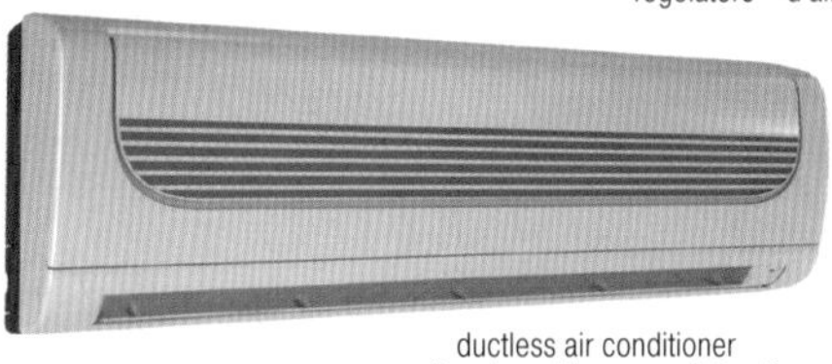

ductless air conditioner
climatiseur ^{M} sans conduites ^{F}
aparato ^{M} de aire ^{M} acondicionado interior
mobile Klimaanlage ^{F}
unità ^{F} interna del condizionatore ^{M}

canister vacuum cleaner
aspirateur-traîneau ^{M}
aspiradora ^{F}
Kanister-Staubsauger ^{M}
aspirapolvere ^{M}

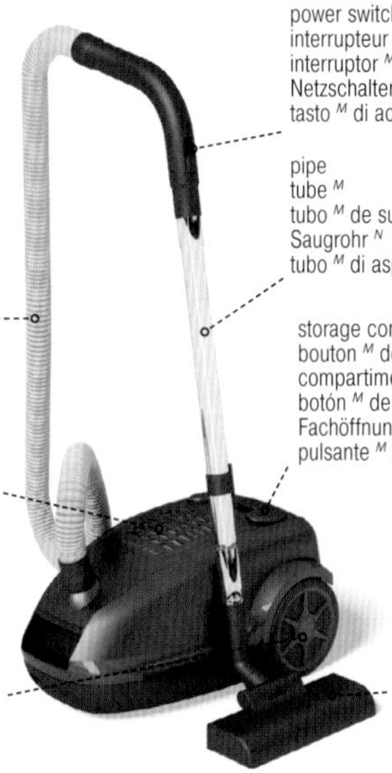

power switch
interrupteur d'alimentation ^{M}
interruptor ^{M}
Netzschalter ^{M}
tasto ^{M} di accensione ^{F}

pipe
tube ^{M}
tubo ^{M} de succión ^{F}
Saugrohr ^{N}
tubo ^{M} di aspirazione ^{F}

hose
tuyau ^{M}
manguera ^{F}
Schlauch ^{M}
tubo ^{M}

storage compartment release button
bouton ^{M} déclencheur ^{M} du compartiment ^{M} de rangement ^{M}
botón ^{M} de apertura ^{F} del depósito ^{M}
Fachöffnungsknopf ^{M}
pulsante ^{M} di rilascio ^{M} del vano ^{M}

ventillation grille
grille ^{F} de ventilation ^{F}
rejilla ^{F} de ventilación ^{F}
Lüftungsgitter ^{N}
valvola ^{F} di sfiato ^{M}

wheel
roue ^{F}
rueda ^{F}
Rad ^{N}
ruota ^{F}

rug and floor brush
brosse ^{F} à tapis ^{M} et planchers ^{M}
cepillo ^{M} para pisos ^{M} y alfombras ^{F}
Teppich- und Fußbodenbürste ^{F}
spazzola ^{F}

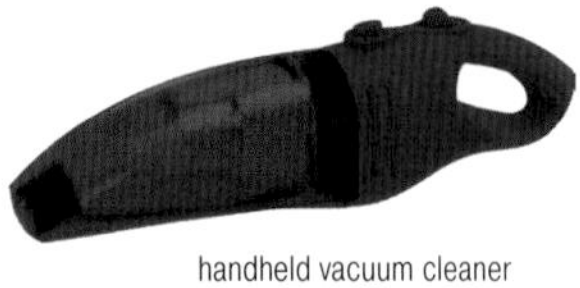

handheld vacuum cleaner
aspirateur ^{M} portatif
aspiradora ^{F} de mano ^{F}
Akkusauger ^{M}
aspirapolvere ^{M} portatile

robotic vacuum cleaner
aspirateur ^{M} robot ^{M}
aspiradora ^{F} automática
Roboterstaubsauger ^{M}
aspirapolvere ^{M} robot

upright vacuum cleaner
aspirateur ^{M} vertical/balai
aspiradora ^{F} vertical
Bürststaubsauger ^{M}
aspirapolvere ^{M} verticale

Audiovisual equipment

Matériel [M] audiovisuel | Equipo [M] audiovisual | Audiovisuelle Geräte [N] | Apparecchiature [F] audiovisive

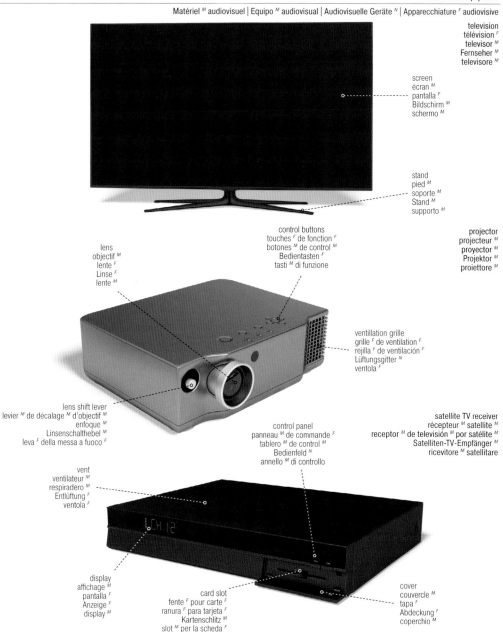

television
télévision [F]
televisor [M]
Fernseher [M]
televisore [M]
screen
écran [M]
pantalla [F]
Bildschirm [M]
schermo [M]
stand
pied [M]
soporte [M]
Stand [M]
supporto [M]

projector
projecteur [M]
proyector [M]
Projektor [M]
proiettore [M]
lens
objectif [M]
lente [F]
Linse [F]
lente [M]
control buttons
touches [F] de fonction [F]
botones [M] de control [M]
Bedientasten [F]
tasti [M] di funzione
ventillation grille
grille [F] de ventilation [F]
rejilla [F] de ventilación [F]
Lüftungsgitter [N]
ventola [F]
lens shift lever
levier [M] de décalage [M] d'objectif [M]
enfoque [M]
Linsenschalthebel [M]
leva [F] della messa a fuoco [F]

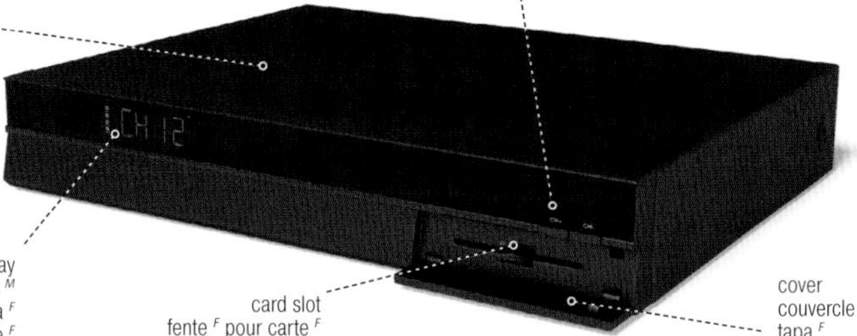
satellite TV receiver
récepteur [M] satellite [M]
receptor [M] de televisión [M] por satélite [M]
Satelliten-TV-Empfänger [M]
ricevitore [M] satellitare
control panel
panneau [M] de commande [F]
tablero [M] de control [M]
Bedienfeld [N]
annello [M] di controllo
vent
ventilateur [M]
respiradero [M]
Entlüftung [F]
ventola [F]
display
affichage [M]
pantalla [F]
Anzeige [F]
display [M]
card slot
fente [F] pour carte [F]
ranura [F] para tarjeta [F]
Kartenschlitz [M]
slot [M] per la scheda [F]
cover
couvercle [M]
tapa [F]
Abdeckung [F]
coperchio [M]

sound system
chaîne F audio
sistema M de sonido M
Lautsprecheranlage F
impianto M acustico

main speaker
haut-parleur M principal
altavoz M principal
Hauptlautsprecher M
colonna F frontale

subwoofer
haut-parleur M d'extrêmes graves M
subwoofer M
Subwoofer M
subwoofer M

stand
support M
soporte M
Ständer M
supporto M

surround speaker
haut-parleur M ambiophonique
altavoz M central
Surround-Lautsprecher M
colonna F posteriore

base
base F
base F
Fußteil N
base F

headphones
écouteurs M
auriculares M
Kopfhörer M
cuffie F

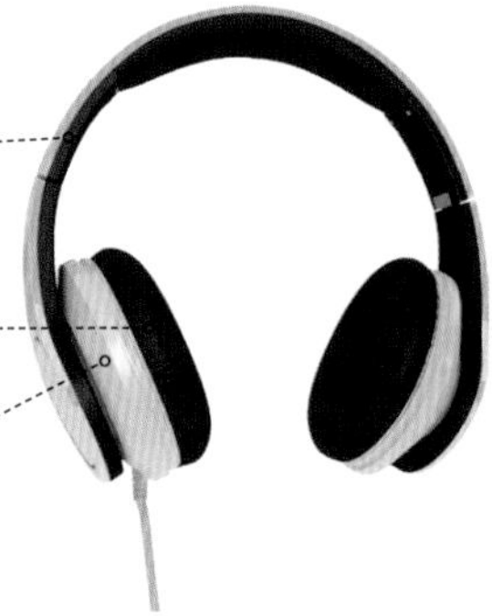

headband
serre-tête M
montura F
Kopfhörerbügel M
archetto M

ear cushion
coussinet M d'oreille F
almohadilla F acústica
Ohrpolster N
cuscinetto M

earphone
écouteur M
auricular M
Hörer M
auricolari M

remote control
télécommande F
control M remoto
Fernbedienung F
telecomando M

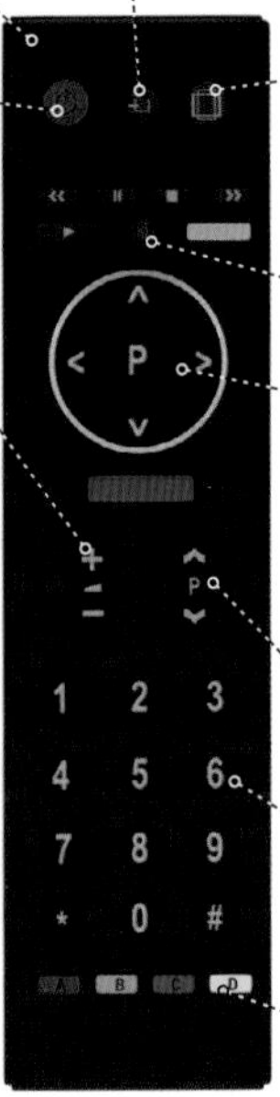

casing
boîtier M
revestimiento M
Gehäuse N
involucro M

input button
bouton M d'entrée F
botón M de entrada F
Eingabeknopf M
tasto M input M

image format button
bouton M de format M de l'image F
botón M de formato M de imagen F
Bildformatknopf M
tasto M formato M immagine F

standby button
bouton M de veille F
botón M de standby M
Standby-Knopf M
tasto M standby M

play button
bouton M de lecture F
botón M de reproducción M
Abspielknopf M
tasto M play M

volume control
contrôle M du volume M
control M de volumen M
Lautstärkeregler M
controllo M volume M

control pad
touche F de commande F
rueda F de control M
Schaltregler M
pulsantiera F di comando M

channel scan button
bouton M de recherche F de canal M
botón M de búsqueda F de canales
Tasten F für Programmwechsel M
tasto M scelta F canali M

channel selector buttons
boutons M de sélection F de canal
botones M selectores M de canales
Programmtaste F
tasti M dei canali M

function button
bouton M de fonction F
botón M de selección F de modo M
Funktionstaste F
tasto M funzione F

DVD player and amplifier
lecteur M DVD M et amplificateur M
reproductor M de DVD M
DVD-Player M mit Verstärker M
lettore M DVD e amplificatore M

DVD slot
fente F pour le DVD M
ranura F para DVD M
DVD-Einschub M
slot M per DVD M

DVD player
lecteur M DVD
reproductor M de DVD M
DVD-Spieler M
lettore M DVD M

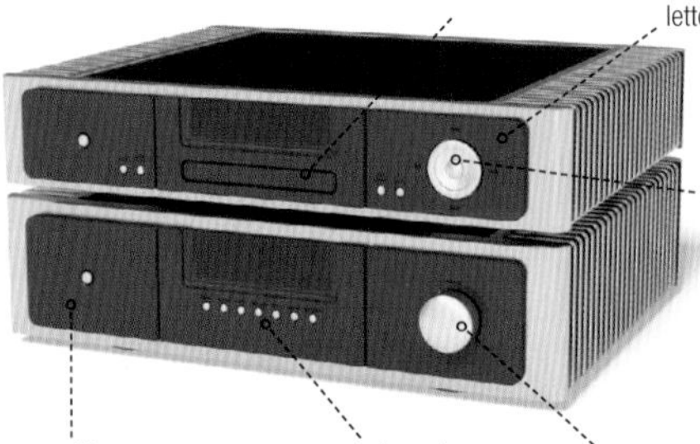

control pad
touche F de commande F
teclado M de control M
Schaltregler M
pulsantiera F di comando M

amplifier
amplificateur M
amplificador M
Verstärker M
amplificatore M

control panel
panneau M de commande F
tablero M de control M
Bedienfeld N
pannello M di controllo M

volume control
contrôle M du volume M
control M de volumen M
Lautstärkeregler M
controllo M volume M

Lightbulbs

Ampoules F | Bombillas F | Glühbirnen F | Lampadine F

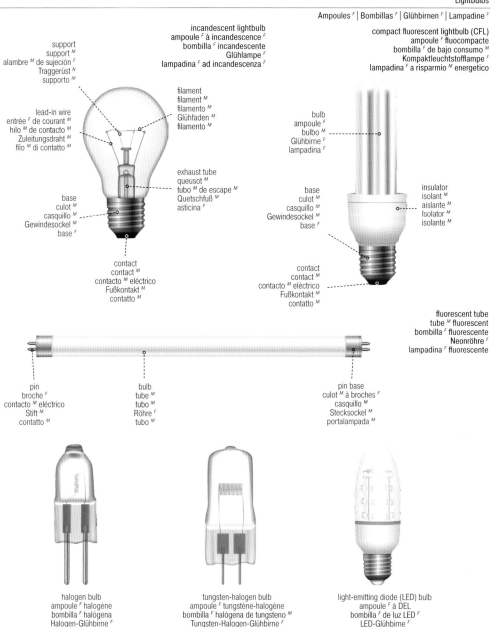

incandescent lightbulb
ampoule F à incandescence F
bombilla F incandescente
Glühlampe F
lampadina F ad incandescenza F

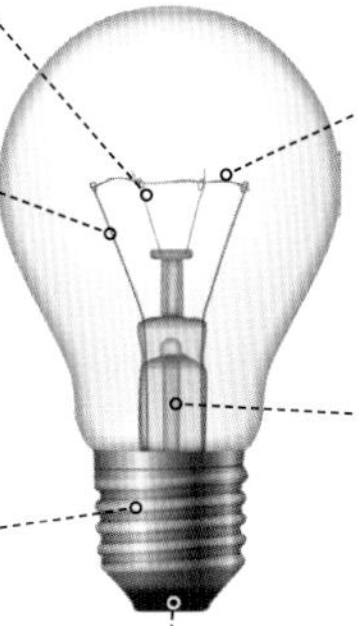
support
support M
alambre M de sujeción F
Traggerüst N
supporto M
lead-in wire
entrée F de courant M
hilo M de contacto M
Zuleitungsdraht M
filo M di contatto M
filament
filament M
filamento M
Glühfaden M
filamento M
exhaust tube
queusot M
tubo M de escape M
Quetschfuß M
asticina F
base
culot M
casquillo M
Gewindesockel M
base F
contact
contact M
contacto M eléctrico
Fußkontakt M
contatto M

compact fluorescent lightbulb (CFL)
ampoule F fluocompacte
bombilla F de bajo consumo M
Kompaktleuchtstofflampe F
lampadina F a risparmio M energetico

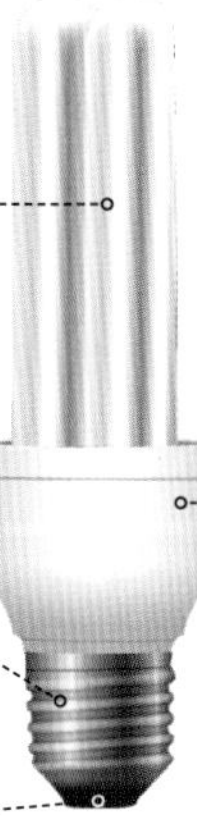
bulb
ampoule F
bulbo M
Glühbirne F
lampadina F
base
culot M
casquillo M
Gewindesockel M
base F
insulator
isolant M
aislante M
Isolator M
isolante M
contact
contact M
contacto M eléctrico
Fußkontakt M
contatto M

fluorescent tube
tube M fluorescent
bombilla F fluorescente
Neonröhre F
lampadina F fluorescente

pin
broche F
contacto M eléctrico
Stift M
contatto M
bulb
tube M
tubo M
Röhre F
tubo M
pin base
culot M à broches F
casquillo M
Stecksockel M
portalampada M

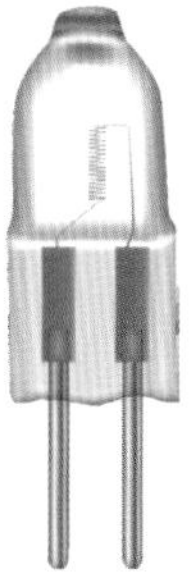

halogen bulb
ampoule F halogène
bombilla F halógena
Halogen-Glühbirne F
lampadina F alogena

tungsten-halogen bulb
ampoule F tungstène-halogène
bombilla F halógena de tungsteno M
Tungsten-Halogen-Glühbirne F
lampada F alogena al tungsteno M

light-emitting diode (LED) bulb
ampoule F à DEL
bombilla F de luz LED F
LED-Glühbirne F
lampada F a LED

Light fixtures and lamps

Luminaires ^{M} et lampes ^{F} | Lámparas ^{F} e iluminación ^{F} | Leuchtkörper ^{M} und Lampen ^{F} | Impianti ^{M} d'illuminazione ^{F} e lampade ^{F}

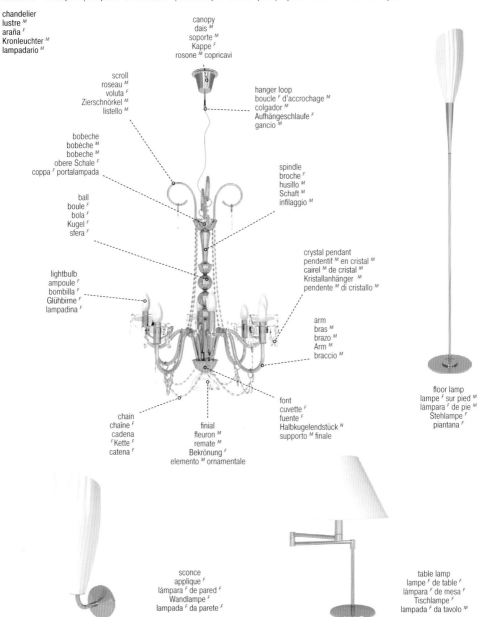

chandelier
lustre ^{M}
araña ^{F}
Kronleuchter ^{M}
lampadario ^{M}

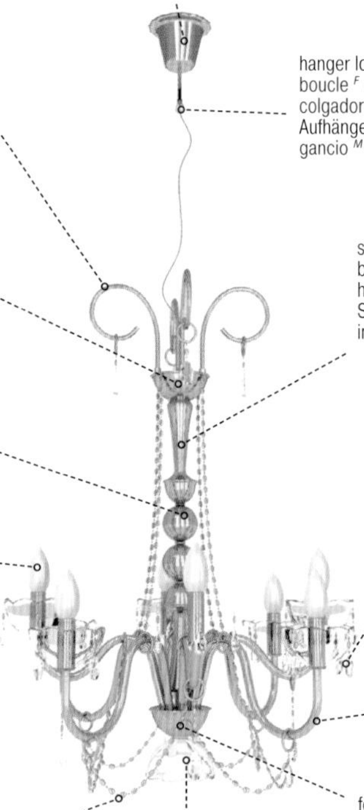

canopy
dais ^{M}
soporte ^{M}
Kappe ^{F}
rosone ^{M} copricavi

scroll
roseau ^{M}
voluta ^{F}
Zierschnörkel ^{M}
listello ^{M}

hanger loop
boucle ^{F} d'accrochage ^{M}
colgador ^{M}
Aufhängeschlaufe ^{F}
gancio ^{M}

bobeche
bobèche ^{M}
bobeche ^{M}
obere Schale ^{F}
coppa ^{F} portalampada

spindle
broche ^{F}
husillo ^{M}
Schaft ^{M}
infilaggio ^{M}

ball
boule ^{F}
bola ^{F}
Kugel ^{F}
sfera ^{F}

crystal pendant
pendentif ^{M} en cristal ^{M}
cairel ^{M} de cristal ^{M}
Kristallanhänger ^{M}
pendente ^{M} di cristallo ^{M}

lightbulb
ampoule ^{F}
bombilla ^{F}
Glühbirne ^{F}
lampadina ^{F}

arm
bras ^{M}
brazo ^{M}
Arm ^{M}
braccio ^{M}

chain
chaîne ^{F}
cadena
^{F} Kette ^{F}
catena ^{F}

finial
fleuron ^{M}
remate ^{M}
Bekrönung ^{F}
elemento ^{M} ornamentale

font
cuvette ^{F}
fuente ^{F}
Halbkugelendstück ^{N}
supporto ^{M} finale

floor lamp
lampe ^{F} sur pied ^{M}
lámpara ^{F} de pie ^{M}
Stehlampe ^{F}
piantana ^{F}

sconce
applique ^{F}
lámpara ^{F} de pared ^{F}
Wandlampe ^{F}
lampada ^{F} da parete ^{F}

table lamp
lampe ^{F} de table ^{F}
lámpara ^{F} de mesa ^{F}
Tischlampe ^{F}
lampada ^{F} da tavolo ^{M}

floor lamp
lampe [F] sur pied [M]
lámpara [F] de pie [M]
Stehlampe [F]
piantana [F]

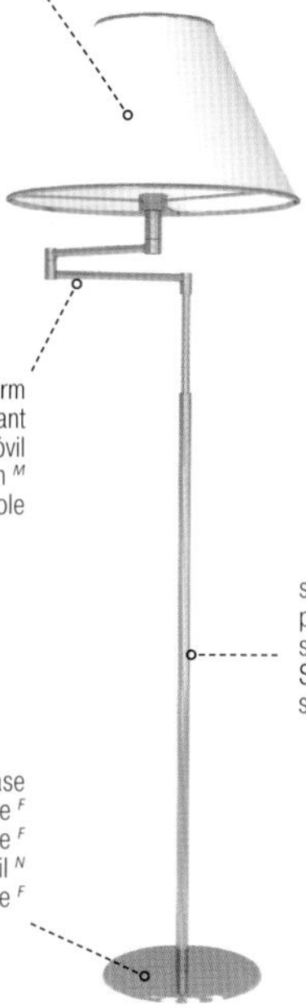

lampshade
abat-jour [M]
pantalla [F]
Lampenschirm [M]
paralume [M]

swivel arm
bras [M] pivotant
brazo [M] móvil
Schwenkarm [M]
braccio [M] girevole

stand
pied [M]
soporte [M]
Stiel [M]
supporto [M]

base
base [F]
base [F]
Fußteil [N]
base [F]

hanging pendant
luminaire [M] suspendu
lámpara [F] colgante
Hängelampe [F]
lampada [F] a sospensione [F]

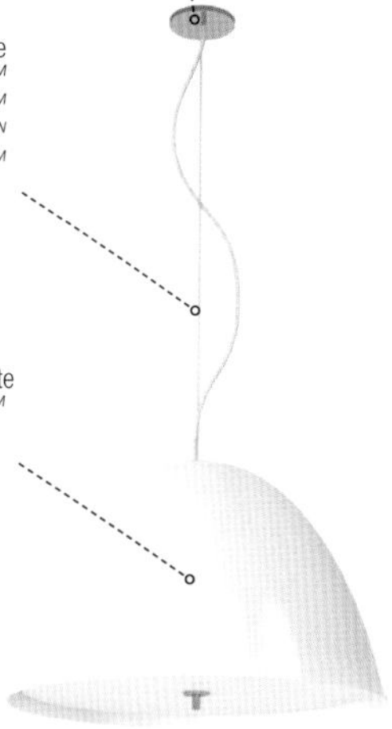

ceiling mount
support [M] de plafond [M]
soporte [M] de techo [M]
Deckenhalterung [F]
calotta [F]

wire
fil [M]
cable [M]
Kabel [N]
cavo [M]

shade
abat-jour [M]
pantalla [F] colgante
Lampenschirm [M]
paralume [M]

ceiling fixture
plafonnier [M]
lámpara [F] de techo [M]
Deckenlampe [F]
plafoniera [F]

hanging track lighting
éclairage [M] sur rail [M] suspendu
lámpara [F] de guía [F] suspendida
hängende Lichtschiene [F]
lampada [F] su binario [M] a sospensione [F]

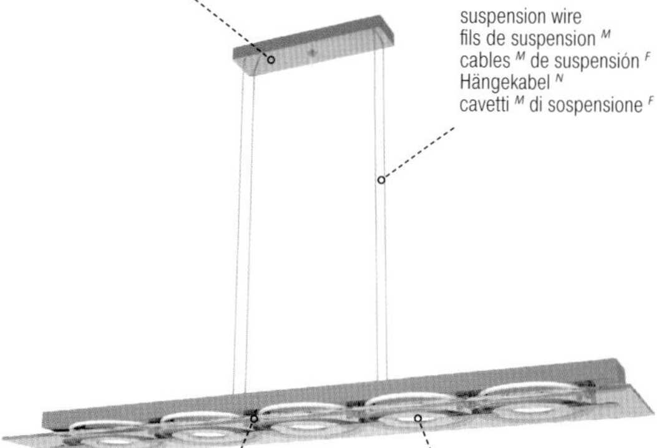

ceiling mount
support [M] de plafond [M]
soporte [M] de techo [M]
Deckenhalterung [F]
calotta [F]

suspension wire
fils de suspension [M]
cables [M] de suspensión [F]
Hängekabel [N]
cavetti [M] di sospensione [F]

track
rail [M]
carril [M]
Schiene [F]
binario [M]

lightbulb
ampoule [F]
foco [M]
Glühbirne [F]
lampadina [F]

Electrical fittings

Raccords [M] électriques | Accesorios [M] eléctricos | Stromarmaturen [F] | Impianti [M] elettrici

light socket
douille [F] de lampe [F]
portalámparas [M]
Birnenfassung [F]
faretto [M]

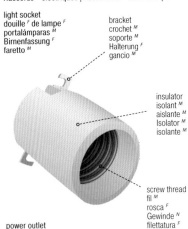

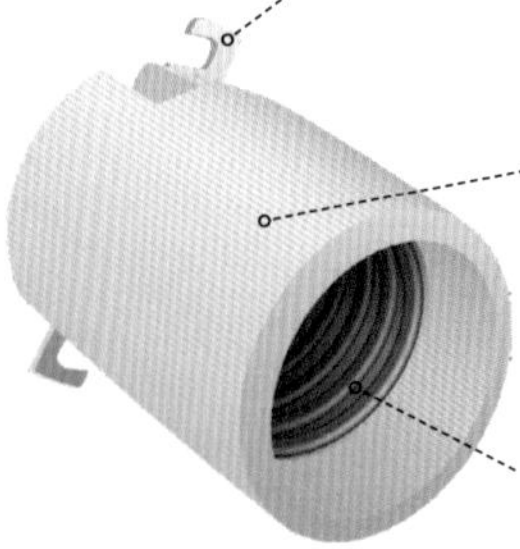
bracket
crochet [M]
soporte [M]
Halterung [F]
gancio [M]
insulator
isolant [M]
aislante [M]
Isolator [M]
isolante [M]
screw thread
fil [M]
rosca [F]
Gewinde [N]
filettatura [F]

cross section of a plug
vue [F] en coupe [F] d'une fiche [F] mâle
sección [F] transversal de un enchufe [M]
Querschnitt eines Steckers [M]
sezione [F] trasversale di una spina [F]

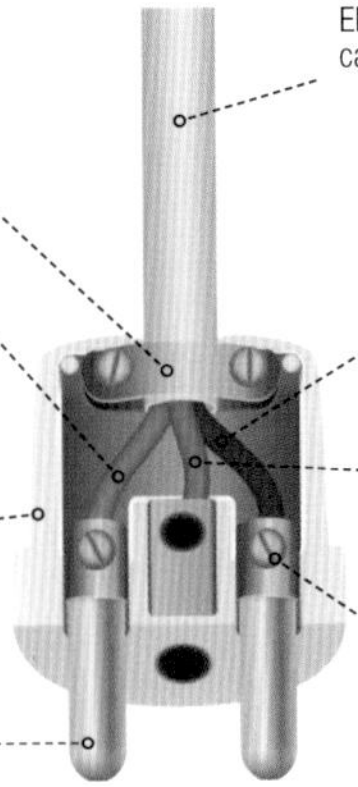
cord
cordon [M]
cable [M] eléctrico
Elektrokabel [N]
cavo [M] elettrico
clamp
étrier [M]
abrazadera [F]
Kabelklemme [F]
fermacavo [M]
neutral wire
fil [M] neutre
cable [M] neutro
Neutralleiter [M]
filo [M] neutro
hot wire
fil [M] sous-tension
cable [M] de fase [F]
Hitzdraht [M]
filo [M] caldo
ground wire
fil [M] de terre [F]
cable [M] de tierra [M]
Erdleiter [M]
filo [M] di terra [F]
cover
couvercle [M]
cuerpo [M]
Gehäuse [N]
corpo [M]
terminal
vis [M]
terminal [M]
Klemmschraube [F]
vite [F]
pin
broche [F]
clavija [F]
Kontakt [M]
polo [M]

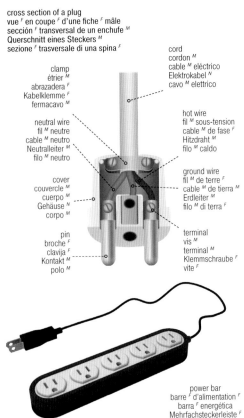

power outlet
prise [F] de courant [M]
enchufe [M]
amerikanische Steckdose [F]
presa [F] elettrica

cover plate
plaque [F] de recouvrement [M]
tapa [F]
Abdeckplatte [F]
piastra [F] copripresa
socket contact
contact [M] femelle
agujero [M] para clavija [F]
Kontaktloch [N]
foro [M] per la spina [F] di corrente [F]

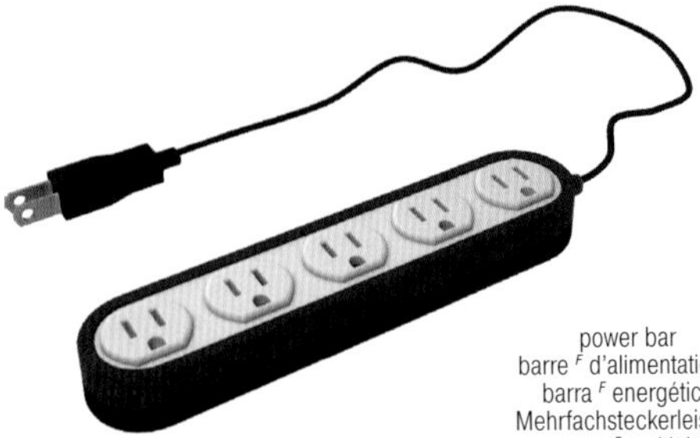

power bar
barre [F] d'alimentation [F]
barra [F] energética
Mehrfachsteckerleiste [F]
presa [F] multipla

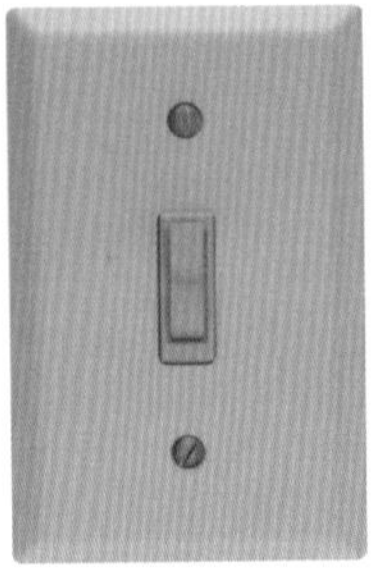

switch
interrupteur [M]
interruptor [M]
Schalter [M]
interruttore [M]

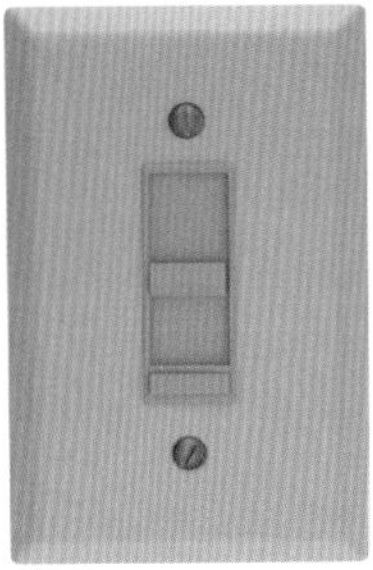

dimmer switch
gradateur [M]
interruptor [M] con regulador [M]
Dimmer [M]
variatore [M] di luminosità [F]

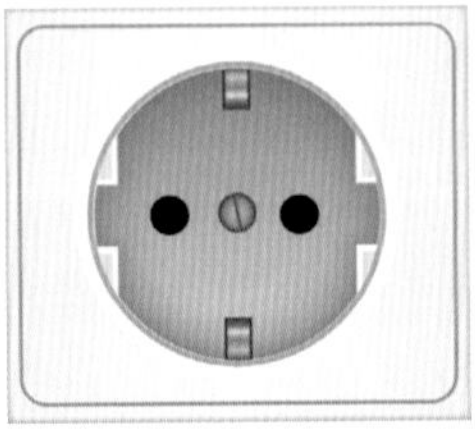

European power outlet
prise [F] de courant [M] européenne
enchufe [M] europeo
Europäische Steckdose [F]
presa [F] elettrica europea

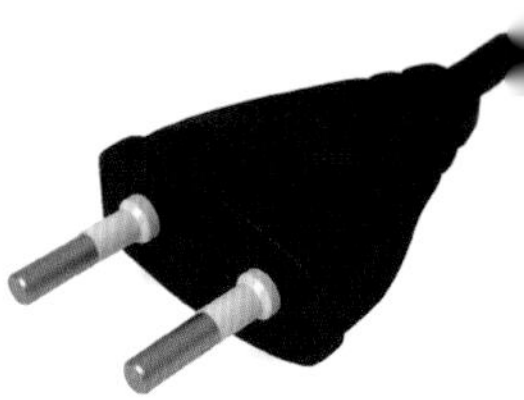

European/round-pin plug
fiche [F] mâle européen
enchufe [M] europeo
Europäischer / Rundstecker [M]
spina [F]

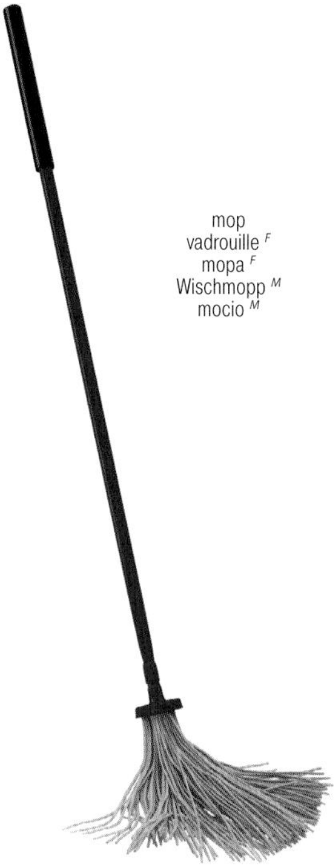

mop
vadrouille [F]
mopa [F]
Wischmopp [M]
mocio [M]

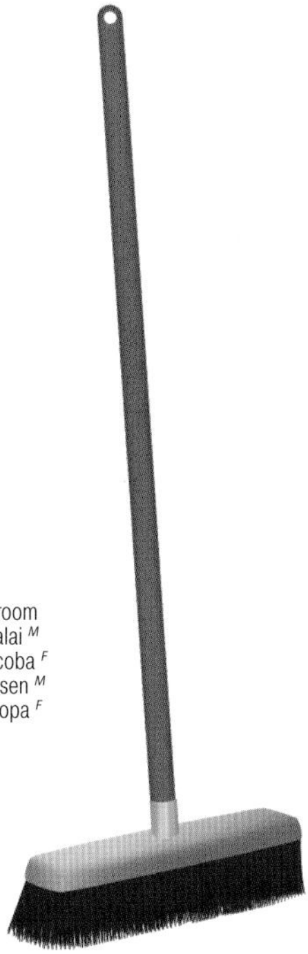

broom
balai [M]
escoba [F]
Besen [M]
scopa [F]

flat mop
balai [M] à laver plat
mopa [F]
Flachmopp [M]
scopa [F] lavapavimenti

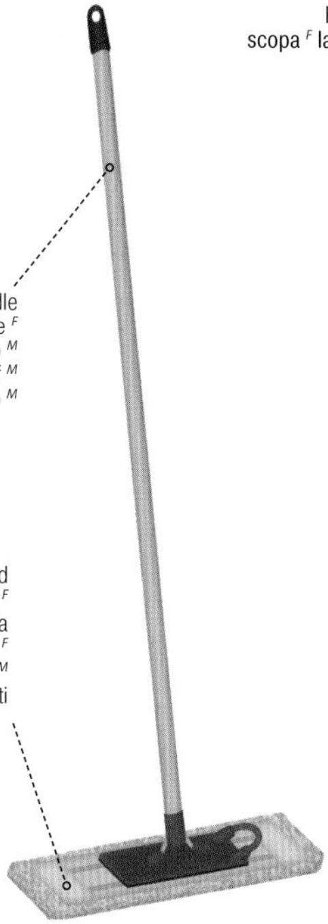

handle
manche [F]
palo [M]
Griff [M]
manico [M]

mop head
tête [F] de vadrouille [F]
cabeza [F] de la mopa [F]
Moppkopf [M]
testa [F] lavapavimenti

bucket
seau [M]
cubo [M]
Eimer [M]
secchio [M]

scrub brush
brosse [F] à récurage [M]
cepillo [M] de cerdas [F]
Scheuerbürste [F]
spazzola [F]

dustpan
porte-poussière [M]
recogedor [M]
Kehrblech [N]
paletta [F]

wastebasket
poubelle [F]
cesto [M] de basura [F]
Abfalleimer [M]
bidoncino [M]

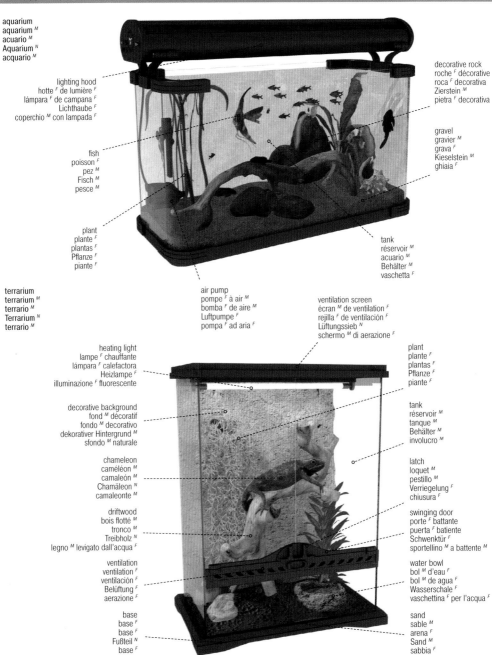

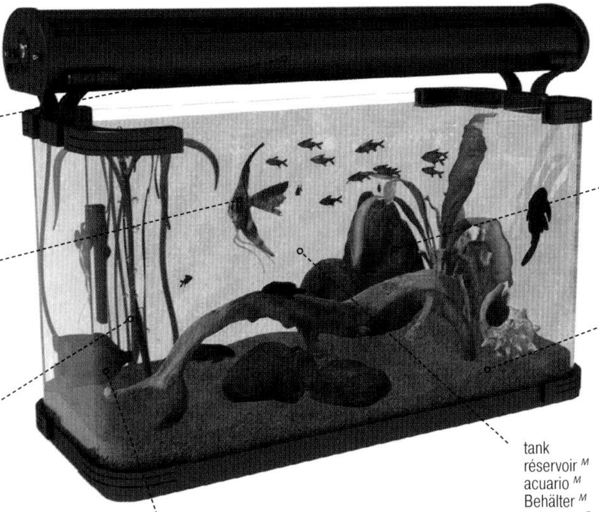
aquarium
aquarium [M]
acuario [M]
Aquarium [N]
acquario [M]
lighting hood
hotte [F] de lumière [F]
lámpara [F] de campana [F]
Lichthaube [F]
coperchio [M] con lampada [F]
fish
poisson [F]
pez [M]
Fisch [M]
pesce [M]
plant
plante [F]
plantas [F]
Pflanze [F]
piante [F]
air pump
pompe [F] à air [M]
bomba [F] de aire [M]
Luftpumpe [F]
pompa [F] ad aria [F]
decorative rock
roche [F] décorative
roca [F] decorativa
Zierstein [M]
pietra [F] decorativa
gravel
gravier [M]
grava [F]
Kieselstein [M]
ghiaia [F]
tank
réservoir [M]
acuario [M]
Behälter [M]
vaschetta [F]

terrarium
terrarium [M]
terrario [M]
Terrarium [N]
terrario [M]
ventilation screen
écran [M] de ventilation [F]
rejilla [F] de ventilación [F]
Lüftungssieb [N]
schermo [M] di aerazione [F]
heating light
lampe [F] chauffante
lámpara [F] calefactora
Heizlampe [F]
illuminazione [F] fluorescente
decorative background
fond [M] décoratif
fondo [M] decorativo
dekorativer Hintergrund [M]
sfondo [M] naturale
chameleon
caméléon [M]
camaleón [M]
Chamäleon [N]
camaleonte [M]
driftwood
bois flotté [M]
tronco [M]
Treibholz [N]
legno [M] levigato dall'acqua [F]
ventilation
ventilation [F]
ventilación [F]
Belüftung [F]
aerazione [F]
base
base [F]
base [F]
Fußteil [N]
base [F]
plant
plante [F]
plantas [F]
Pflanze [F]
piante [F]
tank
réservoir [M]
tanque [M]
Behälter [M]
involucro [M]
latch
loquet [M]
pestillo [M]
Verriegelung [F]
chiusura [F]
swinging door
porte [F] battante
puerta [F] batiente
Schwenktür [F]
sportellino [M] a battente [M]
water bowl
bol [M] d'eau [F]
bol [M] de agua [F]
Wasserschale [F]
vaschettina [F] per l'acqua [F]
sand
sable [M]
arena [F]
Sand [M]
sabbia [F]

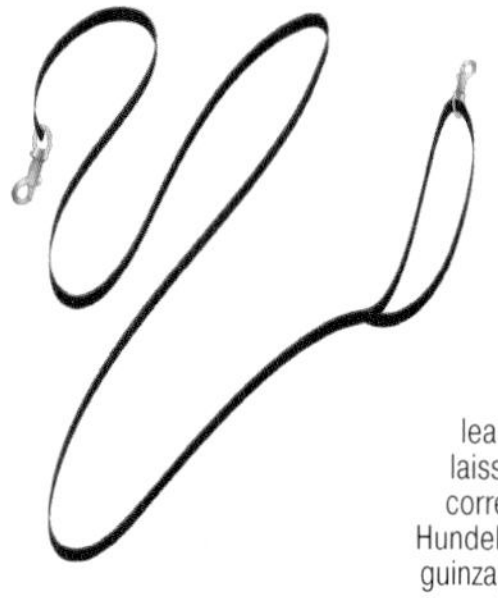

leash
laisse [F]
correa [F]
Hundeleine [F]
guinzaglio [M]

hanging ring
anneau [M] de suspension [F]
anilla [F] colgante
Aufhängring [M]
anello [M] di sospensione [F]
wire bar
fil [M] de fer [M]
estructura [F] de alambre [M]
Drahtstange [F]
barra [F] della gabbia
access door
porte d'accès [F]
puerta [F] de acceso [M]
Käfigtür [F]
ingresso [M]
parrot
perroquet [M]
loro [M]
Papagei [M]
pappagallo [M]
feeding dish
mangeoire [F]
recipiente [M] de comida [F]
Futternapf [M]
mangiatoia [F]
perch
perchoir [M]
percha [F]
Sitzstange [F]
posatoio [M]

birdcage
cage [F] à oiseaux [M]
jaula [F] de pájaro [M]
Vogelkäfig [M]
gabbia [M] per uccelli [M]

food and water bowls
bols [M] pour eau [F] et nourriture [F]
cuencos [M] de agua [F] y comida [F]
Futter- und Wassernapf [M]
ciotole [F] per cane [M]

collar
collier [M]
collar [M]
Halsband [N]
collare [M] per cane [M]

muzzle
muselière [F]
bozal [M]
Maulkorb [M]
museruola [F]

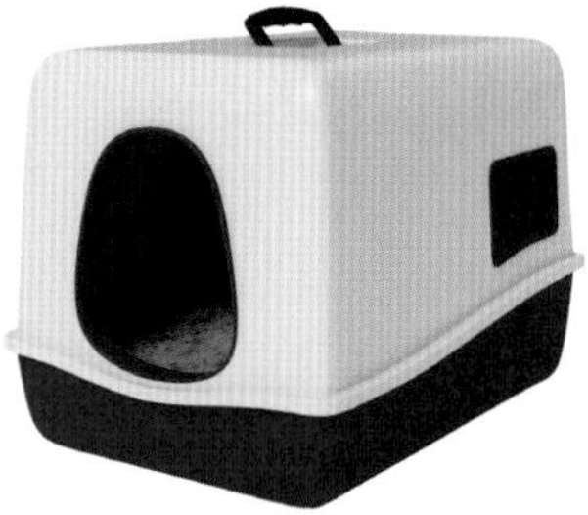

covered litter box
bac [M] à litière [F] couvert
arenero cubierto [M]
Katzentoilette [F]
cuccia [F] trasportabile

pet carrier
cage [F] de transport [M]
transporte [M] para perros [M]
Transportbox [F]
trasportino [M]

small animal cage
petite cage [F] pour animaux [M]
jaula [F] pequeña
kleiner Tierkäfig [M]
gabbietta [F]

Curtain rods

Tringles [F] à rideaux [M] | Barras [F] de cortina [F] | Vorhangstangen [F] | Bastoni [M] per tende [F]

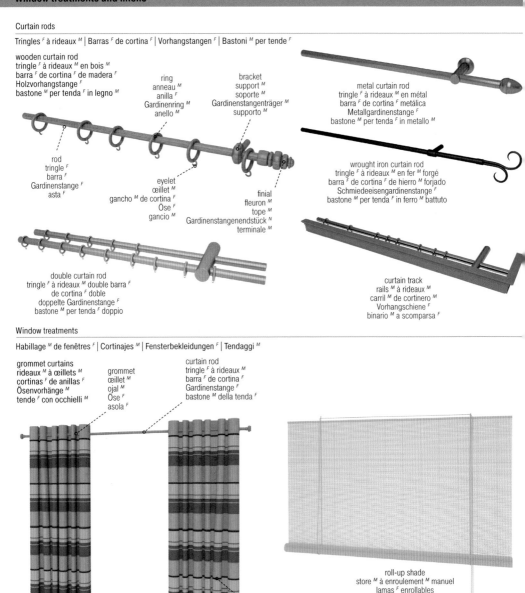

wooden curtain rod
tringle [F] à rideaux [M] en bois [M]
barra [F] de cortina [F] de madera [F]
Holzvorhangstange [F]
bastone [M] per tenda [F] in legno [M]

ring
anneau [M]
anilla [F]
Gardinenring [M]
anello [M]

bracket
support [M]
soporte [M]
Gardinenstangenträger [M]
supporto [M]

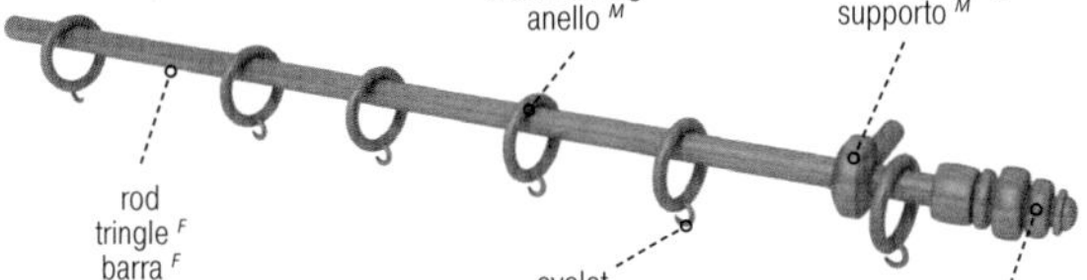

rod
tringle [F]
barra [F]
Gardinenstange [F]
asta [F]

eyelet
œillet [M]
gancho [M] de cortina [F]
Öse [F]
gancio [M]

finial
fleuron [M]
tope [M]
Gardinenstangenendstück [N]
terminale [M]

metal curtain rod
tringle [F] à rideaux [M] en métal
barra [F] de cortina [F] metálica
Metallgardinenstange [F]
bastone [M] per tenda [F] in metallo [M]

wrought iron curtain rod
tringle [F] à rideaux [M] en fer [M] forgé
barra [F] de cortina [F] de hierro [M] forjado
Schmiedeeisengardinenstange [F]
bastone [M] per tenda [F] in ferro [M] battuto

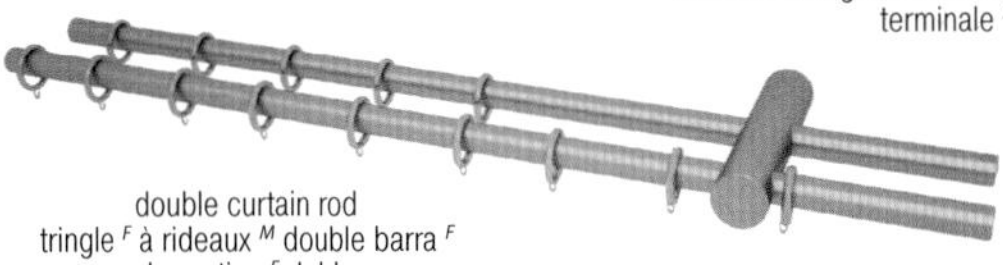

double curtain rod
tringle [F] à rideaux [M] double barra [F] de cortina [F] doble
doppelte Gardinenstange [F]
bastone [M] per tenda [F] doppio

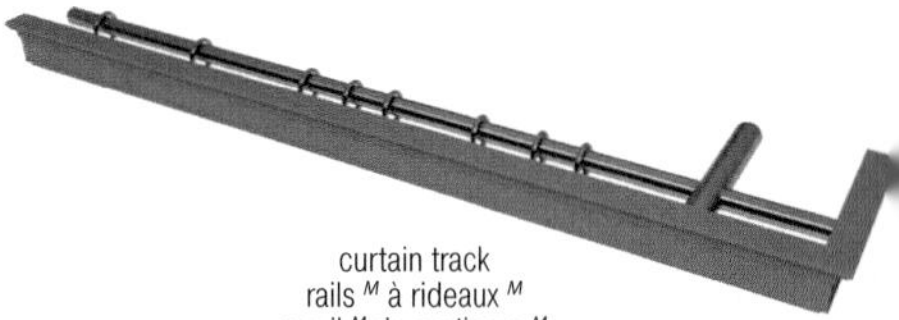

curtain track
rails [M] à rideaux [M]
carril [M] de cortinero [M]
Vorhangschiene [F]
binario [M] a scomparsa [F]

Window treatments

Habillage [M] de fenêtres [F] | Cortinajes [M] | Fensterbekleidungen [F] | Tendaggi [M]

grommet curtains
rideaux [M] à œillets [M]
cortinas [F] de anillas [F]
Ösenvorhänge [M]
tende [F] con occhielli [M]

grommet
œillet [M]
ojal [M]
Öse [F]
asola [F]

curtain rod
tringle [F] à rideaux [M]
barra [F] de cortina [F]
Gardinenstange [F]
bastone [M] della tenda [F]

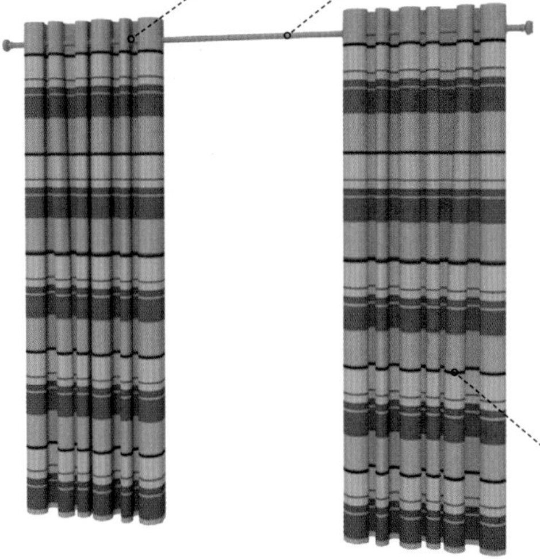

curtain
rideau [M]
cortina [F]
Vorhang [M]
tenda [F]

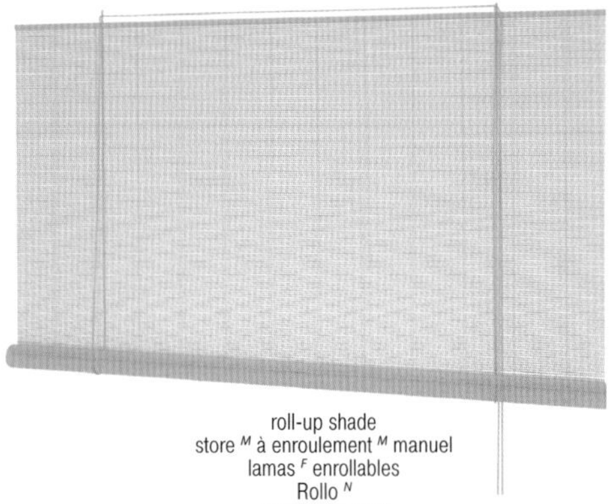

roll-up shade
store [M] à enroulement [M] manuel
lamas [F] enrollables
Rollo [N]
tenda [F] a rullo [M]

drapery
draperie F
cortinas F
Vorhänge M
tende F

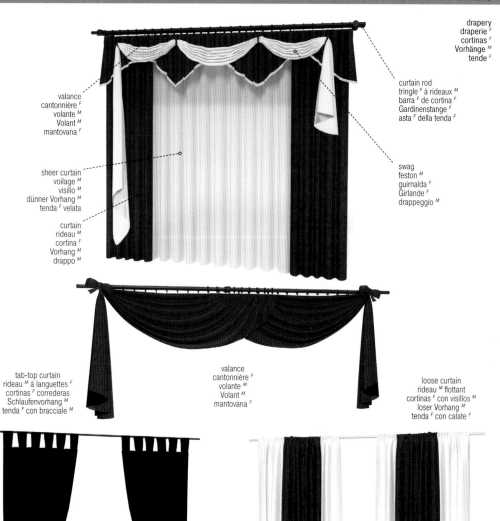

valance
cantonnière F
volante M
Volant M
mantovana F

curtain rod
tringle F à rideaux M
barra F de cortina F
Gardinenstange F
asta F della tenda F

sheer curtain
voilage M
visillo M
dünner Vorhang M
tenda F velata

swag
feston M
guirnalda F
Girlande F
drappeggio M

curtain
rideau M
cortina F
Vorhang M
drappo M

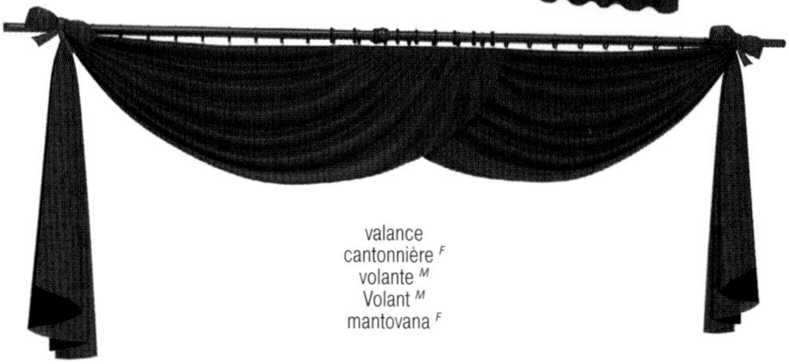

valance
cantonnière F
volante M
Volant M
mantovana F

tab-top curtain
rideau M à languettes F
cortinas F correderas
Schlaufenvorhang M
tenda F con bracciale M

loose curtain
rideau M flottant
cortinas F con visillos M
loser Vorhang M
tenda F con calate F

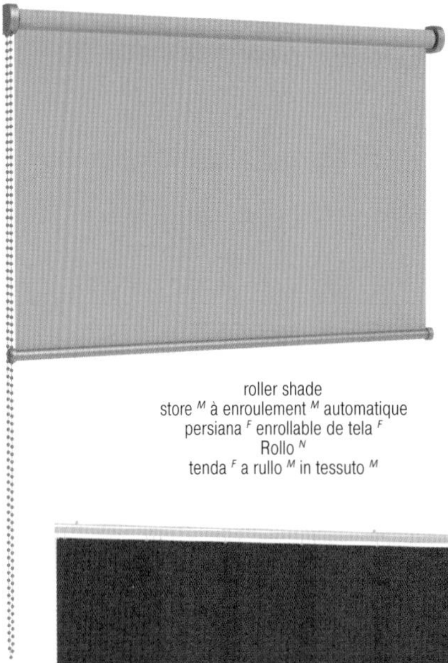

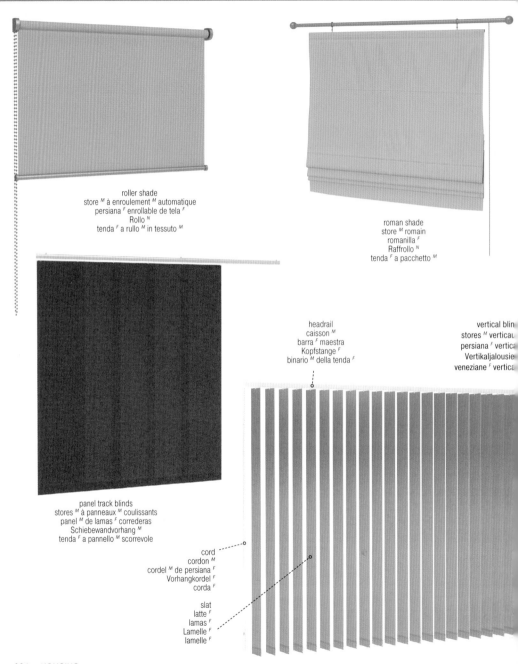

roller shade
store ^{M} à enroulement ^{M} automatique
persiana ^{F} enrollable de tela ^{F}
Rollo ^{N}
tenda ^{F} a rullo ^{M} in tessuto ^{M}

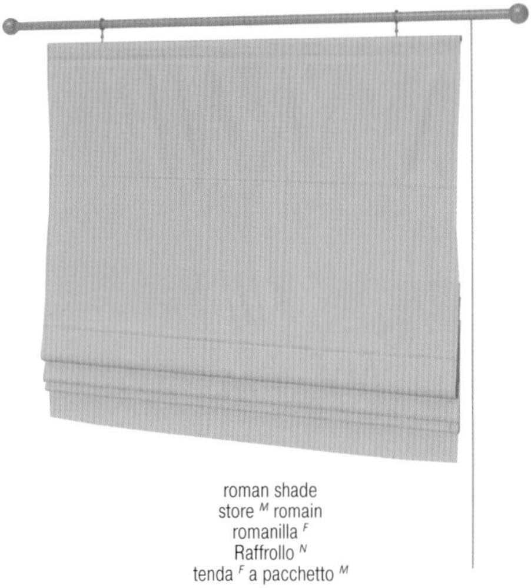

roman shade
store ^{M} romain
romanilla ^{F}
Raffrollo ^{N}
tenda ^{F} a pacchetto ^{M}

panel track blinds
stores ^{M} à panneaux ^{M} coulissants
panel ^{M} de lamas ^{F} correderas
Schiebewandvorhang ^{M}
tenda ^{F} a pannello ^{M} scorrevole

vertical blin
stores ^{M} verticau
persiana ^{F} vertica
Vertikaljalousie
veneziane ^{F} vertica

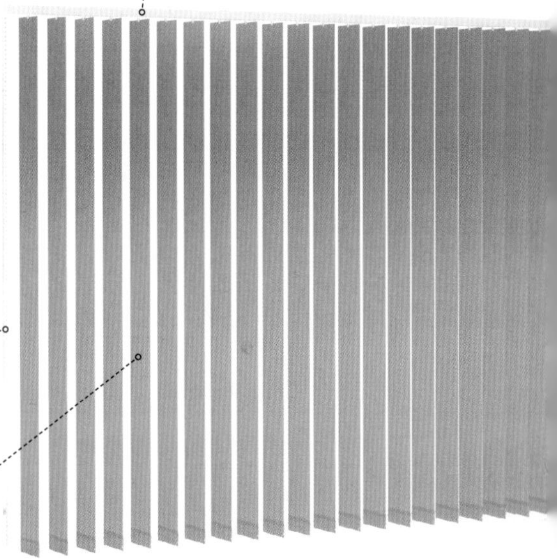
headrail
caisson ^{M}
barra ^{F} maestra
Kopfstange ^{F}
binario ^{M} della tenda ^{F}
cord
cordon ^{M}
cordel ^{M} de persiana ^{F}
Vorhangkordel ^{F}
corda ^{F}
slat
latte ^{F}
lamas ^{F}
Lamelle ^{F}
lamelle ^{F}

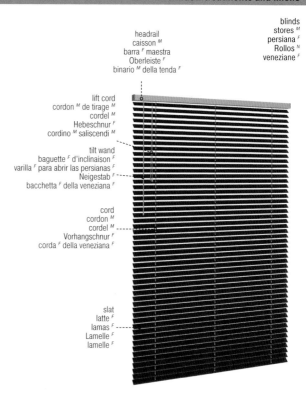

kitchen curtains
rideaux M de cuisine F
cortinillas F de cocina F
Küchenvorhänge M
tende F da cucina F

blinds
stores M
persiana F
Rollos N
veneziane F

headrail
caisson M
barra F maestra
Oberleiste F
binario M della tenda F

lift cord
cordon M de tirage M
cordel M
Hebeschnur F
cordino M saliscendi M

tilt wand
baguette F d'inclinaison F
varilla F para abrir las persianas F
Neigestab F
bacchetta F della veneziana F

cord
cordon M
cordel M
Vorhangschnur F
corda F della veneziana F

slat
latte F
lamas F
Lamelle F
lamelle F

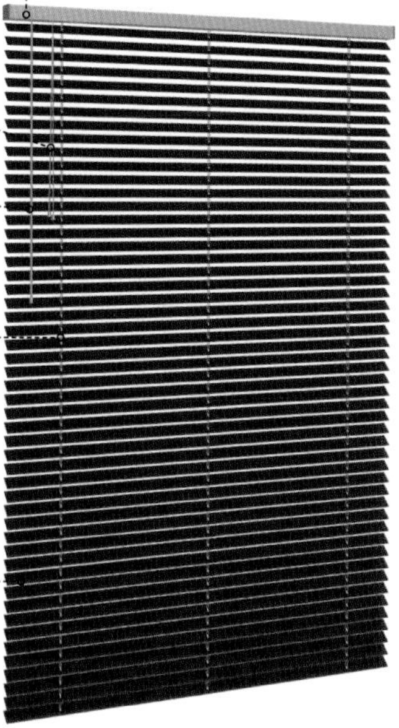

Linens

Linge M de maison F | Lencería F | Textilien N | Tessili M

bed linens
literie F
ropa F de cama F
Bettwäwsche F
biancheria F da letto M

duvet
édredon M
funda F de cobertor M
Steppdecke F
piumone M

pillowcase
taie F d'oreiller M
funda F de almohada F
Kopfkissenbezug M
cuscino M

sheet
drap M
sábana F
Bettlaken N
lenzuolo M

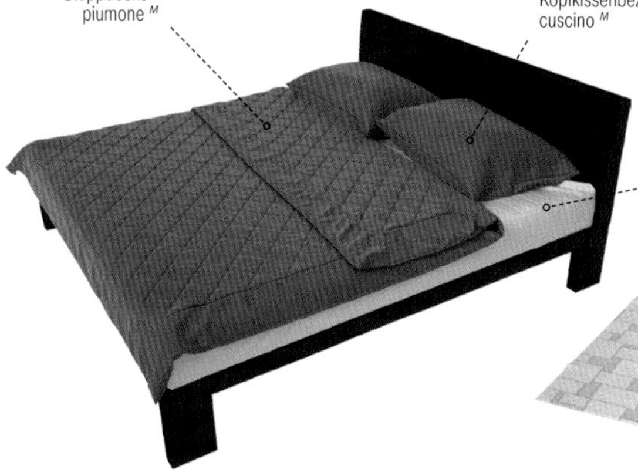

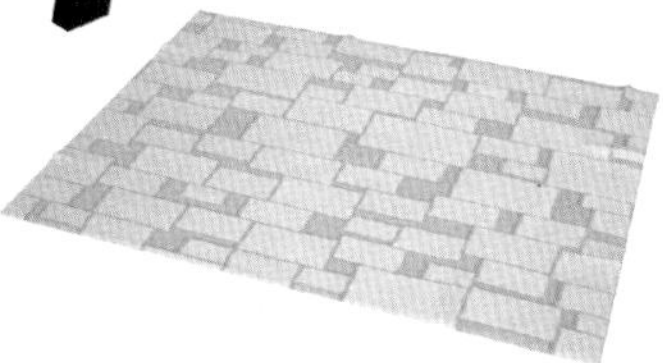

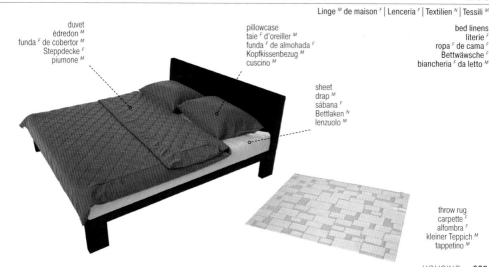

throw rug
carpette F
alfombra F
kleiner Teppich M
tappetino M

brick house
maison [F] de brique [F]
casa [F] de ladrillo [M]
Backsteinhaus [N]
casa [F] in mattoni [M]

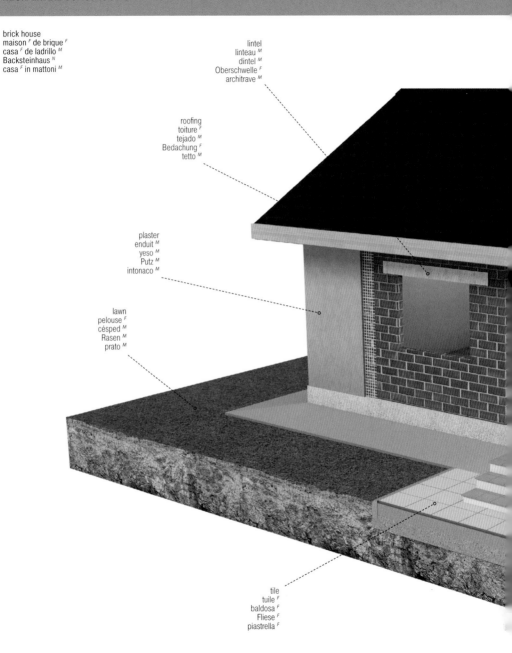

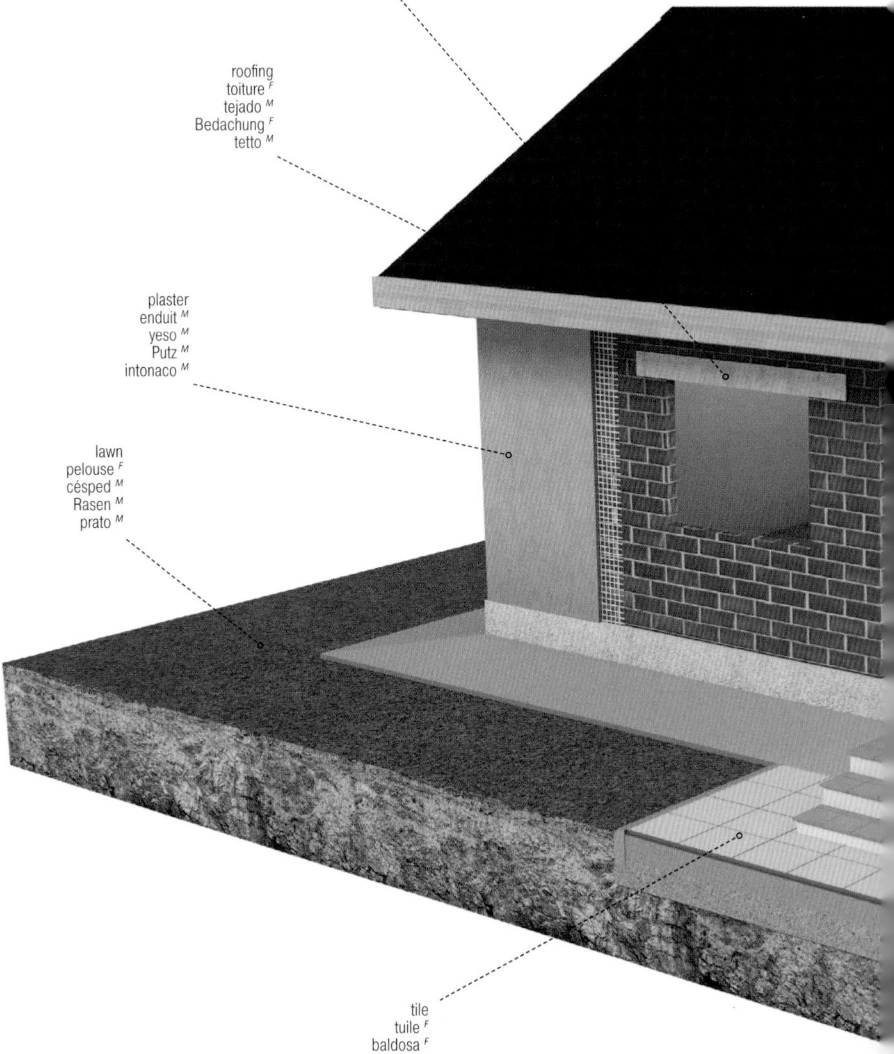
lintel
linteau [M]
dintel [M]
Oberschwelle [F]
architrave [M]
roofing
toiture [F]
tejado [M]
Bedachung [F]
tetto [M]
plaster
enduit [M]
yeso [M]
Putz [M]
intonaco [M]
lawn
pelouse [F]
césped [M]
Rasen [M]
prato [M]
tile
tuile [F]
baldosa [F]
Fliese [F]
piastrella [F]

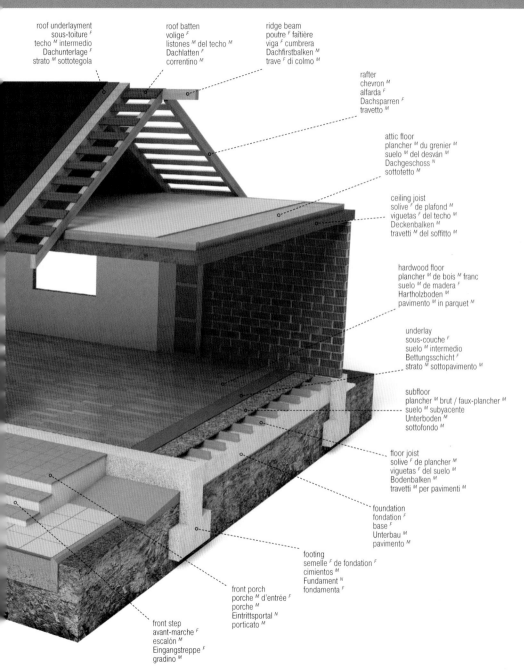

roof underlayment
sous-toiture F
techo M intermedio
Dachunterlage F
strato M sottotegola
roof batten
volige F
listones M del techo M
Dachlatten F
correntino M
ridge beam
poutre F faîtière
viga F cumbrera
Dachfirstbalken M
trave F di colmo M
rafter
chevron M
alfarda F
Dachsparren F
travetto M
attic floor
plancher M du grenier M
suelo M del desván M
Dachgeschoss N
sottotetto M
ceiling joist
solive F de plafond M
viguetas F del techo M
Deckenbalken M
travetti M del soffitto M
hardwood floor
plancher M de bois M franc
suelo M de madera F
Hartholzboden M
pavimento M in parquet M
underlay
sous-couche F
suelo M intermedio
Bettungsschicht F
strato M sottopavimento M
subfloor
plancher M brut / faux-plancher M
suelo M subyacente
Unterboden M
sottofondo M
floor joist
solive F de plancher M
viguetas F del suelo M
Bodenbalken M
travetti M per pavimenti M
foundation
fondation F
base F
Unterbau M
pavimento M
footing
semelle F de fondation F
cimientos M
Fundament N
fondamenta F
front porch
porche M d'entrée F
porche M
Eintrittsportal N
porticato M
front step
avant-marche F
escalón M
Eingangstreppe F
gradino M

reinforced concrete house
maison F en béton M armé
casa F de hormigón M armado
Stahlbetonhaus N
casa F in cemento M armato

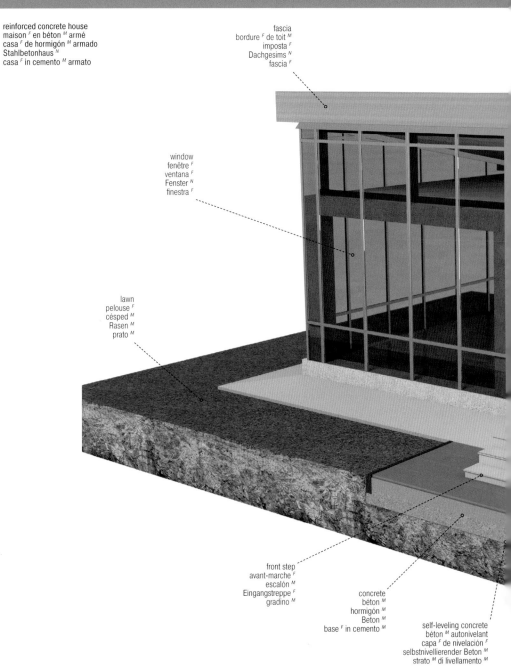

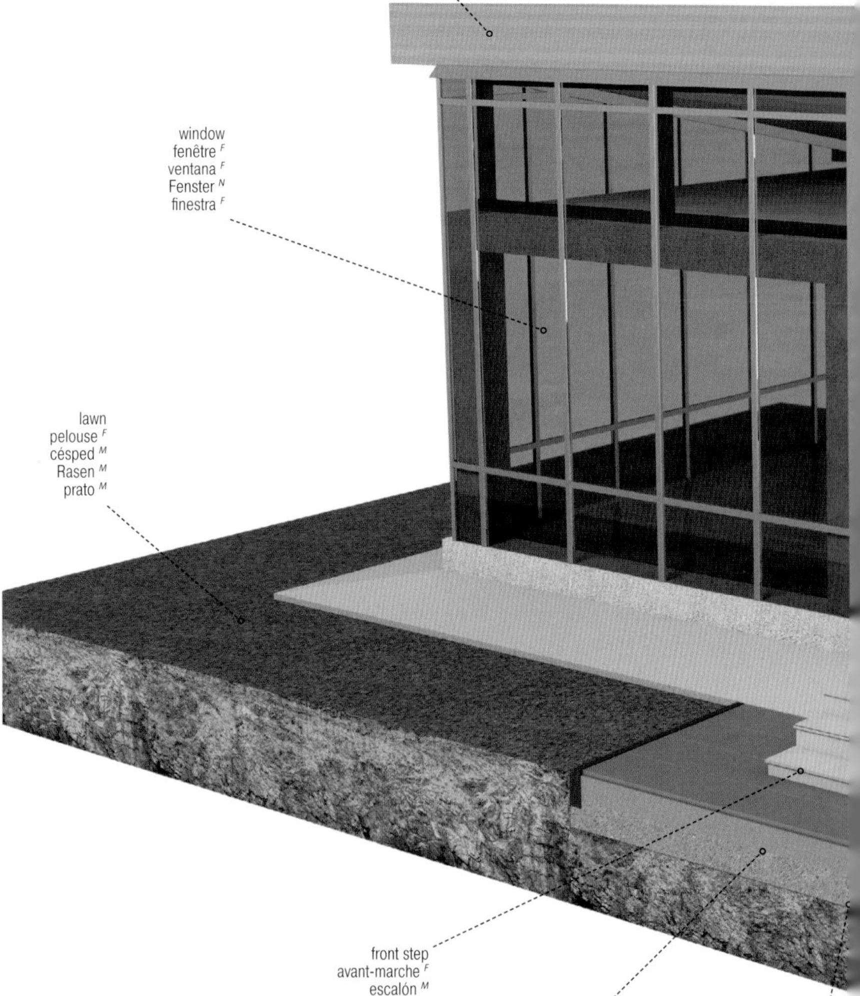
fascia
bordure F de toit M
imposta F
Dachgesims N
fascia F
window
fenêtre F
ventana F
Fenster N
finestra F
lawn
pelouse F
césped M
Rasen M
prato M
front step
avant-marche F
escalón M
Eingangstreppe F
gradino M
concrete
béton M
hormigón M
Beton M
base F in cemento M
self-leveling concrete
béton M autonivelant
capa F de nivelación F
selbstnivellierender Beton M
strato M di livellamento M

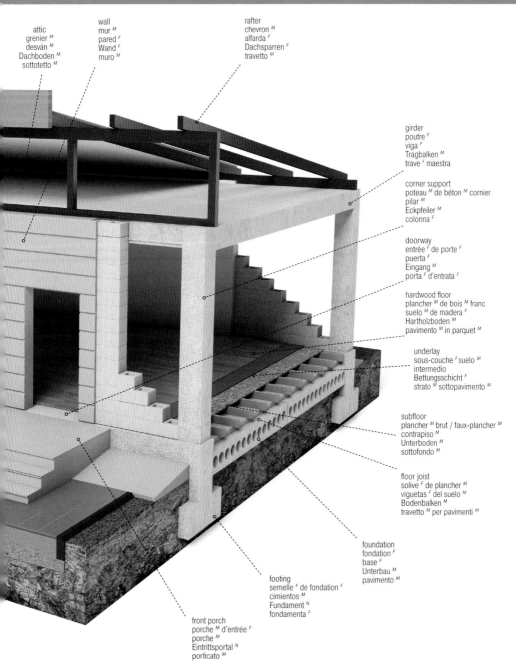

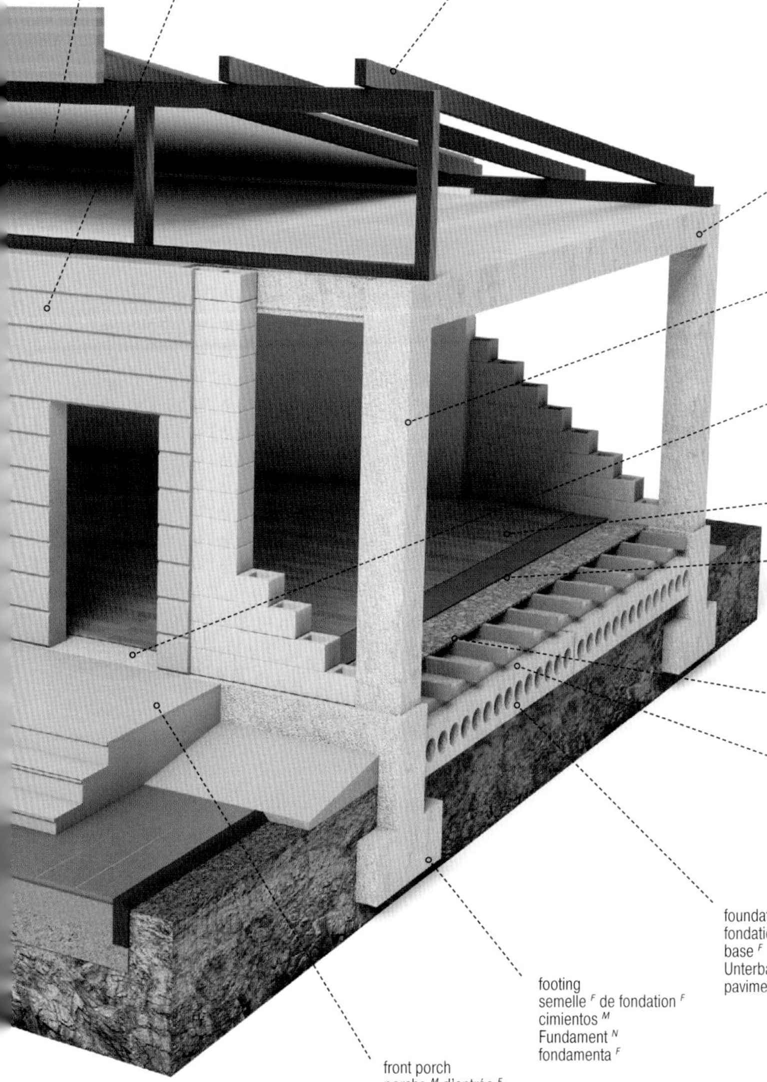
attic
grenier ^{M}
desván ^{M}
Dachboden ^{M}
sottotetto ^{M}
wall
mur ^{M}
pared ^{F}
Wand ^{F}
muro ^{M}
rafter
chevron ^{M}
alfarda ^{F}
Dachsparren ^{F}
travetto ^{M}
girder
poutre ^{F}
viga ^{F}
Tragbalken ^{M}
trave ^{F} maestra
corner support
poteau ^{M} de béton ^{M} cornier
pilar ^{M}
Eckpfeiler ^{M}
colonna ^{F}
doorway
entrée ^{F} de porte ^{F}
puerta ^{F}
Eingang ^{M}
porta ^{F} d'entrata ^{F}
hardwood floor
plancher ^{M} de bois ^{M} franc
suelo ^{M} de madera ^{F}
Hartholzboden ^{M}
pavimento ^{M} in parquet ^{M}
underlay
sous-couche ^{F} suelo ^{M}
intermedio
Bettungsschicht ^{F}
strato ^{M} sottopavimento ^{M}
subfloor
plancher ^{M} brut / faux-plancher ^{M}
contrapiso ^{M}
Unterboden ^{M}
sottofondo ^{M}
floor joist
solive ^{F} de plancher ^{M}
viguetas ^{F} del suelo ^{M}
Bodenbalken ^{M}
travetto ^{M} per pavimenti ^{M}
foundation
fondation ^{F}
base ^{F}
Unterbau ^{M}
pavimento ^{M}
footing
semelle ^{F} de fondation ^{F}
cimientos ^{M}
Fundament ^{N}
fondamenta ^{F}
front porch
porche ^{M} d'entrée ^{F}
porche ^{M}
Eintrittsportal ^{N}
porticato ^{M}

wooden-frame house
maison F à ossature F en bois M
casa F de madera F
Holzrahmenhaus N
casa F con struttura F in legno M

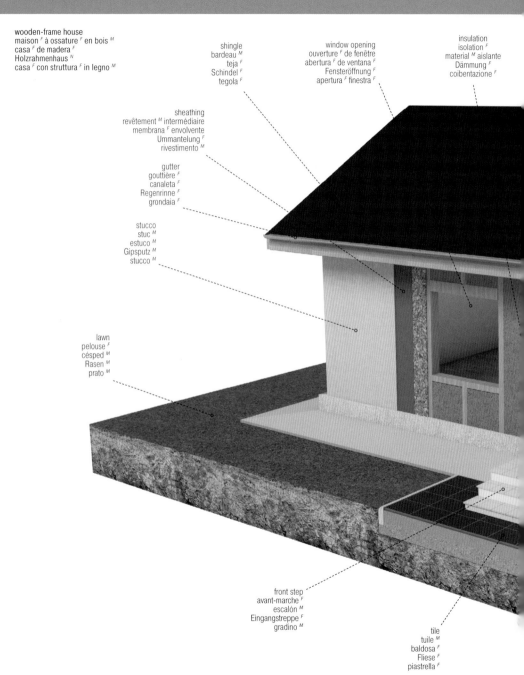

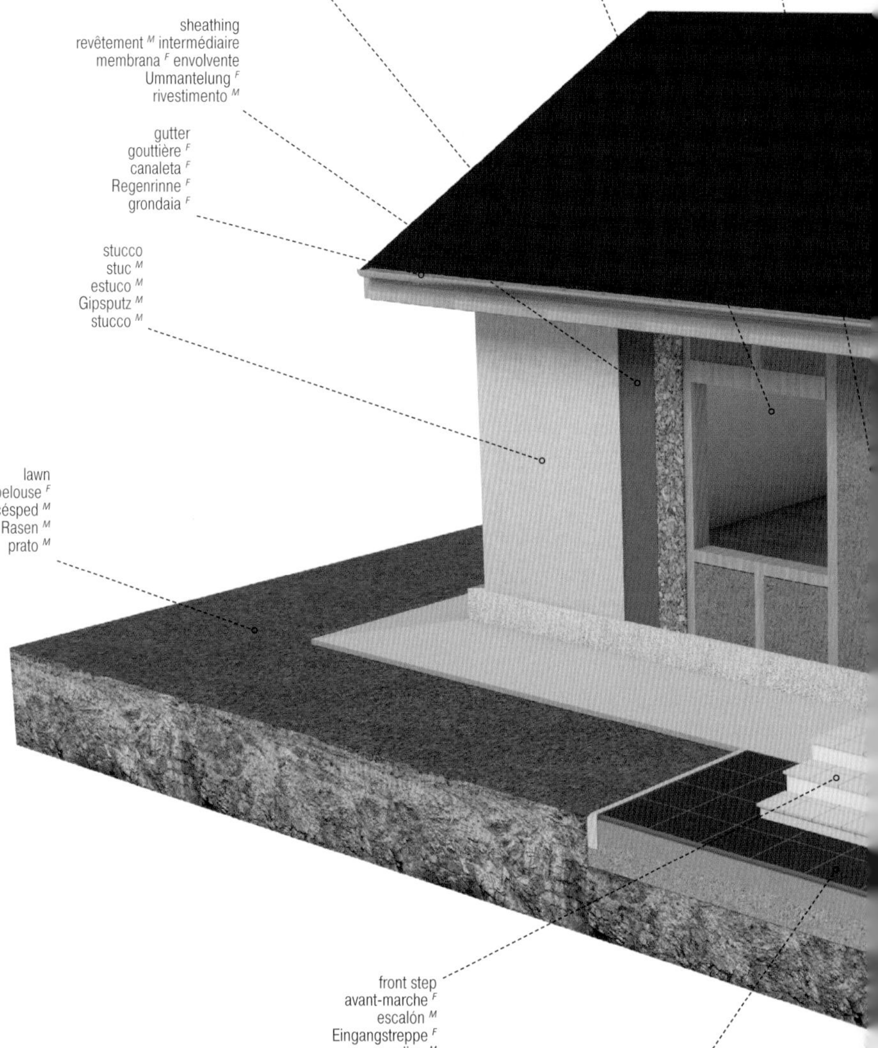
shingle
bardeau M
teja F
Schindel F
tegola F
window opening
ouverture F de fenêtre
abertura F de ventana F
Fensteröffnung F
apertura F finestra F
insulation
isolation F
material M aislante
Dämmung F
coibentazione F
sheathing
revêtement M intermédiaire
membrana F envolvente
Ummantelung F
rivestimento M
gutter
gouttière F
canaleta F
Regenrinne F
grondaia F
stucco
stuc M
estuco M
Gipsputz M
stucco M
lawn
pelouse F
césped M
Rasen M
prato M
front step
avant-marche F
escalón M
Eingangstreppe F
gradino M
tile
tuile M
baldosa F
Fliese F
piastrella F

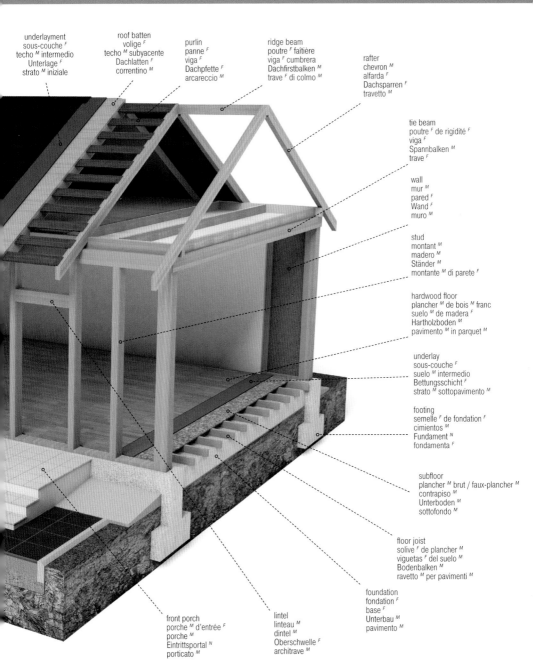

underlayment
sous-couche F
techo M intermedio
Unterlage F
strato M iniziale
roof batten
volige F
techo M subyacente
Dachlatten F
correntino M
purlin
panne F
viga F
Dachpfette F
arcareccio M
ridge beam
poutre F faîtière
viga F cumbrera
Dachfirstbalken M
trave F di colmo M
rafter
chevron M
alfarda F
Dachsparren F
travetto M
tie beam
poutre F de rigidité F
viga F
Spannbalken M
trave F
wall
mur M
pared F
Wand F
muro M
stud
montant M
madero M
Ständer M
montante M di parete F
hardwood floor
plancher M de bois M franc
suelo M de madera F
Hartholzboden M
pavimento M in parquet M
underlay
sous-couche F
suelo M intermedio
Bettungsschicht F
strato M sottopavimento M
footing
semelle F de fondation F
cimientos M
Fundament N
fondamenta F
subfloor
plancher M brut / faux-plancher M
contrapiso M
Unterboden M
sottofondo M
floor joist
solive F de plancher M
viguetas F del suelo M
Bodenbalken M
ravetto M per pavimenti M
foundation
fondation F
base F
Unterbau M
pavimento M
front porch
porche M d'entrée F
porche M
Eintrittsportal N
porticato M
lintel
linteau M
dintel M
Oberschwelle F
architrave M

solid brick
brique [F] pleine
ladrillo [M] sólido
Vollziegel [M]
mattone [M] pieno

perforated brick
brique [F] perforée
ladrillo [M] perforado
Lochziegel [M]
mattone [M] forato

concrete block
bloc [M] de béton [M]
bloque [M] de hormigón [M]
Betonblock [M]
blocco [M] di calcestruzzo [M]

paver
pavé [M]
adoquín [M]
Pflasterklinker [M]
lastrame [M]

board insulation
panneau [M] d'isolation [F]
placa [F] aislante
Plattenisolierung [F]
pannello [M] isolante

roof tiles
tuile [F] pour le toit [M]
teja [F] para tejado [M]
Dachziegel [M]
tegola [F]

tar paper
papier [M] goudronné
tela [F] asfáltica
Teerpappe [F] carta [F]
catramata

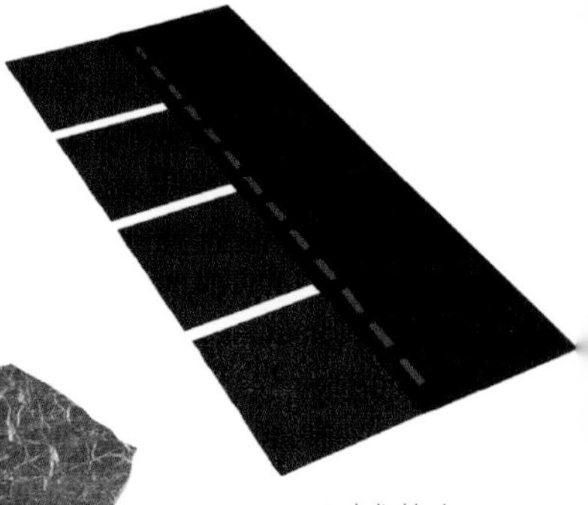

asphalt shingle
bardeau [M] d'asphalte [M]
teja [F] de asfalto [M]
Asphaltschindel [F]
listello [M] di cartonfeltro [M]
bitumato

foam weather stripping
bouchon [M]
burlete [M] de espuma [F]
Wärmedämmband [N]
pellicola [F] in schiuma [F]

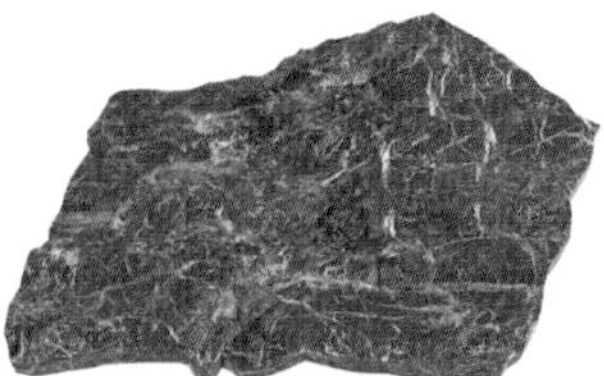

flagstone
dalle [F]
adoquines [M]
Steinplatte [F]
pietra [F] da lastrico [M]

fireplace
cheminée [F]
chimenea [F]
Kamin [M]
camino [M]

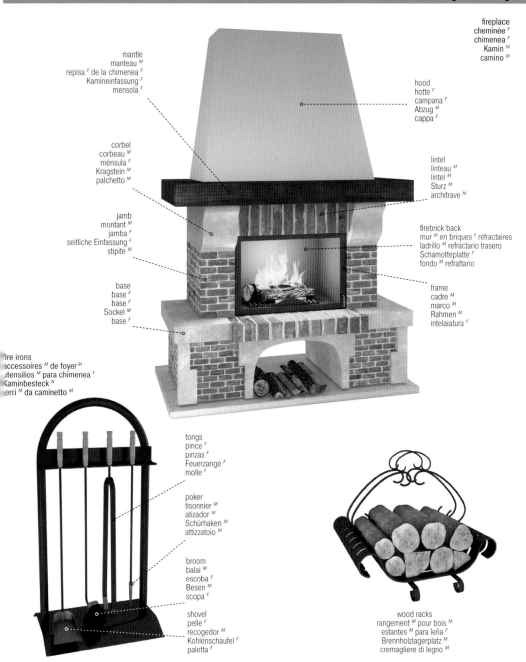

mantle
manteau [M]
repisa [F] de la chimenea [F]
Kamineinfassung [F]
mensola [F]

hood
hotte [F]
campana [F]
Abzug [M]
cappa [F]

corbel
corbeau [M]
ménsula [F]
Kragstein [M]
palchetto [M]

lintel
linteau [M]
lintel [M]
Sturz [M]
architrave [M]

jamb
montant [M]
jamba [F]
seitliche Einfassung [F]
stipite [M]

firebrick back
mur [M] en briques [F] réfractaires
ladrillo [M] refractario trasero
Schamotteplatte [F]
fondo [M] refrattario

base
base [F]
base [F]
Sockel [M]
base [F]

frame
cadre [M]
marco [M]
Rahmen [M]
intelaiatura [F]

ire irons
ccessoires [M] de foyer [M]
tensilios [M] para chimenea [F]
aminbesteck [N]
erri [M] da caminetto [M]

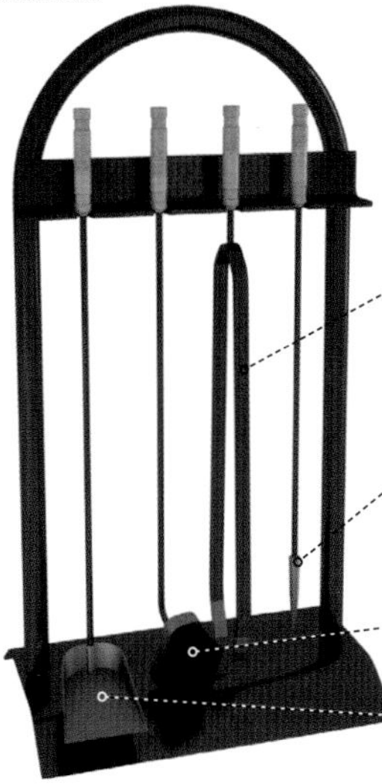

tongs
pince [F]
pinzas [F]
Feuerzange [F]
molle [F]

poker
tisonnier [M]
atizador [M]
Schürhaken [M]
attizzatoio [M]

broom
balai [M]
escoba [F]
Besen [M]
scopa [F]

shovel
pelle [F]
recogedor [M]
Kohlenschaufel [F]
paletta [F]

wood racks
rangement [M] pour bois [M]
estantes [M] para leña [F]
Brennholzlagerplatz [M]
cremagliere di legno [M]

forced-air heating and air-conditioning system
système ^{M} de chauffage ^{M} et de climatisation ^{F} à air ^{M} forcé
sistema ^{M} forzado de calefacción ^{F} y aire ^{M} acondicionado
Warmluftheizung ^{F} und Klimaanlage ^{F}
riscaldamento ^{M} ad aria ^{F} forzata e sistema ^{F} ad aria ^{F} condizionata

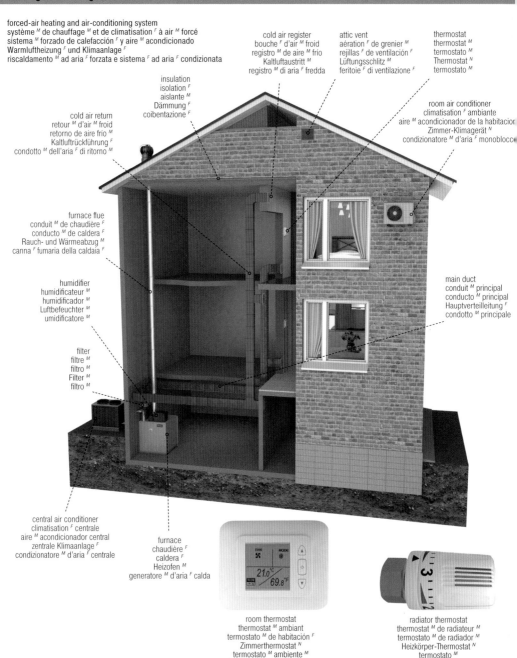

cold air register
bouche ^{F} d'air ^{M} froid
registro ^{M} de aire ^{M} frío
Kaltluftaustritt ^{M}
registro ^{M} di aria ^{F} fredda

attic vent
aération ^{F} de grenier ^{M}
rejillas ^{F} de ventilación ^{F}
Lüftungsschlitz ^{M}
feritoie ^{F} di ventilazione ^{F}

thermostat
thermostat ^{M}
termostato ^{M}
Thermostat ^{N}
termostato ^{M}

insulation
isolation ^{F}
aislante ^{M}
Dämmung ^{F}
coibentazione ^{F}

room air conditioner
climatisation ^{F} ambiante
aire ^{M} acondicionador de la habitacior
Zimmer-Klimagerät ^{N}
condizionatore ^{M} d'aria ^{F} monoblocc

cold air return
retour ^{M} d'air ^{M} froid
retorno de aire frío ^{M}
Kaltluftrückführung ^{F}
condotto ^{M} dell'aria ^{F} di ritorno ^{M}

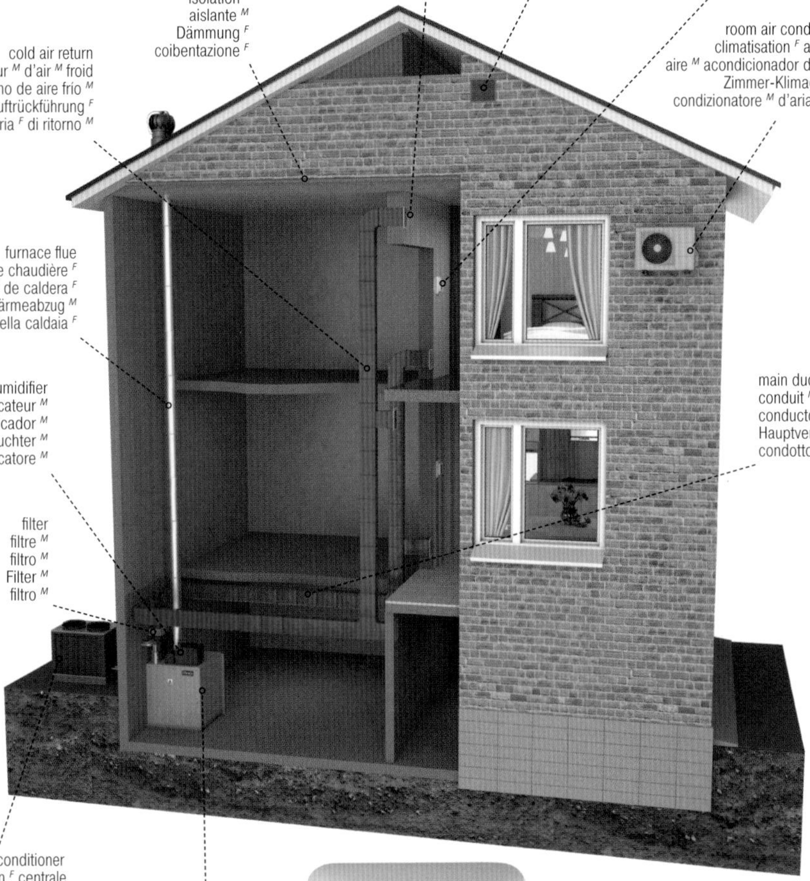

furnace flue
conduit ^{M} de chaudière ^{F}
conducto ^{M} de caldera ^{F}
Rauch- und Wärmeabzug ^{M}
canna ^{F} fumaria della caldaia ^{F}

humidifier
humidificateur ^{M}
humidificador ^{M}
Luftbefeuchter ^{M}
umidificatore ^{M}

main duct
conduit ^{M} principal
conducto ^{M} principal
Hauptverteilleitung ^{F}
condotto ^{M} principale

filter
filtre ^{M}
filtro ^{M}
Filter ^{M}
filtro ^{M}

central air conditioner
climatisation ^{F} centrale
aire ^{M} acondicionador central
zentrale Klimaanlage ^{F}
condizionatore ^{M} d'aria ^{F} centrale

furnace
chaudière ^{F}
caldera ^{F}
Heizofen ^{M}
generatore ^{M} d'aria ^{F} calda

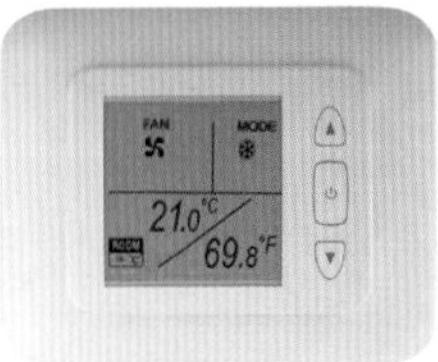
FAN
MODE
21.0°C
69.8°F

room thermostat
thermostat ^{M} ambiant
termostato ^{M} de habitación ^{F}
Zimmerthermostat ^{N}
termostato ^{M} ambiente ^{M}

3

radiator thermostat
thermostat ^{M} de radiateur ^{M}
termostato ^{M} de radiador ^{M}
Heizkörper-Thermostat ^{N}
termostato ^{M}

column radiator
radiateur [M] à colonnes [F]
radiador [M] de columna [F]
Röhrenheizkörper [M]
radiatore [M] a colonna [F]

cover grille
grille [F] couvrante
rejilla [F] de cubierta [F]
Abdeckungsgitter [N]
griglia [F] di rivestimento [M]

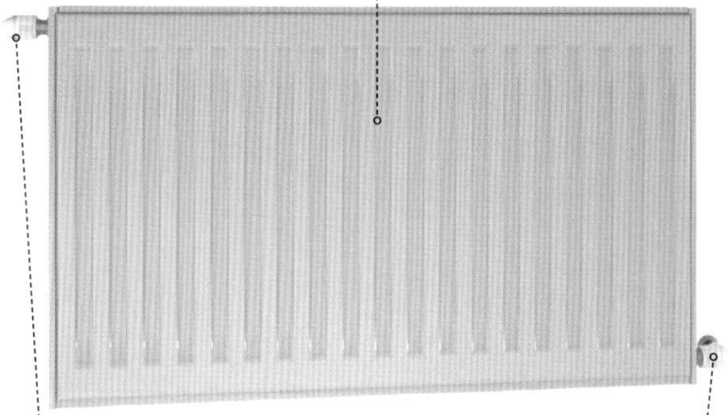

thermostat
thermostat [M]
termostato [M]
Regulierverntil [N]
valvola [F] di regolazione [F]

hot-water outlet
sortie [F] d'eau [F] chaude
salida [F] de agua [F] caliente
Rücklaufverschraubung [F]
uscita [F] dell'acqua [F] calda

towel rail
sèche-serviettes [M]
toallero [M]
Handtuchhalter [M]
portasciugamani [M]

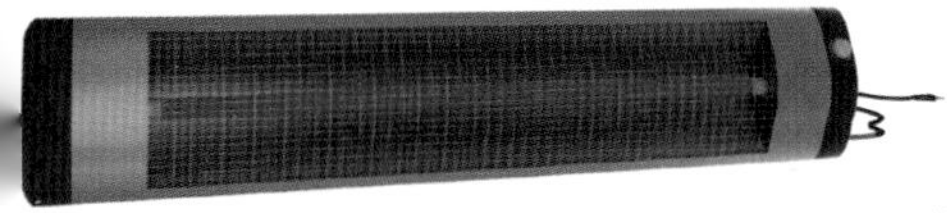

infrared heater
radiateur [M] infrarouge
calefactor [M] infrarrojo
Infrarotheizkörper [M]
riscaldatore [M] a infrarossi [M]

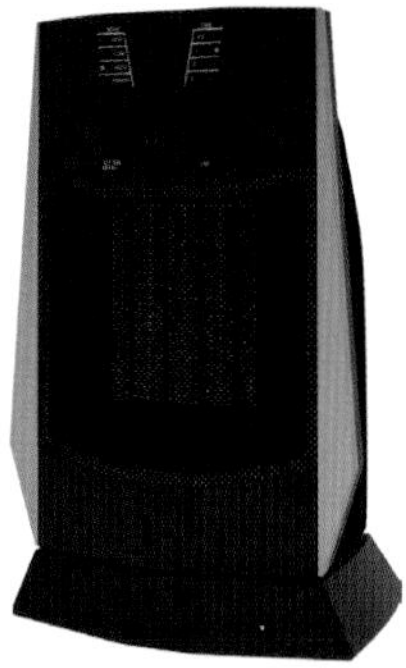

radiant heater
chauffage [M] rayonnant
calefactor [M] de energía [F] radiante
Heizstrahler [M]
stufa [F] radiante

oil-filled radiant heater
radiateur [M] au mazout [M]
radiador [M] de aceite [M]
Ölradiator [M]
radiatore [M] a olio [M]

on/off switches
commutateurs [M]
interruptores [M] de encendido [M]/apagado [M]
Ein-/Aus-Tasten [F]
interruttori [M] di accensione [F]/spegnimento [M]

handle
poignée [F]
mango [M]
Griff [M]
manico [M]

pilot light
témoin [M] lumineux
luz [F] piloto [M]
Kontrolllampe [F]
spia [F] luminosa

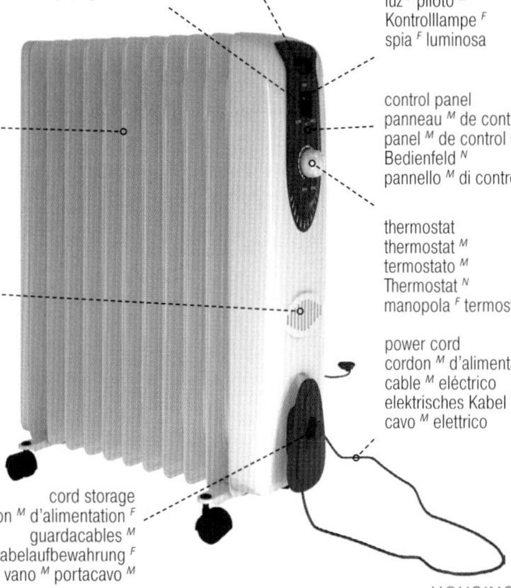

fin
ailette [F]
alerón [M]
Teilkammer [F]
aletta [F]

control panel
panneau [M] de contrôle [M]
panel [M] de control [M]
Bedienfeld [N]
pannello [M] di controllo [M]

thermostat
thermostat [M]
termostato [M]
Thermostat [N]
manopola [F] termostato [M]

vent
aération [F]
ventilación [F]
Lüftung [F]
sfiato [M]

power cord
cordon [M] d'alimentation [F]
cable [M] eléctrico
elektrisches Kabel [N]
cavo [M] elettrico

cord storage
compartiment [M] de rangement [M] du cordon [M] d'alimentation [F]
guardacables [M]
Kabelaufbewahrung [F]
vano [M] portacavo [M]

plumbing system
tuyauterie F
sistema M de fontanería F
Wasserleitungssystem N
impianto M idraulico

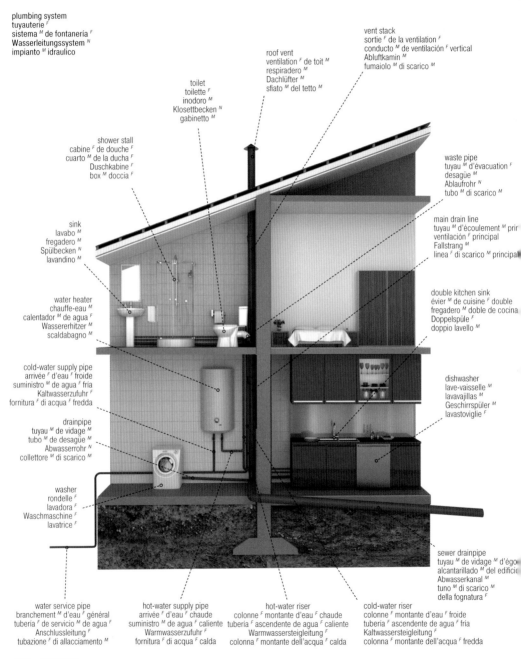

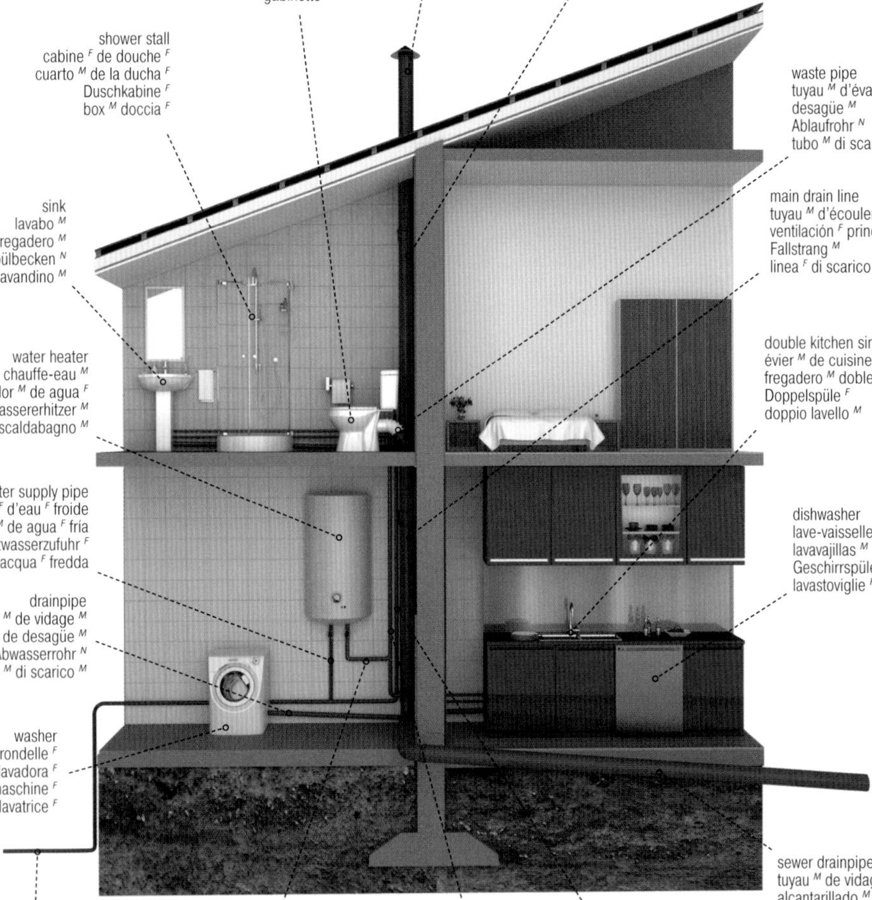
vent stack
sortie F de la ventilation F
conducto M de ventilación F vertical
Abluftkamin M
fumaiolo M di scarico M
roof vent
ventilation F de toit M
respiradero M
Dachlüfter M
sfiato M del tetto M
toilet
toilette F
inodoro M
Klosettbecken N
gabinetto M
shower stall
cabine F de douche F
cuarto M de la ducha F
Duschkabine F
box M doccia F
waste pipe
tuyau M d'évacuation F
desagüe M
Ablaufrohr N
tubo M di scarico M
sink
lavabo M
fregadero M
Spülbecken N
lavandino M
main drain line
tuyau M d'écoulement M prir
ventilación F principal
Fallstrang M
linea F di scarico M principal
double kitchen sink
évier M de cuisine F double
fregadero M doble de cocina
Doppelspüle F
doppio lavello M
water heater
chauffe-eau M
calentador M de agua F
Wassererhitzer M
scaldabagno M
cold-water supply pipe
arrivée F d'eau F froide
suministro M de agua F fría
Kaltwasserzufuhr F
fornitura F di acqua F fredda
dishwasher
lave-vaisselle M
lavavajillas M
Geschirrspüler M
lavastoviglie F
drainpipe
tuyau M de vidage M
tubo M de desagüe M
Abwasserrohr N
collettore M di scarico M
washer
rondelle F
lavadora F
Waschmaschine F
lavatrice F
sewer drainpipe
tuyau M de vidage M d'égo
alcantarillado M del edificio
Abwasserkanal M
tuno M di scarico M
della fognatura F
water service pipe
branchement M d'eau F général
tubería F de servicio M de agua F
Anschlussleitung F
tubazione F di allacciamento M
hot-water supply pipe
arrivée F d'eau F chaude
suministro M de agua F caliente
Warmwasserzufuhr F
fornitura F di acqua F calda
hot-water riser
colonne F montante d'eau F chaude
tubería F ascendente de agua F caliente
Warmwassersteigleitung F
colonna F montante dell'acqua F calda
cold-water riser
colonne F montante d'eau F froide
tubería F ascendente de agua F fría
Kaltwassersteigleitung F
colonna F montante dell'acqua F fredda

cartridge faucet
robinet [M] à cartouche [F]
grifo [M] de cartucho [M]
Mischbatterie [F] mit Kartuschendichtung [F]
rubinetto [M] senza valvola [F]

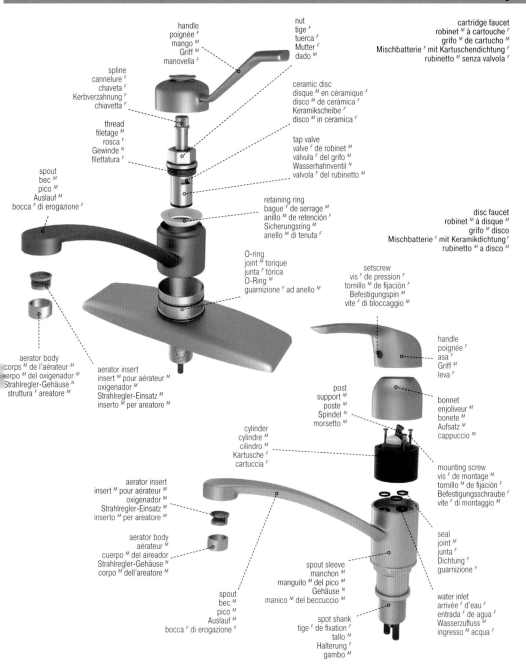

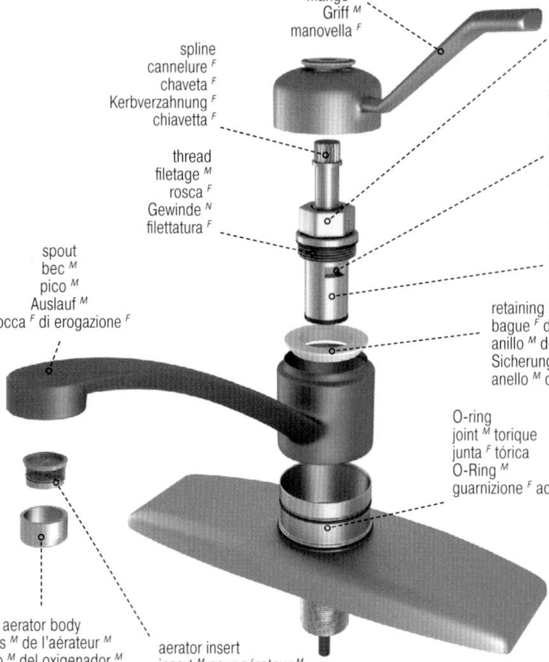
handle
poignée [F]
mango [M]
Griff [M]
manovella [F]
nut
tige [F]
tuerca [F]
Mutter [F]
dado [M]
spline
cannelure [F]
chaveta [F]
Kerbverzahnung [F]
chiavetta [F]
ceramic disc
disque [M] en céramique [F]
disco [M] de cerámica [F]
Keramikscheibe [F]
disco [M] in ceramica [F]
thread
filetage [M]
rosca [F]
Gewinde [N]
filettatura [F]
tap valve
valve [F] de robinet [M]
válvula [F] del grifo [M]
Wasserhahnventil [N]
valvola [F] del rubinetto [M]
spout
bec [M]
pico [M]
Auslauf [M]
bocca [F] di erogazione [F]
retaining ring
bague [F] de serrage [M]
anillo [M] de retención [F]
Sicherungsring [M]
anello [M] di tenuta [F]
O-ring
joint [M] torique
junta [F] tórica
O-Ring [M]
guarnizione [F] ad anello [M]
aerator body
corps [M] de l'aérateur [M]
uerpo [M] del oxigenador [M]
Strahlregler-Gehäuse [N]
struttura [F] areatore [M]
aerator insert
insert [M] pour aérateur [M]
oxigenador [M]
Strahlregler-Einsatz [M]
inserto [M] per areatore [M]

disc faucet
robinet [M] à disque [M]
grifo [M] disco
Mischbatterie [F] mit Keramikdichtung [F]
rubinetto [M] a disco [M]

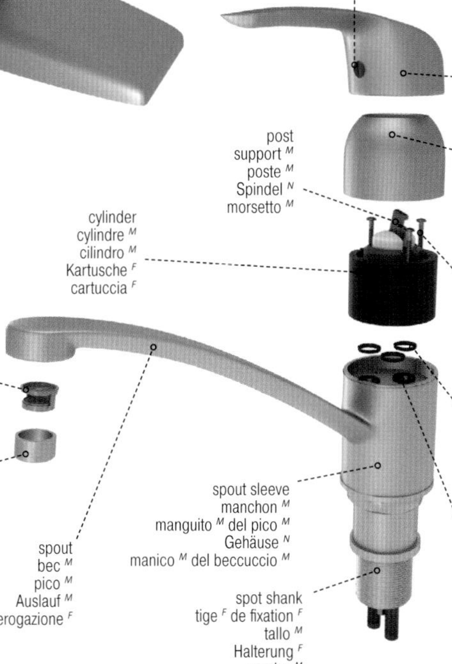
setscrew
vis [F] de pression [F]
tornillo [M] de fijación [F]
Befestigungspin [M]
vite [F] di bloccaggio [M]
handle
poignée [F]
asa [F]
Griff [M]
leva [F]
post
support [M]
poste [M]
Spindel [N]
morsetto [M]
bonnet
enjoliveur [M]
bonete [M]
Aufsatz [M]
cappuccio [M]
cylinder
cylindre [M]
cilindro [M]
Kartusche [F]
cartuccia [F]
mounting screw
vis [F] de montage [M]
tornillo [M] de fijación [F]
Befestigungsschraube [F]
vite [F] di montaggio [M]
aerator insert
insert [M] pour aérateur [M]
oxigenador [M]
Strahlregler-Einsatz [M]
inserto [M] per areatore [M]
seal
joint [M]
junta [F]
Dichtung [F]
guarnizione [F]
aerator body
aérateur [M]
cuerpo [M] del aireador
Strahlregler-Gehäuse [N]
corpo [M] dell'areatore [M]
spout sleeve
manchon [M]
manguito [M] del pico [M]
Gehäuse [N]
manico [M] del beccuccio [M]
spout
bec [M]
pico [M]
Auslauf [M]
bocca [F] di erogazione [F]
water inlet
arrivée [F] d'eau [F]
entrada [F] de agua [F]
Wasserzufluss [M]
ingresso [M] acqua [F]
spot shank
tige [F] de fixation [F]
tallo [M]
Halterung [F]
gambo [M]

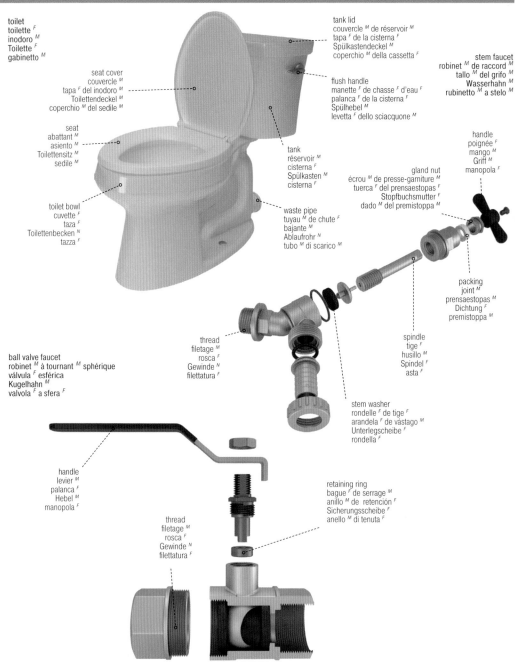

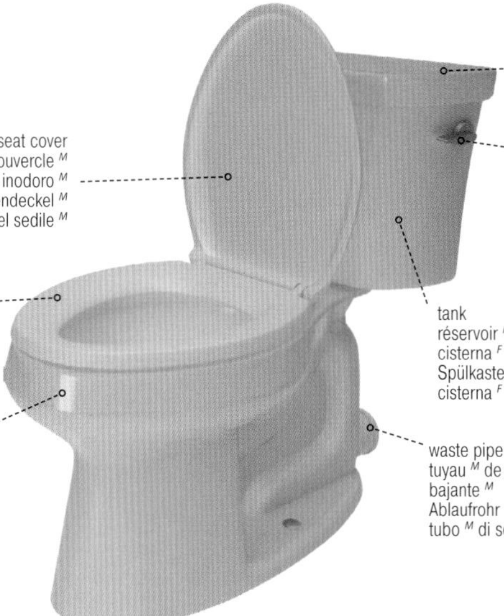
toilet
toilette [F]
inodoro [M]
Toilette [F]
gabinetto [M]
tank lid
couvercle [M] de réservoir [M]
tapa [F] de la cisterna [F]
Spülkastendeckel [M]
coperchio [M] della cassetta [F]
seat cover
couvercle [M]
tapa [F] del inodoro [M]
Toilettendeckel [M]
coperchio [M] del sedile [M]
flush handle
manette [F] de chasse [F] d'eau [F]
palanca [F] de la cisterna [F]
Spülhebel [M]
levetta [F] dello sciacquone [M]
seat
abattant [M]
asiento [M]
Toilettensitz [M]
sedile [M]
tank
réservoir [M]
cisterna [F]
Spülkasten [M]
cisterna [F]
toilet bowl
cuvette [F]
taza [F]
Toilettenbecken [N]
tazza [F]
waste pipe
tuyau [M] de chute [F]
bajante [M]
Ablaufrohr [N]
tubo [M] di scarico [M]

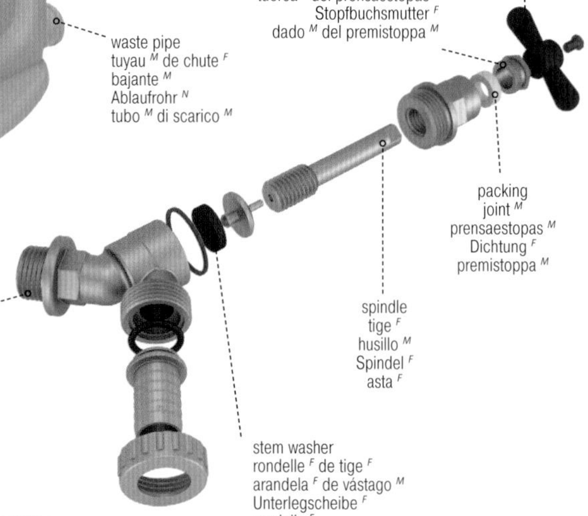
stem faucet
robinet [M] de raccord [M]
tallo [M] del grifo [M]
Wasserhahn [M]
rubinetto [M] a stelo [M]
handle
poignée [F]
mango [M]
Griff [M]
manopola [F]
gland nut
écrou [M] de presse-garniture [M]
tuerca [F] del prensaestopas [F]
Stopfbuchsmutter [F]
dado [M] del premistoppa [M]
packing
joint [M]
prensaestopas [M]
Dichtung [F]
premistoppa [M]
spindle
tige [F]
husillo [M]
Spindel [F]
asta [F]
thread
filetage [M]
rosca [F]
Gewinde [N]
filettatura [F]
stem washer
rondelle [F] de tige [F]
arandela [F] de vástago [M]
Unterlegscheibe [F]
rondella [F]

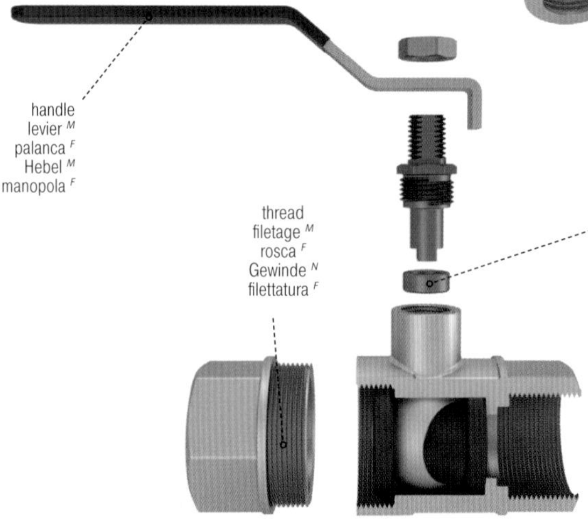
ball valve faucet
robinet [M] à tournant [M] sphérique
válvula [F] esférica
Kugelhahn [M]
valvola [F] a sfera [F]
handle
levier [M]
palanca [F]
Hebel [M]
manopola [F]
retaining ring
bague [F] de serrage [M]
anillo [M] de retención [F]
Sicherungsscheibe [F]
anello [M] di tenuta [F]
thread
filetage [M]
rosca [F]
Gewinde [N]
filettatura [F]

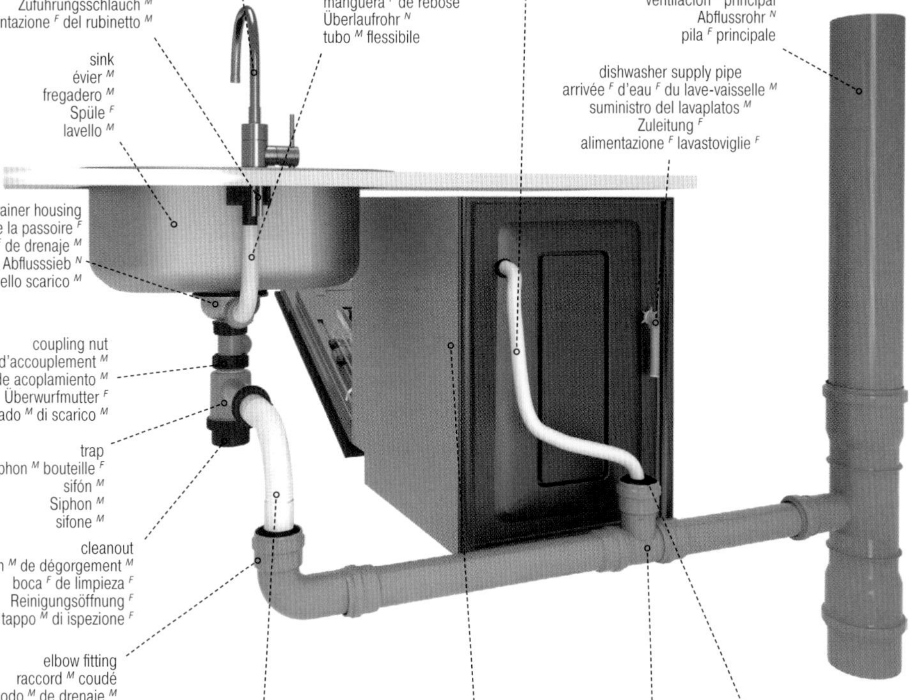

single-handle kitchen faucet
robinet ^{M} mitigeur pour la cuisine ^{F}
grifo ^{M} de cocina ^{F} monomando
Einhand-Mischbatterie ^{F}
miscelatore ^{M} a una leva ^{F}

dishwasher drainpipe
tuyau ^{M} d'évacuation ^{F} du lave-vaisselle ^{M}
manguera ^{F} de drenaje ^{M} del lavaplatos ^{M}
Abflussrohr ^{N} vom Geschirrspüler ^{M}
tubo ^{M} di scarico ^{M} della lavastoviglie ^{F}

kitchen drainage
tuyauterie ^{F} d'évier ^{M}
drenaje ^{M} de cocina ^{F}
Küchenabfluss ^{M}
drenaggio ^{M} della cucina ^{F}

faucet supply pipe
tuyau ^{M} d'alimentation ^{F} du robinet ^{M}
tubo ^{M} de suministro del grifo ^{M}
Zuführungsschlauch ^{M}
tubo ^{M} di alimentazione ^{F} del rubinetto ^{M}

overflow pipe
tuyau ^{M} de trop-plein ^{M}
manguera ^{F} de rebose
Überlaufrohr ^{N}
tubo ^{M} flessibile

main drain line
tuyau ^{M} d'écoulement ^{M} principal
ventilación ^{F} principal
Abflussrohr ^{N}
pila ^{F} principale

sink
évier ^{M}
fregadero ^{M}
Spüle ^{F}
lavello ^{M}

dishwasher supply pipe
arrivée ^{F} d'eau ^{F} du lave-vaisselle ^{M}
suministro del lavaplatos ^{M}
Zuleitung ^{F}
alimentazione ^{F} lavastoviglie ^{F}

strainer housing
boîtier ^{M} de la passoire ^{F}
se ^{F} de la cesta ^{F} de drenaje ^{M}
Abflusssieb ^{N}
filtro ^{M} dello scarico ^{M}

coupling nut
écrou ^{M} d'accouplement ^{M}
tuerca ^{F} de acoplamiento ^{M}
Überwurfmutter ^{F}
dado ^{M} di scarico ^{M}

trap
siphon ^{M} bouteille ^{F}
sifón ^{M}
Siphon ^{M}
sifone ^{M}

cleanout
bouchon ^{M} de dégorgement ^{M}
boca ^{F} de limpieza ^{F}
Reinigungsöffnung ^{F}
tappo ^{M} di ispezione ^{F}

elbow fitting
raccord ^{M} coudé
codo ^{M} de drenaje ^{M}
Ablaufbogen ^{N}
gomito ^{M} di scarico ^{M}

kitchen sink drain hose
tuyau ^{M} d'évacuation ^{F} de l'évier ^{M}
tubería de drenaje ^{F} del fregadero ^{M} de la cocina ^{F}
Küchenbeckenablaufrohr ^{N}
tubo ^{M} di scarico ^{M} del lavello ^{M}

dishwasher
lave-vaisselle ^{M}
lavavajillas ^{M}
Geschirrspüler ^{M}
lavastoviglie ^{F}

tee fitting
raccord ^{M} en té
connector T ^{M}
T-Stück ^{N}
raccordo ^{M} a T

rubber gasket
joint ^{M} en caoutchouc ^{M}
junta ^{F} de caucho ^{M}
Gummidichtung ^{F}
guarnizione ^{F} in gomma ^{F}

Fittings

Joints ^{M} | Uniones ^{M} de cañería ^{F} | Verbindungsstücke ^{N} | Raccordi ^{M}

double wye
té ^{M} double
unión ^{F} de doble Y
Y-Verteiler ^{M}
doppia Y ^{F}

cross
raccord ^{M} en forme ^{F} de croix ^{F}
cruz ^{M}
Kreuz ^{M}
croce ^{F}

coupling
raccord ^{M}
acoplamiento ^{M}
Kupplung ^{F}
accoppiamento ^{M}

45-degree elbow
coude ^{M} à 45 degrés
codo ^{M} de 45 grados ^{M}
Winkel ^{M} 45°
gomito ^{M} a 45°

tee connector
raccord ^{M} en té
conector T ^{M}
T-Stück ^{N}
raccordo ^{M} a T

connector coupling
raccord ^{M} de couplage ^{M}
conector ^{M} de acoplamiento ^{M}
Verbindungskupplung ^{F}
connettore ^{M} di accoppiamento ^{M}

staircase
escalier M
escalera F con descansillo M
Treppe F
scala F

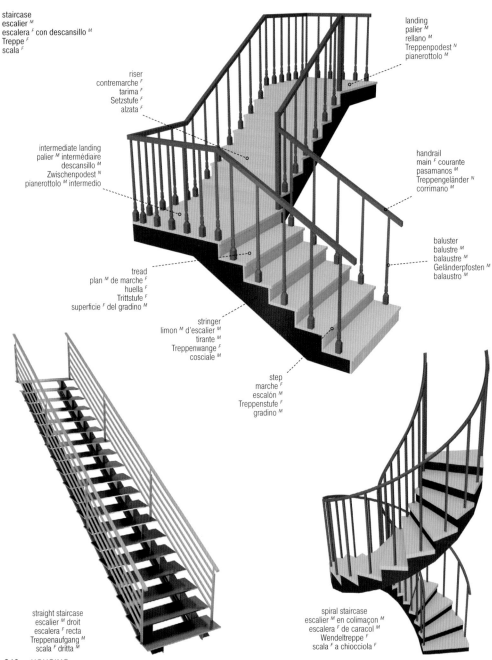

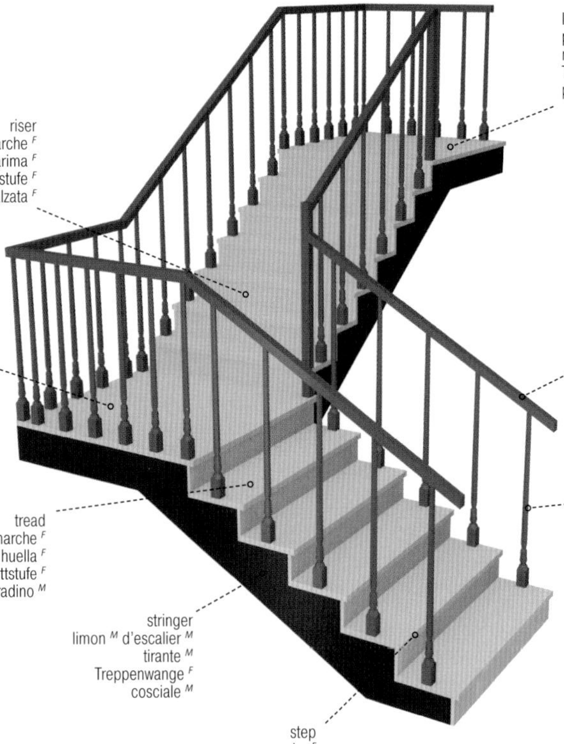
landing
palier M
rellano M
Treppenpodest N
pianerottolo M
riser
contremarche F
tarima F
Setzstufe F
alzata F
intermediate landing
palier M intermédiaire
descansillo M
Zwischenpodest N
pianerottolo M intermedio
handrail
main F courante
pasamanos M
Treppengeländer N
corrimano M
baluster
balustre M
balaustre M
Geländerpfosten M
balaustro M
tread
plan M de marche F
huella F
Trittstufe F
superficie F del gradino M
stringer
limon M d'escalier M
tirante M
Treppenwange F
cosciale M
step
marche F
escalón M
Treppenstufe F
gradino M

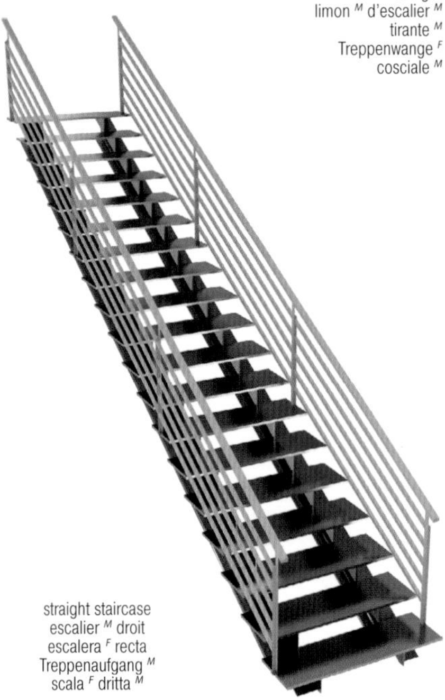

straight staircase
escalier M droit
escalera F recta
Treppenaufgang M
scala F dritta M

spiral staircase
escalier M en colimaçon M
escalera F de caracol M
Wendeltreppe F
scala F a chiocciola F

gabled roof
toit ^{M} à deux versants ^{M}
tejado ^{M} de pendiente ^{F} inclinada
Giebeldach ^{N}
tetto ^{M} a due falde ^{F} molto inclinato

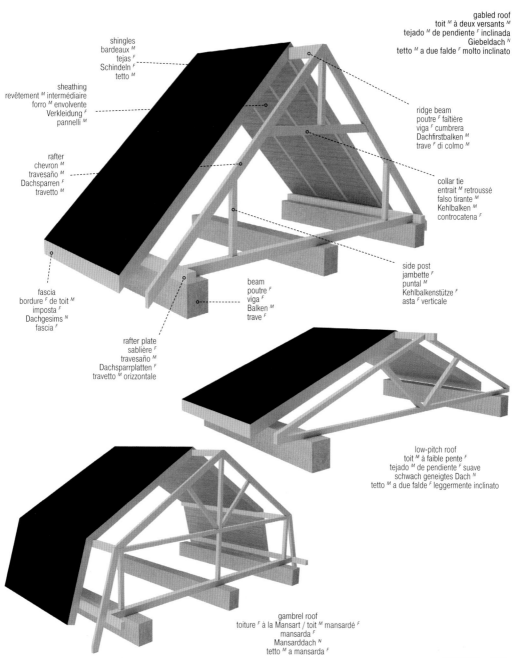

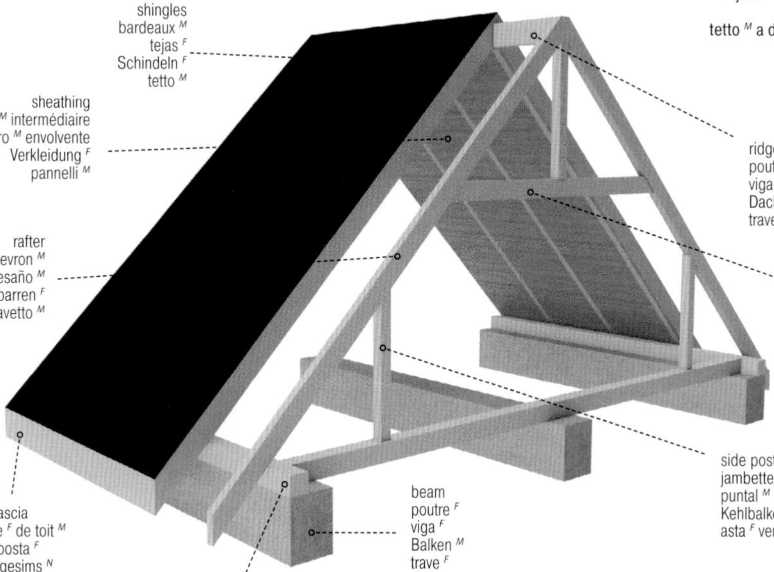
shingles
bardeaux ^{M}
tejas ^{F}
Schindeln ^{F}
tetto ^{M}
sheathing
revêtement ^{M} intermédiaire
forro ^{M} envolvente
Verkleidung ^{F}
pannelli ^{M}
rafter
chevron ^{M}
travesaño ^{M}
Dachsparren ^{F}
travetto ^{M}
fascia
bordure ^{F} de toit ^{M}
imposta ^{F}
Dachgesims ^{N}
fascia ^{F}
rafter plate
sablière ^{F}
travesaño ^{M}
Dachsparrplatten ^{F}
travetto ^{M} orizzontale
beam
poutre ^{F}
viga ^{F}
Balken ^{M}
trave ^{F}
ridge beam
poutre ^{F} faîtière
viga ^{F} cumbrera
Dachfirstbalken ^{M}
trave ^{F} di colmo ^{M}
collar tie
entrait ^{M} retroussé
falso tirante ^{M}
Kehlbalken ^{M}
controcatena ^{F}
side post
jambette ^{F}
puntal ^{M}
Kehlbalkenstütze ^{F}
asta ^{F} verticale

low-pitch roof
toit ^{M} à faible pente ^{F}
tejado ^{M} de pendiente ^{F} suave
schwach geneigtes Dach ^{N}
tetto ^{M} a due falde ^{F} leggermente inclinato

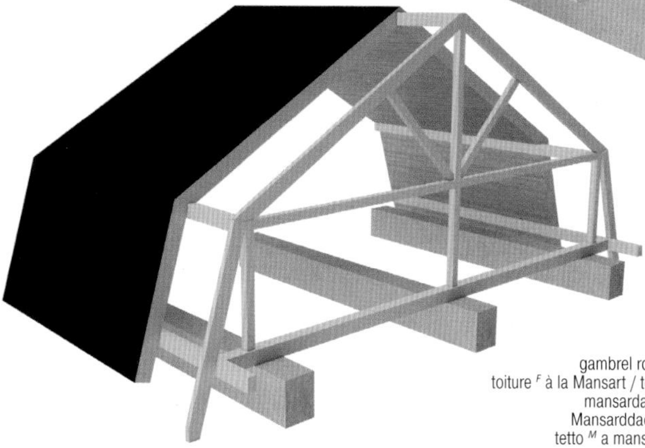

gambrel roof
toiture ^{F} à la Mansart / toit ^{M} mansardé ^{F}
mansarda ^{F}
Mansarddach ^{N}
tetto ^{M} a mansarda ^{F}

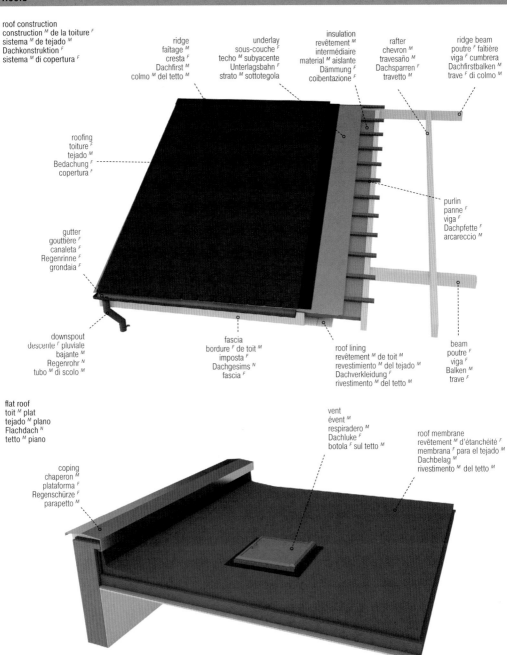

roof construction
construction [M] de la toiture [F]
sistema [M] de tejado [M]
Dachkonstruktion [F]
sistema [M] di copertura [F]

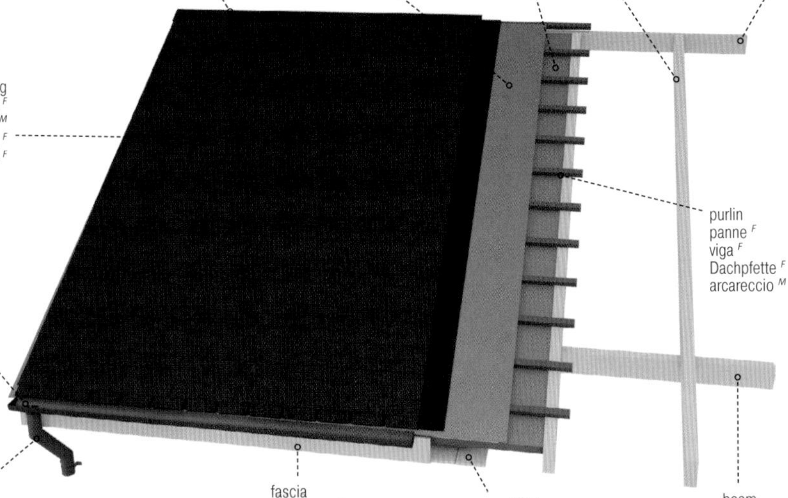
ridge
faîtage [M]
cresta [F]
Dachfirst [M]
colmo [M] del tetto [M]
underlay
sous-couche [F]
techo [M] subyacente
Unterlagsbahn [F]
strato [M] sottotegola
insulation
revêtement [M] intermédiaire
material [M] aislante
Dämmung [F]
coibentazione [F]
rafter
chevron [M]
travesaño [M]
Dachsparren [F]
travetto [M]
ridge beam
poutre [F] faîtière
viga [F] cumbrera
Dachfirstbalken [M]
trave [F] di colmo [M]
roofing
toiture [F]
tejado [M]
Bedachung [F]
copertura [F]
purlin
panne [F]
viga [F]
Dachpfette [F]
arcareccio [M]
gutter
gouttière [F]
canaleta [F]
Regenrinne [F]
grondaia [F]
downspout
descente [F] pluviale
bajante [M]
Regenrohr [N]
tubo [M] di scolo [M]
fascia
bordure [F] de toit [M]
imposta [F]
Dachgesims [N]
fascia [F]
roof lining
revêtement [M] de toit [M]
revestimiento [M] del tejado [M]
Dachverkleidung [F]
rivestimento [M] del tetto [M]
beam
poutre [F]
viga [F]
Balken [M]
trave [F]

flat roof
toit [M] plat
tejado [M] plano
Flachdach [N]
tetto [M] piano

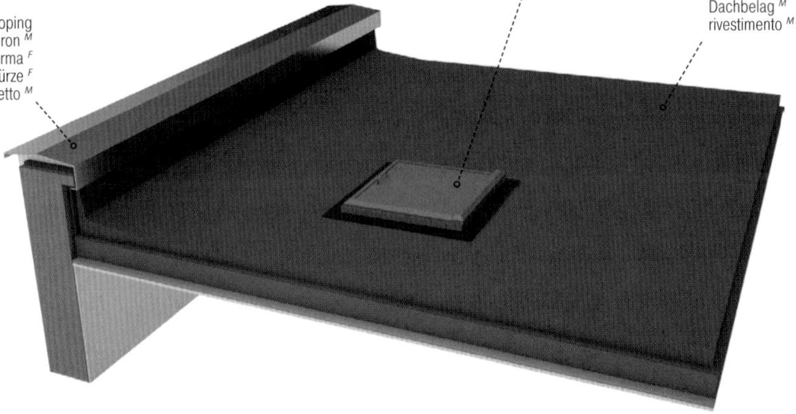
vent
évent [M]
respiradero [M]
Dachluke [F]
botola [F] sul tetto [M]
roof membrane
revêtement [M] d'étanchéité [F]
membrana [F] para el tejado [M]
Dachbelag [M]
rivestimento [M] del tetto [M]
coping
chaperon [M]
plataforma [F]
Regenschürze [F]
parapetto [M]

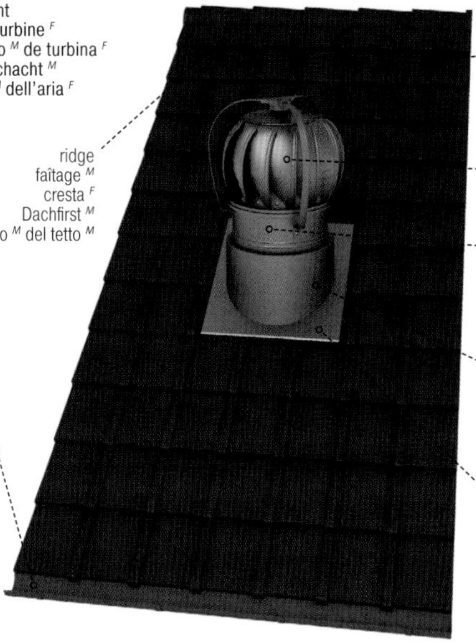
turbine vent
évent M à turbine F
respiradero M de turbina F
Lüftungsschacht M
condotto M dell'aria F
ridge
faîtage M
cresta F
Dachfirst M
colmo M del tetto M
gutter
gouttière F
canaleta F
egenrinne F
grondaia F
roofing
toiture F
tejado M
Bedachung F
tetto M
fan blade
pale F de ventilateur M
hoja F de turbina F
Laubfänger M
comignolo M
rotating cap
chapeau M rotatif
tapa F giratoria
Fassung F
pannello M modulare rotante
skirt
collet M
falda F
Einfassung F
canna F
flashing
solin M
tapajuntas M
Dichtungsblech N
scossalina F

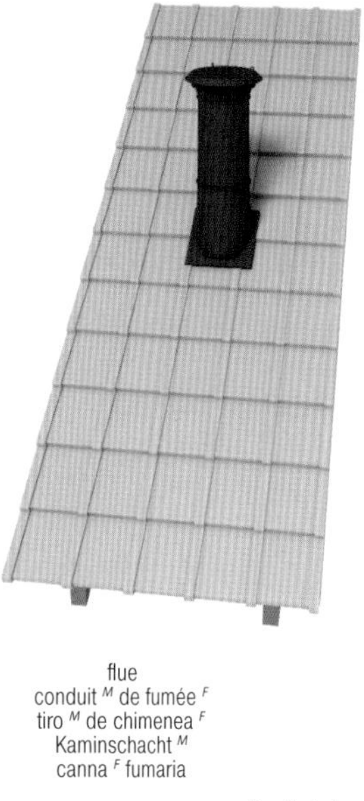
flue
conduit M de fumée F
tiro M de chimenea F
Kaminschacht M
canna F fumaria

Roof windows

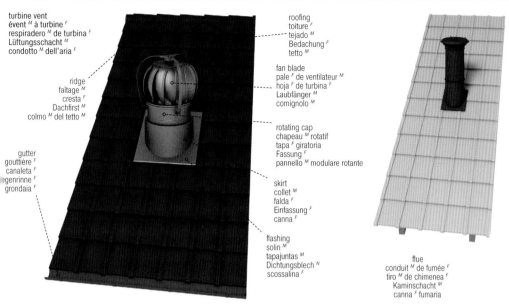

Fenêtres F de toit M | Ventanas F de tejado M | Dachfenster N | Finestre F da mansarda F

skylights
puits M de lumière F
tragaluzes M
Dachfenster N
lucernari M

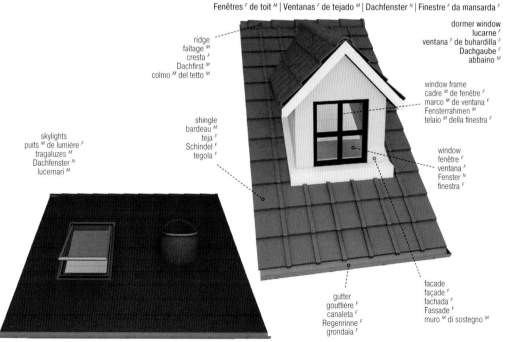

ridge
faîtage M
cresta F
Dachfirst M
colmo M del tetto M
shingle
bardeau M
teja F
Schindel F
tegola F
dormer window
lucarne F
ventana F de buhardilla F
Dachgaube F
abbaino M
window frame
cadre M de fenêtre F
marco M de ventana F
Fensterrahmen M
telaio M della finestra F
window
fenêtre F
ventana F
Fenster N
finestra F
gutter
gouttière F
canaleta F
Regenrinne F
grondaia F
facade
façade F
fachada F
Fassade F
muro M di sostegno M

swimming pool
piscine [F]
pileta [F] / piscina [F]
Schwimmbecken [N]
piscina [F]

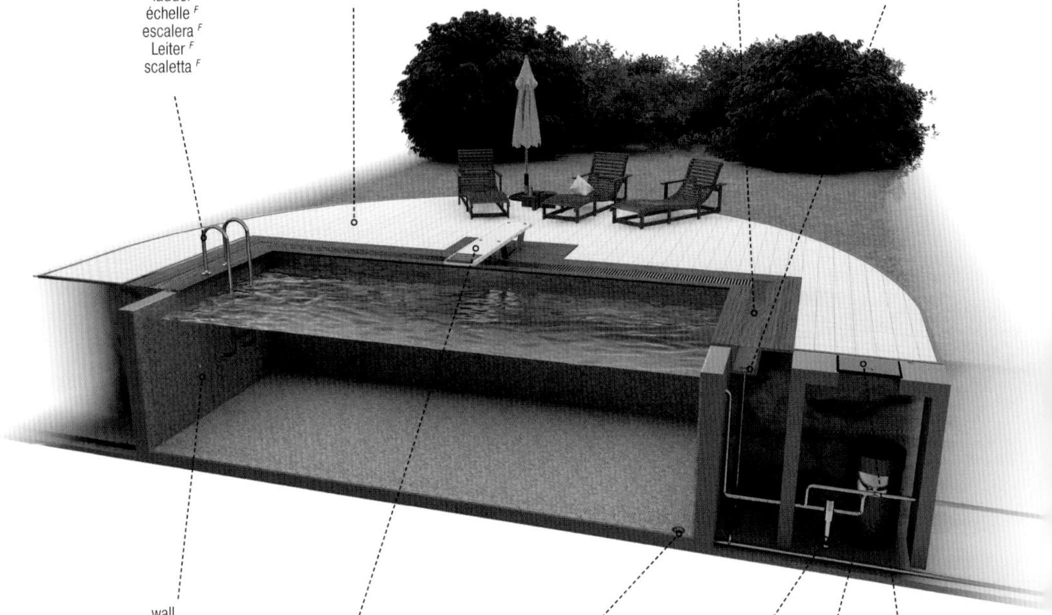

overflow drain
vidange [F] de trop-plein [M]
drenaje [M]
Überlaufablass [M]
canale [M] di sfioro [M]

gutter
trop-plein [M]
canaleta [F]
Abflussrinne [F]
canaletta [F]

deck
terrasse [F]
cubierta [F]
Sonnenterasse [F]
terrazza [F] della piscina [F]

ladder
échelle [F]
escalera [F]
Leiter [F]
scaletta [F]

wall
mur [M]
muro [M]
Beckenwand [F]
parete [F]

diving board
tremplin [M]
trampolín [M]
Sprungbrett [N]
trampolino [M]

drain
bonde [F] de fond [M]
desagüe [M]
Abfluss [M]
scarico [M]

pump
pompe [F]
bomba [F]
Pumpe [F]
pompa [F]

filter
filtre [M]
filtro [M]
Wasserfilter [M]
filtro [M]

hatch
trappe [F]
trampilla [F]
Luke [F]
sportello [M]

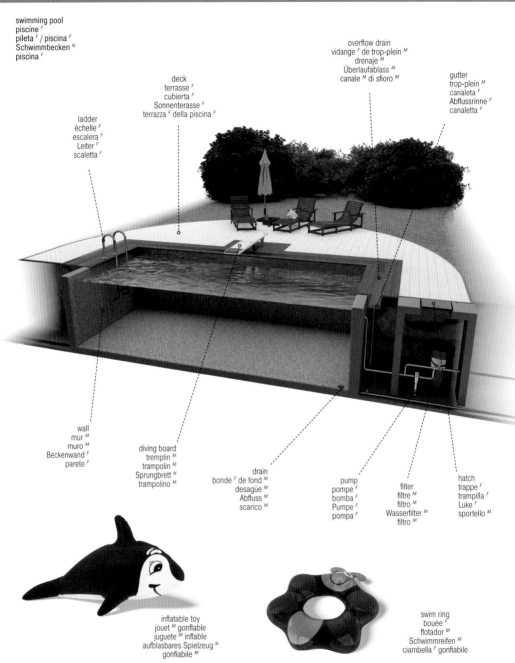

inflatable toy
jouet [M] gonflable
juguete [M] inflable
aufblasbares Spielzeug [N]
gonfiabile [M]

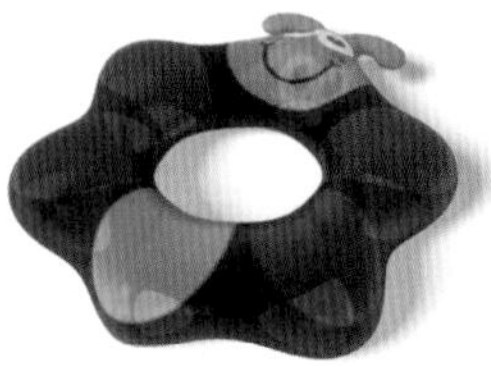

swim ring
bouée [F]
flotador [M]
Schwimmreifen [M]
ciambella [F] gonfiabile

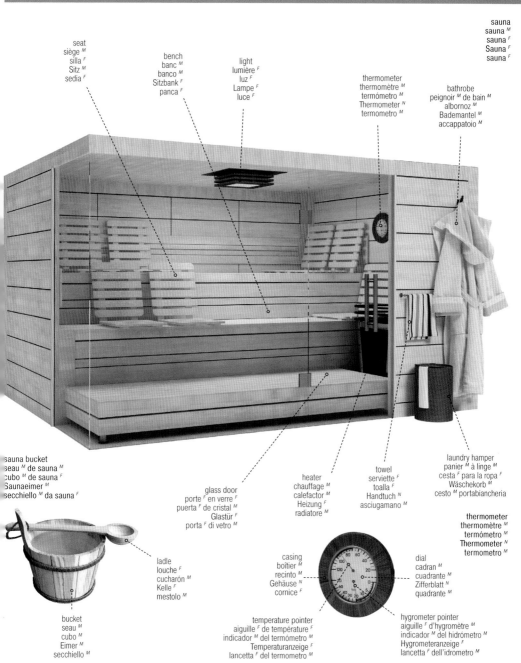

sauna
sauna [M]
sauna [F]
Sauna [F]
sauna [F]

seat
siège [M]
silla [F]
Sitz [M]
sedia [F]

bench
banc [M]
banco [M]
Sitzbank [F]
panca [F]

light
lumière [F]
luz [F]
Lampe [F]
luce [F]

thermometer
thermomètre [M]
termómetro [M]
Thermometer [N]
termometro [M]

bathrobe
peignoir [M] de bain [M]
albornoz [M]
Bademantel [M]
accappatoio [M]

sauna bucket
seau [M] de sauna [M]
cubo [M] de sauna [F]
Saunaeimer [M]
secchiello [M] da sauna [F]

glass door
porte [F] en verre [F]
puerta [F] de cristal [M]
Glastür [F]
porta [F] di vetro [M]

heater
chauffage [M]
calefactor [M]
Heizung [F]
radiatore [M]

towel
serviette [F]
toalla [F]
Handtuch [N]
asciugamano [M]

laundry hamper
panier [M] à linge [M]
cesta [F] para la ropa [F]
Wäschekorb [M]
cesto [M] portabiancheria

ladle
louche [F]
cucharón [M]
Kelle [F]
mestolo [M]

bucket
seau [M]
cubo [M]
Eimer [M]
secchiello [M]

thermometer
thermomètre [M]
termómetro [M]
Thermometer [N]
termometro [M]

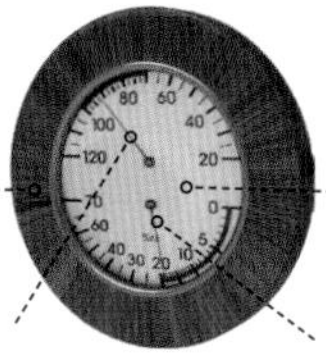

casing
boîtier [M]
recinto [M]
Gehäuse [N]
cornice [F]

dial
cadran [M]
cuadrante [M]
Zifferblatt [N]
quadrante [M]

temperature pointer
aiguille [F] de température [F]
indicador [M] del termómetro [M]
Temperaturanzeige [F]
lancetta [F] del termometro [M]

hygrometer pointer
aiguille [F] d'hygromètre [M]
indicador [M] del hidrómetro [M]
Hygrometeranzeige [F]
lancetta [F] dell'idrometro [M]

deck chair
transatlantique M
silla F de terraza F
Liegestuhl M
sedia F a sdraio

gazebo
belvédère M
glorieta F
Pavillion M
gazebo M

roof
toit M
techo M
Dach N
tetto M
table
table F
mesa F
Tisch M
tavolo M
bench
banc M
banco M
Sitzbank F
panca F
support beam
poutre F de soutien M
puntal M
Stützbalken M
trave F di sostegno M
floor
plancher M
suelo M
Boden M
pavimento M

bistro set
ensemble M bistro
muebles M de exterior M
Bistroset N
set M da giardino M

table
table F
mesa F de exterior M
Tisch M
tavolo M
chair
chaise F
silla F de exterior M
Stuhl M
sedia F

bench
banc M
banco M
Sitzbank F
panca F

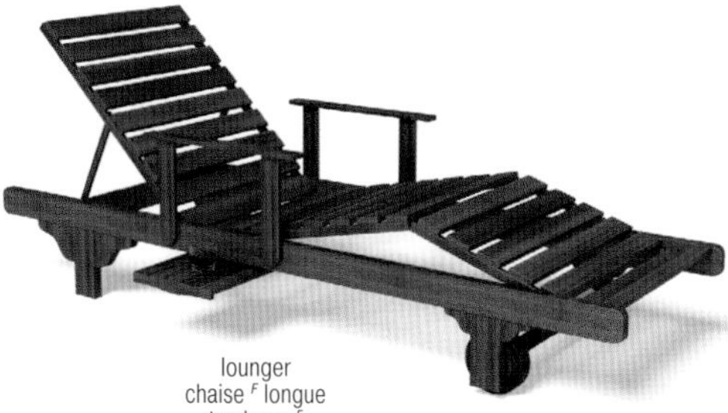

lounger
chaise [F] longue
tumbona [F]
Liege [F]
lettino [M]

sofa
canapé [M]
sofá [M]
Couch [F]
divano [M]

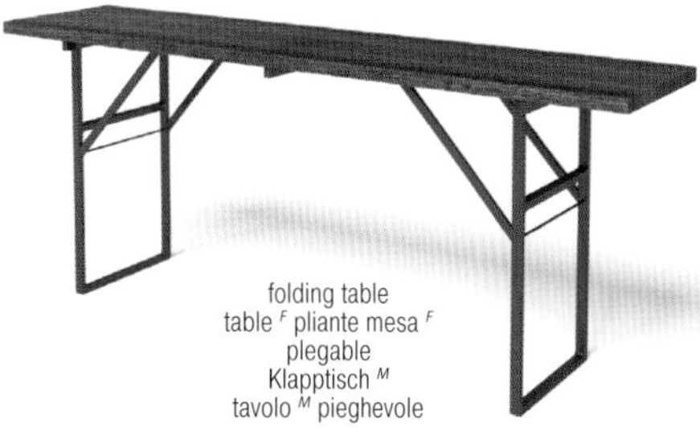

folding table
table [F] pliante mesa [F]
plegable
Klapptisch [M]
tavolo [M] pieghevole

folding bench
banc [M] pliant
banco [M] plegable
Klappbank [F]
panca [F] pieghevole

porch swing
balancelle [F]
balancín [M]
Hollywoodschaukel [F]
dondolo [M] da giardino [M]

bridge
pont [M]
puente [M]
Brücke [F]
ponte [M]

patio umbrella
parasol [M]
sombrilla [F] para terraza [F]
Verandaschirm [M]
ombrellone [M] da giardino [M]

fountain
fontaine [F]
fuente [F]
Springbrunnen [M]
fontana [F]

fence
clôture [F]
valla [F]
Zaun [M]
staccionata [F]

patio heater
radiateur [M] d'extérieur [M]
calefactor [M] de terraza [F]
Terrassenheizer [M]
lampada [F] a gas [M]

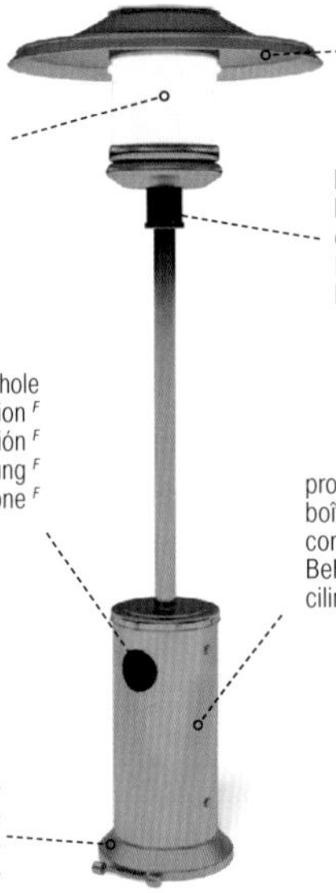

reflector
réflecteur [M]
reflector [M]
Reflektor [M]
riflettore [M]

shade
abat-jour [M]
pantalla [F]
Lampenschirm [M]
paralume [M]

burner
brûleur [M]
quemador [M]
Brenner [M]
bruciatore [M]

ventilation hole
trou [M] de ventilation [F]
abertura [F] de ventilación [F]
Lüftungsöffnung [F]
apertura [F] di ventilazione [F]

propane tank housing
boîtier [M] de la bonbonne [F] de propane [M]
compartimiento [M] del tanque [M] de gas [M]
Behälter [M]
cilindro [M] del propano [M]

base
base [F]
base [F]
Fußteil [N]
base [F]

decorative light
lumière [F] décorative
lámpara [F] decorativa
Zierlicht [N]
luce [F] decorativa

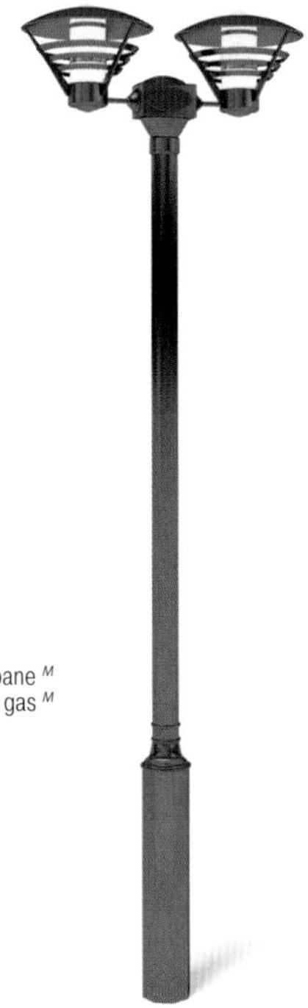

lamppost
lampadaire [M]
poste [M] de luz [F]
Laternenpfahl [M]
palo [M] della luce [F]

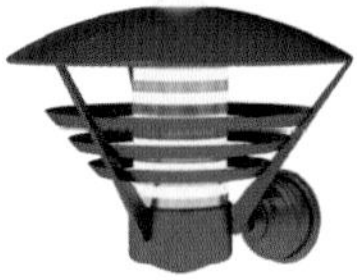

sconce
applique [F]
farola [F]
Wandlicht [N]
applique [F]

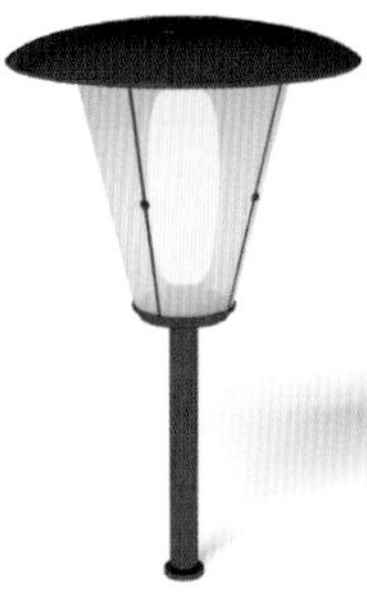

stake light
lampe [F] sur piquet [M]
lámpara [F] de suelo [M]
Rasenlampe [F]
lampada [F] da giardino [M]

barbecue
barbecue M
barbacoa F / parrilla F
Grill M
barbecue M

outdoor fireplace
foyer M extérieur
parrilla F para exteriores M
Außenfeuerstelle F
forno M da esterno M

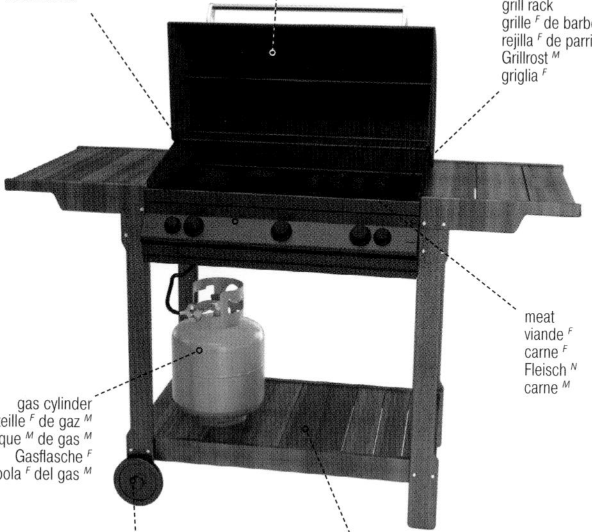

control pad
touche F de commande F
panel M de control M
Schaltregler M
pannello M di controllo M

lid
couvercle M
tapa F
Deckel M
coperchio M

grill rack
grille F de barbecue M
rejilla F de parrilla F
Grillrost M
griglia F

meat
viande F
carne F
Fleisch N
carne M

gas cylinder
bouteille F de gaz M
tanque M de gas M
Gasflasche F
bombola F del gas M

wheel
roue F
rueda F
Rad N
ruota F

storage rack
étagère F de rangement M
estante M de almacenamiento M
Ablageregal N
rastrelliera F di appoggio M

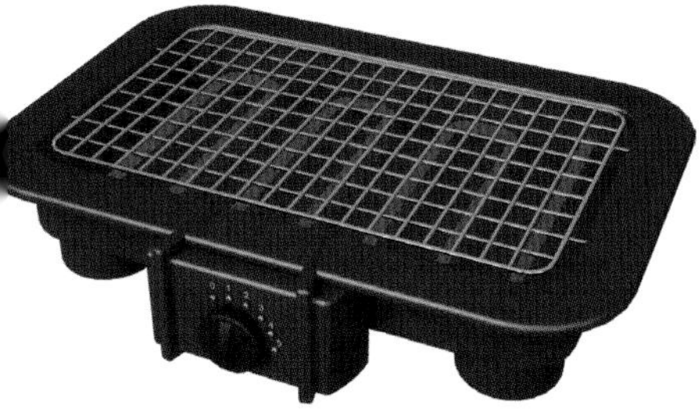

electric grill
gril M électrique
parrilla F eléctrica
Elektrogrill M
griglia F elettrica

hibachi
gril M
barbacoa F de picnic M
Hibachi-Grill M
barbecue M da picnic M

lid
couvercle M
tapa F
Deckel M
coperchio M

grill
grille F
parrilla F
Grillrost M
griglia F

bowl
cuve F
depósito M de carbón M
Schale F
alloggiamento M per la carbonella F

barbecue utensils
ustensiles M de barbecue M
utensilios M de barbacoa F
Grillutensilien N
utensili M da barbecue M

fork
fourchette F
tenedor M
Gabel F
forchetta F

knife
couteau M
cuchillo M
Messer N
coltello M

basting brush
pinceau M
pincel M de cocina F
Küchenpinsel M
pennello M per barbecue M

corn holder
pique-épi M
soporte M para mazorcas F
Maiskolbenhalter M
reggi-pannocchie M

tongs
pinces F
pinzas F
Zange F
pinze F

spatula
spatule F
espátula F
Pfannenwender M
spatola F

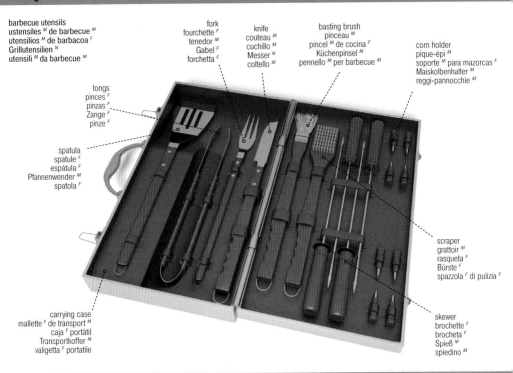

scraper
grattoir M
rasqueta F
Bürste F
spazzola F di pulizia F

carrying case
mallette F de transport M
caja F portátil
Transportkoffer M
valigetta F portatile

skewer
brochette F
brocheta F
Spieß M
spiedino M

TOOLS
Gardening tools

wheelbarrow
brouette F
carretilla F
Schubkarre F
carriola F

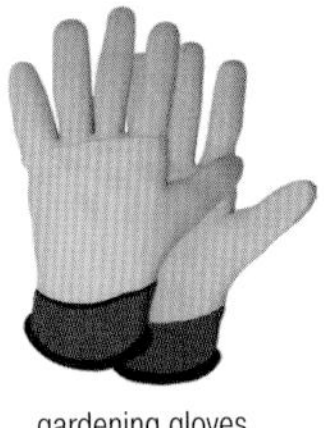

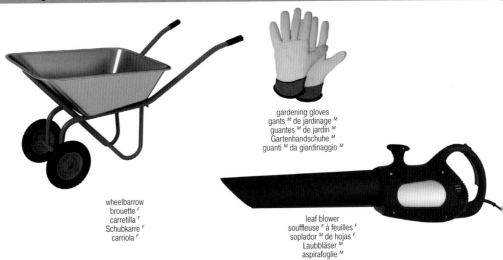

gardening gloves
gants M de jardinage M
guantes M de jardín M
Gartenhandschuhe M
guanti M da giardinaggio M

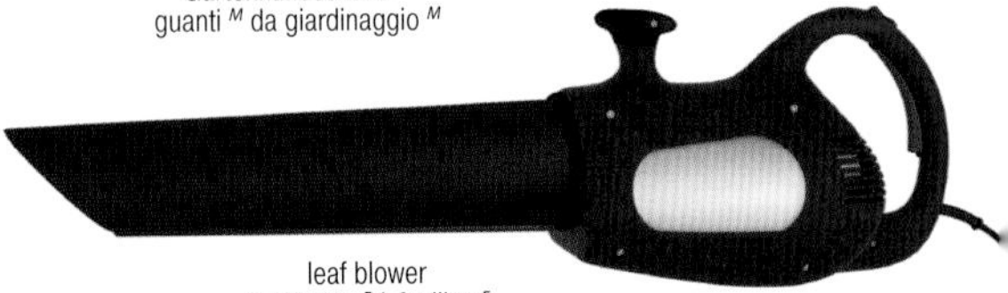

leaf blower
souffleuse F à feuilles F
soplador M de hojas F
Laubbläser M
aspirafoglie M

snow scoop
pousse-neige [M]
quitanieves [M]
Schneewanne [F]
pala [F] da neve [F] professionale

plastic snow shovel
pelle [F] à neige [F] en plastique [M]
pala [F] de nieve [F] de plástico [M]
Plastikschneeschaufel [F]
pala [F] da neve [F] in plastica [F]

metal snow shovel
pelle [F] à neige [F] en métal [M]
pala [F] de nieve [F] metálica
Metallschneeschaufel [F]
pala [F] da neve [F] in metallo [M]

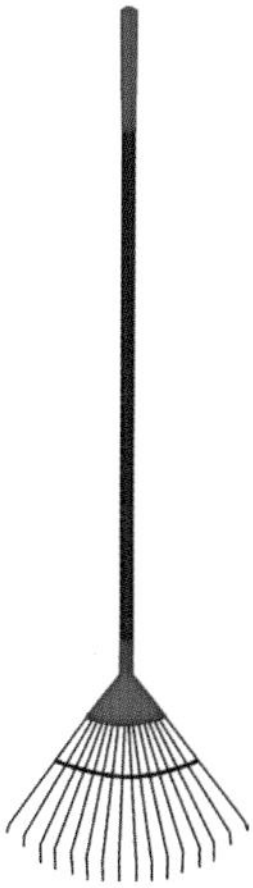

leaf rake
râteau [M] à feuilles [F]
rastrillo [M] de jardín [M]
Laubrechen [M]
rastrello [M] per foglie [F]

level rake
râteau [M] à niveler
rastrillo [M]
Harke [F]
rastrello [M] per terreno [M]

garden fork
fourche [F] à bêcher
horca [F] de jardín [M]
Forke [F]
forcone [M] da giardino [M]

hoe
houe [F]
azada [F]
Hacke [F]
zappa [F]

weeder
truelle [F]
palita [F] de jardín [M]
Unkrautstecher [M]
trapiantatore [M]

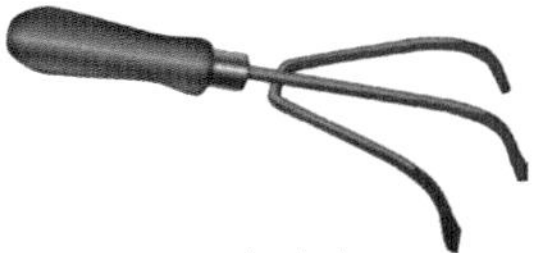

hand rake
râteau [M] à main [F]
cultivador [M] de mano [F]
Handharke [F]
rastrello [M] a mano

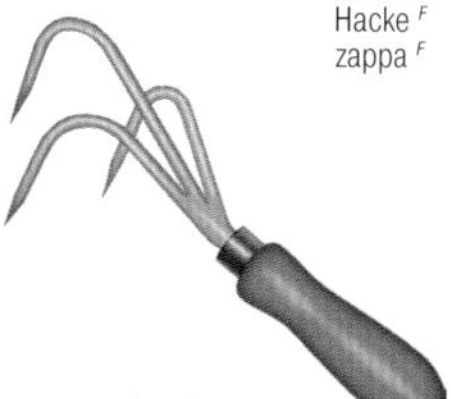

hand cultivator
cultivateur [M] à main [F]
cultivador [M] de mano [F]
Handgrubber [M]
sarchiello [M]

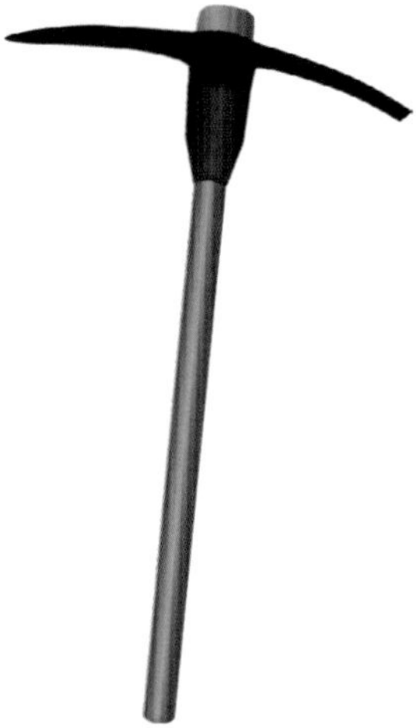

pick
pioche [F]
pico [M]
Spitzhacke [F]
piccone [M]

spade
bêche [F]
pala [F] cuadrada
Spaten [M]
pala [F]

shovel
pelle [F]
pala [F] con punta [F]
Schaufel [F]
vanga [F]

double-headed hoe
houe [F] double tête [F] / bêchard [M]
azada [F] doble
Doppelhacke [F]
doppia zappa [F]

hand fork
fourche [F] à fleurs [F]
horquilla [F] de jardín [M]
Handforke [F]
forcella [F]

garden trowel
transplantoir [M]
pala [F] de jardín [M]
Gartenkelle [F]
paletta [F] da giardiniere [M]

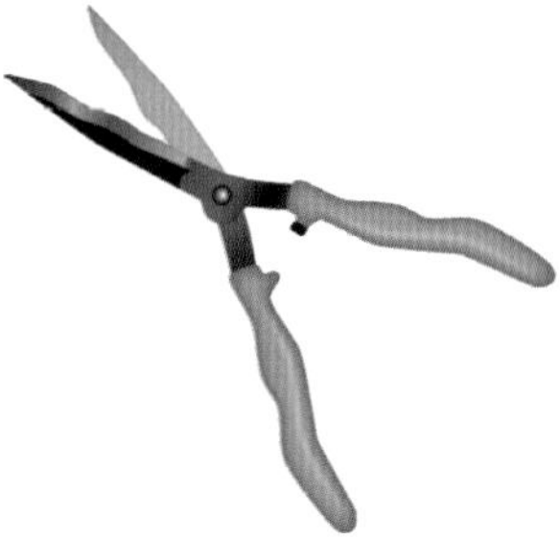

garden shears
cisailles [F] de jardin [M]
tijeras [F] de jardín [M]
Gartenschere [F]
forbici [F] da giardino [M]

ax
hache [F]
hacha [M]
Axt [F]
ascia [F]

pruning saw
scie [F] d'élagage [M]
cortarramas [M]
Astsäge [F]
troncarami [M]

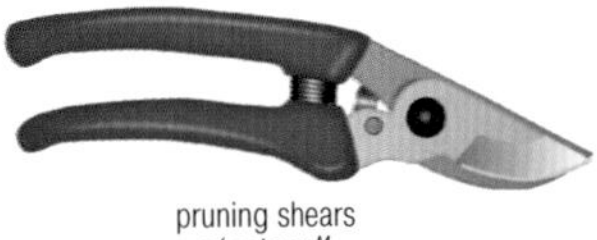

pruning shears
sécateur [M]
podadora [F] de mano [F]
Rebschere [F]
cesoie [F]

chainsaw
scie [F] à chaîne [F]
motosierra [F]
Kettensäge [F]
motosega [F]

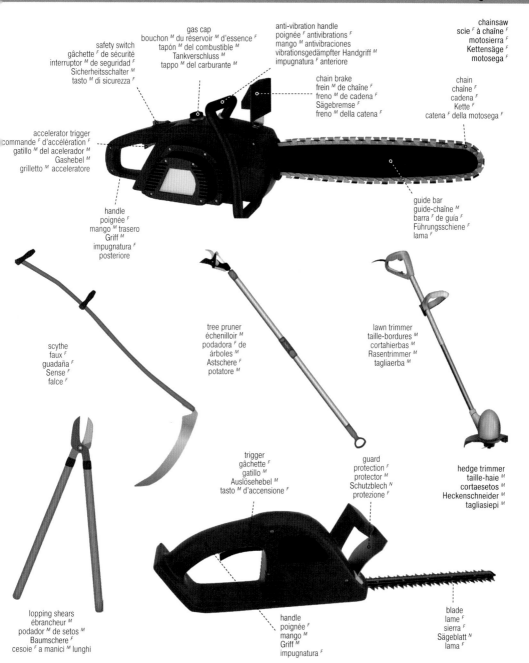

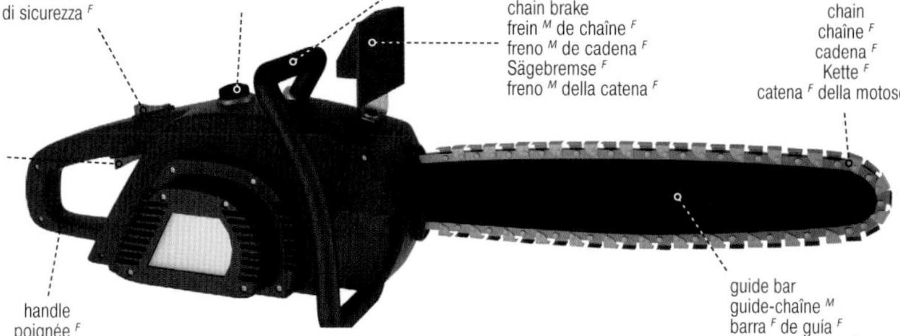
safety switch
gâchette [F] de sécurité
interruptor [M] de seguridad [F]
Sicherheitsschalter [M]
tasto [M] di sicurezza [F]
gas cap
bouchon [M] du réservoir [M] d'essence [F]
tapón [M] del combustible [M]
Tankverschluss [M]
tappo [M] del carburante [M]
anti-vibration handle
poignée [F] antivibrations [F]
mango [M] antivibraciones
vibrationsgedämpfter Handgriff [M]
impugnatura [F] anteriore
chain brake
frein [M] de chaîne [F]
freno [M] de cadena [F]
Sägebremse [F]
freno [M] della catena [F]
chain
chaîne [F]
cadena [F]
Kette [F]
catena [F] della motosega [F]
accelerator trigger
commande [F] d'accélération [F]
gatillo [M] del acelerador [M]
Gashebel [M]
grilletto [M] acceleratore
handle
poignée [F]
mango [M] trasero
Griff [M]
impugnatura [F]
posteriore
guide bar
guide-chaîne [M]
barra [F] de guía [F]
Führungsschiene [F]
lama [F]

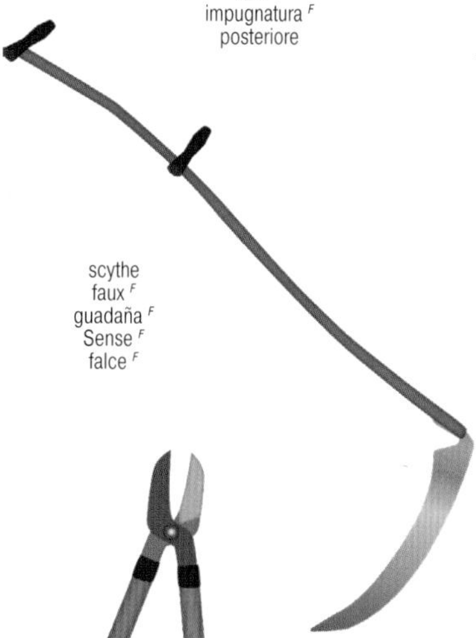

scythe
faux [F]
guadaña [F]
Sense [F]
falce [F]

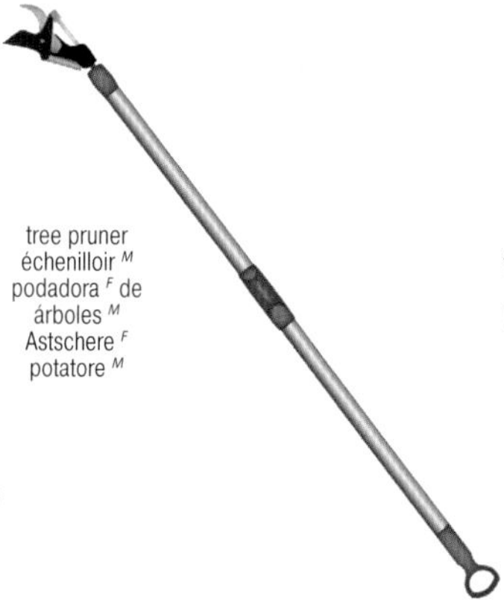

tree pruner
échenilloir [M]
podadora [F] de árboles [M]
Astschere [F]
potatore [M]

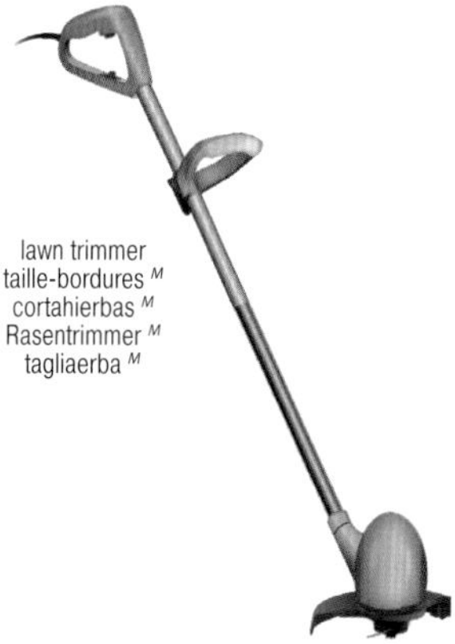

lawn trimmer
taille-bordures [M]
cortahierbas [M]
Rasentrimmer [M]
tagliaerba [M]

lopping shears
ébrancheur [M]
podador [M] de setos [M]
Baumschere [F]
cesoie [F] a manici [M] lunghi

hedge trimmer
taille-haie [M]
cortaesetos [M]
Heckenschneider [M]
tagliasiepi [M]

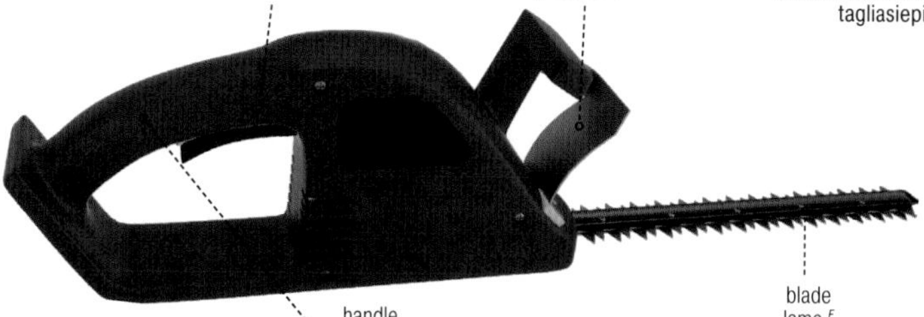
trigger
gâchette [F]
gatillo [M]
Auslösehebel [M]
tasto [M] d'accensione [F]
guard
protection [F]
protector [M]
Schutzblech [N]
protezione [F]
handle
poignée [F]
mango [M]
Griff [M]
impugnatura [F]
blade
lame [F]
sierra [F]
Sägeblatt [N]
lama [F]

lawn mower
tondeuse ^{F} à gazon ^{M}
cortacésped ^{M}
Rasenmäher ^{M}
tagliaerba ^{F}

grass catcher
collecteur ^{M} d'herbe ^{M}
depósito ^{M} de césped ^{M}
Grasfangkorb ^{M}
raccoglierba ^{M}

handle
poignée ^{F}
mango ^{M}
Griff ^{M}
impugnatura ^{F}

gas tank
réservoir ^{M} de carburant ^{M}
depósito ^{M} de combustible ^{M}
Benzintank ^{M}
coperchio ^{M} del serbatoio ^{M}

safety handle
poignée ^{F} de sécurité ^{F}
barra ^{F} de control ^{M}
Sicherheitsgriff ^{M}
barra ^{F} di controllo ^{M}

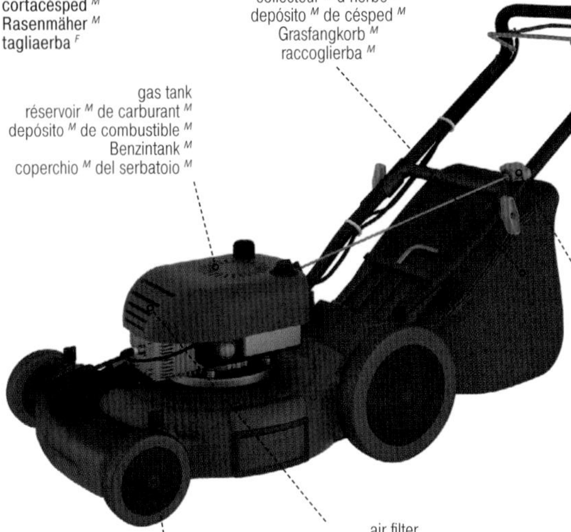

control lever
levier ^{M} de commande ^{F}
palanca ^{F} de control ^{M} del acelerador ^{M}
Bedienhebel ^{M}
leva ^{F} di comando ^{M}

air filter
filtre ^{M} à air ^{M}
filtro ^{M} de aire ^{M}
Luftfilter ^{M}
filtro ^{M} dell'aria ^{F}

wheel
roue ^{F}
rueda ^{F}
Rad ^{N}
ruota ^{F}

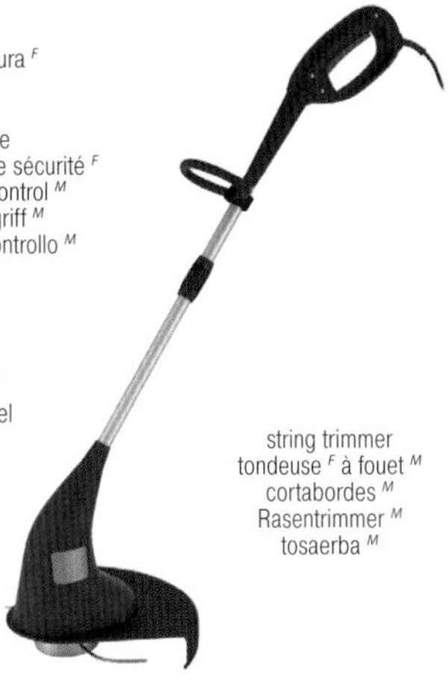

string trimmer
tondeuse ^{F} à fouet ^{M}
cortabordes ^{M}
Rasentrimmer ^{M}
tosaerba ^{M}

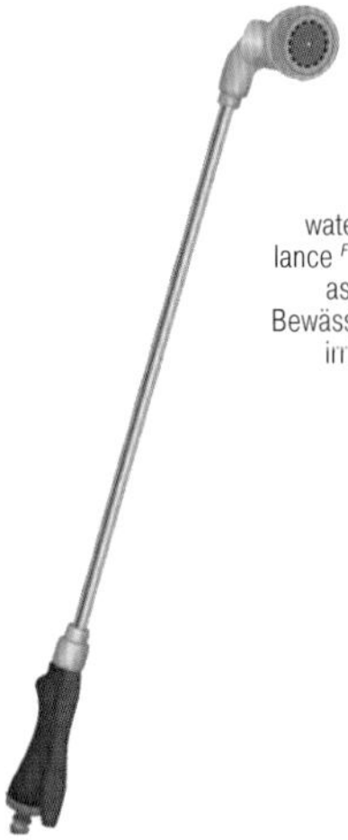

watering wand
lance ^{F} d'arrosage ^{M}
aspersor ^{M}
Bewässerungsstab ^{M}
irrigatore ^{M}

impulse sprinkler
arroseur ^{M} canon ^{M}
aspersor ^{M} de impacto ^{M}
Impuls-Sprinkler ^{M}
irrigatore ^{M} ad impatto ^{M}

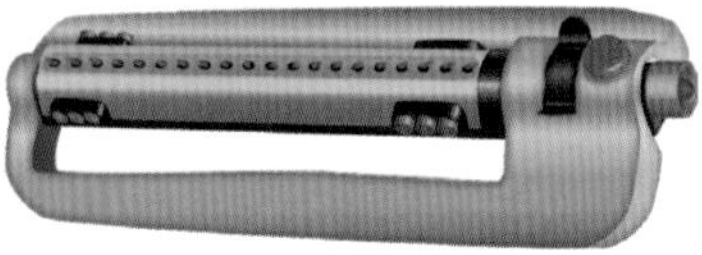

oscillating sprinkler
arroseur ^{M} oscillant
aspersor ^{M} oscilante
Schwingsprinkler ^{M}
irrigatore ^{M} oscillante

pistol nozzle
pistolet ^{M} d'arrosage ^{M}
boquilla ^{F} de pistola ^{F}
Spritze ^{F}
nebulizzatore ^{M}

watering can
arrosoir ^{M}
regadera ^{F}
Gießkanne ^{F}
innaffiatoio ^{M}

garden hose
tuyau ^{M} d'arrosage ^{M}
manguera ^{F} de jardín ^{M}
Gartenschlauch ^{M}
tubo ^{M} da giardino ^{M}

hose reel
enrouleur ^{M}
carrete portamangueras ^{M}
Schlauchwinde ^{F}
avvolgitubo ^{M}

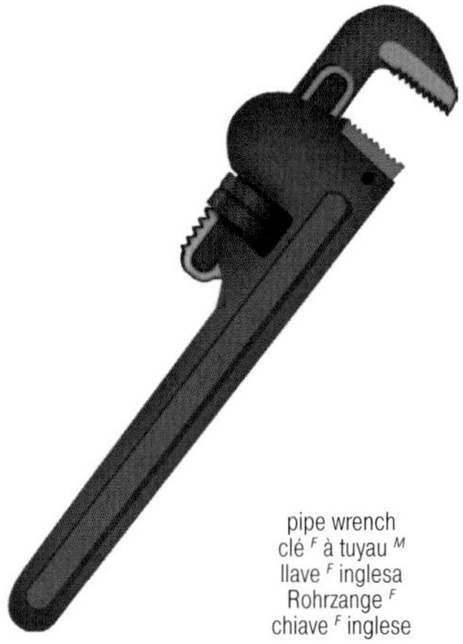

pipe wrench
clé [F] à tuyau [M]
llave [F] inglesa
Rohrzange [F]
chiave [F] inglese

flaring tool
outil [M] à évaser
expansor [M] de tubos [M]
Bördelgerät [N]
spina [F] allargatubi

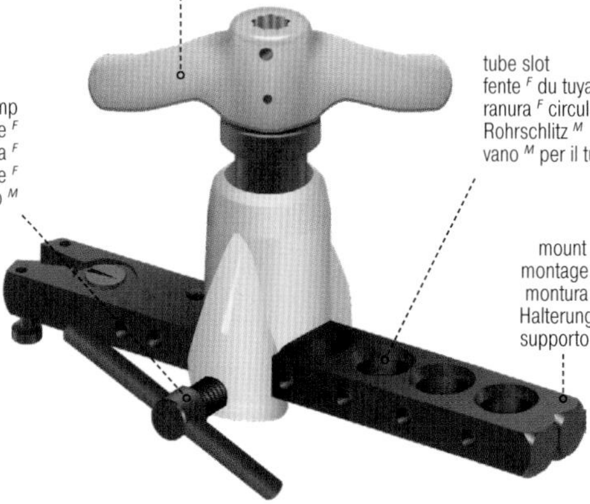

wing nut
écrou [M] à oreilles [F]
tuerca [F] de mariposa [F]
Flügelmutter [F]
dado [M] ad alette [F]

clamp
pince [F]
abrazadera [F]
Klemme [F]
morsetto [M]

tube slot
fente [F] du tuyau [M]
ranura [F] circular
Rohrschlitz [M]
vano [M] per il tubo [M]

mount
montage [M]
montura [F]
Halterung [F]
supporto [M]

pipe cutter
coupe-tuyau [M]
tijera [F] cortatubos
Rohrschneider [M]
tagliatubi [M]

plunger
ventouse [F]
desatascador [M]
Saugglocke [F]
sturalavandini [M]

plumber's snake
furet [M]
sistema [M] de limpieza [F] de alcantarillas [F]
Rohrreinigungsspirale [F]
sturato [M] a molla [F]

tongue-and-groove pliers
pince [F] multiprise
alicate [M] de unión [F] deslizante
Wasserpumpenzange [F] mit Rillen-Gleitgelenk [N]
chiave [F] a ganasce [F] per tubi [M]

pipe threader
fileteuse [F] de tuyaux [M]
machuelo [M]
Rohrgewindeschneider [F]
filiera [F] per tubi [M]

crescent wrench
clé [F] anglaise
llave [F] inglesa
Rollgabelschlüssel [M]
chiave [F] inglese

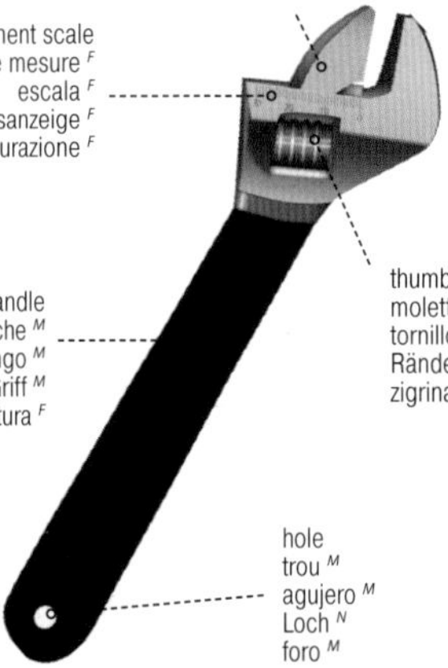
jaw
mâchoire [F]
quijada [F]
Klemmbacken [F]
ganasce [F]
measurement scale
échelle [F] de mesure [F]
escala [F]
Messanzeige [F]
scala [F] di misurazione [F]
thumbscrew
molette [F]
tornillo [M] de ajuste [M]
Rändel [N]
zigrinatura [F]
handle
manche [M]
mango [M]
Griff [M]
impugnatura [F]
hole
trou [M]
agujero [M]
Loch [N]
foro [M]

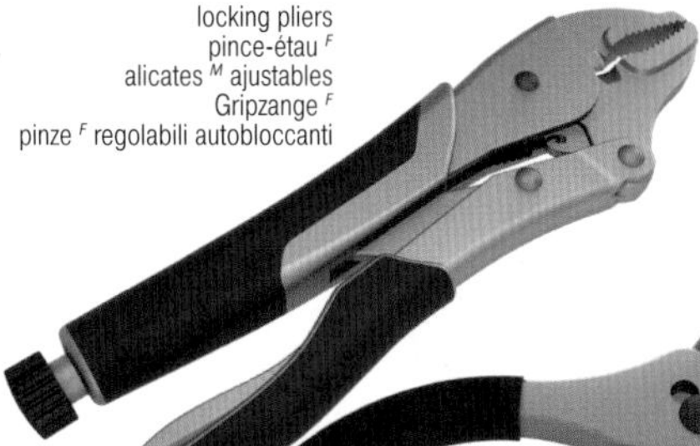

locking pliers
pince-étau [F]
alicates [M] ajustables
Gripzange [F]
pinze [F] regolabili autobloccanti

slip-joint pliers
pinces [F] à joint [M] coulissant
alicates [M] de muela [F] deslizante
Wasserpumpenzange [F]
pinze [F] regolabili

faucet seat wrench
rectifieuse [F]
llave [F] de ajuste [M] de válvula [F]
Standhahnschlüssel [M]
chiave [F] torx

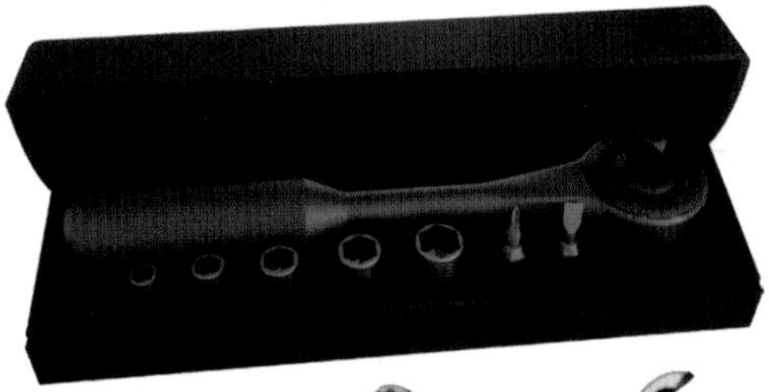

socket set
jeu [M] de clés [F] à douille [F]
juego [M] de llave [F] de cubos [M]
Steckschlüsselgarnitur [F]
set [M] di chiavi [F] a bussola [F]

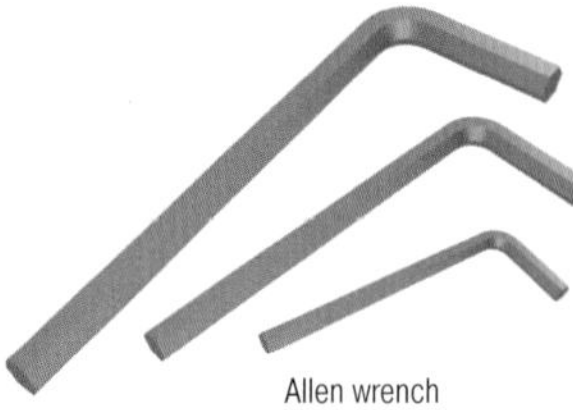

Allen wrench
clé [F] hexagonale
llave [F] hexagonal
Inbusschlüssel [M]
chiave [F] a brugola [F]

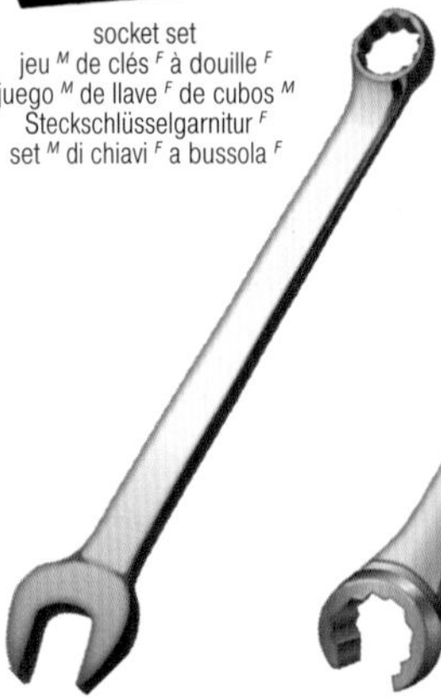

combination wrench
clé [F] mixte
llave [F] combinada
Kombischlüssel [M]
chiave [F] combinata

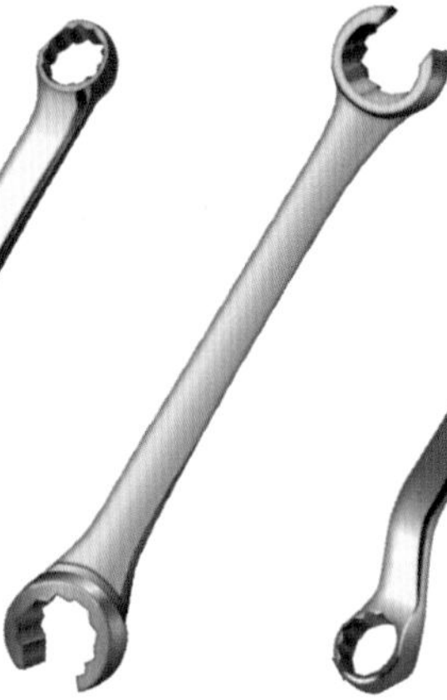

flare nut wrench
clé [F] polygonale à têtes [F] fendue
llave [F] poligonal
offener Ringschlüssel [M]
chiave [F] poligonale

box end wrench
clé [F] polygonale llave [F]
de estrella [F]
Ringschlüssel [M]
chiave [F] ad anello [M]

open end wrench
clé [F] à fourche [F]
llave [F] abierta
Gabelschlüssel [M]
chiave [F] a forchetta [F] doppia

ratchet box end wrench
clé [F] polygonale à cliquet [M]
llave [F] de trinquete [M]
Knarren-Ringschlüssel [M]
chiave [F] a cricchetto [M]

circular saw
scie [F] circulaire
sierra [F] radial
Kreissäge [F]
sega [F] circolare

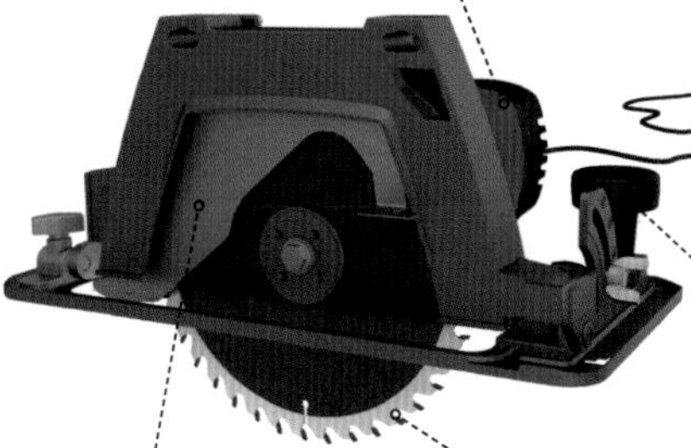

motor housing
boîtier [M] du moteur [M]
compartimento [M] del motor [M]
Motorengehäuse [N]
alloggiamento [M] del motore [M]

handle
poignée [F]
mango [M]
Griff [M]
impugnatura [F]

blade
lame [F]
sierra de disco [M]
Sägeblatt [N]
lama [F]

blade guard
protège-lame [M]
protector [M] de hoja [F]
Schutzhaube [F]
paralama [M]

jigsaw
scie [F] sauteuse
sierra [F] de vaivén [M]
Stichsäge [F]
seghetto [M] da traforo [M]

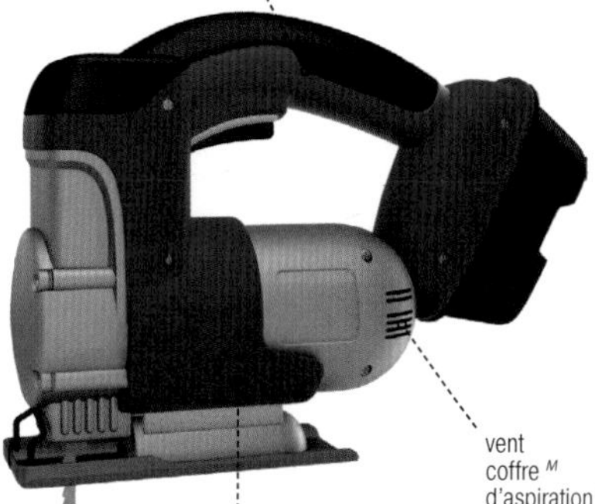

handle
poignée [F]
mango [M]
Griff [M]
impugnatura [F]

vent
coffre [M]
d'aspiration [F]
respiradero [M]
Lüftung [F]
sfiato [M]

blade
lame [F]
hoja [F] de sierra [F]
Sägeblatt [N]
lama [F]

motor housing
boîtier [M] du moteur [M]
compartimento [M] del motor [M]
Motorengehäuse [N]
alloggiamento [M] del motore [M]

hacksaw
scie [F] à métaux [M]
sierra [F] de arco [M]
Bügelsäge [F]
sega [F] a telaio [M]

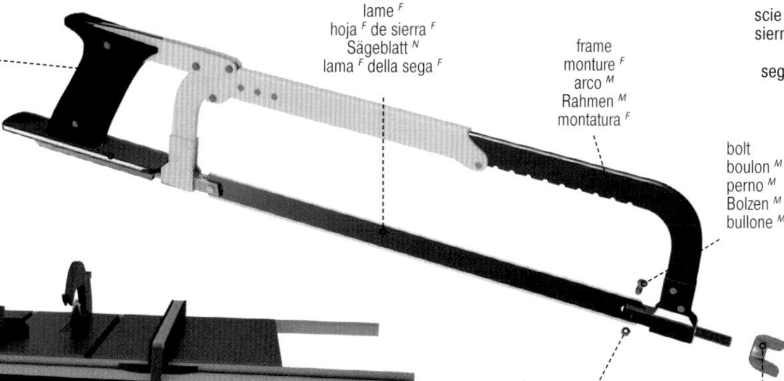

handle
poignée [F]
mango [M]
Griff [M]
impugnatura [F]

blade
lame [F]
hoja [F] de sierra [F]
Sägeblatt [N]
lama [F] della sega [F]

frame
monture [F]
arco [M]
Rahmen [M]
montatura [F]

bolt
boulon [M]
perno [M]
Bolzen [M]
bullone [M]

nut
écrou [M]
tuerca [F]
Mutter [F]
dado [M]

wing nut
écrou [M] à oreilles [F]
tuerca [F] de mariposa [F]
Flügelmutter [F]
dado [M] ad alette [F]

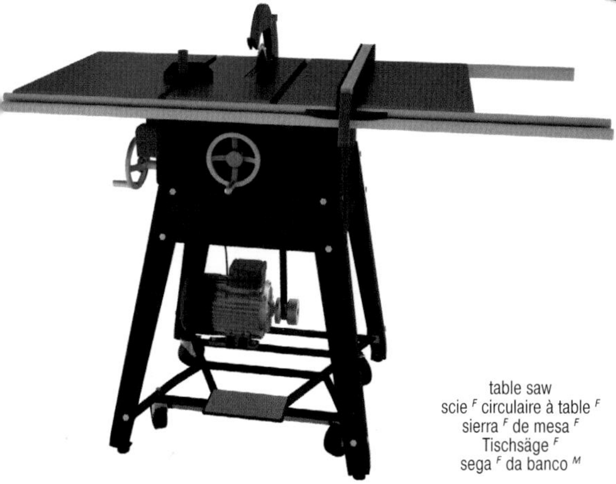

table saw
scie [F] circulaire à table [F]
sierra [F] de mesa [F]
Tischsäge [F]
sega [F] da banco [M]

hand saw
scie ^{M} égoïne
sierra ^{F} de mano ^{F}
Handsäge ^{F}
sega ^{F} a costola ^{F}

backsaw
scie ^{F} à dos ^{M}
serrucho ^{M} de costilla ^{F}
Rückensäge ^{F}
sega ^{F} a dorso ^{M}

compass saw
scie ^{F} à guichet ^{M}
sierra ^{F} de calar
Stichsäge ^{F}
seghetto ^{M} a punta ^{F}

Sanding and polishing tools

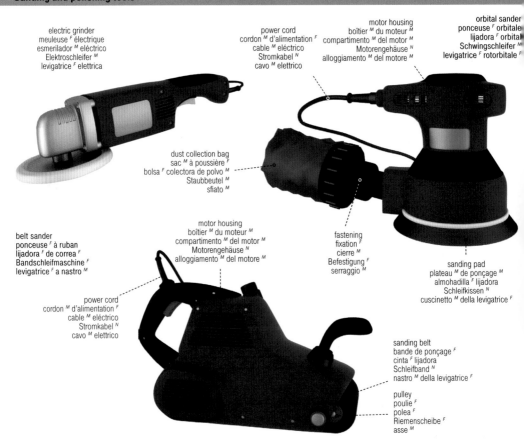

electric grinder
meuleuse ^{F} électrique
esmerilador ^{M} eléctrico
Elektroschleifer ^{M}
levigatrice ^{F} elettrica

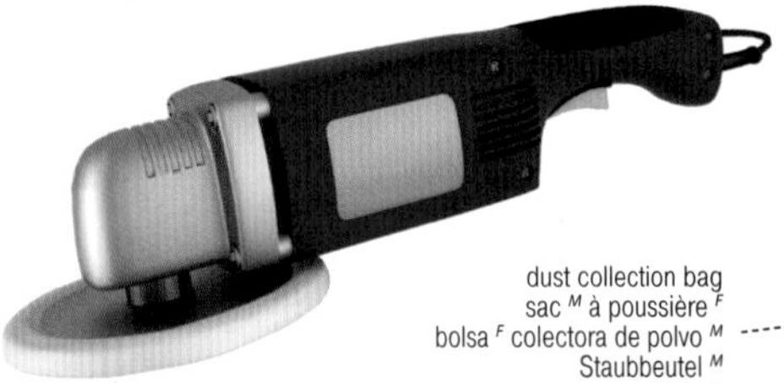

orbital sander
ponceuse ^{F} orbitale
lijadora ^{F} orbital
Schwingschleifer ^{M}
levigatrice ^{F} rotorbitale ^{F}

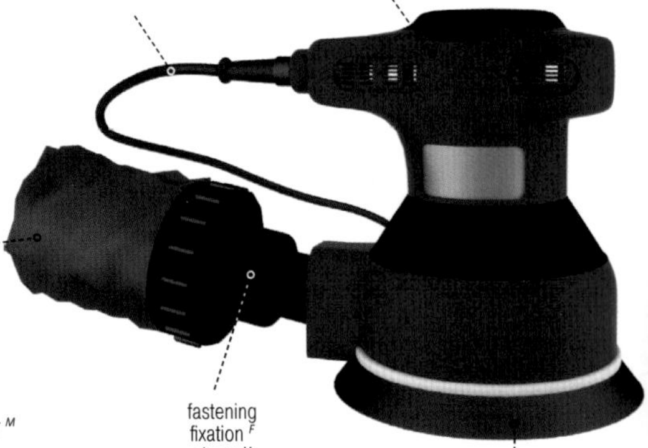
power cord
cordon ^{M} d'alimentation ^{F}
cable ^{M} eléctrico
Stromkabel ^{N}
cavo ^{M} elettrico
motor housing
boîtier ^{M} du moteur ^{M}
compartimento ^{M} del motor ^{M}
Motorengehäuse ^{N}
alloggiamento ^{M} del motore ^{M}
dust collection bag
sac ^{M} à poussière ^{F}
bolsa ^{F} colectora de polvo ^{M}
Staubbeutel ^{M}
sfiato ^{M}
fastening
fixation ^{F}
cierre ^{M}
Befestigung ^{F}
serraggio ^{M}
sanding pad
plateau ^{M} de ponçage ^{M}
almohadilla ^{F} lijadora
Schleifkissen ^{N}
cuscinetto ^{M} della levigatrice ^{F}

belt sander
ponceuse ^{F} à ruban
lijadora ^{F} de correa ^{F}
Bandschleifmaschine ^{F}
levigatrice ^{F} a nastro ^{M}

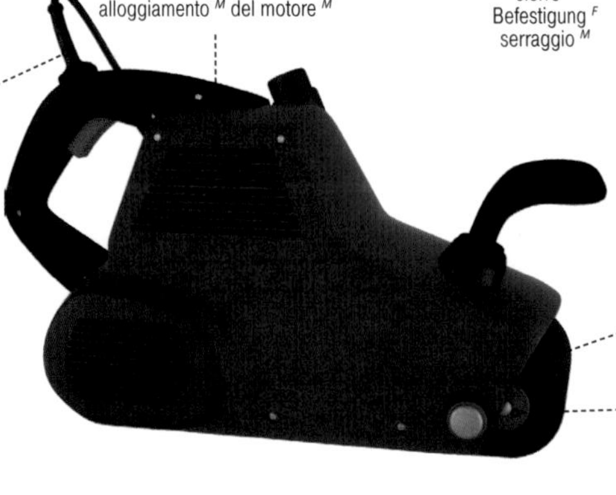
motor housing
boîtier ^{M} du moteur ^{M}
compartimento ^{M} del motor ^{M}
Motorengehäuse ^{N}
alloggiamento ^{M} del motore ^{M}
power cord
cordon ^{M} d'alimentation ^{F}
cable ^{M} eléctrico
Stromkabel ^{N}
cavo ^{M} elettrico
sanding belt
bande de ponçage ^{F}
cinta ^{F} lijadora
Schleifband ^{N}
nastro ^{M} della levigatrice ^{F}
pulley
poulie ^{F}
polea ^{F}
Riemenscheibe ^{F}
asse ^{M}

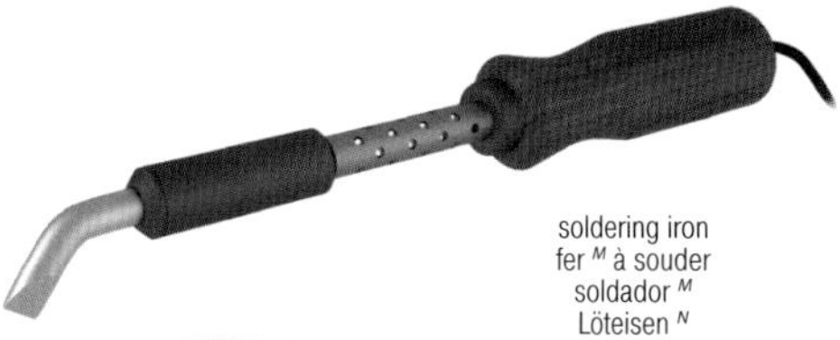

soldering iron
fer [M] à souder
soldador [M]
Löteisen [N]
saldatore [M] per ferro [M]

solder
soudure [F]
soldadura [F]
Lötzinn [M]
stagno [M]

soldering gun
pistolet [M] à souder
soldador [M]
Lötpistole [F]
saldatore [M]

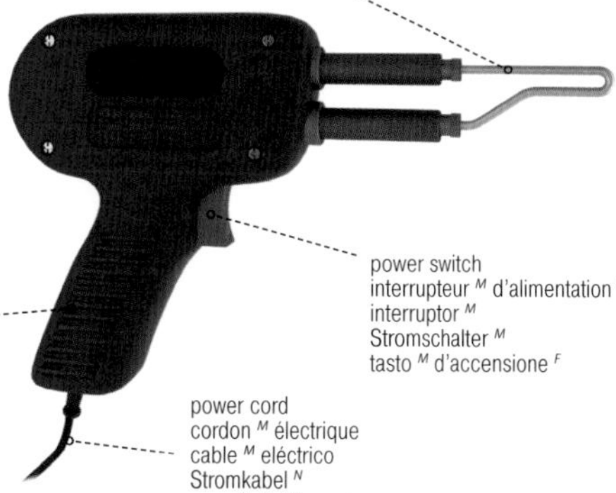

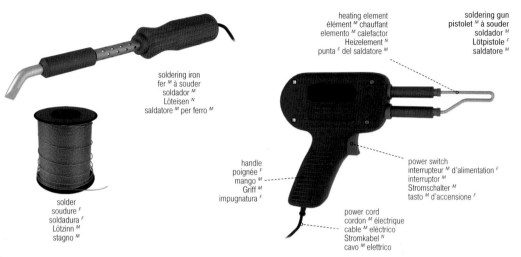

heating element
élément [M] chauffant
elemento [M] calefactor
Heizelement [N]
punta [F] del saldatore [M]

handle
poignée [F]
mango [M]
Griff [M]
impugnatura [F]

power switch
interrupteur [M] d'alimentation [F]
interruptor [M]
Stromschalter [M]
tasto [M] d'accensione [F]

power cord
cordon [M] électrique
cable [M] eléctrico
Stromkabel [N]
cavo [M] elettrico

Electrical tools

multimeter
multimètre [M]
multímetro [M]
Universalmessgerät [N]
multimetro [M]

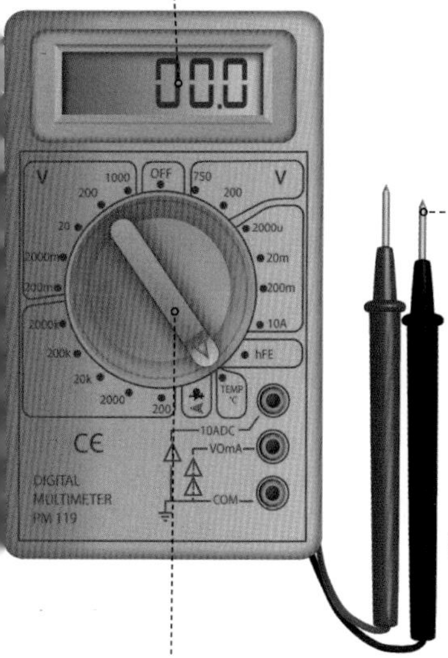
00.0
OFF
1000
750
200
200
V
V
20
2000m
200m
2000k
200k
20k
2000
200
2000u
20m
200m
10A
hFE
TEMP
10ADC
VΩmA
COM
CE
DIGITAL
MULTIMETER
DM 119

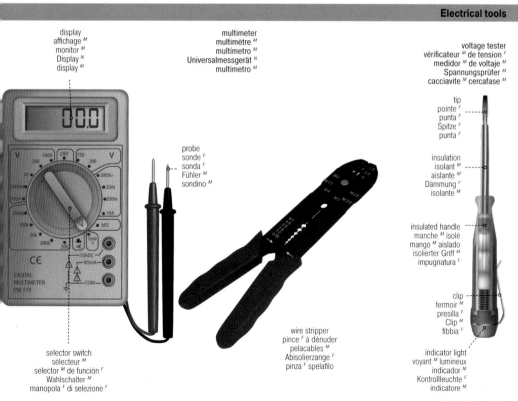

display
affichage [M]
monitor [M]
Display [N]
display [M]

selector switch
sélecteur [M]
selector [M] de función [F]
Wahlschalter [M]
manopola [F] di selezione [F]

probe
sonde [F]
sonda [F]
Fühler [M]
sondino [M]

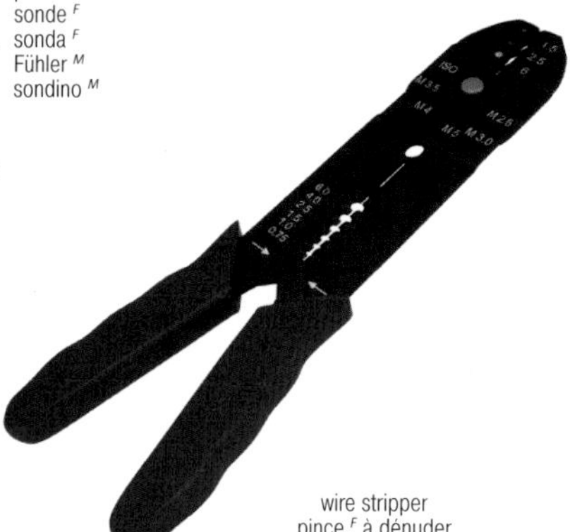

wire stripper
pince [F] à dénuder
pelacables [M]
Abisolierzange [F]
pinza [F] spelafilo

voltage tester
vérificateur [M] de tension [F]
medidor [M] de voltaje [M]
Spannungsprüfer [M]
cacciavite [M] cercafase [M]

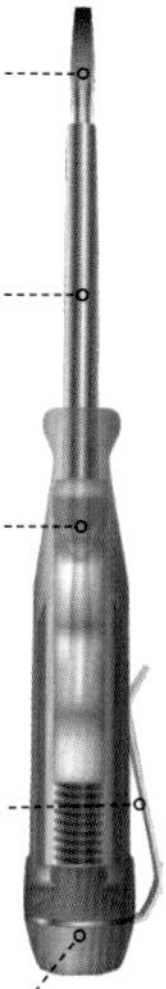

tip
pointe [F]
punta [F]
Spitze [F]
punta [F]

insulation
isolant [M]
aislante [M]
Dämmung [F]
isolante [M]

insulated handle
manche [M] isolé
mango [M] aislado
isolierter Griff [M]
impugnatura [F]

clip
fermoir [M]
presilla [F]
Clip [M]
fibbia [F]

indicator light
voyant [M] lumineux
indicador [M]
Kontrollleuchte [F]
indicatore [M]

electric drill
perceuse [F] électrique
taladro [M] eléctrico
elektrischer Bohrer [M]
trapano [M] senza fili [M]

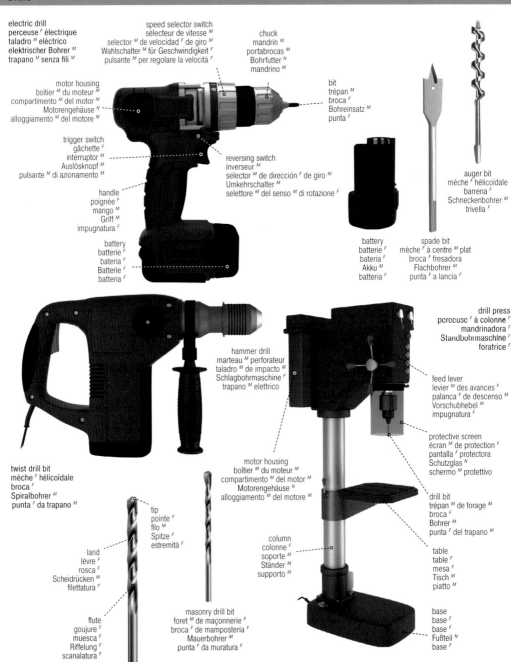

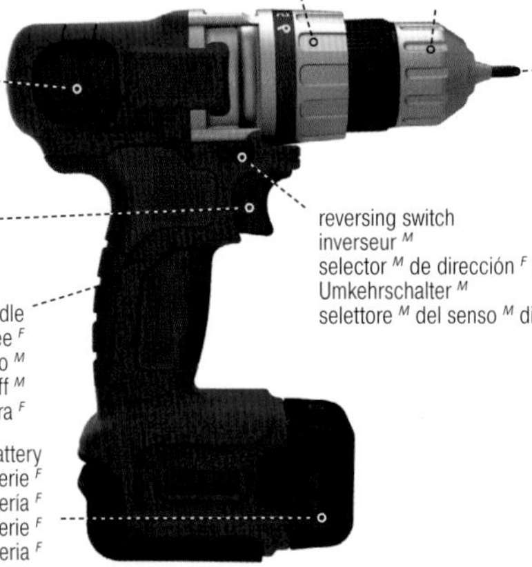

speed selector switch
sélecteur de vitesse [M]
selector [M] de velocidad [F] de giro [M]
Wahlschalter [M] für Geschwindigkeit [F]
pulsante [M] per regolare la velocità [F]

chuck
mandrin [M]
portabrocas [M]
Bohrfutter [N]
mandrino [M]

motor housing
boîtier [M] du moteur [M]
compartimento [M] del motor [M]
Motorengehäuse [N]
alloggiamento [M] del motore [M]

bit
trépan [M]
broca [F]
Bohreinsatz [M]
punta [F]

trigger switch
gâchette [F]
interruptor [M]
Auslösknopf [M]
pulsante [M] di azionamento [M]

reversing switch
inverseur [M]
selector [M] de dirección [F] de giro [M]
Umkehrschalter [M]
selettore [M] del senso [M] di rotazione [F]

handle
poignée [F]
mango [M]
Griff [M]
impugnatura [F]

battery
batterie [F]
batería [F]
Batterie [F]
batteria [F]

battery
batterie [F]
batería [F]
Akku [M]
batteria [F]

spade bit
mèche [F] à centre [M] plat
broca [F] fresadora
Flachbohrer [M]
punta [F] a lancia [F]

auger bit
mèche [F] hélicoïdale
barrena [F]
Schneckenbohrer [M]
trivella [F]

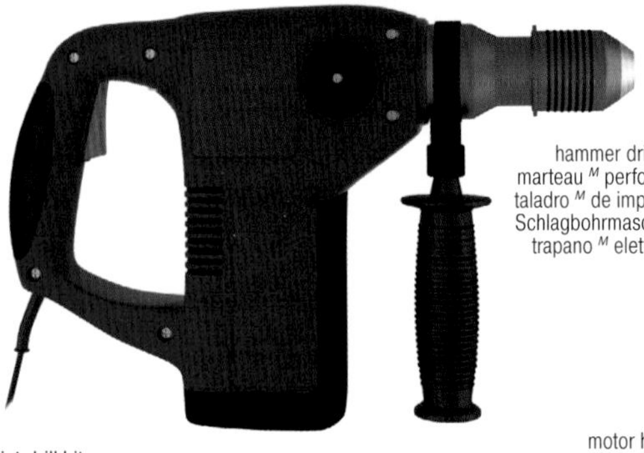

hammer drill
marteau [M] perforateur
taladro [M] de impacto [M]
Schlagbohrmaschine [F]
trapano [M] elettrico

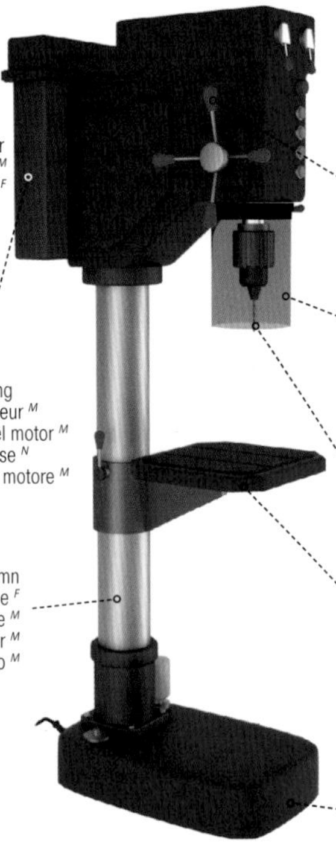

drill press
perceuse [F] à colonne [F]
mandrinadora [F]
Standbohrmaschine [F]
foratrice [F]

feed lever
levier [M] des avances [F]
palanca [F] de descenso [M]
Vorschubhebel [M]
impugnatura [F]

protective screen
écran [M] de protection [F]
pantalla [F] protectora
Schutzglas [N]
schermo [M] protettivo

motor housing
boîtier [M] du moteur [M]
compartimento [M] del motor [M]
Motorengehäuse [N]
alloggiamento [M] del motore [M]

drill bit
trépan [M] de forage [M]
broca [F]
Bohrer [M]
punta [F] del trapano [M]

column
colonne [F]
soporte [M]
Ständer [M]
supporto [M]

table
table [F]
mesa [F]
Tisch [M]
piatto [M]

base
base [F]
base [F]
Fußteil [N]
base [F]

twist drill bit
mèche [F] hélicoïdale
broca [F]
Spiralbohrer [M]
punta [F] da trapano [M]

tip
pointe [F]
filo [M]
Spitze [F]
estremità [F]

land
lèvre [F]
rosca [F]
Scheidrücken [M]
filettatura [F]

flute
goujure [F]
muesca [F]
Riffelung [F]
scanalatura [F]

masonry drill bit
foret [M] de maçonnerie [F]
broca [F] de mampostería [F]
Mauerbohrer [M]
punta [F] da muratura [F]

aw hammer
arteau M de charpentier M
artillo M sacaclavos
schlerhammer M
artello M da carpentiere M

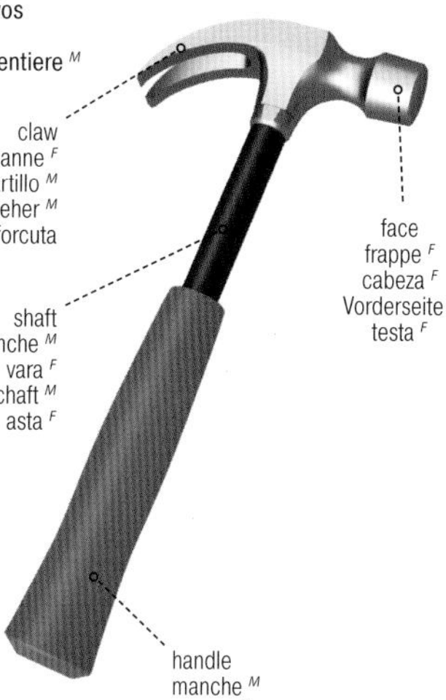
claw
panne F
oreja F de martillo M
Nagelzieher M
estremità F biforcuta
face
frappe F
cabeza F
Vorderseite F
testa F
shaft
manche M
vara F
Schaft M
asta F
handle
manche M
mango M
Griff M
impugnatura F

crowbar
pied-de-biche M
pata F de cabra F
Brecheisen N
piede M di porco M

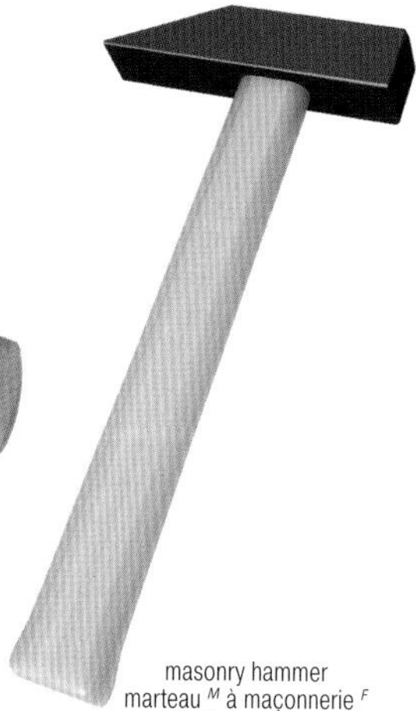

masonry hammer
marteau M à maçonnerie F
martillo M de albañilería F
Maurerhammer M
martello M

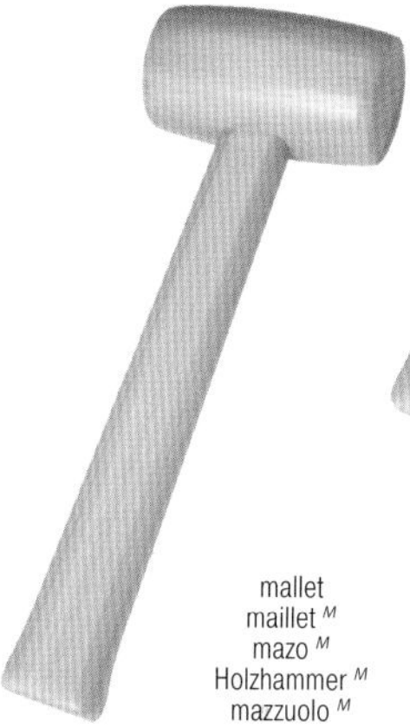

mallet
maillet M
mazo M
Holzhammer M
mazzuolo M

nail gun
cloueuse F
pistola F de clavos M
Nagelpistole F
pistola F sparachiodi

nail set
chasse-clou M
punzón M
Nageltreiber M
set M di punzoni M

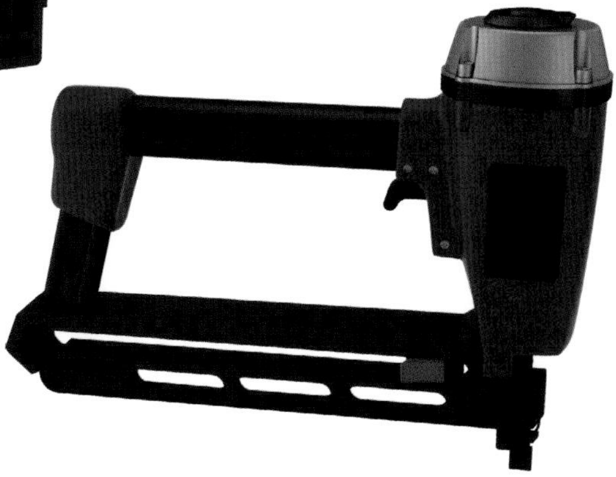

electric stapler
agrafeuse F électrique
grapadora F eléctrica
Elektrotacker M
graffettatrice F elettrica

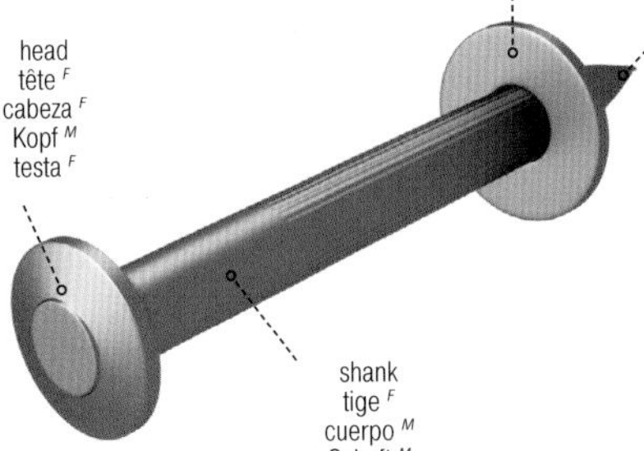
masonry nail
clou [M] à maçonnerie [F]
clavo [M] de mampostería [F]
Maurernagel [M]
chiodo [M] per calcestruzzo [M]
washer
rondelle [F]
arandela [F]
Unterlegscheibe [F]
rondella [F]
tip
pointe [F]
punta [F]
Spitze [F]
punta [F]
head
tête [F]
cabeza [F]
Kopf [M]
testa [F]
shank
tige [F]
cuerpo [M]
Schaft [M]
gambo [M]

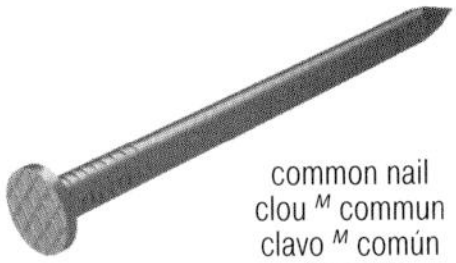
common nail
clou [M] commun
clavo [M] común
Nagel [M]
chiodo [M]

screw and nut
vis [M] et écrou [M]
tornillo [M] y tuerca [F]
Schraube und Mutter [F]
vite [F] e bullone [M]

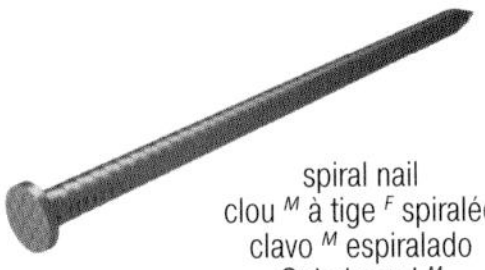
spiral nail
clou [M] à tige [F] spiralée
clavo [M] espiralado
Spiralnagel [M]
chiodo [M] a spirale [F]

screw
vis [F]
tornillo [M]
Schraube [F]
vite [F]

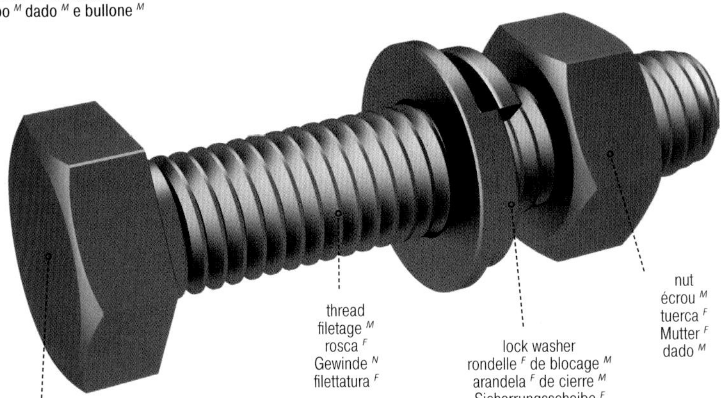
nut and bolt
écrou [M] et boulon [M]
tuerca [F] y perno [M]
Schraube [F] und Mutter [F]
gruppo [M] dado [M] e bullone [M]
thread
filetage [M]
rosca [F]
Gewinde [N]
filettatura [F]
lock washer
rondelle [F] de blocage [M]
arandela [F] de cierre [M]
Sicherrungsscheibe [F]
fermadado [M]
nut
écrou [M]
tuerca [F]
Mutter [F]
dado [M]
head
tête [F]
cabeza [F]
Kopf [M]
testa [F]

anchor
ancrage [M]
taco [M]
Dübel [M]
tassello [M]

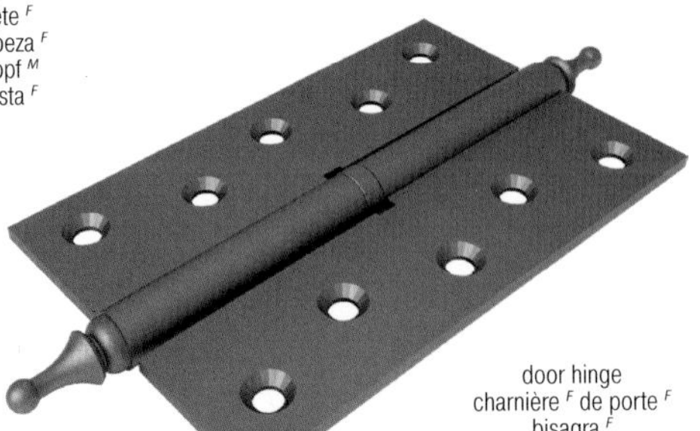
door hinge
charnière [F] de porte [F]
bisagra [F]
Türscharnier [N]
cerniera [F] per porte [F]

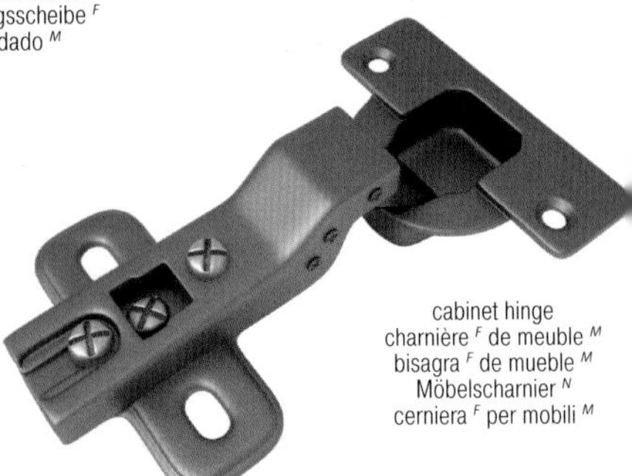
cabinet hinge
charnière [F] de meuble [M]
bisagra [F] de mueble [M]
Möbelscharnier [N]
cerniera [F] per mobili [M]

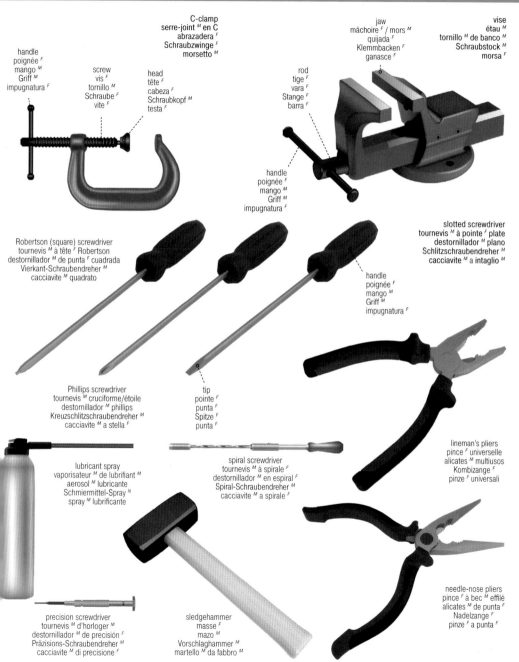

C-clamp
serre-joint [M] en C
abrazadera [F]
Schraubzwinge [F]
morsetto [M]

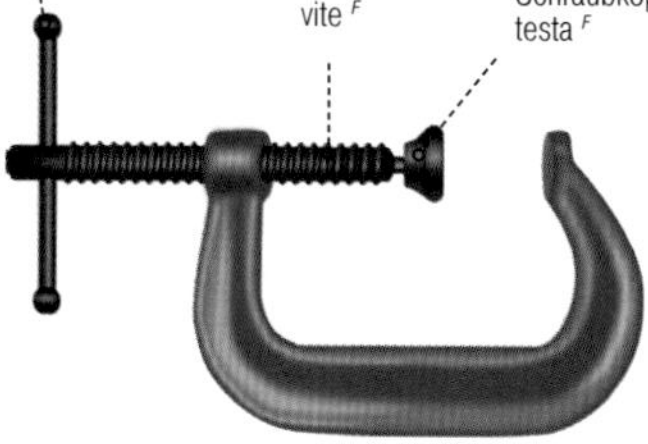

handle
poignée [F]
mango [M]
Griff [M]
impugnatura [F]

screw
vis [F]
tornillo [M]
Schraube [F]
vite [F]

head
tête [F]
cabeza [F]
Schraubkopf [M]
testa [F]

vise
étau [M]
tornillo [M] de banco [M]
Schraubstock [M]
morsa [F]

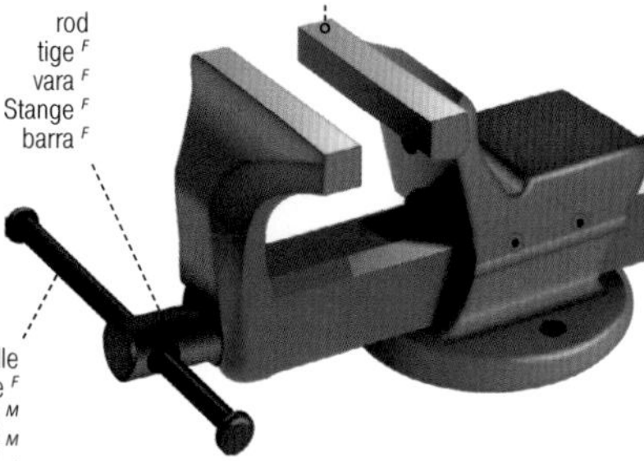

jaw
mâchoire [F] / mors [M]
quijada [F]
Klemmbacken [F]
ganasce [F]

rod
tige [F]
vara [F]
Stange [F]
barra [F]

handle
poignée [F]
mango [M]
Griff [M]
impugnatura [F]

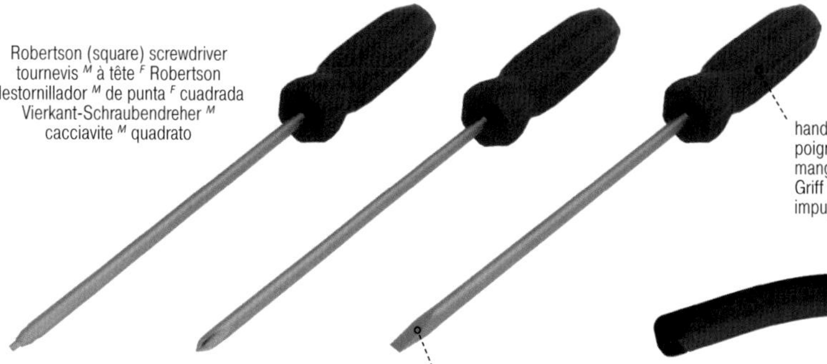

Robertson (square) screwdriver
tournevis [M] à tête [F] Robertson
destornillador [M] de punta [F] cuadrada
Vierkant-Schraubendreher [M]
cacciavite [M] quadrato

slotted screwdriver
tournevis [M] à pointe [F] plate
destornillador [M] plano
Schlitzschraubendreher [M]
cacciavite [M] a intaglio [M]

handle
poignée [F]
mango [M]
Griff [M]
impugnatura [F]

Phillips screwdriver
tournevis [M] cruciforme/étoile
destornillador [M] phillips
Kreuzschlitzschraubendreher [M]
cacciavite [M] a stella [F]

tip
pointe [F]
punta [F]
Spitze [F]
punta [F]

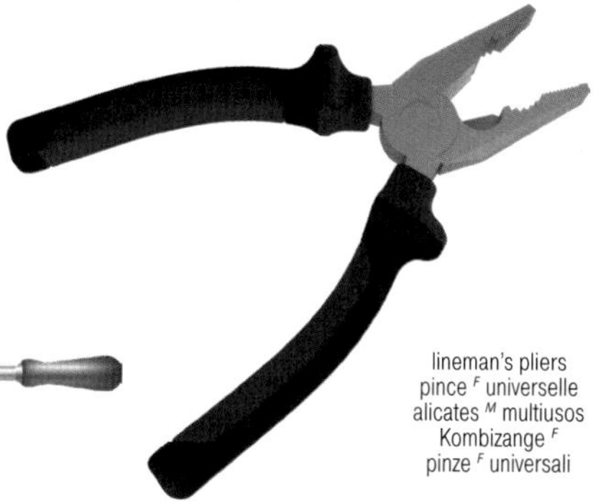

lineman's pliers
pince [F] universelle
alicates [M] multiusos
Kombizange [F]
pinze [F] universali

lubricant spray
vaporisateur [M] de lubrifiant [M]
aerosol [M] lubricante
Schmiermittel-Spray [N]
spray [M] lubrificante

spiral screwdriver
tournevis [M] à spirale [F]
destornillador [M] en espiral [F]
Spiral-Schraubendreher [M]
cacciavite [M] a spirale [F]

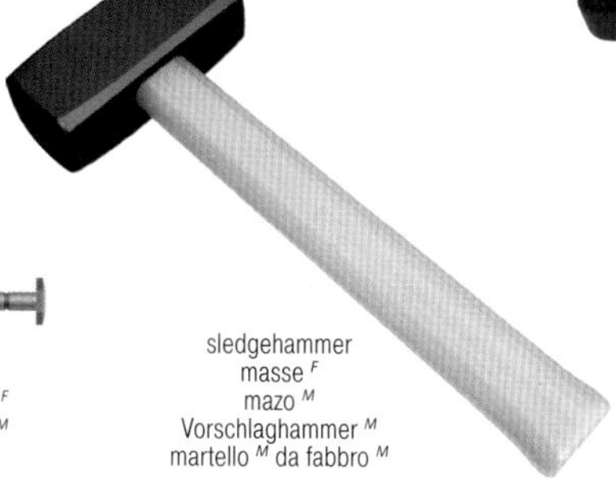

sledgehammer
masse [F]
mazo [M]
Vorschlaghammer [M]
martello [M] da fabbro [M]

needle-nose pliers
pince [F] à bec [M] effilé
alicates [M] de punta [F]
Nadelzange [F]
pinze [F] a punta [F]

precision screwdriver
tournevis [M] d'horloger [M]
destornillador [M] de precisión [F]
Präzisions-Schraubendreher [M]
cacciavite [M] di precisione [F]

caulking gun
pistolet [M] à calfeutrer
pistola [F] de calafateo [M]
Fugenspritze [F]
pistola [F] per silicone [M]

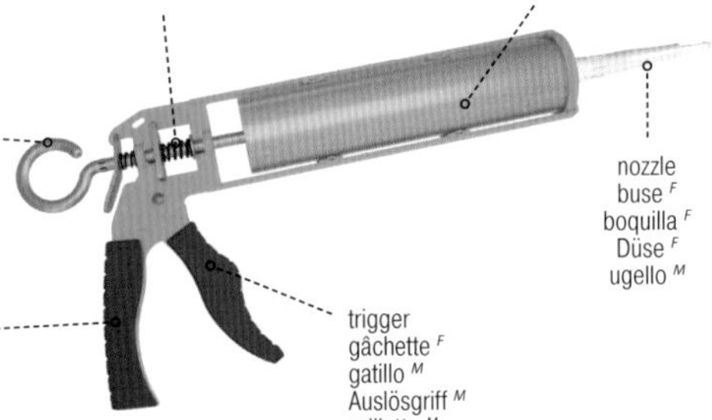
spring
ressort [M]
resorte [M]
Feder [F]
molla [F]
tube
tube [M]
tubo [M]
Röhre [F]
tubo [M]
plunger
piston [M]
émbolo [M]
Pümpel [M]
stantuffo [M]
nozzle
buse [F]
boquilla [F]
Düse [F]
ugello [M]
handle
poignée [F]
mango [M]
Griff [M]
impugnatura [F]
trigger
gâchette [F]
gatillo [M]
Auslösgriff [M]
grilletto [M]

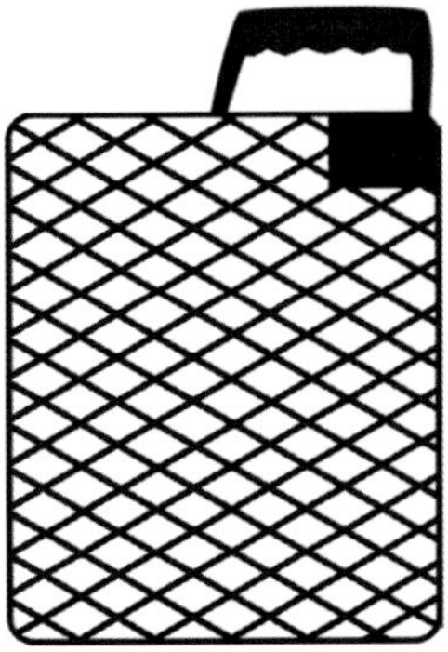

roller grid
grille [M] pour rouleau [M] de peinture [F]
malla [F]
Abstreifgitter [N]
rete [F]

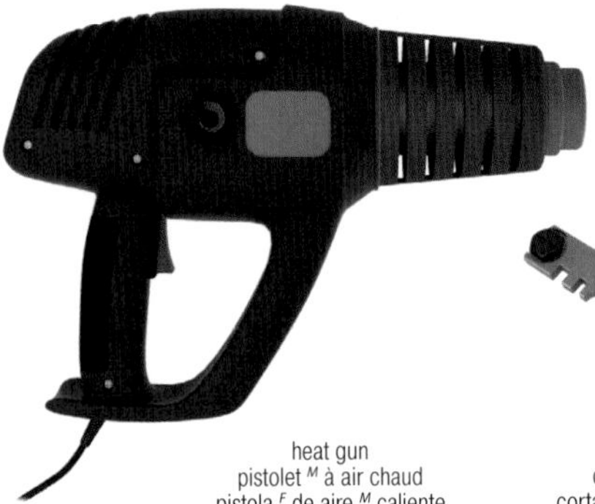

heat gun
pistolet [M] à air chaud
pistola [F] de aire [M] caliente
Heißluftpistole [F]
pistola [F] a caldo [M]

glass cutter
coupe-verre [M]
cortador [M] de cristal [M]
Glasschneider [M]
tagliavetro [M]

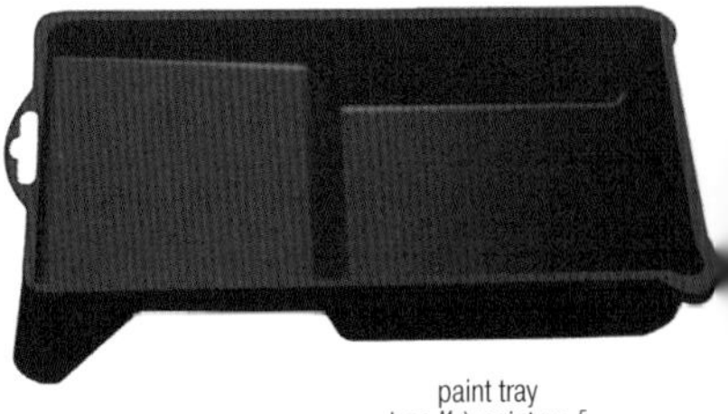

paint tray
bac [M] à peinture [F]
cubeta [F] de pintura [F]
Farbtablett [N]
vaschetta [F] per rullo [M]

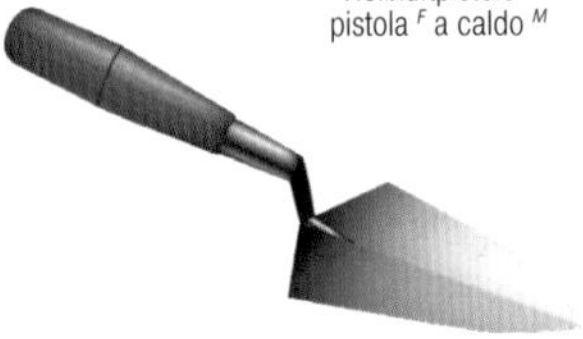

mason's trowel
truelle [F] de maçon [M]
paleta [F]
Kelle [F]
cazzuola [F]

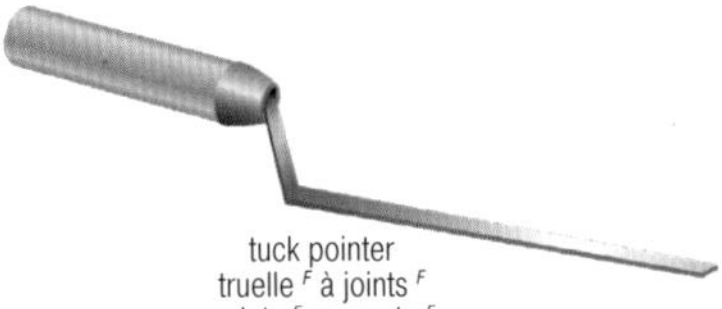

tuck pointer
truelle [F] à joints [F]
paleta [F] en punta [F]
Fugenkelle [F]
cazzuolino [M] marcafughe [M]

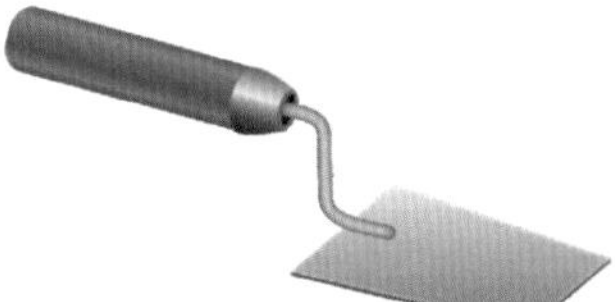

square trowel
truelle [F] carrée
paleta [F] cuadrada
rechteckige Maurerkelle [F]
cazzuola [F] a punta [F] quadra

digital caliper
pied [M] à coulisse [F] numérique
calibrador [M] digital
digitaler Messschieber [M]
squadra [F] digitale

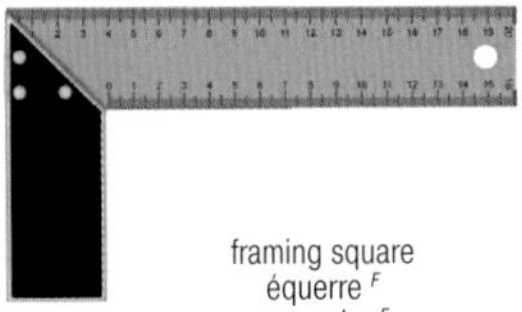

framing square
équerre [F]
escuadra [F]
Winkelmaß [N]
squadra [F]

scraper
grattoir [M]
rasqueta [F]
Spachtel [M]
raschietto [M]

cement mixer
bétonnière ^{F}
hormigonera ^{F}
Betonmischmaschine ^{F}
betoniera ^{F}

extension ladder
échelle ^{F} à coulisse ^{F}
escalera ^{F} extensible
Verlängerungsleiter ^{F}
scala ^{F} telescopica

platform stepladder
escabeau ^{M}
escalera ^{F} de plataforma ^{F}
Trittleiter ^{F}
scaletta ^{F} con pedana ^{F}

shelf
tablette ^{F}
soporte ^{M}
Stütze ^{F}
supporto ^{M}

leg
montant ^{M}
pata ^{F}
Standbein ^{N}
gamba ^{F}

leg tip
embout ^{M} du montant ^{M}
almohadilla ^{F}
Leiterfuß ^{M} appoggio ^{M}
della scaletta ^{F}

step
marche ^{F}
escalón ^{M}
Stufe ^{F}
scalino ^{M}

bricklayer's hammer
marteau ^{M} de briqueteur ^{M}
martillo ^{M} de mampostería ^{F}
Maurerhammer ^{M}
martello ^{M} da muratore ^{M}

paintbrush
pinceau ^{M}
brocha ^{F}
Farbpinsel ^{M}
pennello ^{M}

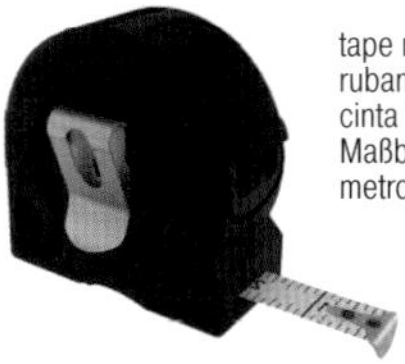

tape measure
ruban ^{M} à mesurer
cinta ^{F} métrica
Maßband ^{N}
metro ^{M} a nastro ^{M}

spirit level
niveau ^{M} à bulle ^{F}
nivel ^{M}
Wasserwaage ^{F}
livella ^{F}

paint roller
rouleau ^{M} à peindre
rodillo ^{M} de pintor ^{M}
Farbroller ^{M}
rullo ^{M} per pittura ^{F}

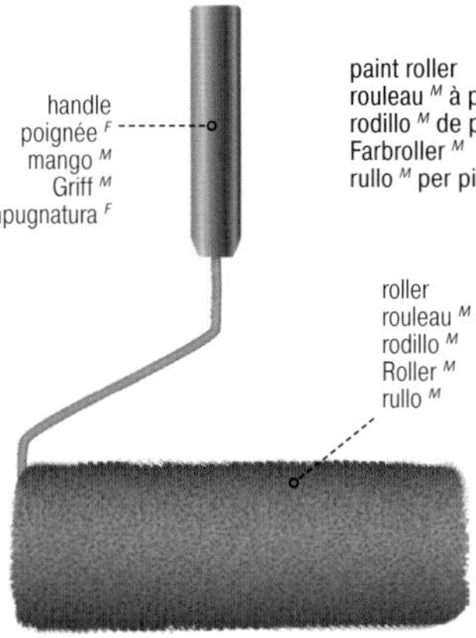

handle
poignée ^{F}
mango ^{M}
Griff ^{M}
impugnatura ^{F}

roller
rouleau ^{M}
rodillo ^{M}
Roller ^{M}
rullo ^{M}

paint sprayer
pistolet ^{M} à peindre
pistola ^{F} de pintura ^{F}
Farbsprayer ^{M}
verniciatore ^{M} a spruzzo ^{M}

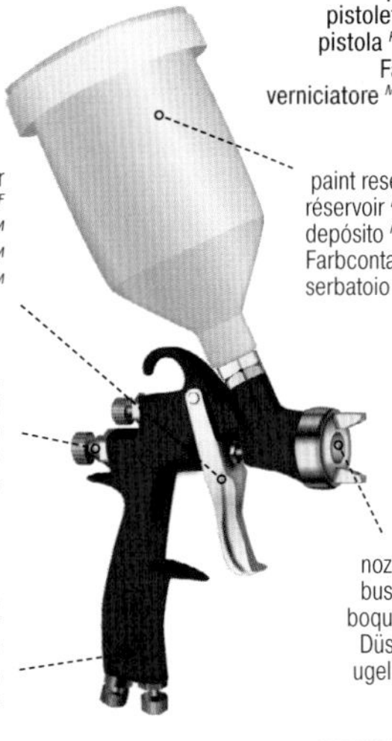

paint reservoir
réservoir ^{M} de peinture ^{F}
depósito ^{M} de pintura ^{F}
Farbcontainer ^{M}
serbatoio ^{M} per vernice ^{F}

trigger
gâchette ^{F}
gatillo ^{M}
Auslöser ^{M}
grilletto ^{M}

fluid adjustment screw
vis ^{F} de réglage ^{M} du fluide ^{M}
tornillo ^{M} de ajuste ^{M}
Verstellschraube ^{F}
vite ^{F} di regolazione ^{F}

nozzle
buse ^{F}
boquilla ^{F}
Düse ^{F}
ugello ^{M}

handle
poignée ^{F}
mango ^{M}
Griff ^{M}
impugnatura ^{F}

LEXI24

FOOD

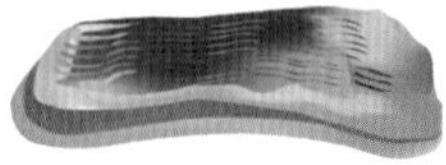

bacon
bacon [M]
tocino [M]
Speck [M]
pancetta [F]

bologna
bologne [M]
salchicha [F] boloñesa
Lyoner [F]
mortadella [F]

cooked sausage
saucisse [F] cuite
salchicha [F] ahumada cocida
Kochwurst [F]
salsiccia [F] affumicata

foie gras
foie [M] gras
foie gras [M]
Stopfleber [F]
fegato [M] d'oca [F]

breakfast sausage
saucisse [F]
salchicha [F] fresca
Breakfast Sausage [F]
salsiccia [F] fresca

sausage meat
chair [F] à saucisse [F]
salchicha [F] ahumada fresca
Brät [N]
salsiccia [F] fresca affumicata

kielbasa sausage
saucisse [F] kielbasa
salchicha [F] polaca
Krakauer [F]
salsiccia [F] kielbasa

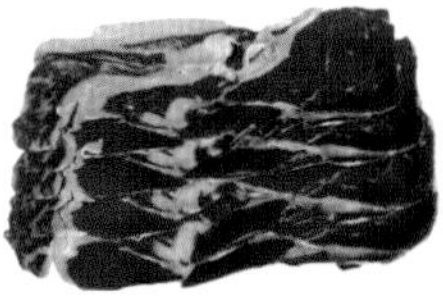

prosciutto
prosciutto [M]
jamón [M] prosciutto [M]
Rohschinken [M]
prosciutto [M] crudo

bratwurst sausage
saucisse [F] bratwurst
embutido [M] crudo
Bratwurst [F]
salsiccia [F] bratwurst

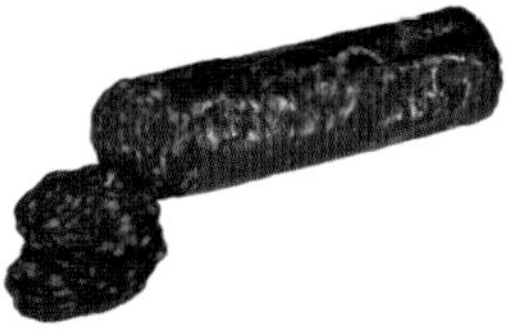

salami
salami [M]
embutido [M] seco
Salami [F]
salame [M]

pâté
pâté [M]
paté [M]
Pastete [F]
paté [M]

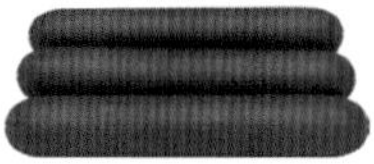

wiener
saucisse [F] fumée
salchicha [F] vienesa
Wiener Würstchen [N]
würstel [M]

Variety meats

beef liver
foie [M] de bœuf [M]
hígado [M] de res [F]
Rinderleber [F]
fegato [M] di manzo [M]

chicken liver
foie [M] de poulet [M]
hígado [M] de pollo [M]
Hähnchenleber [F]
fegato [M] di pollo [M]

heart
cœur [M]
corazón [M]
Herz [N]
cuore [M]

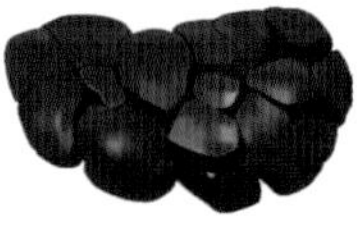

kidney
rein [M]
riñón [M]
Niere [F]
rognone [M]

tongue
langue [F]
lengua [F]
Zunge [F]
lingua [F]

chicken
poulet [M]
pollo [M]
Hähnchen [N]
pollo [M]

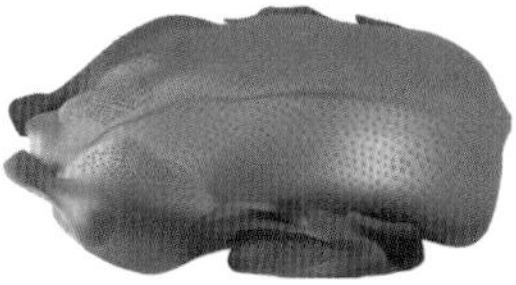

duck
canard [M]
pato [M]
Ente [F]
anatra [F]

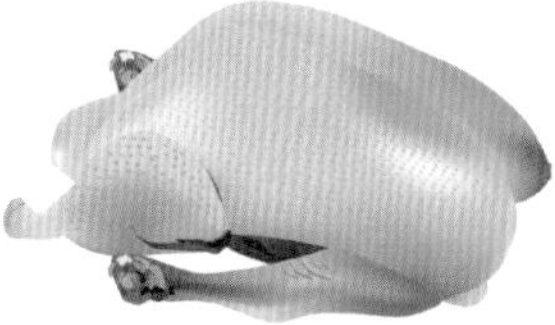

goose
oie [F]
ganso [M]
Gans [F]
oca [F]

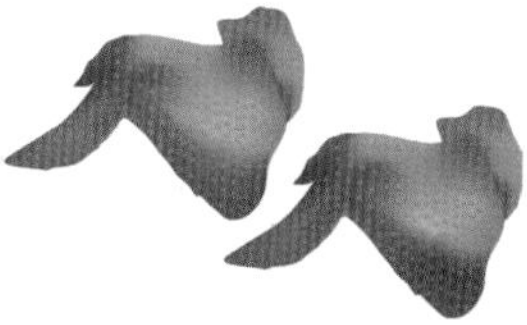

chicken wing
aile [F] de poulet [M]
alitas [F] de pollo [M]
Hähnchenflügel [M]
ali [F] di pollo [M]

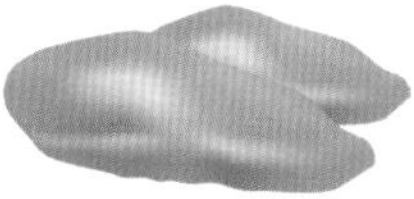

chicken breast
poitrine [F] de poulet [M]
pechuga [F] de pollo [M]
Hühnerbrust [F]
petto [M] di pollo [M]

chicken egg
œuf [M] de poule [F]
huevos [M] de gallina [F]
Hühnerei [N]
uovo [M] di gallina [F]

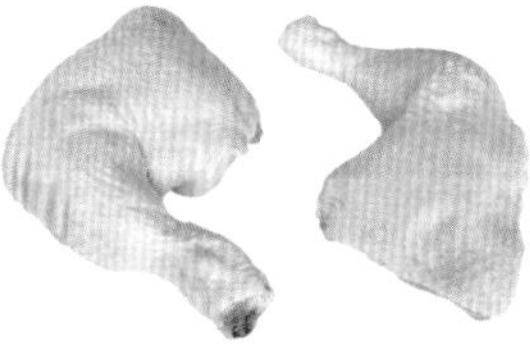

chicken leg
cuisse [F] de poulet [M]
muslos [M] de pollo [M]
Hähnchenkeule [F]
coscia [F] di pollo [M]

Game meats

quail
caille [F]
codorniz [F]
Wachtel [F]
quaglia [F]

quail egg
œuf [M] de caille [F]
huevo [M] de codorniz [F]
Wachtelei [N]
uovo [M] di quaglia [F]

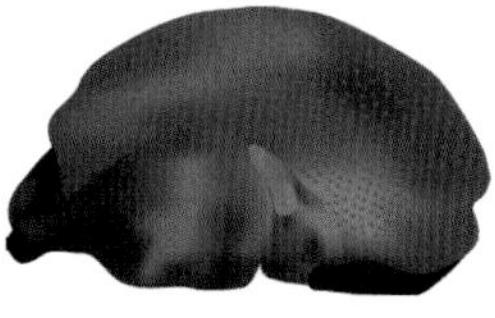

pheasant
faisan [M]
faisán [M]
Fasan [M]
fagiano [M]

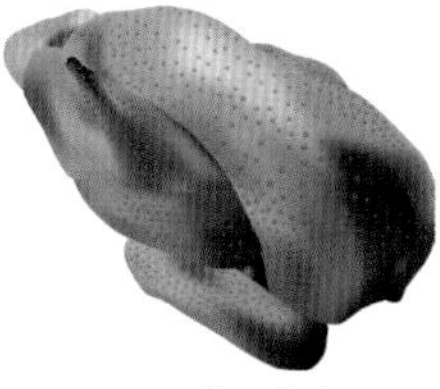

guinea fowl
pintade [F]
pintada [F]
Perlhuhn [N]
faraona [F]

rabbit
lapin [M]
conejo [M]
Kaninchen [N]
coniglio [M]

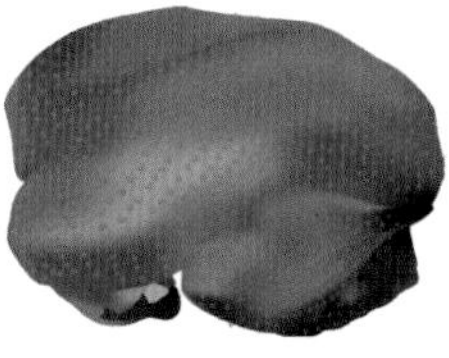

partridge
perdrix [F]
perdiz [F]
Rebhuhn [N]
pernice [F]

Lamb

Agneau M | Cordero M | Lamm N | Agnello M

cuts of lamb
coupes F d'agneau M
cortes M de cordero M
Teilstücke vom Lamm N
tagli M dell'agnello M

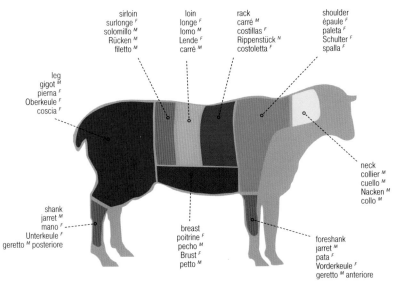

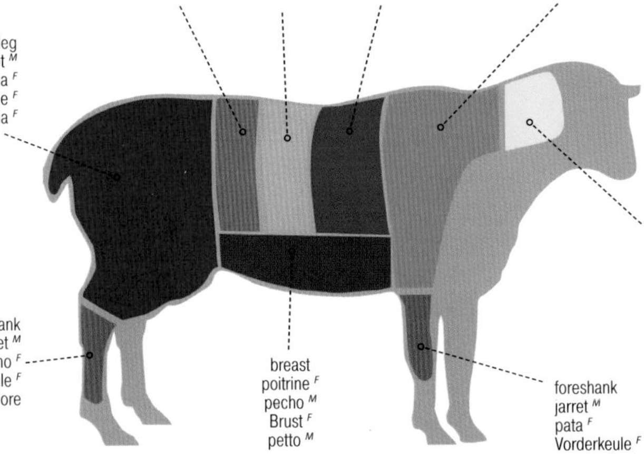
sirloin
surlonge F
solomillo M
Rücken M
filetto M
loin
longe F
lomo M
Lende F
carré M
rack
carré M
costillas F
Rippenstück N
costoletta F
shoulder
épaule F
paleta F
Schulter F
spalla F
leg
gigot M
pierna F
Oberkeule F
coscia F
neck
collier M
cuello M
Nacken M
collo M
shank
jarret M
mano F
Unterkeule F
geretto M posteriore
breast
poitrine F
pecho M
Brust F
petto M
foreshank
jarret M
pata F
Vorderkeule F
geretto M anteriore

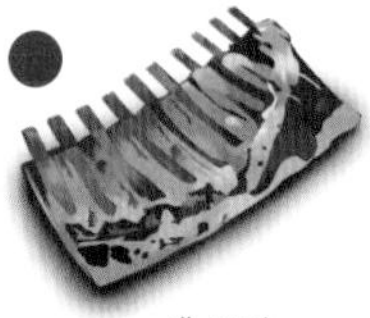
rib roast
rôti M de côte F
chuletas F de costilla F
Lammrippenbraten M
costolette F

loin roast
rôti M de longe F
lomo M de cordero asado
Lammlendenbraten M
sella F di agnello M

strip loin
contre-filet M
solomillo M
Lammlendenstück N
controfiletto M di agnello M

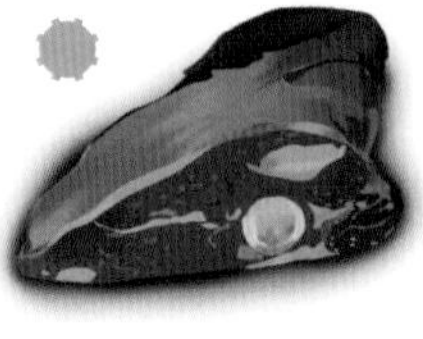
shank
jarret M
pata F
Lammschenkel M
stinco M

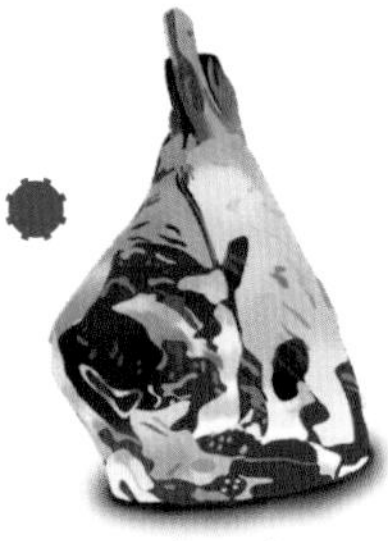
leg roast
gigot M
pata F de cordero
Lammkeule F
cosciotto M di agnello M

Pork

Porc ^{M} | Cerdo ^{M} | Schweinefleisch ^{N} | Maiale ^{M}

cuts of pork
coupes ^{F} de porc ^{M}
cortes ^{M} de cerdo ^{M}
Teilstücke vom Schwein ^{N}
tagli ^{M} del maiale ^{M}

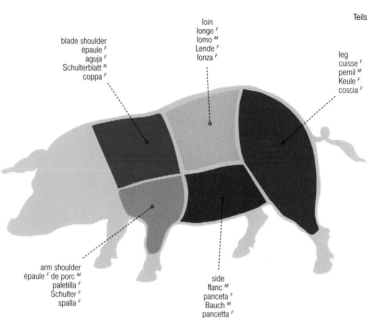

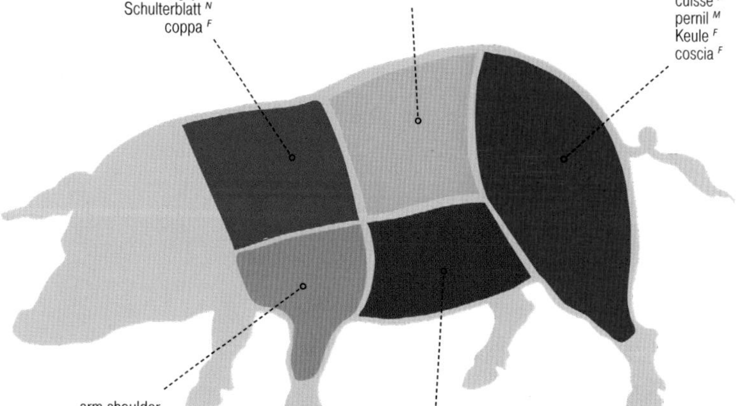
blade shoulder
épaule F
aguja F
Schulterblatt N
coppa F
loin
longe F
lomo M
Lende F
lonza F
leg
cuisse F
pernil M
Keule F
coscia F
arm shoulder
épaule F de porc M
paletilla F
Schulter F
spalla F
side
flanc M
panceta F
Bauch M
pancetta F

pork hock
jarret ^{M} de porc ^{M}
jarrete ^{M} de cerdo ^{M}
Schweinshachse ^{F}
stinco ^{M} di maiale ^{M}

pork chop
côtelette ^{F} de porc ^{M}
chuleta ^{M} de cerdo ^{F}
Schweinekotelett ^{N}
cotoletta ^{F} di maiale ^{M}

spare ribs
côtes ^{F} levées
costillas ^{F} de cerdo ^{M}
Schweinerippchen ^{N}
costolette ^{F} di maiale ^{M}

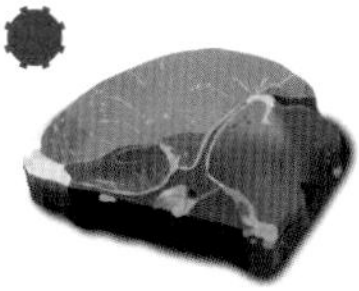

blade steak
tranche ^{F} de palette ^{F}
carne ^{M} de cerdo ^{M}
Schweinesteak ^{N}
braciola ^{F} di maiale ^{M}

tenderloin
filet ^{M}
lomo ^{M} de cerdo ^{M}
Schweinsfilet ^{N}
filetto ^{M} di maiale ^{M}

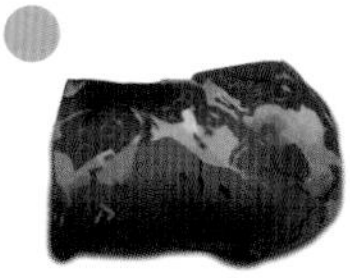

picnic roast
rôti ^{M} d'épaule ^{F} picnic
corte ^{M} para asado ^{M}
Schweinebraten ^{M}
arrosto ^{M} di maiale ^{M}

Beef

Bœuf [M] | Carne [F] de res [F] | Rindfleisch [M] | Manzo [M]

cuts of beef
coupes [F] de bœuf [M]
cortes [M] de carne [F] de res [F]
Teilstücke vom Rind [N]
tagli [M] del manzo [M]

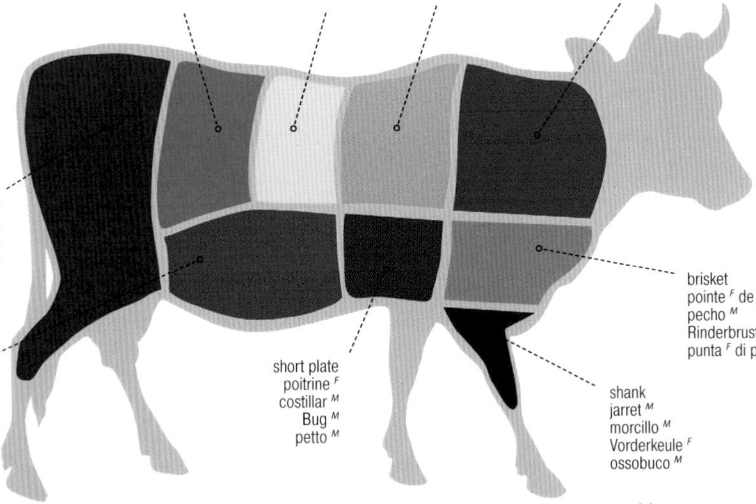
sirloin
surlonge [F]
solomillo [M]
Rinderrücken [M]
lombata [F]
short loin
longe [F] courte
lomo [F]
Filet [N]
controfiletto [M]
rib
côte [F]
costilla [F]
Rippe [F]
costata [F]
chuck
bloc [M] d'épaule [F]
morrillo [M]
Kamm [M]
spalla [F]
round
ronde [F]
redondo [M]
Blume [F]
coscia [F]
brisket
pointe [F] de poitrine [F]
pecho [M]
Rinderbrust [F]
punta [F] di petto [M]
flank
flanc [M]
falda [F]
Schenkel [M]
fianco [M]
short plate
poitrine [F]
costillar [M]
Bug [M]
petto [M]
shank
jarret [M]
morcillo [M]
Vorderkeule [F]
ossobuco [M]

skirt steak
bifteck [M] de hampe [F]
bistec [M]
Kronfleischsteak [N]
bistecca [F]

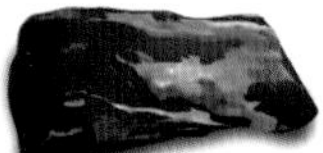

tenderloin roast
rôti [M] de filet [M]
carne [F] asada
Rinderfiletbraten [M]
filetto [M] di manzo [M]

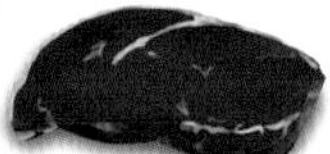

sirloin steak
bifteck [M] de surlonge [F]
solomillo [M]
Sirloin-Steak [N]
bistecca [F] di controfiletto [M]

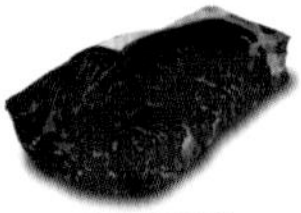

round steak
bifteck [M] de ronde [F]
filete [M]
Round Steak [N]
scamone [M] di manzo [M]

shank
jarret [M]
pierna [F]
Rinderbeinscheibe [F]
garretto [M] di manzo [M]

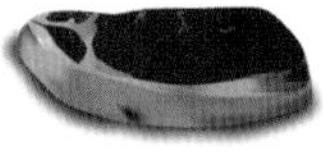

rib eye steak
bifteck [M] de faux-filet [M]
carne [F] para guisar
Rib Eye-Steak [N]
costata [F] di manzo [M]

ground beef
bœuf [M] haché
carne [F] picada
Rinderhackfleisch [N]
macinato [M] di manzo [M]

Chateaubriand
chateaubriand [M]
Chateaubriand [M]
Chateaubriand [N]
Chateubriand [M]

back ribs
côtes [F] levées de dos [M]
costillas [F]
Querrippe [F]
costolette [F] di manzo [M]

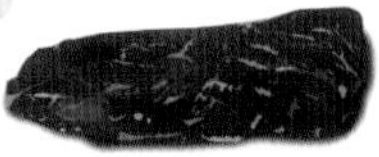

flank steak
bifteck [M] de flanc [M]
filete [M]
Steak [N] aus der Flanke [F]
bavetta [F]

rib roast
rôti [M] de côtes [F]
asado [M] de costilla [F]
Rippenbraten [M]
lombata [F] di manzo [M]

T-bone steak
bifteck [M] d'aloyau [M]
chuletón [M]
T-Bone-Steak [N]
fiorentina [F]

Veal

Veau [M] | Ternera [F] | Kalbfleisch [N] | Vitello [M]

cuts of veal
coupes [F] de veau [M]
cortes [M] de ternera [F]
Teilstücke vom Kalb [N]
tagli [M] del vitello [M]

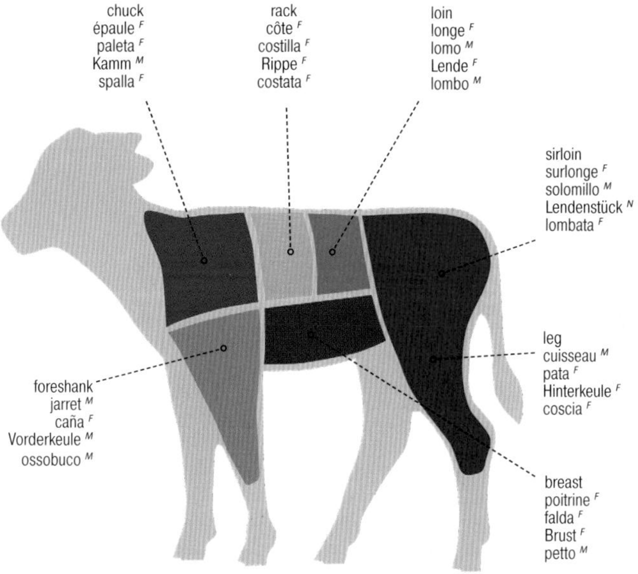
chuck
épaule [F]
paleta [F]
Kamm [M]
spalla [F]
rack
côte [F]
costilla [F]
Rippe [F]
costata [F]
loin
longe [F]
lomo [M]
Lende [F]
lombo [M]
sirloin
surlonge [F]
solomillo [M]
Lendenstück [N]
lombata [F]
leg
cuisseau [M]
pata [F]
Hinterkeule [F]
coscia [F]
breast
poitrine [F]
falda [F]
Brust [F]
petto [M]
foreshank
jarret [M]
caña [F]
Vorderkeule [M]
ossobuco [M]

blade roast
rôti [M] de palette [F]
asado [M] de paleta [F]
Schaufelstückbraten [M]
spalla [F] di vitello [M]

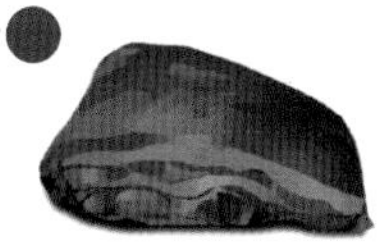

breast
poitrine [F]
falda [F] de ternera [F]
Kalbsbrust [F]
punta [F] di vitello [M]

rib chop
côtelette [F]
chuleta [F] de ternera [F]
Rippenkotelett [N]
costoletta [F] di vitello [M]

shank
jarret [M]
jarrete [M] de ternera [F]
Beinscheibe [F]
stinco [M] di vitello [M]

cutlet
escalope [F]
filete [M] de ternera [F]
Kalbskotelett [N]
fettina [F] di vitello [M]

Milk and cream

Lait [M] et crème [F] | Leche [F] y nata [F] | Milch und Sahne [F] | Latte [M] e panna [F]

cow's milk
lait [M] de vache [F]
leche [F] de vaca [F]
Kuhmilch [F]
latte [M] di mucca [F]

goat's milk
lait [M] de chèvre [F]
leche [F] de cabra [F]
Ziegenmilch [F]
latte [M] di capra [F]

100%
LACTOSE FREE
MILK

lactose-free milk
lait [M] sans lactose [M]
leche [F] sin lactosa [F]
laktosefreie Milch [F]
latte [M] senza lattosio [M]

kefir
kéfir [M]
kéfir [M]
Kefir [M]
kefir [M]

sour cream
crème [F] sure
crema [F] agria
Sauerrahm [M]
panna [F] acida

whipped cream
crème [F] fouettée
crema [F] batida
Schlagsahne [F]
panna [F] montata

yogurt
yogourt [M]
yogur [M]
Joghurt [M]
yogurt [M]

evaporated milk
lait [M] condensé
leche [F] evaporada
Kondensmilch [F]
latte [M] condensato

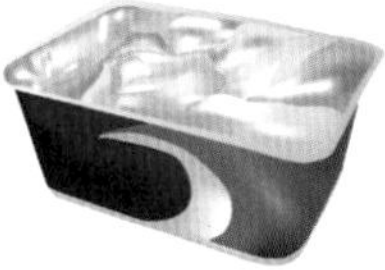

cream cheese
fromage [M] à la crème [F]
queso [M] crema [F]
Frischkäse [M]
formaggio [M] cremoso

butter
beurre [M]
mantequilla [F]
Butter [F]
burro [M]

buttermilk
babeurre [M]
suero [M] de leche [F]
Buttermilch [F]
siero [M] di latte [M]

Cheeses

Fromages [M] | Quesos [M] | Käse [M] | Formaggi [M]

mozzarella
mozzarella [F]
mozzarella [F]
Mozzarella [M]
mozzarella [F]

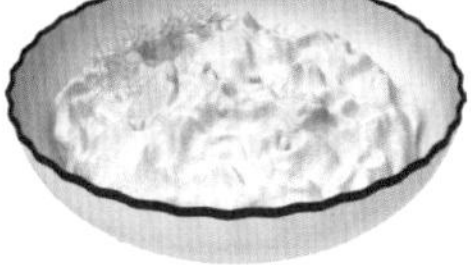

cottage cheese
fromage [M] cottage
requesón [M]
Hüttenkäse [M]
fiocchi [M] di latte [M]

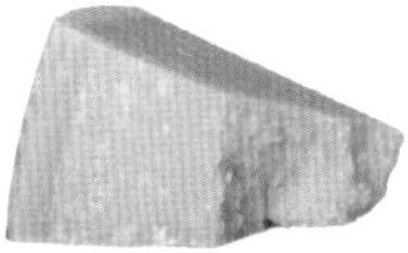

Parmesan
parmesan M
parmesano M
Parmesan M
parmigiano M

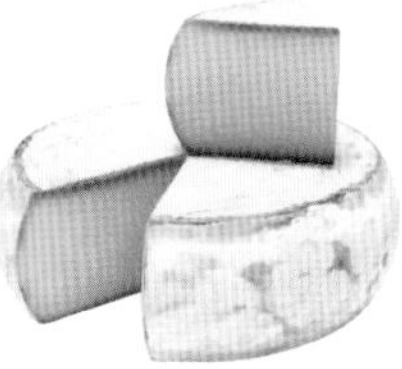

Gouda
gouda M
Gouda M
Gouda M
gouda M

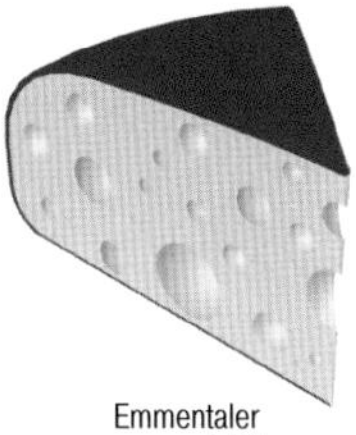

Emmentaler
emmental M
Emmental M
Emmentaler M
Emmenthal M

cheddar
cheddar M
queso M Cheddar M
Cheddar M
cheddar M

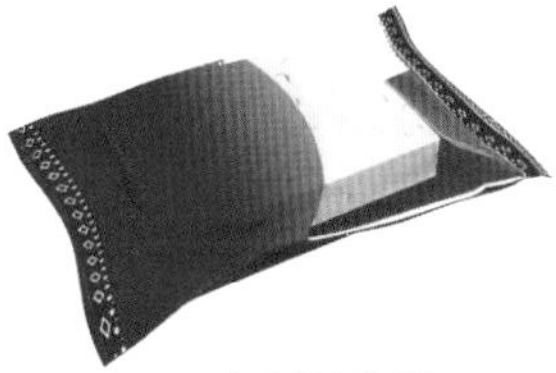

American cheese
fromage M fondu
queso M fundido
amerikanischer Käse M
formaggio M fuso americano

goat cheese
fromage M de chèvre F
queso M de cabra F
Ziegenkäse M
formaggio M di capra F

Gorgonzola
gorgonzola M
Gorgonzola M
Gorgonzola M
gorgonzola M

Danish blue
bleu M danois
queso M danés
dänischer Blauschimmelkäse M
Danablu M

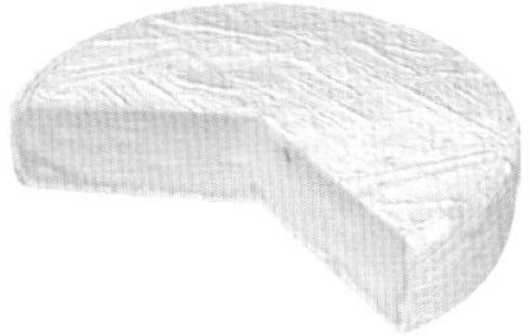

brie
brie M
Brie M
Brie M
brie M

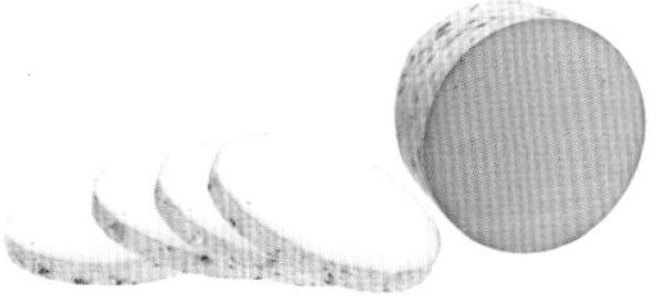

smoked cheese
fromage M fumé
queso M ahumado
Räucherkäse M
formaggio M affumicato

Vegetarian dairy alternatives

Alternatives F laitières végétariennes | Alternativa F vegetariana a productos M lácteos | Vegetarische Lebensmittel N | Prodotti M vegetariani

tofu
tofu M
tofu M
Tofu M
tofu M

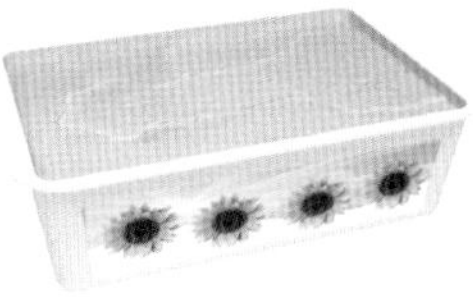

margarine
margarine F
margarina F
Margarine F
margarina F

soy milk
lait M de soja M
leche F de soja F
Sojamilch F
latte M di soia F

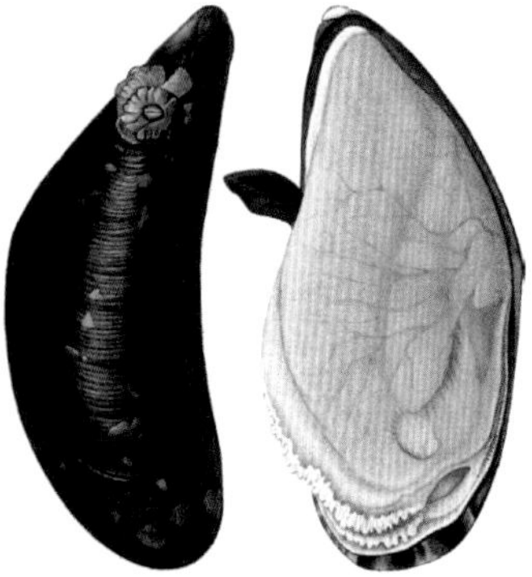

mussel
moule F
mejillón M
Miesmuschel F
cozza F

salmon roe
œufs M de saumon M
huevas F de salmón M
Lachsrogen M
uova F di salmone M

caviar
caviar M
caviar M
Kaviar M
caviale M

scallop
pétoncle M
vieira F
Kammmuschel F
pettine M di mare M

clam
palourde F
almeja F
Muschel F
vongola F

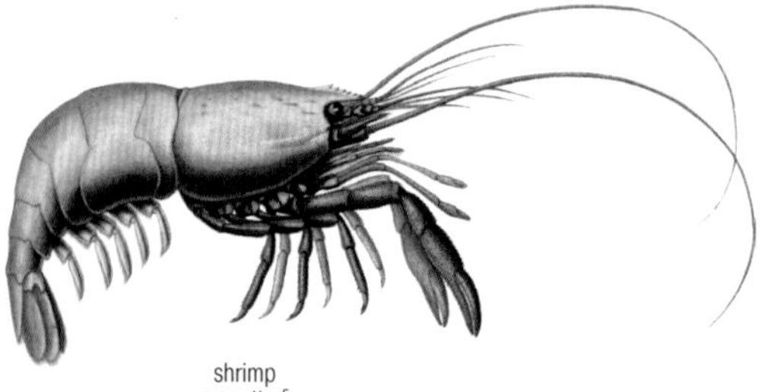

shrimp
crevette F
camarón M
Garnele F
gambero M

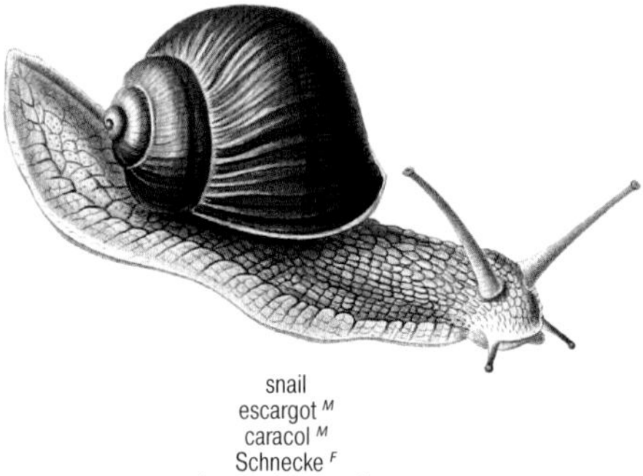

snail
escargot M
caracol M
Schnecke F
lumaca F di mare M

fish
poisson [M]
pescado [M]
Fisch [M]
pesce [M]

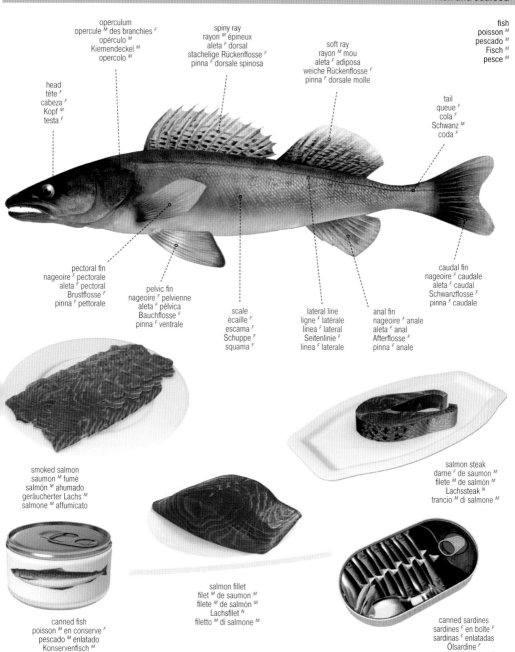

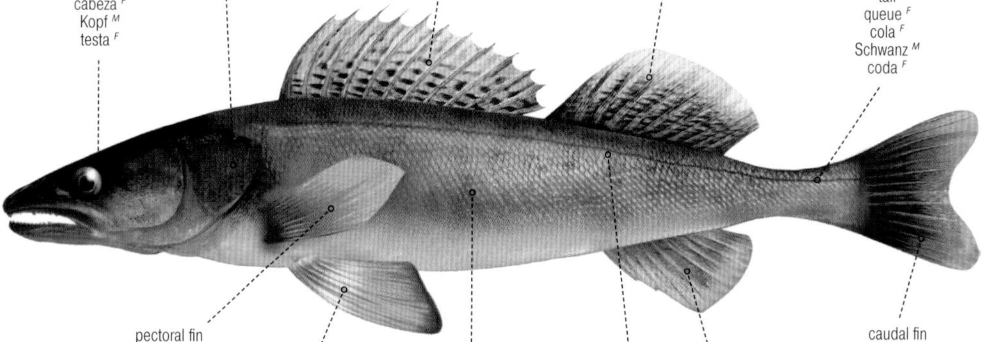
operculum
opercule [M] des branchies [F]
opérculo [M]
Kiemendeckel [M]
opercolo [M]
spiny ray
rayon [M] épineux
aleta [F] dorsal
stachelige Rückenflosse [F]
pinna [F] dorsale spinosa
soft ray
rayon [M] mou
aleta [F] adiposa
weiche Rückenflosse [F]
pinna [F] dorsale molle
head
tête [F]
cabeza [F]
Kopf [M]
testa [F]
tail
queue [F]
cola [F]
Schwanz [M]
coda [F]
pectoral fin
nageoire [F] pectorale
aleta [F] pectoral
Brustflosse [F]
pinna [F] pettorale
pelvic fin
nageoire [F] pelvienne
aleta [F] pélvica
Bauchflosse [F]
pinna [F] ventrale
scale
écaille [F]
escama [F]
Schuppe [F]
squama [F]
lateral line
ligne [F] latérale
linea [F] lateral
Seitenlinie [F]
linea [F] laterale
anal fin
nageoire [F] anale
aleta [F] anal
Afterflosse [F]
pinna [F] anale
caudal fin
nageoire [F] caudale
aleta [F] caudal
Schwanzflosse [F]
pinna [F] caudale

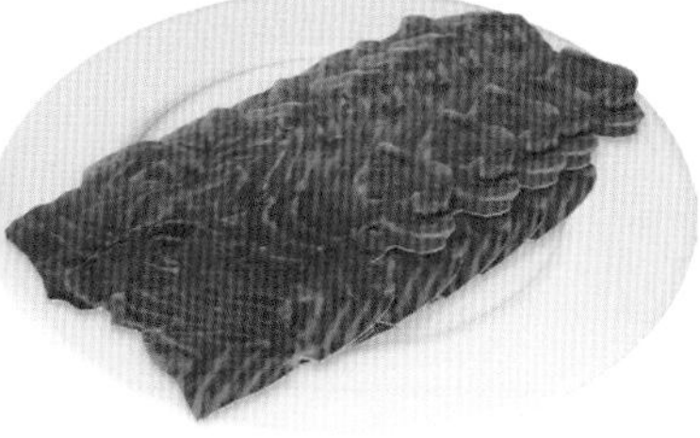

smoked salmon
saumon [M] fumé
salmón [M] ahumado
geräucherter Lachs [M]
salmone [M] affumicato

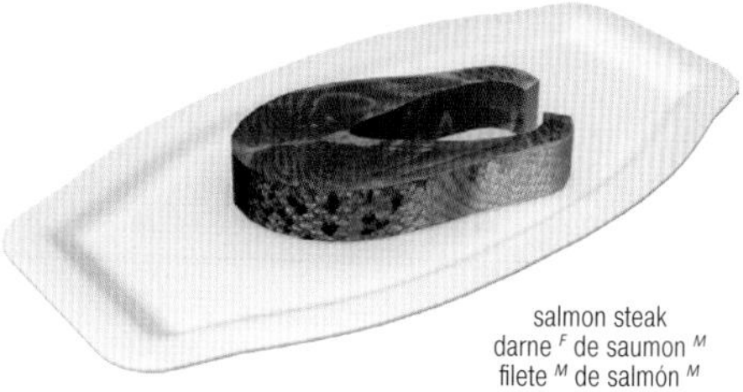

salmon steak
darne [F] de saumon [M]
filete [M] de salmón [M]
Lachssteak [N]
trancio [M] di salmone [M]

salmon fillet
filet [M] de saumon [M]
filete [M] de salmón [M]
Lachsfilet [N]
filetto [M] di salmone [M]

canned fish
poisson [M] en conserve [F]
pescado [M] enlatado
Konservenfisch [M]
pesce [M] in scatola [F]

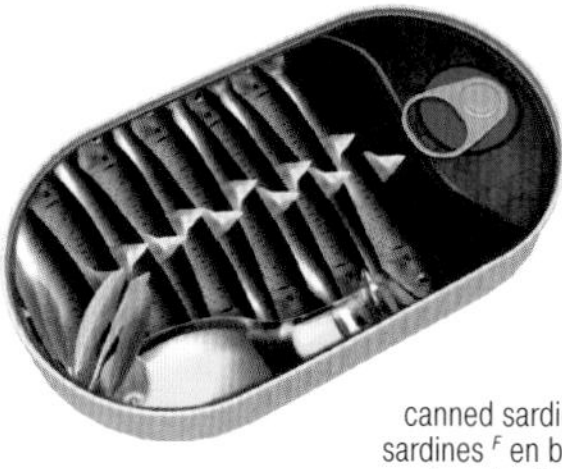

canned sardines
sardines [F] en boîte [F]
sardinas [F] enlatadas
Ölsardine [F]
sardine [F] in scatola [F]

Leaf vegetables

Légumes ^{M} à feuilles ^{F} | Verduras ^{F} de hoja ^{F} | Blattgemüse ^{N} | Ortaggi ^{M} da foglia ^{F}

red cabbage
chou ^{M} rouge
col ^{F} lombarda
Rotkohl ^{M}
cavolo ^{M} rosso

Brussels sprout
chou ^{M} de Bruxelles
coles ^{F} de Bruselas
Rosenkohl ^{M}
cavoletto ^{M} di Bruxelles

white cabbage
chou ^{M} blanc
repollo ^{M}
Weißkraut ^{N}
cavolo ^{M}

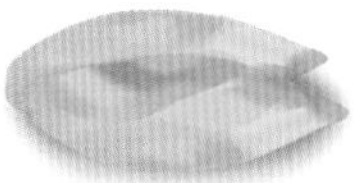

Belgian endive
endive ^{F}
escarola ^{F}
Chicorée ^{M}
insalata ^{F} belga

corn salad
mâche ^{F}
canónigo ^{M}
Feldsalat ^{M}
valeriana ^{F} locusta

curly kale
chou ^{M} frisé
col ^{F} rizada
Grünkohl ^{M}
cavolo ^{M} riccio

garden sorrel
oseille ^{F}
acedera ^{F}
Sauerampfer ^{M}
acetosa ^{F}

Boston lettuce
laitue ^{F} Boston
lechuga ^{F} francesa
Kopfsalat ^{M}
lattuga ^{F} cappuccina

iceberg lettuce
laitue ^{F} iceberg
lechuga ^{F} iceberg
Eisbergsalat ^{M}
lattuga ^{F} iceberg

Chinese cabbage
chou ^{M} chinois
col ^{F} china
Chinakohl ^{M}
cavolo ^{M} cinese

radicchio
radicchio ^{M}
achicoria ^{F} roja
Radicchio ^{M}
radicchio ^{M}

arugula
roquette ^{F}
rúcula ^{F}
Rauke ^{F}
rucola ^{F}

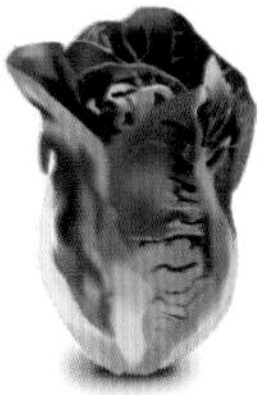

romaine lettuce
laitue ^{F} romaine
lechuga ^{F} romana
Römersalat ^{M}
lattuga ^{F} romana

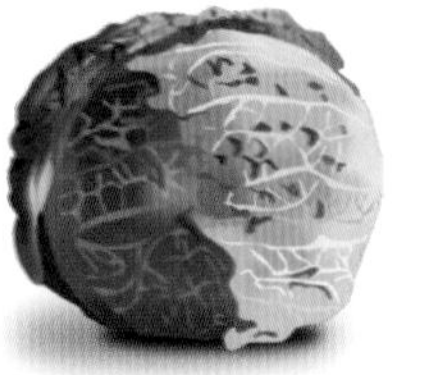

green cabbage
chou ^{M} pommé vert
col ^{F} Savoy
Wirsing ^{M}
verza ^{F}

spinach
épinards ^{M}
espinaca ^{F}
Spinat ^{M}
spinaci ^{M}

bok choy
bok choy ^{M}
bok choy ^{M}
Pak Choi ^{M}
bietola ^{F}

Bulb vegetables

Légumes [M] à bulbes [M] | Verduras [F] de bulbo [M] | Zwiebelgemüse [N] | Ortaggi [M] a bulbo [M]

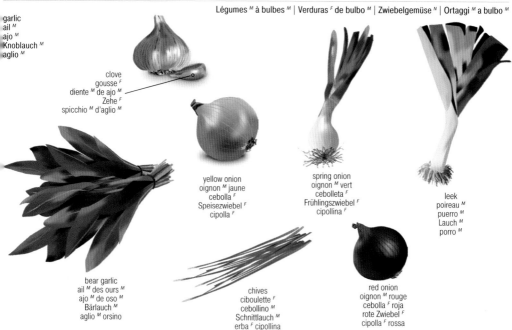

garlic
ail [M]
ajo [M]
Knoblauch [M]
aglio [M]

clove
gousse [F]
diente [M] de ajo [M]
Zehe [F]
spicchio [M] d'aglio [M]

bear garlic
ail [M] des ours [M]
ajo [M] de oso [M]
Bärlauch [M]
aglio [M] orsino

yellow onion
oignon [M] jaune
cebolla [F]
Speisezwiebel [F]
cipolla [F]

spring onion
oignon [M] vert
cebolleta [F]
Frühlingszwiebel [F]
cipollina [F]

leek
poireau [M]
puerro [M]
Lauch [M]
porro [M]

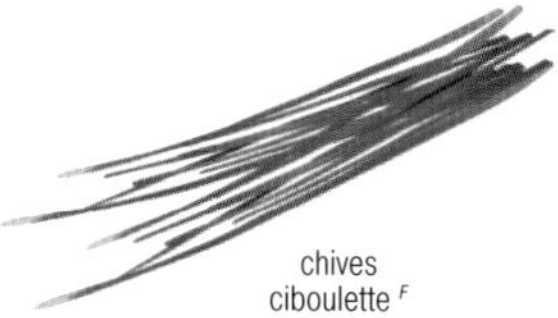

chives
ciboulette [F]
cebollino [M]
Schnittlauch [M]
erba [F] cipollina

red onion
oignon [M] rouge
cebolla [F] roja
rote Zwiebel [F]
cipolla [F] rossa

Inflorescence vegetables

Légumes fleurs [M] | Verduras [F] de flor [F] | Blütengemüse [N] | Ortaggi [M] da infiorescenza [F]

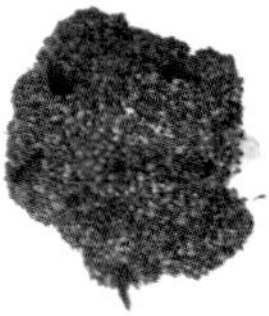

broccoli
brocoli [M]
brócoli [M]
Brokkoli [M]
broccoli [M]

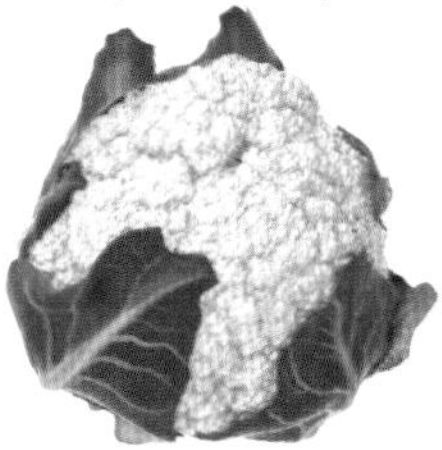

cauliflower
chou-fleur [M]
coliflor [F]
Blumenkohl [M]
cavolfiore [M]

artichoke
artichaut [M]
alcachofa [F]
Artischocke [F]
carciofo [M]

Seaweed

Algues [F] | Algas [F] | Meeresalgen [F] | Alghe [F]

nori
nori [F]
nori [F]
Nori [N]
nori [F]

sea lettuce
laitue [F] de mer [F]
lechuga [F] de mar
Meersalat [M]
lattuga [F] marina

Fruit vegetables

Légumes-fruits M | Hortalizas F de fruto M | Fruchtgemüse N | Frutta F / verdura F

olives
olives F
aceitunas F
Oliven F
olive F

black olive
olives F noires
aceitunas F negras
schwarze Oliven F
olive F nere

green olive
olives F vertes
aceitunas F verdes
grüne Oliven F
olive F verdi

avocado
avocat M
aguacate M / palta F
Avocado F
avocado M

tomatoes on the vine
tomate M en grappe F
tomate M en rama F
Strauchtomate F
pomodoro M a grappolo M

vine
vigne F
rama F
Stängel M
grappolo M

zucchini
zucchini M
calabacín M
Zucchini F
zucchina F

pattypan squash
pâtisson M
calabaza F pattypan
Patisson M
zucca F bianca

okra
gombo M
quimbombó M
Okraschote F
gombo M

green chili pepper
piment M vert chile M
verde largo
grüner Chili M
peperoncino M verde

tomato
tomate F
tomate M
Tomate F
pomodoro M

red chili pepper
piment M de Cayenne
chiles M
roter Chili M
peperoncini M

buttercup squash
courge [F] Buttercup
calabaza [F] buttercup
Riesen-Kürbis [M]
zucca [F] buttercup

pumpkin
citrouille [F]
calabaza [F]
Kürbis [M]
zucca [F]

acorn squash
courge [M] poivrée
calabacín [M]
Eichelkürbis [M]
zucca [F] acorn

sweet pepper
poivron [M]
pimiento [M]
Paprikaschote [F]
peperone [M]

yellow pepper
poivron [M] jaune
pimiento [M] amarillo
gelber Paprika [M]
peperone [M] giallo

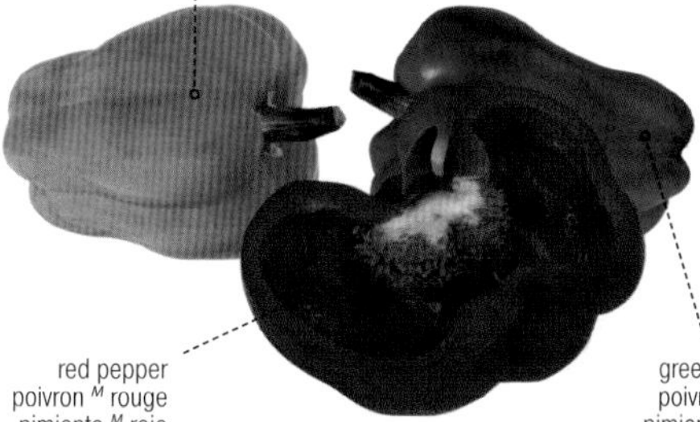

red pepper
poivron [M] rouge
pimiento [M] rojo
roter Paprika [M]
peperone [M] rosso

green pepper
poivron [M] vert
pimiento [M] verde
grüner Paprika [M]
peperone [M] verde

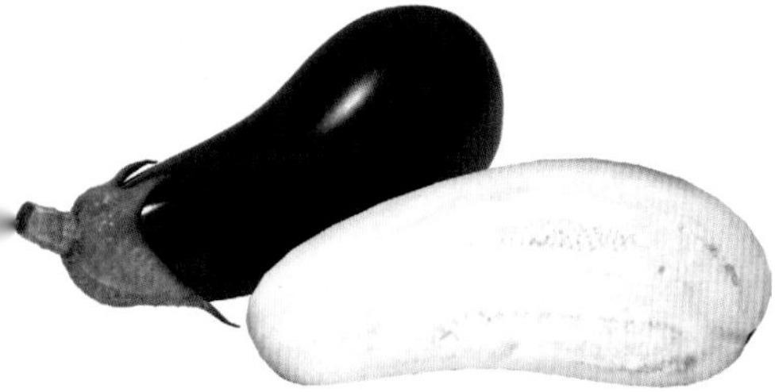

eggplant
aubergine [F]
berenjena [F]
Aubergine [F]
melanzana [F]

cucumber
concombre [M]
pepino [M]
Gurke [F]
cetriolo [M]

Root vegetables

Légumes-racines ^{M} | Verduras ^{F} de raíz ^{F} | Wurzelgemüse ^{N} | Ortaggi ^{M} da radice ^{F}

carrot
carotte ^{F}
zanahoria ^{F}
Karrote ^{F}
carota ^{F}

carrot tops
fanes ^{F} de carottes ^{F}
hojas ^{F} de zanahoria ^{F}
Karottengrün ^{N}
foglie ^{F} di carota ^{F}

beet
betterave ^{F}
remolacha ^{F}
Rote Bete ^{F}
barbabietola ^{F}

horseradish
raifort ^{M}
rábano ^{M} picante
Meerrettich ^{M}
rafano ^{M}

radish
radis ^{M}
rábano ^{M}
Radieschen ^{N}
ravanello ^{M}

black radish
radis ^{M} noir
rábano ^{M} negro
Schwarzrettich ^{M}
ravanello ^{M} nero

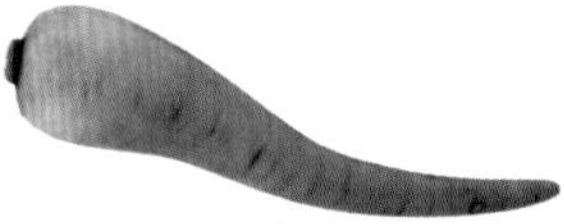

parsnip
panais ^{M}
chirivía ^{F}
Pastinak ^{M}
pastinaca ^{F}

watermelon radish
radis ^{M} melon ^{M} d'eau ^{F}
rábano ^{M} blanco
weißer Rettich ^{M}
ravanello ^{M} bianco

turnip
navet ^{M}
nabo ^{M}
Rübe ^{F}
rapa ^{F}

rutabaga
rutabaga ^{M}
colinabo ^{M}
Kohlrübe ^{F}
rutabaga ^{F}

daikon
radis ^{M} du Japon ^{M}
rábano ^{M} japonés
Daikon-Rettich ^{M}
daikon ^{M}

Stalk vegetables

Légumes-tiges ^{M} | Verduras ^{F} de tallo ^{M} | Stangengemüse ^{N} | Ortaggi ^{M} a fusto ^{M}

rhubarb
rhubarbe ^{F}
ruibarbo ^{M}
Rhabarber ^{M}
rabarbaro ^{M}

fennel
fenouil ^{M}
hinojo ^{M}
Fenchel ^{M}
finocchio ^{M}

asparagus
asperge ^{F}
espárrago ^{M}
Spargel ^{M}
asparagi ^{M}

celery
céleri ^{M}
apio ^{M}
Stangensellerie ^{M}
sedano ^{M}

Tuber vegetables

Légumes-tubercules ^{M} | Tubérculos ^{M} | Knollengemüse ^{N} | Ortaggi ^{M} da tubero ^{M}

Jerusalem artichoke
topinambour ^{M}
alcachofa ^{F} de Jerusalén
Topinambur $^{M/F}$
topinambur ^{M}

kohlrabi
chou-rave ^{M}
colirrábano ^{M}
Kohlrabi ^{M}
cavolo ^{M} rapa ^{F}

potato
pomme ^{F} de terre ^{F}
patata ^{F}
Kartoffel ^{F}
patata ^{F}

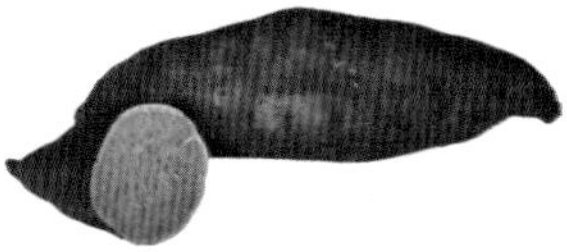

sweet potato
patate ^{F} douce
boniato ^{M}
Süßkartoffel ^{F}
patata ^{F} dolce

Legumes

Légumineuses ^{F} | Leguminosas ^{F} | Hülsenfrüchte ^{F} | Legumi ^{M}

white kidney bean
haricot ^{M} blanc
judía ^{F}
weiße Kidneybohne ^{F}
fagiolo ^{M}

black-eyed pea
haricot ^{M} à œil ^{M} noir
frijol ^{M} de ojo ^{M} negro
Augenbohne ^{F}
fagiolo ^{M} dell'occhio ^{M}

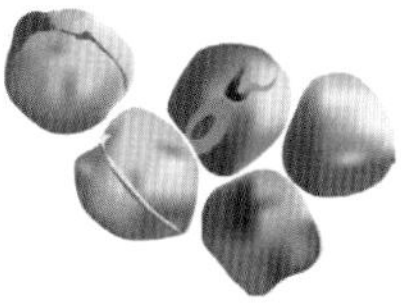

chickpea
pois ^{M} chiche
garbanzos ^{M}
Kichererbse ^{F}
cece ^{M}

lentil
lentille ^{F}
lentejas ^{F}
Linse ^{F}
lenticchia ^{F}

adzuki bean
haricot ^{M} adzuki
frijol ^{M} rojo
Adzukibohne ^{F}
fagiolo ^{M} azuki

red kidney bean
haricot ^{M} rouge
alubias ^{F} rojas
rote Kidneybohne ^{F}
fagiolo ^{M} rosso

pinto bean
haricot ^{M} pinto
frijol ^{M} pintado
Wachtelbohne ^{F}
fagiolo ^{M} pinto

peanut
arachide ^{F}
cacahuete ^{M} / maní ^{M}
Erdnuss ^{F}
arachide ^{F}

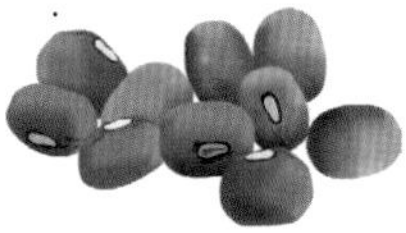

mung bean
haricot ^{M} mungo
frijol ^{M} chino
Mungbohne ^{F}
fagiolo ^{M} mungo

green bean
haricot ^{M} vert
judias ^{F} verdes
Brechbohne ^{F}
fagiolino ^{M}

pea
pois ^{M}
guisantes ^{M}
Erbse ^{F}
pisello ^{M}

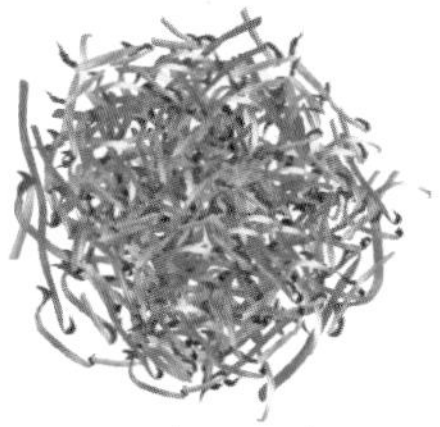

bean sprouts
germes ^{M} de haricot ^{M}
brotes ^{M} / germinados ^{M}
Bohnensprossen ^{F}
germogli ^{M} di soia ^{F}

porcini mushroom
cèpes [M]
hongo [M] porcini
Steinpilz [M]
funghi [M] porcini

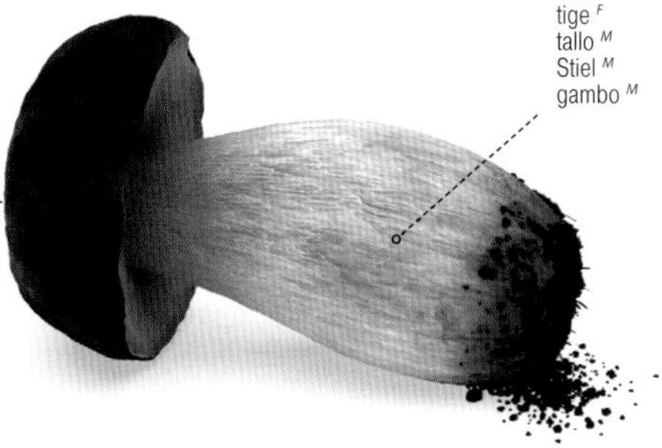
cap
chapeau [M]
sombrero [M]
Hut [M]
cappella [F]
stem
tige [F]
tallo [M]
Stiel [M]
gambo [M]

oyster mushroom
pleurote [M] en forme [F] d'huître [F]
champiñón [M] ostra
Austernpilz [M]
gelone [M]

enoki mushroom
collybie [F] à pied [M] velouté
Enokitake [M]
Samtfußrübling [M]
fungo [M] enoki

cremini
champignon [M] de Paris
champiñón [M] marrón
Brauner Champignon [M]
fungo [M] cremino

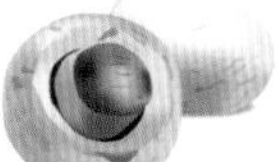
button mushroom
champignon [M] en bouton [M]
champiñón [M] común
Champignon [M]
prataiolo [M]

chanterelle
chanterelle [F]
rebozuelo [M]
Pfifferling [M]
gallinaccio [M]

honey mushroom
armillaire [F] couleur [F] de miel [M]
hongo [M] de miel
Hallimasch [M]
chiodino [M]

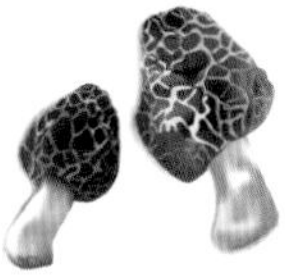
morel
morille [F]
colmenilla [F]
Morchel [F]
spugnola [F]

wood ear
oreille-de-Judas [M]
oreja [F] de Judas
Mu-Err [M]
orecchio [M] di Giuda [M]

truffle
truffe [F]
trufa [F]
Trüffel [M]
tartufo [M]

russula
russule [F]
rúsula [F]
Täubling [M]
rossola [F]

saffron milk cap
lactaire [M] délicieux
níscalo [M]
Edel-Reizker [M]
lapacendro [M] buono

shiitake
shiitake [M]
shiitake [M]
Shiitake [M]
shiitake [M]

slippery jack
bolet [M] jaune
boleto [M] anillado
Butterpilz [M]
pinarolo [M]

bay bolete
bolet ^{M} bai
boleto ^{M} bayo
Maronen-Röhrling ^{M}
boleto ^{M} baio

red aspen bolete
bolet ^{M} orangé
boleto ^{M} anaranjado
Weißstielige Rotkappe ^{F}
porcinello ^{M} rosso

birch bolete
bolet ^{M} rude
boleto ^{M} birch
Birken-Röhrling ^{M}
porcinello ^{M} grigio

suede bolete
bolet ^{M} subtomenteux
boleto ^{M} gamuza
Ziegenlippe ^{F}
boleto ^{M} subtomentoso

Nuts

alnut
oix ^{F}
uez ^{F}
alnuss ^{F}
oce ^{F}

shell
coquille ^{F}
cáscara ^{F} de nuez ^{F}
Schale ^{F}
guscio ^{M}

coconut
noix ^{F} de coco ^{M}
coco ^{M}
Kokosnuss ^{F}
noce ^{F} di cocco ^{M}

almond
amande ^{F}
almendra ^{F}
Mandel ^{F}
mandorla ^{F}

hazelnut
noisette ^{F}
avellana ^{F}
Haselnuss ^{F}
nocciola ^{F}

pine nut
pignon ^{M} de pin ^{M}
piñón ^{M}
Pinienkern ^{M}
pinolo ^{M}

Brazil nut
noix ^{F} du Brésil ^{F}
nuez ^{F} de Brasil
Paranuss ^{F}
noce ^{F} del Brasile ^{M}

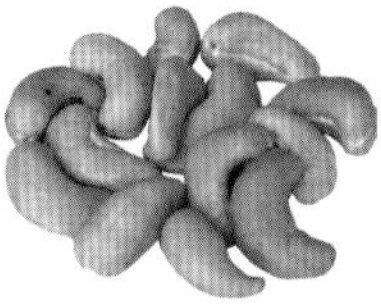

cashew
noix ^{F} de cajou ^{M}
merey ^{M} / nuez ^{F} de cajú
Cashewnuss ^{F}
anacardio ^{M}

macadamia nut
noix ^{F} de macadam ^{M}
nuez ^{F} de macadamia
Macadamia ^{F}
noce ^{F} di macadamia ^{F}

chestnut
châtaigne ^{F}
castaña ^{F}
Esskastanie ^{F}
castagna ^{F}

pistachio
pistache ^{F}
pistacho ^{M}
Pistazie ^{F}
pistacchio ^{M}

pecan
pacane ^{F}
nuez ^{F} pacana
Pekannuss ^{F}
noce ^{F} di pecan ^{M}

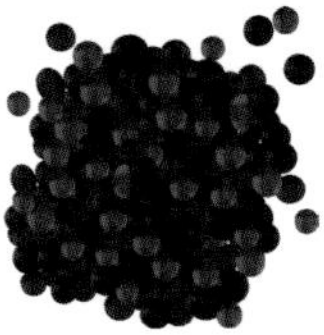

black mustard
moutarde [F] noire
grano [M] de mostaza [F] negra
schwarzer Senf [M]
seme [M] di senape [F] nera

black pepper
poivre [M] noir
pimienta [F] negra
schwarzer Pfeffer [M]
pepe [M] nero

caraway
carvi [M]
comino [M]
Kümmel [M]
cumino [M]

cardamom
cardamome [F]
cardamomo [M]
Kardamom [M/N]
cardamomo [M]

white pepper
poivre [M] blanc
pimienta [F] blanca
weißer Pfeffer [M]
pepe [M] bianco

cinnamon
cannelle [F]
canela [F]
Zimt [M]
cannella [F]

bird's eye chili pepper
piment [M] oiseau [M]
pimiento [M] rojo
Bird's Eye Chili [M]
peperoncino [M]

dried chili
piment [F] séché
pimiento [M] seco
getrocknete Chilischote [F]
peperoncino [M] essiccato

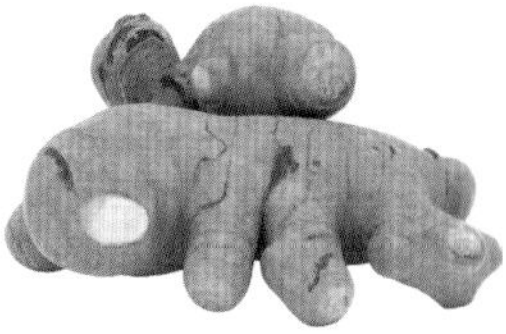

ginger
gingembre [M]
jengibre [M]
Ingwer [M]
zenzero [M]

ground pepper
poivre [M] moulu
pimienta [F] molida
gemahlener Pfeffer [M]
pepe [M] macinato

jalapeño
jalapeño [M]
jalapeño [M]
Jalapeño-Chilischote [F]
jalapeño [M]

juniper berry
baie [F] de genévrier [M]
bayas [F] de enebro [M]
Wacholderbeere [F]
bacca [F] di ginepro [M]

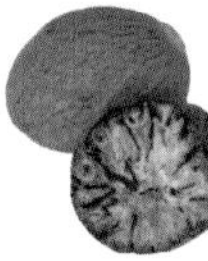

nutmeg
noix [F] de muscade [F]
nuez [F] moscada
Muskat [M]
noce [F] moscata

paprika
paprika [M]
pimentón [M]
Paprikapulver [N]
paprika [F]

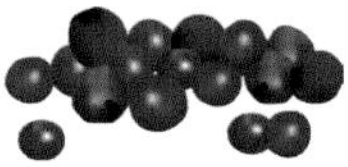

pink peppercorn
poivre [M] rose
pimienta [F] rosa
Rosenpfeffer [M]
pepe [M] rosa

poppy seed
graines [F] de pavot [M]
semillas [F] de amapola [F]
Mohn [M]
seme [M] di papavero [M]

clove
clou [M] de girofle [F]
clavo [M] de olor
Nelke [F]
chiodo [M] di garofano [M]

saffron
safran [M]
azafrán [M]
Safran [M]
zafferano [M]

white mustard
moutarde [F] blanche
grano [M] de mostaza [F] blan
weißer Senf [M]
seme [M] di senape [F] bianc

cayenne pepper
piment [M] de Cayenne [F]
pimienta [F] de Cayena
Cayennepfeffer [M]
pepe [M] di Caienna [F]

table salt
sel [M] de table [F]
sal [F] de mesa [F]
Speisesalz [N]
sale [M] marino

turmeric
curcuma [M]
cúrcuma [F]
Gelbwurz [F]
curcuma [F]

sea salt
sel [M] de mer [F]
sal [F] de mar
Meersalz [N]
sale [M]

curry powder
poudre [F] de curry [M]
polvo [M] de curry
Currypulver [N]
curry [M]

anise
anis [M]
anís [M]
Anis [M]
anice [F]

basil
basilic [M]
albahaca [F]
Basilikum [M]
basilico [M]

bay leaf
feuille [F] de laurier [M]
hojas [F] de laurel [M]
Lorbeerblatt [N]
foglia [M] di alloro [M]

caper
câpres [F]
alcaparra [F]
Kaper [F]
cappero [M]

cilantro
coriandre [M]
cilantro [M]
Koriander [M]
coriandolo [M]

dill
aneth [M]
eneldo [M]
Dill [M]
aneto [M]

rosemary
romarin [M]
romero [M]
Rosmarin [M]
rosmarino [M]

fennel
fenouil [M]
hinojo [M]
Fenchel [M]
finocchio [M]

garden cress
cresson [M] alénois
mastuerzo [M]
Gartenkresse [F]
crescione [M]

parsley
persil [M]
perejil [M]
Petersilie [F]
prezzemolo [M]

lemongrass
citronnelle [F]
citronela [F]
Zitronengras [N]
citronella [F]

mint
menthe [F]
menta [F]
Minze [F]
menta [F]

mugwort
armoise [F]
artemisa [F]
Beifuß [M]
artemisia [F]

sage
sauge [F]
salvia [F]
Salbei [M]
salvia [F]

thyme
thym [M]
tomillo [M]
Thymian [M]
timo [M]

tarragon
estragon [M]
estragón [M]
Estragon [M]
dragoncello [M]

oregano
origan [M]
orégano [M]
Oregano [M]
origano [M]

purple basil
basilic [M] pourpre
albahaca [F] morada
Roter Basilikum [M]
basilico [M] viola

lemon balm
mélisse [F]
melisa [F]
Melisse [F]
melissa [F]

Tea and coffee

black tea
thé [M] noir
té [M] negro
schwarzer Tee [M]
tè [M] nero

herbal tea
tisane [F]
té [M] de hierbas [F]
Kräutertee [M]
tisana [F]

green coffee bean
grain [M] de café [M] vert
granos [M] de café [M] verde
grüne Kaffeebohne [F]
chicchi [M] di caffè [M] verde

ground coffee
café [M] moulu
café [M] molido
gemahlener Kaffee [M]
caffè [M] macinato

instant coffee
café [M] instantané
café [M] instantáneo
Pulverkaffee [M]
caffè [M] istantaneo

oolong tea
thé [M] oolong
té [M] oolong
Oolong-Tee [M]
tè [M] oolong

green tea
thé [M] vert
té [M] verde
grüner Tee [M]
tè [M] verde

white tea
thé [M] blanc
té [M] blanco
weißer Tee [M]
tè [M] bianco

roasted coffee bean
grains [M] de café [M] torréfiés
granos [M] de café [M] tostado
geröstete Kaffeebohne [F]
chicco [M] di caffè [M] tostato

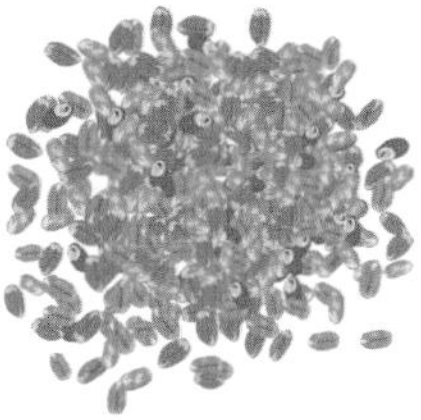

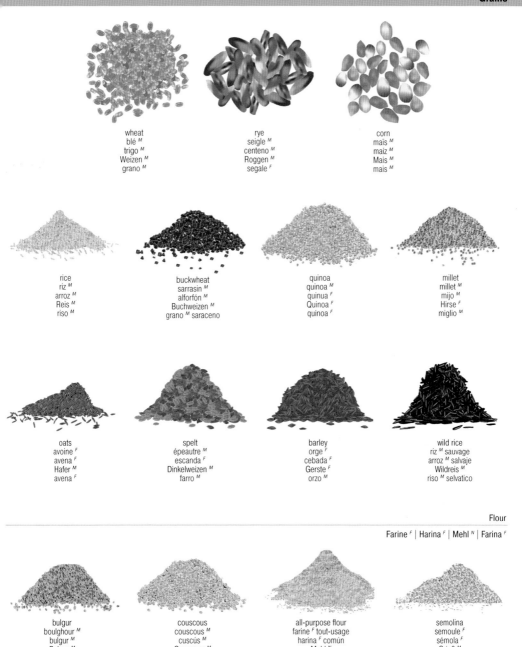

wheat
blé [M]
trigo [M]
Weizen [M]
grano [M]

rye
seigle [M]
centeno [M]
Roggen [M]
segale [F]

corn
maïs [M]
maíz [M]
Mais [M]
mais [M]

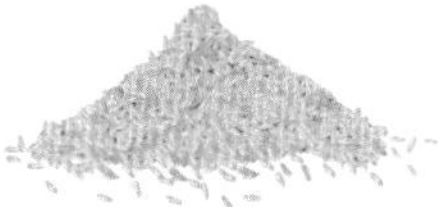

rice
riz [M]
arroz [M]
Reis [M]
riso [M]

buckwheat
sarrasin [M]
alforfón [M]
Buchweizen [M]
grano [M] saraceno

quinoa
quinoa [M]
quinua [F]
Quinoa [F]
quinoa [F]

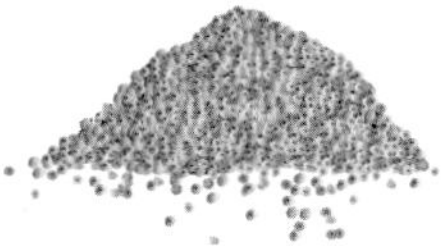

millet
millet [M]
mijo [M]
Hirse [F]
miglio [M]

oats
avoine [F]
avena [F]
Hafer [M]
avena [F]

spelt
épeautre [M]
escanda [F]
Dinkelweizen [M]
farro [M]

barley
orge [F]
cebada [F]
Gerste [F]
orzo [M]

wild rice
riz [M] sauvage
arroz [M] salvaje
Wildreis [M]
riso [M] selvatico

Flour

Farine [F] | Harina [F] | Mehl [N] | Farina [F]

bulgur
boulghour [M]
bulgur [M]
Bulgur [M]
bulgur [M]

couscous
couscous [M]
cuscús [M]
Couscous [M]
cuscus [M]

all-purpose flour
farine [F] tout-usage
harina [F] común
Mehl [N]
farina [F] di grano [M] tenero

semolina
semoule [F]
sémola [F]
Grieß [M]
semola [M]

Tropical fruits

Fruits ^{M} tropicaux | Frutas ^{F} tropicales | Tropenfrüchte ^{F} | Frutta ^{F} tropicale

banana
banane ^{F}
banana ^{F}
Banane ^{F}
banana ^{F}

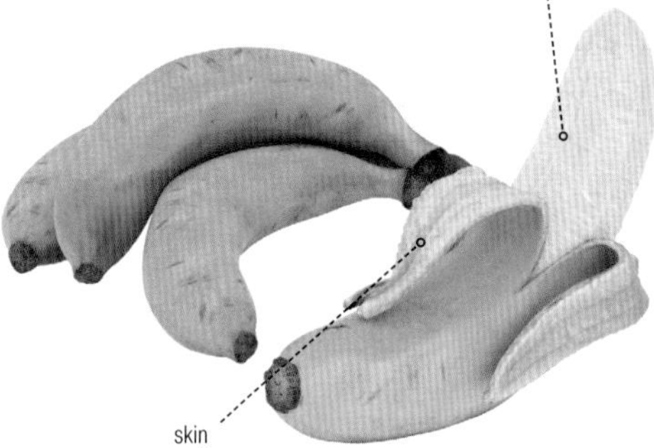
flesh
chair ^{F}
pulpa ^{F}
Fruchtfleisch ^{N}
polpa ^{F}
skin
peau ^{F}
piel ^{F}
Bananenschale ^{F}
buccia ^{F}

papaya
papaye ^{F}
papaya ^{F}
Papaya ^{F}
papaya ^{F}

flesh
chair ^{F}
pulpa ^{F}
Fruchtfleisch ^{N}
polpa ^{F}
seeds
graines ^{F}
semillas ^{F}
Samen ^{M}
semi ^{M}

lychee
litchi ^{M}
lichi ^{M}
Litschi ^{F}
litchi ^{M}

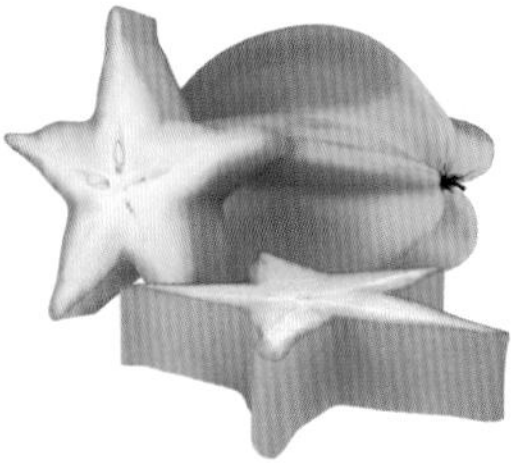

carambola
carambole ^{F}
fruta ^{F} de estrella
Sternfrucht ^{F}
carambola ^{F}

cherimoya
chérimole ^{F}
chirimoya ^{F}
Cherimoya ^{F}
cerimolia ^{F}

durian
durian ^{M}
durián ^{M}
Durianfrucht ^{F}
durian ^{M}

fig
figue ^{F}
higo ^{M}
Feige ^{F}
fico ^{M}

guava
goyave ^{F}
guayaba ^{F}
Guave ^{F}
guava ^{F}

Asian pear
pomme-poire ^{F}
pera ^{F} oriental
Nashi-Birne ^{F}
pera ^{F} cinese

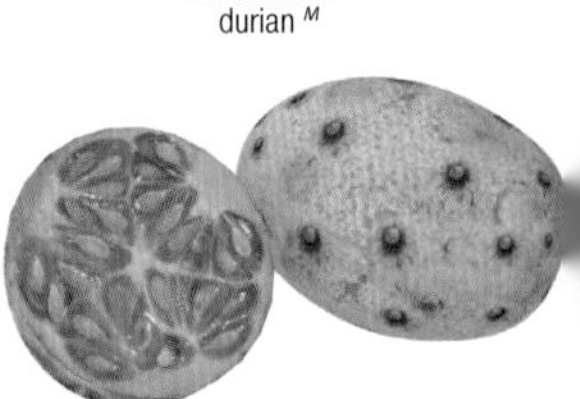

horned melon
melon ^{M} à cornes ^{F}
melón ^{M} africano
Horngurke ^{F}
kiwano ^{M}

pomegranate
grenade [F]
granada [F]
Granatapfel [M]
melagrana [F]

pineapple
ananas [M]
piña [F]
Ananas [F]
ananas [M]

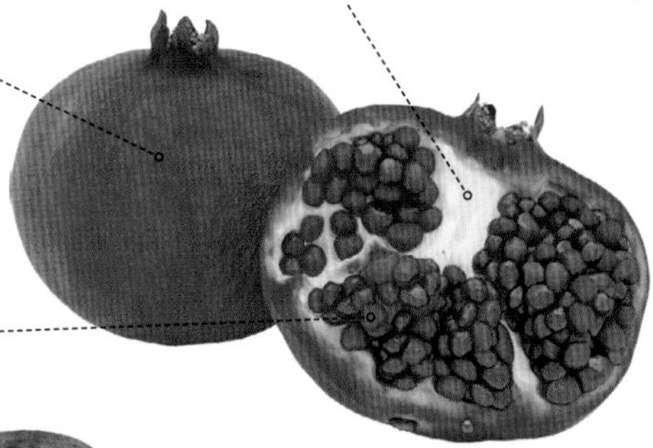
skin
peau [F]
piel [F]
Schale [F]
buccia [F]
membrane
membrane [F]
mesocarpio [M]
Haut [F]
albedo [M]
aril
graine [F]
semilla [F]
Samenmantel [M]
arillo [M]

feijoa
feijoa [M]
feijoa [F]
brasiliansiche Guave [F]
feijoa [F]

kiwifruit
kiwi [M]
kiwi [M]
Kiwi [F]
kiwi [M]

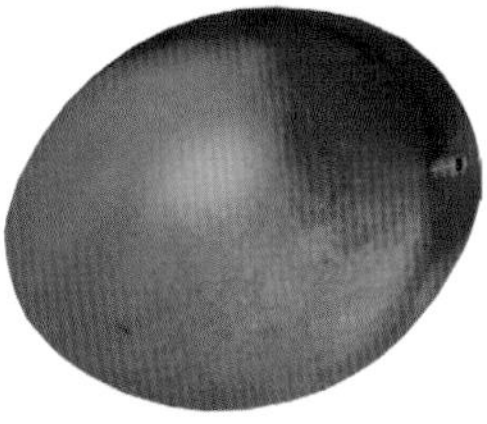

mango
mangue [F]
mango [M]
Mango [F]
mango [M]

mangosteen
mangoustan [M]
mangostán [M]
Mangostane [F]
mangostano [M]

dragon fruit
pitaya [M]
fruta [F] del dragón [M]
Drachenfrucht [F]
frutto [M] del drago [M]

persimmon
kaki [M]
caqui [M]
Kaki [F]
cachi [M]

passion fruit
fruit [M] de la passion [F]
maracuyá [M] / parchita [F]
Maracuja [F]
frutto [M] della passione [F]

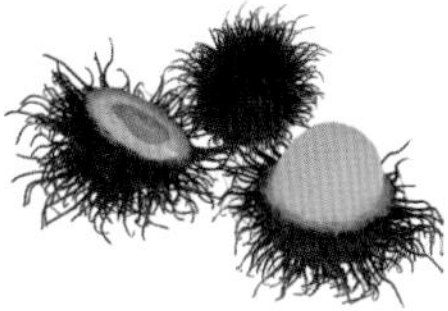

rambutan
ramboutan [M]
rambután [M]
Rambutan [M]
rambutan [M]

tamarillo
tamarillo [M]
tamarillo [M]
Baumtomate [F]
tamarindo [M]

Citrus fruits

Agrumes M | Cítricos M | Zitrusfrüchte F | Agrumi M

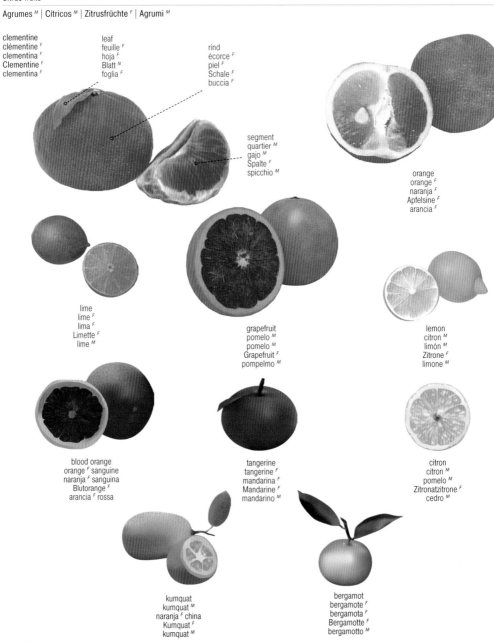

clementine
clémentine F
clementina F
Clementine F
clementina F

leaf
feuille F
hoja F
Blatt N
foglia F

rind
écorce F
piel F
Schale F
buccia F

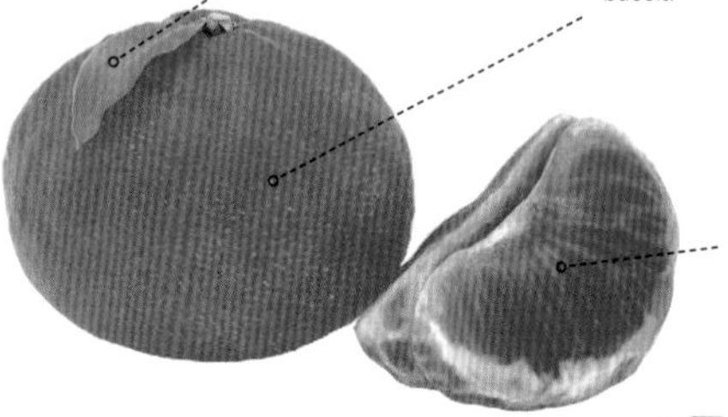

segment
quartier M
gajo M
Spalte F
spicchio M

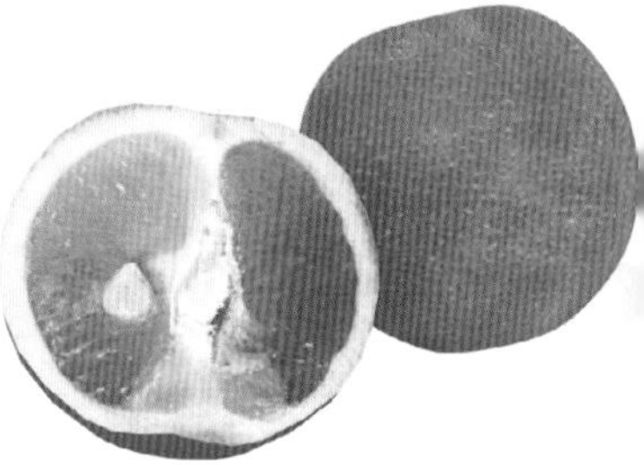

orange
orange F
naranja F
Apfelsine F
arancia F

lime
lime F
lima F
Limette F
lime M

grapefruit
pomelo M
pomelo M
Grapefruit F
pompelmo M

lemon
citron M
limón M
Zitrone F
limone M

blood orange
orange F sanguine
naranja F sanguina
Blutorange F
arancia F rossa

tangerine
tangerine F
mandarina F
Mandarine F
mandarino M

citron
citron M
pomelo M
Zitronatzitrone F
cedro M

kumquat
kumquat M
naranja F china
Kumquat F
kumquat M

bergamot
bergamote F
bergamota F
Bergamotte F
bergamotto M

Berries

Baies [F] | Bayas [F] | Beeren [F] | Bacche [F]

cranberry
canneberge [F]
arándano [M] agrio
Moosbeere [F]
ossicocco [M] americano

red grape
raisin [M] rouge
uva [F] negra
rote Weintraube [F]
uva [F] rossa

white grape
raisin [M] blanc
uva [F] blanca
weiße Weintraube [F]
uva [F] bianca

red currant
groseille [F] rouge
grosella [F] roja
rote Johannisbeere [F]
ribes [M] rosso

cloudberry
chicouté [F]
mora [F] de los pantanos [M]
Moltebeere [F]
lampone [M] artico

raspberry
framboise [F]
frambuesa [F]
Himbeere [F]
lampone [M]

strawberry
fraise [F]
fresa [F]
Erdbeere [F]
fragola [F]

blackberry
mûre [F]
mora [F]
Brombeere [F]
mora [F]

gooseberry
groseille [F] à maquereau [M]
grosella [F]
Stachelbeere [F]
uva [F] spina [F]

black currant
cassis [M]
grosella [F] negra
chwarze Johannisbeere [F]
ribes [M] nero

blueberry
bleuet [M]
arándano [M] azul
Heidelbeere [F]
mirtillo [M]

cape gooseberry
groseille [F] du Cap [M]
uchuva [F]
Andenbeere [F]
alchechengi [M]

elderberry
sureau [M]
saúco [M]
Holunderbeere [F]
bacca [F] di sambuco [M]

lingonberry
airelles [F] rouges
arándano [M] rojo
Preiselbeere [F]
mirtillo [M] rosso

Melons

Melons ^{M} | Melones ^{M} | Melonen ^{F} | Meloni ^{M}

watermelon
melon ^{M} d'eau ^{F}
sandía ^{F}
Wassermelone ^{F}
cocomero ^{M}

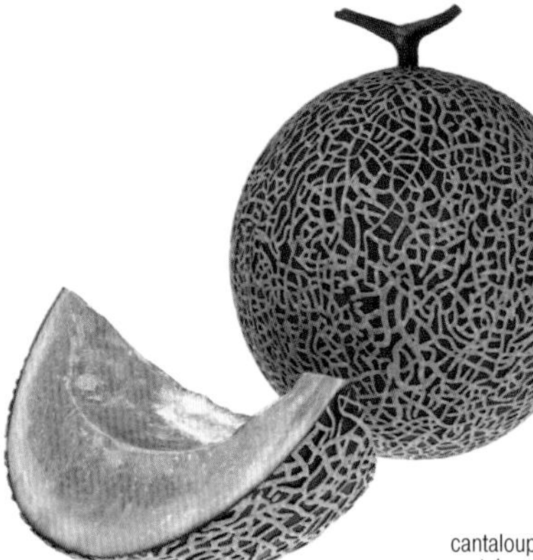

cantaloupe
cantaloup ^{M}
melón ^{M}
Cantaloupe-Melone ^{F}
melone ^{M} di Cantalupo

yellow watermelon
melon ^{M} à chair ^{F} jaune
sandía ^{F} amarilla
gelbe Wassermelone ^{F}
cocomero ^{M} giallo

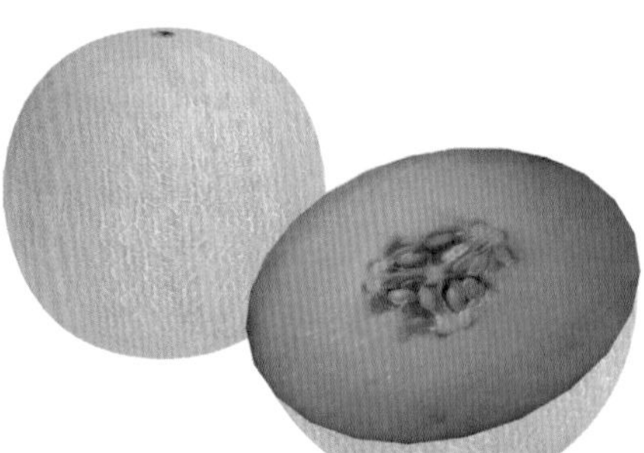

honeydew melon
melon ^{M} miel
melón ^{M} de almizcle ^{M}
Honigmelone ^{F}
melone ^{M} verde

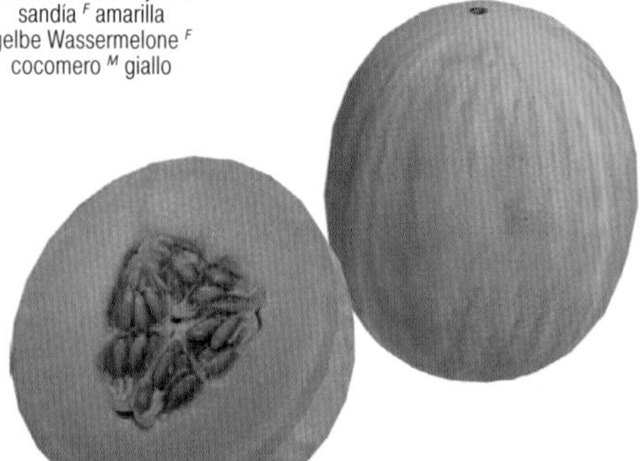

canary melon
melon ^{M} brésilien
melón ^{M} dulce
Gelbe Honigmelone ^{F}
melone ^{M} d'inverno ^{M}

Pome fruits

Fruits [M] à pépins [M] | Frutas [F] de pepita [F] | Kernobst [N] | Pomacee [F]

pear
poire [F]
pera [F]
Birne [F]
pera [F]

leaf
feuille [F]
hoja [F]
Blatt [N]
foglia [F]

stalk
tige [F]
tallo [M]
Stiel [M]
torsolo [M]

red apple
pomme [F] rouge
manzana [F] roja
roter Apfel [M]
mela [F] rossa

flesh
chair [F]
pulpa [F]
Fruchtfleisch [N]
polpa [F]

seed
pépin [M]
pepita [F]
Kern [M]
seme [M]

skin
peau [F]
piel [F]
Schale [F]
buccia [F]

stamen
étamine [F]
estambre [M]
Blütenrest [M]
stame [M]

loquat
nèfle [F] du Japon [M]
níspero [M]
japanische Wollmispel [F]
nespola [F]

green apple
pomme [F] verte
manzana [F] verde
grüner Apfel [M]
mela [F] verde

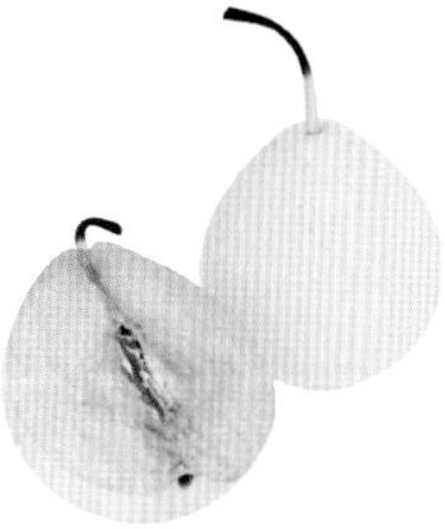

ya pear
poire [F] Yali
nashi [M]
Nashi-Birne [F]
pera [F] Nashi

Stone fruits

Fruits [M] à noyau [M] | Frutas [F] de hueso [M] | Steinfrüchte [F] | Frutti [M] a nocciolo [M]

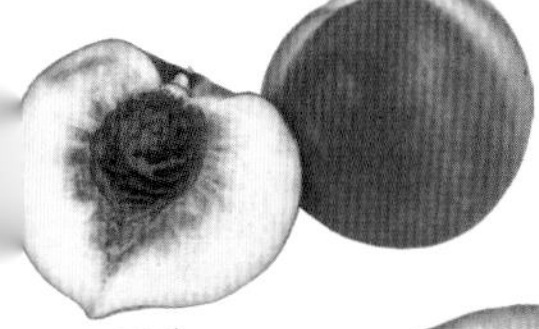

peach
pêche [F]
melocotón [M]
Pfirsich [M]
pesca [F]

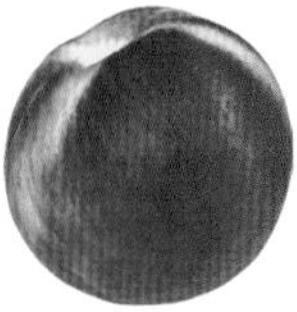

nectarine
nectarine [F]
nectarina [F]
Nektarine [F]
pescanoce [F]

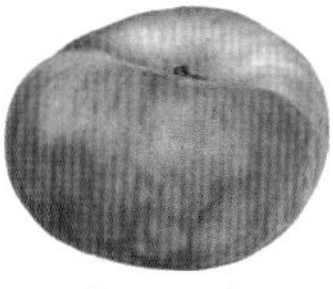

Saturn peach
pêche [F] plate
paraguayo [M]
Plattpfirsich [M]
pesca [F] tabacchiera

apricot
abricot [M]
albaricoque [M]
Aprikose [F]
albicocca [F]

black cherry
cerise [F] noire
cereza [F] negra
späte Traubenkirsche [F]
ciliegia [F] nera

plum
prune [F]
ciruela [F]
Pflaume [F]
prugna [F]

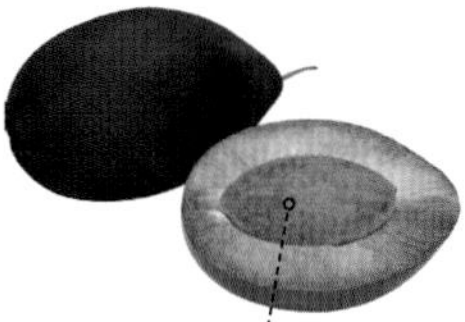

seed
noyau [M]
hueso [M]
Stein [M]
nocciolo [M]

acerola
cerise [F] des Antilles [F]
acerola [F]
Acerolakirsche [F]
acerola [F]

greengage
reine-claude [F]
ciruela [F] claudia
Reneklode [F]
prugna [F] regina [F] Claudia [F]

cherry
cerise [F]
cereza [F]
Kirsche [F]
ciliegia [F]

sour cherry
cerise [F] acide
cereza [F] ácida
Sauerkirsche [F]
amarena [F]

date
datte [F]
dátil [M]
Dattel [F]
dattero [M]

aioli
aïoli [M]
alioli [M]
Knoblauchmayonnaise [F]
aioli [F]

barbecue sauce
sauce [F] barbecue
salsa [F] barbacoa
Barbecuesoße [F]
salsa [F] barbecue [M]

salsa
salsa [F]
salsa [F]
Salsa [F]
salsa [F]

mustard
moutarde [F]
mostaza [F]
Senf [M]
senape [F]

Italian dressing
vinaigrette [F] italienne
aderezo [M] italiano
Italienisches Dressing [N]
salsa [F] all'italiana

ketchup
ketchup [M]
salsa [F] de tomate [M] / cátsup [M]
Ketchup [N/M]
ketchup [M]

mayonnaise
mayonnaise [F]
mayonesa [F]
Mayonnaise [F]
maionese [F]

French dressing
vinaigrette [F] française
aderezo [M] francés
French dressing [N]
vinaigrette [F]

harissa
harissa [F]
harissa [F]
Harissa [F/N]
harissa [F]

pesto
pesto [M]
pesto [M]
Pesto [N]
pesto [M]

rémoulade
rémoulade [F]
remoulade [F]
Remoulade [F]
remoulade [F]

sambal oelek
sambal oelek [M]
sambal [M]
Sambal Oelek [N]
sambal oelek [M]

tomato paste
purée [F] de tomates [F]
concentrado [M] de tomate [M]
Tomatenmark [N]
concentrato [M] di pomodoro [M]

tamarind paste
pâte [F] de tamarin [M]
pasta [F] de tamarindo [M]
Tamarinde-Paste [F]
pasta [F] di tamarindo [M]

wasabi
wasabi [M]
wasabi [M]
Wasabi [N]
wasabi [M]

tomato puree
coulis [M] de tomates [F]
puré [M] de tomate [M]
Tomatenmark [N]
passata [F] di pomodoro [M]

balsamic vinegar
vinaigre [M] balsamique
vinagre [M] balsámico
Balsamicoessig [M]
aceto [M] balsamico

cider vinegar
vinaigre [M] de cidre [M]
vinagre [M] de manzana [F]
Apfelessig [M]
aceto [M] di sidro [M]

chili oil
sauce [F] piquante
salsa [F] picante
Chiliöl [N]
olio [M] piccante

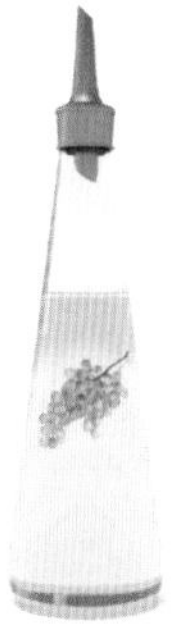

white wine vinegar
vinaigre [M] de vin [M] blanc
vinagre [M] de vino blanco [M]
Weißweinessig [M]
aceto [M] di vino [M] bianco

soy sauce
sauce [F] de soja [M]
salsa [F] de soja [F]
Sojasoße [F]
salsa [F] di soia [F]

white vinegar
vinaigre blanc
vinagre [M] destilado
weißer Essig [M]
aceto [M] bianco

Oils

sunflower oil
huile [F] de tournesol [M]
aceite [M] de girasol [M]
Sonnenblumenöl [N]
olio [M] di girasole [M]

walnut oil
huile [F] de noix [F]
aceite [M] de nuez [F]
Walnussöl [N]
olio [M] di noci [F]

soybean oil
huile [F] de soja [M]
aceite [M] de soja [F]
Sojaöl [N]
olio [M] di soia [F]

sesame oil
huile [F] de sésame [M]
aceite [M] de ajonjolí [M]
Sesamöl [N]
olio [M] di sesamo [M]

corn oil
huile [F] de maïs [M]
aceite [M] de maíz [M]
Maiskeimöl [N]
olio [M] di mais [M]

olive oil
huile [F] d'olive [F]
aceite [M] de oliva [F]
Olivenöl [N]
olio [M] di oliva [F]

peanut oil
huile [F] d'arachide [F]
aceite [M] de cacahuete [M]
Erdnussöl [N]
olio [M] di arachidi [F]

pumpkin seed oil
huile [F] de pépins [M] de citrouille [F]
aceite [M] de semillas [F] de calabaza [F]
Kürbiskernöl [N]
olio [M] di semi [M] di zucca [F]

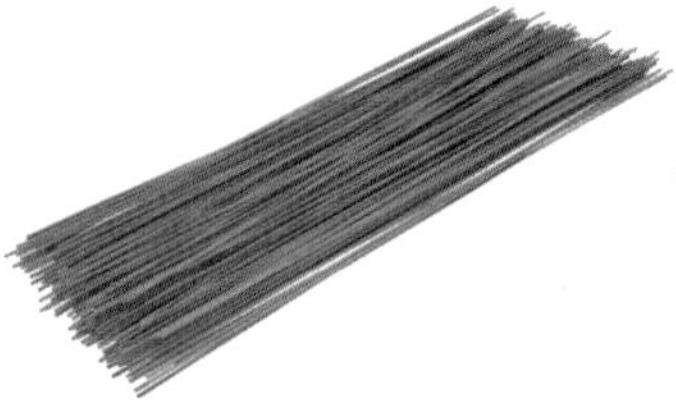

spaghetti
spaghetti [M]
espaguetis [M]
Spaghetti [F]
spaghetti [M]

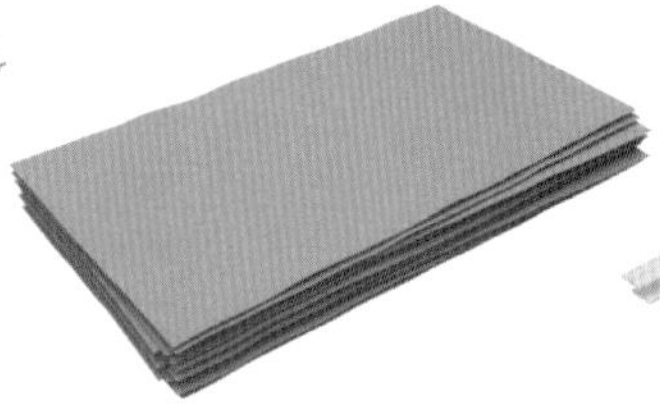

lasagna
lasagne [F]
lasaña [F]
Lasagne [F]
lasagne [F]

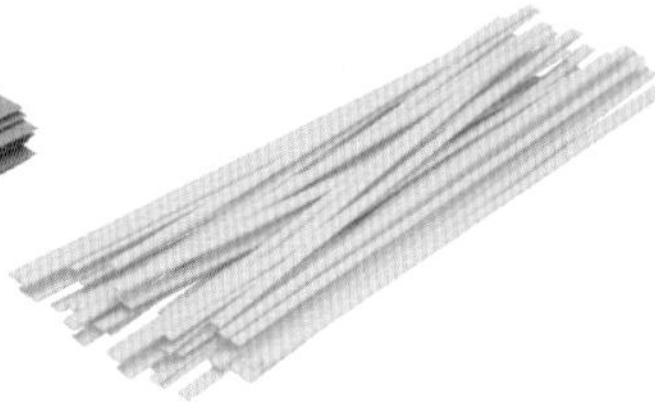

udon
udon [M]
udon [M]
Udon-Nudel [F]
udon [M]

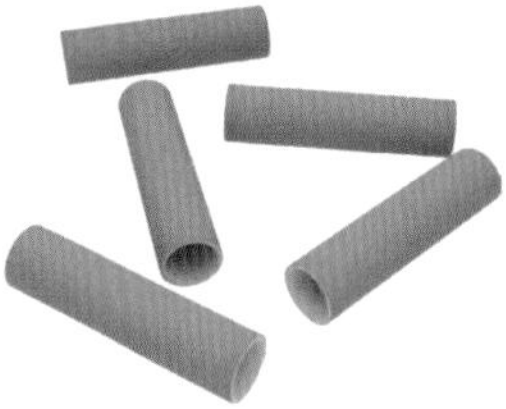

cannelloni
cannelloni [M]
canelones [M]
Cannelloni [F]
cannelloni [M]

ramen
ramen [M]
fideos [M] de huevo [M]
Ramen-Nudel [F]
ramen [M]

tagliatelle
tagliatelle [F]
tagliatelle [F]
Tagliatelle [F]
tagliatelle [F]

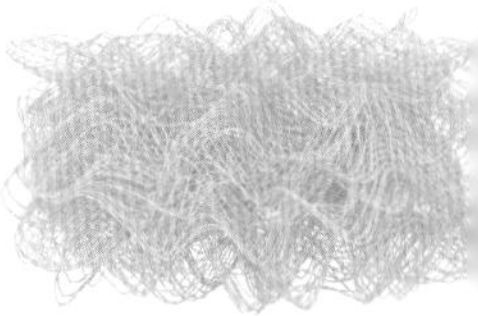

rice noodles
nouilles [F] de riz [M]
fideos [M] de arroz [M]
Reisnudeln [F]
spaghetti [M] di riso [M]

fusilli
fusilli [M]
tornillos [M]
Fusilli [M]
fusilli [M]

penne
penne [F]
plumitas [F]
Penne [F]
penne [F]

conchiglie
coquille [F]
conchas [F]
Conchiglie [F]
conchiglie [F]

rigatoni
rigatoni [M]
rigatoni [M]
Rigatoni [M]
rigatoni [M]

gnocchi
gnocchi [M]
ñoquis [M]
Gnocchi [M]
gnocchi [M]

ravioli
ravioli [M]
ravioles [M]
Ravioli [M]
ravioli [M]

tortellini
tortellini [M]
tortellini [M]
Tortellini [F]
tortellini [M]

farfalle
farfalle [F]
mariposas [M]
Farfalle [F]
farfalle [F]

baguette
baguette [F]
baguette [F]
Baguette [N]
baguette [F]

crust
croûte [F]
corteza [F]
Kruste [F]
crosta [F]

multi-grain bread
pain [M] multicéréales
pan [M] multi grano [M]
Mehrkornbrot [N]
pane [M] multicereale

slice
tranche [F]
rebanada [F]
Scheibe [F]
fetta [F]

sunflower seed
graine [F] de tournesol [M]
semillas [F] de girasol [M]
Sonnenblumenkern [M]
semi [M] di girasole [M]

white bread
pain [M] blanc
pan [M] blanco
Weißbrot [N]
pane [M] bianco

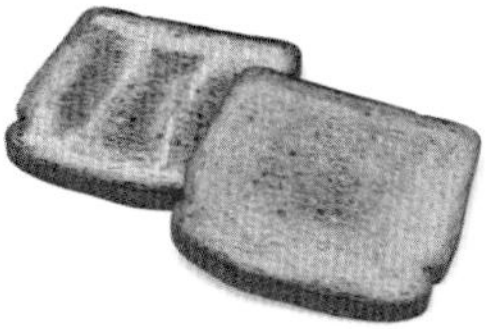

toast
rôtie [F]
tostada [F]
Toastbrot [N]
pane [M] tostato

challah
hallah [F]
jalá [M]
Hefezopf [M]
challah [F]

bagel
bagel [M]
bagel [M]
Bagel [M]
bagel [M]

pretzel
bretzel [M]
pretzel [M]
Brezel [F]
pretzel [M]

stuffed pastry
pâtisserie [F] farcie
pastelito [M] relleno
Teigtasche [F]
panzerotto [M]

whole wheat roll
petit pain [M] de blé [M] entier
panecillo [M] integral
Vollkornbrötchen [N]
panino [M] integrale

coarse rye bread
pain [M] de seigle [M]
pan [M] de centeno [M]
Roggenbrot [N]
pane [M] di segale [F]

sourdough bread
pain [M] au levain [M]
pan [M] de centeno [M] grueso
Sauerteigbrot [N]
pane [M] con lievito [M] madre [F]

jelly doughnut
beigne [M] à la gelée [F]
dónut [M] de mermelada [F]
Berliner [M]
krapfen [M] con marmellata [F]

powdered sugar
sucre [M] à glacer
azúcar [M] glas
Puderzucker [M]
zucchero [M] a velo [M]

doughnut
beigne [M]
dónut [M]
Donut [M]
ciambella [F]

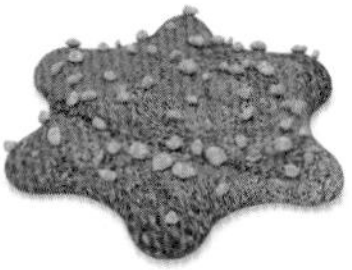

sugar cookie
biscuit [M] au sucre [M]
galleta [F]
Keks [M]
biscotto [M]

chocolate cookie
biscuit [M] au chocolat [M]
galleta [F] de chocolate [F]
Schokoladenplätzchen
biscotto [M] al cioccolato

kifli
kifli [M]
kifli [M]
Hörnchen [N]
kifli [M]

Spritzkuchen
Spritzkuchen [M]
Spritzkuchen [M]
Spritzgebäck [N]
Spritzkuchen [M]

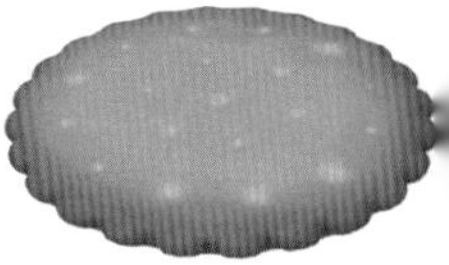

butter cookie
biscuit [M] au beurre [M]
galleta [F] de mantequilla [F]
Butterkeks [M]
biscotto [M] al burro [M]

layer cake
gâteau [M] étagé
pastel [M] de varias capas [F]
Sahneschnitte [F]
torta [F] a strati [M]

jelly roll
roulé [M] à la gelée [F]
brazo [M] de gitano
Biskuitrolle [F]
rotolo [M] dolce

bread roll
petit pain [M]
panecillo [M]
Brötchen [N]
panino [M]

oatmeal cookie
biscuit [M] à l'avoine [F]
galleta [F] de avena [F]
Haferflockenkeks [M]
biscotto [M] alla farina [F] d'avena [F]

vatrushka
vatrouchka [F]
vatrushka [F]
Watruschka [F]
vatrushka [F]

croissant
croissant [M]
cruasán [M]
Croissant [N]
croissant [M]

waffle
gaufre [F]
gofre [M]
Waffel [F]
waffle [M]

rusk
biscotte [F]
bizcocho [M]
Zwieback [M]
fetta [F] biscottata

Bundt cake
gâteau [M] Bundt
pastel [M] para café [M]
Napfkuchen [M]
torta [F] Bundt

cupcake
petit gâteau [M]
magdalena [F]
Cupcake [N]
cupcake [M]

fruit tartlet
tartelette [F] aux fruits [M]
tartaleta [F] de frutas [F]
Fruchttörtchen [N]
tortina [F] alla frutta [F]

cheesecake
gâteau [M] au fromage [M]
tarta [F] de queso [M]
Käsekuchen [M]
torta [F] al formaggio [M]

fruit sauce
sauce [F] aux fruits [M]
cobertura [F] de mermelada [F]
Fruchtsauce [F]
salsa [F] alla frutta [F]

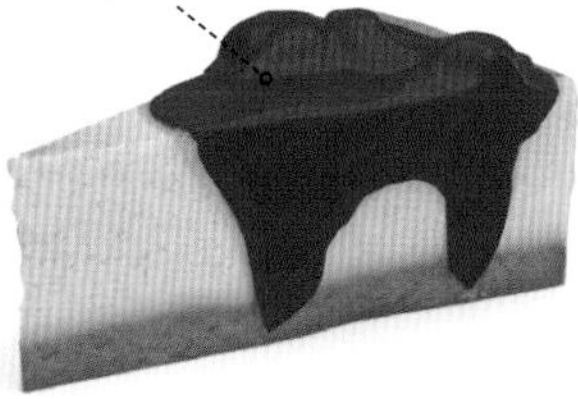

blueberry pie
tarte [F] aux bleuets [M]
tarta [F] de arándanos [M]
Heidelbeerkuchen [M]
torta [F] ai frutti di bosco [M]

cherry tart
clafoutis [M] aux cerises
tartaleta [F] de cerezas [F]
Kirschkuchen [M]
torta [F] alle ciliegie [F]

banana bread
pain [M] aux bananes [F]
pan [M] de plátano [M]
Bananenbrot [N]
pane [M] alla banana [F]

cake
gâteau [M]
pastel [M]
Torte [F]
torta [F]

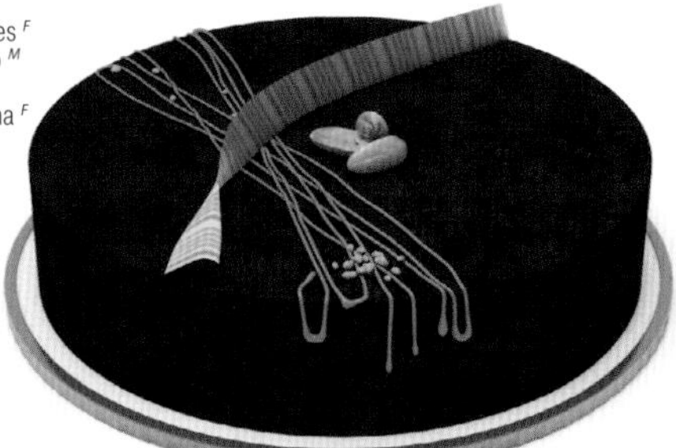

chocolate torte
torte [F] au chocolat [M]
pastel [M] de chocolate [M]
Schokoladentorte [F]
torta [F] al cioccolato [M]

ice cream cone
cornet ^{M} de crème ^{F}
glacée barquilla ^{F} de helado ^{M}
Eiswaffel ^{F}
cono ^{M} gelato

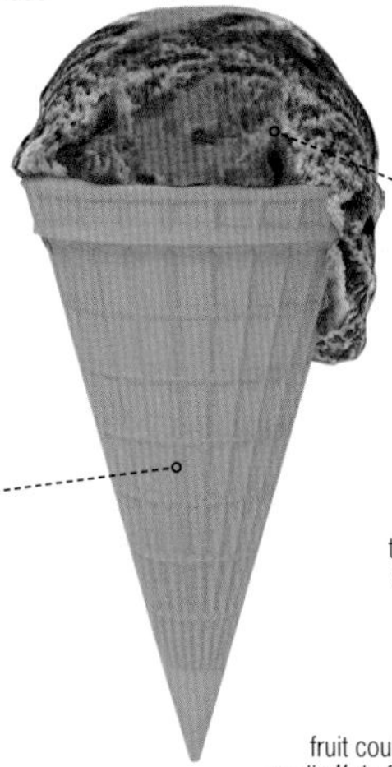

ice cream
crème ^{F} glacée
helado ^{M}
Eis ^{N}
gelato ^{M}

cone
cornet ^{M}
barquilla ^{F}
Waffel ^{F}
cono ^{M}

sundae
coupe ^{F} glacée
copa ^{M} de helado ^{M}
Eisbecher ^{M}
gelato ^{M} guarnito

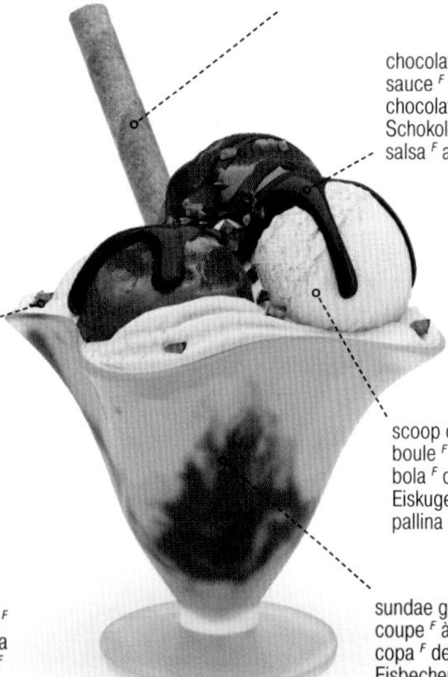

wafer
gaufrette ^{F}
barquillo ^{M}
Waffel ^{F}
wafer ^{M}

chocolate sauce
sauce ^{F} au chocolat ^{M}
chocolate ^{M} fundido
Schokoladensauce ^{F}
salsa ^{F} al cioccolato ^{M}

crushed nut
noix ^{F} concassée
trocito ^{M} de nueces ^{F}
zerkleinerte Nüsse ^{F}
granella ^{F} di noci ^{F}

scoop of ice cream
boule ^{F} de crème ^{F} glacée
bola ^{F} de helado ^{M}
Eiskugel ^{F}
pallina ^{F} di gelato ^{M}

sundae glass
coupe ^{F} à crème ^{F} glacée
copa ^{F} de helado ^{M}
Eisbecher ^{M}
coppa ^{F} di gelato ^{M}

dessert
dessert ^{M}
postre ^{M}
Dessert ^{M}
dolce ^{M}

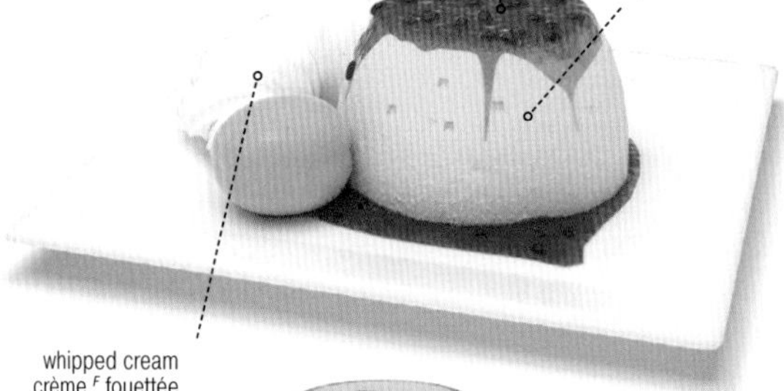

fruit coulis
coulis ^{M} de fruits ^{M}
coulis ^{M} de frutas ^{F}
Frucht-Coulis ^{F}
coulis ^{F} di frutta ^{F}

panna cotta
panna cotta ^{F}
panna ^{F} cotta
Pannacotta ^{F}
panna ^{F} cotta

whipped cream
crème ^{F} fouettée
crema ^{F} batida
Schlagsahne ^{F}
panna ^{F} montata

honey
miel ^{M}
miel ^{F}
Honig ^{M}
miele ^{M}

jam
confiture
mermelada
Marmelade
marmellata

jar
pot ^{M}
bote ^{M}
Glas ^{N}
barattolo ^{M}

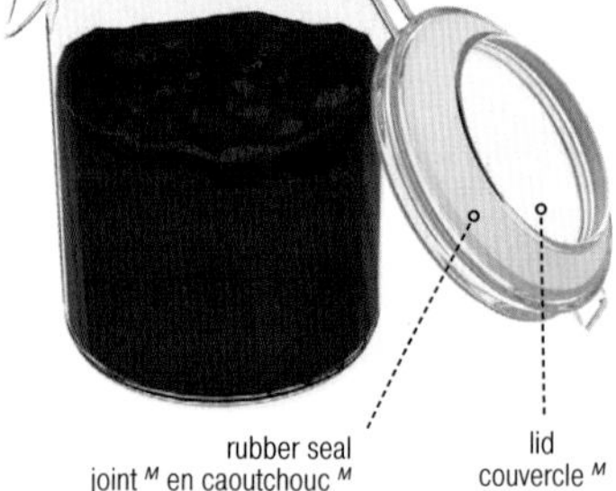

rubber seal
joint ^{M} en caoutchouc ^{M}
sello ^{M} de goma ^{M}
Gummidichtung ^{F}
guarnizione ^{F} in gomma ^{F}

lid
couvercle ^{M}
tapa ^{F}
Deckel ^{M}
coperchio ^{M}

candy-coated chocolates
chocolats [M] enrobés de bonbons [M]
pastillas [F] de chocolate [M]
Schokolinsen [F]
confetti [M] di cioccolato [M]

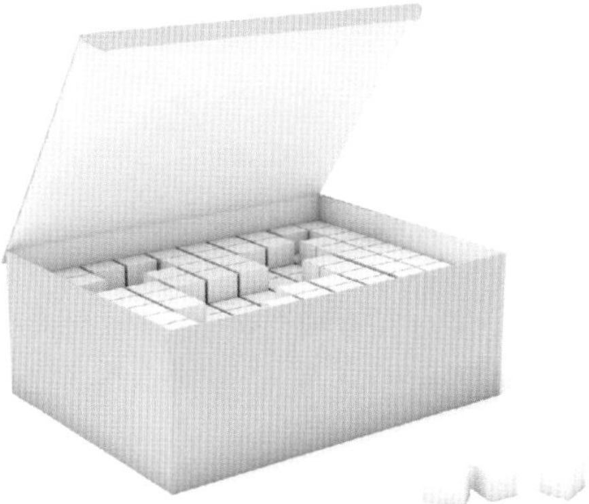

sugar cubes
carrés [M] de sucre [M]
terrones [M] de azúcar [M]
Würfelzucker [M]
zollette [F] di zucchero [M]

chocolate truffle
truffe [M] au chocolat [M]
praliné [M]
Praline [F]
pralina [F]

hard candy
bonbons [M] durs
caramelos [M]
Bonbon [N]
caramella [F]

sugar crystals
cristaux [M] de sucre [M]
cristales [M] de azúcar [M]
Kandiszucker [M]
zucchero [M] cristallizzato [M]

gummy candy
bonbons [M] gommeux
gomitas [F]
Fruchtgummi-Süßwaren [F]
gelatina [F]

chocolate candy
confiserie [F] au chocolat [M]
chocolate [M]
Pralinee [N]
cioccolatino [M]

chocolate coating
enrobage [M] de chocolat [M]
cobertura [F] de chocolate [M]
Schokoladenüberzug [M]
copertura [F] di cioccolato [M]

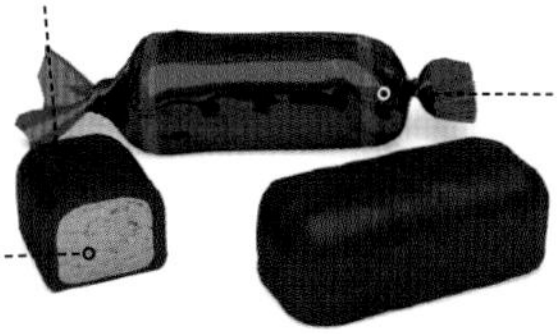

wrapper
emballage [M]
envoltorio [M]
Bonbonpapier [N]
incarto [F]

filling
garniture [F]
relleno [M]
Füllung [F]
ripieno [M]

Chocolate

Chocolat [M] | Chocolate [M] | Schokolade [F] | Cioccolato [M]

cocoa
cacao [M]
cacao [M]
Kakao [M]
cacao [M]

aerated chocolate
chocolat [M] aéré
chocolate [M] aireado
Luftschokolade [F]
cioccolato [M] soffiato

dark chocolate
chocolat [M] noir
chocolate [M] negro
Bitterschokolade [F]
cioccolato [M] fondente

milk chocolate
chocolat [M] au lait [M]
chocolate [M] con leche [F]
Milchschokolade [F]
cioccolato [M] al latte [M]

white chocolate
chocolat [M] blanc
chocolate [M] blanco
weiße Schokolade [F]
cioccolato [M] bianco

hot dog
hot-dog [M]
perro [M] caliente
Hotdog [M]
hot dog [M]

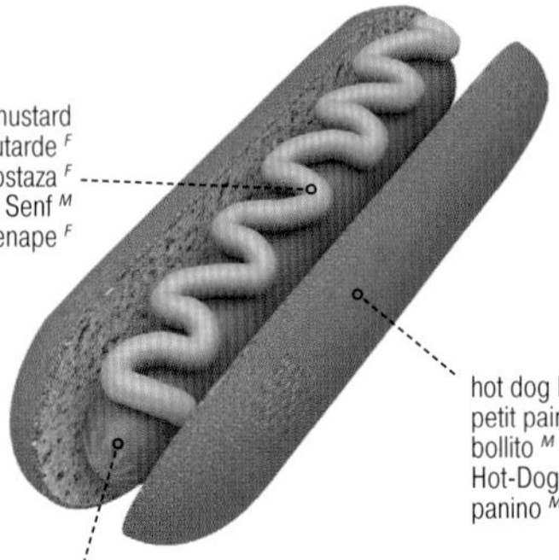

mustard
moutarde [F]
mostaza [F]
Senf [M]
senape [F]

hot dog bun
petit pain [M]
bollito [M]
Hot-Dog-Brötchen [N]
panino [M] per hot dog [M]

wiener
saucisse [F]
salchicha [F] vienesa
Wiener Würstchen [N]
wurstel [M]

Greek salad
salade [F] grecque
ensalada [F] griega
griechischer Salat [M]
insalata [F] greca

chips
croustilles [F]
patatas [F] chips
Chips [M]
patatine [F]

french fries
frites [F]
papas [F] fritas
Pommes frites [F]
patatine [F] fritte

pizza
pizza [F]
pizza [F]
Pizza [F]
pizza [F]

toppings
garnitures [F]
ingredientes [M] extra
Belag [M]
condimento [M]

crust
croûte [F]
borde [M]
Kruste [F]
crosta [F]

slice of pizza
pointe [F] de pizza [F]
porción [M] de pizza [M]
Pizzastück [N]
trancio [M] di pizza [F]

pizza peel
pelle [F] à pizza [F]
paleta [F] para pizza [F]
Pizzabrett [N]
tagliere [M] per pizza [F]

cola
cola [M]
refresco [M]
Cola [F]
bibita [F] analcolica

chips and dip
croustilles [F] et trempette [F]
nachos [M]
Chips [M] und Dip [M]
tortilla [F] e salsa [F]

salsa
salsa [F]
salsa [F]
Salsa [F]
salsa [F]

sandwich
sandwich [M]
bocadillo [M] / sándwich [M]
Sandwich [N]
panino [M]

wrap
roulé [M]
burrito [M]
Wrap [M]
piadina [F] arrotolata

coffee
café [M]
café [M]
Kaffee [M]
caffè [M]

hamburger
hamburger [M]
hamburguesa [F]
Hamburger [M]
hamburger [M]

popcorn
maïs [M] soufflé
palomitas [F] de maíz [M]
Popcorn [N]
popcorn [M]

doner kebab / shawarma / gyro
doner kébab [M] / chawarma [M] / gyros [M]
shawarma [M]
Döner Kebab [M] / Schawarma [N] / Gyros [N]
kebab [M]

breakfast cereal
céréales F pour petit déjeuner M
cereal M de desayuno M
Müsli N
muesli M

milk
lait M
leche F
Milch F
latte M

rolled oats
flocons M d'avoine F
copos M de avena F
Haferflocken F
fiocchi M d'avena F

blueberry
bleuet M
arándanos M
Heidelbeere F
mirtillo M

soft-boiled egg
œuf M à la coque F
huevo M pasado por agua F
weichgekochtes Ei N
uovo M alla coque F

cream of vegetable soup
crème F de légumes M
crema F de verduras F
Gemüsecremesuppe F
vellutata F di verdure F

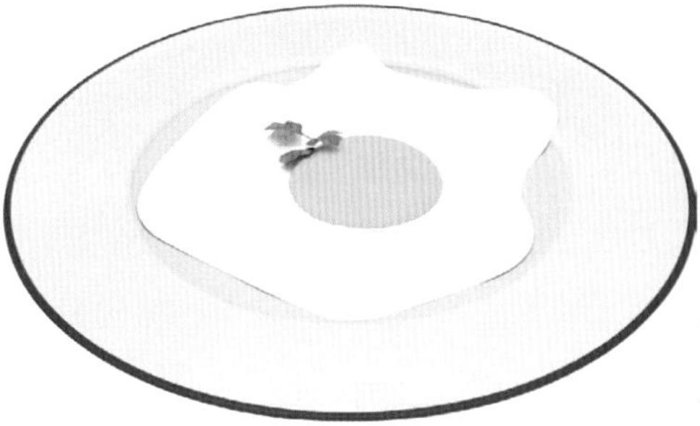

fried egg
œuf M poêlé
huevo M frito
Spiegelei N
uovo M al tegamino M

appetizer
hors-d'œuvre M
aperitivo M
Vorspeise F
stuzzichini M

olive oil
huile F d'olive F
aceite M de oliva F
Olivenöl N
olio M d'oliva F

dipping bowl
pot M à tremper
tazón M de salsa F
Dippschale F
ciotolina F

bread
pain M
pan M
Brot N
pane M

green olive
olive F verte
aceitunas F verdes
grüne Olive F
oliva F verde

black olive
olive F noire
aceitunas F negras
schwarze Olive F
oliva F nera

serving board
plateau M de service M
tabla F para cortar
Schneidebrett N
tagliere M

tomato soup
soupe ^{F} de tomate ^{F}
sopa ^{F} de tomate ^{M}
Tomatensuppe ^{F}
zuppa ^{F} di pomodoro ^{M}

roast turkey dinde ^{F} rôtie
pavo ^{M} asado
Putenbraten ^{M}
tacchino ^{M} arrosto

breast
poitrine ^{F}
pechuga ^{F}
Brust ^{F}
petto ^{M}

leg
cuisse ^{F}
muslo ^{M}
Keule ^{F}
coscia ^{F}

stuffing
farce ^{F}
relleno ^{M}
Füllung ^{F}
ripieno ^{M}

wing
aile ^{F}
alita ^{F}
Flügel ^{M}
ala ^{F}

spaghetti and sauce
spaghetti ^{M} et sauce ^{F}
pasta ^{F} con salsa ^{F}
Spaghetti ^{F} mit Sauce ^{F}
spaghetti ^{M} al sugo ^{M}

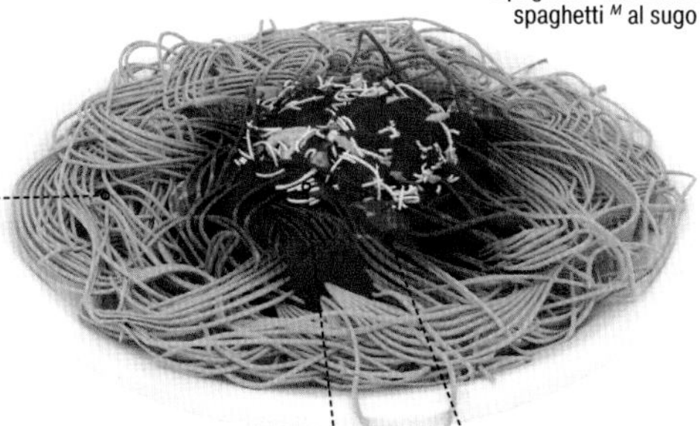

spaghetti
spagettis ^{M}
espaguetis ^{M}
Spaghetti ^{F}
spaghetti ^{M}

grated cheese
fromage ^{M} râpé
queso ^{M} rallado
geriebener Käse ^{M}
formaggio ^{M} grattugiato

tomato sauce
sauce ^{F} tomate ^{F}
salsa ^{F} de tomate ^{M}
Tomatensauce ^{F}
sugo ^{M} di pomodoro ^{m}

ors d'œuvre
ors-d'œuvre ^{M}
anapé ^{M}
ppetithäppchen ^{N}
ntipasto ^{M}

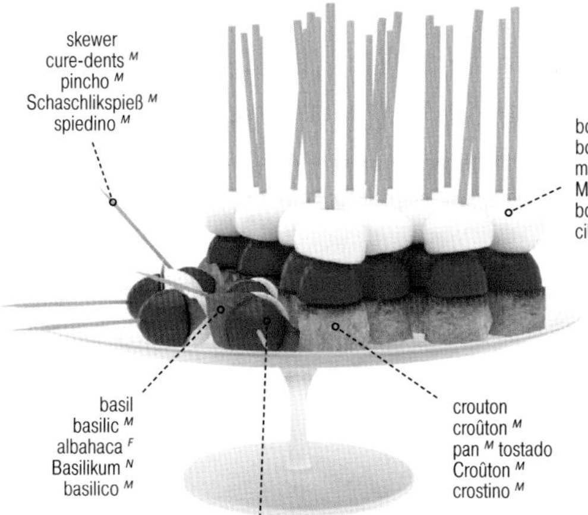

skewer
cure-dents ^{M}
pincho ^{M}
Schaschlikspieß ^{M}
spiedino ^{M}

bocconcini
bocconcini ^{M}
mozzarella ^{F}
Mozzarellakugel ^{F}
bocconcino ^{M} di ciliegina ^{F} di mozzarella ^{F}

basil
basilic ^{M}
albahaca ^{F}
Basilikum ^{N}
basilico ^{M}

crouton
croûton ^{M}
pan ^{M} tostado
Croûton ^{M}
crostino ^{M}

cherry tomato
tomate ^{F} cerise ^{F}
tomate ^{M} cherry
Kirschtomate ^{F}
pomodoro ^{M} ciliegino

pancakes
crêpes ^{F}
panquecas ^{F}
Pfannkuchen ^{M}
pancake ^{M}

whipped cream
crème ^{F} fouettée
crema ^{F} batida
Schlagsahne ^{F}
panna ^{F} montata

pancake
crêpes ^{F}
panqueca ^{F}
Pfannkuchen ^{M}
pancake ^{M}

green tea
thé [M] vert té [F] verde
grüner Tee [M]
tè [M] verde

teapot
théière [F]
tetera [F]
Teekanne [F]
teiera [F]

tea
thé [M]
té [M]
Tee [M]
tè [M]

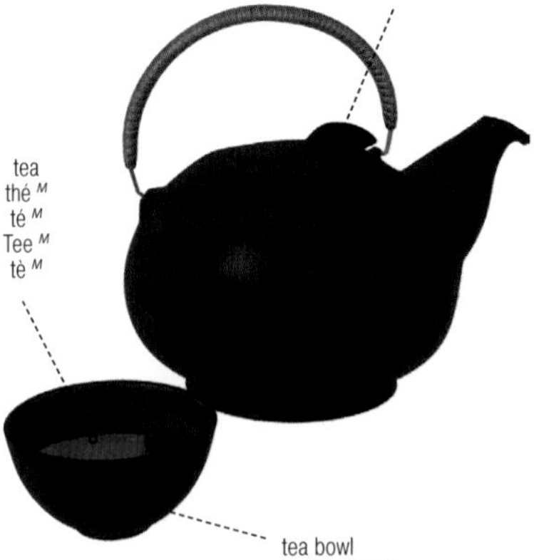

tea bowl
bol [M] à thé [M]
taza [F] de té [M]
Teeschale [F]
tazza [F] da tè [M]

sushi
sushi [M]
sushi [M]
Sushi [N]
sushi [M]

avocado
avocat [M]
aguacate [M] / palta [F]
Avocado [F]
avocado [M]

rice
riz [M]
arroz [M]
Reis [M]
riso [M]

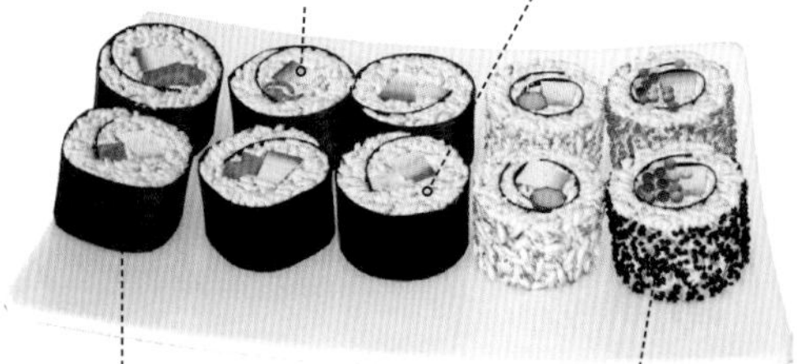

nori
nori [M]
alga [F] nori
Nori [N]
nori [M]

tobiko (flying fish roe)
tobiko (œufs [M] de poisson [M] volant
huevas [F] de pez [M] volador
Fliegenfischrogen (Tobiko) [M]
uova [M] di pesce [M] volante (tobiko)

chopsticks
baguettes [F] chinoises
palillos [M]
Essstäbchen [N]
bacchette [F]

chopstick
baguette [F]
palillo [M] chino
Essstäbchen [N]
bacchetta [F]

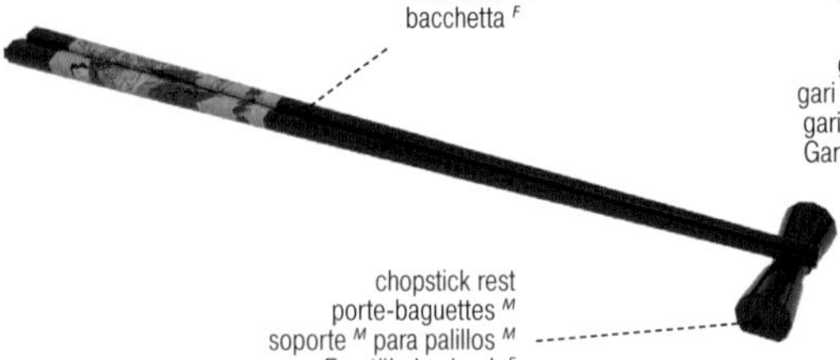

chopstick rest
porte-baguettes [M]
soporte [M] para palillos [M]
Essstäbchenbank [F]
poggiabacchette [M]

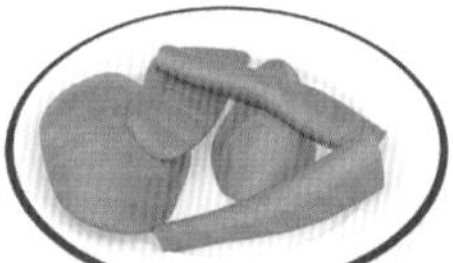

gari (pickled ginger)
gari [M] (gingembre [M] mariné)
gari (gengibre [M] encurtido)
Gari (eingelegter Ingwer) [M]
gari [M]

soy sauce
sauce [F] soya
salsa [F] de soja [F]
Sojasoße [F]
salsa [F] di soia [F]

chow mei
chow mein
fideos [M] chino
Chow-Mein
spaghetti [M] cine

chopstick
baguette [F] chinoise
palillos [M]
Essstäbchen [N]
bacchette [F]

miso soup
soupe [F] de tofu [M]
sopa [F] miso [M]
Tofusuppe [F]
zuppa [F] di miso [M]

fortune cookie
biscuit [M] chinois
galleta [F] de la suerte [F]
Glückskeks [M]
biscotto [M] della fortuna [F]

cappuccino
cappuccino [M]
capuchino [M]
Cappuccino [M]
cappuccino [M]

espresso
espresso [M]
espresso [M]
Espresso [M]
espresso [M]

black tea
thé [M] noir
té [M] negro
schwarzer Tee [M]
tè [M] nero

hot chocolate
chocolat [M] chaud
chocolate [M] caliente
Heiße Schokolade [F]
cioccolata [F] calda

creamer
crémier [M]
jarrita [F] de leche [F]
Sahne [F]
bricco [M] del latte [M]

coffee
café [M]
taza [F] de café [M]
Kaffee [M]
caffè [M]

beverage with ice and lime
boisson [F] avec glace [F] et lime [M]
bebida [F] con lima [F] y hielo [M]
Getränk [N] mit Eis [N] und Limette [F]
bibita [F] con ghiaccio [M] e limone [m]

milkshake
lait [M] frappé
batido [M]
Milchshake [M]
frappè [M]

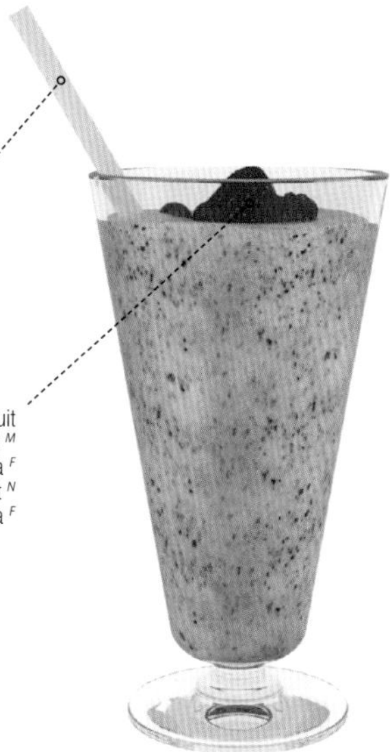

straw
paille [F]
pajita [F] / pitillo [M]
Strohhalm [M]
cannuccia [F]

fruit
fruit [M]
fruta [F]
Obst [N]
frutta [F]

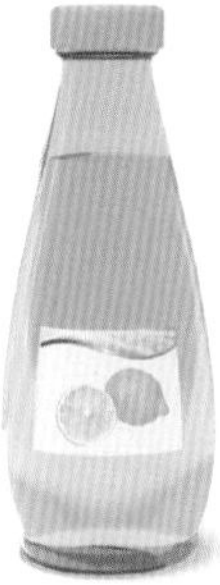

lemonade
limonade ^{F}
limonada ^{F}
Zitronenlimonade ^{F}
limonata ^{F}

pineapple juice
jus ^{M} d'ananas ^{M}
zumo ^{M} de piña ^{F}
Ananassaft ^{M}
succo ^{M} d'ananas ^{M}

orange juice
jus ^{M} d'orange ^{F}
zumo ^{M} de naranja ^{F}
Orangensaft ^{M}
succo ^{M} d'arancia ^{F}

peach juice
jus ^{M} de pêche ^{F}
zumo ^{M} de melocotón ^{M}
Pfirsichsaft ^{M}
succo ^{M} di pesca ^{F}

pomegranate juice
jus ^{M} de grenade ^{F}
zumo ^{M} de granada ^{F}
Granatapfelsaft ^{M}
succo ^{M} di melograno ^{M}

apple juice
jus ^{M} de pomme ^{F}
zumo ^{M} de manzana ^{F}
Apfelsaft ^{M}
succo ^{M} di mela ^{F}

grape juice
jus ^{M} de raisin ^{M}
zumo ^{M} de uva ^{F}
Traubensaft ^{M}
succo ^{M} d'uva ^{F}

tomato juice
jus ^{M} de tomate ^{F}
zumo ^{M} de tomate ^{M}
Tomatensaft ^{M}
succo ^{M} di pomodoro ^{M}

bottled water
eau ^{F} embouteillée
agua ^{F} de mesa ^{F}
Tafelwasser ^{N}
acqua ^{F} da tavola ^{F}

cap
bouchon ^{M}
tapón ^{M}
Flaschenverschluss ^{M}
tappo ^{M}

label
étiquette ^{F}
etiqueta ^{F}
Etikett ^{N}
etichetta ^{F}

barcode
code-barres ^{M}
código ^{M} de barras ^{F}
Strichcode ^{M}
codice ^{M} a barre ^{F}

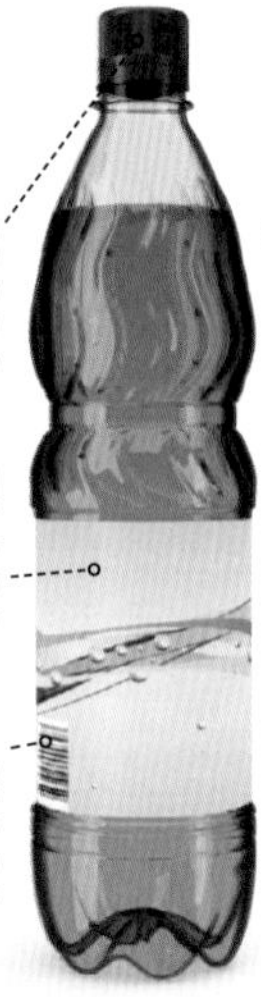

sparkling water
eau ^{F} gazeuse
agua ^{F} mineral con gas ^{M}
Mineralwasser ^{N} mit Kohlensäure ^{F}
acqua ^{F} minerale frizzante

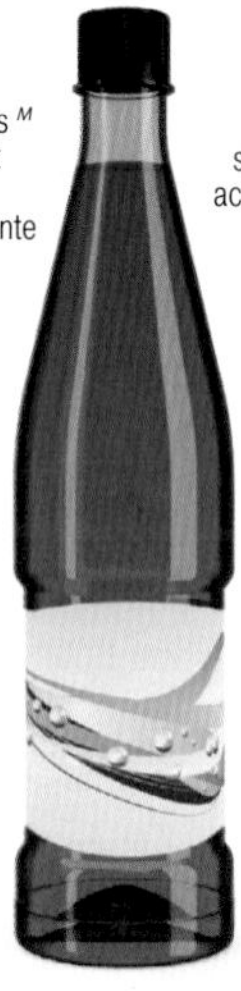

still mineral water
eau ^{F} minérale
agua ^{F} mineral
stilles Mineralwasser ^{N}
acqua ^{F} minerale naturale

canned pop
canette ^{F} de boisson ^{F} ga
refresco ^{M} enlatado
Getränkedose ^{F}
bibita ^{F} in lattina ^{F}

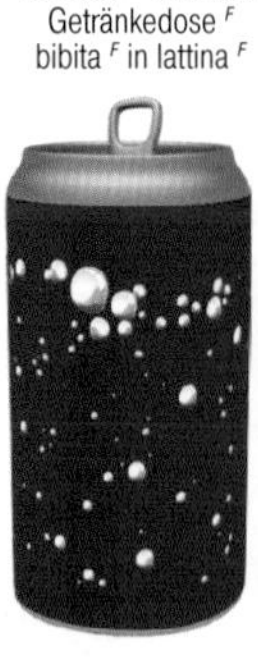

wine stopper
bouchon ^{M} à vin ^{M}
tapón ^{M} para vino ^{M}
Weinflaschenverschluss ^{M}
tappo ^{M} per vino ^{M}

red wine
vin ^{M} rouge
vino ^{M} tinto
Rotwein ^{M}
vino ^{M} rosso

white wine
vin ^{M} blanc
vino ^{M} blanco
Weißwein ^{M}
vino ^{M} bianco

champagne
champagne ^{M}
champán ^{M}
Champagner ^{M}
champagne ^{M}

vodka
vodka ^{F}
vodka ^{M}
Wodka ^{M}
vodka ^{F}

cognac
cognac ^{M}
coñac ^{M}
Cognac ^{M}
cognac ^{M}

whiskey
whisky ^{M}
whisky ^{M}
Whisky ^{M}
whisky ^{M}

beer
bière ^{F}
cerveza ^{F}
Bier ^{N}
birra ^{F}

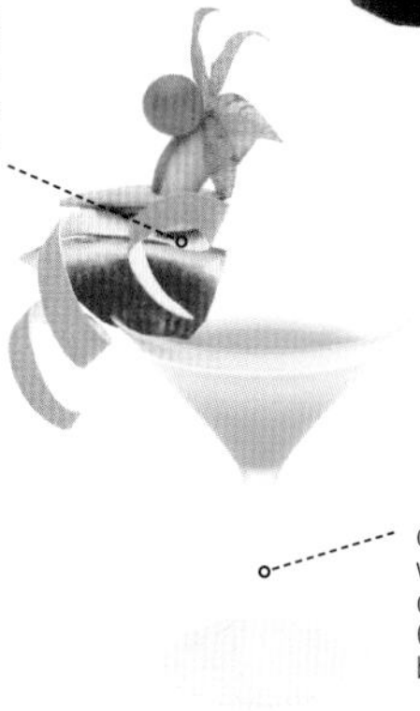

garnish
garniture ^{F}
guarnición ^{F}
Garnierung ^{F}
guarnizione ^{F}

cocktail
cocktail ^{M}
cóctel ^{F}
Cocktail ^{M}
cocktail ^{M}

cocktail glass
verre ^{M} à cocktail ^{M}
copa ^{F} de cóctel ^{M}
Cocktailglas ^{N}
bicchiere ^{M} da cocktail ^{M}

CLOTHING AND ACCESSORIES

fashion show
défilé M de mode F
desfile M de moda F
Modenschau F
sfilata F di moda F

truss
structure F
andamiaje M
Gerüst N
impalcatura F
spotlight
projecteur M
reflector M
Scheinwerfer M
riflettore M
designer
styliste M
diseñador M de moda F
Modedesigner M
stilista M
cameraman
caméraman M
camarógrafo M
Kameramann M
cameraman M
video camera
caméra F
cámara F de vídeo M
Kamera F
videocamera F
audience
spectateur M
público M
Zuschauer M
pubblico M

WEEK
ON · MILAN

sign
panneau M
panel M publicitario
Werbetafel F
cartello M

model
mannequin M
modelo M
Modell N
modella F

photographer
photographe M
fotógrafo M
Fotograf M
fotografo M

uplight
éclairage M vers le haut M
luces F de suelo M
Bodenleuchte F
illuminazione F dal basso

runway
passerelle F
pasarela F
Laufsteg M
passerella F

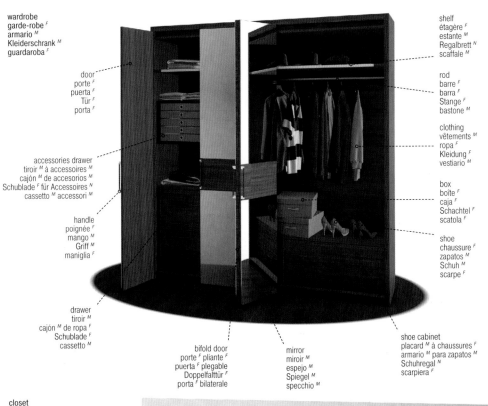

wardrobe
garde-robe F
armario M
Kleiderschrank M
guardaroba F
door
porte F
puerta F
Tür F
porta F
accessories drawer
tiroir M à accessoires M
cajón M de accesorios M
Schublade F für Accessoires N
cassetto M accessori M
handle
poignée F
mango M
Griff M
maniglia F
drawer
tiroir M
cajón M de ropa F
Schublade F
cassetto M
bifold door
porte F pliante F
puerta F plegable
Doppelfalttür F
porta F bilaterale
mirror
miroir M
espejo M
Spiegel M
specchio M
shoe cabinet
placard M à chaussures F
armario M para zapatos M
Schuhregal N
scarpiera F
shelf
étagère F
estante M
Regalbrett N
scaffale M
rod
barre F
barra F
Stange F
bastone M
clothing
vêtements M
ropa F
Kleidung F
vestiario M
box
boîte F
caja F
Schachtel F
scatola F
shoe
chaussure F
zapatos M
Schuh M
scarpe F

closet
placard M
armario M empotrado
Ankleidezimmer N
armadio M
glass door
porte F en verre M
mampara F de cristal M
Glastür F
porta F in vetro M
drawer
tiroir M
cajón M corredero
Schublade F
cassetto M

oat
ıanteau M
brigo M
lantel M
appotto M

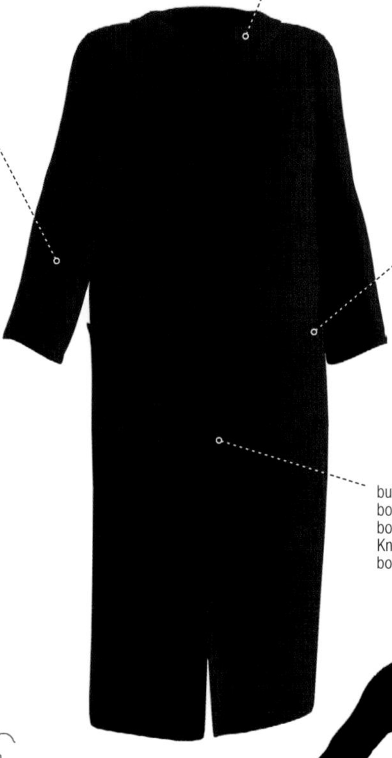
collar
col M
cuello M
Kragen M
collo M
sleeve
manche F
manga F
Ärmel M
manica F
pocket
poche F
bolsillo M
Tasche F
tasca F
button
bouton M
botón M
Knopf M
bottone M

jacket
veste F
chaqueta F
Jacke F
giacca F

trench coat
trench-coat M
impermeable M
Trenchcoat M
impermeabile M

fleece jacket
veste F polaire
chaqueta F acolchada
Fleecejacke F
giacca F di pile M

sweat suit
survêtement M
chándal M
Trainingsanzug M
ta F da ginnastica F

Suits and formal accessories

suit
costume [M]
traje [M]
Anzug [M]
completo [M] da uomo [M]

vest
gilet [M]
chaleco [M]
Weste [F]
gilet [M]

double-breasted jacket
veston [M] croisé
abrigo [M] de doble botonadura [F]
doppelreihige Jacke [F]
cappotto [M] a doppio petto [M]

bow tie
nœud [M] papillon [M]
pajarita [F]
Fliege [F]
papillon [M]

necktie
cravate [F]
corbata [F]
Krawatte [F]
cravatta [M]

Pants

jeans
jean [M]
vaqueros [M]
Jeans [F]
jeans [M]

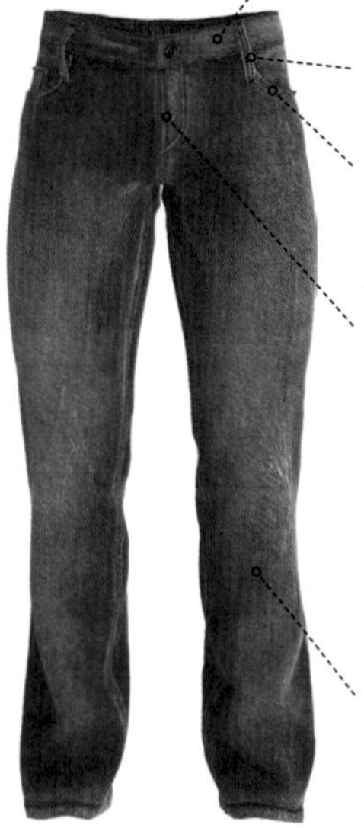

waistband
ceinture [F] montée
pretina [F]
Hosenbund [M]
cintura [F]

belt loop
passant [M] de pantalon [M]
trabilla [F] para el cinturón [M]
Gürtelschlaufe [F]
passante [M]

pocket
poche [F]
bolsillo [M]
Hosentasche [F]
tasca [F]

zipper
braguette [F]
bragueta [F]
Reißverschluss [M]
cerniera [F], zip [F]

pant leg
jambe [F] de pantalon [M]
pernera [F] del pantalón [M]
Hosenbein [N]
gamba [F] dei pantaloni [M]

belt
ceinture [F]
cinturón [M]
Gürtel [M]
cinta [F]

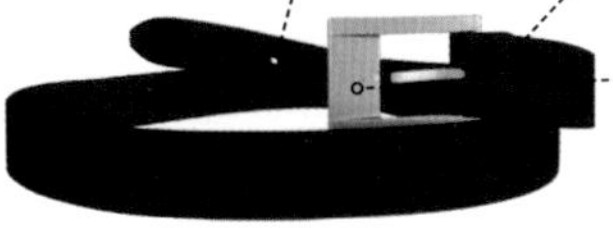

punch hole
trou [M] de poinçon [M]
agujero [M]
Loch [N]
foro [M]

belt loop
passant [M] de ceinture [F]
trabilla [F]
Gürtelschlaufe [F]
passante [M]

buckle
boucle [F] de ceinture [F]
hebilla [F]
Schnalle [F]
fibbia [F]

Bermuda shorts
bermuda [M]
bermudas [F]
Bermudashorts [F]
bermuda [M]

suspenders
bretelles [F]
tirantes [M]
Hosenträger [M]
bretelle [F]

pants
pantalon [M]
pantalones [M]
Hose [F]
pantaloni [M]

hoodie
chandail ^{M} à capuchon ^{M}
sudadera ^{F}
Kapuzen-Shirt ^{N}
felpa ^{F} con cappuccio ^{M}

sweatshirt
chandail ^{M} en molleton ^{M}
jersey ^{M} de punto
Sweatshirt ^{N}
felpa ^{F}

three-button sweater
chandail ^{M} à trois boutons ^{M}
jersey ^{M}
Pullover ^{M} mit drei Knöpfen ^{M}
maglia ^{F}

zip-front cardigan
veste ^{F} à fermeture ^{F} éclair frontale
chaqueta ^{F}
Jacke ^{F} mit Reißverschluss ^{M}
cardigan ^{M} con cerniera ^{F}

sweater
chandail ^{M}
suéter ^{M}
Pullover ^{M}
maglione ^{M}

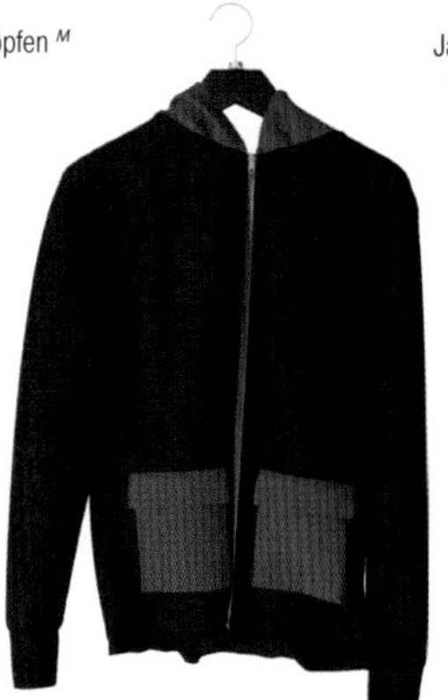

zip hoodie
veste ^{F} zippée à capuche ^{F}
sudadera ^{F} con capucha ^{F}
Kapuzenjacke ^{F}
felpa ^{F} con cerniera ^{F} e cappuccio ^{M}

cardigan
cardigan ^{M}
cárdigan ^{M} de caballero ^{M}
Herrenstrickjacke ^{F}
cardigan ^{M}

dress shirt
chemise ^{F} habillée
camisa ^{F} con puños ^{M}
Oberhemd ^{N}
camicia ^{F}

collar
col ^{M}
cuello ^{M}
Kragen ^{M}
collo ^{M}

button
bouton ^{M}
botón ^{M}
Knopf ^{M}
bottone ^{M}

sleeve
manche ^{F}
manga ^{F}
Ärmel ^{M}
manica ^{F}

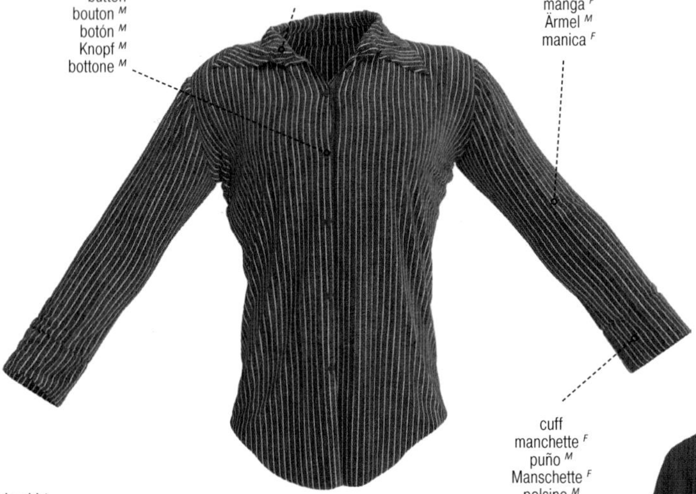

cuff
manchette ^{F}
puño ^{M}
Manschette ^{F}
polsino ^{M}

plaid shirt
chemise ^{F} à carreaux ^{M}
camisa ^{F} de cuadritos ^{M}
Holzfällerhemd ^{N}
camicia ^{F} scozzese

polo shirt
polo ^{F}
camisa ^{F} estilo ^{M} polo
Polohemd ^{N}
polo ^{F}

V-neck
col ^{M} en V
cuello ^{M} en V
V-Ausschnitt ^{M}
scollatura ^{F} a V

short sleeve
manches ^{F} courtes
manga ^{F} corta
kurzer Ärmel ^{M}
manica ^{F} corta

T-shirt
t-shirt ^{M}
camiseta ^{F}
T-Shirt ^{N}
maglietta ^{F}

double-pocket shirt
chemise ^{F} à doubles poches ^{F}
camisa ^{F} con bolsillos ^{M}
Hemd ^{N} mit Brusttaschen ^{F}
camicia ^{F} con due tasche ^{F}

short-sleeved shirt
chemise ^{F} à manches ^{F} courtes ^{F}
camisa ^{F} de manga ^{F} corta
kurzärmliges Hemd ^{N}
camicia ^{F} a maniche ^{F} corte

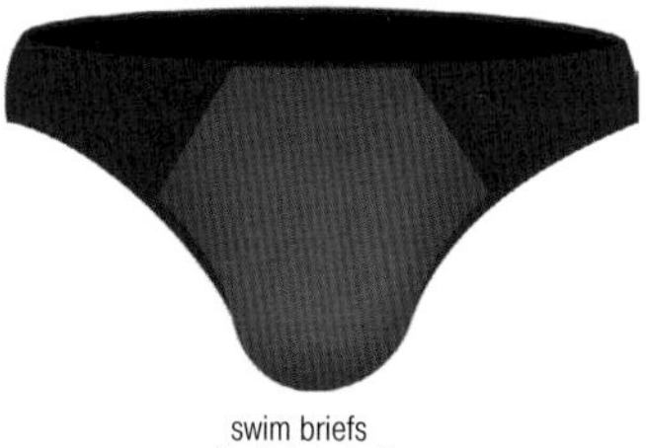

swim briefs
slip [M] de bain [M]
bañador [M] de slip
Badehose [F]
slip [M] da mare [M] per uomo [M]

trunks
maillot [M] de bain [M]
short de baño [M]
Badehose [F] / Sportshorts [F]
calzoncini [M] da bagno [M]

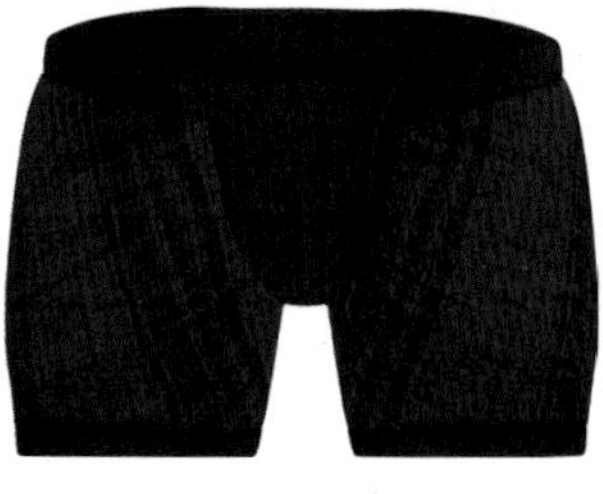

square-cut trunks
maillot [M] boxer
bañador [M] largo
Square-Cut Shorts [F]
pantaloncini [M] da bagno [M] da uomo [M]

boxer shorts
caleçon [M] boxeur
calzoncillos [M] bóxer
Boxershorts [F]
boxer [M]

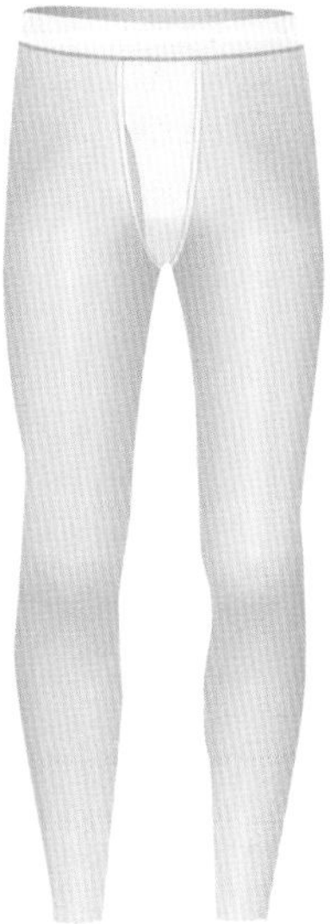

long underwear
sous-vêtements [M] longs
calzoncillos [M] largos
lange Unterhose [F]
calzamaglie [F] termiche

briefs
caleçon [M] pour homme [M]
calzoncillos [M] de slip
Unterhose [F]
slip [M]

ocks
aussettes [F]
lcetines [M]
ocken [F]
lzini [M]

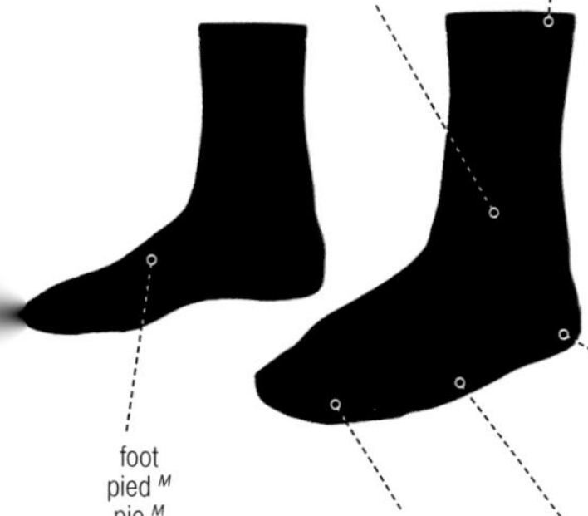

ribbed top
bord-côte [F]
tobillo [M] de canalé [M]
Rippenbündchen [N]
bordo [M] elastico

leg
jambe [F]
pierna [F]
Bein [N]
gamba [F]

heel
talon [M]
talón [M]
Ferse [F]
calcagno [M]

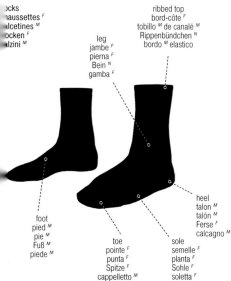

foot
pied [M]
pie [M]
Fuß [M]
piede [M]

toe
pointe [F]
punta [F]
Spitze [F]
cappelletto [M]

sole
semelle [F]
planta [F]
Sohle [F]
soletta [F]

undershirt
maillot [M] de corps [M]
camiseta [F] interior
Unterhemd [N]
canottiera [F]

trench coat
trench-coat ^{F}
trenca ^{F} larga
Trenchcoat ^{M}
impermeabile ^{M}

collar
col ^{M}
cuello ^{M}
Kragen ^{M}
collo ^{M}

button
bouton ^{M}
botón ^{M}
Knopf ^{M}
bottone ^{M}

belt
ceinture ^{F}
cinturón ^{M}
Gürtel ^{M}
cintura ^{F}

sleeve
manche ^{F}
manga ^{F}
Ärmel ^{M}
manica ^{F}

parka
parka ^{M}
chaqueta ^{F} acolchada
Anorak ^{M}
parka ^{M}

biker jacket
veste ^{F} de motard ^{M}
chaqueta ^{F} de motorista $^{M/F}$
Biker-Jacke ^{F}
giacca ^{F} da moto ^{F}

peacoat
caban ^{M}
abrigo ^{M} de marinero ^{M}
Caban-Mantel ^{M}
caban ^{M}

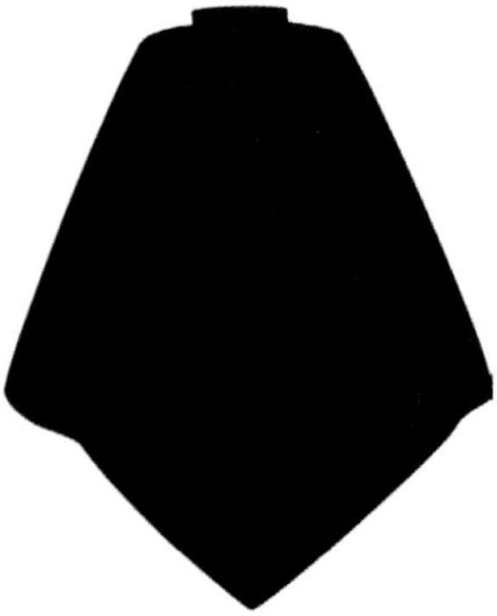

poncho
poncho ^{M}
poncho ^{M}
Poncho ^{M}
poncho ^{M}

fur coat
manteau ^{M} de fourrure ^{F}
abrigo ^{M} de piel ^{F}
Pelzmantel ^{M}
pelliccia ^{F}

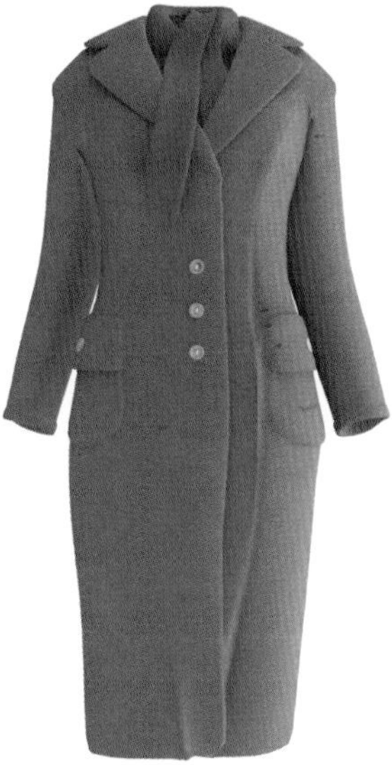

wool coat
manteau ^{M} en laine ^{F}
abrigo ^{M} de lana ^{F}
Wollmantel ^{M}
cappotto ^{M} in lana ^{F}

denim jacket
veste ^{F} en denim ^{M}
chaqueta ^{F} vaquera
Jeansjacke ^{F}
giacchetto ^{M} di jeans ^{M}

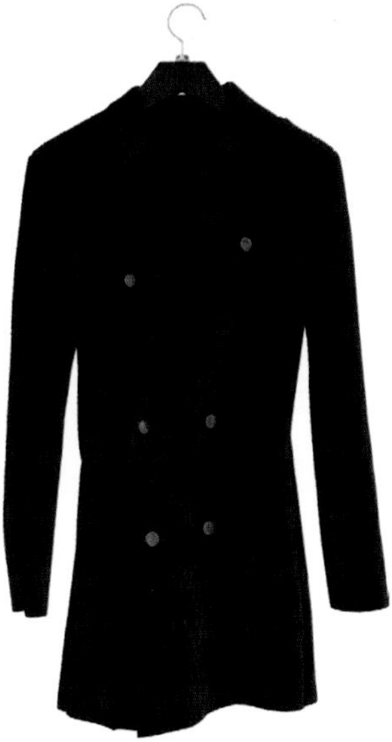

double-breasted overcoat
pardessus ^{M} croisé
abrigo ^{M} de doble botonadura
zweireihiger Mantel ^{M}
soprabito ^{M} a doppio ^{M} petto ^{M}

sheepskin jacket
veste ^{F} en peau ^{F} de mouton ^{M}
abrigo ^{M} de piel ^{F} de borrego ^{M}
Lammfelljacke ^{F}
giacca ^{M} di montone ^{M}

overcoat
pardessus ^{M}
trenca ^{F}
Mantel ^{M}
soprabito ^{M}

down coat
manteau ^{M} de duvet ^{M}
abrigo ^{M} de plumón ^{M}
Daunenmantel ^{M}
piumino ^{M}

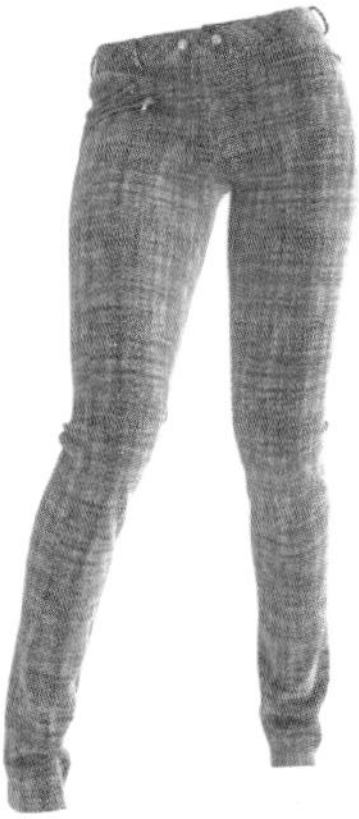

slim-fit pants
pantalon [M] à coupe [F] étroite
pantalones [M] ajustados
schmal geschnittene Hose [F]
pantaloni [M] aderenti

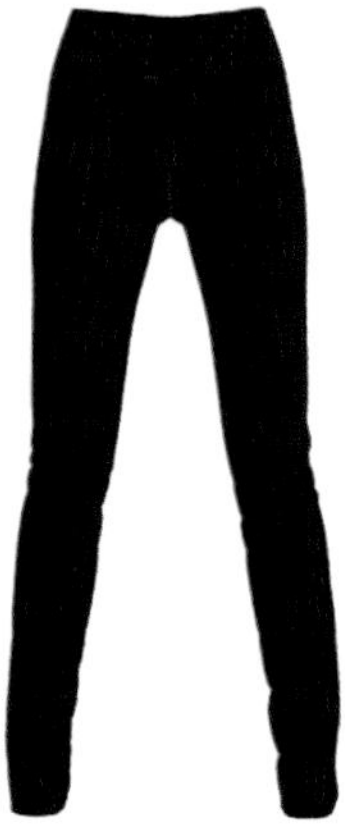

jeggings
collant-jean [M]
jeggings [M]
Jeggings [F]
jeggings [M]

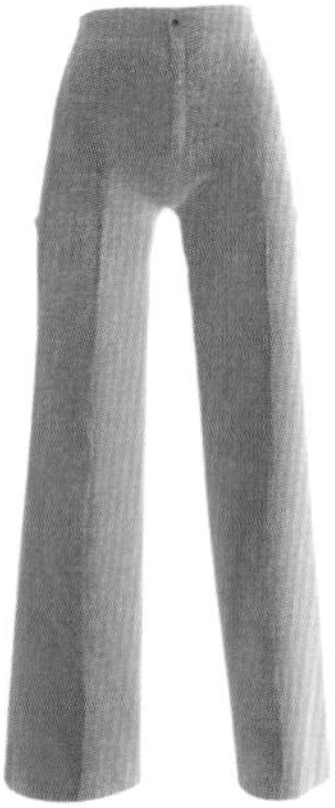

wide-leg pants
pantalon [M] coupe [F] ample
pantalones [M] de pierna [F] ancha
Hose [F] mit weitem Bein [N]
pantaloni [M] a palazzo [M]

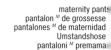

maternity pants
pantalon [M] de grossesse
pantalones [M] de maternidad
Umstandshose
pantaloni [M] premamá

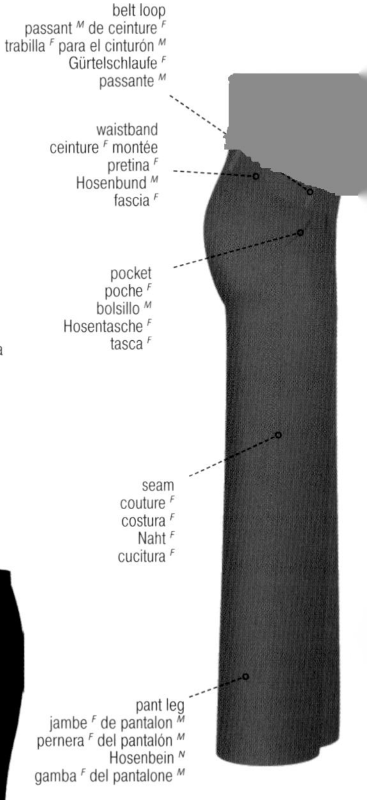
belt loop
passant [M] de ceinture [F]
trabilla [F] para el cinturón [M]
Gürtelschlaufe [F]
passante [M]
waistband
ceinture [F] montée
pretina [F]
Hosenbund [M]
fascia [F]
pocket
poche [F]
bolsillo [M]
Hosentasche [F]
tasca [F]
seam
couture [F]
costura [F]
Naht [F]
cucitura [F]
pant leg
jambe [F] de pantalon [M]
pernera [F] del pantalón [M]
Hosenbein [N]
gamba [F] del pantalone [M]

bell-bottomed jeans
jean [M] à pattes [F] d'éléphant [M]
vaqueros [M] de campana [F]
Jeans [F] mit Schlag [M]
jeans [M] a zampa [F] di elefante [M]

straight-leg jeans
jean [M] droit [M]
vaqueros [M] rectos
klassische gerade Jeans [F]
jeans [M] a sigaretta [F]

slim-fit jeans
jean [M] à coupe [F] étroite
vaqueros [M] ajustados
Röhrenjeans [F]
jeans [M] aderenti

shorts
short [M]
pantalones [M] cortos
klassische Shorts
pantaloncini [M]

spaghetti strap dress
robe ^{F} à bretelles ^{F} fines
vestido ^{M} con correa ^{F} de espagueti
Spaghettiträgerkleid ^{N}
abito ^{M} con spalline ^{F} sottili

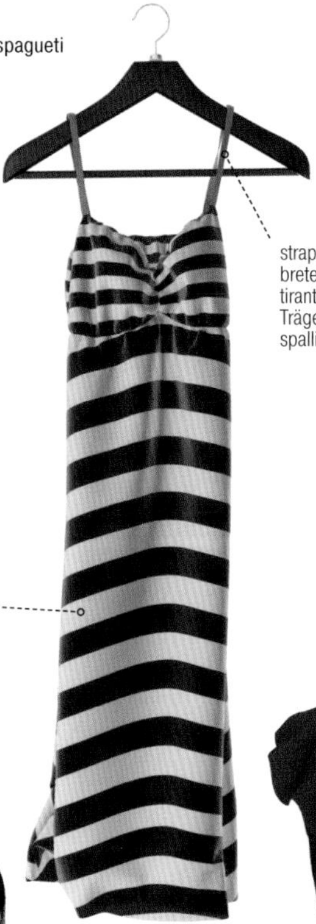

strap
bretelle ^{F}
tirante ^{M}
Träger ^{M}
spallina ^{F}

skirt
jupe ^{F}
falda ^{F}
Rock ^{M}
gonna ^{F}

sheath dress
robe ^{F} fourreau ^{M}
vestido ^{M} de una pieza ^{F}
Etuikleid ^{N}
tubino ^{M}

draped neckline
décolleté ^{M} drapé
escote ^{M} drapeado
drapierter Ausschnitt ^{M}
scollatura ^{F}
drappeggiata

belt
ceinture ^{F}
cinturón ^{M}
Gürtel ^{M}
cinta ^{F}

halter dress
robe ^{F} à dos ^{M} nu
vestido ^{M} atado al cuello ^{M}
Kleid ^{N} mit Nackenband ^{N}
vestito ^{M} scollato ^{M} sul retro ^{M}

drop-waist dress
robe ^{F} à taille ^{F} basse
vestido ^{M} de cintura ^{F} suelta ^{F}
Kleid ^{N} mit tiefer Taille ^{F}
abito ^{M} con vita ^{F} a goccia ^{F}

shirtdress
robe-chemisier ^{F}
vestido ^{M} camisero ^{M}
Hemdblusenkleid ^{N}
chemisier ^{M}

A-line dress
robe ^{F} silhouette ^{F} trapèze
vestido ^{M} con línea ^{F} en A
A-Linien-Kleid ^{N}
abito ^{M} a trapezio ^{M}

sleeve
manche ^{F}
manga ^{F}
Ärmel ^{M}
manica ^{F}

jersey dress
robe ^{F} de cocktail ^{M}
vestido ^{M} de tela ^{F} de jersey
Strickkleid ^{N}
abito ^{M} da cocktail ^{M}

strapless gown
robe-bustier ^{F}
vestido ^{M} sin tirantes
trägerloses Kleid ^{N}
abito ^{F} da sera ^{M} senza spalline ^{F}

maxi skirt
jupe ^{F} longue
falda ^{F} larga
langer Rock ^{M}
gonna ^{F} lunga

jumpsuit
combinaison ^{F}
mono ^{M}
Overall ^{M}
tuta ^{F}

sundress
robe ^{F} d'été ^{M}
vestido ^{M} veraniego
leichtes Sommerkleid ^{N}
prendisole ^{M}

cap-sleeve dress
robe ^{F} à manches ^{F} capes
vestido ^{M} de mangas ^{F} cortas
Kleid ^{N} mit Flügelärmel ^{M}
abito ^{M} a maniche ^{F} corte

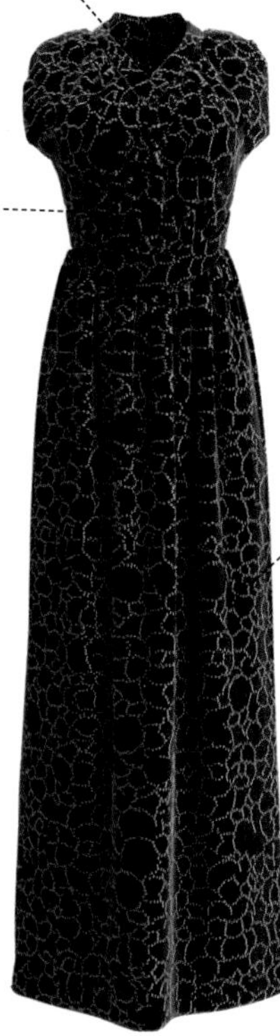
V-neck
encolure ^{F} en V
cuello ^{M} en V
V-Ausschnitt ^{M}
scollatura ^{F} a V
bodice
corsage ^{M}
corpiño ^{M}
Taille ^{F}
busto ^{M}
skirt
jupe ^{F}
falda ^{F}
Rock ^{M}
gonna ^{F}

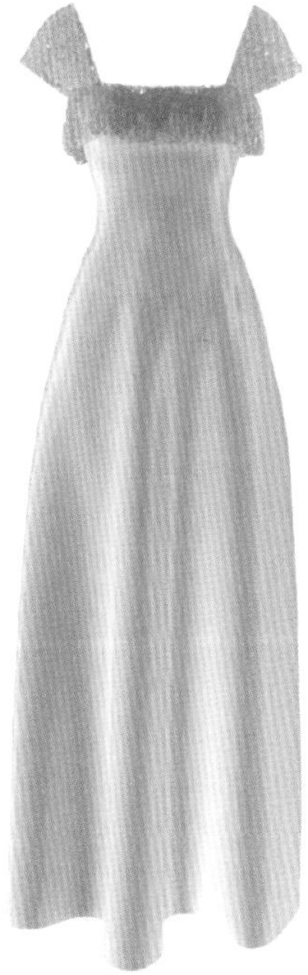

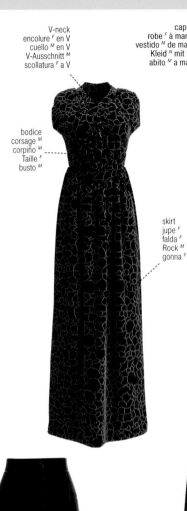

wedding dress
robe ^{F} de mariée ^{F}
vestido ^{M} de novia ^{F}
Hochzeitskleid ^{N}
abito ^{M} da sposa ^{F}

pencil skirt
jupe ^{F} droite
falda ^{F} tubo ^{M}
Bleistiftrock ^{M}
gonna ^{F} con spacco ^{M}

maxi dress
robe ^{F} longue
vestido ^{M} largo
Maxikleid ^{N}
abito ^{F} lungo

minidress
minirobe ^{F}
minivestido ^{M}
Minikleid ^{N}
miniabito ^{M}

short-sleeved shirt
chandail [M] à manches [F] courtes
blusa [F] de manga [F] corta
kurzärmlige Bluse [F]
camicia [F] a maniche [F] corte

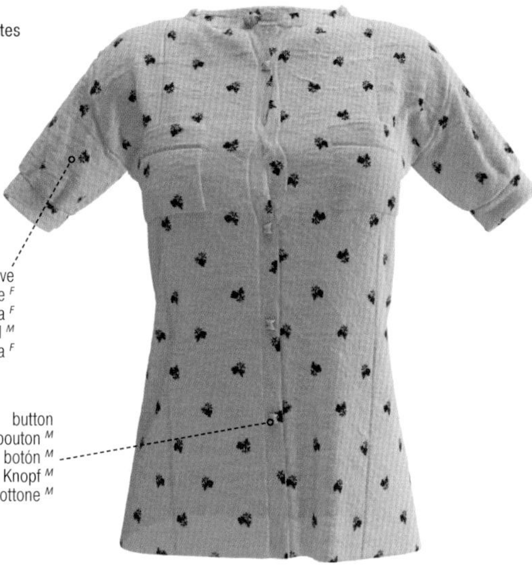

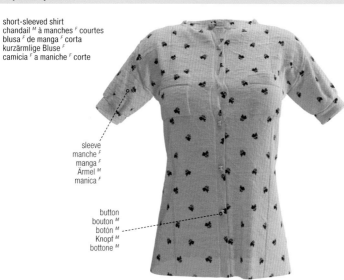

sleeve
manche [F]
manga [F]
Ärmel [M]
manica [F]

button
bouton [M]
botón [M]
Knopf [M]
bottone [M]

bolero
boléro [M]
bolero [M]
Bolero [M]
bolero [M]

tunic sweater
chandail tunique [M]
suéter [M]
Tunika-Pullover [M]
maglione [M]

tank top
débardeur [M]
top [M]
ärmelloses Oberteil [N]
top [M]

ruffled top
chemisier [M] à volants [M]
blusa [F] drapeada
Rüschenbluse [F]
blusa [F] arricciata

spencer
spencer [M]
blazer [M] corto
Spenzer [M]
spencer [M]

peasant blouse
blouse [F] paysanne
blusa [F] campesina
Tunika [F]
tunica [F]

blouse
robe-chemisier [F]
vestido [M] mini
lange Bluse [F]
camicetta [F]

batwing-sleeve top
chandail [M] à manches [F] chauve-souris [F]
jersey [M] de mangas [F] de murciélago [M]
Pullover [M] mit Fledermausärmeln [M]
maglione [M] a pipistrello [M]

pocket
poche [F]
bolsillo [M]
Tasche [F]
tasca [F]

blazer
blazer [M]
blazer [M] clásico
Blazer [M]
blazer [M]

long cardigan
cardigan [M]
long cárdigan [M] largo
lange Strickjacke [F]
cardigan [M] lungo

T-shirt
t-shirt [M]
camiseta [F]
T-Shirt [N]
maglietta [F]

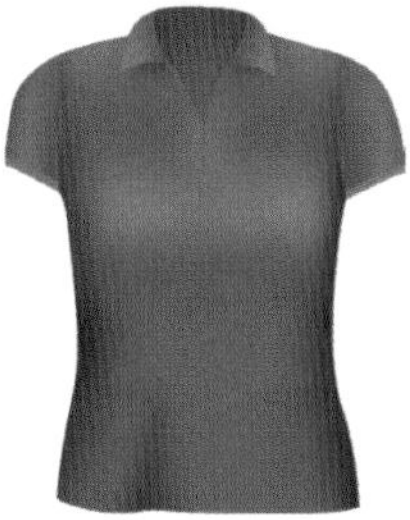

polo shirt
polo [M]
camisa [F] polo [M] de señora [F]
Polohemd [N]
polo [F]

three-quarter sleeve top
haut [M] à manches [F] trois-quarts
top [M] de manga [F] larga
Oberteil [N] mit Dreiviertelarm [M]
maglia [F] con maniche ¾

short cardigan
cardigan [M] court
cárdigan [M] corto
kurze Strickjacke [F]
cardigan [M] corto

sweater vest
gilet [M] en tricot [M]
chaleco [M] tejido [M]
Pullunder [M]
smanicato [M]

elastic-waist top
haut [M] avec taille [F] élastique
top [M] con cintura [F] elástica
Top [N] mit Gummizug [M] im Taillenbereich [M]
maglia [F] arricciata in vita [F]

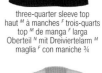

cover-up
cache-maillot [M]
túnica [F] de playa [F]
Tunika [F]
copricostume [M]

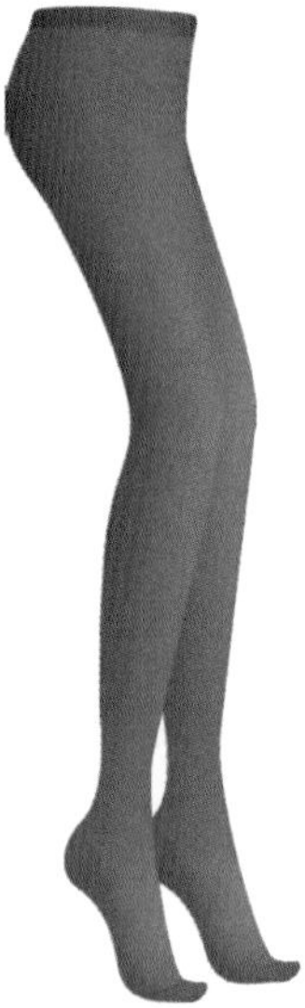

tights
collants M
mallas F
Strumpfhose F
calzamaglie F

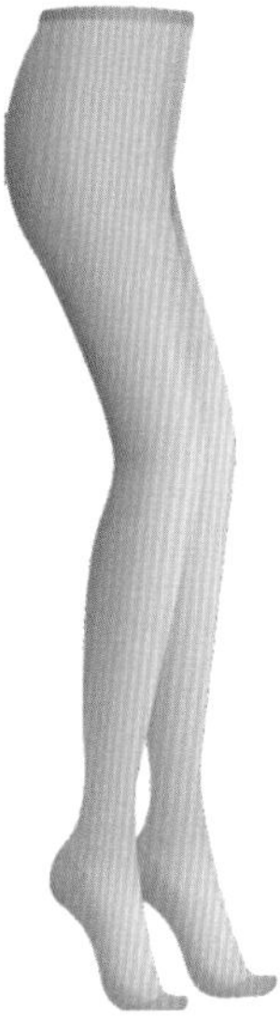

pantyhose
collants M
medias F panty
Strumpfhose F
collant F

leggings
collants M sans pieds M
leggings M
Leggins M
pantacollant M

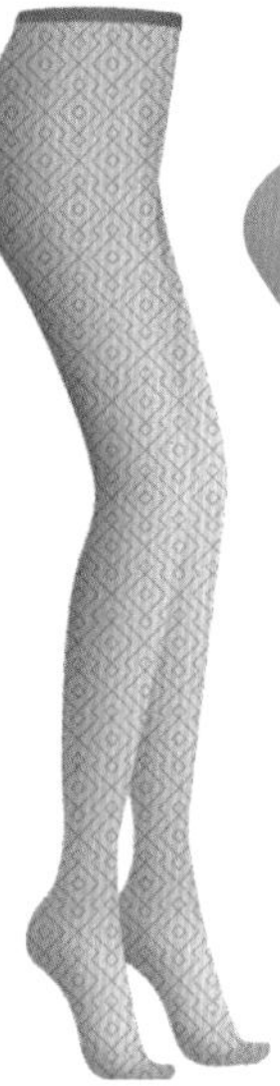

fishnets tights
bas M résille F
medias F de redecilla F
Netzstrumpfhose F
collant M a rete F

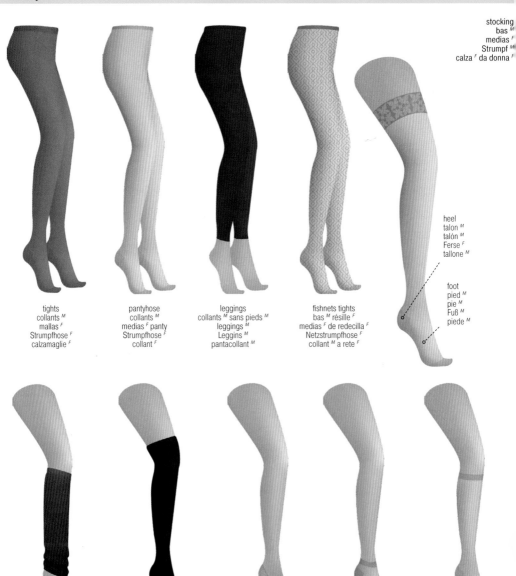

stocking
bas M
medias F
Strumpf M
calza F da donna F

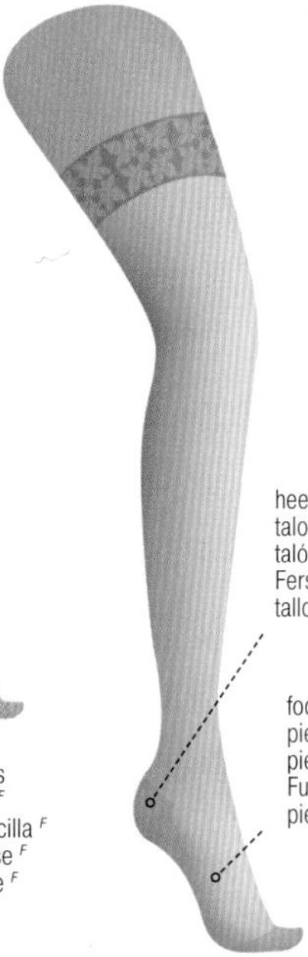
heel
talon M
talón M
Ferse F
tallone M
foot
pied M
pie M
Fuß M
piede M

leg warmer
jambière F
calentador M
Stulpe F
scaldamuscoli M

over-the-knee sock
chaussettes F montantes
calcetines M por encima de la rodilla F
Überkniestrumpf M
parigine F

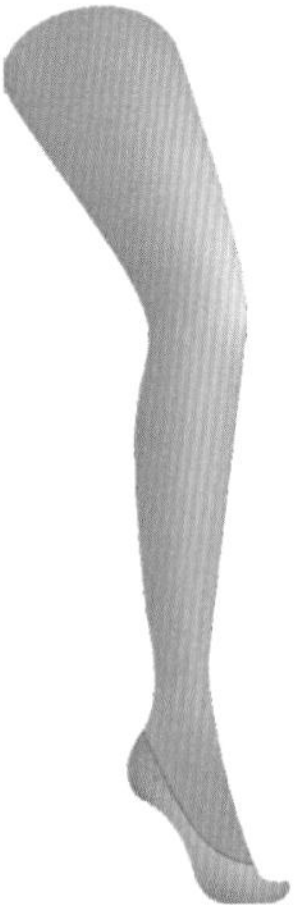

liner sock
protège-bas M
medias F sin puño M
Füßling M
fantasmino M

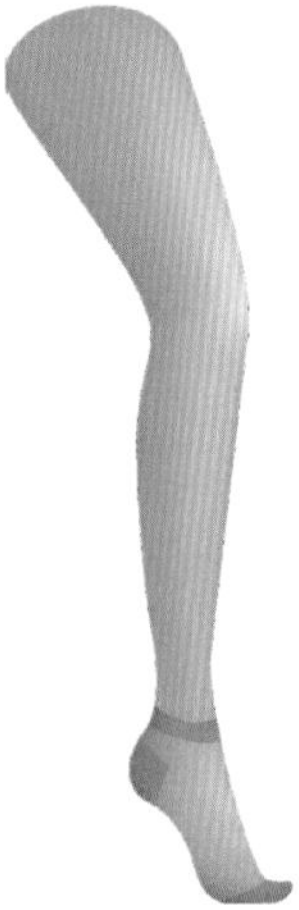

ankle sock
socquettes F
calcetines M tobilleros
Sneaker Socke F
calzini M corti

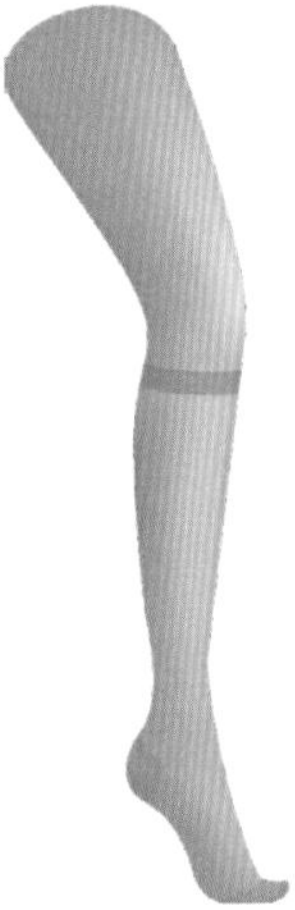

kneesock
bas M aux genoux M
calcetines M hasta la rodilla F
Kniestrumpf M
gambaletto M

corselet
combiné [M]
corsé [M]
Mieder [N]
bustino [M]

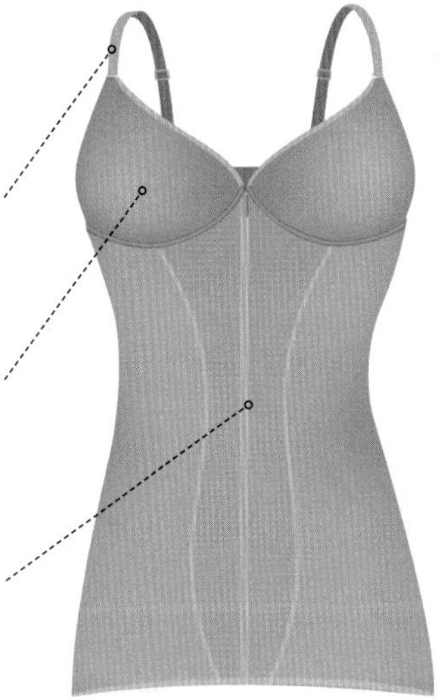

shoulder strap
bretelle [F]
tira [F] para el hombro [M]
Schulterträger [M]
spallina [F]

cup
bonnet [M]
copa [F]
Körbchen [N]
coppa [F]

zipper
fermeture [F] éclair
cremallera [F]
Reißverschluss [M]
cerniera [F]

dressing gown
robe [F] de chambre [F]
negligé [M]
Morgenmantel [M]
vestaglia [F]

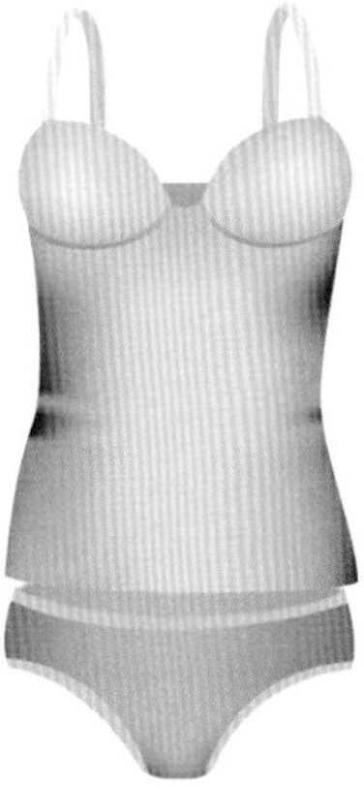

camisole and briefs
camisole [F] et culotte [F]
camiseta [F] de tirantes [M] y bragas [F]
Leibchen [N] und Slip [M]
coordinato [M] canotta [F] e mutandine [F]

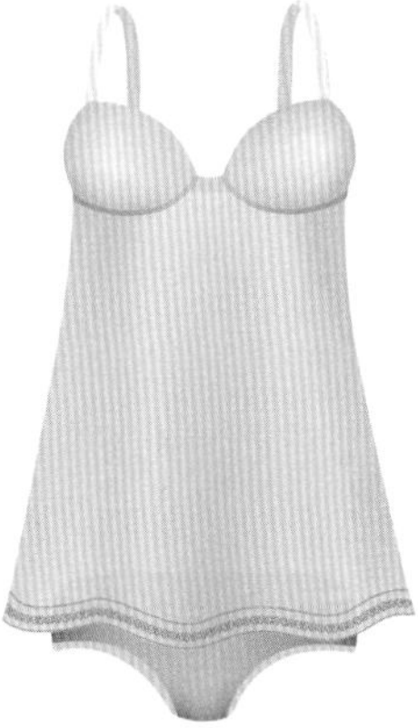

baby-doll
nuisette [F]
picardías [M]
Babydoll [N]
babydoll [M]

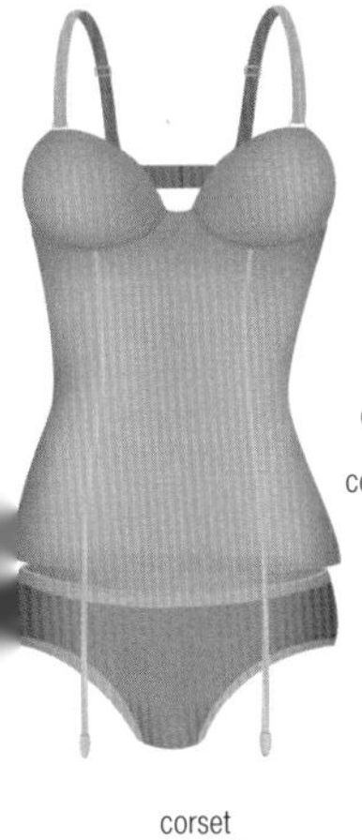

corset
corset [M]
corpiño [M]
Korsett [N]
corsetto [M]

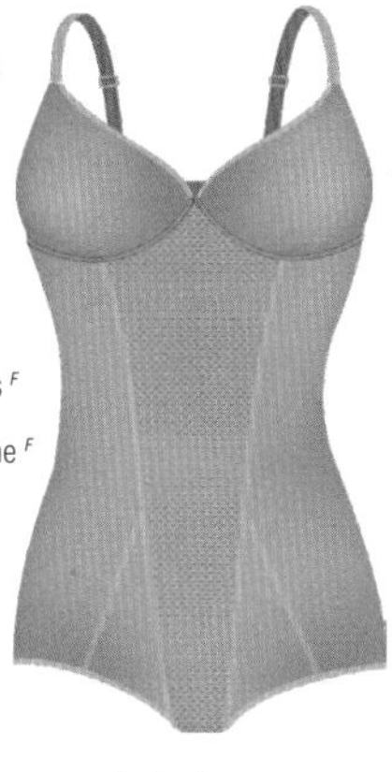

body shaper
combiné [M] galbant de correction [F]
corsé [M] todo en uno
Body Shaper [M]
body [M] modellante

slip
combinaison [F]
combinación [F]
Unterkleid [N]
sottoveste [F]

push-up bra and panties
soutien-gorge ^{M} pigeonnant et culotte ^{F}
sujetador ^{M} y bragas ^{M} push-up
Push-Up-BH ^{M} und Höschen ^{N}
reggiseno ^{M} push-up e mutandine ^{F}

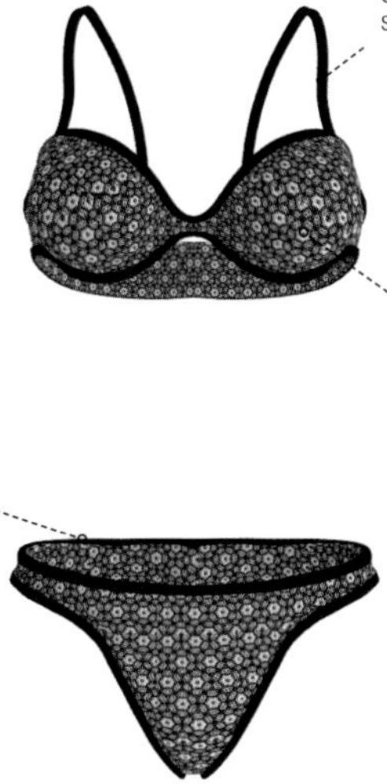

shoulder strap
bretelle ^{F}
tira ^{F} para el hombro ^{M}
Schulterträger ^{M}
spallina ^{F}

bra
soutien-gorge ^{M}
sujetador ^{M}
BH ^{M}
reggiseno ^{M}

cup
bonnet ^{M}
copa ^{F}
Körbchen ^{N}
coppa ^{F}

waistband
ceinture ^{F}
cintura ^{F}
Höschenbund ^{M}
cintura ^{F}

panties
culotte ^{F}
bragas ^{F}
Höschen ^{N}
mutandine ^{M}

sweat suit
survêtement ^{M}
chándal ^{M}
Trainingsanzug ^{M}
tuta ^{F} da ginnastica ^{F}

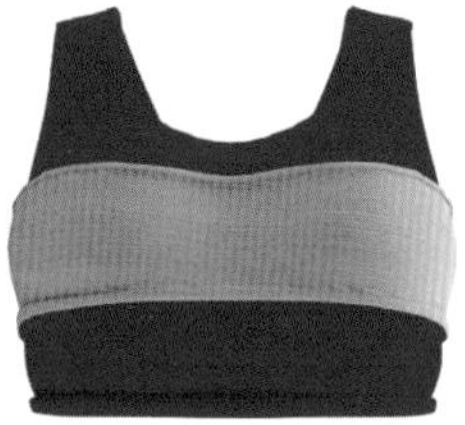

sports bra
soutien-gorge ^{M} de sport ^{M}
sujetador ^{M} deportivo
Sport-BH ^{M}
reggiseno ^{M} sportivo

nightgown
chemise ^{F} de nuit ^{F}
camisón ^{M}
Nachthemd ^{N}
camicia ^{F} da notte ^{F}

teddy
combinaison-culotte ^{F}
body ^{M}
Body ^{M}
body ^{M}

pajamas
pyjama ^{M}
pijama ^{M}
Pyjama ^{M}
pigiama ^{M}

garter belt
porte-jarretelles ^{M}
liguero ^{M}
Strumpfhaltergürtel ^{M}
reggicalze ^{M}

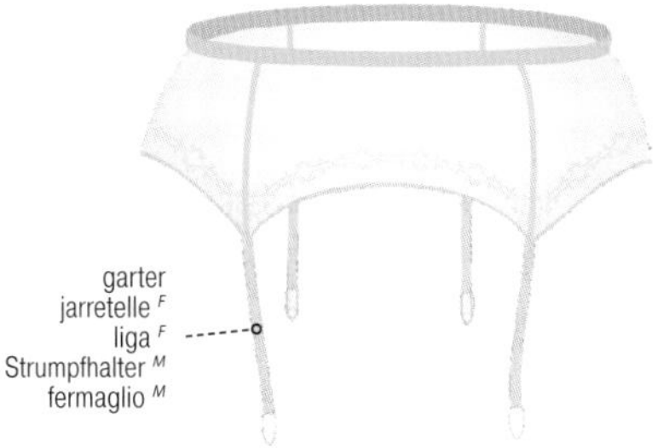
garter
jarretelle ^{F}
liga ^{F}
Strumpfhalter ^{M}
fermaglio ^{M}

camisole
camisole ^{F}
camiseta ^{F} de tirantes ^{M}
Leibchen ^{N}
canotta ^{F}

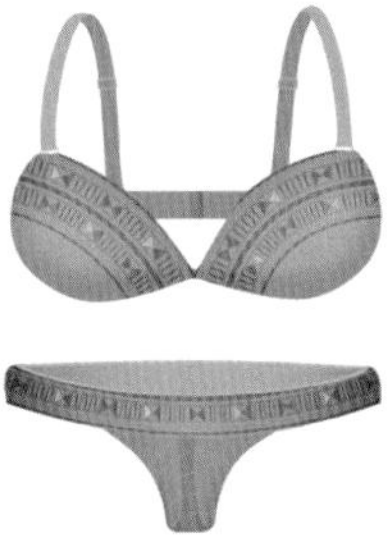

bra and thong set
ensemble ^{M} de soutien-gorge ^{M} et string ^{M}
sujetador ^{M} y tanga ^{M}
BH ^{M} und Tanga ^{M}
coordinato ^{M} reggiseno ^{M} e tanga ^{M}

nursing bra
soutien-gorge ^{M} d'allaitement ^{M}
sujetador ^{M} de lactancia ^{F}
Still-BH ^{M}
reggiseno ^{M} da allattamento ^{M}

bathrobe
peignoir ^{M} de bain ^{M}
albornoz ^{M}
Bademantel ^{M}
accappatoio ^{M}

Swimwear

tankini
tankini ^{M}
tankini ^{M}
Tankini ^{M}
tankini ^{M}

one-piece swimsuit
maillot ^{M} de bain ^{M} une pièce ^{F}
traje ^{M} de baño ^{M} de una pieza ^{F}
Badeanzug ^{M}
costume ^{M} da bagno ^{M} intero

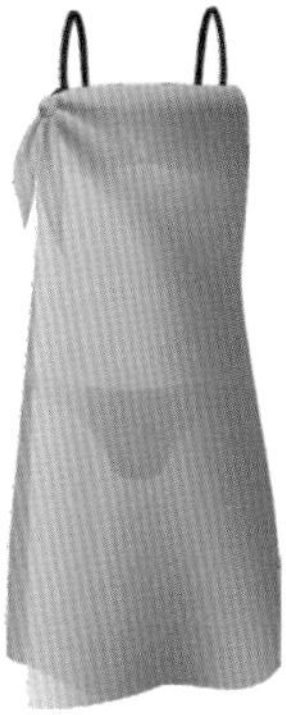

sarong
sarong ^{M}
pareo ^{M}
Sarong ^{M}
sarong ^{M}

bikini
bikini ^{M}
bikini ^{M}
Bikini ^{M}
bikini ^{M}

diaper bag
sac ^{M} à couches ^{F}
bolsa ^{F} portapañales ^{M}
Wickeltasche ^{F}
borsa ^{F} portapannolini

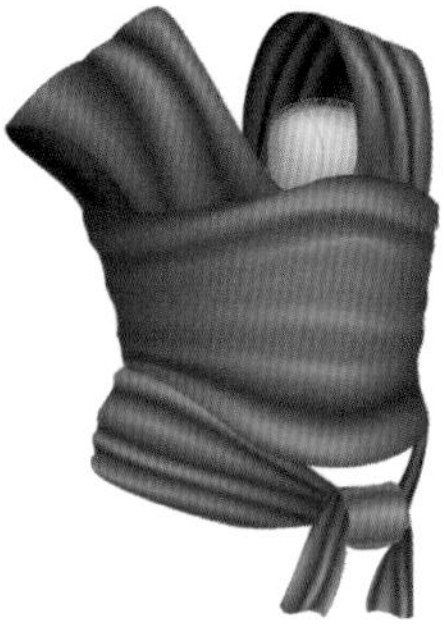

baby sling
écharpe ^{F} porte-bébé ^{M}
fular ^{M} portabebés ^{M}
Babytragetuch ^{N}
fascia ^{F} portabebè

cloth baby carrier
porte-bébé ^{M} en toile ^{F}
portabebés ^{M} de tela ^{F}
Babytrage ^{F}
marsupio ^{M} portabebè

bib
bavoir ^{M}
babero ^{M}
Lätzchen ^{N}
bavaglino ^{M}

nursing pillow
coussin ^{M} d'allaitement ^{M}
cojín ^{M} de lactancia ^{F}
Stillkissen ^{N}
cuscino ^{M} per allattamento ^{M}

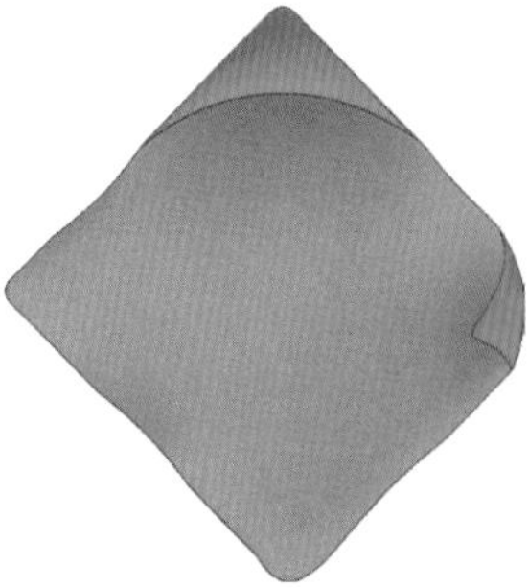

hooded towel
serviette ^{F} à capuchon ^{M}
toalla ^{F} con capucha ^{F}
Kapuzen-Badetuch ^{N}
asciugamano ^{M} con cappuccio ^{M}

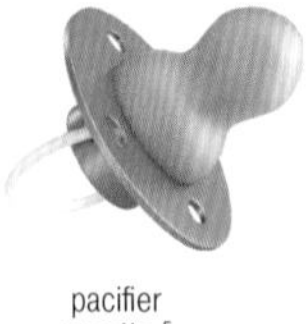

pacifier
sucette ^{F}
chupón ^{M}
Schnuller ^{M}
ciuccio ^{M}

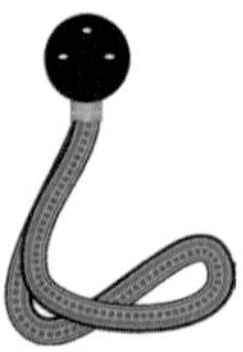

pacifier clip
attache-sucette ^{F}
cinta ^{F} para chupón ^{M}
Schnuller-Clip ^{M}
laccio ^{M} appendiciuccio

teething ring
anneau ^{M} de dentition ^{F}
mordedor ^{M}
Beißring ^{M}
dentaruolo ^{M}

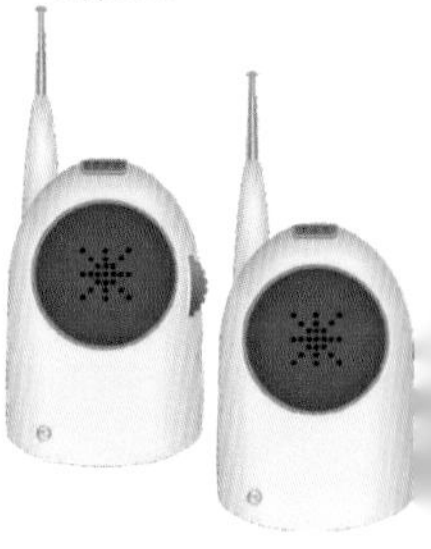

baby monitor
moniteur ^{M} pour bébé ^{M}
monitor ^{M} de bebés ^{M}
Babyphone ^{N}
interfono ^{M}

backpack baby carrier
sac à dos ^{M} porte-bébé ^{M}
mochila ^{F} portabebés ^{M}
Baby-Rückentrage ^{F}
zaino ^{M} portabebè

baby bouncer
exerciseur ^{M} pour bébé ^{M}
mecedora ^{F} para bebé ^{M}
Babywippe ^{F}
sdraietta ^{F} per bambini ^{M}

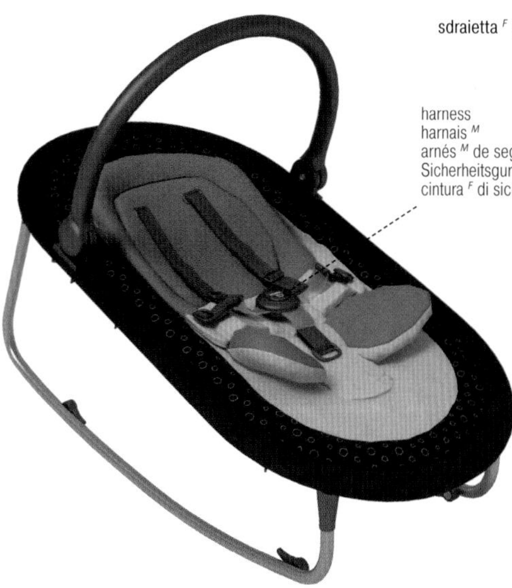

harness
harnais ^{M}
arnés ^{M} de seguridad ^{F}
Sicherheitsgurt ^{M}
cintura ^{F} di sicurezza ^{F}

stroller
landau ^{M} / pousette ^{F}
cochecito ^{M} de paseo ^{M}
Kinderwagen ^{M}
carrozzina ^{F}

handle
poignée ^{F}
manillar ^{M}
Griff ^{M}
impugnatura ^{F}

hood
capote ^{M}
capota ^{F}
Verdeck ^{N}
capottina ^{F}

wheel
roue ^{F}
rueda ^{F}
Rad ^{N}
ruota ^{F}

basket
panier ^{M}
cesta ^{F}
Korb ^{M}
cesto ^{M}

brake
frein ^{M}
freno ^{M}
Bremse ^{F}
freno ^{M}

lightweight stroller
poussette ^{F} / poussette ^{F} pliante
cochecito ^{M} de paseo ^{M}
Buggy ^{M}
passeggino ^{M}

play mat
tapis M de jeu M
manta F de actividades F
Spielmatte F
tappetino M per giocare M

toy
jouet M
juguete M
Spielzeug N
giocattolo M

mat
tapis M
colchoneta F
Matte F
tappetino M

baby bathtub
baignoire F pour bébés M
bañera F para bebé M
Babybadewanne F
vaschetta F da bagno M per neonato

tub
cuve F
bañera F
Badewanne F
vasca F

onesie
onesie M
enterizo M / mameluco M
Babybody M
body M

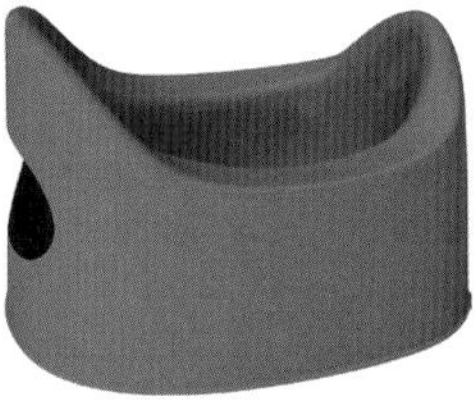

potty chair
pot M
orinal M
Töpfchen N
vasino M

toilet seat reducer
siège M de toilette F réducteur
asiento M adaptador M para inodoro M
Kleinkinder-Toilettensitz M
riduttore M per WC M

disposable diape
couche
pañal M desechabl
Wegwefwindel
pannolino

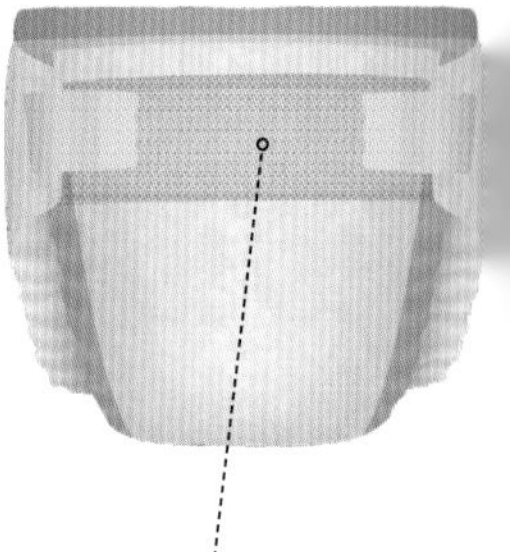

fastener
attache F
cierre M
Klettverschluss M
chiusura F a velcro M

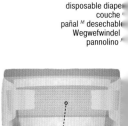

dress shoes
chaussures [F] habillées
zapato [M] de vestir
Anzugschuh [M]
scarpe [F] eleganti

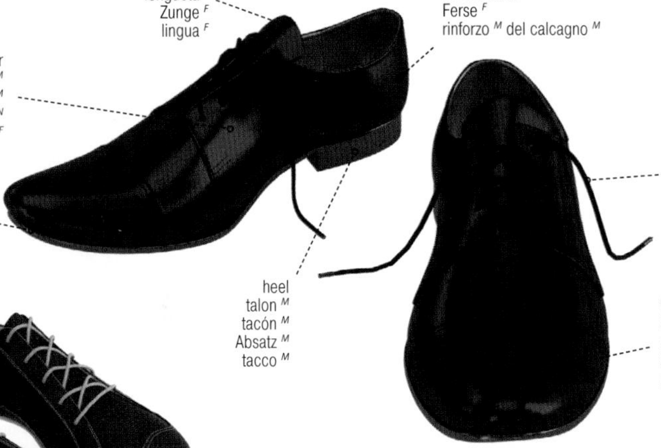
tongue
languette [F]
lengüeta [F]
Zunge [F]
lingua [F]
backstay
contrefort [M]
contrafuerte [M]
Ferse [F]
rinforzo [M] del calcagno [M]
quarter
quartier [M]
cuarto [M]
Quartier [N]
tomaia [F]
lace
lacet [M]
cordón [M]
Schnürsenkel [M]
stringa [F]
sole
semelle [F]
suela [F]
Sohle [F]
suola [F]
heel
talon [M]
tacón [M]
Absatz [M]
tacco [M]
toe cap
bout [M]
puntera [F]
Zehenspitze [F]
punta [F]

sneaker
espadrilles [F]
zapatilla [F] deportiva
Turnschuh [M]
scarpa [F] da ginnastica [F]

cross-trainer
chaussures [F] multisports [M]
zapatillas [F] de deporte [M]
Cross-Trainingsschuh [M]
scarpe [F] da cross-training [M]

basketball shoe
chaussures [F] de basketball [M]
zapatos [M] de baloncesto [M]
Basketballschuh [M]
scarpa [F] da pallacanestro [F]

high-top sneaker
espadrilles [F] hautes
zapatillas [F] deportivas altas
hoher Turnschuh [F]
scarpa [F] da ginnastica alta [F]

oxford
richelieu [M]
Oxfords [M]
Schnürschuh [M]
scarpa [F] oxford

hiking boot
bottes ^{F} de randonnée ^{F}
botas ^{F} de montaña ^{F}
Wanderstiefel ^{M}
scarponi ^{M} da trekking ^{M}

boat shoes
chaussures ^{F} de bateau ^{M}
zapatos ^{M} náuticos ^{M}
Segelschuh ^{M}
scarpa ^{F} da barca ^{F}

moccasins
mocassins ^{M}
mocasines ^{M}
Mokassin ^{M}
mocassini ^{M}

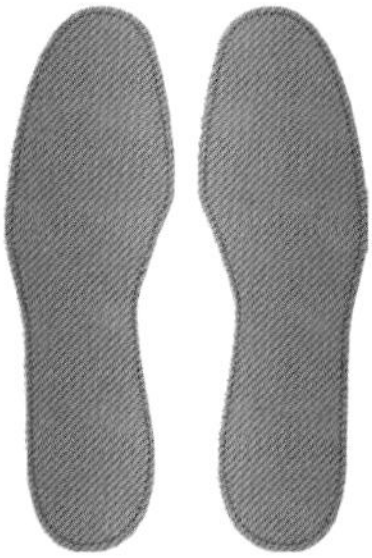

insole
semelle ^{F} intérieure
plantillas ^{F}
Einlegesohle ^{F}
soletta ^{F}

slippers
pantoufles ^{F}
zapatillas ^{F}
Hausschuh ^{M}
ciabatte ^{F}

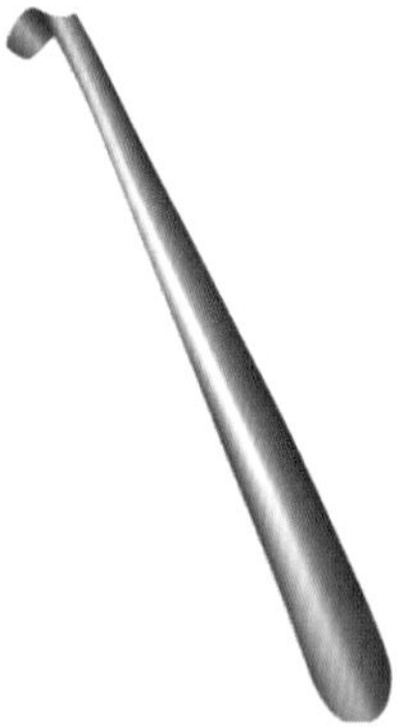

shoehorn
chausse-pied ^{M}
calzador ^{M}
Schuhlöffel ^{M}
calzascarpe ^{M}

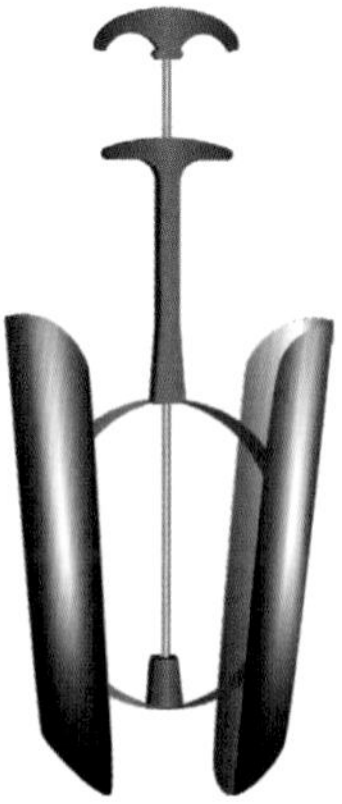

boot tree
tendeur ^{M} pour bottes ^{F}
portabotas ^{M}
Stiefelknecht ^{M}
cavastivali ^{M}

shoe tree
embauchoir ^{M}
horma ^{F} para zapatos ^{M}
Schuhspanner ^{M}
forma ^{F} per scarpe ^{F}

shoe brush
brosse ^{F} à chaussures ^{F}
cepillo ^{M} para zapatos ^{M}
Schuhbürste ^{F}
spazzola ^{F} per scarpe ^{F}

shoe polish
cirage ^{M}
betún ^{M}
Schuhcreme ^{F}
lucido ^{M} da scarpe ^{F}

ankle-strap sandals
sandales [F] à bride [F] de cheville [F]
sandalias [F] con tira [F] en el tobillo [M]
Sandalen [F] mit Knöchelriemchen [N]
sandali [M] con cinturino [M] alla caviglia [F]

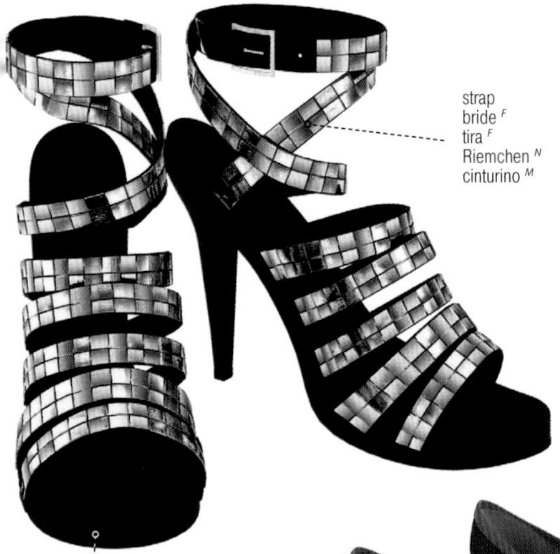

strap
bride [F]
tira [F]
Riemchen [N]
cinturino [M]

sole
semelle [F]
suela [F]
Sohle [F]
suola [F]

platform pumps
escarpins [M] à semelle [F] plate-forme [F]
zapatos [M] de tacón [M]
Pumps [M] mit Plateausohle [F]
zeppe [F]

heel
talon [M]
tacón [M]
Absatz [M]
tacco [M]

platform
semelle [F] plate-forme
plataforma [F]
Plateau [N]
zeppa [F]

toe
bout [M]
puntera [F]
Zehe [F]
punta [F]

ballet flats
chaussons [M] de ballet [M]
zapatillas [F] de bailarina [F]
Ballerinas [F]
ballerina [F]

high-heeled boot
bottes [F] à talons [M] hauts
bota [F] de tacón [M] alto
hochhackiger Stiefel [M]
stivale [M] con tacco [M]

high-heeled sandal
sandales [F] à talons [M] hauts
sandalia [F] de tacón [M] alto
Sandalette [F]
sandalo [F] a tacco [M] alto

sandal
sandales [F]
sandalia [F]
Sandale [F]
sandalo [M]

slippers
pantoufles ^{F}
sandalia ^{F} con tacón ^{M}
Hausschuh ^{M}
ciabatte ^{F}

peep-toe ankle boot
bottines ^{F} à bout ^{M} ouvert
botas ^{F} de tacón ^{M} alto con punta ^{F} abierta
Peeptoe Stiefelette ^{F}
stivaletti ^{M} spuntati alla caviglia ^{F}

peep-toe flat
chaussures ^{F} plates à bout ^{M} ouvert
bailarina ^{F} con punta ^{F} abierta
Peeptoe Ballerinas ^{F}
ballerine ^{F} spuntate

biker boots
bottes ^{F} de motard ^{M}
bota ^{F} de motorista ^{M}
Biker-Stiefel ^{M}
anfibi ^{M}

ankle boots
bottines ^{F}
botín ^{M}
Stiefelette ^{F}
tronchetto ^{M}

wedge boot
bottes ^{F} à talon ^{M} compensé
bota ^{F} con suela ^{F} de cuña ^{F}
Stiefel ^{M} mit Keilabsatz ^{M}
stivali ^{M} con la zeppa ^{F}

peep-toe pump
escarpins ^{M} à bout ^{M} ouvert
zapato ^{M} con punta abierta ^{F}
Peep-Toe-Pumps ^{M}
scarpe ^{F} décolleté spuntate

pump
escarpins ^{M}
zapato ^{M} de salón ^{M}
Pumps ^{M}
décolleté ^{F}

wedge sandal
sandales ^{F} à talon ^{M} compensé
sandalia ^{F} de cuña
Sandale ^{F} mit Keilabsatz ^{M}
sandali ^{M} con la zeppa ^{F}

pom-pom
pompon [M]
pompón [M]
Bommel [M]
pompon [M]

stocking cap
tuque [F]
gorro [M] con pompón [M]
Mütze [F]
berretto [M] con pompon [M]

sun hat
chapeau [M] de soleil [M]
pamela [F]
Sonnenhut [M]
cappello [M] parasole [F]

hatband
ruban [M] de chapeau [M]
banda [F] del sombrero [M]
Hutband [N]
nastro [M] da cappello [M]

crown
calotte [F]
corona [F]
Krone [F]
corona [F]

brim
bord [M]
ala [F]
Krempe [F]
tesa [F]

straw hat
chapeau [M] de paille [F]
sombrero [M] de paja [F]
Strohhut [M]
cappello [M] di paglia [F]

fedora
chapeau [M] mou
sombrero [M] fedora
Filzhut [M]
cappello [M] di feltro [M]

cloche
chapeau [M] cloche [F]
sombrero [M] de señora [F]
Damenhut [M]
cappello [M] cloche [M]

cap
casquette [F]
gorra [F]
Kappe [F]
berretto [M]

earflap cap
casquette [F] avec cache-oreilles [M]
gorro [M] tapaorejas [F]
Mütze [F] mit Ohrenklappen [F]
cappello [M] con paraorecchie [M]

flatcap
casquette [F] plate
gorra [F] irlandesa
Schiebermütze [F]
coppola [F]

baseball cap
casquette [F] de baseball [M]
gorra [F] de béisbol [M]
Baseballkappe [F]
berretto [M] da baseball [M]

scarf
écharpe [F]
pañuelo [M] de señora [F]
Damenschal [M]
sciarpa [F]

gloves
gants [M]
guantes [M]
Handschuhe [M]
guanti [M]

fingerless gloves
gants [M] sans doigt [M]
guantes [M] cortos
Halbfinger-Handschuhe [F]
guanti [M] senza dita [F]

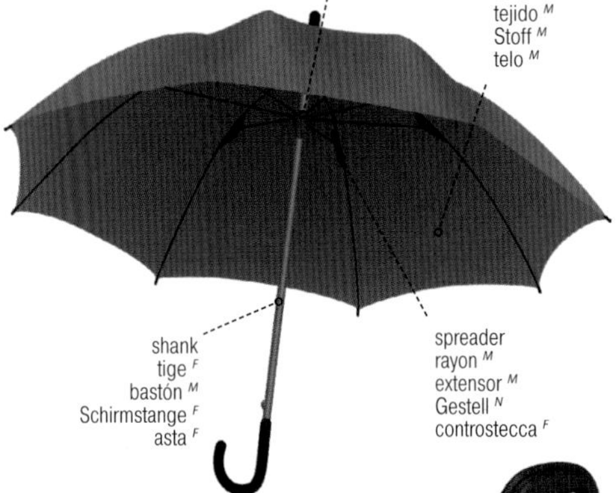

umbrella
parapluie M
paraguas M
Regenschirm M
ombrello M

ring
coulant F
contera F
Gleiter M
collare M

canopy
toile M
tejido M
Stoff M
telo M

shank
tige F
bastón M
Schirmstange F
asta F

spreader
rayon M
extensor M
Gestell N
controstecca F

handle
poignée F
asa F
Griff M
impugnatura F

garment bag
housse F à vêtements M
portatrajes M
Anzug-Tragehülle F
porta abiti M

backpack
sac M à dos M
mochila F deportiva
Sportrucksack M
zaino M sportivo

telescopic umbrella
parapluie M télescopique
paraguas M plegable
Taschenschirm M
ombrello M pieghevole

briefcase
serviette F
portafolio M
Aktentasche F
valigetta F

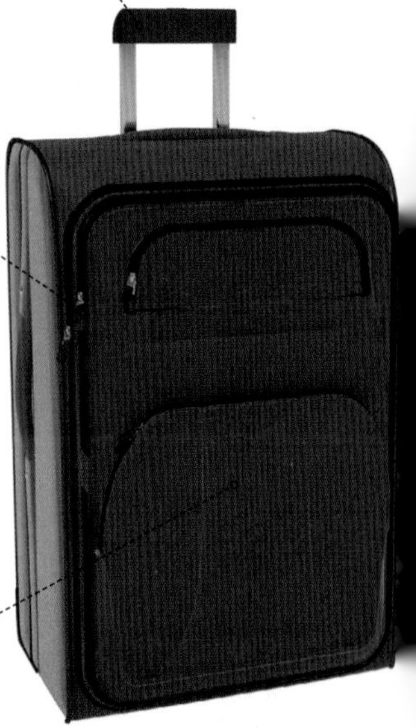

retractable handle
poignée F rétractable
asa F extensible
Ausziehgriff M
manico M estraibile

suitcas
valise
maleta
Koffer
valigia

zipper
fermeture F éclair M
cremallera F
Verschluss M
cerniera F

pocket
pochette F
bolsillo M
Tasche F
tasca F

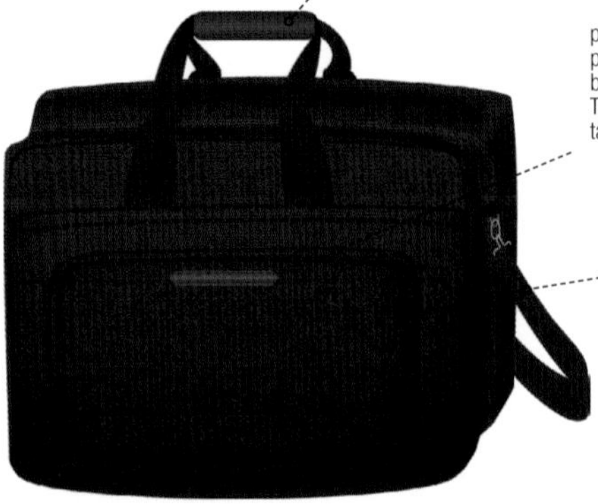

carry-on bag
sac M de vol M
equipaje M de mano F
Handgepäckkoffer M
borsone F a mano M

handle
poignée F
asa F
Griff M
impugnatura F

pocket
pochette F
bolsillo M
Tasche F
tasca F

strap
sangle F
correa F
Gurt M
cinghia F

cell-phone case
étui [F] pour téléphone [M] cellulaire
funda [F] para teléfono [M] móvil
Handyhülle [F]
custodia [F] portacellulare

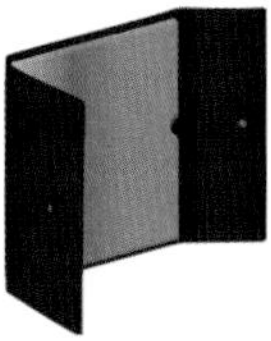

document case
porte-document [M]
portadocumentos [M]
Dokumententasche [F]
portadocumenti [M]

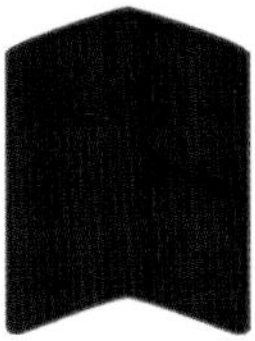

checkbook holder
porte-chéquier [M]
libreta [F] de cheques [M]
Scheckheftetui [N]
portassegni [M]

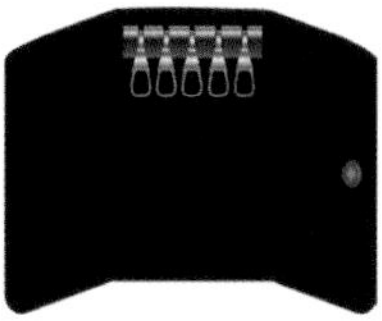

key case
étui [M] porte-clés [M]
cartera [F] con llavero [M]
Schlüsseletui [N]
portachiavi [M]

card case
porte-cartes [M]
tarjetero [M]
Kreditkartenetui [N]
porta carte di credito [F]

coin purse
porte-monnaie [M]
monedero [M]
Portemonnaie [N]
borsellino [M]

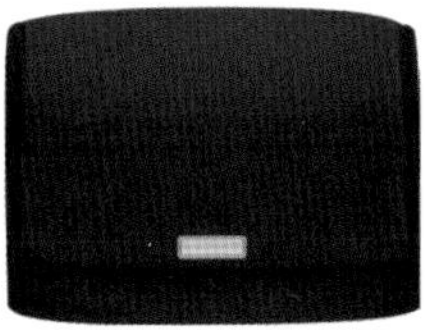

underarm portfolio
porte-documents [M] plat
cartera [F] sin asa [F]
Aktentasche [F]
portadocumenti [M] senza manico [M]

wallet
portefeuille [M]
billetera [F]
Brieftasche [F]
portafoglio [M]

clutch
pochette [F]
clutch [M]
Clutch [F]
pochette [F] senza manico [M]

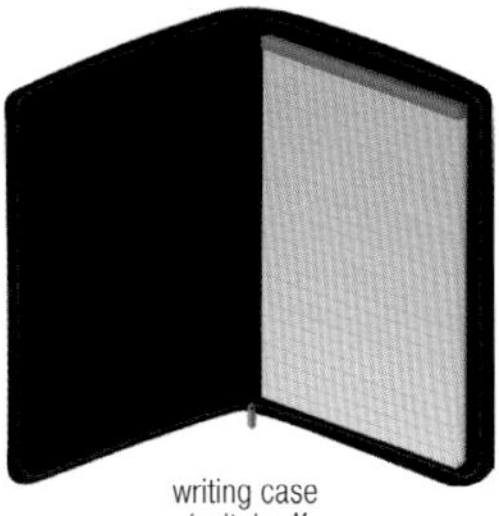

writing case
écritoire [M]
cartera [F] portadocumentos [M]
Schreibmappe [F]
astuccio [M] portablocco

evening bag
sac [M] de soirée [F]
bolso [M] de noche [F]
Abendtasche [F]
borsa [F] da sera [F]

passport holder
étui [M] pour passeport [M]
funda [M] para pasaporte [M]
Reisepasshülle [F]
portapassaporto [M]

backpack purse
sac [M] à dos [M] sac [M] à main [M]
mochila [F]
Rucksack [M]
zainetto [M]

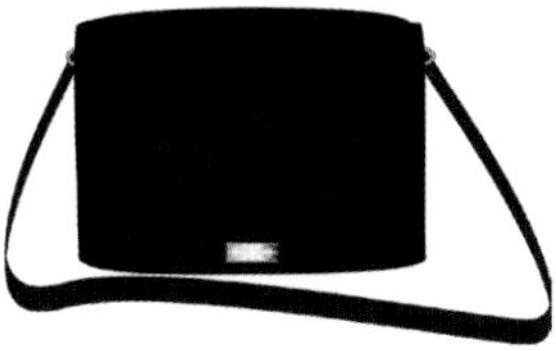

shoulder bag
sac [M] à bandoulière [F]
bandolera [F]
Umhängetasche [F]
borsa [F] a tracolla [F]

men's bag
sac [M] pour hommes [M]
bolso [M] para hombre [M]
Herrentasche [F]
borsello [M]

carrier bag
sac ^{M} à provisions ^{F}
bolsa ^{F} de compras ^{F}
Einkaufstasche ^{F}
borsa ^{F} della spesa ^{F}

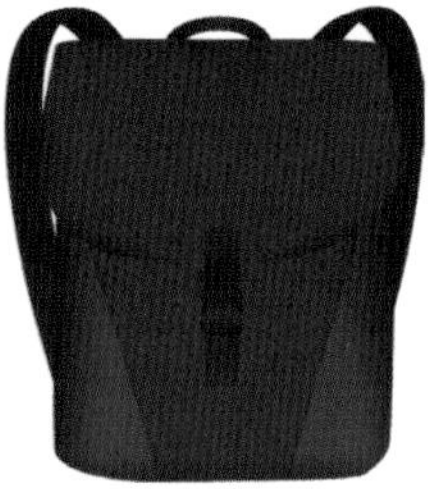

schoolbag
cartable ^{M}
mochila ^{F} escolar
Schultasche ^{F}
cartella ^{F}

sea bag
sac ^{M} marin
petate ^{M}
Seesack ^{M}
sacca ^{F} da viaggio ^{M}

handbag
polochon ^{M}
bolso ^{M} de mano ^{F}
Handtasche ^{F}
borsetta ^{F}

vanity bag
mallette ^{F} de toilette ^{F}
neceser ^{M}
Kosmetikkoffer ^{M}
beauty-case ^{M}

drawstring bag
sac ^{M} à cordonnet ^{M}
bolsito ^{M} con cierre ^{M} de cordón ^{M}
Kordelzugbeutel ^{M}
borsetta ^{F} a secchiello ^{M}

laptop bag
sac ^{M} pour ordinateur ^{M} portatif
bolso ^{M} para computadora ^{F} portátil
Laptoptasche ^{F}
borsa ^{F} porta PC ^{M}

tote purse
sac ^{M} fourre-tout
bolso ^{M} capazo
Tragetasche ^{F}
spallaccio ^{M}

attaché case
attaché-case ^{M}
maletín ^{M}
Aktenkoffer ^{M}
ventiquattrore ^{F}

pocket watch
montre [F] de poche [F]
reloj [M] de bolsillo
Taschenuhr [F]
orologio [M] da tasca

case
boîtier [M]
estuche [M]
Gehäuse [N]
cassa [F]

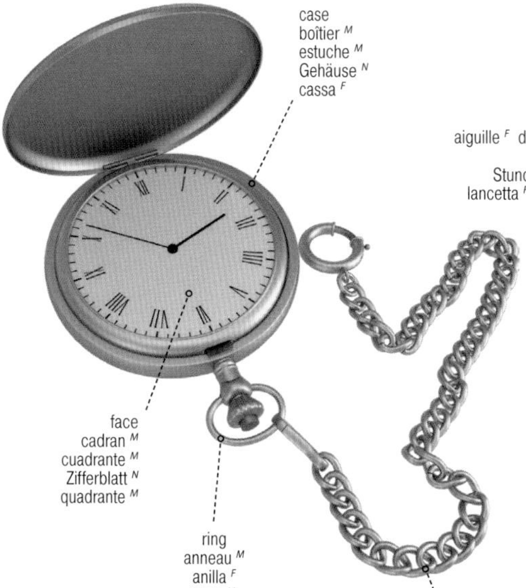

face
cadran [M]
cuadrante [M]
Zifferblatt [N]
quadrante [M]

ring
anneau [M]
anilla [F]
Ring [M]
anello [M]

chain
chaîne [F]
cadena [F]
Kette [F]
catena [F]

analog watch
montre [F] à affichage [M] analogique
reloj [M] analógico
Analoguhr [F]
orologio [M] analogico

watchband
bracelet [M] de montre [F]
correa [F]
Uhrband [N]
cinturino [M]

hour hand
aiguille [F] des heures [F]
horario [M]
Stundenzeiger [M]
lancetta [F] delle ore [F]

crown
couronne [F]
corona [F]
Krone [F]
corona [F]

12
9
6
FRI 25

second hand
trotteuse [F]
segundero [M]
Sekundenzeiger [M]
lancetta [F] dei secondi [M]

minute hand
grande aiguille [F]
minutero [M]
Minutenzeiger [M]
lancetta [F] dei minuti [M]

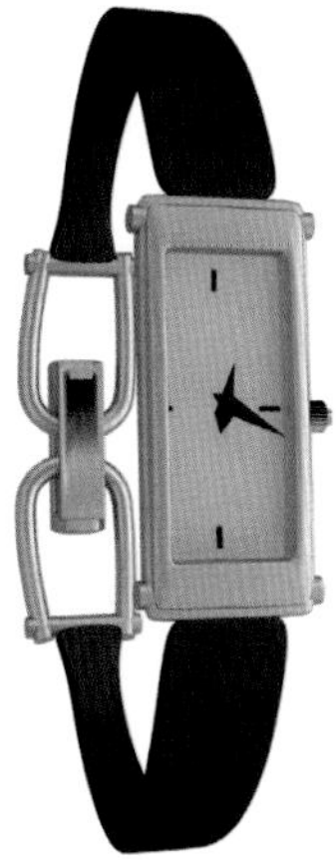

women's watch
montre [F] pour femme
reloj [M] para mujer [F]
Damenuhr [F]
orologio [M] da donna [F]

17:10
FRI 25

digital watch
montre [F] digitale
reloj [M] digital
Digitaluhr [F]
orologio [M] digitale

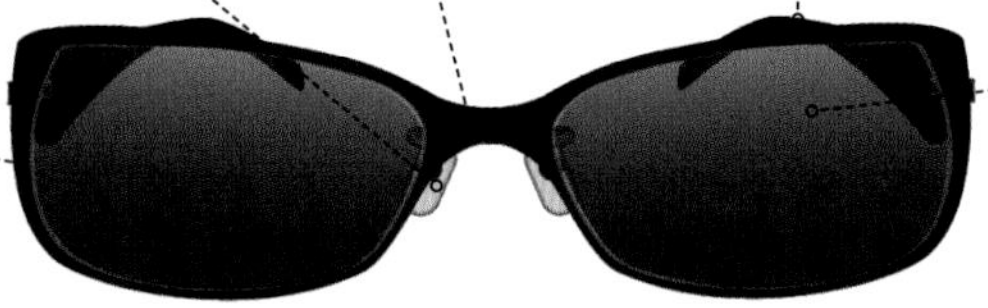
nose pad
plaquette F
plaqueta F
Seitensteg M
nasello M
bridge
arête F nasale
puente M
Brücke F
ponte M
temple
branche F
patilla F
Bügel M
stanghetta F
frame
cercle M
montura F
Rahmen M
montatura F
lens
verre M
lente F
Glas N
lenti F

sunglasses
lunettes F de soleil M
gafas F de sol M
Sonnenbrille F
occhiali M da sole M

eyeglasses
lunettes F
gafas F
Brille F
occhiali M

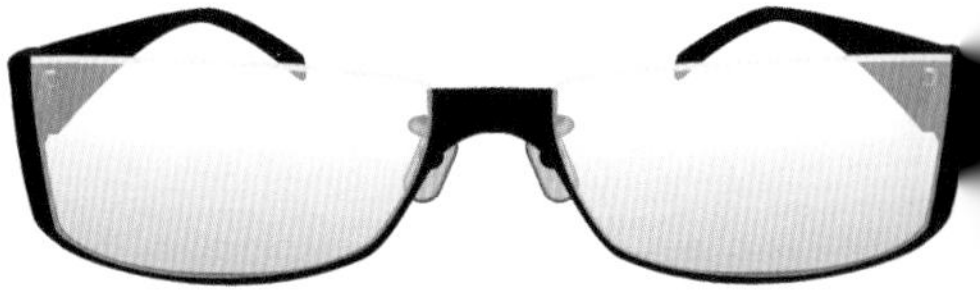

half-rimmed glasses
lunettes F à demi-monture F
gafas F de media montura F
Halbrandbrille F
occhiali M con montatura F a semi-giorno

clip-on sunglasses
clip solaire M
lentes F de sol M enganchables
Sonnenbrillen-Clip M
occhiali M da sole M clip-on

bifocal lens
lentille F à double foyer M
lentes F bifocales
bifokale Linse F
lenti F bifocali

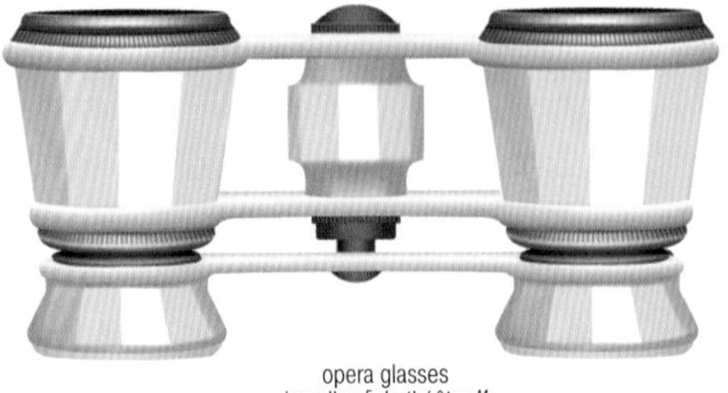

opera glasses
jumelles F de théâtre M
binoculares M para ópera F
Opernglas N
binocoli M da teatro M

monocle
monocle M
monóculo M
Monokel N
monocolo M

soft contact lenses
lentilles F de contact M souples
lentes M de contacto blandos M
weiche Kontaktlinse F
lenti F a contatto M morbide

hard contact lenses
lentilles F de contact M dures
lentes M de contacto duros
harte Kontaktlinse F
lenti F a contatto M rigide

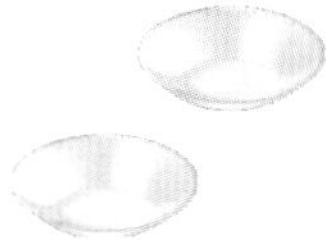

disposable contact lenses
lentilles F de contact M jetables
lentes M de contacto desechables
Einweg-Kontaktlinse F
lenti F a contatto M monouso

lens case
étui M pour lentilles F de contact M
estuche M para lentes M de contacto
Kontaktlinsenbehälter M
portalenti M

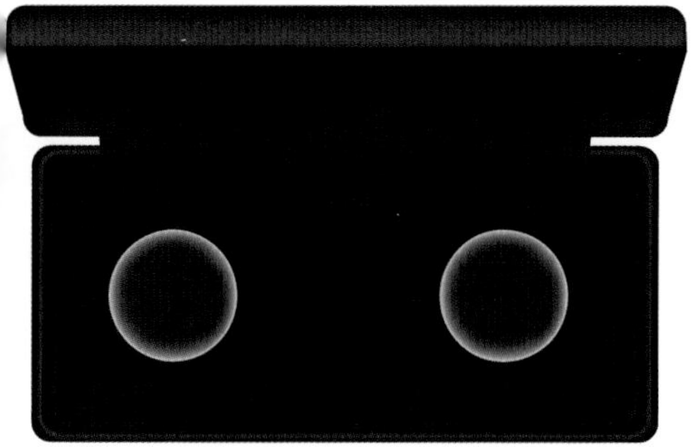

antique lens case
étui M antique pour lentilles F de contact M
estuche M antiguo M para lentes M de contacto
Antiker Kontaktlinsenbehälter M
portalenti M d'epoca

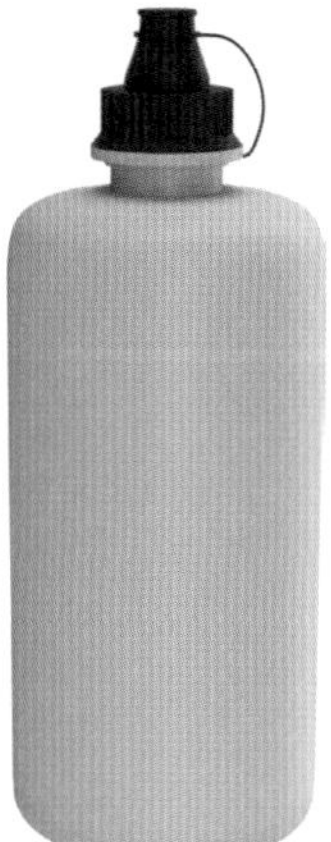

multipurpose solution
solution F multiusage
solución F multiusos
Mehrzwecklösung F
soluzione F multiuso

lubricant eye drops
gouttes F lubrifiantes pour les yeux M
gotas F oculares lubricantes
Augentropfen M
collirio M lubrificante

cleaning cloth
chiffon M de nettoyage M
paño M para limpiar las gafas F
Brillenputztuch N
panno M pulisci-occhiali

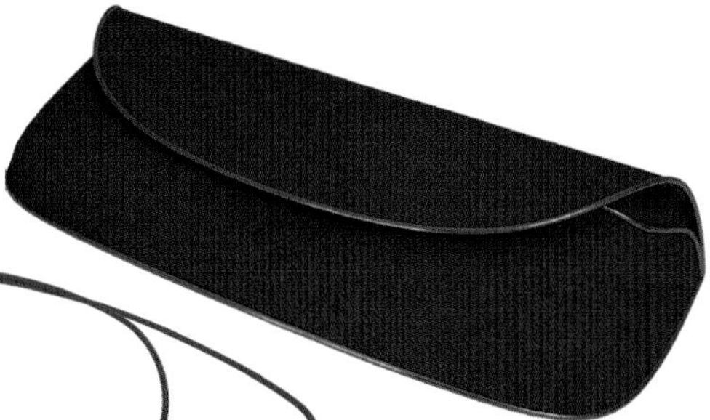

glasses case
étui M à lunettes F
estuche M para gafas F
Brillenetui N
portaocchiali M

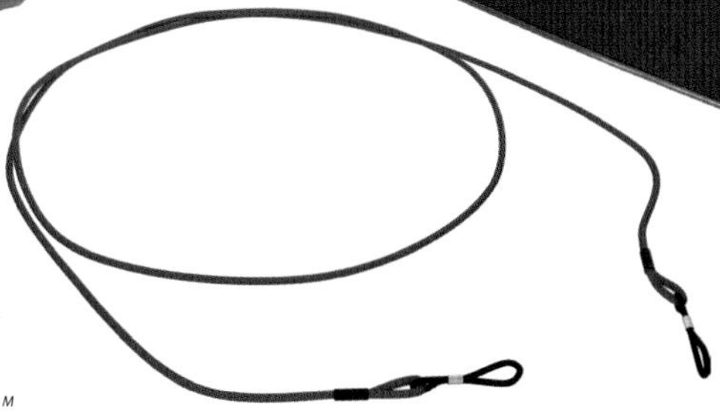

glasses cord
cordon M pour lunettes F
tira F para las gafas F
Brillenband N
cordoncino M per occhiali M

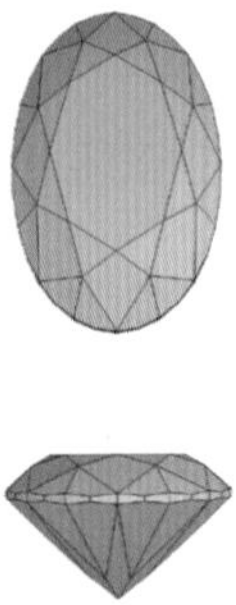

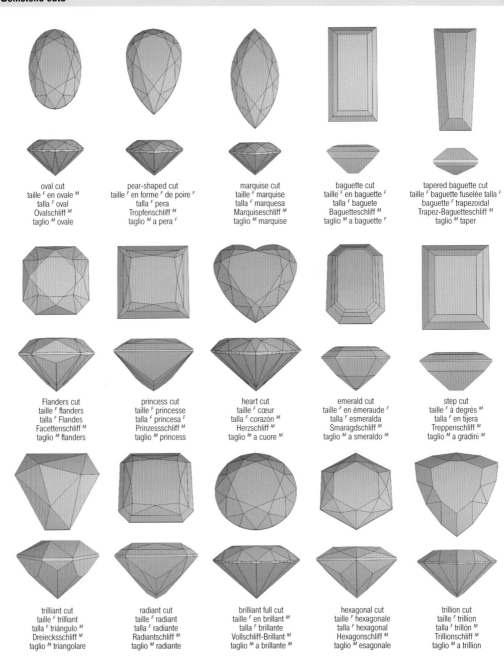

oval cut
taille [F] en ovale [M]
talla [F] oval
Ovalschliff [M]
taglio [M] ovale

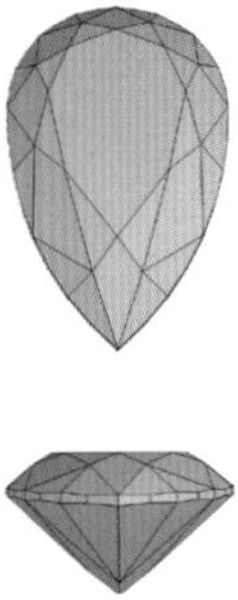

pear-shaped cut
taille [F] en forme [F] de poire [F]
talla [F] pera
Tropfenschliff [M]
taglio [M] a pera [F]

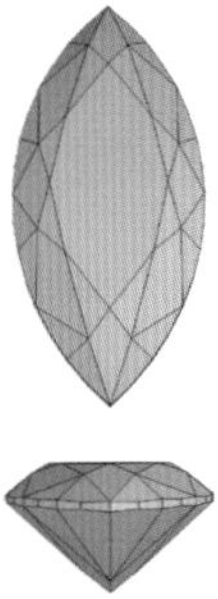

marquise cut
taille [F] marquise
talla [F] marquesa
Marquiseschliff [M]
taglio [M] marquise

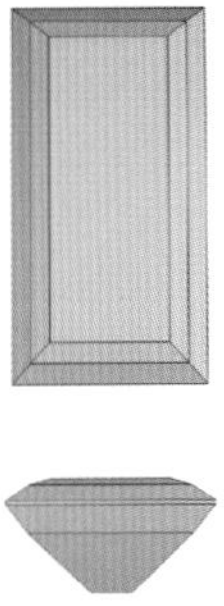

baguette cut
taille [F] en baguette [F]
talla [F] baguete
Baguetteschliff [M]
taglio [M] a baguette [F]

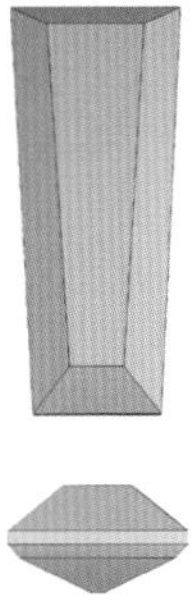

tapered baguette cut
taille [F] baguette fuselée talla [F]
baguette [F] trapezoidal
Trapez-Baguetteschliff [M]
taglio [M] taper

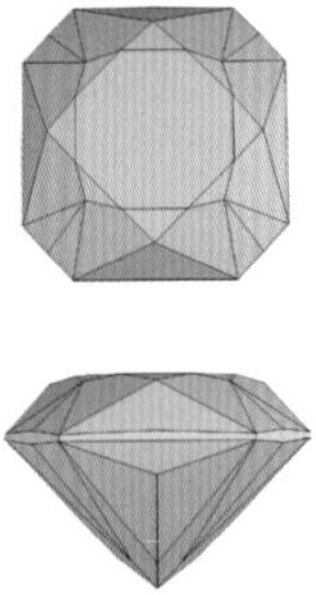

Flanders cut
taille [F] flanders
talla [F] Flandes
Facettenschliff [M]
taglio [M] flanders

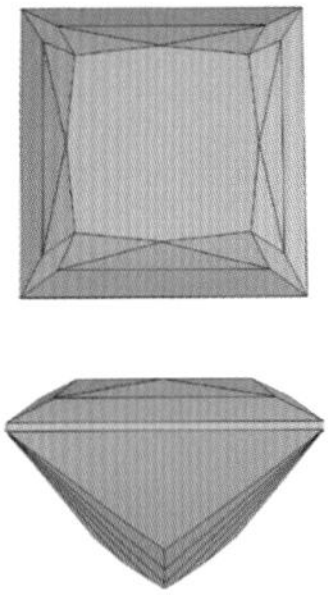

princess cut
taille [F] princesse
talla [F] princesa [F]
Prinzessschliff [M]
taglio [M] princess

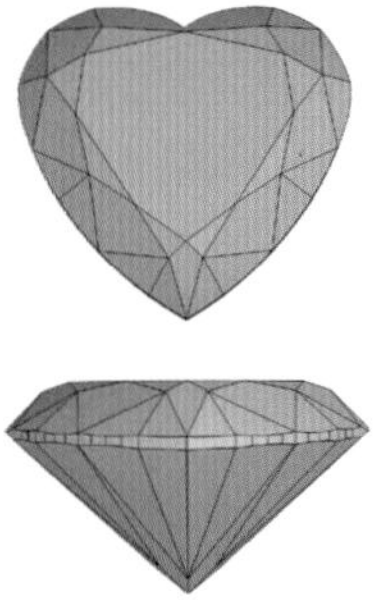

heart cut
taille [F] cœur
talla [F] corazón [M]
Herzschliff [M]
taglio [M] a cuore [M]

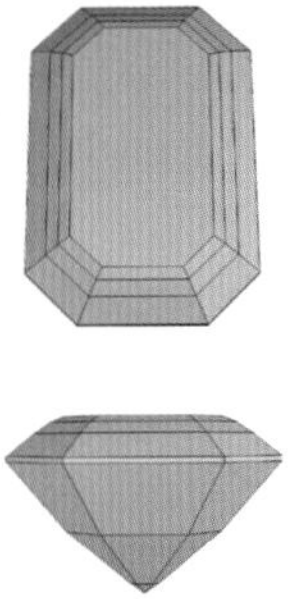

emerald cut
taille [F] en émeraude [F]
talla [F] esmeralda
Smaragdschliff [M]
taglio [M] a smeraldo [M]

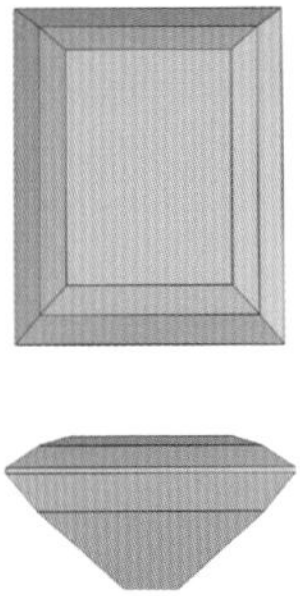

step cut
taille [F] à degrés [M]
talla [F] en tijera
Treppenschliff [M]
taglio [M] a gradini [M]

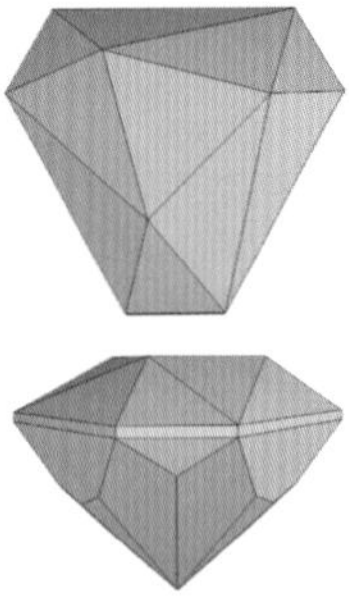

trilliant cut
taille [F] trilliant
talla [F] triángulo [M]
Dreiecksschliff [M]
taglio [M] triangolare

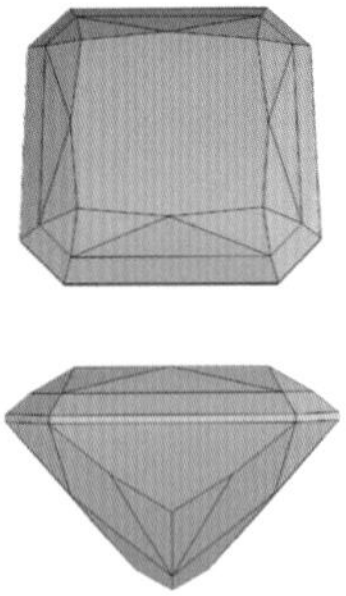

radiant cut
taille [F] radiant
talla [F] radiante
Radiantschliff [M]
taglio [M] radiante

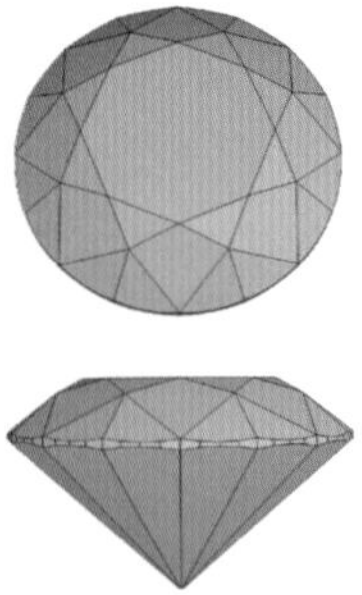

brilliant full cut
taille [F] en brillant [M]
talla [F] brillante
Vollschliff-Brillant [M]
taglio [M] a brillante [M]

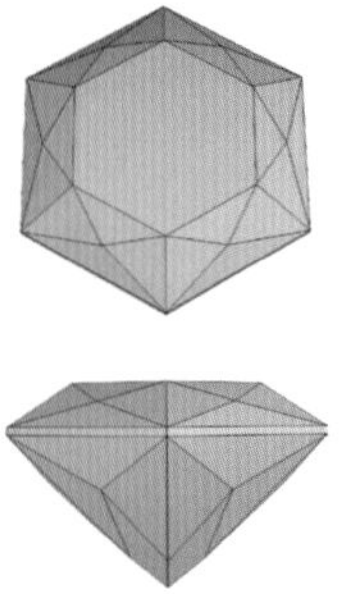

hexagonal cut
taille [F] hexagonale
talla [F] hexagonal
Hexagonschliff [M]
taglio [M] esagonale

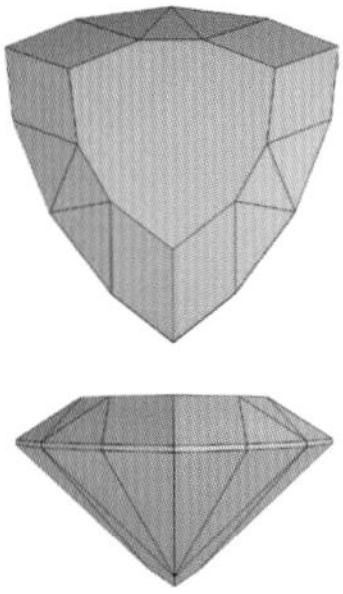

trillion cut
taille [F] trillion
talla [F] trillón [M]
Trillionschliff [M]
taglio [M] a trillion

diamond
diamant ^{M}
diamante ^{M}
Diamant ^{M}
diamante ^{M}

amethyst
améthyste ^{F}
amatista ^{F}
Amethyst ^{M}
ametista ^{F}

aquamarine
aigue-marine ^{F}
aguamarina ^{F}
Aquamarin ^{M}
acquamarina ^{F}

tourmaline
tourmaline ^{F}
turmalina ^{F}
Turmalin ^{M}
tormalina ^{F}

blue topaz
topaze ^{F} bleue
topacio ^{M} azul
Blautopas ^{M}
topazio ^{M} azzurro

ruby
rubis ^{M}
rubí ^{M}
Rubin ^{M}
rubino ^{M}

emerald
émeraude ^{F}
esmeralda ^{F}
Smaragd ^{M}
smeraldo ^{M}

garnet
grenat ^{M}
granate ^{M}
Granat ^{M}
granato ^{M}

sapphire
saphir ^{M}
zafiro ^{M}
Saphir ^{M}
zaffiro ^{M}

quartz crystal
cristal ^{M} de quartz ^{M}
cristal ^{M} de cuarzo ^{M}
Quarzkristall ^{M}
cristallo ^{M} di quarzo ^{M}

malachite
malachite ^{F}
malaquita ^{F}
Malachit ^{M}
malachite ^{F}

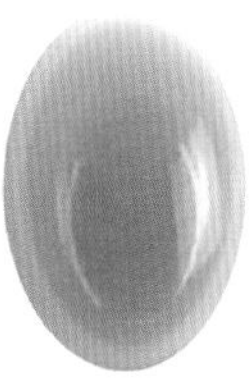

moonstone
pierre ^{F} de lune ^{F}
piedra ^{F} de luna ^{F}
Mondstein ^{M}
pietra ^{F} di luna ^{F}

jade
jade ^{M}
jade ^{M}
Jade ^{M}
giada ^{F}

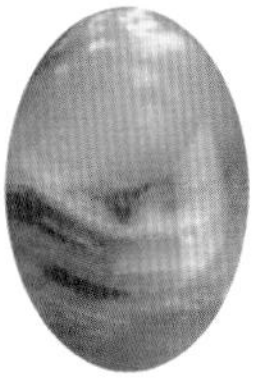

onyx
onyx ^{M}
ónix ^{M}
Onyx ^{M}
onice ^{F}

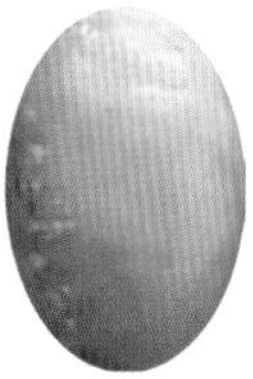

opal
opale ^{F}
ópalo ^{M}
Opal ^{M}
opale ^{M}

ivory
ivoire ^{M}
marfil ^{M}
Elfenbein ^{N}
avorio ^{M}

lapis lazuli
lapis-lazuli ^{M}
lapislázuli ^{M}
Lapislazuli ^{M}
lapislazzuli ^{M}

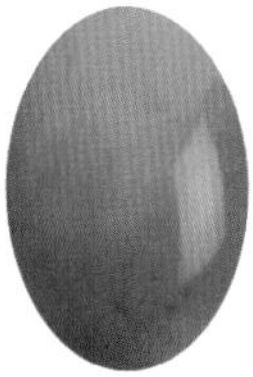

turquoise
turquoise ^{F}
turquesa ^{F}
Türkis ^{M}
turchese ^{M}

tigereye
œil-de-tigre ^{M}
ojo ^{M} de tigre ^{M}
Tigerauge ^{N}
occhio ^{M} di tigre ^{F}

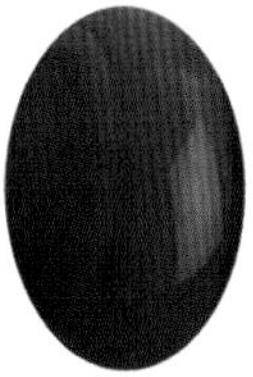

agate
agate ^{F}
ágata ^{F}
Achat ^{M}
agata ^{F}

tiara
tiare [F]
tiara [F]
Diadem [N]
diadema [M]

charm bracelet
bracelet [M] à breloques [F]
pulsera [F] de dijes [M]
Bettelarmband [N]
braccialetto [M] con pendenti [M]

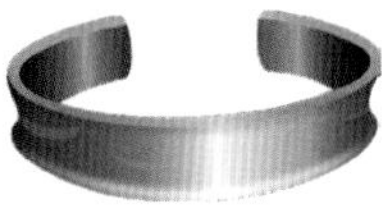

cuff
bracelet-manchette [M]
brazalete [M]
Armreif [M]
braccialetto [M]

leather bangle
bracelet [M] en cuir [M]
brazalete [M] de cuero [M]
Lederarmband [N]
braccialetto [M] in cuoio [M]

locket
médaillon [M]
medallón [M]
Medaillon [N]
medaglione [M]

pearl necklace
collier [M] de perles [F]
collar [M] de perlas [F]
Perlenkette [F]
collana [F] di perle [F]

cameo
camée [M]
camafeo [M]
Kamee [F]
cameo [M]

choker
ras-du-cou [M]
gargantilla [F]
Halsband [N]
girocollo [M]

rhinestone
pierre [F] du Rhin [M]
estrás [M]
Strass [M]
diamante [M] artificiale

brooch
broche [F]
broche [M]
Brosche [F]
spilla [F]

filigree pendant
pendentif [M] filigrane
pendiente [M] de filigrana [F]
Filigranschmuck [M]
filigrana [F]

jewelry box
boîte [F] à bijoux [M]
joyero [M]
Schmuckschatulle [F]
portagioie [M]

pendant
pendentif [M]
pendiente [M]
Anhänger [M]
ciondolo [M]

navel ring stud
boucle [F] de nombril [M]
adorno [M] para piercing [M]
del ombligo [M]
Bauchnabelpiercing [N]
piercing [M]

silver pendant
pendentif [M] en argent [M]
pendiente [M] de plata [F]
Silberanhänger [M]
ciondolo [M] in argento [M]

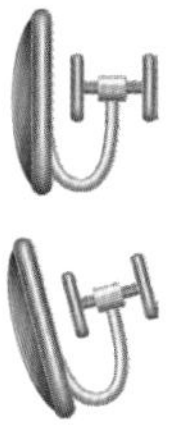

screw earring
boucle [F] d'oreille [F] à vis [F]
pendientes [M] de tornillo [M]
Ohrring mit Schraubverschluss [M]
orecchini [M] a clip [F]

drop earring
pendant [M] d'oreilles [F]
pendientes [M] colgantes
Ohrgehänge [N]
orecchini [M] pendenti

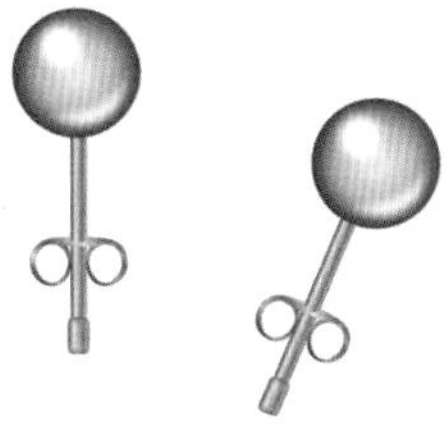

stud
bouton [M] d'oreilles [F]
pendientes [M] con cierre [M] a presión [F]
Ohrstecker [M]
orecchini [M] a bottone [M]

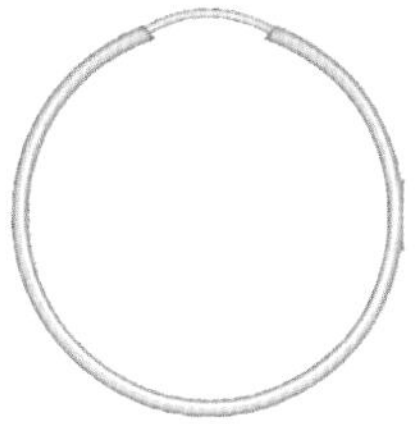

hoop earring
créole [F]
aretes [M]
Creole [F]
orecchini [M] a cerchio [M]

Men's jewelry

tie bar
épingle [F] de cravate [F]
pinza [F] para corbata [F]
Krawattenhalter [M]
fermacravatta [M]

cuff link
bouton [M] de manchette [F]
gemelos [M]
Manschettenknöpfe [M]
gemelli [M]

tiepin
épingle [F] de cravate [F]
pisacorbatas [M]
Krawattennadel [F]
spillo [M] per cravatta [F]

Rings

band
jonc [M]
anillo [M] tipo banda [F]
Ring [M]
anello [M] a fascia [F]

class ring
bague [F] d'étudiant [M]
anillo [M] de graduación [F]
Absolventenring [M]
anello [M] scolastico

engagement ring
bague [F] de fiançailles [F]
anillo [M] de compromiso [M]
Verlobungsring [M]
anello [M] di fidanzamento [M]

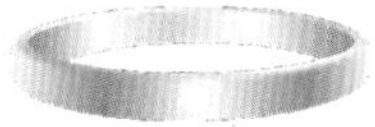

platinum ring
anneau [M] en platine [M]
anillo [M] de platino [M]
Platinring [M]
anello [M] di platino [M]

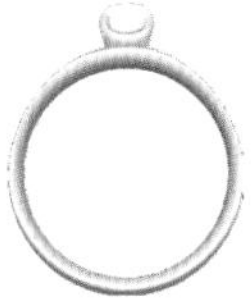

solitaire ring
solitaire [M]
anillo [M] solitario
Solitär-Ring [M]
anello [M] con solitario [M]

wedding ring
anneau [M] de mariage [M]
alianza [F] de boda [F]
Ehering [M]
fede [F] nuziale

signet ring
chevalière [F]
anillo [M] de sello [M]
Siegelring [M]
anello [M] con sigillo [M]

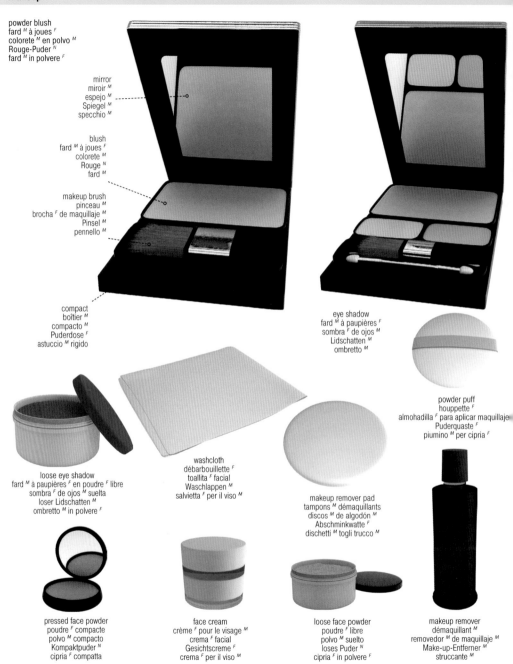

powder blush
fard [M] à joues [F]
colorete [M] en polvo [M]
Rouge-Puder [N]
fard [M] in polvere [F]

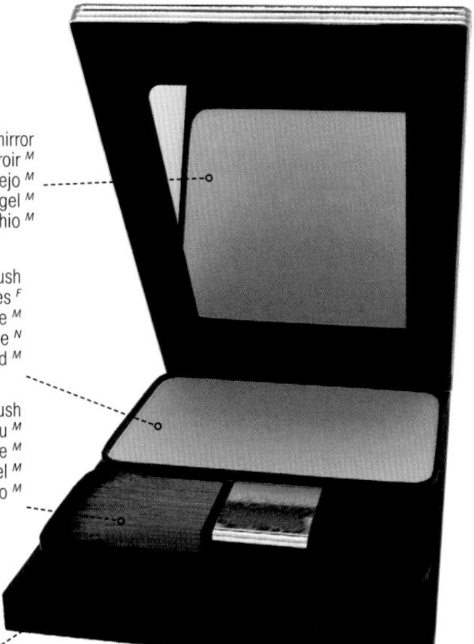

mirror
miroir [M]
espejo [M]
Spiegel [M]
specchio [M]

blush
fard [M] à joues [F]
colorete [M]
Rouge [N]
fard [M]

makeup brush
pinceau [M]
brocha [F] de maquillaje [M]
Pinsel [M]
pennello [M]

compact
boîtier [M]
compacto [M]
Puderdose [F]
astuccio [M] rigido

eye shadow
fard [M] à paupières [F]
sombra [F] de ojos [M]
Lidschatten [M]
ombretto [M]

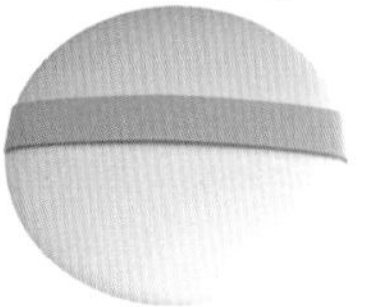

powder puff
houppette [F]
almohadilla [F] para aplicar maquillaje
Puderquaste [F]
piumino [M] per cipria [F]

loose eye shadow
fard [M] à paupières [F] en poudre [F] libre
sombra [F] de ojos [M] suelta
loser Lidschatten [M]
ombretto [M] in polvere [F]

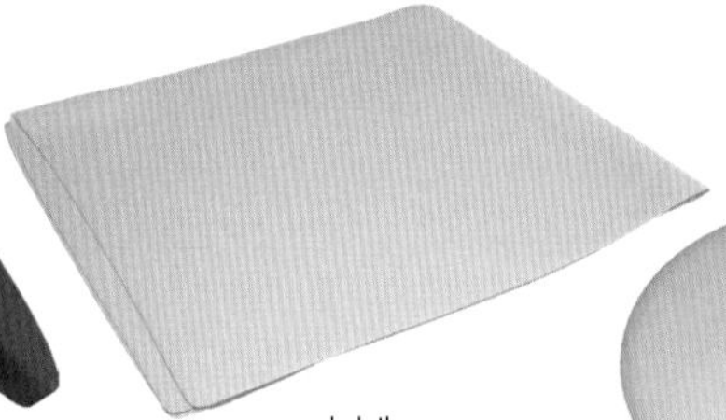

washcloth
débarbouillette [F]
toallita [F] facial
Waschlappen [M]
salvietta [F] per il viso [M]

makeup remover pad
tampons [M] démaquillants
discos [M] de algodón [M]
Abschminkwatte [F]
dischetti [M] togli trucco [M]

pressed face powder
poudre [F] compacte
polvo [M] compacto
Kompaktpuder [N]
cipria [F] compatta

face cream
crème [F] pour le visage [M]
crema [F] facial
Gesichtscreme [F]
crema [F] per il viso [M]

loose face powder
poudre [F] libre
polvo [M] suelto
loses Puder [N]
cipria [F] in polvere [F]

makeup remover
démaquillant [M]
removedor [M] de maquillaje [M]
Make-up-Entferner [M]
struccante [M]

brow brush and lash comb
brosse[F] pour sourcils[M] et peigne-cils[M]
cepillo[M] para cejas[F] y peine[M] para pestañas[F]
Augenbrauen- und Wimpernbürstchen[N]
pettine[M] per ciglia[F] e sopracciglia[F]

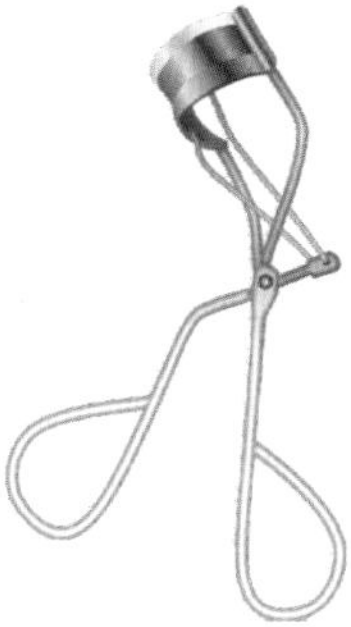

eyelash curler
courbe-cils[M]
rizador[M] de pestañas[F]
Wimpernzange[F]
piegaciglia[M]

cotton swab
coton-tiges[M]
hisopo[M] de algodón[M]
Wattestäbchen[N]
cotton fioc[M]

tweezers
pinces[F] à épiler
pinzas[F] de depilar
Pinzette[F]
pinzette[F]

lip gloss
brillant[M] à lèvres[F]
brillo[M] de labios[M]
Lipgloss[N]
lucidalabbra[M]

eye cream
crème[F] pour les yeux[M]
crema[F] para los ojos[M]
Augencreme[F]
crema[F] per il contorno[M] occhi[M]

concealer
cache-cernes[M]
corrector[M]
Abdeckstift[M]
correttore[M]

lipstick
rouge[M] à lèvres[F]
pintura[F] de labios[M]
Lippenstift[M]
rossetto[M]

lip balm
baume[M] pour les lèvres[F]
crema[F] de labios[M]
Lippenbalsam[M]
burrocacao[M]

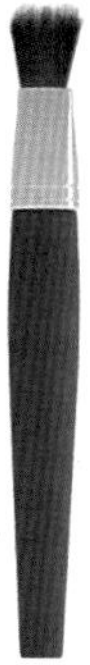

loose powder brush
pinceau[M] pour poudre[F] libre
brocha[F] para polvo[M] suelto
Pinsel[M] für loses Puder[N]
pennello[M] per cipria[F]

liquid eye shadow
fard[M] à paupières[F] liquide
sombra[F] de ojos[M] líquida
flüssiger Lidschatten[M]
ombretto[M] liquido

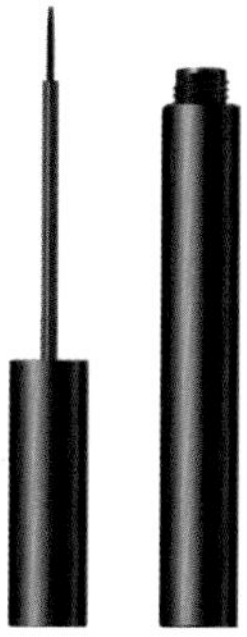

liquid eyeliner
eyeliner[M] liquide
delineador[M] de ojos[M] líquido
flüssiger Eyeliner[M]
eyeliner[M] liquido

mascara
mascara[M]
rímel[M]
Wimperntusche[F]
mascara[M]

Makeup

fan brush
pinceau [M] en éventail [M]
pincel [M] facial
Fächerpinsel [M]
pennello [M] a ventaglio [M]

lip brush
pinceau [M] pour les lèvres [F]
pincel [M] para labios [M]
Lippenpinsel [M]
pennello [M] per labbra [F]

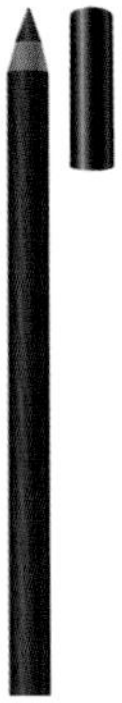

lip liner
crayon [M] contour [M] des lèvres [F]
perfilador [M] de labios [M]
Lippenkonturenstift [M]
matita [F] per le labbra [F]

eyebrow pencil
crayon [M] à sourcils [M]
lápiz [M] de cejas [M]
Augenbrauenstift [M]
matita [F] per sopracciglia [F]

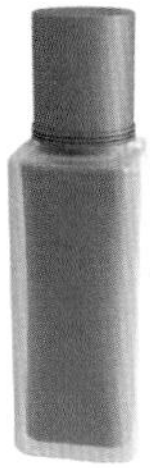

liquid foundation
fond [M] de teint [M] liquide
base [F] líquida
flüssiges Make-up [N]
fondotinta [M] fluido

Manicure and pedicure

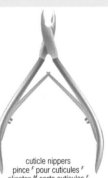

nail polish
vernis [M] à ongles [M]
esmalte [M] de uñas [F]
Nagellack [M]
smalto [M]

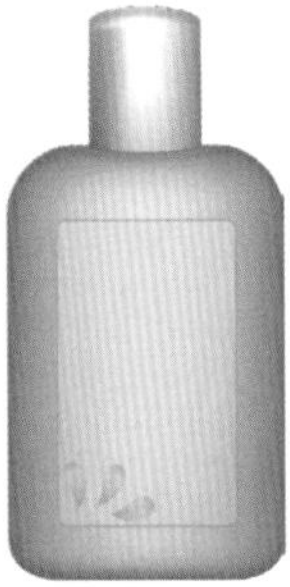

nail polish remover
dissolvant [M] à vernis [M] à ongles [M]
quitaesmalte [M]
Nagellackentferner [M]
acetone [M]

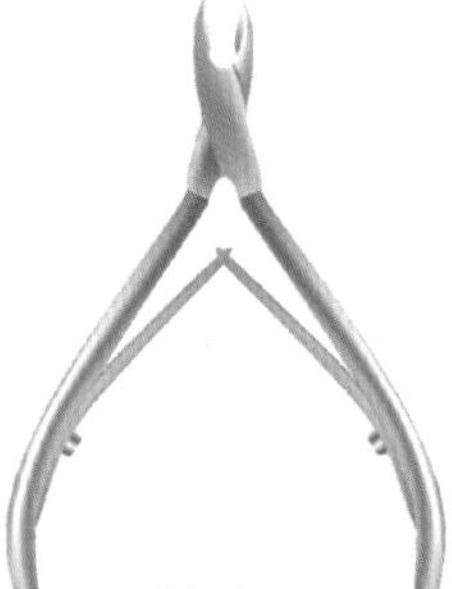

cuticle nippers
pince [F] pour cuticules [F]
alicates [M] corta cutículas [F]
Nagelhautzange [F]
tronchesina [F]

nail clippers
coupe-ongles [M]
cortaúñas [M]
Nagelzange [F]
tagliaunghie [M]

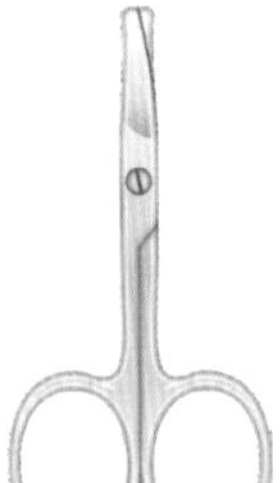

safety scissors
ciseaux [M] de sureté [F]
tijeras [F] de seguridad [F]
Sicherheitsschere [F]
forbici [F] di sicurezza [F]

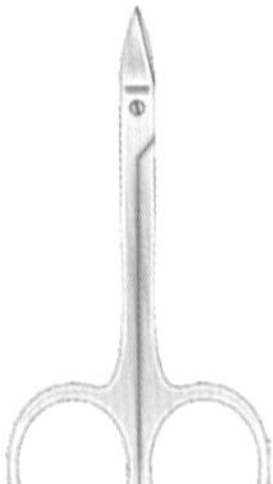

toenail scissors
ciseaux [M] pour ongles [M] des pieds [M]
tijeras [F] para pedicura [F]
Zehennagelschere [F]
forbici [F] per unghie [F] dei piedi [M]

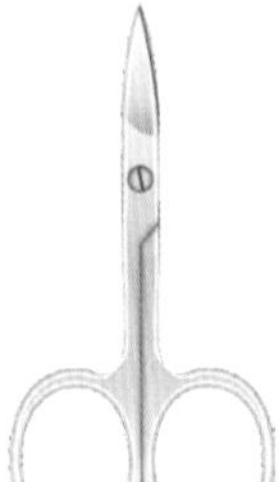

nail scissors
ciseaux [M] à ongles [M]
tijeras [F] para uñas [F]
Nagelschere [F]
forbicine [F] per unghie [F]

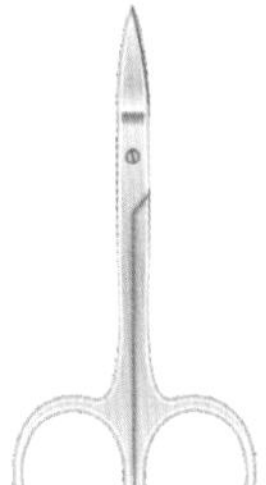

cuticle scissors
ciseaux [M] pour cuticules [F]
tijeras [F] para cutículas [F]
Nagelhautschere [F]
forbicine [F] per cuticole [F]

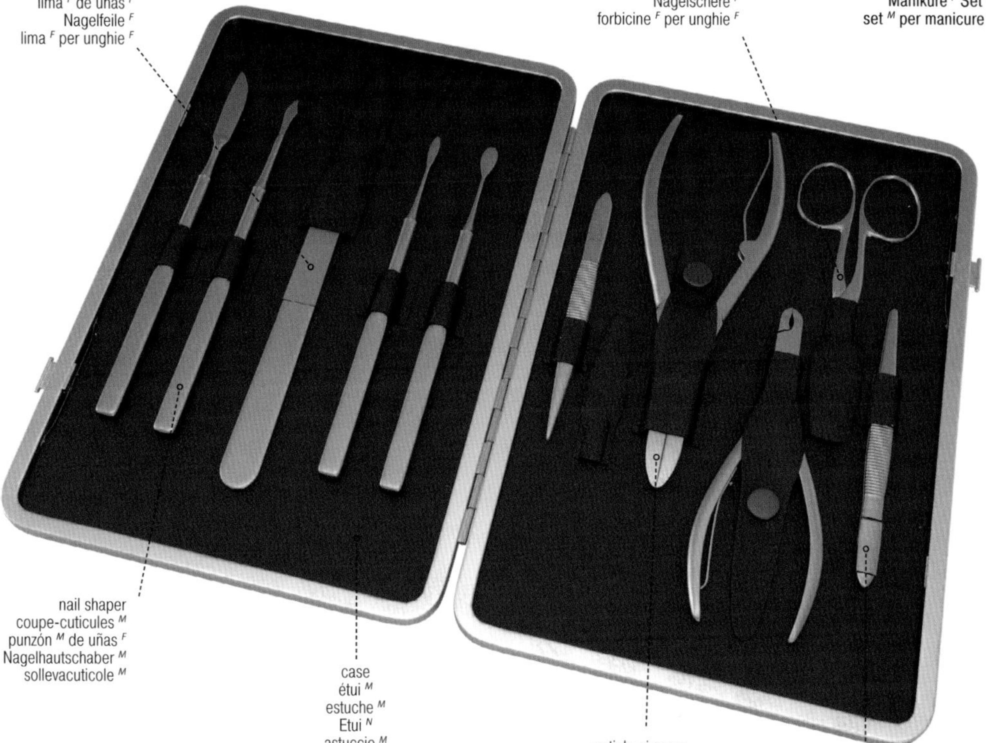
nail file
lime [F] à ongles [M]
lima [F] de uñas [F]
Nagelfeile [F]
lima [F] per unghie [F]
nail scissors
ciseaux [M] pour ongles [M]
tijeras [F] para uñas [F]
Nagelschere [F]
forbicine [F] per unghie [F]
manicure set
trousse [F] à manucure [F]
estuche [M]
Maniküre [F] Set [N]
set [M] per manicure [F]
nail shaper
coupe-cuticules [M]
punzón [M] de uñas [F]
Nagelhautschaber [M]
sollevacuticole [M]
case
étui [M]
estuche [M]
Etui [N]
astuccio [M]
cuticle nippers
ciseaux [M] de manucure [F]
cortacutículas [M]
Nagelhautzange [F]
tronchesina [F] per cuticole [F]
tweezers
pince [F] à épiler
pinza [F] para depilar las cejas [F]
Augenbraunenpinzette [F]
pinzette [F] per sopracciglia [F]

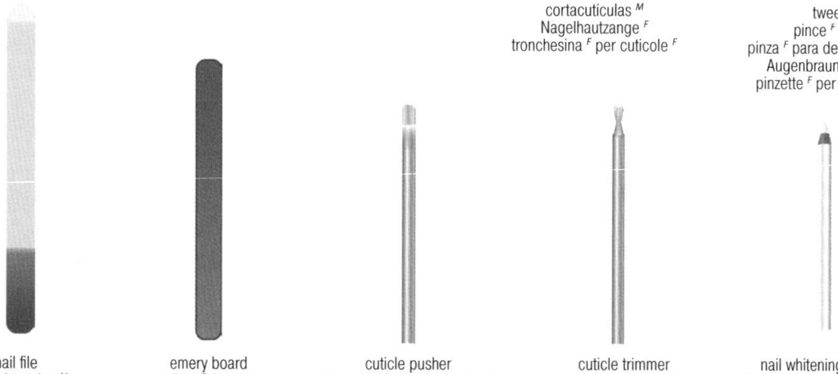
nail file
lime [F] à ongles [M]
lima [F] de uñas [F]
Nagelfeile [F]
lima [F] per unghie [F]
emery board
lime [F] émeri
lima [F] de cartón [M]
Sandblattfeile [F]
lima [F] in cartone [M]
cuticle pusher
poussoir [M] pour cuticules [F]
empujador [M] de cutículas [F]
Nagelhautschieber [M]
spingicuticole [M]
cuticle trimmer
coupe-cuticules [M]
cortacutículas [M]
Nagelhauttrimmer [M]
tagliacuticole [M]
nail whitening pencil
crayon [M] de blanchiment [M] des ongles [M]
lápiz [M] blanqueador [M] de uñas [F]
Nagelaufhellstift [M]
matita [F] sbiancante per unghie [F]

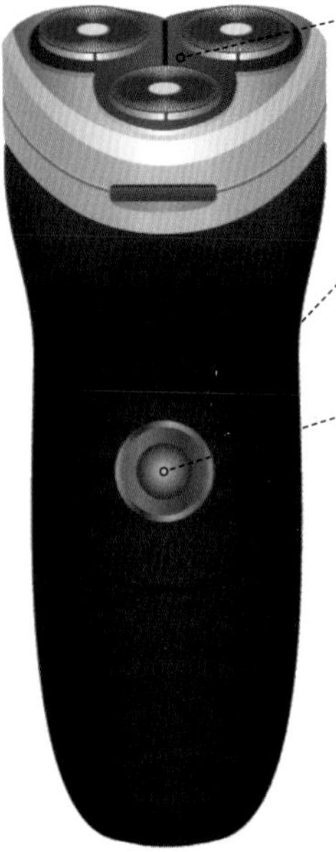

electric shaver
rasoir ^{M} électrique
máquina ^{F} de afeitar eléctrica
elektrischer Rasierapparat ^{M}
rasoio ^{M} elettrico

head
tête ^{F}
cabezal ^{M}
Rasierkopf ^{M}
testina ^{F}

housing
boîtier ^{M}
cuerpo ^{M}
Gehäuse ^{N}
corpo ^{M}

power button
bouton ^{M} d'alimentation ^{F}
botón ^{M} de encendido ^{M}
An-/Ausschalter ^{M}
pulsante ^{M} di accensione ^{F}

flexible power cord
cordon ^{M} d'alimention ^{F} flexible
cable ^{M} flexible
flexibles Netzkabel ^{N}
cavo ^{M} a spirale

shaving cream
crème ^{F} à raser
espuma ^{F} de afeitar
Rasierschaum ^{M}
schiuma ^{F} da barba ^{F}

disposable razor blade
lame ^{F} de rasoir ^{M} jetable
hojilla ^{F} de afeitar desechable
Einwegrasierklinge ^{F}
lametta ^{F} usa e getta

aftershave
lotion ^{F} après-rasage ^{M}
loción ^{M} para después del afeitado
Rasierwasser ^{N}
dopobarba ^{M}

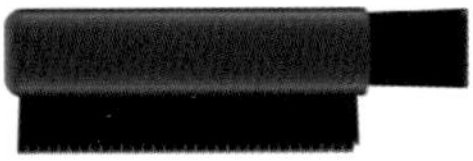

cleaning brush
brosse ^{F} de nettoyage ^{M}
cepillo ^{M} de limpieza ^{F}
Reinigungspinsel ^{M}
spazzolino ^{M} per rasoio ^{M}

disposable razor
rasoir ^{M} jetable
hojilla ^{F} de afeitar desechable
Einwegrasierer ^{M}
rasoio ^{M} usa e getta

men's razor
rasoir ^{M} pour hommes ^{M}
afeitadora ^{M} para hombre ^{M}
Herren-Rasierapparat ^{M}
rasoio ^{M} multilama ^{F}

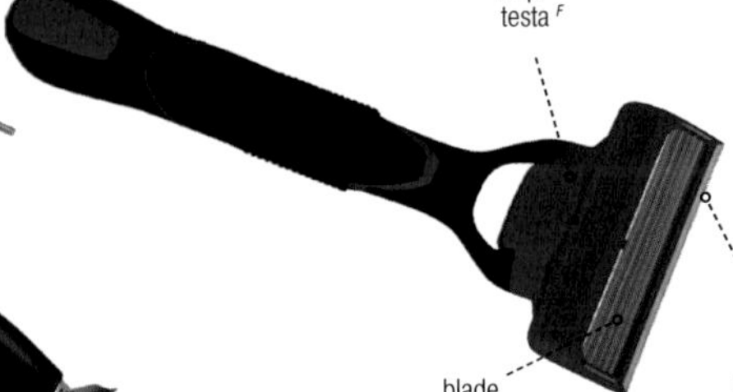

head
tête ^{F}
cabezal ^{M}
Kopf ^{M}
testa ^{F}

blade
lame ^{F}
cuchilla ^{F}
Klinge ^{F}
lama ^{F}

lubricating strip
bande ^{F} hydratante
banda ^{F} lubricante
Lubra-Strip ^{F} striscia ^{F}
lubrificante

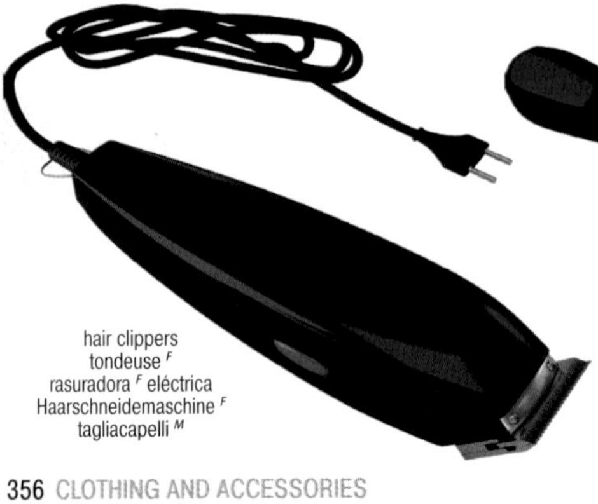

hair clippers
tondeuse ^{F}
rasuradora ^{F} eléctrica
Haarschneidemaschine ^{F}
tagliacapelli ^{M}

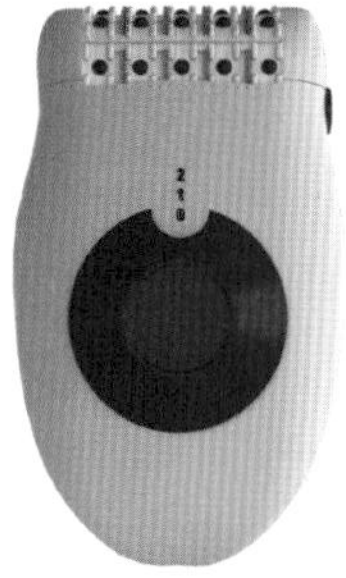

epilator
épilateur M
depiladora F
Epilierer M
epilatore M

shaving brush
blaireau M
brocha F de afeitar
Rasierpinsel M
pennello M da barba F

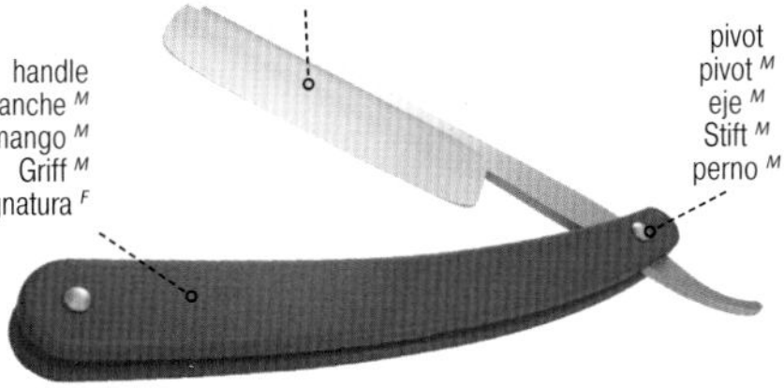

straight razor
rasoir M droit
navaja F de afeitar de barbero M
offenes Rasiermesser N
rasoio M da barbiere M

blade
lame F
hoja F
Klinge F
lama F

handle
manche M
mango M
Griff M
impugnatura F

pivot
pivot M
eje M
Stift M
perno M

Hair care

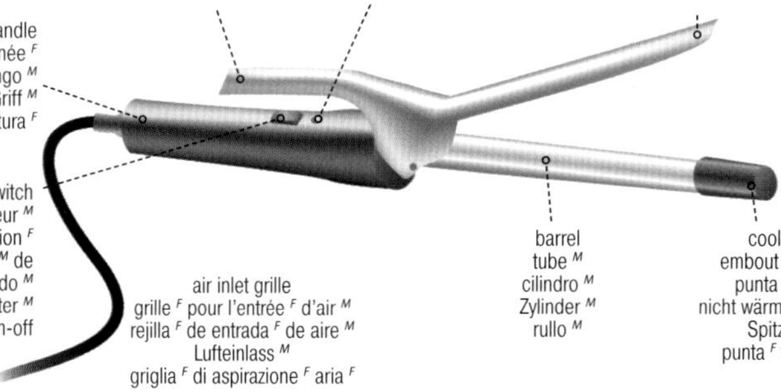

curling iron
fer M à friser
tenacillas F
Lockenstab M
ferro M arricciacapelli

clamp lever
levier M
palanca F
Hebel M für den Klemmbügel M
leva F della pinza F

indicator light
voyant M lumineux
indicador M de encendido M/apagado M
Kontrolllampe F
spia F luminosa

clamp
pince F
pinza F
Klemmbügel M
pinza F

handle
poignée F
mango M
geformter Griff M
impugnatura F

power switch
interrupteur M d'alimentation F
interruptor M de encendido M/apagado M
An-/Ausschalter M
interruttore M on-off

barrel
tube M
cilindro M
Zylinder M
rullo M

cool tip
embout M froid
punta F fría
nicht wärmeleitende Spitze F
punta F fredda

headband
serre-tête M
cintillo M
Haarreif M
cerchietto M

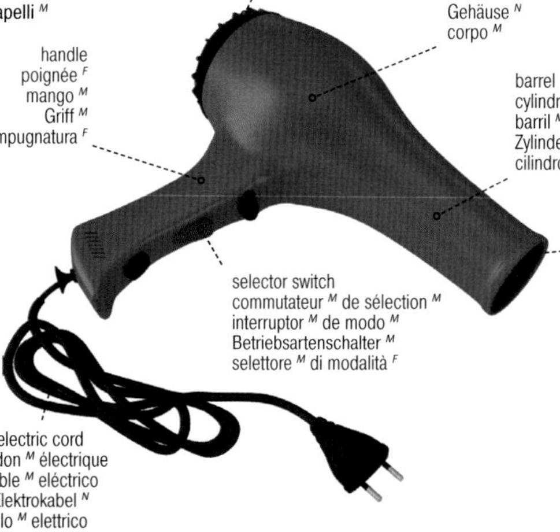

blow-dryer
sèche-cheveux M
secador M de pelo M
Haartrockner M
asciugacapelli M

air inlet grille
grille F pour l'entrée F d'air M
rejilla F de entrada F de aire M
Lufteinlass M
griglia F di aspirazione F aria F

fan housing
boîtier M du ventilateur M
cubierta F del ventilador M
Gehäuse N
corpo M

handle
poignée F
mango M
Griff M
impugnatura F

barrel
cylindre M
barril M
Zylinder M
cilindro M

air outlet grille
grille F de sortie F d'air M
rejilla F de salida F de aire
Düse F
bocchetta M

selector switch
commutateur M de sélection M
interruptor M de modo M
Betriebsartenschalter M
selettore M di modalità F

electric cord
cordon M électrique
cable M eléctrico
Elektrokabel N
filo M elettrico

barrette
barrette F
pasador M para el pelo M
Haarspange F
fermacapelli M

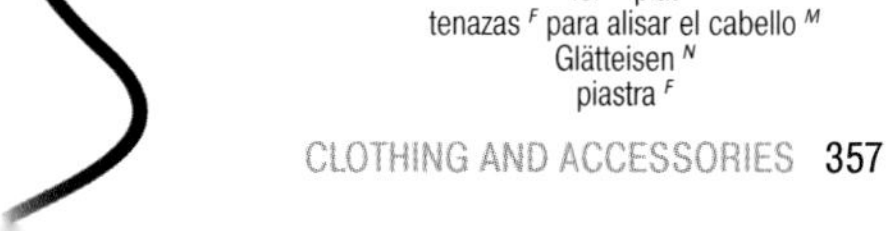

straightening iron
fer M plat
tenazas F para alisar el cabello M
Glätteisen N
piastra F

self-grip roller
bigoudi ^{M} autoagrippant
rulo ^{M} regulable
Klettlockenwickler ^{M}
bigodino ^{M} adesivo

roller
bigoudi ^{M}
rulo ^{M}
Lockenwickler ^{M}
bigodino ^{M}

hair tie
serre-cheveux ^{M}
goma ^{F} para el pelo ^{M}
Haargummi $^{M/N}$
elastico ^{M} per capelli ^{M}

hair gel
gel ^{M} pour les cheveux ^{M}
gel ^{M} para el pelo ^{M}
Haargel ^{N}
gel ^{M}

hair spray
fixatif ^{M}
laca ^{F}
Haarspray ^{N}
lacca ^{F}

hair conditioner
revitalisant ^{M}
acondicionador ^{M}
Haarspülung ^{F}
balsamo ^{M}

hair dye
colorant ^{M} pour cheveux ^{M}
tinte ^{M} para el pelo ^{M}
Haarfarbe ^{F}
tintura ^{F} per capelli ^{M}

shampoo
shampooing ^{M}
champú ^{M}
Shampoo ^{N}
shampoo ^{M}

mousse
mousse ^{F}
espuma ^{F}
Schaumfestiger ^{M}
spuma ^{F}

single-edged thinning scissors
ciseaux ^{M} dentés à effiler à simple tranchant ^{M}
tijeras ^{F} de entresacar dentadas con hoja ^{F} única
einseitig gezahnte Effilierschere ^{F}
forbici ^{F} per sfoltire a doppia lama ^{F} dentata

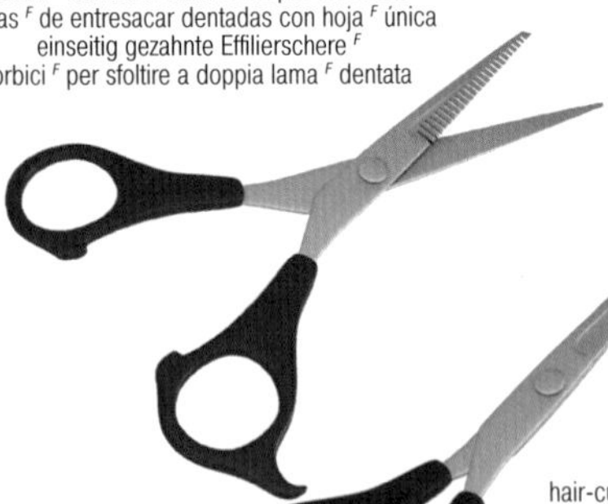

hair-cutting scissors
ciseaux ^{M} de coupe ^{F}
tijeras ^{F} de peluquería ^{F}
Haarschneideschere ^{F}
forbici ^{F} per tagliare i capelli

double-edged thinning scissors
ciseaux ^{M} dentés à effiler à double tranchant ^{M}
tijeras ^{F} para rebajar con doble hoja ^{F}
zweiseitig gezahnte Effilierschere ^{F}
forbici ^{M} per sfoltire a doppia lama ^{F}

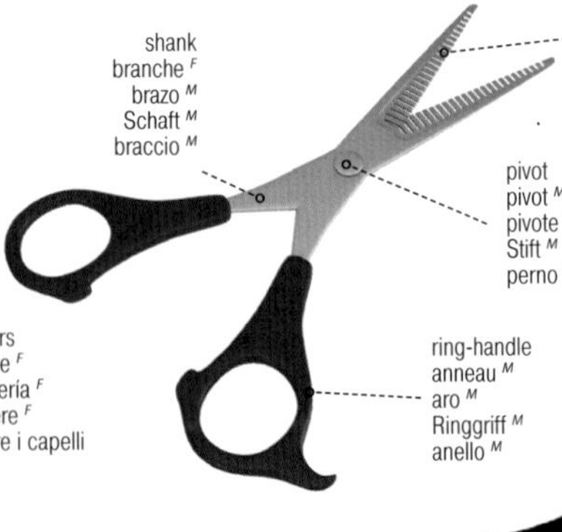
tooth
dent F
diente M
Zahn M
dente M
shank
branche F
brazo M
Schaft M
braccio M
pivot
pivot M
pivote M
Stift M
perno M
ring-handle
anneau M
aro M
Ringgriff M
anello M

bobby pin
pince ^{F} à cheveux ^{M}
horquilla ^{F}
Haarklemme ^{F}
ferrettino ^{M} per capelli ^{M}

hairpin
épingle ^{F} à cheveux ^{M}
horquilla ^{F} de moño ^{M}
Haarnadel ^{F}
forcina ^{F}

alligator hair clip
pince ^{F} à cheveux ^{M}
pinza ^{F} para el pelo ^{M}
Haarquetschklemme ^{F}
molletta ^{F}

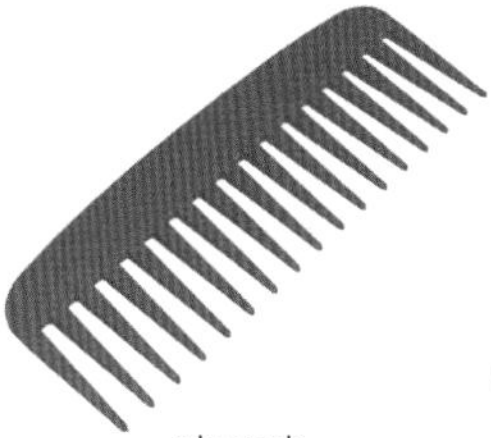

rake comb
peigne [M] râteau [M]
peine [M] rastrillo
Rechenkamm [M]
pettine [M] a denti [M] larghi

quill brush
brosse [F] anglaise
cepillo [M] redondo
Massage-Haarbürste [F]
spazzola [F] con punte [F]

vent brush
brosse-arraignée [F]
cepillo [M] esqueleto [M]
Skelettbürste [F]
spazzola [F] forata

round brush
brosse [F] ronde
cepillo [M] redondo
Rundbürste [F]
spazzola [F] rotonda

tint brush
pinceau [M] pour coloration [F]
brocha [F] para teñir
Färbepinsel [M]
pennello [M] per colore [M]

wave clip
pince [F] pour cheveux [M]
pinza [F] para el pelo [M]
Haarklammer [F]
pinza [F] per capelli [M]

hair pick
peigne [M] fourchette [F]
peine [M] Afro
Afro-Kamm [M]
pettine [M] afro

paddle brush
brosse [F] plate
cepillo [M] plano
Flachbürste [F]
spazzola [F] piatta

tail comb
peigne [M] à queue [F]
peine [M] púa [F]
Stielkamm [M]
pettine [M] a coda [F]

pitchfork comb
peigne [M] fourche
peine [M] ahuecador
Gabelkamm [M]
pettine [M] a forchetta [F]

barber comb
peigne [M] de barbier [M]
peine [M] de peluquero [M]
Barbierkamm [M]
pettine [M] da barbiere [M]

teaser comb
peigne [M] à crêper
peine [M] para cardado [M]
Toupierkamm [M]
pettine [M] per cotonare

battery-operated toothbrush
brosse [F] à dents [F] électrique
cepillo [M] de dientes [M] eléctrico
elektrische Zahnbürste [F]
spazzolino [M] elettrico

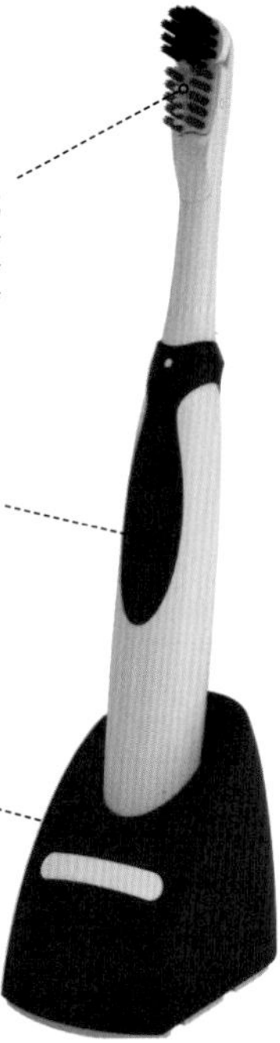

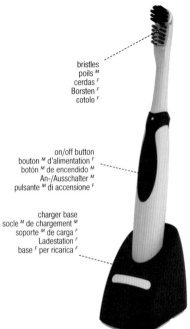

bristles
poils [M]
cerdas [F]
Borsten [F]
cotolo [F]

on/off button
bouton [M] d'alimentation [F]
botón [M] de encendido [M]
An-/Ausschalter [M]
pulsante [M] di accensione [F]

charger base
socle [M] de chargement [M]
soporte [M] de carga [F]
Ladestation [F]
base [F] per ricarica [F]

toothbrush
brosse [F] à dents [F]
cepillo [M] de dientes [M]
Zahnbürste [F]
spazzolino [M] da denti [M]

gum stimulator
stimulateur [M] de gencives [F]
estimulador [M] de encías [F]
Zahnfleischstimulator [M]
stimolatore [M] gengivale

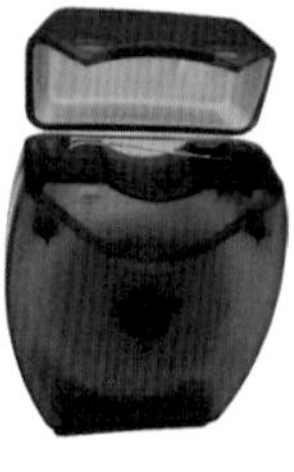

dental floss
soie [F] dentaire [F]
hilo [M] dental
Zahnseide [F]
filo [M] interdentale

toothpaste
dentifrice [M]
pasta [F] dentífrica
Zahnpasta [F]
dentifricio [M]

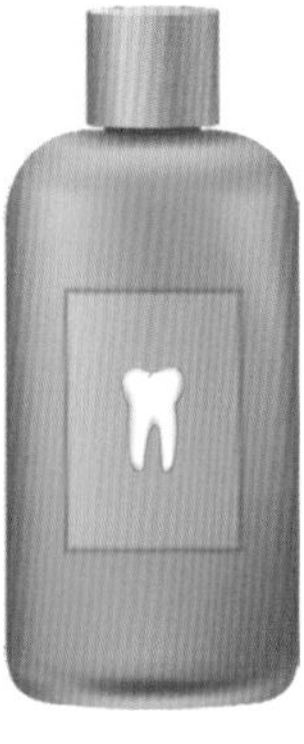

mouthwash
rince-bouche [M]
enjuague [M] bucal
Mundwasser [N]
colluttorio [M]

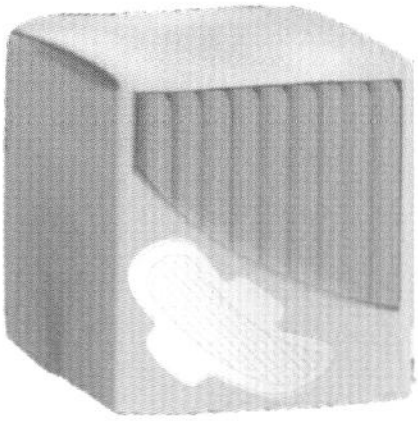

sanitary pad
serviette [F] hygiénique
toallas [F] sanitarias
Damenbinde [F]
assorbenti [M]

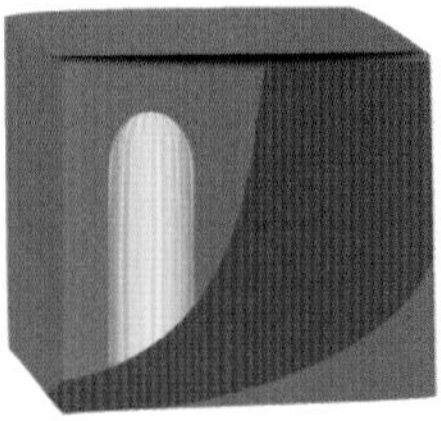

tampon
tampon [M]
tampones [M]
Tampon [M]
assorbenti [M] interni

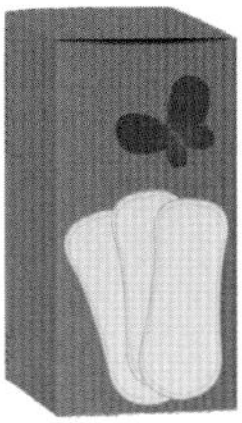

pantyliner
protège-dessous [M]
salva slips [M]
Slipeinlage [F]
salvaslip [M]

wipe
lingette [F]
toallitas [F]
Feuchttuch [N]
salviettine [F]

natural sponge
éponge [F] naturelle
esponja [F] natural
Naturschwamm [M]
spugna [F] naturale

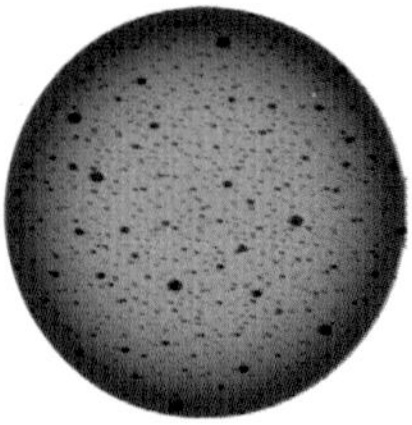

synthetic sponge
éponge [F] synthétique
esponja [F] sintética
Schaumstoffschwamm [M]
spugna [F] sintetica

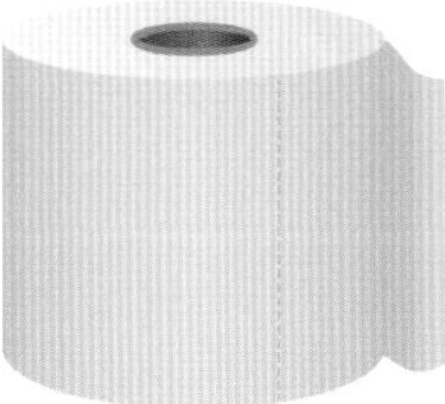

toilet paper
papier [M] de toilette [F]
papel [M] higiénico
Toilettenpapier [N]
carta [F] igienica

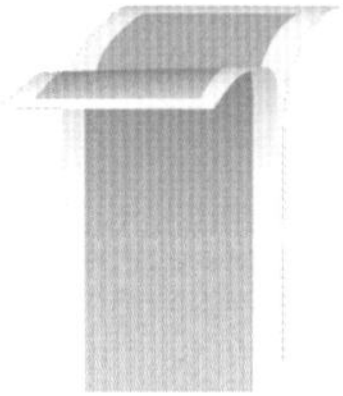

wax strip
bande [F] de cire [F]
bandas [F] de cera [F]
Wachsstreifen [M]
strisce [F] depilatorie

soap dish
porte-savon [M]
jabonera [F]
Seifenschale [F]
portasapone [M]

soap
savon [M]
jabón [M]
Seife [F]
saponetta [F]

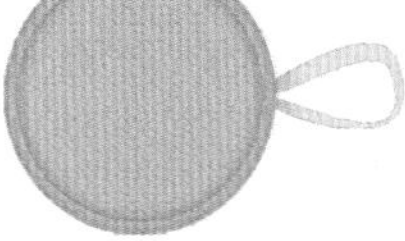

loofah
luffa [M]
esponja [F] vegetal
Luffa [F]
spugna [F] vegetale

condom
préservatif [M]
preservativo [M]
Kondom [M/N]
preservativo [M]

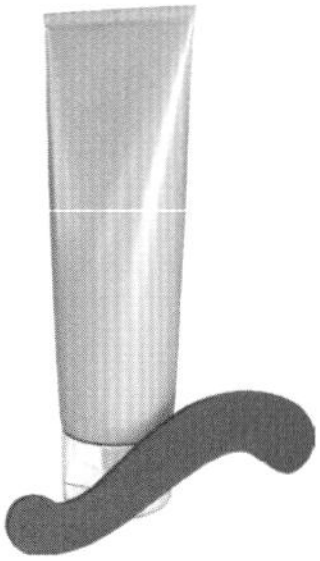

depilatory cream
crème [F] dépilatoire
crema [F] depilatoria
Enthaarungscreme [F]
crema [F] depilatoria

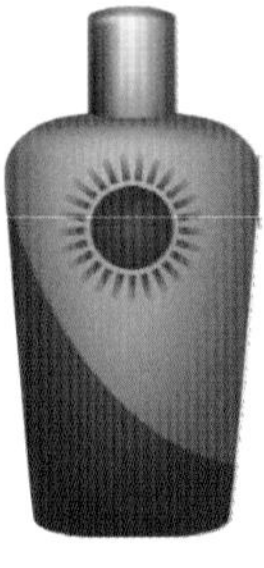

sunscreen
écran [M] solaire
protector [M] solar
Sonnencreme [F]
protezione [F] solare

bronzer
lotion [F] de bronzage [M]
bronceador [M] corporal
Körperbräuner [M]
abbronzante [M] per il corpo [M]

liquid soap
savon [M] liquide
jabón [M] líquido
Flüssigseife [F]
sapone [M] liquido

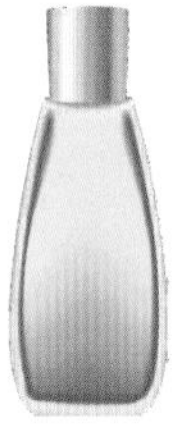

eau de parfum
eau [F] de parfum [M]
eau de parfum [F]
Eau de Parfum [N]
profumo [M]

bubble bath
bain [M] moussant
baño [M] de espuma [F]
Badeschaum [M]
bagnoschiuma [M]

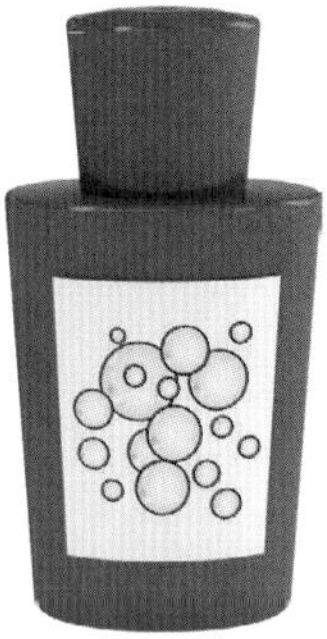

shower gel
gel [M] douche
gel [M] de ducha [F]
Duschgel [N]
gel [M] doccia [F]

spray-on deodorant
désodorisant [M] en aérosol [M]
desodorante [M] en espray [M]
Deospray [N]
deodorante [M] spray [M]

eau de toilette
eau [F] de toilette [F]
eau de toilette [F]
Eau de Toilette [N]
eau [F] de toilette [F]

nail brush
brosse [F] à ongles [M]
cepillo [M] de baño [M]
Nagelbürste [F]
spazzolino [M] da unghie [F]

moisturizer
hydratant [M]
humectante [M]
Feuchtigkeitscreme [F]
idratante [M]

solid deodorant
désodorisant [M]
desodorante [M] sólido
Deodorant [N]
deodorante stick [M]

bath bomb
bombe [F] pour le bain [M]
bomba [F] de baño [M]
Badebombe [F]
bombe [F] da bagno [M]

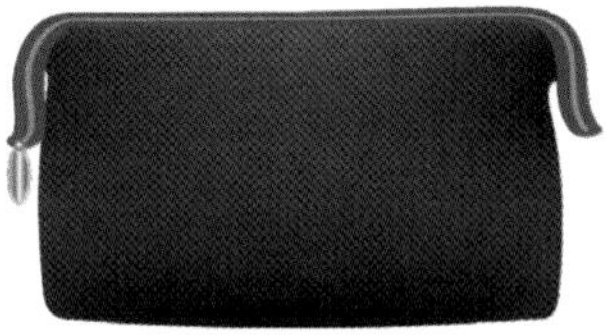

toiletry bag
trousse [F] de toilette [F]
bolsa [F] de aseo [M]
Kulturbeutel [M]
astuccio [M] da toilette [F]

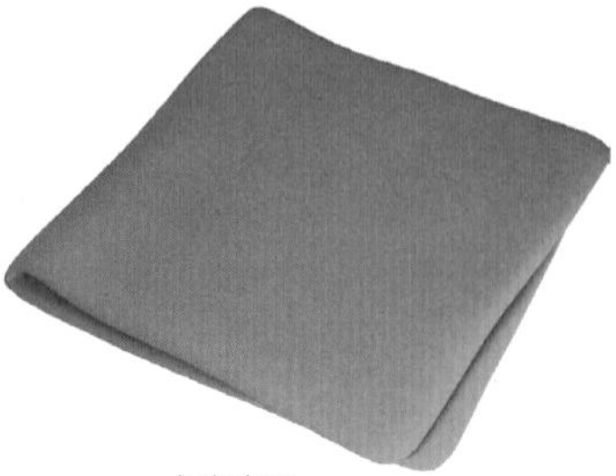

bath sheet
drap [M] de bain [M]
toalla [F] de baño [M] grande
Badelaken [N]
asciugamano [M] da bagno [M]

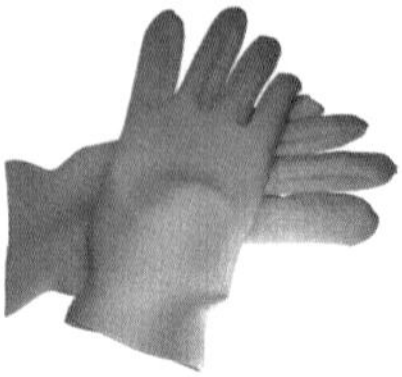

exfoliating glove
gant [M] exfoliant
guante [M] de masaje [M]
Peelinghandschuh [M]
guanto [M] esfoliante [M]

bath towel
serviette [F] de bain [M]
toalla [F] de baño [M]
Badetuch [N]
telo [M] da bagno [M]

washing symbols
lavage [M]
símbolos [M] de lavandería [F]
Waschsymbole [N]
Lavaggio [M]

drying symbols
séchage [M]
símbolos [M] de secado [M]
Trocknersymbole [N]
Asciugatura [F]

do not wash
ne pas laver
no lavar
Nicht waschen
Non lavare

hand wash
laver à la main [F]
lavar a mano [M]
Handwäsche [F]
lavare a mano [F]

wash in warm water
laver à l'eau [F] tiède
lavar en agua [F] tibia
In warmen Wasser [N] waschen
lavare in acqua [F] calda

tumble dry at any heat
sécher par culbutage [M] à toute température [F]
secadora [F] a cualquier temperatura [F]
Symbol für Trommeltrocknen
asciugare a qualsiasi temperatura [F]

tumble dry at low heat
sécher par culbutage [M] à basse température [F]
secar en secadora [F] a baja temperatura [F]
Trommeltrocknen (niedrige Temperatur)
asciugare a temperatura [F] bassa

tumble dry at medium heat
sécher par culbutage [M] à moyenne température [F]
secar en secadora [F] a temperatura media [F]
Trommeltrocknen (mittlere Tempeartur)
asciugare a temperatura [F] media

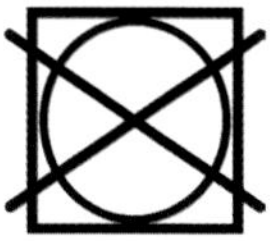

do not tumble dry
ne pas sécher par culbutage [M]
no secar en la secadora [F]
Nicht im Trommeltrockner trocknen
non asciugare in asciugatrice [F]

ironing symbols
repassage [M]
símbolos [M] de planchado [M]
Bügelsymbole [N]
stiratura [F]

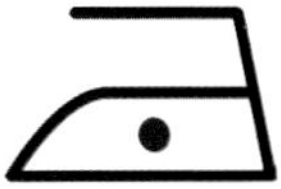

iron at low setting
repasser à basse température [F]
planchar a baja temperatura [F]
Bügeln mit geringer Temperatur
stirare a bassa [F] temperatura [F]

iron at medium setting
repasser à moyenne température [F]
planchar a temperatura [F] media
Bügeln mit mittlerer Temperatur
stirare a media [F] temperatura [F]

iron at high setting
repasser à haute température [F]
planchar a alta temperatura [F]
Bügeln mit hoher Temperatur
stirare ad alta [F] temperatura [F]

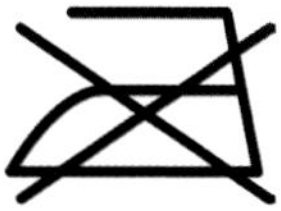

do not iron
ne pas repasser
no planchar
Nicht bügeln
non stirare

bleaching symbols
blanchiment [M]
símbolos [M] de uso [M] de lejía [F]
Bleichsymbole [N]
candeggio [M]

use any bleach
utiliser tout agent [M] de blanchiment [M]
se puede usar lejía [F]
Jegliches Bleichen erlaubt
candeggio [M] consentito

use non-chlorine bleach only
utiliser un agent [M] de blanchiment [M] non chloré seulement
solo lejía sin cloro [M]
Nur chlorfreie Bleiche
solo candeggio [M] senza cloro [M]

do not bleach
ne pas utiliser d'agent [M] de blanchiment [M]
no usar lejía [F]
Bleichen nicht erlaubt
Non candeggiare

dry cleaning
nettoyage [M] à sec
limpieza [F] al seco [M]
Chemische Reinigung [F]
lavaggio [M] a secco

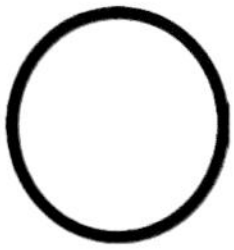

dry clean
faire nettoyer à sec
lavar en seco [M]
Symbol für professionelle Reinigung
lavare a secco [M]

do not dry clean
ne pas faire nettoyer à sec
no lavar en seco
Nicht chemisch reinigen
non lavare a secco [M]

SOCIETY

parents and children
parents [M] et enfants [M]
padres [M] e hijos [M]
Eltern und Kinder [N]
genitori [M] e figli [M]

parents
parents [M]
padres [M]
Eltern
genitori [M]

father
père [M]
padre [M]
Vater [M]
padre [M]

mother
mère [F]
madre [F]
Mutter [F]
madre [F]

daughter
fille [F]
hija [F]
Tochter [F]
figlia [F]

son
fils [M]
hijo [M]
Sohn [M]
figlio [M]

children
enfants [M]
niños [M]
Kinder [N]
bambini [M]

grandparents and grandchildren
grands-parents [M] et petits-enfants [M]
abuelos [M] y nietos [M]
Großeltern und Enkelkinder [N]
nonni [M] e nipoti [M]

grandparents
grands-parents [M]
abuelos [M]
Großeltern
nonni [M]

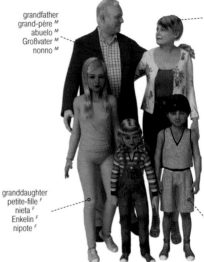

grandfather
grand-père [M]
abuelo [M]
Großvater [M]
nonno [M]

grandmother
grand-mère [F]
abuela [F]
Großmutter [F]
nonna [F]

granddaughter
petite-fille [F]
nieta [F]
Enkelin [F]
nipote [F]

grandson
petit-fils [M]
nieto [M]
Enkel [M]
nipote [M]

grandchildren
petits-enfants [M]
nietos [M]
Enkelkinder [N]
nipoti [M]

twins
jumeaux [M]
gemelos [M]
Zwillinge [M]
gemelle [F]

baby
bébé [M]
bebé [M]
Baby [N]
bambino [M]

brothers and sisters
frères [M] et sœurs [F]
hermanos [M] y hermanas [F]
Brüder [M] und Schwestern [F]
fratelli [M] e sorelle [F]

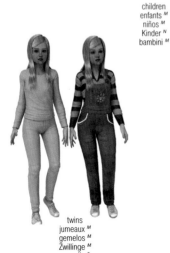

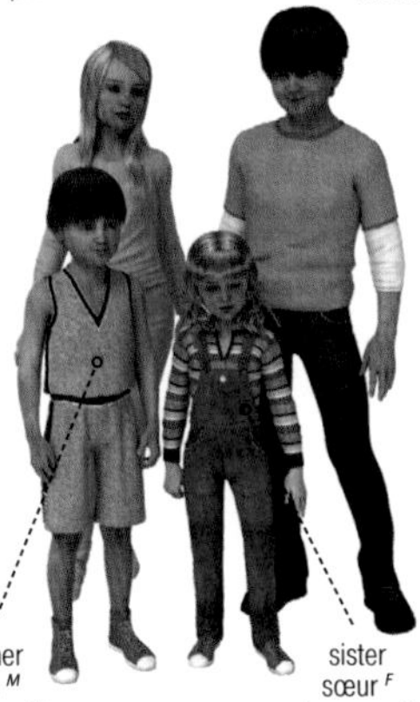

brother
frère [M]
hermano [M]
Bruder [M]
fratello [M]

sister
sœur [F]
hermana [F]
Schwester [F]
sorella [F]

stages of life: female
les étapes [F] de la vie [F]: femme [F]
etapas [F] de la vida [F]: mujeres [F]
Lebensabschnitte [M]: Frau [F]
fasi [F] della vita [F]: femmine [F]

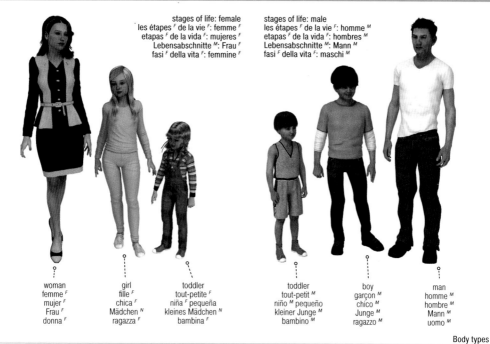

stages of life: male
les étapes [F] de la vie [F]: homme [M]
etapas [F] de la vida [F]: hombres [M]
Lebensabschnitte [M]: Mann [M]
fasi [F] della vita [F]: maschi [M]

woman
femme [F]
mujer [F]
Frau [F]
donna [F]

girl
fille [F]
chica [F]
Mädchen [N]
ragazza [F]

toddler
tout-petite [F]
niña [F] pequeña
kleines Mädchen [N]
bambina [F]

toddler
tout-petit [M]
niño [M] pequeño
kleiner Junge [M]
bambino [M]

boy
garçon [M]
chico [M]
Junge [M]
ragazzo [M]

man
homme [M]
hombre [M]
Mann [M]
uomo [M]

Body types

Types [M] de morphologies [F] | Tipos [M] de cuerpos [M] | Verschiedene Körpertypen [M] | Tipi [M] di corporatura [F]

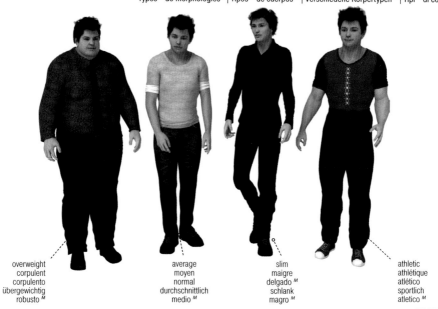

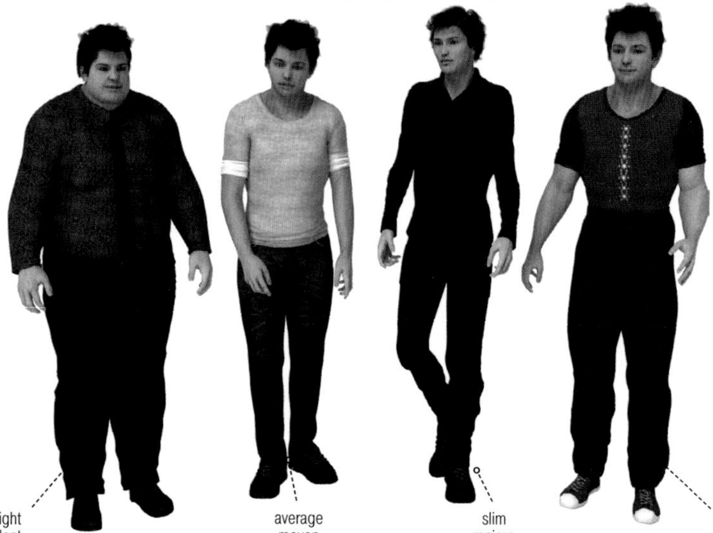

overweight
corpulent
corpulento
übergewichtig
robusto [M]

average
moyen
normal
durchschnittlich
medio [M]

slim
maigre
delgado [M]
schlank
magro [M]

athletic
athlétique
atlético
sportlich
atletico [M]

classroom
salle ^{F} de classe ^{F}
salón ^{M} de clase ^{F}
Schulklassenzimmer ^{N}
Aula ^{F} scolastica

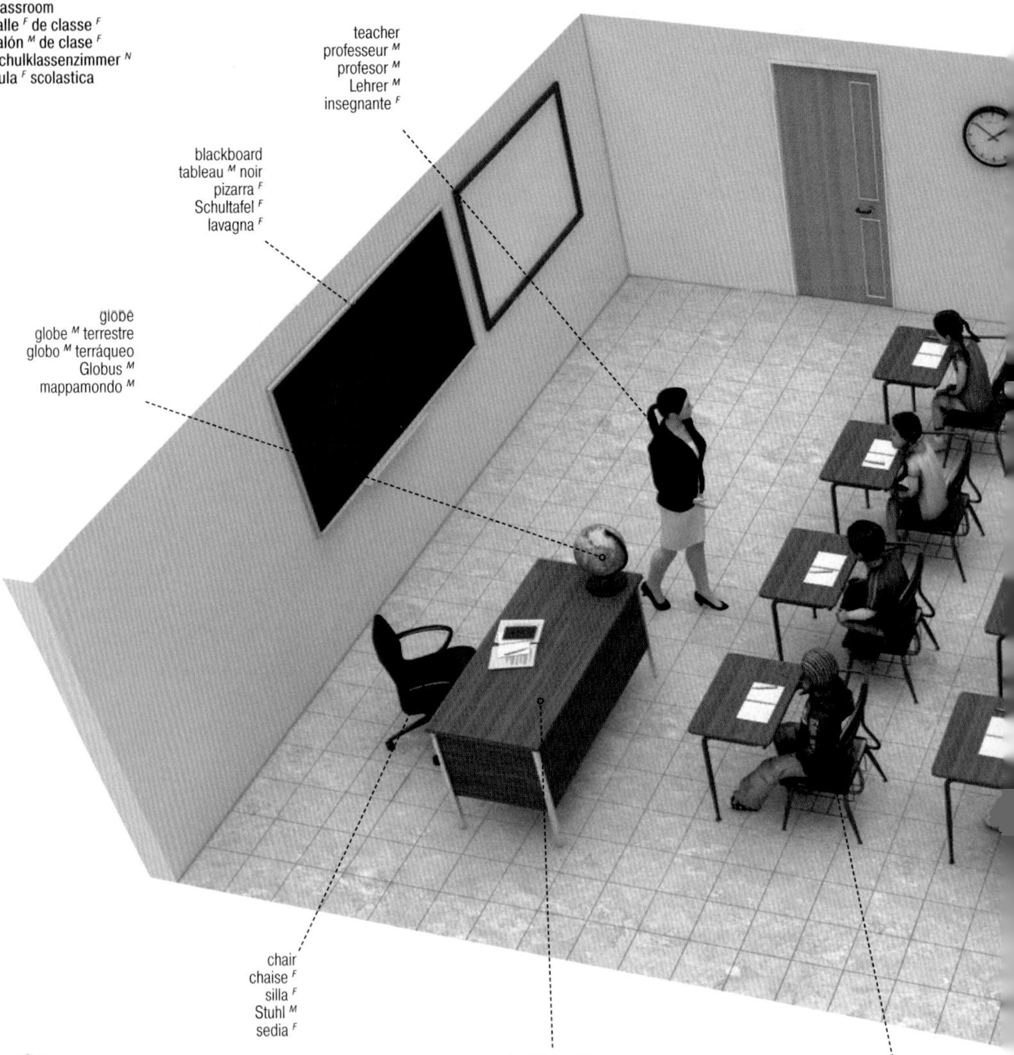

teacher
professeur ^{M}
profesor ^{M}
Lehrer ^{M}
insegnante ^{F}

blackboard
tableau ^{M} noir
pizarra ^{F}
Schultafel ^{F}
lavagna ^{F}

globe
globe ^{M} terrestre
globo ^{M} terráqueo
Globus ^{M}
mappamondo ^{M}

chair
chaise ^{F}
silla ^{F}
Stuhl ^{M}
sedia ^{F}

teacher's desk
bureau ^{M} du professeur ^{M}
mesa ^{F} del profesor ^{M}
Lehrerpult ^{N}
cattedra ^{F}

student
élève ^{M}
estudiante ^{M}
Schüler ^{M}
studente ^{M}

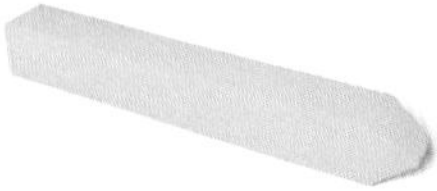

chalk
craie ^{F}
tiza ^{F}
Kreide ^{F}
gesso ^{M}

bulletin board
panneau M d'affichage M
tablón M de anuncios M
Anschlagtafel F
bacheca F
bookcase
bibliothèque F
librero M
Bücherregal N
libreria F
desk
bureau M
escritorio M
Schulbank F
banco M

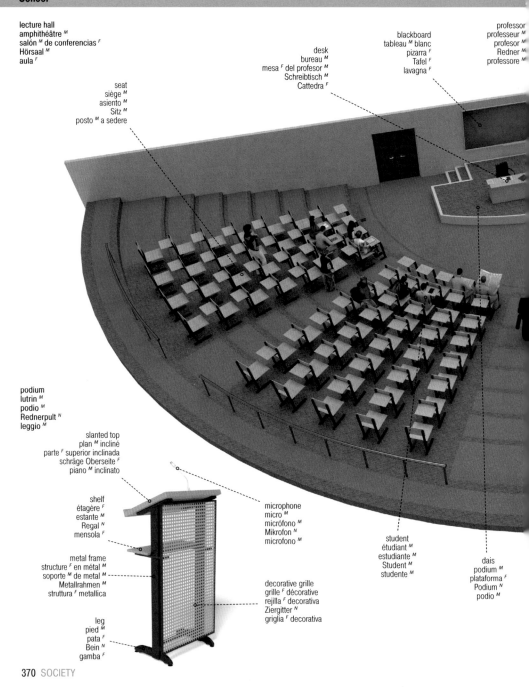

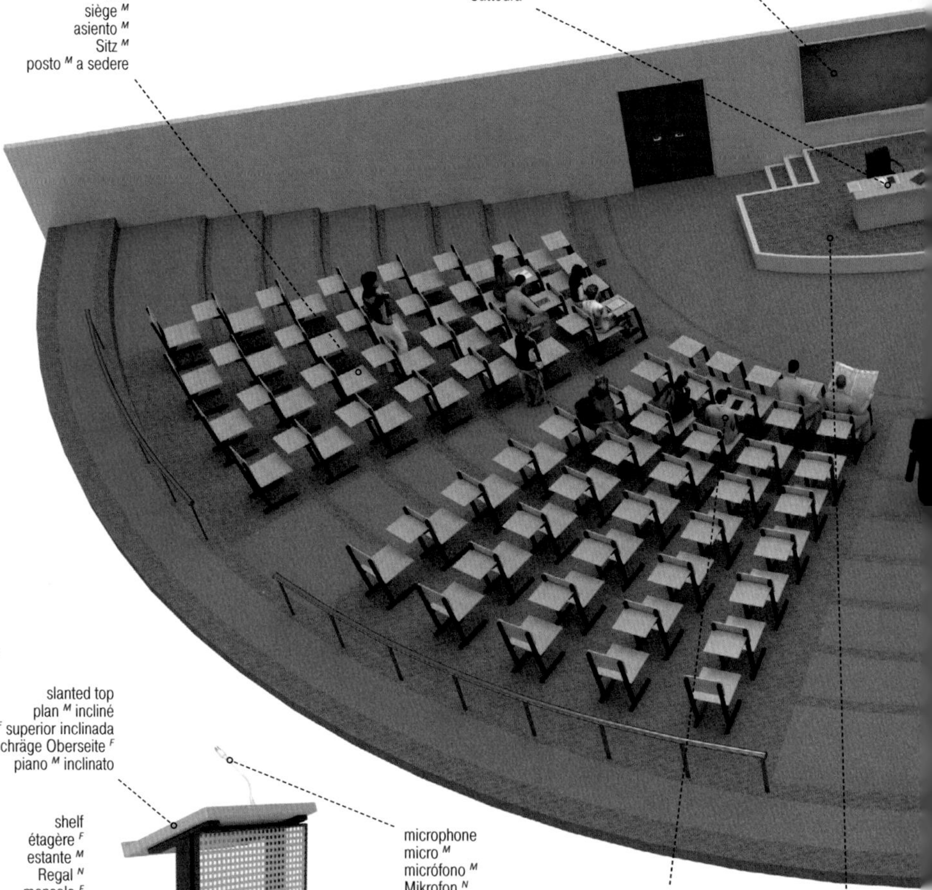
lecture hall
amphithéâtre [M]
salón [M] de conferencias [F]
Hörsaal [M]
aula [F]
professor
professeur [M]
profesor [M]
Redner [M]
professore [M]
blackboard
tableau [M] blanc
pizarra [F]
Tafel [F]
lavagna [F]
desk
bureau [M]
mesa [F] del profesor [M]
Schreibtisch [M]
Cattedra [F]
seat
siège [M]
asiento [M]
Sitz [M]
posto [M] a sedere
student
étudiant [M]
estudiante [M]
Student [M]
studente [M]
dais
podium [M]
plataforma [F]
Podium [N]
podio [M]

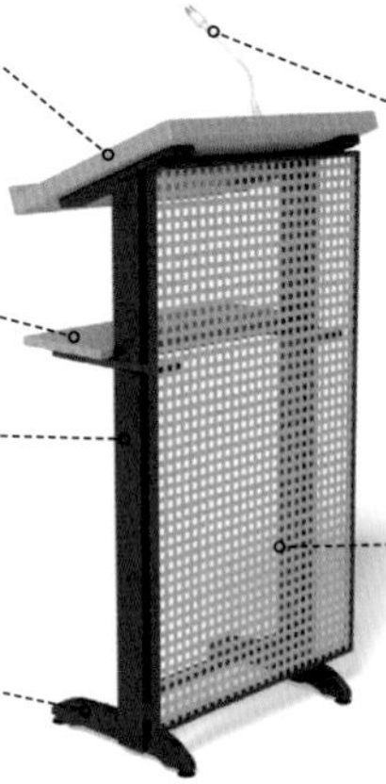
podium
lutrin [M]
podio [M]
Rednerpult [N]
leggio [M]
slanted top
plan [M] incliné
parte [F] superior inclinada
schräge Oberseite [F]
piano [M] inclinato
microphone
micro [M]
micrófono [M]
Mikrofon [N]
microfono [M]
shelf
étagère [F]
estante [M]
Regal [N]
mensola [F]
metal frame
structure [F] en métal [M]
soporte [M] de metal [M]
Metallrahmen [M]
struttura [F] metallica
decorative grille
grille [F] décorative
rejilla [F] decorativa
Ziergitter [N]
griglia [F] decorativa
leg
pied [M]
pata [F]
Bein [N]
gamba [F]

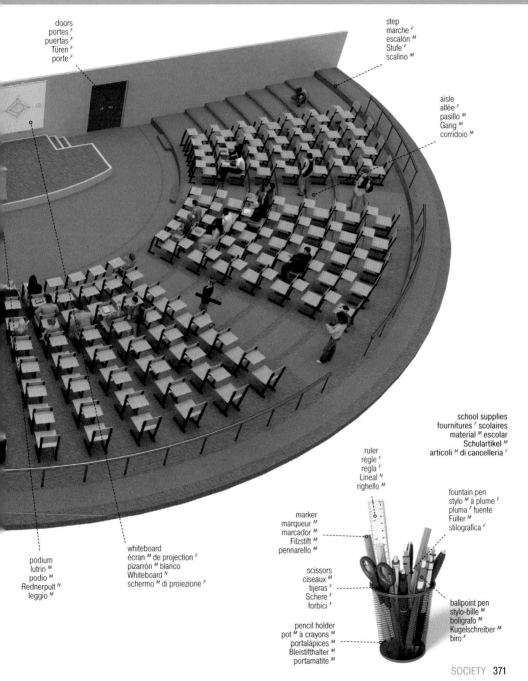

doors
portes [F]
puertas [F]
Türen [F]
porte [F]
step
marche [F]
escalón [M]
Stufe [F]
scalino [M]
aisle
allée [F]
pasillo [M]
Gang [M]
corridoio [M]
podium
lutrin [M]
podio [M]
Rednerpult [N]
leggio [M]
whiteboard
écran [M] de projection [F]
pizarrón [M] blanco
Whiteboard [N]
schermo [M] di proiezione [F]

school supplies
fournitures [F] scolaires
material [M] escolar
Schulartikel [M]
articoli [M] di cancelleria [F]

ruler
règle [F]
regla [F]
Lineal [N]
righello [M]
fountain pen
stylo [M] à plume [F]
pluma [F] fuente
Füller [M]
stilografica [F]
marker
marqueur [M]
marcador [M]
Filzstift [M]
pennarello [M]
scissors
ciseaux [M]
tijeras [F]
Schere [F]
forbici [F]
ballpoint pen
stylo-bille [M]
bolígrafo [M]
Kugelschreiber [M]
biro [F]
pencil holder
pot [M] à crayons [M]
portalápices [M]
Bleistifthalter [M]
portamatite [M]

residential neighborhood
quartier M résidentiel
área F residencial
Wohngebiet N
zona F residenziale

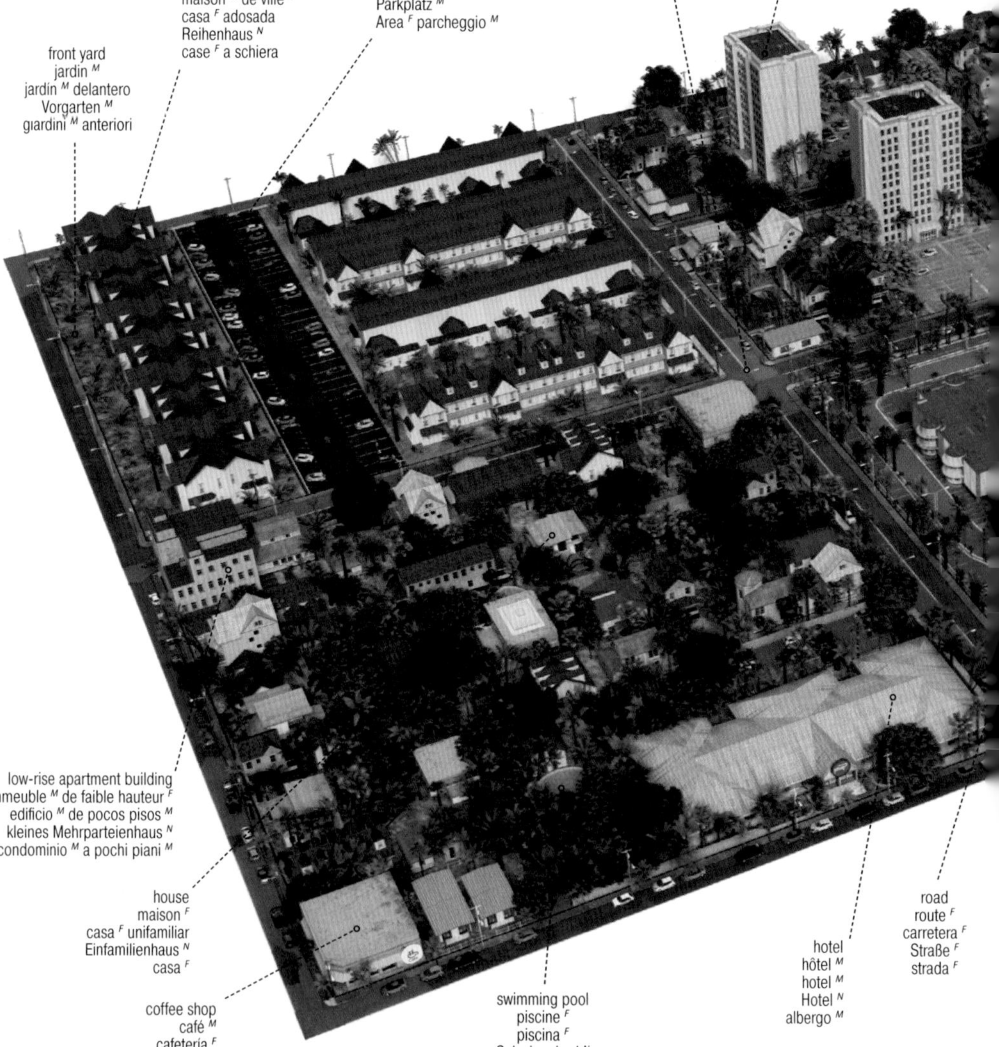
high-rise apartment building
tour F d'habitation F
bloque M de apartamentos M
Wohnhochhaus N
grattacielo-condominio M
intersection
intersection F
intersección F
Kreuzung F
incrocio M
parking lot
parc M de stationnement M
playa F de estacionamiento M
Parkplatz M
Area F parcheggio M
townhouse
maison M de ville F
casa F adosada
Reihenhaus N
case F a schiera
front yard
jardin M
jardín M delantero
Vorgarten M
giardini M anteriori
low-rise apartment building
immeuble M de faible hauteur F
edificio M de pocos pisos M
kleines Mehrparteienhaus N
condominio M a pochi piani M
house
maison F
casa F unifamiliar
Einfamilienhaus N
casa F
coffee shop
café M
cafetería F
Café N
bar M
swimming pool
piscine F
piscina F
Schwimmbad N
piscina F
hotel
hôtel M
hotel M
Hotel N
albergo M
road
route F
carretera F
Straße F
strada F

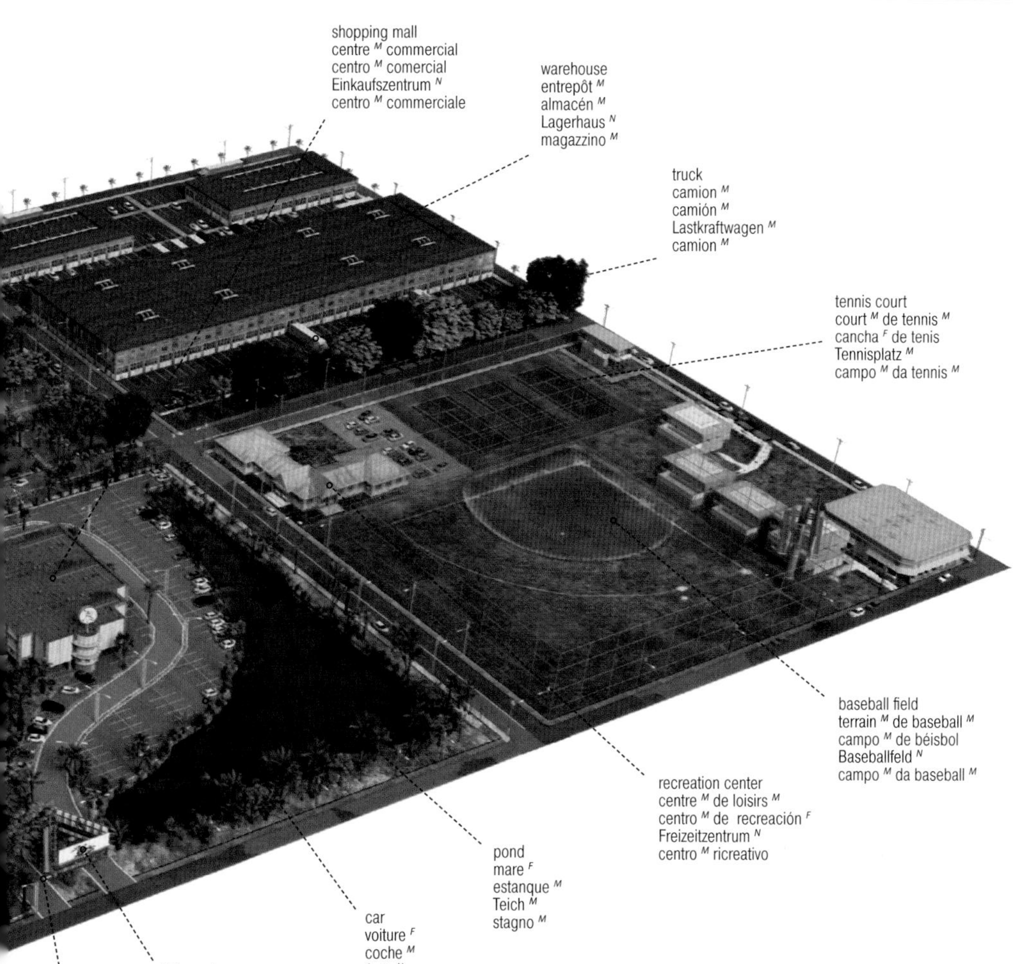
shopping mall
centre ^{M} commercial
centro ^{M} comercial
Einkaufszentrum ^{N}
centro ^{M} commerciale
warehouse
entrepôt ^{M}
almacén ^{M}
Lagerhaus ^{N}
magazzino ^{M}
truck
camion ^{M}
camión ^{M}
Lastkraftwagen ^{M}
camion ^{M}
tennis court
court ^{M} de tennis ^{M}
cancha ^{F} de tenis
Tennisplatz ^{M}
campo ^{M} da tennis ^{M}
baseball field
terrain ^{M} de baseball ^{M}
campo ^{M} de béisbol
Baseballfeld ^{N}
campo ^{M} da baseball ^{M}
recreation center
centre ^{M} de loisirs ^{M}
centro ^{M} de recreación ^{F}
Freizeitzentrum ^{N}
centro ^{M} ricreativo
pond
mare ^{F}
estanque ^{M}
Teich ^{M}
stagno ^{M}
car
voiture ^{F}
coche ^{M}
Auto ^{N}
auto ^{F}
billboard
panneau ^{M} d'affichage ^{M}
valla ^{F} publicitaria
Werbetafel ^{F}
cartellone ^{M} pubblicitario
street light
éclairage ^{M} public
farola ^{F}
Straßenbeleuchtung ^{F}
lampione ^{M}

trash can
poubelle ^{F}
papelera ^{F}
Mülleimer ^{M}
cestino ^{M} dei rifiuti ^{M}

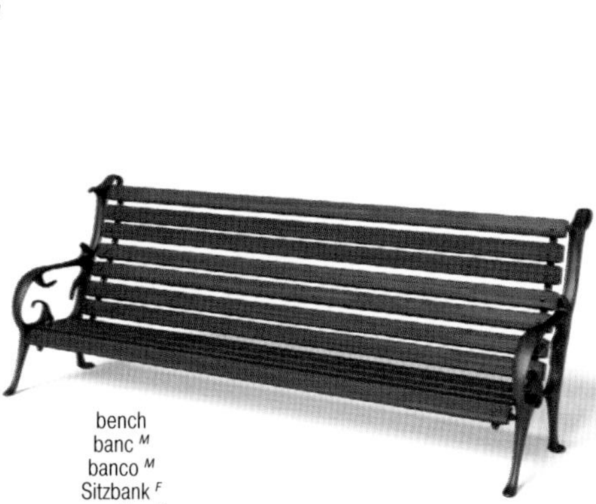

bench
banc ^{M}
banco ^{M}
Sitzbank ^{F}
panchina ^{F}

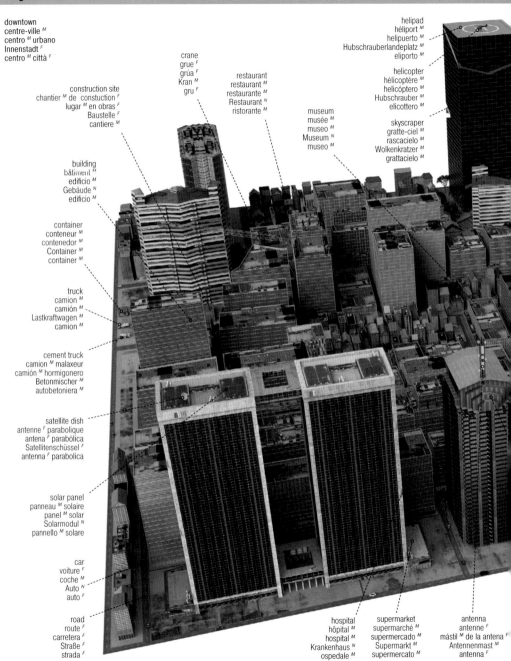

downtown
centre-ville M
centro M urbano
Innenstadt F
centro M città F
crane
grue F
grúa F
Kran M
gru F
construction site
chantier M de constuction F
lugar M en obras F
Baustelle F
cantiere M
restaurant
restaurant M
restaurante M
Restaurant N
ristorante M
helipad
héliport M
helipuerto M
Hubschrauberlandeplatz M
eliporto M
helicopter
hélicoptère M
helicóptero M
Hubschrauber M
elicottero M
museum
musée M
museo M
Museum N
museo M
skyscraper
gratte-ciel M
rascacielo M
Wolkenkratzer M
grattacielo M
building
bâtiment M
edificio M
Gebäude N
edificio M
container
conteneur M
contenedor M
Container M
container M
truck
camion M
camión M
Lastkraftwagen M
camion M
cement truck
camion M malaxeur
camión M hormigonero
Betonmischer M
autobetoniera M
satellite dish
antenne F parabolique
antena F parabólica
Satellitenschüssel F
antenna F parabolica
solar panel
panneau M solaire
panel M solar
Solarmodul N
pannello M solare
car
voiture F
coche M
Auto N
auto F
road
route F
carretera F
Straße F
strada F
hospital
hôpital M
hospital M
Krankenhaus N
ospedale M
supermarket
supermarché M
supermercado M
Supermarkt M
supermercato M
antenna
antenne F
mástil M de la antena F
Antennenmast M
antenna F

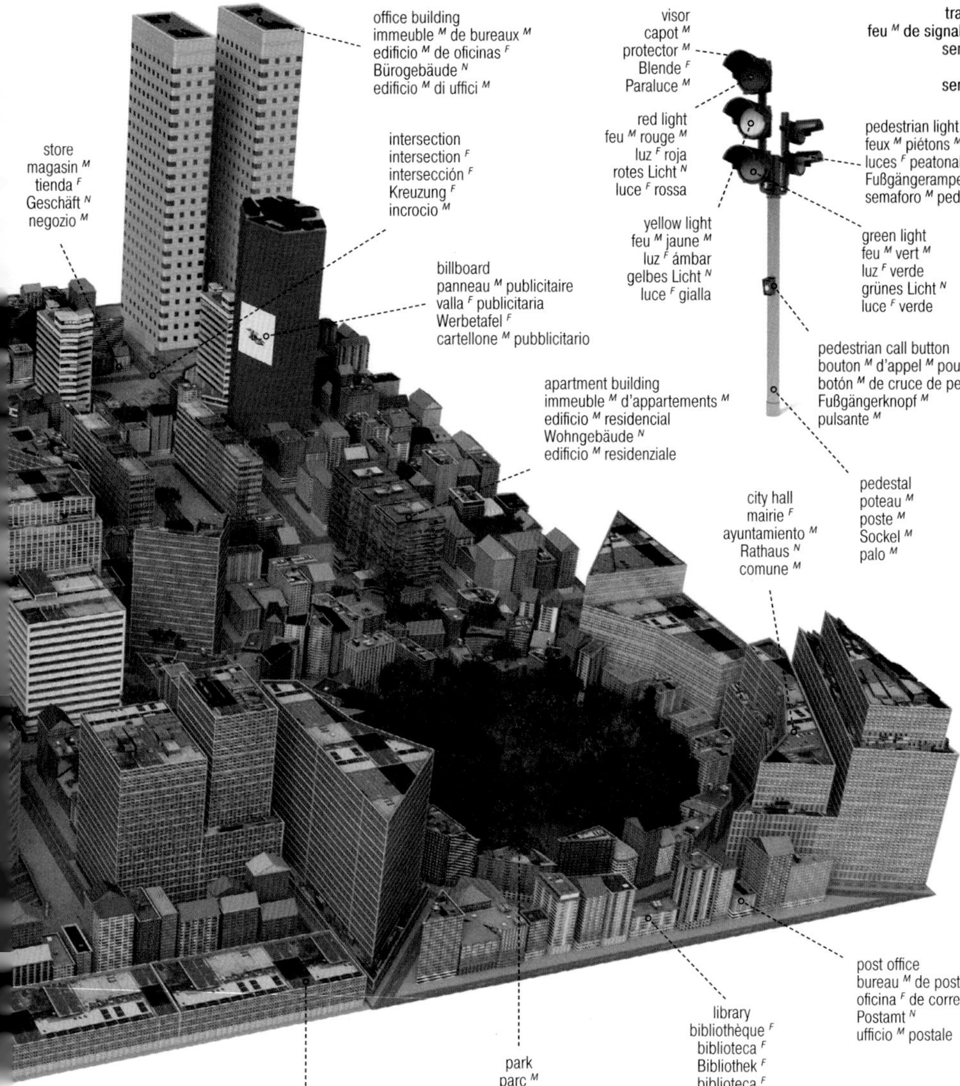
office building
immeuble M de bureaux M
edificio M de oficinas F
Bürogebäude N
edificio M di uffici M
visor
capot M
protector M
Blende F
Paraluce M
traffic light
feu M de signalisation F
semáforo M
Ampel F
semaforo M
store
magasin M
tienda F
Geschäft N
negozio M
intersection
intersection F
intersección F
Kreuzung F
incrocio M
red light
feu M rouge M
luz F roja
rotes Licht N
luce F rossa
pedestrian light
feux M piétons M
luces F peatonales
Fußgängerampel F
semaforo M pedonale
yellow light
feu M jaune M
luz F ámbar
gelbes Licht N
luce F gialla
green light
feu M vert M
luz F verde
grünes Licht N
luce F verde
billboard
panneau M publicitaire
valla F publicitaria
Werbetafel F
cartellone M pubblicitario
pedestrian call button
bouton M d'appel M pour piétons M
botón M de cruce de peatones M
Fußgängerknopf M
pulsante M
apartment building
immeuble M d'appartements M
edificio M residencial
Wohngebäude N
edificio M residenziale
pedestal
poteau M
poste M
Sockel M
palo M
city hall
mairie F
ayuntamiento M
Rathaus N
comune M
post office
bureau M de poste F
oficina F de correos M
Postamt N
ufficio M postale
library
bibliothèque F
biblioteca F
Bibliothek F
biblioteca F
park
parc M
parque M
Park M
parco M
factory
usine F
fábrica F
Fabrik F
fabbrica F
penthouse
penthouse M
penthouse M
Penthaus N
attico M

shopping mall
centre ^{M} commercial
centro ^{M} comercial
Einkaufszentrum ^{N}
centro ^{M} commerciale

cosmetics store
boutique ^{F} de produits ^{M} de beauté ^{F}
tienda ^{F} de cosméticos ^{M}
Kosmetikgeschäft ^{N}
negozio ^{M} di cosmetici ^{M}

maintenance worker
préposé ^{M} à l'entretien ^{M}
empleado ^{M} de mantenimiento ^{M}
Wartungsarbeiter ^{M}
custode ^{M}

sporting goods store
magasin ^{M} d'articles ^{M} de sport ^{M}
tienda ^{F} de artículos ^{M} deportivos
Sportgeschäft ^{N}
negozio ^{M} di articoli ^{M} sportivi

jewelry store
bijouterie ^{F}
joyería ^{F}
Juweliergeschäft ^{N}
gioielleria ^{F}

skylight
lucarne ^{F}
tragaluz ^{M}
Dachflächenfenster ^{N}
lucernario ^{M}

travel agency
agence ^{F} de voyage ^{M}
agencia ^{F} de viajes ^{M}
Reisebüro ^{N}
agenzia ^{F} di viaggi ^{M}

railing
garde-corps ^{M}
barandilla ^{F}
Geländer ^{N}
ringhiera ^{F}

potted plant
plante ^{F} en pot
planta ^{F} decorativa
Topfpflanze ^{F}
pianta ^{F} decorativa

bridge
passerelle ^{F}
puente ^{M}
Brücke ^{F}
ponte ^{M}

clothing store
magasin ^{M} de vêtements ^{M}
tienda ^{F} de ropa ^{F}
Bekleidungsgeschäft ^{N}
negozio ^{M} di abbigliamento ^{M}

housewares store
magasin ^{M} d'articles ^{M} ménagers
tienda ^{F} de artículos ^{M} para el hogar ^{M}
Haushaltswarengeschäft ^{F}
negozio ^{M} di articoli ^{M} per la casa ^{F}

vending machine
distributrice ^{F} automatique
máquina ^{F} expendedora
Verkaufsautomat ^{M}
distributore ^{M} automatico

security guard
agent ^{M} de sécurité ^{F}
vigilante ^{M}
Sicherheitsbediensteter ^{M}
addetto ^{M} alla sicurezza ^{F}

bench
banc ^{M}
banco ^{M}
Sitzbank ^{F}
panchina ^{F}

-70%

menswear store
magasin ^{M} de vêtements ^{M} pour homme ^{M}
tienda ^{F} de ropa ^{F} de hombre ^{M}
Herrenausstatter ^{M}
negozio ^{M} di abbigliamento ^{M} maschile

department store
grand magasin ^{M}
tienda ^{F} por departamentos ^{M}
Kaufhaus ^{N}
supermercato ^{M}

trash can
poubelle ^{F}
cesto ^{M} de basura ^{F}
Mülleimer ^{M}
cestino ^{M} per la spazzatura ^{F}

customer
cliente ^{F}
cliente ^{M}
Kunde ^{M}
cliente ^{M}

information stand
kiosque ^{M} d'informatior
puesto ^{M} de informació
Informationsstand ^{M}
putno ^{M} informazioni

toy store
magasin ^{M} de jouets ^{M}
juguetería ^{F}
Spielzeuggeschäft ^{N}
negozio ^{M} di giocattoli ^{M}

electronics store
magasin ^{M} d'électronique ^{F}
tienda ^{F} de electrónica ^{F}
Elektronikgeschäft ^{N}
negozio ^{M} di computer ^{M}

lighting store
magasin ^{M} de luminaires ^{M}
tienda ^{F} de lámparas ^{F}
Beleuchtungsgeschäft ^{N}
negozio ^{M} di illuminazione ^{F}

information display
kiosque ^{M} d'information ^{F}
panel ^{M} de información ^{F}
Informationsanzeige ^{F}
display ^{M} informazioni ^{F}

coffee shop
café ^{M}
cafetería ^{F}
Café ^{N}
bar ^{M}

newsstand
kiosque ^{M} à journaux ^{M}
puesto ^{M} de venta ^{F} de periódicos ^{M}
Zeitungskiosk ^{M}
edicola ^{F}

automated teller machine (ATM)
guichet ^{M} automatique bancaire
cajero ^{M} automático
Geldautomat ^{M}
bancomat ^{M}

bakery
boulangerie ^{F}
panadería ^{F}
Bäckerei ^{F}
panetteria ^{F}

table and chairs
table ^{F} et chaises ^{F}
mesa ^{F} y sillas ^{F}
Tisch ^{M} und Stühle ^{M}
tavolo ^{M} e sedie ^{F}

baby-changing room
table ^{F} à langer
cuarto ^{M} para cambiar al bebé ^{M}
Wickelraum ^{M}
stanza ^{F} per cambio neonati ^{M}

restroom
toilettes ^{F}
baño ^{M}
Toilette ^{F}
bagno ^{M}

janitor
concierge ^{M}
empleado ^{M} de limpieza ^{M}
Hausmeisterin ^{F}
addetto ^{M} alle pulizie ^{F}

supermarket
supermarché [M]
supermercado [M]
Supermarkt [M]
supermercato [M]

baked goods
rayon [M] boulangerie [F]
productos [M] de panadería [F]
Backwaren [F]
prodotti [M] da forno [M]

drinks fridge
boissons [F] réfrigérées
nevera [F] de bebidas [F]
Getränkekühlschrank [M]
frigo [M] bevande [F]

display freezer
rayon [M] surgelés [M]
exhibidor [M] de comida [F] congelada
Gefrievitrine [F]
banco [M] freezer [M]

prepared foods
plats [M] préparés
mostrador [M] de comida [F] preparada
Fertiggerichte [N]
gastronomia [F]

locker
consigne [F] automatique
casillero [M]
Schließfach [N]
deposito [M] bagagli a cassette

frozen foods
produits [M] congelés
productos [M] congelados
Tiefkühlkost [F]
surgelati [M]

drinks
boissons [F]
bebidas [F]
Getränke [N]
bevande [F]

security guard
agent [M] de sécurité [M]
vigilante [M] de seguridad [F]
Sicherheitswachmann [M]
addetto [M] alla sicurezza [F]

conveyor belt
tapis [M] roulant
banda [F] transportadora
Fließband [N]
nastro [M] trasportatore

cashier
caissière [F]
cajero [M]
Kassiererin [F]
cassiera [F]

chair
chaise [F]
silla [F]
Stuhl [M]
sedia [F]

counter
comptoir [M]
mostrador [M]
Theke [F]
bancone [M]

basket
panier [M]
cesta [F]
Warenkorb [M]
cestino [M]

customer
cliente [F]
cliente [M]
Kundin [F]
cliente [F]

railing
rampe [F]
barandilla [F]
Geländer [N]
barra [F] divisoria

store entrance/exit
entrée [F]/sortie [F] du magasin [M]
entrada [F]/salida [F] de la tienda [F]
Ladeneingang /Ausgang [M]
ingresso [M]/uscita [F] del negozio [M]

anti-theft sensor
portique [M] anti-vol
sensor [M] antirrobo
Antidiebstahlsensor [M]
sensore [M] antifurto

fruits and vegetables
fruits [M] et légumes [M]
frutas [F] y vegetales [M]
Obst [N] und Gemüse [N]
frutta [F] e verdura [F]

shopping cart
chariot [M]
carrito [M] de la compra [F]
Einkaufswagen [M]
carrello [M]

magazine stand
porte-revues [M]
estante [M] para revistas [F]
Zeitschriftenständer [M]
portariviste [M]

newspaper and magazin
présentoir à revues [M]
journaux [M]
estante [M] de periódicos
revistas [F]
Regal [N] für Zeitungen [F]
Zeitschriften [F]
giornali [M] e riviste

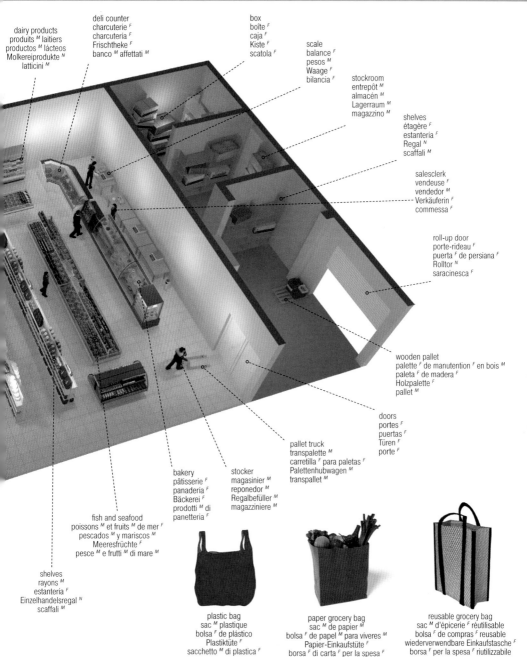

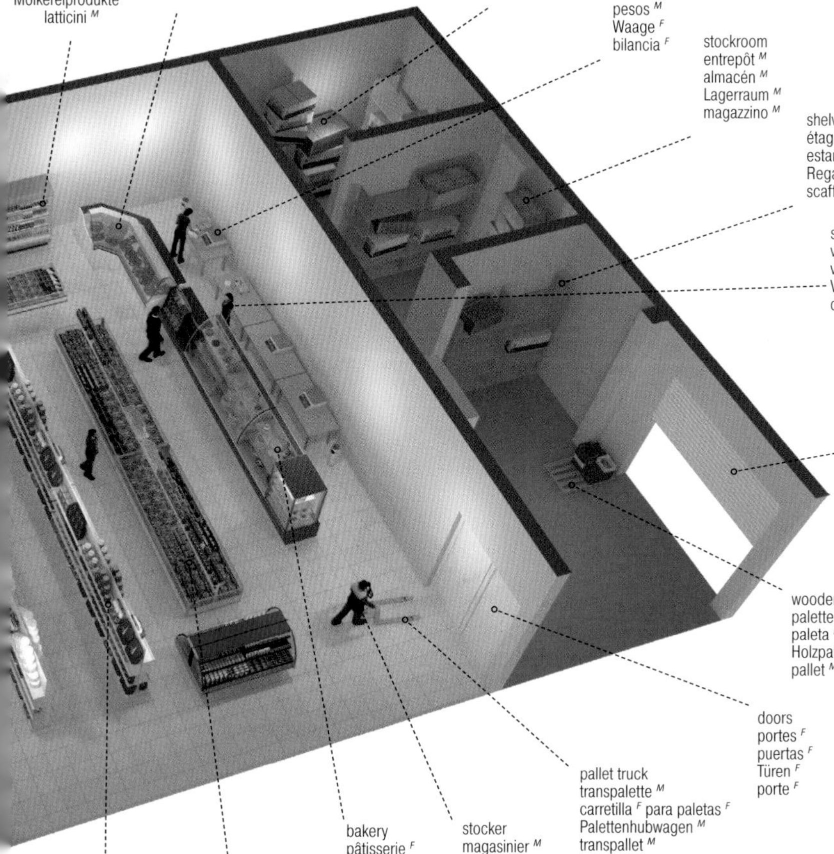
dairy products
produits ^{M} laitiers
productos ^{M} lácteos
Molkereiprodukte ^{N}
latticini ^{M}
deli counter
charcuterie ^{F}
charcutería ^{F}
Frischtheke ^{F}
banco ^{M} affettati ^{M}
box
boîte ^{F}
caja ^{F}
Kiste ^{F}
scatola ^{F}
scale
balance ^{F}
pesos ^{M}
Waage ^{F}
bilancia ^{F}
stockroom
entrepôt ^{M}
almacén ^{M}
Lagerraum ^{M}
magazzino ^{M}
shelves
étagère ^{F}
estantería ^{F}
Regal ^{N}
scaffali ^{M}
salesclerk
vendeuse ^{F}
vendedor ^{M}
Verkäuferin ^{F}
commessa ^{F}
roll-up door
porte-rideau ^{F}
puerta ^{F} de persiana ^{F}
Rolltor ^{N}
saracinesca ^{F}
wooden pallet
palette ^{F} de manutention ^{F} en bois ^{M}
paleta ^{F} de madera ^{F}
Holzpalette ^{F}
pallet ^{M}
doors
portes ^{F}
puertas ^{F}
Türen ^{F}
porte ^{F}
pallet truck
transpalette ^{M}
carretilla ^{F} para paletas ^{F}
Palettenhubwagen ^{M}
transpallet ^{M}
stocker
magasinier ^{M}
reponedor ^{M}
Regalbefüller ^{M}
magazziniere ^{M}
bakery
pâtisserie ^{F}
panadería ^{F}
Bäckerei ^{F}
prodotti ^{M} di panetteria ^{F}
fish and seafood
poissons ^{M} et fruits ^{M} de mer ^{F}
pescados ^{M} y mariscos ^{M}
Meeresfrüchte ^{F}
pesce ^{M} e frutti ^{M} di mare ^{M}
shelves
rayons ^{M}
estantería ^{F}
Einzelhandelsregal ^{N}
scaffali ^{M}

plastic bag
sac ^{M} plastique
bolsa ^{F} de plástico
Plastiktüte ^{F}
sacchetto ^{M} di plastica ^{F}

paper grocery bag
sac ^{M} de papier ^{M}
bolsa ^{F} de papel ^{M} para víveres ^{M}
Papier-Einkaufstüte ^{F}
borsa ^{F} di carta ^{F} per la spesa ^{F}

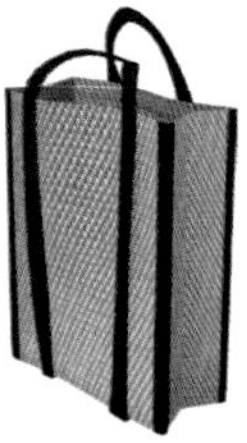

reusable grocery bag
sac ^{M} d'épicerie ^{F} réutilisable
bolsa ^{F} de compras ^{F} reusable
wiederverwendbare Einkaufstasche ^{F}
borsa ^{F} per la spesa ^{F} riutilizzabile

coffee house
café [M]
cafetería [F]
Café [N]
bar [M]

menu display
affichage [M] du menu [M]
expositor [M]
Menüanzeige [F]
display [M] del menù [M]

restroom
toilettes [F]
baño [M]
Toilette [F]
bagno [M]

customer
cliente [F]
cliente [M]
Kundin [F]
cliente [F]

counter
comptoir [M]
barra [F]
Theke [F]
bancone [M]

chair
chaise [F]
silla [F]
Stuhl [M]
sedia [F]

bakery
boulangerie [F]
panadería [F]
Bäckerei [F]
panetteria [F]

door
porte [F]
puerta [F]
Tür [F]
porta [F]

salesclerk
vendeuse [F]
vendedora [F]
Verkäuferin [F]
commessa [F]

refrigerated display case
vitrine [F] réfrigérée
vitrina [F] con refrigeración [F]
Kühlvitrine [F]
espositore [M] refrigerato

counter
comptoir [M]
mostrador [M]
Tresen [M]
bancone [M]

cake
gâteau [M]
pastel [M]
Kuchen [M]
torta [F]

storefront sign
enseigne F de vitrine F
letrero M
Fassadenschild N
insegna F del negozio M

exhaust fan
aération F
extractor M
Abluftventilator M
cappa F aspirante

pendant light
suspension F
lámpara F colgante
Hängeleuchte F
lampadario M

barista
barista M
encargado M de la cafetería F
Barista M
barista M

waitress
serveuse F
camarera F
Kellnerin F
cameriera F

table
table F
mesa F
Tisch M
tavolo M

light
éclairage M
luz F
Lampe F
luce M

tile
carrelage M
azulejos M
Fliese F
piastrella F

menu display
affichage M du menu M
expositor M
Menüanzeige F
display M del menù M

bread loaf
miche F de pain M
pan M
Brot N
pane M

bread roll
petit pain M
panecillo M
Brötchen N
panino M

customer
client M
cliente M
Kunde M
cliente M

cosmetics store
boutique F de produits M de beauté F
tienda F de cosméticos M
Kosmetikgeschäft N
negozio M di cosmetici M

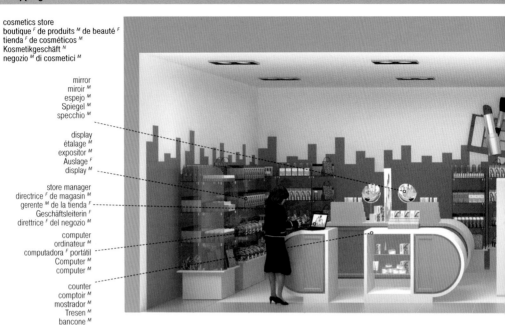

mirror
miroir M
espejo M
Spiegel M
specchio M

display
étalage M
expositor M
Auslage F
display M

store manager
directrice F de magasin M
gerente M de la tienda F
Geschäftsleiterin F
direttrice F del negozio M

computer
ordinateur M
computadora F portátil
Computer M
computer M

counter
comptoir M
mostrador M
Tresen M
bancone M

electronics store
magasin M d'électronique F
tienda F de electrónica F
Elektronikgeschäft N
negozio M di elettronica F

tablet
tablette F
tableta F
Tablet N
tablet M

monitor
laveur M de vitres F
monitor M
Monitor M
schermo M

cellular phone
cellulaire M
teléfono M móvil
Handy N
cellulare M

counter
comptoir M
mostrador M
Beratungstheke F
bancone M

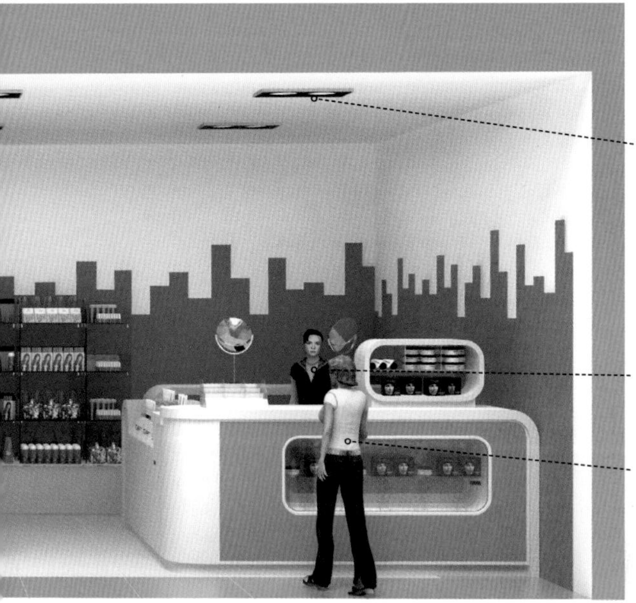

light
lumière [F]
luz [F]
Lampe [F]
luce [F]

sales assistant
assistante [F] aux ventes [F]
vendedora [F]
Verkäuferin [F]
assistente [F] alle vendite

customer
cliente [F]
cliente [M]
Kundin [F]
cliente [F]

shampoo
shampooing [M]
champú [M]
Shampoo [N]
shampoo [M]

perfume
parfum [M]
perfume [M]
Parfüm [N]
profumo [M]

lipstick
rouge [M] à lèvres [F]
lápiz [M] labial
Lippenstift [M]
rossetto [M]

light
lumière [F]
luz [F]
Lampe [F]
luce [F]

display
présentoir [M]
puesto [M]
Display [N]
espositore [M]

sales assistant
assistant [M] aux ventes [M]
asistente [M] de ventas [F]
Verkäufer [M]
assistente [M] alle vendite [F]

customer
client [M]
cliente [M]
Kunde [M]
cliente [M]

laptop
ordinateur [M]
portatif computadora [F]
portátil Laptop [M]
computer [M] portatile

clothing store
magasin M de vêtements M
tienda F de ropa F
Bekleidungsgeschäft N
negozio M di abbigliamento M

hooks
crochets M
perchero M
Kleiderhaken M
appendiabiti M
curtain
rideau M
cortina F
Vorhang M
tenda F
hangers
cintres M
ganchos M de ropa F
Kleiderbügel M
grucce F
fitting room
cabine F d'essayage M
probador M
Umkleidekabine F
camerino M di prova F
bench
banc M
banco M
Sitzbank F
panchina F
full-length mirror
miroir M de plain-pied M
espejo M de cuerpo M entero
großer Spiegel M
specchio M intero F
display table
table F de présentation F
mesa F de exhibición M
Präsentationstisch M
tavolo M d'esposizione F

clothes rod
tringle F à vêtements M
barra F para colgar ropa F
Kleiderstange F
bastoni M appendiabiti M

mannequin
mannequin M
maniquí M
Mannequin N
manichino M

shelves
étagères F
estantería F
Regale N
scaffali M

checkout computer
caisse F
terminal M de caja F
Kassencomputer M
computer M della cassa F

sales and merchandise area
zone F de vente F et d'exposition F
área F de ventas F y mercancías F
Verkaufs- und Warenbereich M
area F vendite F e merci F

counter
comptoir M
caja F
Kasse F
cassa F

bar
bar M
bar M
Bar F
bar M

draft beer taps
robinets M de bière F pression F
tiradores M de cerveza F
Bierzapfanlage F
spillatori M per birra F

patron
cliente F
cliente M
Gast M
cliente F

waitress
serveuse F
camarera F
Kellnerin F
cameriera F

bar counter
comptoir M du bar M
barra F
Bartresen M
bancone M del bar M

bar stool
tabouret M de bar M
taburete M
Barhocker M
sgabello M del bar M

liquor bottle
bouteille ^{F} d'alcool ^{M}
botella ^{F} de licor ^{M}
Spirituosenflasche ^{F}
bottiglia ^{F} di liquore ^{M}

coffee machine
machine ^{F} à café ^{M}
máquina ^{f} de café ^{M}
Kaffeemaschine ^{F}
macchina ^{F} del caffè ^{M}

point-of-sale computer
ordinateur ^{M} de point ^{M} de vente ^{F}
computadora ^{F} de punto ^{M} de venta ^{F}
Kassen-Computer ^{M}
computer ^{M} della cassa ^{F}

wine rack
casier ^{M} à vin ^{M}
botellero ^{M}
Weinregal ^{N}
portabottiglie ^{M} da vino ^{M}

bartender
barman ^{M}
barman ^{M}
Barkeeper ^{M}
barista ^{F}

rack of glasses
égouttoir ^{M} pour verres ^{M}
estante ^{M} de copas ^{F} de cristal ^{M}
Ablage ^{F} für Gläser ^{N}
rastrelliera ^{F} per bicchieri ^{M}

napkin dispenser
distributeur ^{M} de serviettes ^{F}
servilletero ^{M}
Serviettenhalter ^{M}
portatovaglioli ^{M}

refrigerator
réfrigérateur ^{M}
nevera ^{F}
Kühlschrank ^{M}
frigorifero ^{M}

restaurant
restaurant [M]
restaurante [M]
Restaurant [N]
ristorante [M]

prep table
table [F] de préparation [F]
encimera [F]
Arbeitsplatte [F]
piano [M] di lavoro [M]

chef
chef [M]
chef [M]
Koch [M]
capocuoco [M]

kitchen
cuisine [F]
cocina [F]
Küche [F]
cucina [F]

bus cart
desserte [F]
carrito [M]
Servierwagen [M]
carrello [M]

storage room
chambre [F] d'entreposage [M]
almacén [M]
Lagerraum [M]
ripostiglio [M]

walk-in cooler
chambre [F] froide
cámara [F] frigorífica
Kühlraum [M]
cella [F] frigorifera

grand piano
piano [M] à queue [F]
piano [M] de cola [F]
Flügel [M]
pianoforte [M] a coda [F]

bartender
barman [M]
barman [M]
Barkeeper [M]
barista [M]

piano bar
piano-bar [M]
salón [M] del piano [M]
Pianobar [F]
piano-bar [M]

bar counter
comptoir [M] du bar [M]
barra [F]
Bartresen [M]
bancone [M] del bar [M]

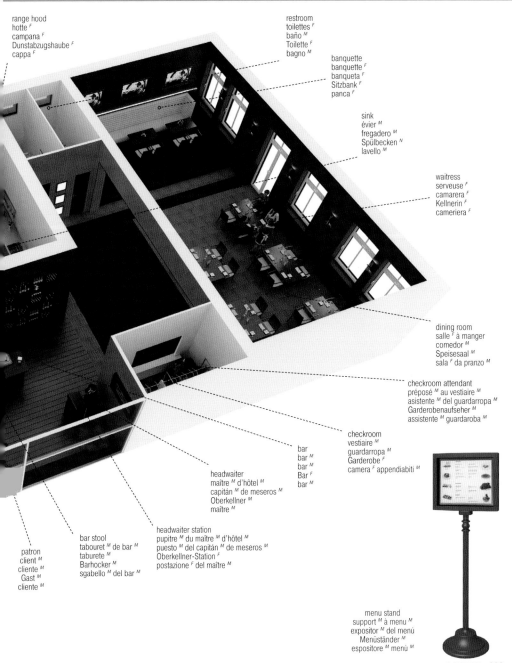

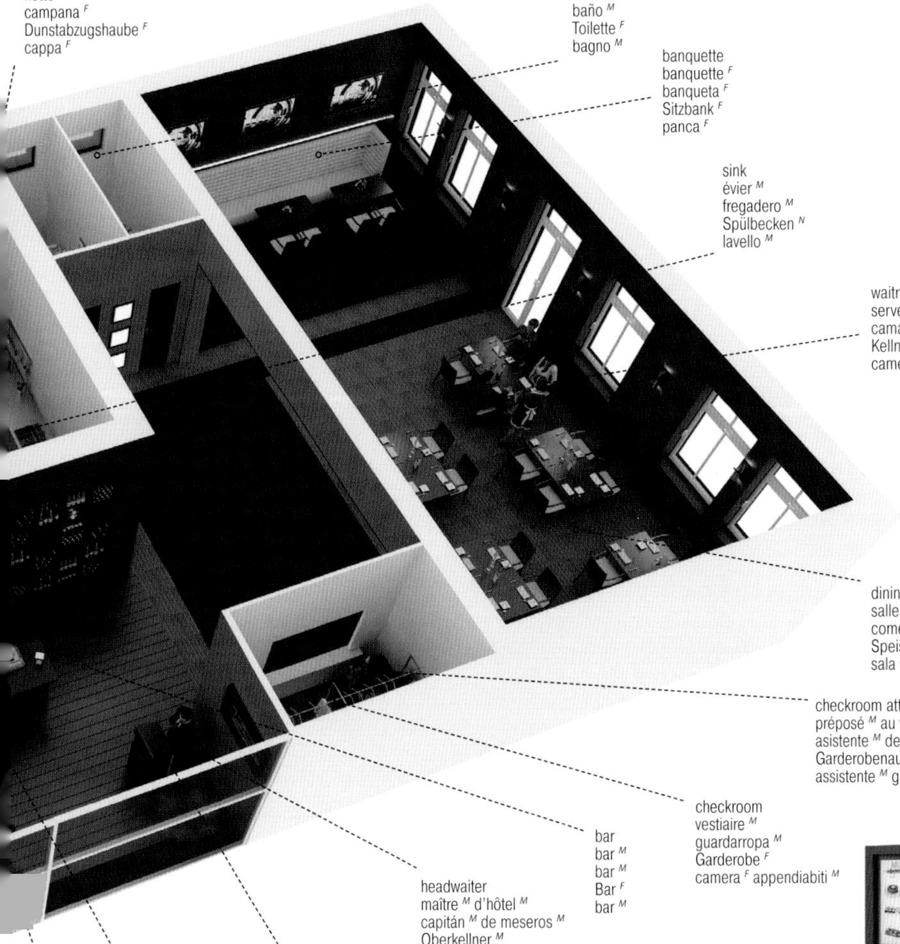
range hood
hotte [F]
campana [F]
Dunstabzugshaube [F]
cappa [F]
restroom
toilettes [F]
baño [M]
Toilette [F]
bagno [M]
banquette
banquette [F]
banqueta [F]
Sitzbank [F]
panca [F]
sink
évier [M]
fregadero [M]
Spülbecken [N]
lavello [M]
waitress
serveuse [F]
camarera [F]
Kellnerin [F]
cameriera [F]
dining room
salle [F] à manger
comedor [M]
Speisesaal [M]
sala [F] da pranzo [M]
checkroom attendant
préposé [M] au vestiaire [M]
asistente [M] del guardarropa [M]
Garderobenaufseher [M]
assistente [M] guardaroba [M]
checkroom
vestiaire [M]
guardarropa [M]
Garderobe [F]
camera [F] appendiabiti [M]
bar
bar [M]
bar [M]
Bar [F]
bar [M]
headwaiter
maître [M] d'hôtel [M]
capitán [M] de meseros [M]
Oberkellner [M]
maître [M]
headwaiter station
pupitre [M] du maître [M] d'hôtel [M]
puesto [M] del capitán [M] de meseros [M]
Oberkellner-Station [F]
postazione [F] del maître [M]
bar stool
tabouret [M] de bar [M]
taburete [M]
Barhocker [M]
sgabello [M] del bar [M]
patron
client [M]
cliente [M]
Gast [M]
cliente [M]

menu stand
support [M] à menu [M]
expositor [M] del menú
Menüständer [M]
espositore [M] menù [M]

fast-food restaurant
restaurant M rapide
restaurante M de comida F rápida
Fastfood-Restaurant N
ristorante M fast-food

cash register
caisse M enregistreuse
caja F registradora
Registrierkasse F
cassa F

beverage dispenser
distributrice F de boissons F
dispensador M de bebidas
Getränkeautomat M
erogatore M di bevande F

menu board
panneau M d'affichage M du menu M
pantalla F de menú M
Menütafel F
menu M digitale

salt and pepper shakers
salière F et poivrière F
salero M y pimentero M
Salz- und Pfefferstreuer M
set M di sale M e pepe M

counter
comptoir M
mostrador M
Tresen M
bancone M

napkin dispenser
distributeur M de serviettes
servilletero M
Serviettenhalter M
portatovaglioli M

waitress
serveuse F
camarera F
Kellnerin F
cameriera F

glasses
verres M
cristalería F
Gläser N
bicchieri M

light
luminaire ^{M}
lámpara ^{F}
Lampe ^{F}
luce ^{F}

table
table ^{F}
mesa ^{F}
Tisch ^{M}
tavolo ^{M}

patron
client ^{M}
cliente ^{M}
Gast ^{M}
cliente ^{M}

window
fenêtre ^{F}
ventana ^{F}
Fenster ^{N}
finestra ^{F}

chair
chaise ^{F}
silla ^{F}
Stuhl ^{M}
sedia ^{F}

squeeze bottle
flacon ^{M} pressable
bote ^{M} de salsa ^{F}
Quetschflasche ^{F}
bottiglia ^{F} di salsa ^{F}

napkin holder
support ^{M} pour serviettes ^{F}
servilletero ^{M}
Serviettenhalter ^{M}
portatovaglioli ^{M}

banquette
banquette ^{F}
banqueta ^{F}
Sitzbank ^{F}
panca ^{F}

reception
réception [F]
recepción [M]
Rezeption [F]
reception [F]

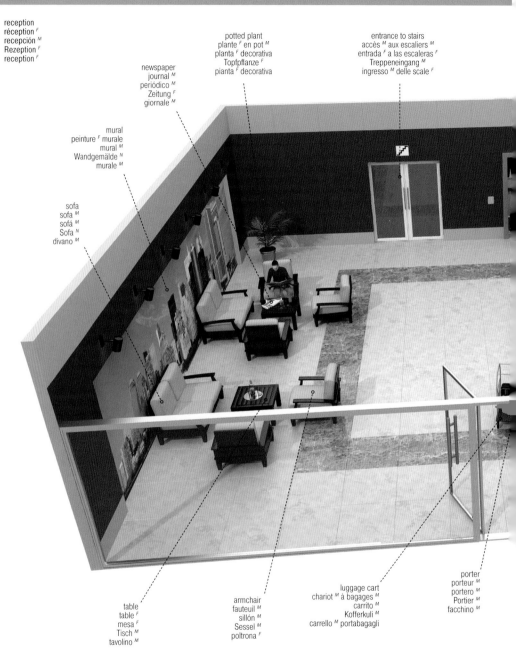

newspaper
journal [M]
periódico [M]
Zeitung [F]
giornale [M]

potted plant
plante [F] en pot [M]
planta [F] decorativa
Topfpflanze [F]
pianta [F] decorativa

entrance to stairs
accès [M] aux escaliers [M]
entrada [F] a las escaleras [F]
Treppeneingang [M]
ingresso [M] delle scale [F]

mural
peinture [F] murale
mural [M]
Wandgemälde [N]
murale [M]

sofa
sofa [M]
sofá [M]
Sofa [N]
divano [M]

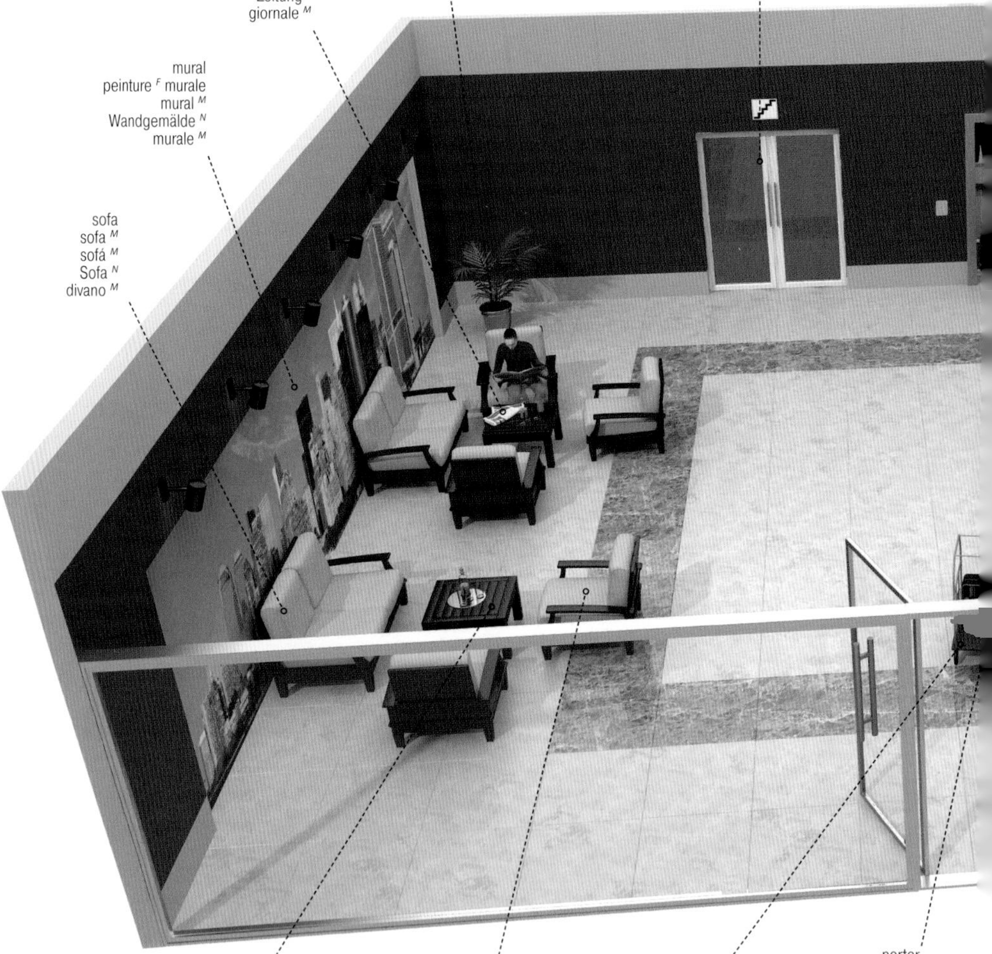

table
table [F]
mesa [F]
Tisch [M]
tavolino [M]

armchair
fauteuil [M]
sillón [M]
Sessel [M]
poltrona [F]

luggage cart
chariot [M] à bagages [M]
carrito [M]
Kofferkuli [M]
carrello [M] portabagagli

porter
porteur [M]
portero [M]
Portier [M]
facchino [M]

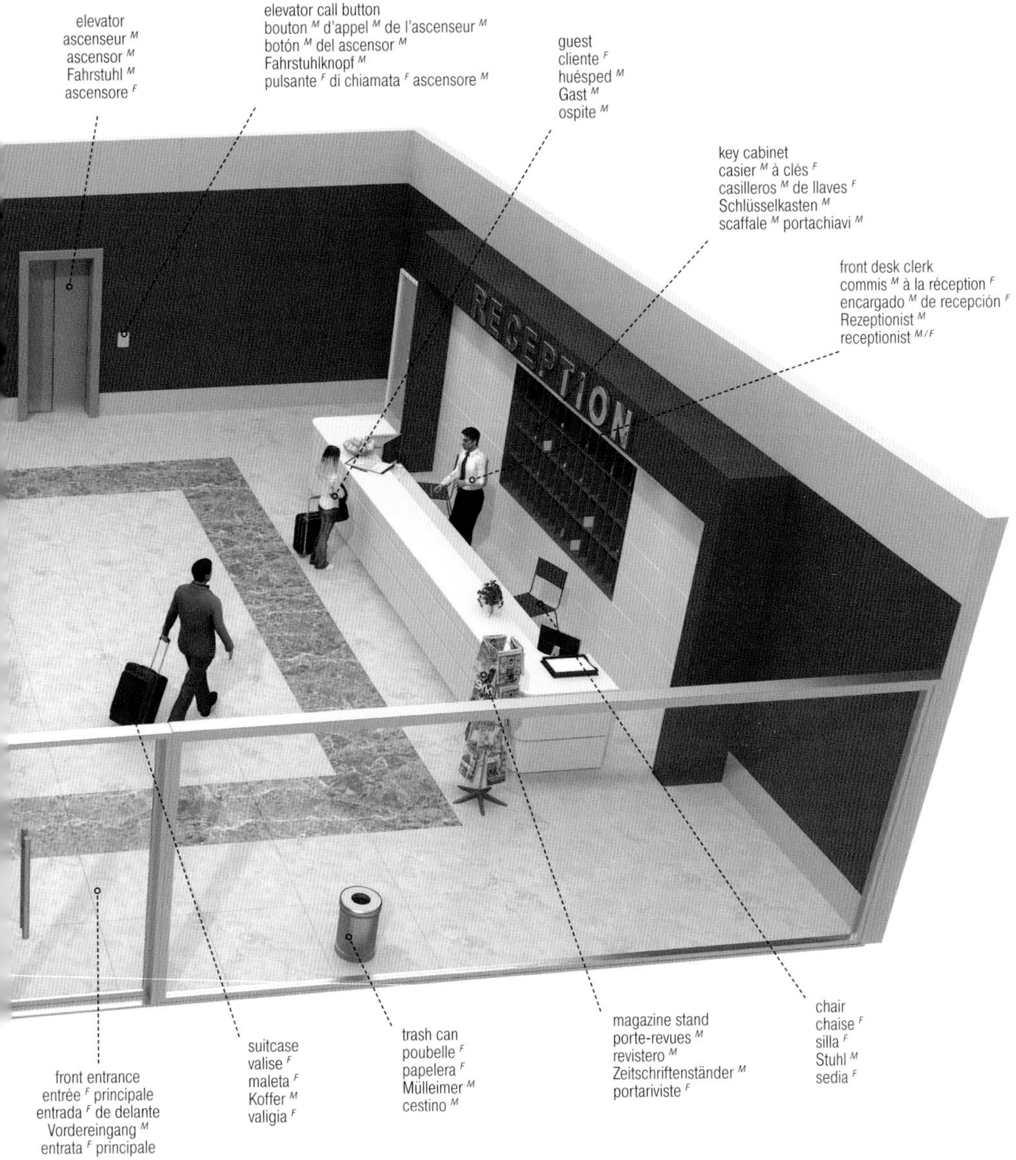
elevator
ascenseur M
ascensor M
Fahrstuhl M
ascensore F
elevator call button
bouton M d'appel M de l'ascenseur M
botón M del ascensor M
Fahrstuhlknopf M
pulsante F di chiamata F ascensore M
guest
cliente F
huésped M
Gast M
ospite M
key cabinet
casier M à clés F
casilleros M de llaves F
Schlüsselkasten M
scaffale M portachiavi M
front desk clerk
commis M à la réception F
encargado M de recepción F
Rezeptionist M
receptionist M/F
RECEPTION
front entrance
entrée F principale
entrada F de delante
Vordereingang M
entrata F principale
suitcase
valise F
maleta F
Koffer M
valigia F
trash can
poubelle F
papelera F
Mülleimer M
cestino M
magazine stand
porte-revues M
revistero M
Zeitschriftenständer M
portariviste F
chair
chaise F
silla F
Stuhl M
sedia F

hotel room
chambre [F] d'hôtel [M]
habitación [F] de hotel [M]
Hotelzimmer [N]
camera [F] d'albergo

ventilation fan
aération [F]
ventilador [M] extractor
Lüftung [F]
ventola [F]

toilet
toilette [F]
inodoro [M]
Toilette [F]
gabinetto [M]

toilet paper
papier [M] toilette [F]
papel [M] higiénico
Toilettenpapier [N]
carta [F] igienica

flush buttons
bouton [M] de chasse [F]
botones [M] para descargar el inodoro [M]
Tasten [F] für [M] Wasserspülung [F]
pulsante [M] dello sciacquone [M]

toilet brush
brosse [F] de toilettes [F]
escobilla [F]
Toilettenbürste [F]
scopino [M]

bathtub
baignoire [F]
tina [F] de baño [M]
Badewanne [F]
vasca [F] da bagno [M]

trash can
poubelle [F]
papelera [F]
Mülleimer [M]
cestino [M]

towel
serviette [F]
toalla [F]
Handtuch [N]
asciugamano [M]

mirror
miroir [M]
espejo [M]
Spiegel [M]
specchio [M]

sink
évier [M]
lavabo [M]
Waschbecken [N]
lavello [M]

bath mat
tapis [M] de bain [M]
alfombrilla [F]
Badematte [F]
tappetino [M] da bagno [M]

front door
porte [F] d'entrée [F]
puerta [F] delantera
Vordertür [F]
porta [F] principale

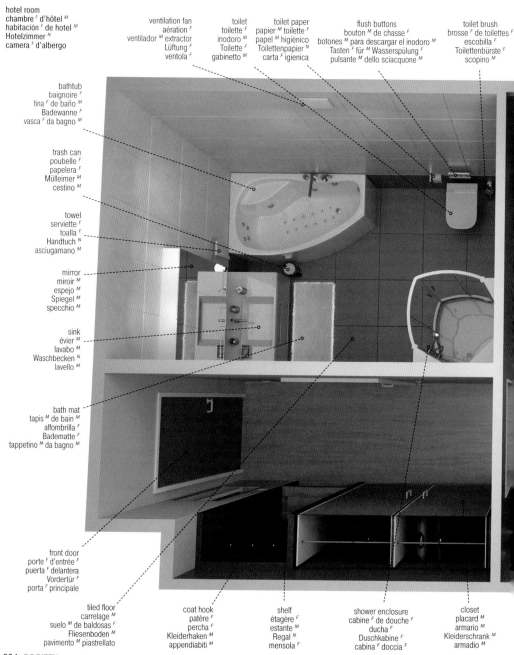

tiled floor
carrelage [M]
suelo [M] de baldosas [F]
Fliesenboden [M]
pavimento [M] piastrellato

coat hook
patère [F]
percha [F]
Kleiderhaken [M]
appendiabiti [M]

shelf
étagère [F]
estante [M]
Regal [N]
mensola [F]

shower enclosure
cabine [F] de douche [F]
ducha [F]
Duschkabine [F]
cabina [F] doccia [F]

closet
placard [M]
armario [M]
Kleiderschrank [M]
armadio [M]

night table
table [F] de nuit [F]
mesita [F] de noche [F]
Nachttisch [M]
comodino [M]

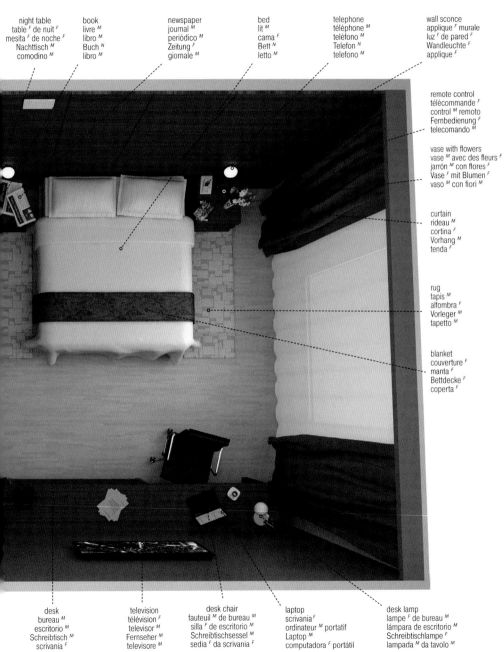

book
livre [M]
libro [M]
Buch [N]
libro [M]

newspaper
journal [M]
periódico [M]
Zeitung [F]
giornale [M]

bed
lit [M]
cama [F]
Bett [N]
letto [M]

telephone
téléphone [M]
teléfono [M]
Telefon [N]
telefono [M]

wall sconce
applique [F] murale
luz [F] de pared [F]
Wandleuchte [F]
applique [F]

remote control
télécommande [F]
control [M] remoto
Fernbedienung [F]
telecomando [M]

vase with flowers
vase [M] avec des fleurs [F]
jarrón [M] con flores [F]
Vase [F] mit Blumen [F]
vaso [M] con fiori [M]

curtain
rideau [M]
cortina [F]
Vorhang [M]
tenda [F]

rug
tapis [M]
alfombra [F]
Vorleger [M]
tapetto [M]

blanket
couverture [F]
manta [F]
Bettdecke [F]
coperta [F]

desk
bureau [M]
escritorio [M]
Schreibtisch [M]
scrivania [F]

television
télévision [F]
televisor [M]
Fernseher [M]
televisore [M]

desk chair
fauteuil [M] de bureau [M]
silla [F] de escritorio [M]
Schreibtischsessel [M]
sedia [F] da scrivania [F]

laptop
scrivania [F]
ordinateur [M] portatif
Laptop [M]
computadora [F] portátil

desk lamp
lampe [F] de bureau [M]
lámpara de escritorio [M]
Schreibtischlampe [F]
lampada [M] da tavolo [M]

auditorium
auditorium ^{M}
auditorio ^{M}
Konferenzsaal ^{M}
sala ^{F} conferenze ^{F}

projector screen
écran ^{M} de projection ^{F}
pantalla ^{F} del proyector ^{M}
Projektionswand ^{F}
schermo ^{M} del proiettore ^{M}

head table
table ^{F} d'honneur ^{M}
mesa ^{F} principal
Podiumstisch ^{M}
tavolo ^{M} presidenziale ^{M}

podium
lutrin ^{M}
podio ^{M}
Rednerpult ^{N}
leggio ^{M}

dais
estrade ^{F}
plataforma ^{F}
Podium ^{N}
podio ^{F}

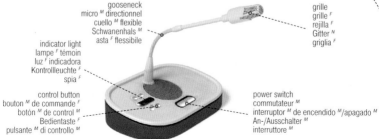

microphone
micro ^{M}
micrófono ^{M}
Mikrofon ^{N}
microfono ^{M}

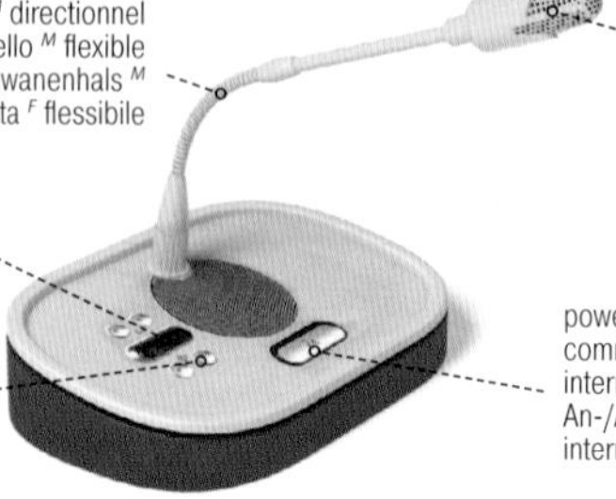

gooseneck
micro ^{M} directionnel
cuello ^{M} flexible
Schwanenhals ^{M}
asta ^{F} flessibile

grille
grille ^{F}
rejilla ^{F}
Gitter ^{N}
griglia ^{F}

indicator light
lampe ^{F} témoin
luz ^{F} indicadora
Kontrollleuchte ^{F}
spia ^{F}

control button
bouton ^{M} de commande ^{F}
botón ^{M} de control ^{M}
Bedientaste ^{F}
pulsante ^{M} di controllo ^{M}

power switch
commutateur ^{M}
interruptor ^{M} de encendido ^{M}/apagado ^{M}
An-/Ausschalter ^{M}
interruttore ^{M}

microphone
micro [M]
micrófono [M]
Mikrofon [N]
microfono [M]

video camera
caméra [F] vidéo [F]
video cámara [F]
Videokamera [F]
videocamera [F]

simultaneous interpretation booth
cabine [F] de traduction [F] simultanée
cabina [F] de interpretación [F] simultánea
Simultandolmetscherkabine [F]
cabina [F] di traduzione [F] simultanea

soundproof window
fenêtre [F] insonorisée
ventana [F] a prueba de sonidos [M]
schalldichtes Fenster [F]
finestra [F] insonorizzata

conference table
table [F] de conférence [F]
mesa [F] de conferencia [F]
Konferenztisch [M]
tavolo [M] da conferenza [F]

desk chair
chaise [F] de bureau [M]
silla [F] de escritorio [M]
Schreibtischsessel [M]
sedia [F] da scrivania [F]

door
porte [F]
puerta [F]
Tür [F]
porta [F]

floor
sol [M]
suelo [M]
Boden [M]
pavimento [M]

Police department

Service ^M de police ^F | Policía ^F | Polizei ^F | Polizia ^F

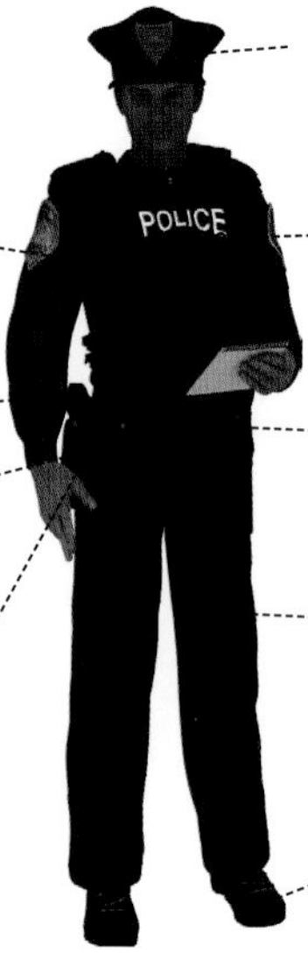
police officer
agent ^M de police ^F
oficial ^M de policía ^F
Polizeibeamter ^M
poliziotto ^M
cap
casquette ^F
gorra ^F
Mütze ^F
berretto ^M
pocket
poche ^F
bolsillo ^M
Tasche ^F
tasca ^F
POLICE
jacket
veste ^F
chaqueta ^F
Jacke ^F
giacca ^F
pistol
pistolet ^M
pistola ^F
Pistole ^F
pistola ^F
buckle
boucle ^F
hebilla ^F
Schnalle ^F
fibbia ^F
belt
ceinture ^F
cinturón ^M
Gürtel ^M
cintura ^F
pants
pantalon ^M
pantalones ^M
Hose ^F
pantaloni ^M
holster
étui ^M de revolver ^M
funda ^F de pistola ^F
Halfter ^N
fondina ^F
boot
botte ^F
bota ^F
Stiefel ^M
stivali ^M

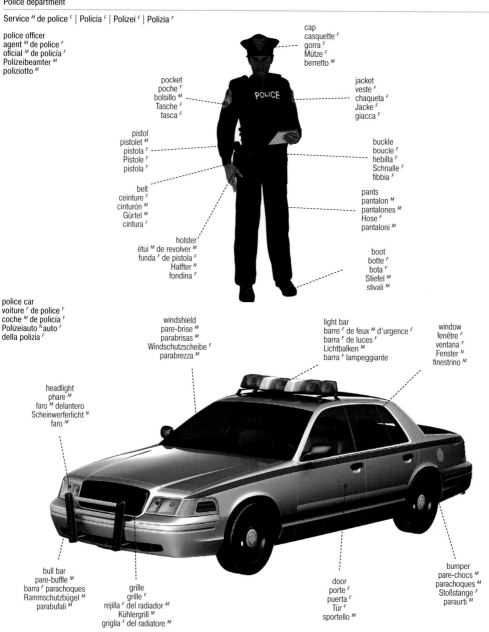

police car
voiture ^F de police ^F
coche ^M de policía ^F
Polizeiauto ^N auto ^F
della polizia ^F
windshield
pare-brise ^M
parabrisas ^M
Windschutzscheibe ^F
parabrezza ^M
light bar
barre ^F de feux ^M d'urgence ^F
barra ^F de luces ^F
Lichtbalken ^M
barra ^F lampeggiante
window
fenêtre ^F
ventana ^F
Fenster ^N
finestrino ^M
headlight
phare ^M
faro ^M delantero
Scheinwerferlicht ^N
faro ^M
bull bar
pare-buffle ^M
barra ^F parachoques
Rammschutzbügel ^M
parabufali ^M
grille
grille ^F
rejilla ^F del radiador ^M
Kühlergrill ^M
griglia ^F del radiatore ^M
door
porte ^F
puerta ^F
Tür ^F
sportello ^M
bumper
pare-chocs ^M
parachoques ^M
Stoßstange ^F
paraurti ^M

police helicopter
hélicoptère M de police F
helicóptero M de policía F
Polizeihubschrauber M
elicottero M della polizia F

rotor blade
pale F de rotor M
aspa F del rotor M
Rotorblatt N
pale F del rotore M
rotor hub
moyeu M de rotor M
mecanismo M de control de aspas F automático
Rotornabe F
mozzo M di motore M
fuselage
fuselage M
fuselaje M
Rumpf M
fusoliera F
anti-torque tail rotor
rotor M anticouple
rotor M de cola F
Heckrotor M
rotore M di coda F
horizontal stabilizer
stabilisateur M horizontal
estabilizador M horizontal
Höhenleitwerk N
ala F
searchlight
projecteur M
proyector M
Suchscheinwerfer M
faro M
door
porte F
puerta F
Tür F
portello M
skid
patin M
patines M de aterrizaje
Kufen F
pattini M
tail boom
poutre M de queue F
estructura F de cola F
Heckausleger M trave F
di coda F

police motorcycle
moto F de police F
motocicleta F de policía F
Polizeimotorrad N
motocicletta F della polizia F

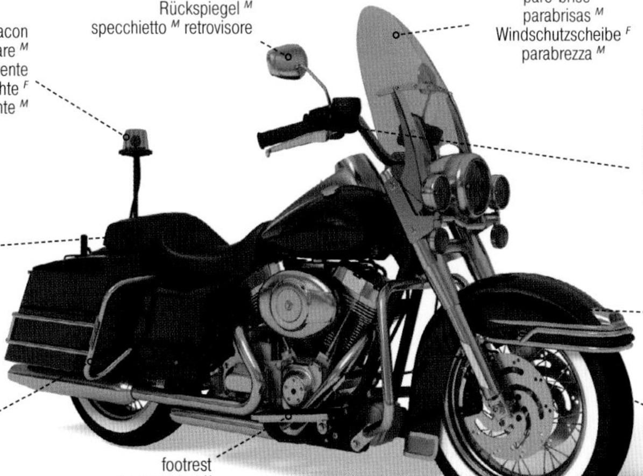
mirror
miroir M
espejo M
Rückspiegel M
specchietto M retrovisore
windshield
pare-brise M
parabrisas M
Windschutzscheibe F
parabrezza M
beacon
gyrophare M
luz F intermitente
Rundumleuchte F
lampeggiante M
handlebars
guidon M
manillar M
Lenker M
manubrio M
seat
siège M
asiento M
Sitz M
sedile M
fender
garde-boue M
guardabarro M
Kotflügel M
parafango M
crash bar
arceau M de sécurité F
barra F parachoques
Sturzbügel M
barre F di protezione F
footrest
repose-pied M
estribo M
Fußablage F
poggiapiedi M
tire
pneu M
neumático M
Reifen M
ruota F

Fire department

Service [M] d'incendie [M] | Bomberos [M] | Feuerwehr [F] | Vigili [M] del fuoco [M]

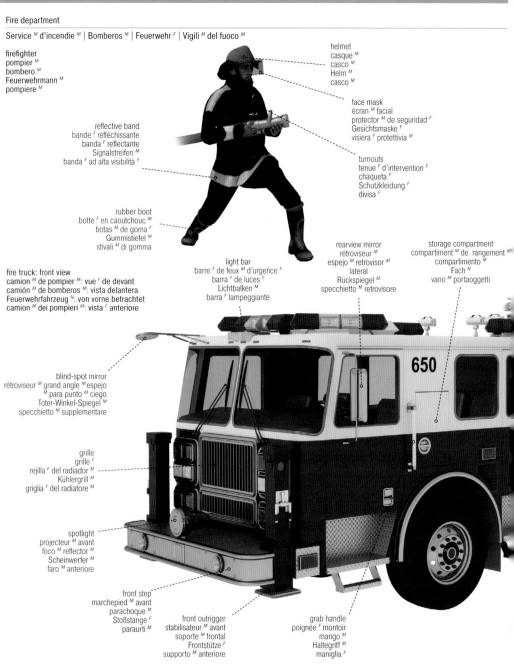

firefighter
pompier [M]
bombero [M]
Feuerwehrmann [M]
pompiere [M]
helmet
casque [M]
casco [M]
Helm [M]
casco [M]
face mask
écran [M] facial
protector [M] de seguridad [F]
Gesichtsmaske [F]
visiera [F] protettivia [M]
reflective band
bande [F] réfléchissante
banda [F] reflectante
Signalstreifen [M]
banda [F] ad alta visibilità [F]
turnouts
tenue [F] d'intervention [F]
chaqueta [F]
Schutzkleidung [F]
divisa [F]
rubber boot
botte [F] en caoutchouc [M]
botas [M] de goma [F]
Gummistiefel [M]
stivali [M] di gomma

fire truck: front view
camion [M] de pompier [M]: vue [F] de devant
camión [M] de bomberos [M]: vista delantera
Feuerwehrfahrzeug [N]: von vorne betrachtet
camion [M] dei pompieri [M]: vista [F] anteriore
light bar
barre [F] de feux [M] d'urgence [F]
barra [F] de luces [F]
Lichtbalken [M]
barra [F] lampeggiante
rearview mirror
rétroviseur [M]
espejo [M] retrovisor [M]
lateral
Rückspiegel [M]
specchietto [M] retrovisore
storage compartment
compartiment [M] de rangement [M]
compartimento [M]
Fach [N]
vano [M] portaoggetti
650
blind-spot mirror
rétroviseur [M] grand angle [M] espejo [M] para punto [M] ciego
Toter-Winkel-Spiegel [M]
specchietto [M] supplementare
grille
grille [F]
rejilla [F] del radiador [M]
Kühlergrill [M]
griglia [F] del radiatore [M]
spotlight
projecteur [M] avant
foco [M] reflector [M]
Scheinwerfer [M]
faro [M] anteriore
front step
marchepied [M] avant
parachoque [M]
Stoßstange [F]
paraurti [M]
front outrigger
stabilisateur [M] avant
soporte [M] frontal
Frontstütze [F]
supporto [M] anteriore
grab handle
poignée [F] montoir
mango [M]
Haltegriff [M]
maniglia [F]

fire truck: back view
camion ^{M} de pompier ^{M}: vue ^{F} de derrière
camión ^{M} de bomberos ^{M}: vista trasera
Feuerwehrfahrzeug ^{N}: von hinten betrachtet
camion ^{M} dei pompieri ^{M}: vista ^{F} posteriore

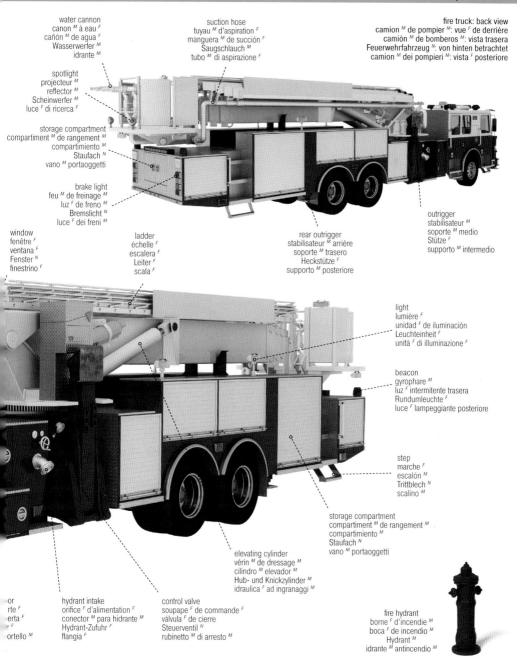

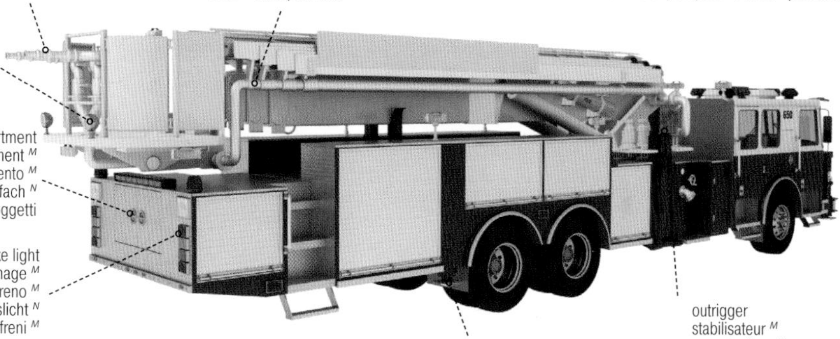
water cannon
canon ^{M} à eau ^{F}
cañón ^{M} de agua ^{F}
Wasserwerfer ^{M}
idrante ^{M}
suction hose
tuyau ^{M} d'aspiration ^{F}
manguera ^{M} de succión ^{F}
Saugschlauch ^{M}
tubo ^{M} di aspirazione ^{F}
spotlight
projecteur ^{M}
reflector ^{M}
Scheinwerfer ^{M}
luce ^{F} di ricerca ^{F}
storage compartment
compartiment ^{M} de rangement ^{M}
compartimiento ^{M}
Staufach ^{N}
vano ^{M} portaoggetti
brake light
feu ^{M} de freinage ^{M}
luz ^{F} de freno ^{M}
Bremslicht ^{N}
luce ^{F} dei freni ^{M}
rear outrigger
stabilisateur ^{M} arrière
soporte ^{M} trasero
Heckstütze ^{F}
supporto ^{M} posteriore
outrigger
stabilisateur ^{M}
soporte ^{M} medio
Stütze ^{F}
supporto ^{M} intermedio

window
fenêtre ^{F}
ventana ^{F}
Fenster ^{N}
finestrino ^{F}
ladder
échelle ^{F}
escalera ^{F}
Leiter ^{F}
scala ^{F}
light
lumière ^{F}
unidad ^{F} de iluminación
Leuchteinheit ^{F}
unità ^{F} di illuminazione ^{F}
beacon
gyrophare ^{M}
luz ^{F} intermitente trasera
Rundumleuchte ^{F}
luce ^{F} lampeggiante posteriore
step
marche ^{F}
escalón ^{M}
Trittblech ^{N}
scalino ^{M}
storage compartment
compartiment ^{M} de rangement ^{M}
compartimiento ^{M}
Staufach ^{N}
vano ^{M} portaoggetti
elevating cylinder
vérin ^{M} de dressage ^{M}
cilindro ^{M} elevador ^{M}
Hub- und Knickzylinder ^{M}
idraulica ^{F} ad ingranaggi ^{M}
or
rte ^{F}
erta ^{F}
^{F}
ortello ^{M}
hydrant intake
orifice ^{F} d'alimentation ^{F}
conector ^{M} para hidrante ^{M}
Hydrant-Zufuhr ^{F}
flangia ^{F}
control valve
soupape ^{F} de commande ^{F}
válvula ^{F} de cierre
Steuerventil ^{N}
rubinetto ^{M} di arresto ^{M}

fire hydrant
borne ^{F} d'incendie ^{M}
boca ^{F} de incendio ^{M}
Hydrant ^{M}
idrante ^{M} antincendio ^{M}

Information signs

Panneaux ^{M} d'information ^{F} | Señales ^{F} informativas | Hinweisschilder ^{N} | Segnali ^{M} standard

telephone
téléphone ^{M}
teléfono ^{M}
Telefon ^{N}
telefono ^{M}

post office
bureau ^{M} de poste ^{M}
correo ^{M}
Post ^{F}
ufficio ^{M} postale

currency exchange
bureau ^{M} de change ^{M}
cambio de divisas ^{F}
Wechselstube ^{F}
cambiovaluta ^{M}

first aid
premiers soins ^{M}
primeros auxilios ^{M}
Erste Hilfe ^{F}
pronto soccorso ^{M}

lost and found
objets ^{M} trouvés
objetos ^{M} perdidos
Fundbüro ^{N}
oggetti ^{M} smarriti

checkroom
vestiaire ^{M}
guardarropa ^{M}
Garderobe ^{F}
guardaroba ^{M}

baggage lockers
consigne ^{F} à bagages ^{M}
guarda equipajes ^{M}
Gepäckschließfächer ^{N}
armadietti ^{M} bagagli ^{M}

down escalator
escalier ^{M} mécanique descendant
escalera ^{F} mecánica, hacia abajo
Rolltreppe ^{F} nach unten
scala ^{F} mobile piano ^{M} inferiore

up escalator
escalier ^{M} mécanique ascendant
escalera ^{F} mecánica, hacia arriba
Rolltreppe ^{F} nach oben
scala ^{F} mobile piano ^{M} superiore

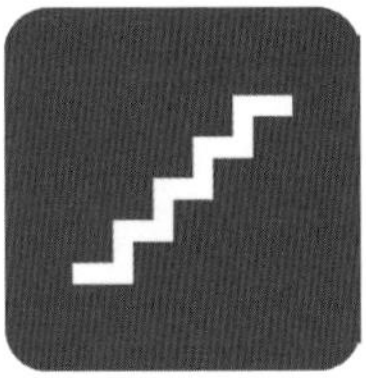

stairs
escaliers ^{M}
escaleras ^{F}
Treppe ^{F}
scale ^{M}

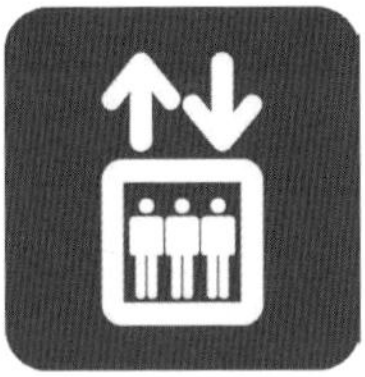

elevator
ascenseur ^{M}
ascensor ^{M}
Fahrstuhl ^{M}
ascensore ^{F}

men's restroom
toilettes ^{F} pour hommes ^{M}
baño ^{M} de caballeros ^{M}
Herrentoilette ^{F}
bagno ^{M} per uomini ^{M}

women's restroom
toilettes ^{F} pour femmes ^{F}
baño ^{M} de damas ^{F}
Damentoilette ^{F}
bagno ^{M} per donne ^{F}

restroom
toilettes ^{F}
baño ^{M}
Toiletten ^{F}
bagni ^{M}

baby changing area
table ^{F} à langer
área ^{F} para cambiar pañales ^{M}
Babywickelraum ^{M}
zonaz ^{F} cambio ^{M} neonati ^{M}

waiting room
salle ^{F} d'attente ^{F}
sala ^{F} de espera ^{F}
Wartezimmer ^{N}
sala ^{F} d'attesa ^{F}

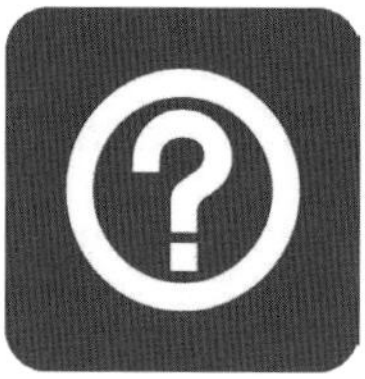

information
information ^{F}
información ^{F}
Information ^{F}
informazioni ^{F}

lodging
hôtel ^{M}
hotel ^{M}
Unterkunft ^{F}
albergo ^{M}

airport
aéroport ^{M}
aeropuerto ^{M}
Flughafen ^{M}
aeroporto ^{M}

litter barrel
poubelle ^{F}
cesto ^{M} de basura ^{F}
Mülleimer ^{M}
Raccolta ^{F} rifiuti ^{M}

taxi stand
station ^{F} de taxi ^{M}
parada ^{F} de taxi ^{M}
Taxistand ^{M}
fermata ^{F} del taxi ^{M}

bus stop
arrêt ^{M} d'autobus ^{M}
parada ^{F} de autobús ^{M}
Bus ^{M}
fermata ^{F} dell'autobus ^{M}

ground transportation
transport ^{M} terrestre
transporte ^{M} terrestre
Bodentransport ^{M}
trasporto ^{M} terrestre

train station
gare ^{F} ferroviaire
estación ^{F} de trenes ^{M}
Bahnhof ^{M}
stazione ^{F} ferroviaria

ferry terminal
gare ^{F} maritime
terminal ^{F} de ferry ^{M}
Fährterminal ^{M}
terminal ^{M} traghetti ^{M}

car rental
location ^{F} de voiture ^{F}
alquiler de coches ^{M}
Autoverleih ^{M}
autonoleggio ^{M}

restaurant
restaurant ^{M}
restaurante ^{M}
Restaurant ^{N}
ristorante ^{M}

coffee shop
café ^{M}
cafetería ^{F}
Café ^{N}
caffè ^{M}

bar
bar ^{M}
bar ^{M}
Bar ^{F}
bar ^{M}

baggage claim
bagages ^{M}
patio ^{M} de equipaje ^{M}
Gepäckausgabe ^{F}
ritiro bagagli ^{M}

parking
stationnement ^{M}
estacionamiento ^{M}
Parkplatz ^{M}
parcheggio ^{M}

smoking area
zone ^{F} fumeur ^{M}
área ^{M} de fumadores ^{M}
Raucherzone ^{F}
area ^{F} fumatori ^{M}

wheelchair access
accès ^{M} pour fauteuils ^{M} roulants
acceso ^{M} para personas ^{F} en sillas ^{F} de ruedas ^{F}
Behindertengerechter Eingang ^{M}
accesso ^{M} disabili ^{M}

tent camping
camping ^{M} sous la tente ^{F}
área ^{F} de campamento ^{M}
Camping ^{N} (Zelt ^{N})
campeggio ^{M} tende ^{F}

trailer camping
campement ^{M} de remorques ^{F}
campamento ^{M} en caravana ^{F}
Camping ^{N} (Wohnwagen ^{M})
campeggio ^{M} roulotte ^{F}

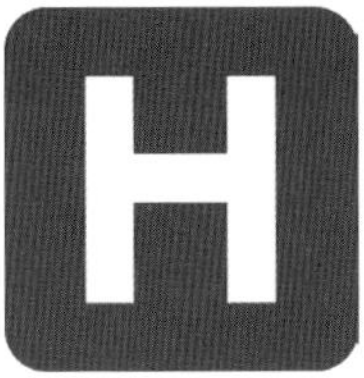
H

hospital
hôpital ^{M}
hospital ^{M}
Krankenhaus ^{N}
hospital ^{M}

picnic area
aire ^{F} de pique-nique ^{M}
área ^{F} de picnic ^{M}
Picknickplatz ^{M}
area ^{F} picnic ^{M}

fire extinguisher
extincteur ^{M}
extintor ^{M}
Feuerlöscher ^{M}
estintore ^{M}

service station
station-service ^{F}
estación ^{F} de servicios ^{M}
Tankstelle ^{F}
stazione ^{F} di servizio ^{M}

Wi-Fi zone
zone ^{F} Wi-Fi ^{M}
zona ^{F} Wi-Fi
WiFi-Zone ^{F}
zona ^{F} Wi-Fi

campfire area
zone ^{F} de feux ^{M} de camp ^{M}
área ^{F} para fogatas ^{F}
Feuerstelle ^{N}
area ^{F} falò ^{M}

$

automatic teller machine (ATM)
guichet ^{M} automatique bancaire
cajero ^{M} automático
Geldautomat ^{M}
bancomat ^{M}

dog-walking area
aire ^{F} d'exercice ^{M} pour chiens ^{M}
área ^{F} para perros ^{M}
Hundeauslaufzone ^{F}
area ^{F} per passeggio ^{M} cani ^{M}

swimming area
baignade ^{F}
área ^{F} de natación ^{F}
Schwimmbereich ^{M}
area ^{F} per nuotare

drinking water
eau ^{F} potable
agua ^{F} potable
Trinkwasser ^{N}
acqua ^{F} potabile

video surveillance
vidéosurveillance ^{F}
vídeo ^{M} de vigilancia
Videoüberwachung ^{F}
videosorveglianza ^{F}

hiking trail
sentier ^{M} de randonnée ^{F} pédestre
sendero ^{M}
Wanderweg ^{M}
sentiero ^{M}

auto mechanic
mécanicien ^{M}
taller ^{M} de reparación ^{F}
Automechaniker ^{M}
officina ^{F} meccanica

Hazard signs

Panneaux ^{M} indicateurs de danger ^{M} | Símbolos ^{M} de peligro ^{M} | Warnschilder ^{N} | Segnali ^{M} di pericolo ^{M}

corrosive to skin and metals
corrosif pour la peau ^{F} et les métaux ^{M}
corrosivo ^{M} para la piel ^{F} y los metales ^{M}
Hautätzend, auf Metall ^{N} korrosiv wirkend
corrosivo per pelle ^{F} e metalli ^{M}

gases under pressure
gaz ^{M} sous pression ^{F}
gases ^{M} comprimidos
Gas ^{N} unter Druck ^{M}
gas ^{M} compresso

explosives, self-reactives
explosifs, ^{M} autoréactifs ^{M}
explosivos ^{M}
Sprengstoffe ^{M}
esplosivi ^{M}

aquatic toxicity
toxicité ^{F} aquatique
tóxico ^{M} para el medio acuático ^{M}
mweltgefahr ^{F} mit Baum ^{M} und Fisch ^{M}
ossicità ^{F} per l'ambiente ^{M} acquatico

oxidizers
agents ^{M} oxydants
agentes ^{M} oxidantes
Oxidationsmittel ^{N}
agenti ^{M} ossidanti

health hazard
danger ^{M} pour la santé ^{F}
peligro ^{M} para la salud ^{F}
Gesundheitsgefahr ^{F}
sostanze ^{M} tossiche

acute toxicity
toxicité ^{F} aiguë
altamente tóxico
hochgiftig
altamente tossico

Workplace safety signs

Panneaux ^{M} de sécurité ^{F} au travail ^{M} | Señales ^{F} de precaución ^{F} | Warnschilder ^{F} am Arbeitsplatz ^{M} | Segnali ^{M} di precauzione ^{F}

eye protection
protection ^{F} des yeux ^{M}
obligatorio el uso de gafas ^{F} protectoras
Augenschutz ^{M} benutzen
occhiali ^{M} di protezione ^{F} obbligatori

respiratory system protection
protection ^{F} respiratoire
obligatorio el uso de protección ^{F} respiratoria
Atemschutz ^{M} benutzen
respiratore ^{M} obbligatorio

hand protection
protection ^{F} des mains ^{F}
obligatorio el uso de guantes ^{M} protectores
Handschutz ^{M} benutzen
guanti ^{M} di protezione ^{F} obbligatori

head protection
protection ^{F} de la tête ^{F}
ligatorio el uso de casco ^{M}
Kopfschutz ^{M} benutzen
) ^{M} di protezione ^{F} obbligatorio

protective clothing
vêtements ^{M} de protection ^{F}
obligatorio el uso de ropa ^{F} de seguridad ^{F}
Schutzkleidung ^{F} benutzen
tuta ^{F} di protezione ^{F} obbligatoria

face shield
écran ^{M} facial
obligatorio el uso de pantalla ^{F} facial
Gesichtsschutz ^{M} benutzen
maschera ^{F} di protezione ^{F} obbligatoria

ear protection
protection ^{F} auditive
obligatorio el uso de protectores ^{M} auditivos
Gehörschutz ^{M} benutzen
protezione ^{F} obbligatoria per le orecchie ^{F}

Warning signs

Panneaux M d'avertissement M | Señales F de advertencia F | Warnschilder N | Segnali M di pericolo M

poison
poison
veneno M
Warnung F vor giftigen Stoffen M
sostanze F velenose

radioactive
radioactif
sustancia F radioactiva
Warnung F vor radioaktiven Stoffen M
materiali M radioattivi

irritant
irritant
irritante M
Gesundheitsschädliche oder reizende Stoffe M
sostanze F irritanti

flammable
inflammable
inflamable M
Warnung F vor feuergefährlichen Stoffen M
sostanze F infiammabili

magnetic field
champ M magnétique
campo M magnético
Warnung F vor magnetischem Feld N
campo M magnetico

high voltage
haute tension F
alto voltaje M
Warnung F vor gefährlicher elektrischer Spannung F
alto voltaggio M

slippery
glissant
superficie F resbaladiza
Warnung F vor Rutschgefahr F
superficie F scivolosa

Prohibition signs

Panneaux M d'interdiction F | Símbolos M de prohibición | Verbotsschilder F | Segni M di regolamentazione F

not drinking water
eau F non potable
no es agua F potable
Kein Trinkwasser N
acqua F non potabile

cell phone use prohibited
cellulaire M interdit
prohibido usar teléfonos M móviles
Mobilfunk M verboten
vietato usare il cellulare M

no open flame
flamme F nue interdite
prohibido fumar y encender fuego M
Feuer N, offenes Licht N und Rauchen verboten
utilizzare fiamme F libere

photography prohibited
interdiction F de prendre des photos
prohibido tomar fotos F
Fotografieren N verboten
vietato scattare foto F

no smoking
interdiction F de fumer
prohibido fumar
Rauchen N verboten
vietato fumare

pets prohibited
animaux M interdits
no se permiten las mascotas F
Keine Haustiere N erlaubt
non sono ammessi animali M

no access
accès M interdit
acceso M cerrado
Betreten N verboten
accesso M vietato

stop
arrêt M
alto M
Zutritt M für Unbefugte F verboten
stop M

Emergency signs

Panneaux [M] d'urgence | Señales [F] de emergencia [F] | Notfallschilder [N] | Segni [M] di evacuazione [F]

first aid
premiers soins [M]
primeros auxilios [M]
Erste Hilfe [F]
pronto soccorso [M]

emergency telephone
téléphone [M] d'urgence
teléfono [M] de emergencias [F]
Notruftelefon [N]
telefono [M] di emergenza [F]

assembly point
point [M] de rassemblement [M]
punto [M] de encuentro [M]
Sammelstelle [F]
punto [M] di raccolta [F]

automated external defibrillator (AED)
défibrillateur [M] externe automatique
desfibrilador [M] externo automático (DEA)
Automatisierter externer Defibrillator (AED) [M]
defibrillatore [M] automatico esterno (AED)

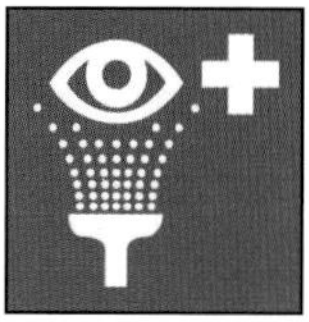

eye wash station
bassin [M] oculaire
estación [F] para lavar los ojos [M]
Augenspüleinrichtung [F]
Stazione [F] di lavaggio degli occhi [M]

doctor
médecin [M]
médico [M]
Arzt [M]
medico [M]

in case of emergency break glass
briser la vitre [F] en cas [M] d'urgence [F]
en caso [M] de emergencia [F] rompa el cristal [M]
Im Notfall [M] Scheibe [F] einschlagen
in caso di emergenza [F] rompere il vetro [M]

emergency exit
sortie [F] de secours [M]
salida [F] de emergencia [F]
Notausgang [M]
uscita [F] di emergenza [F]

Fire safety signs

Panneaux [M] de sécurité [F] incendie [M] | Señales [F] de prevención [F] de incendios [M] | Brandschutzschilder [N] | Cartelli [M] per la prevenzione [F] d' incendi [M]

fire hose
tuyau [M] d'incendie [M]
manguera [F] de incendios [M]
Löschschlauch [M]
lancia [F] antincendio

ladder
échelle [F]
escalera [F]
Leiter [F]
scala [F]

fire extinguisher
extincteur [M]
extintor [M]
Feuerlöscher [M]
estintore [F]

fire alarm
alarme [F] incendie [M]
alarma [F] contra incendio [M]
Brandmelder [M]
rilevatore [M] di incendio [M]

fire-fighting equipment
matériel [M] d'incendie [M]
equipo [M] contra incendio [M]
Brandbekämpfungsgerät [N]
attrezzatura [F] antincendio

emergency phone
téléphone [M] d'urgence
teléfono [M] de emergencia [F]
Notruftelefon [N]
telefono [M] di emergenza [F]

directional arrow
flèche [F] de direction [F]
indicador [M] de dirección [F]
Richtungsangabe [F]
indicatore [M] di direzione [F]

Asia

Asie [F] | Asia [F] | Asien [N] | Asia [F]

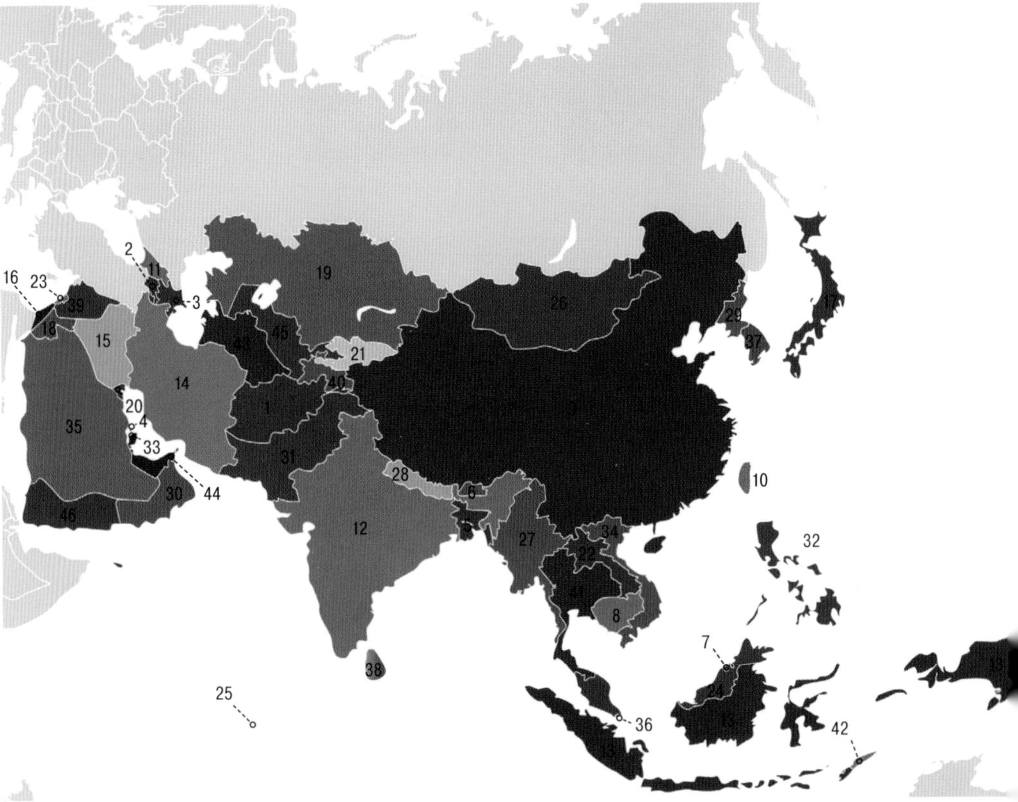
2
11
16
23
3
39
18
15
19
45
43
21
26
29
17
37
14
40
20
4
1
9
35
33
31
28
10
44
30
46
6
12
5
27
34
32
22
41
8
38
7
24
13
25
36
42

1

Afghanistan
Afghanistan [M]
Afganistán [M]
Afghanistan [N]
Afghanistan [M]

2

Armenia
Arménie [F]
Armenia [F]
Armenien [N]
Armenia [F]

3

Azerbaijan
Azerbaïdjan [M]
Azerbaiyán [M]
Aserbaidschan [N]
Azerbaijan [M]

4
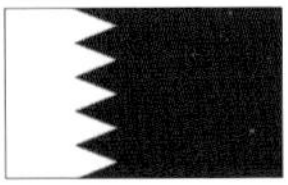

Bahrain
Bahreïn [M]
Reino de Bahréin [M]
Bahrain [N]
Bahrain [M]

5

Bangladesh
Bangladesh [M]
Bangladesh [M]
Bangladesch [N]
Bangladesh [M]

6

Bhutan
Bhoutan [M]
Bután [M]
Bhutan [N]
Bhutan [M]

7

Brunei
Brunei [M]
Brunei [M]
Brunei [N]
Brunei [M]

8

Cambodia
Cambodge [M]
Camboya [F]
Kambodscha [N]
Cambogia [F]

9

Republic of China
République [F] populaire de Chine [F]
China [F]
China [N]
Cina [F]

10

Taiwan
Taïwan
Taiwán [M]
Taiwan [N]
Taiwan [M]

11

Georgia
Géorgie [F]
Georgia [F]
Georgien [N]
Georgia [F]

12

India
Inde [F]
India [F]
Indien [N]
India [F]

13

Indonesia
Indonésie [F]
Indonesia [F]
Indonesien [N]
Indonesia [F]

14

Iran
Iran [M]
Irán [M]
Iran [M]
Iran [M]

15

الله أكبر
Iraq
Irak [M]
Iraq [M]
Irak [M]
Iraq [M]

16

Israel
Israël [M]
Israel [M]
Israel [N]
Israele [M]

17

Japan
Japon [M]
Japón [M]
Japan [N]
Giappone [M]

18

Jordan
Jordanie [F]
Jordania [M]
Jordanien [N]
Giordania [F]

19

Kazakhstan
Kazakhstan [M]
Kazajstán [M]
Kasachstan [N]
Kazakistan [M]

20

Kuwait
Koweït [M]
Kuwait [M]
Kuwait [N]
Kuwait [M]

21

Kyrgyzstan
Kirghizistan [M]
Kirguistán [M]
Kirgisistan [N]
Kirghizistan [M]

22
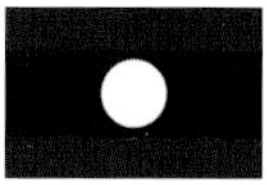
Laos
Laos [M]
Laos [M]
Laos [N]
Laos [M]

23

Lebanon
Liban [M]
Líbano [M]
Libanon [M]
Libano [M]

24

Federation of Malaysia
Fédération [F] de Malaisie [F]
Malasia [F]
Malaysia [N]
Malesia [F]

25

Maldives
Maldives [F]
Maldivas [F]
Malediven [F]
Maldive [F]

26

Mongolia
Mongolie [F]
Mongolia [F]
Mongolei [F]
Mongolia [F]

27

Myanmar
Myanmar [M]
Myanmar [M]
Myanmar [N]
Myanmar [M]

28

Nepal
Népal [M]
Nepal [M]
Nepal [N]
Nepal [M]

29

North Korea
Corée [F] du Nord [M]
Corea del Norte [F]
Nordkorea [N] Corea del Nord [F]

30
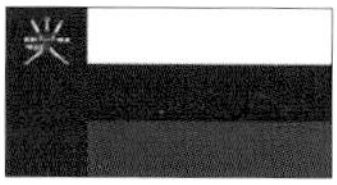
Oman
Oman [M]
Omán [M]
Oman [N]
Oman [M]

31

Pakistan
Pakistan [M]
Pakistán [M]
Pakistan [N]
Pakistan [M]

32

Philippines
Philippines [F]
Filipinas [F]
Philippinen
Filippine [F]

33

Qatar
Qatar [M]
Qatar [M]
Katar [N]
Qatar [M]

34

Vietnam
Vietnam [M]
Vietnam [M]
Vietnam [N]
Vietnam [M]

35

Saudi Arabia
Arabie Saoudite [F]
Arabia Saudí [M]
Saudi Arabien [N]
Arabia Saudita [F]

36

Singapore
Singapour [M]
Singapur [M]
Singapur [N]
Singapore [M]

37

South Korea
Corée [F] du Sud [M]
Corea del Sur [F]
Südkorea [N] Corea del Sud [F]

38

Sri Lanka
Sri Lanka [M]
Sri Lanka [F]
Sri Lanka [N]
Sri Lanka [M]

39

Syria
Syrie [F]
Siria [F]
Syrien [N]
Siria [F]

40

Tajikistan
Tadjikistan [M]
Tayikistán [M]
Tadschikistan [N]
Tajikistan [M]

41

Thailand
Thaïlande [F]
Tailandia [F]
Thailand [N]
Thailandia [F]

42

East Timor
Timor oriental [M]
Timor Oriental [M]
Osttimor [N]
Timor Est [M]

43

Turkmenistan
Turkménistan [M]
Turkmenistán [M]
Turkmenistan [N]
Turkmenistan [M]

44

United Arab Emirates
Émirats [M] arabes unis
Emiratos Árabes Unidos [M]
Vereinigte Arabische Emirate [N]
Emirati Arabi Uniti [M]

45

Uzbekistan
Ouzbékistan [M]
Uzbekistán [M]
Usbekistan [N]
Uzbekistan [M]

46

Yemen
Yémen [M]
Yemen [M]
Jemen [M]
Yemen [M]

Europe

Europe [F] | Europa [F] | Europa [N] | Europa [F]

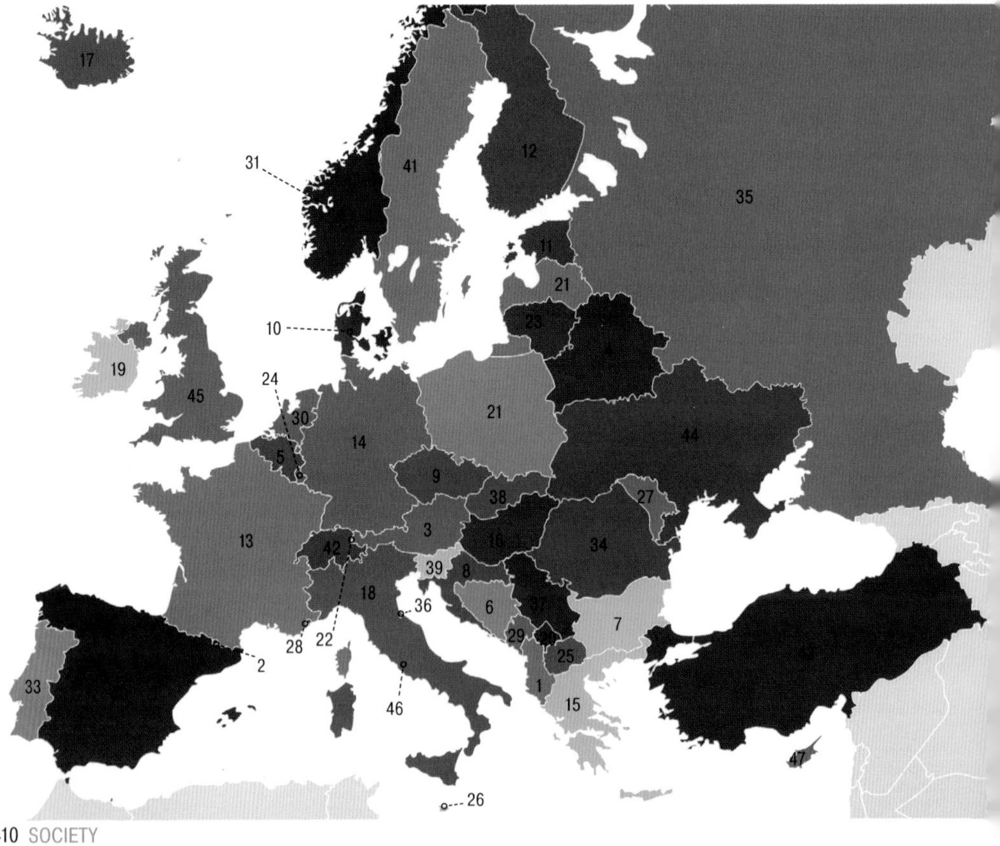
17
31
41
12
35
11
21
10
23
19
24
45
30
21
14
5
9
44
38
27
3
13
42
16
34
39
8
18
36
6
37
7
28
22
29
25
2
33
1
15
46
47
26

1

Albania
Albanie [F]
Albania [F]
Albanien [N]
Albania [F]

2

Andorra
Andorre [F]
Andorra [F]
Andorra [N]
Andorra [F]

3

Austria
Autriche [F]
Austria [F]
Österreich [N]
Austria [F]

4

Belarus
Biélorussie [F]
Bielorrusia [F]
Weißrussland [N]
Bielorussia [F]

5
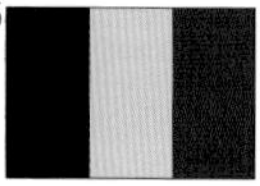

Belgium
Belgique [F]
Bélgica [F]
Belgien [N]
Belgio [M]

6

Bosnia and Herzegovina
Bosnie-Herzégovine [F]
Bosnia y Herzegovina [F]
Bosnien [N] und Herzegowina [N]
Bosnia-Erzegovina [F]

7
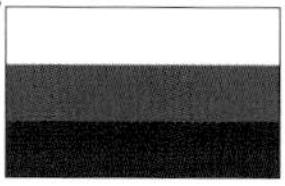

Bulgaria
Bulgarie [F]
Bulgaria [F]
Bulgarien [N]
Bulgaria [F]

8

Croatia
Croatie [F]
Croacia [F]
Kroatien [N]
Croazia [F]

9
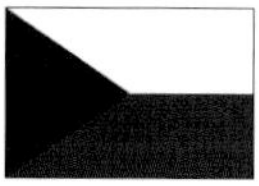

Czech Republic
République [F] tchèque
Republica Checa [F]
Tschechische Republik [F]
Repubblica Ceca [F]

10
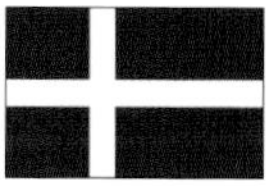

Denmark
Danemark [M]
Dinamarca [F]
Dänemark [N]
Danimarca [F]

11

Estonia
Estonie [F]
Estonia [F]
Estland [N]
Estonia [F]

12
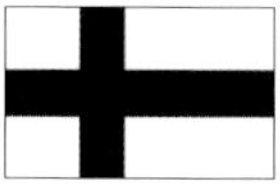

Finland
Finlande [F]
Finlandia [F]
Finnland [N]
Finlandia [F]

13
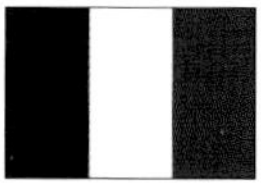

France
France [F]
Francia [F]
Frankreich [N]
Francia [F]

14
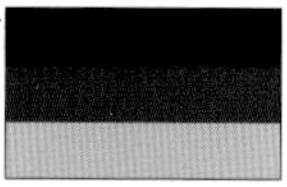

Germany
Allemagne [F]
Alemania [F]
Deutschland [N]
Germania [F]

15
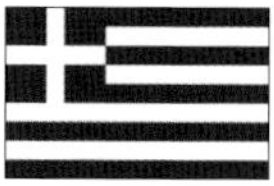

Greece
Grèce [F]
Grecia [F]
Griechenland [N]
Grecia [F]

16

Hungary
Hongrie [F]
Hungría [F]
Ungarn [N]
Ungheria [F]

17

Iceland
Islande [F]
Islandia [F]
Island [N]
Islanda [F]

18

Italy
Italie [F]
Italia [F]
Italien [N]
Italia [F]

19

Ireland
Irlande [F]
Irlanda [F]
Irland [N]
Irlanda [F]

20

Kosovo
Kosovo [M]
Kosovo [M]
Kosovo [M]
Kosovo [M]

Latvia
Lettonie [F]
Letonia [F]
Lettland [N]
Lettonia [F]

22

Liechtenstein
Liechtenstein [M]
Liechtenstein [M]
Liechtenstein [N]
Liechtenstein [M]

23

Lithuania
Lituanie [F]
Lituania [F]
Litauen [N]
Lituania [F]

24

Luxembourg
Luxembourg [M]
Luxemburgo [M]
Luxemburg [N]
Lussemburgo [M]

25

Macedonia
Macédoine [F]
Macedonia [F]
Mazedonien [N]
Macedonia [F]

26

Malta
Malte [F]
Malta [F]
Malta [N]
Malta [F]

27

Moldova
Moldavie [F]
Moldavia [F]
Moldawien [N]
Moldova [F]

28

Monaco
Monaco [M]
Mónaco [M]
Monaco [N]
Monaco [M]

29

Montenegro
Monténégro [M]
Montenegro [M]
Montenegro [N]
Montenegro [M]

30

Netherlands
Pays-Bas [M]
Países Bajos [M]
Niederlande
Paesi Bassi [M]

31

Norway
Norvège F
Noruega F
Norwegen N
Norvegia F

32

Poland
Pologne F
Polonia F
Polen N
Polonia F

33

Portugal
Portugal M
Portugal M
Portugal N
Portogallo M

34

Romania
Roumanie F
Rumania F
Rumänien N
Romania F

35
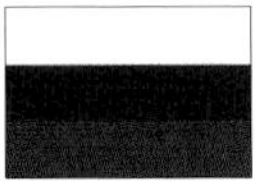
Russia
Russie F
Rusia F
Russland N
Russia F

36

San Marino
Saint-Marin M
San Marino M
San Marino N
San Marino M

37

Serbia
Serbie F
Serbia F
Serbien N
Serbia F

38

Slovakia
Slovaquie F
Eslovaquia F
Slowakei F
Slovacchia F

39

Slovenia
Slovénie F
Eslovenia F
Slowenien N
Slovenia F

40

Spain
Espagne F
España F
Spanien N
Spagna F

41

Sweden
Suède F
Suecia F
Schweden N
Svezia F

42

Switzerland
Suisse F
Suiza F
Schweiz F
Svizzera F

43

Turkey
Turquie F
Turquía F
Türkei F
Turchia F

44
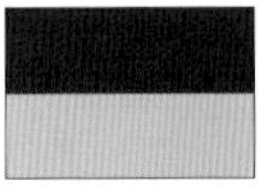
Ukraine
Ukraine F
Ucrania F
Ukraine F
Ucraina F

45

United Kingdom
Royaume-Uni M
Reino Unido M
Vereinigtes Königreich N
Regno Unito M

46

Vatican City
Cité F du Vatican M
Ciudad del Vaticano F
Vatikanstadt F
Città del Vaticano F

47

Cyprus
Chypre F
Chipre M
Zypern N
Cipro M

Africa

Afrique F | África F | Afrika N | Africa F

1

Algeria
Algérie F
Argelia F
Algerien N
Algeria F

2

Angola
Angola M
Angola F
Angola N
Angola F

3

Benin
Bénin M
Benín M
Benin N
Benin M

4
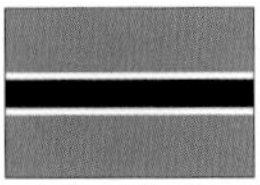
Botswana
Botswana M
Botsuana F
Botswana N
Botswana M

5

Burkina Faso
Burkina Faso M
Burkina Faso F
Burkina Faso N
Burkina Faso M

6

Burundi
Burundi M
Burundi M
Burundi N
Burundi M

7

Cameroon
Cameroun M
Camerún M
Kamerun N
Camerun M

8

Cape Verde
Cap-Vert M
Cabo Verde M
Kap Verde N
Capo Verde M

9

Central African Republic
République F centrafricaine
República de África Central F
Zentralafrikanische Republik F
Repubblica Centrafricana F

10

Chad
Tchad M
Chad M
Tschad M
Ciad M

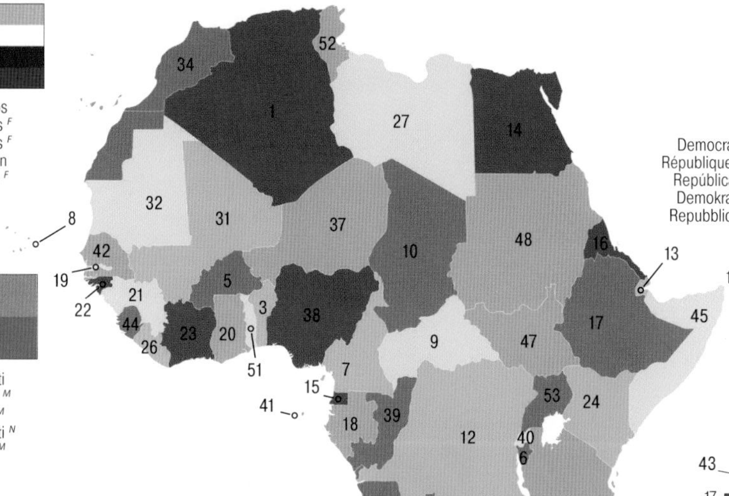
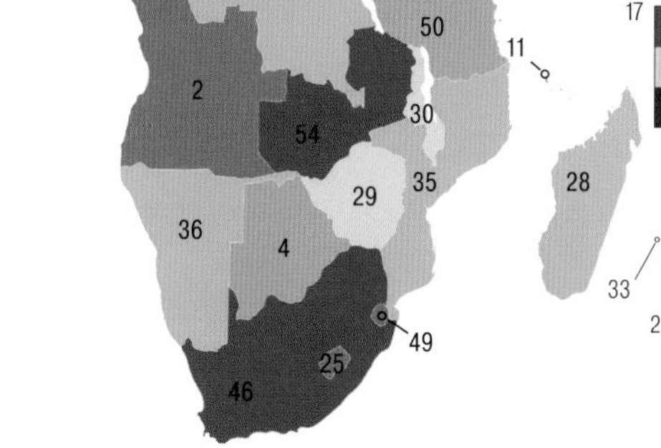
52
34
1
27
14
32
31
37
10
48
16
8
42
13
19
5
21
3
22
38
44
23
20
17
45
47
9
26
51
7
53
24
15
41
18
39
12
40
6
43
50
11
2
30
54
29
35
28
36
4
33
49
25
46

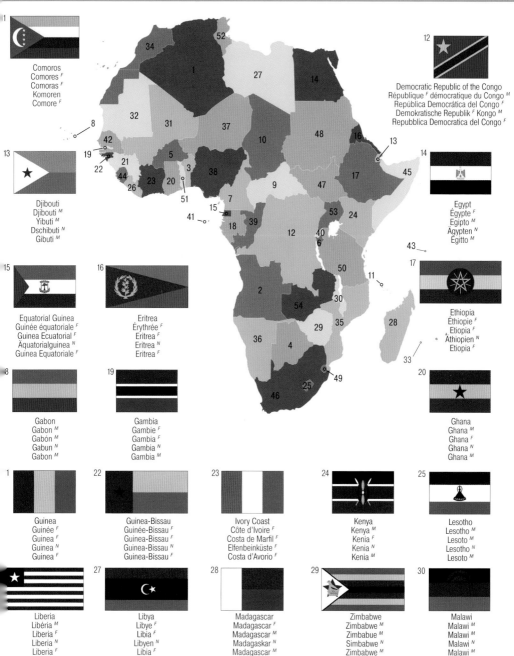

1

Comoros
Comores [F]
Comoras [F]
Komoren
Comore [F]

12

Democratic Republic of the Congo
République [F] démocratique du Congo [M]
República Democrática del Congo [F]
Demokratische Republik [F] Kongo [M]
Repubblica Democratica del Congo [F]

13

Djibouti
Djibouti [M]
Yibuti [M]
Dschibuti [N]
Gibuti [M]

14

Egypt
Égypte [F]
Egipto [M]
Ägypten [N]
Egitto [M]

15

Equatorial Guinea
Guinée équatoriale [F]
Guinea Ecuatorial [F]
Äquatorialguinea [N]
Guinea Equatoriale [F]

16

Eritrea
Érythrée [F]
Eritrea [F]
Eritrea [N]
Eritrea [F]

17

Ethiopia
Éthiopie [F]
Etiopía [F]
Äthiopien [N]
Etiopia [F]

18

Gabon
Gabon [M]
Gabón [M]
Gabun [N]
Gabon [M]

19

Gambia
Gambie [F]
Gambia [F]
Gambia [N]
Gambia [M]

20

Ghana
Ghana [M]
Ghana [F]
Ghana [N]
Ghana [M]

21

Guinea
Guinée [F]
Guinea [F]
Guinea [N]
Guinea [F]

22

Guinea-Bissau
Guinée-Bissau [F]
Guinea-Bissau [F]
Guinea-Bissau [N]
Guinea-Bissau [F]

23

Ivory Coast
Côte d'Ivoire [F]
Costa de Marfil [F]
Elfenbeinküste [F]
Costa d'Avorio [F]

24
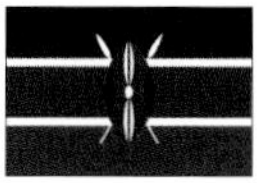
Kenya
Kenya [M]
Kenia [F]
Kenia [N]
Kenia [M]

25

Lesotho
Lesotho [M]
Lesoto [M]
Lesotho [N]
Lesoto [M]

Liberia
Libéria [M]
Liberia [F]
Liberia [N]
Liberia [F]

27

Libya
Libye [F]
Libia [F]
Libyen [N]
Libia [F]

28

Madagascar
Madagascar [F]
Madagascar [M]
Madagaskar [N]
Madagascar [M]

29

Zimbabwe
Zimbabwe [M]
Zimbabue [M]
Simbabwe [N]
Zimbabwe [M]

30

Malawi
Malawi [M]
Malawi [M]
Malawi [N]
Malawi [M]

31

Mali
Mali [M]
Mali [M]
Mali [N]
Mali [M]

32

Mauritania
Mauritanie [F]
Mauritania [F]
Mauretanien [N]
Mauritania [F]

33
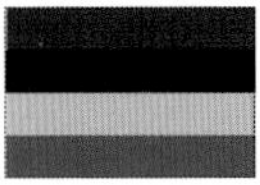
Mauritius
Ile Maurice [F]
Islas Mauricios [F]
Mauritius [N]
Mauritius [F]

34

Morocco
Maroc [M]
Marruecos [M]
Marokko [N]
Marocco [M]

35

Mozambique
Mozambique [M]
Mozambique [M]
Mosambik [N]
Mozambico [M]

36

Namibia
Namibie [F]
Namibia [F]
Namibia [N]
Namibia [F]

37

Niger
Niger [M]
Níger [M]
Niger [M]
Niger [M]

38

Nigeria
Nigéria [M]
Nigeria [F]
Nigeria [N]
Nigeria [F]

39

Republic of the Congo
République [F] du Congo [M]
República del Congo [F]
Republik [F] Kongo [M]
Repubblica [F] del Congo [M]

40

Rwanda
Rwanda [M]
Ruanda [F]
Ruanda [N]
Ruanda [M]

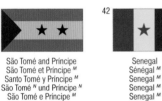

41

São Tomé and Príncipe
São Tomé et Príncipe [M]
Santo Tomé y Príncipe [M]
São Tomé [N] und Príncipe [N]
São Tomé e Príncipe [M]

42

Senegal
Sénégal [M]
Senegal [M]
Senegal [M]
Senegal [M]

43

Seychelles
Seychelles [F]
Seychelles [F]
Seychellen
Seychelles [F]

44

Sierra Leone
Sierra Leone [F]
Sierra Leona [F]
Sierra Leone [N]
Sierra Leone [F]

45

Somalia
Somalie [F]
Somalia [F]
Somalia [N]
Somalia [F]

46
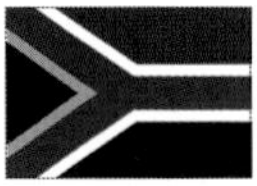
South Africa
Afrique du Sud [F]
Sudáfrica [F]
Südafrika [N]
Sudafrica [M]

47

South Sudan
sud [M] du Soudan [M]
Sudán del Sur [M]
Südsudan [M]
Sudan [M] del Sud

48

Sudan
Soudan [M]
Sudán [M]
Sudan [M]
Sudan [M]

49

Swaziland
Swaziland [M]
Suazilandia [F]
Swasiland [N]
Swaziland [M]

50

Tanzania
Tanzanie [F]
Tanzania [F]
Tansania [N]
Tanzania [F]

51

Togo
Togo [M]
Togo [M]
Togo [N]
Togo [M]

52

Tunisia
Tunisie [F]
Túnez [M]
Tunesien [N]
Tunisia [F]

53

Uganda
Ouganda [M]
Uganda [F]
Uganda [N]
Uganda [F]

54

Zambia
Zambie [F]
Zambia [F]
Sambia [N]
Zambia [M]

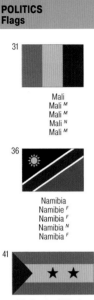

North America

Amérique [F] du Nord [M] | Norteamérica [F] | Nordamerika [N] | America [F] del Nord [M]

1

Antigua & Barbuda
Antigua-et-Barbuda [F]
Antigua y Barbuda [F]
Antigua [N] und Barbuda [N]
Antigua [F] e Barbuda [F]

2

Bahamas
Bahamas [F]
Bahamas [M]
Bahamas [F]
Bahamas [F]

3

Barbados
Barbade [F]
Barbados [F]
Barbados [N]
Barbados [F]

4

Belize
Bélize [M]
Belice [M]
Belize [N]
Belize [M]

5

Canada
Canada [M]
Canadá [M]
Kanada [N]
Canada [M]

5
22
16
2
13
7
9
4
15
1
8
19
20
12
14
3
10
17
6
11
21
18

6

Costa Rica
Costa Rica ^{M}
Costa Rica ^{F}
Costa Rica ^{N}
Costa Rica ^{F}

7

Cuba
Cuba ^{M}
Cuba ^{F}
Kuba ^{N}
Cuba ^{F}

8

Dominica
Dominique ^{F}
Dominica ^{F}
Dominica ^{N}
Dominica ^{F}

9

Dominican Republic
République ^{F} dominicaine
República Dominicana ^{F}
Dominikanische Republik ^{F}
Repubblica Dominicana ^{F}

10

El Salvador
Salvador ^{M}
El Salvador ^{M}
El Salvador ^{N}
El Salvador ^{M}

11

Grenada
Grenade ^{F}
Granada ^{F}
Grenada ^{N}
Grenada ^{M}

12

Guatemala
Guatemala ^{M}
Guatemala ^{F}
Guatemala ^{N}
Guatemala ^{M}

13

Haiti
Haïti ^{M}
Haití ^{M}
Haiti ^{N}
Haiti ^{M}

14

Honduras
Honduras ^{M}
Honduras ^{F}
Honduras ^{N}
Honduras ^{M}

15
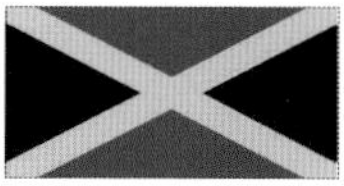

Jamaica
Jamaïque ^{F}
Jamaica ^{F}
Jamaika ^{N}
Giamaica ^{F}

16

Mexico
Mexique ^{M}
México ^{M}
Mexiko ^{N}
Messico ^{M}

17

Nicaragua
Nicaragua ^{M}
Nicaragua ^{F}
Nicaragua ^{N}
Nicaragua ^{M}

18

Panama
Panama ^{M}
Panamá ^{F}
Panama ^{N}
Panama ^{M}

19

Saint Kitts-Nevis
Saint-Kitts-et-Nevis ^{F}
San Cristóbal ^{M} y Nieves ^{F}
St. Kitts ^{N} und Nevis ^{N}
San Kitts e Nevis ^{F}

20

Saint Lucia
Sainte-Lucie ^{F}
Santa Lucía ^{F}
St. Lucia ^{N}
Santa Lucia ^{F}

21

Saint Vincent and the Grenadines
Saint-Vincent-et-les Grenadines ^{F}
San Vicente y las Granadinas ^{M}
St. Vincent ^{N} und die Grenadinen
San Vincenzo e Grenadine ^{F}

22

United States of America
États-Unis ^{M} d'Amérique ^{F}
Estados Unidos de América ^{M}
Vereinigte Staaten ^{F} von
Amerika ^{N}
Stati Uniti d'America ^{M}

South America

Amérique ^F^ du Sud ^M^ | Sudamérica ^F^ | Südamerika ^N^ | Sud America ^M^

11
13
7
10
5
6
9
3
2
8
12
1
4

1

Argentina
Argentine ^F^
Argentina ^F^
Argentinien ^N^
Argentina ^F^

2

Bolivia
Bolivie ^F^
Bolivia ^F^
Bolivien ^N^
Bolivia ^F^

3

Brazil
Brésil ^M^
Brasil ^M^
Brasilien ^N^
Brasile ^M^

4

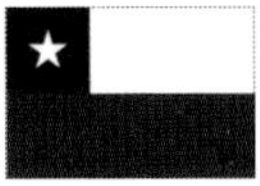

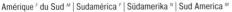

Chile
Chili ^M^
Chile ^M^
Chile ^N^
Cile ^M^

5

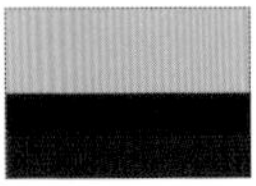

Colombia
Colombie ^F^
Colombia ^F^
Kolumbien ^N^
Colombia ^F^

6

Ecuador
Équateur ^M^
Ecuador ^M^
Ecuador ^N^
Ecuador ^M^

7

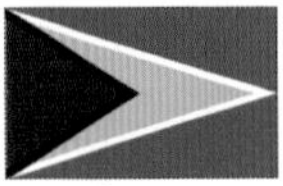

Guyana
Guyana ^M^
Guyana ^F^
Guyana ^N^
Guyana ^F^

8

Paraguay
Paraguay ^M^
Paraguay ^M^
Paraguay ^N^
Paraguay ^M^

9

Peru
Pérou ^M^
Perú ^M^
Peru ^N^
Perù ^M^

10

Suriname
Suriname ^M^
Surinam ^M^
Suriname ^N^
Suriname ^M^

11

Trinidad and Tobago
Trinité-et-Tobago ^F^
Trinidad y Tobago ^F^
Trinidad ^N^ und Tobago ^N^
Trinidad e Tobago ^M^

12

Uruguay
Uruguay ^M^
Uruguay ^M^
Uruguay ^N^
Uruguay ^M^

13

Venezuela
Venezuela ^M^
Venezuela ^F^
Venezuela ^N^
Venezuela ^M^

Australia and Oceania

Australie ^F^ et Océanie ^F^ | Australia y Oceanía ^F^ | Australien ^N^ und Ozeanien ^N^ | Australia ^F^ e Oceania ^F^

2
5
8
6
11
4
13
10
14
3
12
7

1

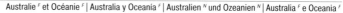

Australia
Australie ^F^
Australia ^F^
Australien ^N^
Australia ^F^

2

Federated States of Micronesia
États ^M^ fédérés de Micronésie ^F^
Estados Federales de Micronesia ^M^
Föderierte Staaten ^M^ von Mikronesien ^N^
Stati ^M^ Federati della Micronesia ^F^

3

Fiji
Fidji ^F^
Fiji ^M^
Fidschi ^N^
Fiji ^F^

4

Kiribati
Kiribati ^M^
Kiribati ^M^
Kiribati ^N^
Kiribati ^M^

5

Marshall Islands
Îles Marshall ^F^
Islas Marshall ^F^
Marshallinseln ^F^
Isole Marshall ^F^

6

Nauru
Nauru ^F^
Nauru ^M^
Nauru ^N^
Nauru ^M^

7

New Zealand
Nouvelle-Zélande ^F^
Nueva Zelanda ^F^
Neuseeland ^N^ Nuova
Zelanda ^F^

8
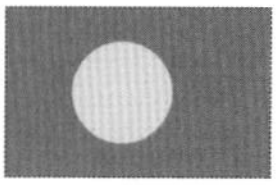

Palau
Palau ^M^
Palau ^M^
Palau ^N^
Palau ^M^

9

Papua New Guinea
Papouasie-Nouvelle-Guinée ^F^
Papua Nueva Guinea ^F^
Papua-Neuguinea ^N^
Papua Nuova Guinea ^F^

10

Samoa
Samoa ^F^
Samoa ^F^
Samoa ^N^
Samoa ^F^

11

Solomon Islands
Îles Salomon ^F^
Islas Salomón ^F^
Salomon-Inseln ^F^
Isole Salomone ^F^

12

Tonga
Tonga ^M^
Tonga ^F^
Tonga ^N^
Tonga ^M^

13

Tuvalu
Tuvalu ^M^
Tuvalu ^M^
Tuvalu ^N^
Tuvalu ^M^

14

Vanuatu
Vanuatu ^M^
Vanuatu ^M^
Vanuatu ^N^
Vanuatu ^M^

International organizations

Organisations ^F^ internationales | Organizaciones ^M^ internacionales | Internationale Organisationen ^F^ | Organizzazioni ^F^ internazionali

United Nations
Nations ^F^ unies
Naciones Unidas ^M^
Vereinte Nationen ^F^
Nazioni Unite ^F^

European Union
Union ^F^ européenne ^F^
Unión Europea ^F^
Europäische Union ^F^
Unione Europea ^F^

International Olympic Committee
Comité ^M^ international olympique
Comité Olímpico Internacional ^M^
Internationales Olympisches Komitee ^N^
Comitato ^M^ Olimpico Internazionale

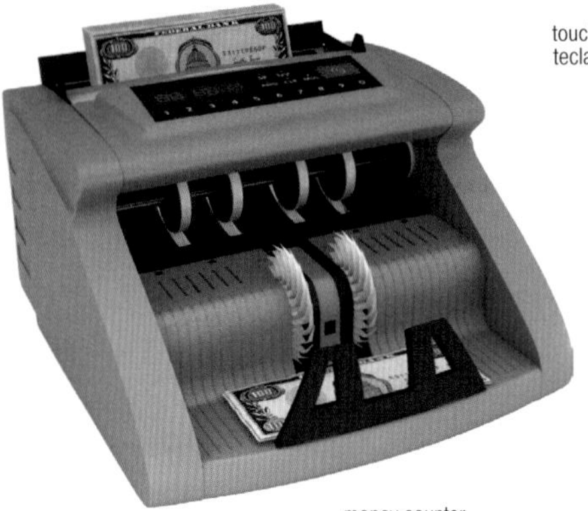

money counter
compteur [M] d'argent [M]
contador de dinero [M]
Geldzählmaschine [F]
contatore [M] di denaro [M]

$	€	£
dollar dollar [M] dólar [M] Dollar [M] dollaro [M]	euro euro [M] euro [M] Euro [M] euro [M]	pound livre [F] libra [F] Pfund [N] sterlina [F]

automatic teller machine (ATM)
guichet [M] automatique bancaire
cajero [M] automático
Bankautomat [M]
bancomat [M]

function keys
touches [F] d'opération [F]
teclas [F] de operación [F]
Funktionstasten [F]
tasti [M] funzione [F]

deposit slot
fente [F] de dépôt [M]
ranura [F] de depósito [M]
Einzahlungsschlitz [M]
fessura [F] per il deposito [M]

LEXI24 Cashpoint
Cashpoint
Please insert your card

alphanumeric keypad
clavier [M] alphanumérique
teclado [M] alfanumérico
alphanumerische Tastatur [F]
tastiera [F] alfanumerica

cash dispenser
sortie [F] des billets [M]
emisión [F] de billetes [M]
Geldscheinausgabe [F]
sportello [M] banconote [F]

card reader slot
fente [F] du lecteur [M] de carte
ranura [F] lector de tarjeta
Kartenlese-Slot [M]
fessura [F] per lettura [F] carta

check
chèque [M]
cheque [M]
Scheck [M]
assegno [M]

financial institution
institution [F] financière
institución [F] financiera
Finanzinstitut [N]
ente [M] finanziario

date of issue
date [F] de délivrance [F]
fecha [F] de emisión [F]
Ausstellungsdatum [N]
data di rilascio [M]

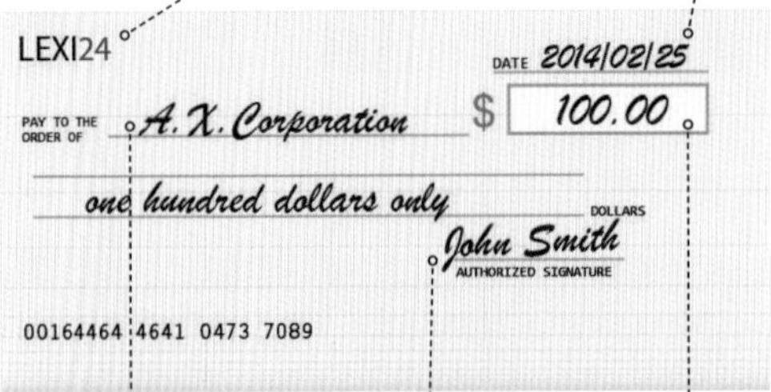
LEXI24
DATE 2014/02/25
PAY TO THE ORDER OF A. X. Corporation
$ 100.00
one hundred dollars only
DOLLARS
John Smith
AUTHORIZED SIGNATURE
00164464 4641 0473 7089

payee
bénéficiaire [M]
beneficiario [M]
Zahlungsempfänger [M]
beneficiario [M]

signature of drawer
signature [F] du débiteur [M]
firma [F] del librador
Unterschrift [F] des Ausstellers [M]
firma [F] del traente [M]

amount of currency
montant [M] en devise [F]
cantidad [F] de dinero [M]
Währungsbetrag [M]
importo [M]

stack of bills
pile [F] de billets [M]
fajo [M] de billetes [M]
Geldscheinstapel [M]
mazzetta [F] di banconote [F]

FEDERAL BANK
100
E31119560F
ONE HUNDRED DOLLARS

paper money
billet [M] de banque [F]
billete [M]
Banknote [F]
banconota [F]

50 PENNIES 50¢

roll of pennies
rouleau [M] de sous [M] noi
rollo [M] de peniques [M]
Münzrolle [F]
rotolo [M] di monetine [F]

chip
puce F
chip M
Chip M
chip M

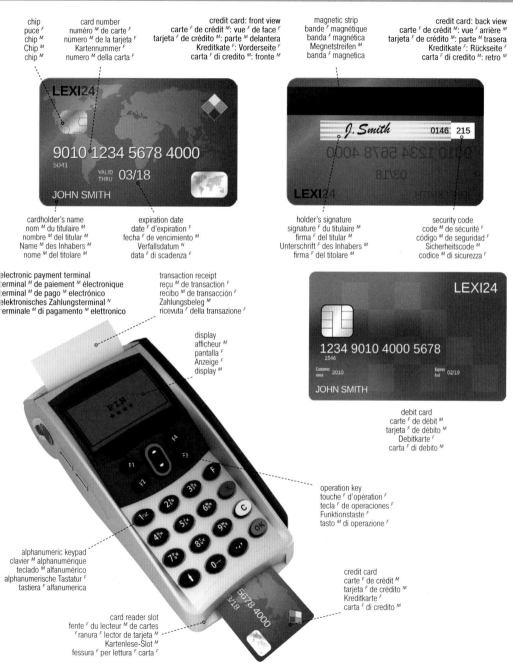

card number
numéro M de carte F
número M de la tarjeta F
Kartennummer F
numero M della carta F

credit card: front view
carte F de crédit M: vue F de face F
tarjeta F de crédito M: parte M delantera
Kreditkate F: Vorderseite F
carta F di credito M: fronte M

LEXI24
9010 1234 5678 4000
5041
VALID THRU 03/18
JOHN SMITH

cardholder's name
nom M du titulaire M
nombre M del titular M
Name M des Inhabers M
nome M del titolare M

expiration date
date F d'expiration F
fecha F de vencimiento M
Verfallsdatum N
data F di scadenza F

magnetic strip
bande F magnétique
banda F magnética
Megnetstreifen M
banda F magnetica

credit card: back view
carte F de crédit M: vue F arrière M
tarjeta F de crédito M: parte M trasera
Kreditkate F: Rückseite F
carta F di credito M: retro M

J. Smith
0146 215
LEXI24

holder's signature
signature F du titulaire M
firma F del titular M
Unterschrift F des Inhabers M
firma F del titolare M

security code
code M de sécurité F
código M de seguridad F
Sicherheitscode M
codice M di sicurezza F

electronic payment terminal
terminal M de paiement M électronique
terminal M de pago M electrónico
elektronisches Zahlungsterminal N
terminale M di pagamento M elettronico

transaction receipt
reçu M de transaction F
recibo M de transacción F
Zahlungsbeleg M
ricevuta F della transazione F

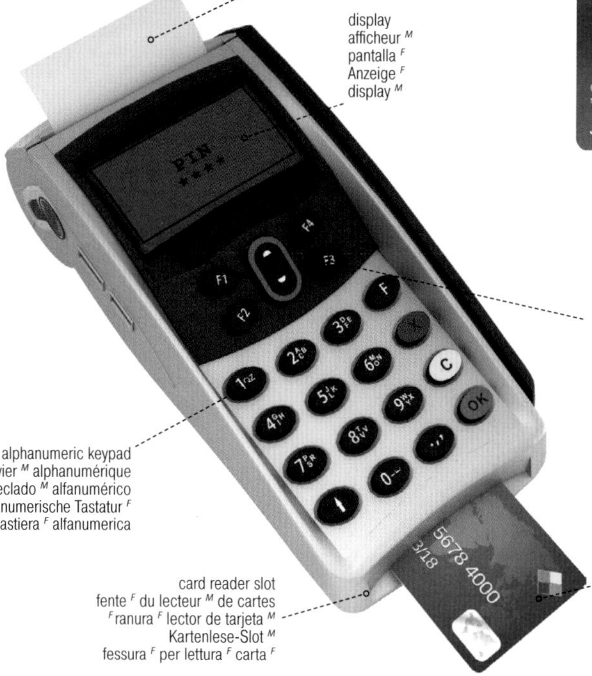
PIN
F1
F2
F3
F4
OK

display
afficheur M
pantalla F
Anzeige F
display M

operation key
touche F d'opération F
tecla F de operaciones F
Funktionstaste F
tasto M di operazione F

alphanumeric keypad
clavier M alphanumérique
teclado M alfanumérico
alphanumerische Tastatur F
tastiera F alfanumerica

card reader slot
fente F du lecteur M de cartes
F ranura F lector de tarjeta M
Kartenlese-Slot M
fessura F per lettura F carta F

credit card
carte F de crédit M
tarjeta F de crédito M
Kreditkarte F
carta F di credito M

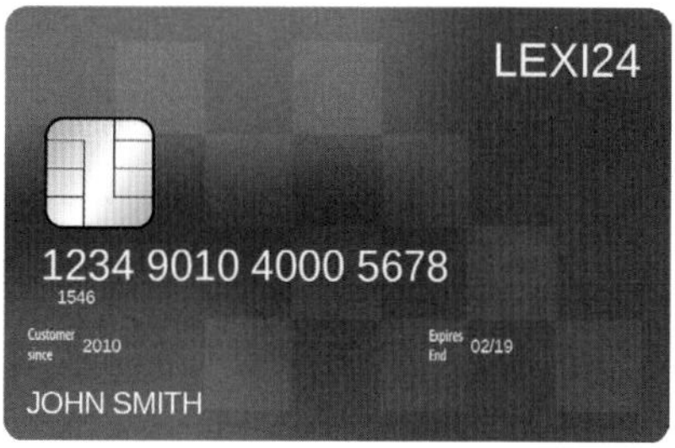
LEXI24
1234 9010 4000 5678
1546
Customer since 2010
Expires End 02/19
JOHN SMITH

debit card
carte F de débit M
tarjeta F de débito M
Debitkarte F
carta F di debito M

pistol
pistolet [M]
pistola [F]
Pistole [F]
pistola [F]

front sight
guidon [M]
punto [M] de mira [F]
Korn [N]
mirino [M]

barrel
baril [M]
barril [M]
Lauf [M]
canna [F]

takedown lever
levier [M] de démontage [M]
palanca [F] para desmontar
Take-Down-Hebel [M]
leva [F] di smontaggio [M]

rear sight
hausse [F]
alza [F] de mira [F] trasera
Kimme [F]
tacca [F] di mira

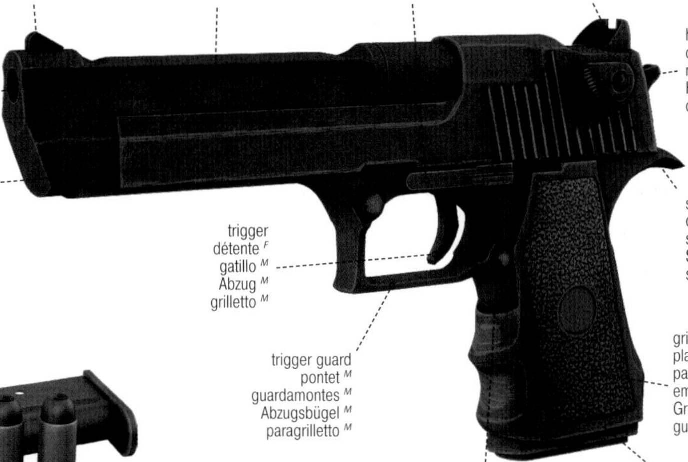

hammer
chien [M]
martillo [M]
Hahn [M]
cane [M]

muzzle
canon [M]
boca [F]
Mündung [F]
bocca [F]

slide
cadre [M]
estructura [F]
Verschluss [M]
telaio [M]

safety catch
cran [M] d'arrêt [M]
seguro [M]
Sicherung [F]
sicura [F]

trigger
détente [F]
gatillo [M]
Abzug [M]
grilletto [M]

magazine
chargeur [M]
cargador [M]
Magazin [N]
clip [F]

trigger guard
pontet [M]
guardamontes [M]
Abzugsbügel [M]
paragrilletto [M]

grip panel
plaquette [F]
panel [M] de empuñadura [F]
Grifffeld [N]
guancetta [F]

cartridge case
douille [F]
envoltura [F]
Patronenhülse [F]
cartucciera [F]

magazine catch
arrêtoir [M] de chargeur [M]
retén [M] del cargador [M]
Magazinhalter [M]
pulsante [M] di rilascio [M] del caricatore [M]

butt
manche [M]
mango [M]
Griff [M]
impugnatura [F]

magazine
chargeur [M]
cargador [M]
Magazin [N]
clip [F]

bullet
balle [F]
bala [F]
Kugel [F]
proiettile [M]

revolver
revolver [M]
revólver [M]
Revolver [M]
rivoltella [F]

front sight
guidon [M]
mira [F] delantera
Korn [N]
mirino [M]

barrel
barillet [M]
cañón [M]
Lauf [M]
canna [F]

cylinder
cylindre [M]
cilindro [M]
Zylinder [M]
cilindro [M]

hammer
chien [M]
martillo [M]
Hahn [M]
cane [M]

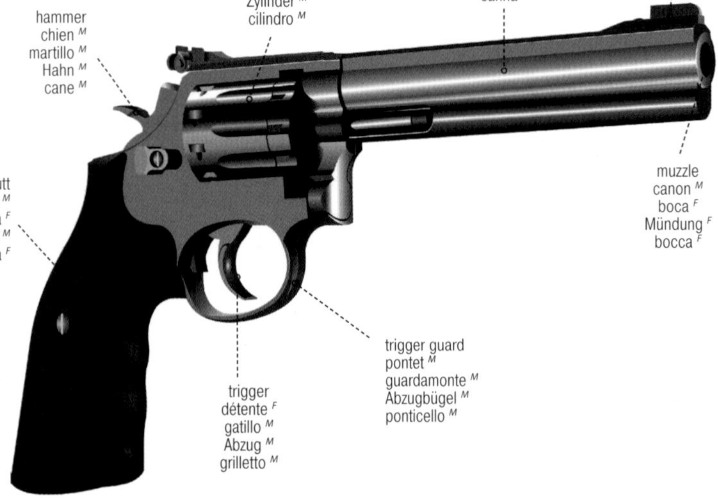

muzzle
canon [M]
boca [F]
Mündung [F]
bocca [F]

butt
manche [M]
empuñadura [F]
Griff [M]
impugnatura [F]

trigger guard
pontet [M]
guardamonte [M]
Abzugbügel [M]
ponticello [M]

trigger
détente [F]
gatillo [M]
Abzug [M]
grilletto [M]

assault rifle
fusil [M] d'assaut [M]
fusil [M] automático de asalto [M]
Sturmgewehr [N]
fucile [M] d'assalto [M]

front sight housing
protège-guidon [M]
punto [M] de mira [F]
Kornhalter [M]
mirino [M] anteriore

gas tube
tube [M] à gaz [M]
respiradero [M]
Antriebsstange [F]
sfiato [M] del gas [M]

rear sight
hausse [F]
alza [F] de mira [F]
Visier [N]
mirino [M] posteriore

trigger
détente [F]
gatillo [M]
Abzug [M]
grilletto [M]

safety lever
verrou [M] de sureté [F]
bloqueo [M] de seguridad [F]
Sicherheitsschloss [N] und Feuerhebel [M]
sicura [F]

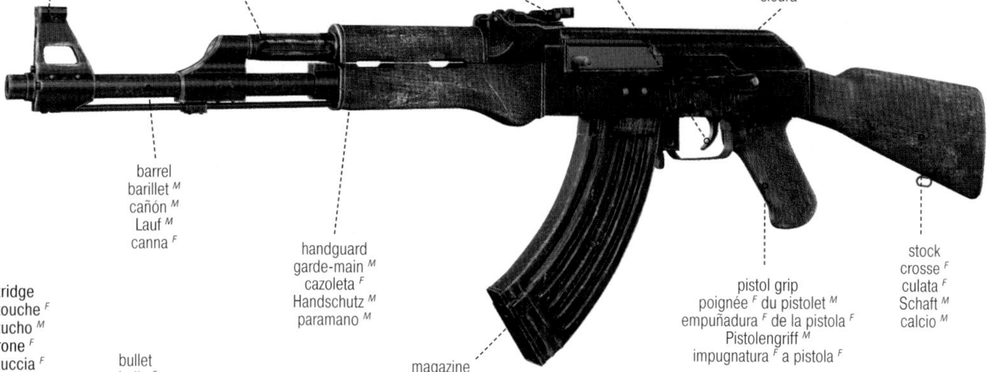

barrel
barillet [M]
cañón [M]
Lauf [M]
canna [F]

handguard
garde-main [M]
cazoleta [F]
Handschutz [M]
paramano [M]

magazine
chargeur [M]
cargador [M]
Magazin [N]
caricatore [M]

pistol grip
poignée [F] du pistolet [M]
empuñadura [F] de la pistola [F]
Pistolengriff [M]
impugnatura [F] a pistola [F]

stock
crosse [F]
culata [F]
Schaft [M]
calcio [M]

artridge
artouche [F]
artucho [M]
'atrone [F]
artuccia [F]

bullet
balle [F]
bala [F]
Kugel [F]
proiettile [M]

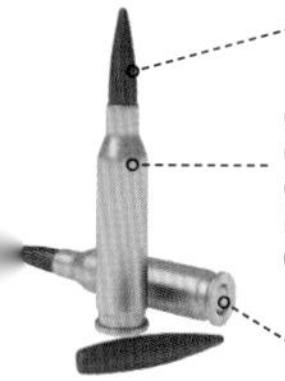

cartridge case
douille [F]
cartuchera [F]
Patronenhülse [F]
cartucciera [F]

primer
amorce [F]
pistón [M]
Zündkapsel [F]
innesco [M]

assault rifle with folding stock
fusil [M] d'assaut [M] avec crosse [F] repliable
rifle [M] de asalto [M] con culata [F] plegable
Sturmgewehr [N] mit Klappschaft [M]
fucile [M] d'assalto [M] con calcio [M] pieghevole

light machine gun
mitrailleuse [F] légère
ametralladora [F] ligera
leichtes Maschinengewehr [N]
mitragliatore [M] leggero

rocket-propelled grenade (RPG) and launcher
grenade [F] propulsée par roquette [F] et rampe [F] de lancement [M]
granada [F] propulsada por cohete [M] y lanzacohetes [M]
Panzerfaust [F]
RPG lanciarazzi [F]

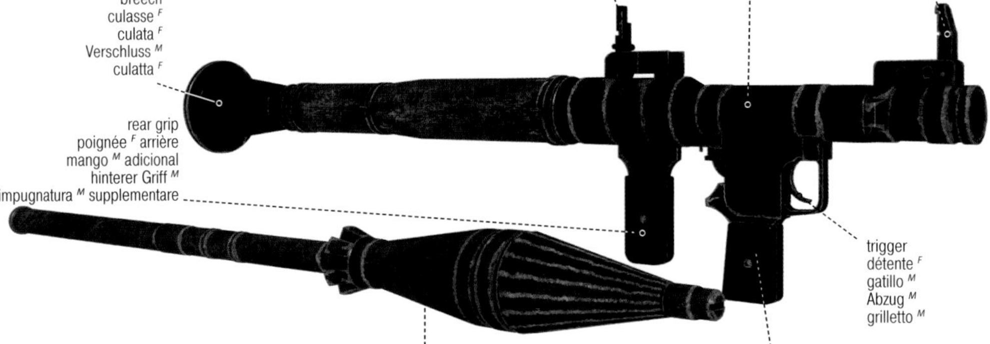

optical sight
lunette [F] de tir [M]
alza [F] de mira [F] mecánico
optisches Visier [N]
mirino [M] ottico

barrel
barillet [M]
cañón [M]
Lauf [M]
canna [F]

front sight
guidon [M]
punto [M] de mira [F]
Korn [N]
mirino [M]

breech
culasse [F]
culata [F]
Verschluss [M]
culatta [F]

rear grip
poignée [F] arrière
mango [M] adicional
hinterer Griff [M]
impugnatura [M] supplementare

trigger
détente [F]
gatillo [M]
Abzug [M]
grilletto [M]

grenade
grenade [F]
granada [F]
Granate [F]
granata [F]

front grip
poignée [F] avant
mango [M]
Griff [M]
maniglia [F]

shotgun
fusil [M] à pompe [F]
escopeta [F]
Flinte [F]
fucile [M] a pompa [F]

sniper rifle
fusil [M] de sniper [M]
rifle [M] de francotirador [M]
Scharfschützengewehr [N]
fucile [M] di precisione [F]

optical sight
lunette [F] de tir [M]
alza [M] de mira [F] óptico
optisches Visier [N]
mirino [M] ottico

rear sight
hausse [F]
alza [M] de mira [F] mecánico
Kimme [F]
mirino [M] posteriore

barrel
barillet [M]
cañón [M]
Lauf [M]
canna [F]

front sight
viseur [M]
punto [M] de mira [F]
Korn [N]
mirino [M] anteriore

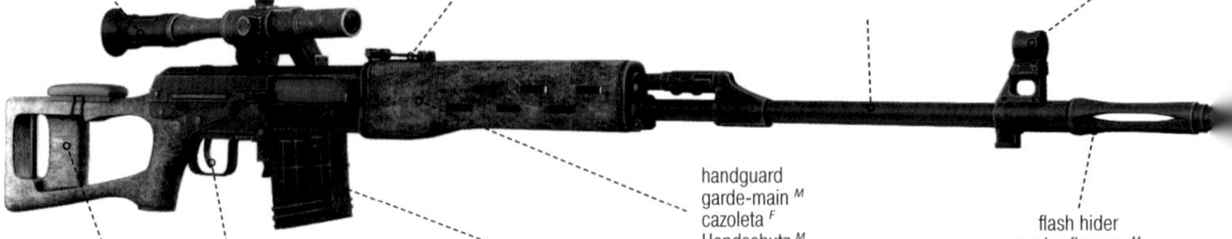

handguard
garde-main [M]
cazoleta [F]
Handschutz [M]
paramano [M]

flash hider
cache-flamme [M]
soporte [M] del punto [M] de mira [F]
Feuerdämpfer [M]
bindella [F]

stock
crosse [F]
culata [F]
Schaft [M]
calcio [M]

trigger
détente [F]
gatillo [M]
Abzug [M]
grilletto [M]

magazine
chargeur [M]
cargador [M]
Magazin [N]
caricatore [M]

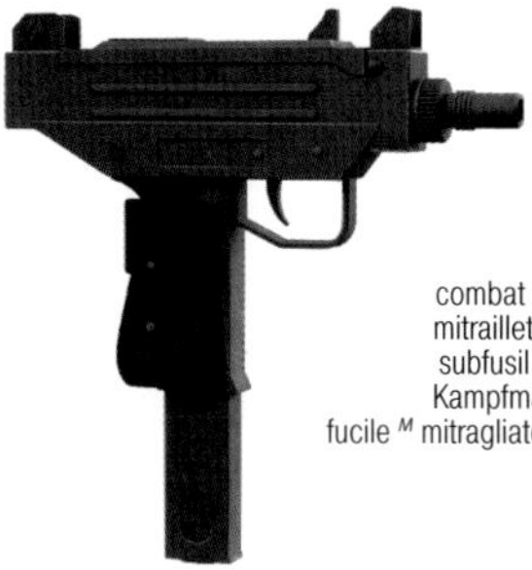

combat submachine gun
mitraillette [F] de combat [M]
subfusil [M] de combate [M]
Kampfmaschinenpistole [F]
fucile [M] mitragliatore [M] da combattimento [M]

submachine gun
mitraillette [F]
subfusil [M]
Maschinenpistole [F]
fucile [M] mitragliatore [M]

aerial bomb
bombe [F] aérienne
bomba [F] aérea
Fliegerbombe [F]
bomba [F] aerea

stun grenade
grenade [F] incapacitante
granada [F] de aturdimiento [M]
Blendgranate [F]
granata [F] stordente

primary pull ring
premier anneau [M]
anilla [F] de tiro [M] principal
Hauptzugring [M]
spoletta [F] principale

secondary pull ring
deuxième anneau [M]
anilla [F] de tiro [M] secundaria
Nebenzugring [M]
spoletta [F] secondaria

safety lever
levier [M] de sécurité [F]
palanca [F] de seguridad [F]
Sicherheitshebel [M]
leva [F] di sicurezza

body
corps [M]
cuerpo [M]
Gehäuse [N]
corpo [M]

charge
charge [F]
carga [F]
Ladung [F]
carica [F]

mine
mine [F]
mina [F]
Mine [F]
mina [F]

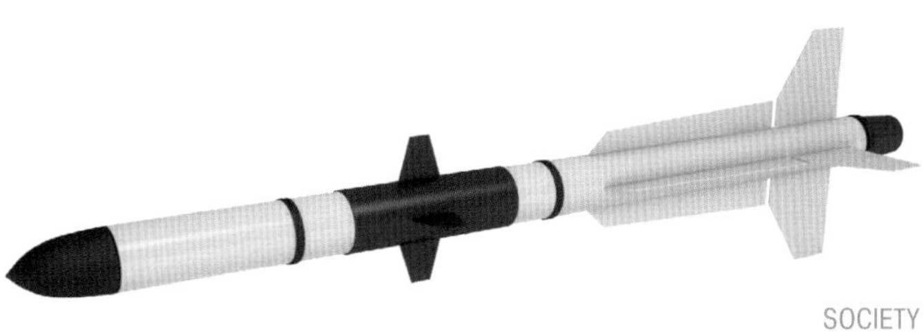

missile
missile [M]
misil [M]
Rakete [F]
missile [M]

soldier
soldat M
soldado M
Soldat M
soldato M

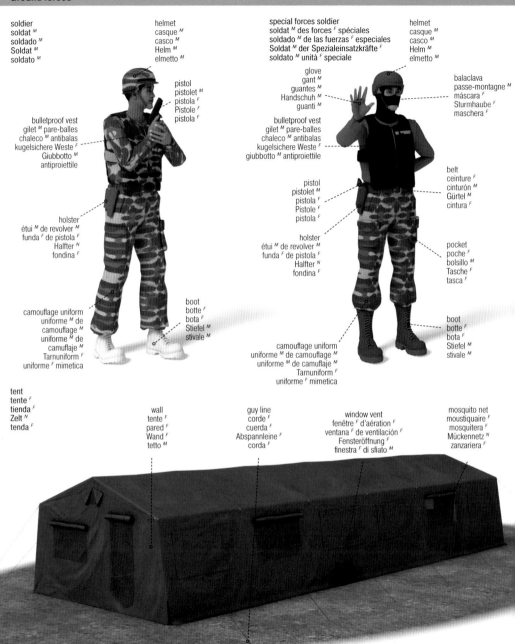

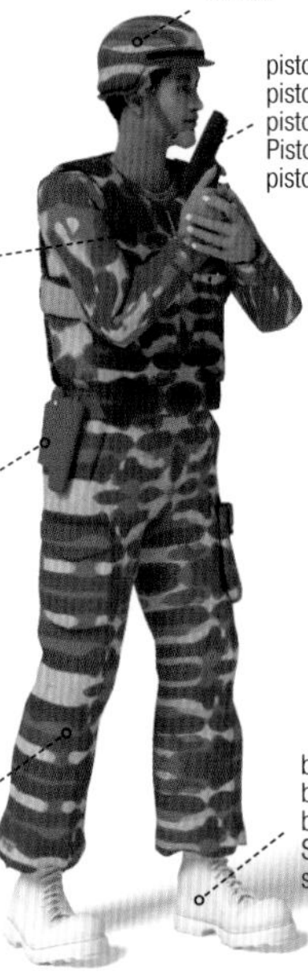
helmet
casque M
casco M
Helm M
elmetto M
pistol
pistolet M
pistola F
Pistole F
pistola F
bulletproof vest
gilet M pare-balles
chaleco M antibalas
kugelsichere Weste F
Giubbotto M
antiproiettile
holster
étui M de revolver M
funda F de pistola F
Halfter N
fondina F
camouflage uniform
uniforme M de
camouflage M
uniforme M de
camuflaje M
Tarnuniform F
uniforme F mimetica
boot
botte F
bota F
Stiefel M
stivale M

special forces soldier
soldat M des forces F spéciales
soldado M de las fuerzas F especiales
Soldat M der Spezialeinsatzkräfte F
soldato M unità F speciale

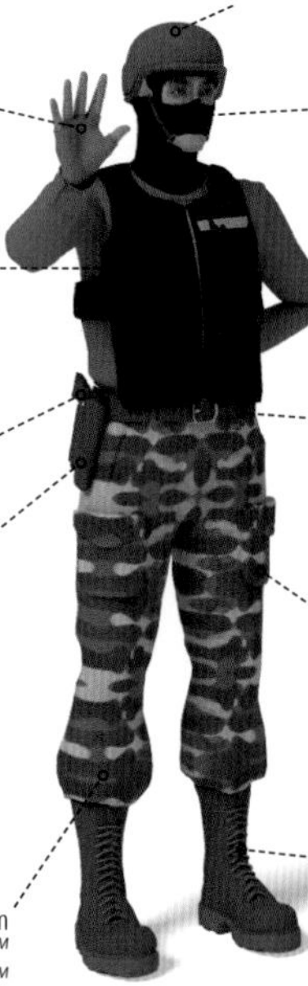
helmet
casque M
casco M
Helm M
elmetto M
glove
gant M
guantes M
Handschuh M
guanti M
balaclava
passe-montagne M
máscara F
Sturmhaube F
maschera F
bulletproof vest
gilet M pare-balles
chaleco M antibalas
kugelsichere Weste F
giubbotto M antiproiettile
pistol
pistolet M
pistola F
Pistole F
pistola F
belt
ceinture F
cinturón M
Gürtel M
cintura F
holster
étui M de revolver M
funda F de pistola F
Halfter N
fondina F
pocket
poche F
bolsillo M
Tasche F
tasca F
boot
botte F
bota F
Stiefel M
stivale M
camouflage uniform
uniforme M de camouflage M
uniforme M de camuflaje M
Tarnuniform F
uniforme F mimetica

tent
tente F
tienda F
Zelt N
tenda F

wall
tente F
pared F
Wand F
tetto M
guy line
corde F
cuerda F
Abspannleine F
corda F
window vent
fenêtre F d'aération F
ventana F de ventilación F
Fensteröffnung F
finestra F di sfiato M
mosquito net
moustiquaire F
mosquitera F
Mückennetz N
zanzariera F

main battle tank (MBT)
char ^{M} de combat ^{M} principal
tanque ^{M} de batalla ^{F}
Kampfpanzer ^{M}
principali ^{M} carri ^{M} armati

turret
tourelle ^{F}
torreta ^{F}
Panzerturm ^{M}
torretta ^{F}
periscope
périscope ^{M}
periscopio ^{M}
Sehrohr ^{N}
periscopio ^{M}
armor
blindage ^{M}
blindaje ^{M}
Panzerung ^{F}
struttura ^{F}
cannon
canon ^{M}
cañón ^{M}
Kanone ^{F}
cannone ^{M}
headlight
phare ^{M}
faro ^{M} delantero
Frontscheinwerfer ^{M}
faro ^{M}
wheel
roue ^{F}
rueda ^{F}
Rad ^{N}
ruota ^{F}
hatch
trappe ^{F}
escotilla ^{F}
Luke ^{F}
portello ^{M}
track
chenille ^{F}
oruga ^{F}
Gleiskette ^{F}
cingolo ^{M}

infantry fighting vehicle (IFV)
véhicule ^{M} de combat ^{M} d'infanterie ^{F}
vehículo ^{M} de combate ^{M} de infantería ^{F}
Schützenpanzer ^{M}
veicolo ^{M} da combattimento della fanteria

heavy tank
char ^{M} lourd
tanque ^{M} pesado
schwerer Panzer ^{M}
carroarmato ^{M}

high mobility multipurpose wheeled vehicle (humvee)
véhicule M sur roues F polyvalent à grande mobilité F
vehículo M todoterreno multiuso
Mehrzweckgeländewveicolo M
veicolo M multifunzione su ruote F ad alta mobilità F (humvee M)

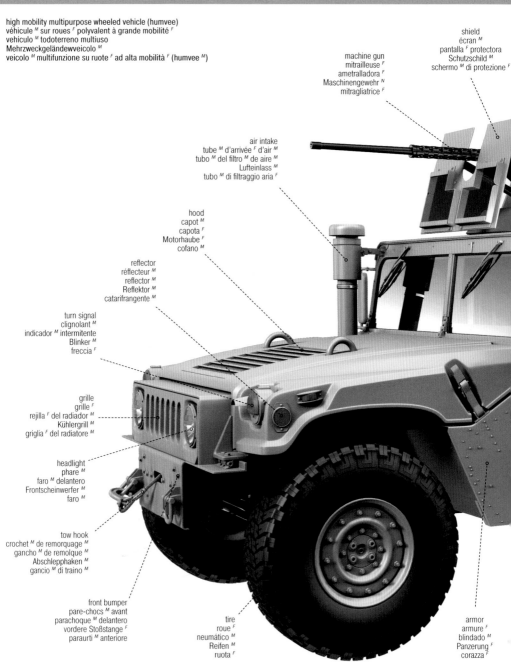

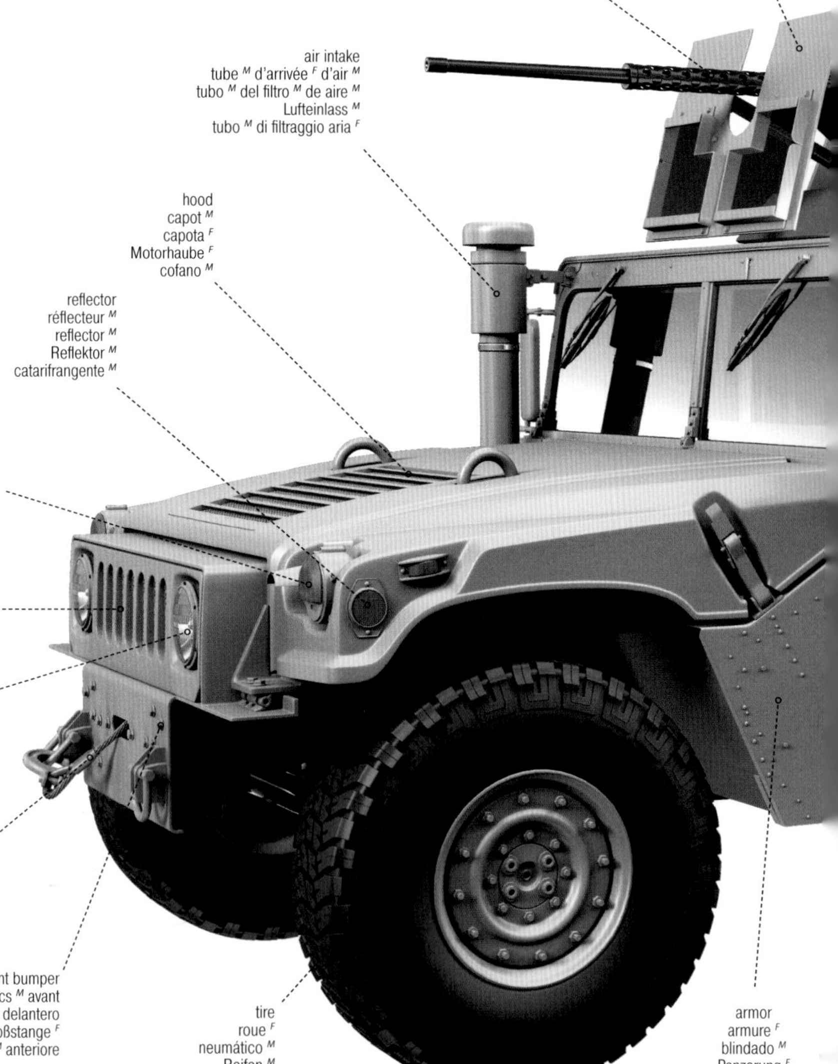
shield
écran M
pantalla F protectora
Schutzschild M
schermo M di protezione F
machine gun
mitrailleuse F
ametralladora F
Maschinengewehr N
mitragliatrice F
air intake
tube M d'arrivée F d'air M
tubo M del filtro M de aire M
Lufteinlass M
tubo M di filtraggio aria F
hood
capot M
capota F
Motorhaube F
cofano M
reflector
réflecteur M
reflector M
Reflektor M
catarifrangente M
turn signal
clignolant M
indicador M intermitente
Blinker M
freccia F
grille
grille F
rejilla F del radiador M
Kühlergrill M
griglia F del radiatore M
headlight
phare M
faro M delantero
Frontscheinwerfer M
faro M
tow hook
crochet M de remorquage M
gancho M de remolque M
Abschlepphaken M
gancio M di traino M
front bumper
pare-chocs M avant
parachoque M delantero
vordere Stoßstange F
paraurti M anteriore
tire
roue F
neumático M
Reifen M
ruota F
armor
armure F
blindado M
Panzerung F
corazza F

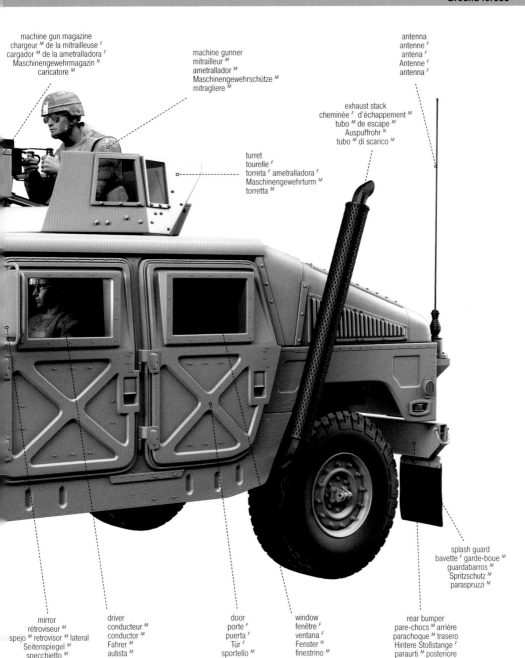

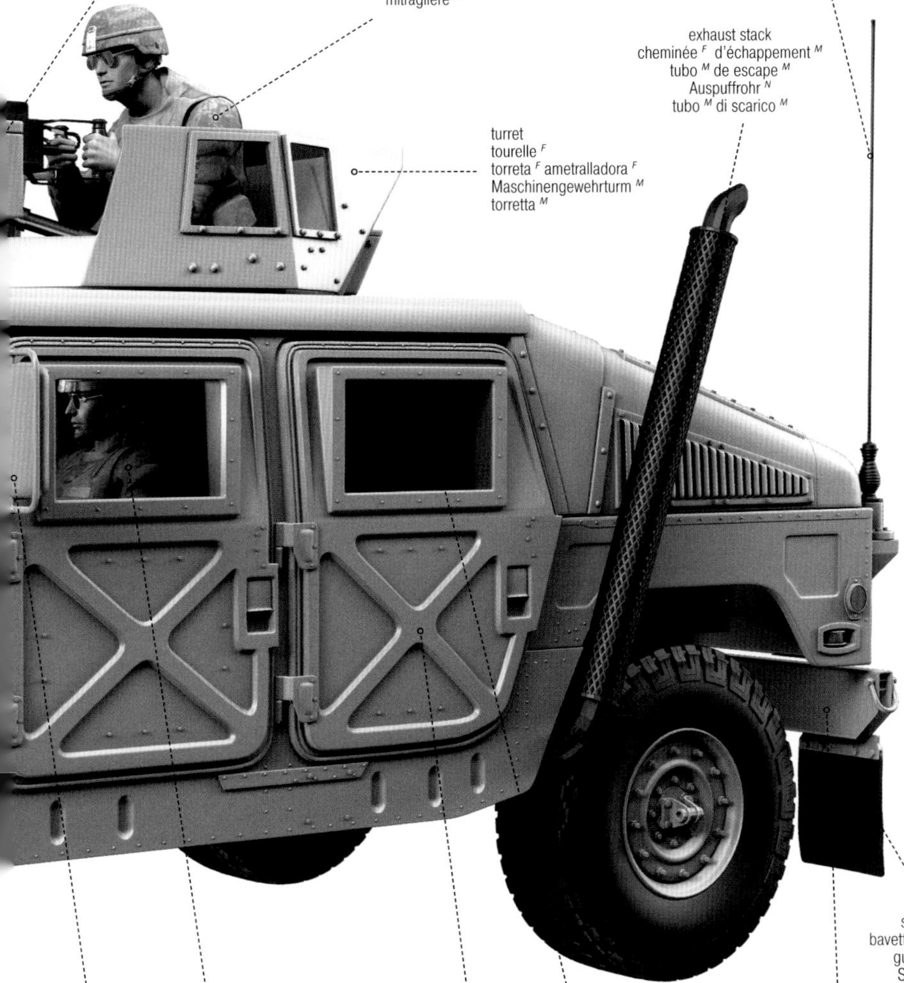
machine gun magazine
chargeur [M] de la mitrailleuse [F]
cargador [M] de la ametralladora [F]
Maschinengewehrmagazin [N]
caricatore [M]
machine gunner
mitrailleur [M]
ametrallador [M]
Maschinengewehrschütze [M]
mitragliere [M]
antenna
antenne [F]
antena [F]
Antenne [F]
antenna [F]
exhaust stack
cheminée [F] d'échappement [M]
tubo [M] de escape [M]
Auspuffrohr [N]
tubo [M] di scarico [M]
turret
tourelle [F]
torreta [F] ametralladora [F]
Maschinengewehrturm [M]
torretta [M]
splash guard
bavette [F] garde-boue [M]
guardabarros [M]
Spritzschutz [M]
paraspruzzi [M]
mirror
rétroviseur [M]
spejo [M] retrovisor [M] lateral
Seitenspiegel [M]
specchietto [M]
driver
conducteur [M]
conductor [M]
Fahrer [M]
autista [M]
door
porte [F]
puerta [F]
Tür [F]
sportello [M]
window
fenêtre [F]
ventana [F]
Fenster [N]
finestrino [M]
rear bumper
pare-chocs [M] arrière
parachoque [M] trasero
Hintere Stoßstange [F]
paraurti [M] posteriore

humvee: bottom view
véhicule [M] militaire tous terrains: vue [F] de dessous [M]
vehículo [M] todoterreno multiuso: vista [F] inferior
Unteransicht [F] auf Geländewagen [M]
humvee [M]: vista [F] dal basso [M]

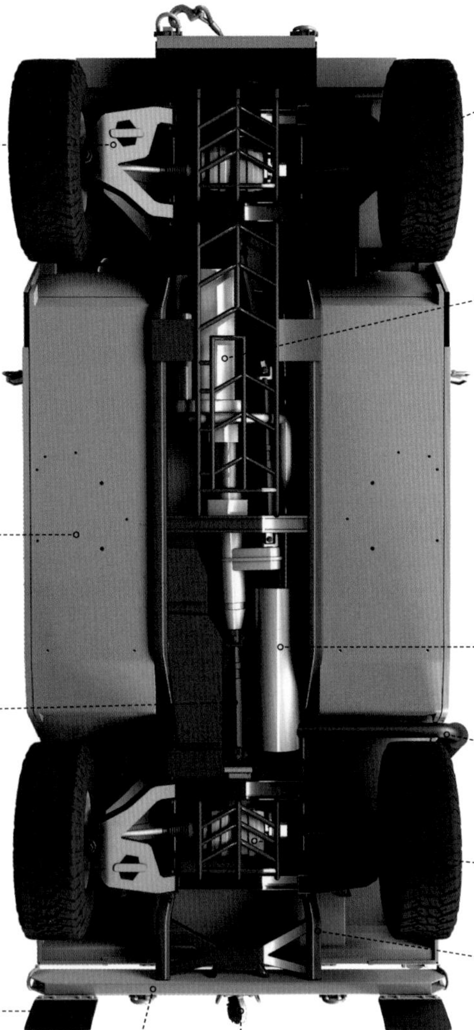

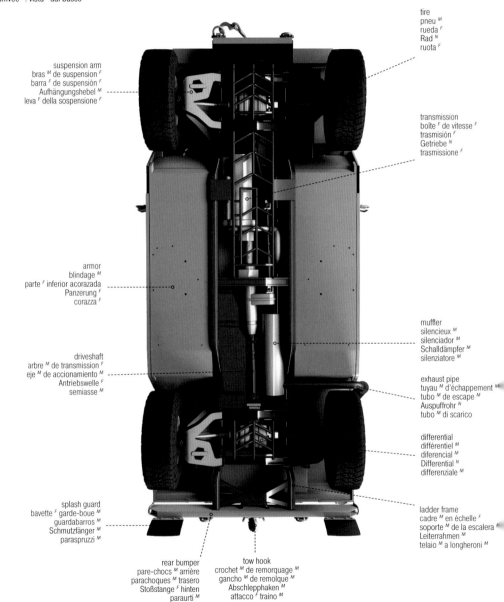

tire
pneu [M]
rueda [F]
Rad [N]
ruota [F]

suspension arm
bras [M] de suspension [F]
barra [F] de suspensión [F]
Aufhängungshebel [M]
leva [F] della sospensione [F]

transmission
boîte [F] de vitesse [F]
trasmisión [F]
Getriebe [N]
trasmissione [F]

armor
blindage [M]
parte [F] inferior acorazada
Panzerung [F]
corazza [F]

muffler
silencieux [M]
silenciador [M]
Schalldämpfer [M]
silenziatore [M]

driveshaft
arbre [M] de transmission [F]
eje [M] de accionamiento [M]
Antriebswelle [F]
semiasse [M]

exhaust pipe
tuyau [M] d'échappement [M]
tubo [M] de escape [M]
Auspuffrohr [N]
tubo [M] di scarico

differential
différentiel [M]
diferencial [M]
Differential [N]
differenziale [M]

ladder frame
cadre [M] en échelle [F]
soporte [M] de la escalera
Leiterrahmen [M]
telaio [M] a longheroni [M]

splash guard
bavette [F] garde-boue [M]
guardabarros [M]
Schmutzfänger [M]
paraspruzzi [M]

rear bumper
pare-chocs [M] arrière
parachoques [M] trasero
Stoßstange [F] hinten
paraurti [M]

tow hook
crochet [M] de remorquage [M]
gancho [M] de remolque [M]
Abschlepphaken [M]
attacco [F] traino [M]

truck
camion [M]
camión [M]
Lastkraftwagen [M]
camion [M]

Czech hedgehog
hérisson [M] tchèque
erizo [M] checo
Tschechenigel [M]
riccio [M] ceco [M]

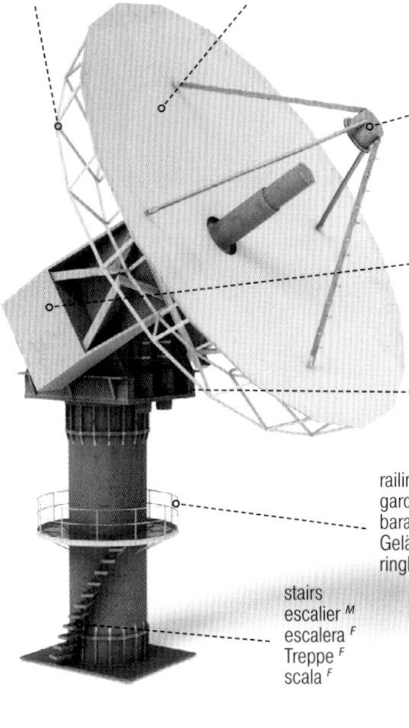
dish antenna
antenne [F]
parabolique antena [F]
Parabolantenne [F]
antenna [F]
load-bearing frame
cadre [M] porteur
armazón [F]
Tragrahmen [M]
struttura [F] portante
parabolic reflector
réflecteur [M] parabolique
reflector [M] principal
Parabolreflektor [M]
riflettore [M] parabolico
feed horn
cornet [M] d'alimentation [F]
bocina [F] de alimentación [F]
Einspeisungshorn [N]
convertitore [M]
elevation adjustment
ajustement [M] d'élévation [F]
mecanismo [M] de elevación [F]
Höhenverstellung [F]
meccanismo [M] di elevazione [F]
azimuth adjustment
ajustement [M] azimut
mecanismo [M] azimutal
Azimutvorrichtung [F]
meccanismo [M] di azimut [M]
railing
garde-corps [M]
barandilla [F]
Geländer [N]
ringhiera [F]
stairs
escalier [M]
escalera [F]
Treppe [F]
scala [F]

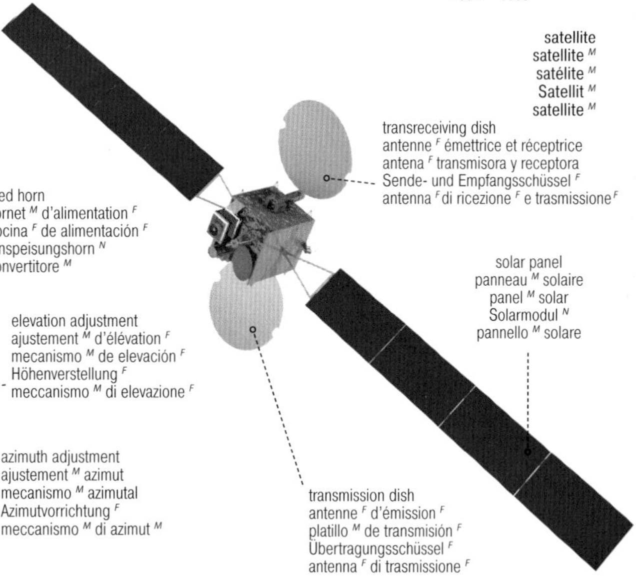
satellite
satellite [M]
satélite [M]
Satellit [M]
satellite [M]
transreceiving dish
antenne [F] émettrice et réceptrice
antena [F] transmisora y receptora
Sende- und Empfangsschüssel [F]
antenna [F] di ricezione [F] e trasmissione [F]
solar panel
panneau [M] solaire
panel [M] solar
Solarmodul [N]
pannello [M] solare
transmission dish
antenne [F] d'émission [F]
platillo [M] de transmisión [F]
Übertragungsschüssel [F]
antenna [F] di trasmissione [F]

Airplanes

Avions M | Aviones M | Flugzeuge N | Aerei M

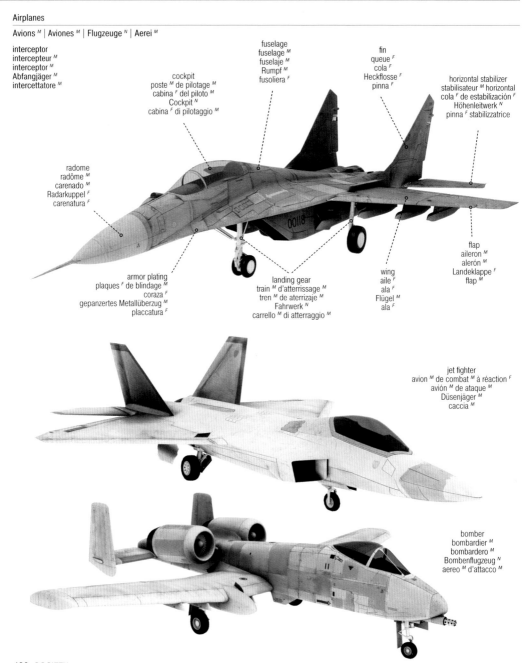

interceptor
intercepteur M
interceptor M
Abfangjäger M
intercettatore M

cockpit
poste M de pilotage M
cabina F del piloto M
Cockpit N
cabina F di pilotaggio M
fuselage
fuselage M
fuselaje M
Rumpf M
fusoliera F
fin
queue F
cola F
Heckflosse F
pinna F
horizontal stabilizer
stabilisateur M horizontal
cola F de estabilización F
Höhenleitwerk N
pinna F stabilizzatrice
radome
radôme M
carenado M
Radarkuppel F
carenatura F
00118
armor plating
plaques F de blindage M
coraza F
gepanzertes Metallüberzug M
placcatura F
landing gear
train M d'atterrissage M
tren M de aterrizaje M
Fahrwerk N
carrello M di atterraggio M
wing
aile F
ala F
Flügel M
ala F
flap
aileron M
alerón M
Landeklappe F
flap M

jet fighter
avion M de combat M à réaction F
avión M de ataque M
Düsenjäger M
caccia M

bomber
bombardier M
bombardero M
Bombenflugzeug N
aereo M d'attacco M

unmanned combat air vehicle (drone)
avion [M] de combat [M] sans équipage [M] (drone [M])
aviones [M] de combate [M] no tripulados
Unbemanntes Kampfflugzeug [N] (Drohne [F])
veicolo [M] da combattimento [M] aereo senza pilota [M] (drone [M])

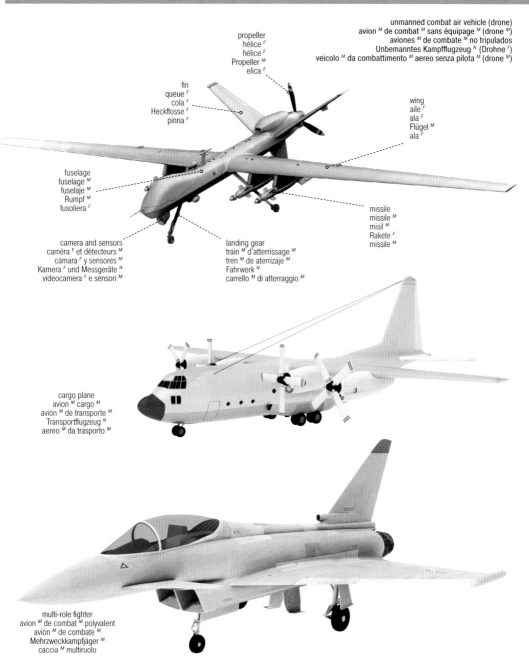

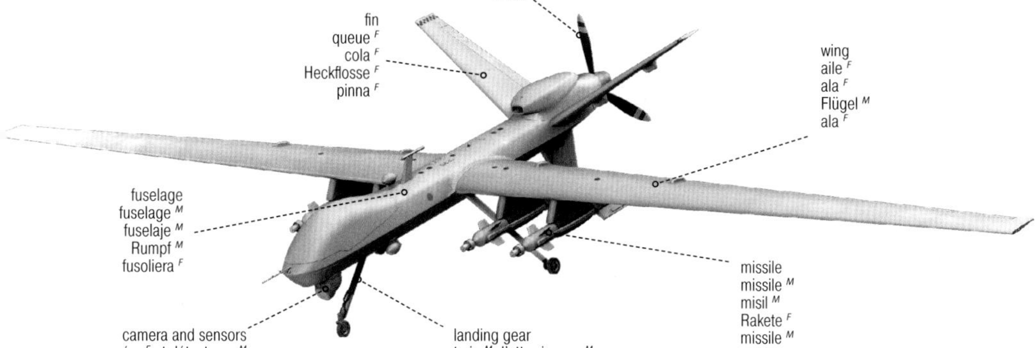
propeller
hélice [F]
hélice [F]
Propeller [M]
elica [F]
fin
queue [F]
cola [F]
Heckflosse [F]
pinna [F]
wing
aile [F]
ala [F]
Flügel [M]
ala [F]
fuselage
fuselage [M]
fuselaje [M]
Rumpf [M]
fusoliera [F]
missile
missile [M]
misil [M]
Rakete [F]
missile [M]
camera and sensors
caméra [F] et détecteurs [M]
cámara [F] y sensores [M]
Kamera [F] und Messgeräte [N]
videocamera [F] e sensori [M]
landing gear
train [M] d'atterrissage [M]
tren [M] de aterrizaje [M]
Fahrwerk [N]
carrello [M] di atterraggio [M]

cargo plane
avion [M] cargo [M]
avión [M] de transporte [M]
Transportflugzeug [N]
aereo [M] da trasporto [M]

multi-role fighter
avion [M] de combat [M] polyvalent
avión [M] de combate [M]
Mehrzweckkampfjäger [M]
caccia [M] multiruolo

Helicopters

Hélicoptère ᴹ | Helicóptero ᴹ | Hubschrauber ᴹ | Elicotteri ᴹ

utility helicopter: side view
hélicoptère ᴹ polyvalent: vue ᶠ de côté
helicóptero ᴹ multi función ᶠ: vista ᶠ lateral
Seitenansicht ᶠ eines Mehrzweckhubschraubers ᴹ
elicottero ᴹ multiuso: vista ᶠ laterale

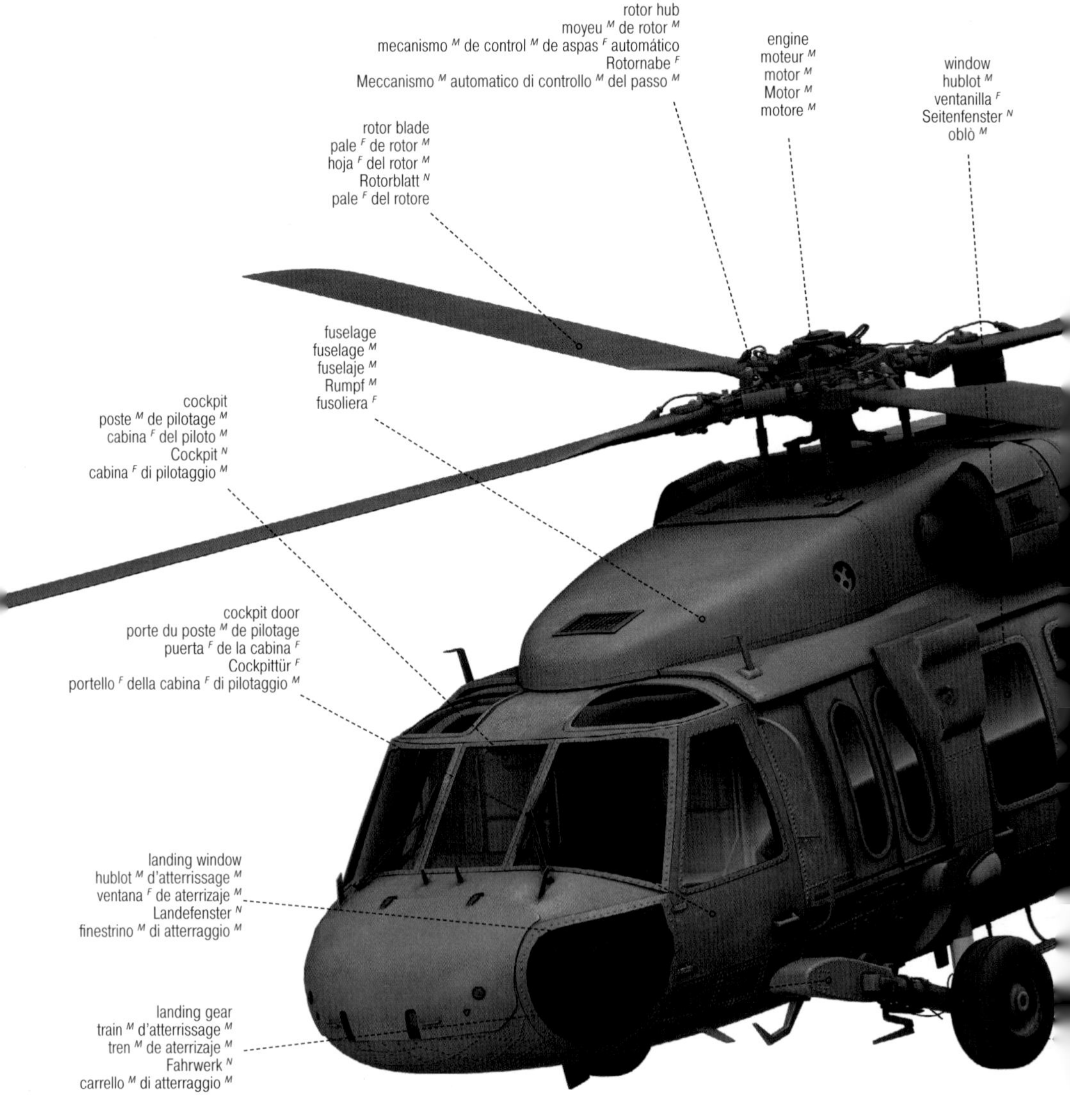
rotor hub
moyeu ᴹ de rotor ᴹ
mecanismo ᴹ de control ᴹ de aspas ᶠ automático
Rotornabe ᶠ
Meccanismo ᴹ automatico di controllo ᴹ del passo ᴹ
engine
moteur ᴹ
motor ᴹ
Motor ᴹ
motore ᴹ
window
hublot ᴹ
ventanilla ᶠ
Seitenfenster ᴺ
oblò ᴹ
rotor blade
pale ᶠ de rotor ᴹ
hoja ᶠ del rotor ᴹ
Rotorblatt ᴺ
pale ᶠ del rotore
fuselage
fuselage ᴹ
fuselaje ᴹ
Rumpf ᴹ
fusoliera ᶠ
cockpit
poste ᴹ de pilotage ᴹ
cabina ᶠ del piloto ᴹ
Cockpit ᴺ
cabina ᶠ di pilotaggio ᴹ
cockpit door
porte du poste ᴹ de pilotage
puerta ᶠ de la cabina ᶠ
Cockpittür ᶠ
portello ᶠ della cabina ᶠ di pilotaggio ᴹ
landing window
hublot ᴹ d'atterrissage ᴹ
ventana ᶠ de aterrizaje ᴹ
Landefenster ᴺ
finestrino ᴹ di atterraggio ᴹ
landing gear
train ᴹ d'atterrissage ᴹ
tren ᴹ de aterrizaje ᴹ
Fahrwerk ᴺ
carrello ᴹ di atterraggio ᴹ

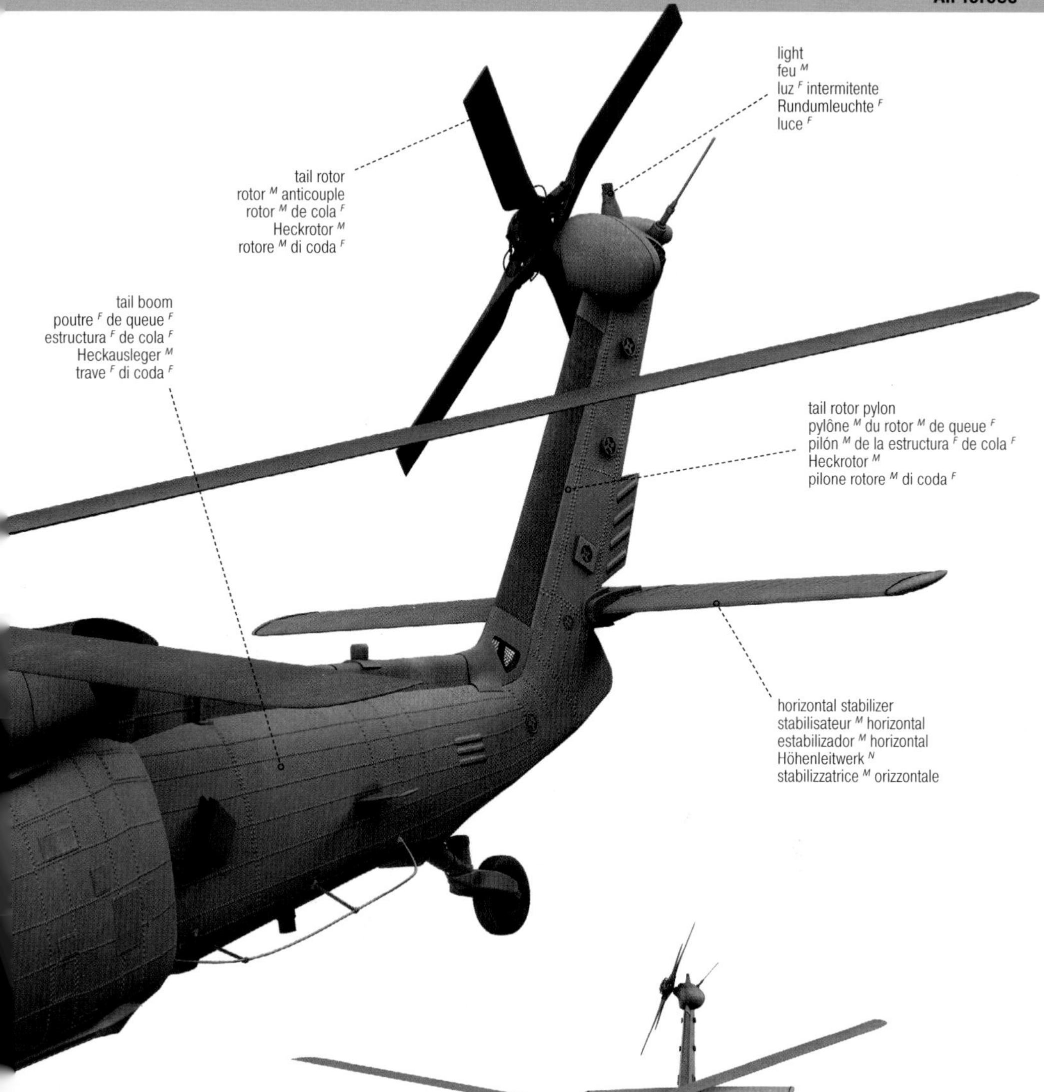
light
feu [M]
luz [F] intermitente
Rundumleuchte [F]
luce [F]
tail rotor
rotor [M] anticouple
rotor [M] de cola [F]
Heckrotor [M]
rotore [M] di coda [F]
tail boom
poutre [F] de queue [F]
estructura [F] de cola [F]
Heckausleger [M]
trave [F] di coda [F]
tail rotor pylon
pylône [M] du rotor [M] de queue [F]
pilón [M] de la estructura [F] de cola [F]
Heckrotor [M]
pilone rotore [M] di coda [F]
horizontal stabilizer
stabilisateur [M] horizontal
estabilizador [M] horizontal
Höhenleitwerk [N]
stabilizzatrice [M] orizzontale
step
marchepied [M]
escalón [M]
Trittstufe [F]
scalino [M]
wheel
roue [F]
rueda [F]
Rad [N]
ruota [F]

utility helicopter: front view
hélicoptère [M]: vue [F] de devant [M]
helicóptero [M]: vista [F] delantera
Vorderansicht [F] des Hubschraubers [M]
elicottero [M]: vista [F] frontale

cockpit
poste M de pilotage M
cabina F de vuelo
Cockpit N
cabina F di pilotaggio M
windshield
pare-brise M
parabrisas M
Windschutzscheibe F
parabrezza M
windshield wiper
essuie-glace M
limpiaparabrisas M
Scheibenwischer M
tergicristallo M
control stick
manche M à balai M
palanca F de control M
Steuerknüppel M
barra F di controllo M
instrument panel
tableau M de bord M
panel M de instrumentos M
Instrumententafel F
cruscotto M
display
affichage M
pantalla F
Anzeige F
display M
anti-torque pedal
palonnier M
pedal M de control M
Pedal N für Drehmomentausgleich M
pedale M di controllo M
gauge
jauge F
manómetro M
Messinstrument N
manometro M
center console
unité F de commande F
unidad F de control M central
Mittelkonsole F
unità F di controllo M

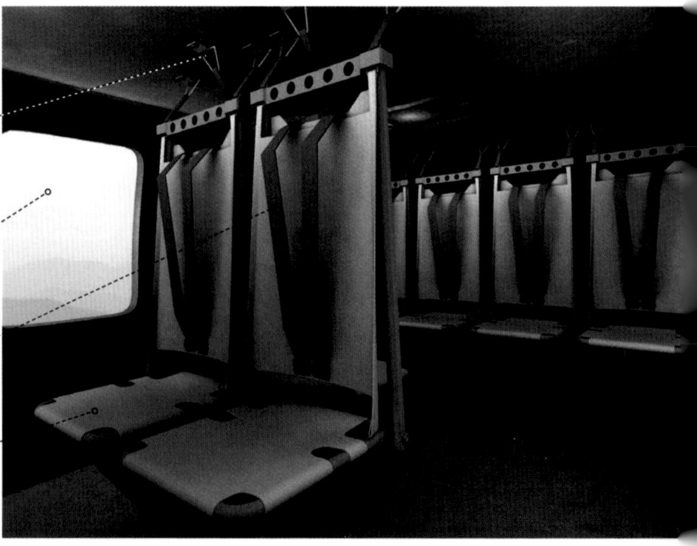
passenger cabin
cabine F des passagers M
compartimento M de pasajeros
Fahrgastraum M des Hubschraubers M
abitacolo M passeggeri M
anchor point
point M d'ancrage M
enganche M del cinturón M de seguridad F
Befestigungspunkt M
punto M di ancoraggio M
window
hublot M
ventanilla F
Seitenfenster N
oblò M
safety belt
ceinture F de sécurité F
cinturón M de seguridad F
Sicherheitsgurt M
cintura F di sicurezza F
seat
siège M
asiento M
Sitz M
sedile M

search and rescue (SAR) helicopter
hélicoptère ᴹ de recherche ᶠ et de sauvetage ᴹ
helicóptero ᴹ de búsqueda ᶠ y rescate ᴹ
Rettungshubschrauber ᴹ
elicottero ᴹ da ricerca ᶠ e soccorso ᴹ

transport helicopter
hélicoptère ᴹ pour le transport ᴹ
helicóptero ᴹ de pasajeros ᴹ
Transporthubschrauber ᴹ
elicottero ᴹ per trasporto ᴹ

attack helicopter
hélicoptère ᴹ d'attaque ᶠ
helicóptero ᴹ de combate ᴹ
Kampfhubschrauber ᴹ
elicottero ᴹ da attacco ᴹ

patrol coastal ship
navire M de patrouille F côtière
buque M de patrulla F
costera Küstenwachschiff N
nave F da pattugliamento M costiera

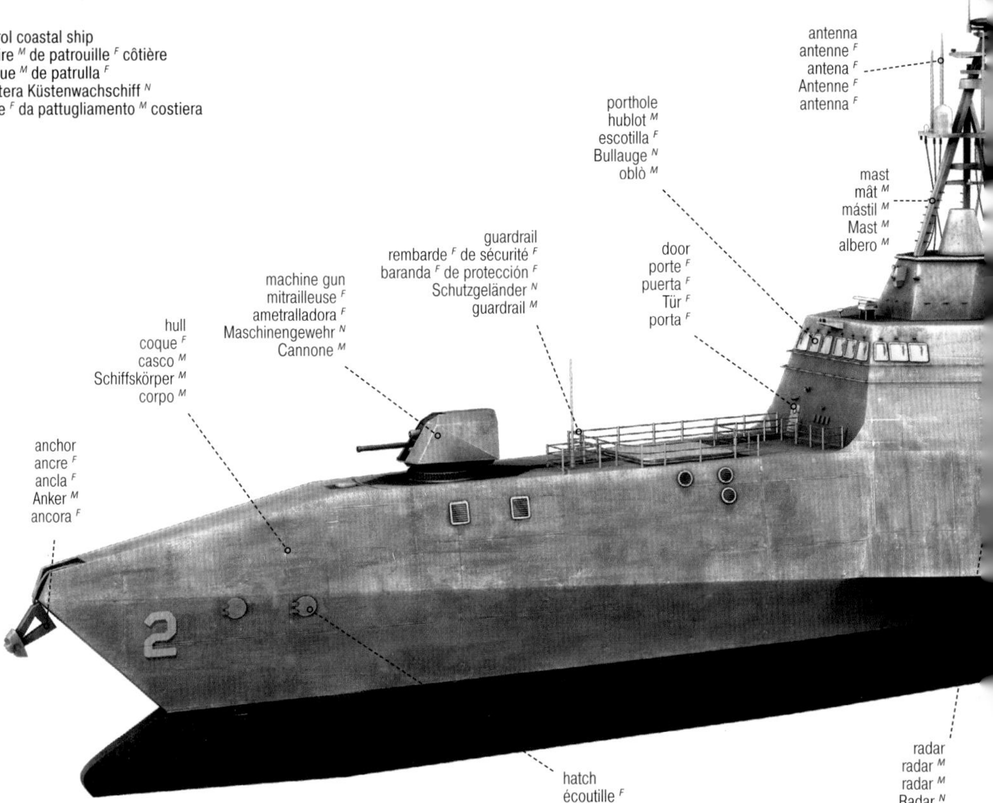
antenna
antenne F
antena F
Antenne F
antenna F
porthole
hublot M
escotilla F
Bullauge N
oblò M
mast
mât M
mástil M
Mast M
albero M
guardrail
rembarde F de sécurité F
baranda F de protección F
Schutzgeländer N
guardrail M
door
porte F
puerta F
Tür F
porta F
machine gun
mitrailleuse F
ametralladora F
Maschinengewehr N
Cannone M
hull
coque F
casco M
Schiffskörper M
corpo M
anchor
ancre F
ancla F
Anker M
ancora F
hatch
écoutille F
escotilla F
Luke F
portello M
radar
radar M
radar M
Radar N
radar M

submarine
sous-marin M
submarino M
U-Boot N
sottomarino M

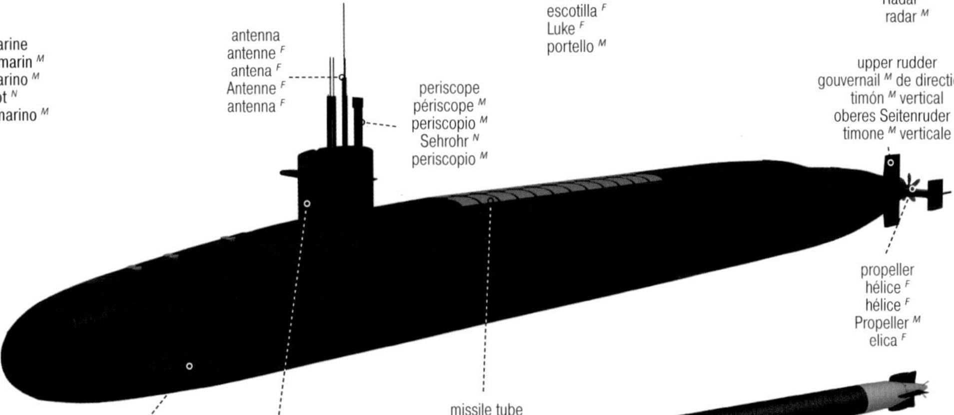
antenna
antenne F
antena F
Antenne F
antenna F
periscope
périscope M
periscopio M
Sehrohr N
periscopio M
upper rudder
gouvernail M de directio
timón M vertical
oberes Seitenruder N
timone M verticale
propeller
hélice F
hélice F
Propeller M
elica F
torpedo tube
tubes M lance-torpilles
tubo M del torpedo M
Torpedorohr N
lanciasiluri M
conning tower
kiosque M de sous-marin M
torre F de mando M
Kommandoturm M
torretta F
missile tube
fosse F à missile M
tubo M de misiles M
Raketenschacht M
tubo M lanciamissili

torpedo
torpille F
torpedo M
Torpedo M
siluro M

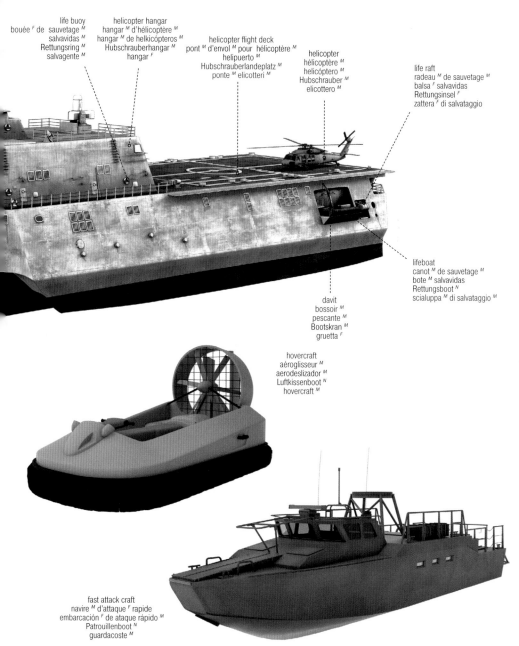

life buoy
bouée [F] de sauvetage [M]
salvavidas [M]
Rettungsring [M]
salvagente [M]
helicopter hangar
hangar [M] d'hélicoptère [M]
hangar [M] de helkicópteros [M]
Hubschrauberhangar [M]
hangar [F]
helicopter flight deck
pont [M] d'envol [M] pour hélicoptère [M]
helipuerto [M]
Hubschrauberlandeplatz [M]
ponte [M] elicotteri [M]
helicopter
hélicoptère [M]
helicóptero [M]
Hubschrauber [M]
elicottero [M]
life raft
radeau [M] de sauvetage [M]
balsa [F] salvavidas
Rettungsinsel [F]
zattera [F] di salvataggio
lifeboat
canot [M] de sauvetage [M]
bote [M] salvavidas
Rettungsboot [N]
scialuppa [M] di salvataggio [M]
davit
bossoir [M]
pescante [M]
Bootskran [M]
gruetta [F]

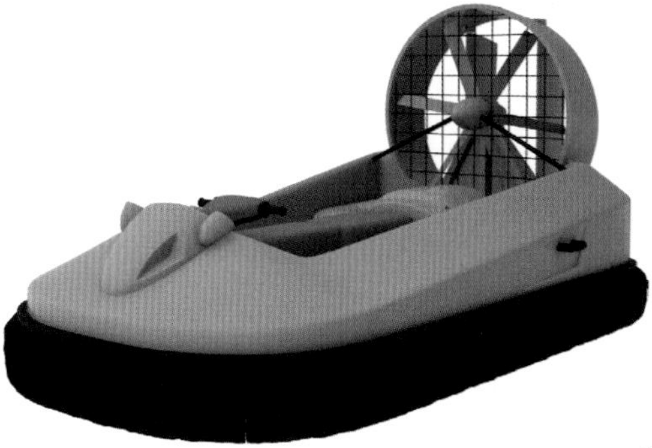
hovercraft
aéroglisseur [M]
aerodeslizador [M]
Luftkissenboot [N]
hovercraft [M]

fast attack craft
navire [M] d'attaque [F] rapide
embarcación [F] de ataque rápido [M]
Patrouillenboot [N]
guardacoste [M]

propeller
hélice [F]
hélice [M] del barco [M]
Schiffspropeller [M]
elica [F]

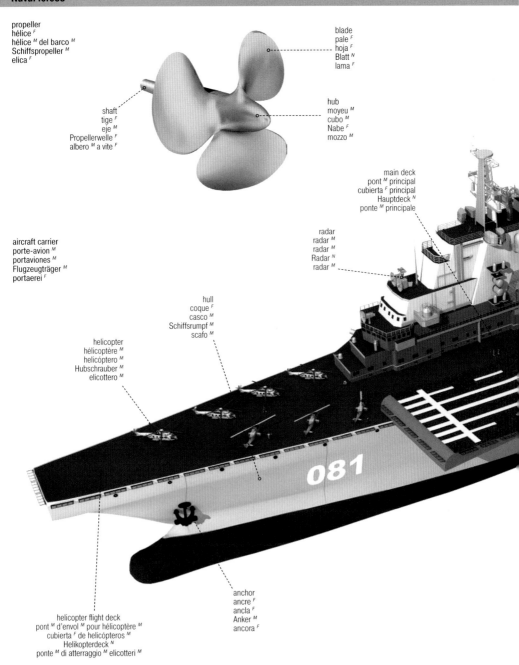

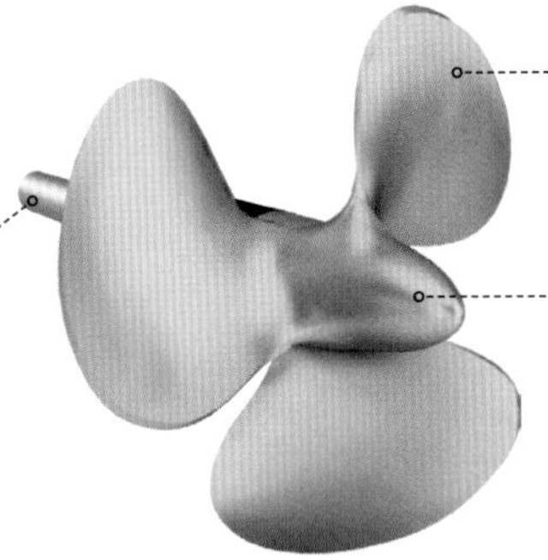
blade
pale [F]
hoja [F]
Blatt [N]
lama [F]
shaft
tige [F]
eje [M]
Propellerwelle [F]
albero [M] a vite [F]
hub
moyeu [M]
cubo [M]
Nabe [F]
mozzo [M]

aircraft carrier
porte-avion [M]
portaviones [M]
Flugzeugträger [M]
portaerei [F]

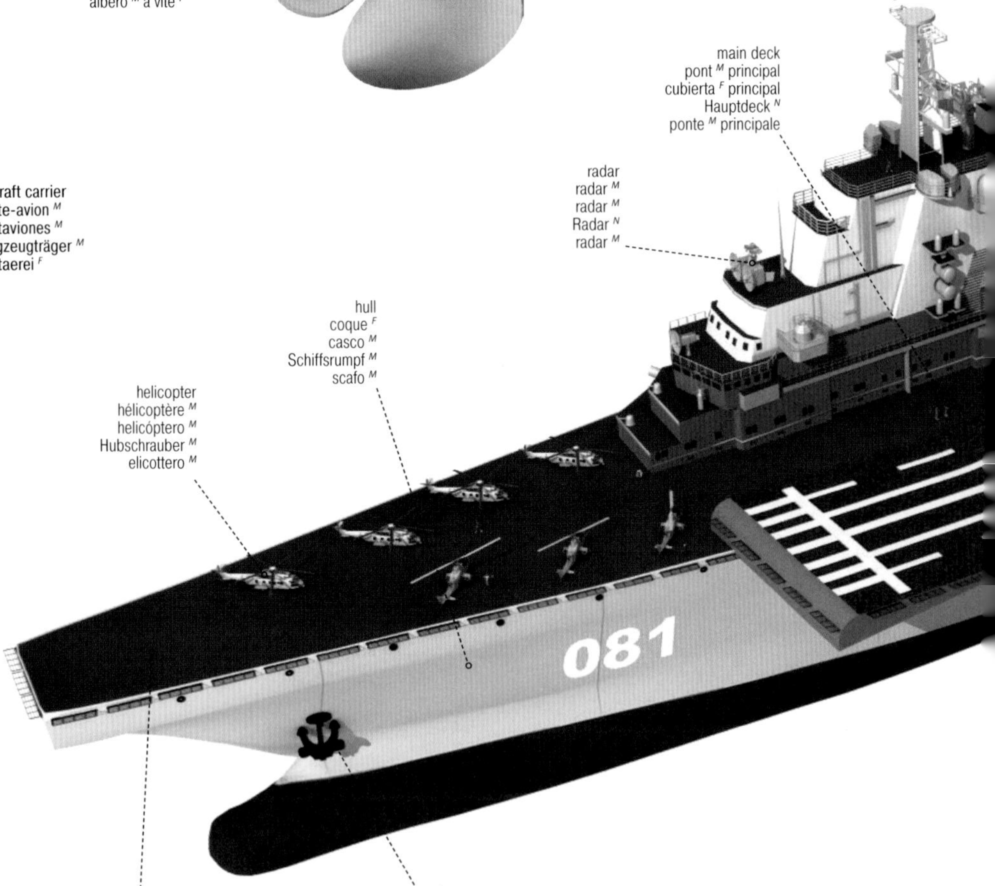
main deck
pont [M] principal
cubierta [F] principal
Hauptdeck [N]
ponte [M] principale
radar
radar [M]
radar [M]
Radar [N]
radar [M]
hull
coque [F]
casco [M]
Schiffsrumpf [M]
scafo [M]
helicopter
hélicoptère [M]
helicóptero [M]
Hubschrauber [M]
elicottero [M]
081
anchor
ancre [F]
ancla [F]
Anker [M]
ancora [F]
helicopter flight deck
pont [M] d'envol [M] pour hélicoptère [M]
cubierta [F] de helicópteros [M]
Helikopterdeck [N]
ponte [M] di atterraggio [M] elicotteri [M]

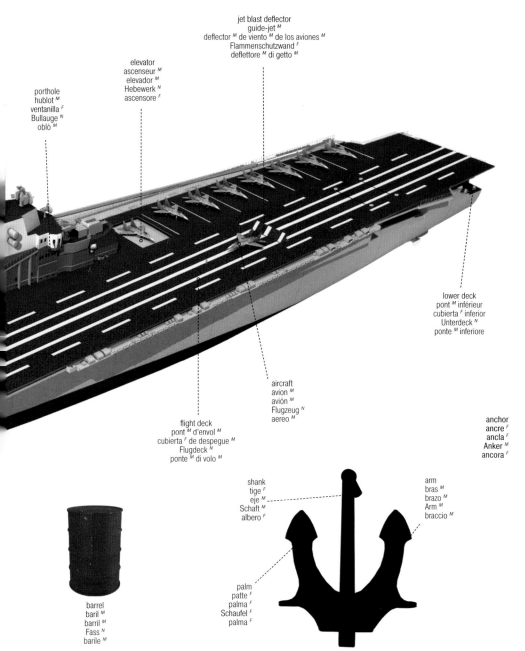

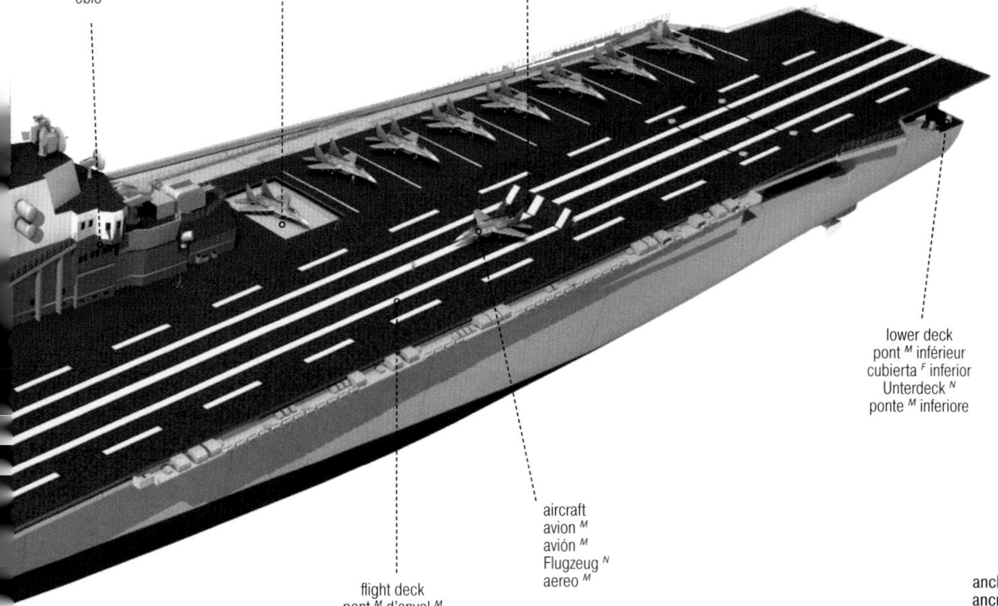
jet blast deflector
guide-jet M
deflector M de viento M de los aviones M
Flammenschutzwand F
deflettore M di getto M
elevator
ascenseur M
elevador M
Hebewerk N
ascensore F
porthole
hublot M
ventanilla F
Bullauge N
oblò M
lower deck
pont M inférieur
cubierta F inferior
Unterdeck N
ponte M inferiore
aircraft
avion M
avión M
Flugzeug N
aereo M
flight deck
pont M d'envol M
cubierta F de despegue M
Flugdeck N
ponte M di volo M

anchor
ancre F
ancla F
Anker M
ancora F

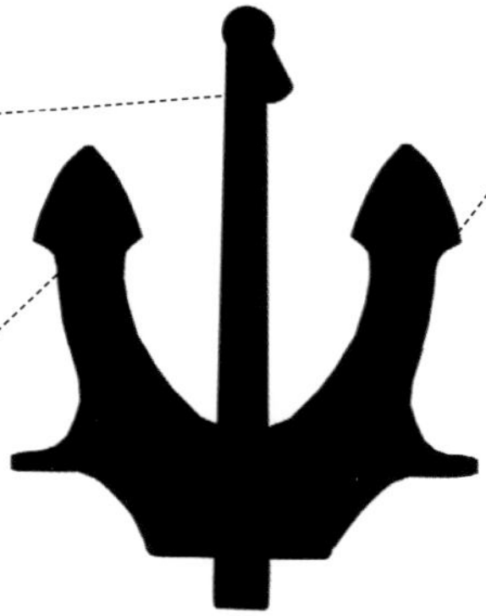
shank
tige F
eje M
Schaft M
albero F
arm
bras M
brazo M
Arm M
braccio M
palm
patte F
palma F
Schaufel F
palma F

barrel
baril M
barril M
Fass N
barile M

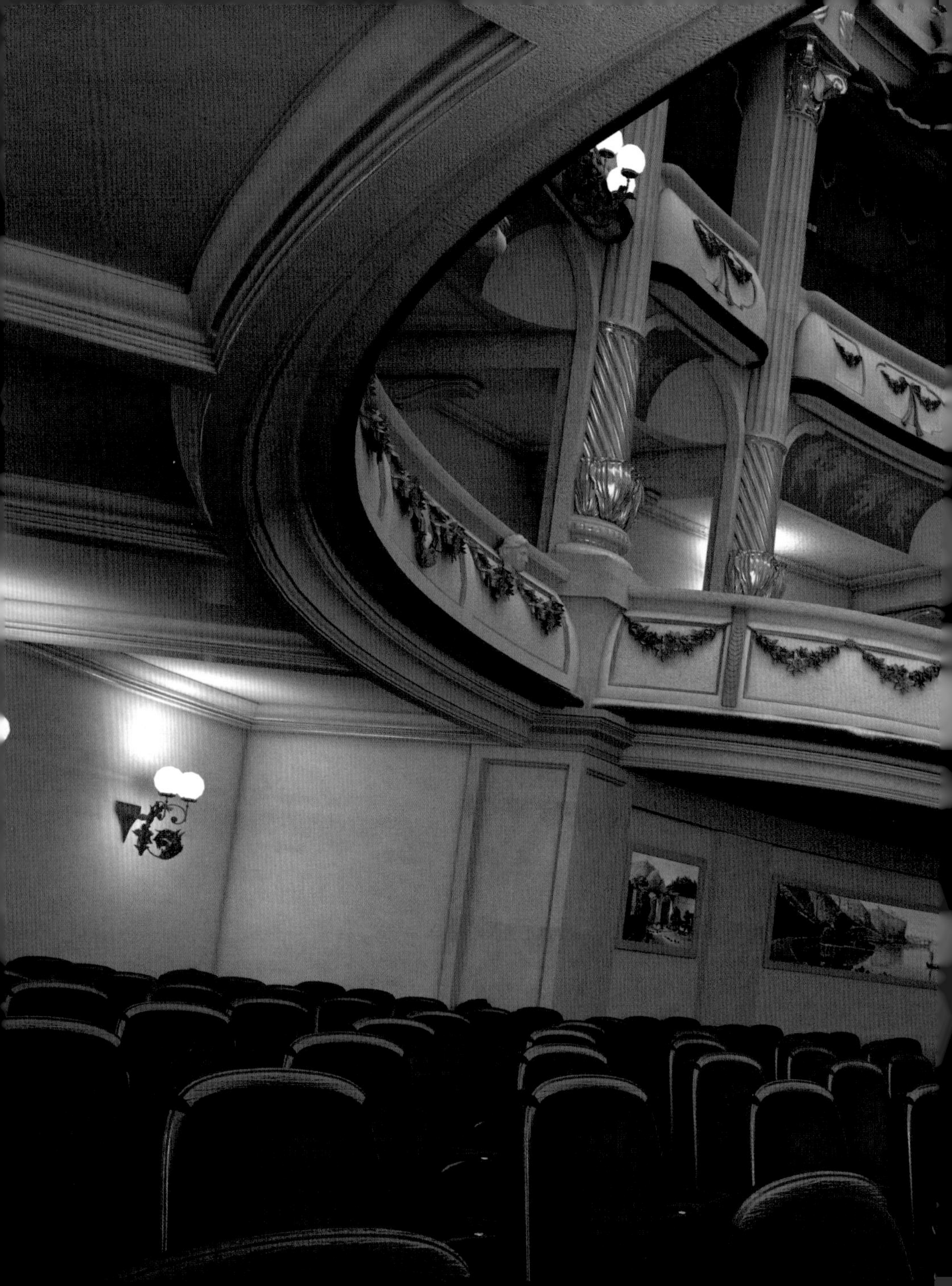

ARTS AND ARCHITECTURE

band
groupe [M] de musique [F]
grupo [M] musical
Musikband [F]
gruppo [M] musicale

block of lights
bloc [M] de projecteurs [M]
panel [M] de iluminación [F]
Lichtset [N]
luci [F] fisse

parabolic aluminized reflector light
lampe [F] à réflecteur [M] parabolique aluminé
reflector parabólico [M] aluminizado
PAR-Scheinwerfer [M]
riflettore [M] parabolico in alluminio [M]

guitarist
guitariste [M]
guitarrista [M]
Gitarrist [M]
chitarrista [M]

electric guitar
guitare [F]
guitarra [F] eléctrica
Gitarre [F]
chitarra [F] elettrica

loudspeaker
haut-parleur [M]
altavoces [M]
Lautsprecher [M]
altoparlanti [M]

cable
câble [M]
cable [M]
Kabel [N]
cavo [M]

monitor
haut-parleur [M] de contrôle [M]
monitor [M]
Monitor [M]
monitor [M]

synthesizer
synthétiseur [M]
sintetizador [M]
Synthesizer [M]
sintetizzatore [M]

keyboardist
claviériste [M]
tecladista [M]
Keyboardspieler [M]
tastierista [M]

audio en
ingénieur [M] du
técnico [M] de so
Toningen
tecnico [M] del s

singer
chanteuse F
cantante M
Sängerin F
cantante M/F
drummer
batteur M
baterista M
Schlagzeuger M
batterista M
drum kit
batterie F
batería F
Schlagzeug N
batteria F
bassist
bassiste M
bajista M
Bassgitarrist M
bassista M
trussing
structure F
andamiaje M
Traverse F
impalcatura F
console
console F
consola F
Mischpult N
console F
chair
chaise F
silla F
Stuhl M
sedia F
laptop computer
ordinateur M portatif
computadora F portátil
Laptop M
computer M portatile
table
table F
mesa F
Tisch M
tavolo M
bass guitar
basse F
bajo M
Bassgitarre F
basso M
stage
scène F
escenario M
Bühne F
palcoscenico M

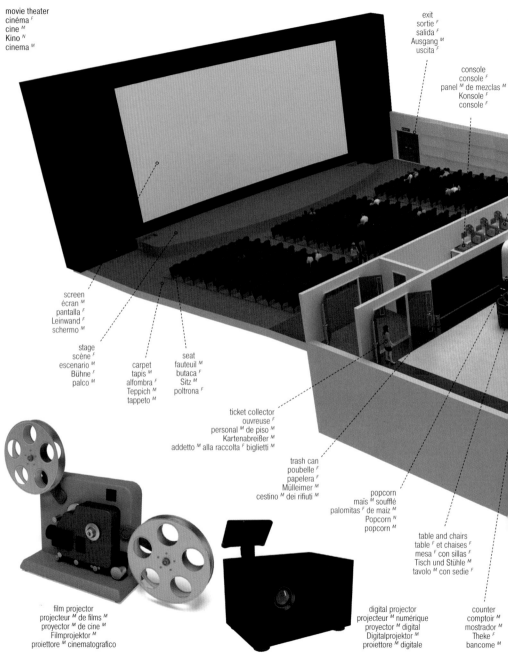

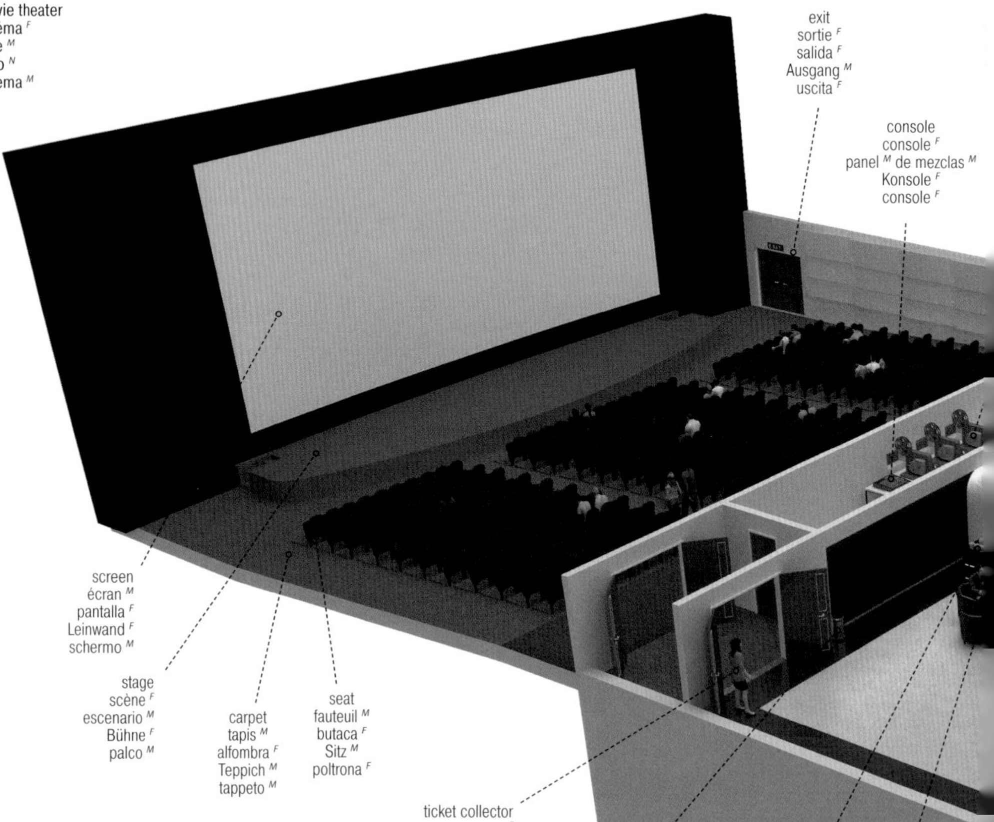
movie theater
cinéma F
cine M
Kino N
cinema M
exit
sortie F
salida F
Ausgang M
uscita F
console
console F
panel M de mezclas M
Konsole F
console F
screen
écran M
pantalla F
Leinwand F
schermo M
stage
scène F
escenario M
Bühne F
palco M
carpet
tapis M
alfombra F
Teppich M
tappeto M
seat
fauteuil M
butaca F
Sitz M
poltrona F
ticket collector
ouvreuse F
personal M de piso M
Kartenabreißer M
addetto M alla raccolta F biglietti M
trash can
poubelle F
papelera F
Mülleimer M
cestino M dei rifiuti M
popcorn
maïs M soufflé
palomitas F de maíz M
Popcorn N
popcorn M
table and chairs
table F et chaises F
mesa F con sillas F
Tisch und Stühle M
tavolo M con sedie F
counter
comptoir M
mostrador M
Theke F
bancome M

film projector
projecteur M de films M
proyector M de cine M
Filmprojektor M
proiettore M cinematografico

digital projector
projecteur M numérique
proyector M digital
Digitalprojektor M
proiettore M digitale

rojector
rojecteur ^{M}
royector ^{M}
ilmprojektor ^{M}
roiettore ^{M}

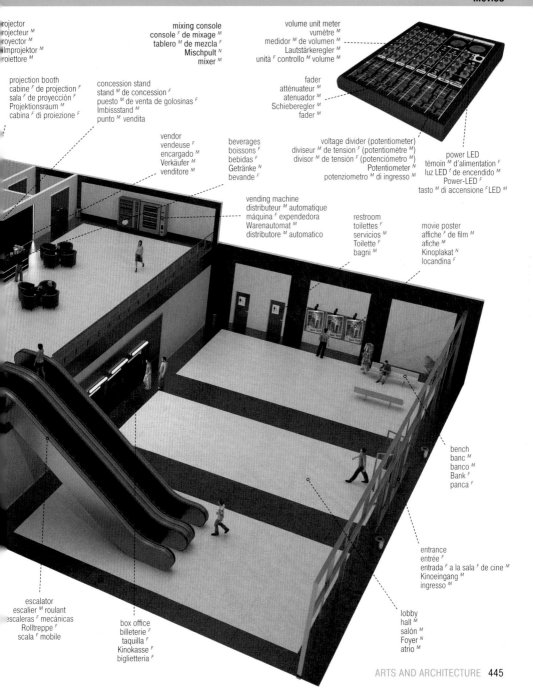

mixing console
console ^{F} de mixage ^{M}
tablero ^{M} de mezcla ^{F}
Mischpult ^{N}
mixer ^{M}

volume unit meter
vumètre ^{M}
medidor ^{M} de volumen ^{M}
Lautstärkeregler ^{M}
unità ^{F} controllo ^{M} volume ^{M}

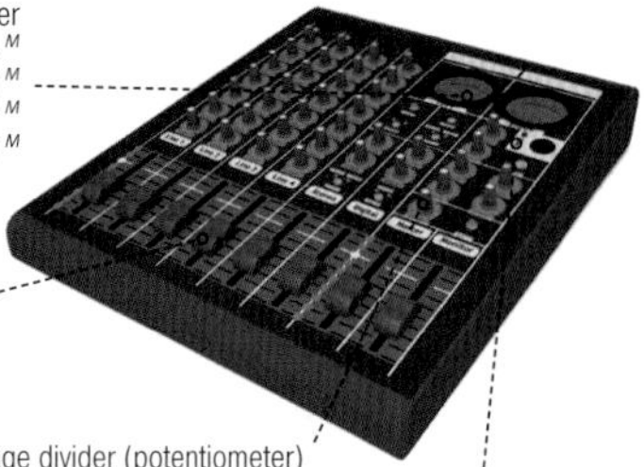

fader
atténuateur ^{M}
atenuador ^{M}
Schieberegler ^{M}
fader ^{M}

voltage divider (potentiometer)
diviseur ^{M} de tension ^{F} (potentiomètre ^{M})
divisor ^{M} de tensión ^{F} (potenciómetro ^{M})
Potentiometer ^{N}
potenziometro ^{M} di ingresso ^{M}

power LED
témoin ^{M} d'alimentation ^{F}
luz LED ^{f} de encendido ^{M}
Power-LED ^{F}
tasto ^{M} di accensione ^{F}LED ^{M}

projection booth
cabine ^{F} de projection ^{F}
sala ^{F} de proyección ^{F}
Projektionsraum ^{M}
cabina ^{F} di proiezione ^{F}

concession stand
stand ^{M} de concession ^{F}
puesto ^{M} de venta de golosinas ^{F}
Imbissstand ^{M}
punto ^{M} vendita

vendor
vendeuse ^{F}
encargado ^{M}
Verkäufer ^{M}
venditore ^{M}

beverages
boissons ^{F}
bebidas ^{F}
Getränke ^{N}
bevande ^{F}

vending machine
distributeur ^{M} automatique
máquina ^{F} expendedora
Warenautomat ^{M}
distributore ^{M} automatico

restroom
toilettes ^{F}
servicios ^{M}
Toilette ^{F}
bagni ^{M}

movie poster
affiche ^{F} de film ^{M}
afiche ^{M}
Kinoplakat ^{N}
locandina ^{F}

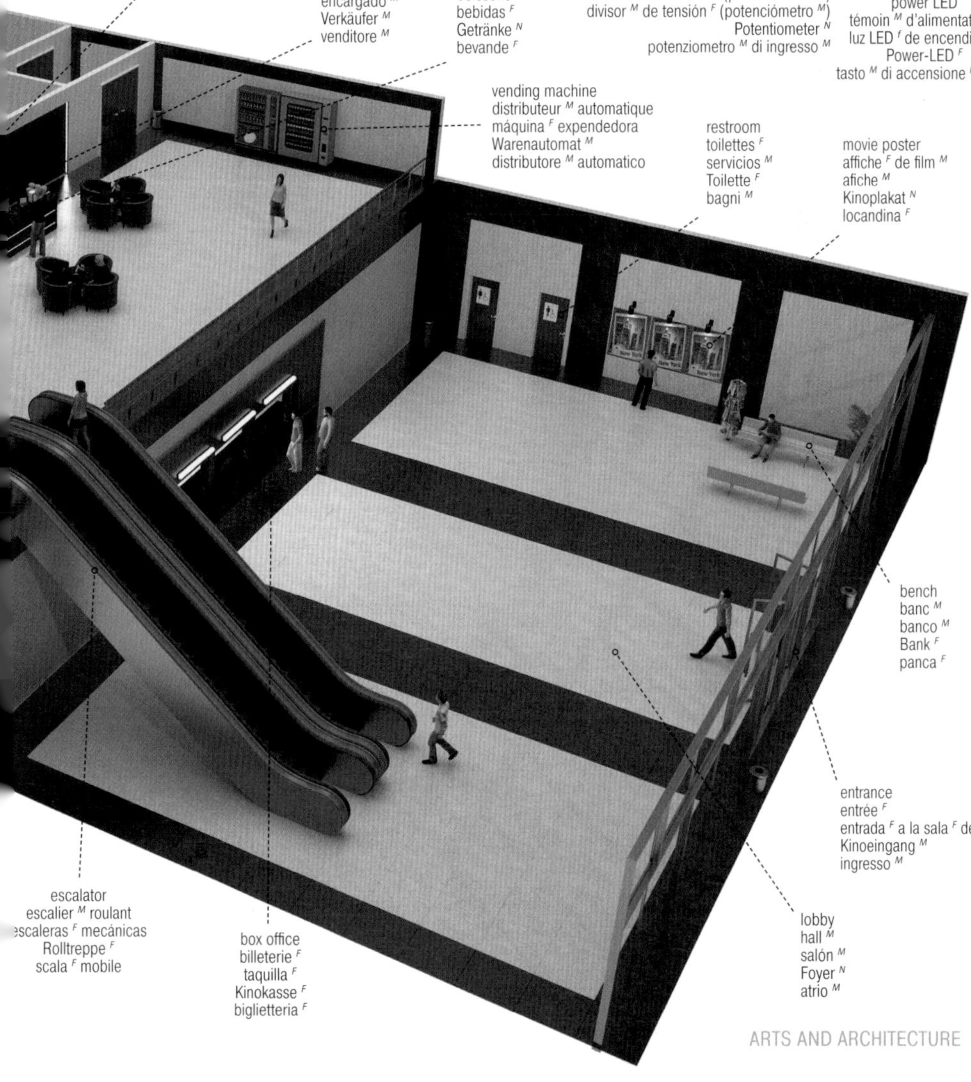

bench
banc ^{M}
banco ^{M}
Bank ^{F}
panca ^{F}

entrance
entrée ^{F}
entrada ^{F} a la sala ^{F} de cine ^{M}
Kinoeingang ^{M}
ingresso ^{M}

escalator
escalier ^{M} roulant
scaleras ^{F} mecánicas
Rolltreppe ^{F}
scala ^{F} mobile

box office
billeterie ^{F}
taquilla ^{F}
Kinokasse ^{F}
biglietteria ^{F}

lobby
hall ^{M}
salón ^{M}
Foyer ^{N}
atrio ^{M}

television show
émission [F] de télévision [F]
programa [M] de televisión [F]
Fernsehshow [F]
spettacolo [M] televisivo

stage
scène [F]
escena [F]
Podium [N]
palco [M]

desk
bureau [M]
mesa [F]
Tisch [M]
tavolo [M]

scenery
décor [M]
decorado [M]
Kulisse [F]
scenario [M]

host
animateur [M]
presentador [M]
Moderator [M]
conduttore [M]

monitor
moniteur [M]
monitor [M]
Bildschirm [M]
monitor [M]

guest
invitée F
invitado M
Studiogast M
ospite M
chair
chaise F
silla F
Stuhl M
poltrona F
electric guitar
guitare F
guitarra F eléctrica
E-Gitarre F
chitarra F elettrica
drum kit
batterie F
batería F
Schlagzeug N
batteria F
microphone
microphone M
micrófono M
Mikrofon N
microfono M

television studio
studio [M] de télévision [F]
estudio [M] de televisión [F]
Fernsehstudio [N]
studio [M] televisivo

scenery
décor [M]
decorado [M]
Kulisse [F]
scenario [M]

light
éclairage [M]
luz [F]
Scheinwerfer [M]
riflettore [M]

monitor
moniteur [M]
monitor [M]
Bildschirm [M]
monitor [M]

truss
grille [F] d'éclairage [M]
entramado [M]
Traverse [F]
impalcatura [F]

host
animateur [M]
presentador [M]
Moderator [M]
conduttore [M]

cable
câble [M]
cable [M]
Kabel [N]
cavo [M]

microphone
microphone [M]
micrófono [M]
Mikrofon [N]
microfono [M]

cameraman
caméraman [M]
camarógrafo [M]
Kameramann [M]
cameraman [M]

script
script [M]
guión [M]
Skript [N]
testo [M]

stage
scène [F]
escena [F]
Podium [N]
palco [M]

guest
invitée F
invitado M
Studiogast M
ospite M
singer
chanteuse F
cantante M
Sängerin F
cantante MF
musician
musicien M
músico M
Musiker M
musicista M
director
réalisatrice M
director M
Regisseur M
regista M
camera
caméra F
cámara F de televisión F
Fernsehkamera F
telecamera F
audience member
membre M de l'auditoire M
espectador M
Zuschauer M
spettatore M

stage
scène [F]
escenario [M]
Bühne [F]
palcoscenico [M]

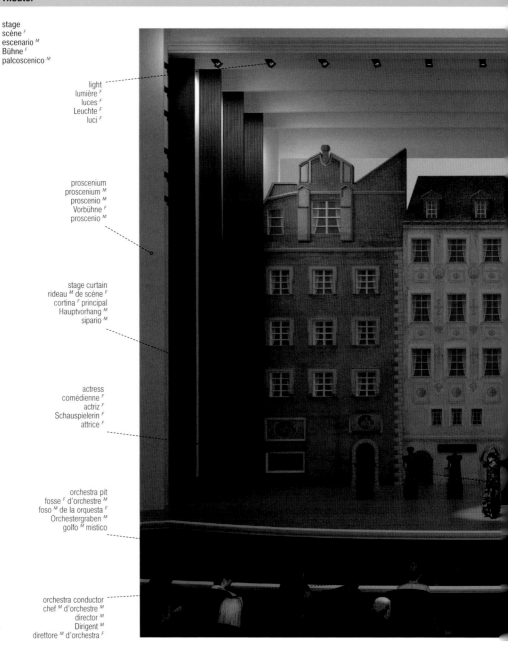

light
lumière [F]
luces [F]
Leuchte [F]
luci [F]

proscenium
proscenium [M]
proscenio [M]
Vorbühne [F]
proscenio [M]

stage curtain
rideau [M] de scène [F]
cortina [F] principal
Hauptvorhang [M]
sipario [M]

actress
comédienne [F]
actriz [F]
Schauspielerin [F]
attrice [F]

orchestra pit
fosse [F] d'orchestre [M]
foso [M] de la orquesta [F]
Orchestergraben [M]
golfo [M] mistico

orchestra conductor
chef [M] d'orchestre [M]
director [M]
Dirigent [M]
direttore [M] d'orchestra [F]

beam
frise [F]
tela [M]
Balken [M]
trave [F]
backdrop
toile [F] de fond [M]
telón [M] de fondo [M]
Hintergrund [M]
fondale [M]
actor
comédien [M]
actor [M]
Schauspieler [M]
attore [M]
stage
scène [F]
escenario [M]
Bühne [F]
palco [M]
audience
public [M]
público [M]
Publikum [N]
pubblico [M]

theater
auditorium [M]
teatro [M]
Theater [N]
teatro [M]

mezzanine
mezzanine [F]
palco [M] de honor [M]
erster Rang [M]
mezzanino [M]

balcony
balcon [M]
palco [M]
Balkon [M]
galleria [F]

seat
siège [M]
butaca [F]
Sitz [M]
posto [M] a sedere

orchestra
orchestre [M]
platea [F]
Orchester [N]
platea [F]

opera glasses
jumelles ^{F} de théâtre ^{M}
binoculares ^{M} de ópera ^{F}
Opernglas ^{N}
binocoli ^{M} da teatro ^{M}

lens
lentille ^{F}
lente ^{F}
Linse ^{F}
lente ^{F}

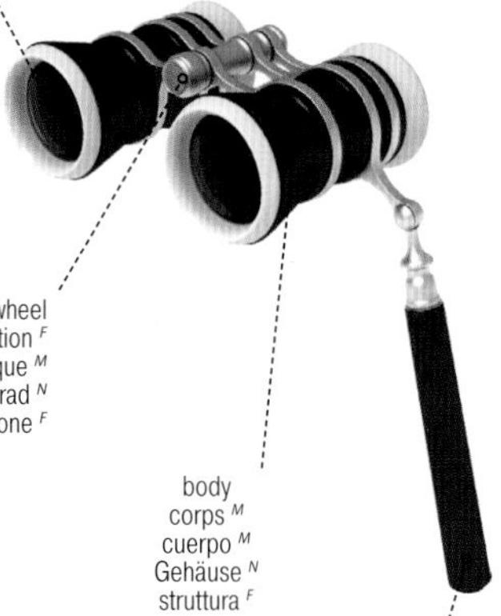

focusing wheel
molette ^{F} de focalisation ^{F}
perilla ^{F} de enfoque ^{M}
Fokussierrad ^{N}
rotella ^{F} di regolazione ^{F}

body
corps ^{M}
cuerpo ^{M}
Gehäuse ^{N}
struttura ^{F}

handle
poignée ^{F}
mango ^{M}
Griff ^{M}
impugnatura ^{F}

flamenco dancer
danseuse ^{F} de flamenco ^{M}
bailarina ^{F} de flamenco ^{M}
Flamencotänzerin ^{F}
ballerina ^{F} di flamenco ^{M}

ruffled sleeve
manches ^{F} à volants ^{M}
mangas ^{F} con volantes ^{M}
Rüschenärmel ^{M}
maniche ^{F} con balze ^{F}

ruffled skirt
jupe ^{F} à volants ^{M}
falda ^{F} con faralaos ^{M}
Rüschenrock mit Volanten ^{M}
gonna ^{F} a balze ^{F}

ctor
omédien ^{M}
ctor ^{M}
chauspieler ^{M}
tore ^{M}

costume
costume ^{M}
traje ^{M}
Kostüm ^{N}
costume ^{M}

Indian dancer
danseuse ^{F} indienne
bailarina ^{F} india
indische Tänzerin ^{F}
ballerina ^{F} indiana

maang tikka
maang tikka ^{M}
maang tikka
Maang-Tikka-Haarschmuck ^{M}
mang tikka ^{M}

bindi
bindi ^{M}
bindi ^{M}
Bindi ^{N}
bindi ^{M}

nose ring
anneau ^{M} de nez ^{M}
pendiente ^{M} de nariz ^{F} nath
Nathnasenring ^{M}
orecchino ^{M} per naso ^{M}

panja bracelet
bracelet ^{M} panja
pulsera ^{F} panja
Panjaarmband ^{N}
bracciale ^{M} panja

choli
choli ^{M}
blusa ^{F} choli
Saribluse ^{F}
camicetta ^{F} choli

bangle
bracelet ^{M}
brazaletes ^{M}
Armreifen ^{M}
braccialetto ^{M}

dupatta
dupatta ^{F}
chal ^{M} dupatta
Dupattaschal ^{M}
dupatta ^{M}

lehenga
lehenga ^{M}
falda ^{F} lehenga
Lehengarock ^{M}
lehenga ^{F}

first position of the arms
première position ^F des bras ^M
primera posición ^F de brazos ^M
Ausgangsposition ^F der Arme ^M
prima posizione ^F

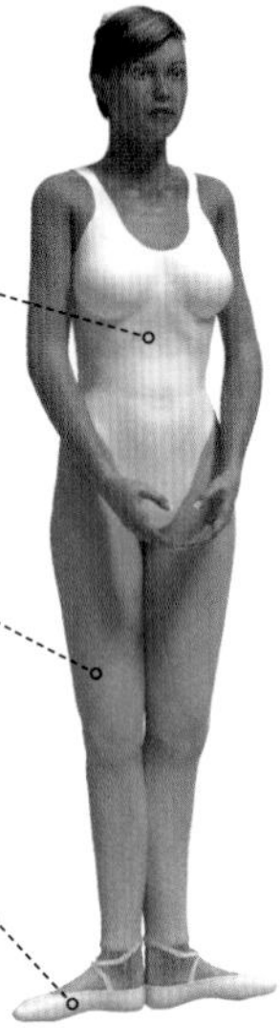

leotard
léotard ^M
maillot ^M
Turnanzug ^M
body ^M

tights
collants ^M
mallas ^F
Strumpfhose ^F
pantacollant ^M

ballet shoes
chaussons ^M de ballet ^M
zapatillas ^F de ballet ^M
Ballettschuhe ^M
scarpette ^F da ballo ^M

arabesque on pointe
arabesque ^F sur pointe ^F
arabesco ^M en punta ^F
Arabesque ^F auf Spitze ^F
arabesque ^F sulla punta ^F

jeté
jeté ^M
jeté ^F
Jeté ^N
jeté ^M

front attitude on pointe
attitude ^F devant en pointe ^F
attitude ^F hacia adelante en punta ^F
Attitude-nach vorne-Spitze ^F
attitude ^F dévant

grand jeté
grand jeté ^M
grand jeté ^F
Grand Jeté ^N
grand jeté ^M

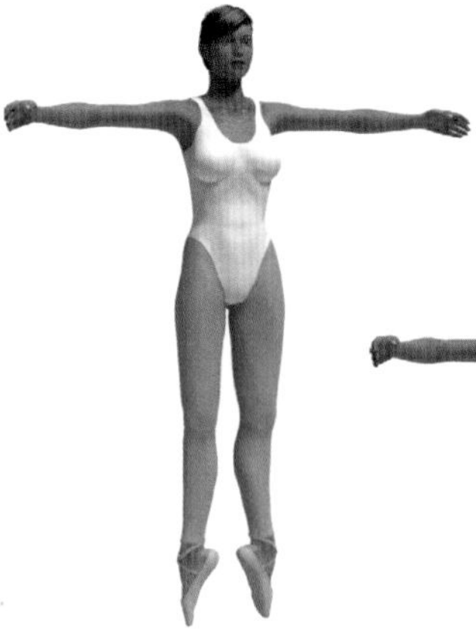

second position of the arms
deuxième position ^F des bras ^M
segunda posición ^F de los brazos ^M
zweite Position ^F der Arme ^M
seconda posizione ^F

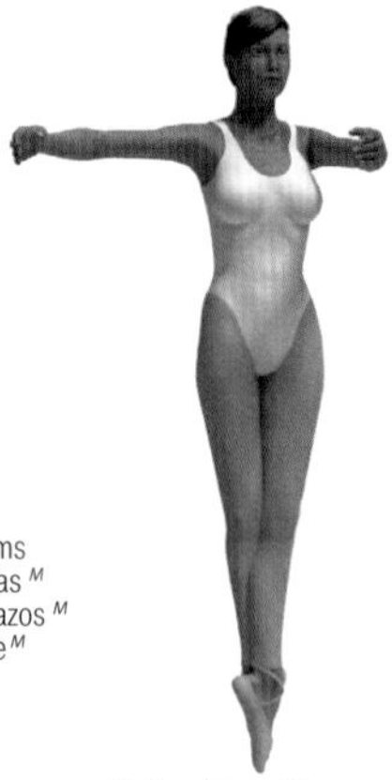

third position of the arms
troisième position ^F des bras ^M
tercera posición ^F de los brazos ^M
dritte Position ^F der Arme ^M
terza posizione ^F

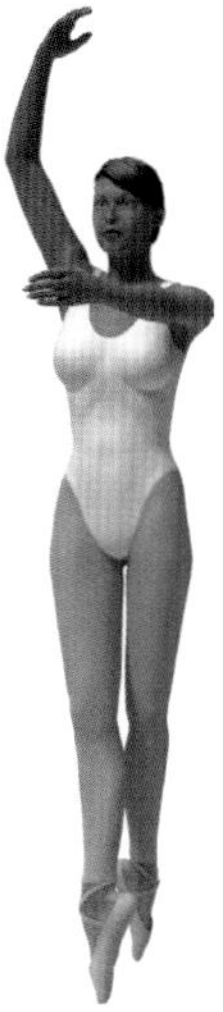

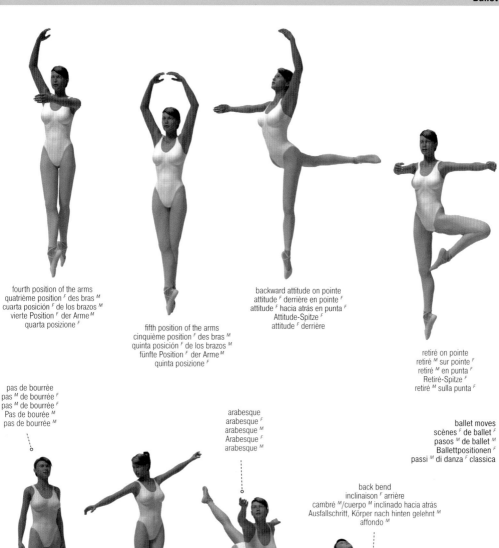

fourth position of the arms
quatrième position ^{F} des bras ^{M}
cuarta posición ^{F} de los brazos ^{M}
vierte Position ^{F} der Arme ^{M}
quarta posizione ^{F}

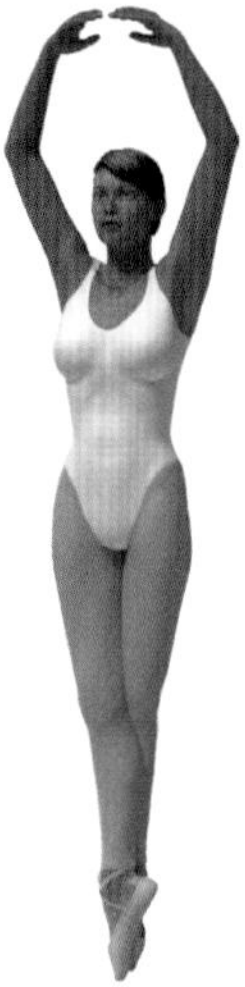

fifth position of the arms
cinquième position ^{F} des bras ^{M}
quinta posición ^{F} de los brazos ^{M}
fünfte Position ^{F} der Arme ^{M}
quinta posizione ^{F}

backward attitude on pointe
attitude ^{F} derrière en pointe ^{F}
attitude ^{F} hacia atrás en punta ^{F}
Attitude-Spitze ^{F}
attitude ^{F} derrière

retiré on pointe
retiré ^{M} sur pointe ^{F}
retiré ^{M} en punta ^{F}
Retiré-Spitze ^{F}
retiré ^{M} sulla punta ^{F}

ballet moves
scènes ^{F} de ballet ^{F}
pasos ^{M} de ballet ^{M}
Ballettpositionen ^{F}
passi ^{M} di danza ^{F} classica

pas de bourrée
pas ^{M} de bourrée ^{F}
pas ^{M} de bourrée ^{F}
Pas de bourée ^{M}
pas de bourrée ^{M}

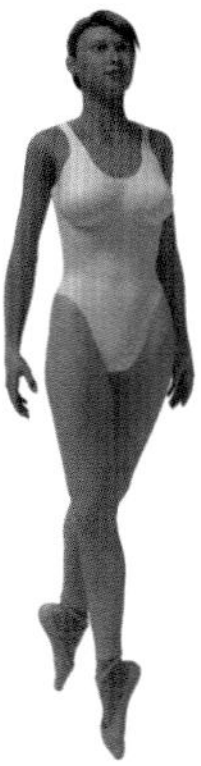

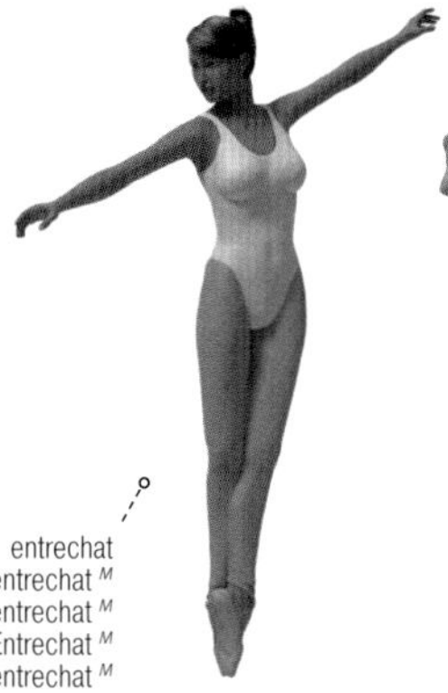

entrechat
entrechat ^{M}
entrechat ^{M}
Entrechat ^{M}
entrechat ^{M}

arabesque
arabesque ^{F}
arabesque ^{M}
Arabesque ^{F}
arabesque ^{M}

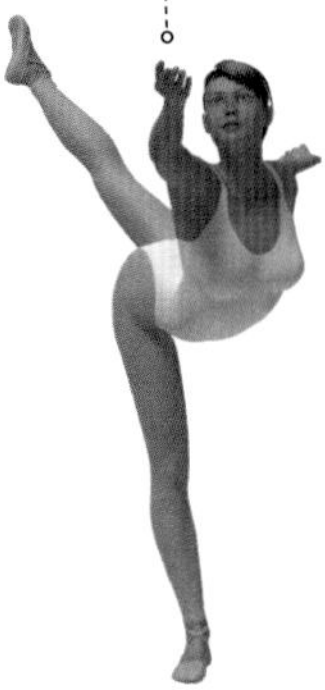

back bend
inclinaison ^{F} arrière
cambré ^{M}/cuerpo ^{M} inclinado hacia atrás
Ausfallschritt, Körper nach hinten gelehnt ^{M}
affondo ^{M}

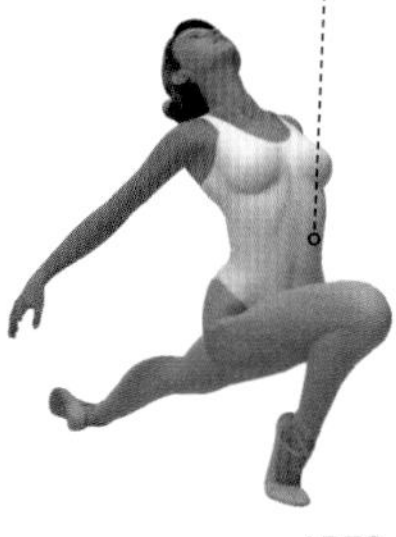

music staff
portée F
Líneas F
Liniensystem N
Pentagramma M

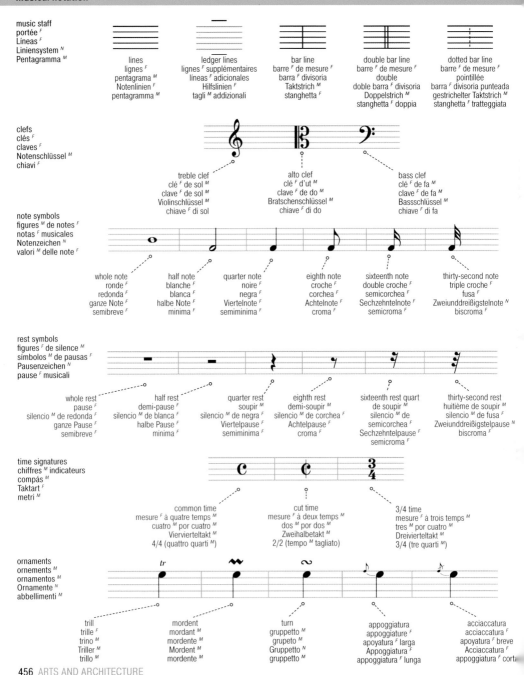

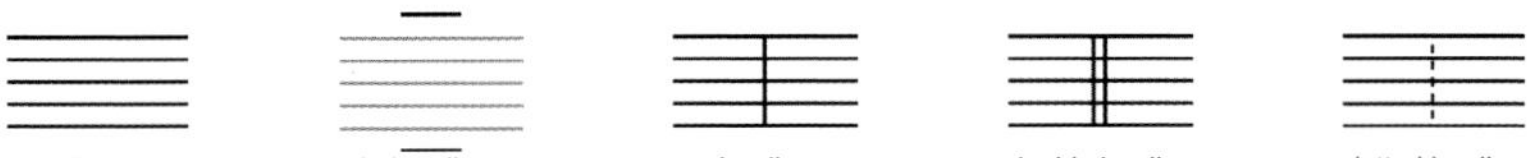

lines
lignes F
pentagrama M
Notenlinien F
pentagramma M

ledger lines
lignes F supplémentaires
líneas F adicionales
Hilfslinien F
tagli M addizionali

bar line
barre F de mesure F
barra F divisoria
Taktstrich M
stanghetta F

double bar line
barre F de mesure F double
doble barra F divisoria
Doppelstrich M
stanghetta F doppia

dotted bar line
barre F de mesure F pointillée
barra F divisoria punteada
gestrichelter Taktstrich M
stanghetta F tratteggiata

clefs
clés F
claves F
Notenschlüssel M
chiavi F

treble clef
clé F de sol M
clave F de sol M
Violinschlüssel M
chiave F di sol

alto clef
clé F d'ut M
clave F de do M
Bratschenschlüssel M
chiave F di do

bass clef
clé F de fa M
clave F de fa M
Bassschlüssel M
chiave F di fa

note symbols
figures M de notes F
notas F musicales
Notenzeichen N
valori M delle note F

whole note
ronde F
redonda F
ganze Note F
semibreve F

half note
blanche F
blanca F
halbe Note F
minima F

quarter note
noire F
negra F
Viertelnote F
semiminima F

eighth note
croche F
corchea F
Achtelnote F
croma F

sixteenth note
double croche F
semicorchea F
Sechzehntelnote F
semicroma F

thirty-second note
triple croche F
fusa F
Zweiunddreißigstelnote N
biscroma F

rest symbols
figures F de silence M
símbolos M de pausas F
Pausenzeichen N
pause F musicali

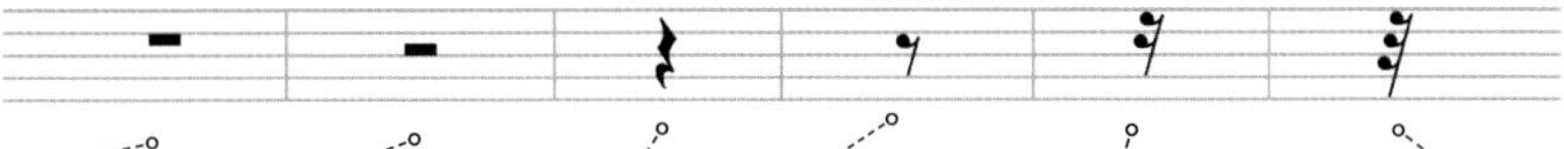

whole rest
pause F
silencio M de redonda F
ganze Pause F
semibreve F

half rest
demi-pause F
silencio M de blanca F
halbe Pause F
minima F

quarter rest
soupir M
silencio M de negra F
Viertelpause F
semiminima F

eighth rest
demi-soupir M
silencio M de corchea F
Achtelpause F
croma F

sixteenth rest quart de soupir M
silencio M de semicorchea F
Sechzehntelpause F
semicroma F

thirty-second rest
huitième de soupir M
silencio M de fusa F
Zweiunddreißigstelpause N
biscroma F

time signatures
chiffres M indicateurs
compás M
Taktart F
metri M

common time
mesure F à quatre temps M
cuatro M por cuatro M
Viervierteltakt M
4/4 (quattro quarti M)

cut time
mesure F à deux temps M
dos M por dos M
Zweihalbetakt M
2/2 (tempo M tagliato)

3/4 time
mesure F à trois temps M
tres M por cuatro M
Dreivierteltakt M
3/4 (tre quarti M)

ornaments
ornements M
ornamentos M
Ornamente N
abbellimenti M

tr

trill
trille F
trino M
Triller M
trillo M

mordent
mordant M
mordente M
Mordent M
mordente M

turn
gruppetto M
grupeto M
Gruppetto N
gruppetto M

appoggiatura
appoggiature F
apoyatura F larga
Appoggiatura F
appoggiatura F lunga

acciaccatura
acciaccatura F
apoyatura F breve
Acciaccatura F
appoggiatura F cort

accidentals
altérations F
alteraciones F
Vorzeichen N
accidenti M

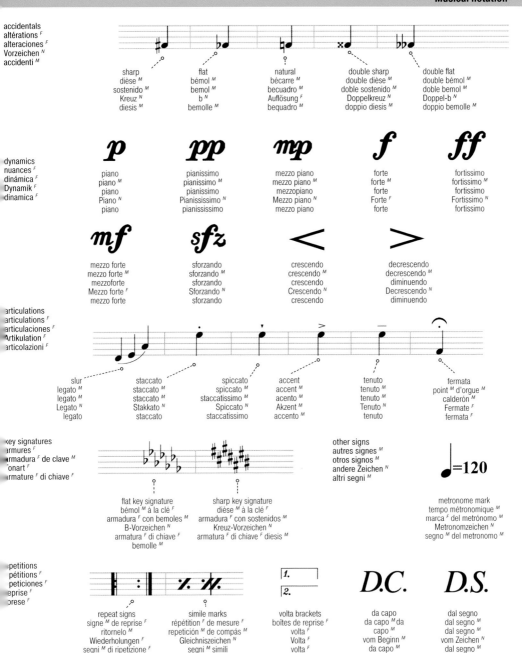

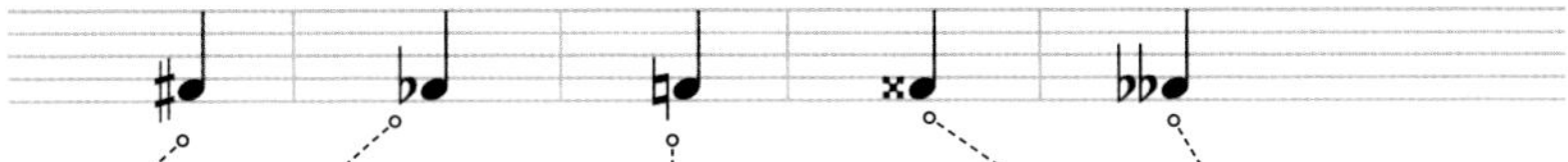

sharp
dièse M
sostenido M
Kreuz N
diesis M

flat
bémol M
bemol M
b N
bemolle M

natural
bécarre M
becuadro M
Auflösung F
bequadro M

double sharp
double dièse M
doble sostenido M
Doppelkreuz N
doppio diesis M

double flat
double bémol M
doble bemol M
Doppel-b N
doppio bemolle M

dynamics
nuances F
dinámica F
Dynamik F
dinamica F

p

piano
piano M
piano
Piano N
piano

pp

pianissimo
pianissimo M
pianissimo
Pianississimo N
pianississimo

mp

mezzo piano
mezzo piano M
mezzopiano
Mezzo piano N
mezzo piano

f

forte
forte M
forte
Forte F
forte

ff

fortissimo
fortissimo M
fortissimo
Fortissimo N
fortissimo

mf

mezzo forte
mezzo forte M
mezzoforte
Mezzo forte F
mezzo forte

sfz

sforzando
sforzando M
sforzando
Sforzando N
sforzando

<

crescendo
crescendo M
crescendo
Crescendo N
crescendo

>

decrescendo
decrescendo M
diminuendo
Decrescendo N
diminuendo

rticulations
rticulations F
rticulaciones F
Artikulation F
rticolazioni F

slur
legato M
legato M
Legato N
legato

staccato
staccato M
staccato M
Stakkato N
staccato

spiccato
spiccato M
staccatissimo M
Spiccato N
staccatissimo

accent
accent M
acento M
Akzent M
accento M

tenuto
tenuto M
tenuto M
Tenuto N
tenuto

fermata
point M d'orgue M
calderón M
Fermate F
fermata F

ey signatures
rmures F
rmadura F de clave M
onart F
rmature F di chiave F

flat key signature
bémol M à la clé F
armadura F con bemoles M
B-Vorzeichen N
armatura F di chiave F
bemolle M

sharp key signature
dièse M à la clé F
armadura F con sostenidos M
Kreuz-Vorzeichen N
armatura F di chiave F diesis M

other signs
autres signes M
otros signos M
andere Zeichen N
altri segni M

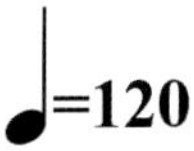

metronome mark
tempo métronomique M
marca F del metrónomo M
Metronomzeichen N
segno M del metronomo M

petitions
pétitions F
peticiones F
eprise F
prese F

repeat signs
signe M de reprise F
ritornelo M
Wiederholungen F
segni M di ripetizione F

simile marks
répétition F de mesure F
repetición M de compás M
Gleichniszeichen N
segni M simili

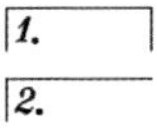
1.
2.

volta brackets
boîtes de reprise F
volta F
Volta F
volta F

D.C.

da capo
da capo M da
capo M
vom Beginn M
da capo M

D.S.

dal segno
dal segno M
dal segno M
vom Zeichen N
dal segno M

upright piano
piano [M] droit
piano [M] vertical
Klavier [N]
pianoforte [M] verticale

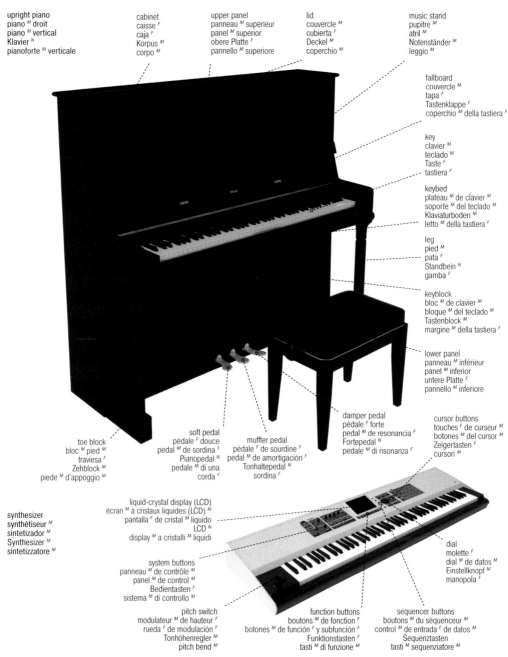

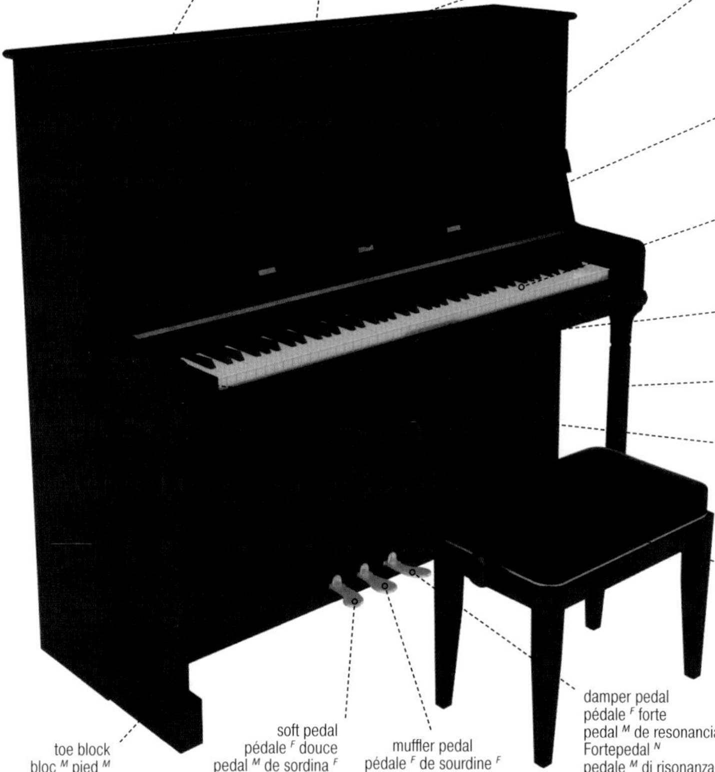
cabinet
caisse [F]
caja [F]
Korpus [M]
corpo [M]
upper panel
panneau [M] supérieur
panel [M] superior
obere Platte [F]
pannello [M] superiore
lid
couvercle [M]
cubierta [F]
Deckel [M]
coperchio [M]
music stand
pupitre [M]
atril [M]
Notenständer [M]
leggio [M]
fallboard
couvercle [M]
tapa [F]
Tastenklappe [F]
coperchio [M] della tastiera [F]
key
clavier [M]
teclado [M]
Taste [F]
tastiera [F]
keybed
plateau [M] de clavier [M]
soporte [M] del teclado [M]
Klaviaturboden [M]
letto [M] della tastiera [F]
leg
pied [M]
pata [F]
Standbein [N]
gamba [F]
keyblock
bloc [M] de clavier [M]
bloque [M] del teclado [M]
Tastenblock [M]
margine [M] della tastiera [F]
lower panel
panneau [M] inférieur
panel [M] inferior
untere Platte [F]
pannello [M] inferiore
damper pedal
pédale [F] forte
pedal [M] de resonancia [F]
Fortepedal [N]
pedale [M] di risonanza [F]
muffler pedal
pédale [F] de sourdine [F]
pedal [M] de amortigación [F]
Tonhaltepedal [N]
sordina [F]
soft pedal
pédale [F] douce
pedal [M] de sordina [F]
Pianopedal [N]
pedale [M] di una
corda [F]
toe block
bloc [M] pied [M]
traviesa [F]
Zehblock [M]
piede [M] d'appoggio [M]

synthesizer
synthétiseur [M]
sintetizador [M]
Synthesizer [M]
sintetizzatore [M]

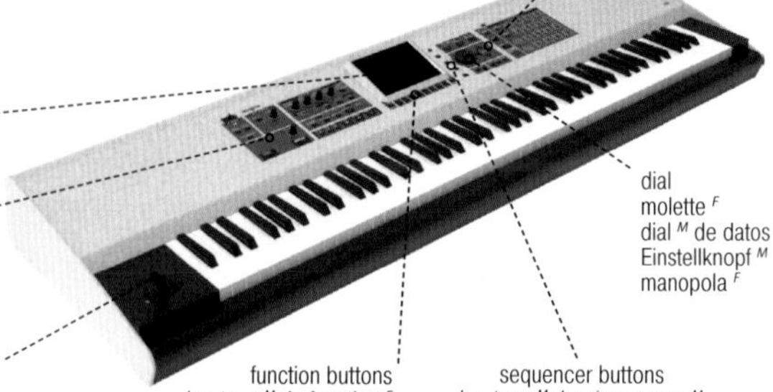
cursor buttons
touches [F] de curseur [M]
botones [M] del cursor [M]
Zeigertasten [F]
cursori [M]
liquid-crystal display (LCD)
écran [M] à cristaux liquides (LCD) [M]
pantalla [F] de cristal [M] liquido
LCD [N]
display [M] a cristalli [M] liquidi
dial
molette [F]
dial [M] de datos [M]
Einstellknopf [M]
manopola [F]
system buttons
panneau [M] de contrôle [M]
panel [M] de control [M]
Bedientasten [F]
sistema [M] di controllo [M]
pitch switch
modulateur [M] de hauteur [F]
rueda [F] de modulación [F]
Tonhöhenregler [M]
pitch bend [M]
function buttons
boutons [M] de fonction [F]
botones [M] de función [F] y subfunción [F]
Funktionstasten [F]
tasti [M] di funzione [M]
sequencer buttons
boutons [M] du séquenceur [M]
control [M] de entrada [F] de datos [M]
Sequenztasten
tasti [M] sequenziatore [M]

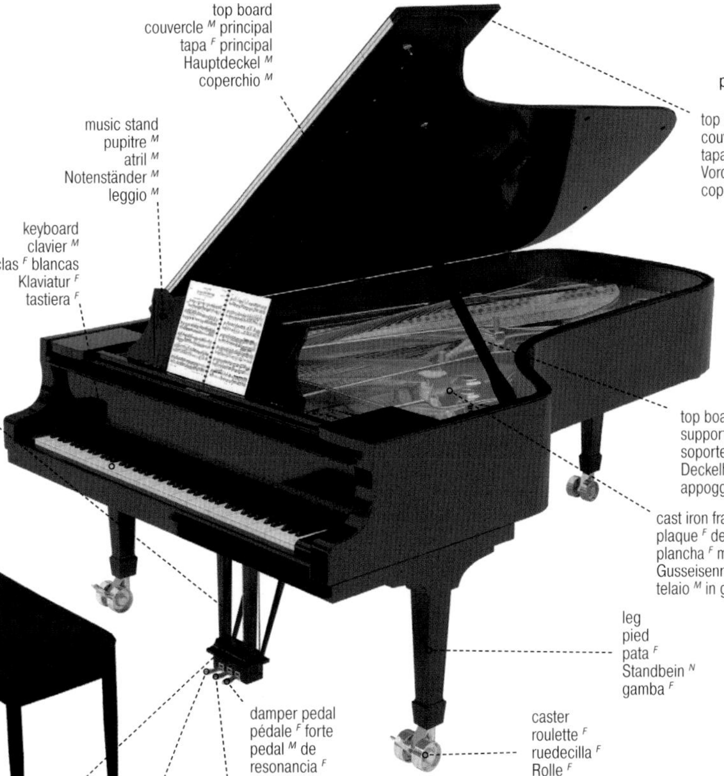

grand piano
piano [M] à queue [M]
piano [M] de cola [F]
Flügel [M]
pianoforte [M] a coda [F]

top board
couvercle [M] principal
tapa [F] principal
Hauptdeckel [M]
coperchio [M]

top board front
couvercle [M] avant
tapa [F] frontal
Vorderdeckel [M]
coperchio [M] frontale

music stand
pupitre [M]
atril [M]
Notenständer [M]
leggio [M]

keyboard
clavier [M]
teclas [F] blancas
Klaviatur [F]
tastiera [F]

lyre post
lyre [F]
lira [F]
Leier [F]
lira [F]

top board prop
support [M] du couvercle [M]
soporte [M] de la tapa [F]
Deckelhalter [M]
appoggio [M] del coperchio [M]

cast iron frame
plaque [F] de fonte [F]
plancha [F] metálica
Gusseisenrahmen [M]
telaio [M] in ghisa [F]

iano bench
abouret [M] de piano [M]
anquillo [M] de piano [M]
lavierbank [F]
anca per pianoforte [M]

leg
pied
pata [F]
Standbein [N]
gamba [F]

caster
roulette [F]
ruedecilla [F]
Rolle [F]
rotella [F]

damper pedal
pédale [F] forte
pedal [M] de
resonancia [F]
Fortepedal [N]
pedale [M] di risonanza [F]

pedal box
pédalier [M]
caja [F] de pedales [M]
Pedalkasten [M]
pedaliera [F]

muffler pedal
pédale [F] de sourdine [F]
pedal [M] de amortigación [F]
Tonhaltepedal [N]
pedale [M] sostenuto

soft pedal
pédale [F] douce
pedal [M] de sordina [F]
Pianopedal [N]
pedale [M] di una corda [F]

electric organ
orgue [M] électrique
órgano [M] eléctrico
Hammondorgel [F]
organo [M] elettrico

harpsichord
clavecin [M]
clavicémbalo [M]
Cembalo [N]
clavicembalo [M]

drum kit
batterie ^{F}
batería ^{F}
Schlagzeug ^{N}
batteria ^{F}

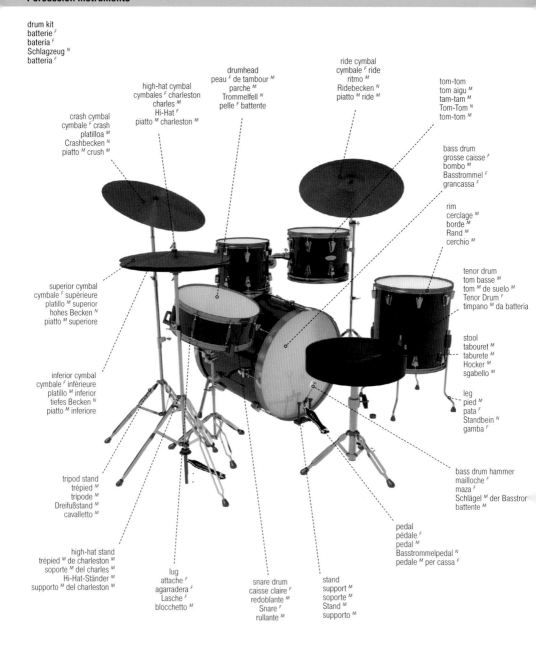

high-hat cymbal
cymbales ^{F} charleston
charles ^{M}
Hi-Hat ^{F}
piatto ^{M} charleston ^{M}
drumhead
peau ^{F} de tambour ^{M}
parche ^{M}
Trommelfell ^{N}
pelle ^{F} battente
ride cymbal
cymbale ^{F} ride
ritmo ^{M}
Ridebecken ^{N}
piatto ^{M} ride ^{M}
tom-tom
tom aigu ^{M}
tam-tam ^{M}
Tom-Tom ^{N}
tom-tom ^{M}
crash cymbal
cymbale ^{F} crash
platilloa ^{M}
Crashbecken ^{N}
piatto ^{M} crush ^{M}
bass drum
grosse caisse ^{F}
bombo ^{M}
Basstrommel ^{F}
grancassa ^{F}
rim
cerclage ^{M}
borde ^{M}
Rand ^{M}
cerchio ^{M}
tenor drum
tom basse ^{M}
tom ^{M} de suelo ^{M}
Tenor Drum ^{F}
timpano ^{M} da batteria
superior cymbal
cymbale ^{F} supérieure
platillo ^{M} superior
hohes Becken ^{N}
piatto ^{M} superiore
stool
tabouret ^{M}
taburete ^{M}
Hocker ^{M}
sgabello ^{M}
inferior cymbal
cymbale ^{F} inférieure
platillo ^{M} inferior
tiefes Becken ^{N}
piatto ^{M} inferiore
leg
pied ^{M}
pata ^{F}
Standbein ^{N}
gamba ^{F}
tripod stand
trépied ^{M}
trípode ^{M}
Dreifußstand ^{M}
cavalletto ^{M}
bass drum hammer
mailloche ^{F}
maza ^{F}
Schlägel ^{M} der Basstror
battente ^{M}
pedal
pédale ^{F}
pedal ^{M}
Basstrommelpedal ^{N}
pedale ^{M} per cassa ^{F}
high-hat stand
trépied ^{M} de charleston ^{M}
soporte ^{M} del charles ^{M}
Hi-Hat-Ständer ^{M}
supporto ^{M} del charleston ^{M}
lug
attache ^{F}
agarradera ^{F}
Lasche ^{F}
blocchetto ^{M}
snare drum
caisse claire ^{F}
redoblante ^{M}
Snare ^{F}
rullante ^{M}
stand
support ^{M}
soporte ^{M}
Stand ^{M}
supporto ^{M}

cymbals
cymbales ^{F}
platillos ^{M}
Becken ^{M}
piatti ^{M}

gong
gong ^{M}
gong ^{M}
Gong ^{M}
gong ^{M}

castanets
castagnettes ^{F}
castañuelas ^{F}
Kastagnetten ^{F}
nacchere ^{F}

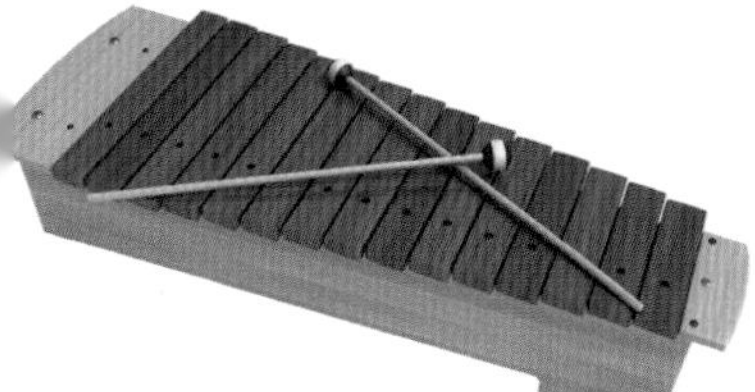

xylophone
xylophone ^{M}
xilófono ^{M}
Xylophon ^{N}
xilofono ^{M}

triangle
triangle ^{M}
triángulo ^{M}
Triangel ^{F}
triangolo ^{M}

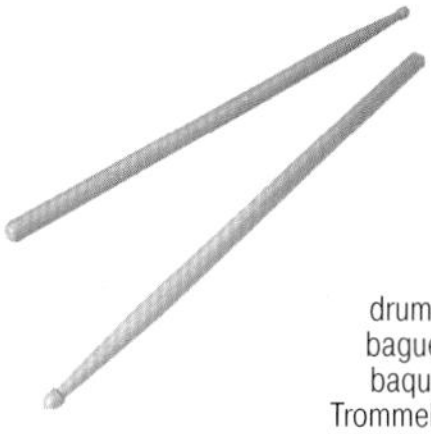

drumsticks
baguettes ^{F}
baquetas ^{F}
Trommelstöcke ^{M}
bacchette ^{F}

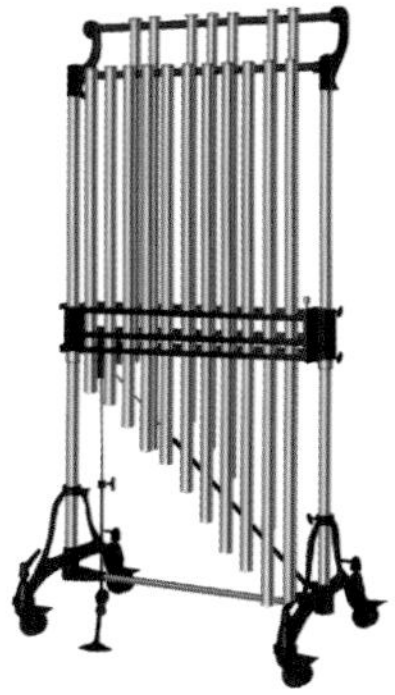

tubular bells
carillons ^{M}
campanas ^{F} tubulares
Röhrenglocken ^{F}
campane ^{F} tubolari

tambourine
tambourin ^{M}
pandereta ^{F}
Tamburin ^{N}
tamburello ^{M}

sleigh bells
grelots ^{M}
cascabeles ^{M}
Schlittenglocke ^{F}
campanelli ^{M} da slitta ^{F}

wire brush
balais ^{M} métallique
cepillos ^{M} de batería ^{F}
Stahlbesen ^{M}
spazzola ^{F} metallica

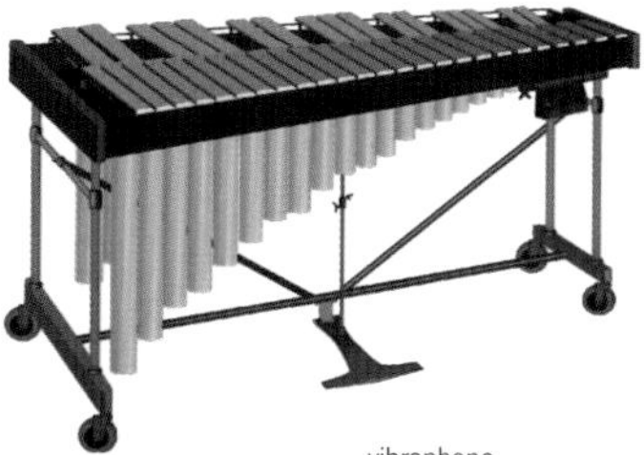

vibraphone
vibraphone ^{M}
vibráfono ^{M}
Vibrafon ^{N}
vibrafono ^{M}

bongos
bongos ^{M}
bongos ^{M}
Bongos ^{F}
bongo ^{M}

djembe
djembé ^{M}
djembe ^{M}
Djembe ^{F}
djembe ^{M}

bass drum hammer
mailloche ^{F} de grosse caisse ^{F}
mazo ^{M} de bombo ^{M}
Basstrommelschlägel ^{M}
pedale ^{M} del battente ^{M}

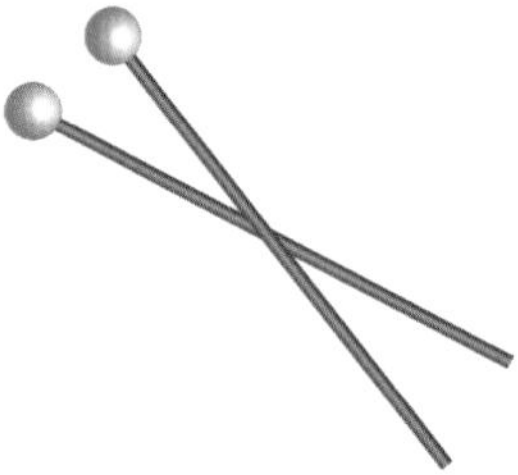

mallet
maillets ^{M}
mazo ^{M}
Schlägel ^{M}
bacchette ^{F}

kettledrum
timbale ^{F}
timbal ^{M}
Kesseltrommel ^{F}
timpano ^{M}

tension rod
barre F de tension F
tornillo M de tensión F
Spannschraube F
vite F di tensione F
drum head
peau F de tambour M
parche M de tambor M
Trommelfell N
pelle F
counterhoop
cercle M
aro M
Metalldruckreifen M
cerchio M in metallo M
caster
roulette F
ruedecita F
Rolle F
pedale M di accordatura F

bass drum
grosse caisse ^{F}
bombo ^{M}
Basstrommel ^{F}
battente ^{M}

Brass instruments

Cuivres [M] | Instrumentos [M] de metal [M] | Blechblasinstrumente [N] | Ottoni [M]

trombone
trombone [M]
trombón [M]
Posaune [F]
trombone [M]

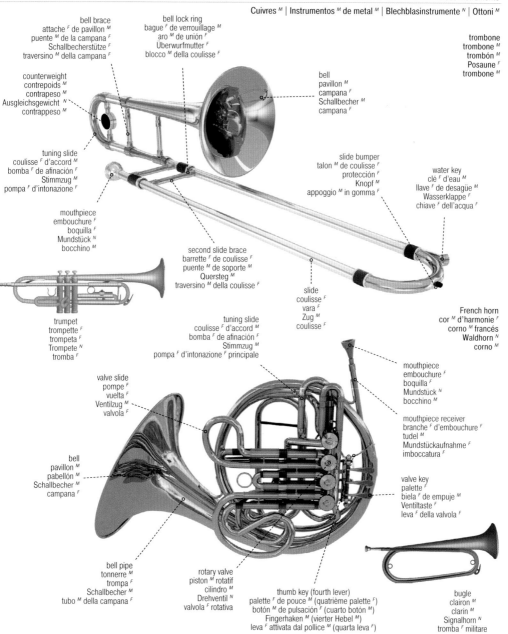

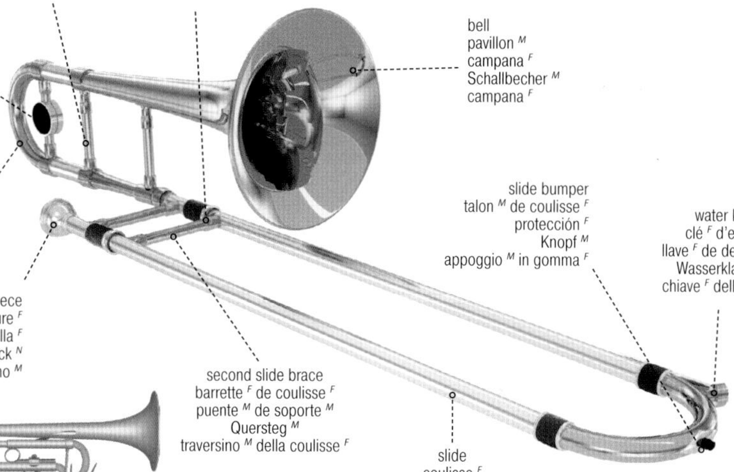
bell brace
attache [F] de pavillon [M]
puente [M] de la campana [F]
Schallbecherstütze [F]
traversino [M] della campana [F]
bell lock ring
bague [F] de verrouillage [M]
aro [M] de unión [F]
Überwurfmutter [F]
blocco [M] della coulisse [F]
counterweight
contrepoids [M]
contrapeso [M]
Ausgleichsgewicht [N]
contrappeso [M]
bell
pavillon [M]
campana [F]
Schallbecher [M]
campana [F]
tuning slide
coulisse [F] d'accord [M]
bomba [F] de afinación [F]
Stimmzug [M]
pompa [F] d'intonazione [F]
slide bumper
talon [M] de coulisse [F]
protección [F]
Knopf [M]
appoggio [M] in gomma [F]
water key
clé [F] d'eau [M]
llave [F] de desagüe [M]
Wasserklappe [F]
chiave [F] dell'acqua [F]
mouthpiece
embouchure [F]
boquilla [F]
Mundstück [N]
bocchino [M]
second slide brace
barrette [F] de coulisse [F]
puente [M] de soporte [M]
Quersteg [M]
traversino [M] della coulisse [F]
slide
coulisse [F]
vara [F]
Zug [M]
coulisse [F]

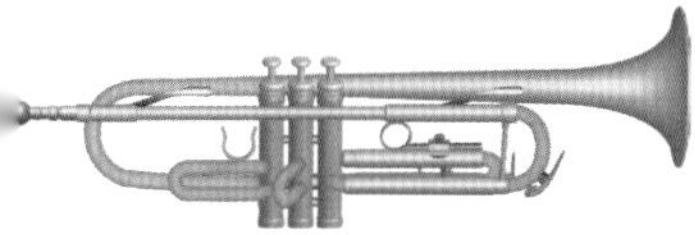

trumpet
trompette [F]
trompeta [F]
Trompete [N]
tromba [F]

French horn
cor [M] d'harmonie [F]
corno [M] francés
Waldhorn [N]
corno [M]

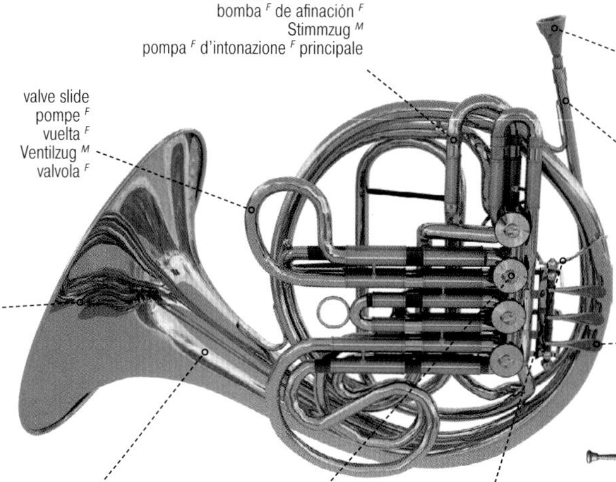
tuning slide
coulisse [F] d'accord [M]
bomba [F] de afinación [F]
Stimmzug [M]
pompa [F] d'intonazione [F] principale
mouthpiece
embouchure [F]
boquilla [F]
Mundstück [N]
bocchino [M]
valve slide
pompe [F]
vuelta [F]
Ventilzug [M]
valvola [F]
mouthpiece receiver
branche [F] d'embouchure [F]
tudel [M]
Mundstückaufnahme [F]
imboccatura [F]
bell
pavillon [M]
pabellón [M]
Schallbecher [M]
campana [F]
valve key
palette [F]
biela [F] de empuje [M]
Ventiltaste [F]
leva [F] della valvola [F]
bell pipe
tonnerre [M]
trompa [F]
Schallbecher [M]
tubo [M] della campana [F]
rotary valve
piston [M] rotatif
cilindro [M]
Drehventil [N]
valvola [F] rotativa
thumb key (fourth lever)
palette [F] de pouce [M] (quatrième palette [F])
botón [M] de pulsación [F] (cuarto botón [M])
Fingerhaken [M] (vierter Hebel [M])
leva [F] attivata dal pollice [M] (quarta leva [F])

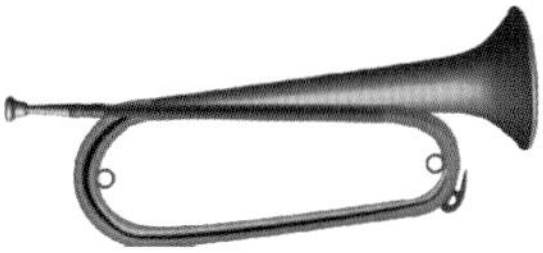

bugle
clairon [M]
clarín [M]
Signalhorn [N]
tromba [F] militare

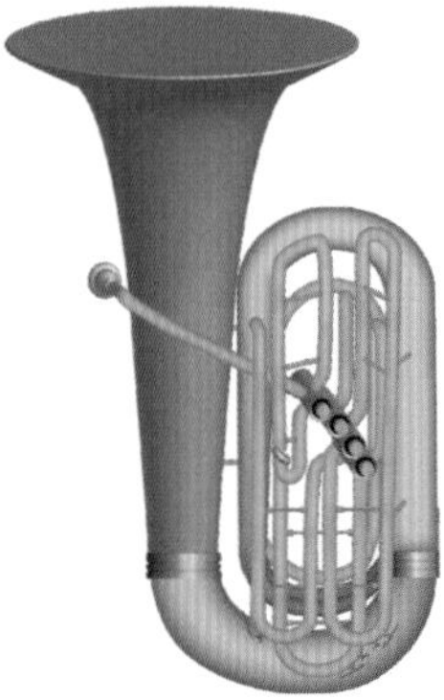

tuba
tuba M
tuba F
Tuba F
tuba F

saxhorn
saxhorn M
saxhorno M
Saxhorn N
flicorno M

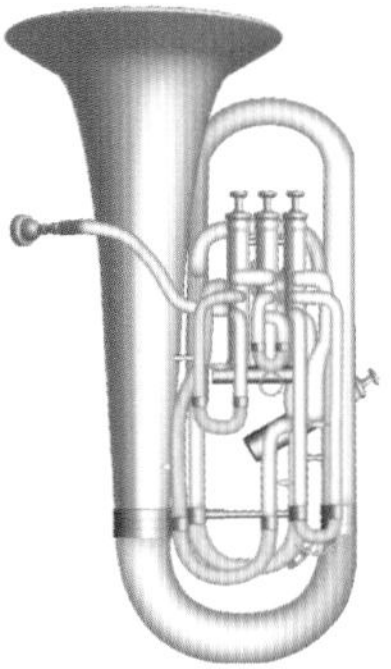

euphonium
euphonium M
bombardino M
Euphonium N
eufonio M

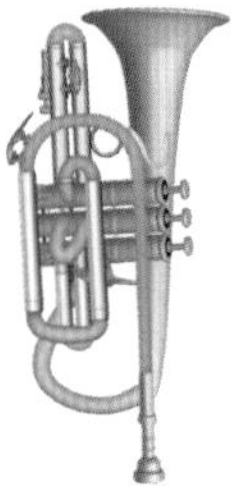

cornet
cornet M
corneta F
Kornett N
cornetta F

Woodwind instruments

Instruments M à vent M en bois M | Instrumentos M de viento M de madera F | Holzblasinstrumente N | Legni M

saxophone
saxophone M
saxofón M
Saxophon N
sassofono M

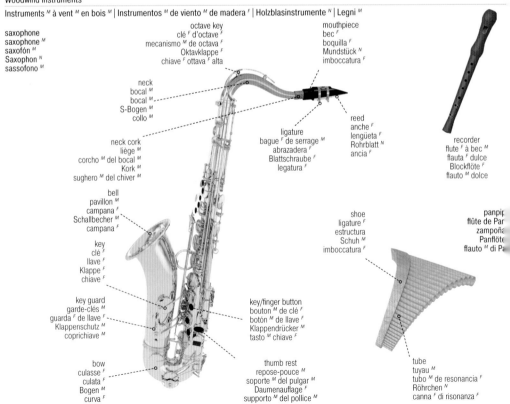

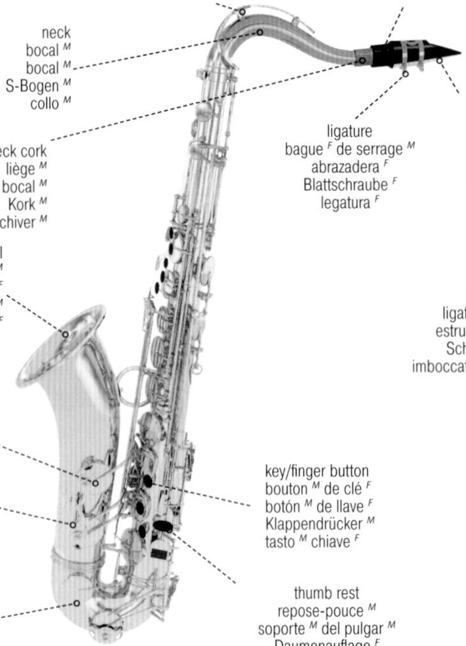
octave key
clé F d'octave F
mecanismo M de octava F
Oktavklappe F
chiave F ottava F alta
mouthpiece
bec F
boquilla F
Mundstück N
imboccatura F
neck
bocal M
bocal M
S-Bogen M
collo M
reed
anche F
lengüeta F
Rohrblatt N
ancia F
ligature
bague F de serrage M
abrazadera F
Blattschraube F
legatura F
neck cork
liège M
corcho M del bocal M
Kork M
sughero M del chiver M
bell
pavillon M
campana F
Schallbecher M
campana F
key
clé F
llave F
Klappe F
chiave F
key guard
garde-clés M
guarda F de llave F
Klappenschutz M
coprichiave M
key/finger button
bouton M de clé F
botón M de llave F
Klappendrücker M
tasto M chiave F
bow
culasse F
culata F
Bogen M
curva F
thumb rest
repose-pouce M
soporte M del pulgar M
Daumenauflage F
supporto M del pollice M

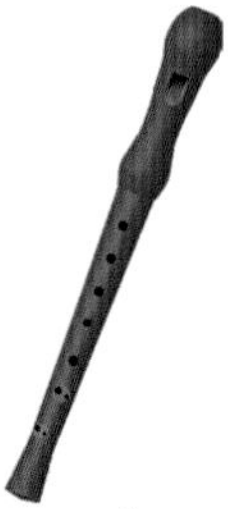

recorder
flute F à bec M
flauta F dulce
Blockflöte F
flauto M dolce

panpip
flûte de Par
zampoña
Panflöte
flauto M di Pa

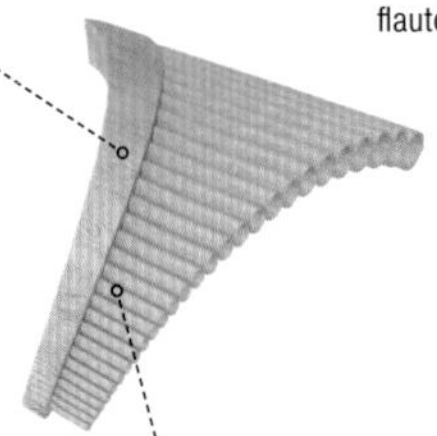
shoe
ligature F
estructura
Schuh M
imboccatura F
tube
tuyau M
tubo M de resonancia F
Röhrchen N
canna F di risonanza F

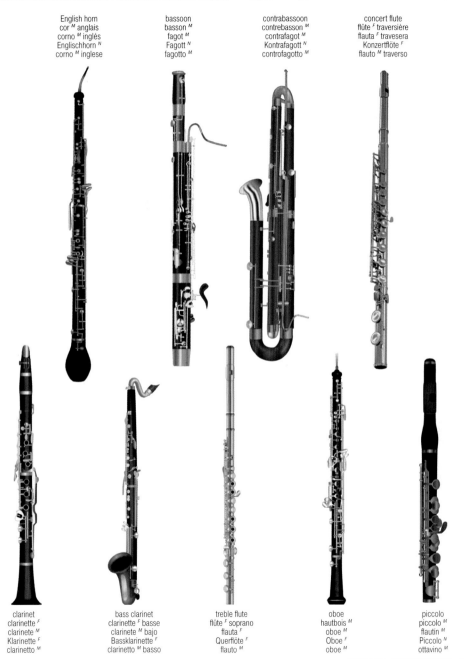

English horn
cor [M] anglais
corno [M] inglés
Englischhorn [N]
corno [M] inglese

bassoon
basson [M]
fagot [M]
Fagott [N]
fagotto [M]

contrabassoon
contrebasson [M]
contrafagot [M]
Kontrafagott [N]
controfagotto [M]

concert flute
flûte [F] traversière
flauta [F] travesera
Konzertflöte [F]
flauto [M] traverso

clarinet
clarinette [F]
clarinete [M]
Klarinette [F]
clarinetto [M]

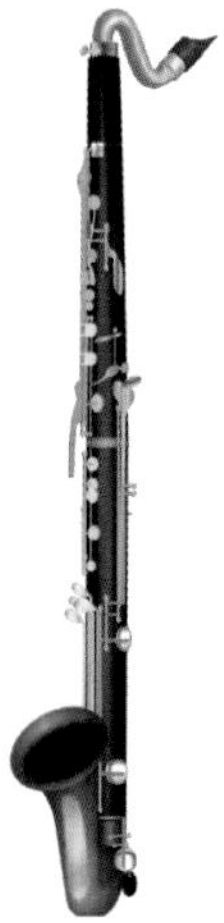

bass clarinet
clarinette [F] basse
clarinete [M] bajo
Bassklarinette [F]
clarinetto [M] basso

treble flute
flûte [F] soprano
flauta [F]
Querflöte [F]
flauto [M]

oboe
hautbois [M]
oboe [M]
Oboe [F]
oboe [M]

piccolo
piccolo [M]
flautín [M]
Piccolo [N]
ottavino [M]

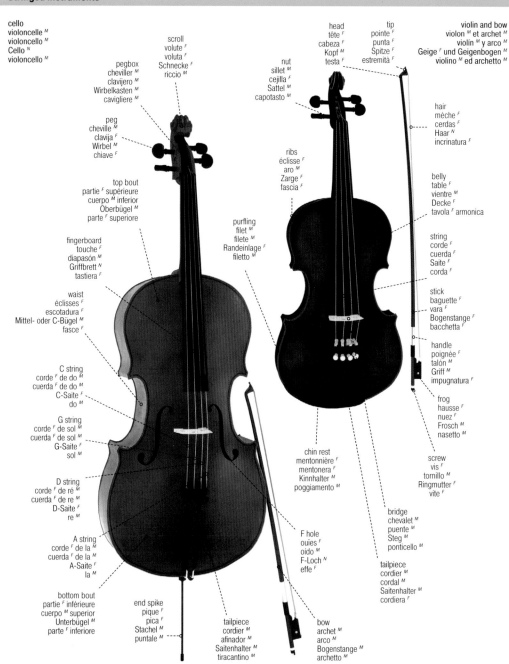

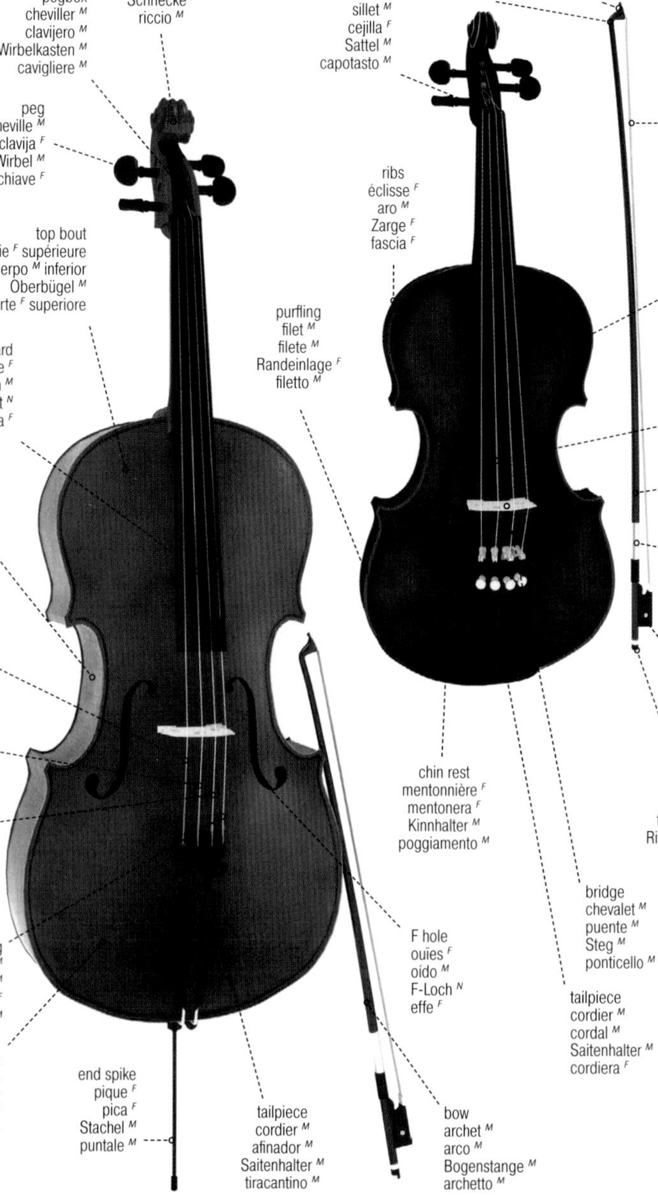
cello
violoncelle M
violoncello M
Cello N
violoncello M

scroll
volute F
voluta F
Schnecke F
riccio M

pegbox
cheviller M
clavijero M
Wirbelkasten M
cavigliere M

peg
cheville M
clavija F
Wirbel M
chiave F

top bout
partie F supérieure
cuerpo M inferior
Oberbügel M
parte F superiore

fingerboard
touche F
diapasón M
Griffbrett N
tastiera F

waist
éclisses F
escotadura F
Mittel- oder C-Bügel M
fasce F

C string
corde F de do M
cuerda F de do M
C-Saite F
do M

G string
corde F de sol M
cuerda F de sol M
G-Saite F
sol M

D string
corde F de ré M
cuerda F de re M
D-Saite F
re M

A string
corde F de la M
cuerda F de la M
A-Saite F
la M

bottom bout
partie F inférieure
cuerpo M superior
Unterbügel M
parte F inferiore

end spike
pique F
pica F
Stachel M
puntale M

tailpiece
cordier M
afinador M
Saitenhalter M
tiracantino M

bow
archet M
arco M
Bogenstange M
archetto M

F hole
ouïes F
oído M
F-Loch N
effe F

purfling
filet M
filete M
Randeinlage F
filetto M

ribs
éclisse F
aro M
Zarge F
fascia F

nut
sillet M
cejilla F
Sattel M
capotasto M

head
tête F
cabeza F
Kopf M
testa F

tip
pointe F
punta F
Spitze F
estremità F

violin and bow
violon M et archet M
violín M y arco M
Geige F und Geigenbogen M
violino M ed archetto M

hair
mèche F
cerdas F
Haar N
incrinatura F

belly
table F
vientre M
Decke F
tavola F armonica

string
corde F
cuerda F
Saite F
corda F

stick
baguette F
vara F
Bogenstange F
bacchetta F

handle
poignée F
talón M
Griff M
impugnatura F

frog
hausse F
nuez F
Frosch M
nasetto M

screw
vis F
tornillo M
Ringmutter F
vite F

chin rest
mentonnière F
mentonera F
Kinnhalter M
poggiamento M

bridge
chevalet M
puente M
Steg M
ponticello M

tailpiece
cordier M
cordal M
Saitenhalter M
cordiera F

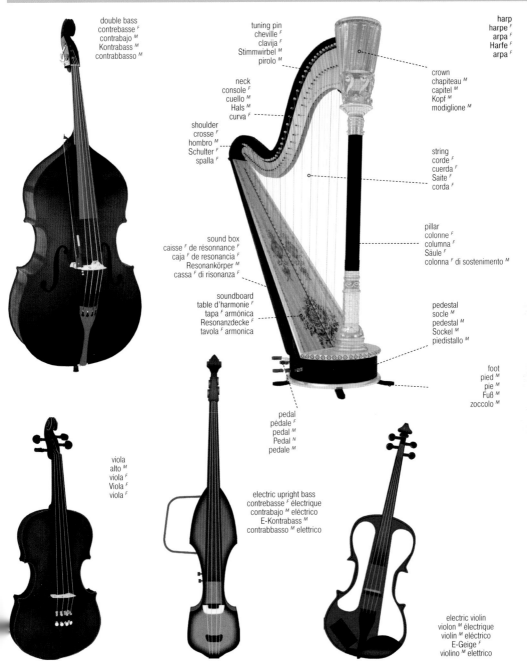

double bass
contrebasse [F]
contrabajo [M]
Kontrabass [M]
contrabbasso [M]

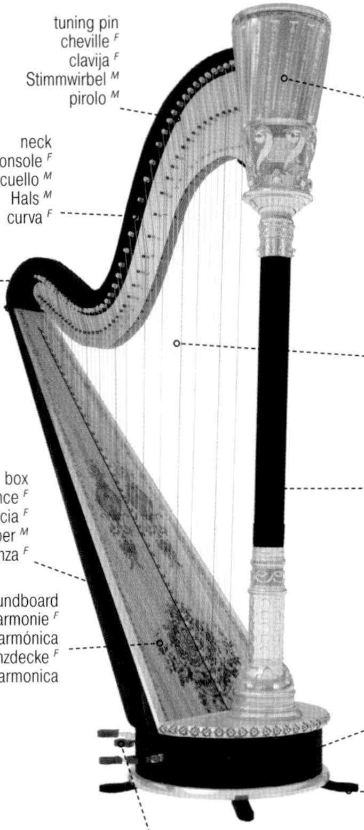
tuning pin
cheville [F]
clavija [F]
Stimmwirbel [M]
pirolo [M]
neck
console [F]
cuello [M]
Hals [M]
curva [F]
shoulder
crosse [F]
hombro [M]
Schulter [F]
spalla [F]
sound box
caisse [F] de résonnance [F]
caja [F] de resonancia [F]
Resonankörper [M]
cassa [F] di risonanza [F]
soundboard
table d'harmonie [F]
tapa [F] armónica
Resonanzdecke [F]
tavola [F] armonica
pedal
pédale [F]
pedal [M]
Pedal [N]
pedale [M]
crown
chapiteau [M]
capitel [M]
Kopf [M]
modiglione [M]
string
corde [F]
cuerda [F]
Saite [F]
corda [F]
pillar
colonne [F]
columna [F]
Säule [F]
colonna [F] di sostenimento [M]
pedestal
socle [M]
pedestal [M]
Sockel [M]
piedistallo [M]
foot
pied [M]
pie [M]
Fuß [M]
zoccolo [M]

harp
harpe [F]
arpa [F]
Harfe [F]
arpa [F]

viola
alto [M]
viola [F]
Viola [F]
viola [F]

electric upright bass
contrebasse [F] électrique
contrabajo [M] eléctrico
E-Kontrabass [M]
contrabbasso [M] elettrico

electric violin
violon [M] électrique
violín [M] eléctrico
E-Geige [F]
violino [M] elettrico

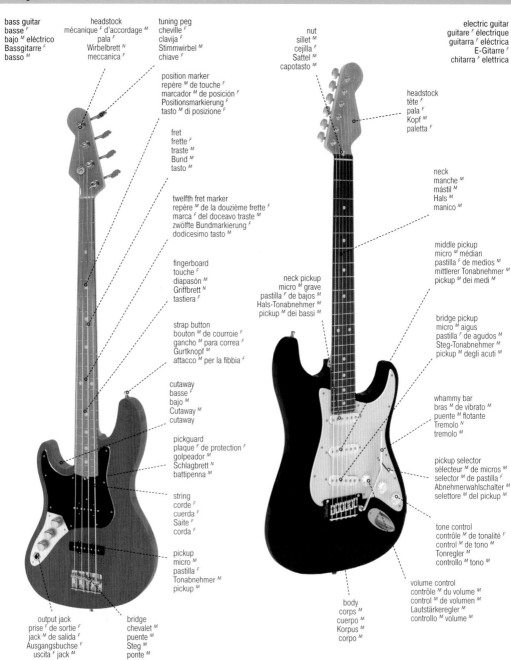

bass guitar
basse ^{F}
bajo ^{M} eléctrico
Bassgitarre ^{F}
basso ^{M}

headstock
mécanique ^{F} d'accordage ^{M}
pala ^{F}
Wirbelbrett ^{N}
meccanica ^{F}

tuning peg
cheville ^{F}
clavija ^{F}
Stimmwirbel ^{M}
chiave ^{F}

position marker
repère ^{M} de touche ^{F}
marcador ^{M} de posición ^{F}
Positionsmarkierung ^{F}
tasto ^{M} di posizione ^{F}

fret
frette ^{F}
traste ^{M}
Bund ^{M}
tasto ^{M}

twelfth fret marker
repère ^{M} de la douzième frette ^{F}
marca ^{F} del doceavo traste ^{M}
zwölfte Bundmarkierung ^{F}
dodicesimo tasto ^{M}

fingerboard
touche ^{F}
diapasón ^{M}
Griffbrett ^{N}
tastiera ^{F}

strap button
bouton ^{M} de courroie ^{F}
gancho ^{M} para correa ^{F}
Gurtknopf ^{M}
attacco ^{M} per la fibbia ^{F}

cutaway
basse ^{F}
bajo ^{M}
Cutaway ^{M}
cutaway

pickguard
plaque ^{F} de protection ^{F}
golpeador ^{M}
Schlagbrett ^{N}
battipenna ^{M}

string
corde ^{F}
cuerda ^{F}
Saite ^{F}
corda ^{F}

pickup
micro ^{M}
pastilla ^{F}
Tonabnehmer ^{M}
pickup ^{M}

output jack
prise ^{F} de sortie ^{F}
jack ^{M} de salida ^{F}
Ausgangsbuchse ^{F}
uscita ^{F} jack ^{M}

bridge
chevalet ^{M}
puente ^{M}
Steg ^{M}
ponte ^{M}

electric guitar
guitare ^{F} électrique
guitarra ^{F} eléctrica
E-Gitarre ^{F}
chitarra ^{F} elettrica

nut
sillet ^{M}
cejilla ^{F}
Sattel ^{M}
capotasto ^{M}

headstock
tête ^{F}
pala ^{F}
Kopf ^{M}
paletta ^{F}

neck
manche ^{M}
mástil ^{M}
Hals ^{M}
manico ^{M}

middle pickup
micro ^{M} médian
pastilla ^{F} de medios ^{M}
mittlerer Tonabnehmer ^{M}
pickup ^{M} dei medi ^{M}

neck pickup
micro ^{M} grave
pastilla ^{F} de bajos ^{M}
Hals-Tonabnehmer ^{M}
pickup ^{M} dei bassi ^{M}

bridge pickup
micro ^{M} aigus
pastilla ^{F} de agudos ^{M}
Steg-Tonabnehmer ^{M}
pickup ^{M} degli acuti ^{M}

whammy bar
bras ^{M} de vibrato ^{M}
puente ^{M} flotante
Tremolo ^{N}
tremolo ^{M}

pickup selector
sélecteur ^{M} de micros ^{M}
selector ^{M} de pastilla ^{F}
Abnehmerwahlschalter ^{M}
selettore ^{M} del pickup ^{M}

tone control
contrôle ^{M} de tonalité ^{F}
control ^{M} de tono ^{M}
Tonregler ^{M}
controllo ^{M} tono ^{M}

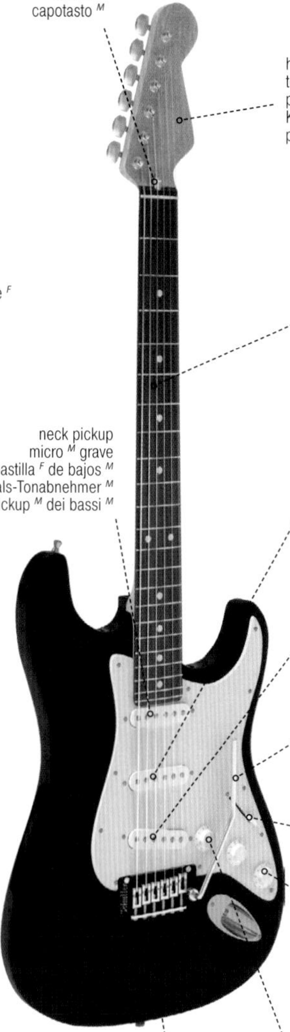

volume control
contrôle ^{M} du volume ^{M}
control ^{M} de volumen ^{M}
Lautstärkeregler ^{M}
controllo ^{M} volume ^{M}

body
corps ^{M}
cuerpo ^{M}
Korpus ^{M}
corpo ^{M}

semi-acoustic guitar
guitare F semi-acoustique
guitarra F semi-acústica
Halbresonanzgitarre F
chitarra F semiacustica

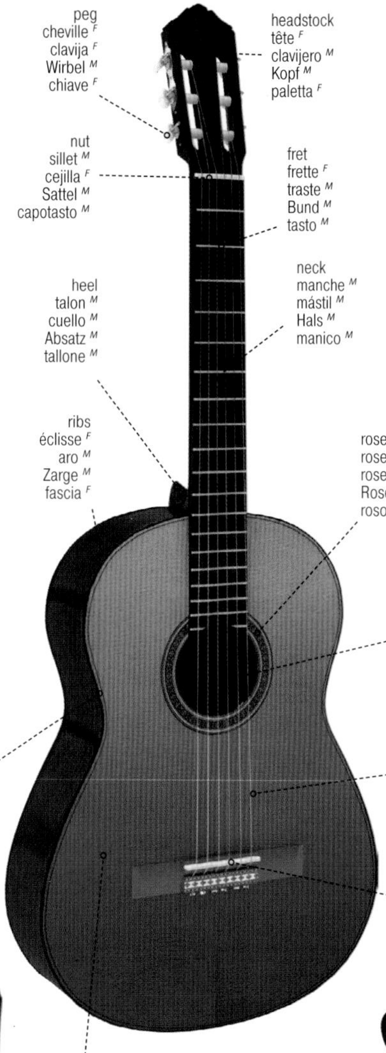
peg
cheville F
clavija F
Wirbel M
chiave F
headstock
tête F
clavijero M
Kopf M
paletta F
nut
sillet M
cejilla F
Sattel M
capotasto M
fret
frette F
traste M
Bund M
tasto M
heel
talon M
cuello M
Absatz M
tallone M
neck
manche M
mástil M
Hals M
manico M
ribs
éclisse F
aro M
Zarge M
fascia F
rosette
rosette F
roseta F
Rosette F
rosone M
sound hole
rosace F
boca F
Schallloch N
buca F
string
corde F
cuerda F
Saite F
corda F
purfling
filet M
ribete M
Randeinlage F
rilegatura F
bridge
sillet M de chevalet M
montura F
Steg M
ponticello M
soundboard
table F d'harmonie F
tapa F armónica
Resonanzboden M
tavola F armonica

acoustic guitar
guitare F acoustique
guitarra F acústica
Akustikgitarre F
chitarra F acustica

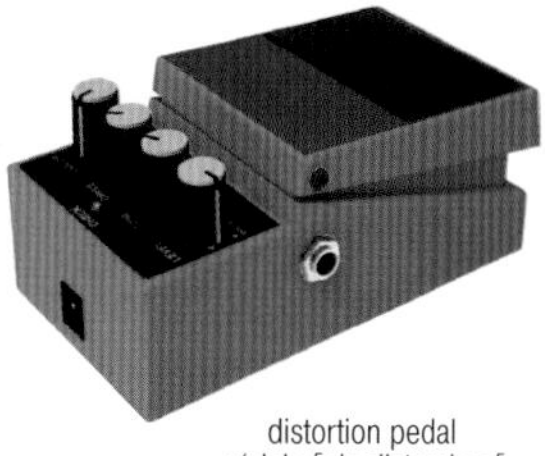

distortion pedal
pédale F de distorsion F
pedal M de distorsión F
Verzerrerpedal N
pedale M di distorsione F

amplifier
amplificateur M
amplificador M de guitarra F
Verstärker M
amplificatore M

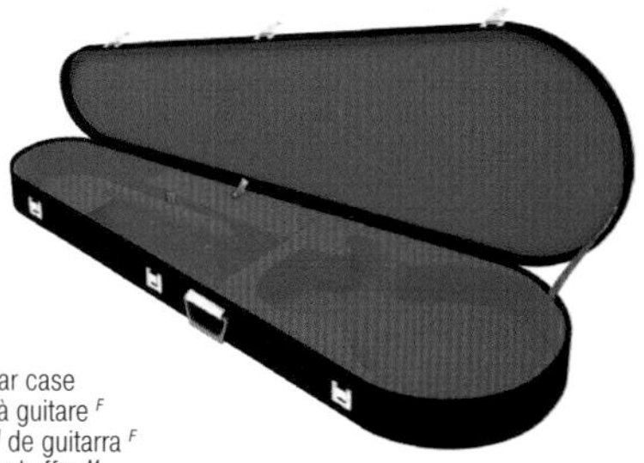

guitar case
étui M à guitare F
estuche M de guitarra F
Gitarrenkoffer M
custodia F per chitarra F

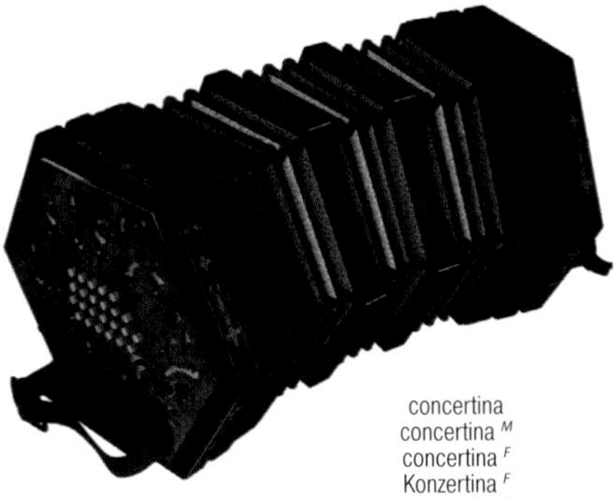

concertina
concertina [M]
concertina [F]
Konzertina [F]
concertina [F]

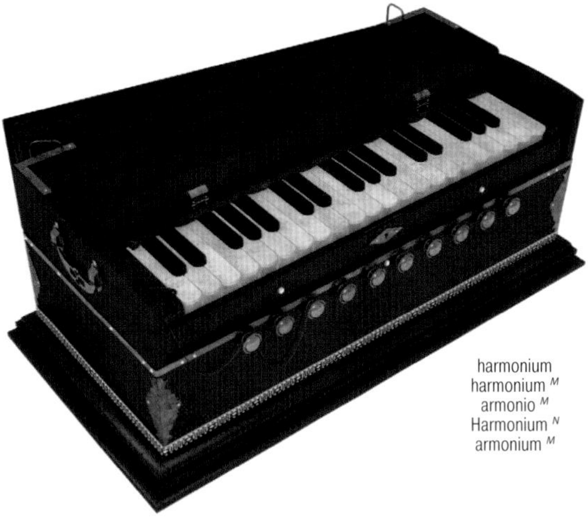

harmonium
harmonium [M]
armonio [M]
Harmonium [N]
armonium [M]

melodica
mélodica [M]
melódica [F]
Melodica [F]
diamonica [F]

harmonica
harmonica [M]
armónica [F]
Harmonika [F]
armonica [F]

accordion
accordéon [M]
acordeón [M]
Akkordeon [N]
fisarmonica [F]

bayan
bayan [M]
bayán [M]
Bajan [N]
bajan [M]

Australian instruments

Instruments ^{M} d'Australie ^{F} | Instrumentos ^{M} australianos | Australien ^{N} | Strumenti ^{M} australiani

didgeridoo
didgeridoo ^{M}
didgeridoo ^{M}
Didgeridoo ^{N}
didgeridoo ^{M}

Middle Eastern instruments

Instruments ^{M} du Moyen-Orient ^{M} | Instrumentos ^{M} europeos del Medio Oriente ^{M} | Instrumente aus dem Nahen Osten ^{M} | Strumenti ^{M} mediorientali

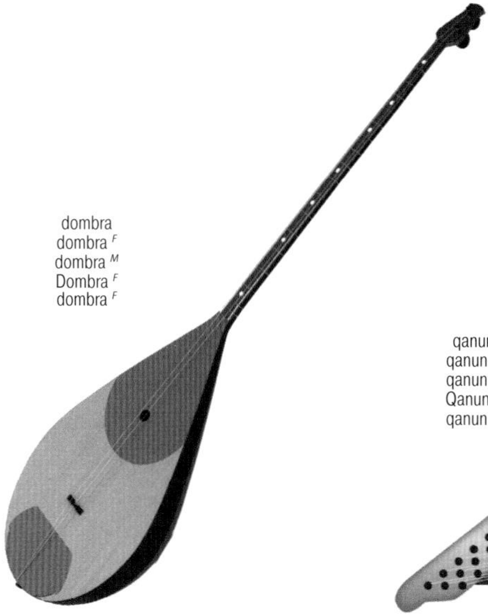

dombra
dombra ^{F}
dombra ^{M}
Dombra ^{F}
dombra ^{F}

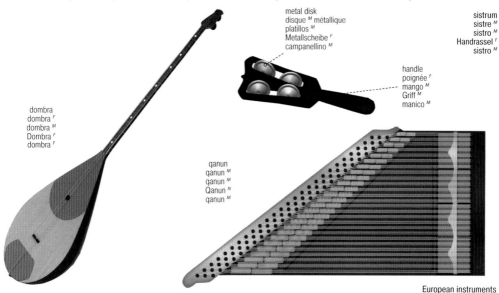

metal disk
disque ^{M} métallique
platillos ^{M}
Metallscheibe ^{F}
campanellino ^{M}
handle
poignée ^{F}
mango ^{M}
Griff ^{M}
manico ^{M}

sistrum
sistre ^{M}
sistro ^{M}
Handrassel ^{F}
sistro ^{M}

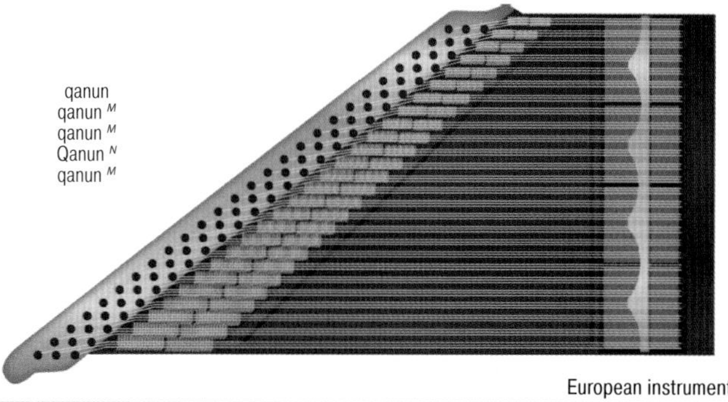

qanun
qanun ^{M}
qanun ^{M}
Qanun ^{N}
qanun ^{M}

European instruments

Instruments ^{M} d'Europe ^{F} | Instrumentos ^{M} europeos | Europäische Instrumente ^{N} | Strumenti ^{M} europei

lyre
lyre ^{F}
lira ^{F}
Leier ^{F}
lira ^{F}

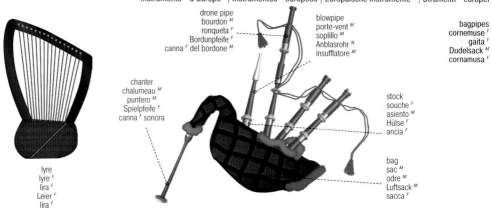

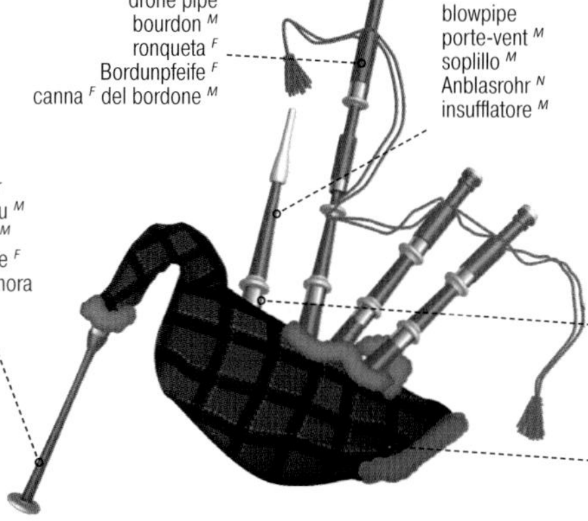
drone pipe
bourdon ^{M}
ronqueta ^{F}
Bordunpfeife ^{F}
canna ^{F} del bordone ^{M}
blowpipe
porte-vent ^{M}
soplillo ^{M}
Anblasrohr ^{N}
insufflatore ^{M}
chanter
chalumeau ^{M}
puntero ^{M}
Spielpfeife ^{F}
canna ^{F} sonora
stock
souche ^{F}
asiento ^{M}
Hülse ^{F}
ancia ^{F}
bag
sac ^{M}
odre ^{M}
Luftsack ^{M}
sacca ^{F}

bagpipes
cornemuse ^{F}
gaita ^{F}
Dudelsack ^{M}
cornamusa ^{F}

mandolin
mandoline F
mandolina F
Mandoline F
mandolino M

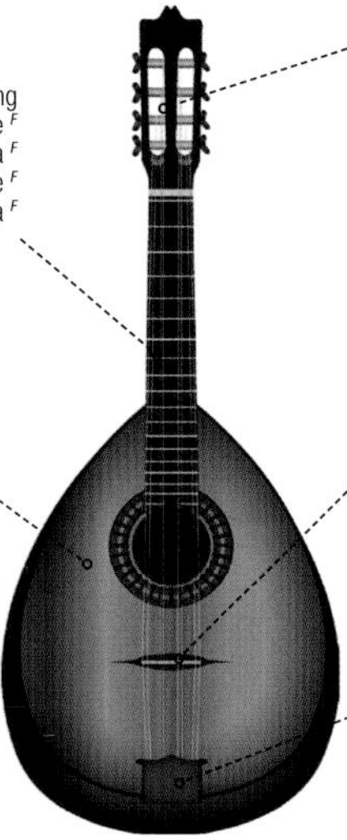

headstock
tête F
cabeza F
Kopf M
testa F

string
corde F
cuerda F
Saite F
corda F

bridge
chevalet M
puente M
Steg M
ponticello M

body
caisse F
cuerpo M
Korpus M
cassa F

tailpiece
cordier M
tiracuerdas M
Saitenhalter M
cordiera F

barrel organ
orgue M de Barbarie
organillo M
Drehorgel F
organetto M

bowed psaltery
psaltérion M **à archet** M
salterio M **de arco** M
Streichpsalter N
salterio M **ad arco** M

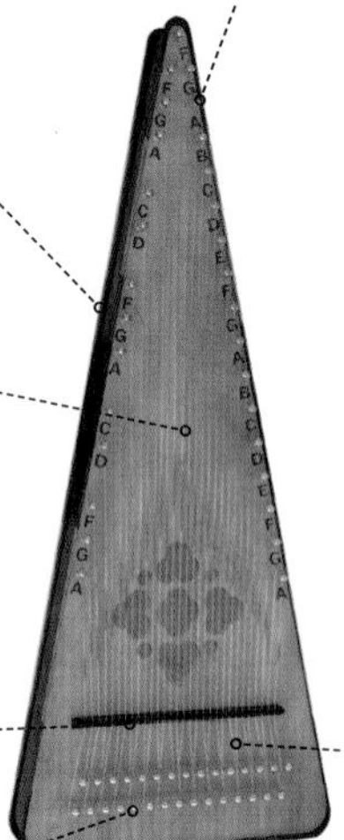

hitch pins
fixation F des cordes F
tornillo M
Hakenstift M
piolo M

body
corps M
cuerpo M triangular
Korpus M
corpo M

soundboard
table F d'harmonie F
tapa F armónica
Resonanzdecke F
tavola F armonica

bridge
chevalet M
puente M
Steg M
ponticello M

string
cordes F
cuerdas F
Saiten F
corda F

tuning pin
cheville F d'accordage M
clavija F
Stimmwirbel M
pirolo M di accordatura F

psaltery bow
archet M semi-circulaire
arco M de salterio M
Psalterbogen M
archetto M semicircolare

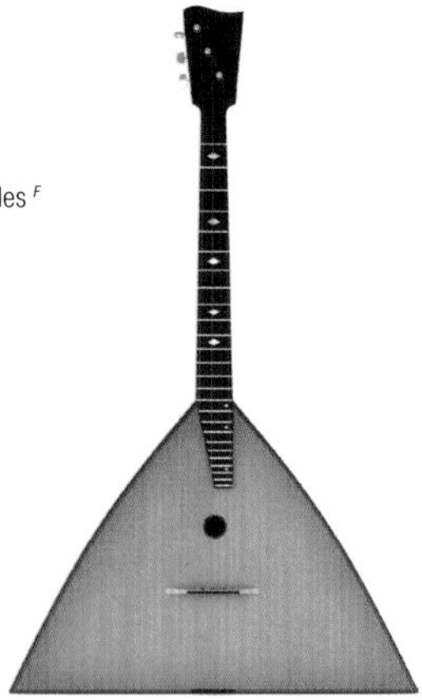

balalaika
balalaïka F
balalaica F
Balalaika F
balalaica F

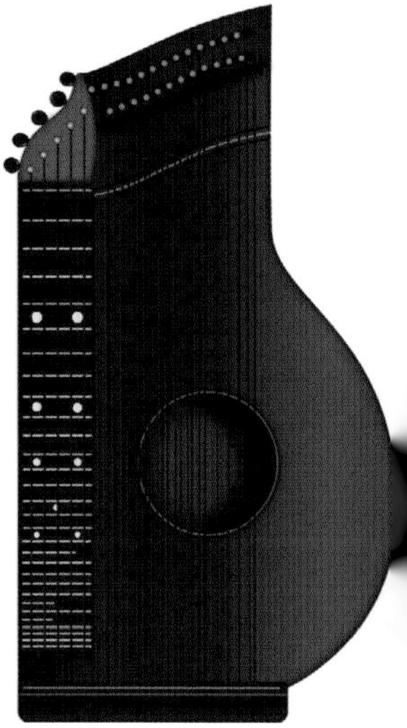

zither
cithare F
cítara F
Zither F
zither M

African instruments

Instruments ᴹ d'Afrique ᶠ | Instrumentos ᴹ africanos | Afrikanische Instrumente ᴺ | Strumenti ᴹ africani

African conga
conga ᴹ africain
djembe ᴹ
afrikanische Congatrommel ᶠ
conga ᶠ africana

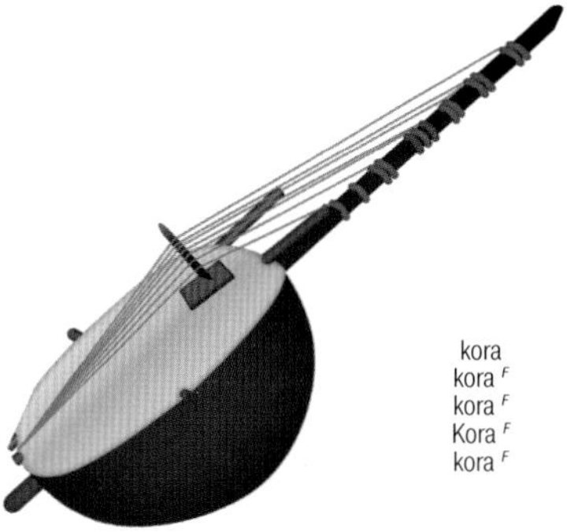

kora
kora ᶠ
kora ᶠ
Kora ᶠ
kora ᶠ

American instruments

Instruments ᴹ d'Amérique ᶠ | Instrumentos ᴹ americanos | Amerikanische Instrumente ᴺ | Strumenti ᴹ americani

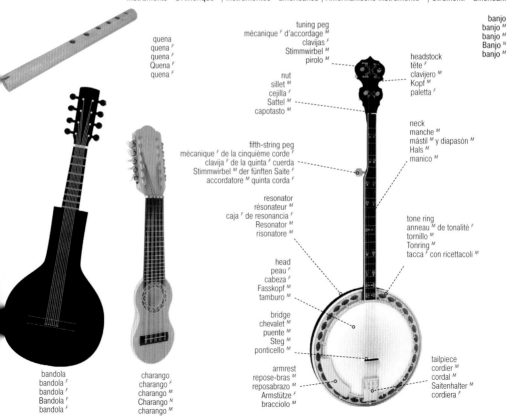

quena
quena ᶠ
quena ᶠ
Quena ᶠ
quena ᶠ

bandola
bandola ᶠ
bandola ᶠ
Bandola ᶠ
bandola ᶠ

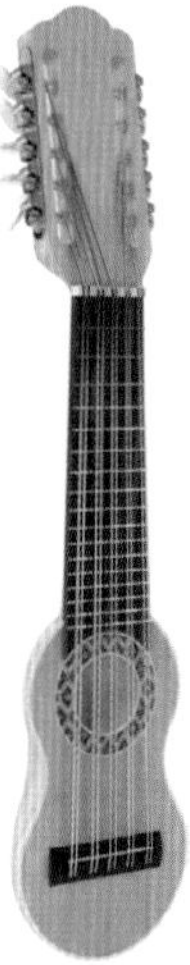

charango
charango ᶠ
charango ᴹ
Charango ᴺ
charango ᴹ

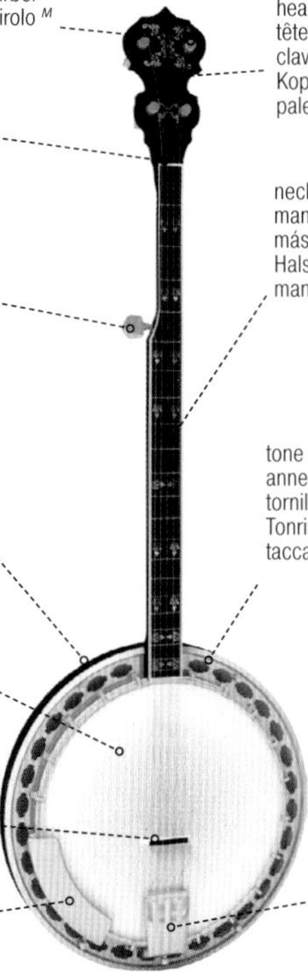

banjo
banjo ᴹ
banjo ᴹ
Banjo ᴺ
banjo ᴹ

tuning peg
mécanique ᶠ d'accordage ᴹ
clavijas ᶠ
Stimmwirbel ᴹ
pirolo ᴹ

headstock
tête ᶠ
clavijero ᴹ
Kopf ᴹ
paletta ᶠ

nut
sillet ᴹ
cejilla ᶠ
Sattel ᴹ
capotasto ᴹ

neck
manche ᴹ
mástil ᴹ y diapasón ᴹ
Hals ᴹ
manico ᴹ

fifth-string peg
mécanique ᶠ de la cinquième corde ᶠ
clavija ᶠ de la quinta ᶠ cuerda
Stimmwirbel ᴹ der fünften Saite ᶠ
accordatore ᴹ quinta corda ᶠ

resonator
résonateur ᴹ
caja ᶠ de resonancia ᶠ
Resonator ᴹ
risonatore ᴹ

tone ring
anneau ᴹ de tonalité ᶠ
tornillo ᴹ
Tonring ᴹ
tacca ᶠ con ricettacoli ᴹ

head
peau ᶠ
cabeza ᶠ
Fasskopf ᴹ
tamburo ᴹ

bridge
chevalet ᴹ
puente ᴹ
Steg ᴹ
ponticello ᴹ

armrest
repose-bras ᴹ
reposabrazo ᴹ
Armstütze ᶠ
bracciolo ᴹ

tailpiece
cordier ᴹ
cordal ᴹ
Saitenhalter ᴹ
cordiera ᶠ

Asian instruments

Instruments M d'Asie F | Instrumentos M asiáticos | Asiatische Instrumente N | Strumenti M asiatici

guzheng
guzheng M
guzheng M
Guzheng M
guhzeng M

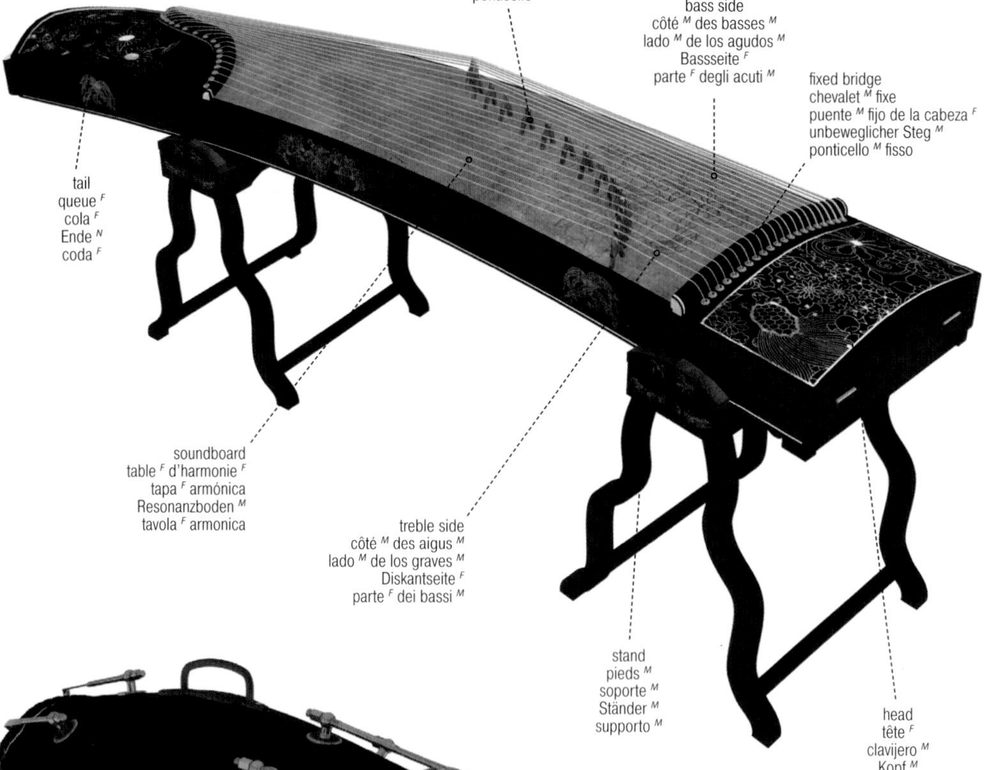
bridge
chevalet M
puente M de afinación F individual
Steg M
ponticello M
bass side
côté M des basses M
lado M de los agudos M
Bassseite F
parte F degli acuti M
fixed bridge
chevalet M fixe
puente M fijo de la cabeza F
unbeweglicher Steg M
ponticello M fisso
tail
queue F
cola F
Ende N
coda F
soundboard
table F d'harmonie F
tapa F armónica
Resonanzboden M
tavola F armonica
treble side
côté M des aigus M
lado M de los graves M
Diskantseite F
parte F dei bassi M
stand
pieds M
soporte M
Ständer M
supporto M
head
tête F
clavijero M
Kopf M
testa F

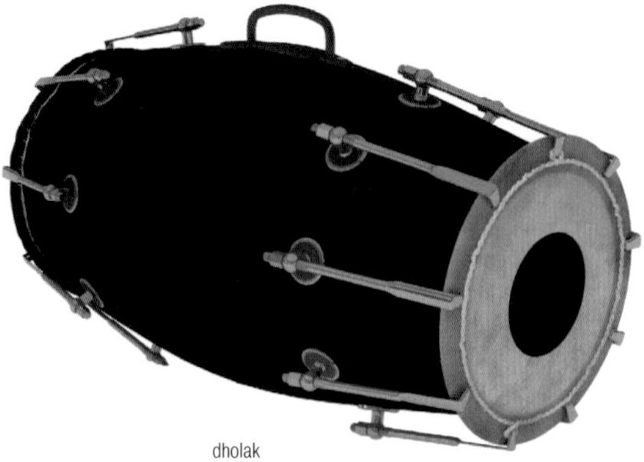

dholak
dholak M
naal M
Dholaktrommel F
dholak M

jew's harp
guimbarde F
arpa F de boca F
Maultrommel F
scacciapensieri M

guqin
qugin [M]
qugin [M]
Qugin [M]
guqin [M]

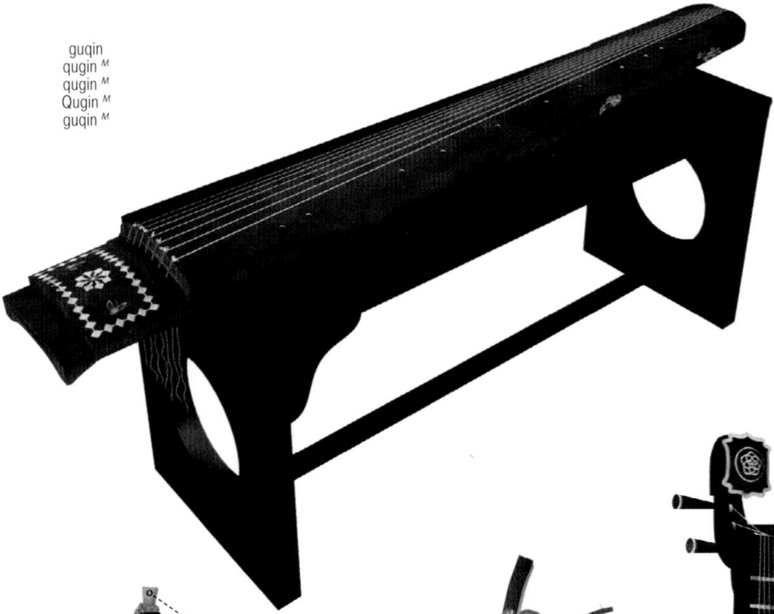

shehnai
shehnai [F]
shenai [M]
Shehnai [F]
shanai [M]

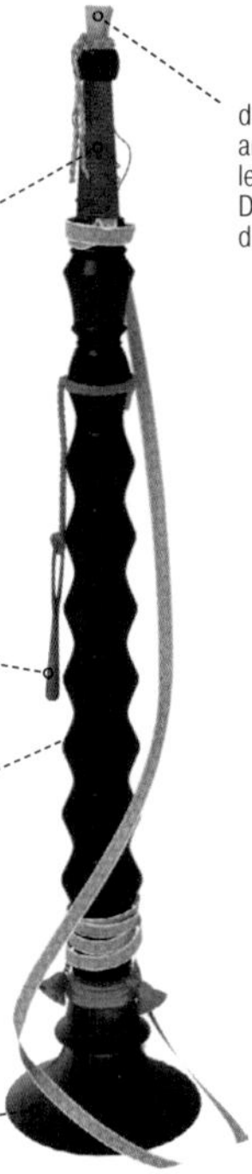
double reed
anche [F] double
lengüeta [F] doble
Doppelrohrblatt [N]
doppia ancia [F]
staple
tube [M]
cabezal [M]
Klammer [F]
supporto [M]
ivory needle
aiguille [F] d'ivoire [M]
aguja [F] de marfil [M]
Elfenbeinnadel [F]
punta [F] d'avorio [M]
finger hole
trou [M] de doigt [M]
agujero [M]
Fingerloch [N]
foro [M] per le dita [F]
bell
pavillon [M]
campana [F]
Schallbecher [M]
campanella [F]

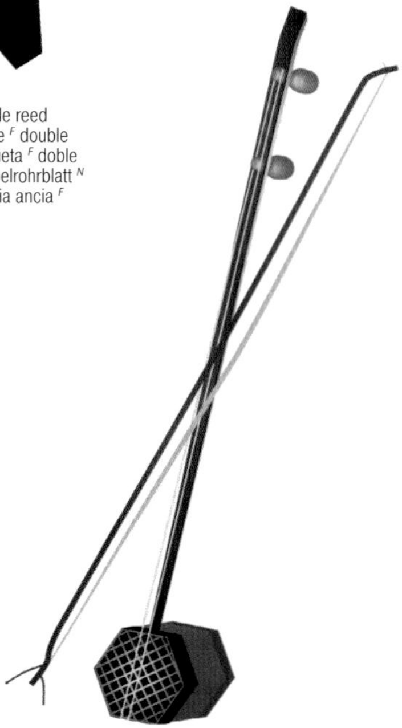

huqin
huqin [M]
huqin [M]
Huqin [F]
huqin [M]

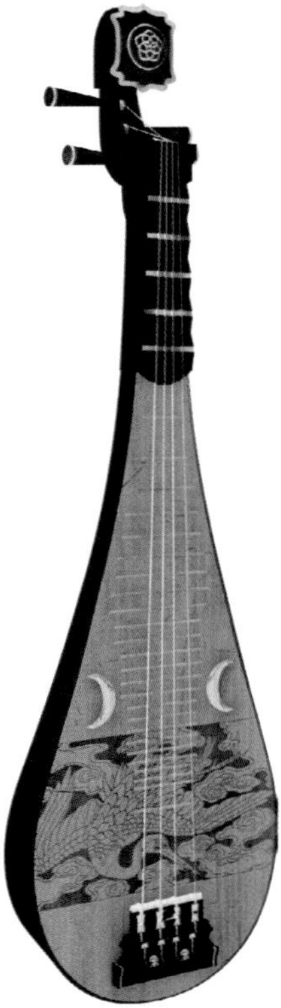

pipa
pipa [M]
pipa [F]
Pipa [F]
pipa [M]

easel
chevalet [M]
caballete [M]
Staffelei [F]
cavalletto [M]

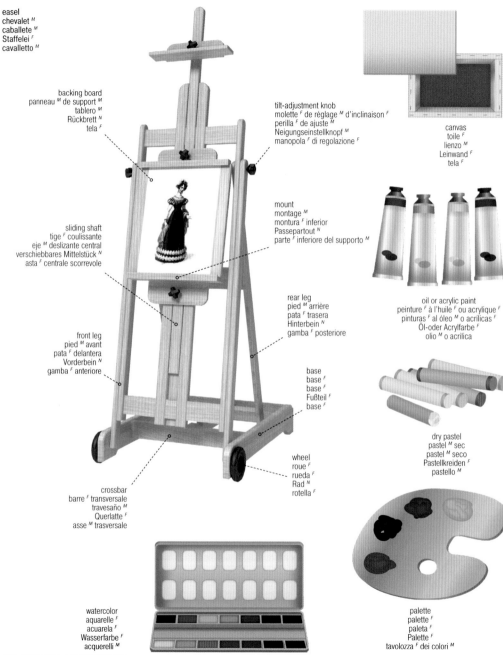

backing board
panneau [M] de support [M]
tablero [M]
Rückbrett [N]
tela [F]

tilt-adjustment knob
molette [F] de réglage [M] d'inclinaison [F]
perilla [F] de ajuste [M]
Neigungseinstellknopf [M]
manopola [F] di regolazione [F]

mount
montage [M]
montura [F] inferior
Passepartout [N]
parte [F] inferiore del supporto [M]

sliding shaft
tige [F] coulissante
eje [M] deslizante central
verschiebbares Mittelstück [N]
asta [F] centrale scorrevole

rear leg
pied [M] arrière
pata [F] trasera
Hinterbein [N]
gamba [F] posteriore

front leg
pied [M] avant
pata [F] delantera
Vorderbein [N]
gamba [F] anteriore

base
base [F]
base [F]
Fußteil [F]
base [F]

wheel
roue [F]
rueda [F]
Rad [N]
rotella [F]

crossbar
barre [F] transversale
travesaño [M]
Querlatte [F]
asse [M] trasversale

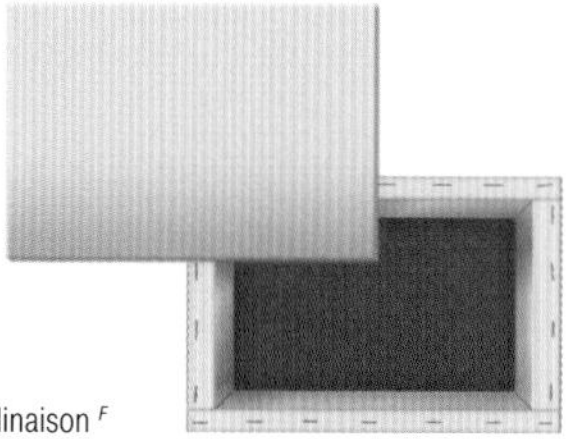

canvas
toile [F]
lienzo [M]
Leinwand [F]
tela [F]

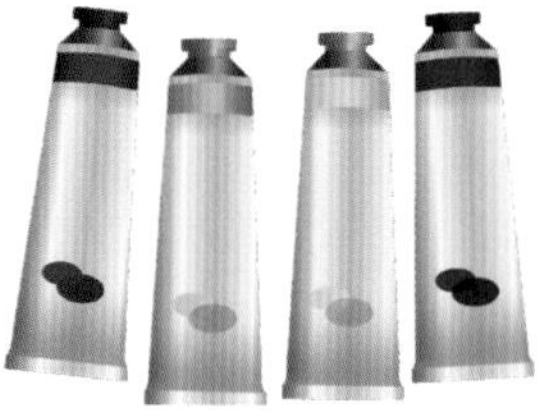

oil or acrylic paint
peinture [F] à l'huile [F] ou acrylique [F]
pinturas [F] al óleo [M] o acrílicas [F]
Öl-oder Acrylfarbe [F]
olio [M] o acrilica

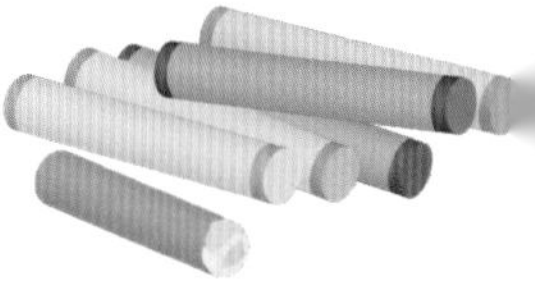

dry pastel
pastel [M] sec
pastel [M] seco
Pastellkreiden [F]
pastello [M]

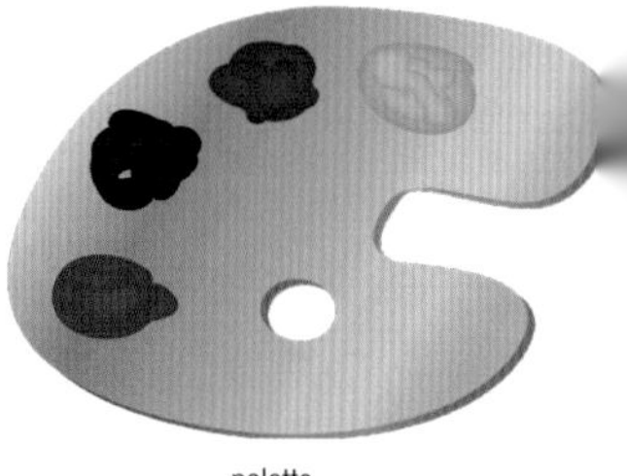

palette
palette [F]
paleta [F]
Palette [F]
tavolozza [F] dei colori [M]

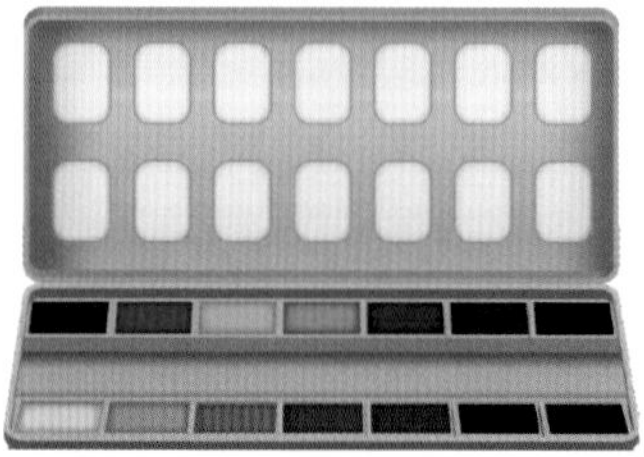

watercolor
aquarelle [F]
acuarela [F]
Wasserfarbe [F]
acquerelli [M]

brush
pinceau [M]
pincel [M]
Pinsel [M]
pennello [M]

flat brush
pinceau [M] plat
pincel [M] plano
Flachpinsel [M]
pennello [M] piatto

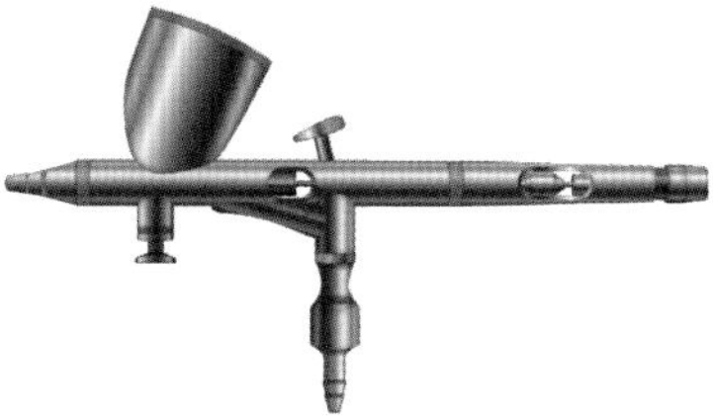

airbrush
aérographe [M]
aerógrafo [M]
Airbrush [F]
aerografo [M]

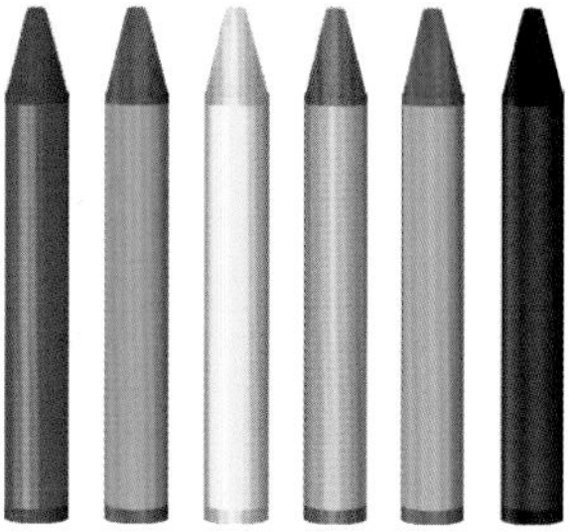

wax crayon
crayon [M] de cire [F]
lápiz [M] de cera [F]
Wachsmalstift [M]
pastelli [M] a cera [F]

colored pencil
crayon [M] de couleur [F]
lápices [M] de colorear
Farbstift [M]
matite [F] colorate

gouache
gouache [F]
gouache [M]
Gouache [F]
pittura [F] a tempera [F]

turpentine
térébenthine [F]
trementina [F]
Terpentin [N]
acquaragia [F]

oil pastel
pastel [M] à l'huile [F]
pastel [M] al aceite [M]
Ölpastell [N]
pastello [M] ad olio [M]

Mosaic work

Mosaïque [F] | Trabajo [M] de mosaico [M] | Mosaik [N] | Mosaico [M]

glue
colle [F]
cola [F]
Mosaikkleber [M]
colla [F]

tessera
tesselles [F]
piedra [F] de mosaico [M]
Mosaikstein [M]
tessera [F]

mosaic
mosaïque [F]
mosaico [M]
Mosaik [N]
mosaico [M]

Embroidery

Broderie ^{F} | Bordado ^{M} | Stickerei ^{F} | Ricamo ^{M}

satin stitch
point ^{M} de satin ^{M}
punto ^{M} de satén ^{M}
Plattstich ^{M}
punto ^{M} raso ^{M}

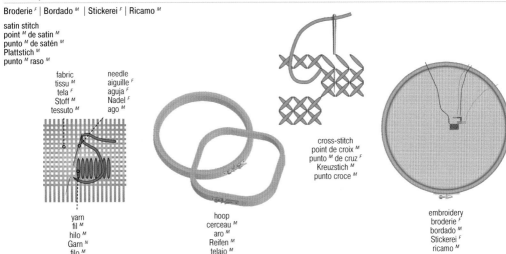

fabric
tissu ^{M}
tela ^{F}
Stoff ^{M}
tessuto ^{M}

needle
aiguille ^{F}
aguja ^{F}
Nadel ^{F}
ago ^{M}

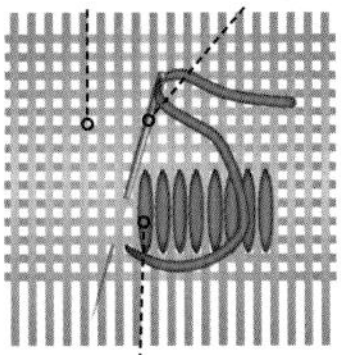

yarn
fil ^{M}
hilo ^{M}
Garn ^{N}
filo ^{M}

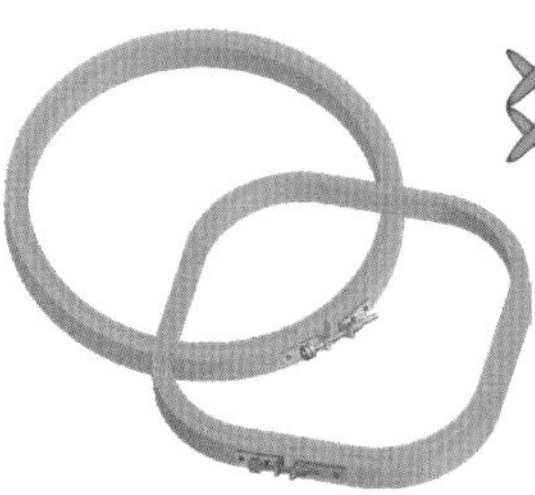

hoop
cerceau ^{M}
aro ^{M}
Reifen ^{M}
telaio ^{M}

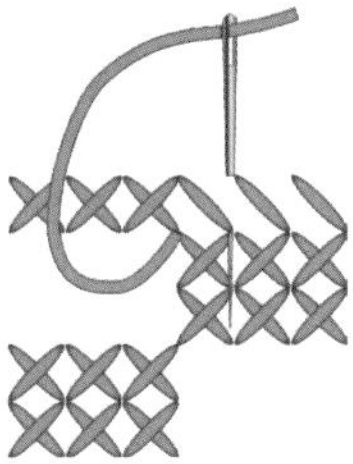

cross-stitch
point de croix ^{M}
punto ^{M} de cruz ^{F}
Kreuzstich ^{M}
punto croce ^{M}

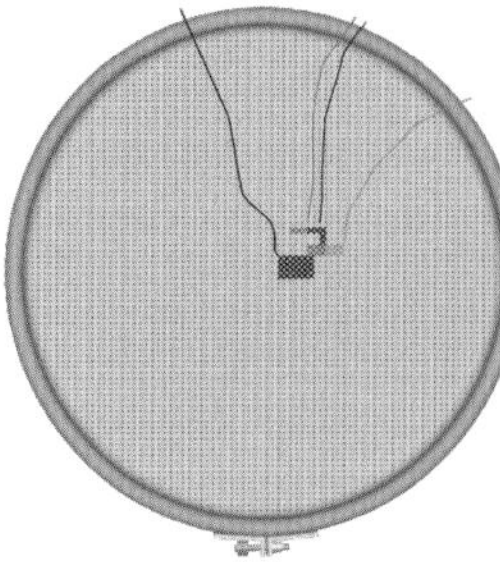

embroidery
broderie ^{F}
bordado ^{M}
Stickerei ^{F}
ricamo ^{M}

Other handwork

Autre travail ^{M} à la main ^{F} | Otras ^{F} labores ^{F} de mano ^{M} | andre Handarbeiten ^{F} | Altro lavoro ^{M}

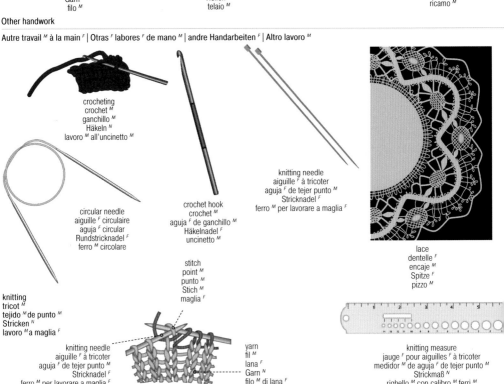

crocheting
crochet ^{M}
ganchillo ^{M}
Häkeln ^{N}
lavoro ^{M} all'uncinetto ^{M}

crochet hook
crochet ^{M}
aguja ^{F} de ganchillo ^{M}
Häkelnadel ^{F}
uncinetto ^{M}

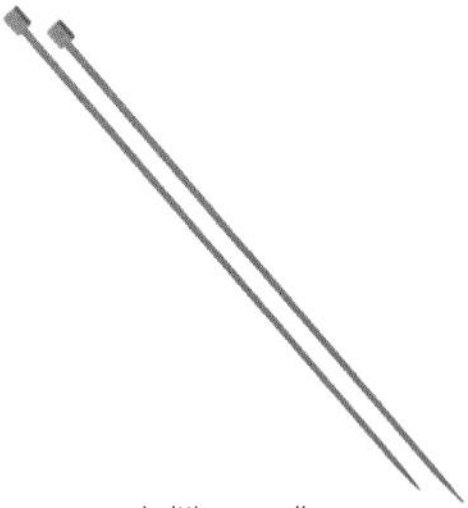

knitting needle
aiguille ^{F} à tricoter
aguja ^{F} de tejer punto ^{M}
Stricknadel ^{F}
ferro ^{M} per lavorare a maglia ^{F}

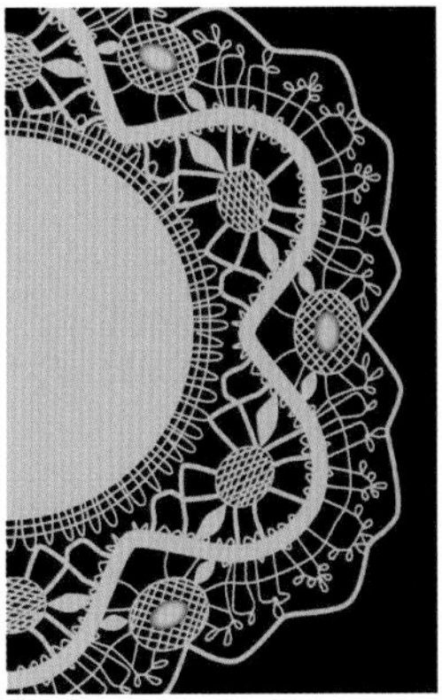

lace
dentelle ^{F}
encaje ^{M}
Spitze ^{F}
pizzo ^{M}

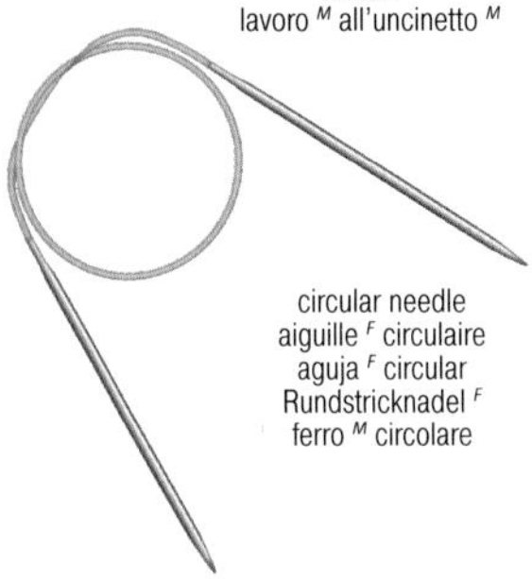

circular needle
aiguille ^{F} circulaire
aguja ^{F} circular
Rundstricknadel ^{F}
ferro ^{M} circolare

stitch
point ^{M}
punto ^{M}
Stich ^{M}
maglia ^{F}

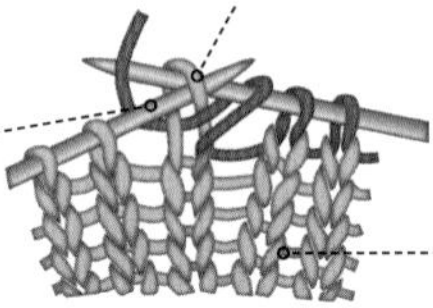

knitting
tricot ^{M}
tejido ^{M} de punto ^{M}
Stricken ^{N}
lavoro ^{M} a maglia ^{F}

knitting needle
aiguille ^{F} à tricoter
aguja ^{F} de tejer punto ^{M}
Stricknadel ^{F}
ferro ^{M} per lavorare a maglia ^{F}

yarn
fil ^{M}
lana ^{F}
Garn ^{N}
filo ^{M} di lana ^{F}

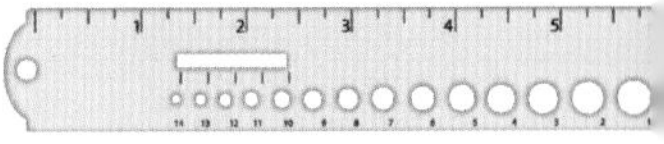

knitting measure
jauge ^{F} pour aiguilles ^{F} à tricoter
medidor ^{M} de aguja ^{F} de tejer punto ^{M}
Strickmaß ^{N}
righello ^{M} con calibro ^{M} ferri ^{M}

Sewing

Couture [F] | Costura [F] | Nähen [N] | Cucito [M]

sewing machine
machine à coudre [F]
máquina [F] de coser
Nähmaschine [F]
macchina [F] per cucire

zipper
fermeture [F] à glissière [F]
cremallera [F]
Reißverschluss [M]
cerniera [F] lampo [M]

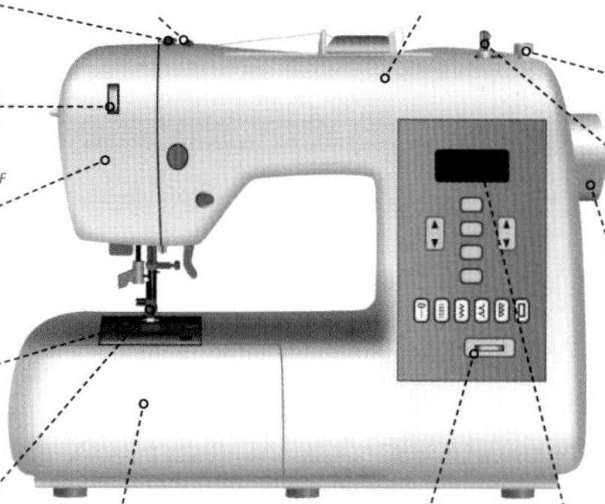

thread take-up lever
levier [M] releveur de fil [M]
palanca [F] tira-hilo [M]
Fadenaufwickelhebel [M]
leva [F] tirafilo

thread guide
guide-fil [M]
guía-hilo [M]
Fadenführung [F]
guidafilo [M]

arm
bras [M]
brazo [M]
Arm [M]
braccio [M]

pressure dial
réglage [M] de la tension [F]
regulador [M] de presión [F]
Druckscheibe [F]
indicatore [M] di pressione [F]

head
tête [F]
cabezal [M]
Kopf [M]
testata [F]

needle plate
plaque [F] à aiguille [F]
placa [F] de la aguja [F]
Stichplatte [F]
placca [F] dell'ago [M]

needle
aiguille [F]
aguja [F]
Nadel [F]
ago [M]

flat bed
plateau [M]
base [F]
Maschinenbett [N]
base [F]

switch
interrupteur [M] éclairage [M]
interruptor [M] de la luz [F]
Schalter [M]
interruttore [M]

display
affichage [M]
monitor [M]
Anzeige [F]
display [M]

bobbin winder
roue [F] de bobine [F]
embobinador [M]
Spuler [M]
spolina [F]

spool release lever
levier [M] de déclenchement [M]
de la bobine [F]
palanca [F] para soltar la bobina [F]
Spulenstopper [M] und
Spulenspindel [F]
portarocchetti [M]

handwheel
volant [M]
rueda [F] volante
Handrad [N]
manopola [F] di selezione [F]
dei punti [M]

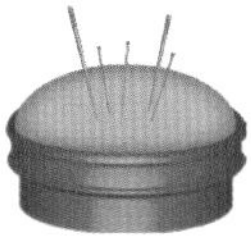

pincushion
pelote [F] à épingles [F]
alfiletero [M]
Nadelkissen [N]
portaspilli [M]

needle threader
enfileur [M] à aiguilles [F]
enhebrador [M]
Nadeleinfädler [M]
infila-ago [M]

snap
bouton-pression [M]
broche [M] a presión [M]
Druckknopf [M]
bottone [M] a pressione [F]

thimble
dé [M] à coudre
dedal [M]
Fingerhut [M]
ditale [M]

tape measure
ruban [M] à mesurer
cinta [F] métrica
Maßband [N]
metro [M] a nastro [M]

sew-through buttons
boutons [M] à trous [M]
botón [M] con agujeros [M]
Durchnähknöpfe [M]
bottoni [M]

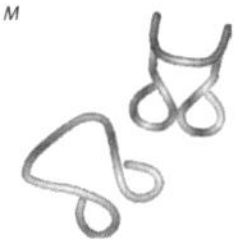

hook and eye
agrafe [F] et porte [F]
gancho [M] y bucle [M]
Haken [M] und Öse [F]
gancetti [M]

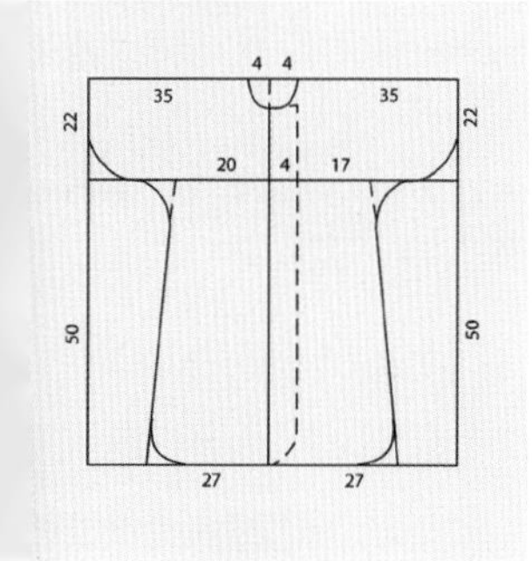
4 4
35
35
22
22
20
4
17
50
50
27
27

pattern
patron [M]
patrón [M]
Muster [N]
cartamodello [M]

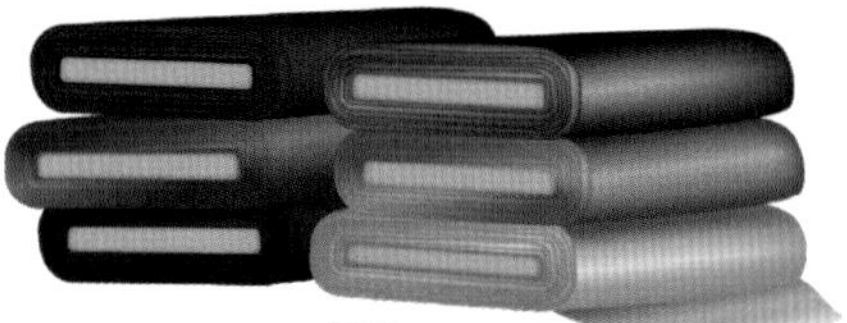

fabric
tissu [M]
tela [F]
Stoff [M]
stoffa [F]

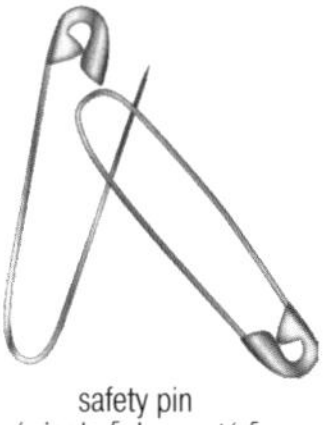

safety pin
épingle [F] de sureté [F]
imperdible [M]
Sicherheitsnadel [F]
spilla [F] da balia [F]

cathedral
cathédrale F
catedral F
Kathedrale F
cattedrale F

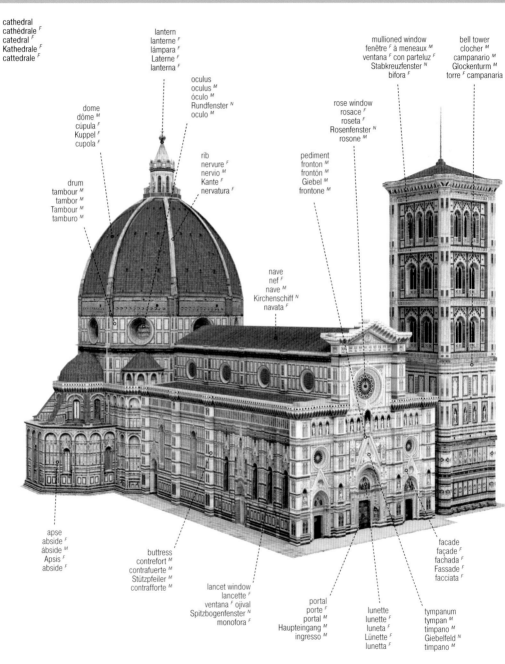

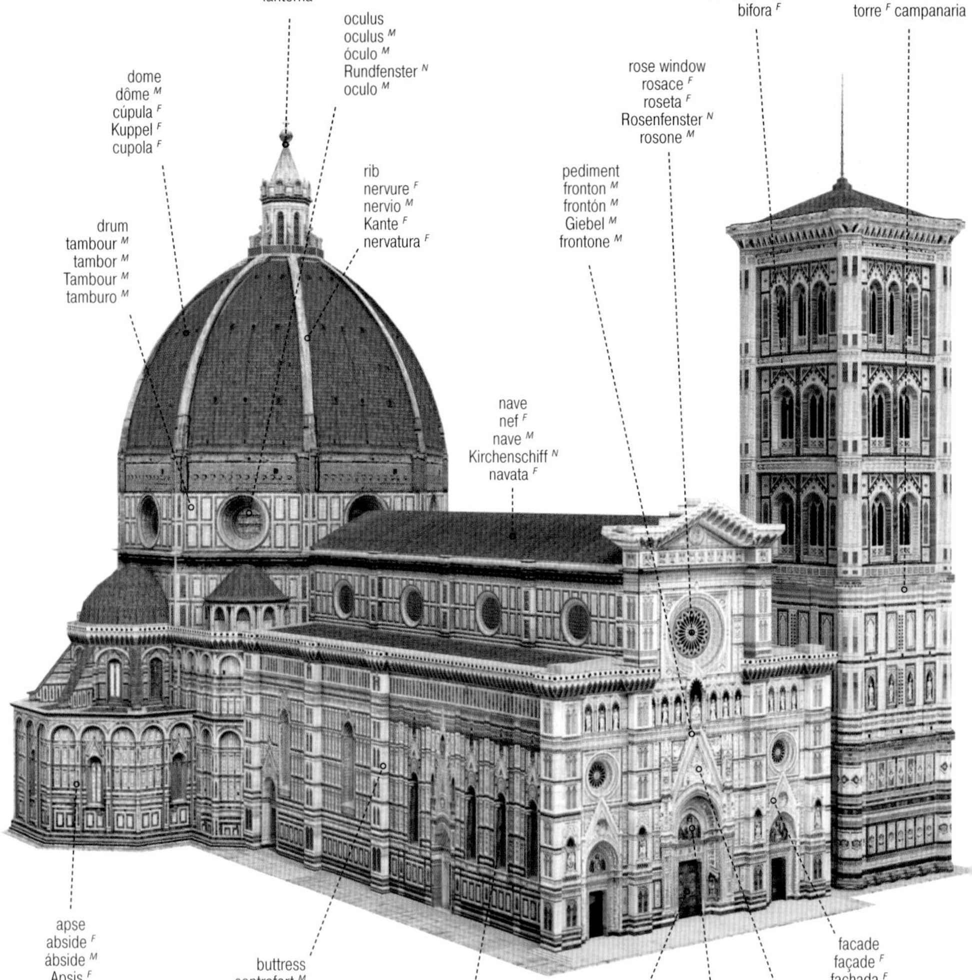
lantern
lanterne F
lámpara F
Laterne F
lanterna F
oculus
oculus M
óculo M
Rundfenster N
oculo M
dome
dôme M
cúpula F
Kuppel F
cupola F
rib
nervure F
nervio M
Kante F
nervatura F
drum
tambour M
tambor M
Tambour M
tamburo M
mullioned window
fenêtre F à meneaux M
ventana F con parteluz F
Stabkreuzfenster N
bifora F
bell tower
clocher M
campanario M
Glockenturm M
torre F campanaria
rose window
rosace F
roseta F
Rosenfenster N
rosone M
pediment
fronton M
frontón M
Giebel M
frontone M
nave
nef F
nave M
Kirchenschiff N
navata F
apse
abside F
ábside M
Apsis F
abside F
buttress
contrefort M
contrafuerte M
Stützpfeiler M
contrafforte M
lancet window
lancette F
ventana F ojival
Spitzbogenfenster N
monofora F
portal
porte F
portal M
Haupteingang M
ingresso M
lunette
lunette F
luneta F
Lünette F
lunetta F
tympanum
tympan M
tímpano M
Giebelfeld N
timpano M
facade
façade F
fachada F
Fassade F
facciata F

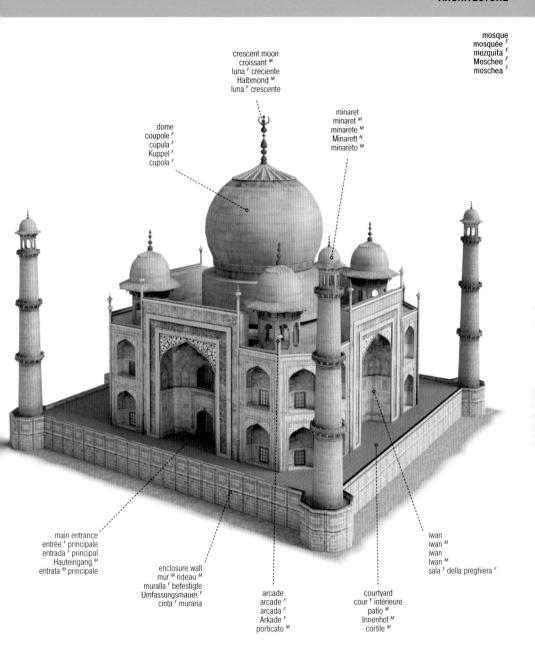

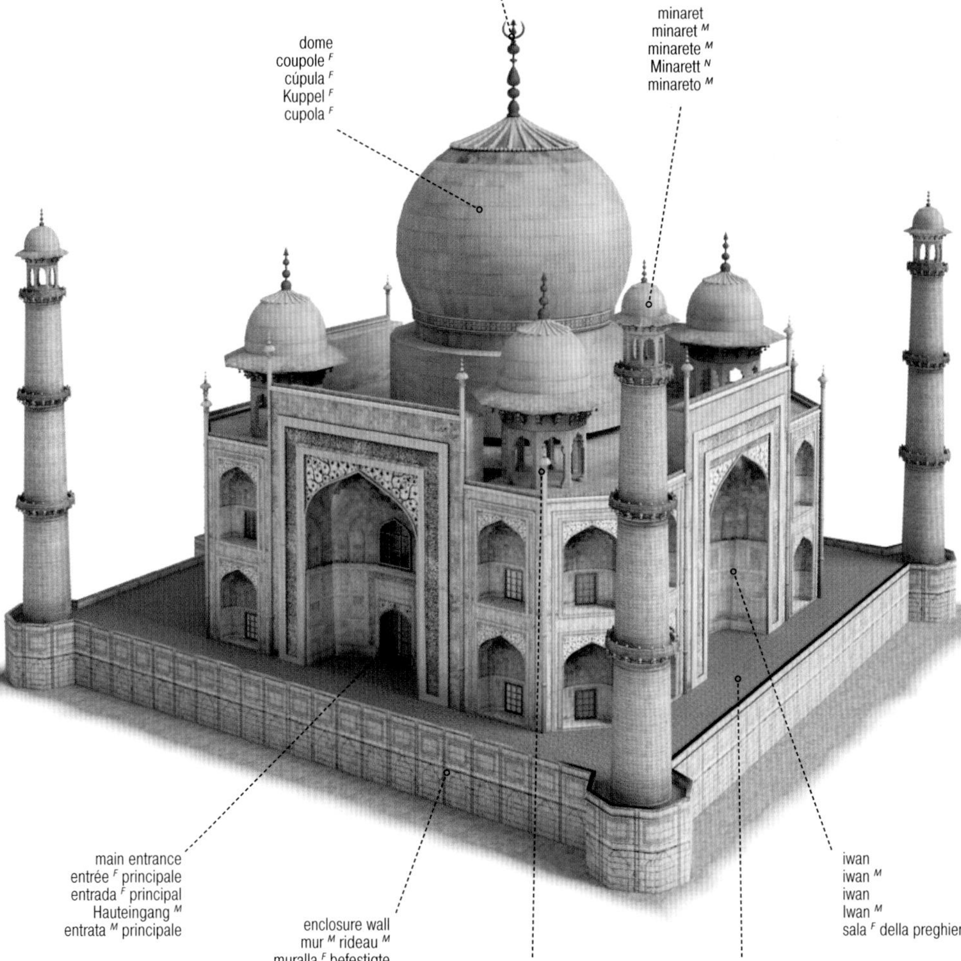
mosque
mosquée F
mezquita F
Moschee F
moschea F
crescent moon
croissant M
luna F creciente
Halbmond M
luna F crescente
dome
coupole F
cúpula F
Kuppel F
cupola F
minaret
minaret M
minarete M
Minarett N
minareto M
main entrance
entrée F principale
entrada F principal
Hauteingang M
entrata M principale
enclosure wall
mur M rideau M
muralla F befestigte
Umfassungsmauer F
cinta F muraria
arcade
arcade F
arcada F
Arkade F
porticato M
courtyard
cour F intérieure
patio M
Innenhof M
cortile M
iwan
iwan M
iwan
Iwan M
sala F della preghiera F

synagogue
synagogue F
sinagoga F
Synagoge F
sinagoga F

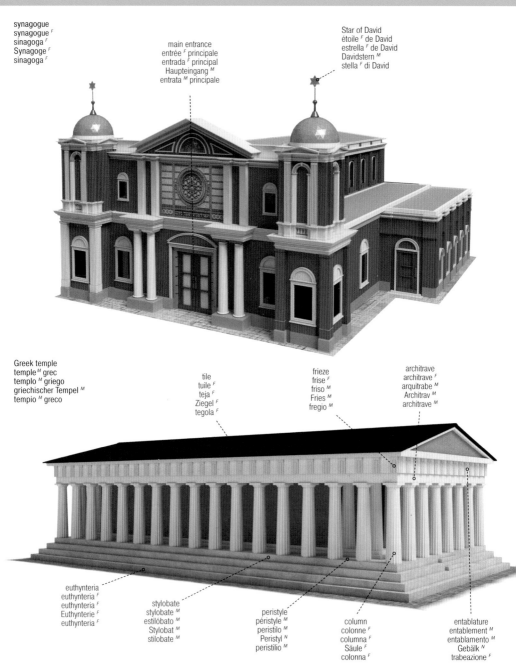

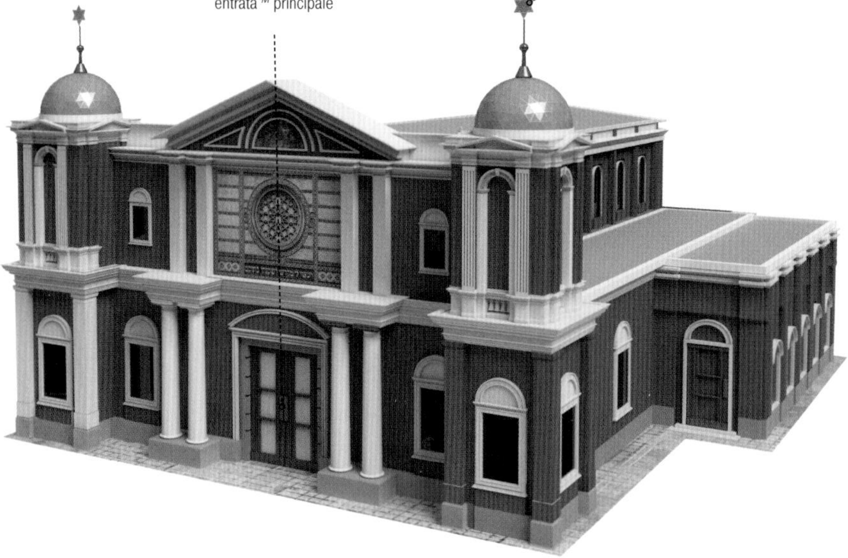
main entrance
entrée F principale
entrada F principal
Haupteingang M
entrata M principale
Star of David
étoile F de David
estrella F de David
Davidstern M
stella F di David

Greek temple
temple M grec
templo M griego
griechischer Tempel M
tempio M greco

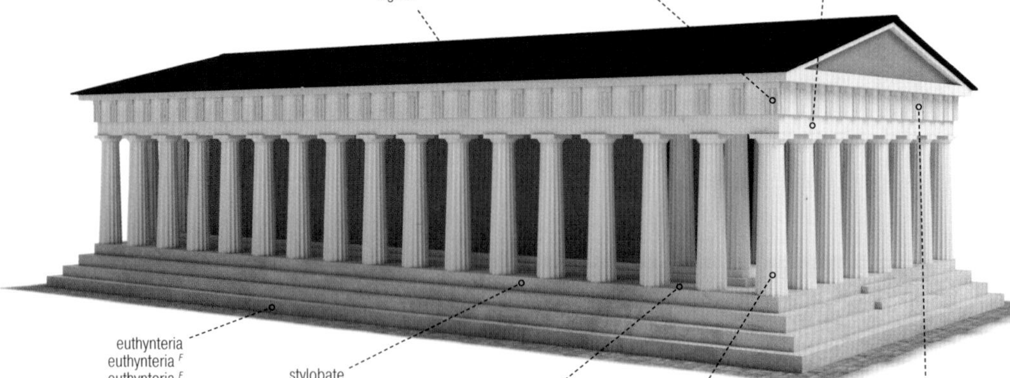
tile
tuile F
teja F
Ziegel F
tegola F
frieze
frise F
friso M
Fries M
fregio M
architrave
architrave F
arquitrabe M
Architrav M
architrave M
euthynteria
euthynteria F
euthynteria F
Euthynterie F
euthynteria F
stylobate
stylobate M
estilóbato M
Stylobat M
stilobate M
peristyle
péristyle M
peristilo M
Peristyl N
peristilio M
column
colonne F
columna F
Säule F
colonna F
entablature
entablement M
entablamento M
Gebälk N
trabeazione F

medieval castle
château ^{M} médiéval
castillo ^{M} medieval
mittelalterliche Burg ^{F}
castello ^{M} medievale

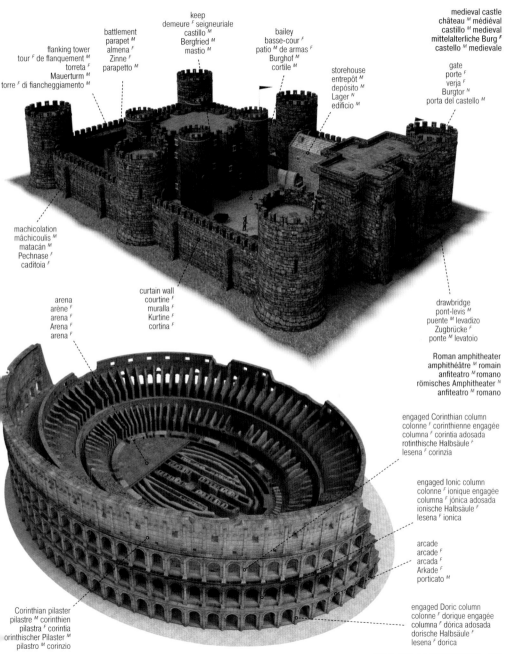

keep
demeure ^{F} seigneuriale
castillo ^{M}
Bergfried ^{M}
mastio ^{M}
battlement
parapet ^{M}
almena ^{F}
Zinne ^{F}
parapetto ^{M}
flanking tower
tour ^{F} de flanquement ^{M}
torreta ^{F}
Mauerturm ^{M}
torre ^{F} di fiancheggiamento ^{M}
bailey
basse-cour ^{F}
patio ^{M} de armas ^{F}
Burghof ^{M}
cortile ^{M}
storehouse
entrepôt ^{M}
depósito ^{M}
Lager ^{N}
edificio ^{M}
gate
porte ^{F}
verja ^{F}
Burgtor ^{N}
porta del castello ^{M}
machicolation
mâchicoulis ^{M}
matacán ^{M}
Pechnase ^{F}
caditoia ^{F}
curtain wall
courtine ^{F}
muralla ^{F}
Kurtine ^{F}
cortina ^{F}
drawbridge
pont-levis ^{M}
puente ^{M} levadizo
Zugbrücke ^{F}
ponte ^{M} levatoio

Roman amphitheater
amphithéâtre ^{M} romain
anfiteatro ^{M} romano
römisches Amphitheater ^{N}
anfiteatro ^{M} romano

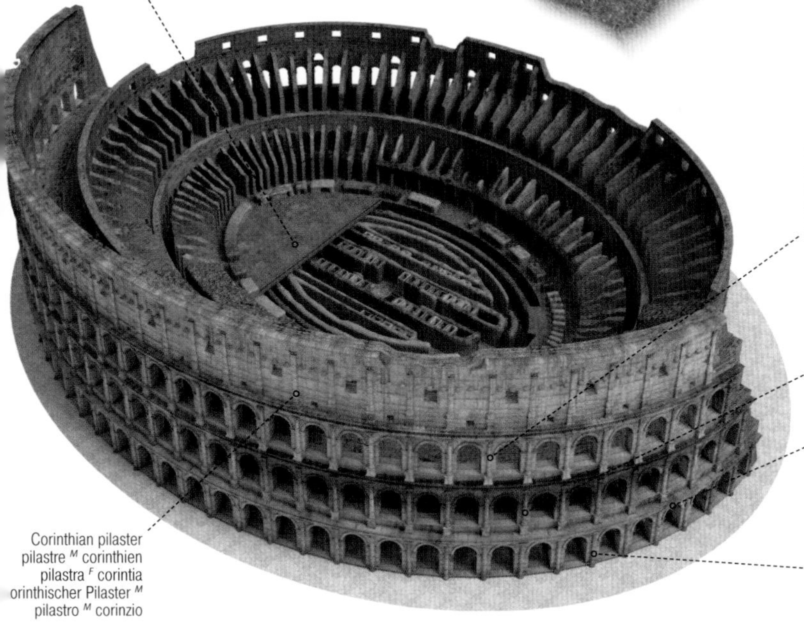
arena
arène ^{F}
arena ^{F}
Arena ^{F}
arena ^{F}
engaged Corinthian column
colonne ^{F} corinthienne engagée
columna ^{F} corintia adosada
rotinthische Halbsäule ^{F}
lesena ^{F} corinzia
engaged Ionic column
colonne ^{F} ionique engagée
columna ^{F} jónica adosada
ionische Halbsäule ^{F}
lesena ^{F} ionica
arcade
arcade ^{F}
arcada ^{F}
Arkade ^{F}
porticato ^{M}
Corinthian pilaster
pilastre ^{M} corinthien
pilastra ^{F} corintia
orinthischer Pilaster ^{M}
pilastro ^{M} corinzio
engaged Doric column
colonne ^{F} dorique engagée
columna ^{F} dórica adosada
dorische Halbsäule ^{F}
lesena ^{F} dorica

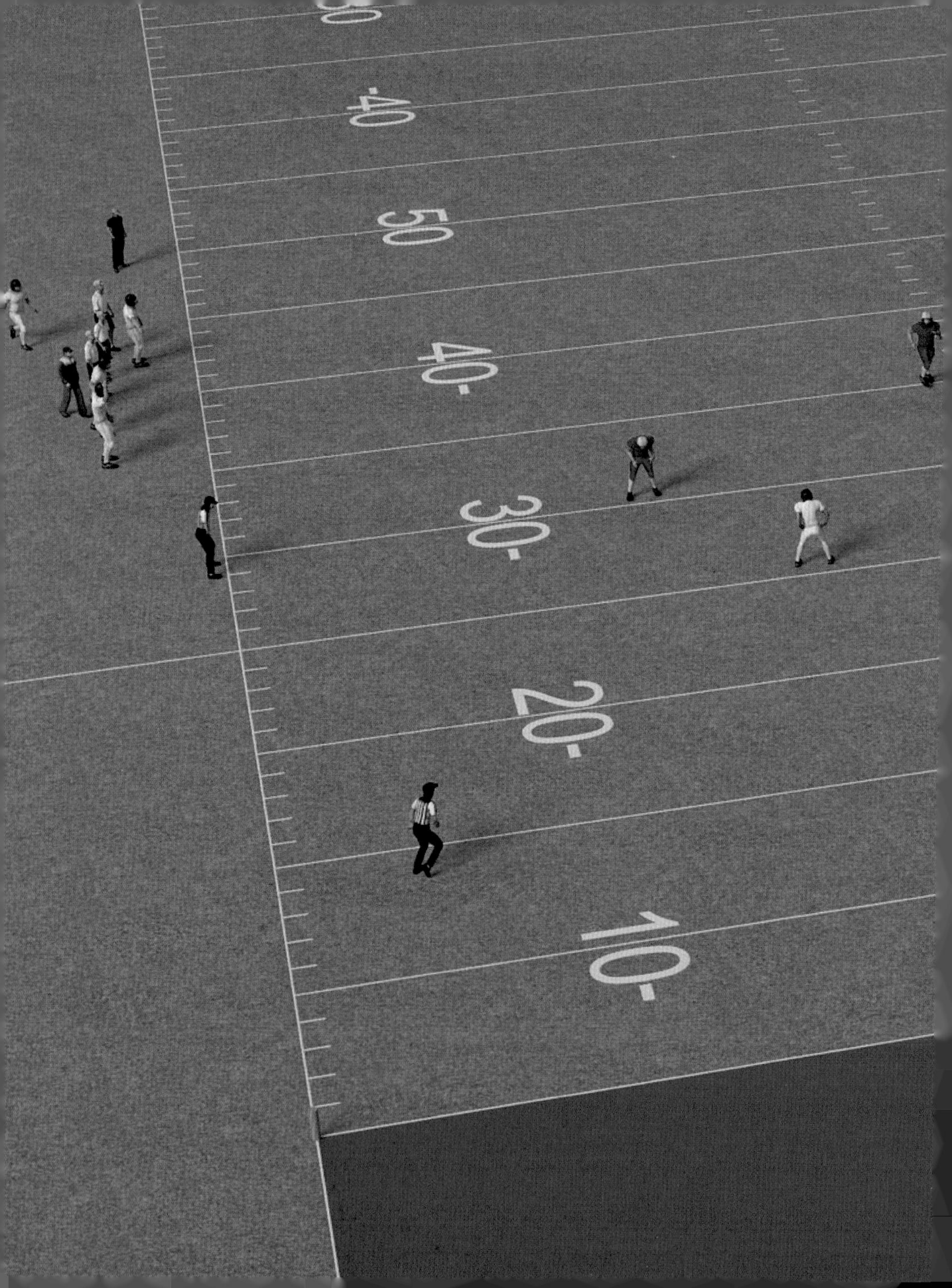

50
40
30

SPORTS

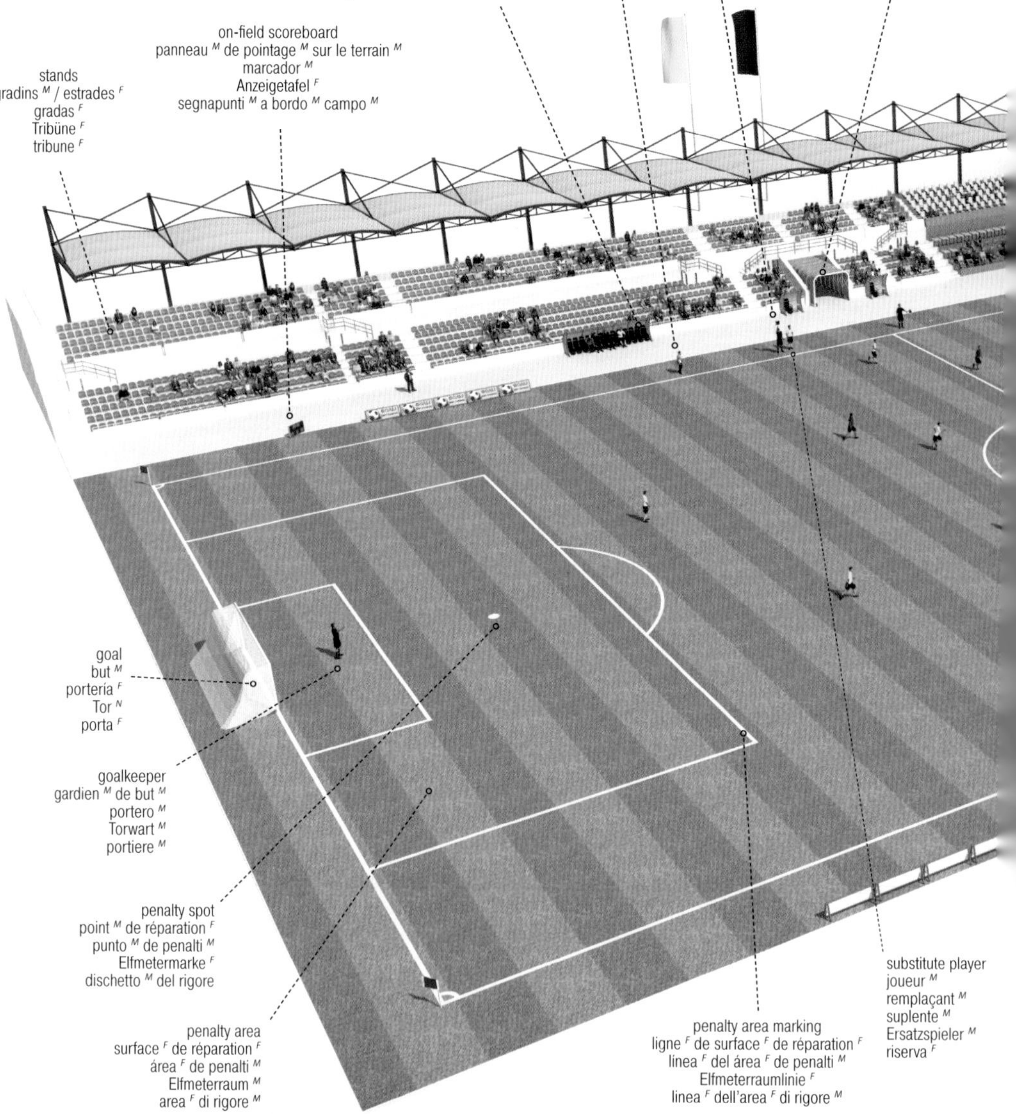
soccer field
terrain M de soccer M
campo M de futbol M
Fußballfeld N
campo M da calcio M
substitutes' bench
banc M des remplaçants M
banquilllo M de suplentes M
Ersatzbank F
panchina F delle riserve F
coach
entraîneur M
entrenador M
Trainer M
allenatore M
fourth official
quatrième M arbitre
cuarto árbitro M
vierte Offizielle M
quarto uomo M
entrance gate to field
porte F d'accès M au terrain M
entrada F del campo M
Spielfeldeingang M
tunnel M di ingresso M in campo
on-field scoreboard
panneau M de pointage M sur le terrain M
marcador M
Anzeigetafel F
segnapunti M a bordo M campo M
stands
gradins M / estrades F
gradas F
Tribüne F
tribune F
goal
but M
portería F
Tor N
porta F
goalkeeper
gardien M de but M
portero M
Torwart M
portiere M
penalty spot
point M de réparation F
punto M de penalti M
Elfmetermarke F
dischetto M del rigore
penalty area
surface F de réparation F
área F de penalti M
Elfmeterraum M
area F di rigore M
penalty area marking
ligne F de surface F de réparation F
línea F del área F de penalti M
Elfmeterraumlinie F
linea F dell'area F di rigore M
substitute player
joueur M
remplaçant M
suplente M
Ersatzspieler M
riserva F

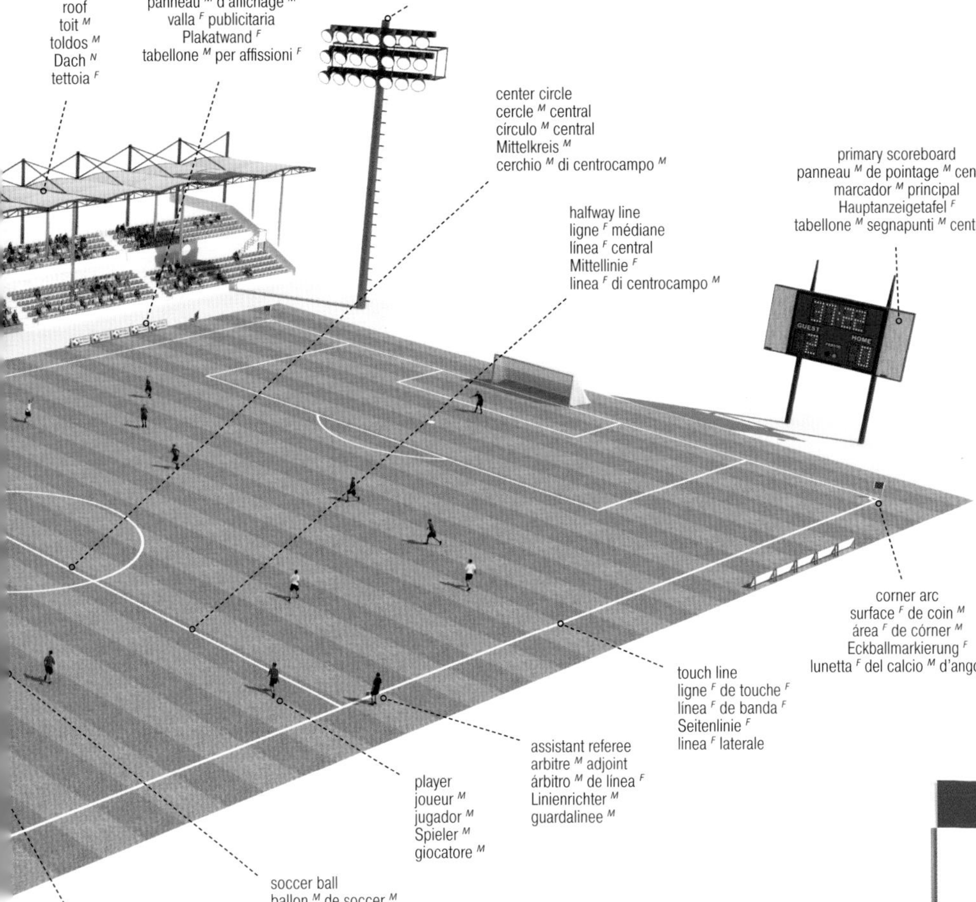
roof
toit ^{M}
toldos ^{M}
Dach ^{N}
tettoia ^{F}
billboard
panneau ^{M} d'affichage ^{M}
valla ^{F} publicitaria
Plakatwand ^{F}
tabellone ^{M} per affissioni ^{F}
floodlights
projecteurs ^{M}
torre ^{F} de iluminación ^{F}
Flutlichtanlage ^{M}
riflettori ^{M}
center circle
cercle ^{M} central
círculo ^{M} central
Mittelkreis ^{M}
cerchio ^{M} di centrocampo ^{M}
halfway line
ligne ^{F} médiane
línea ^{F} central
Mittellinie ^{F}
linea ^{F} di centrocampo ^{M}
primary scoreboard
panneau ^{M} de pointage ^{M} central
marcador ^{M} principal
Hauptanzeigetafel ^{F}
tabellone ^{M} segnapunti ^{M} centrale
GUEST
HOME
corner arc
surface ^{F} de coin ^{M}
área ^{F} de córner ^{M}
Eckballmarkierung ^{F}
lunetta ^{F} del calcio ^{M} d'angolo ^{M}
touch line
ligne ^{F} de touche ^{F}
línea ^{F} de banda ^{F}
Seitenlinie ^{F}
linea ^{F} laterale
assistant referee
arbitre ^{M} adjoint
árbitro ^{M} de línea ^{F}
Linienrichter ^{M}
guardalinee ^{M}
player
joueur ^{M}
jugador ^{M}
Spieler ^{M}
giocatore ^{M}
soccer ball
ballon ^{M} de soccer ^{M}
pelota ^{F} de futbol ^{M}
Fußball ^{M}
pallone ^{M} da calcio ^{M}
referee
arbitre ^{M}
árbitro ^{M} principal
Hauptschiedsrichter ^{M}
arbitro ^{M}

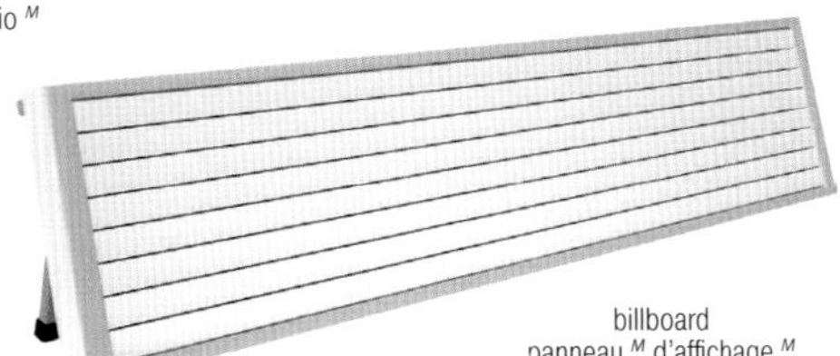
billboard
panneau ^{M} d'affichage ^{M}
valla ^{F} publicitaria
Plakatwand ^{F}
tabellone ^{M} per affissioni ^{F}

corner flag
drapeau ^{M} de coin ^{M}
banderín ^{M} de córner ^{M}
Eckfahne ^{F}
bandierina ^{F} d'angolo ^{M}

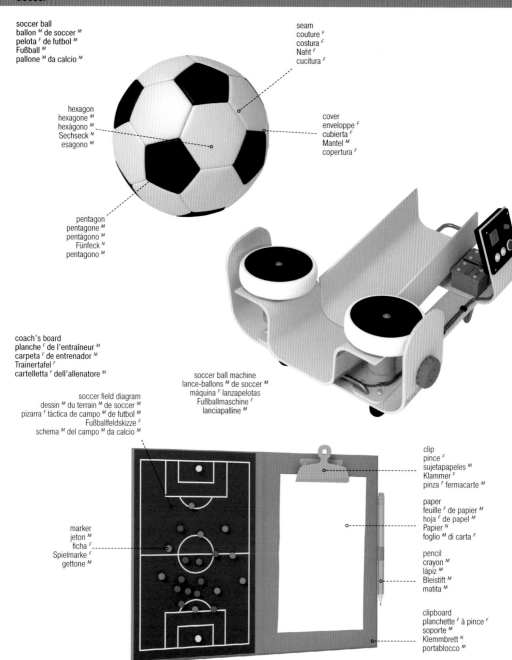

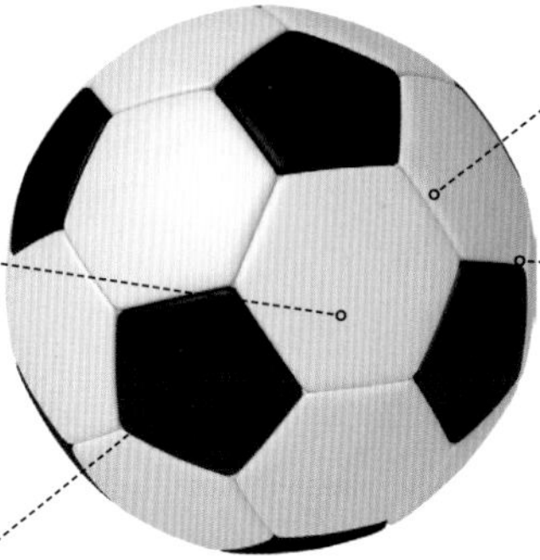
soccer ball
ballon [M] de soccer [M]
pelota [F] de futbol [M]
Fußball [M]
pallone [M] da calcio [M]
seam
couture [F]
costura [F]
Naht [F]
cucitura [F]
hexagon
hexagone [M]
hexágono [M]
Sechseck [N]
esagono [M]
cover
enveloppe [F]
cubierta [F]
Mantel [M]
copertura [F]
pentagon
pentagone [M]
pentágono [M]
Fünfeck [N]
pentagono [M]

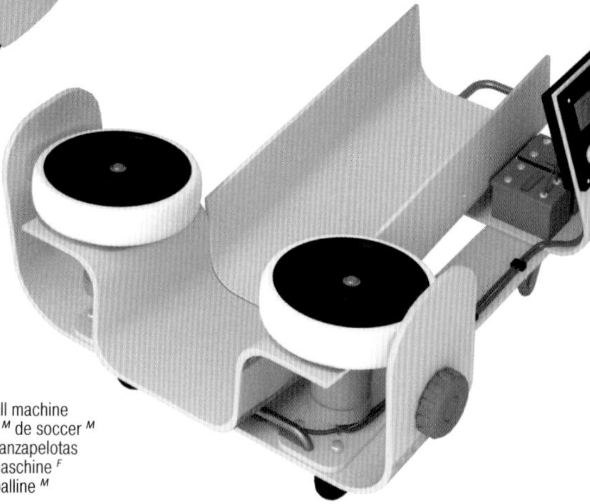
soccer ball machine
lance-ballons [M] de soccer [M]
máquina [F] lanzapelotas
Fußballmaschine [F]
lanciapalline [M]

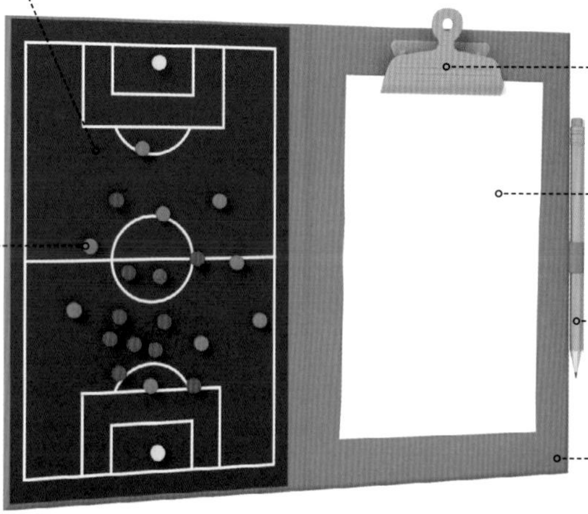
coach's board
planche [F] de l'entraîneur [M]
carpeta [F] de entrenador [M]
Trainertafel [F]
cartelletta [F] dell'allenatore [M]
soccer field diagram
dessin [M] du terrain [M] de soccer [M]
pizarra [F] táctica de campo [M] de futbol [M]
Fußballfeldskizze [F]
schema [M] del campo [M] da calcio [M]
clip
pince [F]
sujetapapeles [M]
Klammer [F]
pinza [F] fermacarte [M]
paper
feuille [F] de papier [M]
hoja [F] de papel [M]
Papier [N]
foglio [M] di carta [F]
marker
jeton [M]
ficha [F]
Spielmarke [F]
gettone [M]
pencil
crayon [M]
lápiz [M]
Bleistift [M]
matita [M]
clipboard
planchette [F] à pince [F]
soporte [M]
Klemmbrett [N]
portablocco [M]

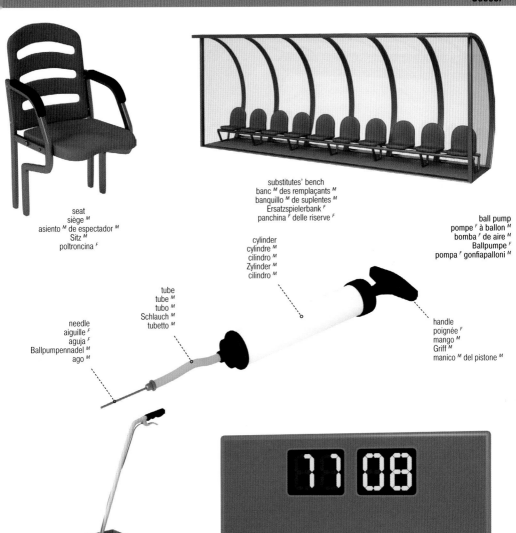

seat
siège M
asiento M de espectador M
Sitz M
poltroncina F

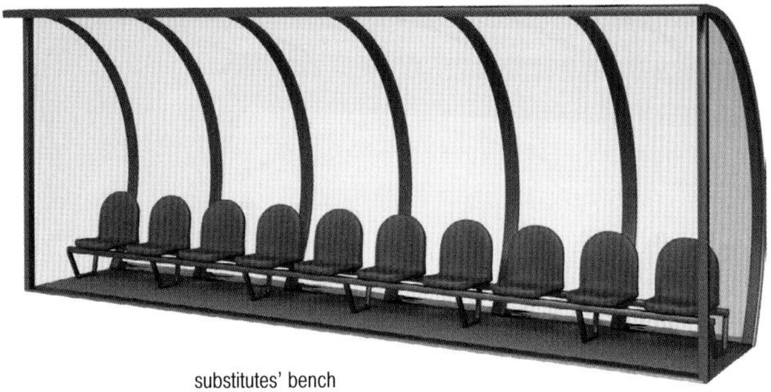

substitutes' bench
banc M des remplaçants M
banquillo M de suplentes M
Ersatzspielerbank F
panchina F delle riserve F

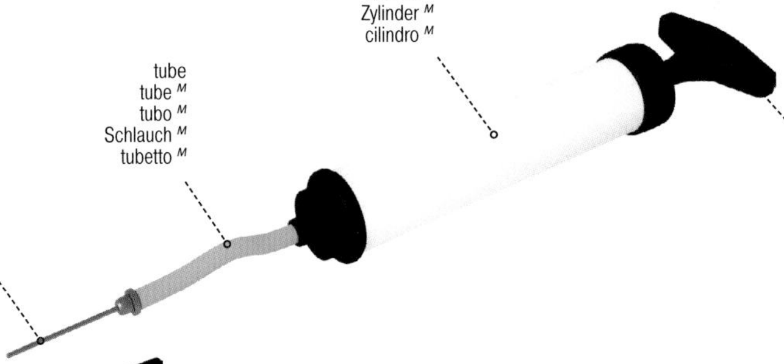
cylinder
cylindre M
cilindro M
Zylinder M
cilindro M
tube
tube M
tubo M
Schlauch M
tubetto M
needle
aiguille F
aguja F
Ballpumpennadel M
ago M
handle
poignée F
mango M
Griff M
manico M del pistone M

ball pump
pompe F à ballon M
bomba F de aire M
Ballpumpe F
pompa F gonfiapalloni M

field marker
traceur M de terrain M
carrito M marcador de lineas F
Markierungswagen M
macchina F traccialinee

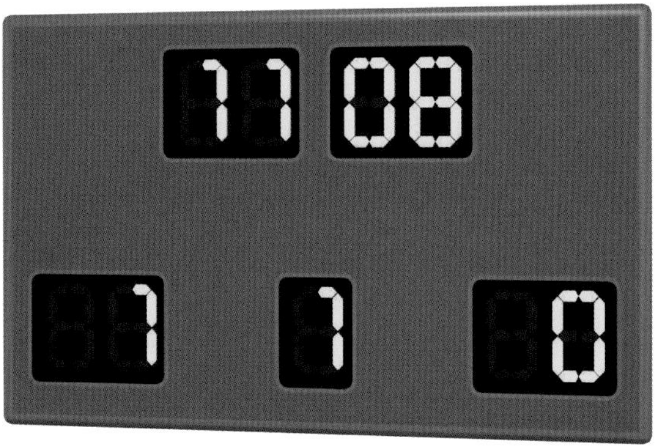
11 08
7 7 0

scoreboard
panneau M de pointage M
marcador M
Anzeigetafel F
tabellone M segnapunti

Referee's equipment

Équipement [M] d'arbitre [M] | Equipo [M] del árbitro [M] | Schiedsrichterausrüstung [F] | Attrezzature [F] dell'arbitro [M]

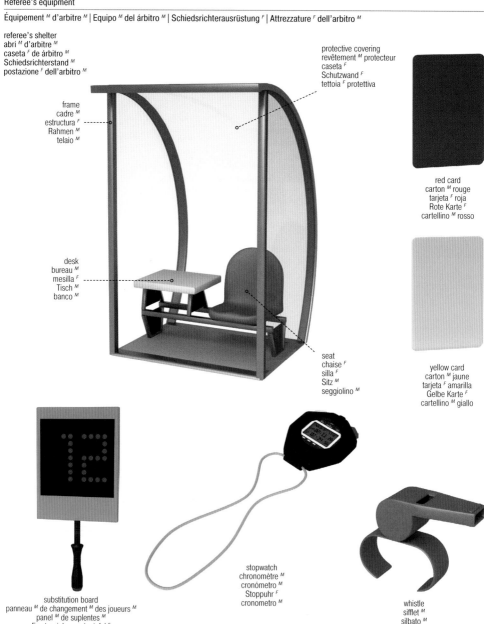

referee's shelter
abri [M] d'arbitre [M]
caseta [F] de árbitro [M]
Schiedsrichterstand [M]
postazione [F] dell'arbitro [M]

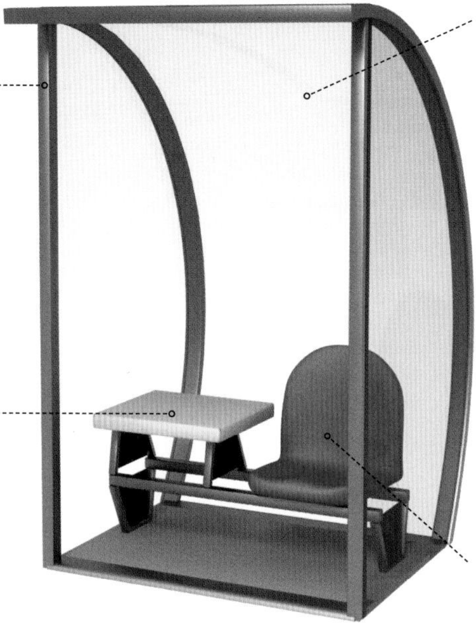
protective covering
revêtement [M] protecteur
caseta [F]
Schutzwand [F]
tettoia [F] protettiva
frame
cadre [M]
estructura [F]
Rahmen [M]
telaio [M]
desk
bureau [M]
mesilla [F]
Tisch [M]
banco [M]
seat
chaise [F]
silla [F]
Sitz [M]
seggiolino [M]

red card
carton [M] rouge
tarjeta [F] roja
Rote Karte [F]
cartellino [M] rosso

yellow card
carton [M] jaune
tarjeta [F] amarilla
Gelbe Karte [F]
cartellino [M] giallo

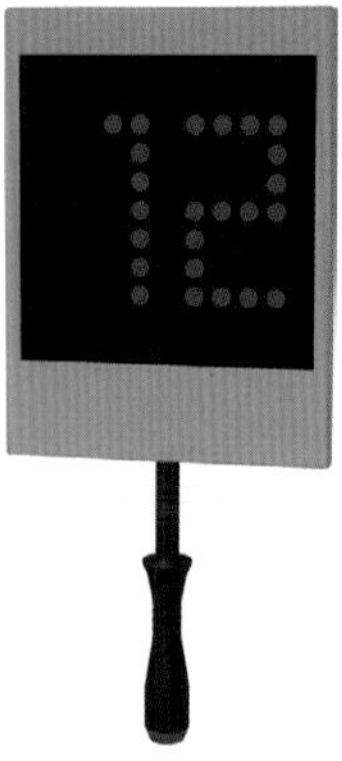

substitution board
panneau [M] de changement [M] des joueurs [M]
panel [M] de suplentes [M]
Ersatzspieleranzeigetafel [F]
tabellone [M] delle sostituzioni [F]

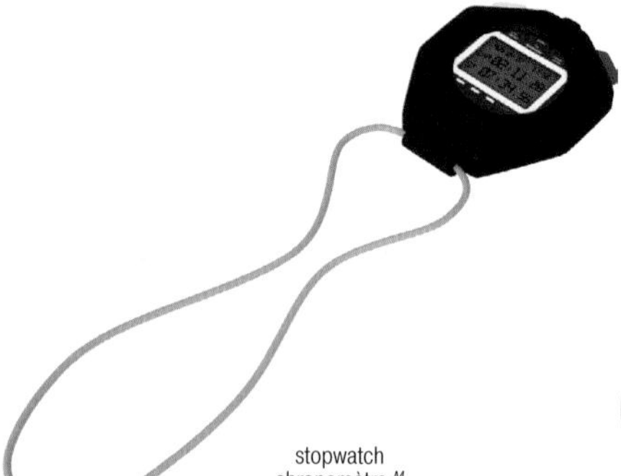

stopwatch
chronomètre [M]
cronómetro [M]
Stoppuhr [F]
cronometro [M]

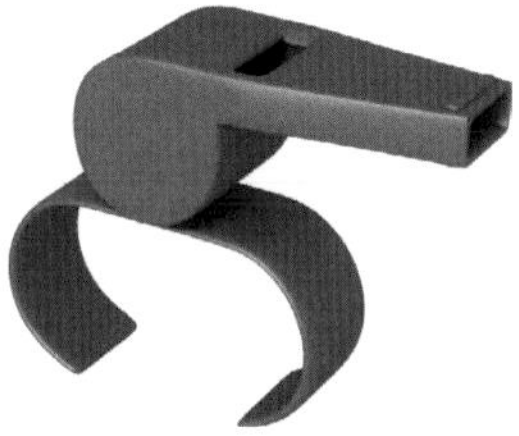

whistle
sifflet [M]
silbato [M]
Pfeife [F]
fischietto [M]

Soccer player and equipment

Joueur [M] et équipement [M] de soccer [M] | Jugador [M] y equipo [M] de futbol [M] | Fußballspieler und -ausrüstung | Giocatore [M] di calcio [M] e attrezzatura [F]

shin guard
protège-tibia [M]
espinilleras [F]
Schienbeinschoner [M]
parastinchi [M]

soccer player
joueur [M] de soccer [M]
jugador [M] de futbol [M]
Fußballspieler [M]
calciatore [M]

jersey
maillot [M]
camiseta [F]
Fußballtrikot [N]
maglia [F]

shorts
short [M]
pantalón [M] corto
Shorts [F]
pantaloncini [M]

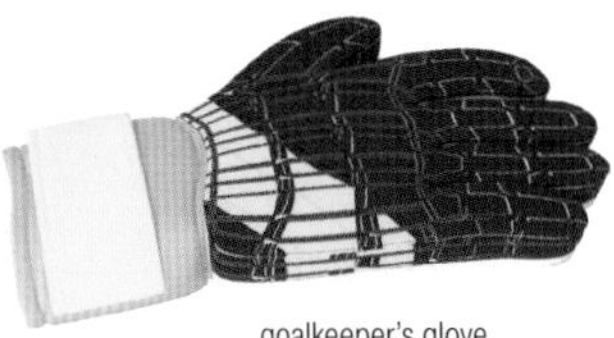

goalkeeper's glove
gant [M] de gardien [M] de but [M]
guantes [M] de portero [M]
Torwarthandschuh [M]
guanti [M] da portiere [M]

soccer cleats
crampons [M]
zapatos [M] de futbol [M]
Fußballschuh [M]
scarpe [F] da calcio [M]

tongue
languette [F]
lengüeta [F]
Zunge [F]
linguetta [F]

lace
lacet [M]
cordones [M]
Schnürsenkel [M]
stringa [F]

stud
pointe [F]
taco [M]
Stollen [M]
chiodo [M]

heel
talon [M]
talón [M]
Ferse [F]
tallone [M]

toe
orteil [M]
puntera [M]
Spitze [F]
punta [F]

American football field
terrain [M] de football [M] américain
campo [M] de futbol [M] americano
Footballfeld [N]
campo [M] da football [M] americano

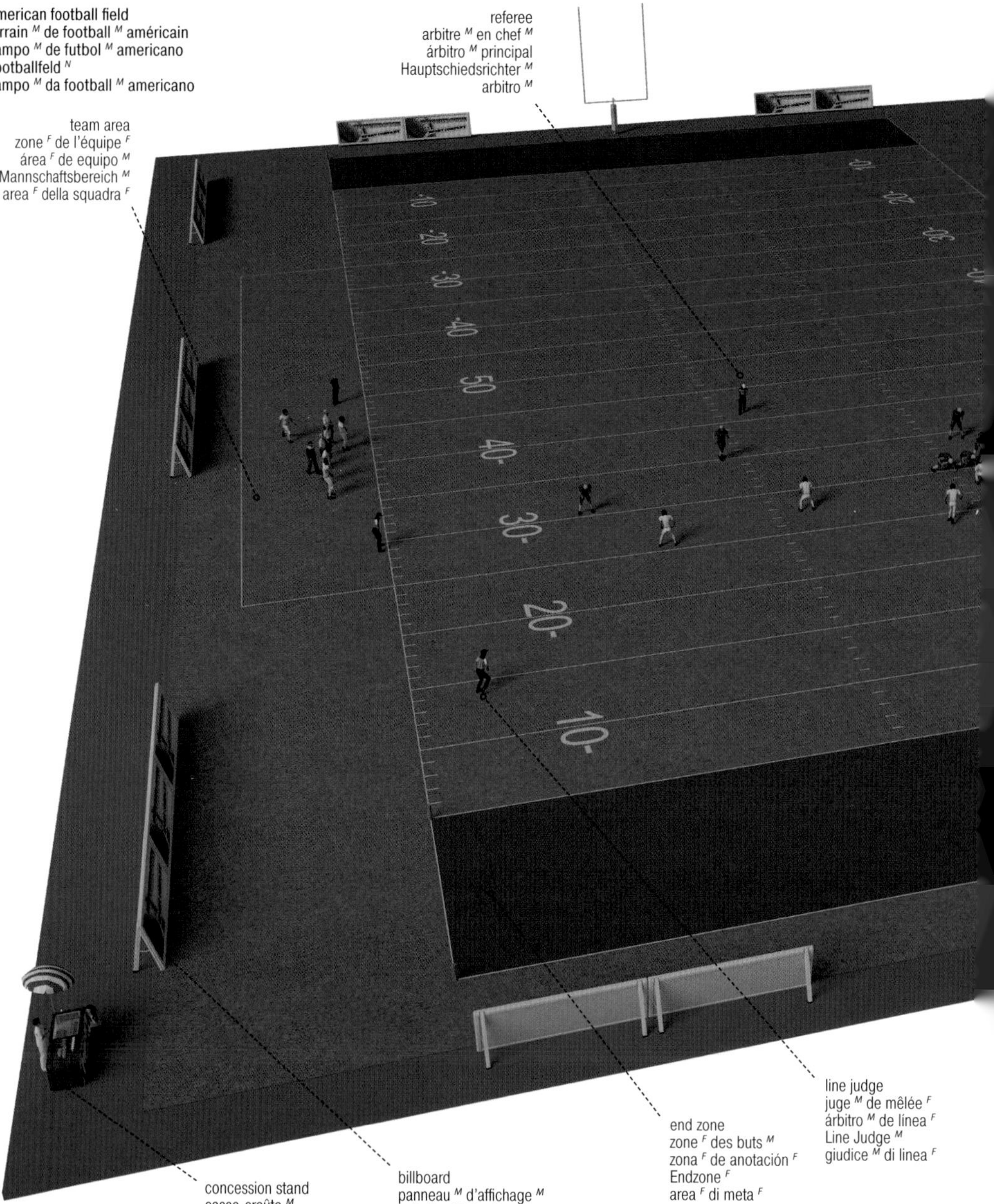
referee
arbitre [M] en chef [M]
árbitro [M] principal
Hauptschiedsrichter [M]
arbitro [M]
team area
zone [F] de l'équipe [F]
área [F] de equipo [M]
Mannschaftsbereich [M]
area [F] della squadra [F]
line judge
juge [M] de mêlée [F]
árbitro [M] de línea [F]
Line Judge [M]
giudice [M] di linea [F]
end zone
zone [F] des buts [M]
zona [F] de anotación [F]
Endzone [F]
area [F] di meta [F]
concession stand
casse-croûte [M]
punto [M] de venta [F]
Imbissstand [M]
chiosco [M]
billboard
panneau [M] d'affichage [M]
valla [F] publicitaria
Plakatwand [F]
tabellone [M] per affissioni [F]

lace
lacets ^{M}
cordón ^{M}
Schnürung ^{F}
laccio ^{M}

football
football ^{M}
pelota ^{F} de futbol ^{M} americano
Football ^{M}
football ^{M}

seam
couture ^{F}
costura ^{F}
Naht ^{F}
cucitura ^{F}

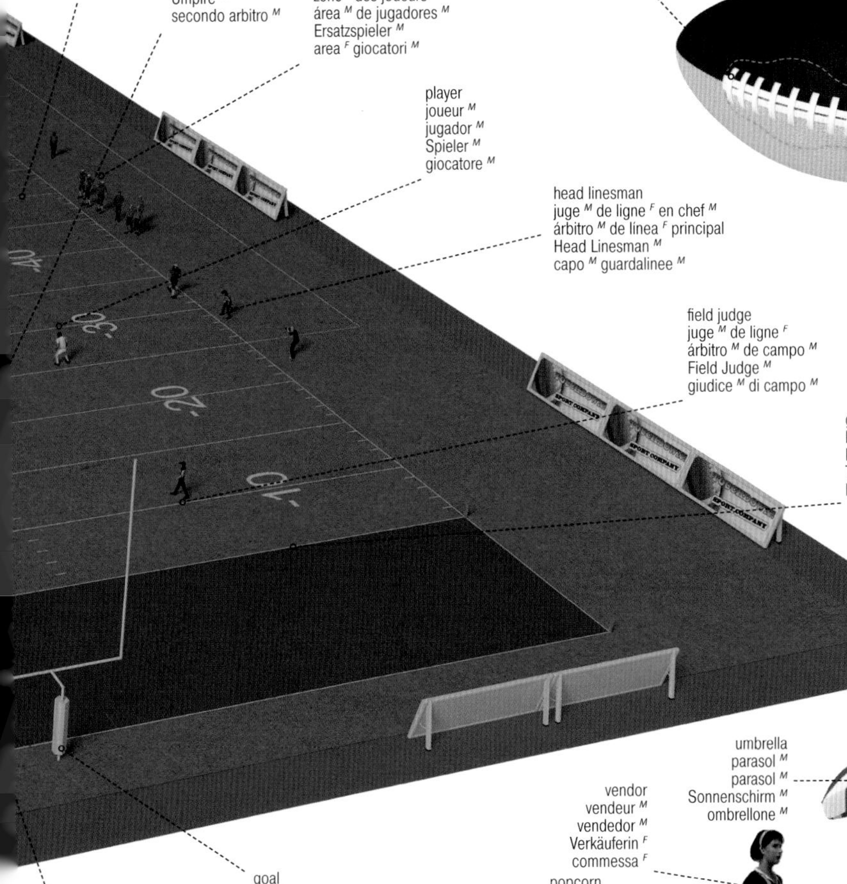

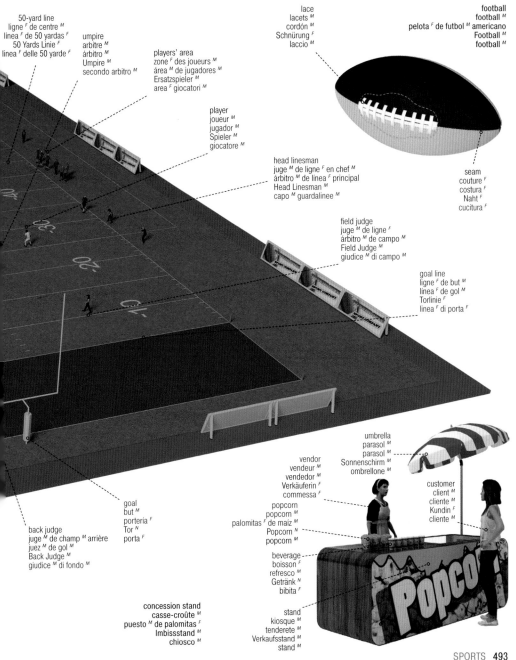

50-yard line
ligne ^{F} de centre ^{M}
línea ^{F} de 50 yardas ^{F}
50 Yards Linie ^{F}
linea ^{F} delle 50 yarde ^{F}

umpire
arbitre ^{M}
árbitro ^{M}
Umpire ^{M}
secondo arbitro ^{M}

players' area
zone ^{F} des joueurs ^{M}
área ^{M} de jugadores ^{M}
Ersatzspieler ^{M}
area ^{F} giocatori ^{M}

player
joueur ^{M}
jugador ^{M}
Spieler ^{M}
giocatore ^{M}

head linesman
juge ^{M} de ligne ^{F} en chef ^{M}
árbitro ^{M} de línea ^{F} principal
Head Linesman ^{M}
capo ^{M} guardalinee ^{M}

field judge
juge ^{M} de ligne ^{F}
árbitro ^{M} de campo ^{M}
Field Judge ^{M}
giudice ^{M} di campo ^{M}

goal line
ligne ^{F} de but ^{M}
línea ^{F} de gol ^{M}
Torlinie ^{F}
linea ^{F} di porta ^{F}

goal
but ^{M}
portería ^{F}
Tor ^{N}
porta ^{F}

back judge
juge ^{M} de champ ^{M} arrière
juez ^{M} de gol ^{M}
Back Judge ^{M}
giudice ^{M} di fondo ^{M}

umbrella
parasol ^{M}
parasol ^{M}
Sonnenschirm ^{M}
ombrellone ^{M}

vendor
vendeur ^{M}
vendedor ^{M}
Verkäuferin ^{F}
commessa ^{F}

customer
client ^{M}
cliente ^{M}
Kundin ^{F}
cliente ^{M}

popcorn
popcorn ^{M}
palomitas ^{F} de maíz ^{M}
Popcorn ^{N}
popcorn ^{M}

beverage
boisson ^{F}
refresco ^{M}
Getränk ^{N}
bibita ^{F}

concession stand
casse-croûte ^{M}
puesto ^{M} de palomitas ^{F}
Imbissstand ^{M}
chiosco ^{M}

stand
kiosque ^{M}
tenderete ^{M}
Verkaufsstand ^{M}
stand ^{M}

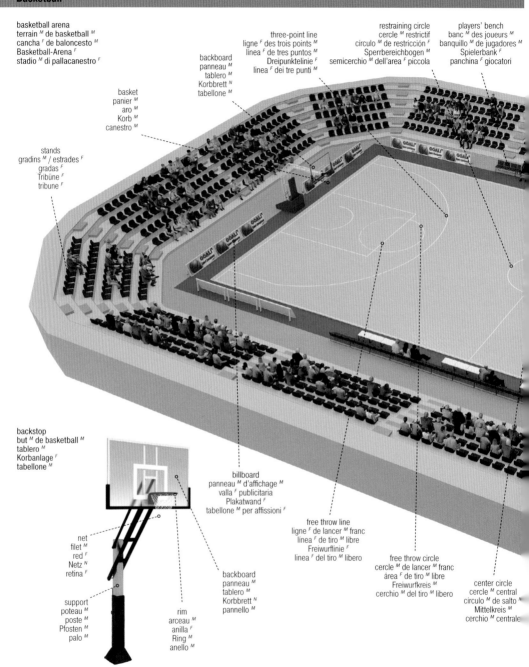

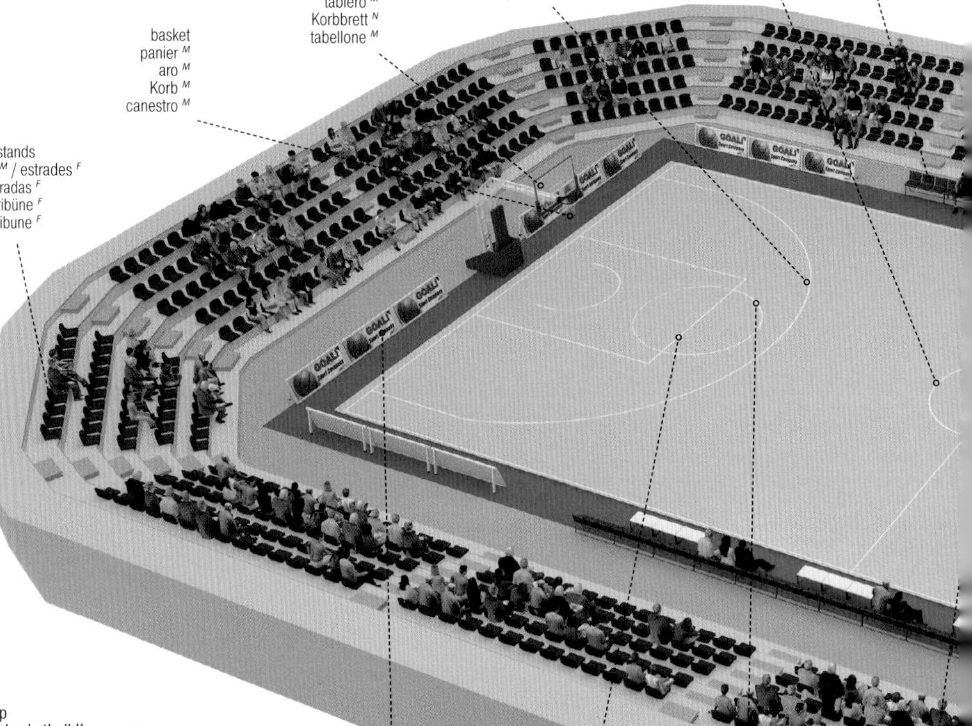
basketball arena
terrain M de basketball M
cancha F de baloncesto M
Basketball-Arena F
stadio M di pallacanestro F
three-point line
ligne F des trois points M
línea F de tres puntos M
Dreipunktelinie F
linea F dei tre punti M
restraining circle
cercle M restrictif
círculo M de restricción F
Sperrbereichbogen M
semicerchio M dell'area F piccola
players' bench
banc M des joueurs M
banquillo M de jugadores M
Spielerbank F
panchina F giocatori
backboard
panneau M
tablero M
Korbbrett N
tabellone M
basket
panier M
aro M
Korb M
canestro M
stands
gradins M / estrades F
gradas F
Tribüne F
tribune F
billboard
panneau M d'affichage M
valla F publicitaria
Plakatwand F
tabellone M per affissioni F
free throw line
ligne F de lancer M franc
línea F de tiro M libre
Freiwurflinie F
linea F del tiro M libero
free throw circle
cercle M de lancer M franc
área F de tiro M libre
Freiwurfkreis M
cerchio M del tiro M libero
center circle
cercle M central
círculo M de salto M
Mittelkreis M
cerchio M centrale

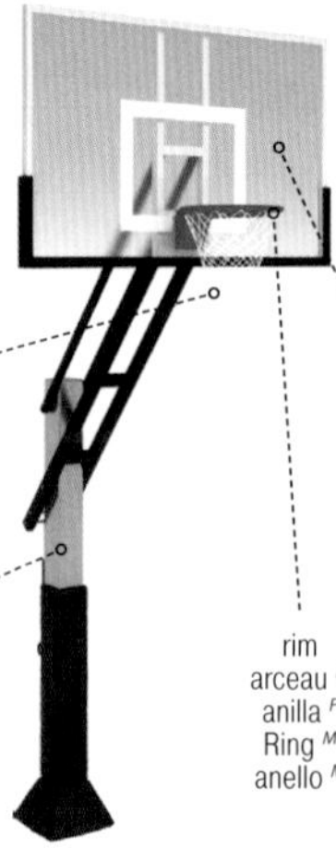
backstop
but M de basketball M
tablero M
Korbanlage F
tabellone M
net
filet M
red F
Netz N
retina F
support
poteau M
poste M
Pfosten M
palo M
rim
arceau M
anilla F
Ring M
anello M
backboard
panneau M
tablero M
Korbbrett N
pannello M

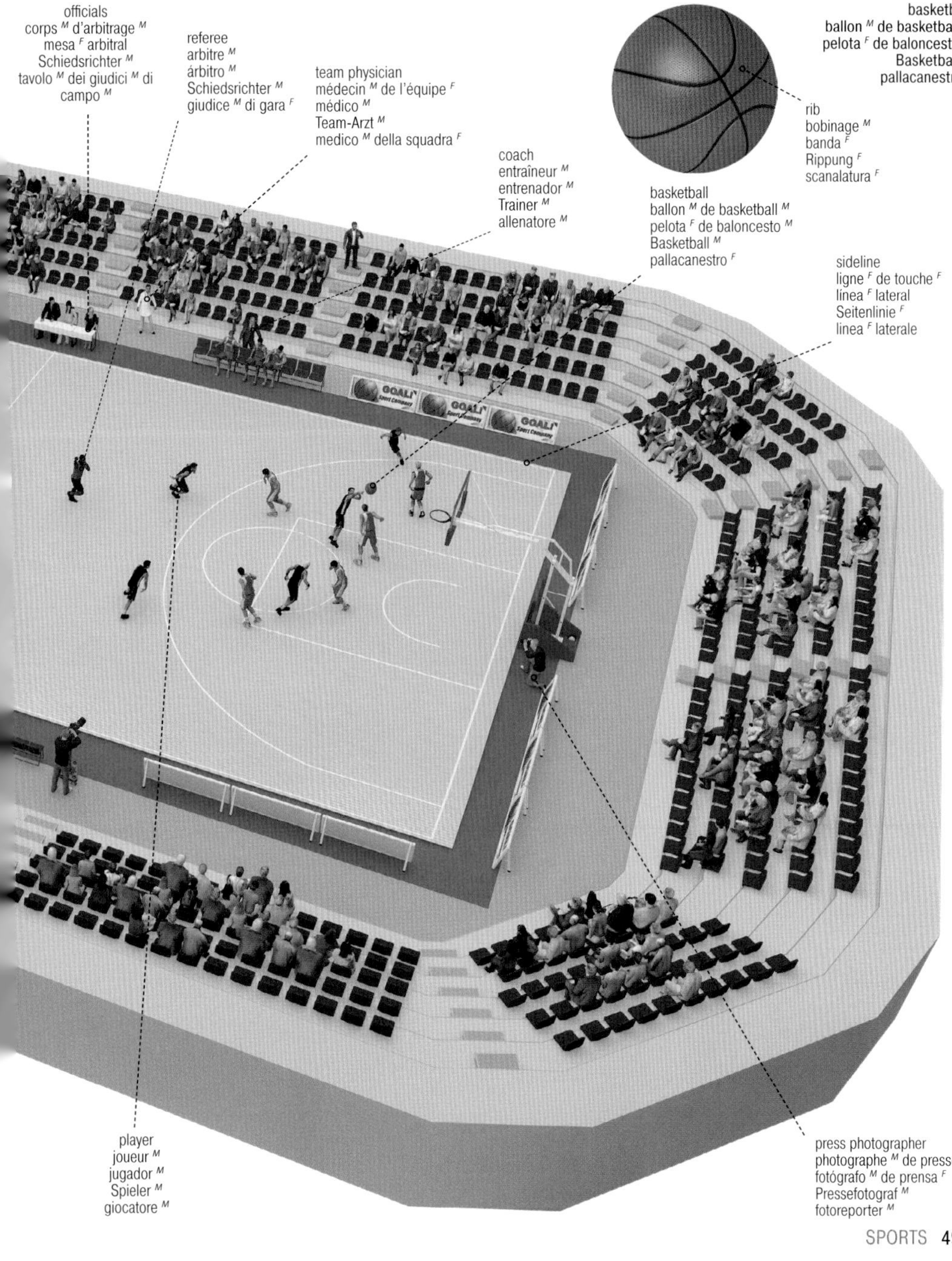
officials
corps M d'arbitrage M
mesa F arbitral
Schiedsrichter M
tavolo M dei giudici M di campo M
referee
arbitre M
árbitro M
Schiedsrichter M
giudice M di gara F
team physician
médecin M de l'équipe F
médico M
Team-Arzt M
medico M della squadra F
coach
entraîneur M
entrenador M
Trainer M
allenatore M
basketball
ballon M de basketball M
pelota F de baloncesto M
Basketball M
pallacanestro F
rib
bobinage M
banda F
Rippung F
scanalatura F
basketball
ballon M de basketball M
pelota F de baloncesto M
Basketball M
pallacanestro F
sideline
ligne F de touche F
línea F lateral
Seitenlinie F
linea F laterale
GOALI Sport Company
player
joueur M
jugador M
Spieler M
giocatore M
press photographer
photographe M de presse F
fotógrafo M de prensa F
Pressefotograf M
fotoreporter M

Basketball moves

Mouvements ᴹ du basketball ᴹ | Movimientos ᴹ de baloncesto ᴹ | Basketballbewegungen ᶠ | Mosse ᶠ di pallacanestro ᶠ

layup
tir ᴹ déposé
tiro ᴹ con una mano ᶠ
Korbleger ᴹ
tiro ᴹ con una mano ᶠ

hook shot
tir ᴹ à bras ᴹ roulé
tiro ᴹ libre
Hakenwurf ᴹ
gancio ᴹ

holding
tenir le ballon ᴹ
aguantar ᴹ la pelota ᶠ
Halten ᴺ des Balls ᴹ
trattenuta ᶠ

dribbling
dribbler
dribleo ᴹ
den Ball dribbeln ᴹ
palleggio ᴹ

pump fake
feinte ᶠ de passe ᶠ
tiro ᴹ falso
Wurffinte ᶠ
finta ᶠ di tiro ᴹ

baseball glove: bottom view
gant [M] de baseball [M]: vue [F] du dessous [M]
guante [M] de béisbol [M]: vista posterior
Baseballhandschuh: Unteransicht [M]
guanto [M] da baseball [M]: vista [F] dal basso [M]

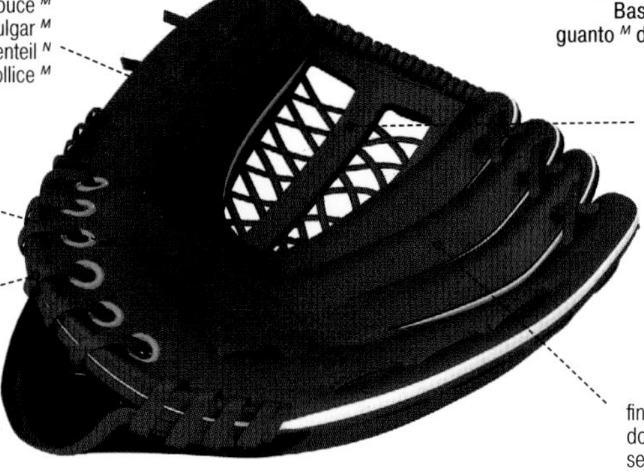
thumb
pouce [M]
sección [F] del pulgar [M]
Daumenteil [N]
sezione [F] del pollice [M]
palm
paume [F]
palma [F]
Handfläche [F]
palmo [M]
lace
lacets [M]
cordón [M]
Schnürung [F]
laccio [M]
strap
patte [F]
correa [F]
Riemen [M]
allacciatura [F]
finger
doigt [M]
sección [F] de los dedos [M]
Finger [M]
dito [M]

baseball glove: top view
gant [M] de baseball [M]: vue [F] du dessus [M]
guante [M] de beisbol [M]: vista [F] superior
Baseballhandschuh: Draufsicht [M]
guanto [M] da baseball [M]: vista [F] dall'alto

cross section of a baseball
coupe [F] de la balle [F]
corte [M] de la pelota [M] de béisbol [M]
Baseball [M] im Querschnitt [M]
sezione [F] trasversale di una palla [F] da baseball [M]

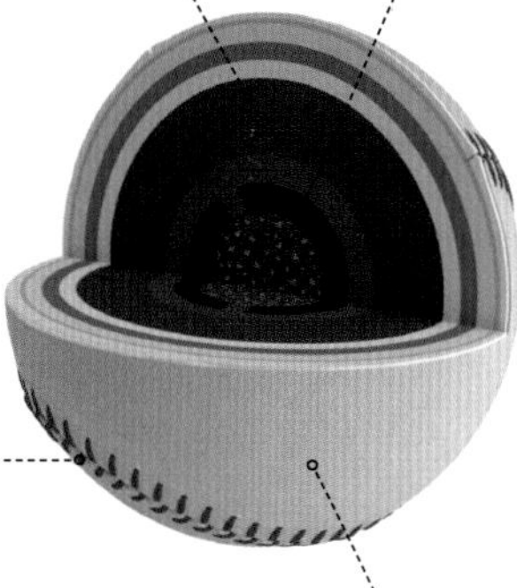
yarn ball
balle [F] de fil [M]
retors bola [F] de hilo [M]
Garnball [M]
gomitolo [M]
cork center
centre [M] de liège [M]
centro [M] de corcho [M]
Korkball [M]
nucleo [M] in sughero [M]
stitches
couture [F]
costura [F]
Nähte [F]
punti [M] di sutura [F]
cover
enveloppe [F]
forro [M]
Außenschicht [F]
copertura [F]

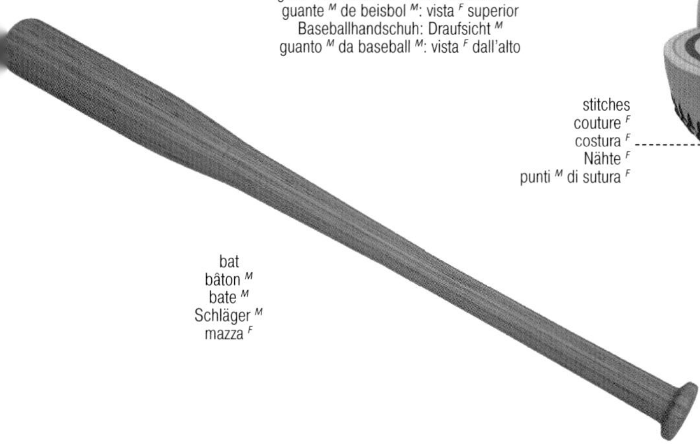
bat
bâton [M]
bate [M]
Schläger [M]
mazza [F]

baseball field (baseball diamond)
terrain ^{M} de baseball ^{M}
campo ^{M} de béisbol ^{M}
Baseballfeld ^{N}
campo ^{M} da baseball ^{M} (diamante ^{M})

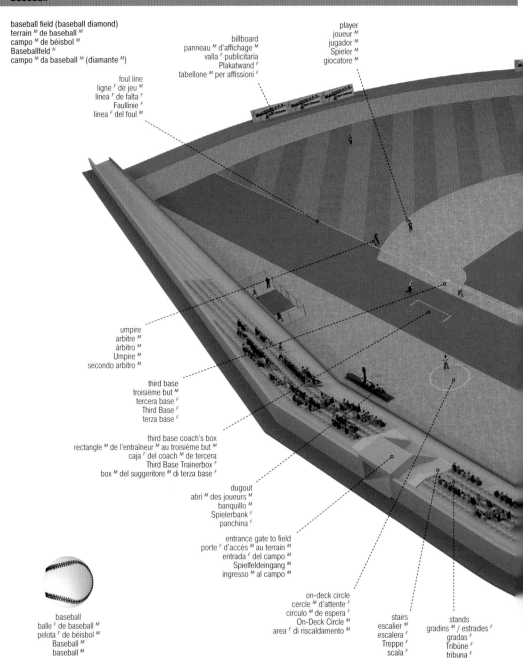

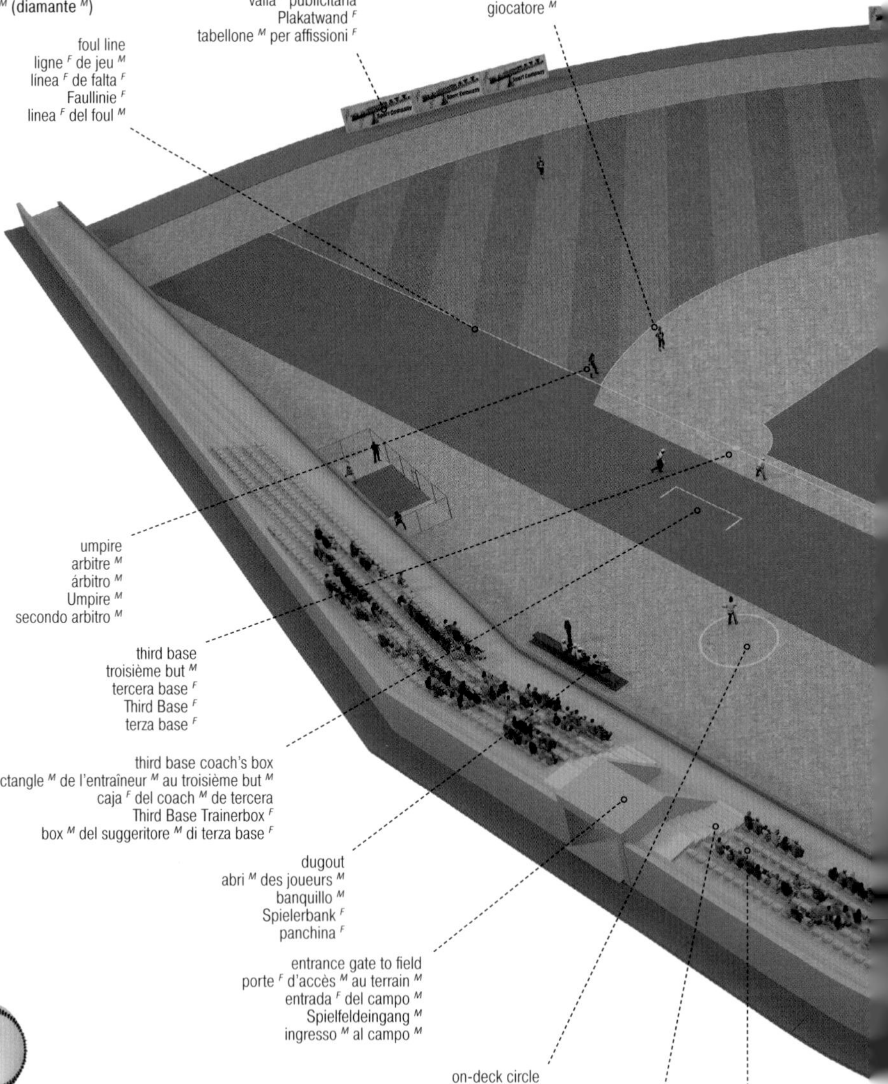

billboard
panneau ^{M} d'affichage ^{M}
valla ^{F} publicitaria
Plakatwand ^{F}
tabellone ^{M} per affissioni ^{F}

player
joueur ^{M}
jugador ^{M}
Spieler ^{M}
giocatore ^{M}

foul line
ligne ^{F} de jeu ^{M}
línea ^{F} de falta ^{F}
Faullinie ^{F}
linea ^{F} del foul ^{M}

umpire
arbitre ^{M}
árbitro ^{M}
Umpire ^{M}
secondo arbitro ^{M}

third base
troisième but ^{M}
tercera base ^{F}
Third Base ^{F}
terza base ^{F}

third base coach's box
rectangle ^{M} de l'entraîneur ^{M} au troisième but ^{M}
caja ^{F} del coach ^{M} de tercera
Third Base Trainerbox ^{F}
box ^{M} del suggeritore ^{M} di terza base ^{F}

dugout
abri ^{M} des joueurs ^{M}
banquillo ^{M}
Spielerbank ^{F}
panchina ^{F}

entrance gate to field
porte ^{F} d'accès ^{M} au terrain ^{M}
entrada ^{F} del campo ^{M}
Spielfeldeingang ^{M}
ingresso ^{M} al campo ^{M}

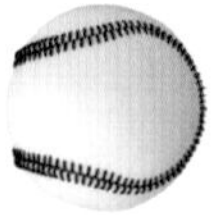

baseball
balle ^{F} de baseball ^{M}
pelota ^{F} de béisbol ^{M}
Baseball ^{M}
baseball ^{M}

on-deck circle
cercle ^{M} d'attente ^{F}
círculo ^{M} de espera ^{F}
On-Deck Circle ^{M}
area ^{F} di riscaldamento ^{M}

stairs
escalier ^{M}
escalera ^{F}
Treppe ^{F}
scala ^{F}

stands
gradins ^{M} / estrades ^{F}
gradas ^{F}
Tribüne ^{F}
tribuna ^{F}

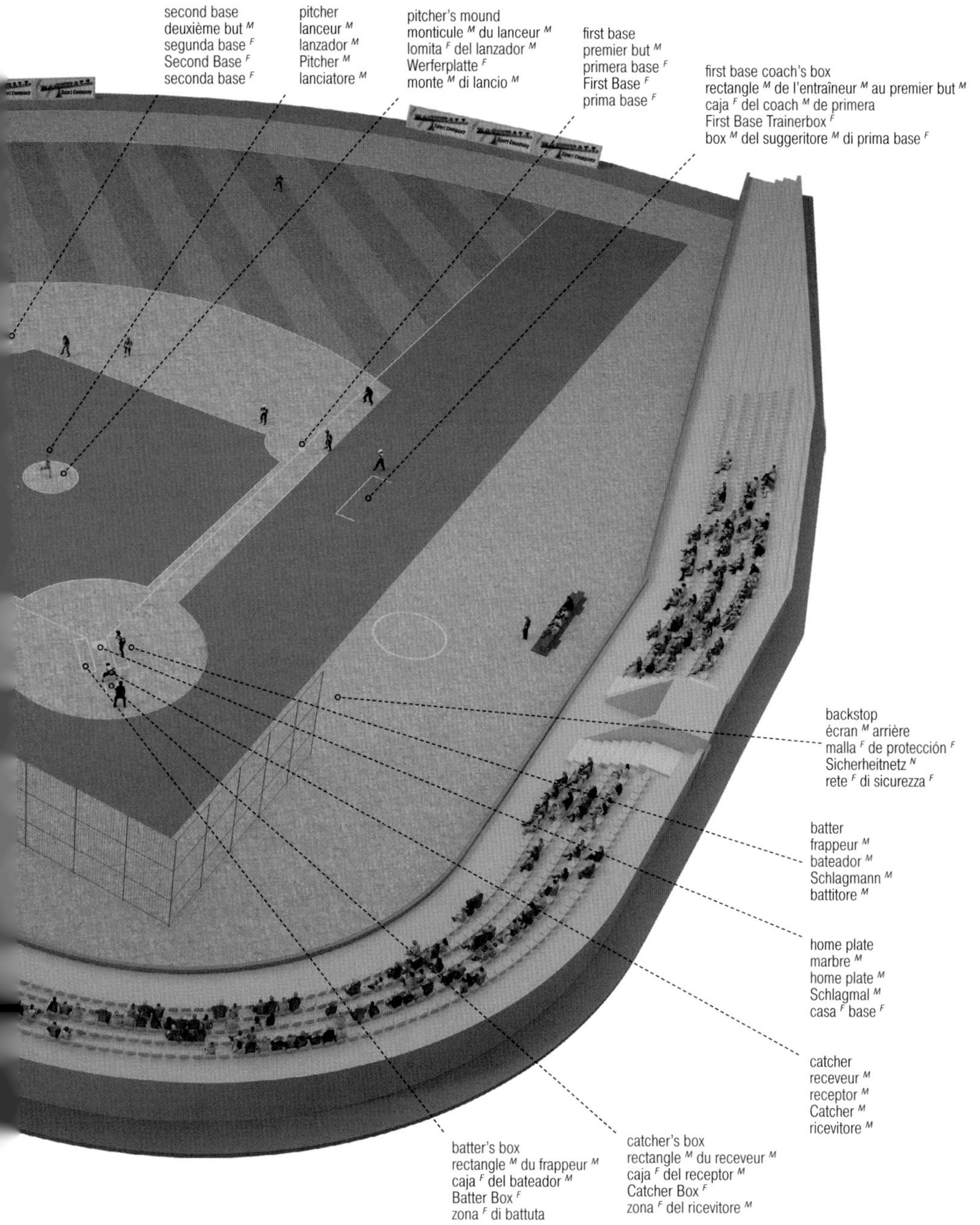
second base
deuxième but [M]
segunda base [F]
Second Base [F]
seconda base [F]
pitcher
lanceur [M]
lanzador [M]
Pitcher [M]
lanciatore [M]
pitcher's mound
monticule [M] du lanceur [M]
lomita [F] del lanzador [M]
Werferplatte [F]
monte [M] di lancio [M]
first base
premier but [M]
primera base [F]
First Base [F]
prima base [F]
first base coach's box
rectangle [M] de l'entraîneur [M] au premier but [M]
caja [F] del coach [M] de primera
First Base Trainerbox [F]
box [M] del suggeritore [M] di prima base [F]
backstop
écran [M] arrière
malla [F] de protección [F]
Sicherheitnetz [N]
rete [F] di sicurezza [F]
batter
frappeur [M]
bateador [M]
Schlagmann [M]
battitore [M]
home plate
marbre [M]
home plate [M]
Schlagmal [M]
casa [F] base [F]
catcher
receveur [M]
receptor [M]
Catcher [M]
ricevitore [M]
batter's box
rectangle [M] du frappeur [M]
caja [F] del bateador [M]
Batter Box [F]
zona [F] di battuta
catcher's box
rectangle [M] du receveur [M]
caja [F] del receptor [M]
Catcher Box [F]
zona [F] del ricevitore [M]

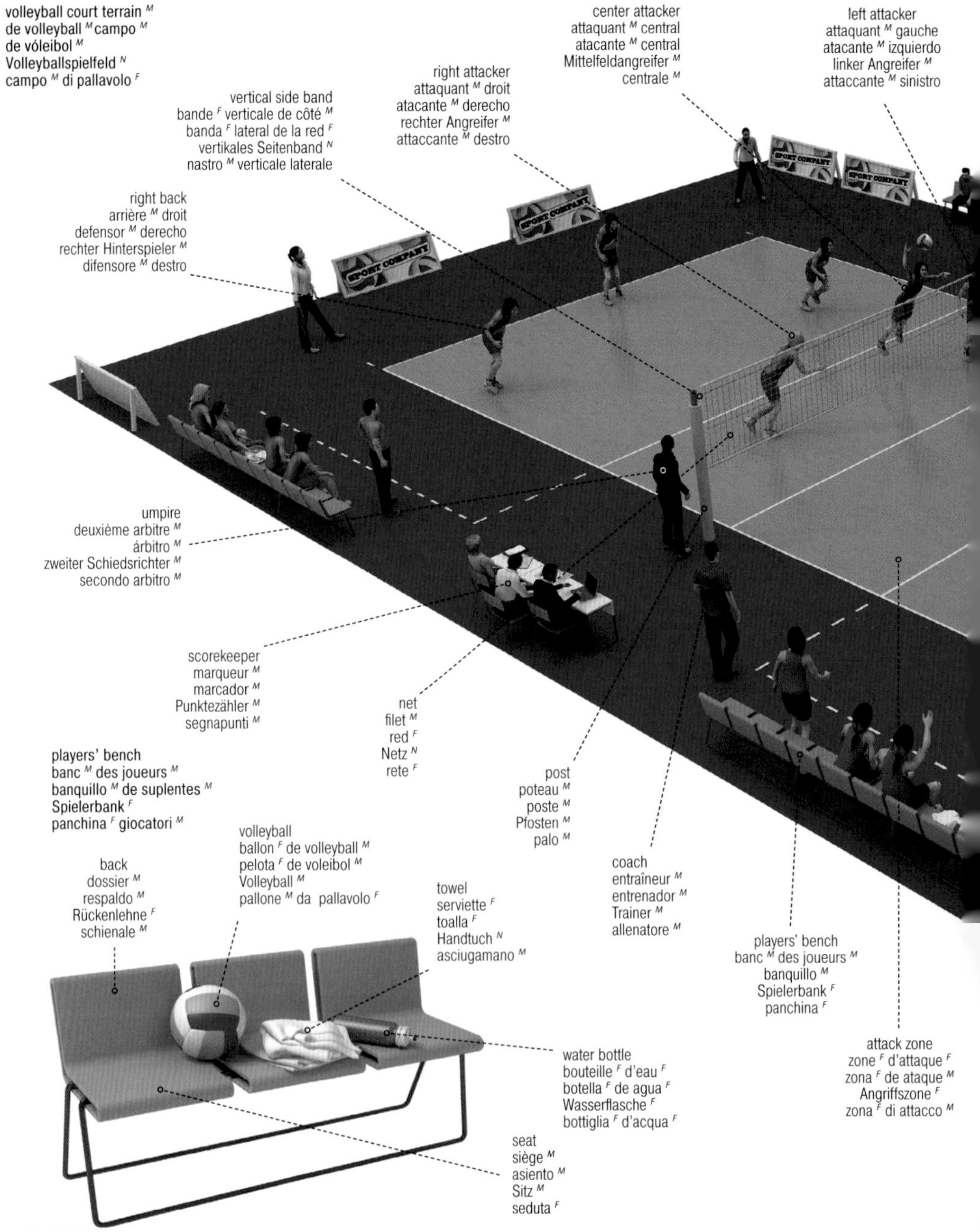
volleyball court terrain M de volleyball M campo M de vóleibol M Volleyballspielfeld N campo M di pallavolo F
center attacker attaquant M central atacante M central Mittelfeldangreifer M centrale M
left attacker attaquant M gauche atacante M izquierdo linker Angreifer M attaccante M sinistro
right attacker attaquant M droit atacante M derecho rechter Angreifer M attaccante M destro
vertical side band bande F verticale de côté M banda F lateral de la red F vertikales Seitenband N nastro M verticale laterale
right back arrière M droit defensor M derecho rechter Hinterspieler M difensore M destro
umpire deuxième arbitre M árbitro M zweiter Schiedsrichter M secondo arbitro M
scorekeeper marqueur M marcador M Punktezähler M segnapunti M
net filet M red F Netz N rete F
players' bench banc M des joueurs M banquillo M de suplentes M Spielerbank F panchina F giocatori M
post poteau M poste M Pfosten M palo M
coach entraîneur M entrenador M Trainer M allenatore M
players' bench banc M des joueurs M banquillo M Spielerbank F panchina F
attack zone zone F d'attaque F zona F de ataque M Angriffszone F zona F di attacco M
volleyball ballon F de volleyball M pelota F de voleibol M Volleyball M pallone M da pallavolo F
back dossier M respaldo M Rückenlehne F schienale M
towel serviette F toalla F Handtuch N asciugamano M
water bottle bouteille F d'eau F botella F de agua F Wasserflasche F bottiglia F d'acqua F
seat siège M asiento M Sitz M seduta F

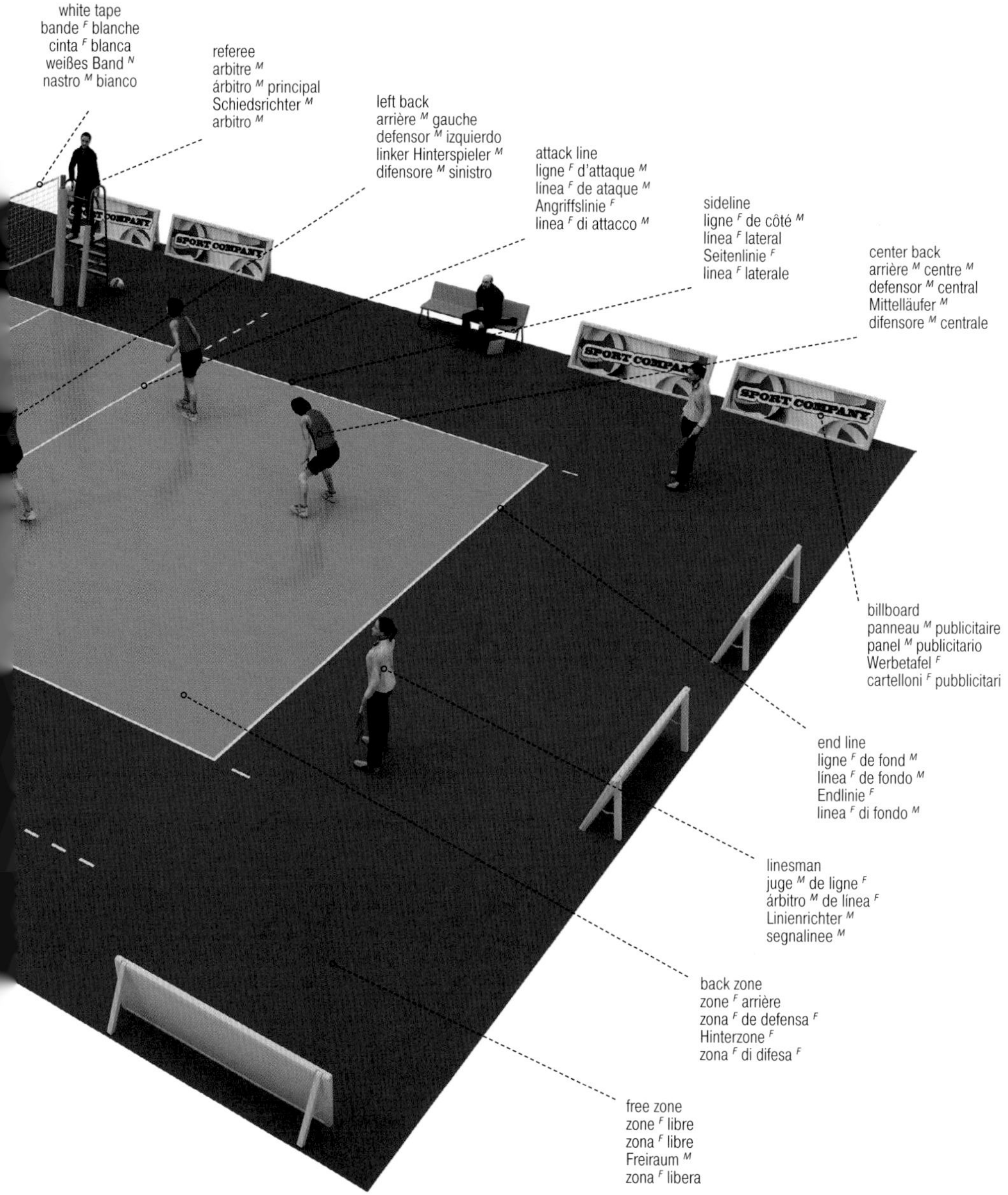
white tape
bande [F] blanche
cinta [F] blanca
weißes Band [N]
nastro [M] bianco
referee
arbitre [M]
árbitro [M] principal
Schiedsrichter [M]
arbitro [M]
left back
arrière [M] gauche
defensor [M] izquierdo
linker Hinterspieler [M]
difensore [M] sinistro
attack line
ligne [F] d'attaque [M]
línea [F] de ataque [M]
Angriffslinie [F]
linea [F] di attacco [M]
sideline
ligne [F] de côté [M]
línea [F] lateral
Seitenlinie [F]
linea [F] laterale
center back
arrière [M] centre [M]
defensor [M] central
Mittelläufer [M]
difensore [M] centrale
SPORT COMPANY
SPORT COMPANY
SPORT COMPANY
SPORT COMPANY
billboard
panneau [M] publicitaire
panel [M] publicitario
Werbetafel [F]
cartelloni [F] pubblicitari
end line
ligne [F] de fond [M]
línea [F] de fondo [M]
Endlinie [F]
linea [F] di fondo [M]
linesman
juge [M] de ligne [F]
árbitro [M] de línea [F]
Linienrichter [M]
segnalinee [M]
back zone
zone [F] arrière
zona [F] de defensa [F]
Hinterzone [F]
zona [F] di difesa [F]
free zone
zone [F] libre
zona [F] libre
Freiraum [M]
zona [F] libera

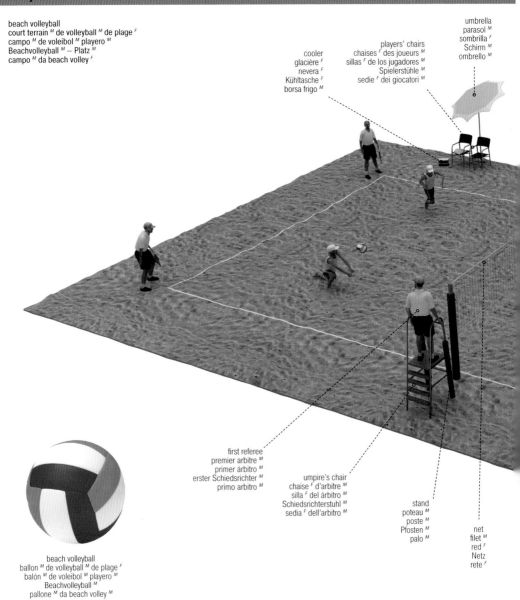

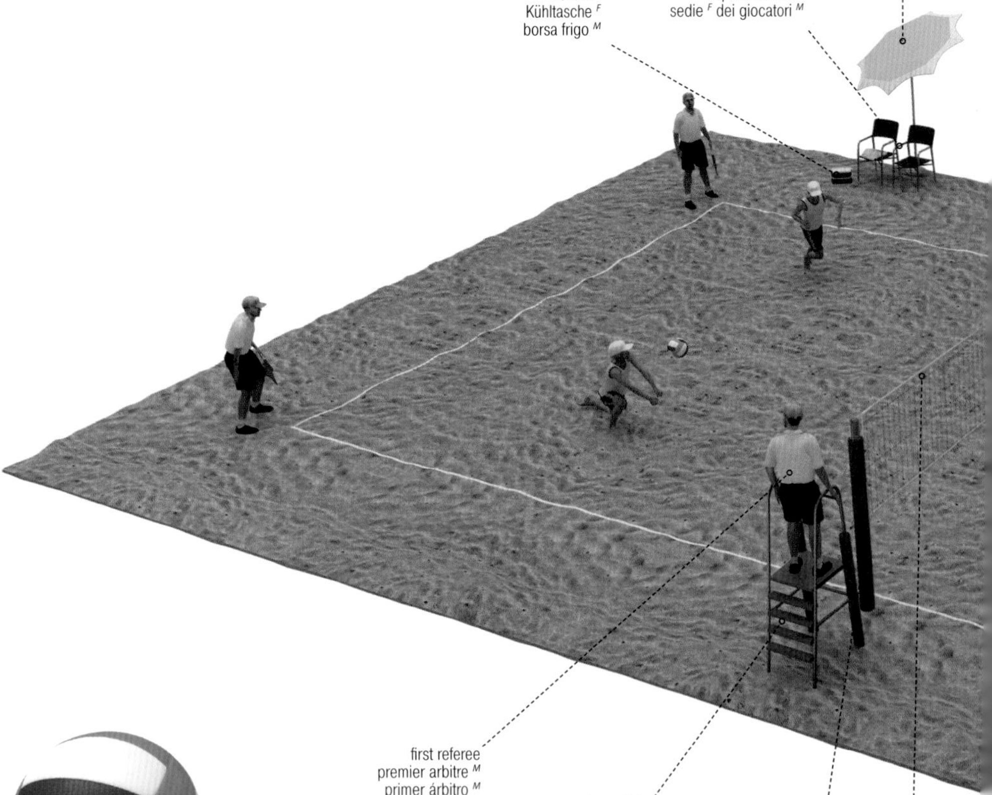
beach volleyball
court terrain [M] de volleyball [M] de plage [F]
campo [M] de voleibol [M] playero [M]
Beachvolleyball [M] – Platz [M]
campo [M] da beach volley [F]
umbrella
parasol [M]
sombrilla [F]
Schirm [M]
ombrello [M]
players' chairs
chaises [F] des joueurs [M]
sillas [F] de los jugadores [M]
Spielerstühle [M]
sedie [F] dei giocatori [M]
cooler
glacière [F]
nevera [F]
Kühltasche [F]
borsa frigo [M]
first referee
premier arbitre [M]
primer árbitro [M]
erster Schiedsrichter [M]
primo arbitro [M]
umpire's chair
chaise [F] d'arbitre [M]
silla [F] del árbitro [M]
Schiedsrichterstuhl [M]
sedia [F] dell'arbitro [M]
stand
poteau [M]
poste [M]
Pfosten [M]
palo [M]
net
filet [M]
red [F]
Netz
rete [F]

beach volleyball
ballon [M] de volleyball [M] de plage [F]
balón [M] de voleibol [M] playero [M]
Beachvolleyball [M]
pallone [M] da beach volley [M]

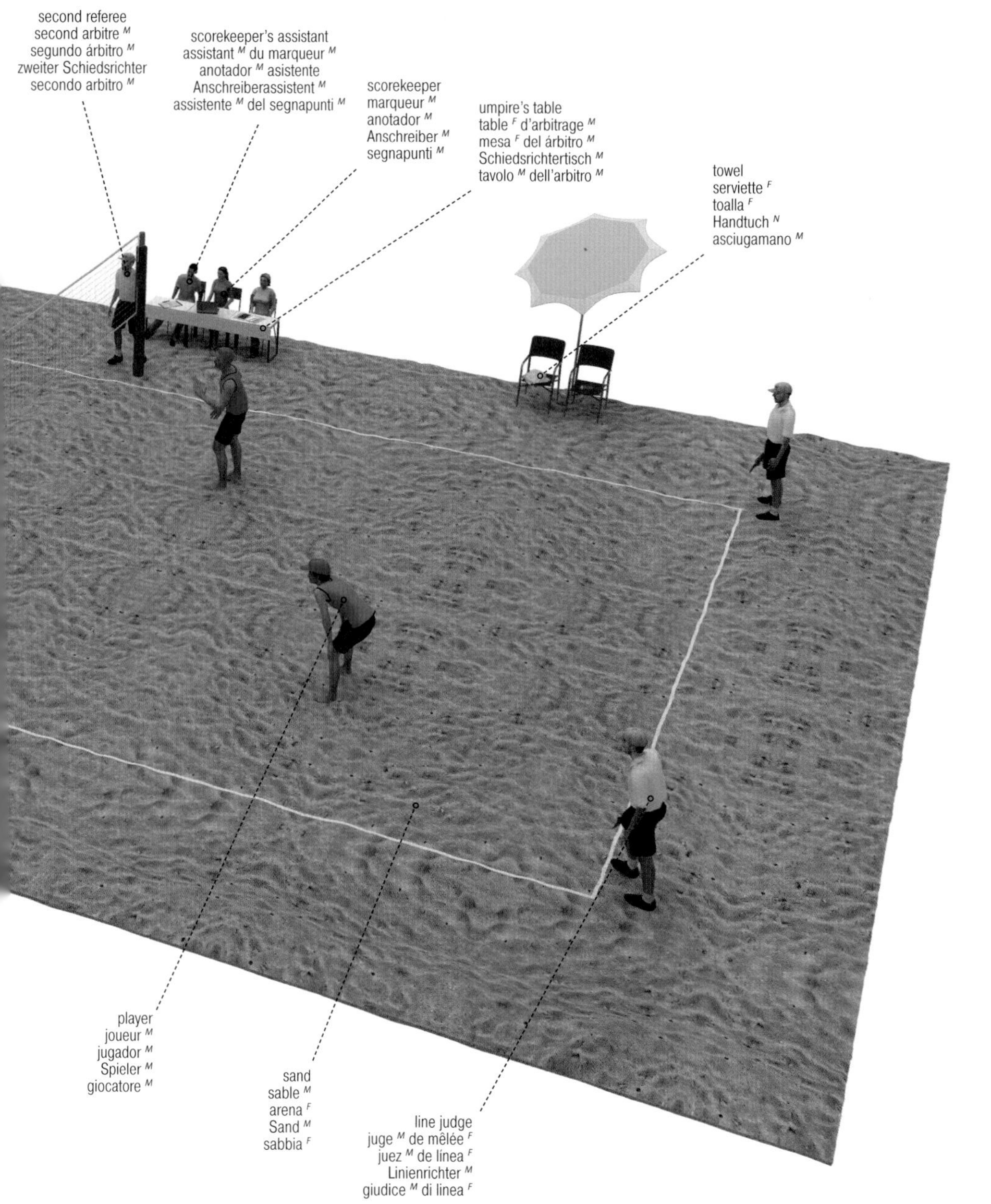
second referee
second arbitre M
segundo árbitro M
zweiter Schiedsrichter
secondo arbitro M
scorekeeper's assistant
assistant M du marqueur M
anotador M asistente
Anschreiberassistent M
assistente M del segnapunti M
scorekeeper
marqueur M
anotador M
Anschreiber M
segnapunti M
umpire's table
table F d'arbitrage M
mesa F del árbitro M
Schiedsrichtertisch M
tavolo M dell'arbitro M
towel
serviette F
toalla F
Handtuch N
asciugamano M
player
joueur M
jugador M
Spieler M
giocatore M
sand
sable M
arena F
Sand M
sabbia F
line judge
juge M de mêlée F
juez M de línea F
Linienrichter M
giudice M di linea F

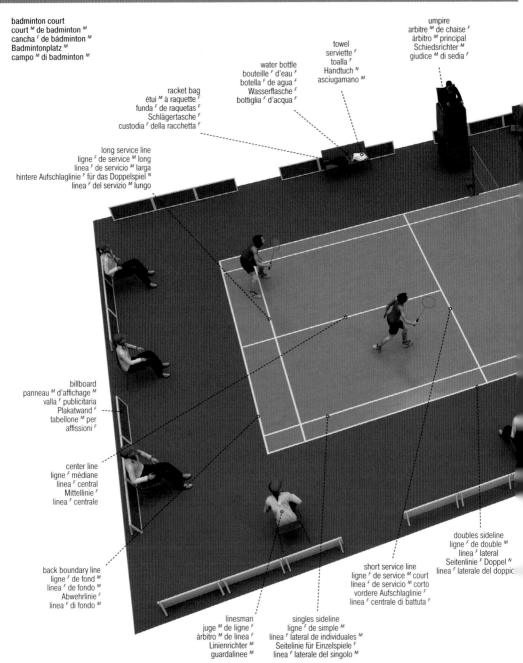

badminton court
court [M] de badminton [M]
cancha [F] de bádminton [M]
Badmintonplatz [M]
campo [M] di badminton [M]
umpire
arbitre [M] de chaise [F]
árbitro [M] principal
Schiedsrichter [M]
giudice [M] di sedia [F]
towel
serviette [F]
toalla [F]
Handtuch [N]
asciugamano [M]
water bottle
bouteille [F] d'eau [F]
botella [F] de agua [F]
Wasserflasche [F]
bottiglia [F] d'acqua [F]
racket bag
étui [M] à raquette [F]
funda [F] de raquetas [F]
Schlägertasche [F]
custodia [F] della racchetta [F]
long service line
ligne [F] de service [M] long
línea [F] de servicio [M] larga
hintere Aufschlaglinie [F] für das Doppelspiel [N]
linea [F] del servizio [M] lungo
billboard
panneau [M] d'affichage [M]
valla [F] publicitaria
Plakatwand [F]
tabellone [M] per affissioni [F]
center line
ligne [F] médiane
línea [F] central
Mittellinie [F]
linea [F] centrale
back boundary line
ligne [F] de fond [M]
línea [F] de fondo [M]
Abwehrlinie [F]
linea [F] di fondo [M]
linesman
juge [M] de ligne [F]
árbitro [M] de línea [F]
Linienrichter [M]
guardalinee [M]
singles sideline
ligne [F] de simple [M]
línea [F] lateral de individuales [M]
Seitenlinie für Einzelspiele [F]
linea [F] laterale del singolo [M]
short service line
ligne [F] de service [M] court
línea [F] de servicio [M] corto
vordere Aufschlaglinie [F]
linea [F] centrale di battuta [F]
doubles sideline
ligne [F] de double [M]
línea [F] lateral
Seitenlinie [F] Doppel [N]
linea [F] laterale del doppic

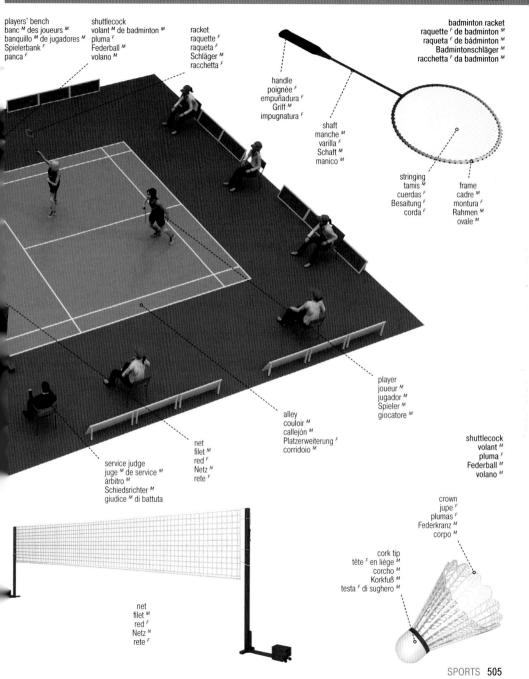

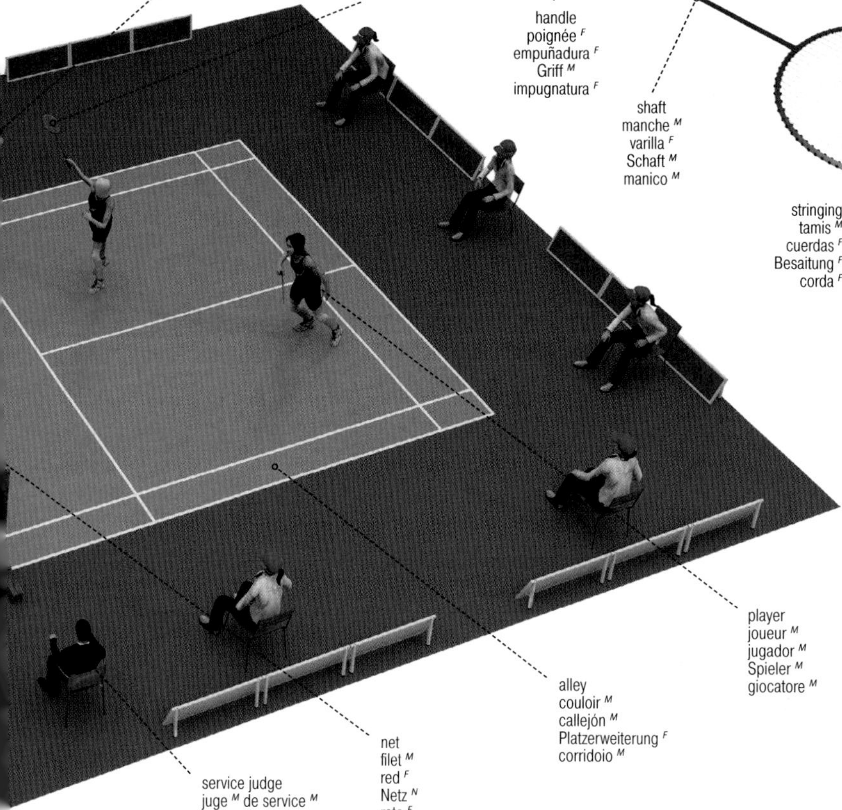
players' bench
banc M des joueurs M
banquillo M de jugadores M
Spielerbank F
panca F
shuttlecock
volant M de badminton M
pluma F
Federball M
volano M
racket
raquette F
raqueta F
Schläger M
racchetta F
player
joueur M
jugador M
Spieler M
giocatore M
alley
couloir M
callejón M
Platzerweiterung F
corridoio M
net
filet M
red F
Netz N
rete F
service judge
juge M de service M
árbitro M
Schiedsrichter M
giudice M di battuta

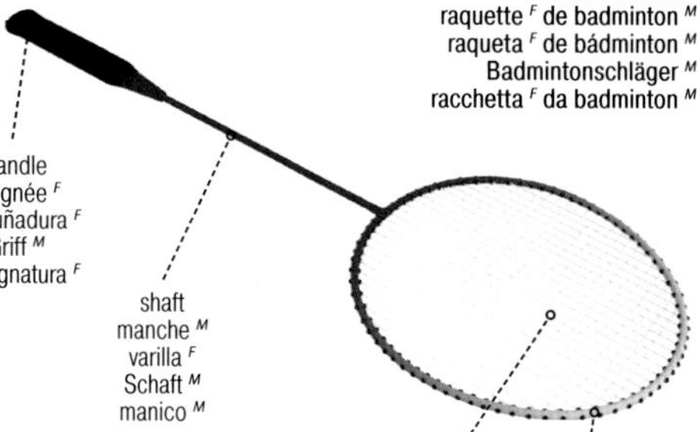
badminton racket
raquette F de badminton M
raqueta F de bádminton M
Badmintonschläger M
racchetta F da badminton M
handle
poignée F
empuñadura F
Griff M
impugnatura F
shaft
manche M
varilla F
Schaft M
manico M
stringing
tamis M
cuerdas F
Besaitung F
corda F
frame
cadre M
montura F
Rahmen M
ovale M

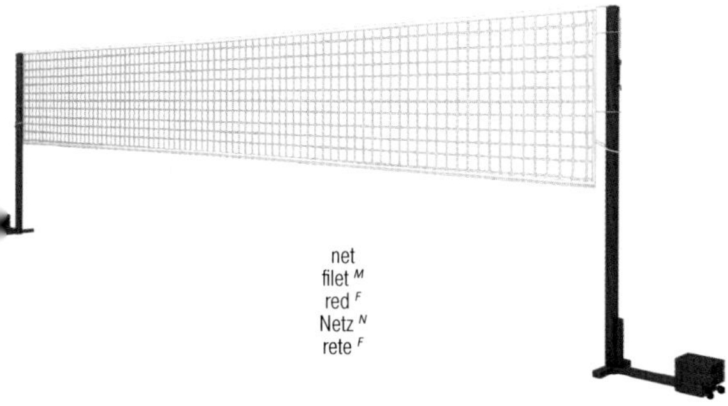
net
filet M
red F
Netz N
rete F

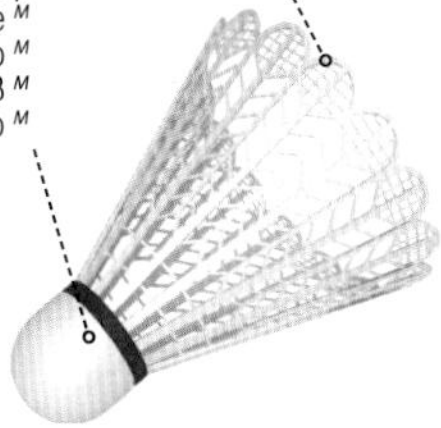
shuttlecock
volant M
pluma F
Federball M
volano M
crown
jupe F
plumas F
Federkranz M
corpo M
cork tip
tête F en liège M
corcho M
Korkfuß M
testa F di sughero M

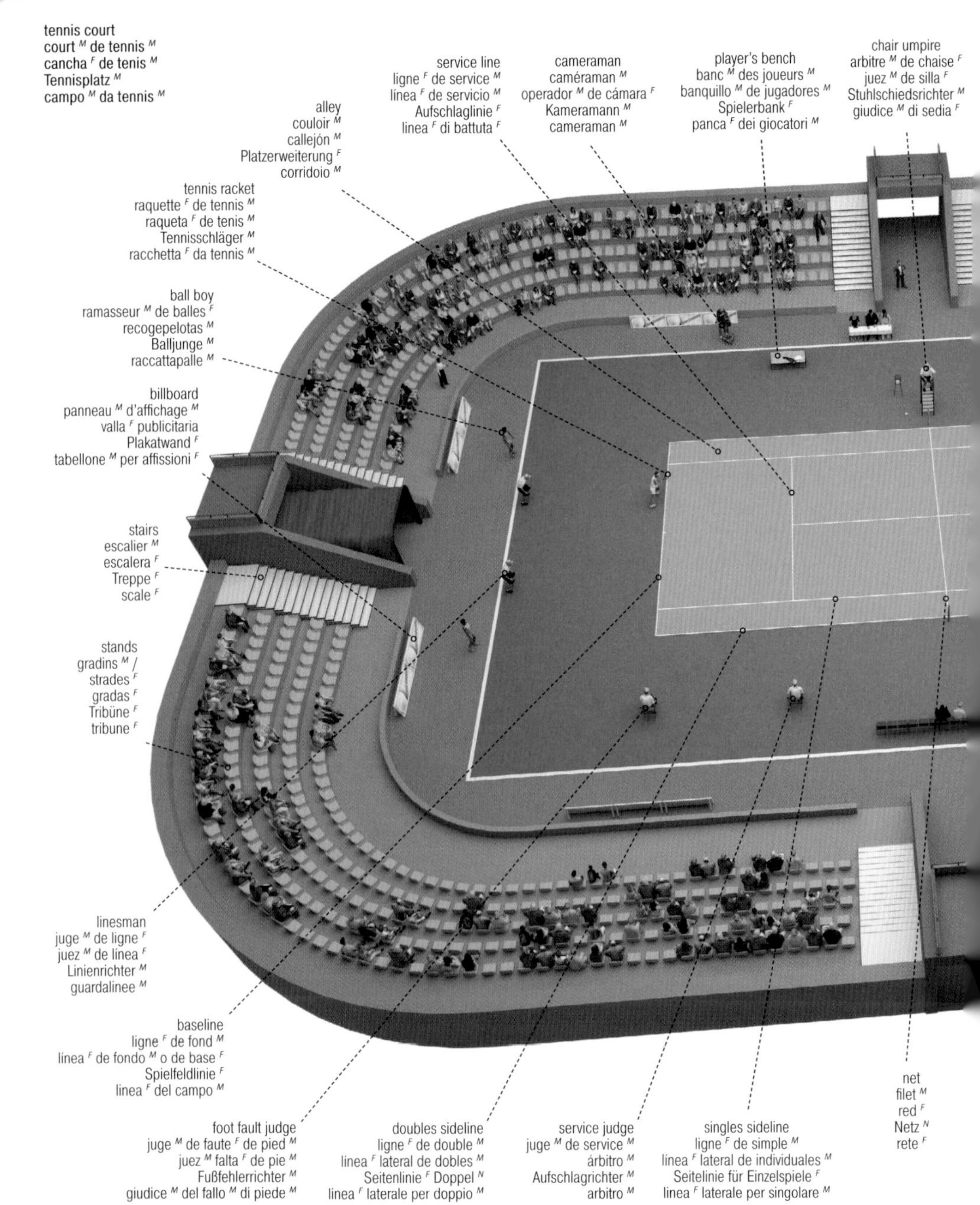
tennis court
court M de tennis M
cancha F de tenis M
Tennisplatz M
campo M da tennis M
alley
couloir M
callejón M
Platzerweiterung F
corridoio M
service line
ligne F de service M
línea F de servicio M
Aufschlaglinie F
linea F di battuta F
cameraman
caméraman M
operador M de cámara F
Kameramann M
cameraman M
player's bench
banc M des joueurs M
banquillo M de jugadores M
Spielerbank F
panca F dei giocatori M
chair umpire
arbitre M de chaise F
juez M de silla F
Stuhlschiedsrichter M
giudice M di sedia F
tennis racket
raquette F de tennis M
raqueta F de tenis M
Tennisschläger M
racchetta F da tennis M
ball boy
ramasseur M de balles F
recogepelotas M
Balljunge M
raccattapalle M
billboard
panneau M d'affichage M
valla F publicitaria
Plakatwand F
tabellone M per affissioni F
stairs
escalier M
escalera F
Treppe F
scale F
stands
gradins M /
strades F
gradas F
Tribüne F
tribune F
linesman
juge M de ligne F
juez M de línea F
Linienrichter M
guardalinee M
baseline
ligne F de fond M
línea F de fondo M o de base F
Spielfeldlinie F
linea F del campo M
net
filet M
red F
Netz N
rete F
foot fault judge
juge M de faute F de pied M
juez M falta F de pie M
Fußfehlerrichter M
giudice M del fallo M di piede M
doubles sideline
ligne F de double M
línea F lateral de dobles M
Seitenlinie F Doppel N
linea F laterale per doppio M
service judge
juge M de service M
árbitro M
Aufschlagrichter M
arbitro M
singles sideline
ligne F de simple M
línea F lateral de individuales M
Seitelinie für Einzelspiele F
linea F laterale per singolare M

right service court
carré [M] de service [M] droit
zona [F] de saque [M] derecha
rechtes Aufschlagfeld [N]
rettangolo [M] destro di servizio [M]

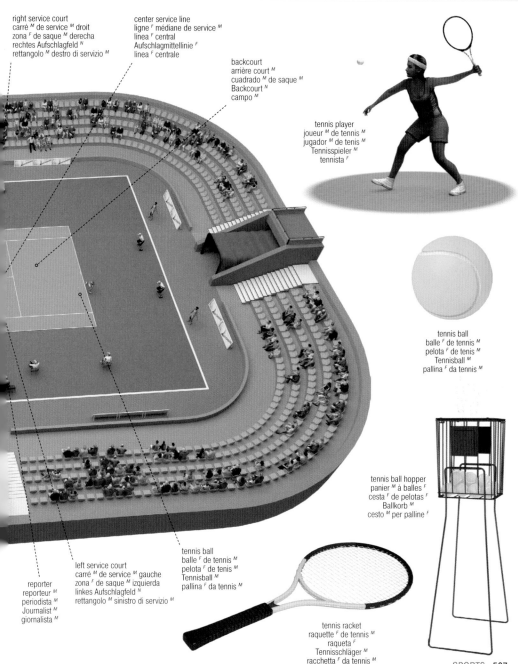

center service line
ligne [F] médiane de service [M]
linea [F] central
Aufschlagmittellinie [F]
linea [F] centrale

backcourt
arrière court [M]
cuadrado [M] de saque [M]
Backcourt [N]
campo [M]

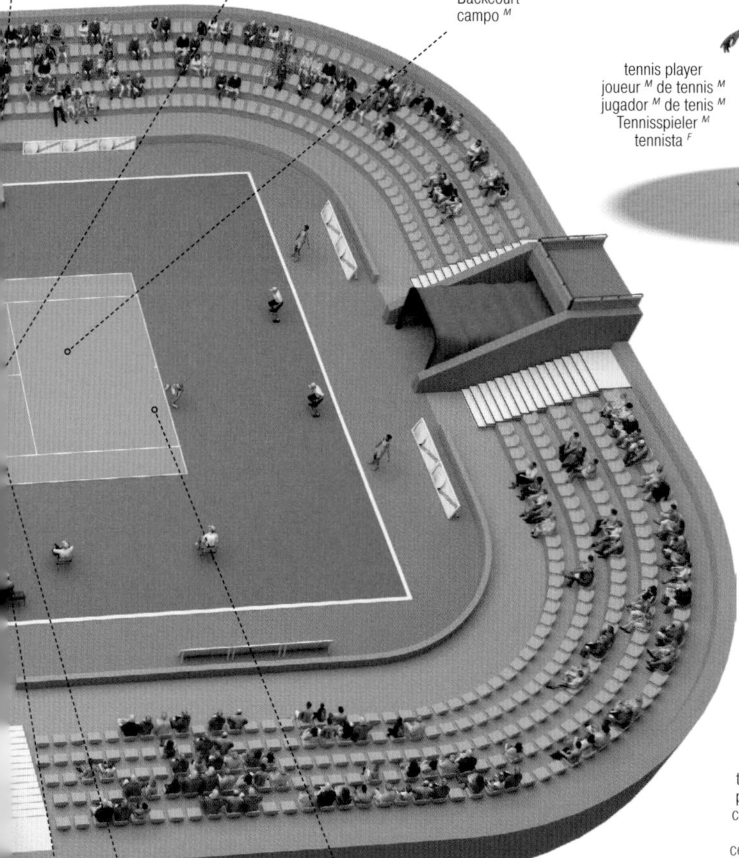

tennis player
joueur [M] de tennis [M]
jugador [M] de tenis [M]
Tennisspieler [M]
tennista [F]

tennis ball
balle [F] de tennis [M]
pelota [F] de tenis [M]
Tennisball [M]
pallina [F] da tennis [M]

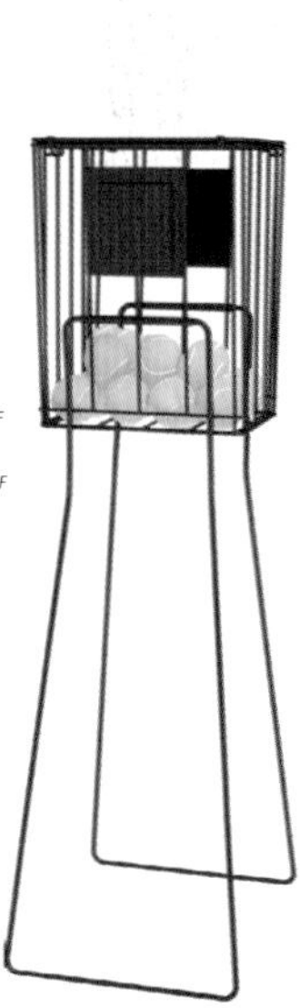

tennis ball hopper
panier [M] à balles [F]
cesta [F] de pelotas [F]
Ballkorb [M]
cesto [M] per palline [F]

tennis ball
balle [F] de tennis [M]
pelota [F] de tenis [M]
Tennisball [M]
pallina [F] da tennis [M]

left service court
carré [M] de service [M] gauche
zona [F] de saque [M] izquierda
linkes Aufschlagfeld [N]
rettangolo [M] sinistro di servizio [M]

reporter
reporteur [M]
periodista [M]
Journalist [M]
giornalista [M]

tennis racket
raquette [F] de tennis [M]
raqueta [F]
Tennisschläger [M]
racchetta [F] da tennis [M]

table tennis court
court ᴹ de tennis ᴹ de table ᶠ
sala ᶠ de tenis ᴹ de mesa ᶠ
Tischtennisplatz ᴹ
campo ᴹ da ping-pong ᴹ

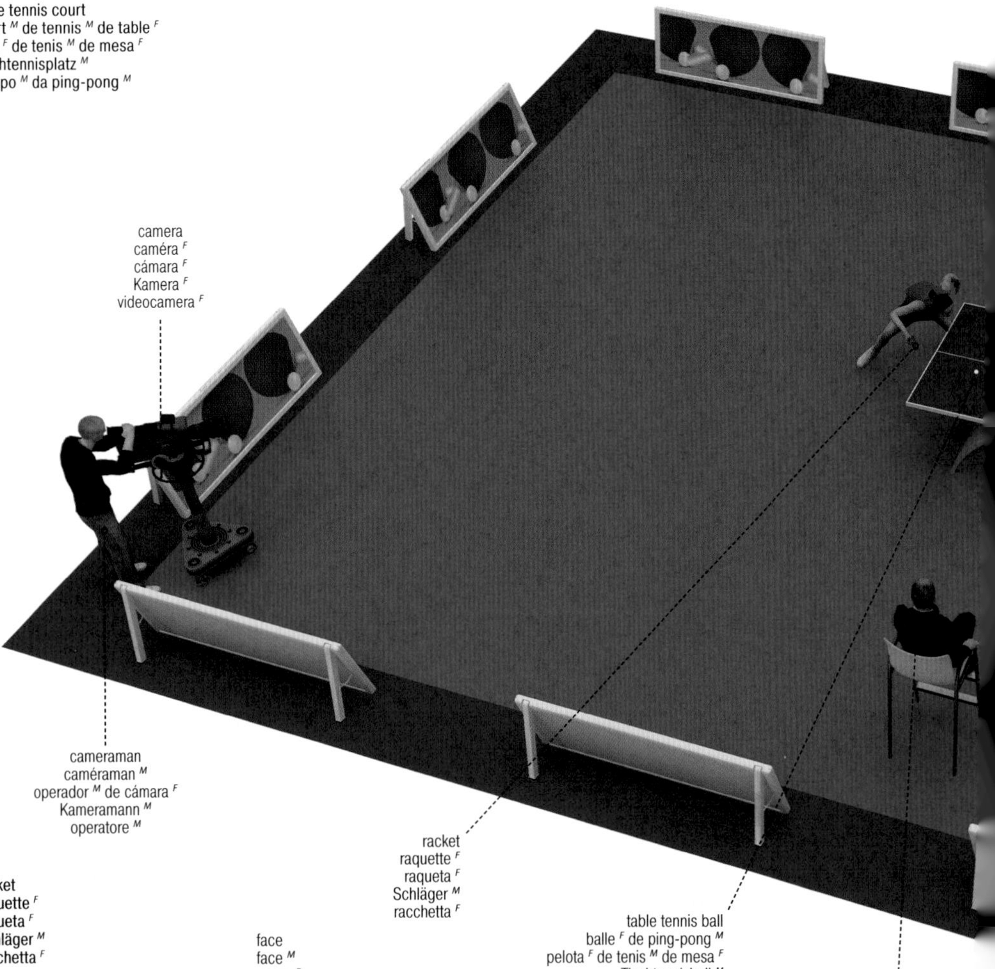
camera
caméra ᶠ
cámara ᶠ
Kamera ᶠ
videocamera ᶠ
cameraman
caméraman ᴹ
operador ᴹ de cámara ᶠ
Kameramann ᴹ
operatore ᴹ
racket
raquette ᶠ
raqueta ᶠ
Schläger ᴹ
racchetta ᶠ
table tennis ball
balle ᶠ de ping-pong ᴹ
pelota ᶠ de tenis ᴹ de mesa ᶠ
Tischtennisball ᴹ
pallina ᶠ da ping-pong ᴹ
umpire
arbitre ᴹ
árbitro ᴹ
Schiedsrichter ᴹ
arbitro ᴹ

racket
raquette ᶠ
raqueta ᶠ
Schläger ᴹ
racchetta ᶠ

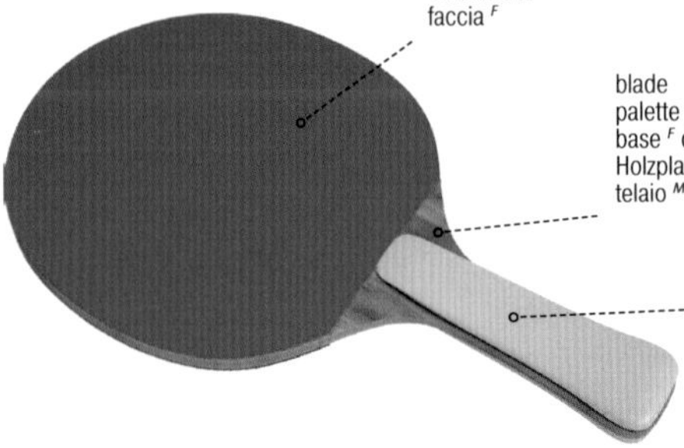
face
face ᴹ
goma ᶠ
Vorderseite ᶠ
faccia ᶠ
blade
palette ᶠ
base ᶠ de madera ᶠ
Holzplatte ᶠ
telaio ᴹ
handle
manche ᴹ
mango ᴹ
Griff ᴹ
impugnatura ᶠ

table tennis ball
balle ᶠ de ping-pong ᴹ
pelota ᶠ de tenis ᴹ de mesa ᶠ
Tischtennisball ᴹ
pallina ᶠ da ping-pong ᴹ

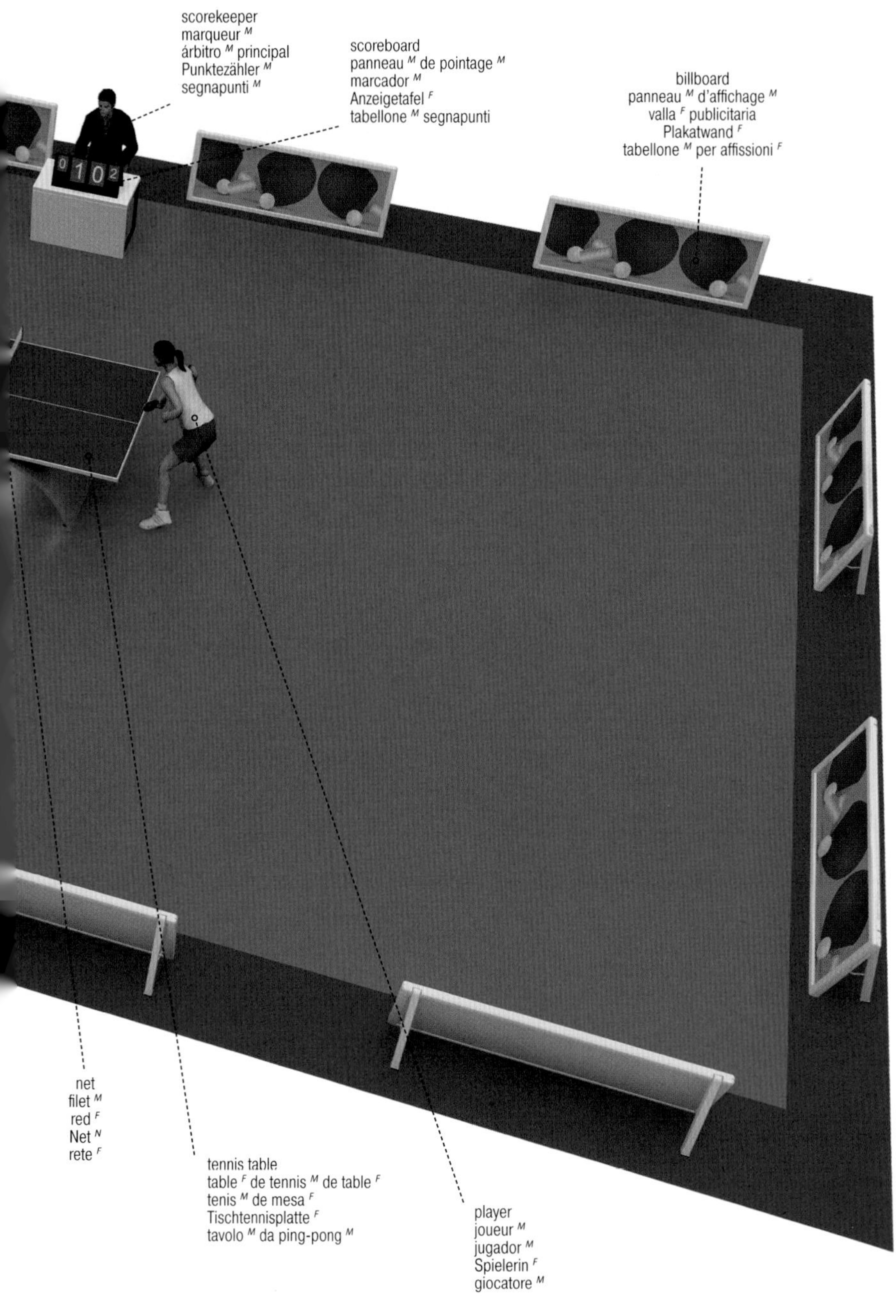
scorekeeper
marqueur M
árbitro M principal
Punktezähler M
segnapunti M
scoreboard
panneau M de pointage M
marcador M
Anzeigetafel F
tabellone M segnapunti
billboard
panneau M d'affichage M
valla F publicitaria
Plakatwand F
tabellone M per affissioni F
net
filet M
red F
Net N
rete F
tennis table
table F de tennis M de table F
tenis M de mesa F
Tischtennisplatte F
tavolo M da ping-pong M
player
joueur M
jugador M
Spielerin F
giocatore M

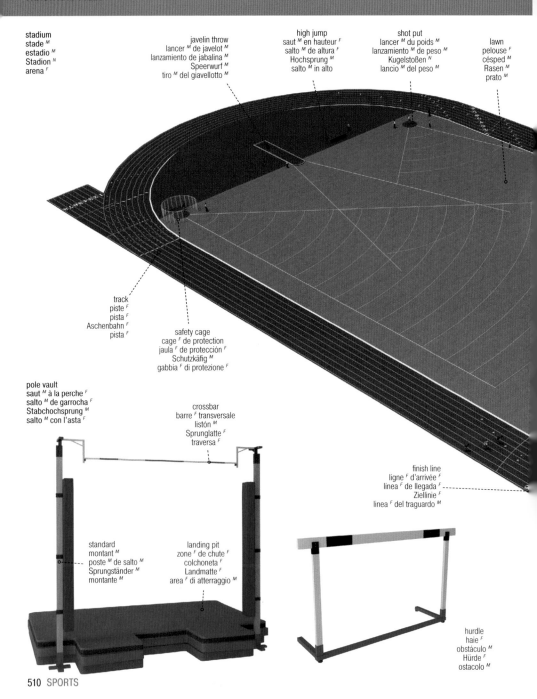

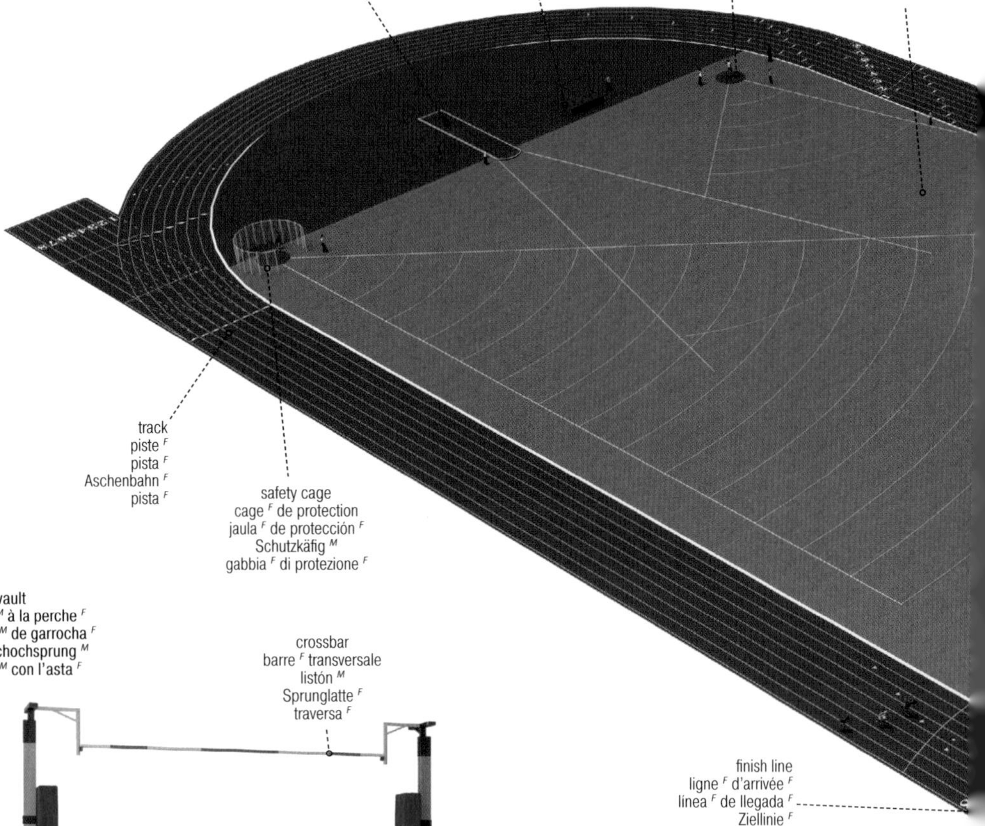
stadium
stade ^{M}
estadio ^{M}
Stadion ^{N}
arena ^{F}
javelin throw
lancer ^{M} de javelot ^{M}
lanzamiento de jabalina ^{M}
Speerwurf ^{M}
tiro ^{M} del giavellotto ^{M}
high jump
saut ^{M} en hauteur ^{F}
salto ^{M} de altura ^{F}
Hochsprung ^{M}
salto ^{M} in alto
shot put
lancer ^{M} du poids ^{M}
lanzamiento ^{M} de peso ^{M}
Kugelstoßen ^{N}
lancio ^{M} del peso ^{M}
lawn
pelouse ^{F}
césped ^{M}
Rasen ^{M}
prato ^{M}
track
piste ^{F}
pista ^{F}
Aschenbahn ^{F}
pista ^{F}
safety cage
cage ^{F} de protection
jaula ^{F} de protección ^{F}
Schutzkäfig ^{M}
gabbia ^{F} di protezione ^{F}
finish line
ligne ^{F} d'arrivée ^{F}
línea ^{F} de llegada ^{F}
Ziellinie ^{F}
linea ^{F} del traguardo ^{M}

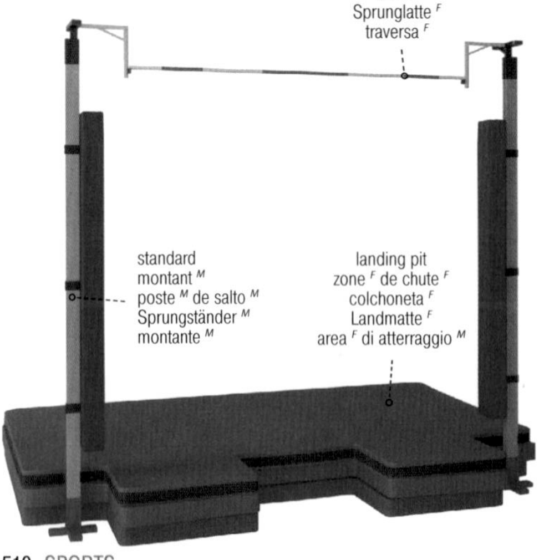
pole vault
saut ^{M} à la perche ^{F}
salto ^{M} de garrocha ^{F}
Stabchochsprung ^{M}
salto ^{M} con l'asta ^{F}
crossbar
barre ^{F} transversale
listón ^{M}
Sprunglatte ^{F}
traversa ^{F}
standard
montant ^{M}
poste ^{M} de salto ^{M}
Sprungständer ^{M}
montante ^{M}
landing pit
zone ^{F} de chute ^{F}
colchoneta ^{F}
Landmatte ^{F}
area ^{F} di atterraggio ^{M}

hurdle
haie ^{F}
obstáculo ^{M}
Hürde ^{F}
ostacolo ^{M}

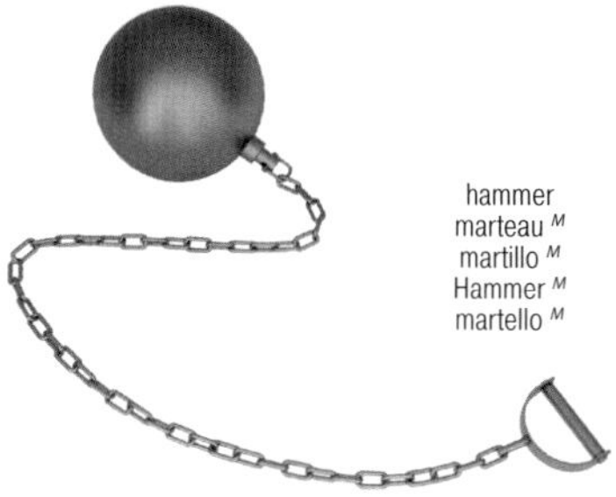

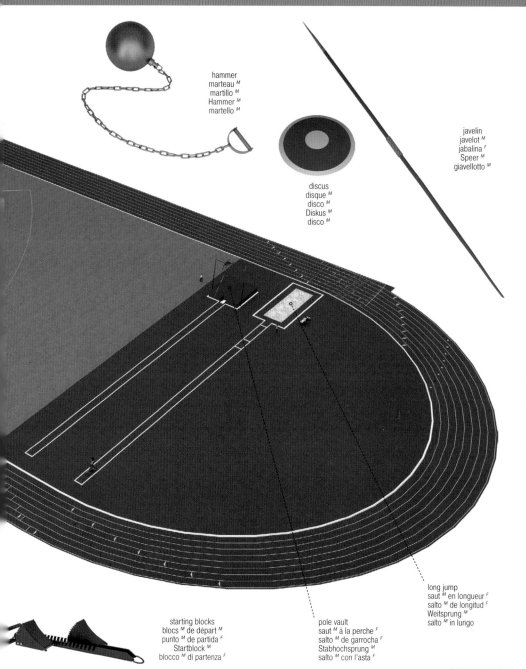

hammer
marteau ^{M}
martillo ^{M}
Hammer ^{M}
martello ^{M}

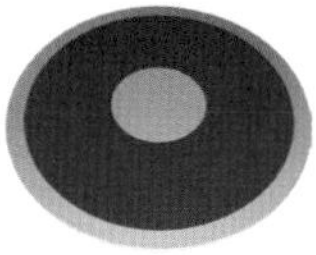

discus
disque ^{M}
disco ^{M}
Diskus ^{M}
disco ^{M}

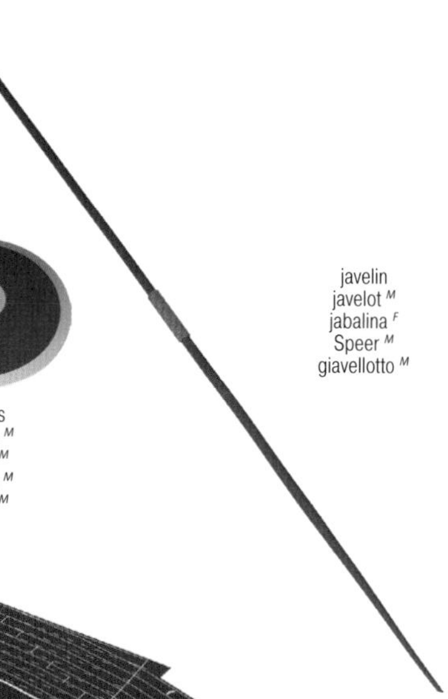

javelin
javelot ^{M}
jabalina ^{F}
Speer ^{M}
giavellotto ^{M}

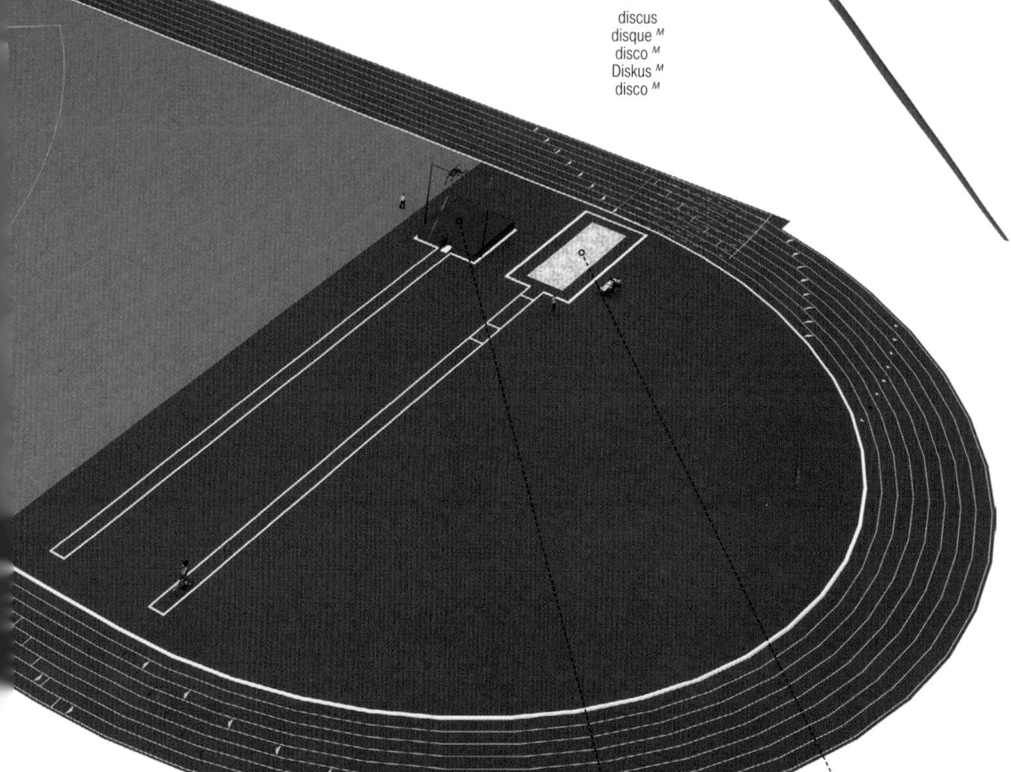

long jump
saut ^{M} en longueur ^{F}
salto ^{M} de longitud ^{F}
Weitsprung ^{M}
salto ^{M} in lungo

pole vault
saut ^{M} à la perche ^{F}
salto ^{M} de garrocha ^{F}
Stabhochsprung ^{M}
salto ^{M} con l'asta ^{F}

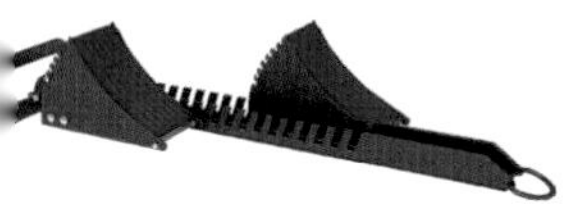

starting blocks
blocs ^{M} de départ ^{M}
punto ^{M} de partida ^{F}
Startblock ^{M}
blocco ^{M} di partenza ^{F}

artistic gymnastics
gymnastique [F] artistique
gimnasia [F] artística
Geräteturnanlage [F]
ginnastica [F] artistica

scoreboard
panneau [M] de pointage [M]
marcador [M]
Anzeigetafel [F]
tabellone [M] segnapunti [M]

coach
entraîneur [M]
entrenador [M]
Trainer [M]
allenatore [M]

chalk
craie [F]
tiza [F]
Kreide [F]
gesso [M]

pommel horse
cheval [M] d'arçons [M]
potro [M]
Seitpferd [N]
cavallo [M] con maniglie [F]

springboard
tremplin [M]
plataforma [F]
Sprungbrett [N]
trampolino [M]

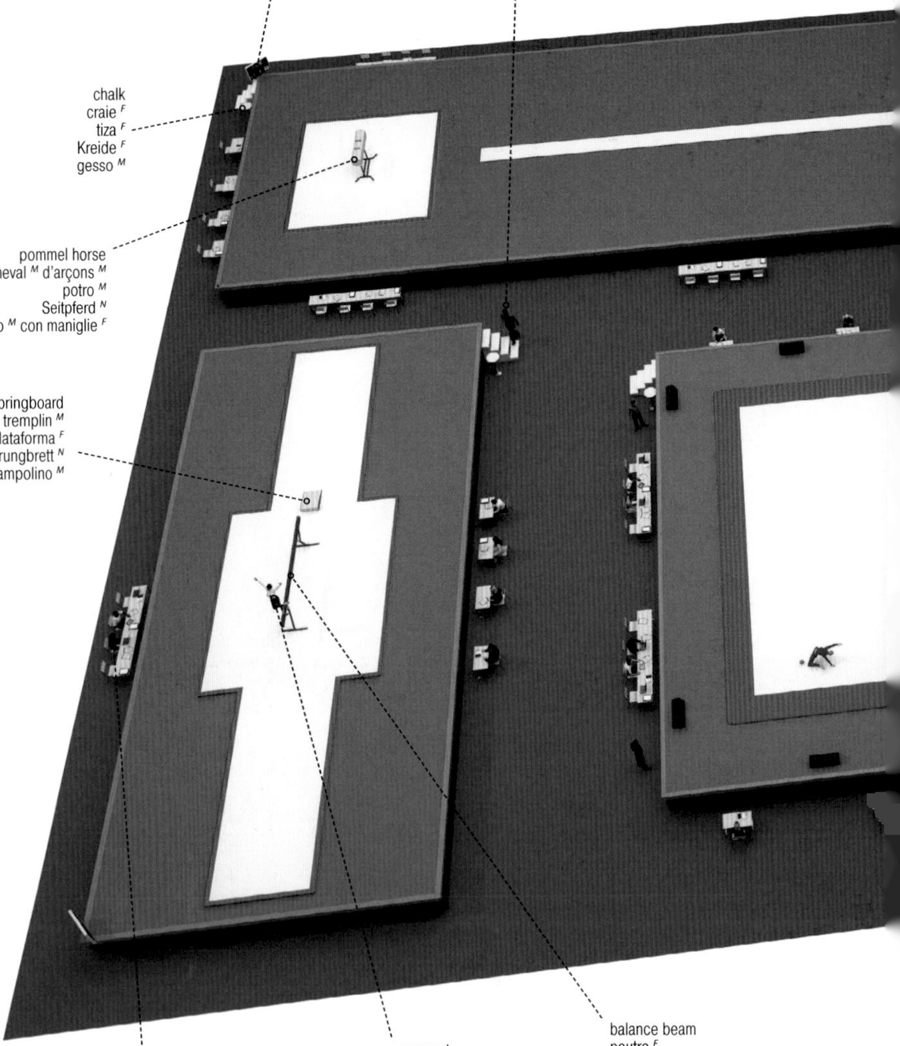

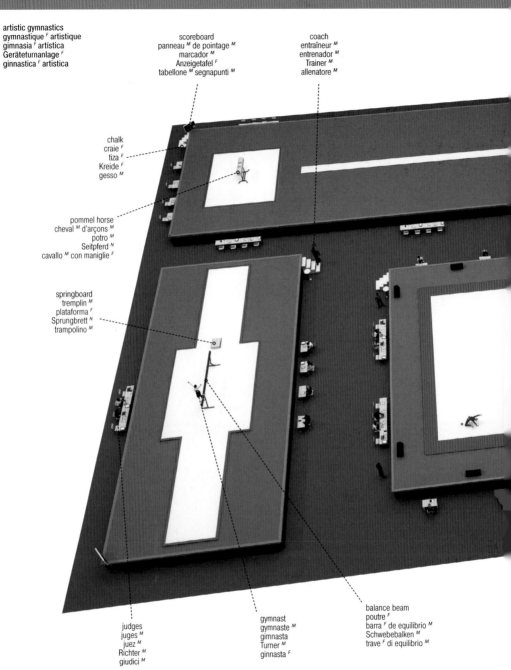

judges
juges [M]
juez [M]
Richter [M]
giudici [M]

gymnast
gymnaste [M]
gimnasta
Turner [M]
ginnasta [F]

balance beam
poutre [F]
barra [F] de equilibrio [M]
Schwebebalken [M]
trave [F] di equilibrio [M]

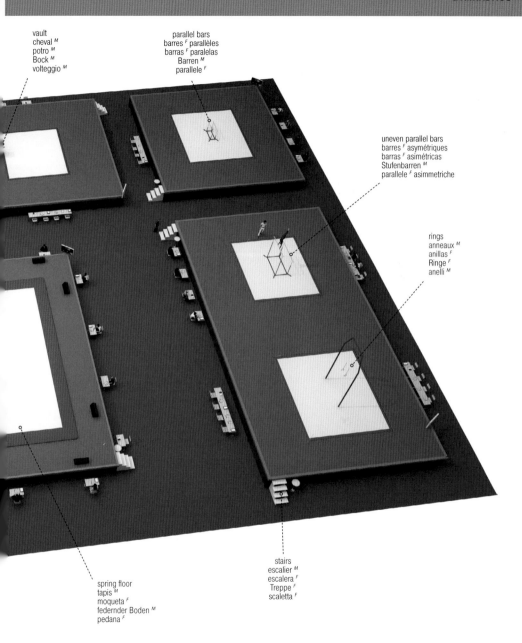

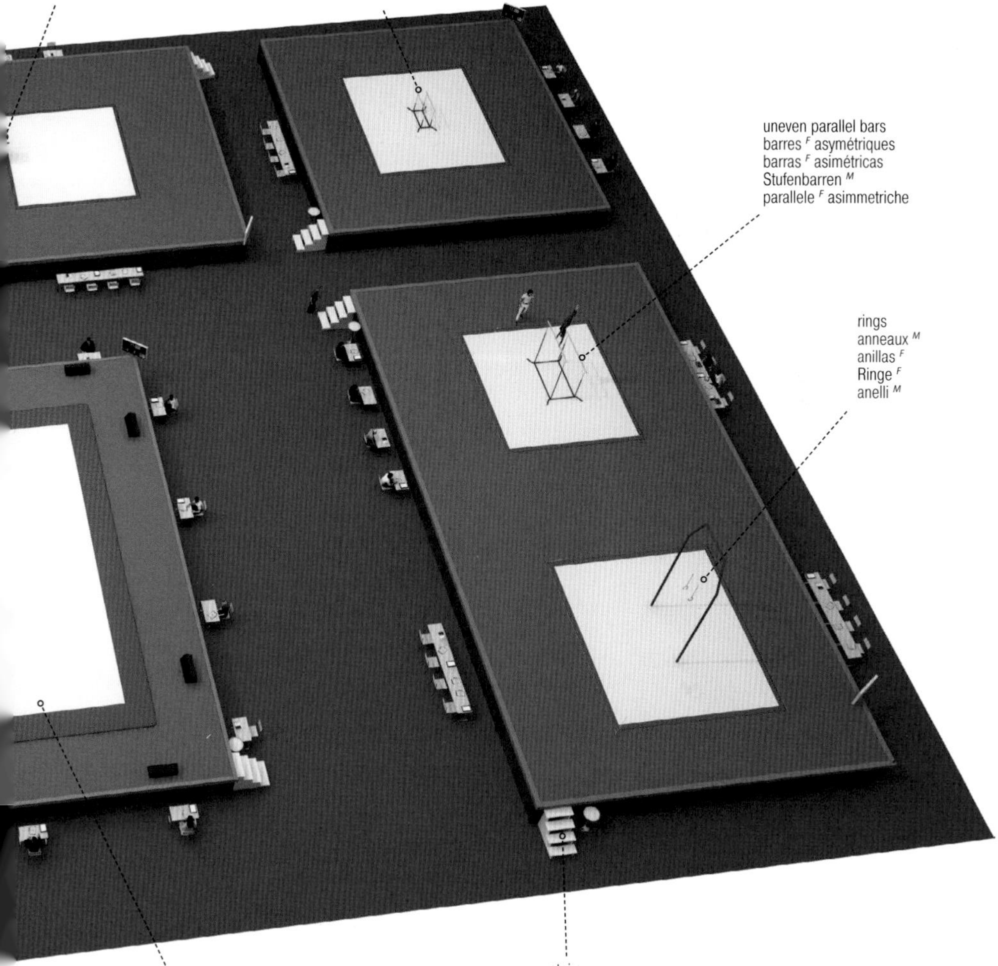
vault
cheval M
potro M
Bock M
volteggio M
parallel bars
barres F parallèles
barras F paralelas
Barren M
parallele F
uneven parallel bars
barres F asymétriques
barras F asimétricas
Stufenbarren M
parallele F asimmetriche
rings
anneaux M
anillas F
Ringe F
anelli M
spring floor
tapis M
moqueta F
federnder Boden M
pedana F
stairs
escalier M
escalera F
Treppe F
scaletta F

Artistic gymnastics equipment

Équipement M pour gymnastique F artistique | Aparatos M de la gimnasia F artística | Turngeräte N | Attrezzature F da ginnastica F artistica

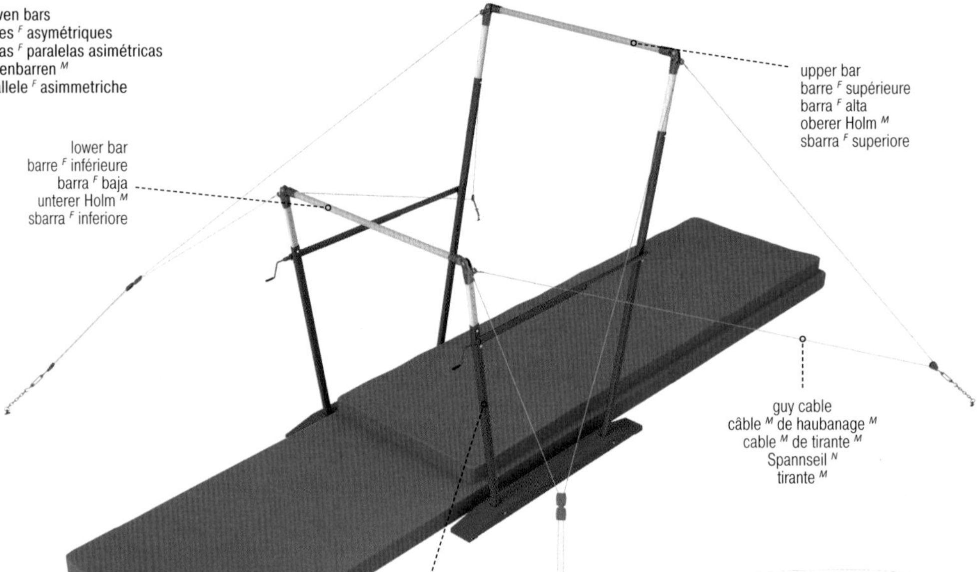

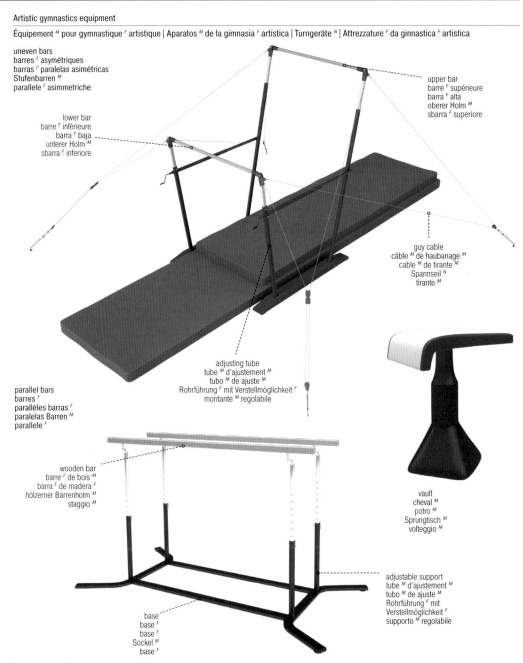

uneven bars
barres F asymétriques
barras F paralelas asimétricas
Stufenbarren M
parallele F asimmetriche

upper bar
barre F supérieure
barra F alta
oberer Holm M
sbarra F superiore

lower bar
barre F inférieure
barra F baja
unterer Holm M
sbarra F inferiore

guy cable
câble M de haubanage M
cable M de tirante M
Spannseil N
tirante M

adjusting tube
tube M d'ajustement M
tubo M de ajuste M
Rohrführung F mit Verstellmöglichkeit F
montante M regolabile

vault
cheval M
potro M
Sprungtisch M
volteggio M

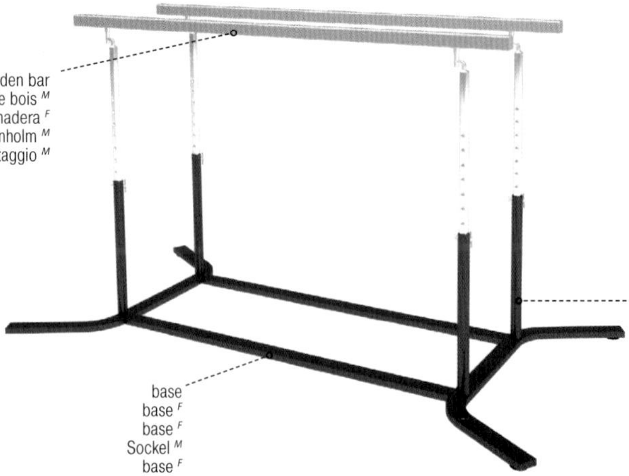

parallel bars
barres F
parallèles barras F
paralelas Barren M
parallele F

wooden bar
barre F de bois M
barra F de madera F
hölzerner Barrenholm M
staggio M

adjustable support
tube M d'ajustement M
tubo M de ajuste M
Rohrführung F mit
Verstellmöglichkeit F
supporto M regolabile

base
base F
base F
Sockel M
base F

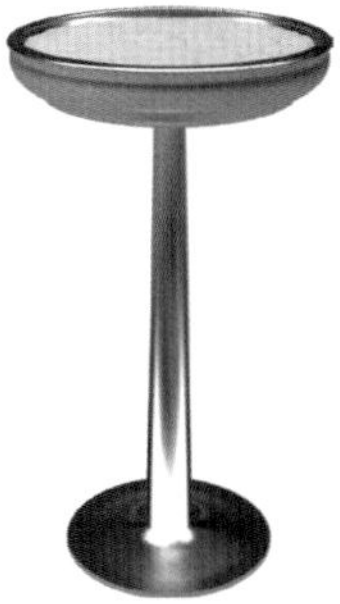

chalk bowl
recipient ᴹ à talc ᴹ
bol ᴹ para talco ᴹ
Kreideschüssel ᶠ
portatalco ᴹ

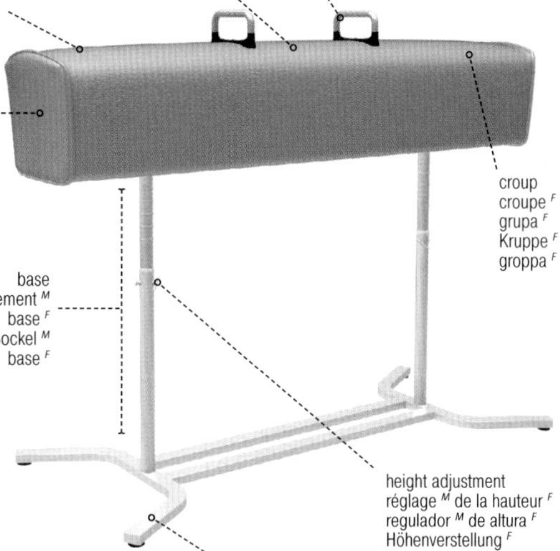
neck
cou M
cabeza F
Hals M
testa F
saddle
selle F
silla F
Sattel M
sella F
pommel
arçon M
arzón M
Pausche F
maniglia F
horse
cheval M
caballo M
Pferd F
cavallo M
croup
croupe F
grupa F
Kruppe F
groppa F
base
piètement M
base F
Sockel M
base F
height adjustment
réglage M de la hauteur F
regulador M de altura F
Höhenverstellung F
sistema M di regolazione F dell'altezza F
anti-slip shoe
patin M antidérapant
zapata F antideslizante
rutschfester Sockel M
piede M antisdrucciolo

pommel horse
cheval M d'arçons M
caballo M con arcos M
Seitpferd N
cavallo M con maniglie F

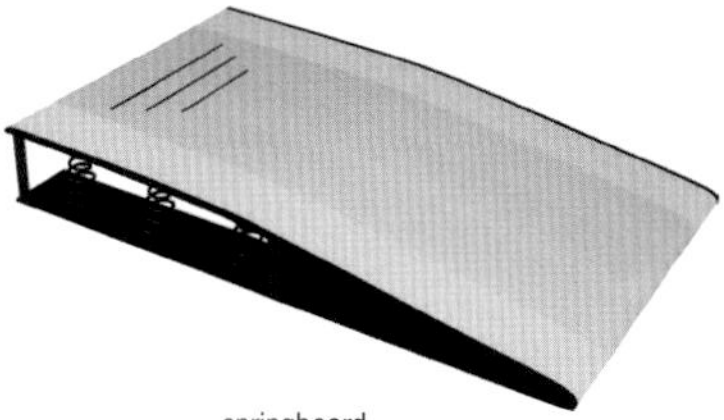

springboard
tremplin M
tabla F de balanceo M
Sprungbrett N pedana F
elastica

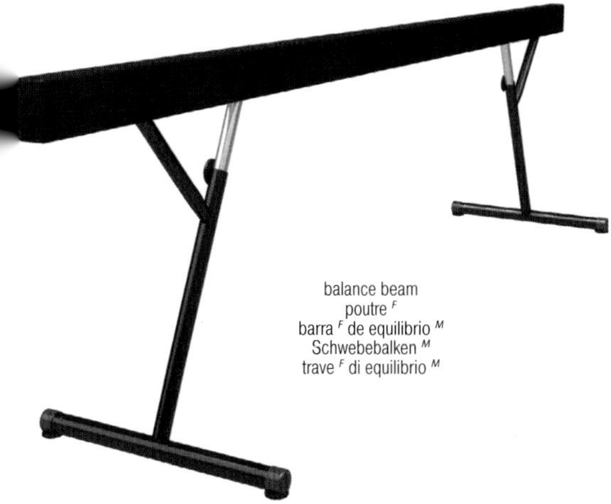

balance beam
poutre F
barra F de equilibrio M
Schwebebalken M
trave F di equilibrio M

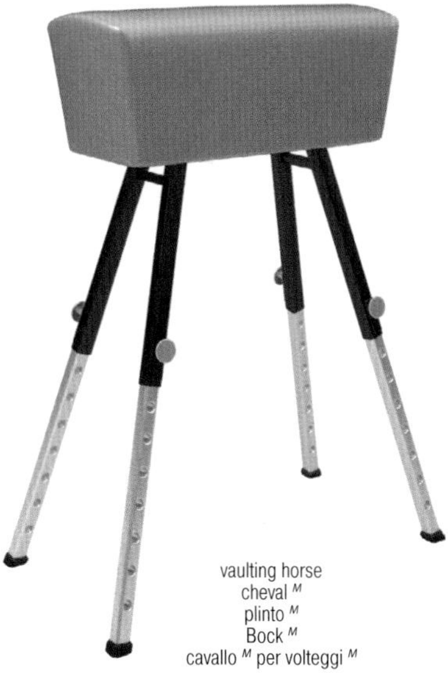

vaulting horse
cheval M
plinto M
Bock M
cavallo M per volteggi M

gymnast
gymnaste F
gimnasta F
Turnerin F
ginnasta F

rhythmic gymnastics
gymnastique F rythmique
gimnasia F rítmica
Rhythmische Sportgymnastik F
ginnastica F ritmica

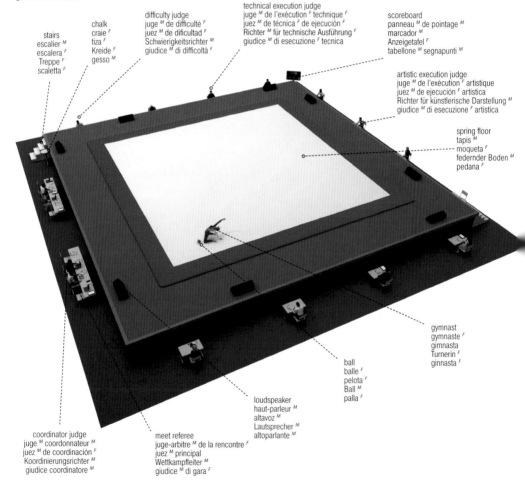

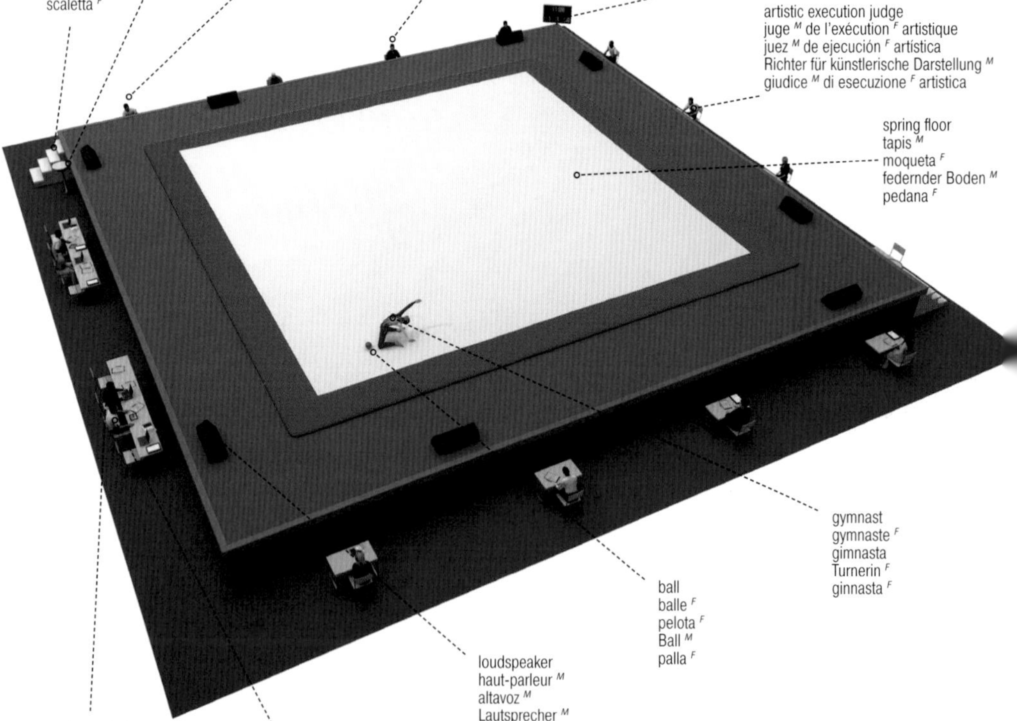
stairs
escalier M
escalera F
Treppe F
scaletta F
chalk
craie F
tiza F
Kreide F
gesso M
difficulty judge
juge M de difficulté F
juez M de dificultad F
Schwierigkeitsrichter M
giudice M di difficoltà F
technical execution judge
juge M de l'exécution F technique F
juez M de técnica F de ejecución F
Richter M für technische Ausführung F
giudice M di esecuzione F tecnica
scoreboard
panneau M de pointage M
marcador M
Anzeigetafel F
tabellone M segnapunti M
artistic execution judge
juge M de l'exécution F artistique
juez M de ejecución F artística
Richter für künstlerische Darstellung M
giudice M di esecuzione F artistica
spring floor
tapis M
moqueta F
federnder Boden M
pedana F
gymnast
gymnaste F
gimnasta
Turnerin F
ginnasta F
ball
balle F
pelota F
Ball M
palla F
loudspeaker
haut-parleur M
altavoz M
Lautsprecher M
altoparlante M
meet referee
juge-arbitre M de la rencontre F
juez M principal
Wettkampfleiter M
giudice M di gara F
coordinator judge
juge M coordonnateur M
juez M de coordinación F
Koordinierungsrichter M
giudice coordinatore M

golf cart: front view
voiturette F de golf M: vue F de face F
carrito M de golf M: vista delantera F
Golfwagen: Vorderansicht M
golf car F: vista frontale

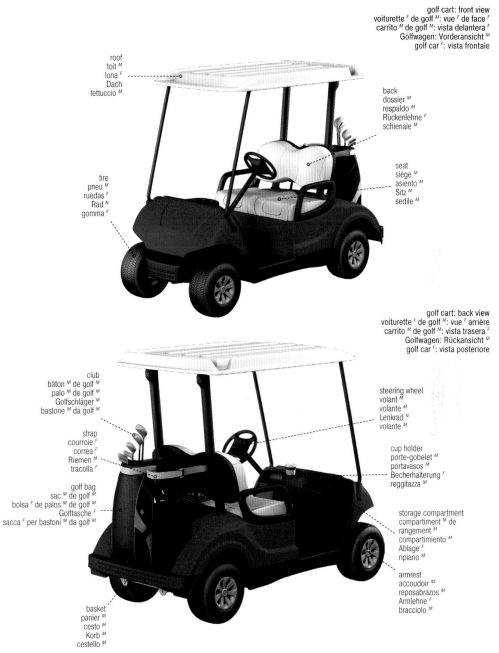

roof
toit M
lona F
Dach
tettuccio M
back
dossier M
respaldo M
Rückenlehne F
schienale M
seat
siège M
asiento M
Sitz M
sedile M
tire
pneu M
ruedas F
Rad N
gomma F

golf cart: back view
voiturette F de golf M: vue F arrière
carrito M de golf M: vista trasera F
Golfwagen: Rückansicht M
golf car F: vista posteriore

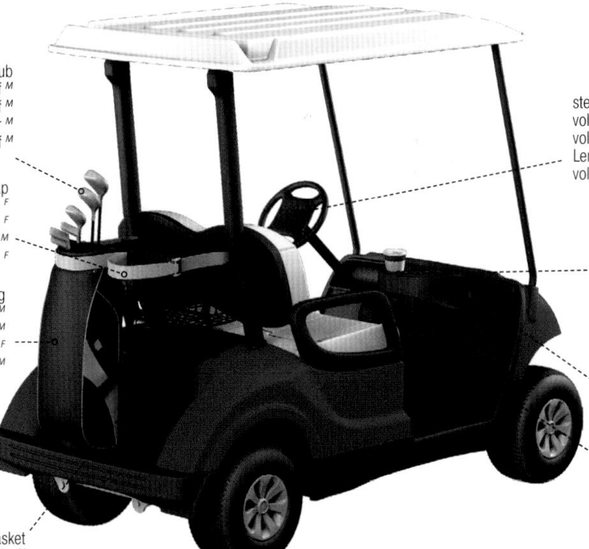
club
bâton M de golf M
palo M de golf M
Golfschläger M
bastone M da golf M
steering wheel
volant M
volante M
Lenkrad N
volante M
strap
courroie F
correa F
Riemen M
tracolla F
cup holder
porte-gobelet M
portavasos M
Becherhalterung F
reggitazza M
golf bag
sac M de golf M
bolsa F de palos M de golf M
Golftasche F
sacca F per bastoni M da golf M
storage compartment
compartiment M de rangement M
compartimiento M
Ablage F
ripiano M
armrest
accoudoir M
reposabrazos M
Armlehne F
bracciolo M
basket
panier M
cesto M
Korb M
cestello M

golfer
golfeur ^{M}
golfista $^{M/F}$
Golfspieler ^{M}
golfista ^{M}

golf club
bâton ^{M} de golf ^{M}
palo ^{M} de golf ^{M}
Golfschläger ^{M}
bastone ^{M} da club ^{M}

golf glove
gant ^{M} de golf ^{M}
guante ^{M} de golf ^{M}
Golfhandschuh ^{M}
guanto ^{M}

golf shoes
chaussures ^{F} de golf ^{M}
zapatos ^{M} de golf ^{M}
Golfschuhe ^{M}
scarpe ^{F}

golf ball
bombe ^{F}
pelota ^{F} de golf ^{M}
Golfball ^{M}
palla ^{F} da golf ^{M}

golf bag
sac ^{M} de golf ^{M}
bolsa ^{F} de palos ^{M}
Golftasche ^{F}
sacca ^{F} per mazze ^{F} da golf ^{M}

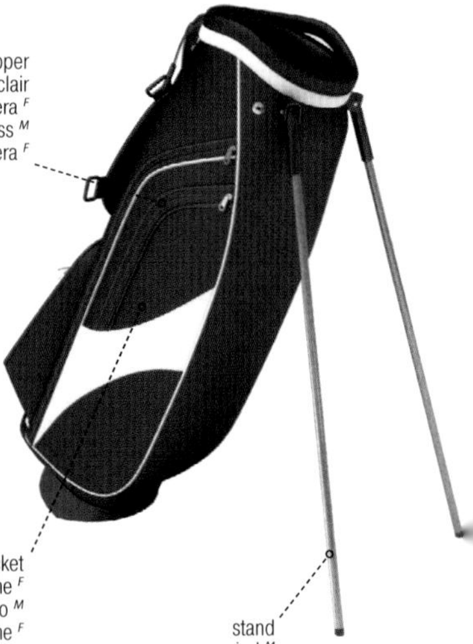

zipper
fermeture ^{F} éclair
cremallera ^{F}
Reißverschluss ^{M}
cerniera ^{F}

pocket
poche ^{F}
bolsillo ^{M}
Tasche ^{F}
tasca ^{F}

stand
pied ^{M}
soporte ^{M}
Standbein ^{N}
sostegno ^{M}

golf course
terrain ^{M} de golf ^{M}
campo ^{M}
Golfspiel ^{N}
campo ^{M} di golf ^{M}

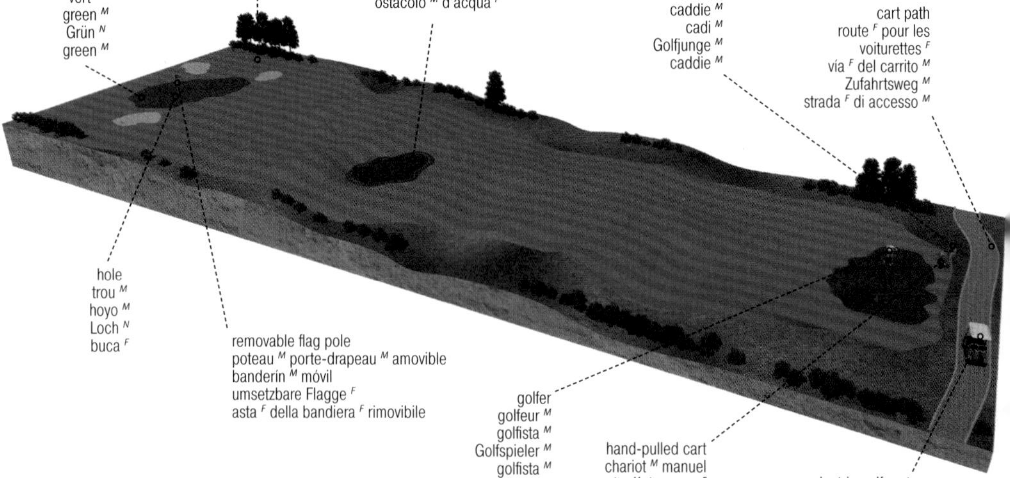

grass
gazon ^{M}
hierba ^{F}
Rasen ^{M}
prato ^{M}

green
vert ^{M}
green ^{M}
Grün ^{N}
green ^{M}

water hazard
obstacle ^{M} d'eau ^{F}
trampa ^{F} de agua ^{F}
Wasserhindernis ^{N}
ostacolo ^{M} d'acqua ^{F}

caddie
caddie ^{M}
cadi ^{M}
Golfjunge ^{M}
caddie ^{M}

cart path
route ^{F} pour les voiturettes ^{F}
vía ^{F} del carrito ^{M}
Zufahrtsweg ^{M}
strada ^{F} di accesso ^{M}

hole
trou ^{M}
hoyo ^{M}
Loch ^{N}
buca ^{F}

removable flag pole
poteau ^{M} porte-drapeau ^{M} amovible
banderín ^{M} móvil
umsetzbare Flagge ^{F}
asta ^{F} della bandiera ^{F} rimovibile

golfer
golfeur ^{M}
golfista ^{M}
Golfspieler ^{M}
golfista ^{M}

hand-pulled cart
chariot ^{M} manuel
carrito ^{M} de mano ^{F}
Golf-Trolley ^{M}
carrello ^{M} da golf ^{M}

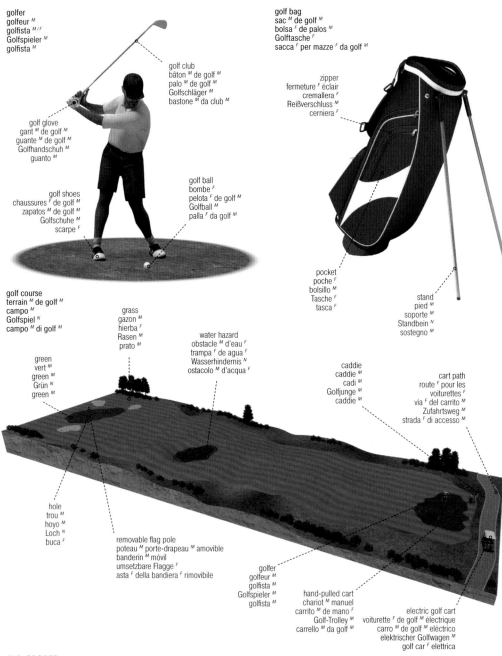

electric golf cart
voiturette ^{F} de golf ^{M} électrique
carro ^{M} de golf ^{M} eléctrico
elektrischer Golfwagen ^{M}
golf car ^{F} elettrica

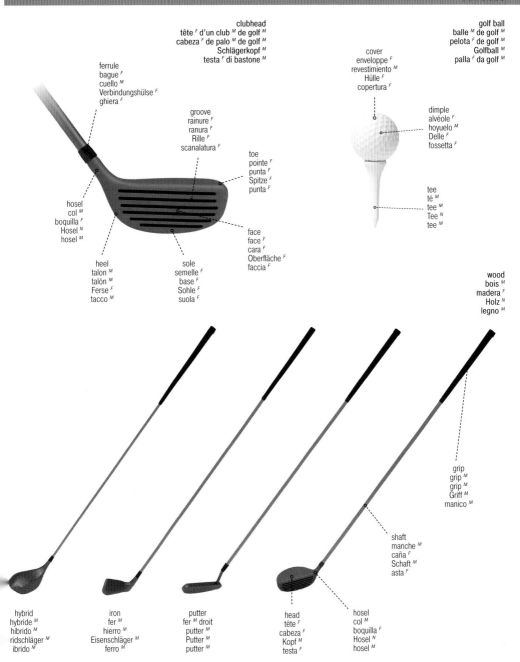

clubhead
tête F d'un club M de golf M
cabeza F de palo M de golf M
Schlägerkopf M
testa F di bastone M

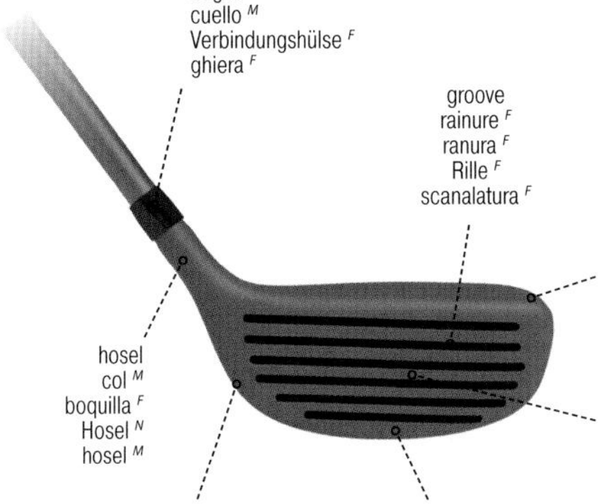
ferrule
bague F
cuello M
Verbindungshülse F
ghiera F
groove
rainure F
ranura F
Rille F
scanalatura F
toe
pointe F
punta F
Spitze F
punta F
hosel
col M
boquilla F
Hosel N
hosel M
face
face F
cara F
Oberfläche F
faccia F
heel
talon M
talón M
Ferse F
tacco M
sole
semelle F
base F
Sohle F
suola F

golf ball
balle M de golf M
pelota F de golf M
Golfball M
palla F da golf M

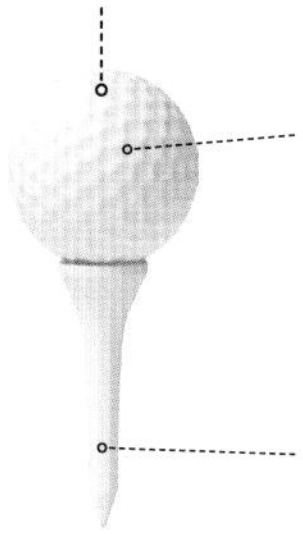
cover
enveloppe F
revestimiento M
Hülle F
copertura F
dimple
alvéole F
hoyuelo M
Delle F
fossetta F
tee
té M
tee M
Tee N
tee M

wood
bois M
madera F
Holz N
legno M

grip
grip M
grip M
Griff M
manico M
shaft
manche M
caña F
Schaft M
asta F
hybrid
hybride M
híbrido M
ridschläger M
ibrido M
iron
fer M
hierro M
Eisenschläger M
ferro M
putter
fer M droit
putter M
Putter M
putter M
head
tête F
cabeza F
Kopf M
testa F
hosel
col M
boquilla F
Hosel N
hosel M

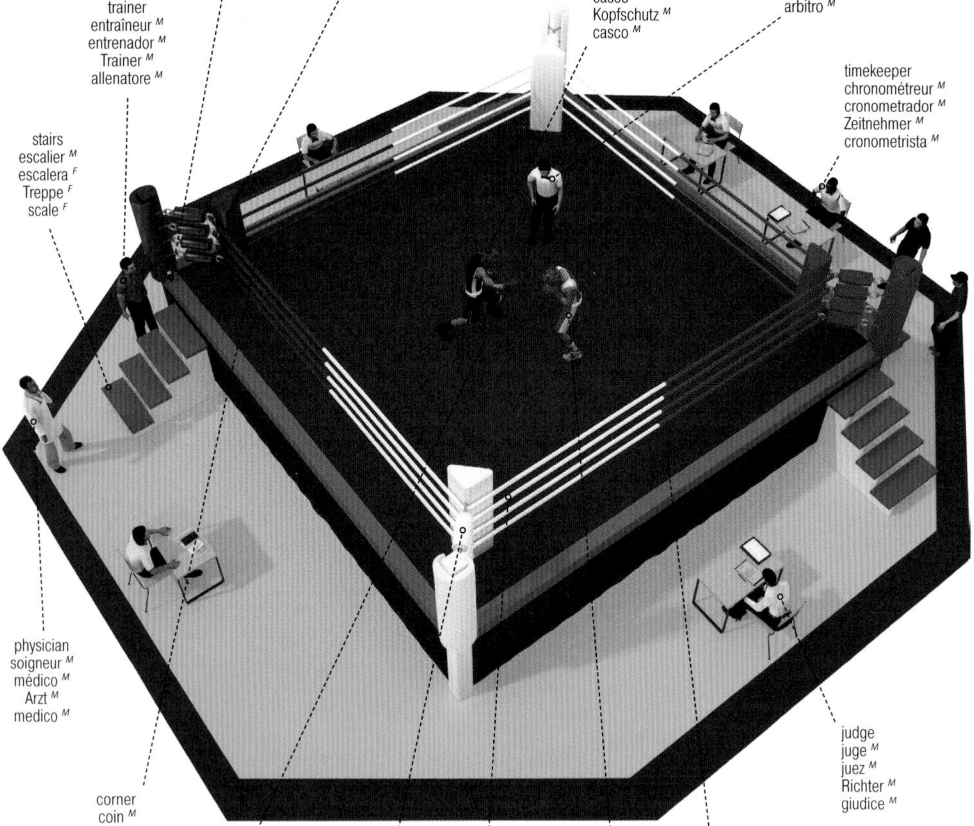

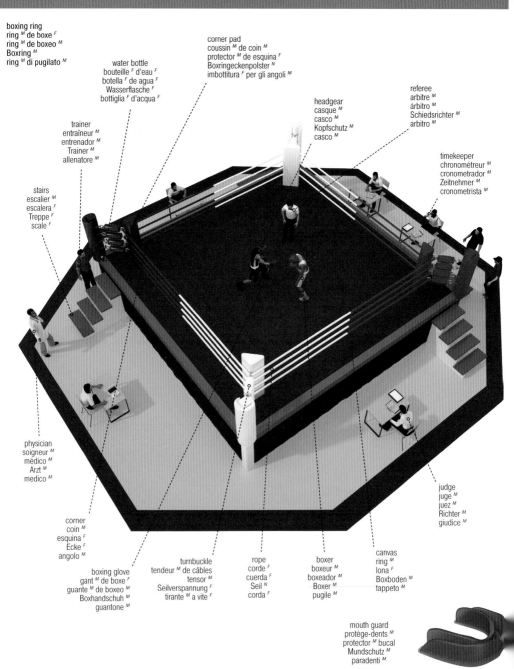

boxing ring
ring M de boxe F
ring M de boxeo M
Boxring M
ring M di pugilato M
water bottle
bouteille F d'eau F
botella F de agua F
Wasserflasche F
bottiglia F d'acqua F
corner pad
coussin M de coin M
protector M de esquina F
Boxringeckenpolster N
imbottitura F per gli angoli M
headgear
casque M
casco M
Kopfschutz M
casco M
referee
arbitre M
árbitro M
Schiedsrichter M
arbitro M
trainer
entraîneur M
entrenador M
Trainer M
allenatore M
timekeeper
chronométreur M
cronometrador M
Zeitnehmer M
cronometrista M
stairs
escalier M
escalera F
Treppe F
scale F
physician
soigneur M
médico M
Arzt M
medico M
judge
juge M
juez M
Richter M
giudice M
corner
coin M
esquina F
Ecke F
angolo M
boxing glove
gant M de boxe F
guante M de boxeo M
Boxhandschuh M
guantone M
turnbuckle
tendeur M de câbles
tensor M
Seilverspannung F
tirante M a vite F
rope
corde F
cuerda F
Seil N
corda F
boxer
boxeur M
boxeador M
Boxer M
pugile M
canvas
ring M
lona F
Boxboden M
tappeto M

mouth guard
protège-dents M
protector M bucal
Mundschutz M
paradenti M

freestanding heavy bag
punching-bag [M] autoportant / sac [M] d'entraînement [M] autoportant
saco [M] de boxeo [M] con base [F]
Fußboden-Sandsack [M]
sacco [M] a pavimento [M]

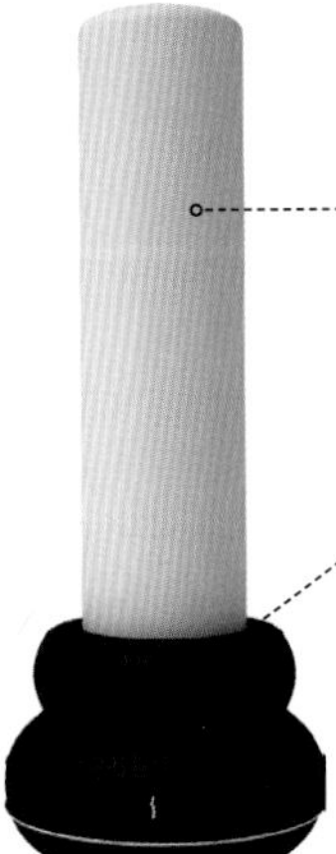

punching bag
punching-bag [M]
saco [M] de boxeo [M]
Boxsack [M]
sacco [M] da pugilato [M]

base
socle [M]
pedestal [M]
Sockel [M]
piedistallo [M]

heavy bag
punching-bag [M] / sac [M] d'entraînement [M]
saco [M] de boxeo [M] colgante
Mehrzweck-Sandsack [M]
sacco [M] sospeso

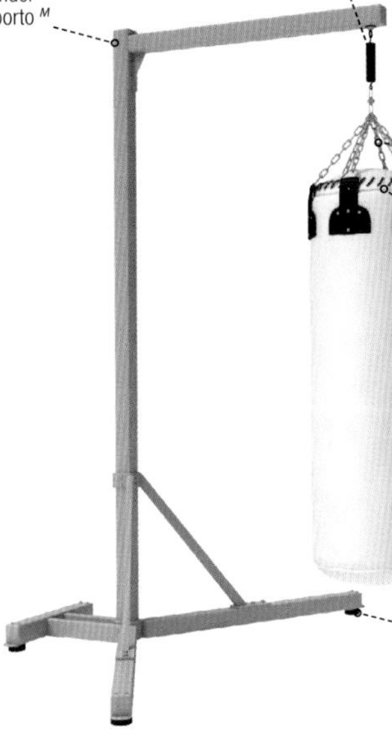

stand
support [M]
soporte [M]
Ständer [M]
supporto [M]

shock-absorbing spring
ressort [M] absorbeur [M] de chocs [M]
amortiguador [M]
Feder [F]
ammortizzatore [M]

chain
chaîne [F]
cadena [F]
Kette [F]
catena [F]

stitching
couture [F]
costura [F]
Naht [F]
cucitura [F]

rubber foot
pied [M] en caoutchouc [M]
pie [M] de goma [F]
Gummifuß [M]
piedino [M] in gomma [F]

boxing gloves
gants [M] de boxe [F]
guantes [M] de boxeo [M]
Boxhandschuhe [M]
guantoni [M]

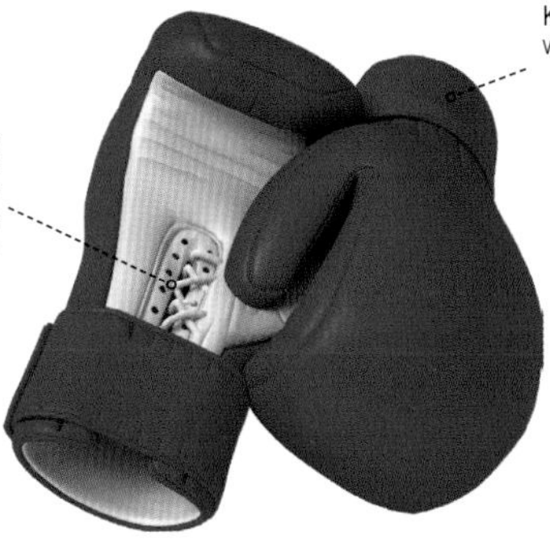

laces
lacets [M]
cordones [M]
Schnürung [F]
laccio [M]

strap
patte [F]
tira [F]
Klettverschluss [M]
velcro [M]

speed bag
ballon [M] rapide
pera [F] de boxeo [M]
Punchingball [M]
sacco [M] veloce

weight room
salle ^{F} de musculation ^{F}
sala ^{F} de pesas ^{F}
Kraftraum ^{M}
sala ^{F} pesi ^{M}

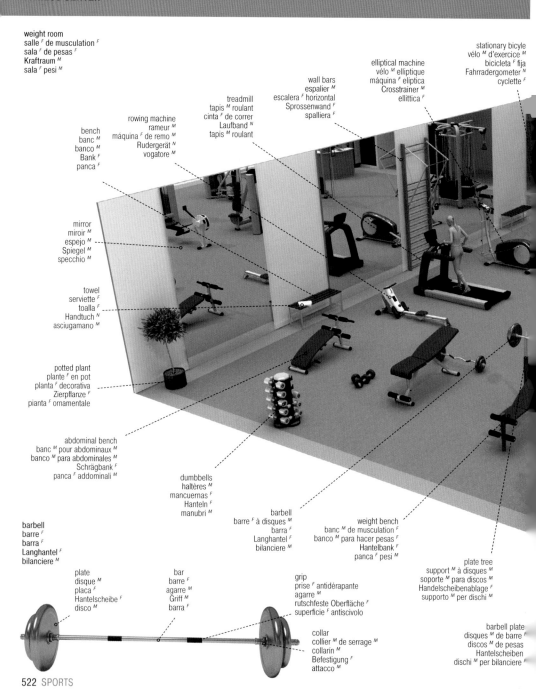

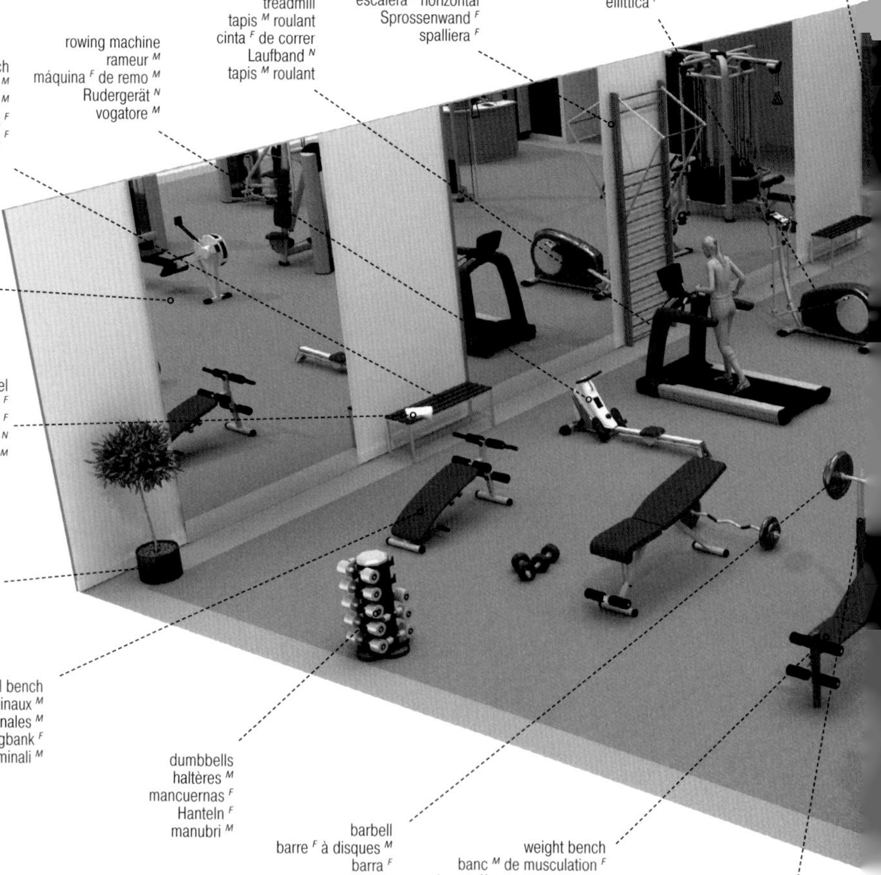

stationary bicyle
vélo ^{M} d'exercice ^{M}
bicicleta ^{F} fija
Fahrradergometer ^{N}
cyclette ^{F}

elliptical machine
vélo ^{M} elliptique
máquina ^{F} elíptica
Crosstrainer ^{M}
ellittica ^{F}

wall bars
espalier ^{M}
escalera ^{F} horizontal
Sprossenwand ^{F}
spalliera ^{F}

treadmill
tapis ^{M} roulant
cinta ^{F} de correr
Laufband ^{N}
tapis ^{M} roulant

rowing machine
rameur ^{M}
máquina ^{F} de remo ^{M}
Rudergerät ^{N}
vogatore ^{M}

bench
banc ^{M}
banco ^{M}
Bank ^{F}
panca ^{F}

mirror
miroir ^{M}
espejo ^{M}
Spiegel ^{M}
specchio ^{M}

towel
serviette ^{F}
toalla ^{F}
Handtuch ^{N}
asciugamano ^{M}

potted plant
plante ^{F} en pot
planta ^{F} decorativa
Zierpflanze ^{F}
pianta ^{F} ornamentale

abdominal bench
banc ^{M} pour abdominaux ^{M}
banco ^{M} para abdominales ^{M}
Schrägbank ^{F}
panca ^{F} addominali ^{M}

dumbbells
haltères ^{M}
mancuernas ^{F}
Hanteln ^{F}
manubri ^{M}

barbell
barre ^{F} à disques ^{M}
barra ^{F}
Langhantel ^{F}
bilanciere ^{M}

weight bench
banc ^{M} de musculation ^{F}
banco ^{M} para hacer pesas ^{F}
Hantelbank ^{F}
panca ^{F} pesi ^{M}

plate tree
support ^{M} à disques ^{M}
soporte ^{M} para discos ^{M}
Handelscheibenablage ^{F}
supporto ^{M} per dischi ^{M}

barbell
barre ^{F}
barra ^{F}
Langhantel ^{F}
bilanciere ^{M}

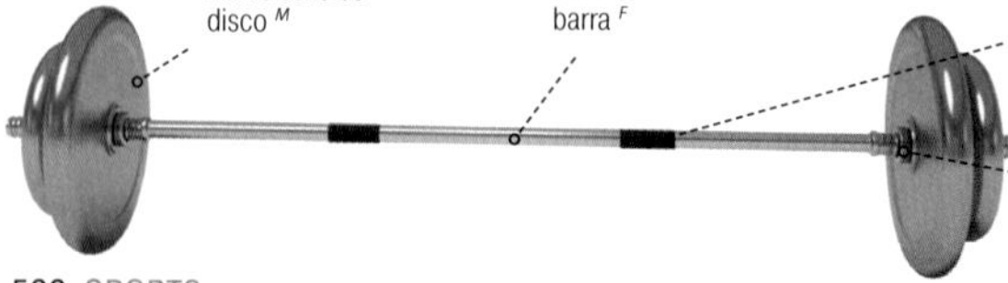

plate
disque ^{M}
placa ^{F}
Hantelscheibe ^{F}
disco ^{M}

bar
barre ^{F}
agarre ^{M}
Griff ^{M}
barra ^{F}

grip
prise ^{F} antidérapante
agarre ^{M}
rutschfeste Oberfläche ^{F}
superficie ^{F} antiscivolo

collar
collier ^{M} de serrage ^{M}
collarín ^{M}
Befestigung ^{F}
attacco ^{M}

barbell plate
disques ^{M} de barre ^{F}
discos ^{M} de pesas
Hantelscheiben
dischi ^{M} per bilanciere ^{F}

weight machine
machine F de musculation F
máqina F de pesas F
ainingsgerät N mit Gewichten N
attrezzo M con pesi M

locker
casier M
casillero M
Spind M
armadietto M

clock
horloge F
reloj M
Uhr F
orologio M

stack machine
machine F à poulies F
máquina F para brazos M
Kabelzuggerät N
attrezzo M multifunzione

entry door
porte F d'entrée F
puerta F de entrada F
Eingangstür F
ingresso M

vending machine
distributrice F
máquina F expendedora
Getränkeautomat M
distributore M automatico

reception
réception M
recepción F
Rezeption F
banco M reception F

table and chairs
table F avec chaises F
mesa F con sillas F
Tisch mit Stühlen M
tavolo M con sedie F

calf machine
appareil M pour les mollets M
máquina F para pantorrillas F
Wadentrainer M
attrezzo M per polpacci M

leg abduction machine
appareil M d'abduction F des jambes F
máquina F de cintura F
Oberschenkelmuskulaturtrainer M
attrezzo M per abduzione F gambe F

cable crossover machine
double poulie F
máquina F cruzada
Kabelzugstation F
macchina F a cavi M incrociati

disinfectants
désinfectants M
desinfectantes M
Desinfektionsmittel N
disinfettanti M

shelving
étagère F
estante M
Regal N
scaffale M

pec machine
machine F à pectoraux M
máquina F de pecho M
Brustmuskeltrainer M
attrezzo M per pettorali M

barbell
barre F à disques M
barra F corta
Hantel F
bilanciere M

leg extension machine
appareil M pour extension F des jambes F
máquina F de piernas F
Beinbeugermaschine F
attrezzo M per potenziamento M gambe F

wastebasket
corbeille F à papier M
papelera F
Papierkorb M
cestino M per la carta F

paper towel
essuie-tout
rollo M de papel M
Papiertuch N
panno M di carta F

reception area
comptoir [M] d'accueil [M]
área [F] de recepción [F]
Rezeption [F]
banco [M] reception [F]

bottled water
bouteille [F] d'eau [F]
botella [F] de agua [F]
Wasserflasche [F]
acqua [F] in bottiglia [F]

flower vase
vase [M] à fleurs [F]
jarrón [M] de flores [F]
Blumenvase [F]
vaso [M] di fiori [M]

laptop computer
ordinateur [M] portatif
computadora [F] portátil
Laptop [M]
computer [M] portatile

desk
comptoir [M]
mostrador [M]
Theke [F]
banco [M]

locker
casier [M]
casillero [M]
Schließfach [N]
armadietto [M]

door
porte [F]
puerta [F]
Tür [F]
sportello [M]

lock
verrou [M]
cierre [M]
Schloss [N]
serratura [F]

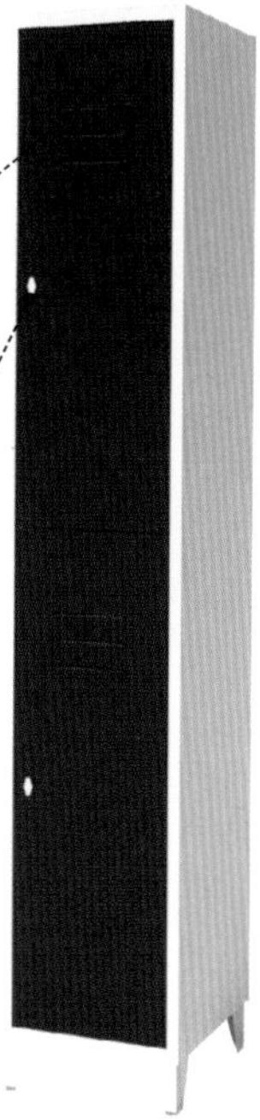

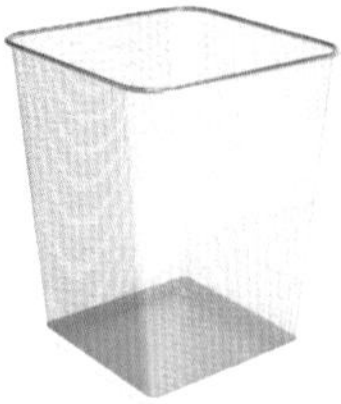

wastebasket
corbeille [F] à papier [M]
papelera [F]
Papierkorb [M]
cestino [M] per la carta [F]

cleaning area
poste [M] de nettoyage [M]
área [F] de limpieza [F]
Reinigungsbereich [M]
area [F] pulizia [F]

disinfectant
désinfectant [M]
desinfectante [M]
Desinfektionsmittel [N]
disinfettante [M]

shelf
étagère [F]
estante [M]
Regal [N]
mensola [F]

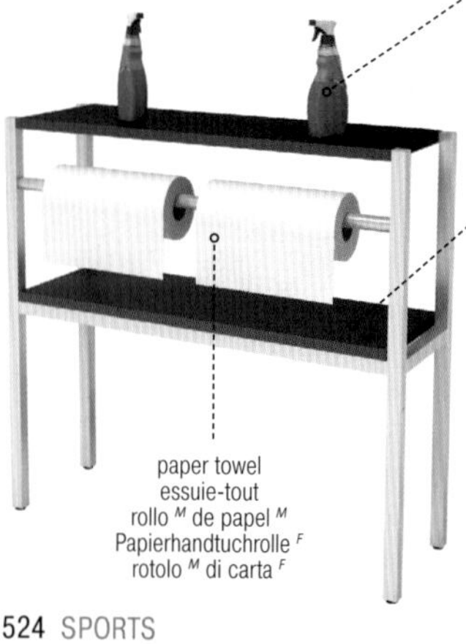

paper towel
essuie-tout
rollo [M] de papel [M]
Papierhandtuchrolle [F]
rotolo [M] di carta [F]

bench
banc [M]
banco [M]
Bank [F]
panca [F]

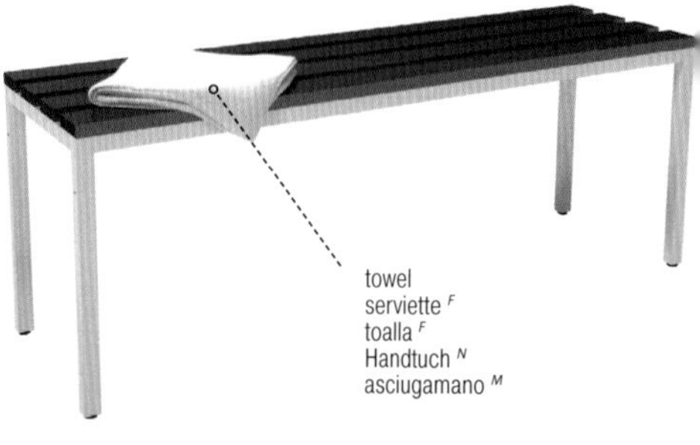

towel
serviette [F]
toalla [F]
Handtuch [N]
asciugamano [M]

fixed dumbbells
haltères ^{M} préchargés
mancuernas ^{F} fijas
Hantelgewichte ^{N}
manubri ^{M} fissi

cable crossover machine
double poulie ^{F}
máquina ^{F} de brazos ^{M} uso ^{M} general
Multikraftstation ^{F}
attrezzo ^{M} a cavi ^{M} incrociati

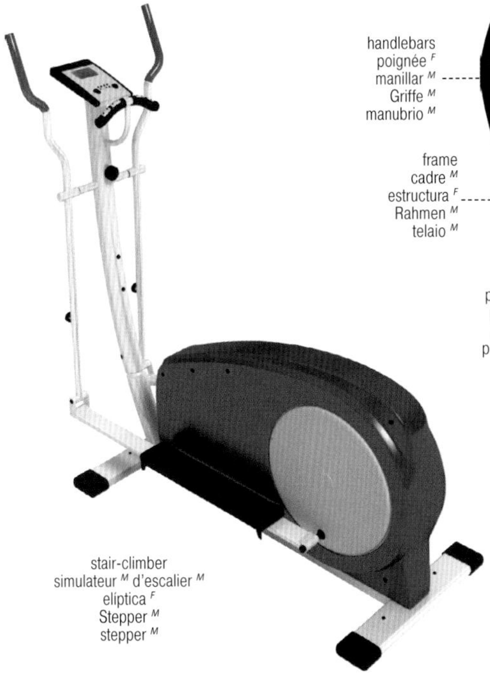

stair-climber
simulateur ^{M} d'escalier ^{M}
elíptica ^{F}
Stepper ^{M}
stepper ^{M}

stationary bicycle
vélo ^{M} d'exercice ^{M}
bicicleta ^{F} fija
Fahrradergometer ^{N}
cyclette ^{F}

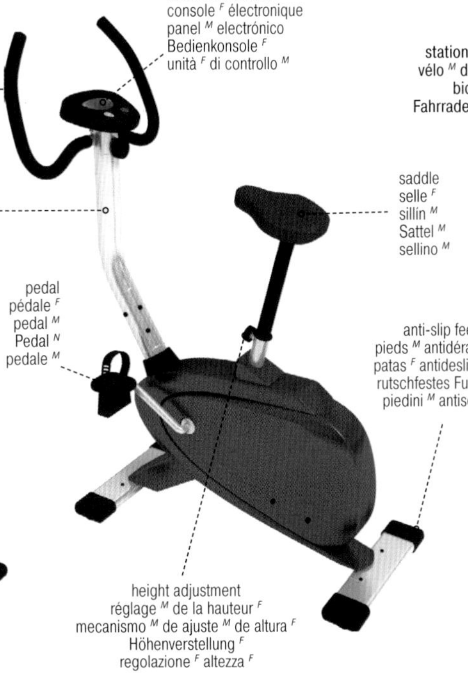
electronic console
console ^{F} électronique
panel ^{M} electrónico
Bedienkonsole ^{F}
unità ^{F} di controllo ^{M}
handlebars
poignée ^{F}
manillar ^{M}
Griffe ^{M}
manubrio ^{M}
frame
cadre ^{M}
estructura ^{F}
Rahmen ^{M}
telaio ^{M}
saddle
selle ^{F}
sillín ^{M}
Sattel ^{M}
sellino ^{M}
pedal
pédale ^{F}
pedal ^{M}
Pedal ^{N}
pedale ^{M}
anti-slip feet
pieds ^{M} antidérapants
patas ^{F} antideslizantes
rutschfestes Fußteil ^{N}
piedini ^{M} antiscivolo
height adjustment
réglage ^{M} de la hauteur ^{F}
mecanismo ^{M} de ajuste ^{M} de altura ^{F}
Höhenverstellung ^{F}
regolazione ^{F} altezza ^{F}

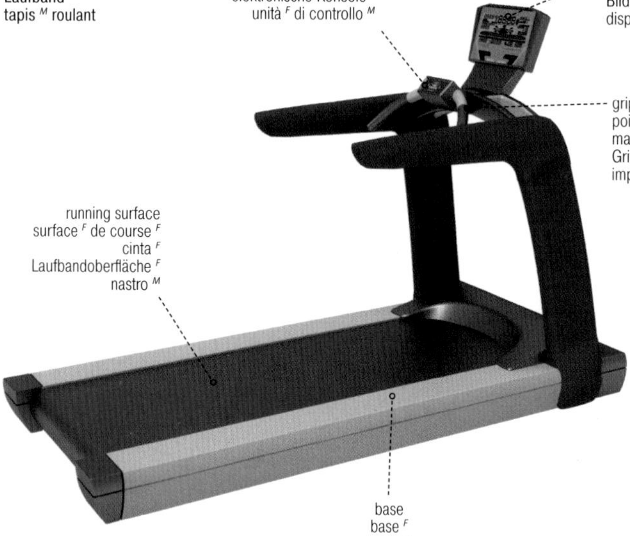
treadmill
tapis^{M} roulant
cinta^{F} de correr
Laufband^{N}
tapis^{M} roulant
electronic console
console^{F} électronique
panel^{M} de control^{M}
elektronische Konsole^{F}
unità^{F} di controllo^{M}
display
écran^{M}
pantalla^{F}
Bildschirm^{M}
display^{M}
grip
poignée^{F}
manillar^{M}
Griff^{M}
impugnatura^{F}
running surface
surface^{F} de course^{F}
cinta^{F}
Laufbandoberfläche^{F}
nastro^{M}
base
base^{F}
base^{F}
Rahmen^{M}
base^{F}

barbell plates and tree
disques^{M} pour barres^{F} et support^{M}
discos^{M} y árbol^{M} de pesas^{F}
Hantelscheiben^{F} und Ständer^{M}
dischi^{M} per bilanciere^{M} con supporto^{M}

adjustable dumbbell
haltère^{M} ajustable
mancuerna^{F} ajustable
verstellbare Hantel^{F}
manubrio^{M} regolabile

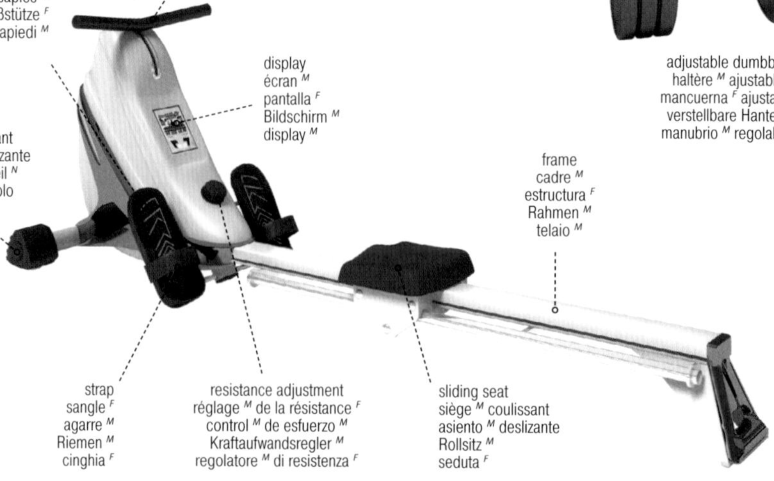
rowing machine
rameur^{M}
máquina^{F} de remo^{M}
Rudergerät^{N}
vogatore^{M}
handle
poignée^{F}
mango^{M}
Griff^{M}
impugnatura^{F}
footrest
repose-pieds^{M}
reposapiés^{M}
Fußstütze^{F}
puntapiedi^{M}
display
écran^{M}
pantalla^{F}
Bildschirm^{M}
display^{M}
anti-slip foot
pied^{M} antidérapant
superficie^{F} antideslizante
rutschfestes Fußteil^{N}
piedini^{M} antiscivolo
frame
cadre^{M}
estructura^{F}
Rahmen^{M}
telaio^{M}
strap
sangle^{F}
agarre^{M}
Riemen^{M}
cinghia^{F}
resistance adjustment
réglage^{M} de la résistance^{F}
control^{M} de esfuerzo^{M}
Kraftaufwandsregler^{M}
regolatore^{M} di resistenza^{F}
sliding seat
siège^{M} coulissant
asiento^{M} deslizante
Rollsitz^{M}
seduta^{F}

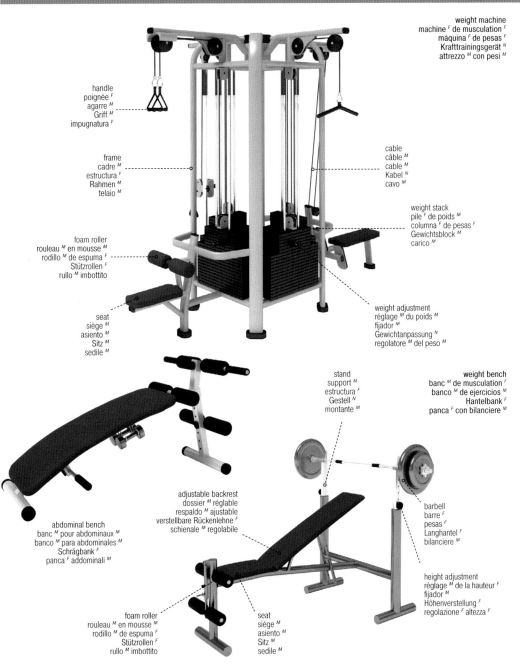

weight machine
machine [F] de musculation [F]
máquina [F] de pesas [F]
Krafttrainingsgerät [N]
attrezzo [M] con pesi [M]
handle
poignée [F]
agarre [M]
Griff [M]
impugnatura [F]
frame
cadre [M]
estructura [F]
Rahmen [M]
telaio [M]
cable
câble [M]
cable [M]
Kabel [N]
cavo [M]
weight stack
pile [F] de poids [M]
columna [F] de pesas [F]
Gewichtsblock [M]
carico [M]
foam roller
rouleau [M] en mousse [M]
rodillo [M] de espuma [F]
Stützrollen [F]
rullo [M] imbottito
seat
siège [M]
asiento [M]
Sitz [M]
sedile [M]
weight adjustment
réglage [M] du poids [M]
fijador [M]
Gewichtanpassung [N]
regolatore [M] del peso [M]

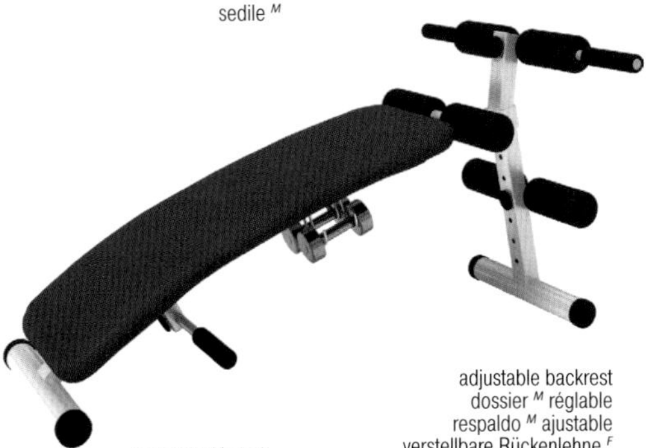
abdominal bench
banc [M] pour abdominaux [M]
banco [M] para abdominales [M]
Schrägbank [F]
panca [F] addominali [M]

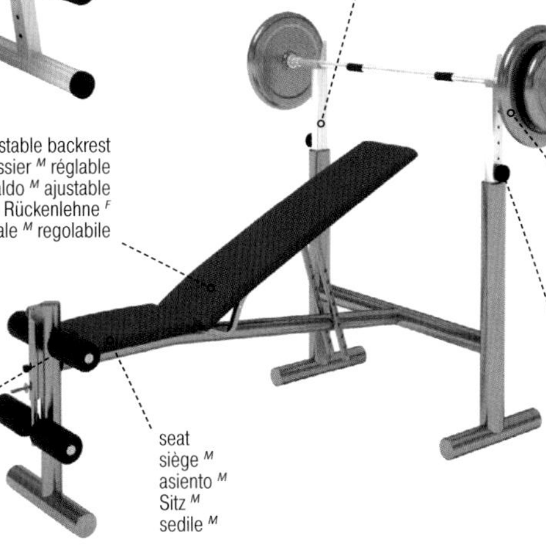
weight bench
banc [M] de musculation [F]
banco [M] de ejercicios [M]
Hantelbank [F]
panca [F] con bilanciere [M]
stand
support [M]
estructura [F]
Gestell [N]
montante [M]
barbell
barre [F]
pesas [F]
Langhantel [F]
bilanciere [M]
adjustable backrest
dossier [M] réglable
respaldo [M] ajustable
verstellbare Rückenlehne [F]
schienale [M] regolabile
height adjustment
réglage [M] de la hauteur [F]
fijador [M]
Höhenverstellung [F]
regolazione [F] altezza [F]
foam roller
rouleau [M] en mousse [M]
rodillo [M] de espuma [F]
Stützrollen [F]
rullo [M] imbottito
seat
siège [M]
asiento [M]
Sitz [M]
sedile [M]

stack machine
machine ^{F} de musculation ^{F} à poulies ^{F}
máquina ^{F} de brazos ^{M}
Kabelzugbaum ^{M}
attrezzo ^{M} multifunzione

pec machine
machine ^{F} à épaules ^{F}
máquina ^{F} de hombros ^{M}
Brustmuskeltrainer ^{M}
attrezzo ^{F} per pettorali ^{M}

barbell stand
porte-haltère ^{M}
barra ^{F} de soporte ^{M}
Langhantelgestell ^{N}
supporto ^{M} bilanciere ^{M}

leg extension machine
appareil ^{M} pour extension ^{F} des jambes ^{F}
máquina ^{F} de piernas ^{F}
Beinbeugermaschine ^{F}
attezzo ^{M} per potenziamento ^{M} gambe ^{F}

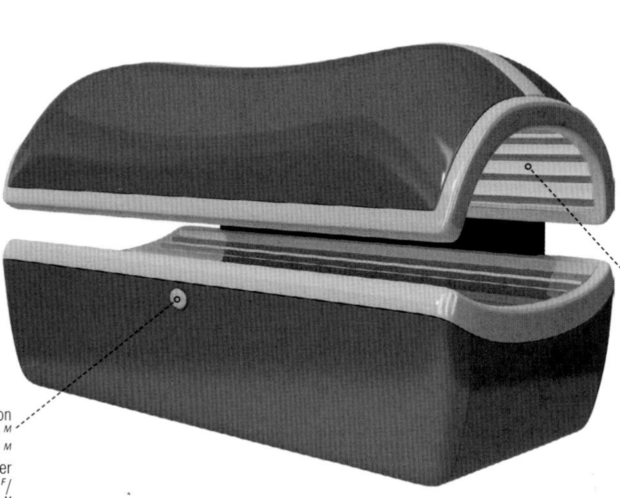
fluorescent lamps
lampes ^{F} fluorescentes
luces ^{F} fluorescentes
Fluoreszierende Lampen ^{F}
lampade ^{F} fluorescenti
on/off button
bouton ^{M} marche ^{F}/arrêt ^{M}
botón ^{M} de encendido ^{M}
An-/Aus-Schalter
pulsante ^{M} di accensione ^{F}/ spegnimento ^{M}

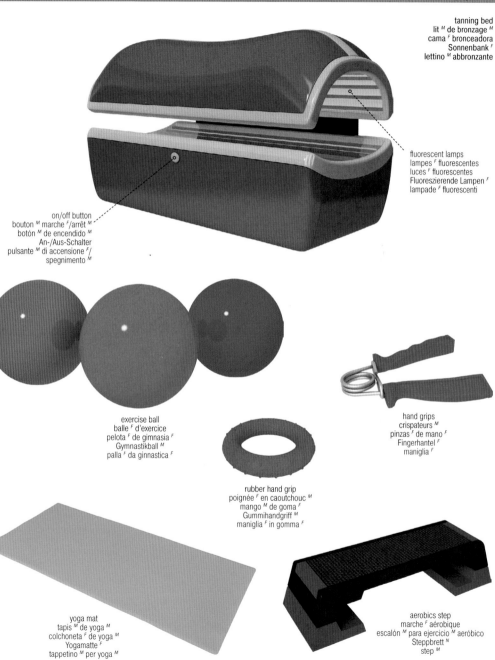

tanning bed
lit ^{M} de bronzage ^{M}
cama ^{F} bronceadora
Sonnenbank ^{F}
lettino ^{M} abbronzante

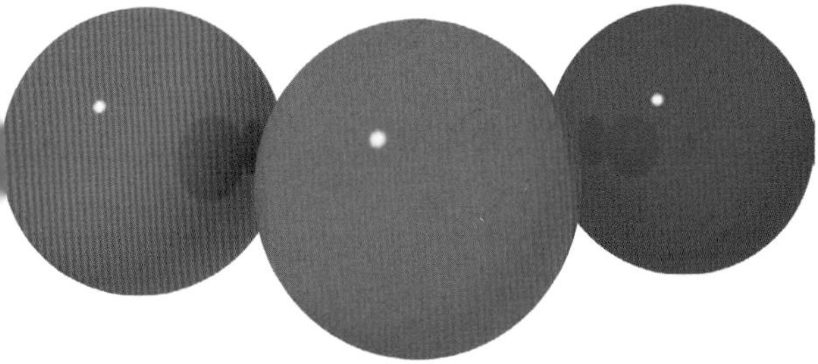

exercise ball
balle ^{F} d'exercice
pelota ^{F} de gimnasia ^{F}
Gymnastikball ^{M}
palla ^{F} da ginnastica ^{F}

hand grips
crispateurs ^{M}
pinzas ^{F} de mano ^{F}
Fingerhantel ^{F}
maniglia ^{F}

rubber hand grip
poignée ^{F} en caoutchouc ^{M}
mango ^{M} de goma ^{F}
Gummihandgriff ^{M}
maniglia ^{F} in gomma ^{F}

yoga mat
tapis ^{M} de yoga ^{M}
colchoneta ^{F} de yoga ^{M}
Yogamatte ^{F}
tappetino ^{M} per yoga ^{M}

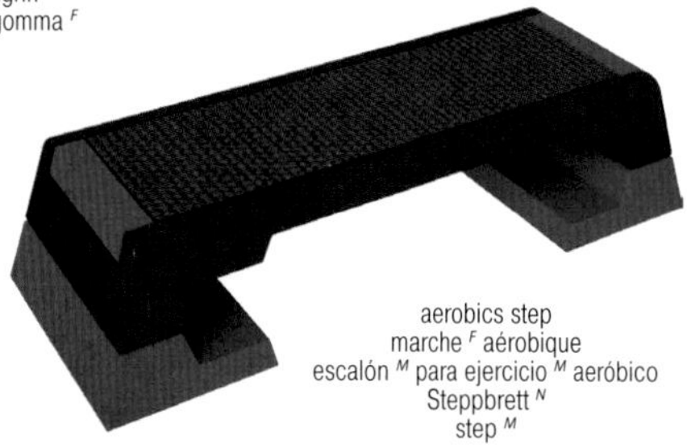

aerobics step
marche ^{F} aérobique
escalón ^{M} para ejercicio ^{M} aeróbico
Steppbrett ^{N}
step ^{M}

shoulder stand
chandelle F sur épaules F
estiramiento M de piernas F sobre los hombros M
Kerze F
candela F

standing leg lift
élévation latérale de la jambe – debou
elevación F sobre una pierna F
Bein seitlich anheben N
sollevamento M di una gamba F

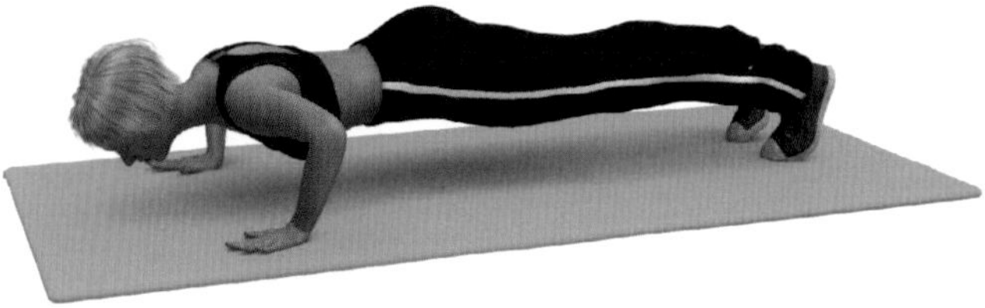

push-up
pompes F
flexiones F
Liegestütz M
flessione F

scissors
ciseaux M
tijeras F
Schere F
forbice F

forward bend
flexion F avant
estiramiento M para adelante
Vorwärtsbeugen N
piegamento M del busto M in avanti

side lunge
étirements [M] latéraux
estiramientos [M] laterales
seitlicher Ausfallschritt [M]
affondo [M] laterale

bra top
haut [M] de sport [M]
sostén [M] deportivo
Bustier [N]
top [M] sportivo

sweatpants
pantalon [M] d'exercice [M]
pantalones [M] de deporte [M]
Jogginghose [F]
pantaloni [M] della tuta [F]

sneakers
espadrilles [F]
zapatillas [F] deportivas
Turnschuhe [M]
scarpe [F] da ginnastica [F]

seated forward bend
fente [F] avant-assis
estiramiento [M] para adelante sentada en el suelo [M]
Vorwärtsbeuge [F] sitzend
piegamento [M] del busto [M] in avanti da seduti

shoulder stand scissors
ciseaux [M] avec chandelle [F] sur épaules [F]
tijereta [F] en posición [F] supina
Schere in Rückenlage [F]
forbice [F] in appoggio sulle spalle [F]

forward lunge
fente [F] avant
estiramiento [M] de piernas [F]
Ausfallschritt [M] nach vorne
allungo [M] avanti

Skateboarding

Planches ᶠ à roulettes ᶠ | Deporte ᴹ de patineta ᶠ | Skateboards ᴺ | skateboard ᴹ

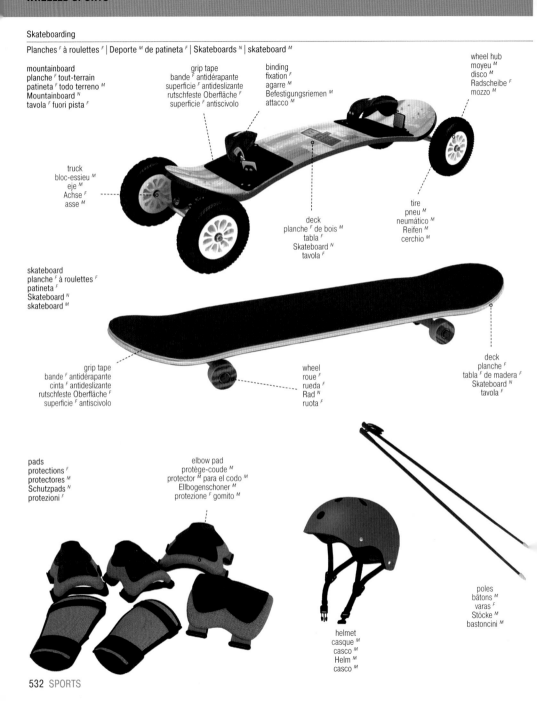

mountainboard
planche ᶠ tout-terrain
patineta ᶠ todo terreno ᴹ
Mountainboard ᴺ
tavola ᶠ fuori pista ᶠ

grip tape
bande ᶠ antidérapante
superficie ᶠ antideslizante
rutschfeste Oberfläche ᶠ
superficie ᶠ antiscivolo

binding
fixation ᶠ
agarre ᴹ
Befestigungsriemen ᴹ
attacco ᴹ

wheel hub
moyeu ᴹ
disco ᴹ
Radscheibe ᶠ
mozzo ᴹ

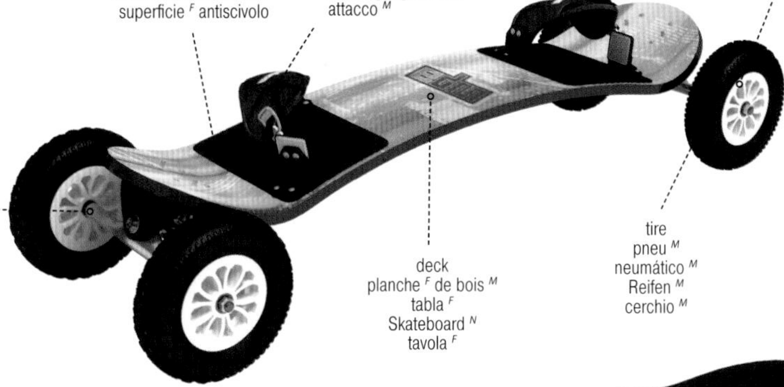

truck
bloc-essieu ᴹ
eje ᴹ
Achse ᶠ
asse ᴹ

deck
planche ᶠ de bois ᴹ
tabla ᶠ
Skateboard ᴺ
tavola ᶠ

tire
pneu ᴹ
neumático ᴹ
Reifen ᴹ
cerchio ᴹ

skateboard
planche ᶠ à roulettes ᶠ
patineta ᶠ
Skateboard ᴺ
skateboard ᴹ

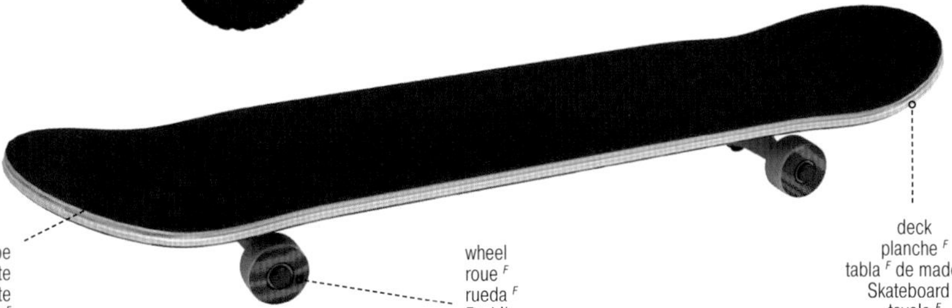

grip tape
bande ᶠ antidérapante
cinta ᶠ antideslizante
rutschfeste Oberfläche ᶠ
superficie ᶠ antiscivolo

wheel
roue ᶠ
rueda ᶠ
Rad ᴺ
ruota ᶠ

deck
planche ᶠ
tabla ᶠ de madera ᶠ
Skateboard ᴺ
tavola ᶠ

pads
protections ᶠ
protectores ᴹ
Schutzpads ᴺ
protezioni ᶠ

elbow pad
protège-coude ᴹ
protector ᴹ para el codo ᴹ
Ellbogenschoner ᴹ
protezione ᶠ gomito ᴹ

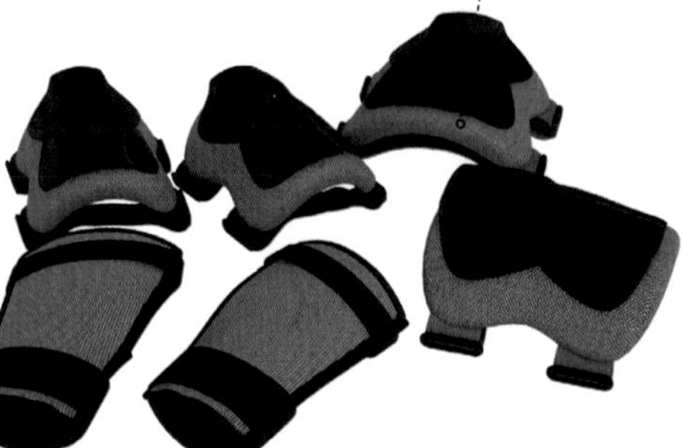

helmet
casque ᴹ
casco ᴹ
Helm ᴹ
casco ᴹ

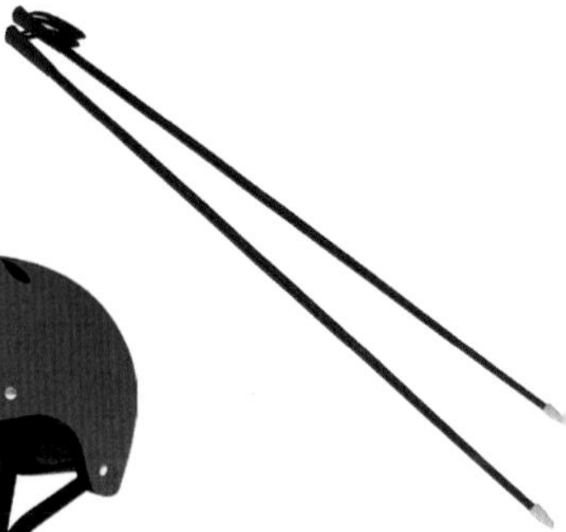

poles
bâtons ᴹ
varas ᶠ
Stöcke ᴹ
bastoncini ᴹ

half-pipe
rampe [F]
medio-tubo [M]
Halfpipe [F]
rampa half-pipe [F]

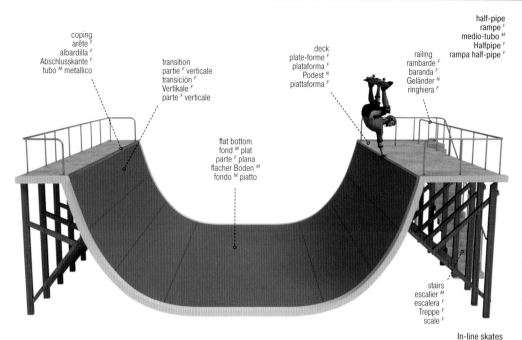

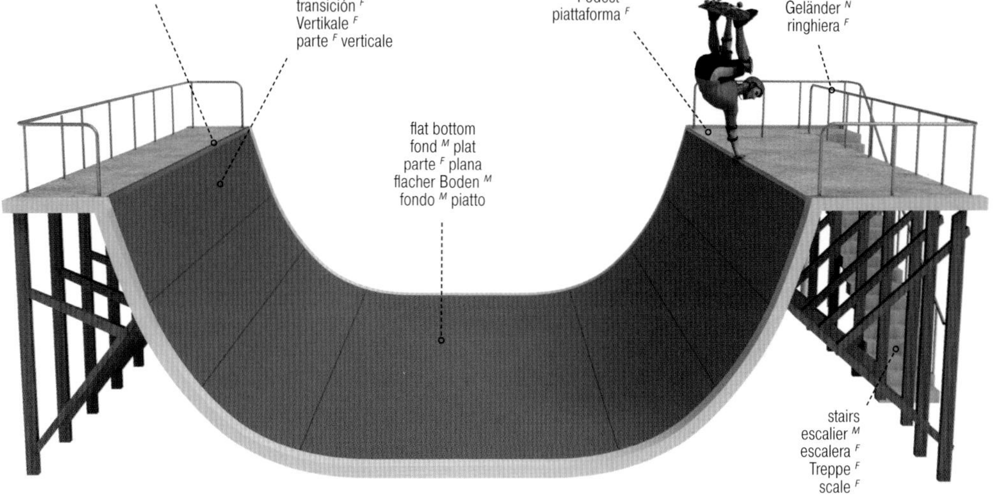
coping
arête [F]
albardilla [F]
Abschlusskante [F]
tubo [M] metallico
transition
partie [F] verticale
transición [F]
Vertikale [F]
parte [F] verticale
deck
plate-forme [F]
plataforma [F]
Podest [N]
piattaforma [F]
railing
rambarde [F]
baranda [F]
Geländer [N]
ringhiera [F]
flat bottom
fond [M] plat
parte [F] plana
flacher Boden [M]
fondo [M] piatto
stairs
escalier [M]
escalera [F]
Treppe [F]
scale [F]

In-line skates

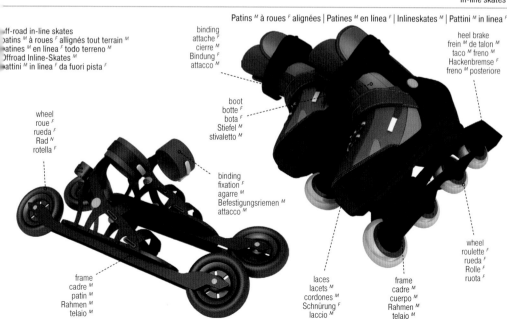

Patins [M] à roues [F] alignées | Patines [M] en línea [F] | Inlineskates [M] | Pattini [M] in linea [F]

ff-road in-line skates
atins [M] à roues [F] allignés tout terrain [M]
atines [M] en línea [F] todo terreno [M]
ffroad Inline-Skates [M]
attini [M] in linea [F] da fuori pista [F]

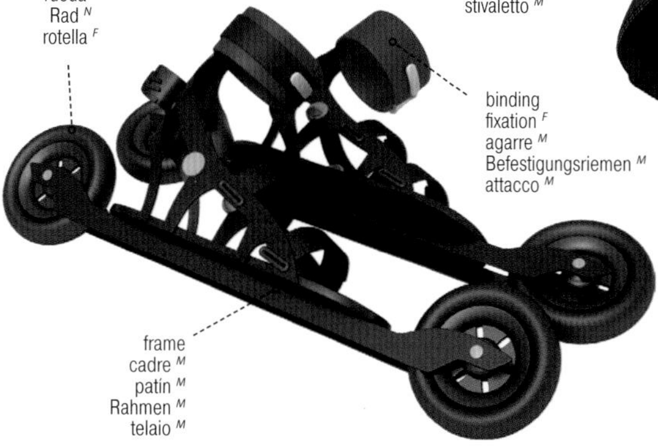
wheel
roue [F]
rueda [F]
Rad [N]
rotella [F]
binding
fixation [F]
agarre [M]
Befestigungsriemen [M]
attacco [M]
frame
cadre [M]
patín [M]
Rahmen [M]
telaio [M]

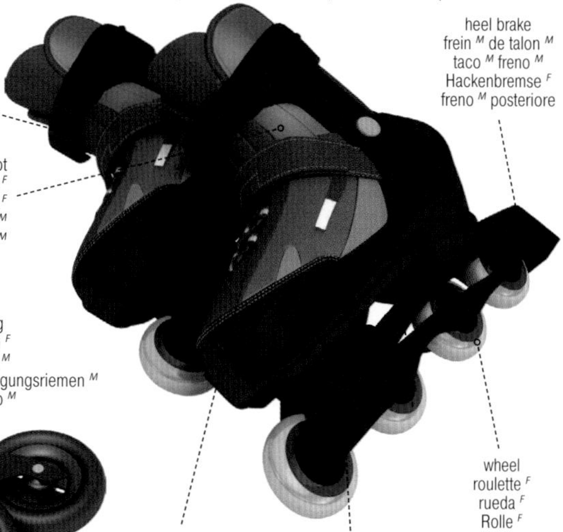
binding
attache [F]
cierre [M]
Bindung [F]
attacco [M]
boot
botte [F]
bota [F]
Stiefel [M]
stivaletto [M]
heel brake
frein [M] de talon [M]
taco [M] freno [M]
Hackenbremse [F]
freno [M] posteriore
laces
lacets [M]
cordones [M]
Schnürung [F]
laccio [M]
frame
cadre [M]
cuerpo [M]
Rahmen [M]
telaio [M]
wheel
roulette [F]
rueda [F]
Rolle [F]
ruota [F]

mountain bicycle
vélo [M] de montagne [F]
bicicleta [F] de montaña [F]
Mountainbike [N]
mountain bike [F]

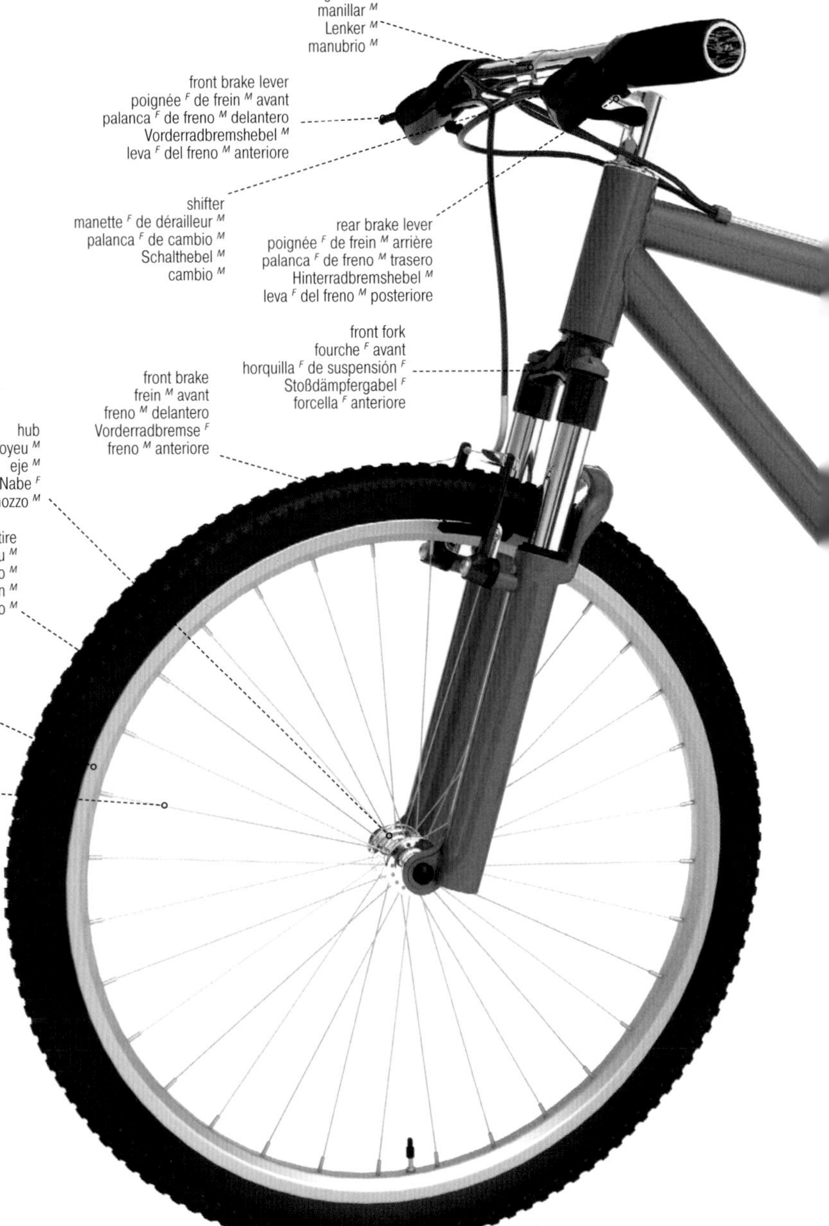

handlebars
guidon [M]
manillar [M]
Lenker [M]
manubrio [M]

front brake lever
poignée [F] de frein [M] avant
palanca [F] de freno [M] delantero
Vorderradbremshebel [M]
leva [F] del freno [M] anteriore

shifter
manette [F] de dérailleur [M]
palanca [F] de cambio [M]
Schalthebel [M]
cambio [M]

rear brake lever
poignée [F] de frein [M] arrière
palanca [F] de freno [M] trasero
Hinterradbremshebel [M]
leva [F] del freno [M] posteriore

front fork
fourche [F] avant
horquilla [F] de suspensión [F]
Stoßdämpfergabel [F]
forcella [F] anteriore

front brake
frein [M] avant
freno [M] delantero
Vorderradbremse [F]
freno [M] anteriore

hub
moyeu [M]
eje [M]
Nabe [F]
mozzo [M]

tire
pneu [M]
neumático [M]
Reifen [M]
pneumatico [M]

rim
jante [F]
llanta [F]
Felge [F]
cerchione [M]

spoke
rayon [M]
radio [M]
Speiche [F]
raggio [M]

road-racing bicycle
vélo ^{M} de course ^{F}
bicicleta ^{F} de carreras ^{F}
Rennrad ^{N}
bicicletta ^{F} da corsa ^{F}

seat
selle ^{F}
sillín ^{M}
Sattel ^{M}
sella ^{F}
frame
cadre ^{M}
armazón ^{M}
Rahmen ^{M}
telaio ^{M}
rear brake
frein ^{M} arrière
freno ^{M} trasero
Hinterradbremse ^{F}
freno ^{M} posteriore
rear derailleur
dérailleur ^{M} arrière
desviador ^{M} trasero
Schalterk ^{N}
deragliatore ^{M}
posteriore
chain
chaîne ^{F}
cadena ^{F}
Kette ^{F}
catena ^{F}
front derailleur
dérailleur ^{M} avant
desviador ^{M} delantero
Umwerfer ^{M}
deragliatore ^{M} anteriore
crankset
pédalier ^{M}
piñón ^{M}
Kurbelgarnitur ^{N}
corona ^{F}
stand
pied ^{M}
caballete ^{M}
Fahrradständer ^{M}
cavalletto ^{M}
pedal
pédale ^{F}
pedal ^{M}
Pedal ^{N}
pedale ^{M}

water jump
fossé [M] d'eau [F]
salto [M] de agua [F]
Wassergraben [M]
salto [M] in acqua [F]

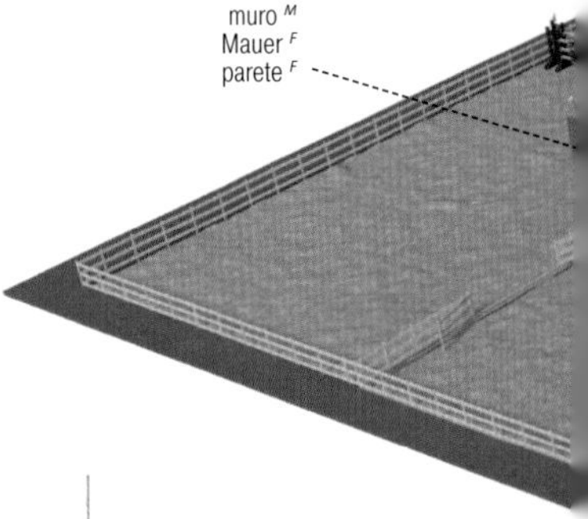

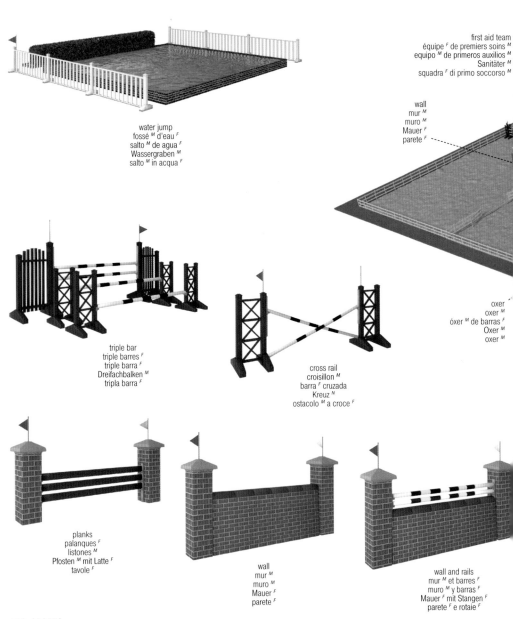

first aid team
équipe [F] de premiers soins [M]
equipo [M] de primeros auxilios [M]
Sanitäter [M]
squadra [F] di primo soccorso [M]

wall
mur [M]
muro [M]
Mauer [F]
parete [F]

oxer
oxer [M]
óxer [M] de barras [F]
Oxer [M]
oxer [M]

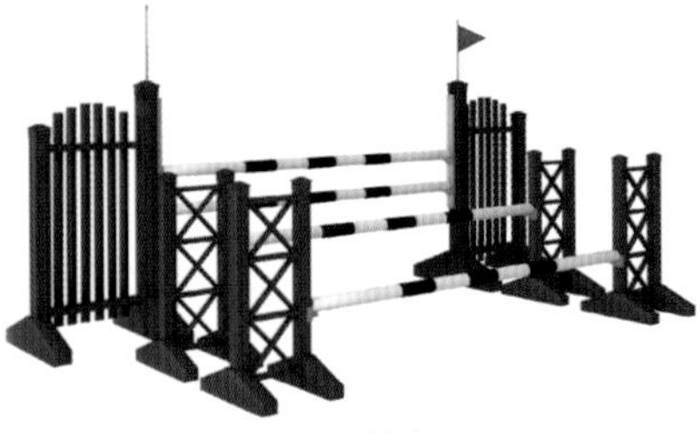

triple bar
triple barres [F]
triple barra [F]
Dreifachbalken [M]
tripla barra [F]

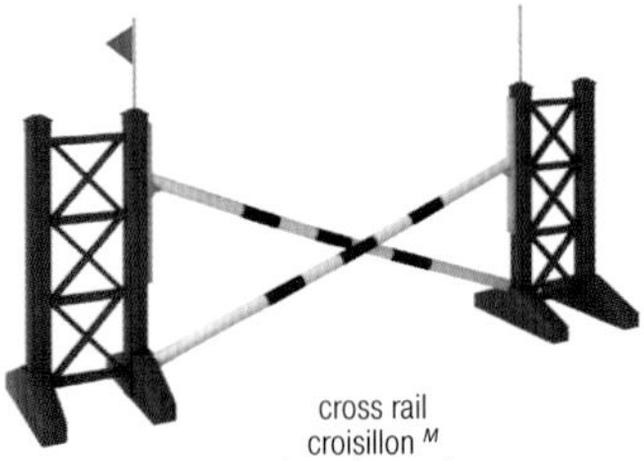

cross rail
croisillon [M]
barra [F] cruzada
Kreuz [N]
ostacolo [M] a croce [F]

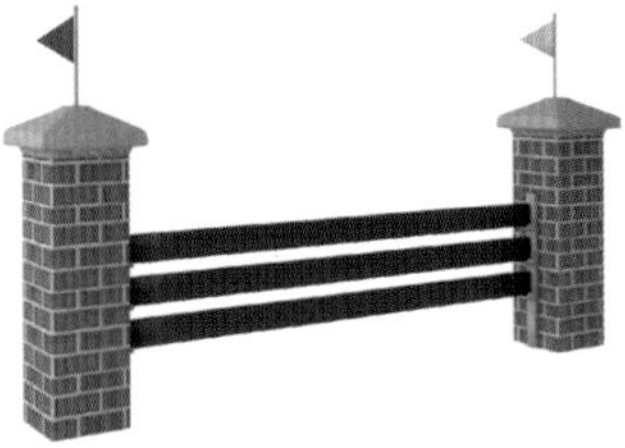

planks
palanques [F]
listones [M]
Pfosten [M] mit Latte [F]
tavole [F]

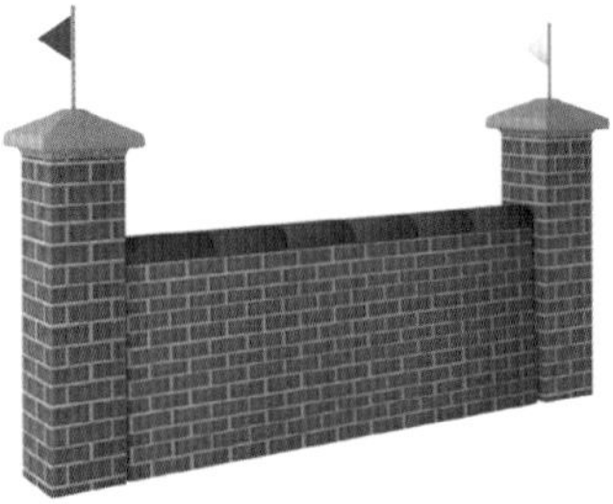

wall
mur [M]
muro [M]
Mauer [F]
parete [F]

wall and rails
mur [M] et barres [F]
muro [M] y barras [F]
Mauer [F] mit Stangen [F]
parete [F] e rotaie [F]

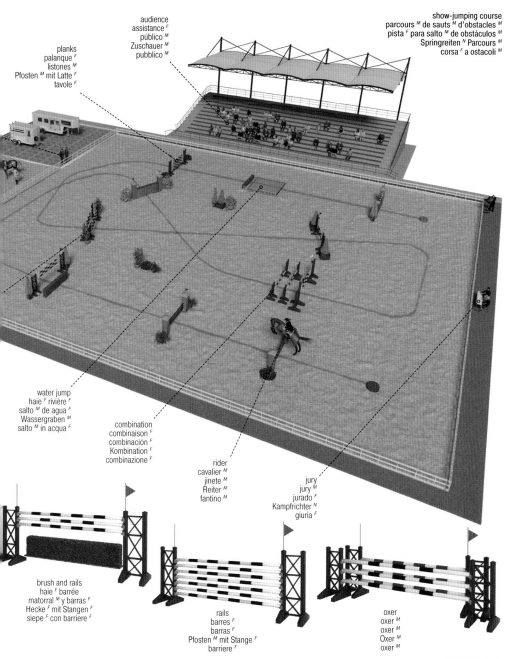

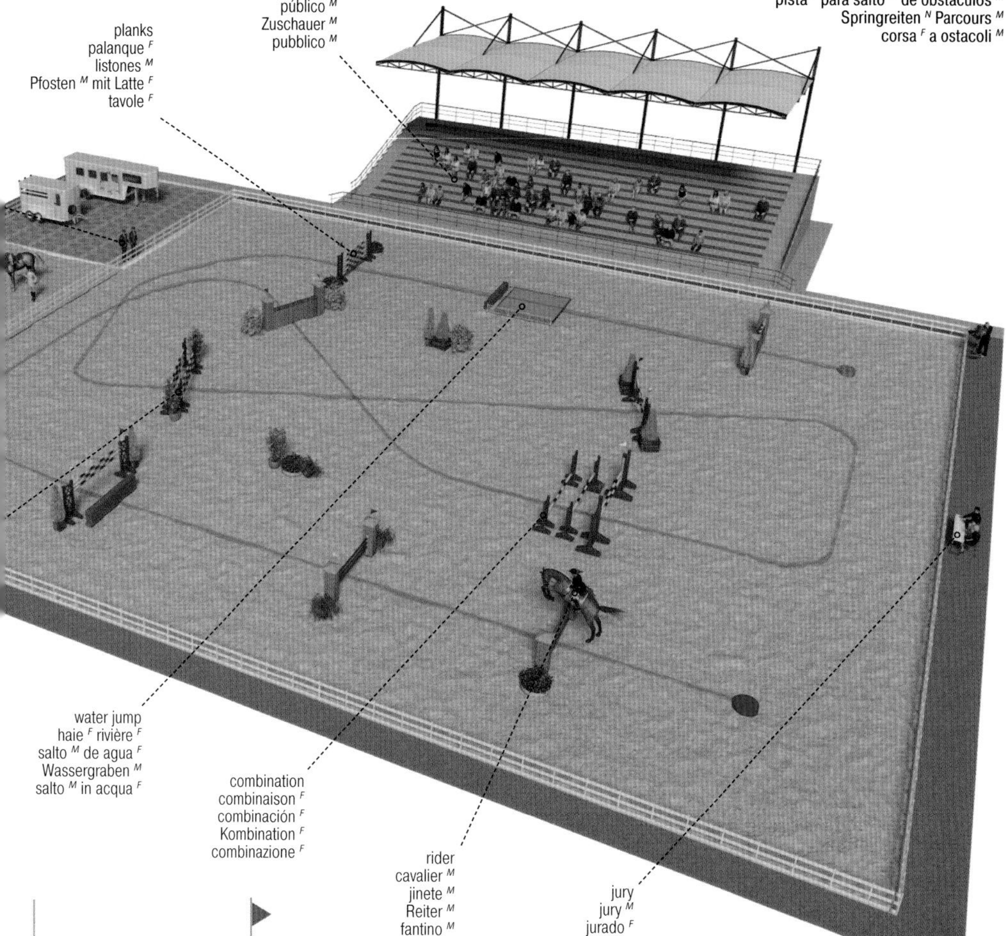
show-jumping course
parcours ^{M} de sauts ^{M} d'obstacles ^{M}
pista ^{F} para salto ^{M} de obstáculos ^{M}
Springreiten ^{N} Parcours ^{M}
corsa ^{F} a ostacoli ^{M}
audience
assistance ^{F}
público ^{M}
Zuschauer ^{M}
pubblico ^{M}
planks
palanque ^{F}
listones ^{M}
Pfosten ^{M} mit Latte ^{F}
tavole ^{F}
water jump
haie ^{F} rivière ^{F}
salto ^{M} de agua ^{F}
Wassergraben ^{M}
salto ^{M} in acqua ^{F}
combination
combinaison ^{F}
combinación ^{F}
Kombination ^{F}
combinazione ^{F}
rider
cavalier ^{M}
jinete ^{M}
Reiter ^{M}
fantino ^{M}
jury
jury ^{M}
jurado ^{F}
Kampfrichter ^{N}
giuria ^{F}

brush and rails
haie ^{F} barrée
matorral ^{M} y barras ^{F}
Hecke ^{F} mit Stangen ^{F}
siepe ^{F} con barriere ^{F}

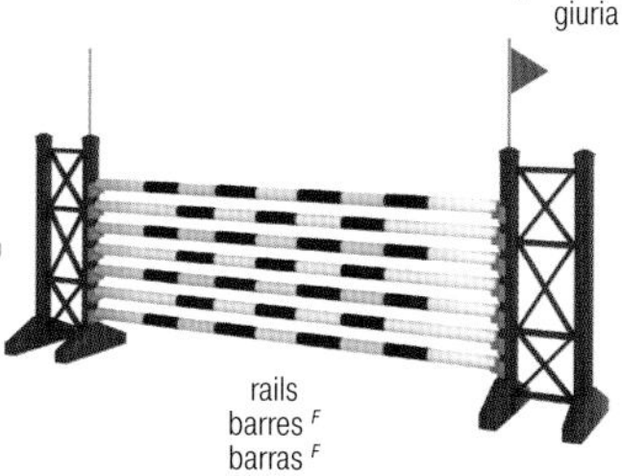

rails
barres ^{F}
barras ^{F}
Pfosten ^{M} mit Stange ^{F}
barriere ^{F}

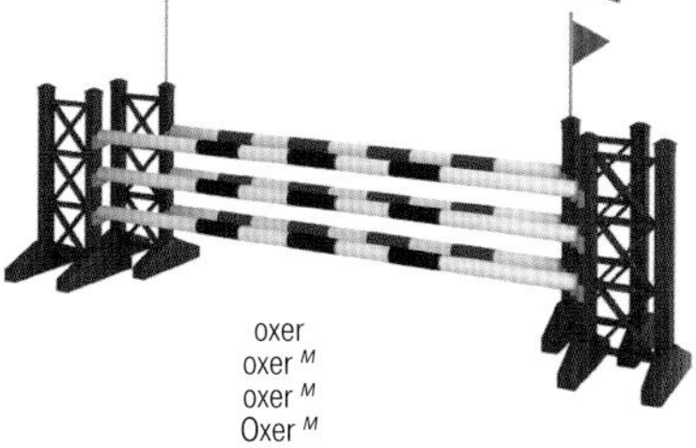

oxer
oxer ^{M}
oxer ^{M}
Oxer ^{M}
oxer ^{M}

English saddle
selle [F] anglaise
silla [F] de montar inglesa
Englischer Sattel [M]
sella [F] inglese

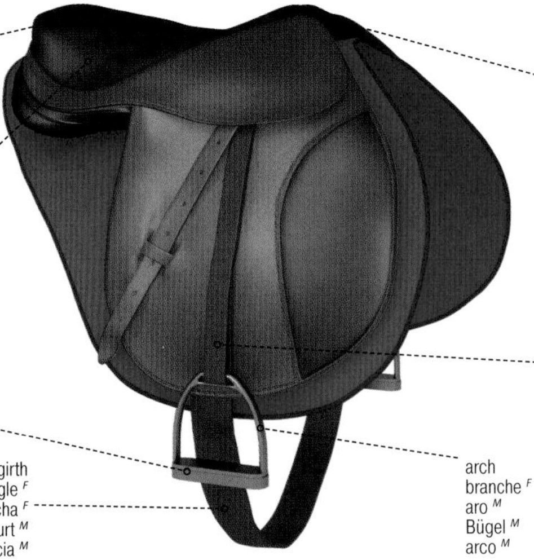
cantle
troussequin [M]
borrén [M] trasero
Hinterzwiesel [M]
paletta [F]
pommel
pommeau [M]
pomo [M]
Vorderzwiesel [M]
pomo [M]
seat
siège [M]
sillín [M]
Sitz [M]
seggio [M]
stirrup leather
étrivière [F]
correa [F]
Bügelriemen [M]
staffile [M]
stirrup
étrier [M]
estribo [M]
Steigbügel [M]
staffa [F]
arch
branche [F]
aro [M]
Bügel [M]
arco [M]
girth
sangle [F]
cincha [F]
Sattelgurt [M]
sottopancia [M]

rider
cavalier [M]
jinete [M]
Reiter [M]
fantino [M]

riding helmet
bombe [F]
casco [M]
Reithelm [M]
cap [M]
riding jacket
jaquette [F]
chaqueta [F] de montar
Reitjacke [F]
giacca [F] da equitazione [F]
saddle pad
tapis [M] de selle [F]
manta [F] de la silla [F]
Schabracke [F]
sottosella [F]
saddle
selle [F]
silla [F]
Sattel [M]
sella [F]
girth
sangle [F]
cincha [F]
Sattelgurt [M]
sottopancia [M]
coronet boot
botte [F] de couronne [F]
bota [F] de la corona [F] del casco [M]
Hufglocke [F]
paranocche [M]
jodhpurs
jodhpurs [M]
pantalones [M] de montar
Reithose [F]
pantaloni [M] da equitazione [F]
stirrup
étrier [M]
estribo [M]
Steigbügel [M]
staffa [F]

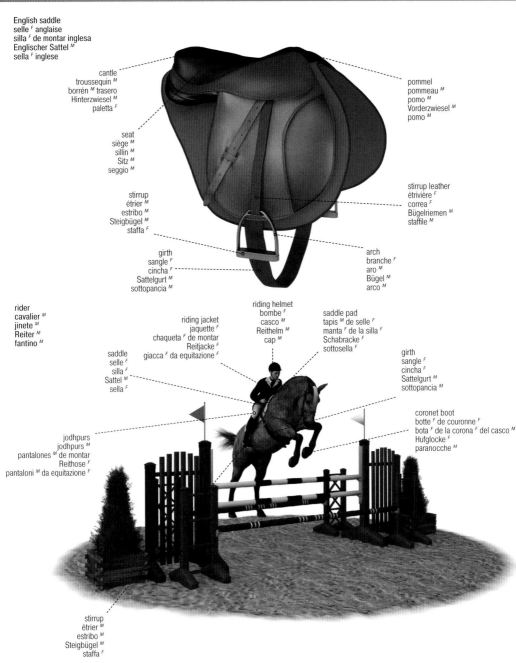

mounted racing
course F équestre
carreras F de caballos M
Pferderennen N
corsa F di cavalli M

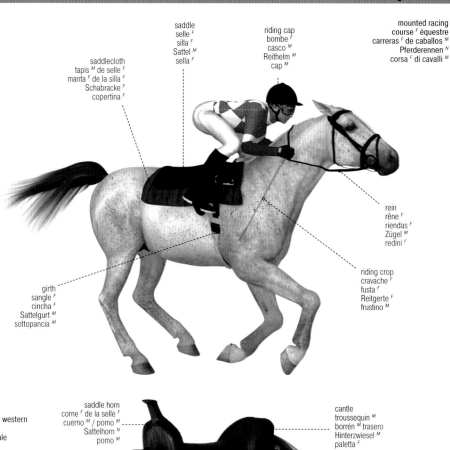

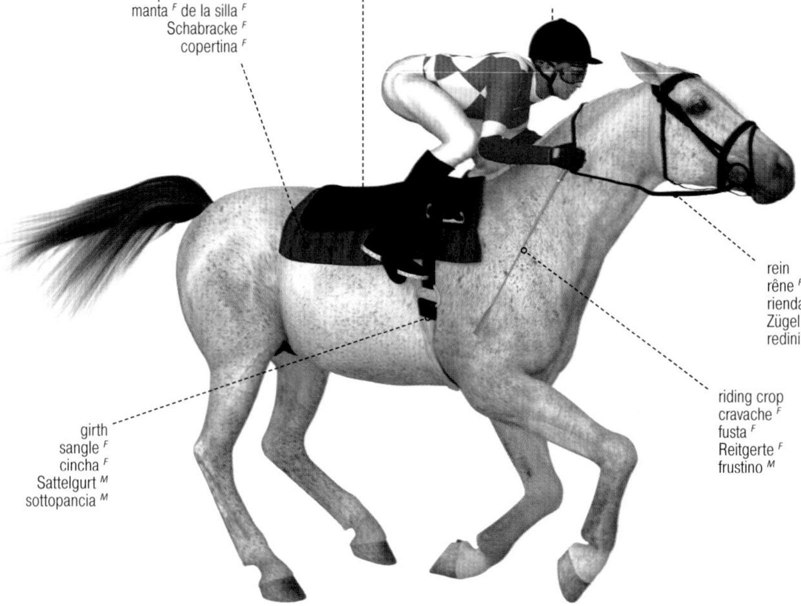
saddle
selle F
silla F
Sattel M
sella F
riding cap
bombe F
casco M
Reithelm M
cap M
saddlecloth
tapis M de selle F
manta F de la silla F
Schabracke F
copertina F
rein
rêne F
riendas F
Zügel M
redini F
riding crop
cravache F
fusta F
Reitgerte F
frustino M
girth
sangle F
cincha F
Sattelgurt M
sottopancia M

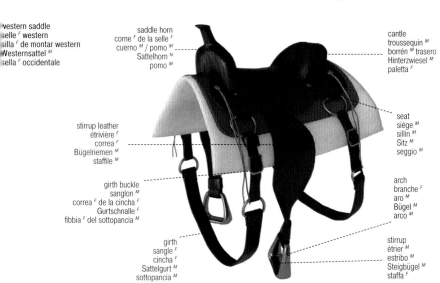

western saddle
selle F western
silla F de montar western
Westernsattel M
sella F occidentale

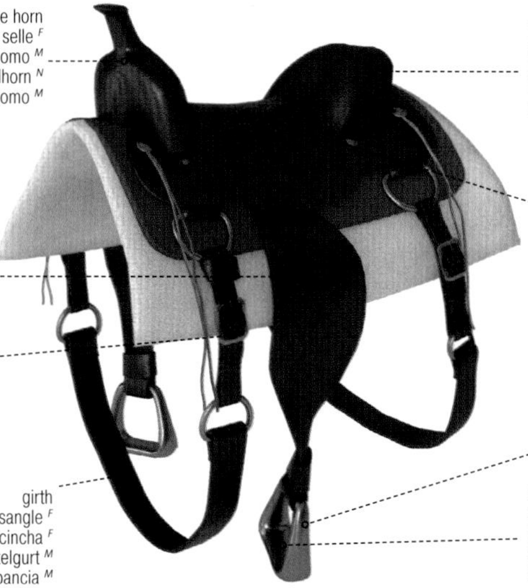
saddle horn
corne F de la selle F
cuerno M / pomo M
Sattelhorn N
pomo M
cantle
troussequin M
borrén M trasero
Hinterzwiesel M
paletta F
seat
siège M
sillín M
Sitz M
seggio M
stirrup leather
étrivière F
correa F
Bügelriemen M
staffile M
girth buckle
sanglon M
correa F de la cincha F
Gurtschnalle F
fibbia F del sottopancia M
arch
branche F
aro M
Bügel M
arco M
girth
sangle F
cincha F
Sattelgurt M
sottopancia M
stirrup
étrier M
estribo M
Steigbügel M
staffa F

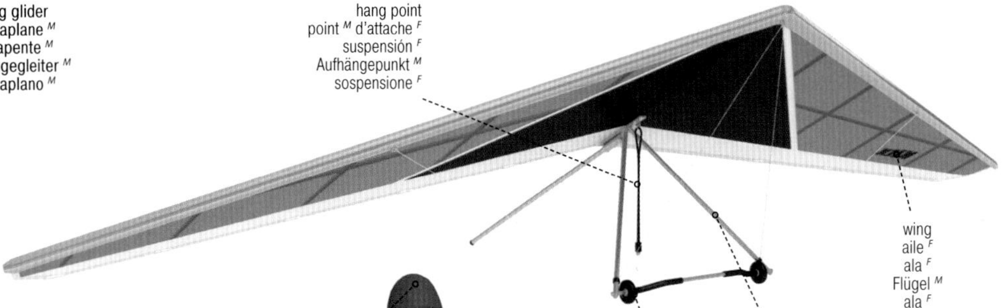
hang glider
deltaplane M
parapente M
Hängegleiter M
deltaplano M
hang point
point M d'attache F
suspensión F
Aufhängepunkt M
sospensione F
wing
aile F
ala F
Flügel M
ala F
wheel
roue F
rueda F
Rad N
ruota F
airframe
cellule F
estructura F
Gestänge N
struttura F

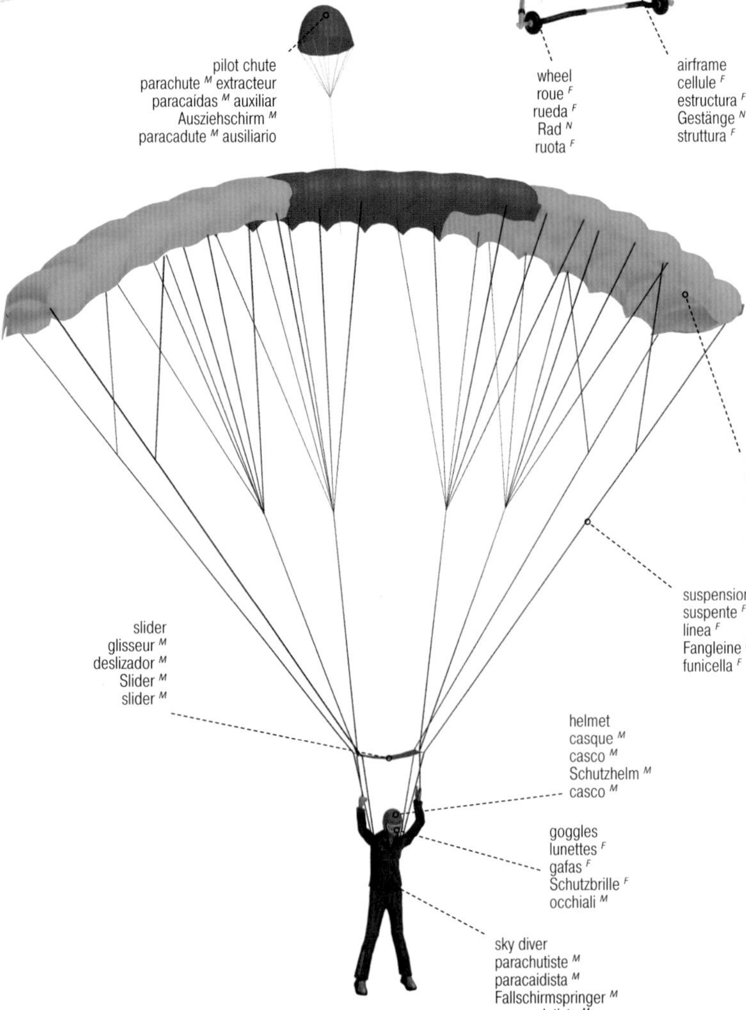
parachute
parachute M
paracaídas M
Fallschirm M
paracadute M
pilot chute
parachute M extracteur
paracaídas M auxiliar
Ausziehschirm M
paracadute M ausiliario
canopy
voile F
ala M
Fallschirmkappe F
paracadute M
suspension line
suspente F
línea F
Fangleine F
funicella F
slider
glisseur M
deslizador M
Slider M
slider M
helmet
casque M
casco M
Schutzhelm M
casco M
goggles
lunettes F
gafas F
Schutzbrille F
occhiali M
sky diver
parachutiste M
paracaidista M
Fallschirmspringer M
paracadutista M

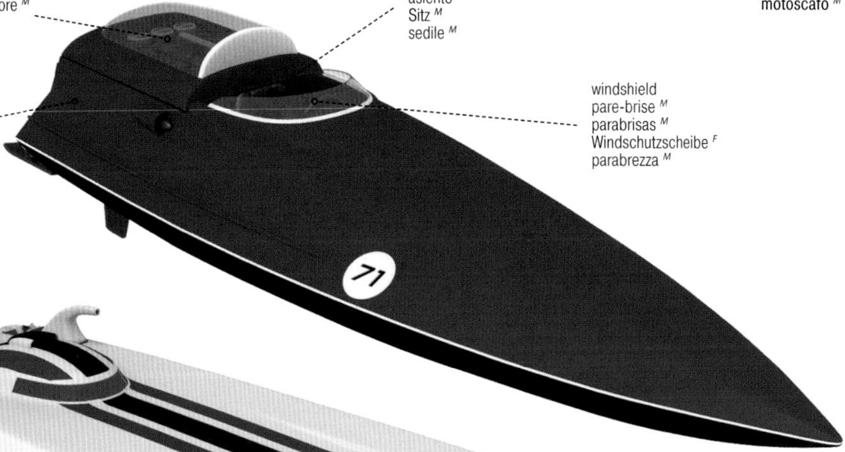
engine compartment
compartiment [M] moteur [M]
compartimiento [M] del motor [M]
Motorraum [M]
vano [M] motore [M]
seat
siège [M]
asiento [M]
Sitz [M]
sedile [M]
powerboat
bateau [M] à moteur [M]
lancha [F]
Powerboot [N]
motoscafo [M]
windshield
pare-brise [M]
parabrisas [M]
Windschutzscheibe [F]
parabrezza [M]
hull
coque [F]
casco [M]
Rumpf [M]
scafo [M]
71

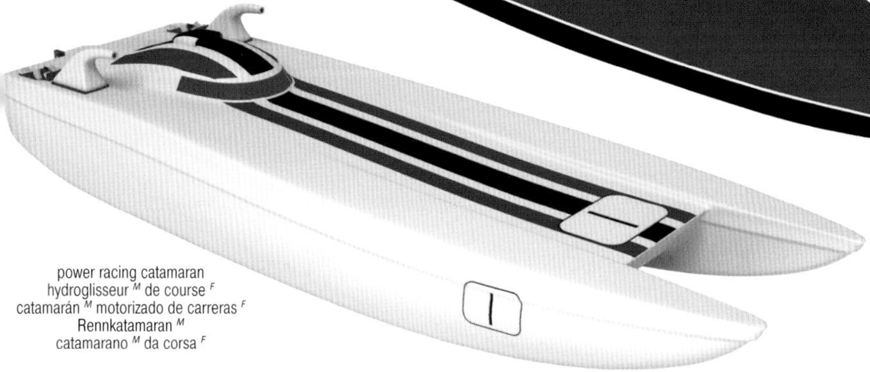
power racing catamaran
hydroglisseur [M] de course [F]
catamarán [M] motorizado de carreras [F]
Rennkatamaran [M]
catamarano [M] da corsa [F]
1

Rowing

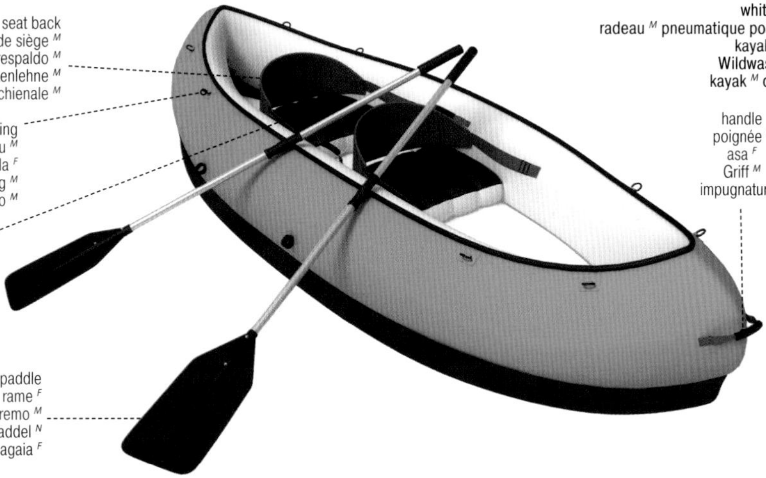
seat back
dossier [M] de siège [M]
respaldo [M]
Rückenlehne [M]
schienale [M]
whitewater raft
radeau [M] pneumatique pour rafting [M]
kayak [M] de río [M]
Wildwasserkajak [N]
kayak [M] da rafting [M]
ring
anneau [M]
anilla [F]
Ring [M]
anello [M]
handle
poignée [F]
asa [F]
Griff [M]
impugnatura [F]
seat
siège [M]
silla [F]
Sitz [M]
sedile [M]
paddle
rame [F]
remo [M]
Paddel [N]
pagaia [F]

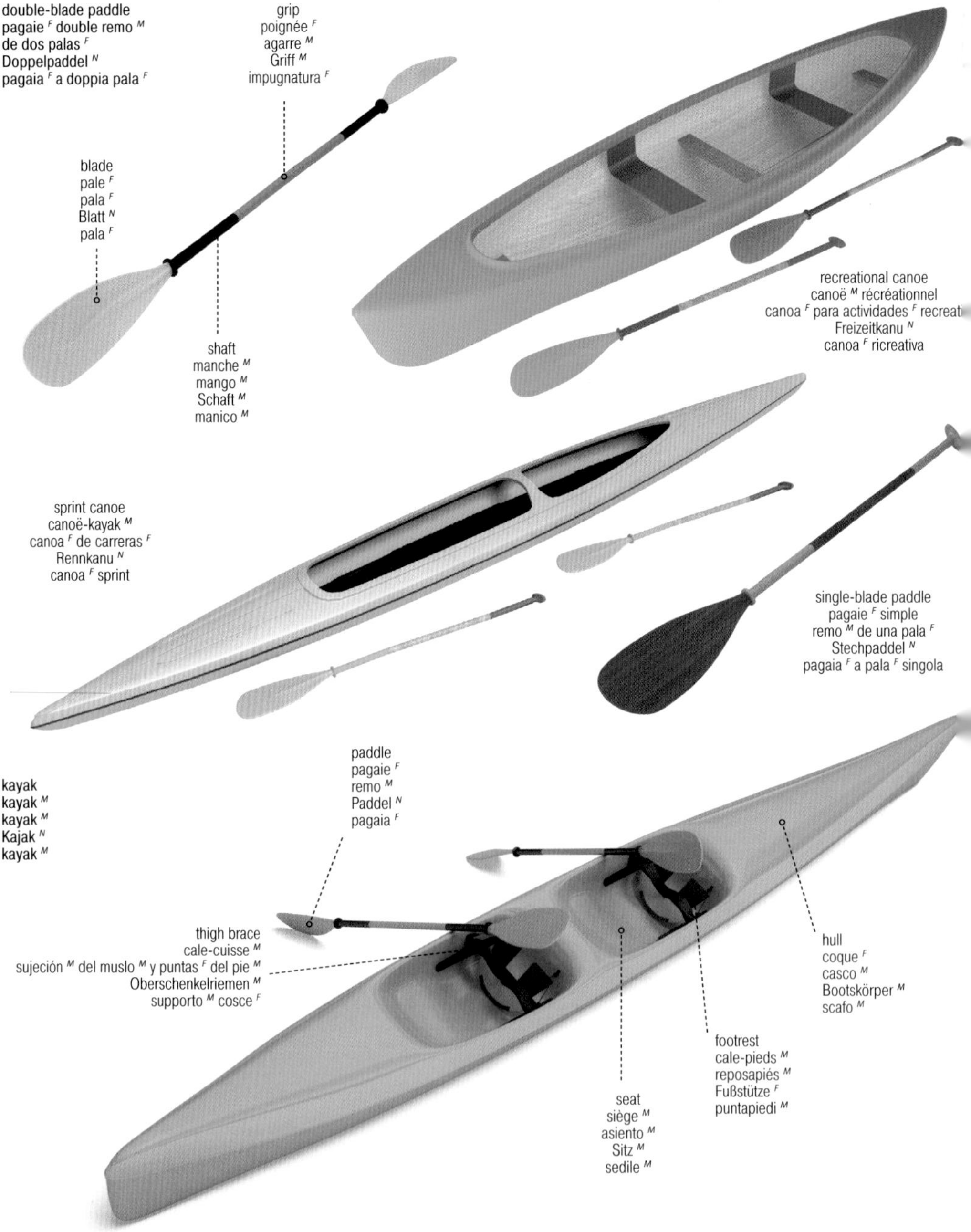
double-blade paddle
pagaie [F] double remo [M]
de dos palas [F]
Doppelpaddel [N]
pagaia [F] a doppia pala [F]
grip
poignée [F]
agarre [M]
Griff [M]
impugnatura [F]
blade
pale [F]
pala [F]
Blatt [N]
pala [F]
shaft
manche [M]
mango [M]
Schaft [M]
manico [M]
recreational canoe
canoë [M] récréationnel
canoa [F] para actividades [F] recreat
Freizeitkanu [N]
canoa [F] ricreativa
sprint canoe
canoë-kayak [M]
canoa [F] de carreras [F]
Rennkanu [N]
canoa [F] sprint
single-blade paddle
pagaie [F] simple
remo [M] de una pala [F]
Stechpaddel [N]
pagaia [F] a pala [F] singola
kayak
kayak [M]
kayak [M]
Kajak [N]
kayak [M]
paddle
pagaie [F]
remo [M]
Paddel [N]
pagaia [F]
thigh brace
cale-cuisse [M]
sujeción [M] del muslo [M] y puntas [F] del pie [M]
Oberschenkelriemen [M]
supporto [M] cosce [F]
hull
coque [F]
casco [M]
Bootskörper [M]
scafo [M]
footrest
cale-pieds [M]
reposapiés [M]
Fußstütze [F]
puntapiedi [M]
seat
siège [M]
asiento [M]
Sitz [M]
sedile [M]

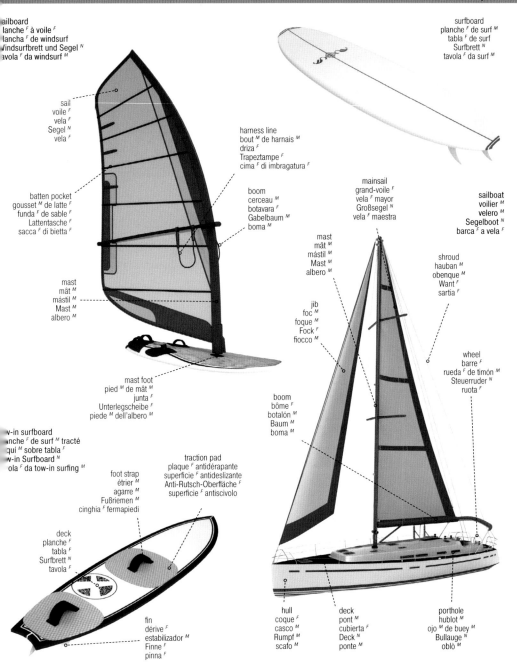

ailboard
lanche [F] à voile [F]
lancha [F] de windsurf
/indsurfbrett und Segel [N]
ɜvola [F] da windsurf [M]

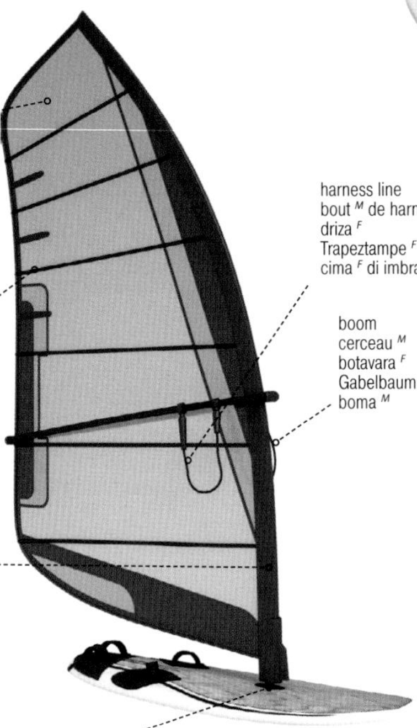
sail
voile [F]
vela [F]
Segel [N]
vela [F]
harness line
bout [M] de harnais [M]
driza [F]
Trapeztampe [F]
cima [F] di imbragatura [F]
batten pocket
gousset [M] de latte [F]
funda [F] de sable [F]
Lattentasche [F]
sacca [F] di bietta [F]
boom
cerceau [M]
botavara [F]
Gabelbaum [M]
boma [M]
mast
mât [M]
mástil [M]
Mast [M]
albero [M]
mast foot
pied [M] de mât [M]
junta [F]
Unterlegscheibe [F]
piede [M] dell'albero [M]

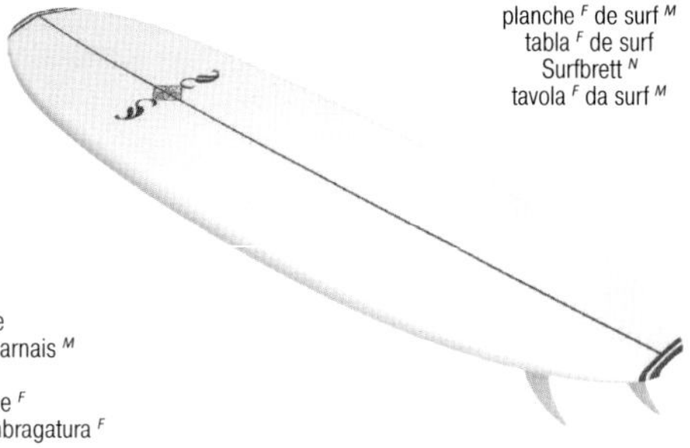
surfboard
planche [F] de surf [M]
tabla [F] de surf
Surfbrett [N]
tavola [F] da surf [M]

sailboat
voilier [M]
velero [M]
Segelboot [N]
barca [F] a vela [F]

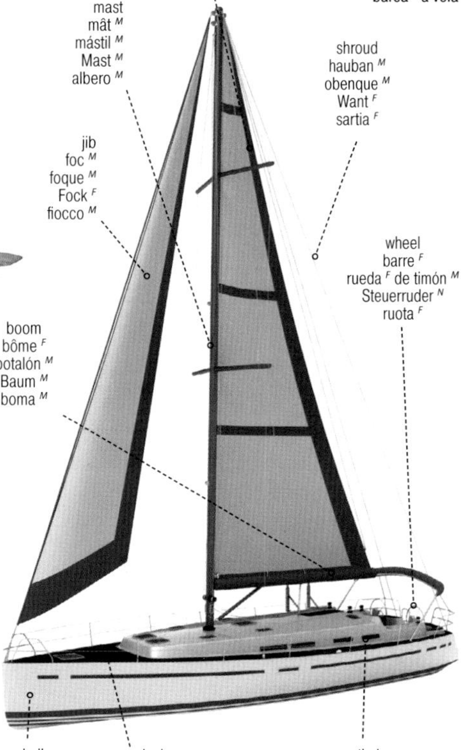
mainsail
grand-voile [F]
vela [F] mayor
Großsegel [N]
vela [F] maestra
mast
mât [M]
mástil [M]
Mast [M]
albero [M]
shroud
hauban [M]
obenque [M]
Want [F]
sartia [F]
jib
foc [M]
foque [M]
Fock [F]
fiocco [M]
wheel
barre [F]
rueda [F] de timón [M]
Steuerruder [N]
ruota [F]
boom
bôme [F]
botalón [M]
Baum [M]
boma [M]
hull
coque [F]
casco [M]
Rumpf [M]
scafo [M]
deck
pont [M]
cubierta [F]
Deck [N]
ponte [M]
porthole
hublot [M]
ojo [M] de buey [M]
Bullauge [N]
oblò [M]

v-in surfboard
ınche [F] de surf [M] tracté
quí [M] sobre tabla [F]
v-in Surfboard [N]
ola [F] da tow-in surfing [M]

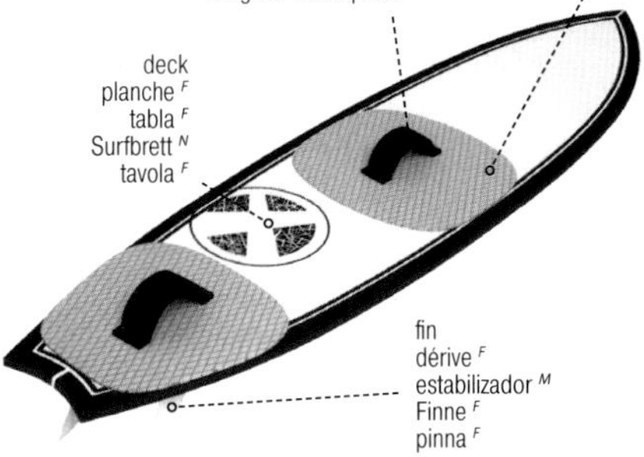
foot strap
étrier [M]
agarre [M]
Fußriemen [M]
cinghia [F] fermapiedi
traction pad
plaque [F] antidérapante
superficie [F] antideslizante
Anti-Rutsch-Oberfläche [F]
superficie [F] antiscivolo
deck
planche [F]
tabla [F]
Surfbrett [N]
tavola [F]
fin
dérive [F]
estabilizador [M]
Finne [F]
pinna [F]

water polo pool
piscine [F] pour water-polo [M]
piscina [F] de waterpolo [M]
Wasserball [M]
piscina [F] per pallanuoto [F]

goal judge
juge [M] de but [M]
juez [M] de gol [M]
Torrichter [M]
giudice [M] di porta [F]

goal
but [M]
portería [F]
Tor [N]
porta [F]

goal line
ligne [F] de but [M]
línea [F] de meta [F]
Torlinie [F]
linea [F] di porta [F]

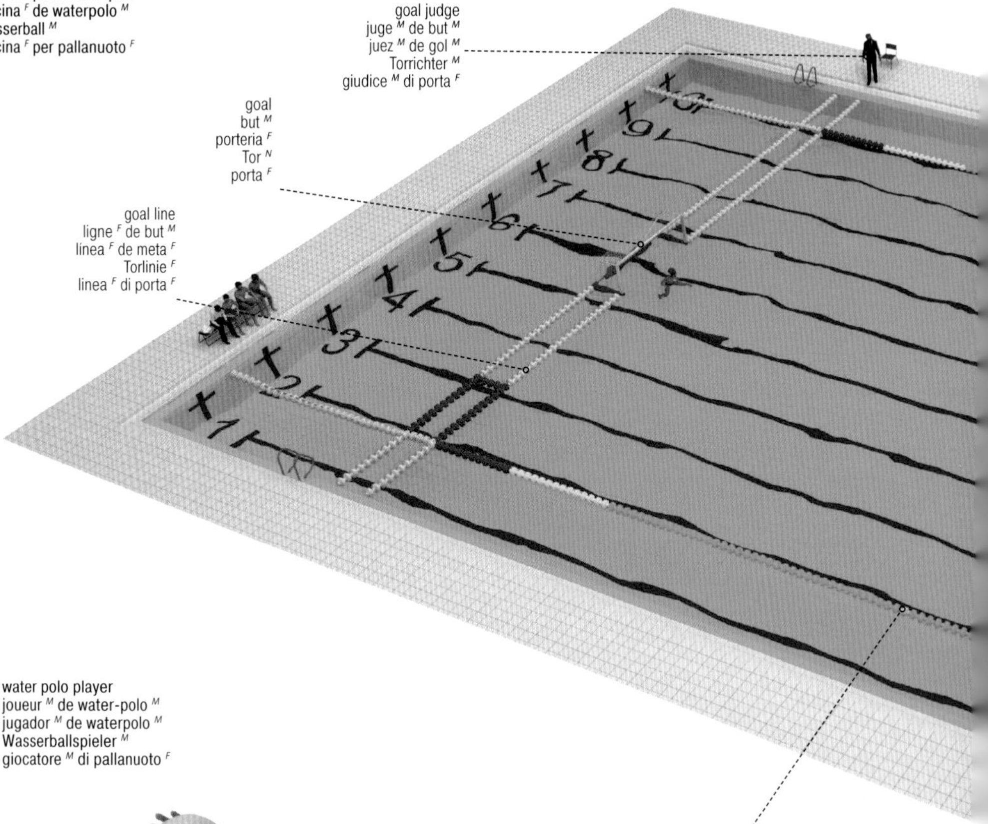

water polo player
joueur [M] de water-polo [M]
jugador [M] de waterpolo [M]
Wasserballspieler [M]
giocatore [M] di pallanuoto [F]

mid-pool line
ligne [F] à la mi-piscine [F]
línea [F] del medio campo [M]
Mittellinie [F]
linea [F] di metà [F] campo [M]

refer
arbitr
árbitro [M] princi
Schiedsrichte
arbitr

water polo ball
ballon [M] de water-polo [M]
balón [M] de waterpolo [M]
Wasserball [M]
pallone [M]

cap
bonnet [M]
gorro [M]
Mütze [F]
cuffia [F]

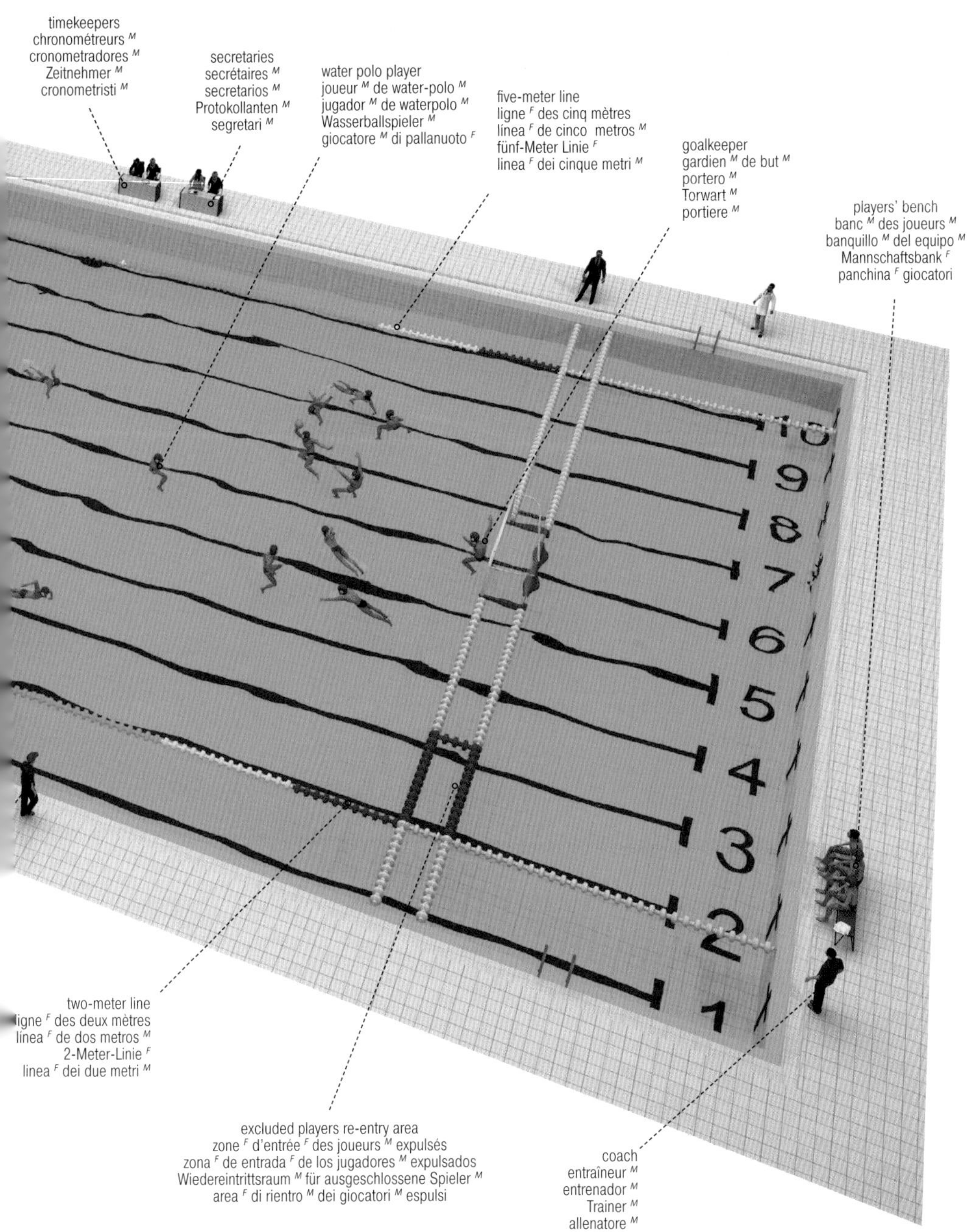
timekeepers
chronométreurs M
cronometradores M
Zeitnehmer M
cronometristi M
secretaries
secrétaires M
secretarios M
Protokollanten M
segretari M
water polo player
joueur M de water-polo M
jugador M de waterpolo M
Wasserballspieler M
giocatore M di pallanuoto F
five-meter line
ligne F des cinq mètres
linea F de cinco metros M
fünf-Meter Linie F
linea F dei cinque metri M
goalkeeper
gardien M de but M
portero M
Torwart M
portiere M
players' bench
banc M des joueurs M
banquillo M del equipo M
Mannschaftsbank F
panchina F giocatori
10
9
8
7
6
5
4
3
2
1
two-meter line
ligne F des deux mètres
línea F de dos metros M
2-Meter-Linie F
linea F dei due metri M
excluded players re-entry area
zone F d'entrée F des joueurs M expulsés
zona F de entrada F de los jugadores M expulsados
Wiedereintrittsraum M für ausgeschlossene Spieler M
area F di rientro M dei giocatori M espulsi
coach
entraîneur M
entrenador M
Trainer M
allenatore M

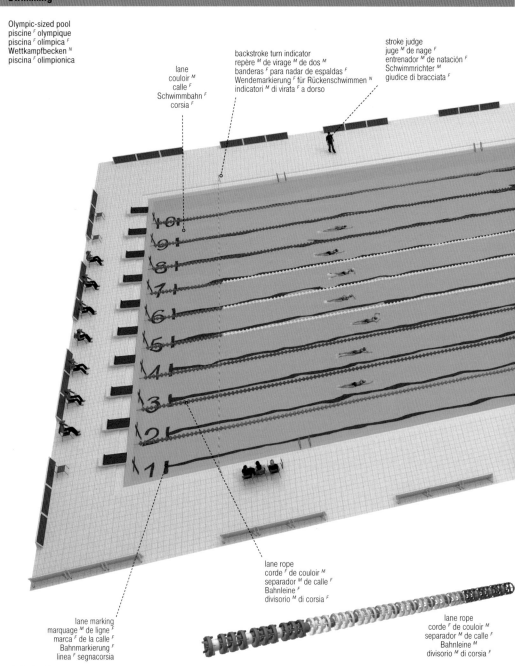

Olympic-sized pool
piscine F olympique
piscina F olímpica F
Wettkampfbecken N
piscina F olimpionica

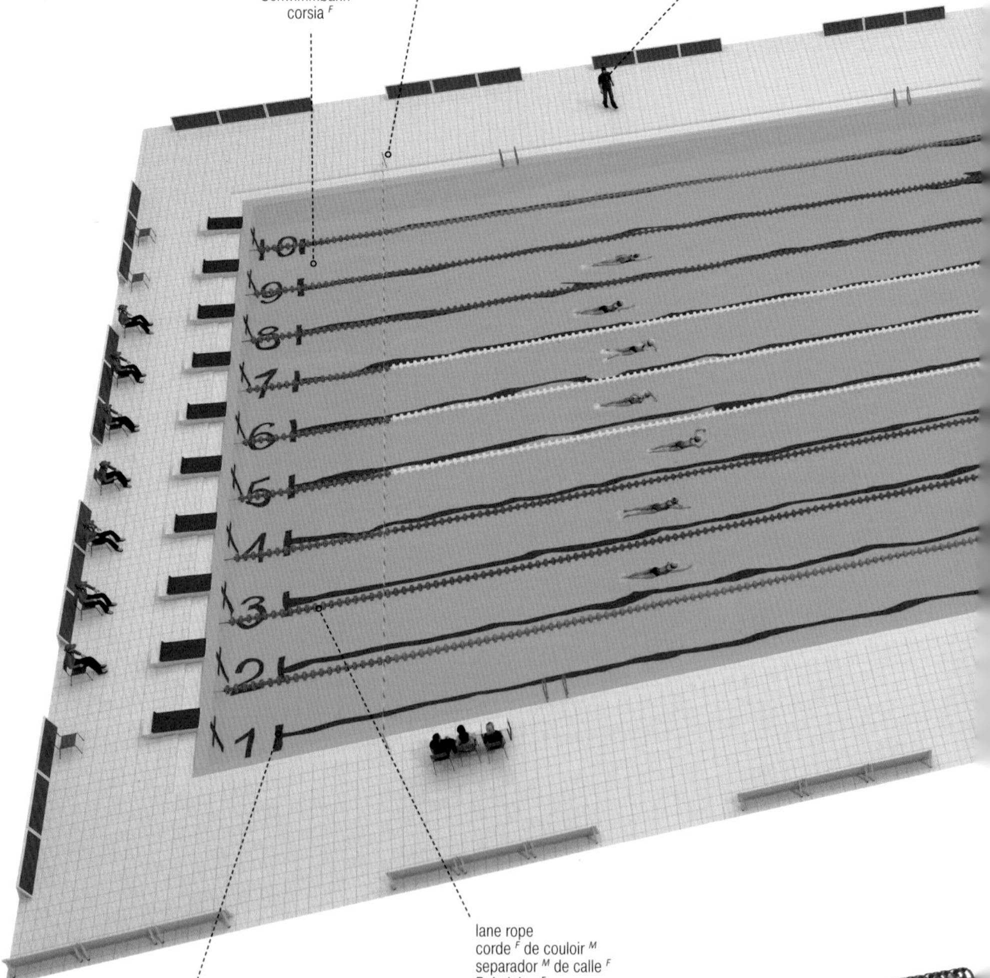
lane
couloir M
calle F
Schwimmbahn F
corsia F
backstroke turn indicator
repère M de virage M de dos M
banderas F para nadar de espaldas F
Wendemarkierung F für Rückenschwimmen N
indicatori M di virata F a dorso
stroke judge
juge M de nage F
entrenador M de natación F
Schwimmrichter M
giudice di bracciata F
lane rope
corde F de couloir M
separador M de calle F
Bahnleine F
divisorio M di corsia F
lane marking
marquage M de ligne F
marca F de la calle F
Bahnmarkierung F
linea F segnacorsia

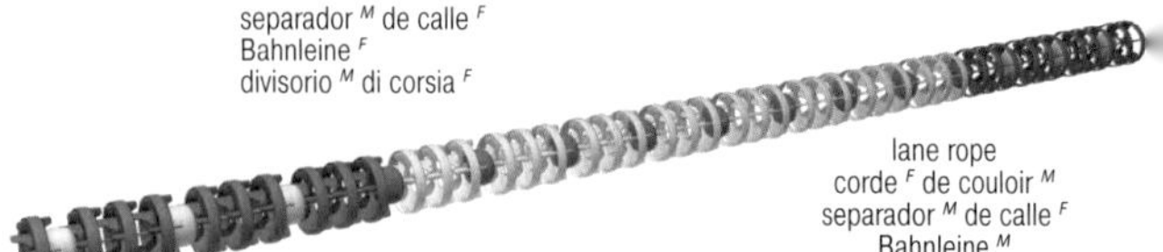
lane rope
corde F de couloir M
separador M de calle F
Bahnleine M
divisorio M di corsia F

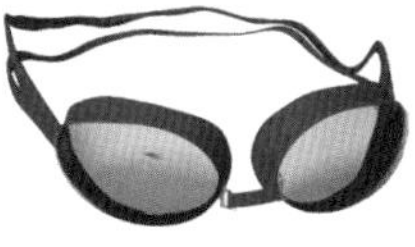

goggles
lunettes F
gafas F de natación F
Schwimmbrille F
occhialini M

swim cap
bonnet M de bain M
gorro M de natación F
Badekappe F
cuffia F

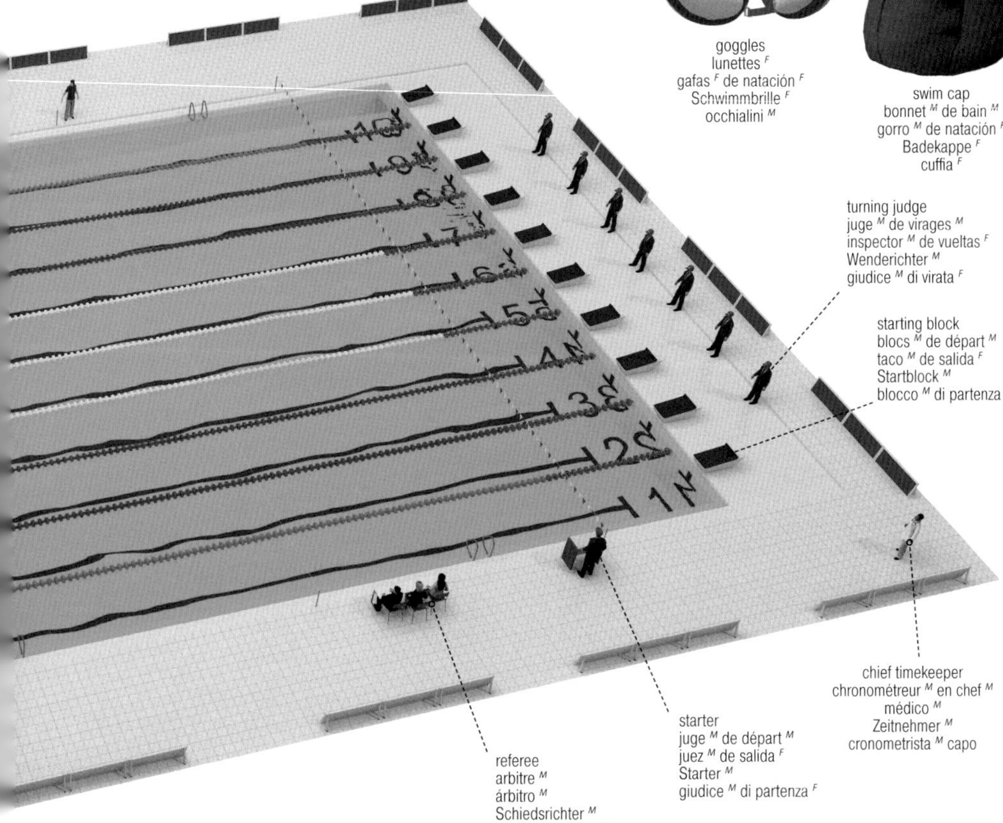
turning judge
juge M de virages M
inspector M de vueltas F
Wenderichter M
giudice M di virata F
starting block
blocs M de départ M
taco M de salida F
Startblock M
blocco M di partenza F
chief timekeeper
chronométreur M en chef M
médico M
Zeitnehmer M
cronometrista M capo
starter
juge M de départ M
juez M de salida F
Starter M
giudice M di partenza F
referee
arbitre M
árbitro M
Schiedsrichter M
giudice M arbitro M

starting block
bloc M de départ M
taco M de salida F
Startblock M
blocco M di partenza F

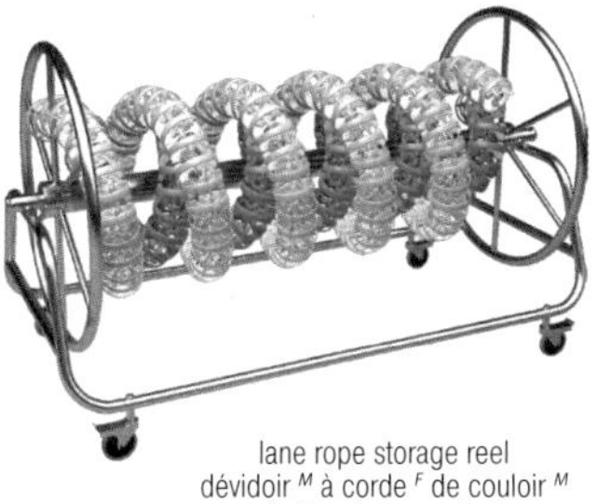

lane rope storage reel
dévidoir M à corde F de couloir M
bobina F de cuerda F
Seilspule F
carrello M avvolgicorsia M

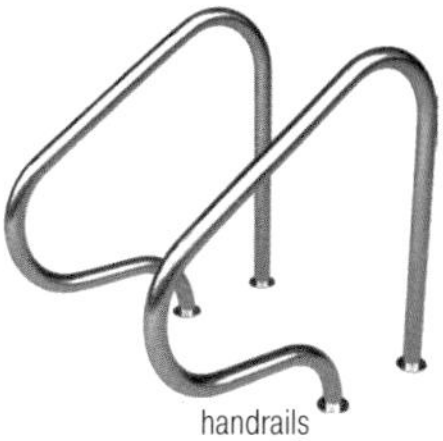

handrails
rampe F
barandillas F
Ausstiegsgeländer N
maniglie F

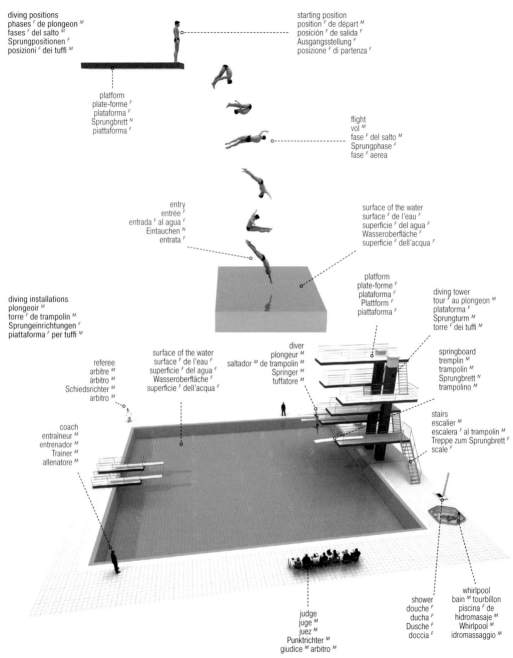

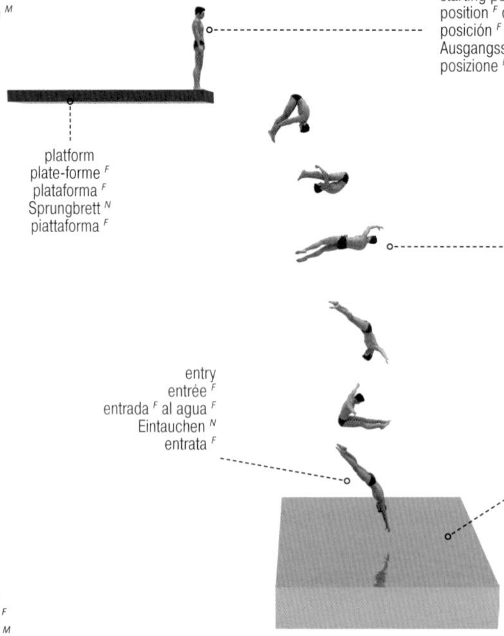
diving positions
phases F de plongeon M
fases F del salto M
Sprungpositionen F
posizioni F dei tuffi M
starting position
position F de départ M
posición F de salida F
Ausgangsstellung F
posizione F di partenza F
platform
plate-forme F
plataforma F
Sprungbrett N
piattaforma F
flight
vol M
fase F del salto M
Sprungphase F
fase F aerea
entry
entrée F
entrada F al agua F
Eintauchen N
entrata F
surface of the water
surface F de l'eau F
superficie F del agua F
Wasseroberfläche F
superficie F dell'acqua F

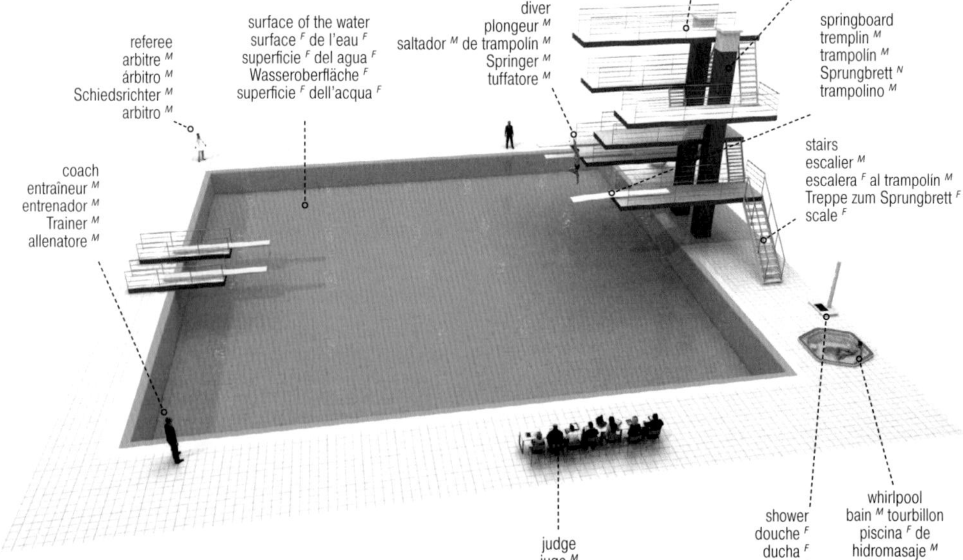
diving installations
plongeoir M
torre F de trampolín M
Sprungeinrichtungen F
piattaforma F per tuffi M
platform
plate-forme F
plataforma F
Plattform F
piattaforma F
diving tower
tour F au plongeon M
plataforma F
Sprungturm M
torre F dei tuffi M
referee
arbitre M
árbitro M
Schiedsrichter M
arbitro M
surface of the water
surface F de l'eau F
superficie F del agua F
Wasseroberfläche F
superficie F dell'acqua F
diver
plongeur M
saltador M de trampolín M
Springer M
tuffatore M
springboard
tremplin M
trampolín M
Sprungbrett N
trampolino M
stairs
escalier M
escalera F al trampolín M
Treppe zum Sprungbrett F
scale F
coach
entraîneur M
entrenador M
Trainer M
allenatore M
judge
juge M
juez M
Punktrichter M
giudice M arbitro M
shower
douche F
ducha F
Dusche F
doccia F
whirlpool
bain M tourbillon
piscina F de
hidromasaje M
Whirlpool M
idromassaggio M

scuba diver
plongeur M
buceador
Taucher M
subacqueo M

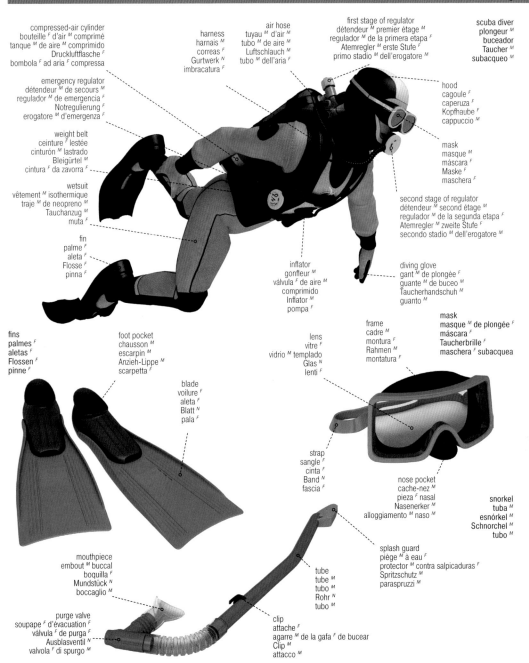

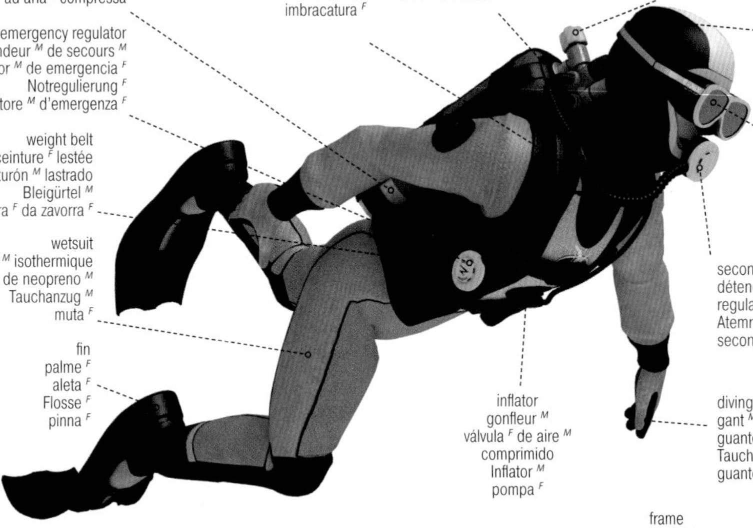
compressed-air cylinder
bouteille F d'air M comprimé
tanque M de aire M comprimido
Druckluftflasche F
bombola F ad aria F compressa
harness
harnais M
correas F
Gurtwerk N
imbracatura F
air hose
tuyau M d'air M
tubo M de aire M
Luftschlauch M
tubo M dell'aria F
first stage of regulator
détendeur M premier étage M
regulador M de la primera etapa F
Atemregler M erste Stufe F
primo stadio M dell'erogatore M
hood
cagoule F
caperuza F
Kopfhaube F
cappuccio M
emergency regulator
détendeur M de secours M
regulador M de emergencia F
Notregulierung F
erogatore M d'emergenza F
weight belt
ceinture F lestée
cinturón M lastrado
Bleigürtel M
cintura F da zavorra F
mask
masque M
máscara F
Maske F
maschera F
wetsuit
vêtement M isothermique
traje M de neopreno M
Tauchanzug M
muta F
second stage of regulator
détendeur M second étage M
regulador M de la segunda etapa F
Atemregler M zweite Stufe F
secondo stadio M dell'erogatore M
fin
palme F
aleta F
Flosse F
pinna F
inflator
gonfleur M
válvula F de aire M
comprimido
Inflator M
pompa F
diving glove
gant M de plongée F
guante M de buceo M
Taucherhandschuh M
guanto M

fins
palmes F
aletas F
Flossen F
pinne F

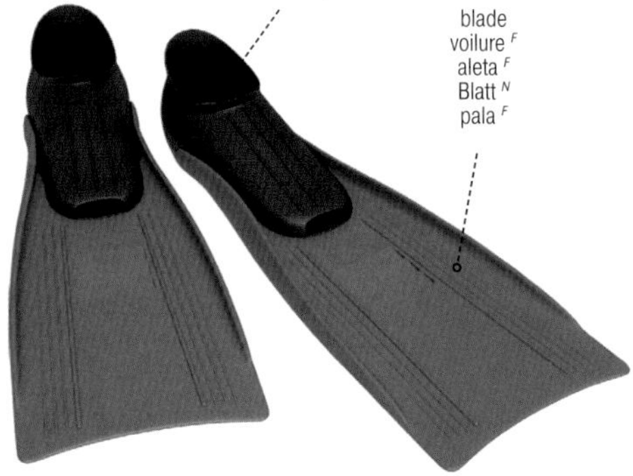
foot pocket
chausson M
escarpín M
Anzieh-Lippe M
scarpetta F
blade
voilure F
aleta F
Blatt N
pala F

mask
masque M de plongée F
máscara F
Taucherbrille F
maschera F subacquea

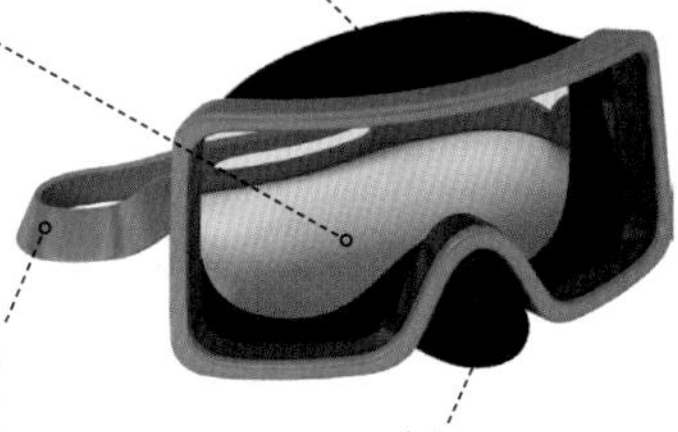
lens
vitre F
vidrio M templado
Glas N
lenti F
frame
cadre M
montura F
Rahmen M
montatura F
strap
sangle F
cinta F
Band N
fascia F
nose pocket
cache-nez M
pieza F nasal
Nasenerker M
alloggiamento M naso M

snorkel
tuba M
esnórkel M
Schnorchel M
tubo M

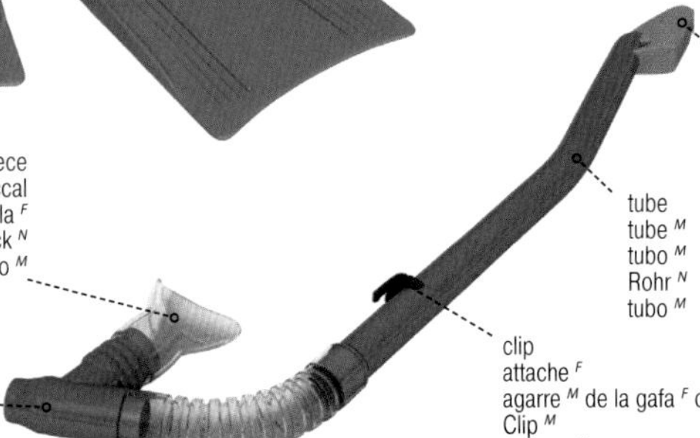
splash guard
piège M à eau F
protector M contra salpicaduras F
Spritzschutz M
paraspruzzi M
mouthpiece
embout M buccal
boquilla F
Mundstück N
boccaglio M
tube
tube M
tubo M
Rohr N
tubo M
purge valve
soupape F d'évacuation F
válvula F de purga F
Ausblasventil N
valvola F di spurgo M
clip
attache F
agarre M de la gafa F de bucear
Clip M
attacco M

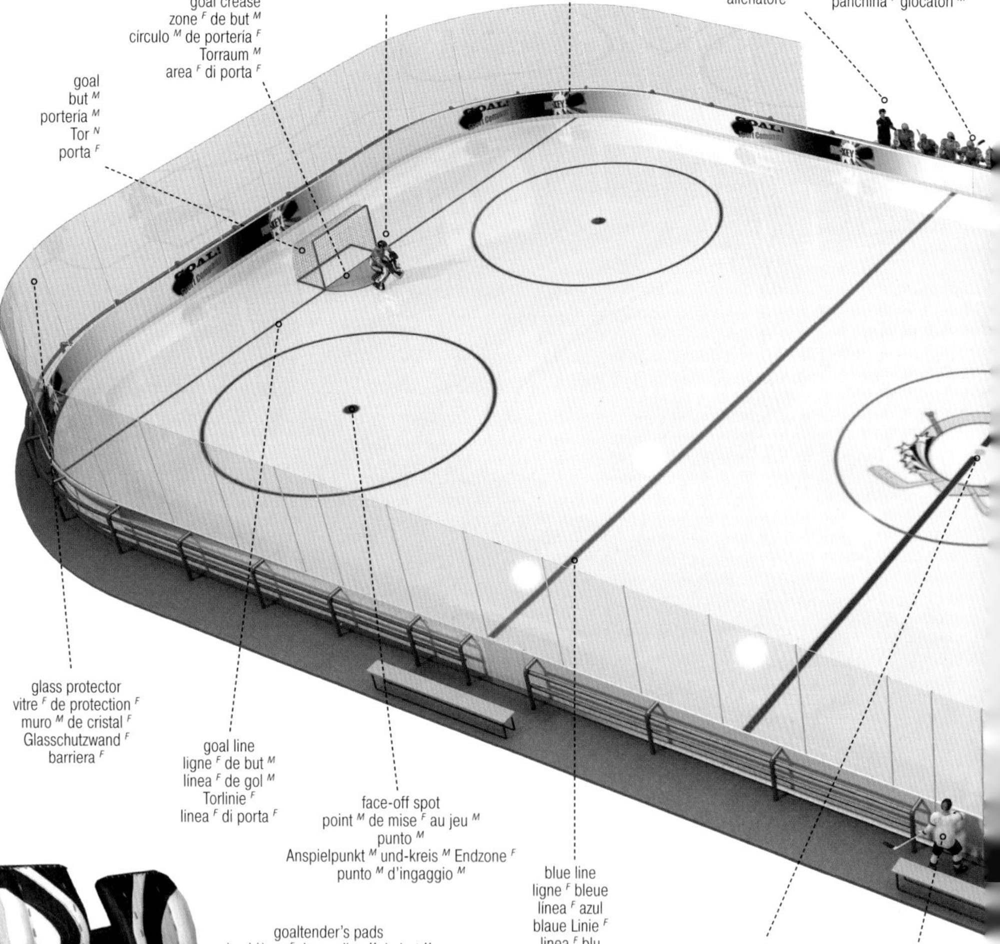
rink
patinoire F
pista F de hielo M
Eisbahn F
pista F di hockey M
goal crease
zone F de but M
círculo M de portería F
Torraum M
area F di porta F
goaltender
gardien M de but M
portero M
Torhüter M
portiere F
boards
bande F
tablas F laterales
Bande F
foro M di ventilazione F
coach
entraîneur M
entrenador M
Trainer M
allenatore M
players' bench
banc M des joueurs M
banco M de jugadores M
Spielerbank F
panchina F giocatori M
goal
but M
portería M
Tor N
porta F
glass protector
vitre F de protection F
muro M de cristal F
Glasschutzwand F
barriera F
goal line
ligne F de but M
línea F de gol M
Torlinie F
linea F di porta F
face-off spot
point M de mise F au jeu M
punto M
Anspielpunkt M und-kreis M Endzone F
punto M d'ingaggio M
blue line
ligne F bleue
línea F azul
blaue Linie F
linea F blu
center face-off circle
cercle M central de mise F au jeu M
punto M central
Anspielpunkt M und-kreis M
Spielfeldmitte F
punto M d'ingaggio M centrale
offending player
joueur M en faute F
jugador M sancionado
Spieler M auf der Strafbank F
giocatore M falloso

goaltender's pads
jambières F de gardien M de but M
protecciones F de portero M
Torhüter-Schutzpolster N
paragambe M del portiere M

puck
rondelle F
disco M
Puck M
disco M

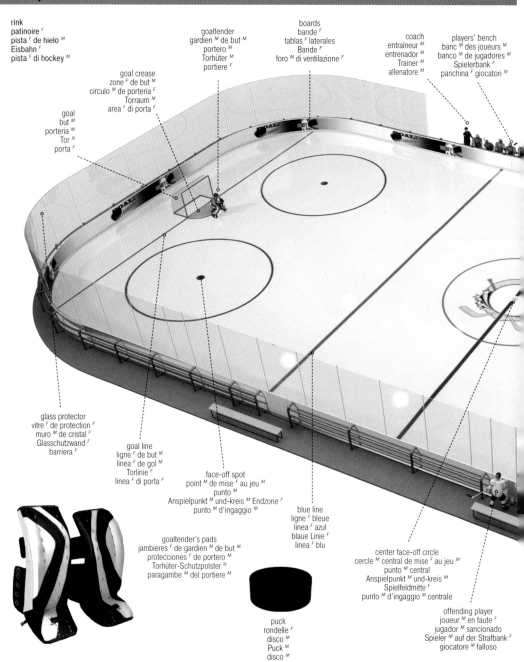

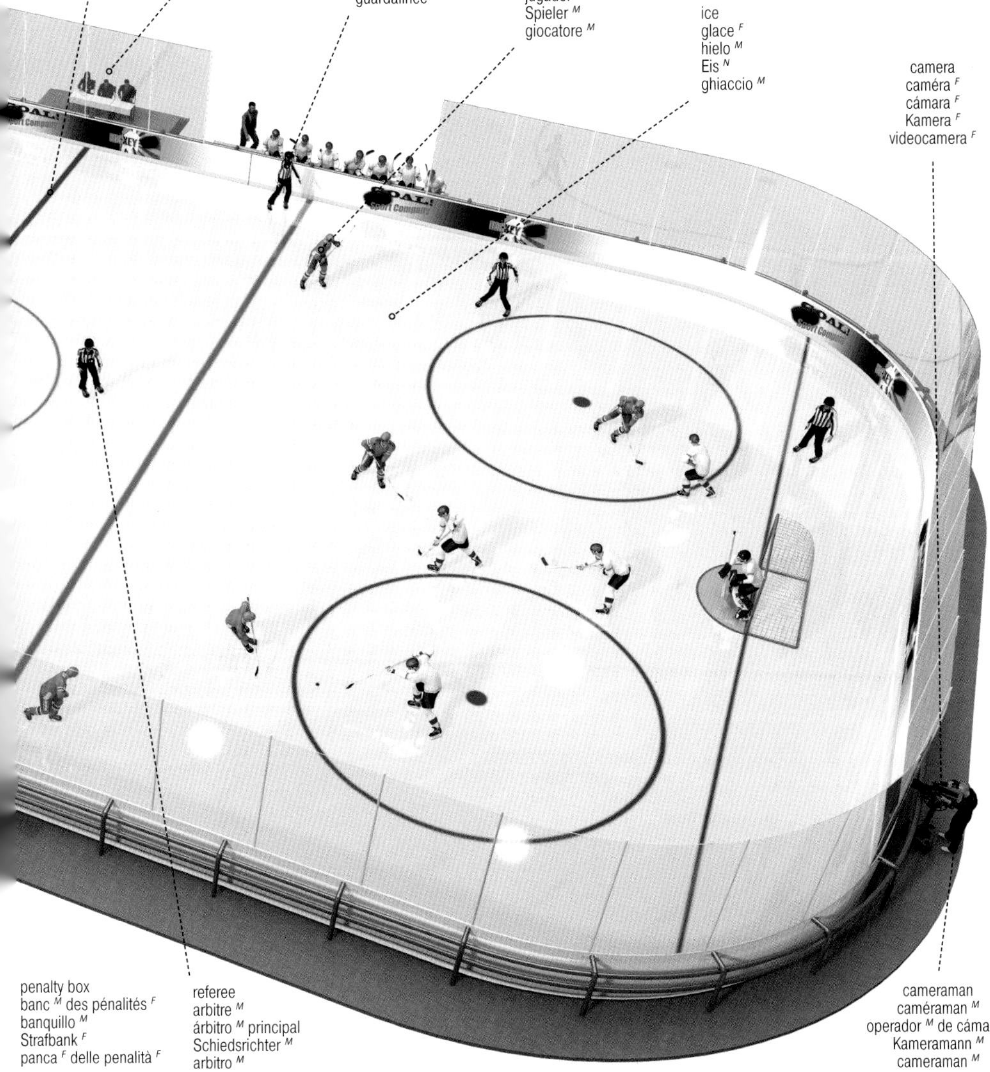
center line
ligne ^{F} centrale
linea ^{F} roja
Mittellinie ^{F}
linea ^{F} rossa
officials' bench
banc ^{M} des officiels ^{M}
banco ^{M} de árbitros ^{M}
Schiedsrichterbank ^{F}
panchina ^{F} arbitri ^{M}
linesman
juge ^{M} de ligne ^{F}
juez ^{M} de línea ^{F}
Linienrichter ^{M}
guardalinee ^{M}
player
joueur ^{M}
jugador ^{M}
Spieler ^{M}
giocatore ^{M}
ice
glace ^{F}
hielo ^{M}
Eis ^{N}
ghiaccio ^{M}
camera
caméra ^{F}
cámara ^{F}
Kamera ^{F}
videocamera ^{F}
penalty box
banc ^{M} des pénalités ^{F}
banquillo ^{M}
Strafbank ^{F}
panca ^{F} delle penalità ^{F}
referee
arbitre ^{M}
árbitro ^{M} principal
Schiedsrichter ^{M}
arbitro ^{M}
cameraman
caméraman ^{M}
operador ^{M} de cámara ^{F}
Kameramann ^{M}
cameraman ^{M}

hockey player
joueur M de hockey M
jugador M de hockey M
Hockeyspieler M
hockeista M

helmet
casque M
casco M
Schutzhelm M
casco M

vent
aération F
agujero M de ventilación F
Belüftungslöcher N
foro M traspirante

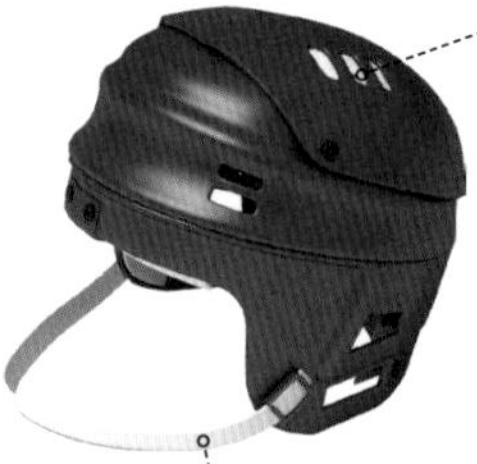

chin strap
jugulaire F
correa F
Riemen M
sottomento M

glove
gant M
guante M
Handschuh M
guanto M

player's stick
bâton M de hockey M
palo M de hockey M
Hockeyschläger M
bastone M del giocatore M

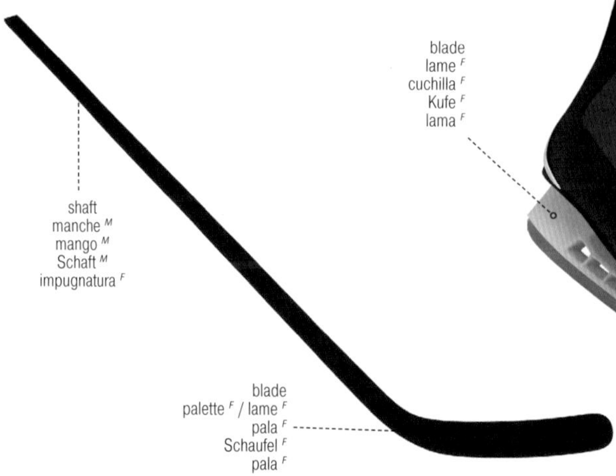

shaft
manche M
mango M
Schaft M
impugnatura F

blade
palette F / lame F
pala F
Schaufel F
pala F

hockey skates
patins M
patines M de hockey M
Eishockeyschuhe M
pattini M da hockey M

tongue
languette F
lengüeta F
Zunge F
linguetta F

blade
lame F
cuchilla F
Kufe F
lama F

lace
lacet M
cordón M
Schnürsenkel M
laccio M

toe
orteil M
punta F
Spitze F
punta F

edge
carre F
filo M
Kante F
filo M

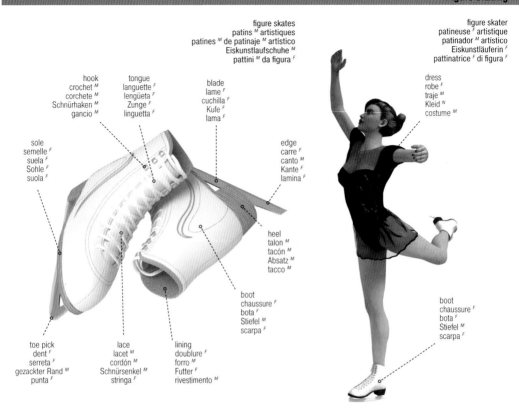

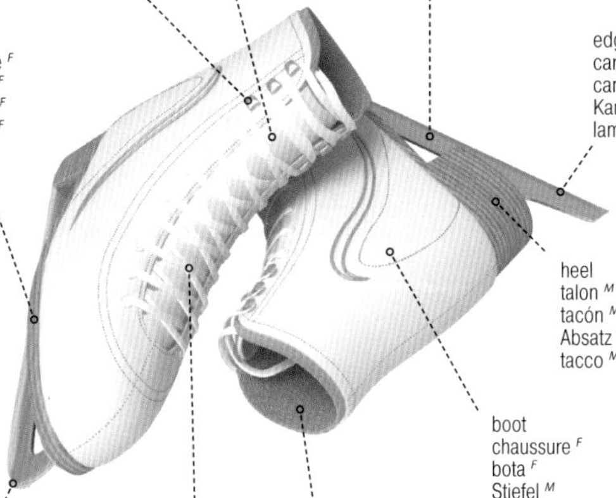
figure skates
patins M artistiques
patines M de patinaje M artístico
Eiskunstlaufschuhe M
pattini M da figura F
hook
crochet M
corchete M
Schnürhaken M
gancio M
tongue
languette F
lengüeta F
Zunge F
linguetta F
blade
lame F
cuchilla F
Kufe F
lama F
sole
semelle F
suela F
Sohle F
suola F
edge
carre F
canto M
Kante F
lamina F
heel
talon M
tacón M
Absatz M
tacco M
boot
chaussure F
bota F
Stiefel M
scarpa F
toe pick
dent F
serreta F
gezackter Rand M
punta F
lace
lacet M
cordón M
Schnürsenkel M
stringa F
lining
doublure F
forro M
Futter F
rivestimento M

figure skater
patineuse F artistique
patinador M artístico
Eiskunstläuferin F
pattinatrice F di figura F
dress
robe F
traje M
Kleid N
costume M
boot
chaussure F
bota F
Stiefel M
scarpa F

Bobsled

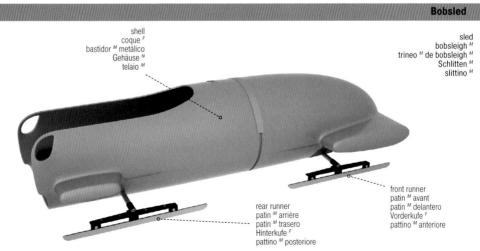

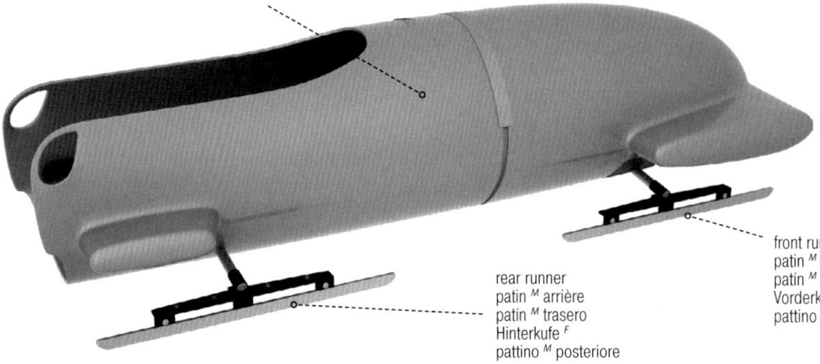
shell
coque F
bastidor M metálico
Gehäuse N
telaio M
sled
bobsleigh M
trineo M de bobsleigh M
Schlitten M
slittino M
front runner
patin M avant
patín M delantero
Vorderkufe F
pattino M anteriore
rear runner
patin M arrière
patín M trasero
Hinterkufe F
pattino M posteriore

curling stone
pierre [F] de curling [M]
piedra [F] de curling [M]
Curlingstein [M]
stone [F] da curling [M]

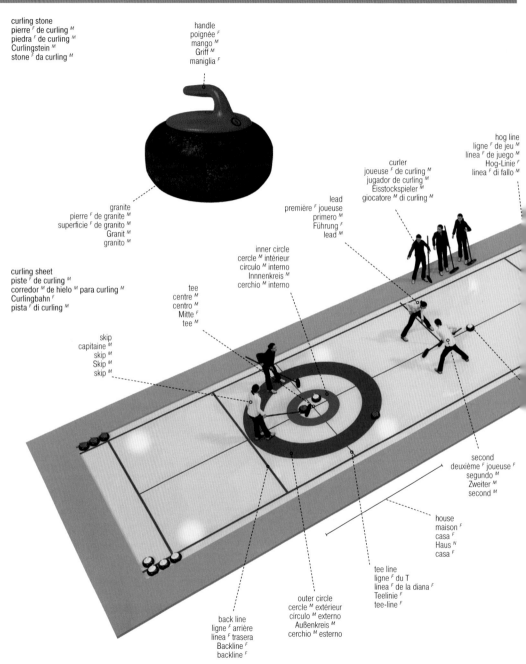

handle
poignée [F]
mango [M]
Griff [M]
maniglia [F]

granite
pierre [F] de granite [M]
superficie [F] de granito [M]
Granit [M]
granito [M]

curling sheet
piste [F] de curling [M]
corredor [M] de hielo [M] para curling [M]
Curlingbahn [F]
pista [F] di curling [M]

hog line
ligne [F] de jeu [M]
línea [F] de juego [M]
Hog-Linie [F]
linea [F] di fallo [M]

curler
joueuse [F] de curling [M]
jugador de curling [M]
Eisstockspieler [M]
giocatore [M] di curling [M]

lead
première [F] joueuse
primero [M]
Führung [F]
lead [M]

inner circle
cercle [M] intérieur
círculo [M] interno
Innnenkreis [M]
cerchio [M] interno

tee
centre [M]
centro [M]
Mitte [F]
tee [M]

skip
capitaine [M]
skip [M]
Skip [M]
skip [M]

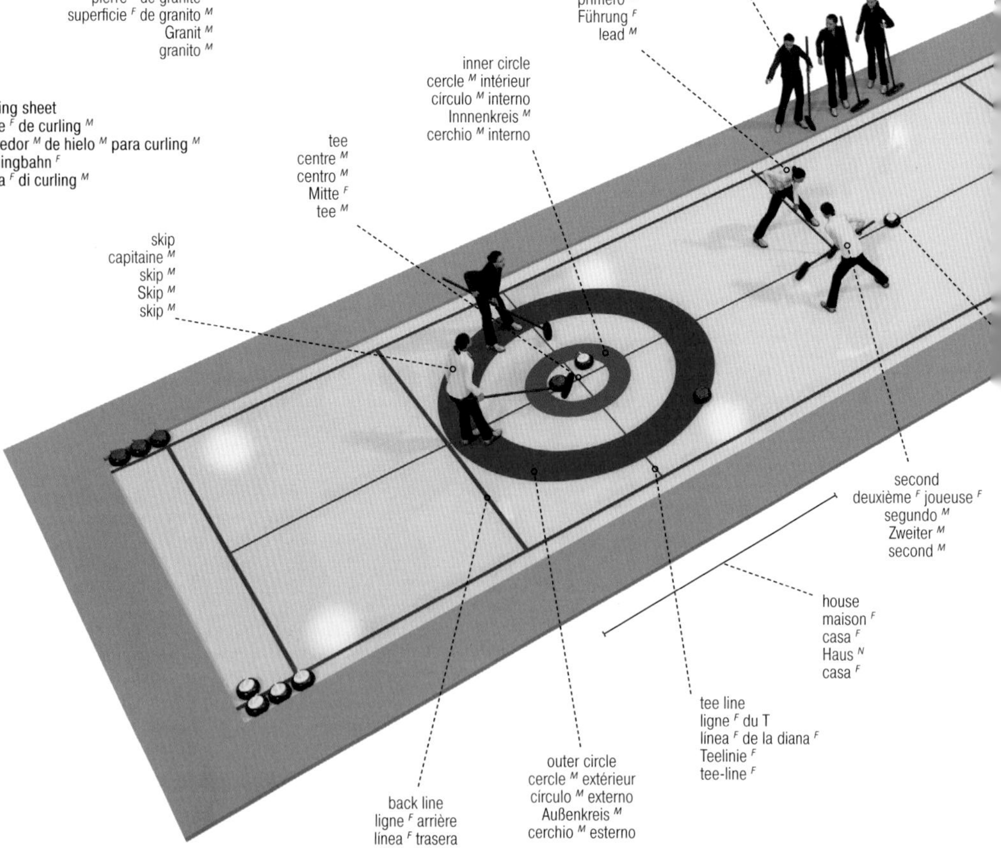

second
deuxième [F] joueuse [F]
segundo [M]
Zweiter [M]
second [M]

house
maison [F]
casa [F]
Haus [N]
casa [F]

tee line
ligne [F] du T
línea [F] de la diana [F]
Teelinie [F]
tee-line [F]

outer circle
cercle [M] extérieur
círculo [M] externo
Außenkreis [M]
cerchio [M] esterno

back line
ligne [F] arrière
línea [F] trasera
Backline [F]
backline [F]

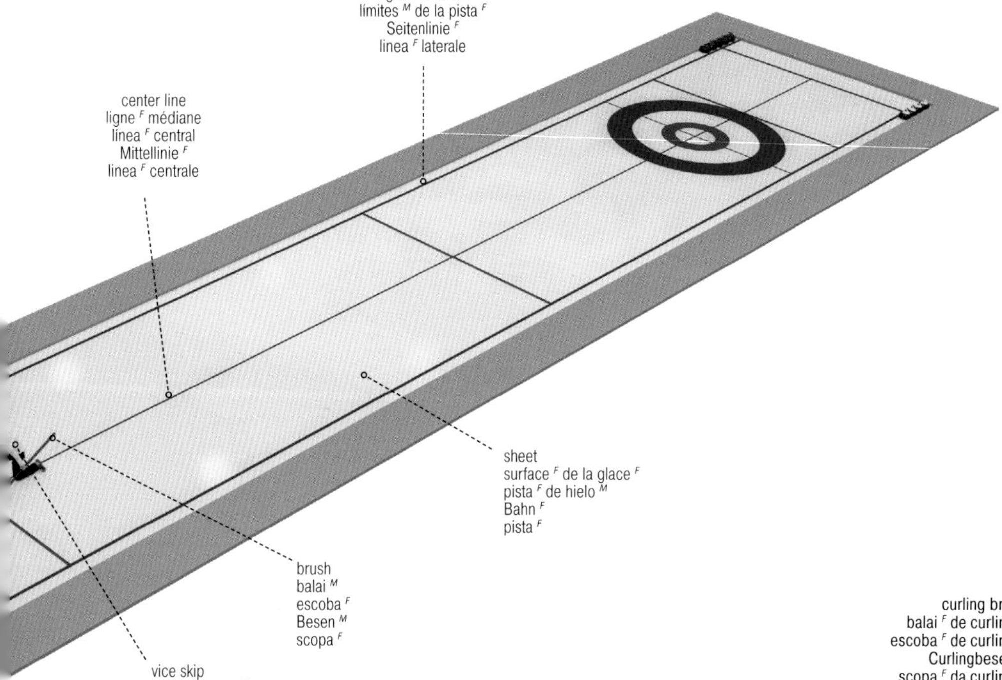
lateral line
ligne [F] latérale
límites [M] de la pista [F]
Seitenlinie [F]
linea [F] laterale
center line
ligne [F] médiane
línea [F] central
Mittellinie [F]
linea [F] centrale
sheet
surface [F] de la glace [F]
pista [F] de hielo [M]
Bahn [F]
pista [F]
brush
balai [M]
escoba [F]
Besen [M]
scopa [F]
vice skip
vice-capitaine [M]
vice skip [M]
Vize-Skip [M]
vice-skip [M]
curling stone
pierre [F] de curling [M]
piedra [F]
Curlingstein [M]
stone [F]

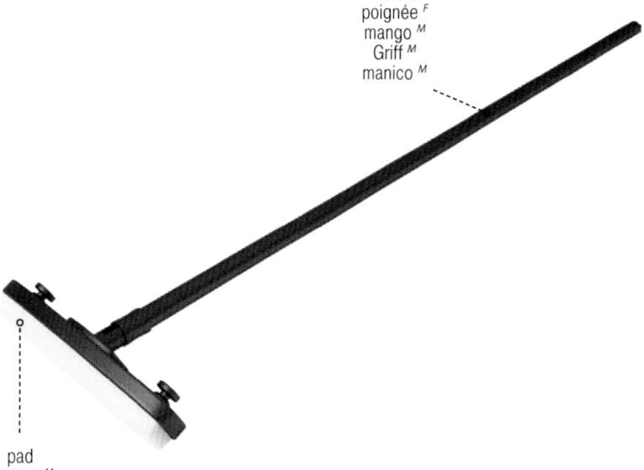
curling brush
balai [F] de curling [M]
escoba [F] de curling [M]
Curlingbesen [M]
scopa [F] da curling [M]
handle
poignée [F]
mango [M]
Griff [M]
manico [M]
pad
tampon [M]
almohadilla [F]
Pad [N]
rivestimento [M] abrasivo

alpine skier
skieur [M] alpin
esquiador [M]
Skiläufer [M]
sciatore [M]

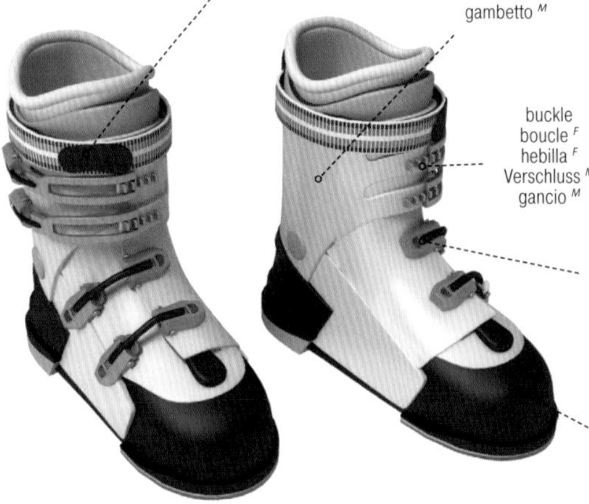
ski boots
bottes [F] de ski [M]
botas [F] de esquí [M]
Skischuhe [M]
scarponi [M] da sci [M]
strap
attache [F]
tira [F]
Riemen [M]
strap [M]
upper shell
coque [F] supérieure
cubierta [F] superior
Hinterteil [N]
gambetto [M]
buckle
boucle [F]
hebilla [F]
Verschluss [M]
gancio [M]
adjustable catch
cran [M] de réglage [M]
gancho [M] ajustable
Klettverschluss [M]
gancio [M] regolabile
lower shell
coque [F] inférieure
cubierta [F] inferior
Spitze [F]
punta [F]

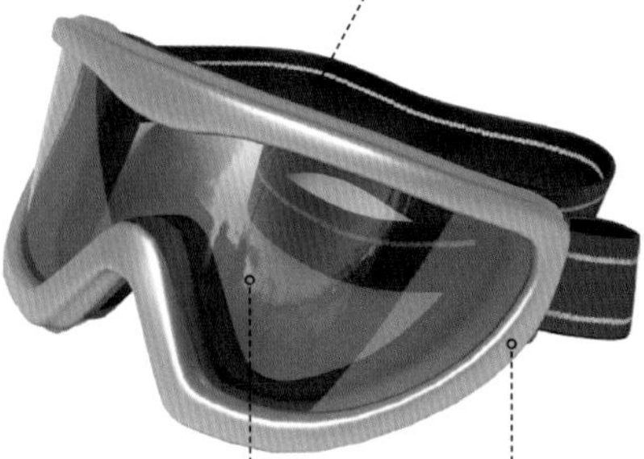
ski goggles
lunettes [F] de ski [M]
gafas [F] de esquí [M]
Skibrille [F]
occhiali [M] da sci [M]
strap
dragonne [F]
correa [F]
Riemen [M]
fascia [F]
lens
verre [M]
cristal [M]
Scheibe [F]
lenti [F]
frame
cadre [M]
montura [F]
Rahmen [M]
montatura [F]

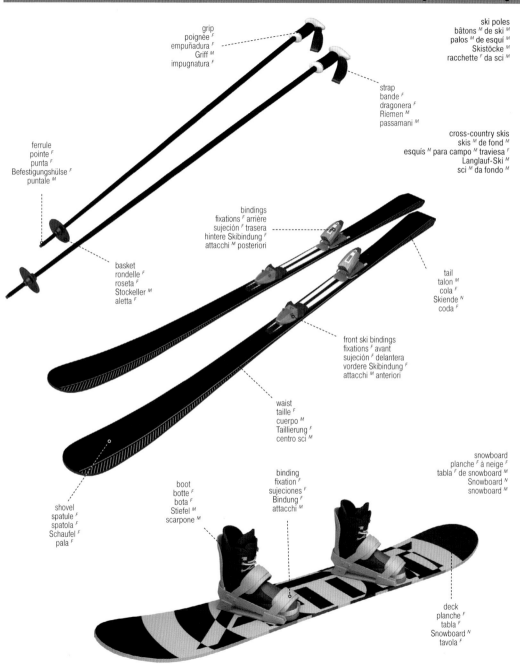

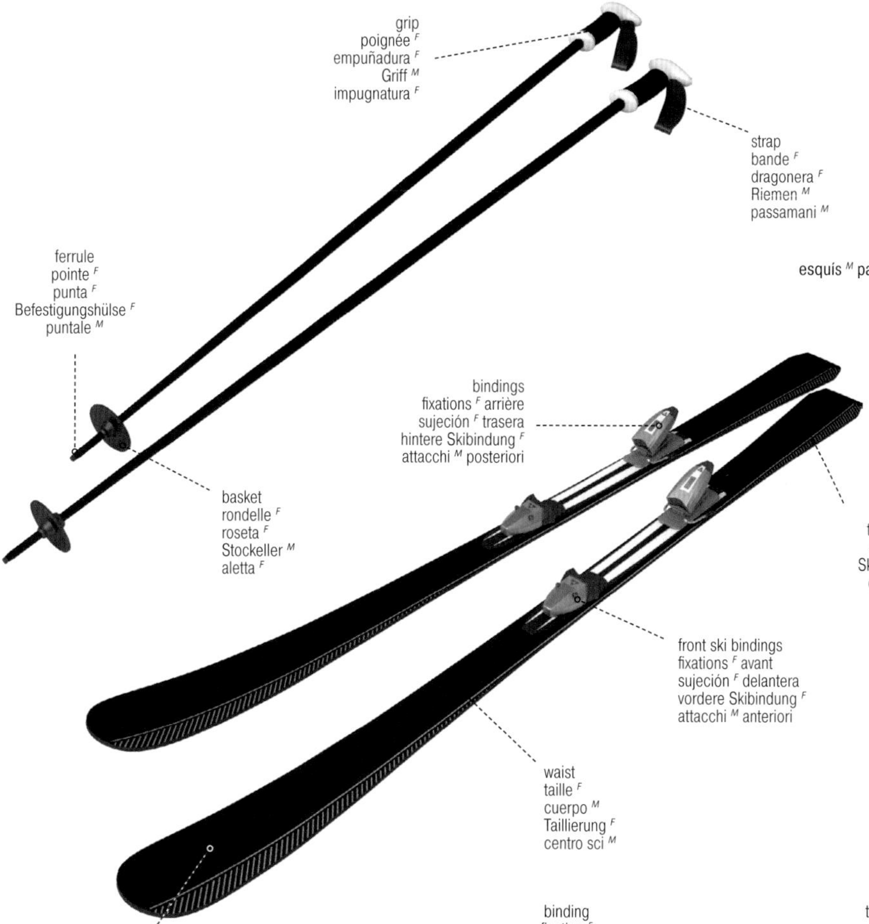
ski poles
bâtons [M] de ski [M]
palos [M] de esquí [M]
Skistöcke [M]
racchette [F] da sci [M]
grip
poignée [F]
empuñadura [F]
Griff [M]
impugnatura [F]
strap
bande [F]
dragonera [F]
Riemen [M]
passamani [M]
ferrule
pointe [F]
punta [F]
Befestigungshülse [F]
puntale [M]
basket
rondelle [F]
roseta [F]
Stockeller [M]
aletta [F]
cross-country skis
skis [M] de fond [M]
esquís [M] para campo [M] traviesa [F]
Langlauf-Ski [M]
sci [M] da fondo [M]
bindings
fixations [F] arrière
sujeción [F] trasera
hintere Skibindung [F]
attacchi [M] posteriori
tail
talon [M]
cola [F]
Skiende [N]
coda [F]
front ski bindings
fixations [F] avant
sujeción [F] delantera
vordere Skibindung [F]
attacchi [M] anteriori
waist
taille [F]
cuerpo [M]
Taillierung [F]
centro sci [M]
shovel
spatule [F]
spatola [F]
Schaufel [F]
pala [F]

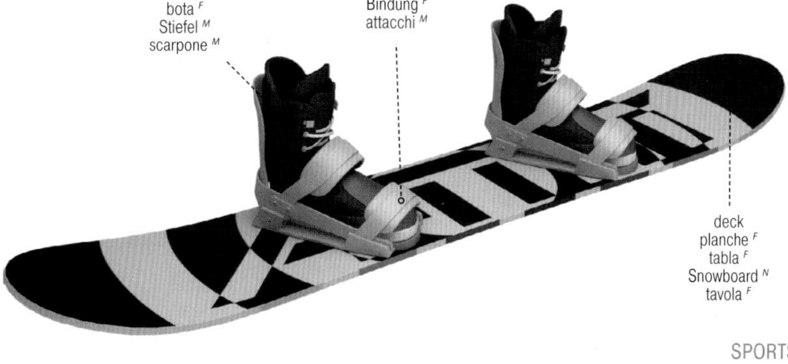
snowboard
planche [F] à neige [F]
tabla [F] de snowboard [M]
Snowboard [N]
snowboard [M]
boot
botte [F]
bota [F]
Stiefel [M]
scarpone [M]
binding
fixation [F]
sujeciones [F]
Bindung [F]
attacchi [M]
deck
planche [F]
tabla [F]
Snowboard [N]
tavola [F]

FOOD
FOOD

LEISURE AND ENTERTAINMENT

plush block
cube ^{M} en peluche ^{F}
dado ^{M} de peluche ^{M}
Plüschwürfel ^{M}
cubo ^{M} di peluche ^{M}

interactive toy
jouet ^{M} interactif
juguete ^{M} interactivo
interaktives Spielzeug ^{N}
gioco ^{M} interattivo

blocks
cubes ^{M}
bloques ^{M}
Würfel ^{M}
cubi ^{M}

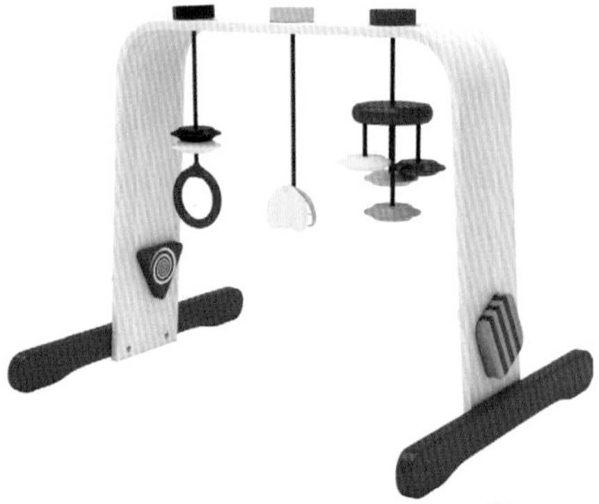

activity gym
portique ^{M} d'éveil ^{M}
gimnasio ^{M} para bebé ^{M}
Babyspielbogen ^{M}
palestrina ^{F}

mobile
mobile ^{M}
móvil ^{M}
Mobile ^{N}
giostrina ^{F}

stuffed animal
animal ^{M} en peluche ^{F}
animal ^{M} de peluche ^{M}
Plüschtier ^{N}
animale ^{M} di peluche ^{M}

dollhouse
maison [F] de poupées [F]
casa [F] de muñecas [F]
Puppenhaus [N]
casa [F] delle bambole [F]

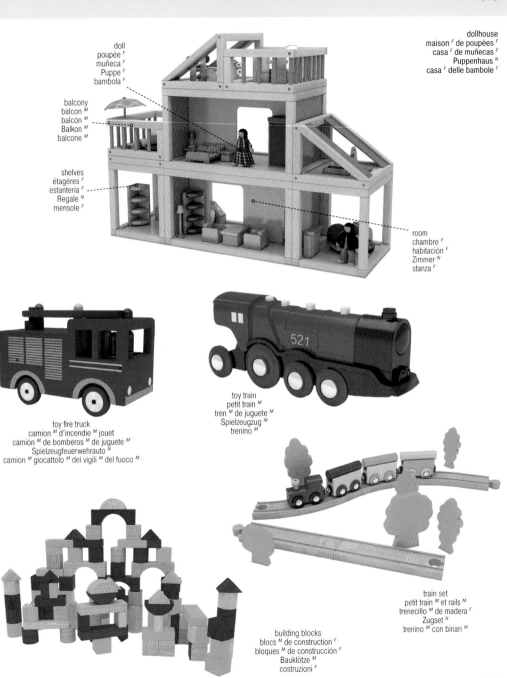

doll
poupée [F]
muñeca [F]
Puppe [F]
bambola [F]
balcony
balcon [M]
balcón [M]
Balkon [M]
balcone [M]
shelves
étagères [F]
estantería [F]
Regale [N]
mensole [F]
room
chambre [F]
habitación [F]
Zimmer [N]
stanza [F]

toy fire truck
camion [M] d'incendie [M] jouet
camión [M] de bomberos [M] de juguete [M]
Spielzeugfeuerwehrauto [N]
camion [M] giocattolo [M] dei vigili [M] del fuoco [M]

521

toy train
petit train [M]
tren [M] de juguete [M]
Spielzeugzug [M]
trenino [M]

train set
petit train [M] et rails [M]
trenecillo [M] de madera [F]
Zugset [N]
trenino [M] con binari [M]

building blocks
blocs [M] de construction [F]
bloques [M] de construcción [F]
Bauklötze [M]
costruzioni [F]

tricycle
tricycle [M]
triciclo [M]
Dreirad [N]
triciclo [M]

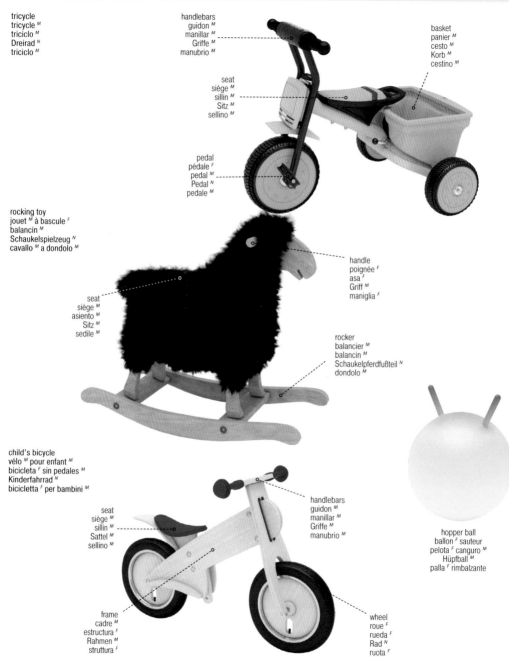

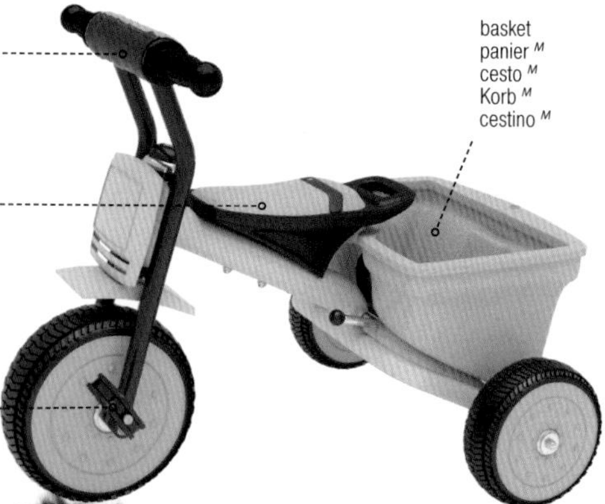
handlebars
guidon [M]
manillar [M]
Griffe [M]
manubrio [M]
basket
panier [M]
cesto [M]
Korb [M]
cestino [M]
seat
siège [M]
sillín [M]
Sitz [M]
sellino [M]
pedal
pédale [F]
pedal [M]
Pedal [N]
pedale [M]

rocking toy
jouet [M] à bascule [F]
balancín [M]
Schaukelspielzeug [N]
cavallo [M] a dondolo [M]

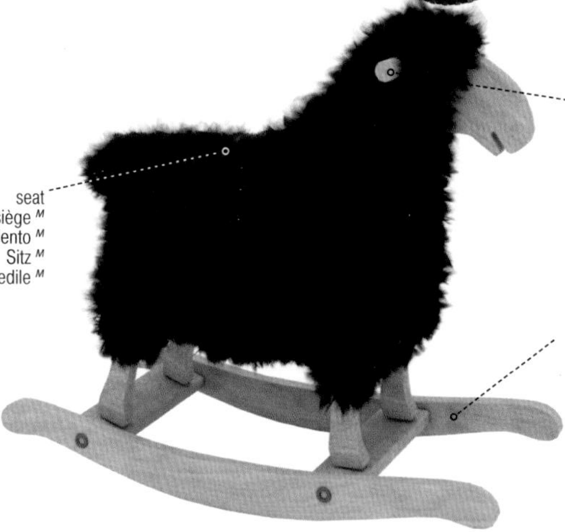
handle
poignée [F]
asa [F]
Griff [M]
maniglia [F]
seat
siège [M]
asiento [M]
Sitz [M]
sedile [M]
rocker
balancier [M]
balancín [M]
Schaukelpferdfußteil [N]
dondolo [M]

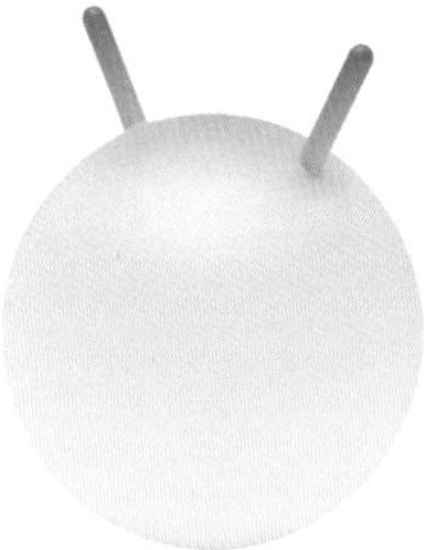

hopper ball
ballon [F] sauteur
pelota [F] canguro [M]
Hüpfball [M]
palla [F] rimbalzante

child's bicycle
vélo [M] pour enfant [M]
bicicleta [F] sin pedales [M]
Kinderfahrrad [N]
bicicletta [F] per bambini [M]

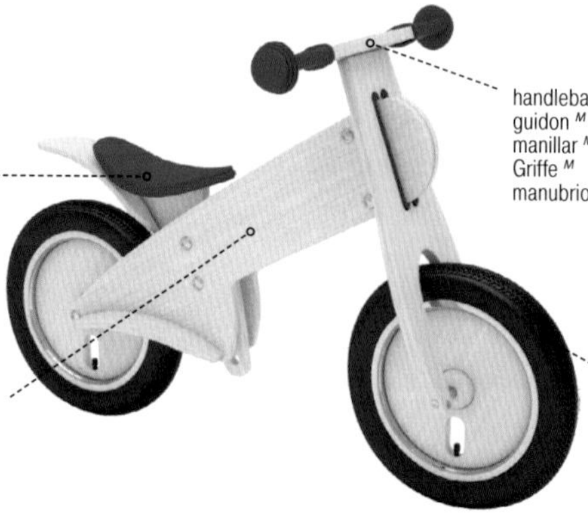
seat
siège [M]
sillín [M]
Sattel [M]
sellino [M]
handlebars
guidon [M]
manillar [M]
Griffe [M]
manubrio [M]
frame
cadre [M]
estructura [F]
Rahmen [M]
struttura [F]
wheel
roue [F]
rueda [F]
Rad [N]
ruota [F]

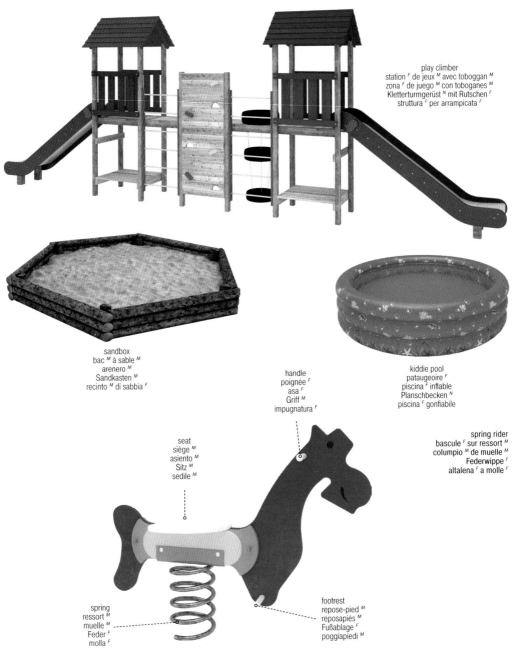

play climber
station ^F^ de jeux ^M^ avec toboggan ^M^
zona ^F^ de juego ^M^ con toboganes ^M^
Kletterturmgerüst ^N^ mit Rutschen ^F^
struttura ^F^ per arrampicata ^F^

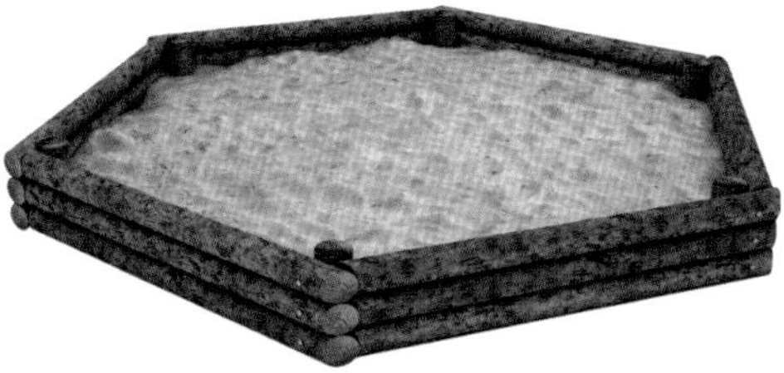

sandbox
bac ^M^ à sable ^M^
arenero ^M^
Sandkasten ^M^
recinto ^M^ di sabbia ^F^

kiddie pool
pataugeoire ^F^
piscina ^F^ inflable
Planschbecken ^N^
piscina ^F^ gonfiabile

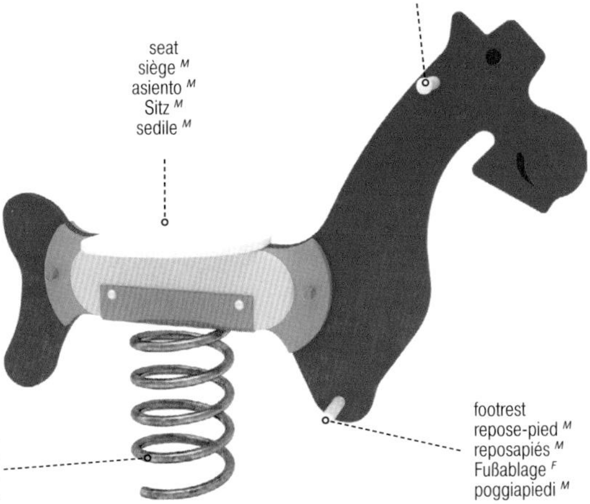
handle
poignée ^F^
asa ^F^
Griff ^M^
impugnatura ^F^
seat
siège ^M^
asiento ^M^
Sitz ^M^
sedile ^M^
spring
ressort ^M^
muelle ^M^
Feder ^F^
molla ^F^
footrest
repose-pied ^M^
reposapiés ^M^
Fußablage ^F^
poggiapiedi ^M^

spring rider
bascule ^F^ sur ressort ^M^
columpio ^M^ de muelle ^M^
Federwippe ^F^
altalena ^F^ a molle ^F^

swing set
portique [M]
columpios [M]
Schaukelset [N]
altalena [F]

top rail
poutre [F]
travesaño [M]
Querbalken [M]
asse [M] trasversale
post
montant [M]
soporte [M]
Pfosten [M]
supporto [M]
seat
siège [M]
asiento [M]
Sitz [M]
sedile [M]
chain
chaîne [F]
cadena [F]
Kette [F]
catena [F]

jungle gym
portique [M] d'escalade [F]
parque infantil [M]
Klettergerüst [N]
struttura [F] per arrampicata [F]

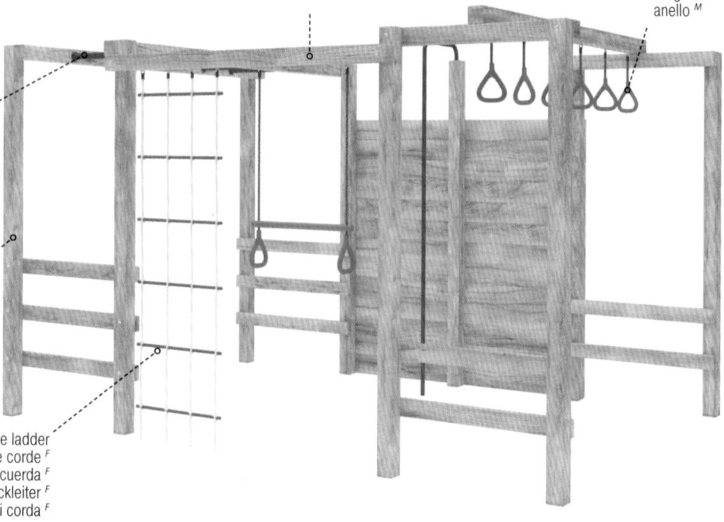
top rail
traverse [F] supérieure
viga [F]
Querbalken [M]
trave [F]
ring
anneau [M]
anilla [F]
Ring [M]
anello [M]
monkey bars
barres [F] de suspension [F]
barra [F] fija
Hangelsprossen [F]
asse [M] trasversale
post
montant [M]
soporte [M]
Pfosten [M]
supporto [M]
rope ladder
échelle [F] de corde [F]
escalera [F] de cuerda [F]
Strickleiter [F]
scaletta [F] di corda [F]

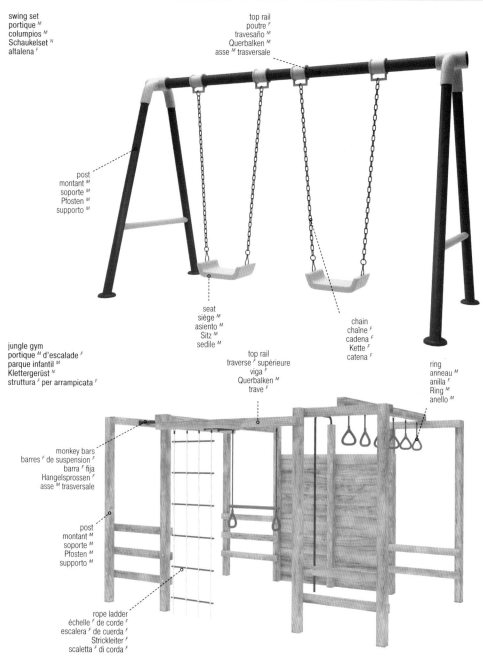

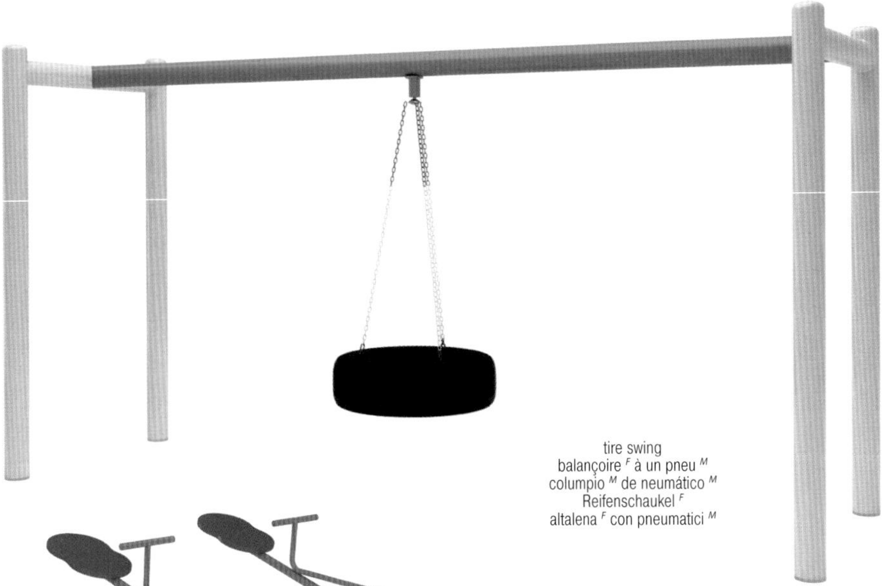

tire swing
balançoire ^{F} à un pneu ^{M}
columpio ^{M} de neumático ^{M}
Reifenschaukel ^{F}
altalena ^{F} con pneumatici ^{M}

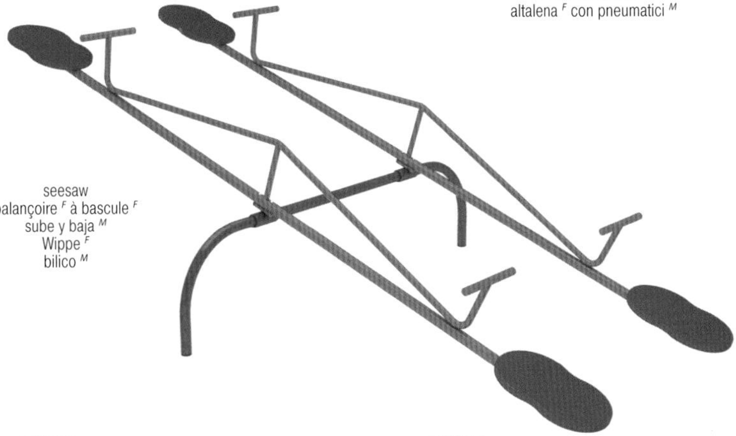

seesaw
balançoire ^{F} à bascule ^{F}
sube y baja ^{M}
Wippe ^{F}
bilico ^{M}

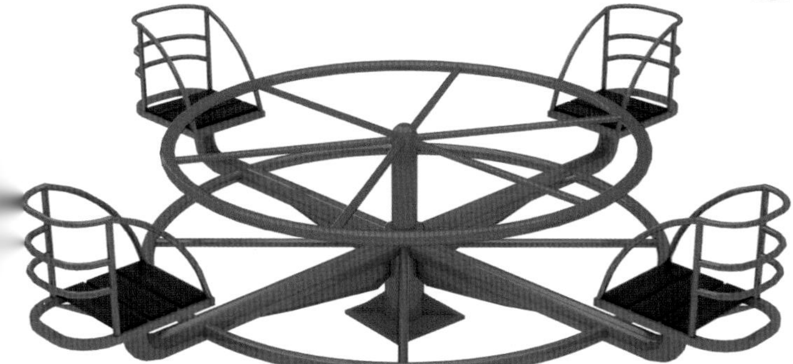

merry-go-round
tourniquet ^{M}
carrusel ^{M}
Karussell ^{N}
giostra ^{F}

amusement park rides
manèges M de parc M d'attractions F
atracciones F
Vergnügungsparkfahrgeschäfte F
parco M divertimenti M

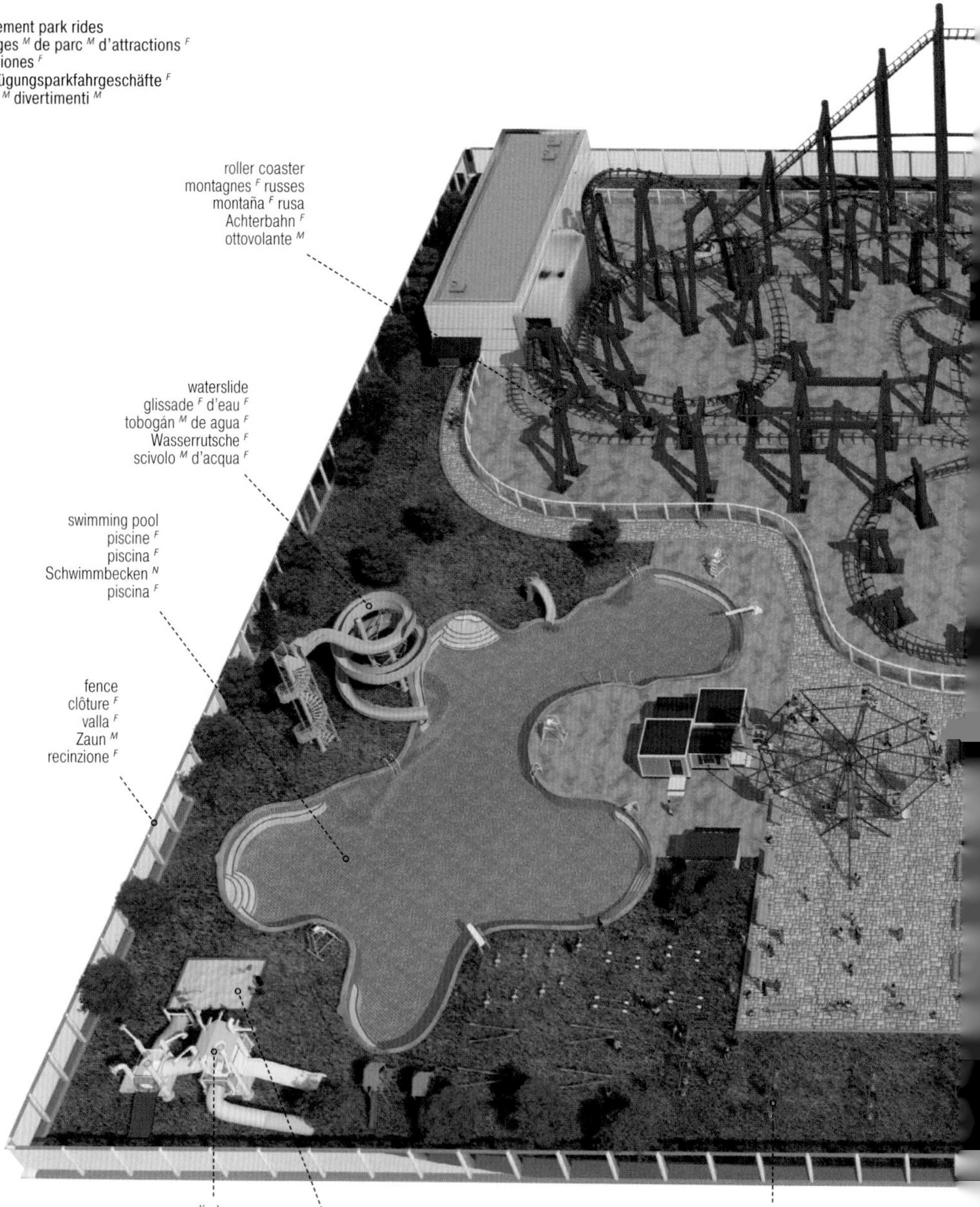
roller coaster
montagnes F russes
montaña F rusa
Achterbahn F
ottovolante M
waterslide
glissade F d'eau F
tobogán M de agua F
Wasserrutsche F
scivolo M d'acqua F
swimming pool
piscine F
piscina F
Schwimmbecken N
piscina F
fence
clôture F
valla F
Zaun M
recinzione F
climber
jeu M à grimper
parque M infantil
Klettergerüst N
struttura F per arrampicata F
sandbox
bac M à sable M
arenero M
Sandkasten M
recinto M di sabbia F
swing set
balançoires F
columpios M
Schaukeln F
altalene F

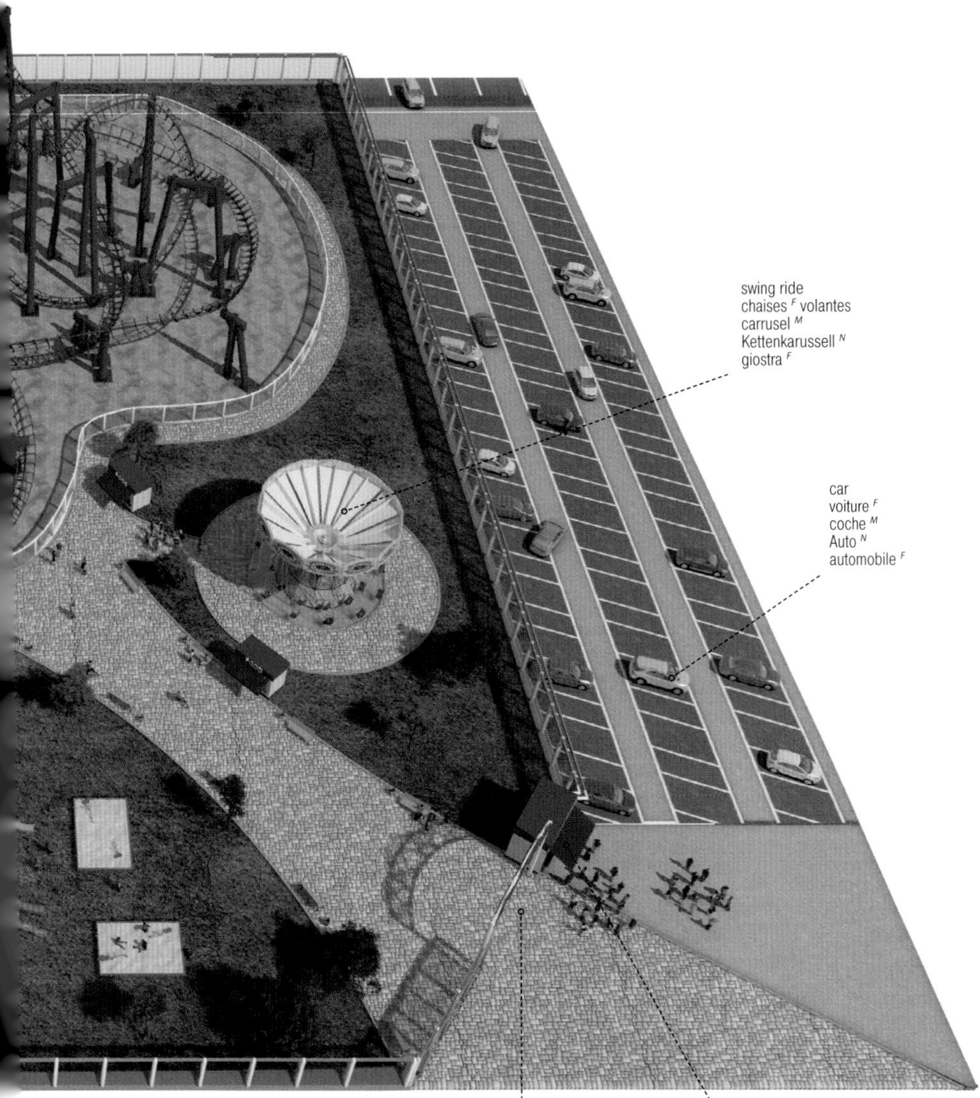
swing ride
chaises F volantes
carrusel M
Kettenkarussell N
giostra F
car
voiture F
coche M
Auto N
automobile F
entrance
entrée F
entrada F
Eingang M
ingresso M
ticket office
billetterie F
taquilla F
Ticketschalter M
biglietteria F

Chess

Échecs ^{M} | Ajedrez ^{M} | Schach ^{N} | Scacchi ^{M}

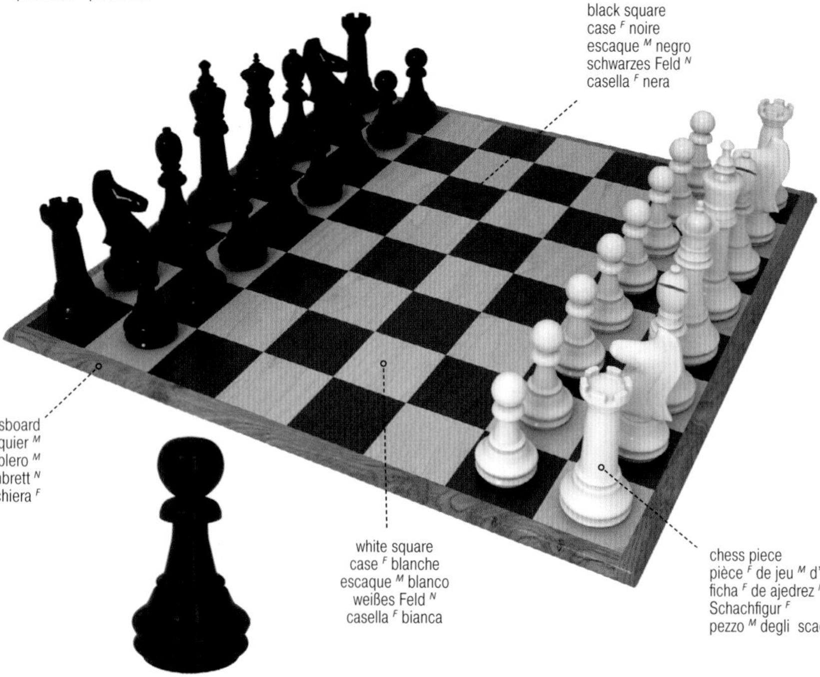

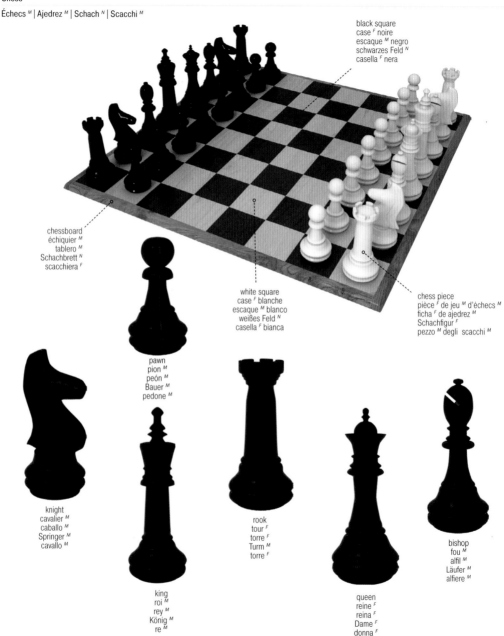

black square
case ^{F} noire
escaque ^{M} negro
schwarzes Feld ^{N}
casella ^{F} nera

chessboard
échiquier ^{M}
tablero ^{M}
Schachbrett ^{N}
scacchiera ^{F}

white square
case ^{F} blanche
escaque ^{M} blanco
weißes Feld ^{N}
casella ^{F} bianca

chess piece
pièce ^{F} de jeu ^{M} d'échecs ^{M}
ficha ^{F} de ajedrez ^{M}
Schachfigur ^{F}
pezzo ^{M} degli scacchi ^{M}

pawn
pion ^{M}
peón ^{M}
Bauer ^{M}
pedone ^{M}

knight
cavalier ^{M}
caballo ^{M}
Springer ^{M}
cavallo ^{M}

rook
tour ^{F}
torre ^{F}
Turm ^{M}
torre ^{F}

king
roi ^{M}
rey ^{M}
König ^{M}
re ^{M}

queen
reine ^{F}
reina ^{F}
Dame ^{F}
donna ^{F}

bishop
fou ^{M}
alfil ^{M}
Läufer ^{M}
alfiere ^{M}

Checkers

Jeu ^{M} de dames ^{F} | Damas ^{F} | Damespiel ^{N} | Dama ^{F}

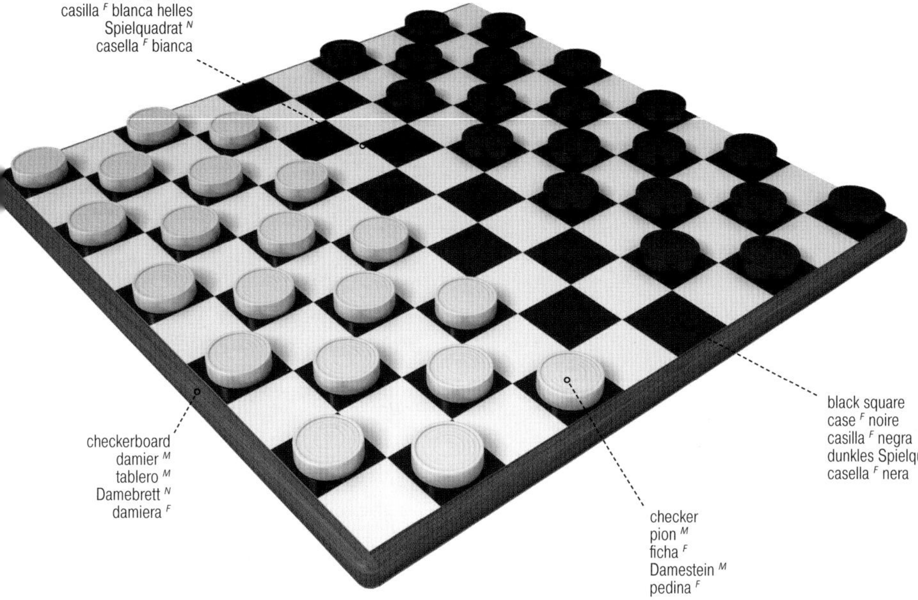
white square
case F blanche
casilla F blanca helles
Spielquadrat N
casella F bianca
black square
case F noire
casilla F negra
dunkles Spielquadrat N
casella F nera
checkerboard
damier M
tablero M
Damebrett N
damiera F
checker
pion M
ficha F
Damestein M
pedina F

Backgammon

Backgammon ^{M} | Backgammon ^{M} | Backgammon ^{N} | Backgammon ^{M}

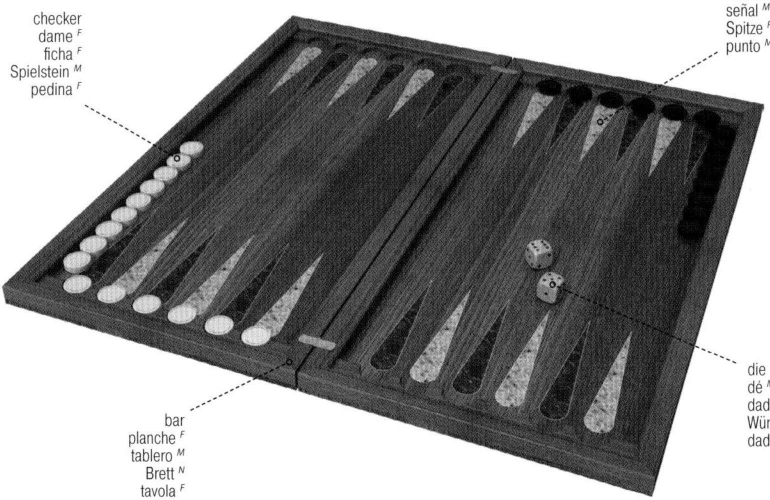
point
flèche F
señal M
Spitze F
punto M
checker
dame F
ficha F
Spielstein M
pedina F
die
dé M
dado M
Würfel M
dado M
bar
planche F
tablero M
Brett N
tavola F

bowling
jeu M de quilles M
bolo M / boliche M
Bowling N
bowling M

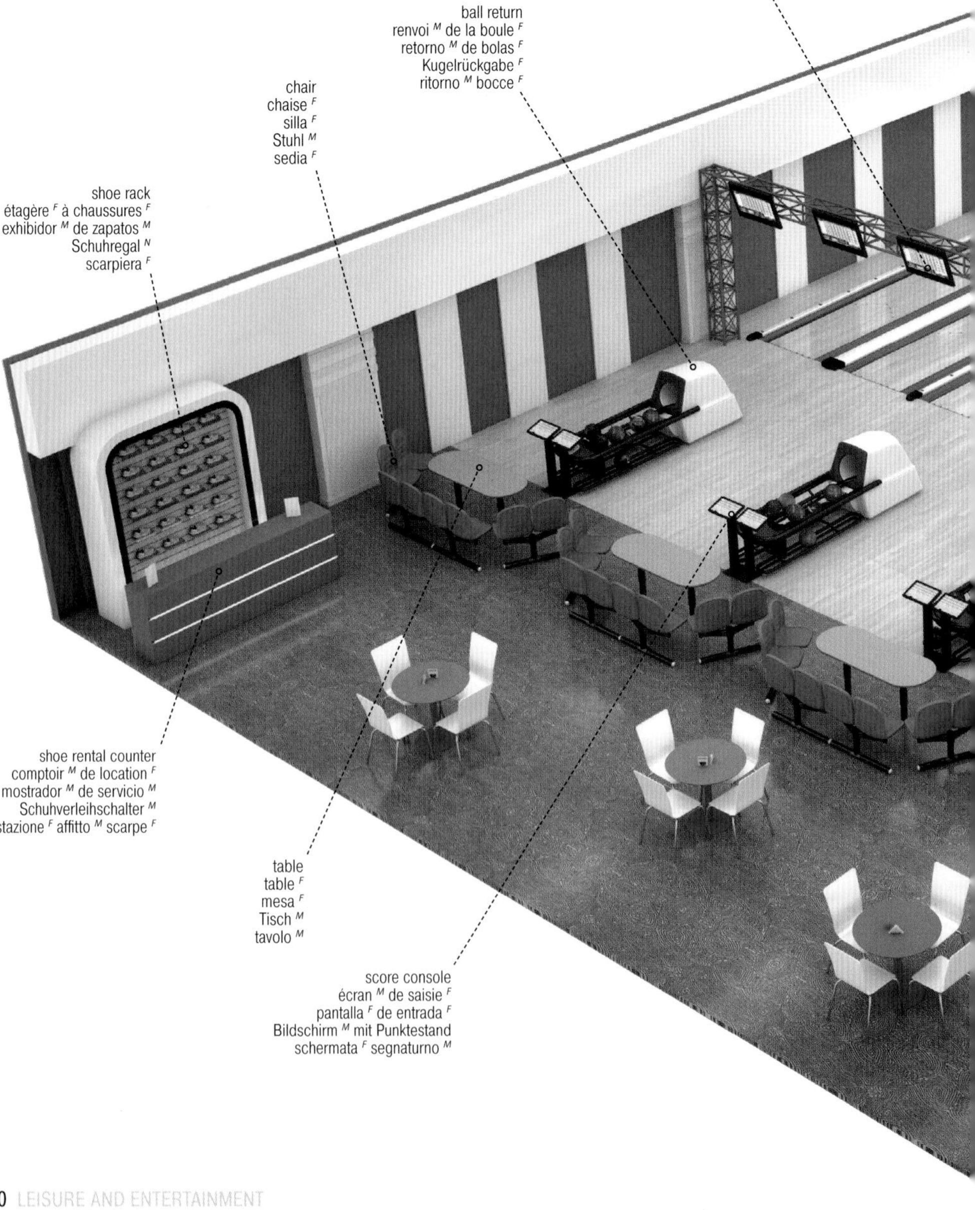
score screen
écran M de pointage M
pantalla F de puntos M
Punktestandanzeige F
schermo M segnapunti M
ball return
renvoi M de la boule F
retorno M de bolas F
Kugelrückgabe F
ritorno M bocce F
chair
chaise F
silla F
Stuhl M
sedia F
shoe rack
étagère F à chaussures F
exhibidor M de zapatos M
Schuhregal N
scarpiera F
shoe rental counter
comptoir M de location F
mostrador M de servicio M
Schuhverleihschalter M
postazione F affitto M scarpe F
table
table F
mesa F
Tisch M
tavolo M
score console
écran M de saisie F
pantalla F de entrada F
Bildschirm M mit Punktestand
schermata F segnaturno M

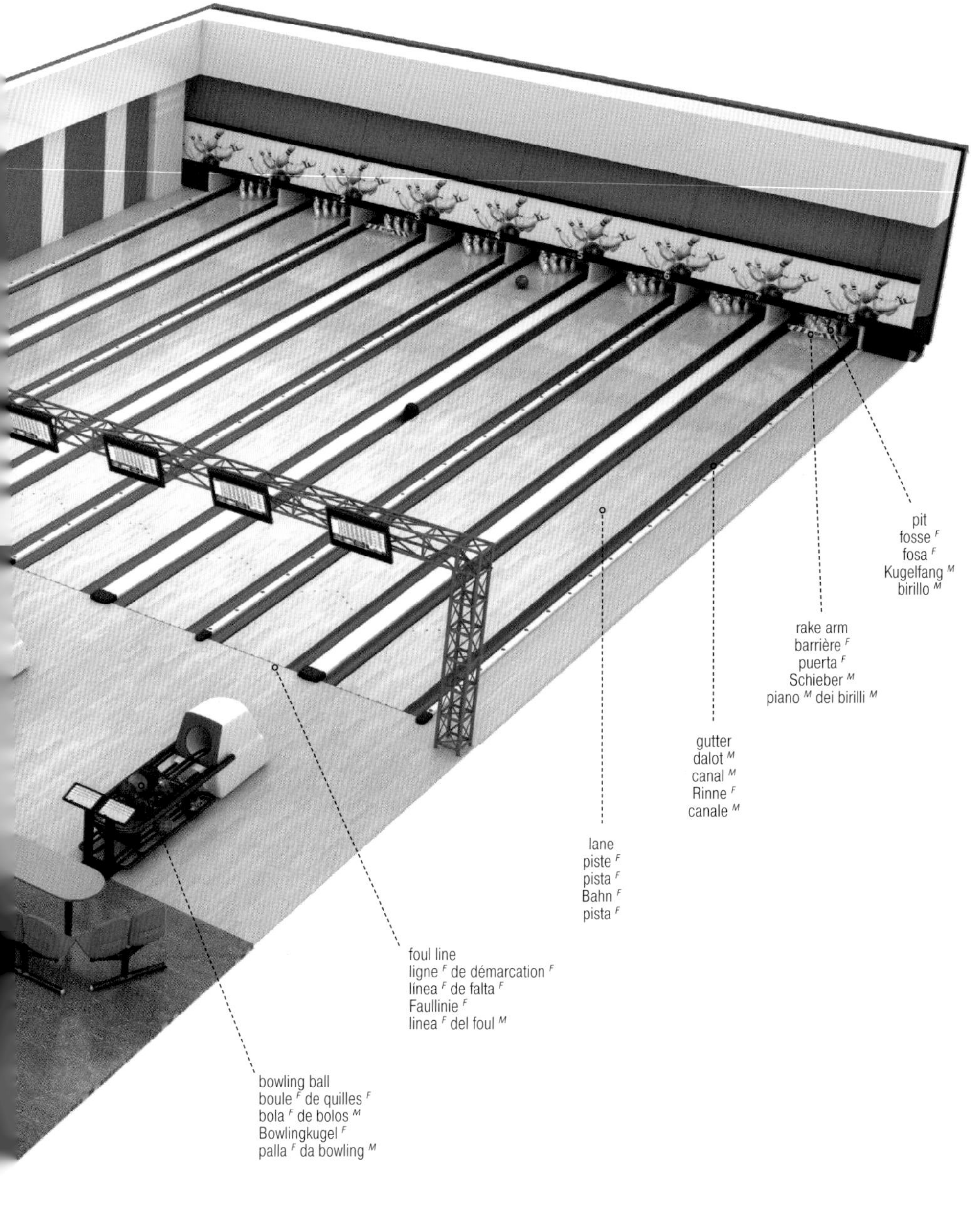
pit
fosse F
fosa F
Kugelfang M
birillo M
rake arm
barrière F
puerta F
Schieber M
piano M dei birilli M
gutter
dalot M
canal M
Rinne F
canale M
lane
piste F
pista F
Bahn F
pista F
foul line
ligne F de démarcation F
línea F de falta F
Faullinie F
linea F del foul M
bowling ball
boule F de quilles F
bola F de bolos M
Bowlingkugel F
palla F da bowling M

ball return
renvoi [M] de la boule [F]
retorno [M] de bolas [F]
Kugelrückgabe [F]
ritorno [M] bocce [F]

ball return window
fenêtre [F] de renvoi [M] de boules [F]
ventana [F] de retorno [M] de bolas [F]
Rückgabefenster [N]
bocchetta [F] di fuoriuscita [F] bocce [F]

track
piste [F]
guía [F]
Bahn [F]
binario [M]

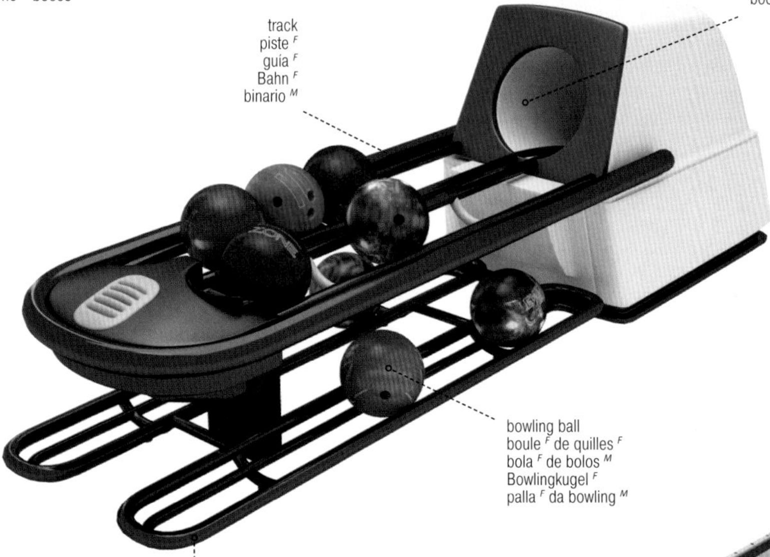

bowling ball
boule [F] de quilles [F]
bola [F] de bolos [M]
Bowlingkugel [F]
palla [F] da bowling [M]

ball stand
support [M] à boules [F]
repisa [F]
Ballablage [F]
griglia [F]

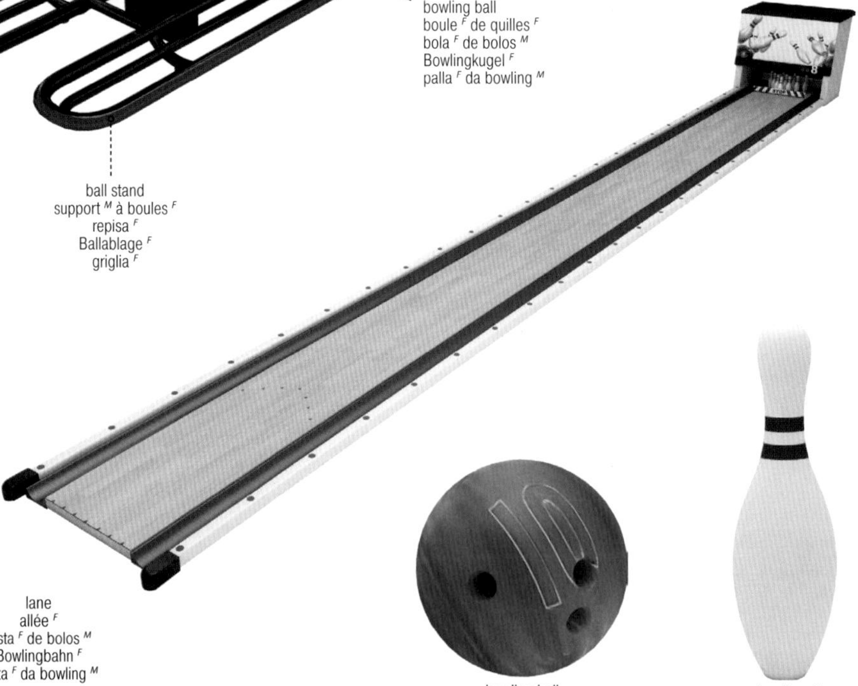

lane
allée [F]
pista [F] de bolos [M]
Bowlingbahn [F]
pista [F] da bowling [M]

bowling ball
boule [F] de quilles [F]
bola [F] de bolos [M]
Bowlingkugel [F]
palla [F] da bowling [M]

bowling pin
quille [F]
bolo [M] / pin [M]
Kegel [M]
birillo [M]

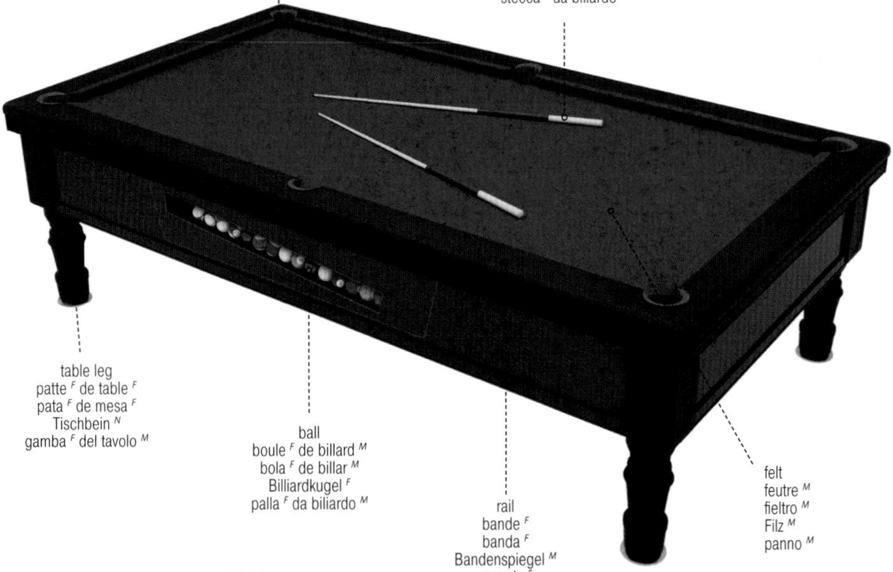
billiard table
table ^{F} de billard ^{M}
mesa ^{F} de billar ^{M}
Billiardtisch ^{M}
tavolo ^{M} da biliardo ^{M}
pocket
poche ^{F}
buchaca ^{F}
Tasche ^{F}
buca ^{F}
pool cue
baguette ^{F} de billard ^{M}
taco ^{M}
Queue ^{N}
stecca ^{F} da biliardo ^{M}
table leg
patte ^{F} de table ^{F}
pata ^{F} de mesa ^{F}
Tischbein ^{N}
gamba ^{F} del tavolo ^{M}
ball
boule ^{F} de billard ^{M}
bola ^{F} de billar ^{M}
Billiardkugel ^{F}
palla ^{F} da biliardo ^{M}
rail
bande ^{F}
banda ^{F}
Bandenspiegel ^{M}
sponda ^{F}
felt
feutre ^{M}
fieltro ^{M}
Filz ^{M}
panno ^{M}

snooker table
table ^{F} de snooker ^{M}
mesa ^{F} de snooker ^{M}
Snookertisch ^{M}
tavolo ^{M} da biliardo ^{M}

billiards rack
support ^{M} de baguettes ^{F} de billard ^{M}
soporte ^{M} de billar
Dreieck ^{N}
triangolo ^{M}

billiards chalk
craie ^{F} de billard ^{M}
tiza ^{F} de billar
Kreide ^{F}
gessetto ^{M}

electronic dartboard
jeu [M] de fléchettes [F] électronique
tablero [M] de dardos [M] electrónico
elektronisches Dartbrett [N]
gioco [M] delle freccette [F] elettronico

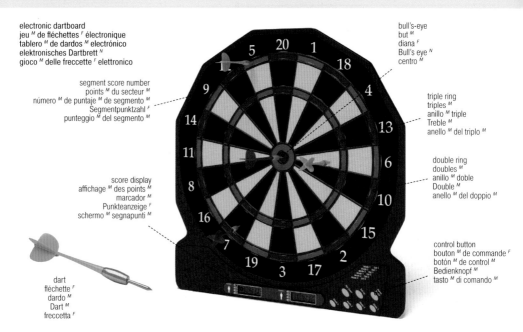

segment score number
points [M] du secteur [M]
número [M] de puntaje [M] de segmento [M]
Segmentpunktzahl [F]
punteggio [M] del segmento [M]

score display
affichage [M] des points [M]
marcador [M]
Punkteanzeige [F]
schermo [M] segnapunti [M]

20
1
18
4
13
6
10
15
2
17
3
19
7
16
8
11
14
9
5

bull's-eye
but [M]
diana [F]
Bull's eye [N]
centro [M]

triple ring
triples [M]
anillo [M] triple
Treble [M]
anello [M] del triplo [M]

double ring
doubles [M]
anillo [M] doble
Double [M]
anello [M] del doppio [M]

control button
bouton [M] de commande [F]
botón [M] de control [M]
Bedienknopf [M]
tasto [M] di comando [M]

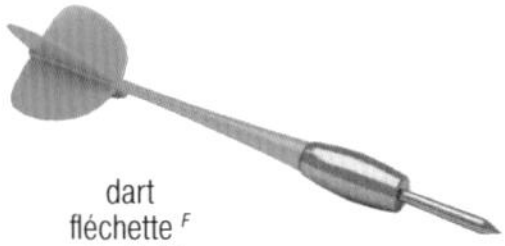

dart
fléchette [F]
dardo [M]
Dart [M]
freccetta [F]

ARCADE GAMES

bowling game
jeu [M] vidéo [F] de quilles [F]
simulador [M] de bolos [M]
Bowlingsimulator [M]
simulatore [M] di bowling [M]

claw crane machine
machine [F] attrape-peluches [F]
máquina [F] atrapa peluches [M]
Greiferspielautomat [M]
macchina [F] da claw crane [M]

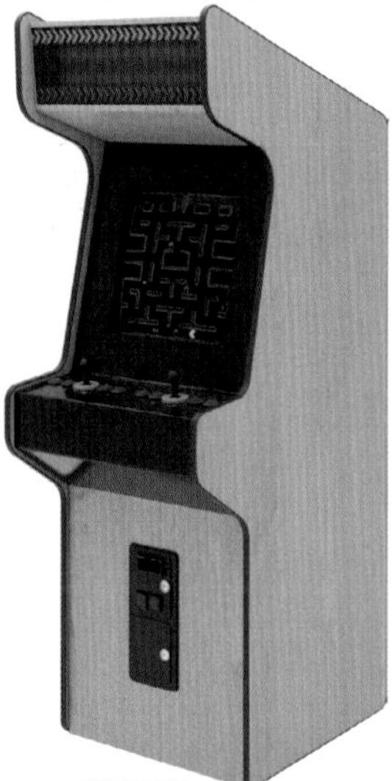

maze game
jeu [M] de labyrinthe [M]
juego laberíntico [M]
Labyrinthspiel [N]
videogioco [M] labirinto [M]

air hockey table
table ^{F} de hockey ^{M} pneumatique
mesa ^{F} de hockey ^{M} de aire ^{M}
Airhockeytisch ^{M}
tavolo ^{M} da air hockey ^{M}

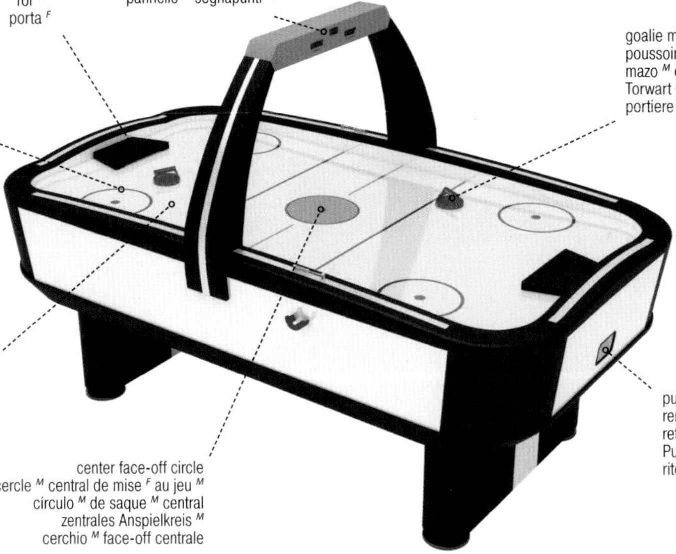

goal
but ^{M}
portería ^{F}
Tor ^{N}
porta ^{F}

score display
tableau ^{M} de pointage ^{M}
marcador ^{M}
Punktestandanzeige ^{F}
pannello ^{M} segnapunti ^{M}

face-off spot
zone ^{F} de mise ^{F} au jeu ^{M}
área ^{M} de saque ^{M}
Bullypunkt ^{M}
punto ^{M} di ingaggio ^{M}

goalie mallet
poussoir ^{M}
mazo ^{M} de portero ^{M}
Torwart ^{M}
portiere ^{M}

playing surface
surface ^{F} de jeu ^{M}
campo ^{M} de juego ^{M}
Spielfeld ^{N}
campo ^{M} da gioco ^{M}

puck return
renvoi ^{M} de la rondelle ^{F}
retorno ^{M} de disco ^{M}
Puckrückgabe ^{F}
ritorno ^{M} del disco ^{M}

center face-off circle
cercle ^{M} central de mise ^{F} au jeu ^{M}
círculo ^{M} de saque ^{M} central
zentrales Anspielkreis ^{M}
cerchio ^{M} face-off centrale

soccer table
table ^{M} de soccer ^{M}
futbolito ^{M}
Tischfußball ^{M}
calcio ^{M} balilla

fighting game
jeu ^{M} de combat ^{M}
simulador ^{M} de combate ^{M}
Kampfsimulator ^{M}
simulatore ^{M} di combattimento ^{M}

table hockey
hockey sur table [M]
hockey [M] de mesa [F]
Tischhockey [N]
hockey [M] da tavolo [M]

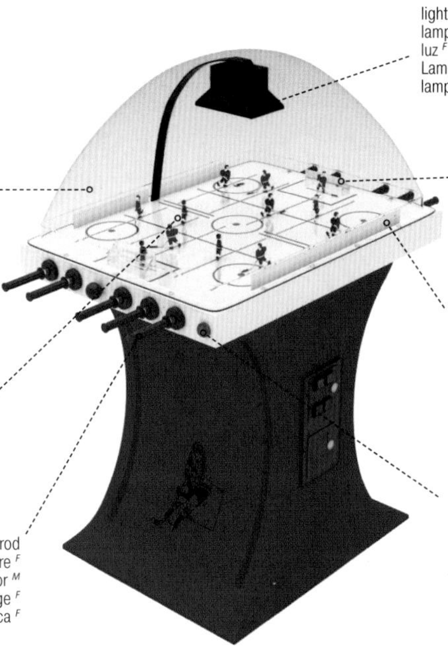
light
lampe [F]
luz [F]
Lampe [F]
lampada [F]
dome
dôme [M]
cristal [M] protector
Schutzkuppel [F]
vetro [M] protettivo
goal
but [M]
portería [F]
Tor [N]
porta [F]
bumper
bande [F]
banda [F]
Bande [F]
sponda [F]
player
joueur [M]
jugador [M]
Spieler [M]
giocatore [M]
start button
bouton [M] de démarrage [M]
botón [M] de inicio [M]
Startknopf [M]
tasto [M] di inizio [M]
rod
barre [F]
control [M] del jugador [M]
Stange [F]
stecca [F]

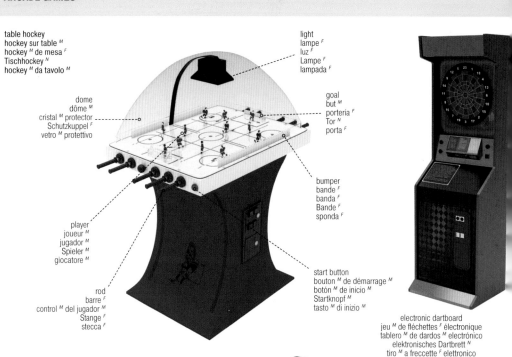

electronic dartboard
jeu [M] de fléchettes [F] électronique
tablero [M] de dardos [M] electrónico
elektronisches Dartbrett [N]
tiro [M] a freccette [F] elettronico

motorcycle racing game
jeu [M] de course [F] de moto [F]
simulador [M] de motos [F]
Motorradrennensimulator [M]
simulatore [M] di corse [F] di motociclette [F]

two-person shooter game
jeu [M] de tir [M] à deux joueurs [M]
simulador [M] de tiro [M] en paralelo
Zweipersonen-Schießsimulator [M]
sparatutto [M] per due persone [F]

boxing simulator
simulateur [M] de boxe
simulador [M] de boxeo
Boxsimulator [M]
simulatore [M] di boxe

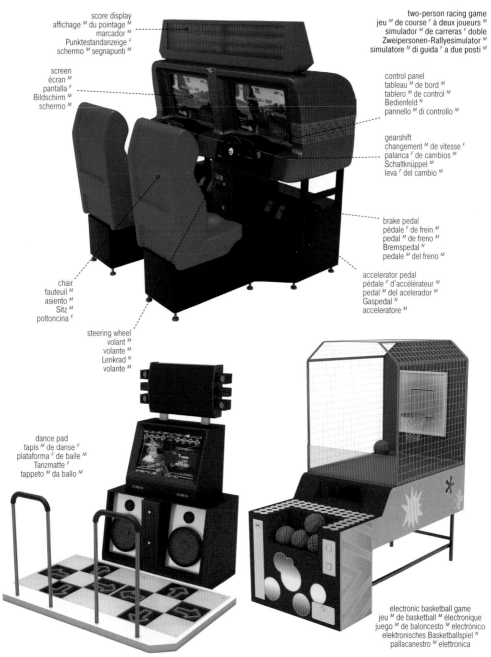

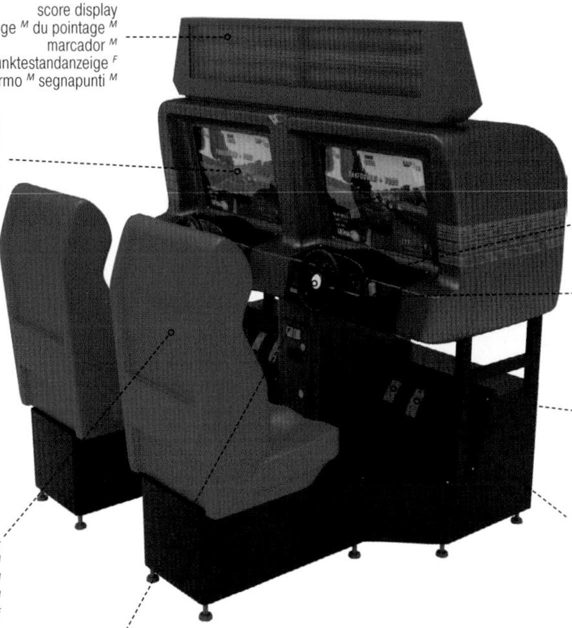
two-person racing game
jeu ^{M} de course ^{F} à deux joueurs ^{M}
simulador ^{M} de carreras ^{F} doble
Zweipersonen-Rallyesimulator ^{M}
simulatore ^{M} di guida ^{F} a due posti ^{M}
score display
affichage ^{M} du pointage ^{M}
marcador ^{M}
Punktestandanzeige ^{F}
schermo ^{M} segnapunti ^{M}
screen
écran ^{M}
pantalla ^{F}
Bildschirm ^{M}
schermo ^{M}
control panel
tableau ^{M} de bord ^{M}
tablero ^{M} de control ^{M}
Bedienfeld ^{N}
pannello ^{M} di controllo ^{M}
gearshift
changement ^{M} de vitesse ^{F}
palanca ^{F} de cambios ^{M}
Schaltknüppel ^{M}
leva ^{F} del cambio ^{M}
brake pedal
pédale ^{F} de frein ^{M}
pedal ^{M} de freno ^{M}
Bremspedal ^{N}
pedale ^{M} del freno ^{M}
accelerator pedal
pédale ^{F} d'accélérateur ^{M}
pedal ^{M} del acelerador ^{M}
Gaspedal ^{N}
acceleratore ^{M}
chair
fauteuil ^{M}
asiento ^{M}
Sitz ^{M}
poltoncina ^{F}
steering wheel
volant ^{M}
volante ^{M}
Lenkrad ^{N}
volante ^{M}

dance pad
tapis ^{M} de danse ^{F}
plataforma ^{F} de baile ^{M}
Tanzmatte ^{F}
tappeto ^{M} da ballo ^{M}

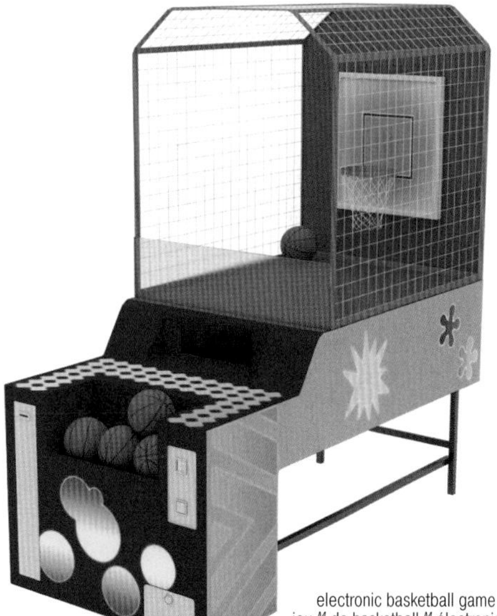
electronic basketball game
jeu ^{M} de basketball ^{M} électronique
juego ^{M} de baloncesto ^{M} electrónico
elektronisches Basketballspiel ^{N}
pallacanestro ^{M} elettronica

roulette table
table ^{F} de roulette ^{F}
ruleta ^{F}
Roulettetisch ^{M}
roulette ^{F}

chip
jeton ^{M}
ficha ^{F} de juego ^{M}
Spielchip ^{M}
fiches ^{F}

croupier's area
place ^{F} du croupier ^{M}
zona ^{F} del crupier ^{M}
Croupierbereich ^{M}
postazione ^{F} del croupier ^{M}

layout
grille ^{F}
zona ^{F} de juego ^{M}
Spielfeld ^{N} area ^{F}
di gioco ^{M}

chip holder
porte-jetons ^{M}
soporte ^{M} para ficha ^{F}
Chiphalter ^{M}
supporto ^{M} per fiches ^{F}

roulette wheel
roulette ^{F}
rueda ^{F} de ruleta ^{F}
Rouletterad ^{N}
ruota ^{F} della roulette ^{F}

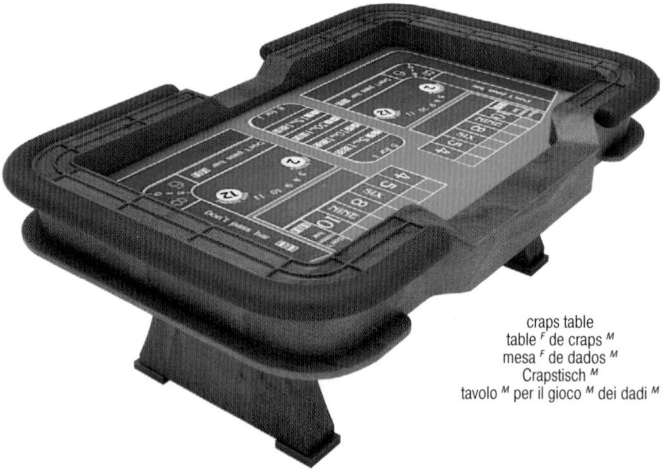
craps table
table ^{F} de craps ^{M}
mesa ^{F} de dados ^{M}
Crapstisch ^{M}
tavolo ^{M} per il gioco ^{M} dei dadi ^{M}

slot machine
machine ^{F} à sous ^{M}
máquina ^{F} tragamonedas ^{F}
Glücksspielautomat ^{M}
slot machine ^{F}

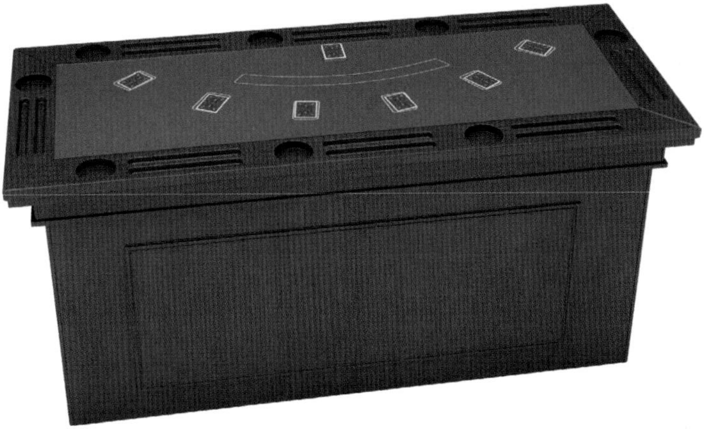

casino poker table
table F de poker M de casino M
mesa F de blackjack M
Casino-Pokertisch M
tavolo M da poker M per casinò M

poker table
table F de poker M
mesa F de póquer M
Pokertisch M
tavolo M da poker M

card table
table F à jeu M de cartes F
mesa F de cartas F
Kartentisch M
tavolo M per il gioco M delle carte F

Suits

Couleurs [F] | Palos [M] | Spielkartenfarben [F] | Semi [M] delle carte [F]

hearts
cœur [M]
corazones [M]
Herz [N]
cuori [M]

diamonds
carreau [M]
diamantes [M]
Karo [N]
quadri [M]

clubs
trèfle [M]
tréboles [M]
Kreuz [N]
fiori [M]

spades
pique [F]
picas [F]
Pik [N]
picche [F]

Face cards and special cards

Figures [F] et cartes [F] spéciales | Cartas [F] de números [M] y cartas [F] de figuras [F] | Bildkarten [F] und spezielle Karten [F] | Facce [F] delle carte [F]

jack
valet [M]
sota [F]
Bube [M]
jack [M]

queen
reine [F]
reina [F]
Dame [F]
regina [F]

king
roi [M]
rey [M]
König [M]
re [M]

ace
as [M]
as [M]
Ass [N]
asso [M]

joker
joker [M]
joker [M]
Joker [M]
jolly [M]

Standard poker hands

Mains [F] de poker [M] standards | Manos [M] de póquer [M] estándar | Pokerkombinationen [F] | Punti [M] del poker [M]

one pair
paire [F]
par [M]
Paar [N]
coppia [F]

two pairs
double paire [F]
dos pares [M]
Zwei Paare [F]
doppia coppia [F]

three of a kind
brelan [M]
trío [M]
Drilling [M]
tris [M]

straight
suite [F]
escalera [F]
Straße [F]
scala [F]

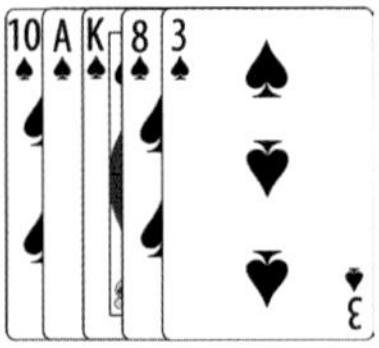

flush
couleur [F]
color [M]
Flush [M]
colore [M]

full house
main [F] pleine
full [M]
Full House [N]
full [M]

four of a kind
carré [M]
póquer [M]
Vierling [M]
poker [M]

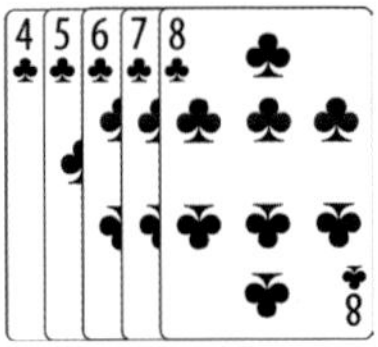

straight flush
quinte [F] couleur [F]
escalera [F] de color [M]
Straße in einer Farbe [F]
scala [F] a colore [M]

royal flush
quinte [F] royale
escalera [F] real
Royal Flush [M]
scala [F] reale

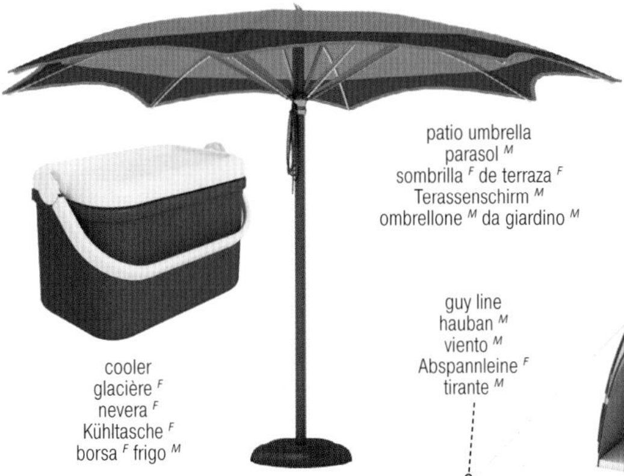
patio umbrella
parasol [M]
sombrilla [F] de terraza [F]
Terassenschirm [M]
ombrellone [M] da giardino [M]
guy line
hauban [M]
viento [M]
Abspannleine [F]
tirante [M]
cooler
glacière [F]
nevera [F]
Kühltasche [F]
borsa [F] frigo [M]

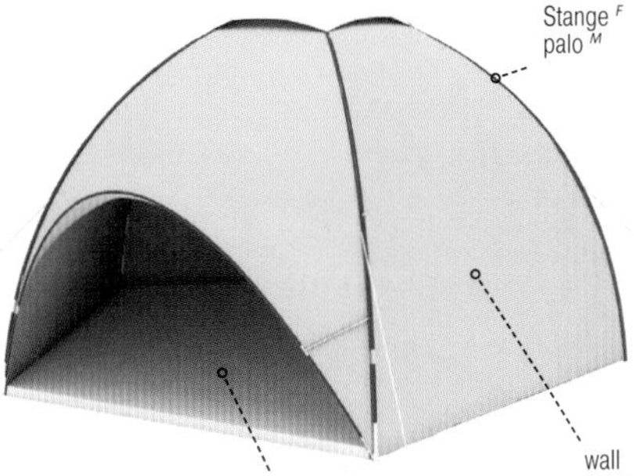
tent
tente [F]
tienda [F] de campaña [F]
Zelt [N]
tenda [F]
pole
arceau [M]
vara [F]
Stange [F]
palo [M]
floor
plancher [M]
suelo [M]
Boden [M]
pavimento [M]
wall
habitacle [M]
tela [F] de tienda [F]
Zeltwand [F]
parete [F] della tenda [F]

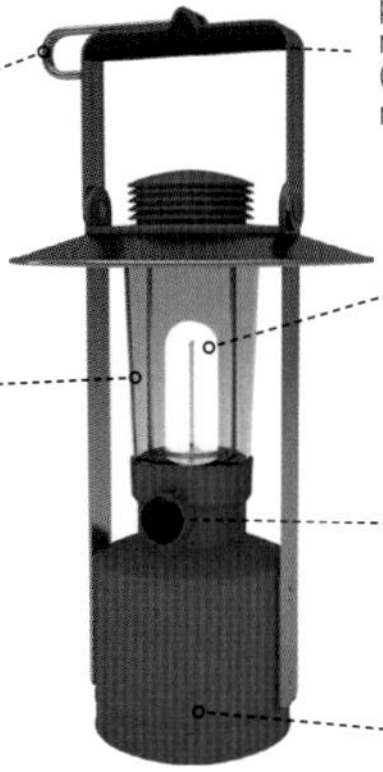
lantern
lanterne [F]
lámpara [F]
Laterne [F]
lanterna [F]
hook
crochet [M]
gancho [F]
Haken [M]
gancio [M]
handle
poignée [F]
mango [M]
Griff [M]
manico [M]
lamp
lampe [F]
lámpara [F]
Lampe [F]
lampada [F]
globe
globe [M]
cristal [M]
Glas [N]
paravento [M]
on/off button
bouton [M] d'alimentation [F]
botón [M] de encendido [M]
An-/Aus-Schalter
pulsante [M] di accensione [F]/ spegnimento [M]
housing
boîtier [M]
cuerpo [M]
Gehäuse [N]
alloggiamento [M]

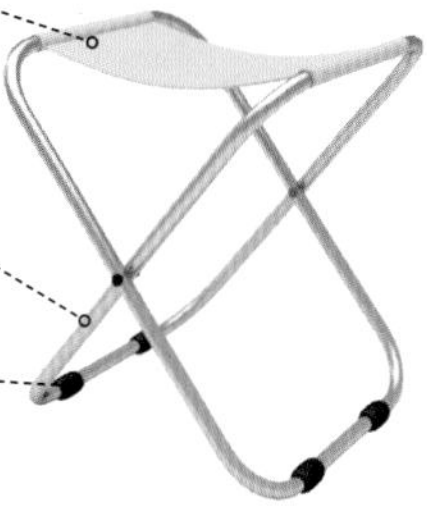
folding camp stool
tabouret [M] de camping [M] pliant
silla [F] plegable
Klappstuhl [M]
sedia [F] pieghevole
seat
siège [M]
asiento [M]
Sitz [M]
seduta [F]
leg
patte [M]
pata [F]
Standbein [N]
gamba [F]
skid-proof foot
patin [FM] antidérapant
banda [F] antideslizante
Rutschschutz [M]
gommini [M] antiscivolo

backpack
sac à dos [M]
mochila [F]
Rucksack [M]
zaino [M]

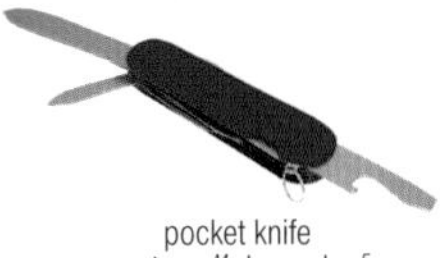
pocket knife
couteau [M] de poche [F]
navaja [F]
Taschenmesser [N]
coltellino [M] da tasca [F]

flashlight
lampe [F] de poche [F]
linterna [F]
Taschenlampe [F]
torcia [F]

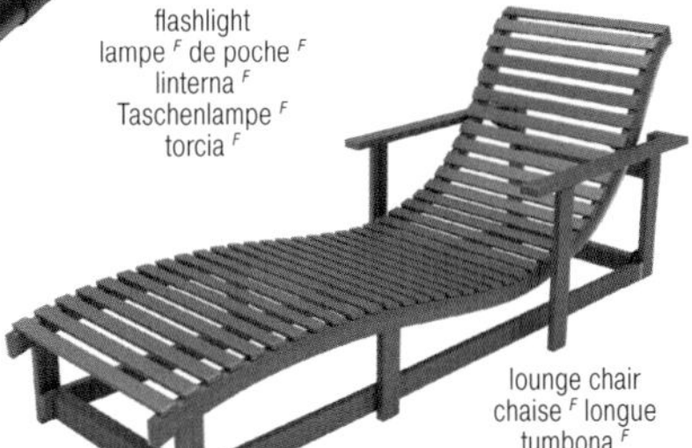
lounge chair
chaise [F] longue
tumbona [F]
Liegestuhl [M]
lettino [M] prendisole

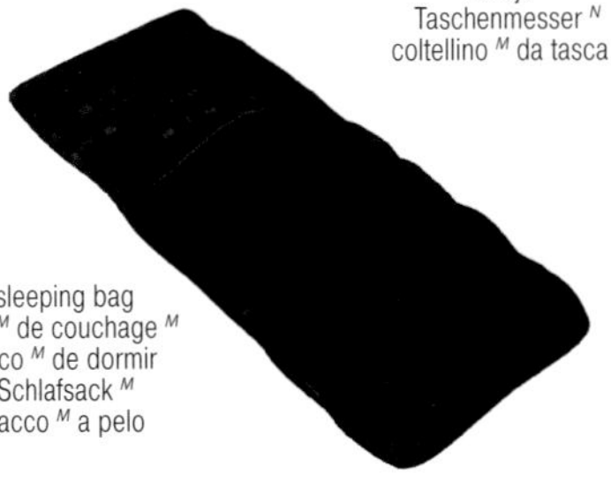
sleeping bag
sac [M] de couchage [M]
saco [M] de dormir
Schlafsack [M]
sacco [M] a pelo

thermal jug
pot [M] isolant
termo [M]
Thermoskanne [F]
thermos [M]

rifle
carabine M
rifle M
Jagdgewehr N
fucile M da caccia F

rifle cartridge
cartouche F de carabine F
cartucho M para rifle M
Gewehrpatrone F
cartuccia F per carabina F

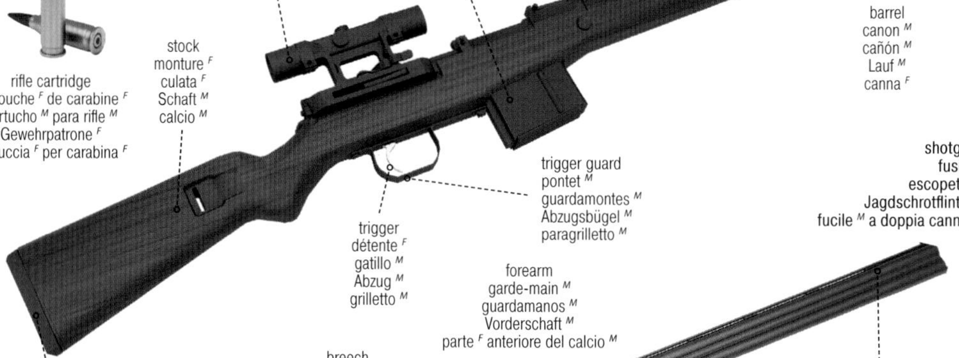
scope
mire F
visor M
Zielfernrohr N
mirino M telescopico
magazine
chargeur M
cargador M
Magazin N
caricatore M
sight
viseur M
mirilla F
Visier N
mirino M
barrel
canon M
cañón M
Lauf M
canna F
stock
monture F
culata F
Schaft M
calcio M
trigger guard
pontet M
guardamontes M
Abzugsbügel M
paragrilletto M
trigger
détente F
gatillo M
Abzug M
grilletto M
butt plate
plaque F de couche F
cantonera F
Kolbenblech N
calciolo M

shotgun
fusil M
escopeta F
Jagdschrotflinte F
fucile M a doppia canna F

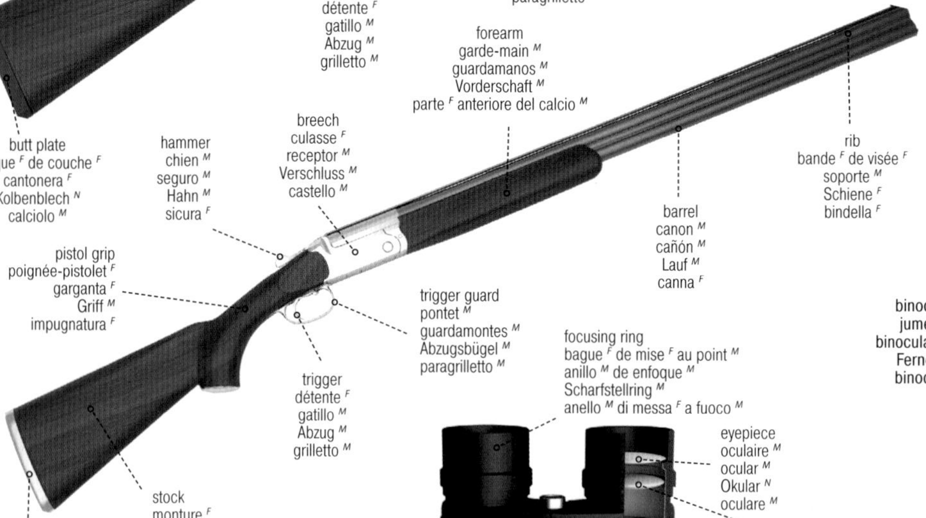
forearm
garde-main M
guardamanos M
Vorderschaft M
parte F anteriore del calcio M
rib
bande F de visée F
soporte M
Schiene F
bindella F
breech
culasse F
receptor M
Verschluss M
castello M
hammer
chien M
seguro M
Hahn M
sicura F
barrel
canon M
cañón M
Lauf M
canna F
pistol grip
poignée-pistolet F
garganta F
Griff M
impugnatura F
trigger guard
pontet M
guardamontes M
Abzugsbügel M
paragrilletto M
trigger
détente F
gatillo M
Abzug M
grilletto M
stock
monture F
culata F
Schaft M
calcio M
butt plate
plaque F de couche F
cantonera F
Kolbenblech N
calciolo M

shotgun cartridge
cartouche F à fusil M
cartucho M para escopeta F
Schrotflintenpatrone F
cartuccia F per fucile M

binocula
jumelle
binoculares
Fernglas
binocolc

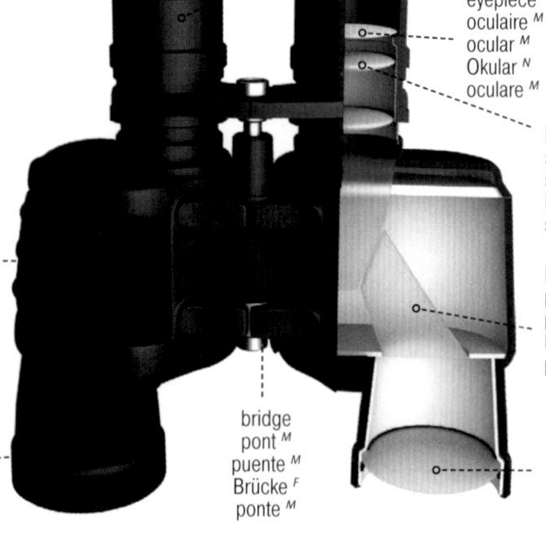
focusing ring
bague F de mise F au point M
anillo M de enfoque M
Scharfstellring M
anello M di messa F a fuoco M
eyepiece
oculaire M
ocular M
Okular N
oculare M
lens system
système M de lentilles F
sistema M de lentes F
Linsensystem N
sistema M di lenti F
central focusing wheel
molette F de mise F au point M centrale
rueda F central de enfoque M
zentrales Scharfstellrad N
rotella F centrale di messa F a fuoco M
Porro prism
prisme M de Porro
prisma M de Porro
Porro-Prisma N
prisma M di Porro
body
tube M
tubo M
Gehäuse N
corpo M
bridge
pont M
puente M
Brücke F
ponte M
objective lens
objectif M
objetivo M
Objektiv N
lente F obiettivo M

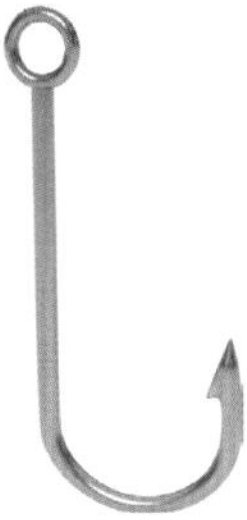

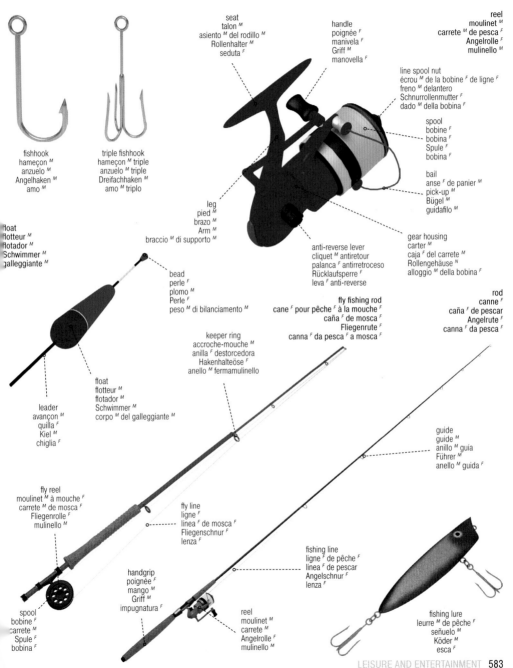

fishhook
hameçon [M]
anzuelo [M]
Angelhaken [M]
amo [M]

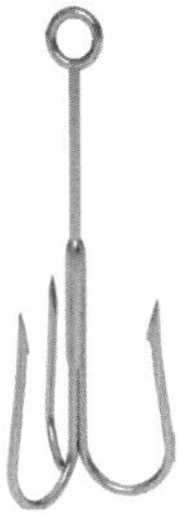

triple fishhook
hameçon [M] triple
anzuelo [M] triple
Dreifachhaken [M]
amo [M] triplo

reel
moulinet [M]
carrete [M] de pesca [F]
Angelrolle [F]
mulinello [M]

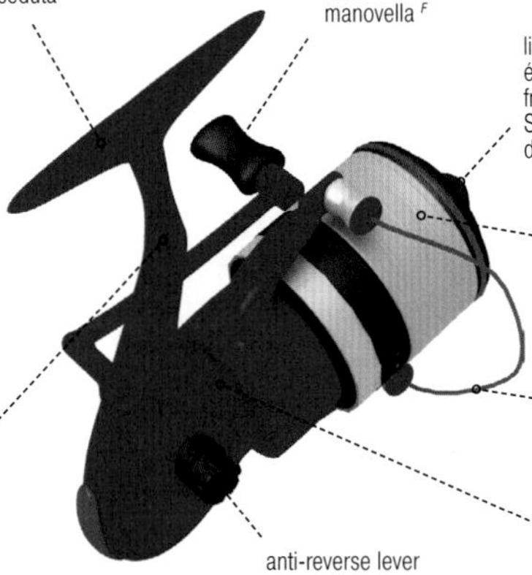

seat
talon [M]
asiento [M] del rodillo [M]
Rollenhalter [M]
seduta [F]

handle
poignée [F]
manivela [F]
Griff [M]
manovella [F]

line spool nut
écrou [M] de la bobine [F] de ligne [F]
freno [M] delantero
Schnurrollenmutter [F]
dado [M] della bobina [F]

spool
bobine [F]
bobina [F]
Spule [F]
bobina [F]

bail
anse [F] de panier [M]
pick-up [M]
Bügel [M]
guidafilo [M]

leg
pied [M]
brazo [M]
Arm [M]
braccio [M] di supporto [M]

anti-reverse lever
cliquet [M] antiretour
palanca [F] antirretroceso
Rücklaufsperre [F]
leva [F] anti-reverse

gear housing
carter [M]
caja [F] del carrete [M]
Rollengehäuse [N]
alloggio [M] della bobina [F]

float
flotteur [M]
flotador [M]
Schwimmer [M]
galleggiante [M]

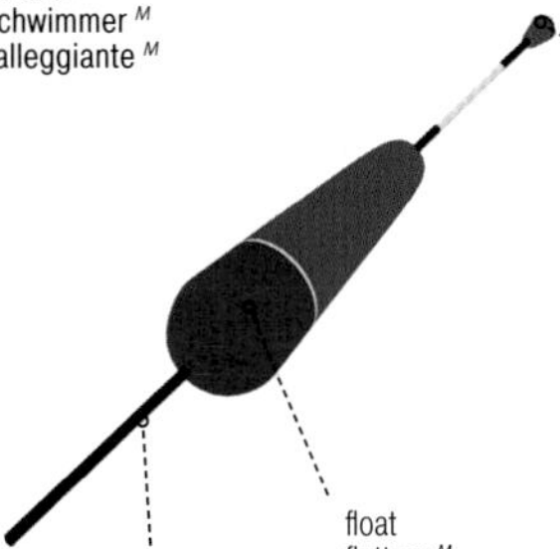

bead
perle [F]
plomo [M]
Perle [F]
peso [M] di bilanciamento [M]

leader
avançon [M]
quilla [F]
Kiel [M]
chiglia [F]

float
flotteur [M]
flotador [M]
Schwimmer [M]
corpo [M] del galleggiante [M]

fly fishing rod
cane [F] pour pêche [F] à la mouche [F]
caña [F] de mosca [F]
Fliegenrute [F]
canna [F] da pesca [F] a mosca [F]

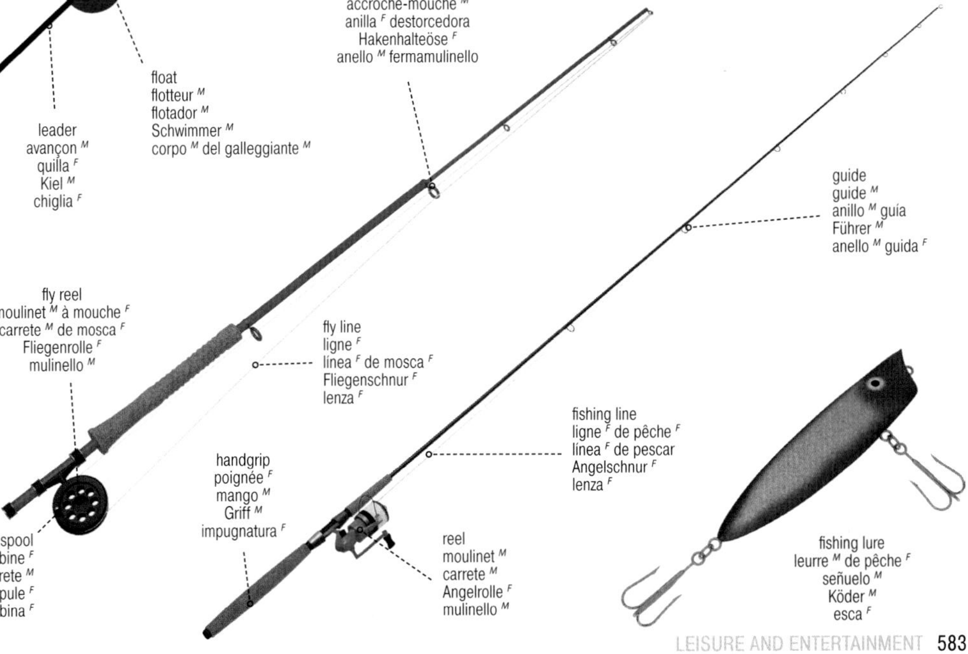

keeper ring
accroche-mouche [M]
anilla [F] destorcedora
Hakenhalteöse [F]
anello [M] fermamulinello

fly reel
moulinet [M] à mouche [F]
carrete [M] de mosca [F]
Fliegenrolle [F]
mulinello [M]

fly line
ligne [F]
línea [F] de mosca [F]
Fliegenschnur [F]
lenza [F]

spool
bobine [F]
carrete [M]
Spule [F]
bobina [F]

rod
canne [F]
caña [F] de pescar
Angelrute [F]
canna [F] da pesca [F]

guide
guide [M]
anillo [M] guía
Führer [M]
anello [M] guida [F]

fishing line
ligne [F] de pêche [F]
línea [F] de pescar
Angelschnur [F]
lenza [F]

handgrip
poignée [F]
mango [M]
Griff [M]
impugnatura [F]

reel
moulinet [M]
carrete [M]
Angelrolle [F]
mulinello [M]

fishing lure
leurre [M] de pêche [F]
señuelo [M]
Köder [M]
esca [F]

(three year moving average)
Mass Supported (kg)
Year

OFFICE

cubicles
postes ^{M} de travail ^{M} modulaires
cubículos ^{M}
Großraumbüro ^{N}
postazioni ^{F} dipendenti ^{M}

file box
boîte-classeur ^{F}
caja ^{F} de documentos ^{M}
scatola ^{F}
portadocumenti ^{M}

sticky note
feuillet ^{M} autoadhésif
nota ^{F} autoadhesiva
Klebezettel ^{M}
foglietto ^{M} adesivo ^{M}

monitor
écran ^{M}
monitor ^{M}
Monitor ^{M}
monitor ^{M}

pen and pencil cup
porte-crayons ^{M}
portalápices ^{M}
Kuli- und Stiftehalter ^{M}
portapenne ^{M}

letter organizer
boîte ^{F} à courrier ^{M}
organizador ^{M} de escritorio ^{M}
Postein- und ausgangsablage ^{F}
supporto ^{M} portadocumenti ^{M}

letter tray
boîte ^{F} à courrier ^{M}
bandeja ^{F}
Ablage ^{F}
vaschetta ^{F} portadocumenti ^{M}

partition
cloison ^{F}
separador ^{M}
Trennwand ^{F}
divisorio ^{M}

desk
bureau ^{M}
escritorio ^{M}
Schreibtisch ^{M}
scrivania ^{F}

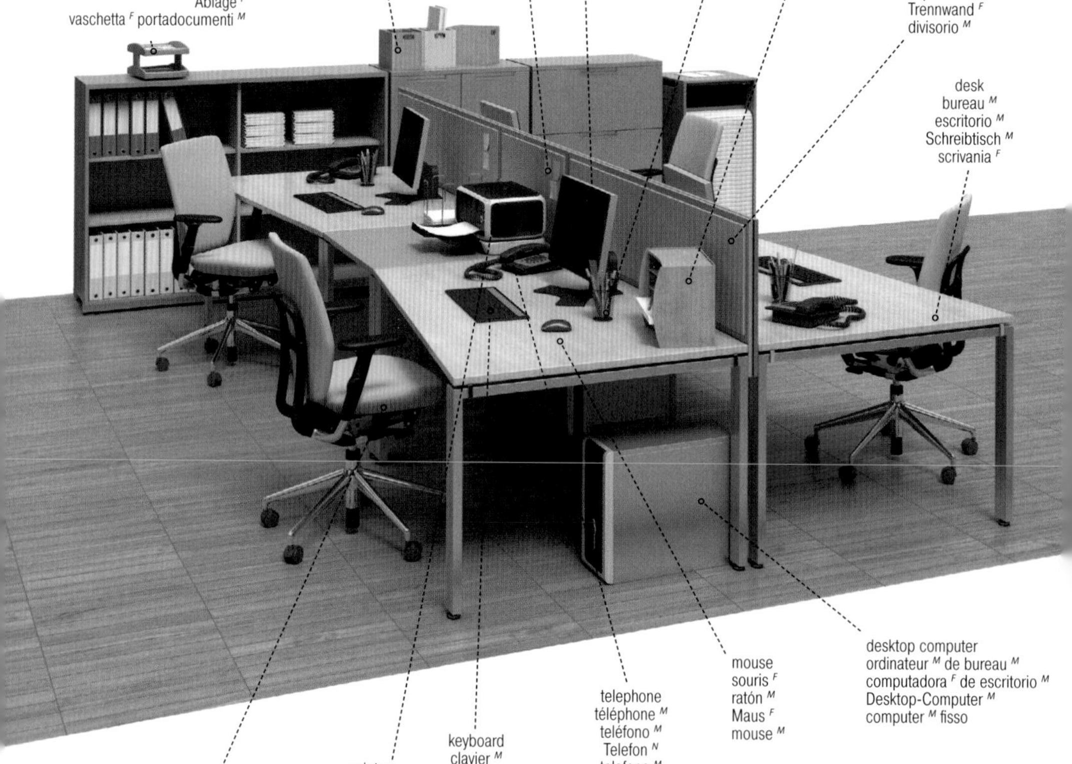

desktop computer
ordinateur ^{M} de bureau ^{M}
computadora ^{F} de escritorio ^{M}
Desktop-Computer ^{M}
computer ^{M} fisso

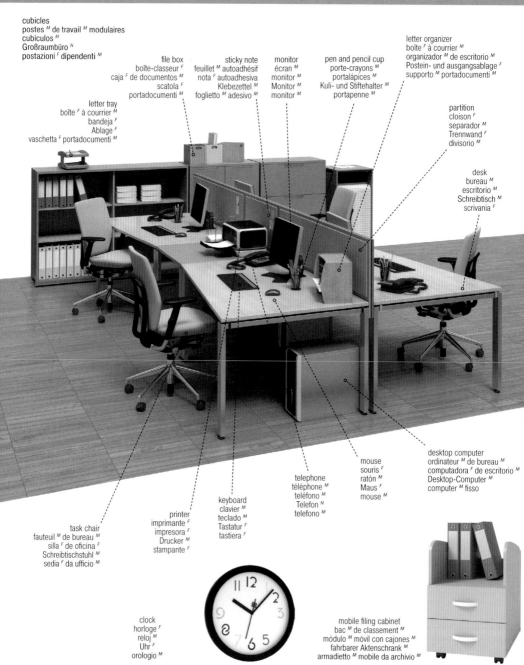

mouse
souris ^{F}
ratón ^{M}
Maus ^{F}
mouse ^{M}

telephone
téléphone ^{M}
teléfono ^{M}
Telefon ^{N}
telefono ^{M}

keyboard
clavier ^{M}
teclado ^{M}
Tastatur ^{F}
tastiera ^{F}

printer
imprimante ^{F}
impresora ^{F}
Drucker ^{M}
stampante ^{F}

task chair
fauteuil ^{M} de bureau ^{M}
silla ^{F} de oficina ^{F}
Schreibtischstuhl ^{M}
sedia ^{F} da ufficio ^{M}

clock
horloge ^{F}
reloj ^{M}
Uhr ^{F}
orologio ^{M}

mobile filing cabinet
bac ^{M} de classement ^{M}
módulo ^{M} móvil con cajones ^{M}
fahrbarer Aktenschrank ^{M}
armadietto ^{M} mobile da archivio ^{M}

call center
centre ᴹ d'appels ᴹ
centro ᴹ de atención telefónica ᶠ
Callcenter ᴺ
call-center ᴹ

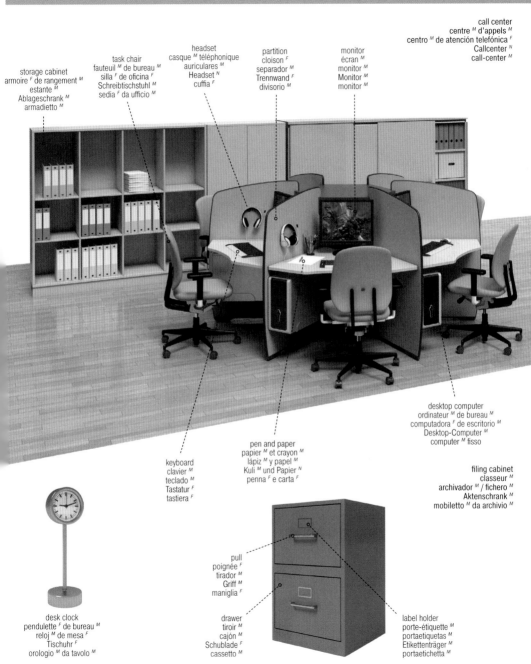

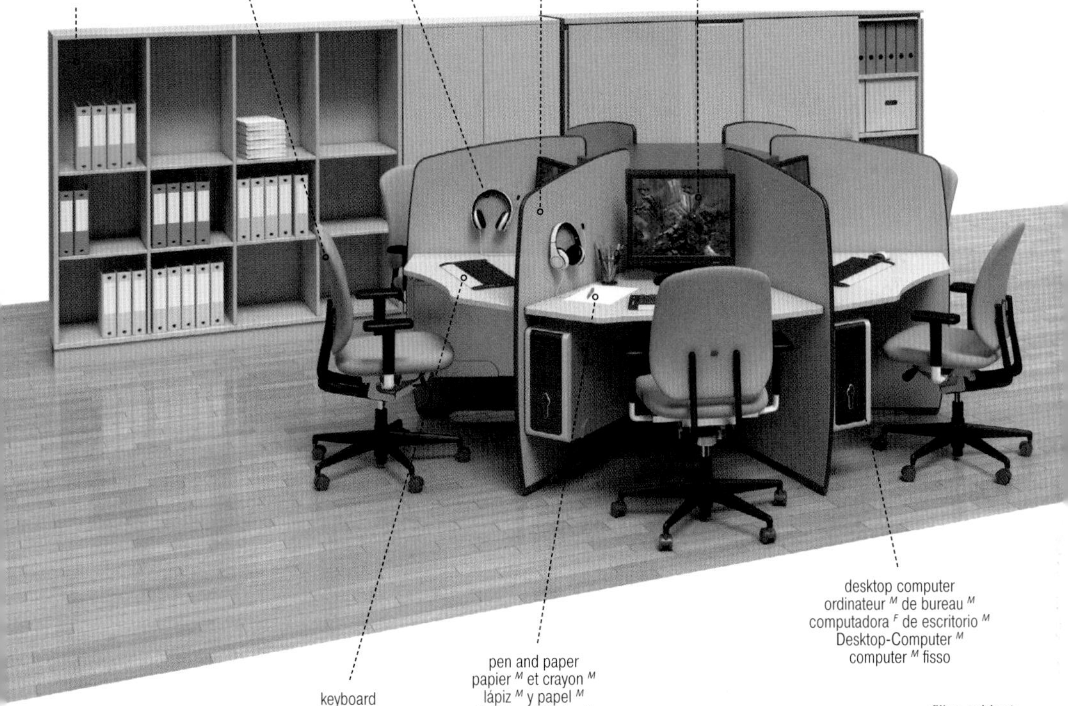
storage cabinet
armoire F de rangement M
estante M
Ablageschrank M
armadietto M
task chair
fauteuil M de bureau M
silla F de oficina F
Schreibtischstuhl M
sedia F da ufficio M
headset
casque M téléphonique
auriculares M
Headset N
cuffia F
partition
cloison F
separador M
Trennwand F
divisorio M
monitor
écran M
monitor M
Monitor M
monitor M
desktop computer
ordinateur M de bureau M
computadora F de escritorio M
Desktop-Computer M
computer M fisso
pen and paper
papier M et crayon M
lápiz M y papel M
Kuli M und Papier N
penna F e carta F
keyboard
clavier M
teclado M
Tastatur F
tastiera F

filing cabinet
classeur M
archivador M / fichero M
Aktenschrank M
mobiletto M da archivio M

desk clock
pendulette F de bureau M
reloj M de mesa F
Tischuhr F
orologio M da tavolo M

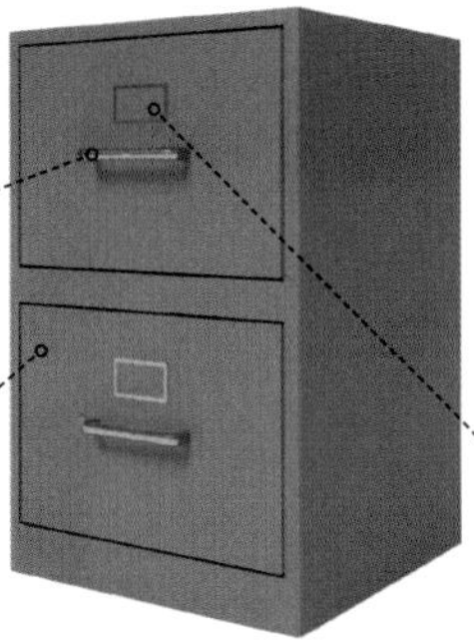
pull
poignée F
tirador M
Griff M
maniglia F
drawer
tiroir M
cajón M
Schublade F
cassetto M
label holder
porte-étiquette M
portaetiquetas M
Etikettenträger M
portaetichetta M

reception
réception M
recepción F
Rezeption F
reception F

binder
reliure F
carpeta F archivadora
Heftmappe F
raccoglitore M
storage cabinet
armoire F de rangement M
estante M
Ablageschrank M
armadietto M
paper
papier M
documento M
Papier N
documento M
armchair
fauteuil M
sillón M
Sessel M
poltroncina F
cup
tasse F
taza F
Tasse F
tazza F
coffee table
table F basse
mesa F de café M
Couchtisch M
tavolino M

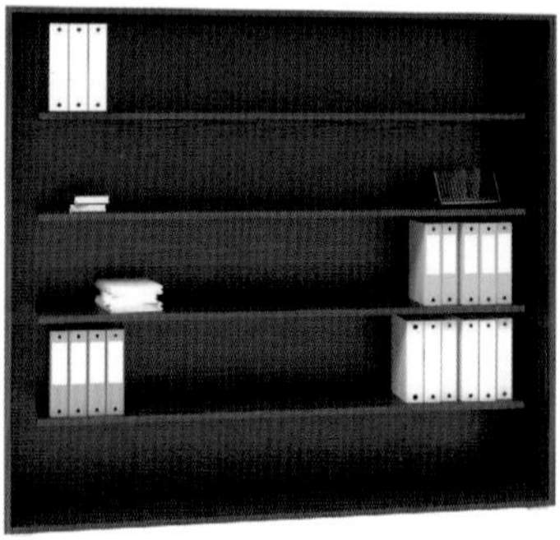
bookcase
bibliothèque F
librero M
Bücherregal N
libreria F

executive armchai
fauteuil M président
silla F ejecutiv
Chefsessel
poltrona F direzional
armrest
accoudoir M
reposabrazos M
Armlehne F
bracciolo M
backrest
dossier M
respaldo M
Rückenlehne F
schienale M
base
base F
base F
Fußteil N
base F
seat
siège M
asiento M
Sitz M
seduta F
height adjustment lever
levier M de réglage M de la hauteur F
regulador M de altura F
Höhenverstellhebel M
leva F per regolare l'altezza F
wheel
roulette F
rueda F
Rad N
ruota F

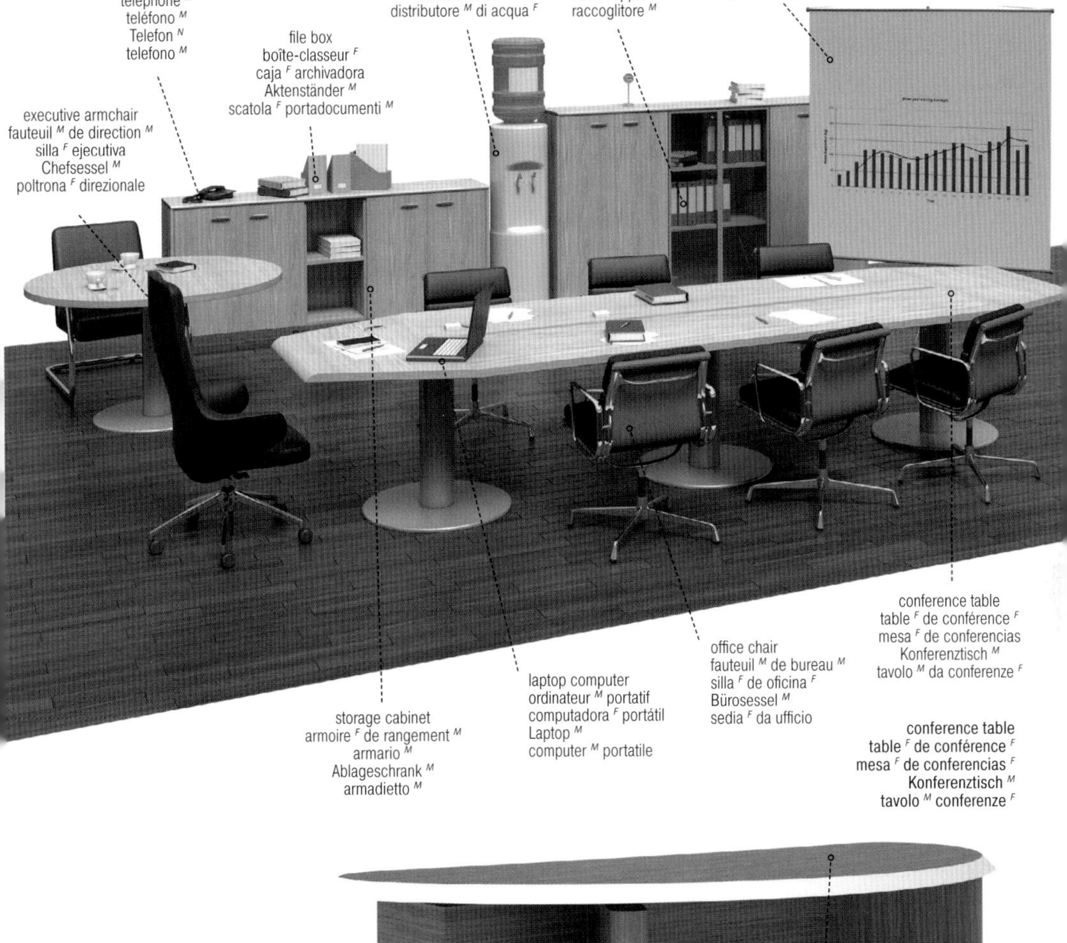
conference room
salle F de conférence F
salón M de conferencias
Konferenzsaal M
sala F conferenze F
telephone
téléphone M
teléfono M
Telefon N
telefono M
watercooler
fontaine F réfrigérée
máquina F de agua F
Wasserkühler M
distributore M di acqua F
binder
reliure F
carpeta F archivadora
Heftmappe F
raccoglitore M
flip chart
tableau M de papier M
rotafolios M
Flipchart N
lavagna F a fogli M mobili
file box
boîte-classeur F
caja F archivadora
Aktenständer M
scatola F portadocumenti M
executive armchair
fauteuil M de direction M
silla F ejecutiva
Chefsessel M
poltrona F direzionale
conference table
table F de conférence F
mesa F de conferencias
Konferenztisch M
tavolo M da conferenze F
office chair
fauteuil M de bureau M
silla F de oficina F
Bürosessel M
sedia F da ufficio
laptop computer
ordinateur M portatif
computadora F portátil
Laptop M
computer M portatile
storage cabinet
armoire F de rangement M
armario M
Ablageschrank M
armadietto M

conference table
table F de conférence F
mesa F de conferencias F
Konferenztisch M
tavolo M conferenze F

leg
patte F
pata F
Bein N
piedino M
top
plateau M/dessus M
tablero M de mesa F
Tischplatte F
piano M

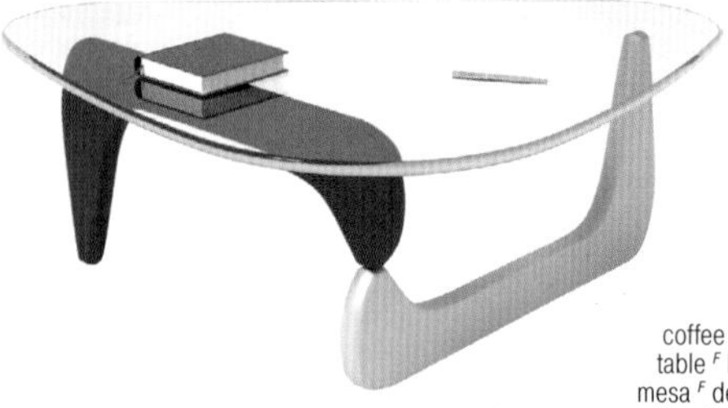
coffee table
table [F] basse
mesa [F] de café [M]
Couchtisch [M]
tavolino [M]

armchair
fauteuil [M]
sillón [M]
Sessel [M]
poltrona [F]

office
bureau [M]
oficina [F]
Büro [N]
ufficio [M]

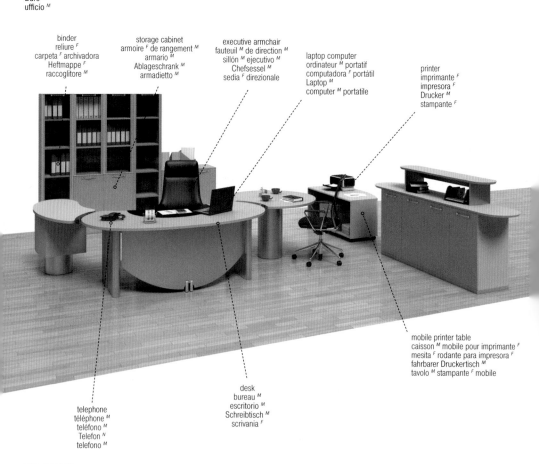

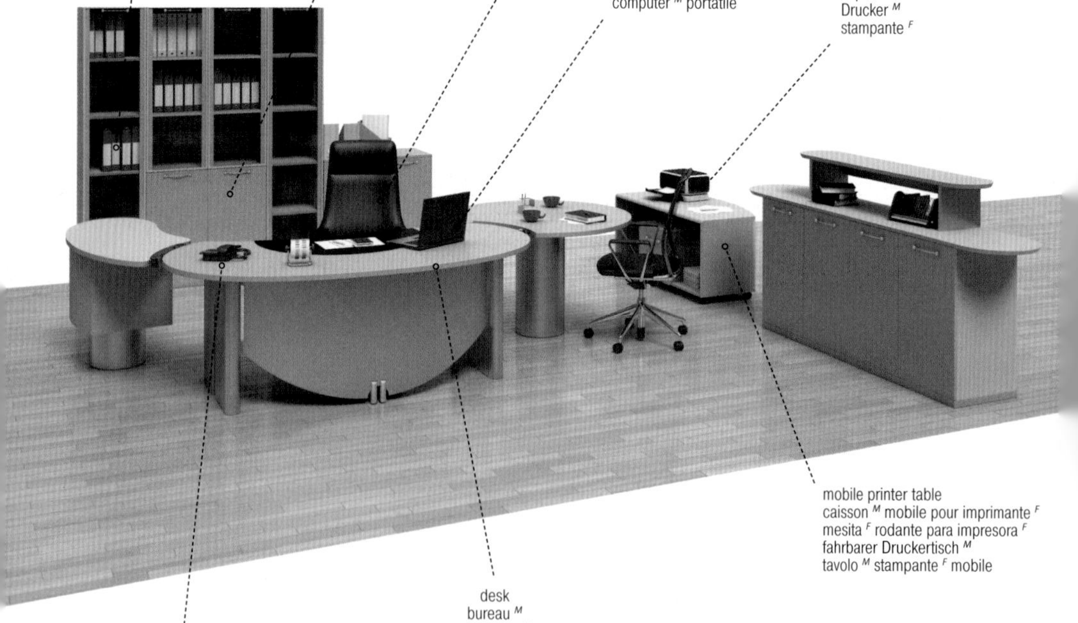
binder
reliure [F]
carpeta [F] archivadora
Heftmappe [F]
raccoglitore [M]
storage cabinet
armoire [F] de rangement [M]
armario [M]
Ablageschrank [M]
armadietto [M]
executive armchair
fauteuil [M] de direction [M]
sillón [M] ejecutivo [M]
Chefsessel [M]
sedia [F] direzionale
laptop computer
ordinateur [M] portatif
computadora [F] portátil
Laptop [M]
computer [M] portatile
printer
imprimante [F]
impresora [F]
Drucker [M]
stampante [F]
mobile printer table
caisson [M] mobile pour imprimante [F]
mesita [F] rodante para impresora [F]
fahrbarer Druckertisch [M]
tavolo [M] stampante [F] mobile
desk
bureau [M]
escritorio [M]
Schreibtisch [M]
scrivania [F]
telephone
téléphone [M]
teléfono [M]
Telefon [N]
telefono [M]

break room
salle [M] de repos [M]
salón [M] de descanso [M]
Pausenraum [M]
zona [F] pausa [F]

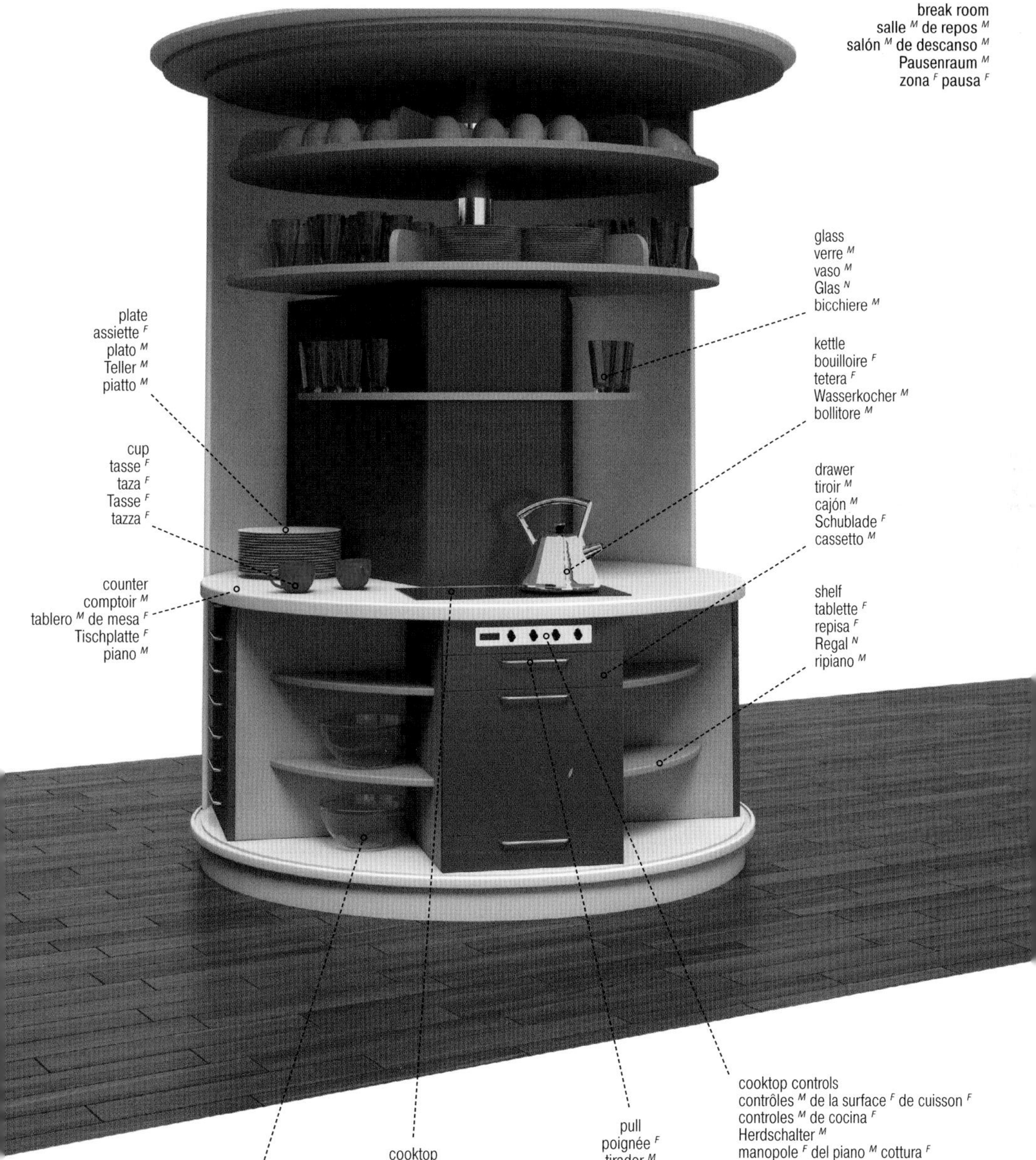
glass
verre [M]
vaso [M]
Glas [N]
bicchiere [M]
kettle
bouilloire [F]
tetera [F]
Wasserkocher [M]
bollitore [M]
drawer
tiroir [M]
cajón [M]
Schublade [F]
cassetto [M]
shelf
tablette [F]
repisa [F]
Regal [N]
ripiano [M]
plate
assiette [F]
plato [M]
Teller [M]
piatto [M]
cup
tasse [F]
taza [F]
Tasse [F]
tazza [F]
counter
comptoir [M]
tablero [M] de mesa [F]
Tischplatte [F]
piano [M]
cooktop controls
contrôles [M] de la surface [F] de cuisson [F]
controles [M] de cocina [F]
Herdschalter [M]
manopole [F] del piano [M] cottura [F]
pull
poignée [F]
tirador [M]
Griff [M]
maniglia [F]
cooktop
surface [F] de cuisson [F]
tapa [F] de cocina [F]
Herdplatte [F]
piano [M] cottura [F]
bowl
saladier [M]
tazón [M]
Schüssel [F]
vaso [M]

filing cabinet
filière ^{F}
archivero ^{M}
Aktenschrank ^{M}
archivio ^{M}

stationary cabinet
armoire ^{F} à papeterie ^{F}
vitrina ^{F} para documentos ^{M}
Schrank ^{M} für Büromaterial ^{N}
armadio ^{M} portadocumenti

Vending machines

Distributrices ^{F} | Máquinas ^{F} expendedoras | Selbstbedienungsautomat ^{M} | Distributori ^{M} automatici

coffeemaker
machine ^{F} à café ^{M}
cafetera ^{F}
Kaffeemaschine ^{F}
macchina ^{F} del caffè ^{M}

coffee hopper
trémie ^{F}
tolva ^{F} para el café ^{M}
Kaffeebehälter ^{M}
tramoggia ^{F} caffè ^{M}

control panel
panneau ^{M} de commande ^{F}
panel ^{M} de control ^{M}
Bedienfeld ^{N}
pannello ^{M} di controllo ^{M}

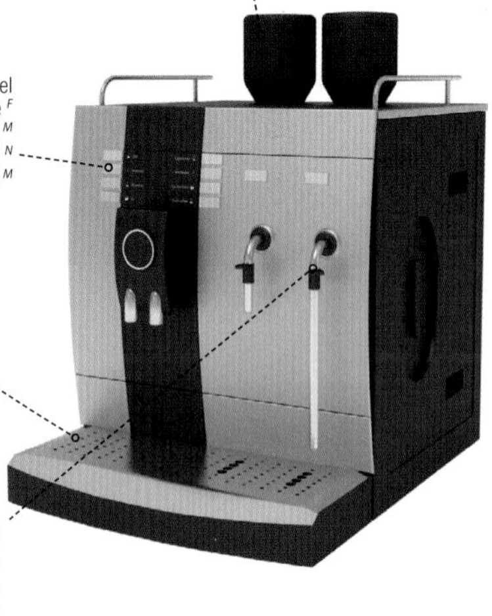

drip tray
plateau ^{M} de trop-plein ^{M}
bandeja ^{F} de goteo ^{M}
Auffangschale ^{F}
raccogligocce ^{M}

nozzle
buse ^{F}
boquilla ^{F}
Düse ^{F}
ugello ^{M}

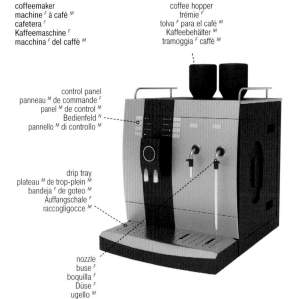

snack food vending machine
distributrice ^{M} automatique à collations ^{F}
máquina ^{F} expendedora
Snackautomat ^{M}
distributore ^{M} automatico di snack ^{M}

coffee machine
machine [F] à café [M]
máquina [F] de café [M]
Kaffeeautomat [M]
macchina [F] del caffè [M]

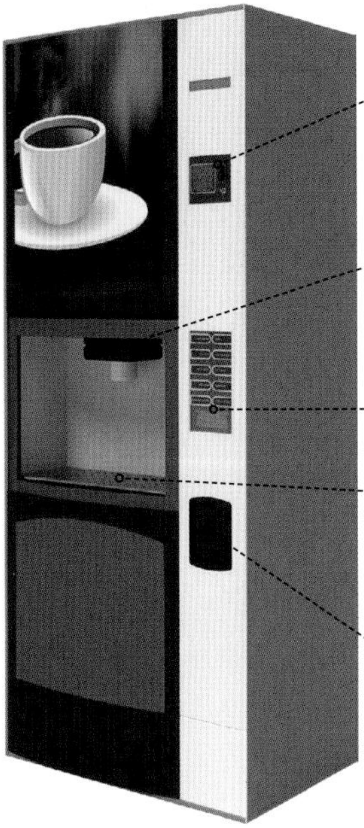

bill acceptor
distributrice [F] acceptant les billets [F]
ranura [F] para dinero [M]
Banknotenannahme [F]
accettatore [M] di monete [F]

nozzle
buse [F]
boquilla [F]
Ausschanköffnung [F]
ugello [M]

drink selection keypad
clavier [M] de sélection [F] de la boisson [F]
teclado [M] para seleccionar bebidas [F]
Getränkeauswahlbereich [M]
tastiera [F] di selezione [F] bevanda [F]

drip tray
plateau [M] de trop-plein [M]
bandeja [F] de goteo [M]
Auffangschale [F]
raccogligocce [M]

change return slot
fenêtre [F] de retour [M] de la monnaie [F]
ventana [F] de entrega [F] de cambio [M]
Wechselgeldausgabe [F]
scomparto [M] per il resto [M]

hot and cold beverage vending machine
distributrice [F] de boissons [F] chaudes et froides
máquina [F] expendedora con bebidas [F] frías y calientes
Automat [M] mit heißen und kalten Getränken [N]
distributore [M] automatico di bevande [F] calde e fredde

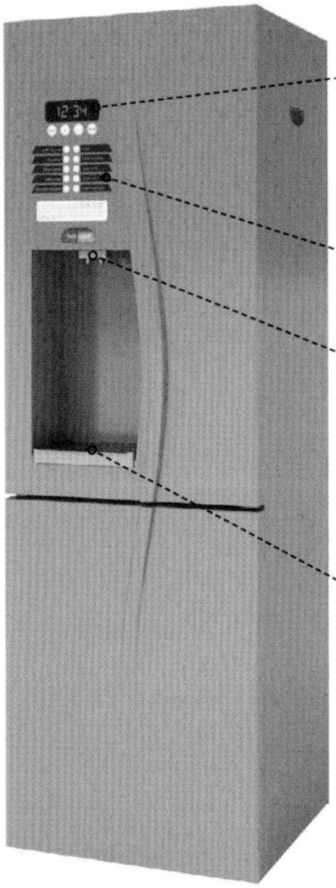

display
écran [M]
pantalla [F]
Anzeige [F]
display [M]

keypad
clavier [M]
teclado [M]
Bedienfeld [N]
tastiera [F]

nozzle
buse [F]
boquilla [F]
Ausschanköffnung [F]
ugello [M]

drip tray
plateau [M] de trop-plein [M]
bandeja [F] de goteo [M]
Auffangschale [F]
raccogligocce [M]

beverage vending machine
distributrice [F] de boissons [F]
máquina [F] expendedora
Getränkeautomat [M]
distributore [M] automatico

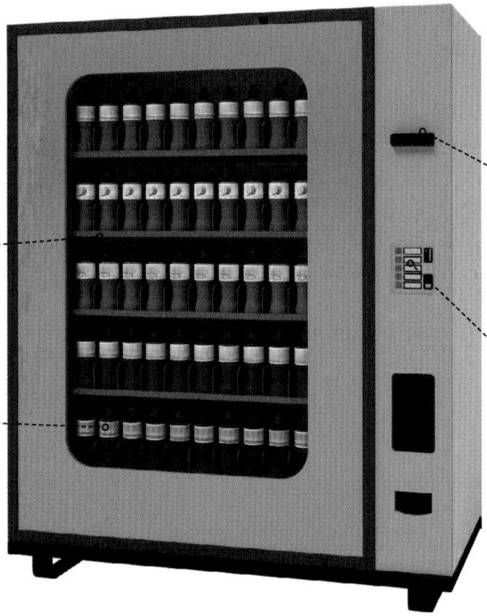

display
présentoir [M]
expositor [M]
Vitrine [F]
vetrina [F]

beverage bottle
bouteille [F]
botella [F]
Getränkeflasche [F]
bottiglia [F] di bevanda [F]

bill acceptor
distributrice [F] acceptant les billets [F]
ranura [F] para dinero [M]
Banknotenannahme [F]
accettatore [M] di monete [F]

keypad
clavier [M]
teclado [M]
Bedieneinheit [F]
tastiera [F]

laptop computer
ordinateur ^{M} portatif ^{M}
computadora ^{F} portátil
Laptop ^{M}
computer ^{M} portatile

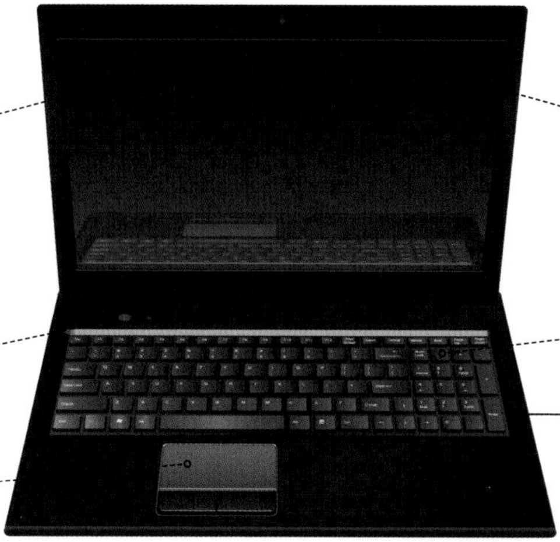

screen
écran ^{M}
pantalla ^{F}
Bildschirm ^{M}
schermo ^{M}

webcam
caméra ^{F} Web
cámara ^{F} web
Webcam ^{F}
webcam ^{F}

power button
bouton ^{M} de mise ^{F} en marche ^{F}
botón ^{M} de encendido ^{M}
An-/Ausschalter ^{M}
pulsante ^{M} di accensione ^{F}

keyboard
clavier ^{M}
teclado ^{M}
Tastatur ^{F}
tastiera ^{F}

touch pad
pavé ^{M} tactile
panel ^{M} táctil
Touchpad ^{N}
touchpad ^{M}

ports
ports ^{M}
puertos ^{M}
Anschlüsse ^{M}
porte ^{F}

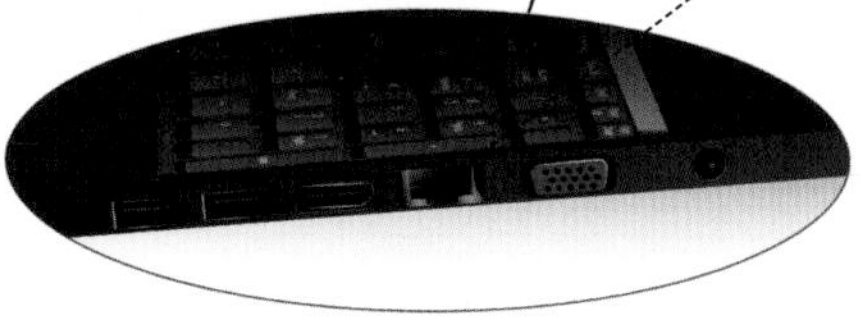

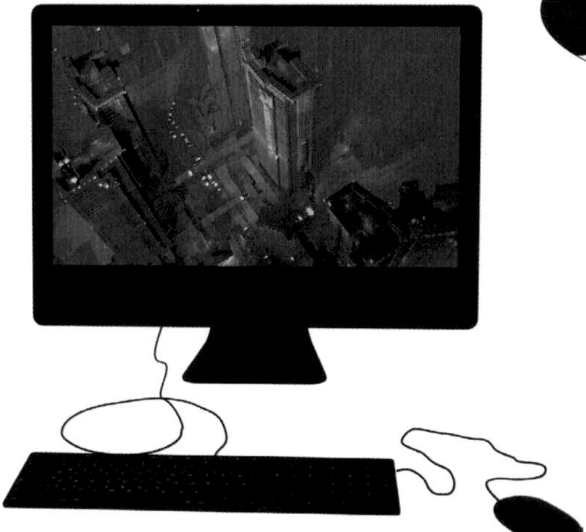

all-in-one computer
ordnateur tout-en-un ^{M}
computadora ^{F} todo en uno ^{M}
All-In-One Computer ^{M}
computer ^{M} all-in-one

tablet computer
tablette ^{F} électronique
tableta ^{F}
Tablet ^{N}
tablet ^{M}

power button
bouton ^{M} de mise ^{F} en marche ^{F}
botón ^{M} de encendido ^{M}
An-/Ausschalter ^{M}
pulsante ^{M} di accensione ^{F}

touch screen
écran ^{M} tactile
pantalla ^{F} táctil
Touchscreen ^{M}
touch screen ^{M}

camera lens
objectif ^{M}
lente ^{F} de la cámara ^{F}
Kameralinse ^{F}
obiettivo ^{M} videocamera

application (app) icon
icône ^{F} d'application ^{F}
icono ^{M} de la aplicación ^{F}
App-Symbol ^{N}
icona ^{F} dell'applicazione ^{F}

17:45
Wed, 17 September
Clock
Internet
Network
Camera
Message
Settings
Shop
Phone
Mail
Calendar
Map
Stocks

volume control
réglage ^{M} du volume ^{M}
botón ^{M} de volumen ^{M}
Lautstärkeregler ^{M}
controllo ^{M} del volume ^{M}

power supply fan
ventilateur [M] d'alimentation [F]
ventilador [M] de fuente [F] de poder [M]
Netzteillüfter [M]
ventola [F] dell'alimentatore [M]

PSU switch
interrupteur [M] du bloc [M] d'alimentation [F]
selector [M] de suministro [M] eléctrico
Netzteilschalter [M]
interruttore [M] alimentatore [M]

power cable connector
connecteur [M] du cordon [M] d'alimentation [F]
puerto [M] de alimentación [F]
Stromanschluss [M]
connettore [M] cavo [M] di alimentazione [F]

desktop computer
ordinateur [M] de bureau [M]
computadora [F] de escritorio [M]
Desktop-Computer [M]
computer [M] fisso

mouse or keyboard port
port [M] pour souris [F] ou clavier [M]
puertos [M] del ratón [M] y del teclado [M]
Anschluss [M] für Maus [F] und Tastatur [F]
porta [F] mouse [M] o tastiera [F]

case fan
ventilateur [M] du boîtier [M]
ventilador [M] del recinto [M]
Gehäuselüfter [M]
griglia [F] di ventilazione

power button
bouton [M] de mise [F] en marche [F]
botón [M] de encendido [M]
An-/Ausschalter [M]
pulsante [M] di accensione [F]

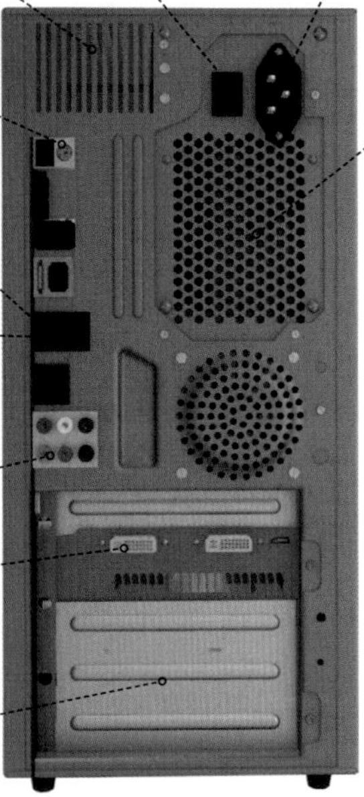

USB port
port [M] USB
puerto [M] USB [M]
USB-Anschluss [M]
porta [F] USB [M]

network port
port [M] réseau
puerto [M] adaptador de red [F]
Netzwerkanschluss [M]
porta [F] di rete [F]

audio jack
prise [F] audio
puerto [M] de audio [M]
Audio-Anschluss [M]
jack [M] audio

video port
port [M] vidéo
puerto [M] de video [M]
Videoanschluss [M]
porta [F] video [M]

expansion slot
emplacement [M] de carte [F]
ranura [F] de expansión [F]
Erweiterungssteckplatz [M]
slot [M] di espansione [F]

keyboard
clavier [M]
teclado [M]
Tastatur [F]
tastiera [F]

cordless mouse
souris [F] sans fil [M]
ratón [M] inalámbrico
kabellose Maus [F]
mouse [M] senza filo [M]

corded mouse
souris [F] avec fil
ratón [M]
Maus [F] mit Kabel [N]
mouse [M] con filo [M]

graphics tablet
tablette [F] graphique
tableta [F] gráfica
Grafiktablett [N]
tavoletta [F] grafica

gaming controller
manette [F] de jeu [M]
control [M] de videojuegos [M]
Spielecontroller [M]
controllore [M] di gioco [M]

Printers, copiers and scanners

Imprimantes, [F] photocopieuses [F] et scanners [M] | Impresoras, [F] fotocopiadoras [F] y escáneres [M] | Drucker, [M] Kopierer [M] und Scanner [M] | Stampanti, [F] fotocopiatrici, [F] scanner [M]

ink cartridge
cartouche [F] d'encre [F]
cartucho [M] de tinta [F] de impresora [F]
Druckerpatrone [F]
cartuccia [F] per stampante [F]

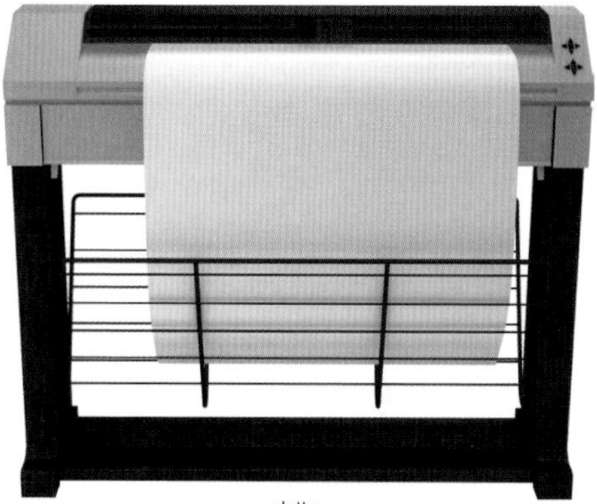

plotter
traceur [M]
trazador [M] de gráficos
Plotter [M]
plotter [M]

laser printer
imprimante [F] laser
impresora [F] láser
Laserdrucker [M]
stampante [F] laser [M]

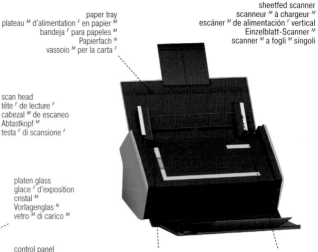

toner cartridge
cartouche [F] de toner [M]
cartucho [M] de impresora [F] láser
Tonerkartusche [F]
cartuccia [F] per stampante [F] laser [M]

flatbed scanner
scanneur [M]
escáner [M] plano [M]
Flachbettscanner [M]
scanner [M] piano

cover
couvercle [M]
tapa [F]
Deckel [M]
coperchio [M]

belt
courroie [F]
cinta [F]
Flachband [N]
cinghia [F]

scan head
tête [F] de lecture [F]
cabezal [M] de escaneo
Abtastkopf [M]
testa [F] di scansione [F]

platen glass
glace [F] d'exposition
cristal [M]
Vorlagenglas [N]
vetro [M] di carico [M]

control panel
panneau [M] de commande [F]
panel [M] de control [M]
Bedienfeld [N]
pannello [M] di controllo [M]

sheetfed scanner
scanneur [M] à chargeur [M]
escáner [M] de alimentación [F] vertical
Einzelblatt-Scanner [M]
scanner [M] a fogli [M] singoli

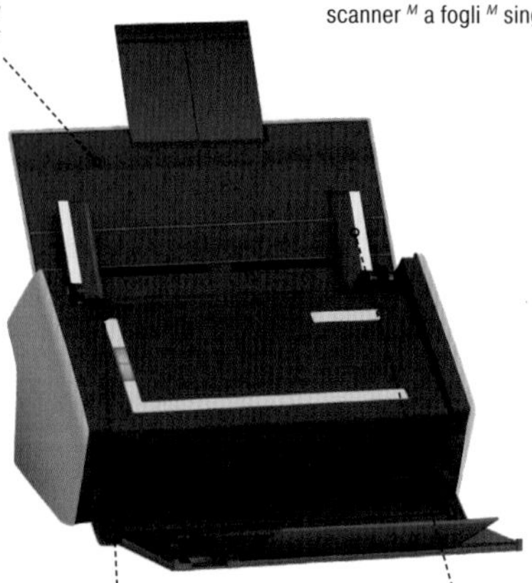

paper tray
plateau [M] d'alimentation [F] en papier [M]
bandeja [F] para papeles [M]
Papierfach [N]
vassoio [M] per la carta [F]

power button
bouton [M] de mise [F] en marche [F]
botón [M] de encendido [M]/apagado [M]
An-/Aus-schalter [M]
interruttore

output tray
plateau [M] de sortie [F]
bandeja [F] de salida [F]
Ausgabefach [N]
vassoio [M] di uscita [F]

ink-jet printer
imprimante [M] à jet [M] d'encre [F]
impresora [F] de chorro [M] de tinta [F]
Tintenstrahldrucker [M]
stampante [F] a getto [M] di inchiostro [M]

control panel
panneau [M] de commande [F]
panel [M] de control [M]
Bedienfeld [N]
pannello [M] di controllo [M]

display
écran [M]
pantalla [F]
Anzeige [F]
display [M]

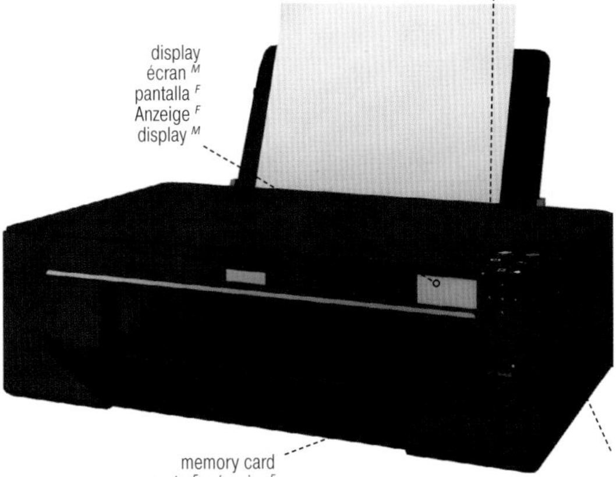

memory card
carte [F] mémoire [F]
tarjeta [F] de memoria [F]
Speicherkarte [F]
scheda [F] di memoria [F]

power button
bouton [M] de mise [F] en marche [F]
botón [M] de encendido [M]
An-/Ausschalter [M]
pulsante [M] di accensione [F]

copier
photocopieur [M]
fotocopiadora [F]
Kopierer [M]
fotocopiatrice [F]

Other electronic devices

headset
casque [M] d'écoute [F]
auriculares [M]
Headset [N]
cuffia [F]

headband
serre-tête [M]
banda [F] de la cabeza [F]
Kopfbügel [M]
archetto [M]

earpiece
écouteur [M]
auricular [M]
Hörer [M]
auricolare [M]

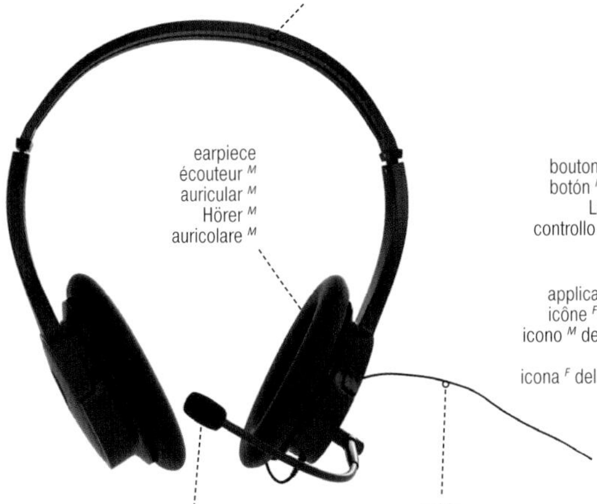

microphone
micro [M]
micrófono [M]
Mikrofon [N]
microfono [M]

cable
câble [M]
cable [M]
Kabel [N]
cavo [M]

power button
bouton [M] de mise [F] en marche [F]
botón [M] de encendido [M]
An-/Aus-schalter [M]
pulsante [M] di accensione [F]

smartphone
téléphone [M] intelligent
teléfono [M] inteligente
Smartphone [N]
smartphone [M]

receiver
récepteur [M]
receptor [M]
Hörer [M]
altoparlante [M]

camera lens
objectif [M]
lente [F] de la cámara [F]
Kameralinse [F]
obiettivo [M]
videocamera

volume control
bouton [M] de volume [M]
botón [M] de volumen [M]
Lautstärketaste [F]
controllo [M] del volume [M]

10:25
24°C
Clock
Internet
Network
Camera
Message
Settings
Shop
Phone
Mail
Calendar
Map
Stocks

touch screen
écran [M] tactile
pantalla [F] táctil
Touchscreen [M]
touch screen [M]

application (app) icon
icône [F] d'application [F]
icono [M] de la aplicación [F]
App-Symbol [N]
icona [F] dell'applicazione [F]

back button
bouton [M] précédent [M]
botón [M] atrás
Zurück-Taste [F]
pulsante [M] Indietro

menu button
bouton [M] de la barre [F] de menus [M]
botón [M] del menú [M]
Menütaste [F]
pulsante [M] del menù [M]

home button
bouton [M] démarrage [M]
botón [M] de inicio [M]
Home-Taste [F]
pulsante [M] di inizio [M]

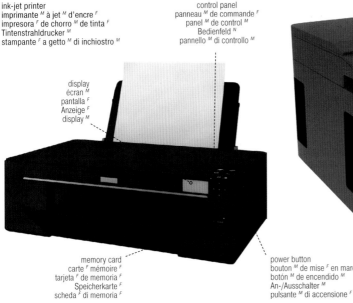

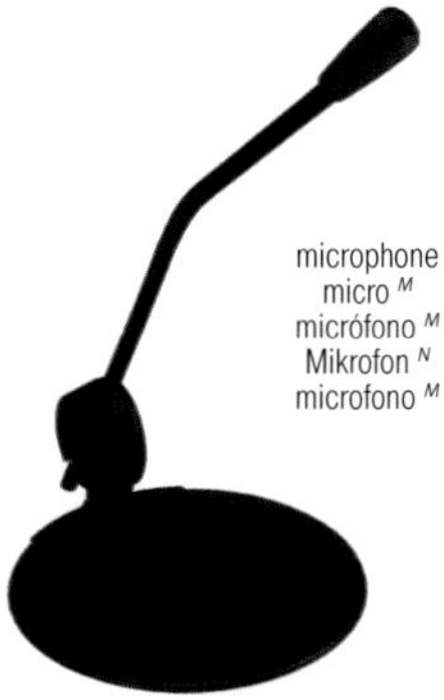

microphone
micro M
micrófono M
Mikrofon N
microfono M

telephone
téléphone M
teléfono M
Telefon N
telefono M

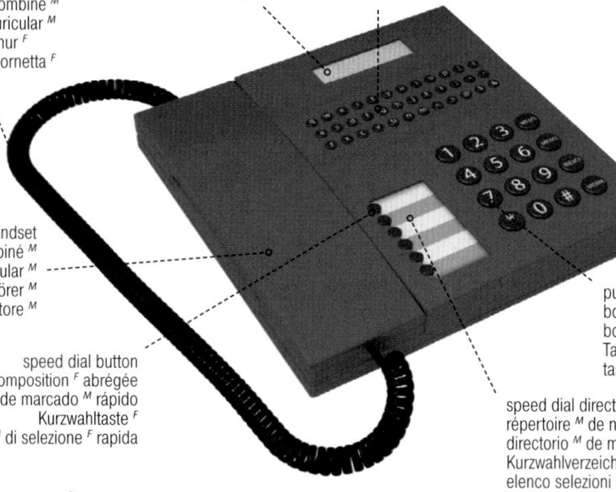

display
écran M
pantalla F
Anzeige F
display M

keypad
clavier M
teclado M
Tastenfeld N
tastiera F

handset cord
cordon M de combiné M
cable M del auricular M
Hörerschnur F
cavo M della cornetta F

handset
combiné M
auricular M
Telefonhörer M
ricevitore M

speed dial button
bouton M de composition F abrégée
botón M de marcado M rápido
Kurzwahltaste F
tasto M di selezione F rapida

push button
bouton-poussoir M
botón M
Taste F
tasto M

speed dial directory
répertoire M de numéros M abrég
directorio M de marcado M rápido
Kurzwahlverzeichnis N
elenco selezioni F rapide

webcam
caméra F Web
cámara F web
Webcam F
webcam F

fax
télécopieur M
fax M
Fax N
fax M

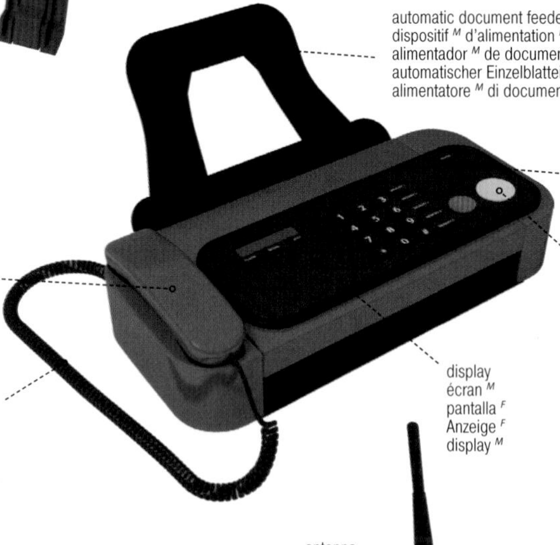

automatic document feeder
dispositif M d'alimentation F automatique
alimentador M de documentos M
automatischer Einzelblatteinzug M
alimentatore M di documenti M automatico

power button
bouton M de mise F en marche F
botón M de encendido M
An-/Ausschalter M
pulsante M di accensione F

handset
combiné M
auricular M
Hörer M
ricevitore M

start button
bouton M démarrer
botón M de enviar fax M
Starttaste F
tasto M di invio M fax M

display
écran M
pantalla F
Anzeige F
display M

handset cord
cordon M de combiné M
cable M del auricular M
Hörerschnur F
cavo M della cornetta F

wireless router
routeur M sans fil M
router M inalámbrico
WLAN-Router M
router M senza fili M

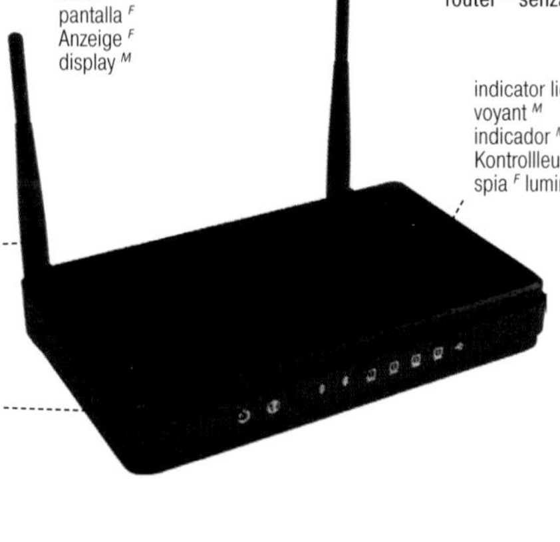

indicator light
voyant M
indicador M
Kontrollleuchte F
spia F luminosa

antenna
antenne F
antena F
Antenne F
antenna F

power button
bouton M de mise F en marche F
botón M de encendido M
An-/Ausschalter M
pulsante M di accensione F

Internet stick
clé F Internet M
módem M USB M
Internet Stick M
chiavetta F internet M

printing calculator
calculatrice [F] à imprimante [F]
calculadora [F] con función [F] de impresión [M]
Rechner [M] mit Druckfunktion [F]
calcolatrice [F] con stampante [F]

paper roll
rouleau [M] de papier [M]
rollo [M] de papel [M]
Papierrolle [F]
rotolo [M] di carta [F]

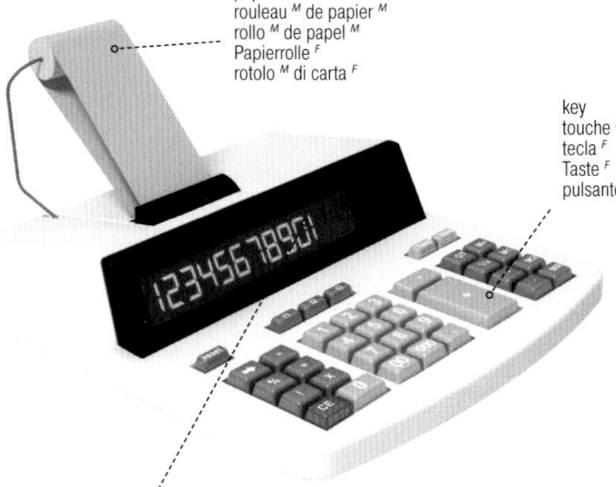
123456789101

key
touche [F]
tecla [F]
Taste [F]
pulsante [M]

screen
écran [M]
pantalla [F]
Display [N]
schermo [M]

calculator
calculatrice [F]
calculadora [F]
Rechner [M]
calcolatrice [F]

69528
TAX-
TAX+
MRC
M-
M+
%
+/_
7
8
9
×
C
4
5
6
AC
1
2
3
+
00
0
=

354
MC
MR
M-
M+
÷
MS
7
8
9
×
%
4
5
6
−
C
1
2
3
+
AC
0
·
=

pocket calculator
calculatrice [F] de poche [F]
calculadora [F] de bolsillo [M]
Taschenrechner [M]
calcolatrice [F] tascabile

shredder
déchiqueteuse [F]
trituradora [F]
Aktenvernichter [M]
distruggidocumenti [M]

lid
couvercle [M]
tapa [F]
Deckel [M]
coperchio [M]

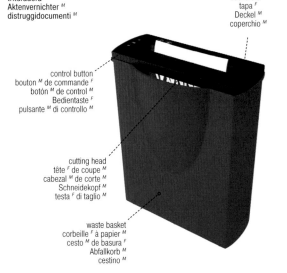

control button
bouton [M] de commande [F]
botón [M] de control [M]
Bedientaste [F]
pulsante [M] di controllo [M]

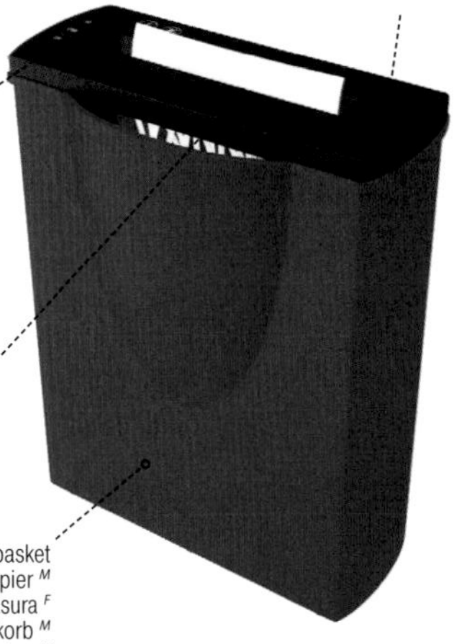

cutting head
tête [F] de coupe [M]
cabezal [M] de corte [M]
Schneidekopf [M]
testa [F] di taglio [M]

waste basket
corbeille [F] à papier [M]
cesto [M] de basura [F]
Abfallkorb [M]
cestino [M]

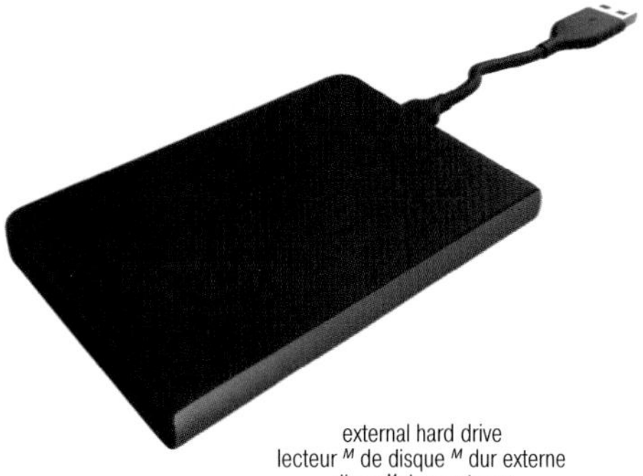

external hard drive
lecteur [M] de disque [M] dur externe
disco [M] duro externo
Externe Festplatte [F]
disco [M] rigido esterno

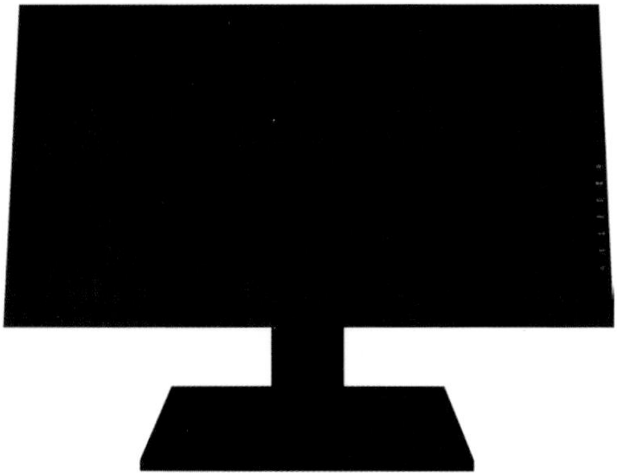

monitor
écran ^{M}
monitor ^{M}
Monitor ^{M}
schermo ^{M}

label maker
étiqueteuse ^{F}
etiquetadora ^{F}
Etikettiergerät ^{N}
etichettatrice ^{F}

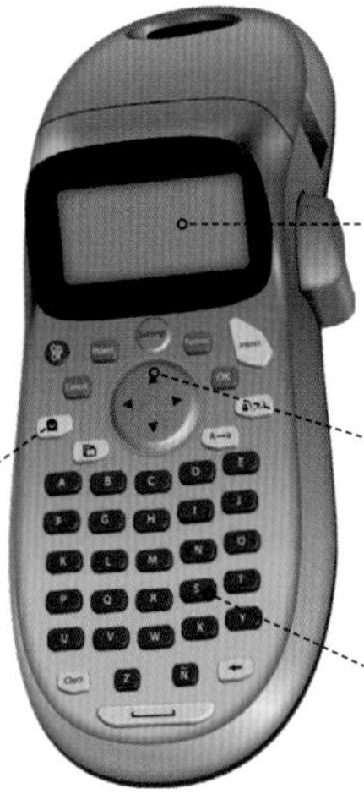

display
écran ^{M}
pantalla ^{F}
Anzeige ^{F}
display ^{M}

control button
bouton ^{M} de commande ^{F}
botón ^{M} de control ^{M}
Bedientaste ^{F}
pulsante ^{M} di controllo ^{M}

navigation buttons
boutons ^{M} de navigation ^{F}
botones ^{M} de navegación ^{F}
Navigationstasten ^{F}
pulsanti ^{M} di navigazione ^{F}

keypad
clavier ^{M}
teclado ^{M}
Tastatur ^{F}
tastiera ^{F}

USB flash drive
clé ^{F} USB ^{M}
memoria ^{F} USB ^{M}
USB-Stick ^{M}
chiave ^{F} USB ^{F}

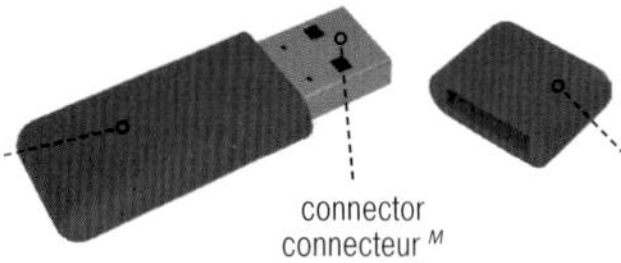

case
boîtier ^{M}
cuerpo ^{M}
Gehäuse ^{N}
involucro ^{M}

connector
connecteur ^{M}
enchufe ^{M}
Stecker ^{M}
connettore ^{M}

cap
bouchon ^{M}
tapón ^{M}
Kappe ^{F}
cappuccio ^{M}

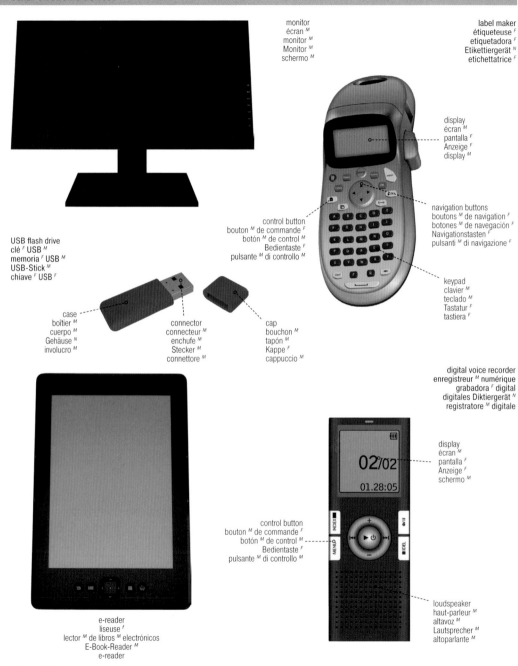

e-reader
liseuse ^{f}
lector ^{M} de libros ^{M} electrónicos
E-Book-Reader ^{M}
e-reader

digital voice recorder
enregistreur ^{M} numérique
grabadora ^{F} digital
digitales Diktiergerät ^{N}
registratore ^{M} digitale

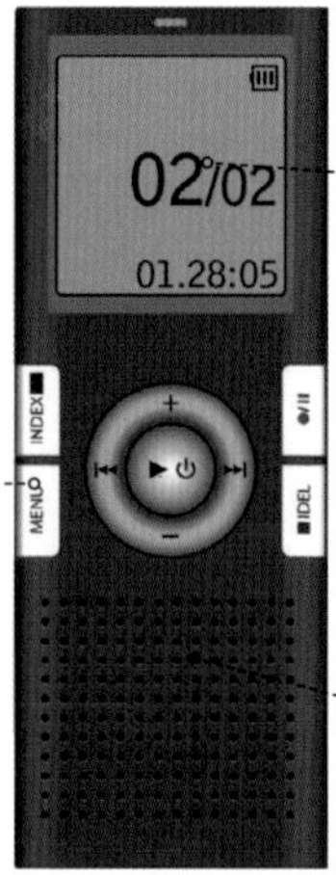
02/02
01.28:05
INDEX
MENU
IDEL

display
écran ^{M}
pantalla ^{F}
Anzeige ^{F}
schermo ^{M}

control button
bouton ^{M} de commande ^{F}
botón ^{M} de control ^{M}
Bedientaste ^{F}
pulsante ^{M} di controllo ^{M}

loudspeaker
haut-parleur ^{M}
altavoz ^{M}
Lautsprecher ^{M}
altoparlante ^{M}

digital clock
horloge F numérique
reloj M digital
Digitaluhr F
orologio M digitale

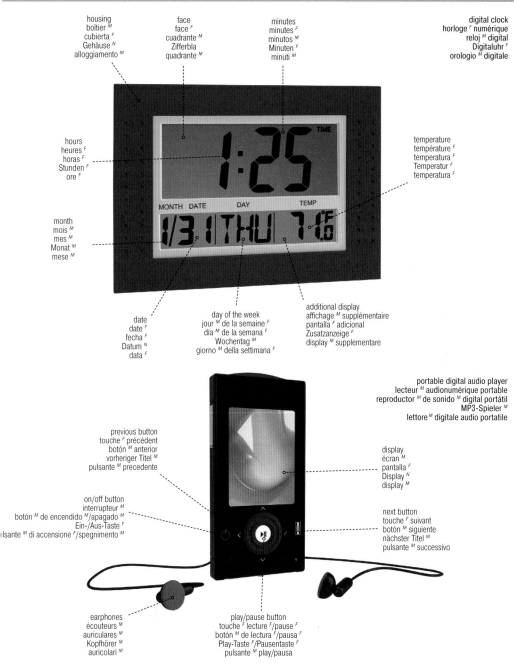

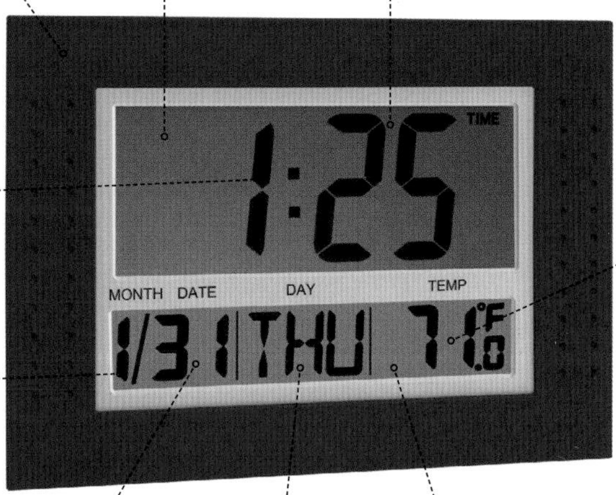
housing
boîtier M
cubierta F
Gehäuse N
alloggiamento M
face
face F
cuadrante M
Zifferbla
quadrante M
minutes
minutes F
minutos M
Minuten F
minuti M
hours
heures F
horas F
Stunden F
ore F
temperature
température F
temperatura F
Temperatur F
temperatura F
month
mois M
mes M
Monat M
mese M
TIME
MONTH DATE
DAY
TEMP
date
date F
fecha F
Datum N
data F
day of the week
jour M de la semaine F
día M de la semana F
Wochentag M
giorno M della settimana F
additional display
affichage M supplémentaire
pantalla F adicional
Zusatzanzeige F
display M supplementare

portable digital audio player
lecteur M audionumérique portable
reproductor M de sonido M digital portátil
MP3-Spieler M
lettore M digitale audio portatile

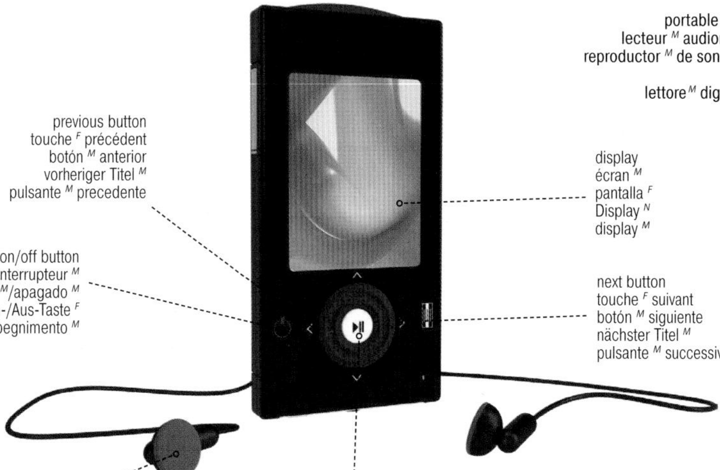
previous button
touche F précédent
botón M anterior
vorheriger Titel M
pulsante M precedente
display
écran M
pantalla F
Display N
display M
on/off button
interrupteur M
botón M de encendido M/apagado M
Ein-/Aus-Taste F
lsante M di accensione F/spegnimento M
next button
touche F suivant
botón M siguiente
nächster Titel M
pulsante M successivo
earphones
écouteurs M
auriculares M
Kopfhörer M
auricolari M
play/pause button
touche F lecture F/pause F
botón M de lectura F/pausa F
Play-Taste F/Pausentaste F
pulsante M play/pausa

single-lens reflex (SLR) digital camera: front view
appareil [M] photo [F] numérique reflex mono-objectif: vue [F] de face [F]
cámara [F] digital reflex de lente [F] única: vista [F] frontal digitale
Spiegelreflexkamera [F] – Vorderseite
fotocamera [F] digitale con singola lente [F] reflex: vista [F] anteriore

data display
écran [M] de données [F]
panel [M] de datos [M]
Kontrolldisplay [N]
display [M] dati [M]

hot-shoe contact
contact [M] électrique
zapata [F] de contacto [M] para flash [M]
Blitzkontakt [M]
contatto [M] caldo

shutter release button
déclencheur [M]
botón [M] disparador
Auslöser [M]
pulsante [M] di scatto [M]

accessory shoe
griffe [F] porte-accessoire
zapata [F] para accesorios [M]
Zubehörschuh [M]
slitta [F] per accessori [M]

mode dial
molette [F] de sélection [M]
selector de modos [M]
Programmwahlrad [M]
selettore [M] programmi [M]

focus setting ring
bague [F] de mise [F] au point [M]
anillo [M] para ajustar el enfoque [M]
Scharfstellring [M]
anello [M] di regolazione [F] del fuoco [M]

neckstrap eyelet
œillet [M] d'attache [F]
anilla [F] para correa [F]
Öse [F] für Tragriemen [M]
asola [F] per tracolla [F]

lens
objectif [M]
objetivos [M]
Objektiv [N]
obiettivo [M]

camery body
boîtier [M] de l'appareil [M] photo
casco [M] de la cámara [F]
Kameragehäuse [N]
corpo [M] della macchina [F] fotografica

lens aperture scale
échelle [F] d'ouverture [F] de l'objectif [M]
escala [F] de abertura [F] de objetivos [M]
Blendenskalaring [M]
scala [F] di apertura [F] della lente [F]

single-lens reflex (SLR) digital camera: back view
appareil [M] photo [F] numérique reflex mono-objectif: vue [F] arrière [F]
cámara [F] digital reflex de lente [F] única: vista trasera
digitale Spiegelreflexkamera [F] – Rückseite
fotocamera [F] digitale con singola lente [F] reflex: vista [F] posteriore

viewfinder
viseur [M]
visor [M]
Sucherokular [N]
mirino [M]

menu button
touche [F] de sélection [F] des menus [M]
botón [M] menú [M]
Menütaste [F]
pulsante [M] del menu [M]

settings display button
bouton [M] d'affichage [M] des paramètres [M]
botón [M] de funciones [F] de visualización [F]
Einstellungsanzeige [F]
pulsante [M] di visualizzazione [F] delle impostazioni [F]

image review button
touche [F] de visualisation [F] des images [F]
botón [M] de revisión [F] de imagen [F]
Bildanzeigeknopf [M]
pulsante [M] di visualizzazione [F] delle immagini [F]

erase button
touche [F] d'effacement [M]
botón [M] de eliminar
Löschtaste [F]
pulsante [M] di cancellazione [F]

display
écran [M]
pantalla [F]
Anzeige [F]
display [M]

enlarge button
bouton [M] d'agrandissement [M]
botón [M] de ampliar
Zoomtaste [F]
pulsante [M] di ingrandimento [M]

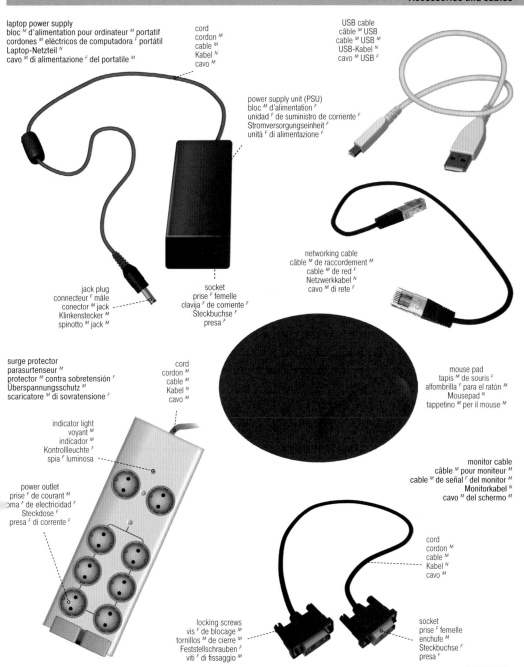

laptop power supply
bloc ^{M} d'alimentation pour ordinateur ^{M} portatif
cordones ^{M} eléctricos de computadora ^{F} portátil
Laptop-Netzteil ^{N}
cavo ^{M} di alimentazione ^{F} del portatile ^{M}

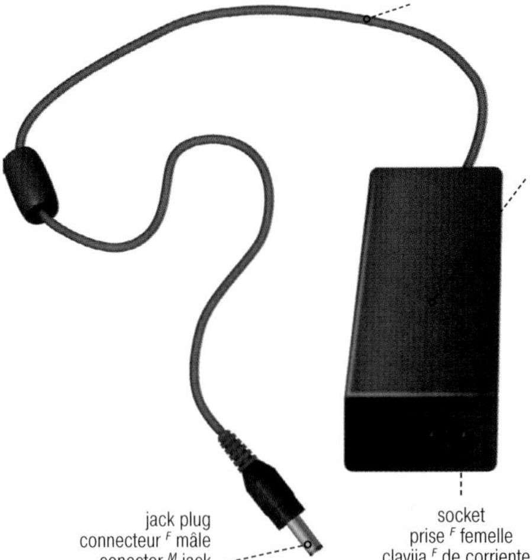
cord
cordon ^{M}
cable ^{M}
Kabel ^{N}
cavo ^{M}
power supply unit (PSU)
bloc ^{M} d'alimentation ^{F}
unidad ^{F} de suministro de corriente ^{F}
Stromversorgungseinheit ^{F}
unità ^{F} di alimentazione ^{F}
jack plug
connecteur ^{F} mâle
conector ^{M} jack
Klinkenstecker ^{M}
spinotto ^{M} jack ^{M}
socket
prise ^{F} femelle
clavija ^{F} de corriente ^{F}
Steckbuchse ^{F}
presa ^{F}

USB cable
câble ^{M} USB
cable ^{M} USB ^{M}
USB-Kabel ^{N}
cavo ^{M} USB ^{F}

networking cable
câble ^{M} de raccordement ^{M}
cable ^{M} de red ^{F}
Netzwerkkabel ^{N}
cavo ^{M} di rete ^{F}

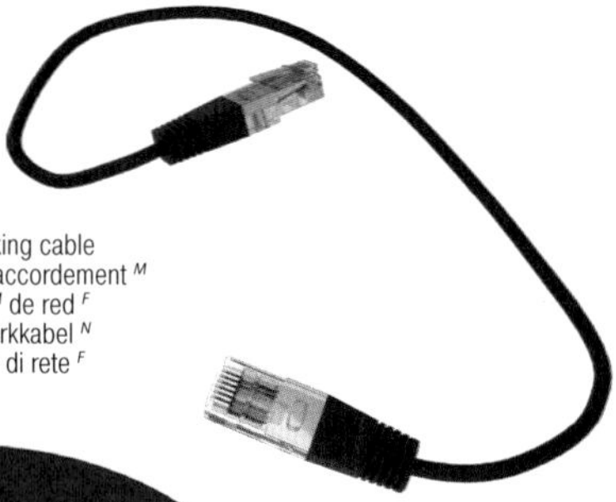

mouse pad
tapis ^{M} de souris ^{F}
alfombrilla ^{F} para el ratón ^{M}
Mousepad ^{N}
tappetino ^{M} per il mouse ^{M}

surge protector
parasurtenseur ^{M}
protector ^{M} contra sobretensión ^{F}
Überspannungsschutz ^{M}
scaricatore ^{M} di sovratensione ^{F}

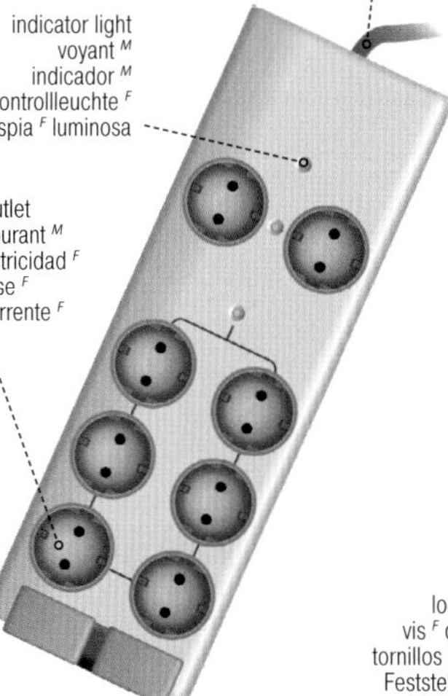
cord
cordon ^{M}
cable ^{M}
Kabel ^{N}
cavo ^{M}
indicator light
voyant ^{M}
indicador ^{M}
Kontrollleuchte ^{F}
spia ^{F} luminosa
power outlet
prise ^{F} de courant ^{M}
oma ^{F} de electricidad ^{F}
Steckdose ^{F}
presa ^{F} di corrente ^{F}

monitor cable
câble ^{M} pour moniteur ^{M}
cable ^{M} de señal ^{F} del monitor ^{M}
Monitorkabel ^{N}
cavo ^{M} del schermo ^{M}

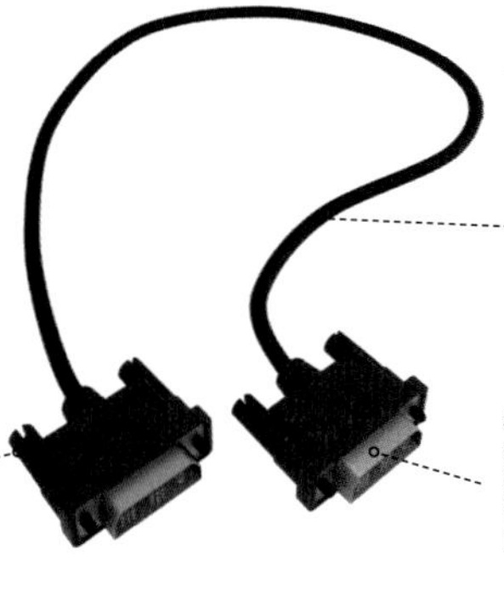
cord
cordon ^{M}
cable ^{M}
Kabel ^{N}
cavo ^{M}
locking screws
vis ^{F} de blocage ^{M}
tornillos ^{M} de cierre ^{M}
Feststellschrauben ^{F}
viti ^{F} di fissaggio ^{M}
socket
prise ^{F} femelle
enchufe ^{M}
Steckbuchse ^{F}
presa ^{F}

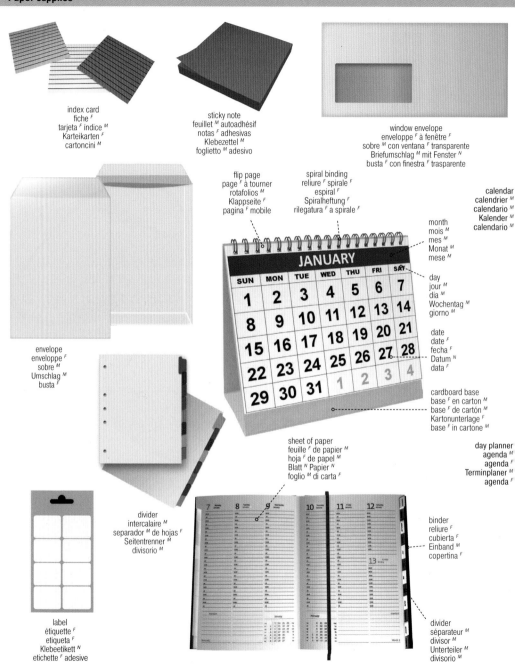

index card
fiche F
tarjeta F índice M
Karteikarten F
cartoncini M

sticky note
feuillet M autoadhésif
notas F adhesivas
Klebezettel M
foglietto M adesivo

window envelope
enveloppe F à fenêtre F
sobre M con ventana F transparente
Briefumschlag M mit Fenster N
busta F con finestra F trasparente

envelope
enveloppe F
sobre M
Umschlag M
busta F

calendar
calendrier M
calendario M
Kalender M
calendario M

flip page
page F à tourner
rotafolios M
Klappseite F
pagina F mobile

spiral binding
reliure F spirale F
espiral F
Spiralheftung F
rilegatura F a spirale F

JANUARY
SUN MON TUE WED THU FRI SAT
1 2 3 4 5 6 7
8 9 10 11 12 13 14
15 16 17 18 19 20 21
22 23 24 25 26 27 28
29 30 31 1 2 3 4

month
mois M
mes M
Monat M
mese M

day
jour M
día M
Wochentag M
giorno M

date
date F
fecha F
Datum N
data F

cardboard base
base F en carton M
base F de cartón M
Kartonunterlage F
base F in cartone M

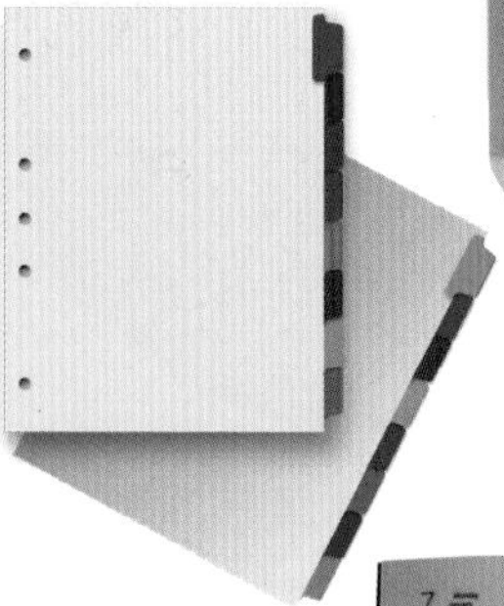

divider
intercalaire M
separador M de hojas F
Seitentrenner M
divisorio M

day planner
agenda M
agenda F
Terminplaner M
agenda F

sheet of paper
feuille F de papier M
hoja F de papel M
Blatt N Papier N
foglio M di carta F

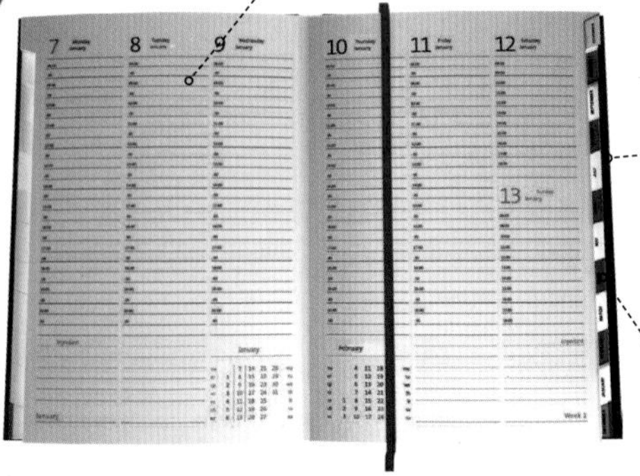

binder
reliure F
cubierta F
Einband M
copertina F

divider
séparateur M
divisor M
Unterteiler M
divisorio M

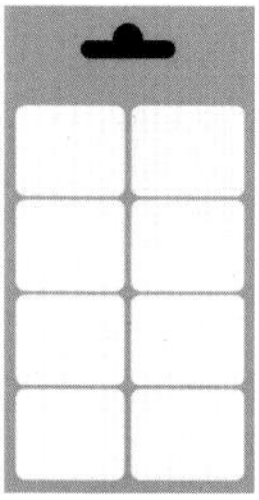

label
étiquette F
etiqueta F
Klebeetikett N
etichette F adesive

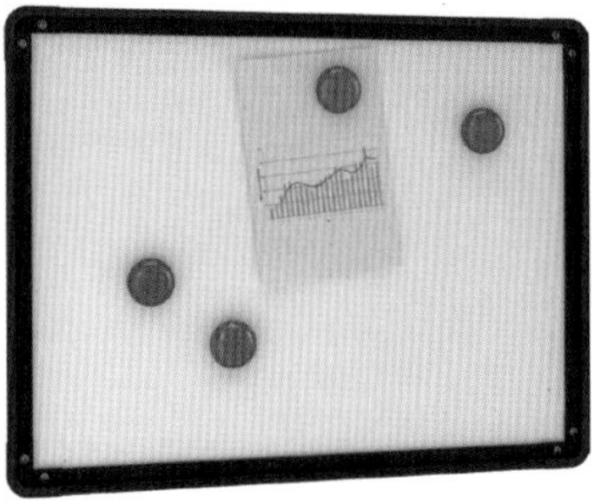

magnetic bulletin board
babillard ^{M} magnétique
tablón ^{M} magnético
Magnettafel ^{F}
bacheca ^{F} magnetica

whiteboard
tableau ^{M} blanc
pizarra ^{F} blanca
Whiteboard ^{N}
lavagna ^{F} bianca

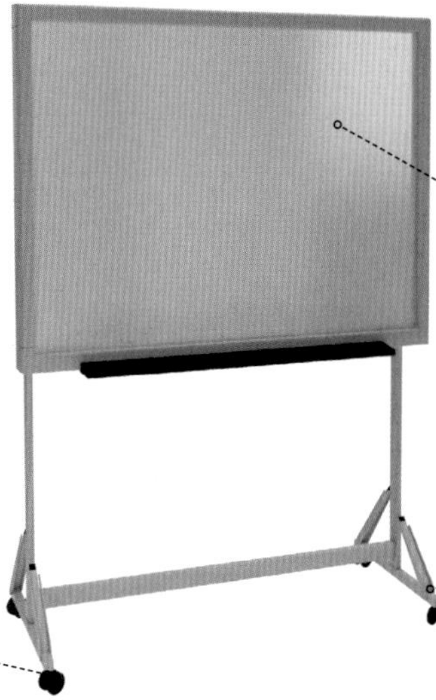
writing surface
surface ^{F} de marquage ^{M}
superficie ^{F} de escritura ^{F}
Schreibfläche ^{F}
superficie ^{F} di scrittura ^{F}
caster
roulette ^{F}
rueda ^{F}
Rolle ^{F}
rotella ^{F}
base
base ^{F}
base ^{F}
Fußteil ^{N}
base ^{F}

Desk supplies

packing tape dispenser
dévidoir ^{M} pistolet ^{M}
soporte ^{M} para cinta ^{F} adhesiva
Klebebandhalter ^{M}
dispenser ^{M} per nastro ^{M} adesivo

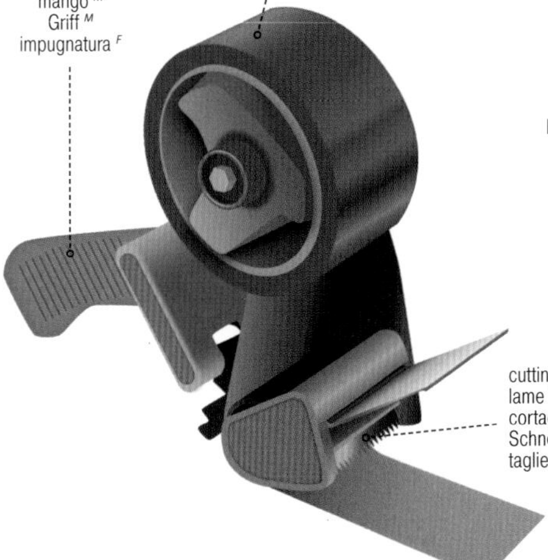
tape
ruban ^{M} adhésif
rollo ^{M} de cinta ^{F} adhesiva
Klebeband ^{N}
rotolo ^{M} di nastro ^{M} adesivo
handle
poignée ^{F}
mango ^{M}
Griff ^{M}
impugnatura ^{F}
cutting blade
lame ^{F} de coupe ^{F}
cortador ^{M}
Schneidemesser ^{N}
taglierina ^{F}

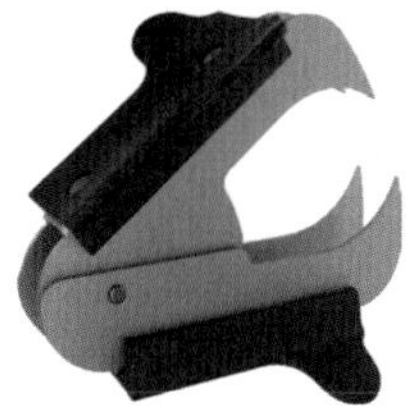

staple remover
dégrafeuse ^{F}
quitagrapas ^{F}
Heftklammerentferner ^{M}
levapunti ^{M}

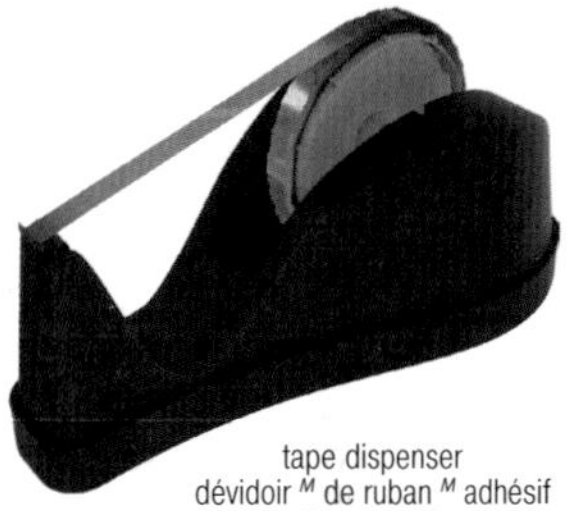

tape dispenser
dévidoir ^{M} de ruban ^{M} adhésif
surtidor ^{M} de cinta ^{F} adhesiva
Klebebandabroller ^{M}
dispenser ^{M} per nastro ^{M} adesivo

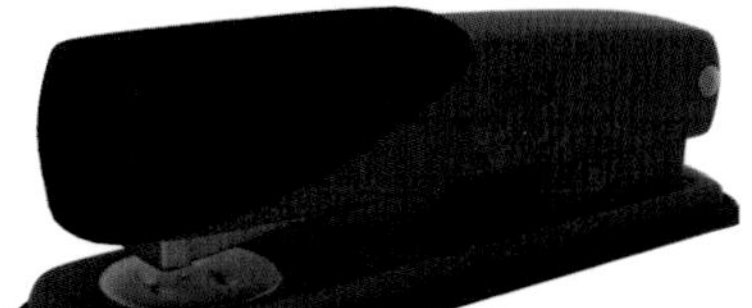

stapler
agrafeuse ^{F} / brocheuse ^{F}
grapadora ^{F} / engrapadora ^{F}
Hefter ^{M}
cucitrice ^{F}

staple
agrafe ^{F}
grapas ^{F}
Heftklammer ^{F}
graffetta ^{F}

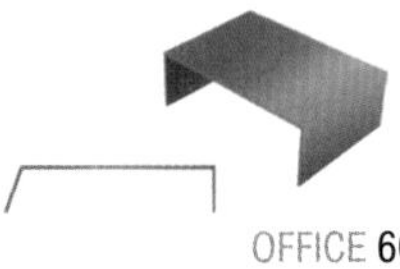

set square
équerre [F]
transportador [M]
Zeichenwinkel [M]
goniometro [M]

paper punch
perforatrice [F]
perforadora [F] de papel [M]
Handlocher [M]
perforatrice [F]

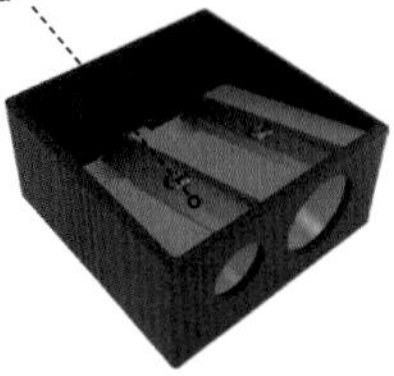

pencil sharpener
taille-crayon [M]
sacapuntas [M]
Bleistiftanspitzer [M]
temperamatite [M]

blade
lame [F]
hoja [F]
Klinge [F]
lama [F]

glue stick
bâton [M] de colle [F]
pegamento [M] en barra [F]
Klebstift [M]
colla [F] stick [M]

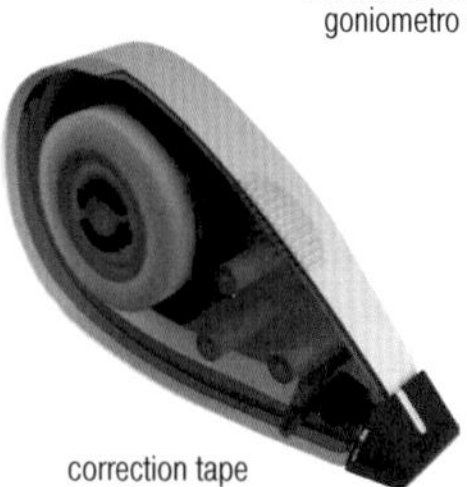

correction tape
ruban [M] correcteur
cinta [F] correctora
Korrekturband [N]
correttore [M] a nastro [M]

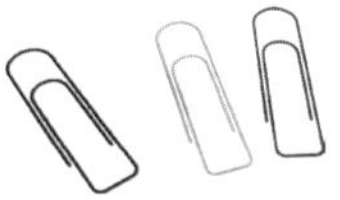

paper clip
trombone [M]
clip [M]
Büroklammer [F]
graffetta [F]

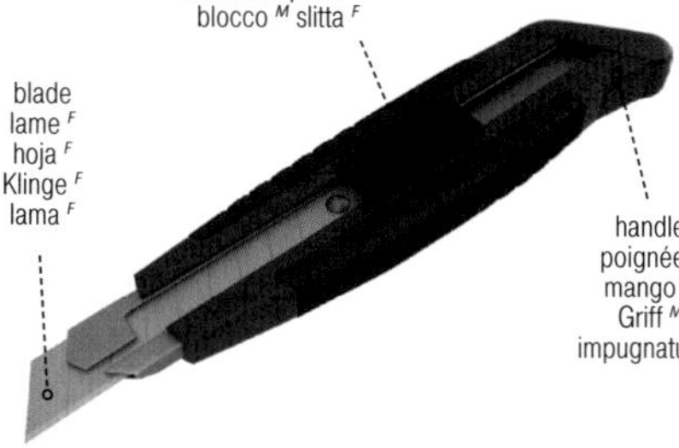

box cutter
couteau [M] à lame [F] rétractable
cúter [M] / cuchillo [M] de trabajo [M]
Teppichmesser [N]
taglierina [F]

slide lock
verrou [M]
marco [M] limitador
Schiebersperre [F]
blocco [M] slitta [F]

blade
lame [F]
hoja [F]
Klinge [F]
lama [F]

handle
poignée [F]
mango [M]
Griff [M]
impugnatura [F]

eraser
gomme [F] à effacer
goma [F] de borrar
Radierer [M]
gomma [F]

pushpin
punaise [F]
chincheta [F]
Reißzwecke [F]
puntina [F]

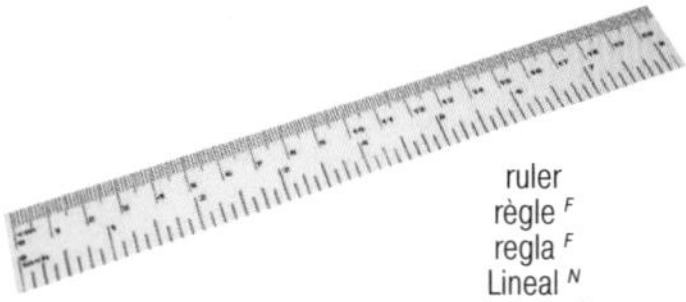

ruler
règle [F]
regla [F]
Lineal [N]
righello [M]

wastebasket
corbeille [F] à papier [M]
papelera [F]
Papierkorb [M]
cestino [M] dei rifiuti [M]

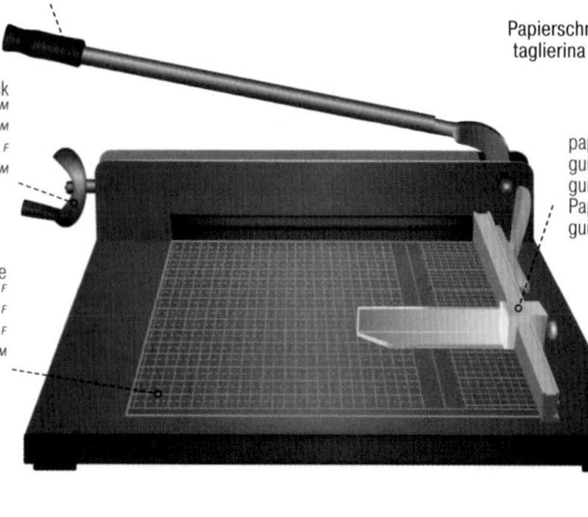

paper cutter
cisaille [F] / massicot [M]
guillotina [F]
Papierschneidemaschine [F]
taglierina [F] a ghigliottina [F]

handle
poignée [F]
manivela [F]
Griff [M]
impugnatura [F]

clamp lock
vis [F] de serrage [M]
regulador [M]
Feststellklemme [F]
dispositivo [M] di serraggio [M]

paper guide
guide-feuille [M]
guía [F] para el papel [M]
Papierführung [F]
guida [F] carta

base
base [F]
base [F]
Papierzufuhrplatte [F]
base [F] appoggio [M]

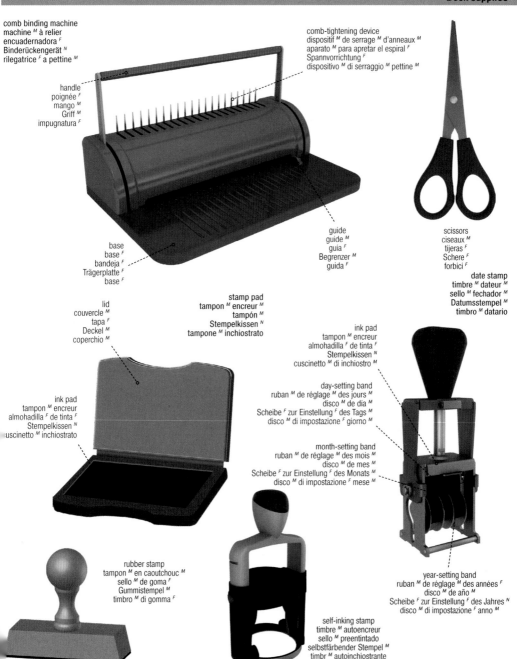

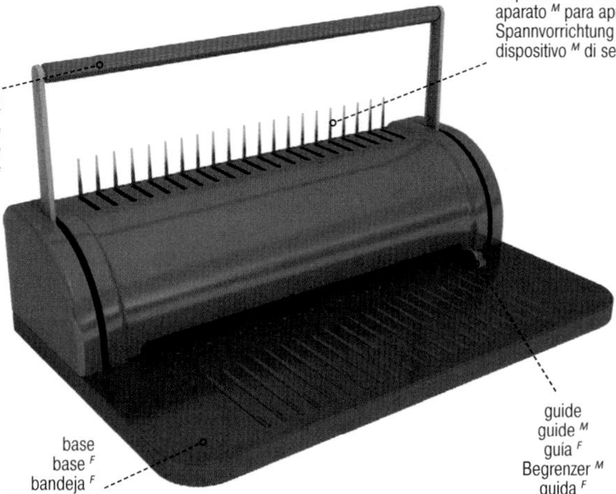
comb binding machine
machine ^{M} à relier
encuadernadora ^{F}
Binderückengerät ^{N}
rilegatrice ^{F} a pettine ^{M}
comb-tightening device
dispositif ^{M} de serrage ^{M} d'anneaux ^{M}
aparato ^{M} para apretar el espiral ^{F}
Spannvorrichtung ^{F}
dispositivo ^{M} di serraggio ^{M} pettine ^{M}
handle
poignée ^{F}
mango ^{M}
Griff ^{M}
impugnatura ^{F}
base
base ^{F}
bandeja ^{F}
Trägerplatte ^{F}
base ^{F}
guide
guide ^{M}
guía ^{F}
Begrenzer ^{M}
guida ^{F}

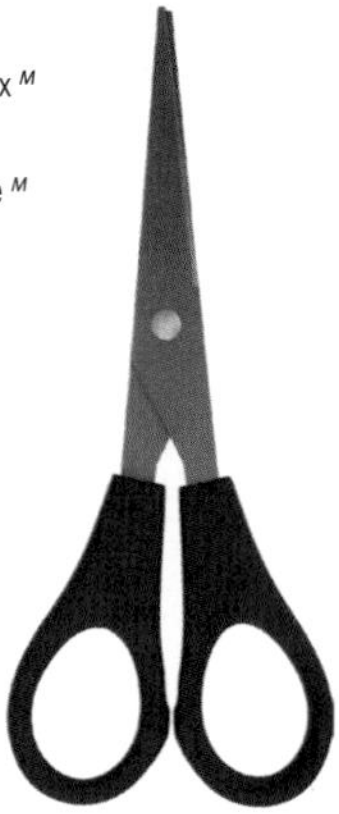
scissors
ciseaux ^{M}
tijeras ^{F}
Schere ^{F}
forbici ^{F}

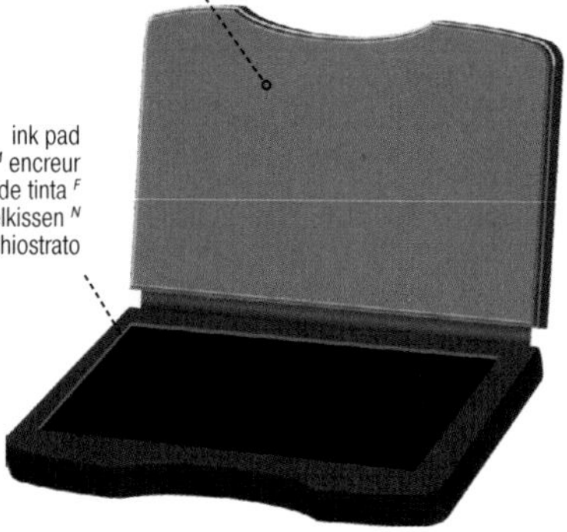
stamp pad
tampon ^{M} encreur ^{M}
tampón ^{M}
Stempelkissen ^{N}
tampone ^{M} inchiostrato
lid
couvercle ^{M}
tapa ^{F}
Deckel ^{M}
coperchio ^{M}
ink pad
tampon ^{M} encreur
almohadilla ^{F} de tinta ^{F}
Stempelkissen ^{N}
cuscinetto ^{M} inchiostrato

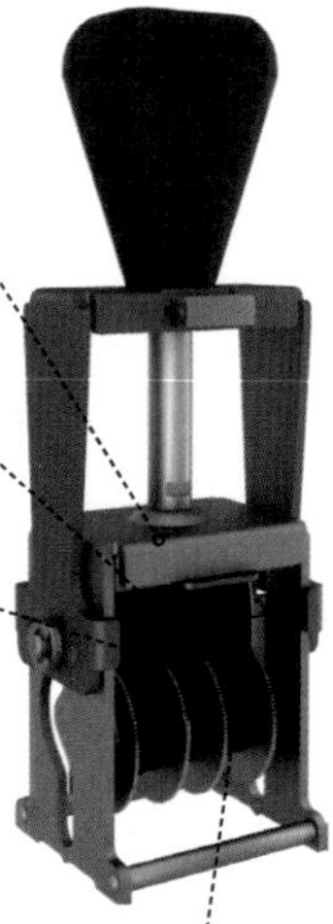
date stamp
timbre ^{M} dateur ^{M}
sello ^{M} fechador ^{M}
Datumsstempel ^{M}
timbro ^{M} datario
ink pad
tampon ^{M} encreur
almohadilla ^{F} de tinta ^{F}
Stempelkissen ^{N}
cuscinetto ^{M} di inchiostro ^{M}
day-setting band
ruban ^{M} de réglage ^{M} des jours ^{M}
disco ^{M} de día ^{M}
Scheibe ^{F} zur Einstellung ^{F} des Tags ^{M}
disco ^{M} di impostazione ^{F} giorno ^{M}
month-setting band
ruban ^{M} de réglage ^{M} des mois ^{M}
disco ^{M} de mes ^{M}
Scheibe ^{F} zur Einstellung ^{F} des Monats ^{M}
disco ^{M} di impostazione ^{F} mese ^{M}
year-setting band
ruban ^{M} de réglage ^{M} des années ^{F}
disco ^{M} de año ^{M}
Scheibe ^{F} zur Einstellung ^{F} des Jahres ^{N}
disco ^{M} di impostazione ^{F} anno ^{M}

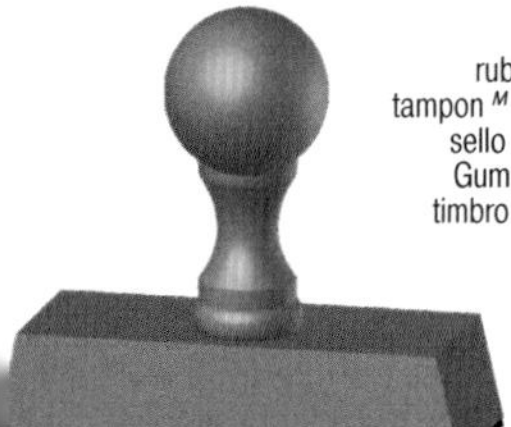
rubber stamp
tampon ^{M} en caoutchouc ^{M}
sello ^{M} de goma ^{F}
Gummistempel ^{M}
timbro ^{M} di gomma ^{F}

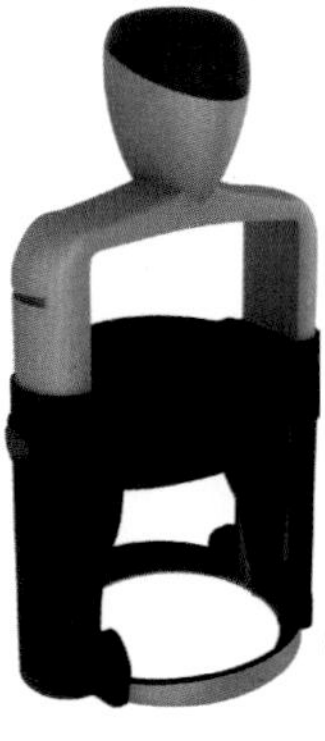
self-inking stamp
timbre ^{M} autoencreur
sello ^{M} preentintado
selbstfärbender Stempel ^{M}
timbr ^{M} autoinchiostrante

correction pen
stylo [M] correcteur
lápiz [M] corrector
Korrekturstift [M]
correttore [M] a penna [F]

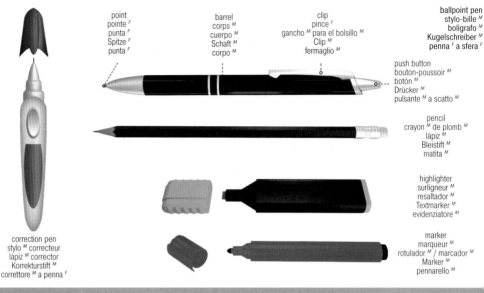

point
pointe [F]
punta [F]
Spitze [F]
punta [F]
barrel
corps [M]
cuerpo [M]
Schaft [M]
corpo [M]
clip
pince [F]
gancho [M] para el bolsillo [M]
Clip [M]
fermaglio [M]
push button
bouton-poussoir [M]
botón [M]
Drücker [M]
pulsante [M] a scatto [M]

ballpoint pen
stylo-bille [M]
bolígrafo [M]
Kugelschreiber [M]
penna [F] a sfera [F]

pencil
crayon [M] de plomb [M]
lápiz [M]
Bleistift [M]
matita [M]

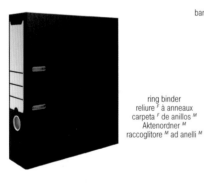

highlighter
surligneur [M]
resaltador [M]
Textmarker [M]
evidenziatore [M]

marker
marqueur [M]
rotulador [M] / marcador [M]
Marker [M]
pennarello [M]

Filing

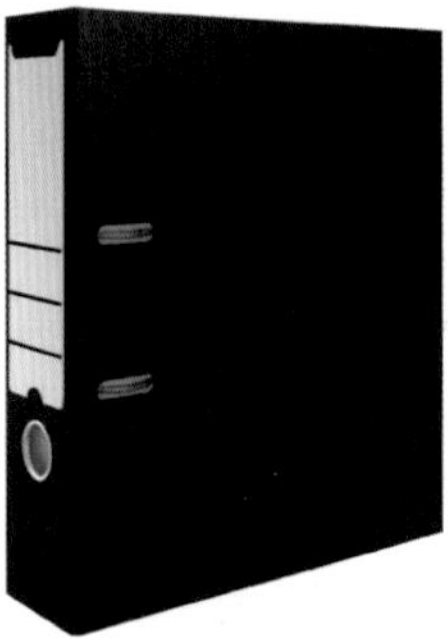

ring binder
reliure [F] à anneaux
carpeta [F] de anillos [M]
Aktenordner [M]
raccoglitore [M] ad anelli [M]

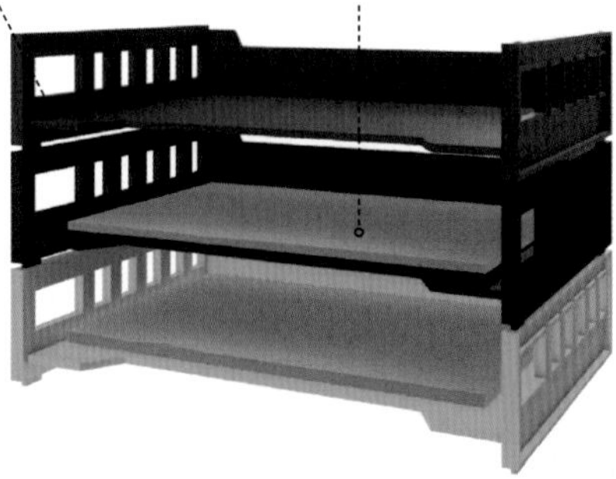
tray
plateau [M]
bandeja [F] para papeles [M]
Ablage [F]
vaschetta [F]
paper
papier [M]
papel [M]
Papier [N]
carta [F]

letter tray
corbeille [F] à courrier [M]
bandeja [F]
Ablagekasten [M]
vaschetta [F] portadocumenti [M]

fastener binder
reliure [F] à glissière [F]
carpeta [F] de gancho [M]
Hefter [M]
raccoglitore [M] con cerniera [F]

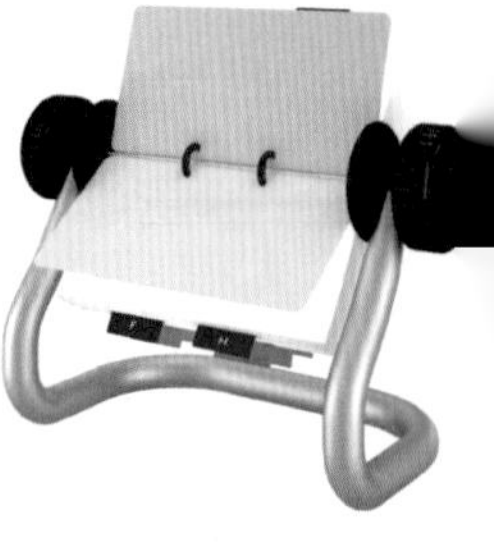

rotary file
fichier [M] rotatif
tarjetero [M] giratorio
Rollkartei [F]
dispositivo [M] voltadocumenti

portable expanding file
pochette F de classement M
portadocumentos M
Dokumententasche F
portadocumenti M allargabile

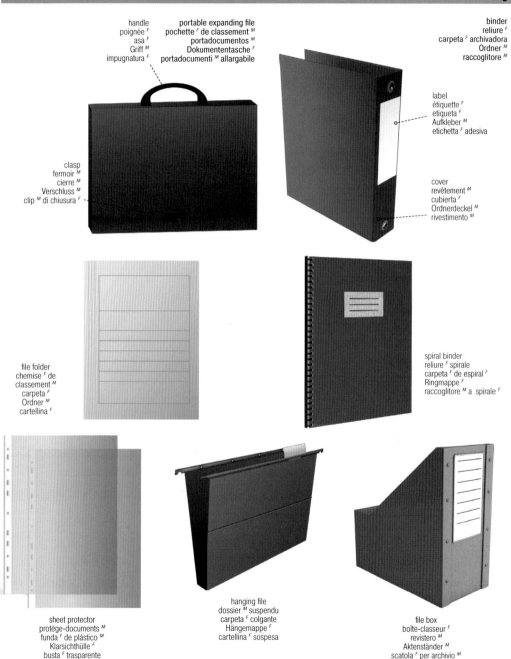

handle
poignée F
asa F
Griff M
impugnatura F
clasp
fermoir M
cierre M
Verschluss M
clip M di chiusura F

binder
reliure F
carpeta F archivadora
Ordner M
raccoglitore M

label
étiquette F
etiqueta F
Aufkleber M
etichetta F adesiva
cover
revêtement M
cubierta F
Ordnerdeckel M
rivestimento M

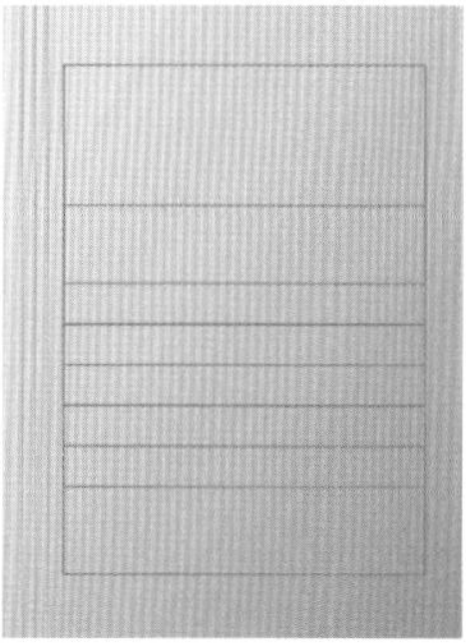

file folder
chemise F de classement M
carpeta F
Ordner M
cartellina F

spiral binder
reliure F spirale
carpeta F de espiral F
Ringmappe F
raccoglitore M a spirale F

sheet protector
protège-documents M
funda F de plástico M
Klarsichthülle F
busta F trasparente

hanging file
dossier M suspendu
carpeta F colgante
Hängemappe F
cartellina F sospesa

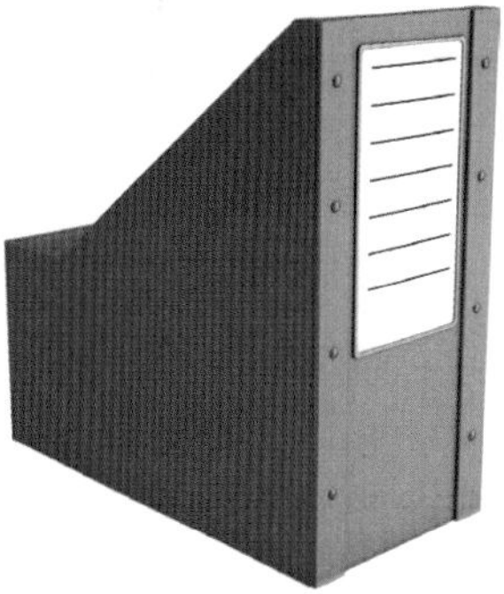

file box
boîte-classeur F
revistero M
Aktenständer M
scatola F per archivio M

diacritics
signes [M] diacritiques
signos [M] diacríticos
Diakritische Zeichen [N]
segni [M] diacritici

é
acute accent
accent [M] aigu
acento [M] agudo
Akut [M]
accento [M] acuto

ă
breve
brève [F]
breve [M]
Breve [N]
breve [M] sopra

ḫ
breve below
brève [F] renversée
breve [M] invertido
Breve [N] Unterzeichen [N]
breve [M] sotto

ç
cedilla
cédille [F]
cedilla [F]
Cédille [F]
cediglia [F]

ģ
cedilla above
cédille [F] en chef [M]
cedilla [F] superior
übergesetzte Cédille [F]
cediglia [F] sopra

ő
double acute accent
double accent [M] aigu
acento [M] agudo doble
Doppelakut [M]
accento [M] doppio acuto

ȁ
double grave accent
double accent [M] grave
acento [M] grave doble
Doppelgravis [M]
doppio accento [M] grave

è
grave accent
accent [M] grave
acento [M] grave
Gravis [M]
accento [M] grave

ả
hook above
crochet [M] en chef [M]
garfio [M] arriba
Haken [M]
gancio [M] sopra

č
hacek
caron [M]
carón [M]
Hatschek [N]
hacek [M]

ơ
horn
corne [F]
cuerno [M]
Horn [N]
corno [M]

ş
hook
virgule [F] souscrite
coma [F] abajo
untergesetzter Haken [M]

ů
ring
rond [M] en chef [M]
anillo [M]
Kreisakzent [M]
anello [M]

ā
macron
macron [M]
macrón [M]
Makron [N]
macron [M]

a̲
underline
ligne [F] souscrite
subrayado [M]
Unterstrich [M]
sottolineatura [F]

l·l
middle dot
point [M] médian
punto [M] medio
Mittelpunkt [M]
punto [M] mediano

ę
ogonek
ogonek [M]
coma [F] abajo invertida
Ogonek [N]
ohonek [F]

ḍ
under dot
point [M] souscrit
punto [M] abajo
Anusvara [M]
punto [M] sotto

ż
over dot
point [M] suscrit
punto [M] arriba
Punkt [M] darüber
punto [M] sopra

Ł
slash
barre [F] oblique
barra [F]
Schrägstrich [M]
barra [F]

ñ
tilde
tilde [F]
tilde [F]
Tilde [M]
tilde [F]

ü
umlaut
tréma [M]
diéresis [F]
Umlaut [M]
dieresi [F]

ê
circumflex accent
accent [M] circonflexe
acento [M] circunflejo
Zirkumflex [M]
accento [M] circonflesso

punctuation marks
signes [M] de ponctuation [F]
signos [M] de puntuación [F]
Satzzeichen [N]
segni [M] di punteggiatura [F]

.
period
point [M]
punto [M]
Punkt [M]
punto [M]

,
comma
virgule [F]
coma [F]
Komma [N]
virgola [F]

;
semicolon
point-virgule [M]
punto [M] y coma [F]
Semikolon [N]
punto [M] e virgola [F]

:
colon
deux-points [M]
dos puntos [M]
Doppelpunkt [M]
due punti [M]

?
question mark
point [M] d'interrogation [F]
signo [M] de interrogación [F]
Fragezeichen [N]
punto [M] interrogativo

!
exclamation mark
point [M] d'exclamation [F]
signo [M] de exclamación [F]
Ausrufezeichen [N]
punto [M] esclamativo

„ " » « « »
quotation marks
guillemets [M]
comillas [F]
Anführungszeichen [N]
virgolette [F]

-
hyphen
trait [M] d'union [M]
guión [M]
Bindestrich [M]
trattino [M]

–
en-dash
tiret [M] demi-cadratin
guión [M] largo
Halbgeviertstrich [M]
trattino [M] breve

—
em-dash
tiret [M] cadratin
guión [M] largo
Geviertstrich [M]
trattino [M] lungo

——
double en-dash
double-cadratin [M]
guión [M] doble
Doppelgeviertstrich [M]
doppio trattino [M] breve

/
slash
barre [F] oblique
barra [F] diagonal
Schrägstrich [M]
barra [F]

****
backslash
barre [F] oblique inverse
barra [F] inversa
Umgekehrter Schrägstrich [M]
barra [F] inversa

( )
parentheses
parenthèses [F]
paréntesis [M]
Runde Klammern [F]
parentesi [F] tonde

[ ]
square brackets
crochets [M]
corchetes [M]
Eckige Klammern [F]
parentesi [F] quadre

{ }
braces
accolades [F]
llaves [F]
Geschweifte Klammern [F]
parentesi [F] graffe

< >
chevrons
chevrons [M]
comillas [F] angulares
Spitze Klammern [F]
parentesi [F] aguzze

…
ellipsis
point [M] de suspension [F]
puntos [M] suspensivos
Auslassungspunkte [M]
ellissi [F]

'
apostrophe
apostrophe [F]
apóstrofe [F]
Apostroph [N]
apostrofo [M]

=
double hyphen
double trait [M]
d'union [M]
guión [M] doble
Doppelbindestrich [M]
doppio trattino [M]

‽
interrobang
point [M] exclarrogatif
interrobang [M]
Interrobang [N]
punto [M] esclarrogativo

~
tilde
tilde [F]
acento [M]
Tilde [F]
tilde [F]

•
bullet
puce [F]
viñeta [F]
Aufzählungszeichen [N]
indicatore [M] di elenco [M]

#
pound
carré [M]
almohadilla [F]
Rautenzeichen [N]
cancelletto [M]

№
number sign
symbole [M] numéro [M]
signo [M] de número [M]
Numero-Zeichen [N]
simbolo [M] del numero [M]

§
section sign
signe [M] de paragraphe [M]
símbolo [M] de sección [F]
Paragraphenzeichen [N]
simbolo [M] di paragrafo [M]

¶
pilcrow
pied-de-mouche [M]
calderón [M]
Absatzzeichen [N]
piede [M] di mosca [F]

@
at
arobase [F]
arroba [F]
At-Zeichen [N]
chiocciola [F]

&
ampersand
esperluette [F]
ampersand [M]
Et-Zeichen [N]
e [F] commerciale

other marks
autres signes [M]
otros signos [M]
sonstige Zeichen [N]
altri segni [M]

′
prime
prime [F]
primo [M]
Minutenzeichen [N]
virgoletta [F] alta

‡
double dagger
croix [F] double
daga [F] doble
Zweibalkenkreuz [N]
doppio obelisco [M]

*****
asterisk
astérisque [M]
asterisco [M]
Sternchen [N]
asterisco [M]

⁂
asterism
astérisme [M]
asterismo [M]
Sterngruppe [F]
triangolo [M] di asterischi [M]

†
dagger
croix [F]
daga [F]
Kreuz [N]
obelisco [M]

″
double prime
double prime [F]
primo [M] doble
Sekundenzeichen [N]
virgolette [F] alte

|
vertical line
barre [F] verticale
línea [F] vertical
Senkrechter Strich [M]
linea [F] verticale

°
degree sign
symbole [M] du degré [M]
signo [M] de grado
Gradzeichen [N]
segno [M] di grado

typesetting
mise [F] en page [F]
composición [F] tipográfica
Schriftsetzen [N]
composizione [F] tipografica

hairline
délié [M]
línea [F] delgada
Haarstrich [M]
asta [F] sottile

angle of stress
axe [M] oblique
angulo [M] de estrés [M]
Schattenachse [F]
asse [M] verticale

counter
contrepoinçon [M]
letra [M] fuerte
Punze [F]
occhiello [M]

ascender
jambage [M] ascendant
ascendente [M]
Oberlänge [F]
asta [F] ascendente

capital letter height
hauteur [F] de majuscule [F]
altura [F] de una letra [F] mayúscula
Versalhöhe [F]
altezza [F] del corpo [M]

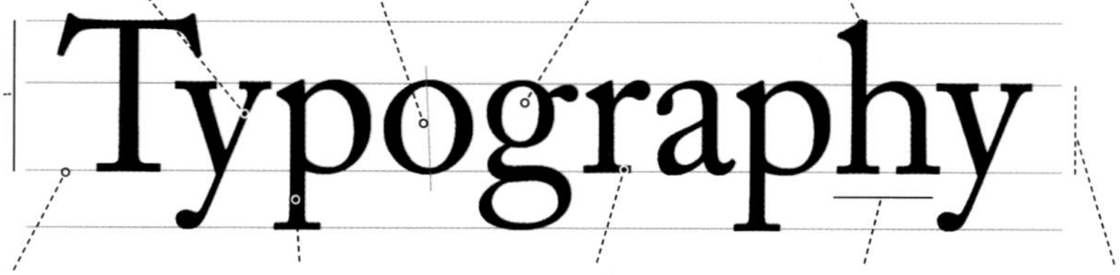
Typography

baseline
ligne [F] de base [F]
línea [F] principal
Grundlinie [F]
linea [F] di base [F]

descender
jambage [M] descendant
descendente [M]
Unterlänge [F]
asta [F] discendente

serif
empattement [M]
serif [M]
Serife [F]
grazia [F]

width
largeur [F]
ancho [M]
Breite [F]
larghezza [F] della lettera [F]

x-height
hauteur [F] x
tamaño [M] del corpus [M]
Mittellänge [F]
dimensioni [F] del corpo [M]

TRANSPORTATION

interchange
échangeur ^{M}
intercambio ^{M} vial
Straßenkreuzung ^{F}
raccordo ^{M} stradale

car
voiture ^{M}
coche ^{M}
Auto ^{N}
auto ^{F}

arch bridge
pont ^{M} à arches ^{F}
puente ^{M} de arco ^{M}
Bogenbrücke ^{F}
ponte ^{M} ad arco ^{M}

road marking
signalisation ^{F} routière
líneas ^{F} de carretera ^{F}
Straßenmarkierung ^{F}
segnaletica ^{M} orizzontale

traffic sign
panneau ^{M} routier
señal ^{F} de tráfico ^{M}
Verkehrszeichen ^{N}
cartello ^{M} stradale

roadway
chaussée ^{F}
carretera ^{F}
Straße ^{F}
fondo ^{M} stradale

billboard (back view)
panneau ^{M} d'affichage ^{M} (vue ^{F} de derrière ^{M})
valla ^{F} publicitaria ^{F} (vista ^{F} posterior)
Plakatwand ^{F}
tabellone ^{M} per affissioni ^{F}

safety railing
rampe ^{F} de sécurité ^{F}
barandilla ^{F}
Schutzgeländer ^{N}
parapetto ^{M}

road worker
travailleur ^{M} routier
trabajador ^{M} de carreteras ^{F}
Straßenbauarbeiter ^{M}
operaio ^{M} stradale

pedestrian
piéton [M]
peatón [M]
Fußgänger [M]
pedone [M]

hard hat
casque [M] de sécurité [F]
casco [M]
Schutzhelm [M]
elmetto [M]

road worker
travailleur [M] routier
trabajador [F] de carreteras [F]
Straßenbauarbeiter [M]
operaio [M] stradale

guardrail
glissière [F] de sécurité [F]
baranda [F]
Leitplanke [F]
guardrail [M]

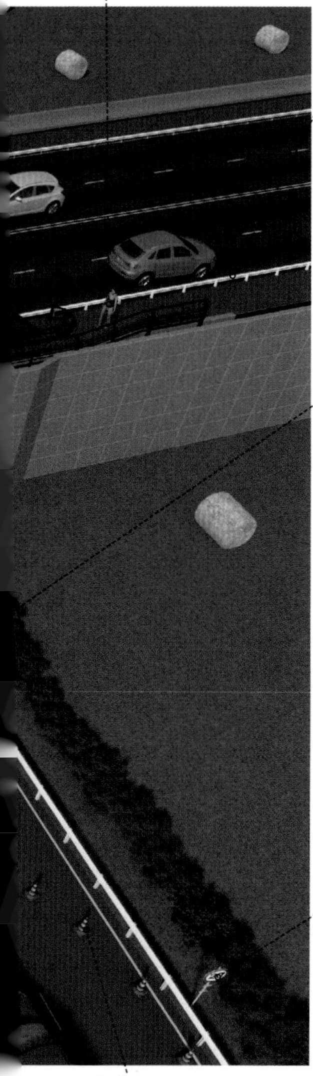

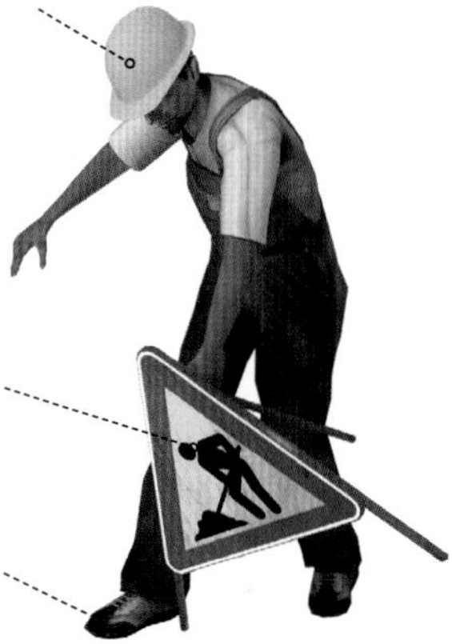

roadwork ahead sign
panneau [M] de travaux [M]
señal [F] de obras [F]
Baustellenschild [N]
segnale [M] di lavori [M] stradali

safety boot
bottes [F] de sécurité [F]
botas [F] de seguridad [F]
Sicherheitsschuhe [M]
stivali [M] con punta [F] in acciaio [M]

sound barrier
mur [M] anti-bruit
barrera [F] de sonido [M]
Schallwand [F]
barriera [F] antirumore

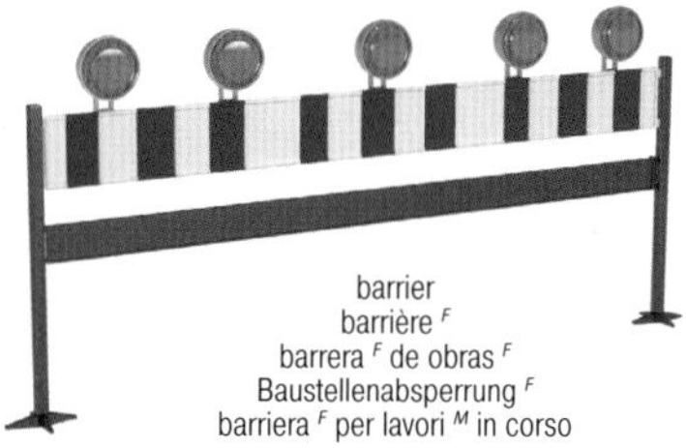

barrier
barrière [F]
barrera [F] de obras [F]
Baustellenabsperrung [F]
barriera [F] per lavori [M] in corso

cross section of road
coupe [F] transversale de la route [F]
vista [F] transversal de carretera [F]
Querschnitt [M] einer Straße
sezione [F] trasversale di una strada [F]

surface course
couche [F] de roulement [M]
asfalto [M]
Straßenbelag [M]
rivestimento [M]

base course
couche [F] de base [F]
capa [F] base
Tragschicht [F]
strato [M] di base [F]

binding course
couche [F] de liaison [F]
capa [F] aglutinante
Binderschicht [F]
manto [M] di pietrischetto [M] botumato

speed limit sign
panneau [M] de limite [F] de vitesse [F]
señal [F] de límite [M] de velocidad [F]
Geschwindigkeitsbegrenzungszeichen [N]
cartello [M] per limite [M] di velocità [F]

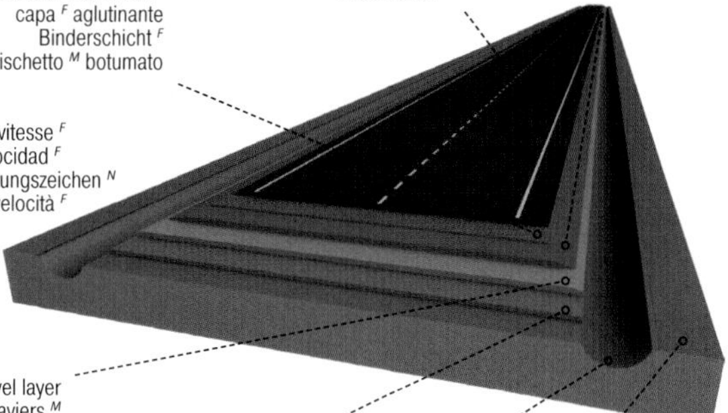

gravel layer
couche [F] de graviers [M]
capa [F] de grava [F]
Kiesschicht [F]
strato [M] di ghiaietto [M]

sand layer
couche [F] de sable [M]
capa [F] de arena [F]
Sandschicht [F]
strato [M] di sabbia [F]

ditch
fossé [M]
drenaje [M]
Straßengraben [M]
fosso [M]

bank
talus [M]
terraplén [M]
Böschung [F]
argine [M]

traffic cone
cône [M] de signalisation [F]
cono [M] de tráfico [M]
Leitkegel [M]
cono [M] stradale

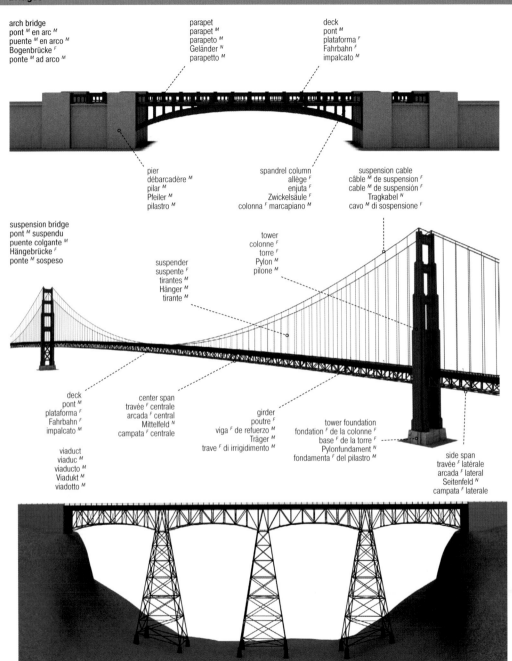

arch bridge
pont M en arc M
puente M en arco M
Bogenbrücke F
ponte M ad arco M
parapet
parapet M
parapeto M
Geländer N
parapetto M
deck
pont M
plataforma F
Fahrbahn F
impalcato M
pier
débarcadère M
pilar M
Pfeiler M
pilastro M
spandrel column
allège F
enjuta F
Zwickelsäule F
colonna F marcapiano M

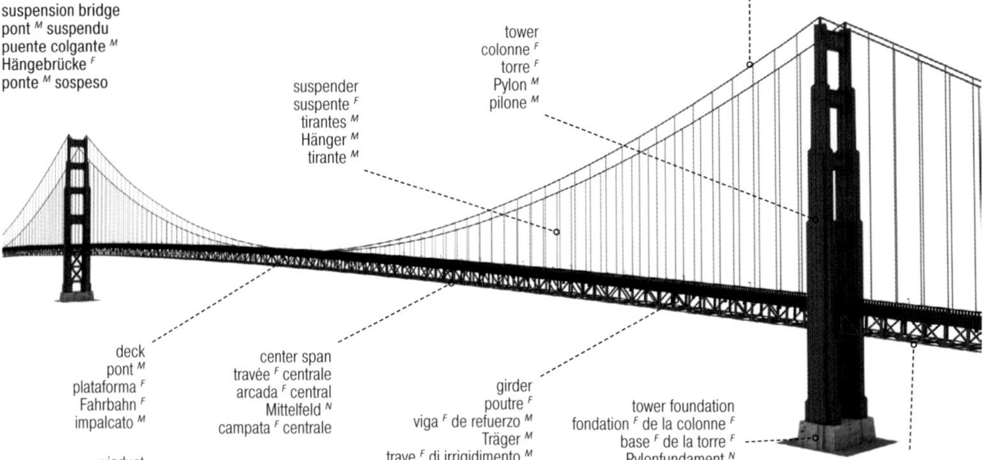
suspension cable
câble M de suspension F
cable M de suspensión F
Tragkabel N
cavo M di sospensione F
suspension bridge
pont M suspendu
puente colgante M
Hängebrücke F
ponte M sospeso
tower
colonne F
torre F
Pylon M
pilone M
suspender
suspente F
tirantes M
Hänger M
tirante M
deck
pont M
plataforma F
Fahrbahn F
impalcato M
center span
travée F centrale
arcada F central
Mittelfeld N
campata F centrale
girder
poutre F
viga F de refuerzo M
Träger M
trave F di irrigidimento M
tower foundation
fondation F de la colonne F
base F de la torre F
Pylonfundament N
fondamenta F del pilastro M
side span
travée F latérale
arcada F lateral
Seitenfeld N
campata F laterale

viaduct
viaduc M
viaducto M
Viadukt M
viadotto M

verview of gas station
ue d'une station [F] libre-service
ista [F] de una estación [F] de servicio [M]
ankstelle [F] Übersicht [F]
anoramica [F] stazione [F] di servizio [M]

car
automobile [F]
coche [M]
Auto [N]
automobile [F]
gas station attendant
employé [M] de station-service [F]
trabajador [M] de estación [F] de servicio [M]
Tankstellenangestellter [M]
benzinaio [M]
driver
conducteur [M]
cliente [M]
Fahrer [M]
guidatore [M]
service bay
aire [F] de service [M]
área [F] de servicio [M]
Servicebucht [F]
piattaforma [M] di servizio
3.10
3.30
3.40
3.55
restroom entrance
entrée [F] des toilettes [F]
entrada [F] al baño [M]
WC-Eingang [M]
entrata [F] del bagno [M]
gasoline pump
pompe [F] à essence [F]
bomba [F] de gasolina [F]
Zapfsäule [F]
pompa [F] del carburante [M]
car wash
lave-auto [M]
tren [M] de lavado [M]
Autowaschanlage [F]
autolavaggio [M]
sign
panneau [M]
panel [M] de información [F]
Anzeigetafel [F]
pannello [M] informativo

gasoline pump
distributeur [M] à essence [F]
omba [F] de gasolina [F]
Zapfsäule [F]
ompa [F] di carburante [M]

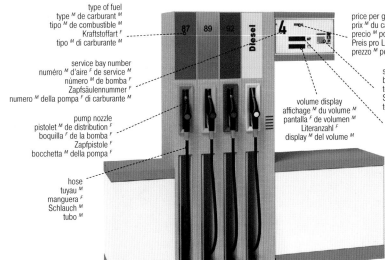

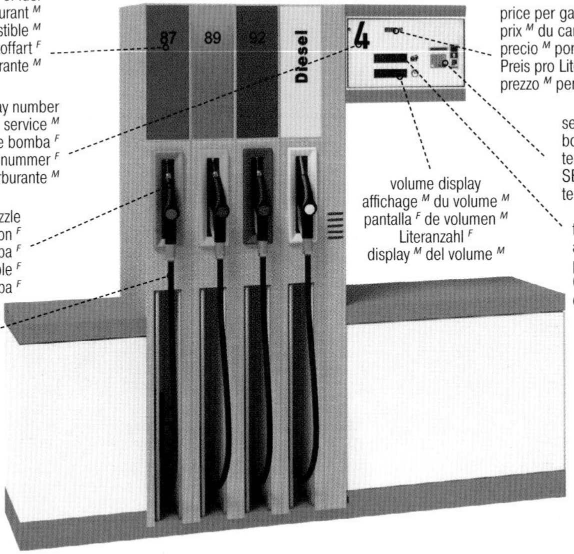
type of fuel
type [M] de carburant [M]
tipo [M] de combustible [M]
Kraftstoffart [F]
tipo [M] di carburante [M]
87
89
92
Diesel
4
price per gallon or liter
prix [M] du carburant [M] par gallon [M] ou par litre [M]
precio [M] por galón [M] o litro [M] de combustible [M]
Preis pro Liter Kraftstoff [M]
prezzo [M] per litro [M] di benzina [F]
service bay number
numéro [M] d'aire [F] de service [M]
número [M] de bomba [F]
Zapfsäulennummer [F]
numero [M] della pompa [F] di carburante [M]
self-service payment terminal
borne [F] de paiement [M] libre-service
terminal [F] de autoservicio [M]
SB-Bezahlterminal [M]
terminale [M] di pagamento self-service
volume display
affichage [M] du volume [M]
pantalla [F] de volumen [M]
Literanzahl [F]
display [M] del volume [M]
pump nozzle
pistolet [M] de distribution [F]
boquilla [F] de la bomba [F]
Zapfpistole [F]
bocchetta [M] della pompa [F]
total sale display
affichage [M] du coût [M] total
pantalla [F] de precio [M] total de venta [F]
Gesamtbetragsanzeige [F]
display [M] del costo [M] totale
hose
tuyau [M]
manguera [F]
Schlauch [M]
tubo [M]

Car accessories

Accessoires ^{M} automobiles | Accesorios ^{M} de automóvil ^{M} | Autozubehör ^{N} | Accessori ^{M} per auto ^{F}

jack
cric ^{M}
gato ^{M}
Wagenheber ^{M}
cric ^{M}

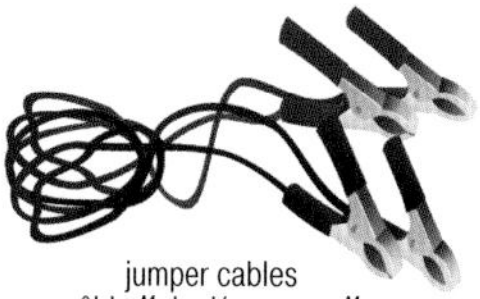

jumper cables
câble ^{M} de démarrage ^{M}
cables ^{M} puente
Starthilfekabel ^{N}
cavi ^{M} di connessione ^{F}

fire extinguisher
extincteur ^{M}
extintor ^{M}
Feuerlöscher ^{M}
estintore ^{M}

bicycle rack
porte-vélo ^{M}
portabicicletas ^{M}
Fahrradträger ^{M}
portabiciclette ^{M}

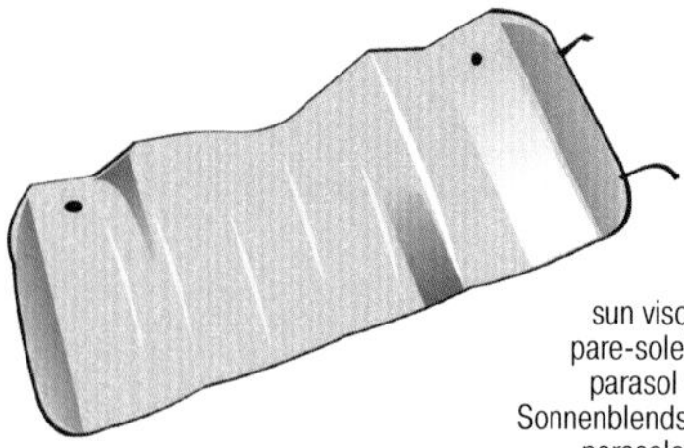

sun visor
pare-soleil ^{M}
parasol ^{M}
Sonnenblendschutz ^{M}
parasole ^{M}

floor mat
tapis ^{M} de sol ^{M}
alfombrilla ^{F}
Gummimatte ^{F}
tappetino ^{M} in gomma ^{F}

snow brush with scraper
balai-neige ^{M} à grattoir ^{M}
cepillo ^{M} para nieve ^{F} con raspador ^{M}
Eiskratzer mit Schneefeger ^{M}
raschiatore ^{M} a spazzola ^{F}

ski rack
porte-ski ^{M}
portaesquís ^{M}
Skiträger ^{M}
portasci ^{M}

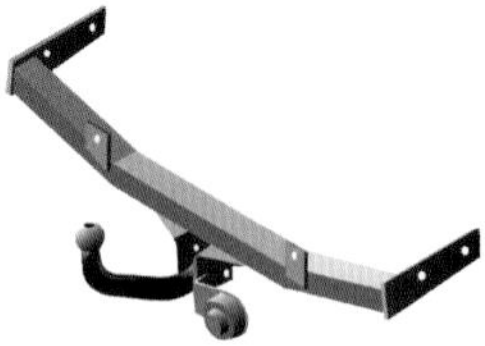

trailer hitch
attelage ^{M} de remorque ^{F}
gancho ^{M} de remolque ^{M}
Anhängerkupplung ^{F}
gancio ^{M} di traino ^{M}

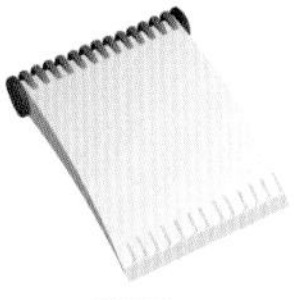

scraper
grattoir ^{M}
rasqueta ^{F}
Eiskratzer ^{M}
raschietto ^{M}

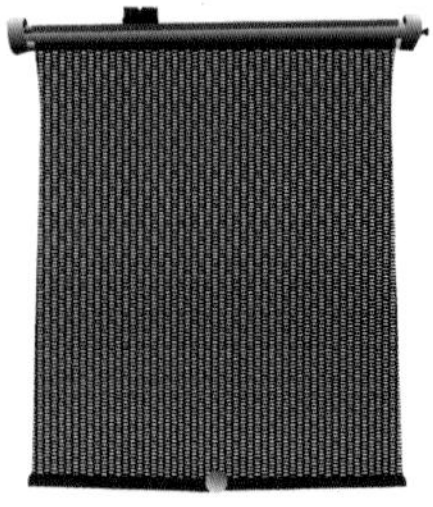

roller shade
store ^{M} à ressort ^{M}
cortinillas ^{F}
Sonnenrollos ^{N}
oscuratori ^{M}

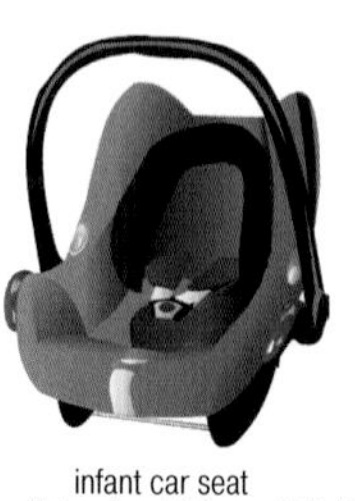

infant car seat
siège ^{M} de sécurité ^{F} pour bébé ^{M}
silla ^{F} de seguridad ^{F} para bebés ^{M}
Babyschale ^{F}
seggiolino ^{M} auto ^{F} per neonati ^{M}

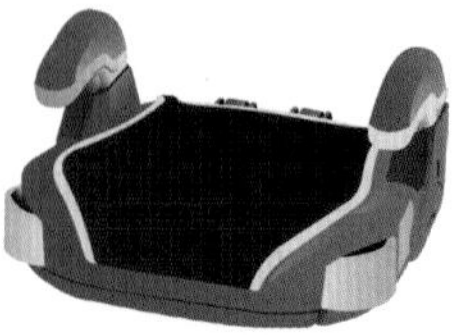

booster car seat
siège ^{M} d'appoint ^{M}
asiento ^{M} elevador ^{M}
Sitzerhöhung ^{F}
seggiolino ^{M} auto ^{F} alzasedia

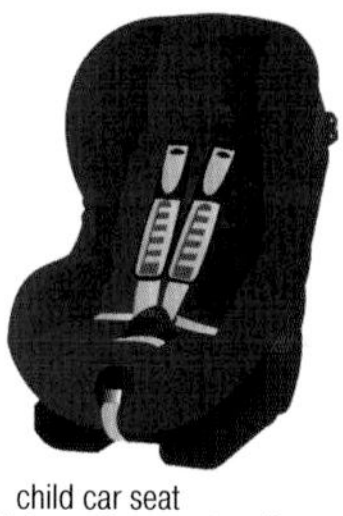

child car seat
siège ^{M} d'auto ^{F} pour enfant ^{M}
silla ^{F} de seguridad ^{F} para niños ^{M}
Kindersicherheitssitz ^{M}
seggiolino ^{M} auto ^{F} per bambini ^{M}

emergency warning triangle
triangle ^{M} de signalisation ^{F}
triángulo ^{M} de seguridad ^{F}
Warndreieck ^{N}
triangolo ^{M} d'emergenza ^{F}

First
Aid Kit

first-aid kit
trousse ^{F} de premiers secours ^{M}
botiquín ^{M} de primeros auxilios ^{M}
Erste-Hilfe -Kasten ^{M}
kit ^{M} di pronto soccorso ^{M}

reflective vest
gilet ^{M} réflécteur
chaleco ^{M} reflector
reflektierende Sicherheitsweste ^{F}
giubbotto ^{M} di sicurezza ^{F} riflettente

lug wrench
démonte-roue ^{M}
llave ^{F} de cruz ^{F}
Radkreuz ^{N}
chiave ^{F} a croce ^{F}

Car systems

Système ^{M} automobile | Sistemas ^{M} del coche ^{M} | Farhzeugsysteme ^{N} | Impianti ^{M} automobilistico

cooling system
système ^{M} de refroidissement ^{M}
sistema ^{M} de refrigeración ^{F}
Kühlungssystem ^{N}
sistema ^{M} di raffreddamento ^{M}

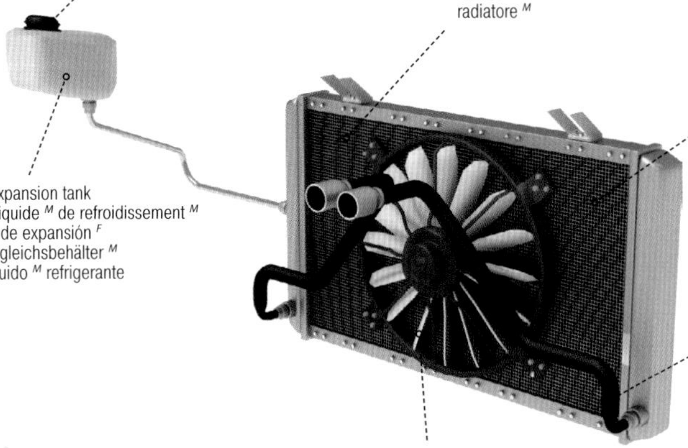

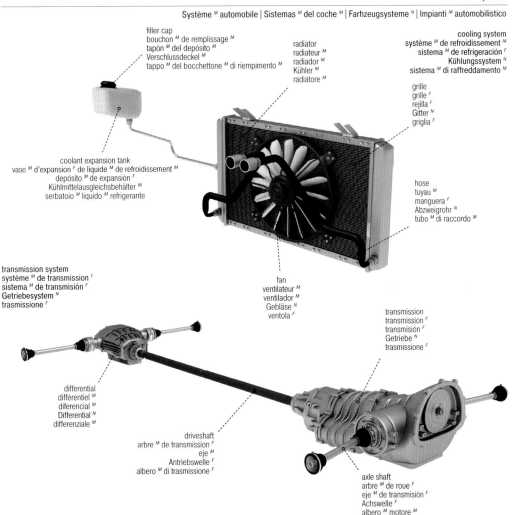

filler cap
bouchon ^{M} de remplissage ^{M}
tapón ^{M} del depósito ^{M}
Verschlussdeckel ^{M}
tappo ^{M} del bocchettone ^{M} di riempimento ^{M}

radiator
radiateur ^{M}
radiador ^{M}
Kühler ^{M}
radiatore ^{M}

grille
grille ^{F}
rejilla ^{F}
Gitter ^{N}
griglia ^{F}

coolant expansion tank
vase ^{M} d'expansion ^{F} de liquide ^{M} de refroidissement ^{M}
depósito ^{M} de expansión ^{F}
Kühlmittelausgleichsbehälter ^{M}
serbatoio ^{M} liquido ^{M} refrigerante

hose
tuyau ^{M}
manguera ^{F}
Abzweigrohr ^{N}
tubo ^{M} di raccordo ^{M}

fan
ventilateur ^{M}
ventilador ^{M}
Gebläse ^{N}
ventola ^{F}

transmission system
système ^{M} de transmission ^{F}
sistema ^{M} de transmisión ^{F}
Getriebesystem ^{N}
trasmissione ^{F}

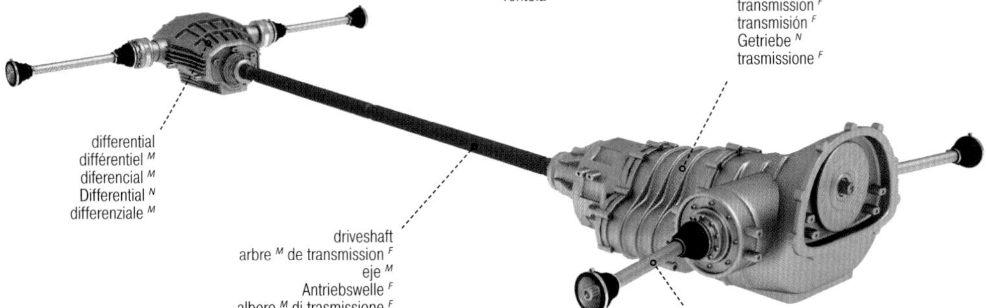

transmission
transmission ^{F}
transmisión ^{F}
Getriebe ^{N}
trasmissione ^{F}

differential
différentiel ^{M}
diferencial ^{M}
Differential ^{N}
differenziale ^{M}

driveshaft
arbre ^{M} de transmission ^{F}
eje ^{M}
Antriebswelle ^{F}
albero ^{M} di trasmissione ^{F}

axle shaft
arbre ^{M} de roue ^{F}
eje ^{M} de transmisión ^{F}
Achswelle ^{F}
albero ^{M} motore ^{M}

braking system
système ^{M} de freinage ^{M}
sistema ^{M} de frenado ^{M}
Bremsanlage ^{F}
sistema ^{M} frenante

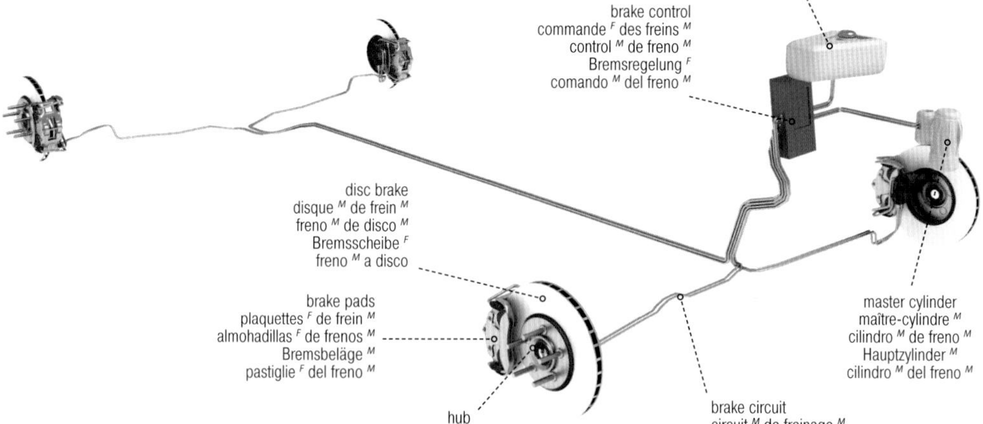
brake fluid reservoir
réservoir ^{M} de liquide ^{M} de frein ^{M}
depósito ^{M} del líquido ^{M} de frenos ^{M}
Bremsflüssigkeitsbehälter ^{M}
serbatoio ^{M} del liquido ^{M} dei freni ^{M}
brake control
commande ^{F} des freins ^{M}
control ^{M} de freno ^{M}
Bremsregelung ^{F}
comando ^{M} del freno ^{M}
disc brake
disque ^{M} de frein ^{M}
freno ^{M} de disco ^{M}
Bremsscheibe ^{F}
freno ^{M} a disco
brake pads
plaquettes ^{F} de frein ^{M}
almohadillas ^{F} de frenos ^{M}
Bremsbeläge ^{M}
pastiglie ^{F} del freno ^{M}
master cylinder
maître-cylindre ^{M}
cilindro ^{M} de freno ^{M}
Hauptzylinder ^{M}
cilindro ^{M} del freno ^{M}
hub
moyeu ^{M}
cubo ^{M}
Radnabe ^{F}
mozzo ^{M}
brake circuit
circuit ^{M} de freinage ^{M}
circuito ^{M} de frenos ^{M}
Bremskreis ^{M}
circuito ^{M} del freno ^{M}

exhaust system
système ^{M} d'échappement ^{M}
sistema ^{M} de escape ^{M}
Auspuffanlage ^{F}
sistema ^{M} di scarico ^{M}

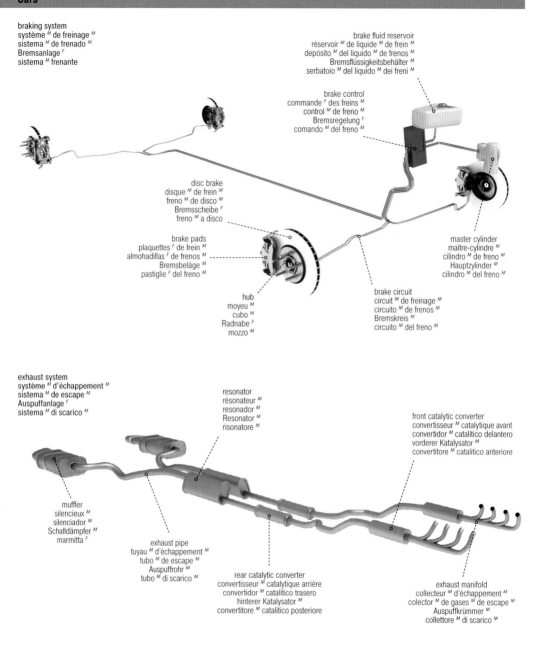

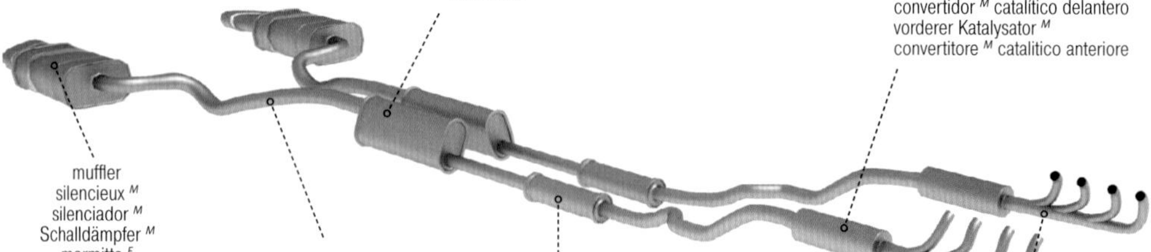
resonator
résonateur ^{M}
resonador ^{M}
Resonator ^{M}
risonatore ^{M}
front catalytic converter
convertisseur ^{M} catalytique avant
convertidor ^{M} catalítico delantero
vorderer Katalysator ^{M}
convertitore ^{M} catalitico anteriore
muffler
silencieux ^{M}
silenciador ^{M}
Schalldämpfer ^{M}
marmitta ^{F}
exhaust pipe
tuyau ^{M} d'échappement ^{M}
tubo ^{M} de escape ^{M}
Auspuffrohr ^{M}
tubo ^{M} di scarico ^{M}
rear catalytic converter
convertisseur ^{M} catalytique arrière
convertidor ^{M} catalítico trasero
hinterer Katalysator ^{M}
convertitore ^{M} catalitico posteriore
exhaust manifold
collecteur ^{M} d'échappement ^{M}
colector ^{M} de gases ^{M} de escape ^{M}
Auspuffkrümmer ^{M}
collettore ^{M} di scarico ^{M}

rear suspension
suspension ᶠ arrière
suspensión ᶠ trasera
Hinterachse ᶠ
sospensione ᶠ posteriore

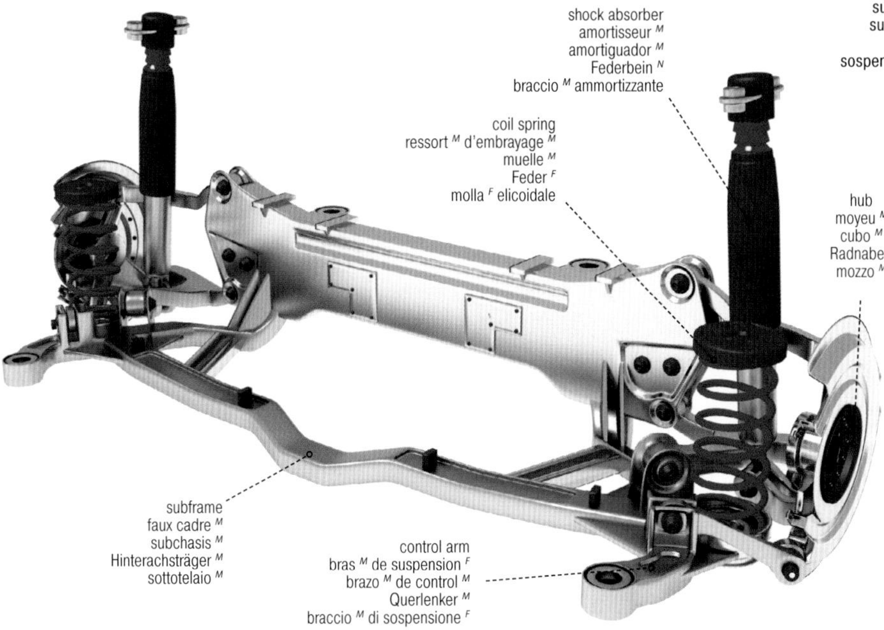
shock absorber
amortisseur ᴹ
amortiguador ᴹ
Federbein ᴺ
braccio ᴹ ammortizzante
coil spring
ressort ᴹ d'embrayage ᴹ
muelle ᴹ
Feder ᶠ
molla ᶠ elicoidale
hub
moyeu ᴹ
cubo ᴹ
Radnabe ᶠ
mozzo ᴹ
subframe
faux cadre ᴹ
subchasis ᴹ
Hinterachsträger ᴹ
sottotelaio ᴹ
control arm
bras ᴹ de suspension ᶠ
brazo ᴹ de control ᴹ
Querlenker ᴹ
braccio ᴹ di sospensione ᶠ

front suspension
suspension ᶠ avant
suspensión ᶠ delantera
Vorderachse ᶠ
sospensione ᶠ anteriore

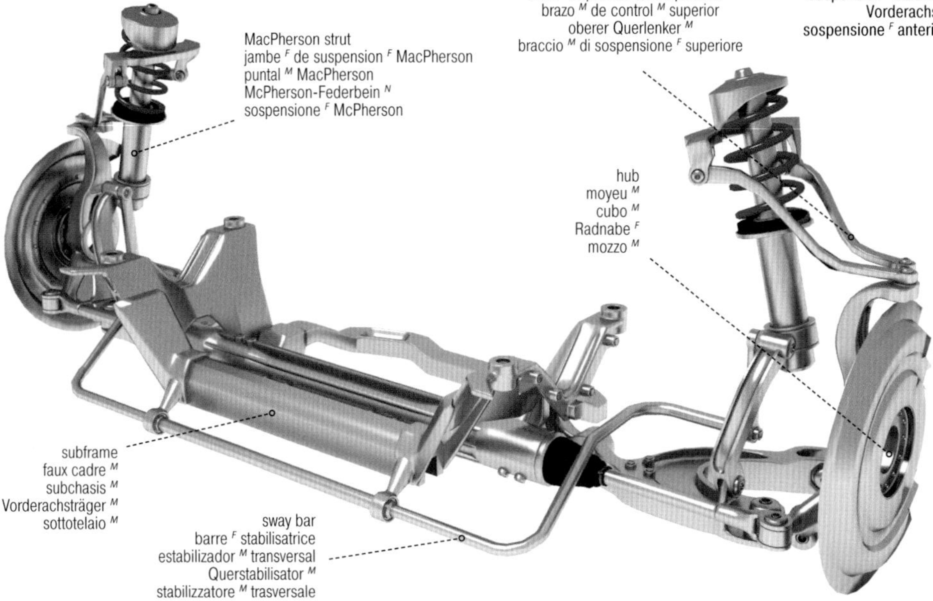
upper control arm
bras ᴹ supérieur de suspension ᶠ
brazo ᴹ de control ᴹ superior
oberer Querlenker ᴹ
braccio ᴹ di sospensione ᶠ superiore
MacPherson strut
jambe ᶠ de suspension ᶠ MacPherson
puntal ᴹ MacPherson
McPherson-Federbein ᴺ
sospensione ᶠ McPherson
hub
moyeu ᴹ
cubo ᴹ
Radnabe ᶠ
mozzo ᴹ
subframe
faux cadre ᴹ
subchasis ᴹ
Vorderachsträger ᴹ
sottotelaio ᴹ
sway bar
barre ᶠ stabilisatrice
estabilizador ᴹ transversal
Querstabilisator ᴹ
stabilizzatore ᴹ trasversale

engine
moteur M
motor M
Motor M
motore M

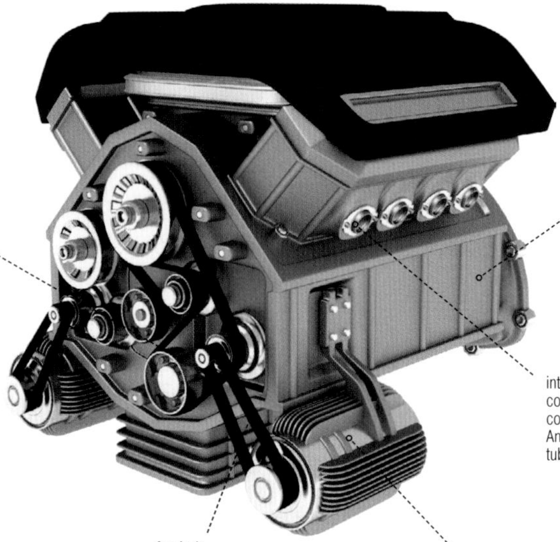
pulley
poulie F
polea F
Riemenscheibe F
puleggia F
engine block
bloc M moteur
bloque del motor M
Motorblock M
blocco M motore M
intake manifold
collecteur M d'échappement M
colector M de admisión F
Ansaugkrümmer M
tubo M collettore M di scarico M
fan belt
courroie F de ventilateur M
correa F del ventilador M
Riemen M
cinghia F della ventola F
alternator
alternateur M
generador M
Lichtmaschine F
alternatore M

four-stroke engine cycle
cycle M d'un moteur M à quatre temps M
ciclo M de un motor M de cuatro tiempos M
Arbeitsprozess M des Viertaktmotors M
motore M a quattro tempi M

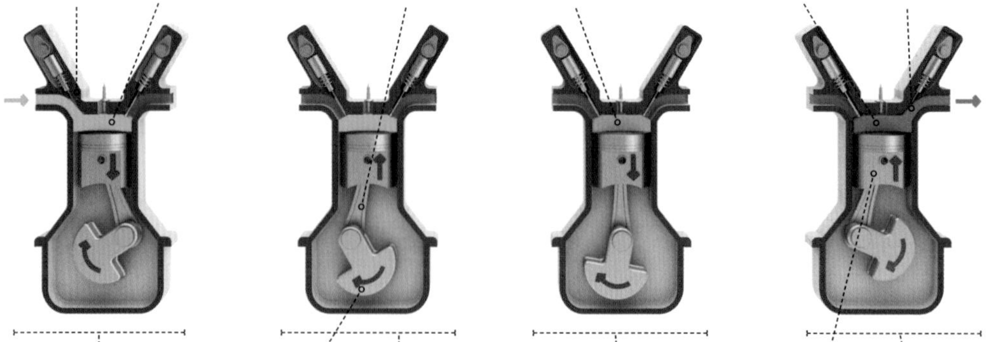
intake valve
soupape F d'admission F
válvula F de admisión F
Einlassventil N
valvola F di aspirazione F
cylinder
cylindre M
cilindro M
Zylinder M
cilindro M
connecting rod
bielle F
biela F
Pleuelstange F
biella F
ignition
explosion F
encendido M
Zündung F
esplosione F
burned gases
gaz M brûlés
gases M quemados
Abgase N
gas M combusti
exhaust valve
soupape F d'échappement M
válvula F de escape M
Auslassventil N
valvola F di scarico M
intake
admission F
admisión F
Ansaugung F
aspirazione F
crankshaft
vilebrequin M
cigüeñal M
Kurbelwelle F
albero M a gomiti M
compression
compression F
compresión F
Verdichtung F
compressione F
power
explosion F
combustión F
Antriebskaft F
scoppio M
piston
piston M
pistón M
Kolben M
pistone M
exhaust
échappement M
escape M
Ausstoß M
scarico M

Car interior and exterior

Intérieur ᴹ et extérieur ᴹ d'une voiture ᶠ | Interior ᴹ y exterior ᴹ del coche ᴹ | Autoteile ᴺ, innen und außen | Parti ᶠ dell'automobile ᶠ

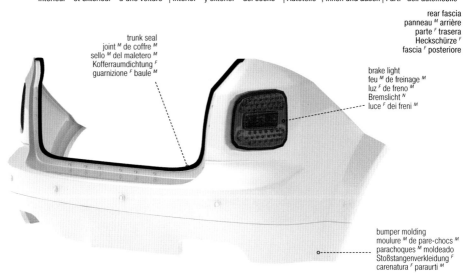

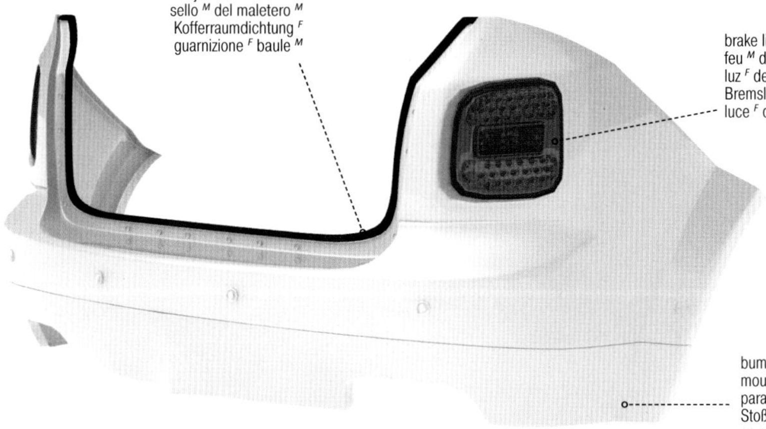
rear fascia
panneau ᴹ arrière
parte ᶠ trasera
Heckschürze ᶠ
fascia ᶠ posteriore
trunk seal
joint ᴹ de coffre ᴹ
sello ᴹ del maletero ᴹ
Kofferraumdichtung ᶠ
guarnizione ᶠ baule ᴹ
brake light
feu ᴹ de freinage ᴹ
luz ᶠ de freno ᴹ
Bremslicht ᴺ
luce ᶠ dei freni ᴹ
bumper molding
moulure ᴹ de pare-chocs ᴹ
parachoques ᴹ moldeado
Stoßstangenverkleidung ᶠ
carenatura ᶠ paraurti ᴹ

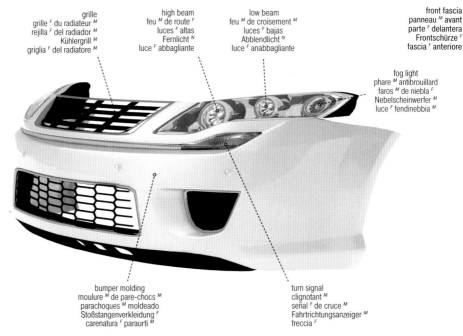

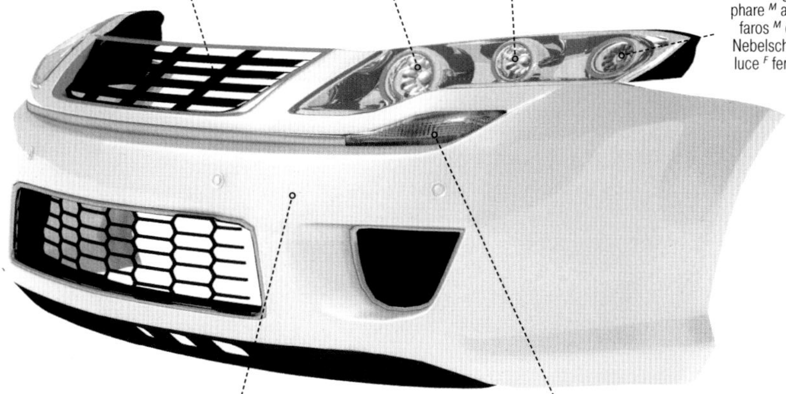
grille
grille ᶠ du radiateur ᴹ
rejilla ᶠ del radiador ᴹ
Kühlergrill ᴹ
griglia ᶠ del radiatore ᴹ
high beam
feu ᴹ de route ᶠ
luces ᶠ altas
Fernlicht ᴺ
luce ᶠ abbagliante
low beam
feu ᴹ de croisement ᴹ
luces ᶠ bajas
Abblendlicht ᴺ
luce ᶠ anabbagliante
front fascia
panneau ᴹ avant
parte ᶠ delantera
Frontschürze ᶠ
fascia ᶠ anteriore
fog light
phare ᴹ antibrouillard
faros ᴹ de niebla ᶠ
Nebelscheinwerfer ᴹ
luce ᶠ fendinebbia ᴹ
bumper molding
moulure ᴹ de pare-chocs ᴹ
parachoques ᴹ moldeado
Stoßstangenverkleidung ᶠ
carenatura ᶠ paraurti ᴹ
turn signal
clignotant ᴹ
señal ᶠ de cruce ᴹ
Fahrtrichtungsanzeiger ᴹ
freccia ᶠ

bucket seats
sièges [M] baquet asientos [M] anatómicos
Schalensitze [M]
sedili [M] anteriori

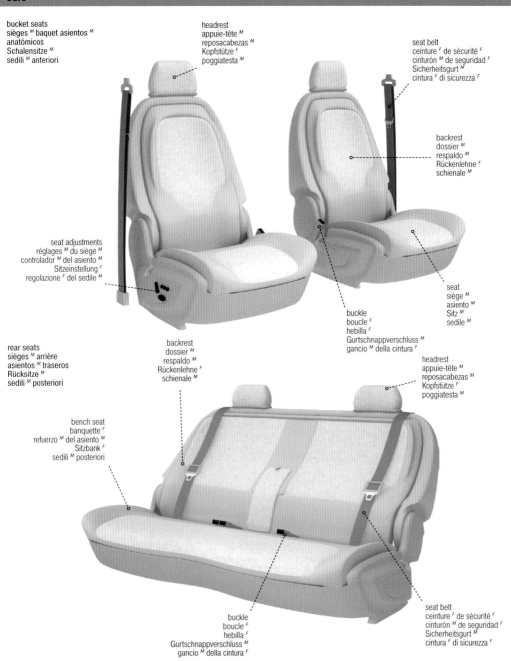

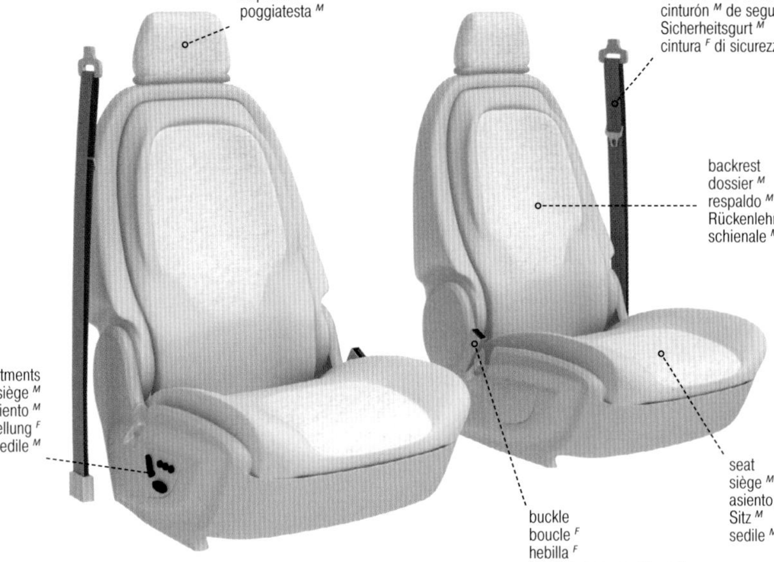
headrest
appuie-tête [M]
reposacabezas [M]
Kopfstütze [F]
poggiatesta [M]
seat belt
ceinture [F] de sécurité [F]
cinturón [M] de seguridad [F]
Sicherheitsgurt [M]
cintura [F] di sicurezza [F]
backrest
dossier [M]
respaldo [M]
Rückenlehne [F]
schienale [M]
seat adjustments
réglages [M] du siège [M]
controlador [M] del asiento [M]
Sitzeinstellung [F]
regolazione [F] del sedile [M]
seat
siège [M]
asiento [M]
Sitz [M]
sedile [M]
buckle
boucle [F]
hebilla [F]
Gurtschnappverschluss [M]
gancio [M] della cintura [F]

rear seats
sièges [M] arrière
asientos [M] traseros
Rücksitze [M]
sedili [M] posteriori

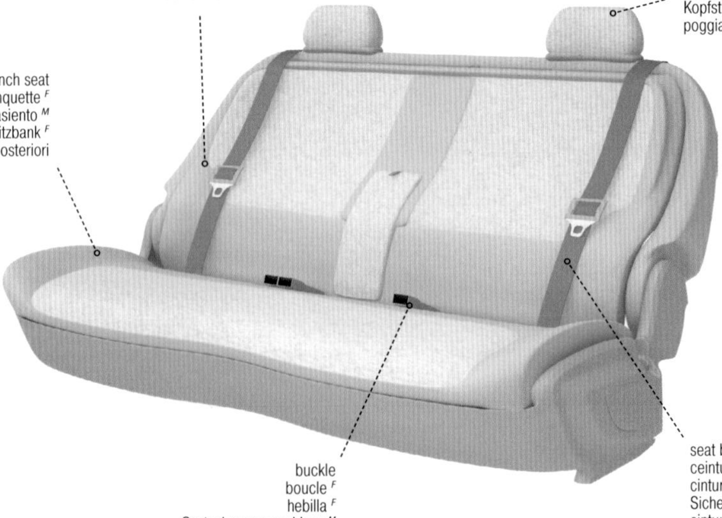
backrest
dossier [M]
respaldo [M]
Rückenlehne [F]
schienale [M]
headrest
appuie-tête [M]
reposacabezas [M]
Kopfstütze [F]
poggiatesta [M]
bench seat
banquette [F]
refuerzo [M] del asiento [M]
Sitzbank [F]
sedili [M] posteriori
buckle
boucle [F]
hebilla [F]
Gurtschnappverschluss [M]
gancio [M] della cintura [F]
seat belt
ceinture [F] de sécurité [F]
cinturón [M] de seguridad [F]
Sicherheitsgurt [M]
cintura [F] di sicurezza [F]

door
porte ^{F}
puerta ^{F}
Tür ^{F}
portiera ^{F}

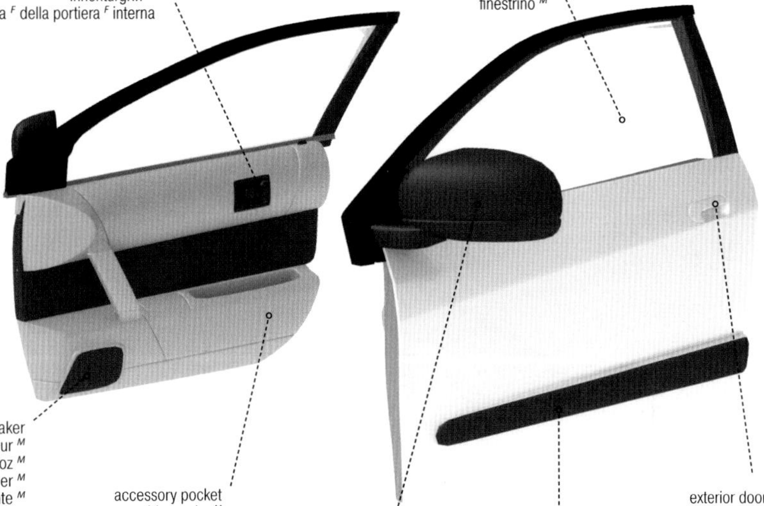

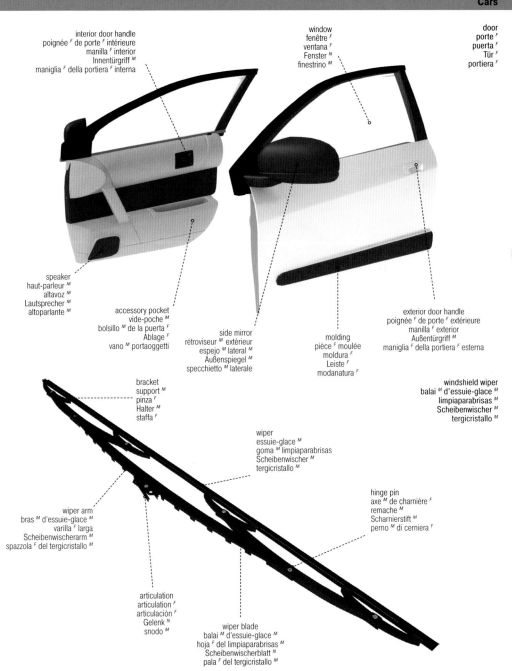

interior door handle
poignée ^{F} de porte ^{F} intérieure
manilla ^{F} interior
Innentürgriff ^{M}
maniglia ^{F} della portiera ^{F} interna

window
fenêtre ^{F}
ventana ^{F}
Fenster ^{N}
finestrino ^{M}

speaker
haut-parleur ^{M}
altavoz ^{M}
Lautsprecher ^{M}
altoparlante ^{M}

accessory pocket
vide-poche ^{M}
bolsillo ^{M} de la puerta ^{F}
Ablage ^{F}
vano ^{M} portaoggetti

side mirror
rétroviseur ^{M} extérieur
espejo ^{M} lateral ^{M}
Außenspiegel ^{M}
specchietto ^{M} laterale

molding
pièce ^{F} moulée
moldura ^{F}
Leiste ^{F}
modanatura ^{F}

exterior door handle
poignée ^{F} de porte ^{F} extérieure
manilla ^{F} exterior
Außentürgriff ^{M}
maniglia ^{F} della portiera ^{F} esterna

windshield wiper
balai ^{M} **d'essuie-glace** ^{M}
limpiaparabrisas ^{M}
Scheibenwischer ^{M}
tergicristallo ^{M}

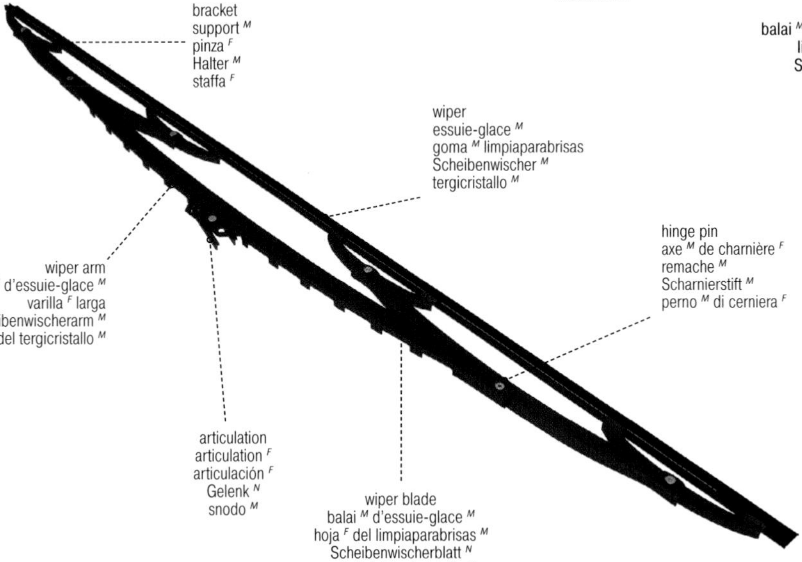

bracket
support ^{M}
pinza ^{F}
Halter ^{M}
staffa ^{F}

wiper
essuie-glace ^{M}
goma ^{M} limpiaparabrisas
Scheibenwischer ^{M}
tergicristallo ^{M}

hinge pin
axe ^{M} de charnière ^{F}
remache ^{M}
Scharnierstift ^{M}
perno ^{M} di cerniera ^{F}

wiper arm
bras ^{M} d'essuie-glace ^{M}
varilla ^{F} larga
Scheibenwischerarm ^{M}
spazzola ^{F} del tergicristallo ^{M}

articulation
articulation ^{F}
articulación ^{F}
Gelenk ^{N}
snodo ^{M}

wiper blade
balai ^{M} d'essuie-glace ^{M}
hoja ^{F} del limpiaparabrisas ^{M}
Scheibenwischerblatt ^{N}
pala ^{F} del tergicristallo ^{M}

instrument panel
tableau ^{M} de bord ^{M}
tablero ^{M} de control ^{M}
Instrumententafel ^{F}
cruscotto ^{M}

warning light
témoin ^{M} lumineux
indicador ^{M} de alerta ^{F}
Warnanzeige ^{F}
spia ^{F} luminosa

alternator warning light
voyant ^{M} de l'alternateur ^{M}
alerta ^{F} de carga ^{F} del alternador ^{M}
Lichtmaschinenwarnanzeige ^{F}
spia ^{F} dell'alternatore ^{M}

left turn signal indicator
témoin ^{M} clignotant ^{M} gauche
señal ^{F} de cruce ^{M} a la izquierda ^{F}
linkes Blinklicht ^{N}
indicatore ^{M} di svolta ^{F} a sinistra

tachometer
compte-tours ^{M}
tacómetro ^{M}
Drehzahlmesser ^{M}
contagiri ^{M}

scale
graduation ^{F}
escala ^{F}
Skala ^{F}
scala ^{F}

needle
aiguille ^{F}
aguja ^{F}
Tachonadel ^{F}
lancetta ^{F}

1 2 3 4 5 6 7 0
1/min x 1000
0 20 40 6
20 40 60 80
km/h
MPH

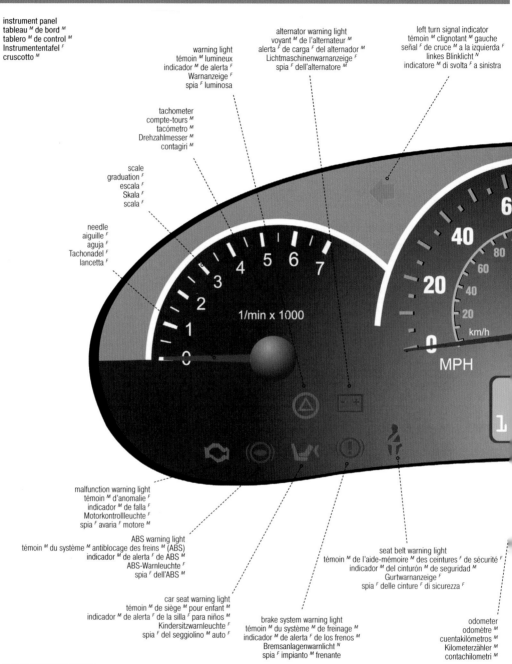

malfunction warning light
témoin ^{M} d'anomalie ^{F}
indicador ^{M} de falla ^{F}
Motorkontrollleuchte ^{F}
spia ^{F} avaria ^{F} motore ^{M}

ABS warning light
témoin ^{M} du système ^{M} antiblocage des freins ^{M} (ABS)
indicador ^{M} de alerta ^{F} de ABS ^{M}
ABS-Warnleuchte ^{F}
spia ^{F} dell'ABS ^{M}

seat belt warning light
témoin ^{M} de l'aide-mémoire ^{M} des ceintures ^{F} de sécurité ^{F}
indicador ^{M} del cinturón ^{M} de seguridad ^{M}
Gurtwarnanzeige ^{F}
spia ^{F} delle cinture ^{F} di sicurezza ^{F}

car seat warning light
témoin ^{M} de siège ^{M} pour enfant ^{M}
indicador ^{M} de alerta ^{F} de la silla ^{F} para niños ^{M}
Kindersitzwarnleuchte ^{F}
spia ^{F} del seggiolino ^{M} auto ^{F}

brake system warning light
témoin ^{M} du système ^{M} de freinage ^{M}
indicador ^{M} de alerta ^{F} de los frenos ^{M}
Bremsanlagenwarnlicht ^{N}
spia ^{F} impianto ^{M} frenante

odometer
odomètre ^{M}
cuentakilómetros ^{M}
Kilometerzähler ^{M}
contachilometri ^{M}

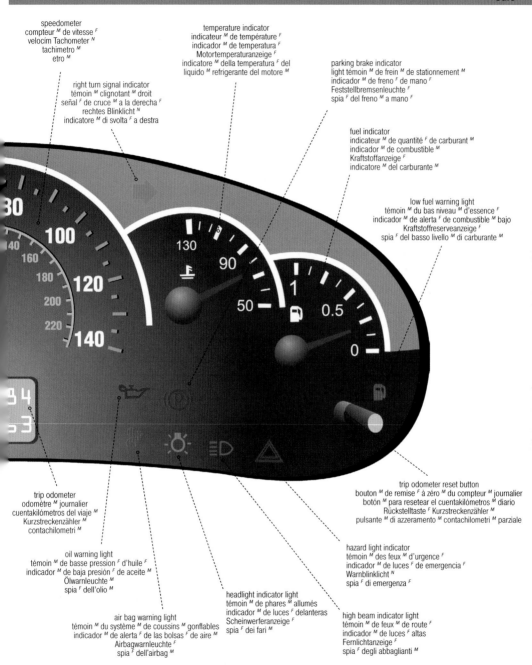

speedometer
compteur [M] de vitesse [F]
velocím Tachometer [N]
tachimetro [M]
etro [M]

temperature indicator
indicateur [M] de température [F]
indicador [M] de temperatura [F]
Motortemperaturanzeige [F]
indicatore [M] della temperatura [F] del liquido [M] refrigerante del motore [M]

right turn signal indicator
témoin [M] clignotant [M] droit
señal [F] de cruce [M] a la derecha [F]
rechtes Blinklicht [N]
indicatore [M] di svolta [F] a destra

parking brake indicator
light témoin [M] de frein [M] de stationnement [M]
indicador [M] de freno [F] de mano [F]
Feststellbremsenleuchte [F]
spia [F] del freno [M] a mano [F]

fuel indicator
indicateur [M] de quantité [F] de carburant [M]
indicador [M] de combustible [M]
Kraftstoffanzeige [F]
indicatore [M] del carburante [M]

low fuel warning light
témoin [M] du bas niveau [M] d'essence [F]
indicador [M] de alerta [F] de combustible [M] bajo
Kraftstoffreserveanzeige [F]
spia [F] del basso livello [M] di carburante [M]

130
90
50
1
0.5
0
100
120
140
160
180
200
220

trip odometer
odomètre [M] journalier
cuentakilómetros del viaje [M]
Kurzstreckenzähler [M]
contachilometri [M]

trip odometer reset button
bouton [M] de remise [F] à zéro [M] du compteur [M] journalier
botón [M] para resetear el cuentakilómetros [M] diario
Rückstelltaste [F] Kurzstreckenzähler [M]
pulsante [M] di azzeramento [M] contachilometri [M] parziale

hazard light indicator
témoin [M] des feux [M] d'urgence [F]
indicador [M] de luces [F] de emergencia [F]
Warnblinklicht [N]
spia [F] di emergenza [F]

oil warning light
témoin [M] de basse pression [F] d'huile [F]
indicador [M] de baja presión [F] de aceite [M]
Ölwarnleuchte [M]
spia [F] dell'olio [M]

headlight indicator light
témoin [M] de phares [M] allumés
indicador [M] de luces [F] delanteras
Scheinwerferanzeige [F]
spia [F] dei fari [M]

air bag warning light
témoin [M] du système [M] de coussins [M] gonflables
indicador [M] de alerta [F] de las bolsas [F] de aire [M]
Airbagwarnleuchte [F]
spia [F] dell'airbag [M]

high beam indicator light
témoin [M] de feux [M] de route [F]
indicador [M] de luces [F] altas
Fernlichtanzeige [F]
spia [F] degli abbaglianti [M]

tires
roues [F]
neumá Räder [N]
ruote [F]
ticos [M]

hubcap
enjoliveur [M]
tapacubos [M]
Radkappe [F]
cerchione [M]
tread
bande [F] de roulement [M]
huella [F]
Reifenprofil [N]
battistrada [M]
bolt
écrou [M]
tornillo [M]
Bolzen [M]
bullone [M]

suspension coil spring
ressort [M] hélicoïdal de suspension [F]
muelle [M] de suspensión [F]
Federaufhängung [F]
molla [F] di sospensione [F]

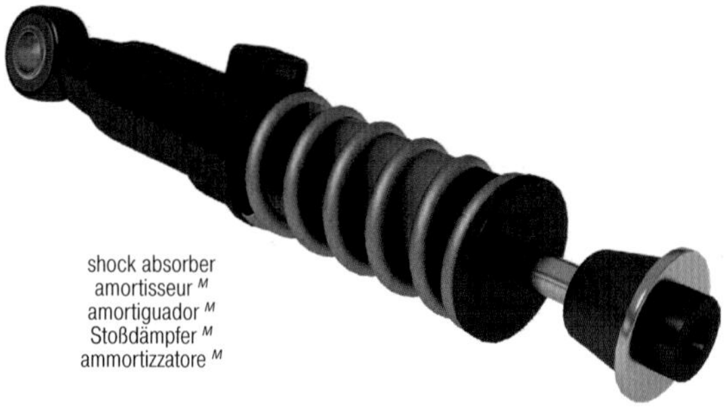

shock absorber
amortisseur [M]
amortiguador [M]
Stoßdämpfer [M]
ammortizzatore [M]

brake pads
plaquettes [F] de frein [M]
pastillas [F] de freno [M]
Bremsbeläge [M]
pastiglie [F] del freno [M]

disc brake
disque [M] de frein [M]
freno [M] de disco [M]
Bremsscheibe [F]
freno [M] a disco

tire
pneu [M]
neumático [M]
Reifen [M]
pneumatico [M]

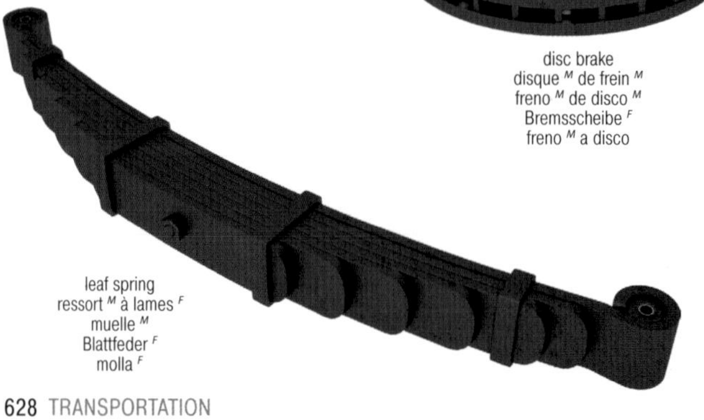

leaf spring
ressort [M] à lames [F]
muelle [M]
Blattfeder [F]
molla [F]

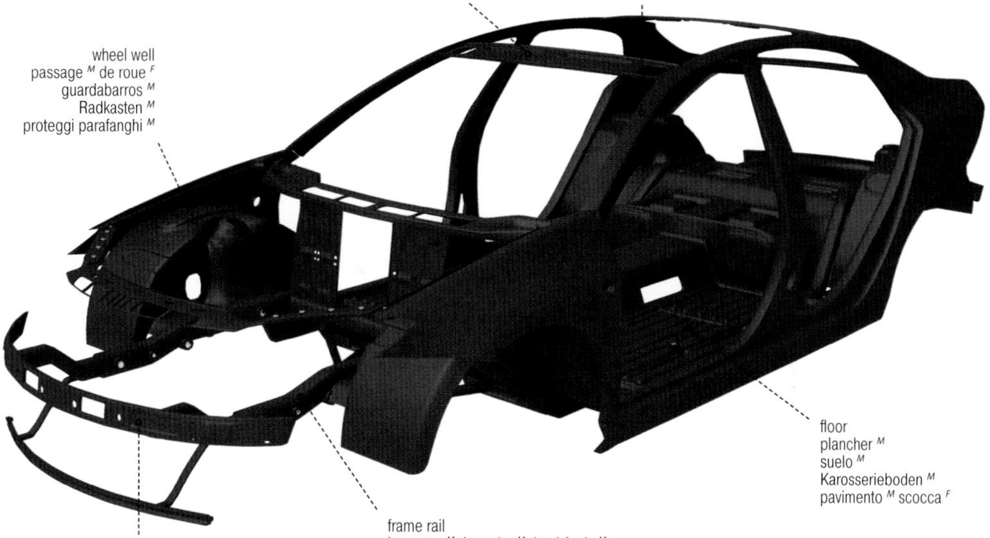
roof rail
longeron [M] de toit [M]
viga [F] de impacto [M] superior
Dachreling [F]
barra [F] di protezione [F] superiore
pillar
montant [M]
pilar [M]
Träger [M]
montante [M]
unibody frame
structure [M] monocoque
mono-chasis [M]
Karosserie [F]
scocca [F]
wheel well
passage [M] de roue [F]
guardabarros [M]
Radkasten [M]
proteggi parafanghi [M]
floor
plancher [M]
suelo [M]
Karosserieboden [M]
pavimento [M] scocca [F]
front bumper
pare-chocs [M] avant
parachoques [M] delantero
Vorderstoßstange [F]
paraurti [M] anteriore
frame rail
longeron [M] de cadre [M] de châssis [M]
viga [F] chasis [M]
Rahmenverstrebung [F]
supporto [M] del telaio [M]

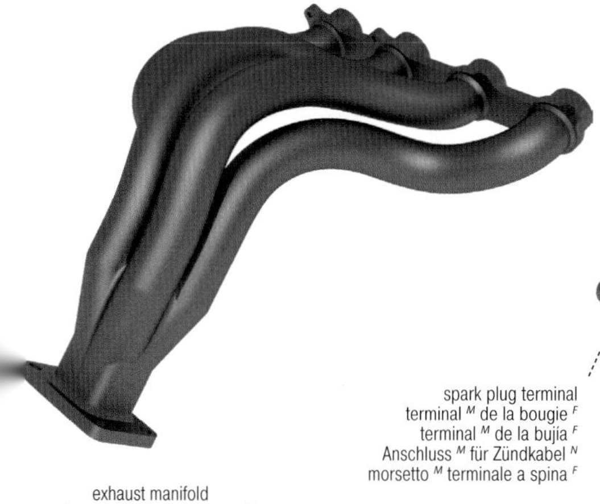
exhaust manifold
collecteur [M] d'échappement [M]
colector [M] de gases [M] de escape [M]
Abgaskrümmer [M]
collettore [M] di scarico [M]

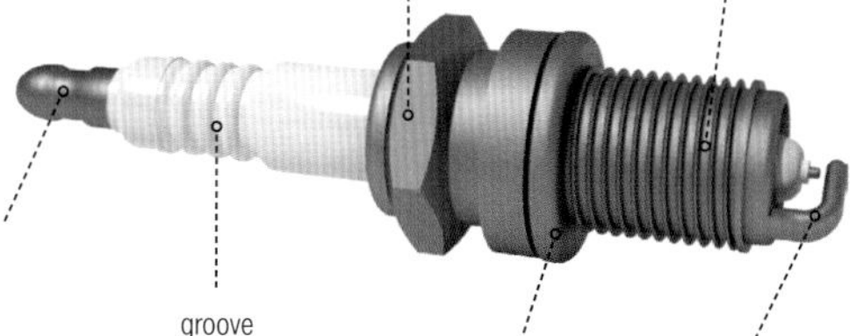
spark plug
bougie [F] d'allumage [M]
bujía [F]
Zündkerze [F]
candela [F]
hex nut
écrou [M] hexagonal
tuerca [F] hexagonal
Sechskantmutter [F]
dado [M] esagonale
body
culot [M]
cuerpo [M] metálico
Zündkerzengehäuse [N]
radice [F] filettata
spark plug terminal
terminal [M] de la bougie [F]
terminal [M] de la bujía [F]
Anschluss [M] für Zündkabel [N]
morsetto [M] terminale a spina [F]
groove
cannelure [F]
ranura [F]
Kriechstrombarriere [F]
scanalatura [F]
gasket
joint [M]
asiento [M]
Zündkerzendichtring [M]
rondella [F] di tenuta [F]
side electrode
électrode [F] de masse [F]
electrodo [M] de masa [F]
Masseeketrode [F]
elettrodo [M] di massa [F]

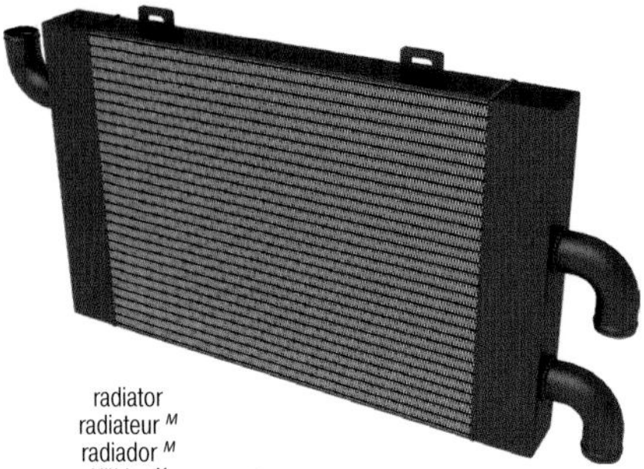

radiator
radiateur M
radiador M
Kühler M
radiatore M

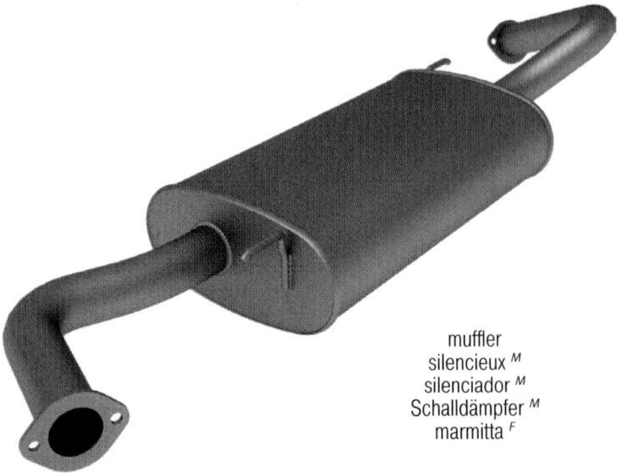

muffler
silencieux M
silenciador M
Schalldämpfer M
marmitta F

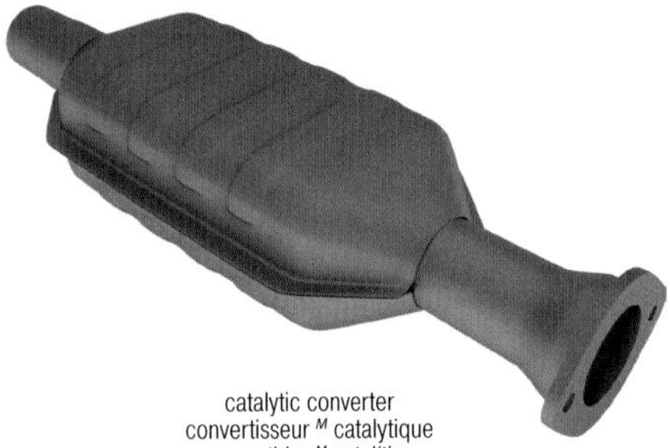

catalytic converter
convertisseur M catalytique
convertidor M catalítico
Katalysator M
convertitore M catalitico

air filter
filtre M à air
filtro M de aire M
Luftfilter M
filtro M dell'aria F

fuel filter
filtre M à carburant M
filtro M de combustible M
Kraftstofffilter M
filtro M del carburante M

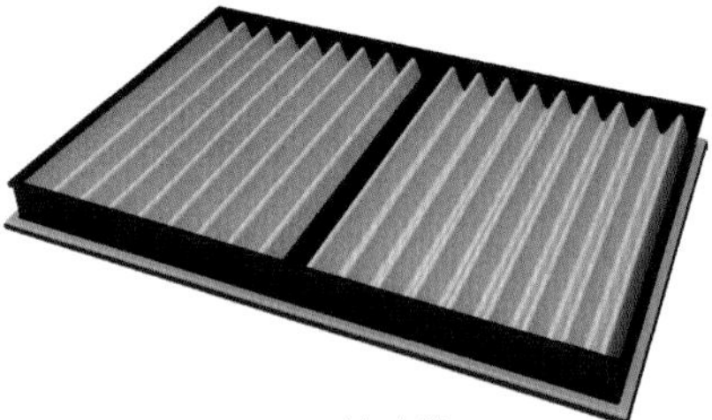

cabin air filter
filtre M à air M d'habitacle M
filtro M de cabina F
Innenraumfilter M
filtro M dell'aria F abitacolo M

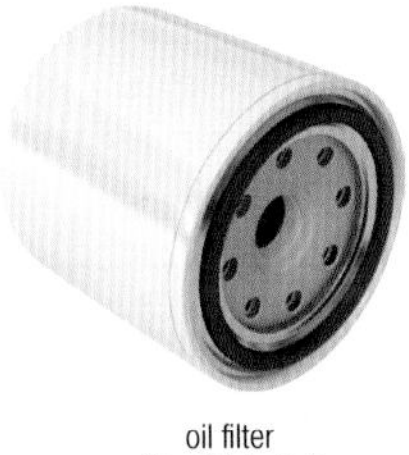

oil filter
filtre M à huile F
filtro M de aceite M
Ölfilter M
filtro M dell'olio M

battery
batterie F
batería F
Batterie F
batteria F

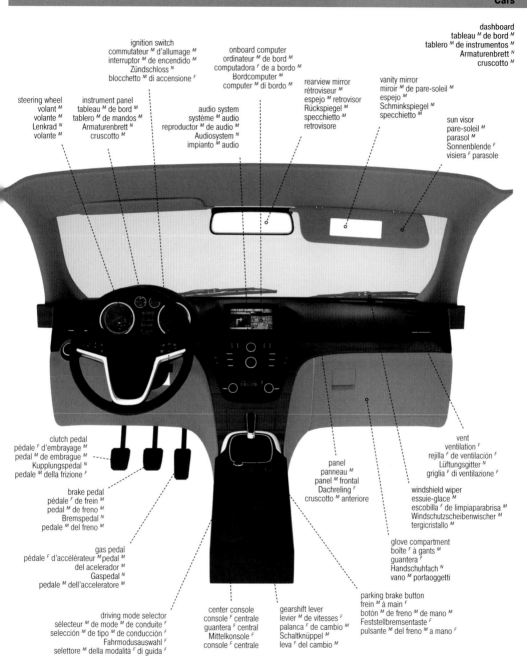

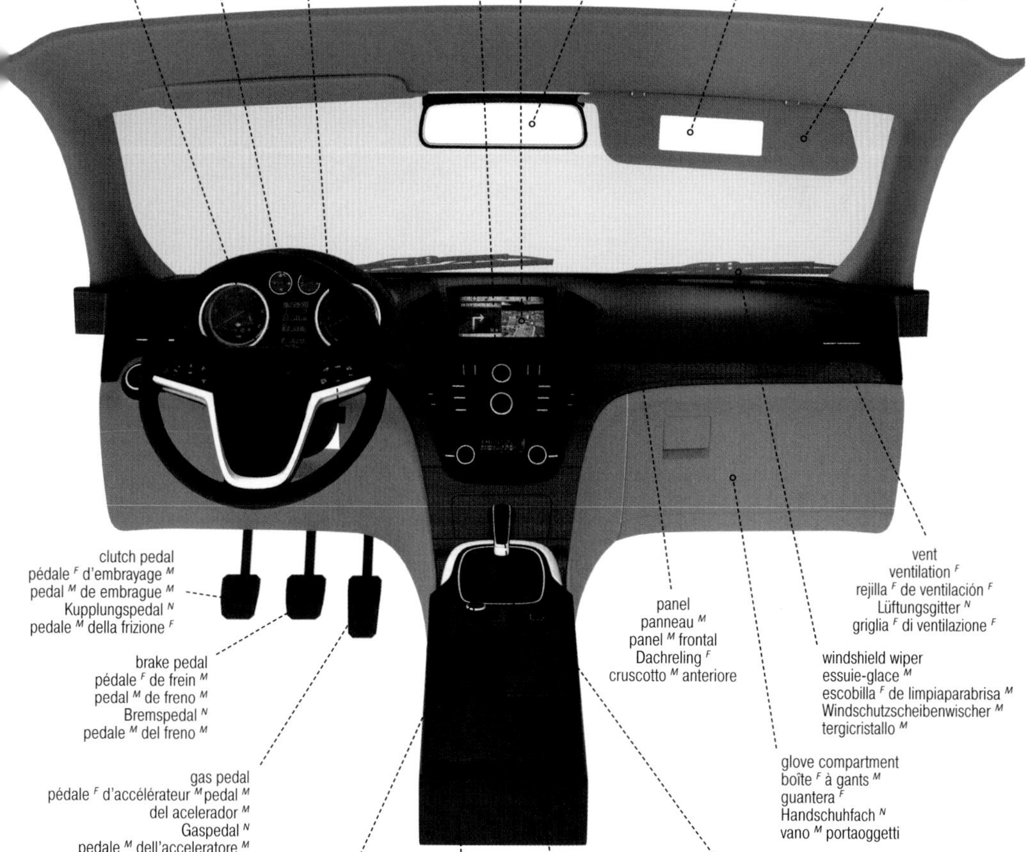
dashboard
tableau M de bord M
tablero M de instrumentos M
Armaturenbrett N
cruscotto M
ignition switch
commutateur M d'allumage M
interruptor M de encendido M
Zündschloss N
blocchetto M di accensione F
onboard computer
ordinateur M de bord M
computadora F de a bordo M
Bordcomputer M
computer M di bordo M
rearview mirror
rétroviseur M
espejo M retrovisor
Rückspiegel M
specchietto M
retrovisore
vanity mirror
miroir M de pare-soleil M
espejo M
Schminkspiegel M
specchietto M
sun visor
pare-soleil M
parasol M
Sonnenblende F
visiera F parasole
steering wheel
volant M
volante M
Lenkrad N
volante M
instrument panel
tableau M de bord M
tablero M de mandos M
Armaturenbrett N
cruscotto M
audio system
système M audio
reproductor M de audio M
Audiosystem N
impianto M audio
clutch pedal
pédale F d'embrayage M
pedal M de embrague M
Kupplungspedal N
pedale M della frizione F
brake pedal
pédale F de frein M
pedal M de freno M
Bremspedal N
pedale M del freno M
gas pedal
pédale F d'accélérateur M pedal M
del acelerador M
Gaspedal N
pedale M dell'acceleratore M
driving mode selector
sélecteur M de mode M de conduite F
selección M de tipo M de conducción F
Fahrmodusauswahl F
selettore M della modalità F di guida F
center console
console F centrale
guantera F central
Mittelkonsole F
console F centrale
gearshift lever
levier M de vitesses F
palanca F de cambio M
Schaltknüppel M
leva F del cambio M
panel
panneau M
panel M frontal
Dachreling F
cruscotto M anteriore
vent
ventilation F
rejilla F de ventilación F
Lüftungsgitter N
griglia F di ventilazione F
windshield wiper
essuie-glace M
escobilla F de limpiaparabrisa M
Windschutzscheibenwischer M
tergicristallo M
glove compartment
boîte F à gants M
guantera F
Handschuhfach N
vano M portaoggetti
parking brake button
frein M à main F
botón M de freno M de mano M
Feststellbremsentaste F
pulsante M del freno M a mano F

exterior
extérieur M
exterior M
Außenansicht F
vista F esterna di un'auto F

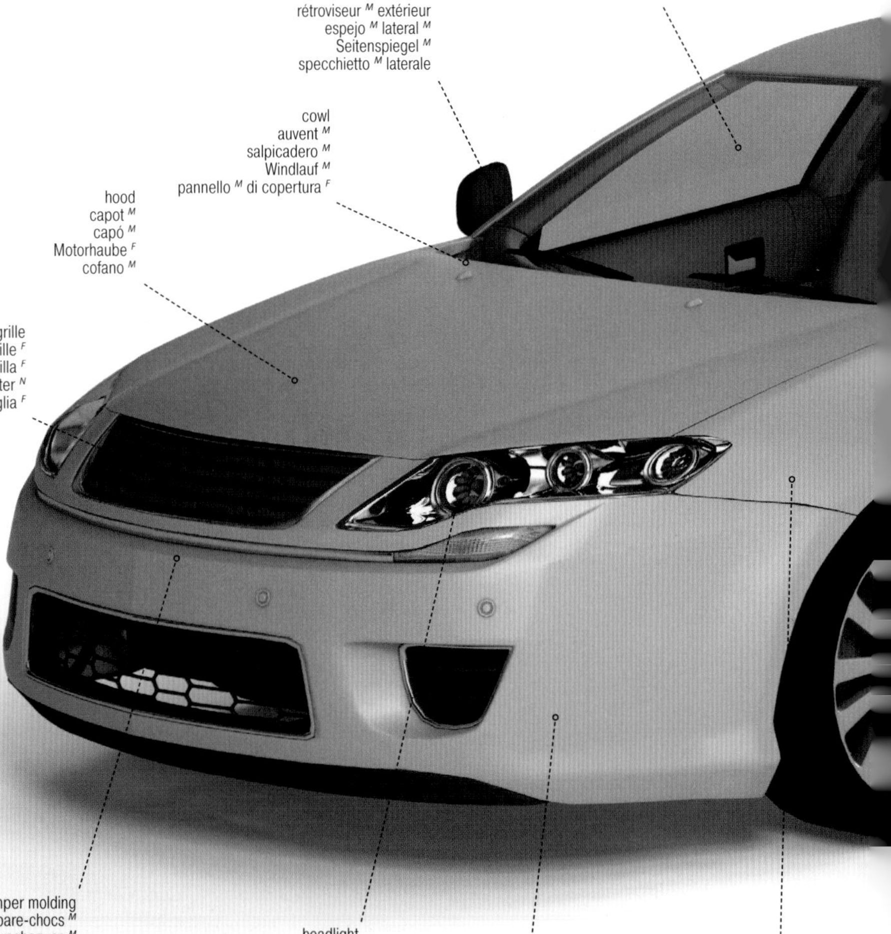
windshield
pare-brise M
parabrisas M
Windschutzscheibe F
parabrezza M
side mirror
rétroviseur M extérieur
espejo M lateral M
Seitenspiegel M
specchietto M laterale
cowl
auvent M
salpicadero M
Windlauf M
pannello M di copertura F
hood
capot M
capó M
Motorhaube F
cofano M
grille
grille F
rejilla F
Gitter N
griglia F
bumper molding
moulure M de pare-chocs M
moldura F del parachoques M
Stoßstangenleiste F
modanatura F paraurti M
headlight
phare M
faro M delantero
Scheinwerfer M
faro M
front fascia
carénage M avant
fascia F delantera
Frontschürze F
fascia F anteriore
fender
aile F
guardabarros M
Kotflügel M
parafango M

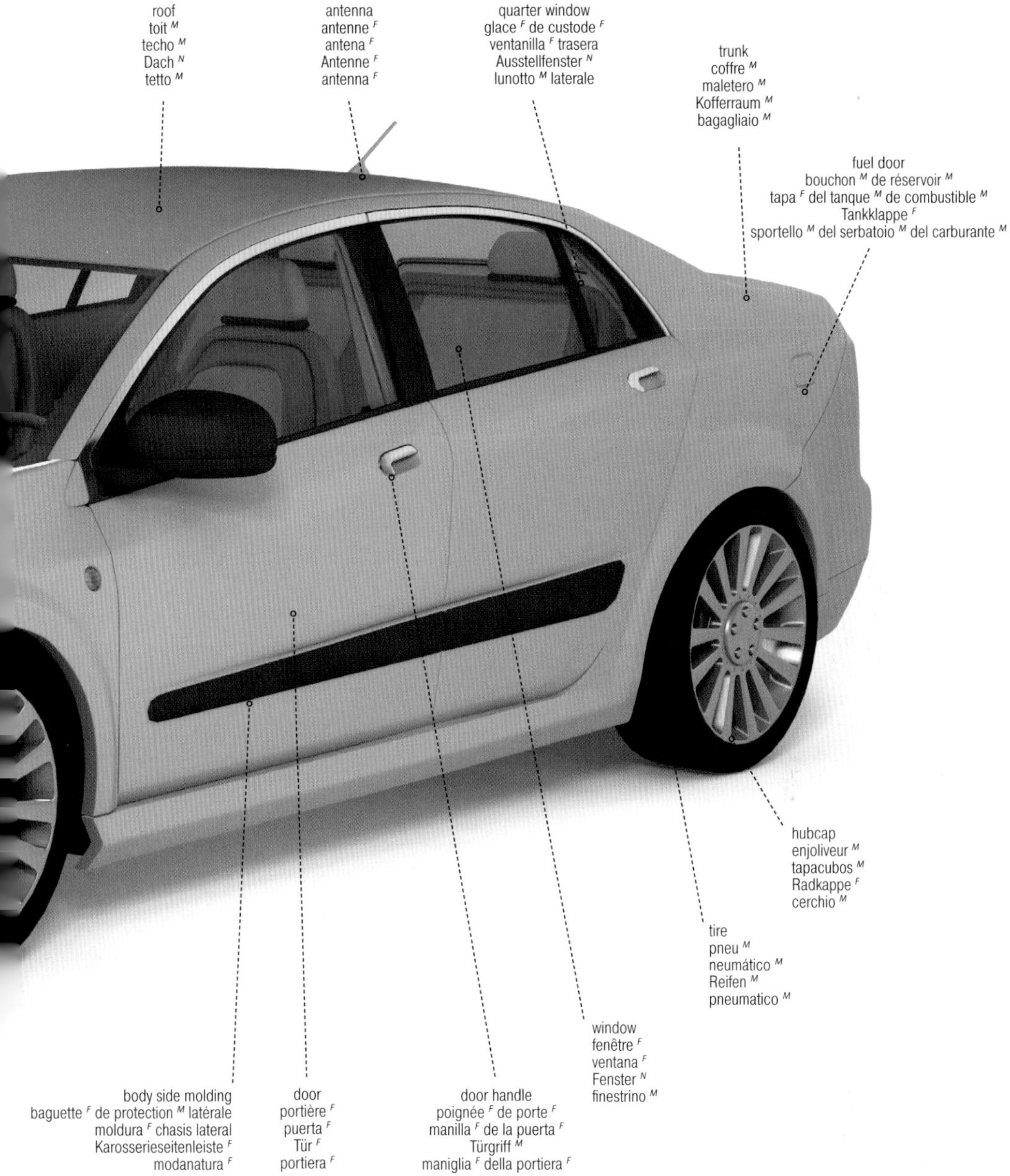
roof
toit M
techo M
Dach N
tetto M
antenna
antenne F
antena F
Antenne F
antenna F
quarter window
glace F de custode F
ventanilla F trasera
Ausstellfenster N
lunotto M laterale
trunk
coffre M
maletero M
Kofferraum M
bagagliaio M
fuel door
bouchon M de réservoir M
tapa F del tanque M de combustible M
Tankklappe F
sportello M del serbatoio M del carburante M
hubcap
enjoliveur M
tapacubos M
Radkappe F
cerchio M
tire
pneu M
neumático M
Reifen M
pneumatico M
window
fenêtre F
ventana F
Fenster N
finestrino M
body side molding
baguette F de protection M latérale
moldura F chasis lateral
Karosserieseitenleiste F
modanatura F
door
portière F
puerta F
Tür F
portiera F
door handle
poignée F de porte F
manilla F de la puerta F
Türgriff M
maniglia F della portiera F

Types of cars

Type ^{M} de carrosserie ^{F} | Tipos ^{M} de coche ^{M} | Fahrzeugarten ^{F} | Tipi ^{M} di auto ^{F}

electric car
voiture ^{F} électrique
coche ^{M} eléctrico
Elektroauto ^{N}
auto ^{F} elettrica

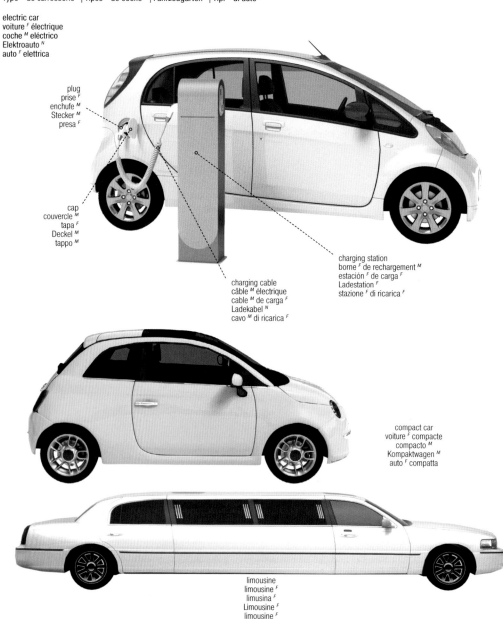

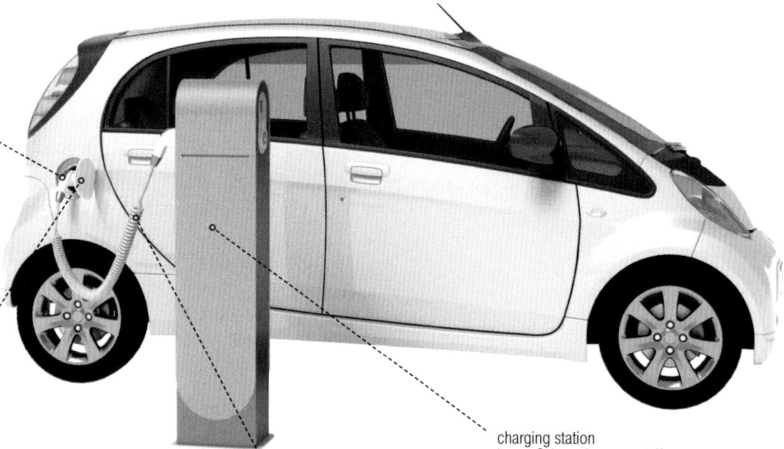
plug
prise ^{F}
enchufe ^{M}
Stecker ^{M}
presa ^{F}
cap
couvercle ^{M}
tapa ^{F}
Deckel ^{M}
tappo ^{M}
charging station
borne ^{F} de rechargement ^{M}
estación ^{F} de carga ^{F}
Ladestation ^{F}
stazione ^{F} di ricarica ^{F}
charging cable
câble ^{M} électrique
cable ^{M} de carga ^{F}
Ladekabel ^{N}
cavo ^{M} di ricarica ^{F}

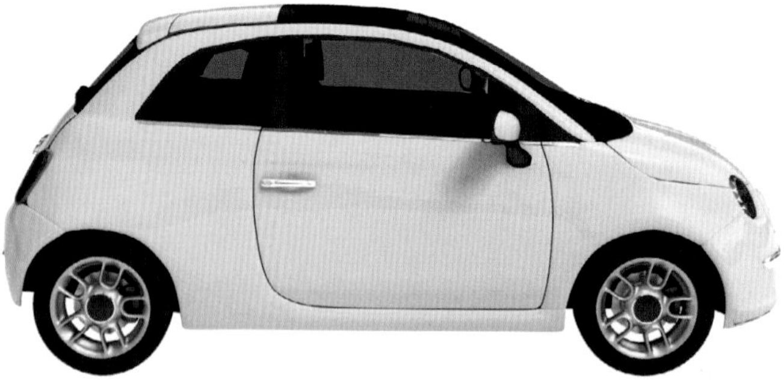

compact car
voiture ^{F} compacte
compacto ^{M}
Kompaktwagen ^{M}
auto ^{F} compatta

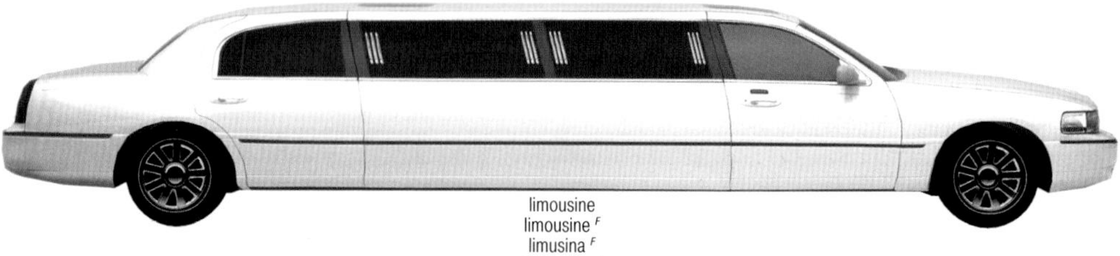

limousine
limousine ^{F}
limusina ^{F}
Limousine ^{F}
limousine ^{F}

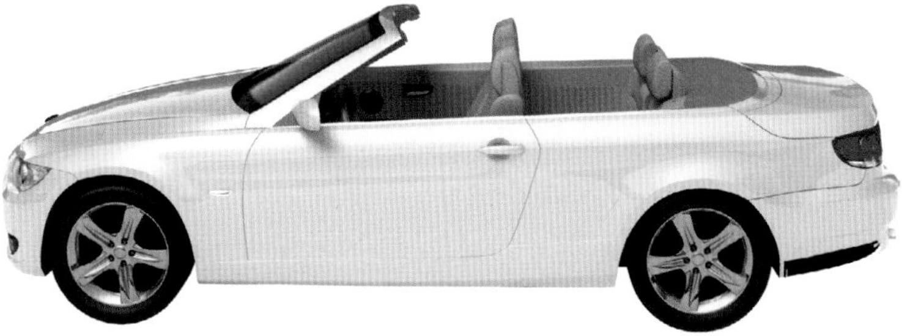

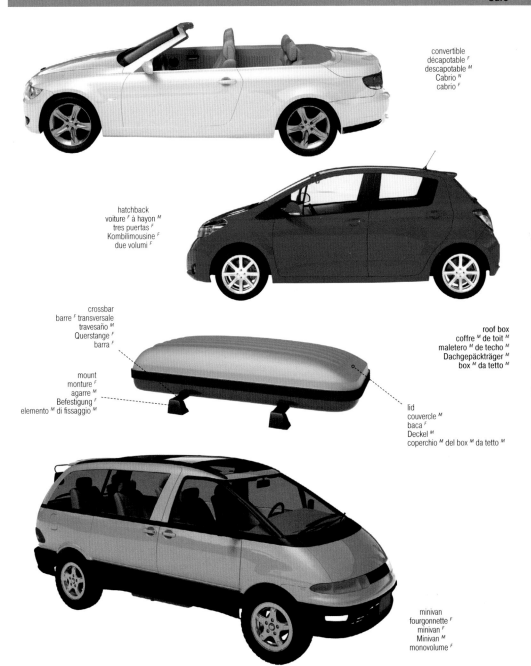

convertible
décapotable [F]
descapotable [M]
Cabrio [N]
cabrio [F]

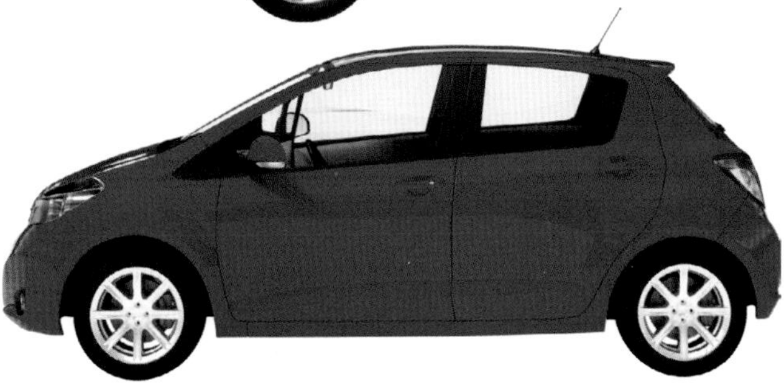

hatchback
voiture [F] à hayon [M]
tres puertas [F]
Kombilimousine [F]
due volumi [F]

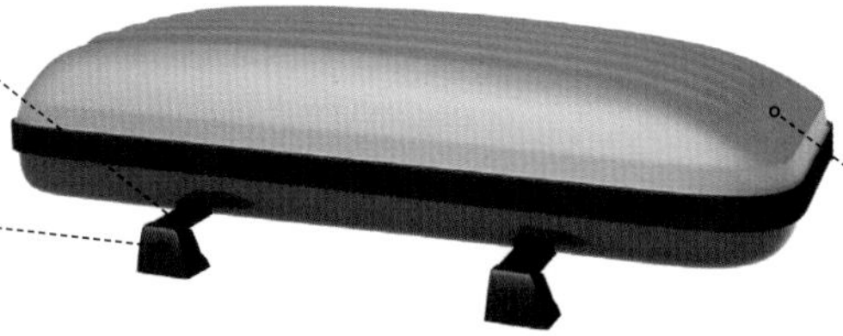
crossbar
barre [F] transversale
travesaño [M]
Querstange [F]
barra [F]
mount
monture [F]
agarre [M]
Befestigung [F]
elemento [M] di fissaggio [M]
lid
couvercle [M]
baca [F]
Deckel [M]
coperchio [M] del box [M] da tetto [M]

roof box
coffre [M] de toit [M]
maletero [M] de techo [M]
Dachgepäckträger [M]
box [M] da tetto [M]

minivan
fourgonnette [F]
minivan [F]
Minivan [M]
monovolume [F]

crossover vehicle
vehicule [M] multisegment
vehículo [M] mixto
Crossover-Fahrzeug [N]
veicolo [M] crossover

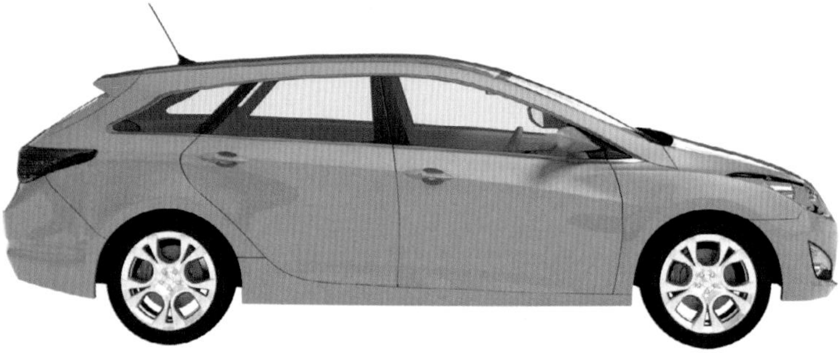

station wagon
familiale [F]
ranchera [F]
Kombi [M]
station wagon [F]

sports car
voiture [F] de sport [M]
deportivo [M]
Sportwagen [M]
auto [F] sportiva

coupe
coupé [F]
cupé [M]
Coupé [N]
coupé [F]

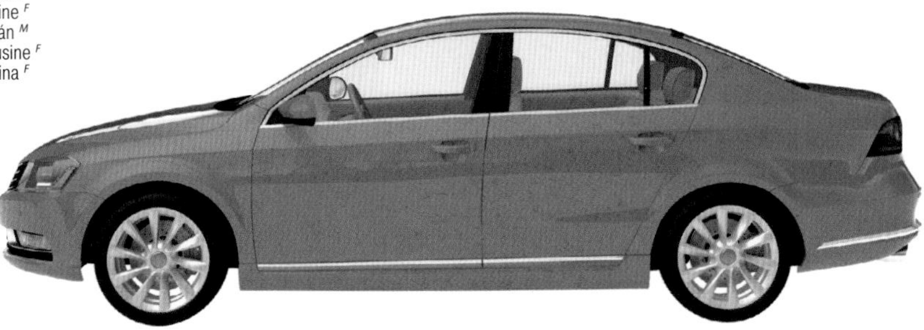

sedan
berline [F]
sedán [M]
Limousine [F]
berlina [F]

sport utility vehicle (SUV)
véhicule [M] utilitaire sport [M]
todoterreno [M]
Geländewagen [M]
suv [M]

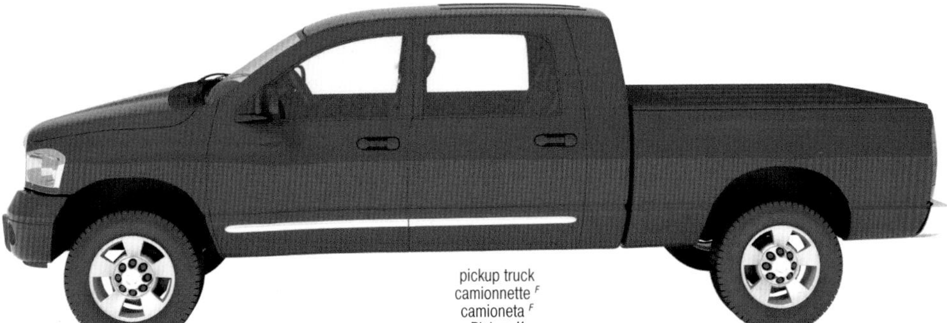

pickup truck
camionnette [F]
camioneta [F]
Pickup [M]
pick-up [M]

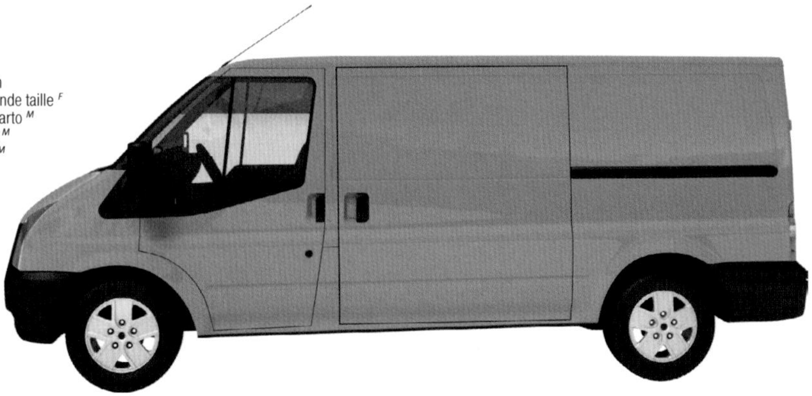
full-size van
fourgonnette F de grande taille F
camión M de reparto M
Lieferwagen M
furgoncino M

Recreational vehicles

Véhicule M récréatif (VR) | Vehículos M recreativos | Wohnmobile N und Anhänger N | Veicoli M ricreativi

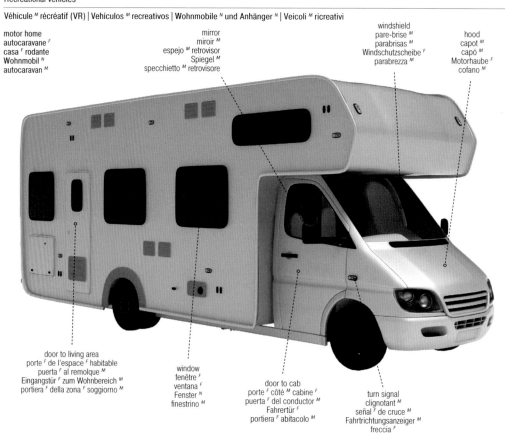

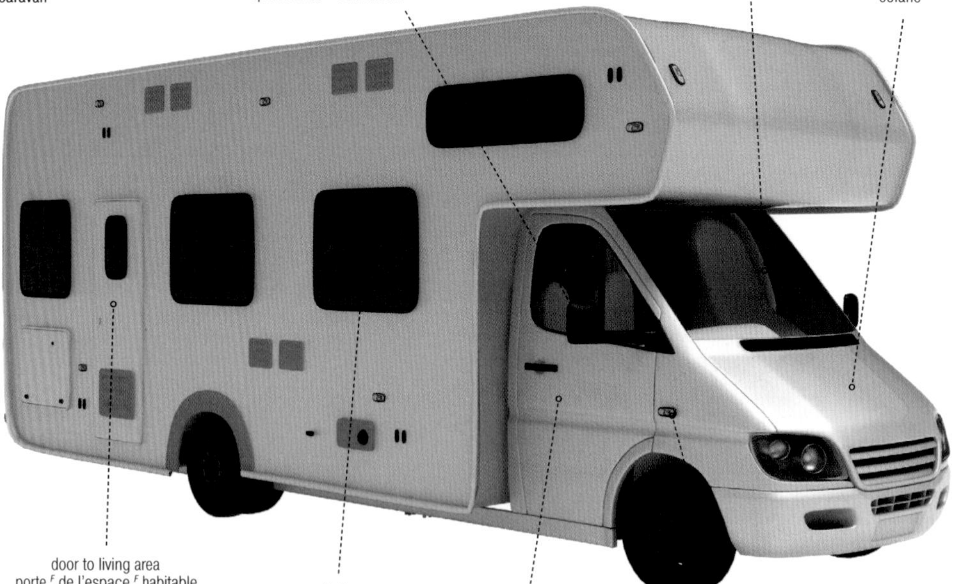
motor home
autocaravane F
casa F rodante
Wohnmobil N
autocaravan M
mirror
miroir M
espejo M retrovisor
Spiegel M
specchietto M retrovisore
windshield
pare-brise M
parabrisas M
Windschutzscheibe F
parabrezza M
hood
capot M
capó M
Motorhaube F
cofano M
door to living area
porte F de l'espace F habitable
puerta F al remolque M
Eingangstür F zum Wohnbereich M
portiera F della zona F soggiorno M
window
fenêtre F
ventana F
Fenster N
finestrino M
door to cab
porte F côté M cabine F
puerta F del conductor M
Fahrertür F
portiera F abitacolo M
turn signal
clignotant M
señal F de cruce M
Fahrtrichtungsanzeiger M
freccia F

teardrop trailer
roulotte ^F^
remolque ^M^ tipo lágrima ^F^
Teardrop-Anhänger ^M^
miniroulotte ^F^

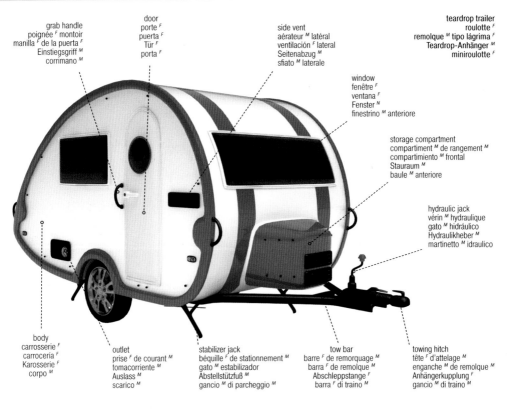

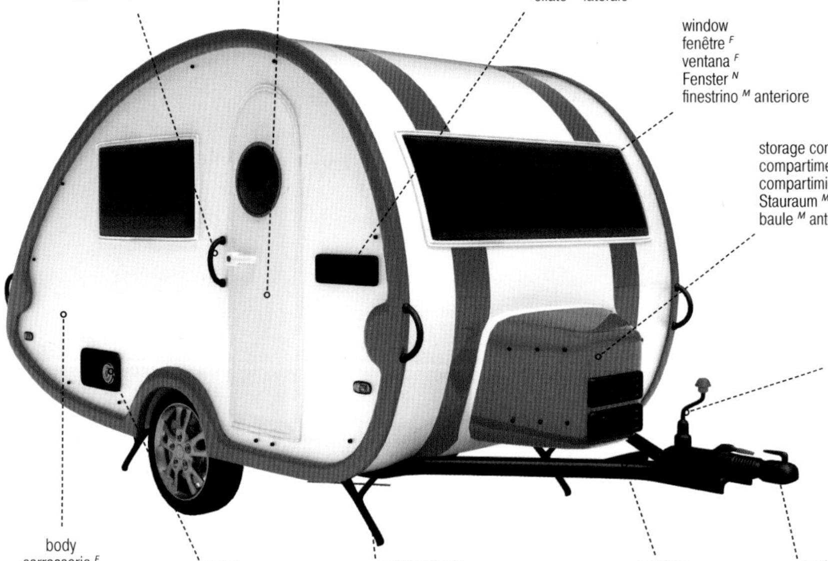
grab handle
poignée F montoir
manilla F de la puerta F
Einstiegsgriff M
corrimano M
door
porte F
puerta F
Tür F
porta F
side vent
aérateur M latéral
ventilación F lateral
Seitenabzug M
sfiato M laterale
window
fenêtre F
ventana F
Fenster N
finestrino M anteriore
storage compartment
compartiment M de rangement M
compartimiento M frontal
Stauraum M
baule M anteriore
hydraulic jack
vérin M hydraulique
gato M hidráulico
Hydraulikheber M
martinetto M idraulico
body
carrosserie F
carrocería F
Karosserie F
corpo M
outlet
prise F de courant M
tomacorriente M
Auslass M
scarico M
stabilizer jack
béquille F de stationnement M
gato M estabilizador
Abstellstützfuß M
gancio M di parcheggio M
tow bar
barre F de remorquage M
barra F de remolque M
Abschleppstange F
barra F di traino M
towing hitch
tête F d'attelage M
enganche M de remolque M
Anhängerkupplung F
gancio M di traino M

trailer
roulotte F
remolque M
Wohnwagen M
rimorchio M

sport bike
moto [F] de sport [M]
motocicleta [F] deportiva
Sportmotorrad [N]
moto [F] sportiva

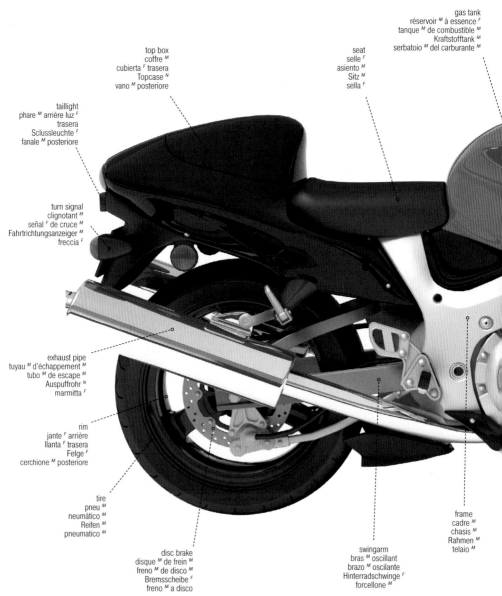

gas tank
réservoir [M] à essence [F]
tanque [M] de combustible [M]
Kraftstofftank [M]
serbatoio [M] del carburante [M]
top box
coffre [M]
cubierta [F] trasera
Topcase [N]
vano [M] posteriore
seat
selle [F]
asiento [M]
Sitz [M]
sella [F]
taillight
phare [M] arrière luz [F]
trasera
Sclussleuchte [F]
fanale [M] posteriore
turn signal
clignotant [M]
señal [F] de cruce [M]
Fahrtrichtungsanzeiger [M]
freccia [F]
exhaust pipe
tuyau [M] d'échappement [M]
tubo [M] de escape [M]
Auspuffrohr [N]
marmitta [F]
rim
jante [F] arrière
llanta [F] trasera
Felge [F]
cerchione [M] posteriore
tire
pneu [M]
neumático [M]
Reifen [M]
pneumatico [M]
frame
cadre [M]
chasis [M]
Rahmen [M]
telaio [M]
disc brake
disque [M] de frein [M]
freno [M] de disco [M]
Bremsscheibe [F]
freno [M] a disco
swingarm
bras [M] oscillant
brazo [M] oscilante
Hinterradschwinge [F]
forcellone [M]

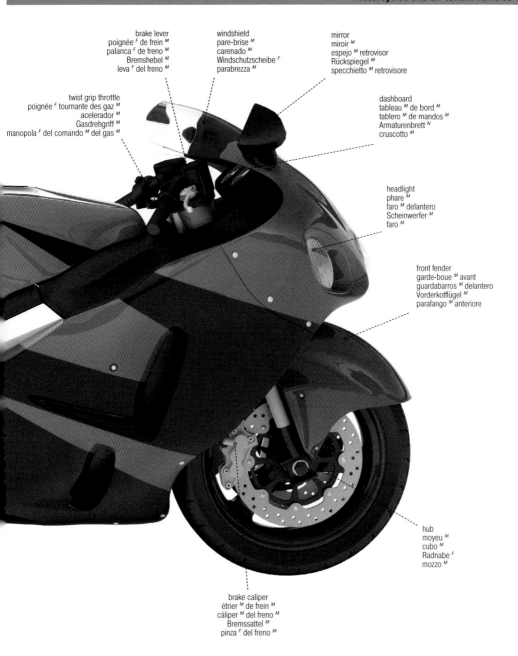

brake lever
poignée F de frein M
palanca F de freno M
Bremshebel M
leva F del freno M
windshield
pare-brise M
carenado M
Windschutzscheibe F
parabrezza M
mirror
miroir M
espejo M retrovisor
Rückspiegel M
specchietto M retrovisore
twist grip throttle
poignée F tournante des gaz M
acelerador M
Gasdrehgriff M
manopola F del comando M del gas M
dashboard
tableau M de bord M
tablero M de mandos M
Armaturenbrett N
cruscotto M
headlight
phare M
faro M delantero
Scheinwerfer M
faro M
front fender
garde-boue M avant
guardabarros M delantero
Vorderkotflügel M
parafango M anteriore
hub
moyeu M
cubo M
Radnabe F
mozzo M
brake caliper
étrier M de frein M
cáliper M del freno M
Bremssattel M
pinza F del freno M

touring motorcycle
moto [F] de route [F]
motocicleta [F] de turismo [M]
Reisemotorrad [N]
moto [F] da turismo [M]

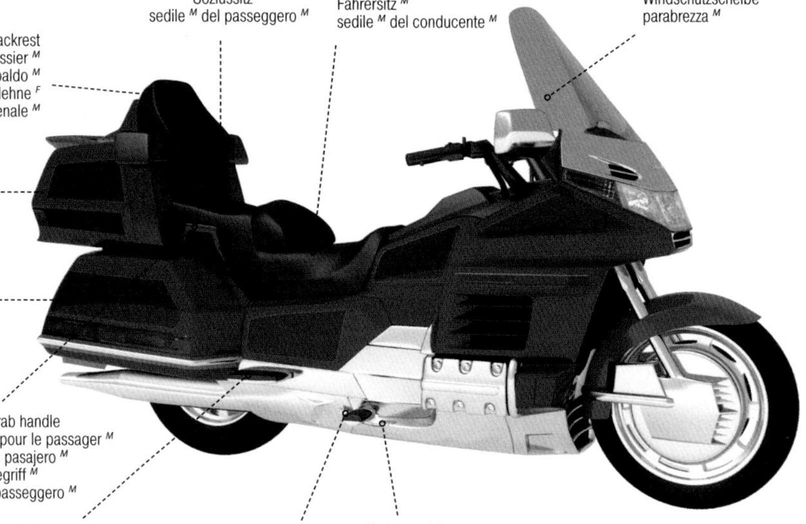
passenger's seat
selle [F] passager [M]
asiento [M] del pasajero [M]
Soziussitz [M]
sedile [M] del passeggero [M]
driver's seat
selle [F] conducteur [M]
asiento [M] del conductor [M]
Fahrersitz [M]
sedile [M] del conducente [M]
windshield
pare-brise [M]
parabrisas [M]
Windschutzscheibe [F]
parabrezza [M]
backrest
dossier [M]
respaldo [M]
Rückenlehne [F]
schienale [M]
top box
coffre [M]
maletero [M]
Topcase [N]
bauletto [M]
saddlebag
sacoche [F]
alforja [F]
Satteltasche [F]
borsa [F]
passenger's grab handle
poignée [F] de soutien [M] pour le passager [M]
agarre [M] para el pasajero [M]
Soziushaltegriff [M]
maniglia [F] per il passeggero [M]
passenger's footrest
repose-pieds [M] passager [M]
reposapiés [M] del pasajero [M]
Soziustrittbrett [N]
poggiapiedi [M] del passeggero [M]
driver's footrest
repose-pieds [M]
reposapiés [M] del conductor [M]
Trittbrett [N]
poggiapiedi [M] del conducente [M/F]
brake pedal
pédale [F] de frein [M]
pedal [M] de freno [M]
Bremspedal [N]
pedale [M] del freno [M]

motor scooter
scooter [M]
motoneta [F]
Motorroller [M]
scooter [M]

off-road motorcycle
moto [F] tout-terrain
moto [F] de enduro [M]
Enduro-Motorrad [N]
moto [F] da enduro

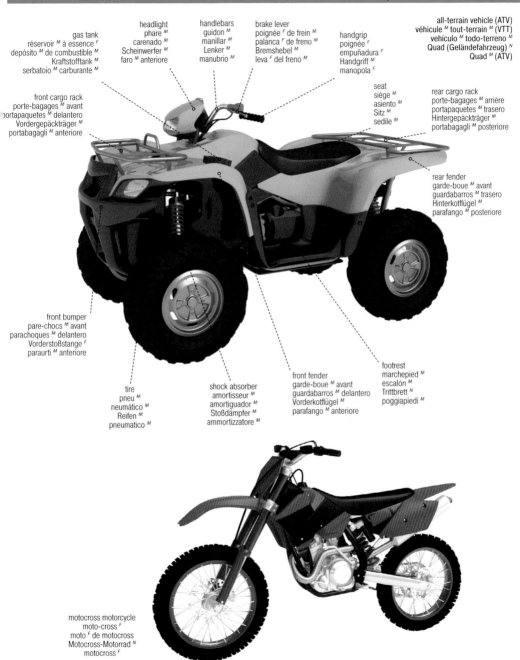

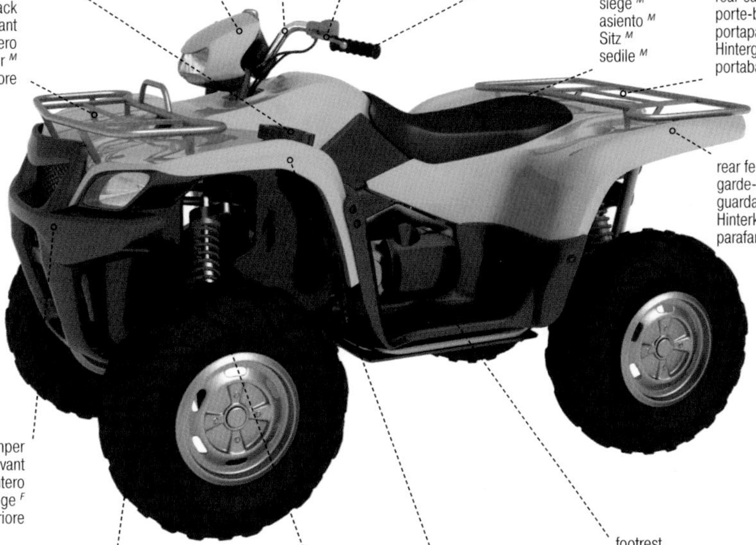
all-terrain vehicle (ATV)
véhicule M tout-terrain M (VTT)
vehículo M todo-terreno M
Quad (Geländefahrzeug) N
Quad M (ATV)
gas tank
réservoir M à essence F
depósito M de combustible M
Kraftstofftank M
serbatoio M carburante M
headlight
phare M
carenado M
Scheinwerfer M
faro M anteriore
handlebars
guidon M
manillar M
Lenker M
manubrio M
brake lever
poignée F de frein M
palanca F de freno M
Bremshebel M
leva F del freno M
handgrip
poignée F
empuñadura F
Handgriff M
manopola F
front cargo rack
porte-bagages M avant
portapaquetes M delantero
Vordergepäckträger M
portabagagli M anteriore
seat
siège M
asiento M
Sitz M
sedile M
rear cargo rack
porte-bagages M arrière
portapaquetes M trasero
Hintergepäckträger M
portabagagli M posteriore
rear fender
garde-boue M avant
guardabarros M trasero
Hinterkotflügel M
parafango M posteriore
front bumper
pare-chocs M avant
parachoques M delantero
Vorderstoßstange F
paraurti M anteriore
tire
pneu M
neumático M
Reifen M
pneumatico M
shock absorber
amortisseur M
amortiguador M
Stoßdämpfer M
ammortizzatore M
front fender
garde-boue M avant
guardabarros M delantero
Vorderkotflügel M
parafango M anteriore
footrest
marchepied M
escalón M
Trittbrett N
poggiapiedi M

motocross motorcycle
moto-cross F
moto F de motocross
Motocross-Motorrad N
motocross F

standard motorcycle
moto [F] standard
motocicleta [F]
Naked Bike
naked

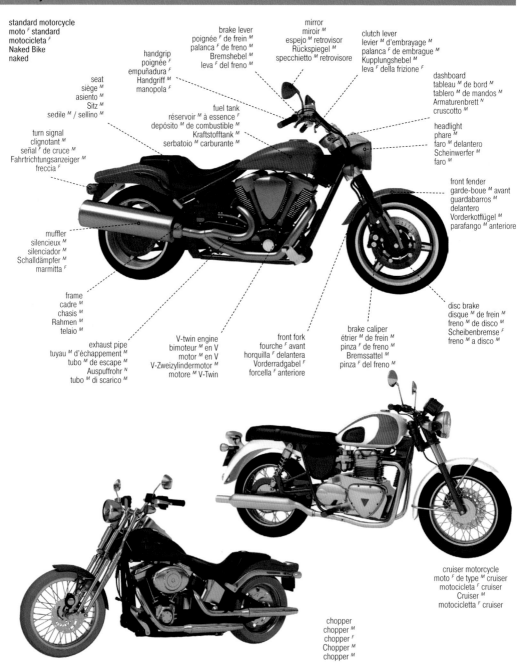

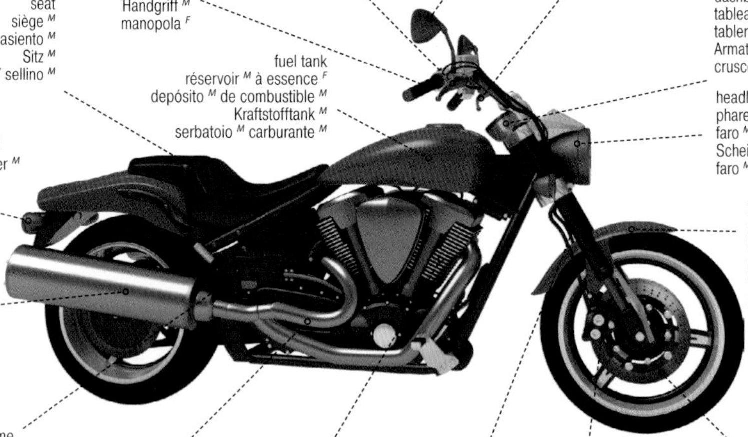
handgrip
poignée [F]
empuñadura [F]
Handgriff [M]
manopola [F]
brake lever
poignée [F] de frein [M]
palanca [F] de freno [M]
Bremshebel [M]
leva [F] del freno [M]
mirror
miroir [M]
espejo [M] retrovisor
Rückspiegel [M]
specchietto [M] retrovisore
clutch lever
levier [M] d'embrayage [M]
palanca [F] de embrague [M]
Kupplungshebel [M]
leva [F] della frizione [F]
seat
siège [M]
asiento [M]
Sitz [M]
sedile [M] / sellino [M]
dashboard
tableau [M] de bord [M]
tablero [M] de mandos [M]
Armaturenbrett [N]
cruscotto [M]
fuel tank
réservoir [M] à essence [F]
depósito [M] de combustible [M]
Kraftstofftank [M]
serbatoio [M] carburante [M]
headlight
phare [M]
faro [M] delantero
Scheinwerfer [M]
faro [M]
turn signal
clignotant [M]
señal [F] de cruce [M]
Fahrtrichtungsanzeiger [M]
freccia [F]
front fender
garde-boue [M] avant
guardabarros [M]
delantero
Vorderkotflügel [M]
parafango [M] anteriore
muffler
silencieux [M]
silenciador [M]
Schalldämpfer [M]
marmitta [F]
frame
cadre [M]
chasis [M]
Rahmen [M]
telaio [M]
disc brake
disque [M] de frein [M]
freno [M] de disco [M]
Scheibenbremse [F]
freno [M] a disco [M]
exhaust pipe
tuyau [M] d'échappement [M]
tubo [M] de escape [M]
Auspuffrohr [N]
tubo [M] di scarico [M]
V-twin engine
bimoteur [M] en V
motor [M] en V
V-Zweizylindermotor [M]
motore [M] V-Twin
front fork
fourche [F] avant
horquilla [F] delantera
Vorderradgabel [F]
forcella [F] anteriore
brake caliper
étrier [M] de frein [M]
pinza [F] de freno [M]
Bremssattel [M]
pinza [F] del freno [M]

cruiser motorcycle
moto [F] de type [M] cruiser
motocicleta [F] cruiser
Cruiser [M]
motocicletta [F] cruiser

chopper
chopper [M]
chopper [F]
Chopper [M]
chopper [M]

balance bicycle
vélo [M] d'apprentissage [M]
bicicleta [F] de equilibrio [M]
Kinderlaufrad [N]
bici [F] da equilibrio [M]

tricycle
tricycle [M]
triciclo [M]
Dreirad [N]
triciclo [M]

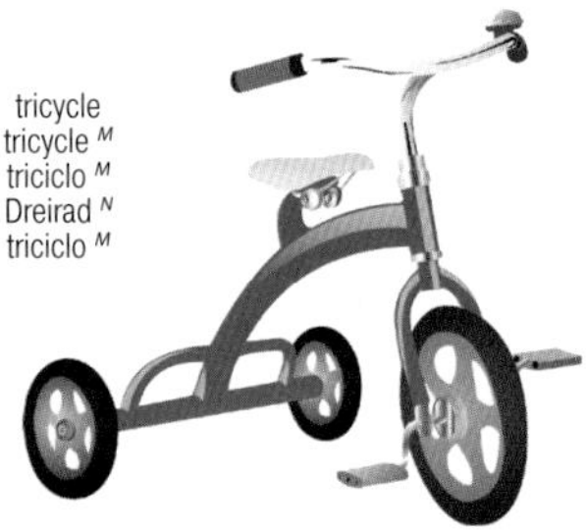

scooter
trottinette [F]
patinete [M]
Roller [M]
monopattino [M]

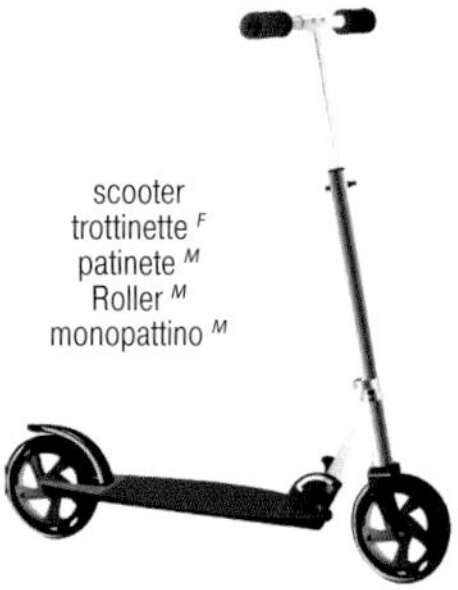

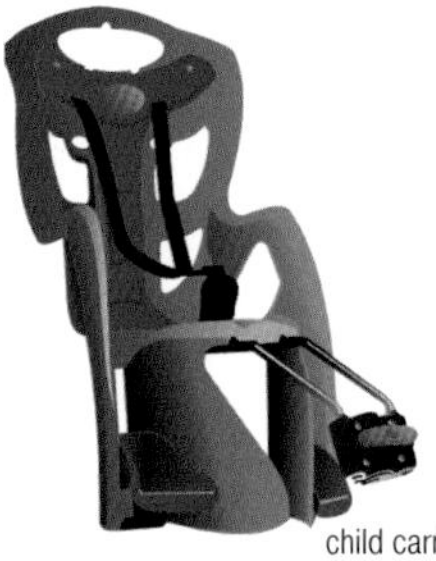

child carrier
siège [M] pour enfant [M]
sillita [F] de niños [M] para bicis [F]
Kinderfahrradsitz [M]
seggiolino [M] per trasporto [M] bambino [M]

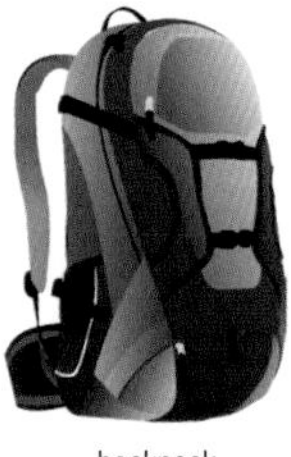

backpack
sac [M] à dos [M]
mochilla [F]
Rucksack [M]
zaino [M]

BMX bicycle
vélocross [M]
bicicleta [F] BMX
BMX-Rad [N]
bicicletta [F] BMX

mountain bicycle
vélo [M] de montagne [F]
bicicleta [F] de montaña [F]
Mountainbike [N]
mountain bike [F]

touring bicycle
vélo [M] de cyclotourisme [M]
bicicleta [F] de paseo [M]
Tourenfahrrad [N]
bicicletta [F] da cicloturismo [M]

tandem bicycle
tandem [M]
tándem [M]
Tandemfahrrad [N]
tandem [M]

child bike trailer
remorque [F] de vélo [M] pour enfant
remolque [M] de bicicleta [F] para niños [M]
Kinderfahrradanhänger [M]
rimorchio [M] per bicicletta [F]

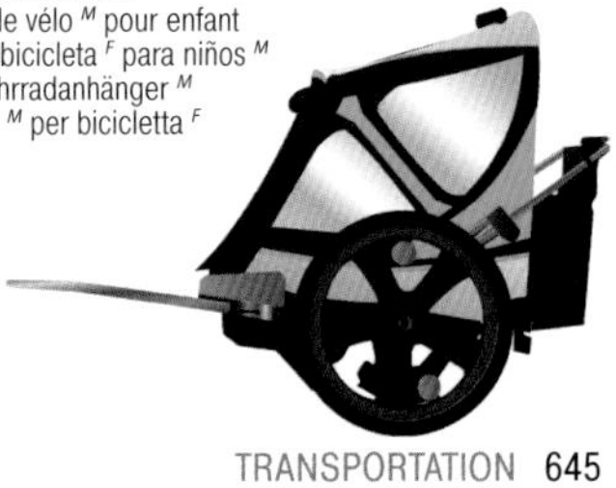

cruiser bicycle
vélo M de plage F
bicicleta F urbana
Cruiser-Fahrrad N
bicicletta F

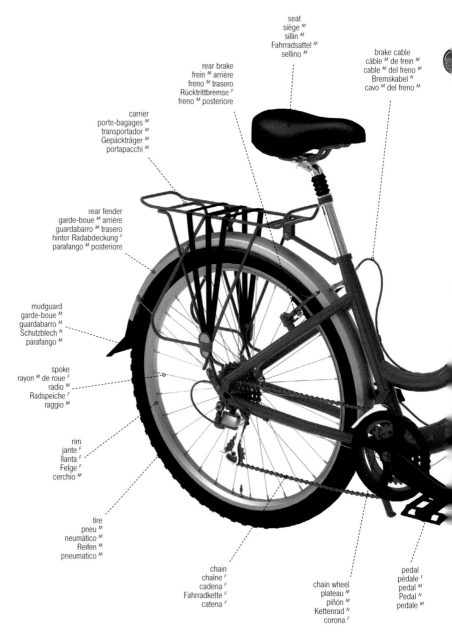

seat
siège M
sillín M
Fahrradsattel M
sellino M
brake cable
câble M de frein M
cable M del freno M
Bremskabel N
cavo M del freno M
rear brake
frein M arrière
freno M trasero
Rücktrittbremse F
freno M posteriore
carrier
porte-bagages M
transportador M
Gepäckträger M
portapacchi M
rear fender
garde-boue M arrière
guardabarro M trasero
hinter Radabdeckung F
parafango M posteriore
mudguard
garde-boue M
guardabarro M
Schutzblech N
parafango M
spoke
rayon M de roue F
radio M
Radspeiche F
raggio M
rim
jante F
llanta F
Felge F
cerchio M
tire
pneu M
neumático M
Reifen M
pneumatico M
chain
chaîne F
cadena F
Fahrradkette F
catena F
chain wheel
plateau M
piñón M
Kettenrad N
corona F
pedal
pédale F
pedal M
Pedal N
pedale M

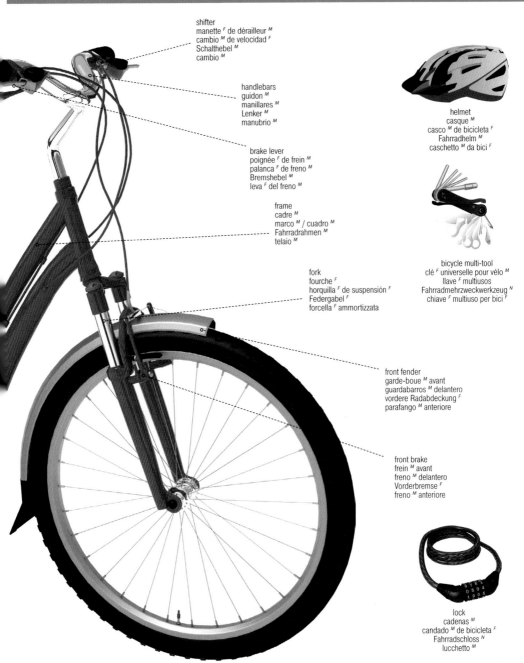

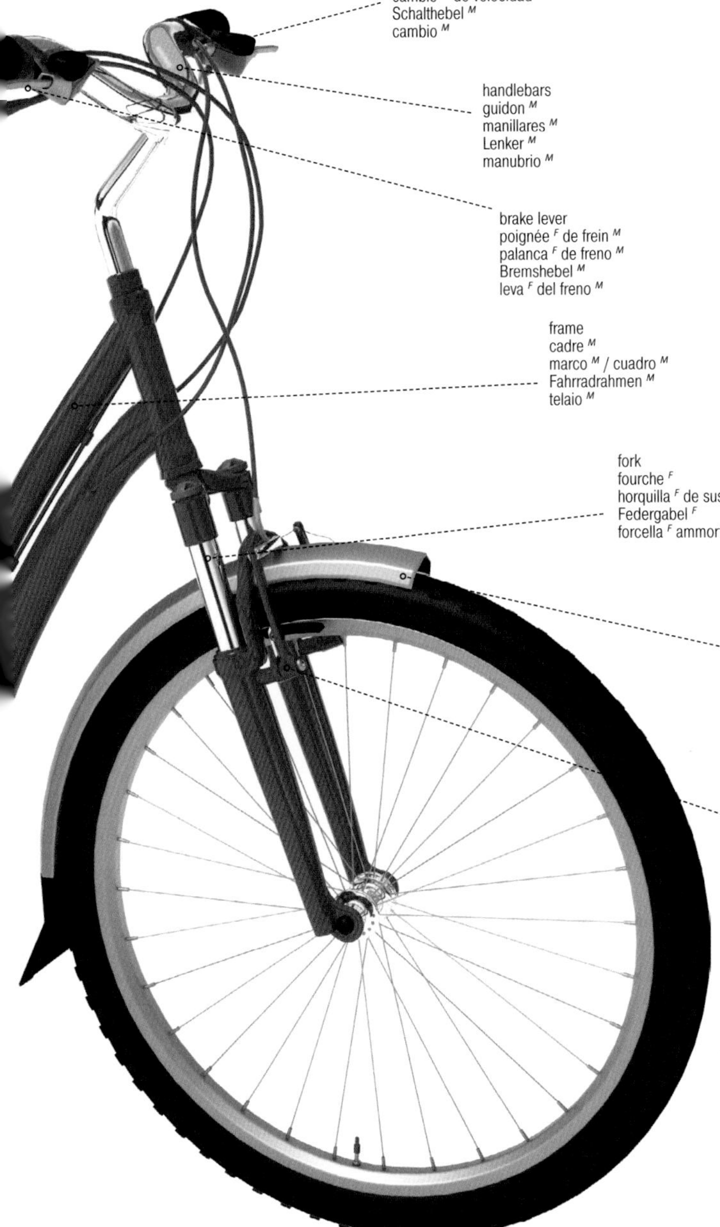
shifter
manette ^{F} de dérailleur ^{M}
cambio ^{M} de velocidad ^{F}
Schalthebel ^{M}
cambio ^{M}

handlebars
guidon ^{M}
manillares ^{M}
Lenker ^{M}
manubrio ^{M}

brake lever
poignée ^{F} de frein ^{M}
palanca ^{F} de freno ^{M}
Bremshebel ^{M}
leva ^{F} del freno ^{M}

frame
cadre ^{M}
marco ^{M} / cuadro ^{M}
Fahrradrahmen ^{M}
telaio ^{M}

fork
fourche ^{F}
horquilla ^{F} de suspensión ^{F}
Federgabel ^{F}
forcella ^{F} ammortizzata

front fender
garde-boue ^{M} avant
guardabarros ^{M} delantero
vordere Radabdeckung ^{F}
parafango ^{M} anteriore

front brake
frein ^{M} avant
freno ^{M} delantero
Vorderbremse ^{F}
freno ^{M} anteriore

helmet
casque ^{M}
casco ^{M} de bicicleta ^{F}
Fahrradhelm ^{M}
caschetto ^{M} da bici ^{F}

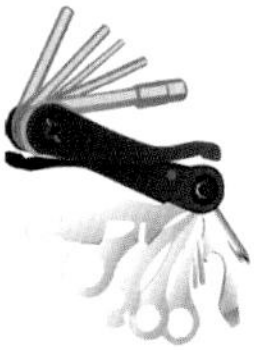

bicycle multi-tool
clé ^{F} universelle pour vélo ^{M}
llave ^{F} multiusos
Fahrradmehrzweckwerkzeug ^{N}
chiave ^{F} multiuso per bici ^{F}

lock
cadenas ^{M}
candado ^{M} de bicicleta ^{F}
Fahrradschloss ^{N}
lucchetto ^{M}

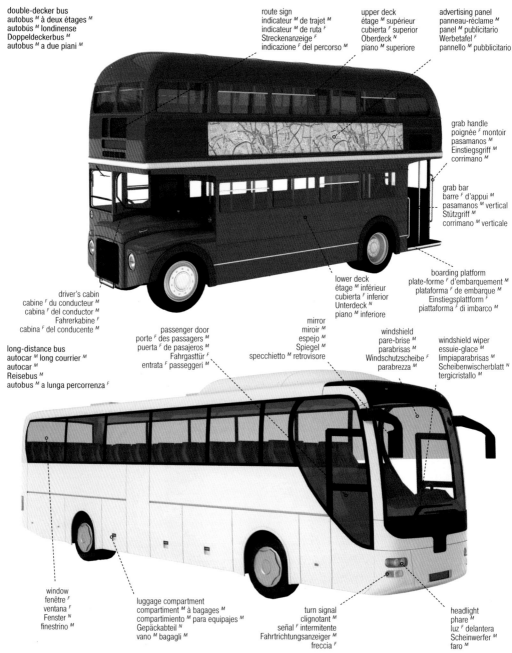

double-decker bus
autobus [M] à deux étages [M]
autobús [M] londinense
Doppeldeckerbus [M]
autobus [M] a due piani [M]

route sign
indicateur [M] de trajet [M]
indicateur [M] de ruta [F]
Streckenanzeige [F]
indicazione [F] del percorso [M]

upper deck
étage [M] supérieur
cubierta [F] superior
Oberdeck [N]
piano [M] superiore

advertising panel
panneau-réclame [M]
panel [M] publicitario
Werbetafel [F]
pannello [M] pubblicitario

grab handle
poignée [F] montoir
pasamanos [M]
Einstiegsgriff [M]
corrimano [M]

grab bar
barre [F] d'appui [M]
pasamanos [M] vertical
Stützgriff [M]
corrimano [M] verticale

boarding platform
plate-forme [F] d'embarquement [M]
plataforma [F] de embarque [M]
Einstiegsplattform [F]
piattaforma [F] di imbarco [M]

lower deck
étage [M] inférieur
cubierta [F] inferior
Unterdeck [N]
piano [M] inferiore

driver's cabin
cabine [F] du conducteur [M]
cabina [F] del conductor [M]
Fahrerkabine [F]
cabina [F] del conducente [M]

long-distance bus
autocar [M] long courrier [M]
autocar [M]
Reisebus [M]
autobus [M] a lunga percorrenza [F]

passenger door
porte [F] des passagers [M]
puerta [F] de pasajeros [M]
Fahrgasttür [F]
entrata [F] passeggeri [M]

mirror
miroir [M]
espejo [M]
Spiegel [M]
specchietto [M] retrovisore

windshield
pare-brise [M]
parabrisas [M]
Windschutzscheibe [F]
parabrezza [M]

windshield wiper
essuie-glace [M]
limpiaparabrisas [M]
Scheibenwischerblatt [N]
tergicristallo [M]

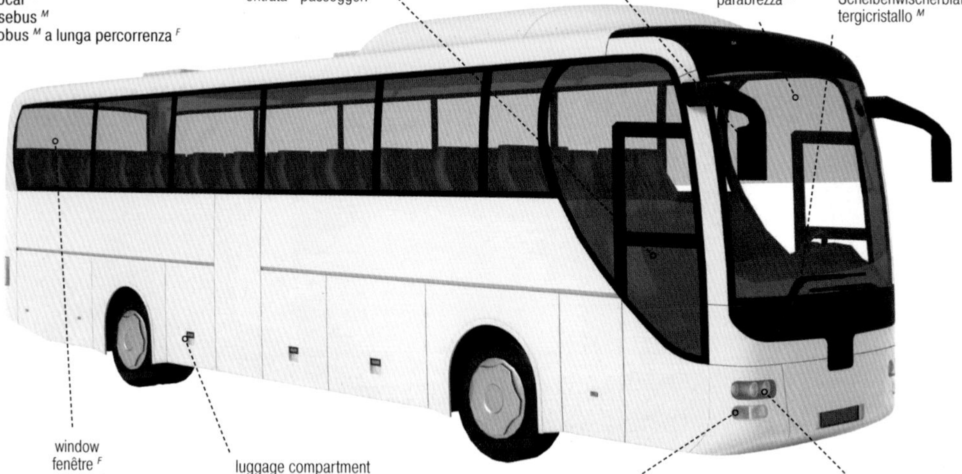

window
fenêtre [F]
ventana [F]
Fenster [N]
finestrino [M]

luggage compartment
compartiment [M] à bagages [M]
compartimiento [M] para equipajes [M]
Gepäckabteil [N]
vano [M] bagagli [M]

turn signal
clignotant [M]
señal [F] intermitente
Fahrtrichtungsanzeiger [M]
freccia [F]

headlight
phare [M]
luz [F] delantera
Scheinwerfer [M]
faro [M]

city bus
autobus ᴹ de ville ᶠ
autobús ᴹ urbano
Stadtbus ᴹ
autobus ᴹ urbano

minibus
minibus ᴹ
minibús ᴹ
Kleinbus ᴹ
minibus ᴹ

double-decker long-distance bus
autobus ᴹ longue distance ᶠ à deux étages ᴹ
autobús ᴹ de viaje ᴹ de dos pisos ᴹ
Doppeldecker-Reisebus ᴹ
autobus ᴹ a lunga percorrenza ᶠ a due piani ᴹ

articulated bus
autobus M articulé
bus M articulado
Gelenkbus M
autobus M articolato

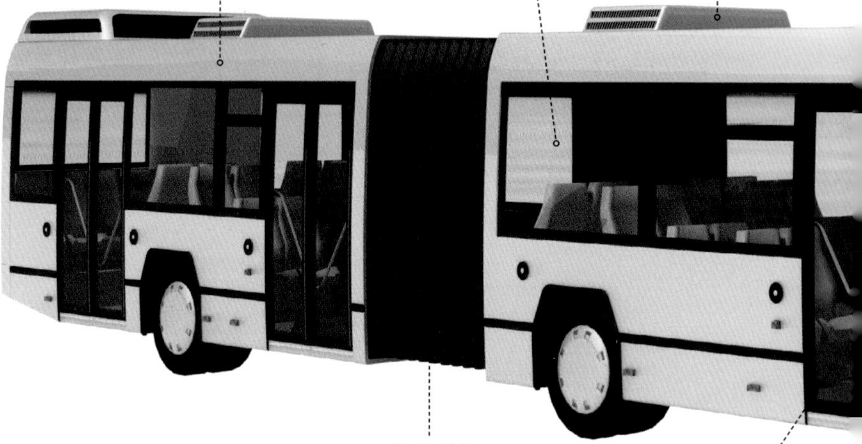
rear rigid section
section F rigide arrière
sección F trasera rígida
starres Fahrzeughinterteil N
sezione F rigida posteriore
window
fenêtre F
ventana F
Fenster N
finestrino M
air conditioner
climatiseur M
aire M acondicionado
Klimaanlage F
condizionatore M
articulated joint
joint M articulé
fuelle M plegable
Faltenbalg M
soffietto M pieghevole
door
porte F
puerta F
Tür F
porta F

bus stop
arrêt M d'autobus M
parada F de autobús M
Bushaltestelle F
fermata F dell'autobus M

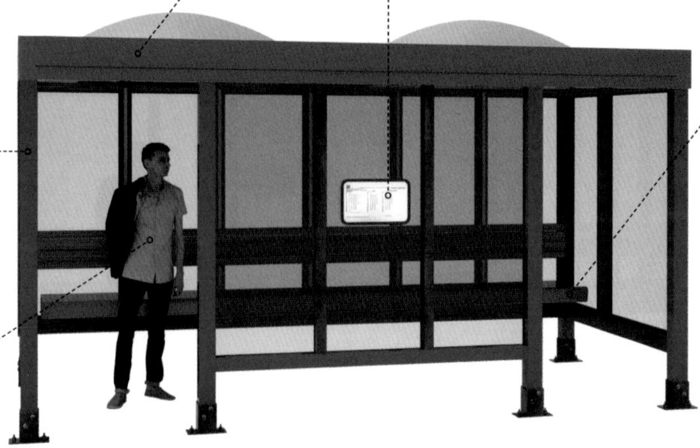
roof
toit M
techo M
Dach N
tetto M
schedule
horaires M
horarios M
Fahrplan M
orari M
bench
banc M
banco M
Bank F
panca F
frame
structure F
estructura F
Gestell N
struttura F
passenger
passager M
pasajero M
Fahrgast M
passeggero M

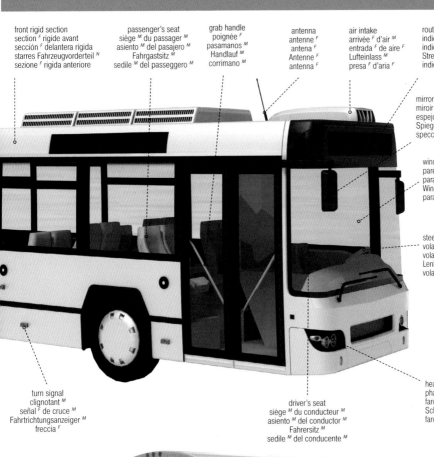

front rigid section
section ^F rigide avant
sección ^F delantera rígida
starres Fahrzeugvorderteil ^N
sezione ^F rigida anteriore
passenger's seat
siège ^M du passager ^M
asiento ^M del pasajero ^M
Fahrgastsitz ^M
sedile ^M del passeggero ^M
grab handle
poignée ^F
pasamanos ^M
Handlauf ^M
corrimano ^M
antenna
antenne ^F
antena ^F
Antenne ^F
antenna ^F
air intake
arrivée ^F d'air ^M
entrada ^F de aire ^F
Lufteinlass ^M
presa ^F d'aria ^F
route sign
indicateur ^M de trajet ^M
indicador ^M de ruta ^F
Streckenanzeige ^M
indicazione ^F del percorso ^M
mirror
miroir ^M
espejo ^M retrovisor
Spiegel ^M
specchietto ^M retrovisore
windshield
pare-brise ^M
parabrisas ^M
Windschutzscheibe ^F
parabrezza ^M
steering wheel
volant ^M
volante ^M
Lenkrad ^N
volante ^M
turn signal
clignotant ^M
señal ^F de cruce ^M
Fahrtrichtungsanzeiger ^M
freccia ^F
driver's seat
siège ^M du conducteur ^M
asiento ^M del conductor ^M
Fahrersitz ^M
sedile ^M del conducente ^M
headlight
phare ^M
faros ^M delanteros
Scheinwerfer ^M
faro ^M

school bus
autobus ^M scolaire
autobús ^M escolar
Schulbus ^M
scuolabus ^M

semitrailer
semi-remorque M
semirremolque M
Sattelschlepper M
autocarro M

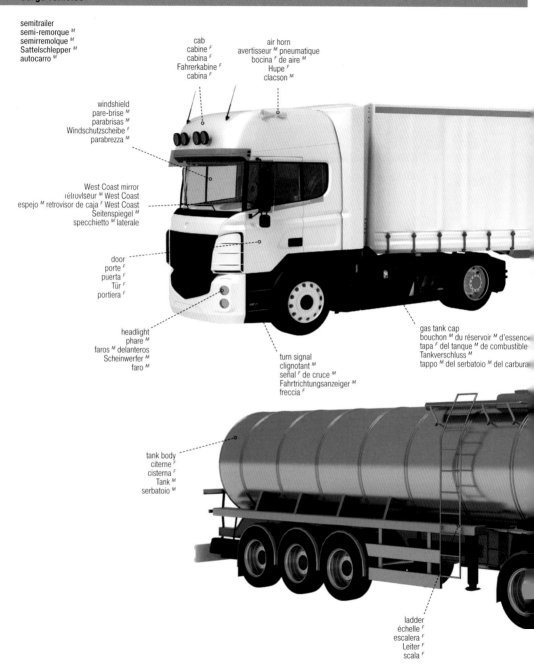

cab
cabine F
cabina F
Fahrerkabine F
cabina F
air horn
avertisseur M pneumatique
bocina F de aire M
Hupe F
clacson M
windshield
pare-brise M
parabrisas M
Windschutzscheibe F
parabrezza M
West Coast mirror
rétroviseur M West Coast
espejo M retrovisor de caja F West Coast
Seitenspiegel M
specchietto M laterale
door
porte F
puerta F
Tür F
portiera F
headlight
phare M
faros M delanteros
Scheinwerfer M
faro M
turn signal
clignotant M
señal F de cruce M
Fahrtrichtungsanzeiger M
freccia F
gas tank cap
bouchon M du réservoir M d'essenc
tapa F del tanque M de combustible
Tankverschluss M
tappo M del serbatoio M del carbura

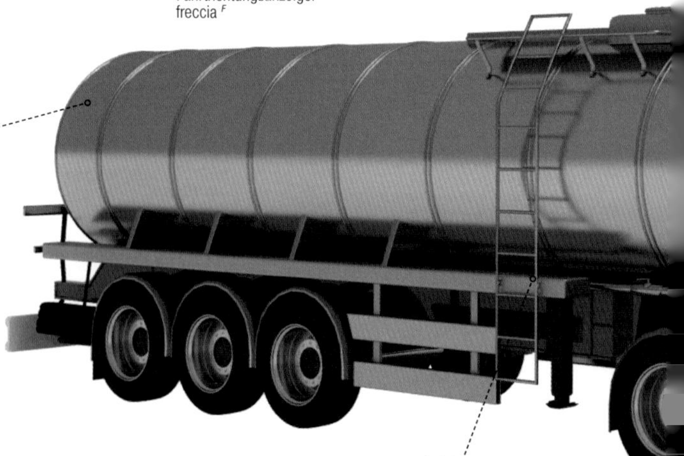
tank body
citerne F
cisterna F
Tank M
serbatoio M
ladder
échelle F
escalera F
Leiter F
scala F

semitrailer
semi-remorque [M]
semirremolque [M]
Sattelanhänger [M]
semirimorchio [M]

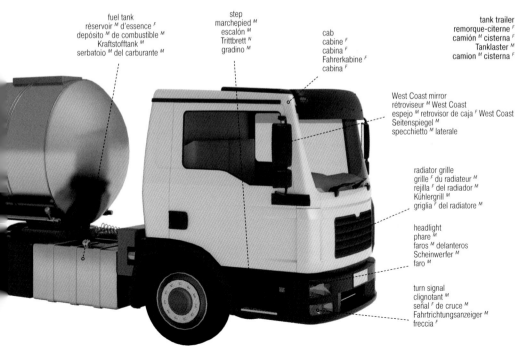

fuel tank
réservoir [M] d'essence [F]
depósito [M] de combustible [M]
Kraftstofftank [M]
serbatoio [M] del carburante [M]
step
marchepied [M]
escalón [M]
Trittbrett [N]
gradino [M]
cab
cabine [F]
cabina [F]
Fahrerkabine [F]
cabina [F]
tank trailer
remorque-citerne [F]
camión [M] cisterna [F]
Tanklaster [M]
camion [M] cisterna [F]
West Coast mirror
rétroviseur [M] West Coast
espejo [M] retrovisor de caja [F] West Coast
Seitenspiegel [M]
specchietto [M] laterale
radiator grille
grille [F] du radiateur [M]
rejilla [F] del radiador [M]
Kühlergrill [M]
griglia [F] del radiatore [M]
headlight
phare [M]
faros [M] delanteros
Scheinwerfer [M]
faro [M]
turn signal
clignotant [M]
señal [F] de cruce [M]
Fahrtrichtungsanzeiger [M]
freccia [F]

semitrailer cab
cabine F de semi-remorque M
cabina F de semirremolque M
Sattelschlepper-Fahrerkabine F
cabina F del camion M

steering wheel
volant M
volante M
Lenkrad N
volante M
speaker
haut-parleur M
altavoz M
Lautsprecher M
altoparlante M
gearshift lever
levier M de vitesse F
palanca F de cambio M
Schaltknüppel M
leva F del cambio M
armrest
accoudoir M
reposabrazos M
Armlehne F
bracciolo M
sleeper cab
cabine F couchette F
camarín M
Lkw-Schlafkabine F
cuccetta F
clutch pedal
pédale F d'embrayage M
pedal M de embrague M
Kupplungspedal N
pedale M della frizione F
brake pedal
pédale F de frein M
pedal M de freno M
Bremspedal N
pedale M del freno M
gas pedal
pédale F d'accélérateur M
pedal M del acelerador M
Gaspedal N
pedale M dell'acceleratore M
instrument panel
tableau M de bord M
tablero M de mandos M
Armaturenbrett N
cruscotto M
seat
siège M
asiento M
Sitz M
sedile M

cement truck
camion-malaxeur ^{M}
hormigonera ^{F}
Betonmischer ^{M}
betoniera ^{F}

dump truck
camion-benne ^{M}
camión ^{M} volteo
Kipplastwagen ^{M}
autocarro ^{M} con cassone ^{M} ribaltabile

truck and tandem trailer
camion ^{M} et remorque ^{F} tandem
camión ^{M} y remolque ^{M} tándem
LKW ^{M} und Tandemanhänger ^{M}
autotreno ^{M}

semitrailer with sleeper cab
semi-remorque ^{M} avec cabine ^{F} couchette
semirremolque ^{M} con camarín ^{M}
Sattelschlepper ^{M} mit Schlafkabine ^{F}
semirimorchio ^{M} con cuccetta ^{F}

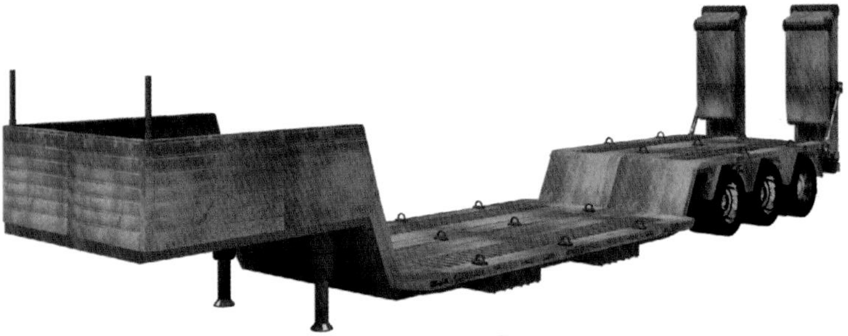

double drop lowbed semitrailer
semi-remorque [F] porte-engins [M] surbaissée
remolque [M] de doble caída [F] y cama [F] baja
Schwanenhalstrailer [M]
semirimorchio [M] basso a doppia cassa [F]

log semitrailer
semi-remorque [F] à bois [M]
semirremolque [M] de troncos [M]
Forstsattelanhänger [M]
semirimorchio [M] per trasporto [M] legname [M]

livestock semitrailer
semi-remorque [F] à bétail [M]
semirremolque [M] de ganado [M]
Viehtransportsattelanhänger [M]
semirimorchio [M] per trasporto [M] bestiame [M]

van body semitrailer
semi-remorque [F] fourgon
semirremolque [M] contenedor
Containersattelanhänger [M]
semirimorchio [M] portacontainer [M]

tank trailer
remorque-citerne [F]
cisterna [F] de remolque
Tanksattelanhänger [M]
semirimorchio [M] cisterna [F]

automobile transport semitrailer
semi-remorque [F] porte-voitures
semirremolque [M] de vehículos [M]
Autotransportanhänger [M]
rimorchio [M] per trasporto [M] autovetture [F]

truck tractor
porteur-remorqueur [M]
camión [M] tractor [M]
Sattelschlepper [M]
motrice [F] per rimorchio [M]

box van
fourgonnette [F] à caisse [F]
furgoneta [F]
Kastenwagen [M]
furgone [M] isotermico

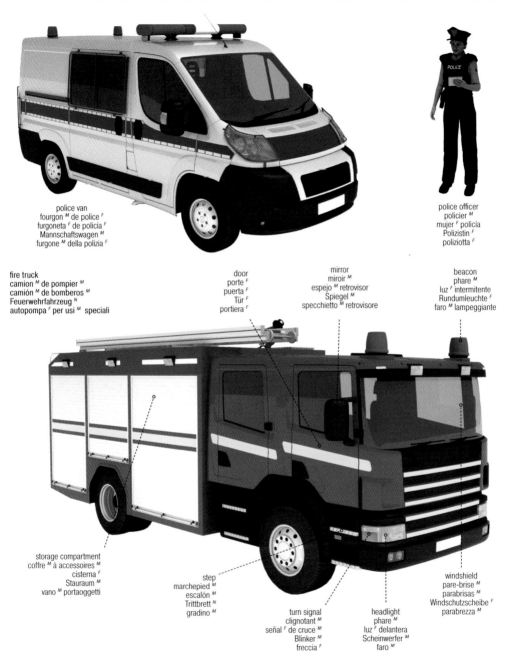

police van
fourgon ^{M} de police ^{F}
furgoneta ^{F} de policía ^{F}
Mannschaftswagen ^{M}
furgone ^{M} della polizia ^{F}

police officer
policier ^{M}
mujer ^{F} policía
Polizistin ^{F}
poliziotta ^{F}

fire truck
camion ^{M} de pompier ^{M}
camión ^{M} de bomberos ^{M}
Feuerwehrfahrzeug ^{N}
autopompa ^{F} per usi ^{M} speciali

door
porte ^{F}
puerta ^{F}
Tür ^{F}
portiera ^{F}

mirror
miroir ^{M}
espejo ^{M} retrovisor
Spiegel ^{M}
specchietto ^{M} retrovisore

beacon
phare ^{M}
luz ^{F} intermitente
Rundumleuchte ^{F}
faro ^{M} lampeggiante

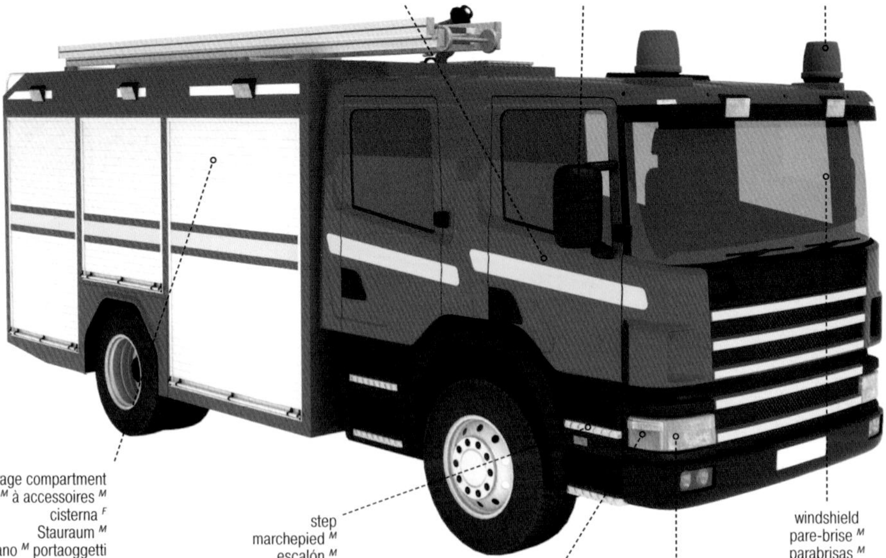

storage compartment
coffre ^{M} à accessoires ^{M}
cisterna ^{F}
Stauraum ^{M}
vano ^{M} portaoggetti

step
marchepied ^{M}
escalón ^{M}
Trittbrett ^{N}
gradino ^{M}

turn signal
clignotant ^{M}
señal ^{F} de cruce ^{M}
Blinker ^{M}
freccia ^{F}

headlight
phare ^{M}
luz ^{F} delantera
Scheinwerfer ^{M}
faro ^{M}

windshield
pare-brise ^{M}
parabrisas ^{M}
Windschutzscheibe ^{F}
parabrezza ^{M}

garbage truck
camion M à ordures F
camión M de basura M
Müllauto N
camion M della nettezza F urbana

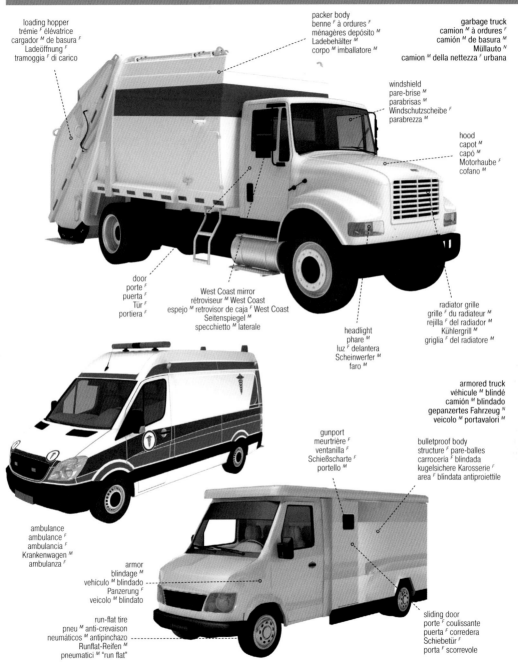

loading hopper
trémie F élévatrice
cargador M de basura F
Ladeöffnung F
tramoggia F di carico

packer body
benne F à ordures F ménagères depósito M
Ladebehälter M
corpo M imballatore M

windshield
pare-brise M
parabrisas M
Windschutzscheibe F
parabrezza M

hood
capot M
capó M
Motorhaube F
cofano M

door
porte F
puerta F
Tür F
portiera F

West Coast mirror
rétroviseur M West Coast
espejo M retrovisor de caja F West Coast
Seitenspiegel M
specchietto M laterale

headlight
phare M
luz F delantera
Scheinwerfer M
faro M

radiator grille
grille F du radiateur M
rejilla F del radiador M
Kühlergrill M
griglia F del radiatore M

ambulance
ambulance F
ambulancia F
Krankenwagen M
ambulanza F

armored truck
véhicule M blindé
camión M blindado
gepanzertes Fahrzeug N
veicolo M portavalori M

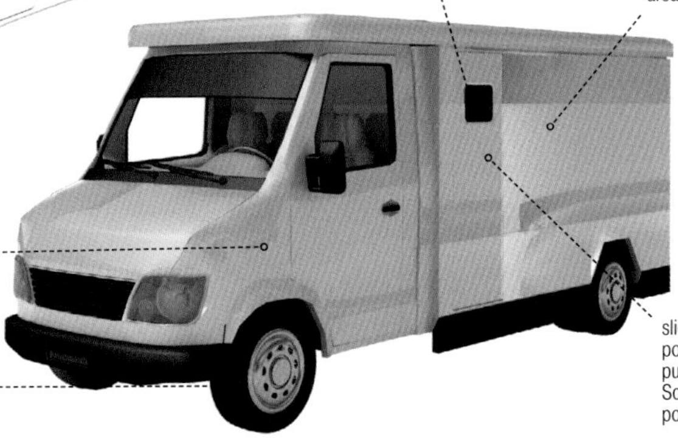

gunport
meurtrière F
ventanilla F
Schießscharte F
portello M

bulletproof body
structure F pare-balles
carrocería F blindada
kugelsichere Karosserie F
area F blindata antiproiettile

armor
blindage M
vehículo M blindado
Panzerung F
veicolo M blindato

run-flat tire
pneu M anti-crevaison
neumáticos M antipinchazo
Runflat-Reifen M
pneumatici M "run flat"

sliding door
porte F coulissante
puerta F corredera
Schiebetür F
porta F scorrevole

street cleaner
camion ^M balayeur
camión ^M limpia calles ^F
Straßenkehrmaschine ^F
spazzatrice ^F

access hatch
trappe ^F d'accès ^M
escotilla ^F de acceso ^M
Zugangsluke ^F
portello ^M di accesso ^M

beacon
gyrophare ^M
luz ^F intermitente
Rundumleuchte ^F
faro ^M lampeggiante

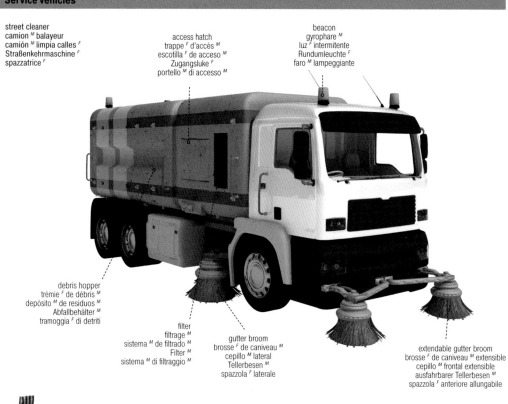

debris hopper
trémie ^F de débris ^M
depósito ^M de residuos ^M
Abfallbehälter ^M
tramoggia ^F di detriti

filter
filtrage ^M
sistema ^M de filtrado ^M
Filter ^M
sistema ^M di filtraggio ^M

gutter broom
brosse ^F de caniveau ^M
cepillo ^M lateral
Tellerbesen ^M
spazzola ^F laterale

extendable gutter broom
brosse ^F de caniveau ^M extensible
cepillo ^M frontal extensible
ausfahrbarer Tellerbesen ^M
spazzola ^F anteriore allungabile

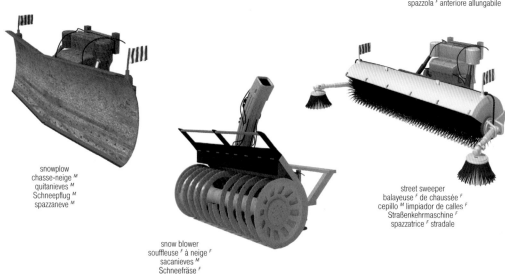

snowplow
chasse-neige ^M
quitanieves ^M
Schneepflug ^M
spazzaneve ^M

snow blower
souffleuse ^F à neige ^F
sacanieves ^M
Schneefräse ^F
spartineve ^M

street sweeper
balayeuse ^F de chaussée ^F
cepillo ^M limpiador de calles ^F
Straßenkehrmaschine ^F
spazzatrice ^F stradale

bulldozer
bouteur M
excavadora F
Planierraupe F
ruspa F

compact excavator
pelle F compacte
excavadora F sobre orugas F compacta
Kompaktraupenbagger M
escavatore M compatto

portable concrete mixer
bétonnière F portative
hormigonera F móvil
fahrbarer Betonmischer M
betoniera F mobile

skid-steer loader
chargeur M à direction F à glissement M
minicargadora F
Kompaktlader M
minipala F compatta

mini road roller
mini rouleau [M] compresseur
apisonadora [F] compacta
Kompakte Doppelwalze [F]
doppio rullo [M] compatto

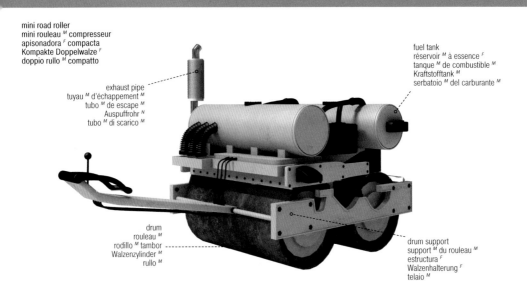

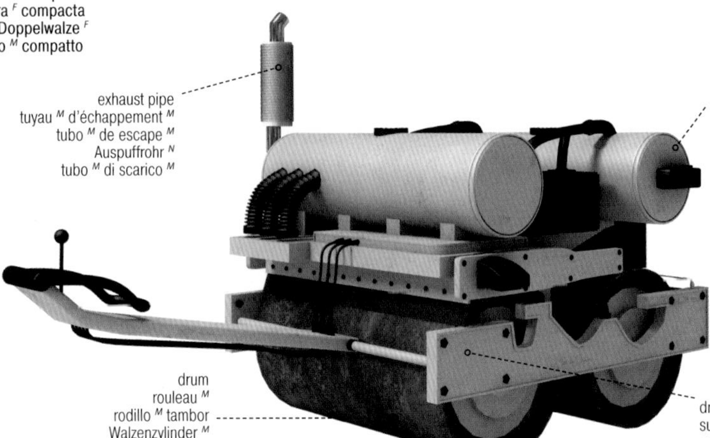
exhaust pipe
tuyau [M] d'échappement [M]
tubo [M] de escape [M]
Auspuffrohr [N]
tubo [M] di scarico [M]
fuel tank
réservoir [M] à essence [F]
tanque [M] de combustible [M]
Kraftstofftank [M]
serbatoio [M] del carburante [M]
drum
rouleau [M]
rodillo [M] tambor
Walzenzylinder [M]
rullo [M]
drum support
support [M] du rouleau [M]
estructura [F]
Walzenhalterung [F]
telaio [M]

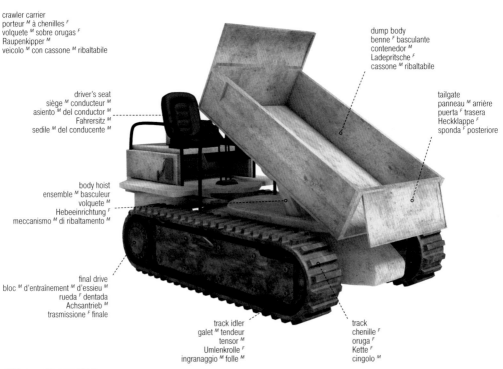

crawler carrier
porteur [M] à chenilles [F]
volquete [M] sobre orugas [F]
Raupenkipper [M]
veicolo [M] con cassone [M] ribaltabile

dump body
benne [F] basculante
contenedor [M]
Ladepritsche [F]
cassone [M] ribaltabile
driver's seat
siège [M] conducteur [M]
asiento [M] del conductor [M]
Fahrersitz [M]
sedile [M] del conducente [M]
tailgate
panneau [M] arrière
puerta [F] trasera
Heckklappe [F]
sponda [F] posteriore
body hoist
ensemble [M] basculeur
volquete [M]
Hebeeinrichtung [F]
meccanismo [M] di ribaltamento [M]
final drive
bloc [M] d'entraînement [M] d'essieu [M]
rueda [F] dentada
Achsantrieb [M]
trasmissione [F] finale
track idler
galet [M] tendeur
tensor [M]
Umlenkrolle [F]
ingranaggio [M] folle [M]
track
chenille [F]
oruga [F]
Kette [F]
cingolo [M]

wheeled bulldozer
bouteur ^{M} à roues ^{F}
excavadora ^{F} rodada
fahrbare Planierraupe ^{F}
pala ^{F} gommata

road roller
rouleau ^{M} compresseur ^{M}
apisonadora ^{F}
Straßenwalze ^{F}
compressore ^{M} stradale

backhoe loader
chargeuse-pelleteuse ^{F}
retroexcavadora ^{F}
Baggerlader ^{M}
terna ^{F}

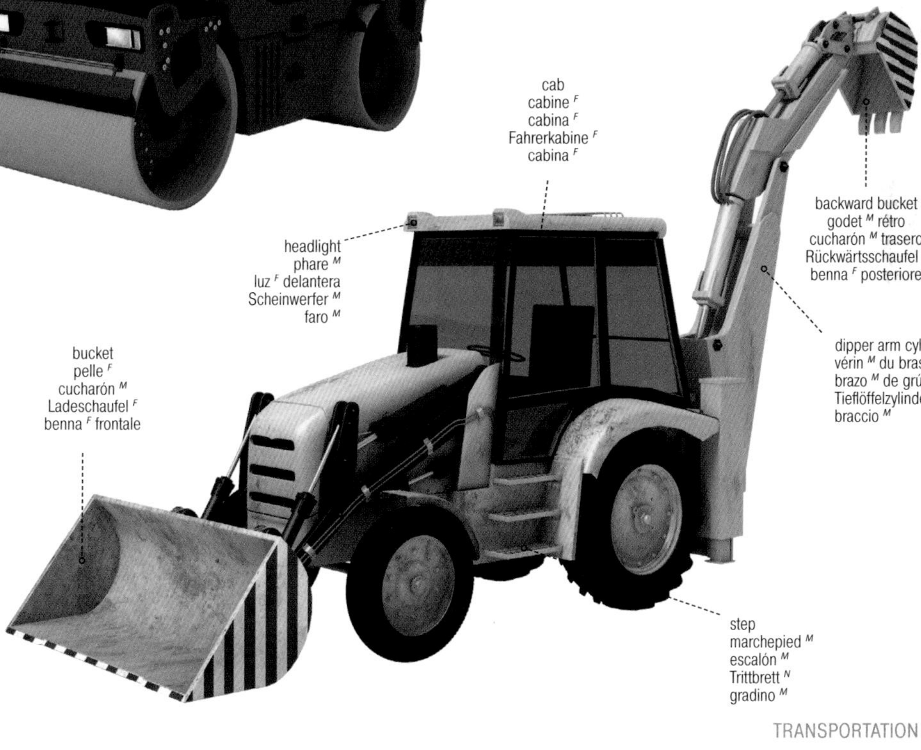
cab
cabine ^{F}
cabina ^{F}
Fahrerkabine ^{F}
cabina ^{F}
headlight
phare ^{M}
luz ^{F} delantera
Scheinwerfer ^{M}
faro ^{M}
backward bucket
godet ^{M} rétro
cucharón ^{M} trasero
Rückwärtsschaufel ^{F}
benna ^{F} posteriore
bucket
pelle ^{F}
cucharón ^{M}
Ladeschaufel ^{F}
benna ^{F} frontale
dipper arm cylinder
vérin ^{M} du bras ^{M}
brazo ^{M} de grúa ^{M}
Tieflöffelzylinder ^{M}
braccio ^{M}
step
marchepied ^{M}
escalón ^{M}
Trittbrett ^{N}
gradino ^{M}

grader
niveleuse ^{F}
niveladora ^{F}
Erdhobel ^{M}
livellatrice ^{F}

concrete mixer
bétonnière ^{F}
hormigonera ^{F}
Betonmischer ^{M}
betoniera ^{F}

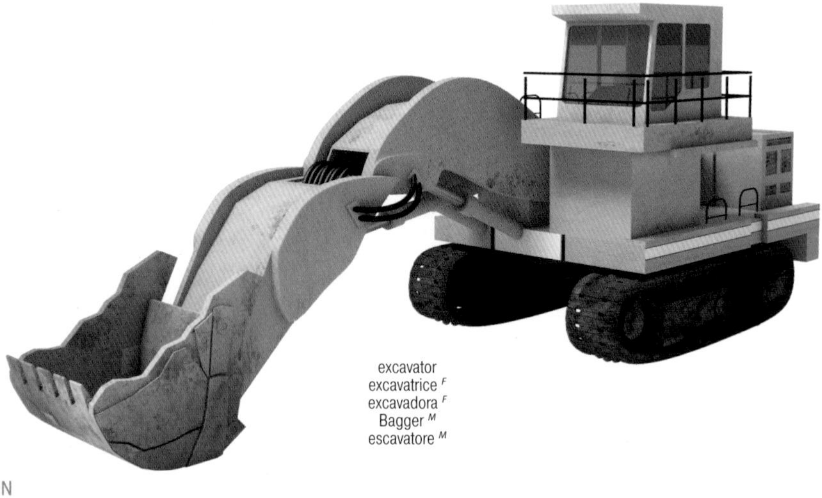

excavator
excavatrice ^{F}
excavadora ^{F}
Bagger ^{M}
escavatore ^{M}

haul truck
camion [M] de transport [M]
camión [M] de volteo [M]
Nutzfahrzeug [N]
camion [M] per il trasporto [M] dei minerali [M]

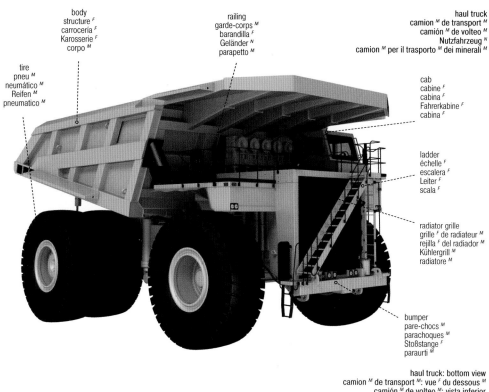

body
structure [F]
carrocería [F]
Karosserie [F]
corpo [M]
railing
garde-corps [M]
barandilla [F]
Geländer [N]
parapetto [M]
tire
pneu [M]
neumático [M]
Reifen [M]
pneumatico [M]
cab
cabine [F]
cabina [F]
Fahrerkabine [F]
cabina [F]
ladder
échelle [F]
escalera [F]
Leiter [F]
scala [F]
radiator grille
grille [F] de radiateur [M]
rejilla [F] del radiador [M]
Kühlergrill [M]
radiatore [M]
bumper
pare-chocs [M]
parachoques [M]
Stoßstange [F]
paraurti [M]

haul truck: bottom view
camion [M] de transport [M]: vue [F] du dessous [M]
camión [M] de volteo [M]: vista inferior
Nutzfahrzeug [N]: Unteransicht [F]
camion [M] per il trasporto [M]
di minerali [M]: vista [F] dal basso

tire
roue [F]
neumático [M]
Reifen [M]
ruota [F]
axle shaft
axe [M] de roue [F] motrice
eje [M] trasero
Achselwelle [F]
semiasse [M]
driveshaft
arbre [M] de transmission [F]
eje [M] de transmisión [M]
Antriebswelle [F]
albero [M] di trasmissione [F]
bumper
pare-chocs [M]
parachoques [M]
Stoßstange [F]
paraurti [M]
crankcase
carter [M] de moteur [M]
cárter [M]
Kurbelwellengehäuse [N]
basamento [M]
transmission
transmission [F]
transmisión [F]
Getriebe [N]
trasmissione [F]

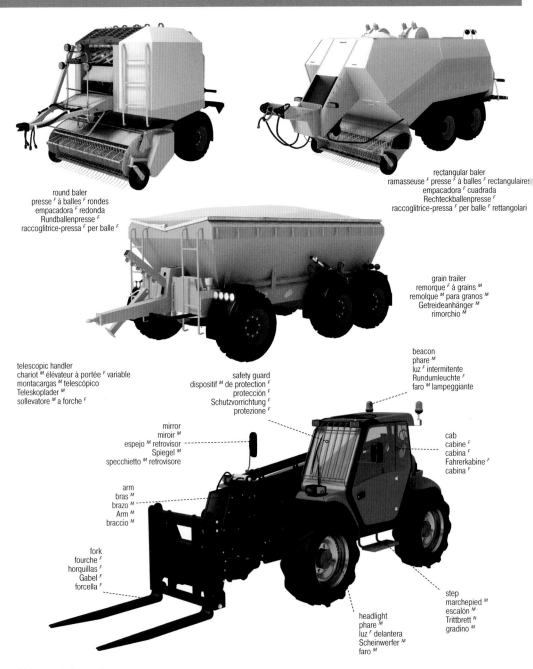

round baler
presse F à balles F rondes
empacadora F redonda
Rundballenpresse F
raccoglitrice-pressa F per balle F

rectangular baler
ramasseuse F presse F à balles F rectangulaires
empacadora F cuadrada
Rechteckballenpresse F
raccoglitrice-pressa F per balle F rettangolari

grain trailer
remorque F à grains M
remolque M para granos M
Getreideanhänger M
rimorchio M

telescopic handler
chariot M élévateur à portée F variable
montacargas M telescópico
Teleskoplader M
sollevatore M a forche F

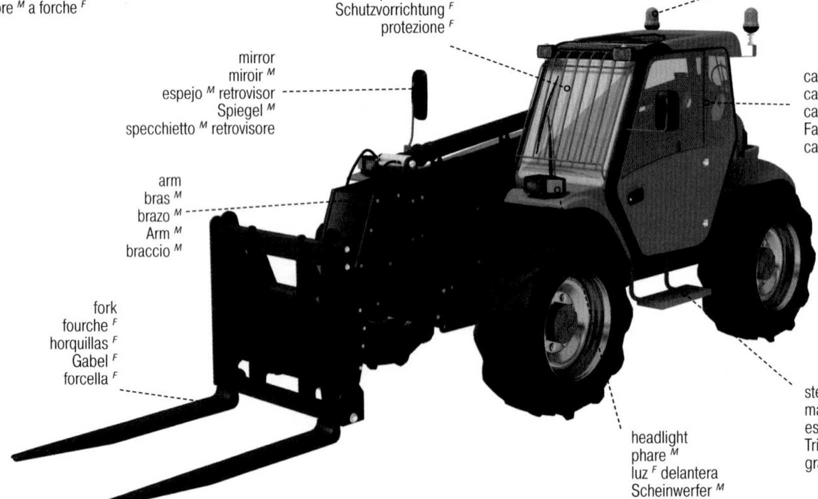
safety guard
dispositif M de protection F
protección F
Schutzvorrichtung F
protezione F
beacon
phare M
luz F intermitente
Rundumleuchte F
faro M lampeggiante
mirror
miroir M
espejo M retrovisor
Spiegel M
specchietto M retrovisore
cab
cabine F
cabina F
Fahrerkabine F
cabina F
arm
bras M
brazo M
Arm M
braccio M
fork
fourche F
horquillas F
Gabel F
forcella F
step
marchepied M
escalón M
Trittbrett N
gradino M
headlight
phare M
luz F delantera
Scheinwerfer M
faro M

harvester
moissonneuse [F]
agavilladora [F]
Erntemaschine [F]
mietitrice [F]

tractor
tracteur [M]
tractor [M]
Traktor [M]
trattore [M]

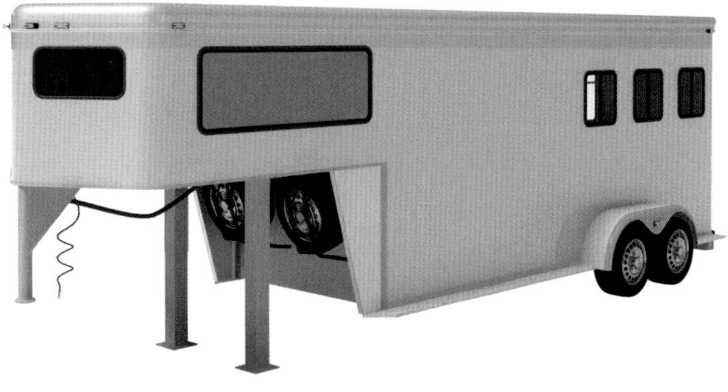

horse trailer
remorque [F] à chevaux [M]
remolque [M] para caballos [M]
Pferdeanhänger [M]
rimorchio [M] per cavalli [M]

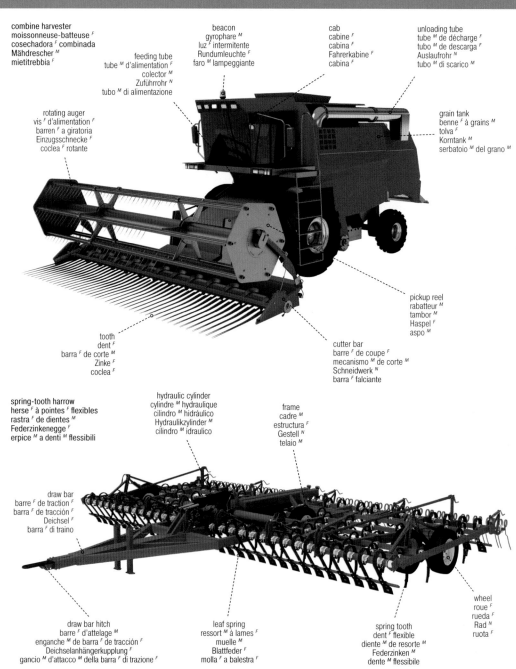

combine harvester
moissonneuse-batteuse F
cosechadora F combinada
Mähdrescher M
mietitrebbia F

beacon
gyrophare M
luz F intermitente
Rundumleuchte F
faro M lampeggiante
cab
cabine F
cabina F
Fahrerkabine F
cabina F
unloading tube
tube M de décharge F
tubo M de descarga F
Auslaufrohr N
tubo M di scarico M
feeding tube
tube M d'alimentation F
colector M
Zuführrohr N
tubo M di alimentazione
rotating auger
vis F d'alimentation F
barren F a giratoria
Einzugsschnecke F
coclea F rotante
grain tank
benne F à grains M
tolva F
Korntank M
serbatoio M del grano M
pickup reel
rabatteur M
tambor M
Haspel F
aspo M
tooth
dent F
barra F de corte M
Zinke F
coclea F
cutter bar
barre F de coupe F
mecanismo M de corte M
Schneidwerk N
barra F falciante

spring-tooth harrow
herse F à pointes F flexibles
rastra F de dientes M
Federzinkenegge F
erpice M a denti M flessibili

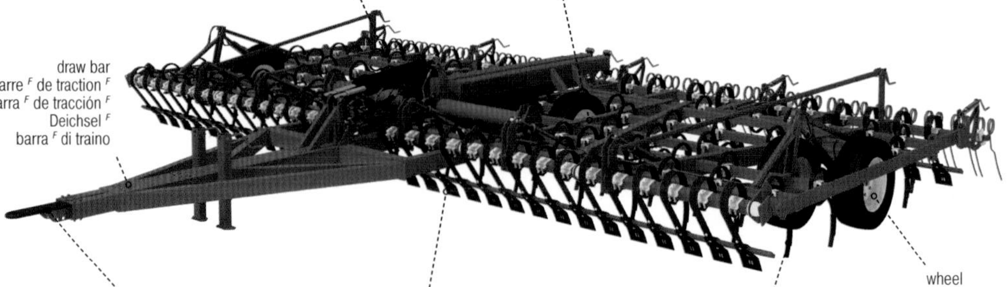
hydraulic cylinder
cylindre M hydraulique
cilindro M hidráulico
Hydraulikzylinder M
cilindro M idraulico
frame
cadre M
estructura F
Gestell N
telaio M
draw bar
barre F de traction F
barra F de tracción F
Deichsel F
barra F di traino
wheel
roue F
rueda F
Rad N
ruota F
draw bar hitch
barre F d'attelage M
enganche M de barra F de tracción F
Deichselanhängerkupplung F
gancio M d'attacco M della barra F di trazione F
leaf spring
ressort M à lames F
muelle M
Blattfeder F
molla F a balestra F
spring tooth
dent F flexible
diente M de resorte M
Federzinken M
dente M flessibile

air seeder
semoir [M] pneumatique
sembradora [F] neumática
Saatmaschine [F]
seminatrice [F]

seed and liquid fertilizer tank
réservoir [M] à graines [F] et à fertilisant [M]
depósito [M] de semillas [F] y fertilizante [M]
Saat- und Flüssigdüngertank [M]
serbatoio [M] per concime [M] liquido e semi [M]

spring-mounted leveling bar
barre [F] de nivellement [M] sur ressorts [M]
barra [F] niveladora con resortes [M]
gefederter Nivellierungsbalken [M]
barra [F] livellatrice montata su molla [F]

serrated disk
disque [M] denté
disco [M] serrado
gezackte Scheibe [F]
disco [M] a denti [M] seghettati

rotary hoe
houe [F] rotative à pointes [F]
motocultor [M]
Bodenfräse [F]
zappatrice [F]

wheel
roue [F]
rueda [F]
Rad [N]
ruota [F]

spring tooth
dent [F] flexible
varilla [F] de rastra
Federzinke [F]
dente [M] flessibile lungo

leveling blade
lame [F] de nivellement [M]
barra [F] niveladora
Nivellierungsblatt [N]
lama [F] livellatrice

disk harrow
herse [F] à disques [M]
rastra [F] de discos [M]
Scheibenegge [F]
erpice [M] frangizolle trainato

hydraulic cylinder
cylindre [M] hydraulique
cilindro [M] hidráulico
hydraulischer Hubzylinder [M]
cilindro [M] a sollevamento [M] idraulico

frame
structure [F]
estructura [F]
Rahmen [M]
telaio [M]

draw bar hitch
barre [F] d'attelage [M]
enganche [M] de barra [F] de tracción [F]
Deichselanhängerkupplung [F]
gancio [M] d'attacco [M] della barra [F] di trazione [F]

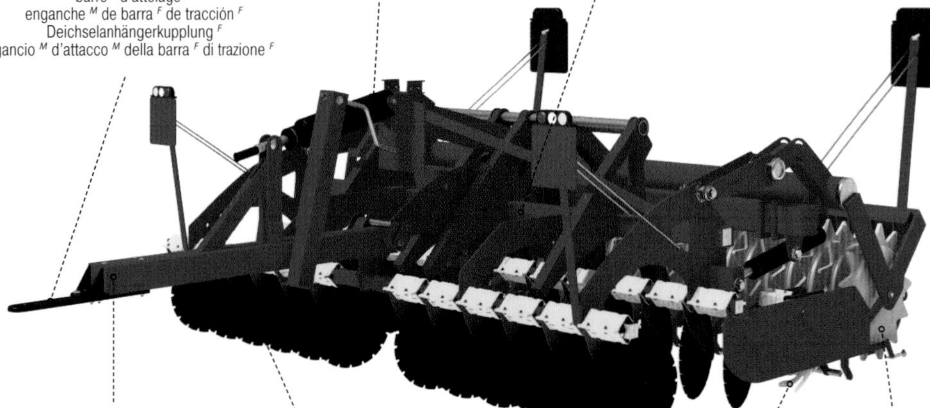

draw bar
barre [F] de traction [F]
barra [F] de tracción [F]
Deichsel [F]
barra [F] di traino

disk
disque [M]
disco [M]
eingekerbte Scheibe [F]
disco [M]

rotary hoe
houe [F] rotative à pointes [F]
motocultor [M]
Bodenfräse [F]
zappatrice [F]

roller
rouleau [M]
rueda [F] dentada
Walze [F]
rullo [M] con ruote [F] a stella [F]

FALLEN
ROCKS

fallen rocks
éboulement [M] de rochers [M]
desprendimeinto [M] de rocas [F]
Steinschlag [M]
caduta massi [M]

PAVEMENT
ENDS

pavement ends
fin [F] de la voie [F] pavée
fin de pavimento [M]
Ende [N] des Straßenbelags [M]
fine [F] manto [M] stradale

LOOSE
GRAVEL

loose gravel
gravillons [M]
gravilla [F]
Schotter [M]
ghiaia [F]

NO
PASSING
ZONE

no passing zone
zone [F] de non-dépassement [M]
zona [F] de no rebasar
Überholverbot [N]
zone [F] di divieto [M] di sorpasso [M]

35
M.P.H.

advisory speed
vitesse [F] conseiller
velocidad [F] aconsejable
Richtgeschwindigkeit [F]
velocità [F] consigliata

SPEED
LIMIT
80
km/h

metric speed limit
limite [F] de vitesse [F] métrique
límite [M] de velocidad [F] metrica
Zulässige Höchstgeschwindigkeit [F] in metrischen
limite [M] di velocità [F] in metri [M]

SPEED
LIMIT
50

speed limit
limite [F] de vitesse [F]
límite [M] de velocidad [F]
Zulässige Höchstgeschwindigkeit [F]
limite [M] di velocità [F]

signal ahead
feux [M] de circulation [F]
semáforo [M] más adelante
Ampel [F]
semaforo [M]

road narrows
rétrécissement [M] de chaussée [F]
estrechamiento [M] de vía [F]
Straßenverengung [F]
strettoia [F]

truck crossing
passage [M] pour camions [M]
cruce [M] de camiones [M]
LKW [M] kreuzen
attraversamento [M] di camion [M]

two-way traffic
circulation [F] dans les deux sens [M]
tráfico [M] en ambas direcciones [F]
Gegenverkehr [M]
doppio senso [M] di circolazione [F]

DIVIDED
HIGHWAY

divided highway crossing
passage [M] d'autoroute [F] à chaussées [F] séparées
cruce [M] de autopista [F]
Geteilte Autobahn [F]
attraversamento [M] divisione autostrada [F]

DETOUR

bicycle and pedestrian detour
détour [M] pour piétons [M] et cyclistes [M]
desvio [M] de bicicletas [F] y peatones [M]
Umleitung [F] für Fahrräder [N] und Fussgänger [M]
deviazione [F] pedoni [M] e biciclette [F]

EXIT
CLOSED

exit closed
sortie [F] barrée
salida [F] cerrada
Ausfahrt [F] geschlossen
uscita [F] chiusa

pedestrian crossing
passage [M] pour piétons [M]
paso [M] de peatones [M]
Fußgängerüberweg [M]
attraversamento [M] pedonale

handicapped crossing
passage [M] pour personnes [F] handicappées
paso de peatones [M] discapacitados
Behinderte [M]
attraversamento [M] disabili [M]

school zone or area
zone [F] d'écoliers [M]
zona [F] escolar
Schulzone [F]
scuola [F]

obstruction to be passed on left
obstruction, [F] passage [M] sur la gauche [F]
obstrucción, [F] pase por la izquierda [F]
Hindernis [N] links
ostruzione [F] passaggio [M] a sinistra [F]

obstruction to be passed on right or left
obstruction, [F] passage [M] sur la gauche [F] ou la droite [F]
obstrucción, [F] pase por la izquierda o la derecha [F]
Hindernis [N] rechts oder links
ostruzione [F] passaggio [M] a destra o a sinistra [F]

obstruction to be passed on right
obstruction, [F] passage [M] sur la droite
obstrucción, [F] pase por la derecha [F]
Hindernis [N] rechts
ostruzione [F] passaggio [M] a destra [F]

ONLY

right turn only
virage [M] à droite [F] uniquement
giro [M] a la derecha [F] únicamente
Abbiegen [N] nach rechts
girare solo a destra [F]

ONLY

intersection lane control
signalisation [F] d'intersection [F]
control [M] de carril [F] de intersección [F]
Vorgeschriebene Spuren [F] an der Kreuzung [F]
controllo [M] corsia [F] di intersezione [F]

ONLY

straight ahead only
aller tout-droit uniquement
sentido [M] obligatorio
Vorgeschriebene Fahrtrichtung [F] geradeaus
direzione [F] obbligatoria diritto

WEIGHT
LIMIT
8T
12T
16T

truck weight limit
poids [M] limite pour camions [M]
limite [M] de peso [M] de camiones [M]
Gewichtsbegrenzung [N] für LKW [N]
limite [M] di peso [M] del camion [M]

RAILROAD
CROSSING

railroad crossing
passage [M] à niveau
cruce [M] de ferrocarril [M]
Bahnübergang [M]
attraversamento [M] ferroviario

HOV
LANE
AHEAD

HOV lane ahead
voie [F] réservée au covoiturage [M]
carril VAO [M] más adelante
Fahrgemeinschaftsspur [F]
corsia [F] HOV più avanti

left or through
tourner à gauche ou avancer tout-droit
izquierda [F] o recto [M]
Nach links oder geradeaus
sinistra [F] o diritto [M]

road ending at T intersection
route [F] finissant en intersection [F] en T
arretera [F] termina en intersección [F] en T
traße [F] endet an T-förmiger Kreuzung [F]
fine strada [F] con intersezione [F] a T

sharp curve to left (arrow)
virage [M] serré à gauche (flèche [F])
curva [F] cerrada a la izquierda [F] (flecha [F])
scharfe Kurve [F] (links)
curva [F] stretta a sinistra [F]

sharp curve to left (chevron)
virage [M] serré à gauce (chevron [M])
curva [F] cerrada a la izquierda [F] (cheurón [M])
scharfe Kurve [F] (links)
curva [F] stretta a destra [F]

DETOUR

detour
détour [M]
desvío [M]
Umleitung [F]
deviazione [F]

DO NOT
ENTER

do not enter
ne pas entrer
prohibido el paso [M]
Einfahrt [F] verboten
non entrare

WRONG
WAY

wrong way
mauvais sens [M]
dirección [F] prohibida
falsche Richtung [F]
direzione [F] errata

YIELD

yield
cédez le passage [M]
ceda el paso [M]
Vorfahrt [F] gewähren
dare precedenza [F]

STOP

stop
arrêt [M]
alto [M]
Halt. Vorfahrt [F] gewähren
stop [M]

divided highway ahead
autoroute ^{F} à chaussées ^{F} séparées
autovía ^{F} más adelante
Geteilte Autobahn ^{F}
autostrada ^{F} divisa più avanti

flagger ahead
signaleur ^{M}
señalizador ^{M} más adelante
Signalmann ^{M}
segnalazioni ^{F} più avanti

road works
travaux ^{M} routiers
obras ^{F}
Baustelle ^{F}
lavori ^{M}

270-degree loop
boucle ^{F} à 270 degrés ^{M}
curva ^{F} de 270 grados ^{M}
270-Grad-Schleife ^{F}
curva ^{F} di 270 gradi ^{M}

curve
virage ^{M}
curva ^{F}
Kurve ^{F}
curva ^{F}

hairpin curve
courbe ^{F} serrée
curva ^{F} de volteo ^{M}
Haarnadelkurve ^{F}
tornante ^{M}

25

curve with speed advisory
courbe ^{F} avec vitesse ^{F} recommandée
curva ^{F} con límite ^{M} de velocidad ^{F}
Kurve ^{F} mit Tempolimit ^{N}
curva ^{F} con velocità ^{F} consigliata

circular intersection ahead
rond-point ^{M}
redoma ^{F} más adelante
Kreisverkehr ^{M}
intersezione ^{M} circolare più avanti

side road (right)
route ^{F} secondaire (à droite)
carretera ^{F} secundaria a la derecha ^{F}
Nebenstraße ^{F} (rechts)
strada ^{F} laterale destra ^{F}

reverse turns
série ^{F} de virages ^{M}
curvas ^{F} peligrosas
Doppelt Abbiegen ^{N}
doppia curva ^{F} la prima a sinistra

road narrows
rétrécissement ^{M} par la droite ^{F}
estrechamiento ^{M} de carretera ^{F}
Straßenverengung ^{F}
strettoia ^{F}

cross road ahead
intersection ^{F}
cruce ^{M} de carretera ^{F} más adelante
Straßenkreuzung ^{F}
incrocio ^{M} più avanti

winding road
virages ^{M}
carretera ^{F} sinuosa
Kurvenreiche Straße ^{F}
strada ^{F} sinuosa

T intersection ahead
intersection ^{F} en T
intersección ^{F} en T más adelante
T-förmige Kreuzung ^{F}
intersezione ^{F} a T più avanti

merging traffic
trafic ^{M} entrant
incorporación ^{F} de tráfico ^{M}
Einmündung ^{F} Zusammenführung ^{F}
zweier Straßen ^{F} zu Einer
confluenza ^{F}

added lane
nouvelle voie ^{F}
incorporación ^{F} de carril ^{M}
Zusammenführung ^{F} Spur von rechts
corsia ^{F} aggiunta

added lane
voie ^{F} supplémentaire
incorporación ^{F} de carril ^{M}
Zusammenführung ^{F} Spur von rechts
corsia ^{F} aggiunta

cattle crossing
passage [M] de bétail [M]
cruce [M] de ganado [M]
Viehtrieb [N] Tiere [N]
attraversamento [M] bestiame [M]

35

trucks rollover warning with speed advisory
risque [M] de renversement [M] et vitesse [F] recommandée
peligro [M] de volcamiento [M] con límite [M] de velocidad [F]
Lkw-Überschlagsgefahr [F] mit Tempolimit [F]
avvertenza [F] di ribaltamento [M] camion [M] con velocità [F] consigliata

12'-6"

low clearance ahead
hauteur [F] limitée
altura [F] baja más adelante
Verbot [N] für Fahrzeuge [N] über der angegebenen Höhe [F] einschließlich Ladung [F]
spazio [M] libero ribassato più avanti

no bicycles
interdit aux vélos [M]
prohibido [M] bicicletas [F]
Verbot [N] für Radfahrer [M]
transito [M] vietato alle biciclette [F]

no pedestrian crossing
traversée [F] de piétons [M] interdite
prohibido [M] el paso de peatones [M]
Kein Fußgängerüberweg [M]
divieto [M] di attraversamento [M] pedonale

P

no parking
stationnement [M] interdit
prohibido [M] estacionar [M]
Eingeschränktes Haltverbot [N]
divieto [M] di parcheggio [M]

no left turn
interdiction [F] de tourner à gauche [F]
giro [M] a la izquierda [F] prohibido
Abbiegen [N] nach links verboten
divieto [M] di svolta [F] a sinistra

no right turn
interdiction [F] de tourner à droite [F]
giro [M] a la derecha [F] prohibido
Abbiegen [N] nach rechts verboten
divieto [M] di svolta [F] a destra

no left or u turns
virages [M] à gauche et demi-tour [M] interdits
giro [M] a la izquierda [F] y media vuelta [F] prohibida
Abbiegen nach links und Wenden [N] verboten
divieto [M] di svolta [F] a sinistra o di inversione [F] ad U

no straight through
interdit d'aller tout droit
prohibido [M] seguir recto
Keine Durchfahrt [F]
divieto [M] di andare dritto

no U turn
demi-tour [M] interdit
media vuelta [F] prohibida
Wendeverbot [N]
divieto [M] di inversione [F] ad U

slippery when wet
risque [M] de chaussée [F] glissante
peligroso [M] al humedecerse
Bei Nässe [F] Rutschgefahr [F]
scivoloso con strada [F] bagnata

R R

railroad crossing
passage [M] à niveau [M]
cruce [M] de ferrocarril [M]
Bahnübergang [M]
attraversamento [M] ferroviario

deer crossing
passage [M] de cerfs [M]
cruce [M] de venado [M]
Wildwechsel [M]
attraversamento [M] di cervi [M]

tow away zone
risque [M] de remorquage [M]
zona [F] de remolque [M]
Abschleppzone [F]
zona [F] rimozione [M]

keep left
serrez à gauche [F]
mantenerse [M] a la izquierda [F]
Linkshalten [N]
tenere la sinistra [F]

ONE WAY

one way traffic
sens [M] unique
tráfico [M] en un solo sentido [M]
Einbahnstraße [F]
senso [M] unico

Airport exterior

Vue ^F^ extérieure de l'aéroport ^M^ | Exterior ^M^ del aeropuerto ^M^ | Flughafenaußenansicht ^F^ | Esterno ^M^ di un aeroporto ^M^

maintenance hangar
hangar ^M^ de maintenance ^F^
hangar ^M^ de mantenimiento ^M^
Flugzeugwartungshalle ^F^
hangar ^M^ di manutenzione ^F^ aeroportuale

runway
piste ^F^ d'envol ^M^
pista ^F^ de aterrizaje o despegue ^M^
Start- und Landebahn ^F^
pista ^F^ di rullaggio ^M^

road
route ^F^
carretera ^F^
Straße ^F^
strada ^F^ carrozzabile

parking lot
stationnement ^M^
playa ^F^ de estacionamiento ^M^
Parkplatz ^M^
area ^F^ di parcheggio ^M^

passenger terminal
aérogare ^F^ passagers ^M^
terminal ^F^ de pasajeros ^M^
Passagierterminal ^M^
terminal ^M^ passeggeri ^M^

taxiway
piste ^F de circulation ^F et d'attente ^F
pista ^F de rodaje ^M
Rollbahn ^F
pista ^F di rullaggio ^M
control tower
tour ^F de contrôle ^M
torre ^F de control ^M
Kontrollturm ^M
torre ^F di controllo ^M
control tower cab
cabine ^F de tour ^F de contrôle ^M
sala ^F de control ^M
Kontrollraum ^M
cabina ^F della torre ^F di controllo ^M
maneuvering area
aire ^F de manœuvre ^F
área ^M de maniobras ^F
Rollfeld ^N
area ^F di manovra ^F
service road
route ^F de service ^M
vía ^F de servicio ^M
Zufahrtsstraße ^F
strada ^F di servizio ^M
taxiway line
ligne ^F de voie ^F de circulation ^F
líneas ^F de pista ^F
Rollbahnmarkierung ^F
segnaletica ^F di pista ^F

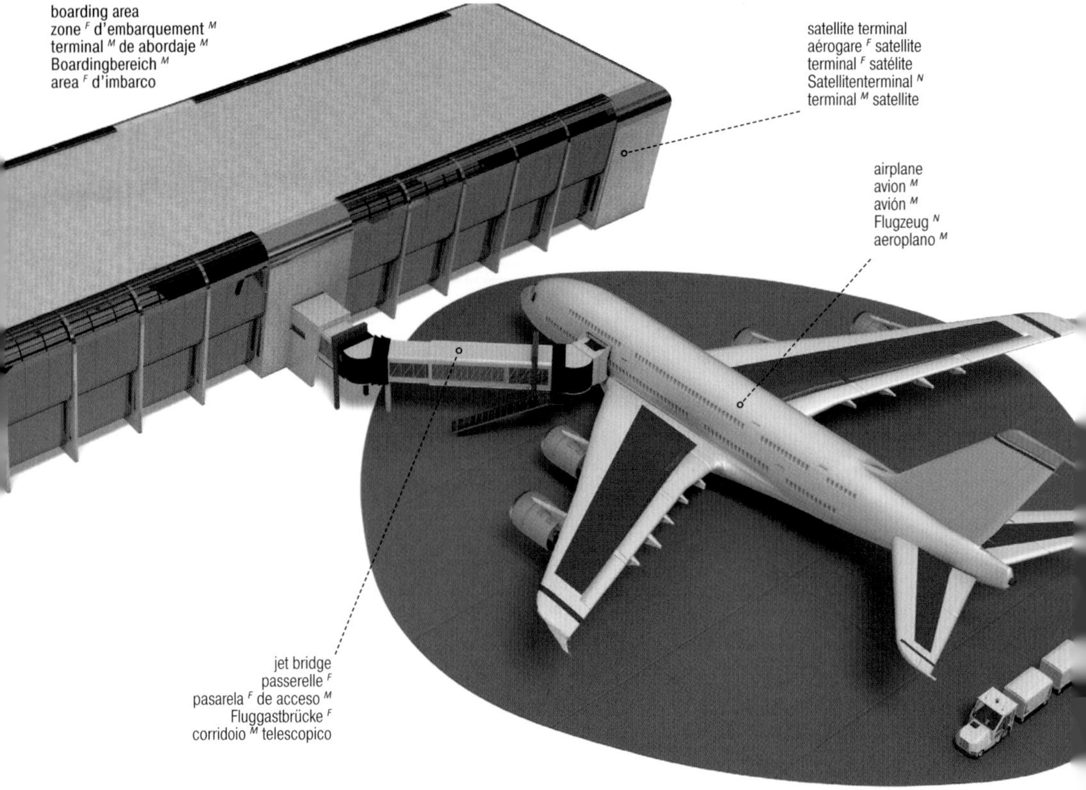
boarding area
zone F d'embarquement M
terminal M de abordaje M
Boardingbereich M
area F d'imbarco
satellite terminal
aérogare F satellite
terminal F satélite
Satellitenterminal N
terminal M satellite
airplane
avion M
avión M
Flugzeug N
aeroplano M
jet bridge
passerelle F
pasarela F de acceso M
Fluggastbrücke F
corridoio M telescopico

Airport interior

Vue F intérieure de l'aéroport M | Interior M del aeropuerto M | Im Innern des Flughafens M | Interno M di un aeroporto M

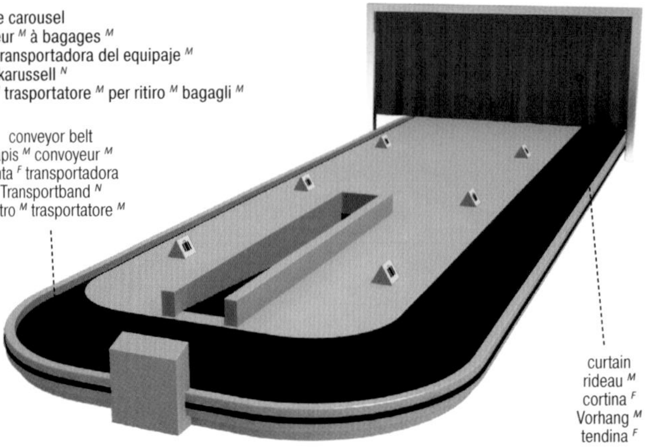
baggage carousel
convoyeur M à bagages M
cinta M transportadora del equipaje M
Gepäckkarussell N
nastro M trasportatore M per ritiro M bagagli M
conveyor belt
tapis M convoyeur M
cinta F transportadora
Transportband N
nastro M trasportatore M
curtain
rideau M
cortina F
Vorhang M
tendina F

baggage cart
chariot M à bagages M
carrito M para equipaje M
Gepäckwagen M
carrello M bagagli M
wheel
roue F
rueda F
Rad N
ruota F

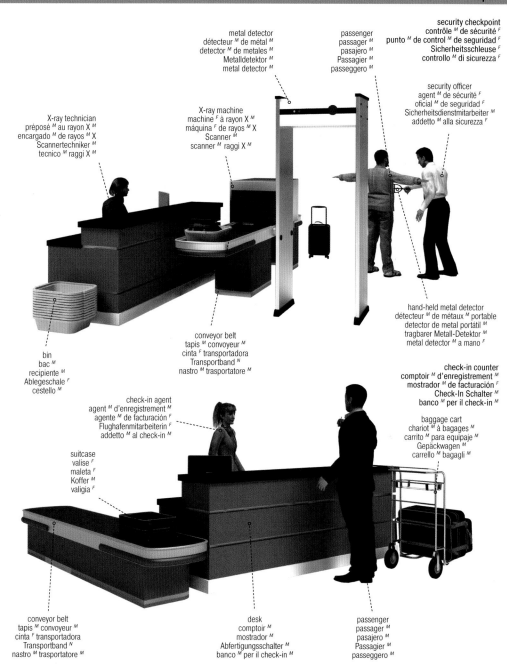

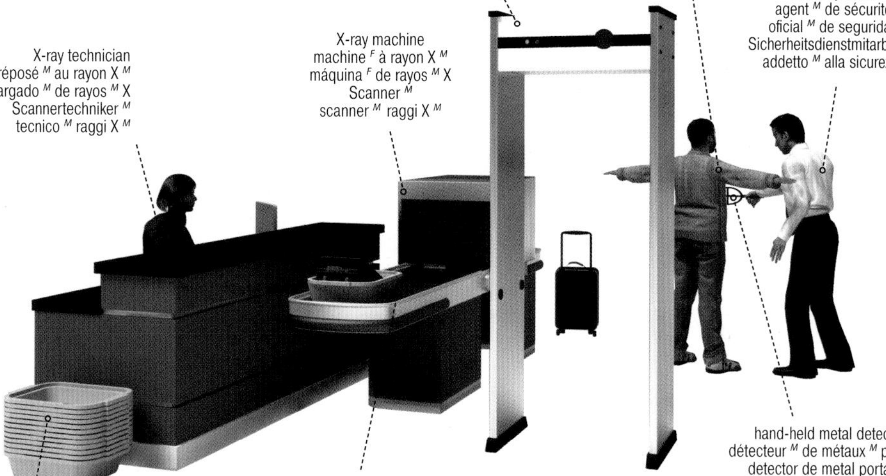
security checkpoint
contrôle M de sécurité F
punto M de control M de seguridad F
Sicherheitsschleuse F
controllo M di sicurezza F
metal detector
détecteur M de métal M
detector M de metales M
Metalldetektor M
metal detector M
passenger
passager M
pasajero M
Passagier M
passeggero M
security officer
agent M de sécurité F
oficial M de seguridad F
Sicherheitsdienstmitarbeiter M
addetto M alla sicurezza F
X-ray technician
préposé M au rayon X M
encargado M de rayos M X
Scannertechniker M
tecnico M raggi X M
X-ray machine
machine F à rayon X M
máquina F de rayos M X
Scanner M
scanner M raggi X M
hand-held metal detector
détecteur M de métaux M portable
detector de metal portátil M
tragbarer Metall-Detektor M
metal detector M a mano F
bin
bac M
recipiente M
Ablegeschale F
cestello M
conveyor belt
tapis M convoyeur M
cinta F transportadora
Transportband N
nastro M trasportatore M

check-in counter
comptoir M d'enregistrement M
mostrador M de facturación F
Check-In Schalter M
banco M per il check-in M
check-in agent
agent M d'enregistrement M
agente M de facturación F
Flughafenmitarbeiterin F
addetto M al check-in M
baggage cart
chariot M à bagages M
carrito M para equipaje M
Gepäckwagen M
carrello M bagagli M
suitcase
valise F
maleta F
Koffer M
valigia F
conveyor belt
tapis M convoyeur M
cinta F transportadora
Transportband N
nastro M trasportatore M
desk
comptoir M
mostrador M
Abfertigungsschalter M
banco M per il check-in M
passenger
passager M
pasajero M
Passagier M
passeggero M

departure area
aire ^{F} de départ ^{M}
área ^{M} de salida ^{F}
Abflugbereich ^{M}
zona ^{F} partenze ^{F}

flight information board
tableau ^{M} d'affichage ^{M} des vols ^{M}
panel ^{M} de información ^{M} de vuelos ^{M}
Fluginformationsanzeige ^{F}
tabellone ^{M} informazioni ^{F} sui voli ^{M}

baggage check-in counter
comptoir ^{M} d'enregistrement ^{M} des bagages ^{M}
facturación ^{F} de equipajes ^{M}
Gepäckabfertigungsschalter ^{M}
banco ^{M} di registrazione ^{F} bagaglio ^{M}

restroom
toilettes ^{F}
baños ^{M}
WC ^{N}
bagno ^{M}

coffee shop
café ^{M}
cafetería ^{F}
Café ^{N}
bar ^{M}

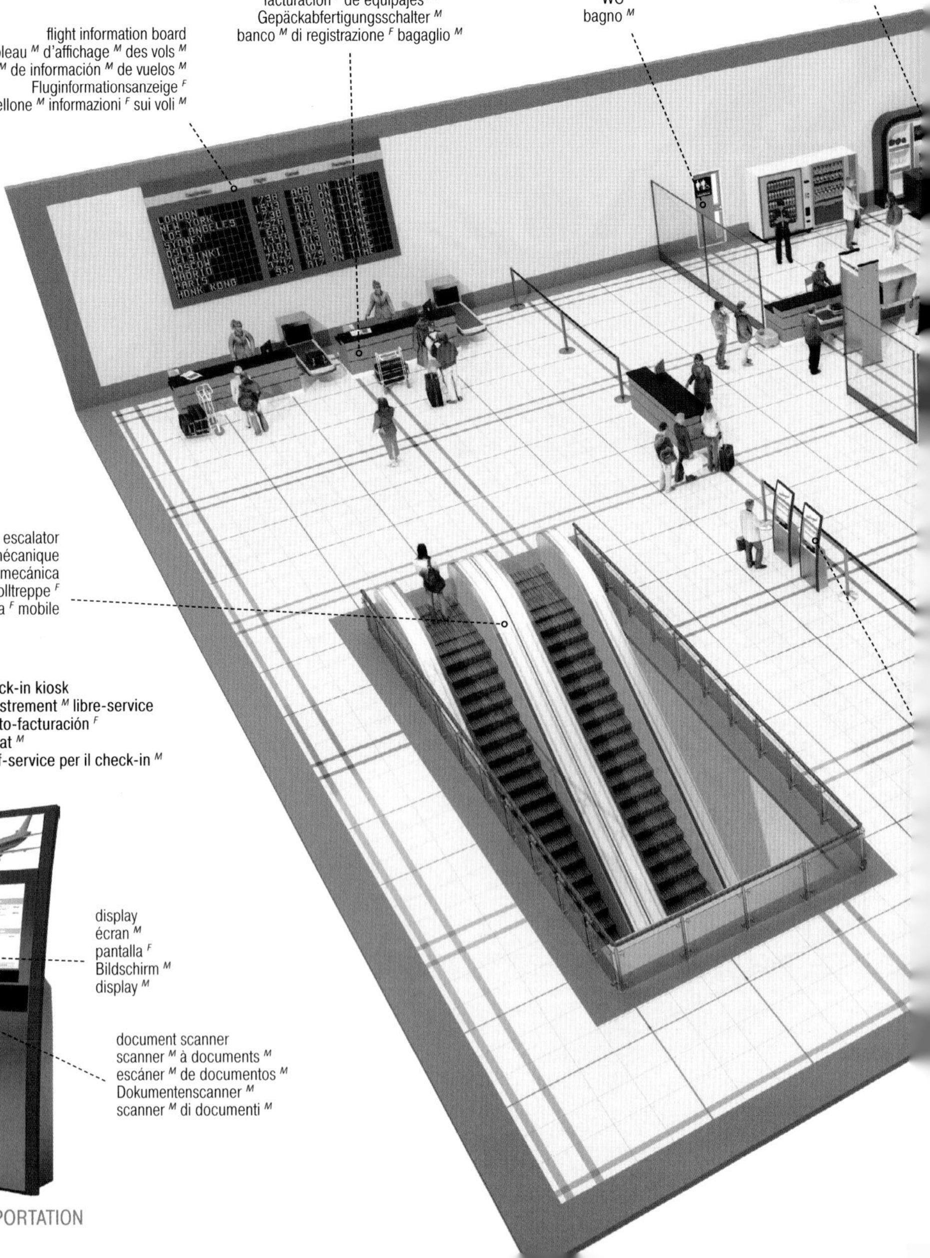

escalator
escalier ^{M} mécanique
escalera ^{F} mecánica
Rolltreppe ^{F}
scala ^{F} mobile

self-service check-in kiosk
borne ^{F} d'enregistrement ^{M} libre-service
quiosco ^{M} de auto-facturación ^{F}
Check-In Automat ^{M}
postazione ^{F} self-service per il check-in ^{M}

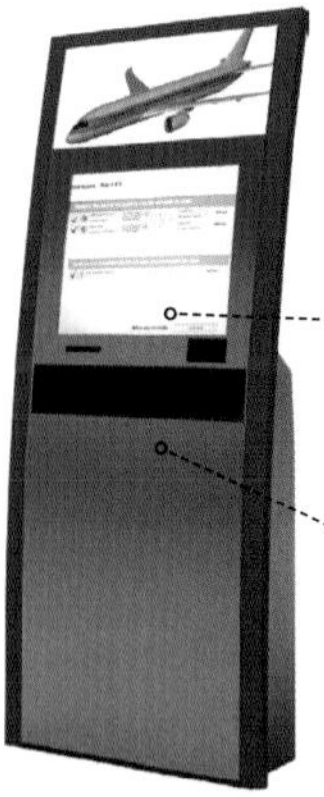

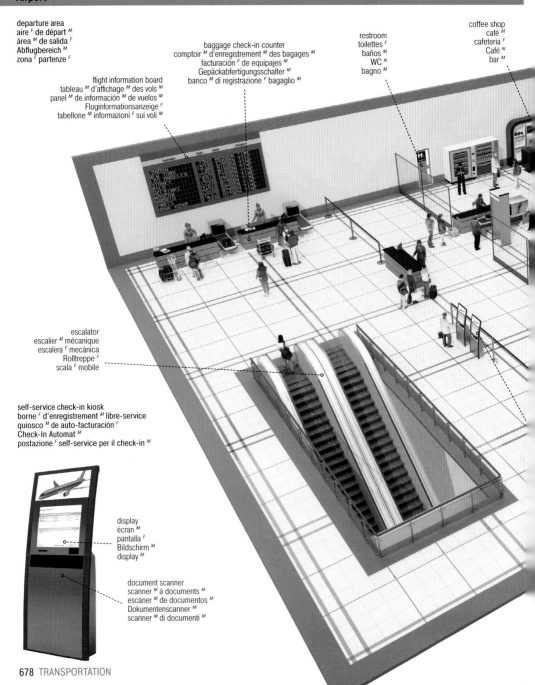

display
écran ^{M}
pantalla ^{F}
Bildschirm ^{M}
display ^{M}

document scanner
scanner ^{M} à documents ^{M}
escáner ^{M} de documentos ^{M}
Dokumentenscanner ^{M}
scanner ^{M} di documenti ^{M}

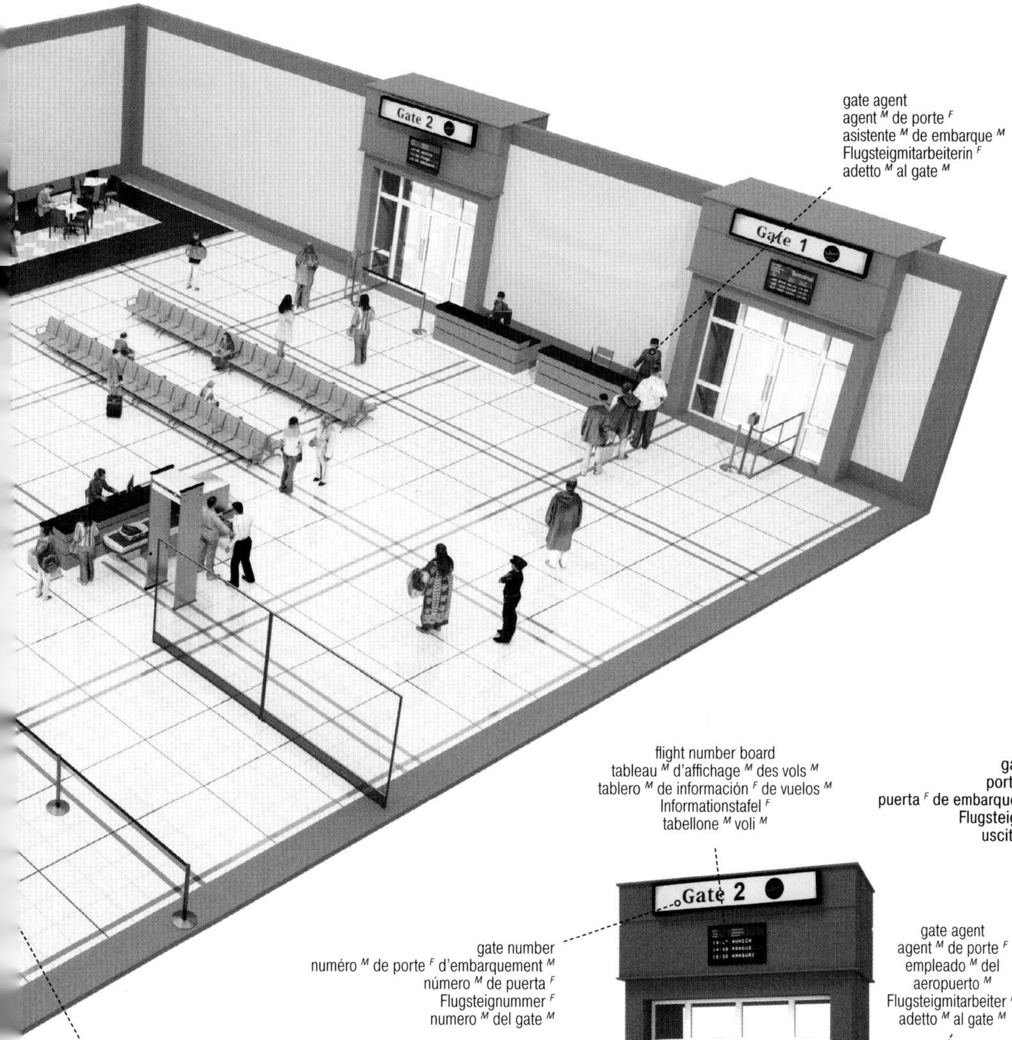

gate agent
agent ^{M} de porte ^{F}
asistente ^{M} de embarque ^{M}
Flugsteigmitarbeiterin ^{F}
adetto ^{M} al gate ^{M}

self-service check-in kiosk
borne ^{F} d'enregistrement ^{M} libre-service
quiosco ^{M} de auto-facturación ^{F}
Check-in-Automat ^{M}
postazione ^{F} self-service per il check-in ^{M}

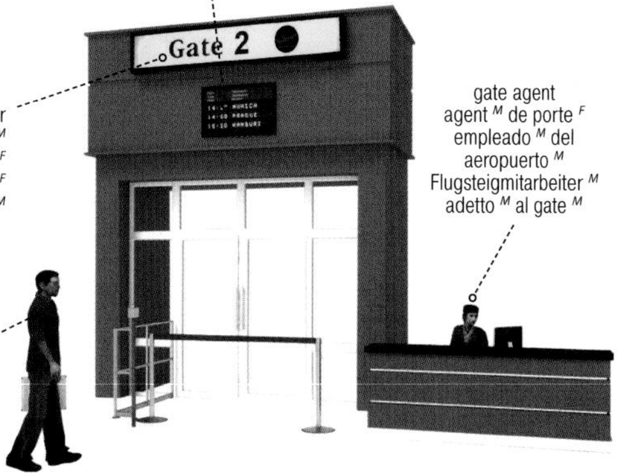

flight number board
tableau ^{M} d'affichage ^{M} des vols ^{M}
tablero ^{M} de información ^{F} de vuelos ^{M}
Informationstafel ^{F}
tabellone ^{M} voli ^{M}

gate
porte ^{F}
puerta ^{F} de embarque ^{M}
Flugsteig ^{M}
uscita ^{F}

gate number
numéro ^{M} de porte ^{F} d'embarquement ^{M}
número ^{M} de puerta ^{F}
Flugsteignummer ^{F}
numero ^{M} del gate ^{M}

gate agent
agent ^{M} de porte ^{F}
empleado ^{M} del aeropuerto ^{M}
Flugsteigmitarbeiter ^{M}
adetto ^{M} al gate ^{M}

passenger
passager ^{M}
pasajero ^{M}
Passagier ^{M}
passeggero ^{M}

arrival area
aire F d'arrivée F
área M de llegada F
Ankunftsbereich M
zona F arrivi M

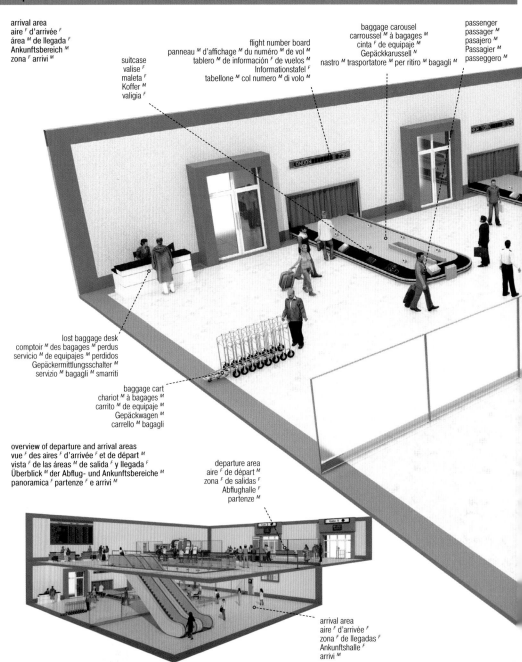

suitcase
valise F
maleta F
Koffer M
valigia F

flight number board
panneau M d'affichage M du numéro M de vol M
tablero M de información F de vuelos M
Informationstafel F
tabellone M col numero M di volo M

baggage carousel
carroussel M à bagages M
cinta F de equipaje M
Gepäckkarussell N
nastro M trasportatore M per ritiro M bagagli M

passenger
passager M
pasajero M
Passagier M
passeggero M

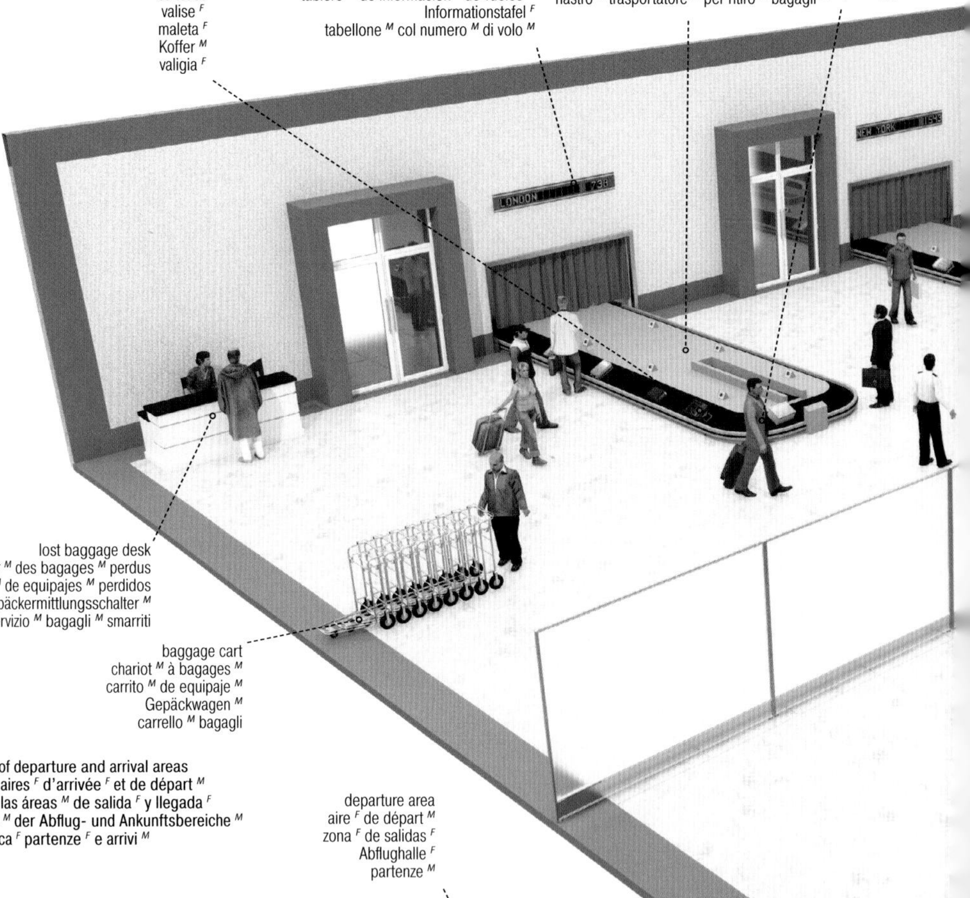

LONDON
738
NEW YORK

lost baggage desk
comptoir M des bagages M perdus
servicio M de equipajes M perdidos
Gepäckermittlungsschalter M
servizio M bagagli M smarriti

baggage cart
chariot M à bagages M
carrito M de equipaje M
Gepäckwagen M
carrello M bagagli

overview of departure and arrival areas
vue F des aires F d'arrivée F et de départ M
vista F de las áreas M de salida F y llegada F
Überblick M der Abflug- und Ankunftsbereiche M
panoramica F partenze F e arrivi M

departure area
aire F de départ M
zona F de salidas F
Abflughalle F
partenze M

Gate 1

arrival area
aire F d'arrivée F
zona F de llegadas F
Ankunftshalle F
arrivi M

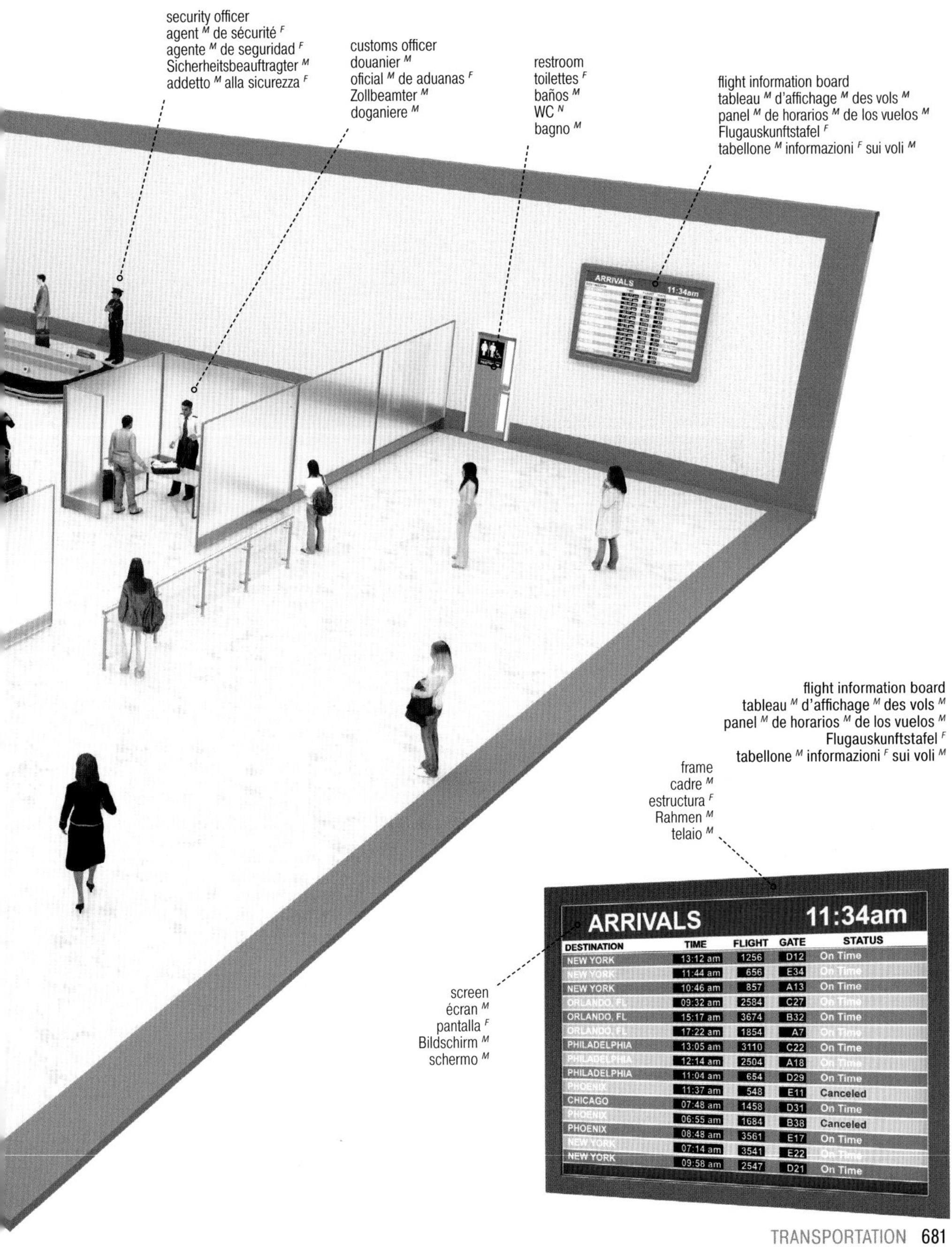
security officer
agent M de sécurité F
agente M de seguridad F
Sicherheitsbeauftragter M
addetto M alla sicurezza F
customs officer
douanier M
oficial M de aduanas F
Zollbeamter M
doganiere M
restroom
toilettes F
baños M
WC N
bagno M
flight information board
tableau M d'affichage M des vols M
panel M de horarios M de los vuelos M
Flugauskunftstafel F
tabellone M informazioni F sui voli M
ARRIVALS
11:34am
flight information board
tableau M d'affichage M des vols M
panel M de horarios M de los vuelos M
Flugauskunftstafel F
tabellone M informazioni F sui voli M
frame
cadre M
estructura F
Rahmen M
telaio M
screen
écran M
pantalla F
Bildschirm M
schermo M
ARRIVALS
11:34am
DESTINATION TIME FLIGHT GATE STATUS
NEW YORK 13:12 am 1256 D12 On Time
NEW YORK 11:44 am 656 E34 On Time
NEW YORK 10:46 am 857 A13 On Time
ORLANDO, FL 09:32 am 2584 C27 On Time
ORLANDO, FL 15:17 am 3674 B32 On Time
ORLANDO, FL 17:22 am 1854 A7 On Time
PHILADELPHIA 13:05 am 3110 C22 On Time
PHILADELPHIA 12:14 am 2504 A18 On Time
PHILADELPHIA 11:04 am 654 D29 On Time
PHOENIX 11:37 am 548 E11 Canceled
CHICAGO 07:48 am 1458 D31 On Time
PHOENIX 06:55 am 1684 B38 Canceled
PHOENIX 08:48 am 3561 E17 On Time
NEW YORK 07:14 am 3541 E22 On Time
NEW YORK 09:58 am 2547 D21 On Time

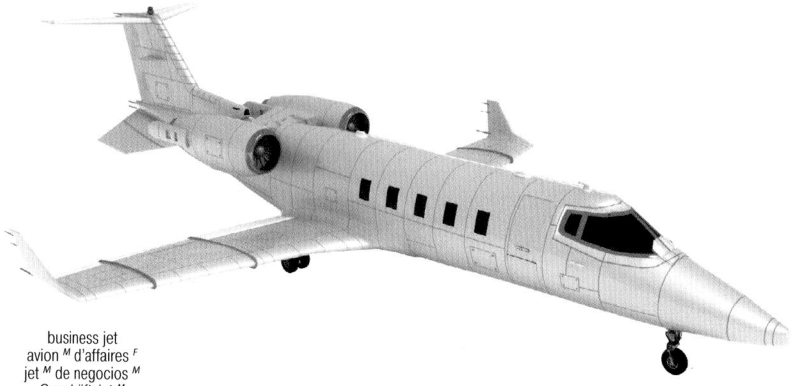

business jet
avion ^{M} d'affaires ^{F}
jet ^{M} de negocios ^{M}
Geschäftsjet ^{M}
jet ^{M} privato

flight attendant
agent de bord ^{M}
azafata ^{F}
Flugbegleiterin ^{F}
assistente $^{M/F}$ di volo ^{M}

light aircraft
avion ^{M} léger
avioneta ^{F}
Leichtfluzeug ^{N}
ultraleggero ^{M}

wide-body airliner
avion ^{M} de ligne ^{F} à fuselage ^{M} large
avión ^{M} de fuselaje ^{M} ancho
Großraumflugzeug ^{N}
aereo ^{M} a fusoliera ^{F} larga

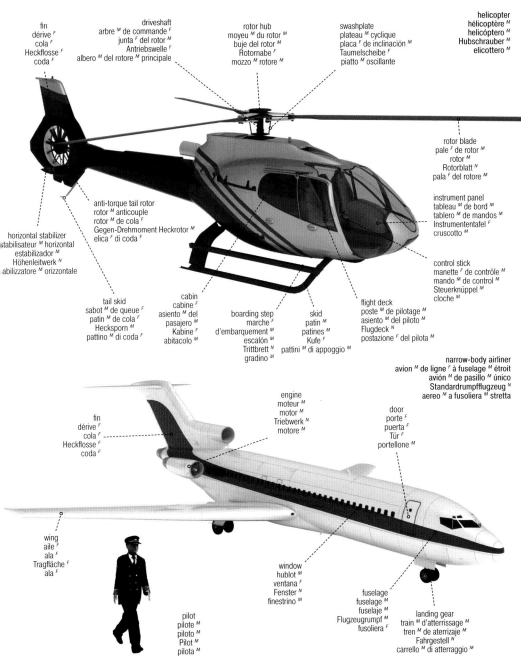

helicopter
hélicoptère M
helicóptero M
Hubschrauber M
elicottero M

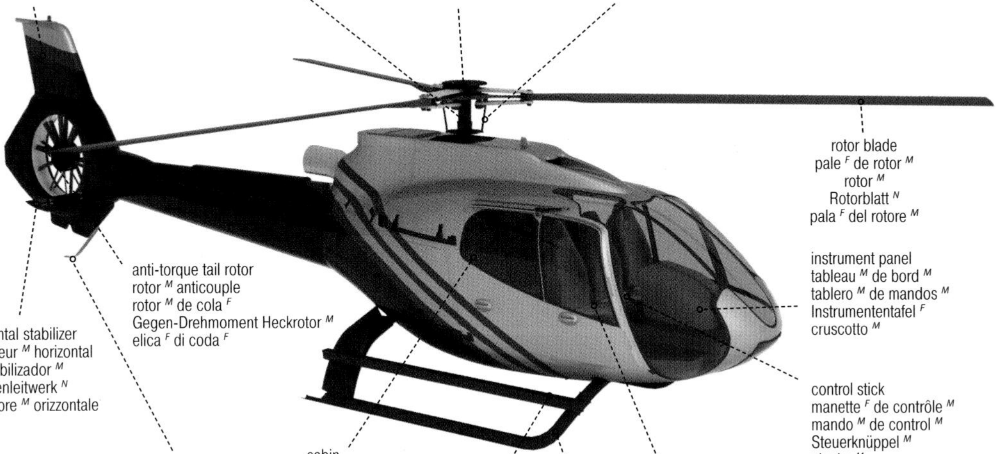
fin
dérive F
cola F
Heckflosse F
coda F
driveshaft
arbre M de commande F
junta F del rotor M
Antriebswelle F
albero M del rotore M principale
rotor hub
moyeu M du rotor M
buje del rotor M
Rotornabe F
mozzo M rotore M
swashplate
plateau M cyclique
placa F de inclinación M
Taumelscheibe F
piatto M oscillante
rotor blade
pale F de rotor M
rotor M
Rotorblatt N
pala F del rotore M
instrument panel
tableau M de bord M
tablero M de mandos M
Instrumententafel F
cruscotto M
anti-torque tail rotor
rotor M anticouple
rotor M de cola F
Gegen-Drehmoment Heckrotor M
elica F di coda F
horizontal stabilizer
tabilisateur M horizontal
estabilizador M
Höhenleitwerk N
abilizzatore M orizzontale
control stick
manette F de contrôle M
mando M de control M
Steuerknüppel M
cloche M
tail skid
sabot M de queue F
patín M de cola F
Hecksporn M
pattino M di coda F
cabin
cabine F
asiento M del pasajero M
Kabine F
abitacolo M
boarding step
marche F d'embarquement M
escalón M
Trittbrett N
gradino M
skid
patin M
patines M
Kufe F
pattini M di appoggio M
flight deck
poste M de pilotage M
asiento M del piloto M
Flugdeck N
postazione F del pilota M

narrow-body airliner
avion M de ligne F à fuselage M étroit
avión M de pasillo M único
Standardrumpfflugzeug N
aereo M a fusoliera M stretta

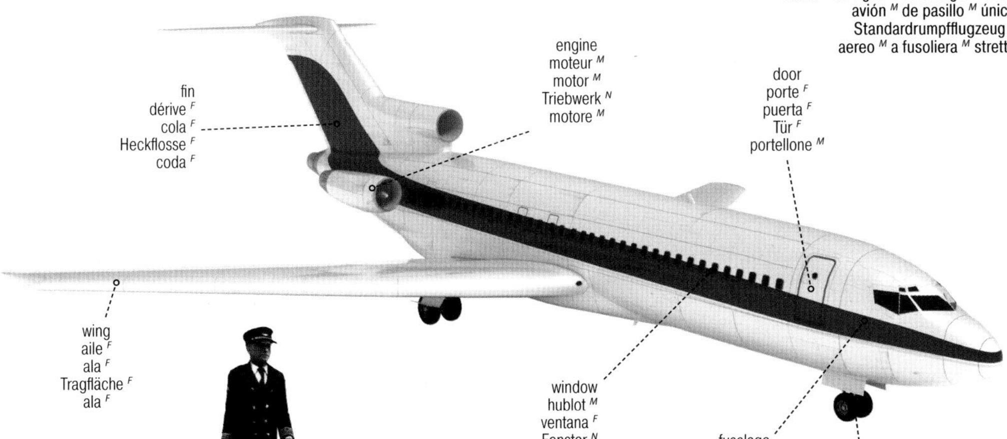
fin
dérive F
cola F
Heckflosse F
coda F
engine
moteur M
motor M
Triebwerk N
motore M
door
porte F
puerta F
Tür F
portellone M
wing
aile F
ala F
Tragfläche F
ala F
window
hublot M
ventana F
Fenster N
finestrino M
fuselage
fuselage M
fuselaje M
Flugzeugrumpf M
fusoliera F
landing gear
train M d'atterrissage M
tren M de aterrizaje M
Fahrgestell N
carrello M di atterraggio M

pilot
pilote M
piloto M
Pilot M
pilota M

catering vehicle
camion ^{M} commissariat ^{M}
camión ^{M} de catering ^{M}
Catering-Lkw ^{M}
camion ^{M} di ristorazione ^{F}

box
boîte ^{F}
caja ^{F}
Box ^{F}
box ^{M}
guardrail
rambarde ^{F}
barandilla ^{F}
Schutzgeländer ^{N}
barriera ^{F} di protezione ^{F}
platform
plate-forme ^{F}
plataforma ^{F}
Bühne ^{F}
piattaforma ^{F}
beacon
phare ^{M}
luz ^{F} intermitente
Rundumleuchte ^{F}
faro ^{M} lampeggiante

jet refueler
ravitailleur ^{M} de jet ^{M}
reabastecedor ^{M} de combustible ^{M}
Flugzeugtankwagen ^{M}
autocisterna ^{F} per rifornimento ^{M} aereo

baggage conveyor
descente F de bagages M
cinta F transportadora F de equipaje M
Gepäckband N
nastro M trasportatore M bagagli M

mobile closed passenger stairs
passerelle F amovible fermée
pasillo M cerrado
fahrbare überdachte Gangway F
passerella F chiusa

mobile passenger stairs
passerelle [F] amovible
escalera [F] de pasajeros [M] móvil
fahrbare Passagiertreppe [F]
scala [F] mobile per passaggeri [M]

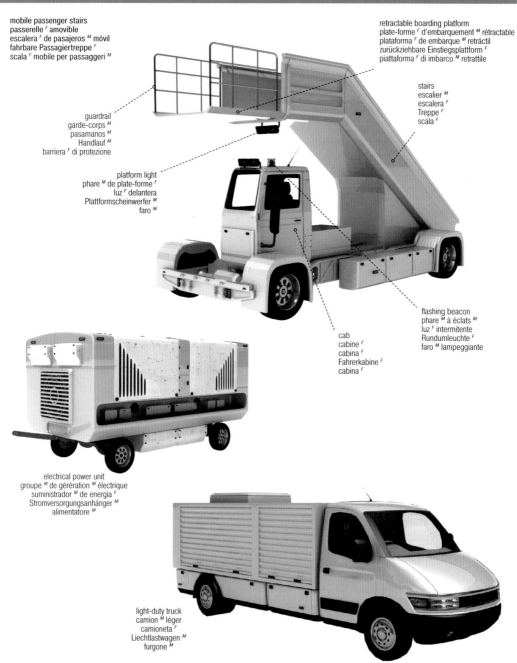

retractable boarding platform
plate-forme [F] d'embarquement [M] rétractable
plataforma [F] de embarque [M] retráctil
zurückziehbare Einstiegsplattform [F]
piattaforma [F] di imbarco [M] retrattile

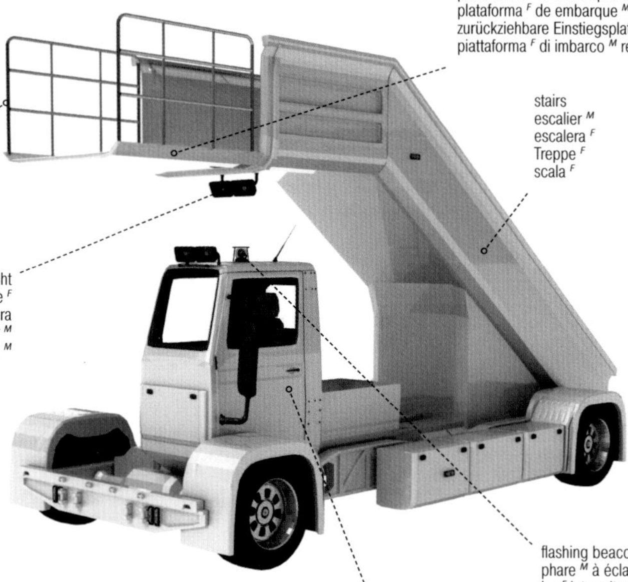

stairs
escalier [M]
escalera [F]
Treppe [F]
scala [F]

guardrail
garde-corps [M]
pasamanos [M]
Handlauf [M]
barriera [F] di protezione

platform light
phare [M] de plate-forme [F]
luz [F] delantera
Plattformscheinwerfer [M]
faro [M]

flashing beacon
phare [M] à éclats [M]
luz [F] intermitente
Rundumleuchte [F]
faro [M] lampeggiante

cab
cabine [F]
cabina [F]
Fahrerkabine [F]
cabina [F]

electrical power unit
groupe [M] de gérération [M] électrique
suministrador [M] de energía [F]
Stromversorgungsanhänger [M]
alimentatore [M]

light-duty truck
camion [M] léger
camioneta [F]
Liechtlastwagen [M]
furgone [M]

escort vehicle
véhicule M d'escorte F
coche M escolta
Begleitfahrzeug N
vettura F di scorta F

service vehicle
véhicule M de service M
vehículo M de servicio M
Servicefahrzeug N
vettura F di servizio M

mobile loading platform
plate-forme F de chargement M
plataforma F de carga F móvil
fahrbare Verladerampe F
piattaforma F di carico M

baggage vehicle
véhicule M de transport M de bagages M
vehículo M de equipajes M
Gepäckfahrzeug N veicolo M
portabagagli M

passenger shuttle
navette M de passagers M
transbordador M de pasajeros M
Passagiershuttle M
navetta F passeggeri M

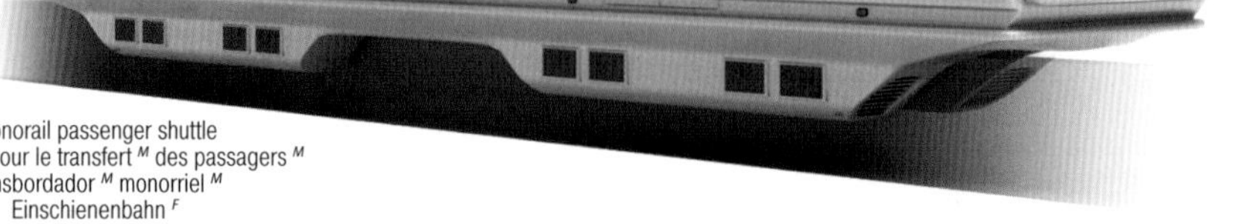

monorail passenger shuttle
monorail M pour le transfert M des passagers M
transbordador M monorriel M
Einschienenbahn F
tram M monorotaia

snowplow
chasse-neige M
quitanieves M
Schneepflug M
spazzaneve M

fire truck
camion M de pompier M
camión M de bomberos M
Feuerwehrfahrzeug N
autopompa F antincendi

pushback tug
camion M de remorquage M
remolcador M
Flugzeugschlepper M
trattore M aragosta F

passenger station
gare F de voyageurs M
estación F de tren M
Flughafen-Bahnhof M
stazione F ferroviaria

clock
horloge F
reloj M
Uhr F
orologio M

exit
sortie F
salida F
Ausgang M
uscita F

store
boutique F
tienda F
Laden M
negozio M

ticket office
billeterie F
oficina F de venta F de billetes M
Fahrkartenschalter M
biglietteria F

schedules information board
tableau M d'affichage M des horaires M
panel M de horarios M
Fahrplananzeigetafel F
tabellone M degli orari M

platform
quai M
andén M
Bahnsteig M
piattaforma F

bench
siège M
asiento M
Bank F
panchina F

stairs
escalier M
escaleras F
Treppe F
scale F

escalator
escalier M mécanique
escalera F mecánica
Rolltreppe F
scala F mobile

ticket vending machine
distributrice F de billets M
máquina F de venta F de billetes M
Fahrscheinautomat M
distributore M automatico di biglietti M

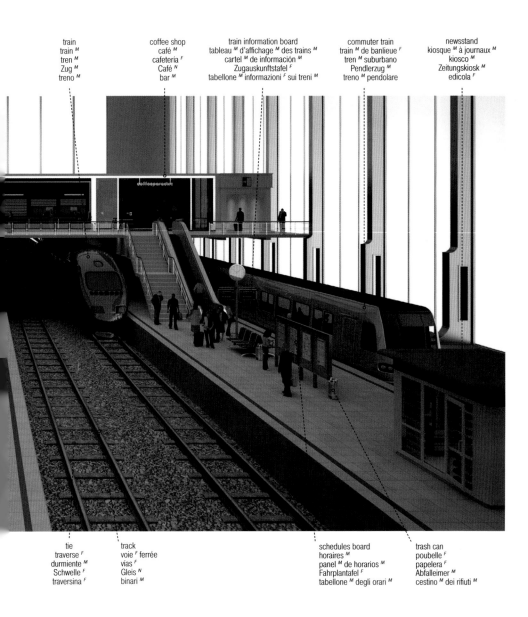

train
train [M]
tren [M]
Zug [M]
treno [M]
coffee shop
café [M]
cafetería [F]
Café [N]
bar [M]
train information board
tableau [M] d'affichage [M] des trains [M]
cartel [M] de información [M]
Zugauskunftstafel [F]
tabellone [M] informazioni [F] sui treni [M]
commuter train
train [M] de banlieue [F]
tren [M] suburbano
Pendlerzug [M]
treno [M] pendolare
newsstand
kiosque [M] à journaux [M]
kiosco [M]
Zeitungskiosk [M]
edicola [F]
tie
traverse [F]
durmiente [M]
Schwelle [F]
traversina [F]
track
voie [F] ferrée
vías [F]
Gleis [N]
binari [M]
schedules board
horaires [M]
panel [M] de horarios [M]
Fahrplantafel [F]
tabellone [M] degli orari [M]
trash can
poubelle [F]
papelera [F]
Abfalleimer [M]
cestino [M] dei rifiuti [M]

junction
correspondace [F]
empalme [M]
Bahnknotenpunkt [M]
snodo [M] ferroviario

water tower
chateau [M] d'eau [F]
torre [F] de agua [F]
Wasserturm [M]
torre [F] del serbatoio [M]

locomotive
locomotive [F]
locomotora [F]
Lokomotive [F]
locomotiva [F]

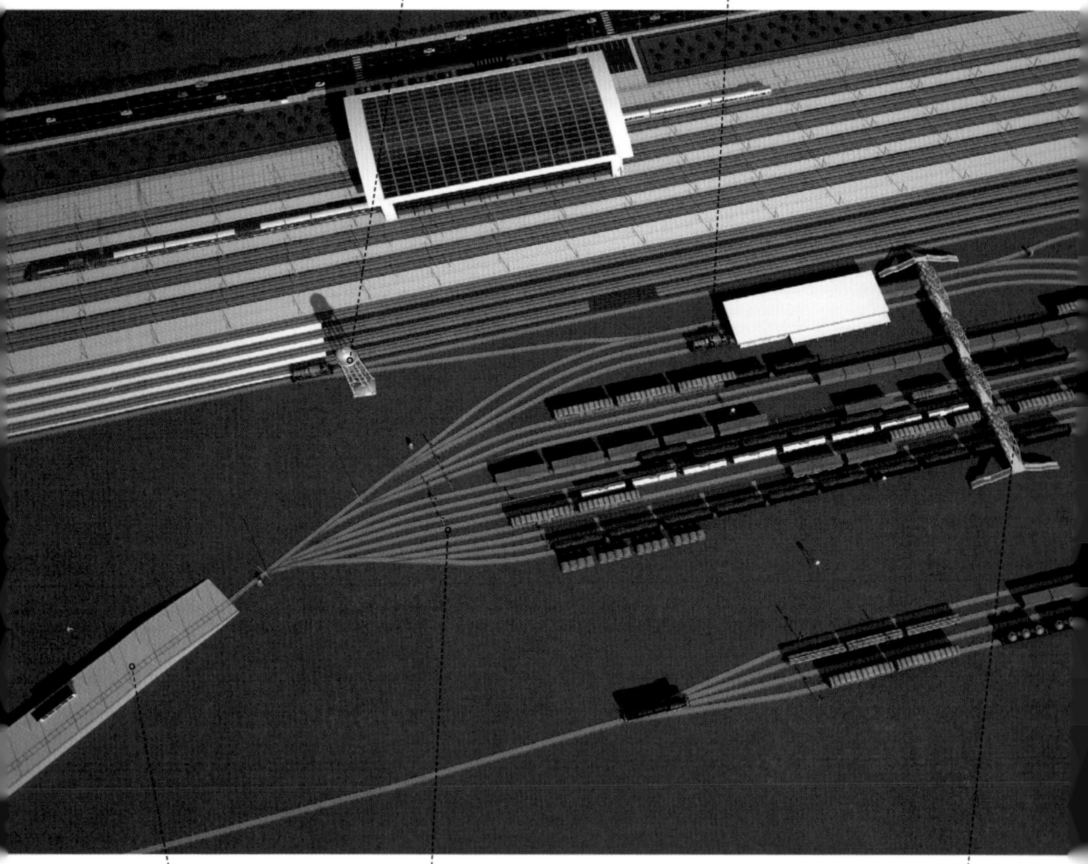

hump
butte [F]
plataforma [F] elevada
Ablaufberg [M]
dosso [M]

signal
signal [M]
semáforo [M]
Signalmast [M]
semaforo [M]

footbridge
passerelle [F]
pasarela [F]
Fußgängerbrücke [F]
ponte [M] pedonale

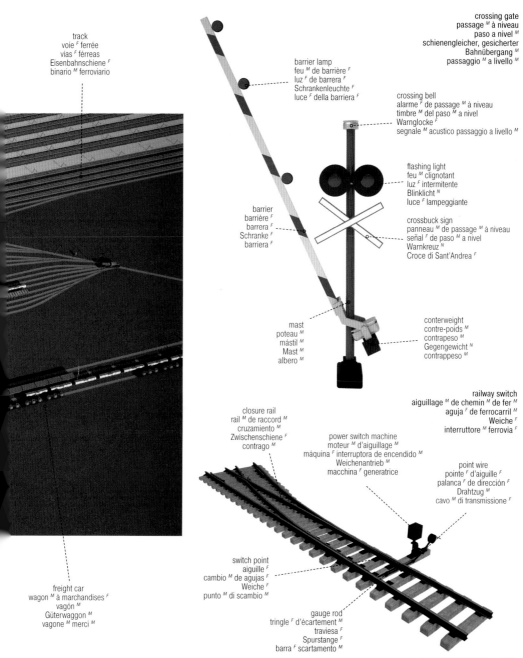

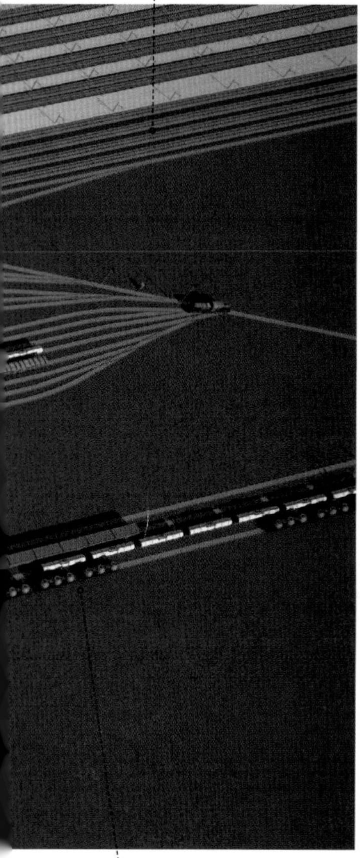
track
voie [F] ferrée
vías [F] férreas
Eisenbahnschiene [F]
binario [M] ferroviario
freight car
wagon [M] à marchandises [F]
vagón [M]
Güterwaggon [M]
vagone [M] merci [M]

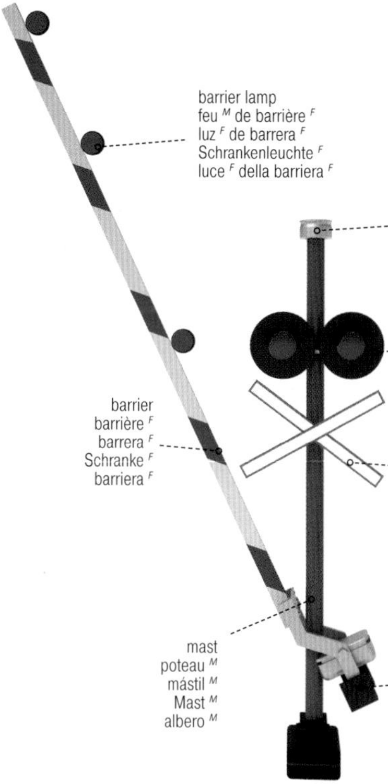
crossing gate
passage [M] à niveau
paso a nivel [M]
schienengleicher, gesicherter Bahnübergang [M]
passaggio [M] a livello [M]
barrier lamp
feu [M] de barrière [F]
luz [F] de barrera [F]
Schrankenleuchte [F]
luce [F] della barriera [F]
crossing bell
alarme [F] de passage [M] à niveau
timbre [M] del paso [M] a nivel
Warnglocke [F]
segnale [M] acustico passaggio a livello [M]
flashing light
feu [M] clignotant
luz [F] intermitente
Blinklicht [N]
luce [F] lampeggiante
barrier
barrière [F]
barrera [F]
Schranke [F]
barriera [F]
crossbuck sign
panneau [M] de passage [M] à niveau
señal [F] de paso [M] a nivel
Warnkreuz [N]
Croce di Sant'Andrea [F]
mast
poteau [M]
mástil [M]
Mast [M]
albero [M]
conterweight
contre-poids [M]
contrapeso [M]
Gegengewicht [N]
contrappeso [M]

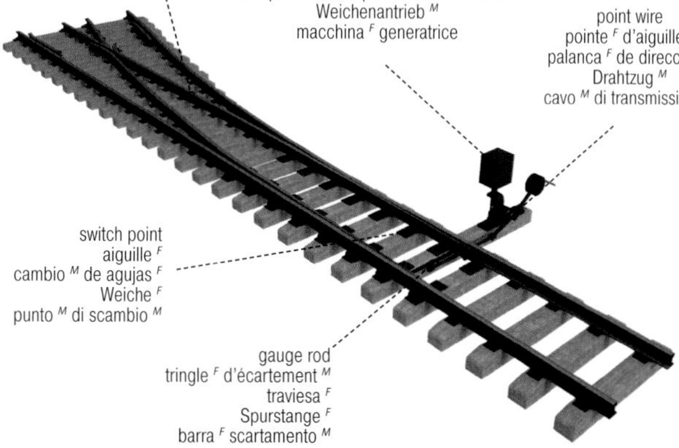
railway switch
aiguillage [M] de chemin [M] de fer [M]
aguja [F] de ferrocarril [M]
Weiche [F]
interruttore [M] ferrovia [F]
closure rail
rail [M] de raccord [M]
cruzamiento [M]
Zwischenschiene [F]
contrago [M]
power switch machine
moteur [M] d'aiguillage [M]
máquina [F] interruptora de encendido [M]
Weichenantrieb [M]
macchina [F] generatrice
point wire
pointe [F] d'aiguille [F]
palanca [F] de dirección [F]
Drahtzug [M]
cavo [M] di transmissione [F]
switch point
aiguille [F]
cambio [M] de agujas [F]
Weiche [F]
punto [M] di scambio [M]
gauge rod
tringle [F] d'écartement [M]
traviesa [F]
Spurstange [F]
barra [F] scartamento [M]

Urban rail transit

Transport ᴹ ferroviaire urbain | Transporte ᴹ ferroviario urbano | Stadtbahn ᶠ | Trasporto ᴹ ferroviario urbano

articulated streetcar
tramway ᴹ
tranvía ᴹ articulado
Gelenktriebwagen ᴹ
tram ᴹ articolato

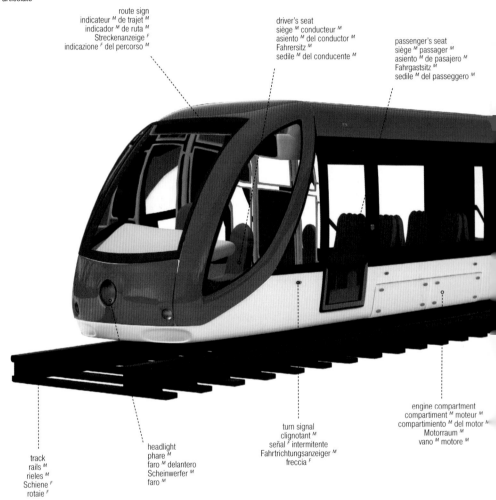

route sign
indicateur ᴹ de trajet ᴹ
indicador ᴹ de ruta ᴹ
Streckenanzeige ᶠ
indicazione ᶠ del percorso ᴹ
driver's seat
siège ᴹ conducteur ᴹ
asiento ᴹ del conductor ᴹ
Fahrersitz ᴹ
sedile ᴹ del conducente ᴹ
passenger's seat
siège ᴹ passager ᴹ
asiento ᴹ de pasajero ᴹ
Fahrgastsitz ᴹ
sedile ᴹ del passeggero ᴹ
engine compartment
compartiment ᴹ moteur ᴹ
compartimiento ᴹ del motor ᴹ
Motorraum ᴹ
vano ᴹ motore ᴹ
turn signal
clignotant ᴹ
señal ᶠ intermitente
Fahrtrichtungsanzeiger ᴹ
freccia ᶠ
headlight
phare ᴹ
faro ᴹ delantero
Scheinwerfer ᴹ
faro ᴹ
track
rails ᴹ
rieles ᴹ
Schiene ᶠ
rotaie ᶠ

subway
métro M
metro M / subterráneo M
Untergrundbahn F
metropolitana F

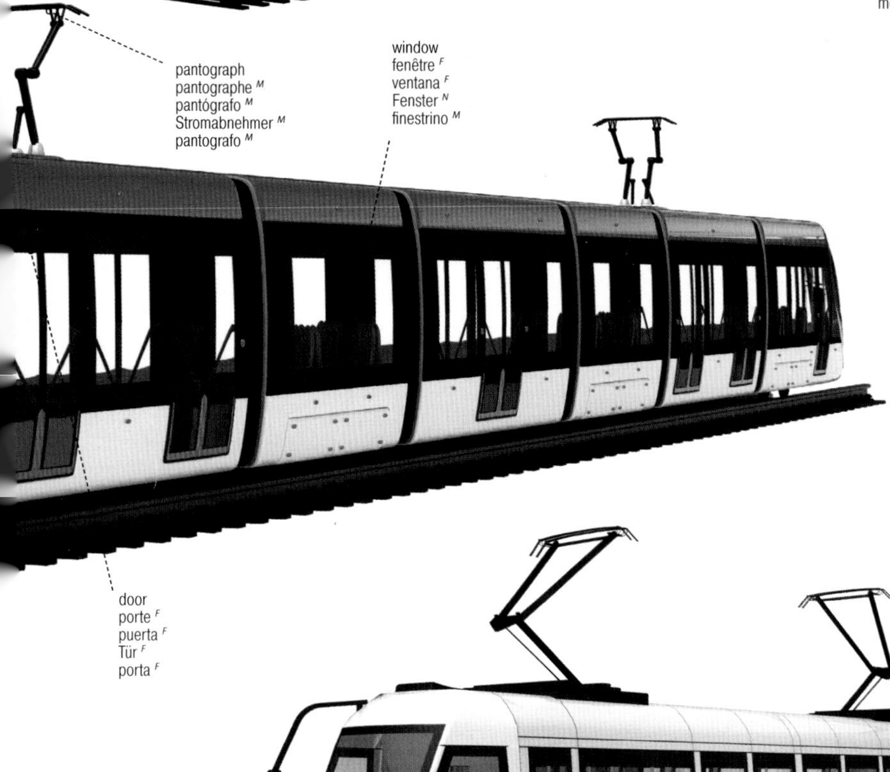
pantograph
pantographe M
pantógrafo M
Stromabnehmer M
pantografo M
window
fenêtre F
ventana F
Fenster N
finestrino M
door
porte F
puerta F
Tür F
porta F

tram
tramway M
tranvía M
Straßenbahn F
tram M

Intercity transport

Transport [M] interurbain | Transporte [M] interurbano | Fernverkehr [M] | Trasporto [M] interurbano

steam locomotive
locomotive [F] à vapeur [F]
locomotora [F] de vapor [M]
Dampflokomotive [F]
locomotiva [F] a vapore [M]

chimney
cheminée [F]
chimenea [F]
Schornstein [M]
camino [M]

driver's cab
cabine [F] du conducteur [M]
cabina [F] del conductor [M]
Fahrerkabine [F]
cabina [F] del conducente [M]

passenger car
wagon [M] de passagers [M]
vagón [M] de pasajeros [M]
Fahrgastwagen [M]
carrozza [F]

smokebox
boîte [F] à vapeur [F]
caja [F] de humos [M]
Rauchkammer [F]
camera [F] a fumo [M]

cylinder
cylindre [M]
mecanismo [M] de biela [F] y manivela [F]
Zylinder [M]
cilindro [M]

tender
tender [M]
ténder [M]
Tender [M]
carro [M] scorta [F]

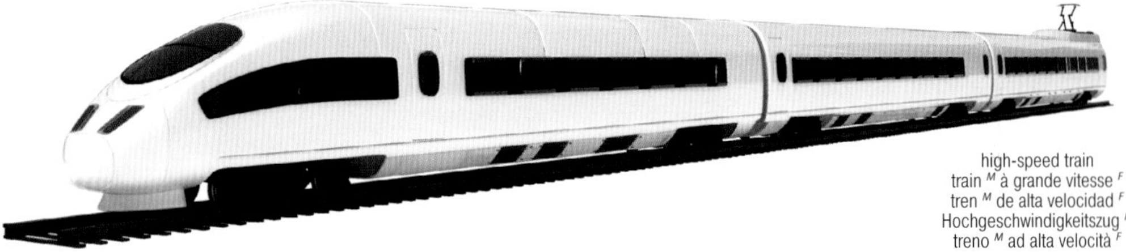

high-speed train
train [M] à grande vitesse [F]
tren [M] de alta velocidad [F]
Hochgeschwindigkeitszug [M]
treno [M] ad alta velocità [F]

electric multiple unit (EMU) train
train [M] avec rames [F] automotrices électriques
tren [M] de unidades eléctricas múltiples
Elektrotriebzug [M]
treno [M] automotore [M]

pantograph
pantographe [M]
pantógrafo [M]
Stromabnehmer [M]
pantografo [M]

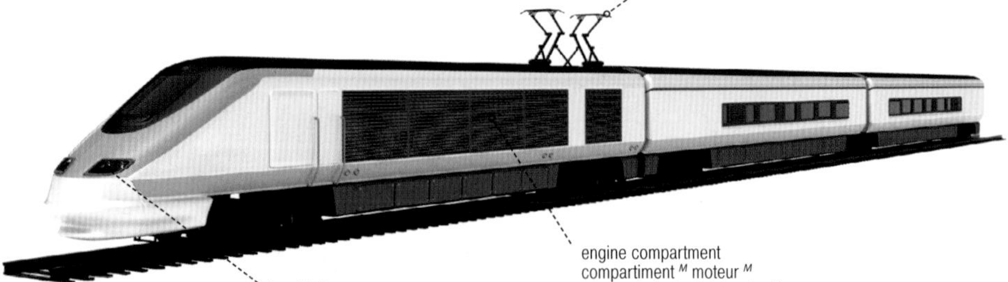

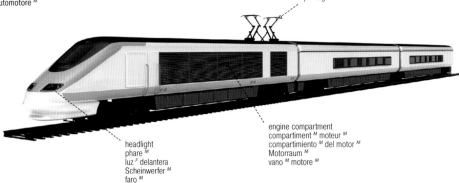

headlight
phare [M]
luz [F] delantera
Scheinwerfer [M]
faro [M]

engine compartment
compartiment [M] moteur [M]
compartimiento [M] del motor [M]
Motorraum [M]
vano [M] motore [M]

Locomotives

Locomotives F | Locomotoras F | Lokomotiven F | Locomotive F

diesel locomotive
locomotive F diesel
locomotora F diesel
Diesellokomotive F
locomotiva F con motore M diesel
headlight
phare M
luz F delantera
Scheinwerfer M
faro M
ventilation grille
grille F de ventilation F
rejilla F de ventilación M
Lüftungsschlitz M
feritoia F di ventilazione F
ditch light
phare M de fossé M
luz F de posición F
Lokscheinwerfer M
luce F di segnalazione F
driver's cab
cabine F du conducteur M
cabina F del conductor M
Fahrerkabine F
cabina F del conducente M
engine compartment
compartiment M moteur M
compartimiento M del motor M
Motorraum M
vano M motore M
buffer
tampon M
tope M
Puffer M
respingente M
guardrail
rambarde F
barandilla F
Handlauf M
barriera F di protezione
automatic coupler
coupleur M automatique
enganche M automático
automatische Kupplung F
gancio M automatico
fuel tank
réservoir M à essence F
depósito M de combustible M
Kraftstofftank M
serbatoio M del carburante M
battery compartment
compartiment M batterie F
compartimiento M de la batería F
Batteriefach N
vano M batteria F
wheel
roue F
rueda F
Zugantriebsrad N
ruota F motrice
truck frame
châssis M de bogie M
chasis M
Drehgestell N
telaio M
side footboard
marchepied M latéral
escalón M
Seitentrittbrett N
pedana F laterale
brake
frein M
freno M
Bremse F
freno M

electric locomotive
locomotive F électrique
locomotora F eléctrica
Elektrolokomotive F
locomotiva F elettrica

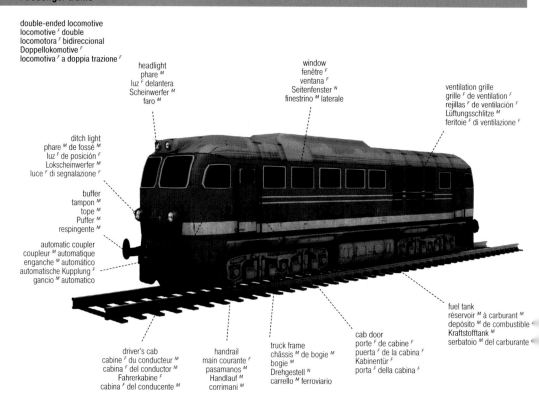

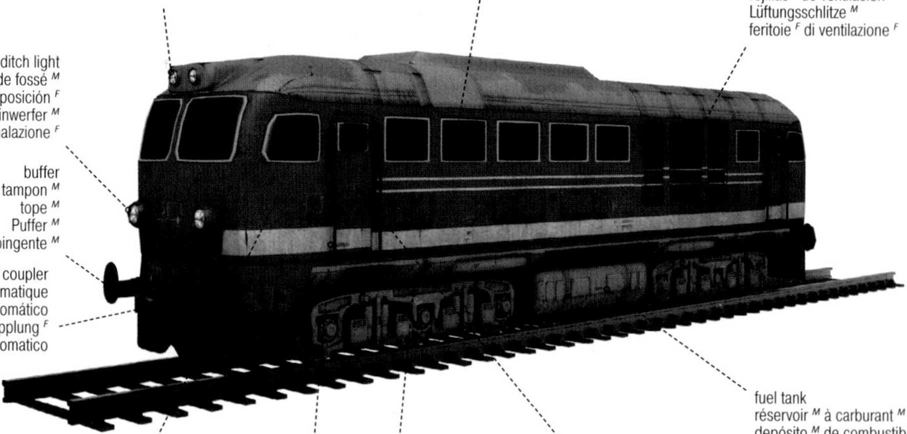
double-ended locomotive
locomotive [F] double
locomotora [F] bidireccional
Doppellokomotive [F]
locomotiva [F] a doppia trazione [F]
headlight
phare [M]
luz [F] delantera
Scheinwerfer [M]
faro [M]
window
fenêtre [F]
ventana [F]
Seitenfenster [N]
finestrino [M] laterale
ventilation grille
grille [F] de ventilation [F]
rejillas [F] de ventilación [F]
Lüftungsschlitze [M]
feritoie [F] di ventilazione [F]
ditch light
phare [M] de fossé [M]
luz [F] de posición [F]
Lokscheinwerfer [M]
luce [F] di segnalazione [F]
buffer
tampon [M]
tope [M]
Puffer [M]
respingente [M]
automatic coupler
coupleur [M] automatique
enganche [M] automático
automatische Kupplung [F]
gancio [M] automatico
fuel tank
réservoir [M] à carburant [M]
depósito [M] de combustible
Kraftstofftank [M]
serbatoio [M] del carburante
driver's cab
cabine [F] du conducteur [M]
cabina [F] del conductor [M]
Fahrerkabine [F]
cabina [F] del conducente [M]
handrail
main courante [F]
pasamanos [M]
Handlauf [M]
corrimani [M]
truck frame
châssis [M] de bogie [M]
bogie [M]
Drehgestell [N]
carrello [M] ferroviario
cab door
porte [F] de cabine [F]
puerta [F] de la cabina [F]
Kabinentür [F]
porta [F] della cabina [F]

Freight cars

double-door boxcar
wagon [M] couvert à double porte [F]
vagón [M] cubierto de doble puerta [F]
Geschlossener Doppeltür-Güterwaggon [M]
carro [M] merci [F] chiuso a doppia porta [F]

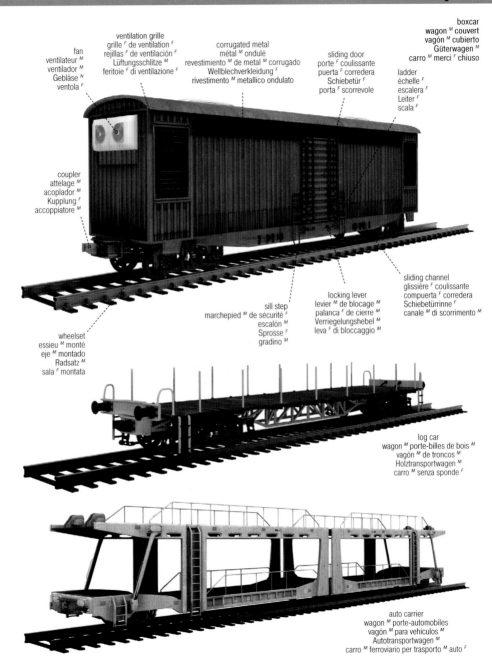

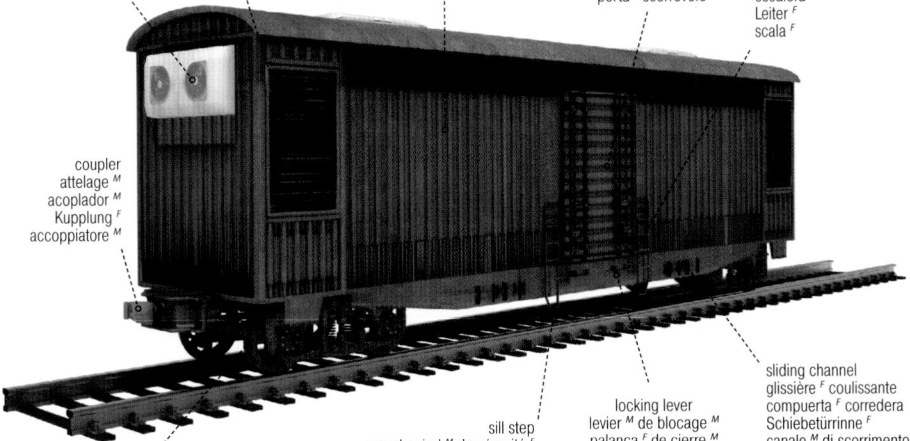
boxcar
wagon M couvert
vagón M cubierto
Güterwagen M
carro M merci F chiuso
fan
ventilateur M
ventilador M
Gebläse N
ventola F
ventilation grille
grille F de ventilation F
rejillas F de ventilación F
Lüftungsschlitze M
feritoie F di ventilazione F
corrugated metal
métal M ondulé
revestimiento M de metal M corrugado
Wellblechverkleidung F
rivestimento M metallico ondulato
sliding door
porte F coulissante
puerta F corredera
Schiebetür F
porta F scorrevole
ladder
échelle F
escalera F
Leiter F
scala F
coupler
attelage M
acoplador M
Kupplung F
accoppiatore M
sliding channel
glissière F coulissante
compuerta F corredera
Schiebetürrinne F
canale M di scorrimento M
locking lever
levier M de blocage M
palanca F de cierre M
Verriegelungshebel M
leva F di bloccaggio M
sill step
marchepied M de sécurité F
escalón M
Sprosse F
gradino M
wheelset
essieu M monté
eje M montado
Radsatz M
sala F montata

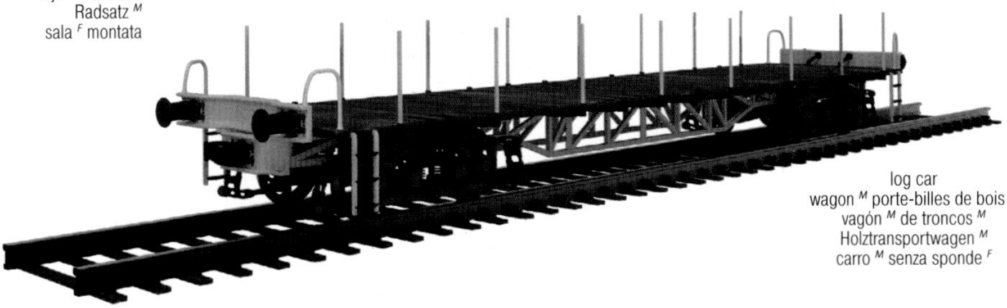
log car
wagon M porte-billes de bois M
vagón M de troncos M
Holztransportwagen M
carro M senza sponde F

auto carrier
wagon M porte-automobiles
vagón M para vehículos M
Autotransportwagen M
carro M ferroviario per trasporto M auto F

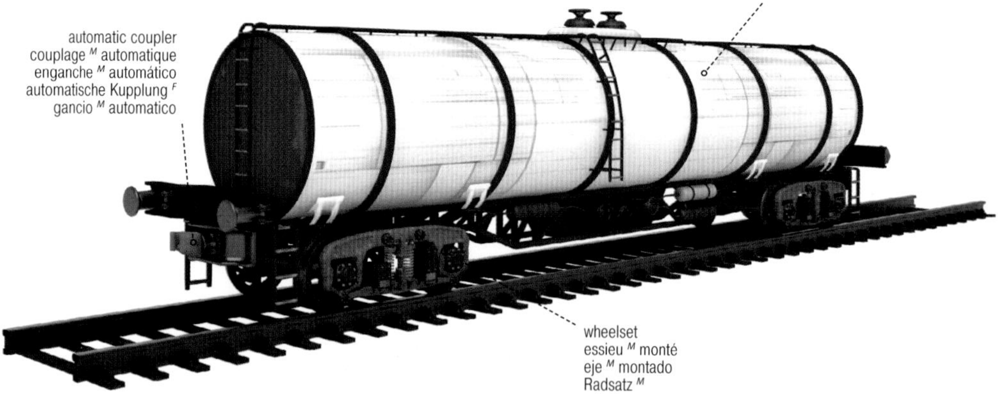
tank car
wagon-citerne M
vagón M cisterna F
Tankwagen M
vagone M cisterna F
tank
réservoir M
cisterna M
Tank M
serbatoio M
automatic coupler
couplage M automatique
enganche M automático
automatische Kupplung F
gancio M automatico
wheelset
essieu M monté
eje M montado
Radsatz M
sala F montata

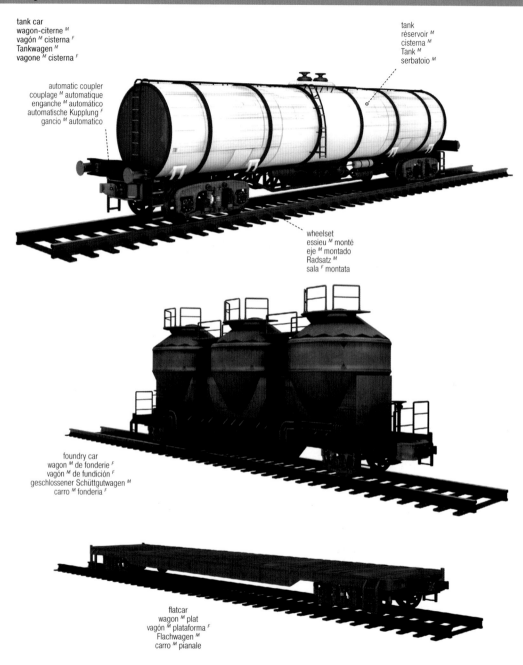

foundry car
wagon M de fonderie F
vagón M de fundición F
geschlossener Schüttgutwagen M
carro M fonderia F

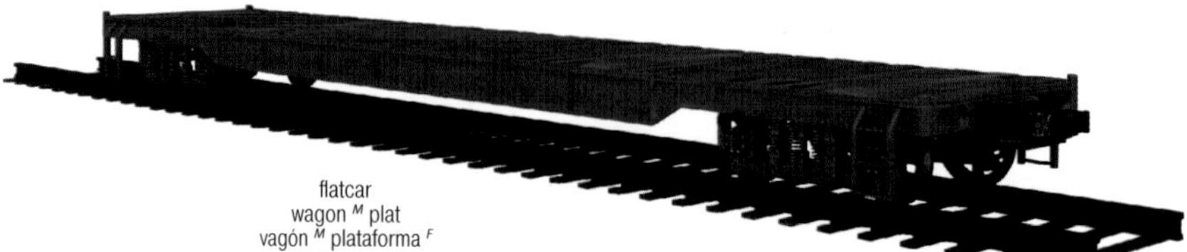
flatcar
wagon M plat
vagón M plataforma F
Flachwagen M
carro M pianale

crane car
wagon-grue ^{M}
grúa ^{F}
Kranwagen ^{M}
gru ^{F} ferroviaria ^{F}

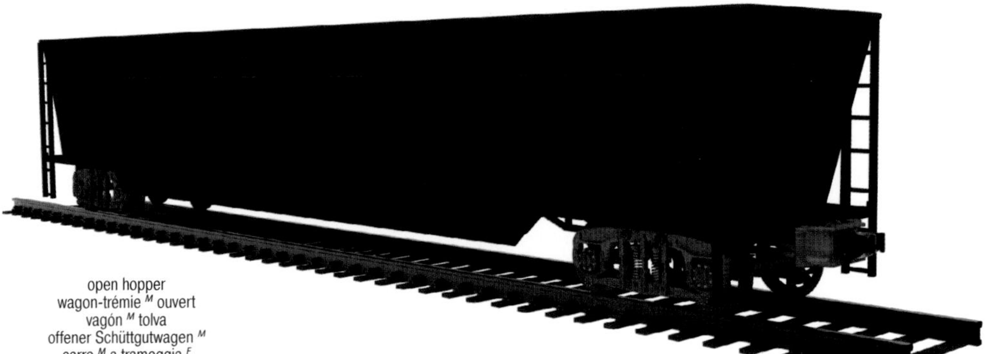

open hopper
wagon-trémie ^{M} ouvert
vagón ^{M} tolva
offener Schüttgutwagen ^{M}
carro ^{M} a tramoggia ^{F}

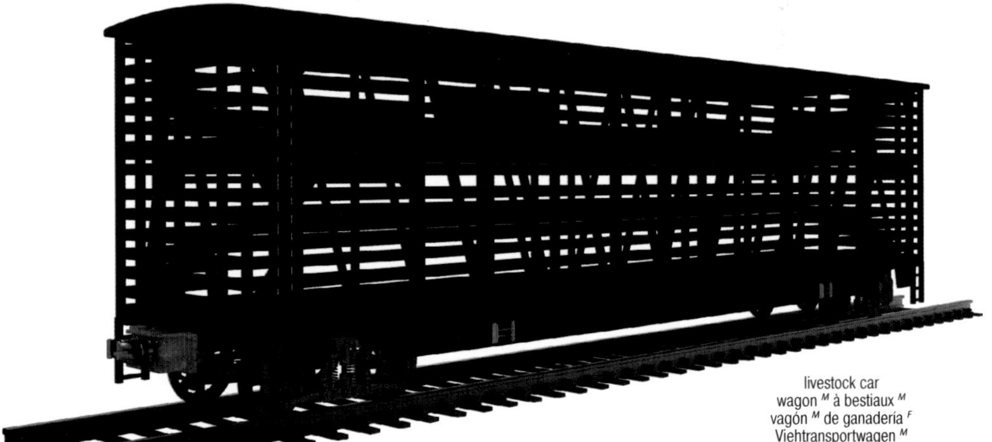

livestock car
wagon ^{M} à bestiaux ^{M}
vagón ^{M} de ganadería ^{F}
Viehtransportwagen ^{M}
carro ^{M} per bestiame ^{M}

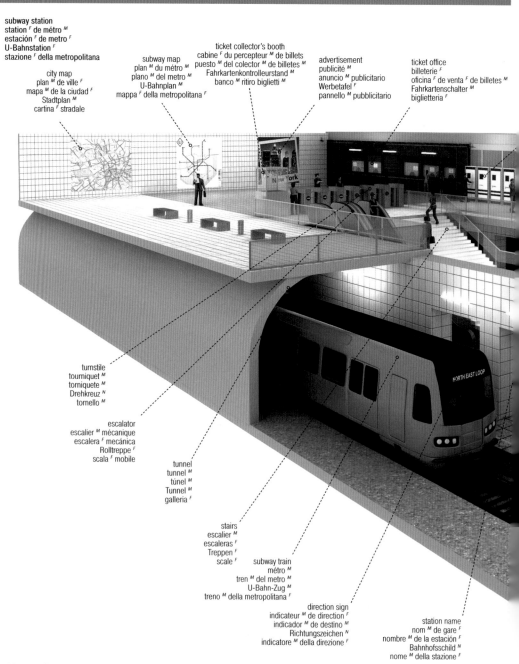

subway station
station ^{F} de métro ^{M}
estación ^{F} de metro ^{F}
U-Bahnstation ^{F}
stazione ^{F} della metropolitana

city map
plan ^{M} de ville ^{F}
mapa ^{M} de la ciudad ^{F}
Stadtplan ^{M}
cartina ^{F} stradale

subway map
plan ^{M} du métro ^{M}
plano ^{M} del metro ^{M}
U-Bahnplan ^{M}
mappa ^{F} della metropolitana ^{F}

ticket collector's booth
cabine ^{F} du percepteur ^{M} de billets
puesto ^{M} del colector ^{M} de billetes ^{M}
Fahrkartenkontrolleurstand ^{M}
banco ^{M} ritiro biglietti ^{M}

advertisement
publicité ^{M}
anuncio ^{M} publicitario
Werbetafel ^{F}
pannello ^{M} pubblicitario

ticket office
billeterie ^{F}
oficina ^{F} de venta ^{F} de billetes ^{M}
Fahrkartenschalter ^{M}
biglietteria ^{F}

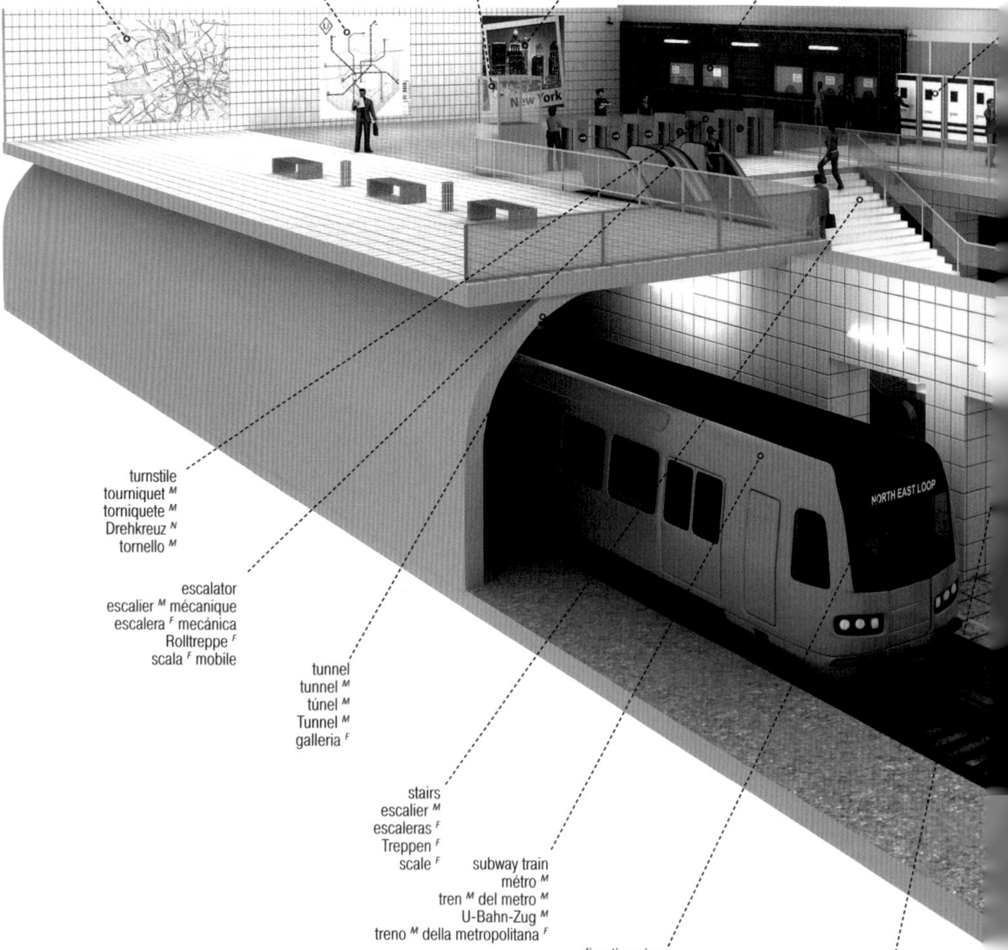
New York
NORTH EAST LOOP

turnstile
tourniquet ^{M}
torniquete ^{M}
Drehkreuz ^{N}
tornello ^{M}

escalator
escalier ^{M} mécanique
escalera ^{F} mecánica
Rolltreppe ^{F}
scala ^{F} mobile

tunnel
tunnel ^{M}
túnel ^{M}
Tunnel ^{M}
galleria ^{F}

stairs
escalier ^{M}
escaleras ^{F}
Treppen ^{F}
scale ^{F}

subway train
métro ^{M}
tren ^{M} del metro ^{M}
U-Bahn-Zug ^{M}
treno ^{M} della metropolitana ^{F}

direction sign
indicateur ^{M} de direction ^{F}
indicador ^{M} de destino ^{M}
Richtungszeichen ^{N}
indicatore ^{M} della direzione ^{F}

station name
nom ^{M} de gare ^{F}
nombre ^{M} de la estación ^{F}
Bahnhofsschild ^{N}
nome ^{M} della stazione ^{F}

ticket vending machine
distributrice F de billets M
máquina F de venta F de billetes M
Fahrkartenautomat M
distributore M automatico di biglietti M

automatic teller machine (ATM)
guichet M automatique bancaire (GAB)
cajero M automático
Bankautomat M
bancomat M

coffee shop
café M
cafetería F
Café N
bar M

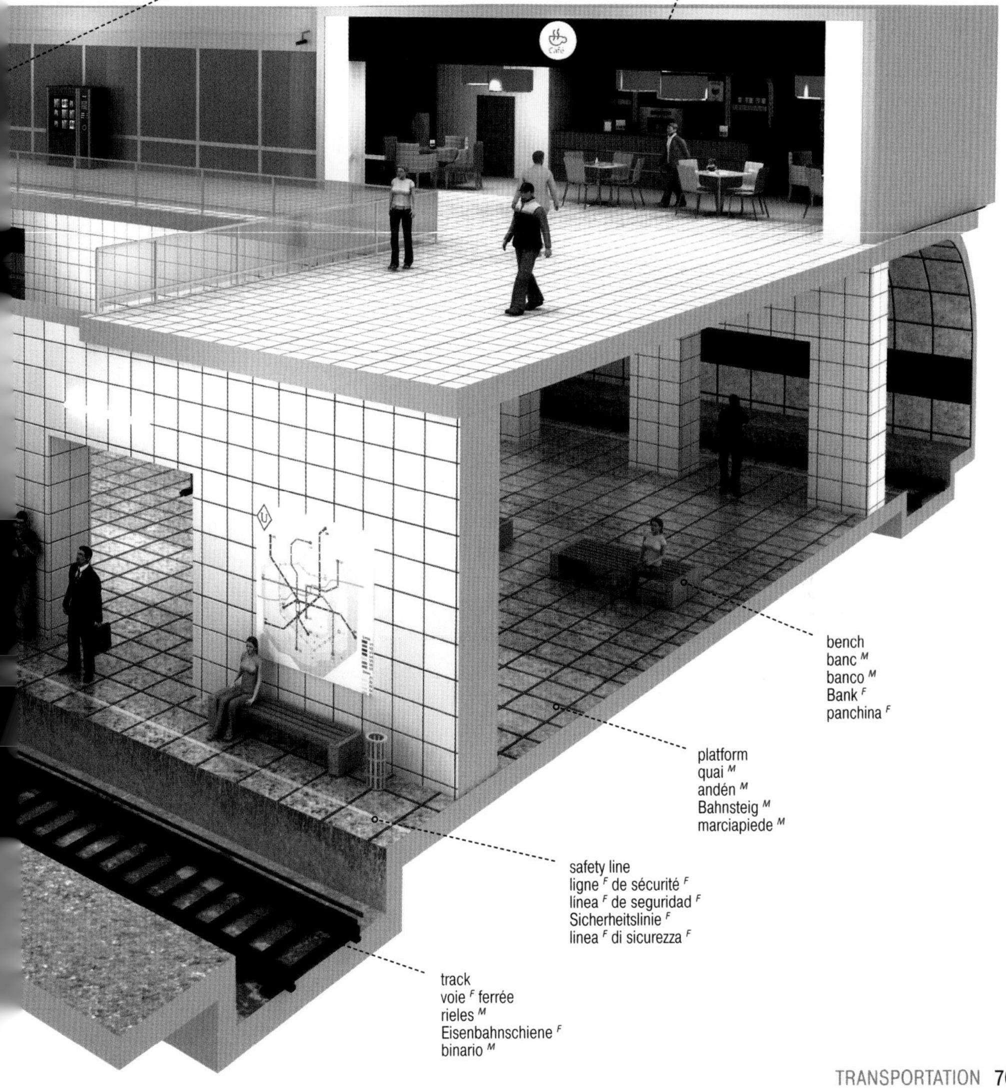
Café

bench
banc M
banco M
Bank F
panchina F

platform
quai M
andén M
Bahnsteig M
marciapiede M

safety line
ligne F de sécurité F
línea F de seguridad F
Sicherheitslinie F
linea F di sicurezza F

track
voie F ferrée
rieles M
Eisenbahnschiene F
binario M

port
port ^{M}
puerto ^{M}
Hafen ^{M}
porto ^{M}

transit shed
entrepôt ^{M} de transit ^{M}
almacén ^{M} de productos ^{M} en tránsito ^{M}
Transitlager ^{N}
deposito ^{M} di transito

tanker
tanker ^{M}
buque ^{M} petrolero
Tanker ^{M}
nave ^{F} cisterna ^{F}

fuel tank
réservoir ^{M} à carburant ^{M}
depósito ^{M} de combustible ^{M}
Kraftstofftank ^{M}
serbatoio ^{M} del carburante ^{M}

train
train ^{M}
locomotora ^{F}
Zug ^{M}
treno ^{M}

slipway
cale ^{F}
gradas ^{F}
Helling ^{F}
scivolo ^{M}

railroad tracks
voies ^{F} ferrées
vías ^{F} del ferrocarril ^{M}
Eisenbahnschienen ^{F}
binario ^{M} ferroviario

tugboat
remorqueur ^{M}
remolcador ^{M}
Schlepper ^{M}
rimorchiatore ^{M}

gantry crane
grue ^{F} à portique ^{M}
grúa ^{F} para contenedores ^{M}
Brückenkran ^{M}
gru ^{F} a cavalletto
customs house
bureau ^{M} des douanes ^{F}
aduana ^{F}
Zollgebäude ^{N}
edificio ^{M} amministrativo
container
conteneur ^{M}
contenedor ^{M}
Container ^{M}
container ^{M}
container ship
navire ^{M} porte-conteneurs ^{M}
buque ^{M} carguero
Containerschiff ^{N}
nave ^{F} container ^{M}
container terminal
terminal ^{M} à conteneurs ^{M}
muelle ^{M} de contenedores ^{M}
Containerterminal ^{M}
banchina ^{F}

lighthouse
phare ^{M}
faro ^{M}
Leuchtturm ^{M}
faro ^{M}
lantern
lanterne ^{F}
faro ^{M}
Laterne ^{F}
faro ^{M} illuminante
gallery
galerie ^{F}
galería ^{F}
Rundgang ^{M}
galleria ^{F}
tower
tour ^{F}
torre ^{F}
Turm ^{M}
torre ^{F}

Passenger vessels

Navires ᴹ de croisière ᶠ | Barcos ᴹ de pasajeros ᴹ | Passagierschiffe ᴺ | Navi ᶠ passeggeri ᴹ

cruise ship
paquebot ᴹ de croisière ᶠ
crucero ᴹ
Kreuzfahrtschiff ᴺ
nave ᶠ da crociera ᶠ

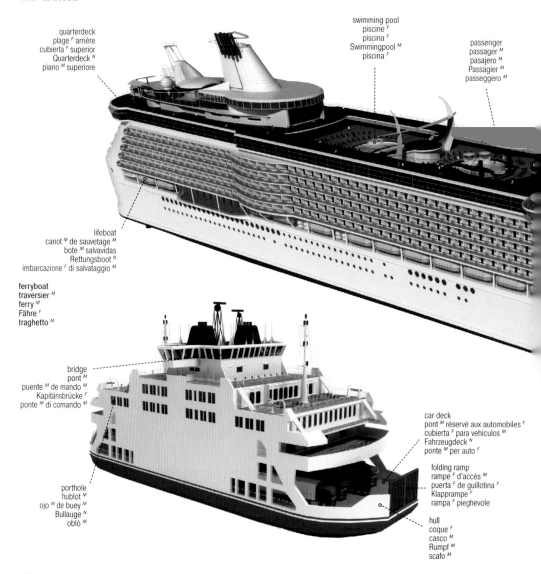

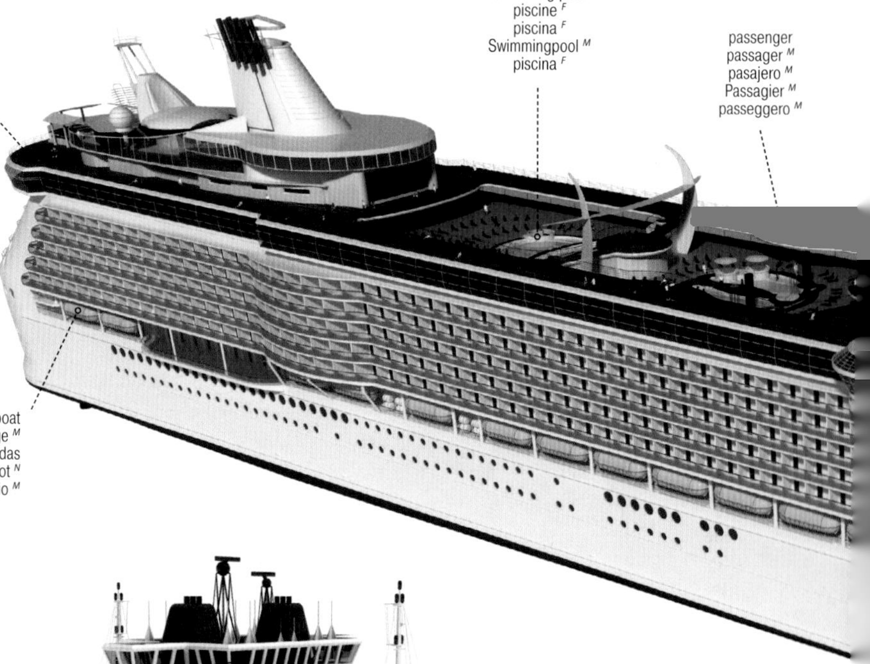
quarterdeck
plage ᶠ arrière
cubierta ᶠ superior
Quarterdeck ᴺ
piano ᴹ superiore
swimming pool
piscine ᶠ
piscina ᶠ
Swimmingpool ᴹ
piscina ᶠ
passenger
passager ᴹ
pasajero ᴹ
Passagier ᴹ
passeggero ᴹ
lifeboat
canot ᴹ de sauvetage ᴹ
bote ᴹ salvavidas
Rettungsboot ᴺ
imbarcazione ᶠ di salvataggio ᴹ

ferryboat
traversier ᴹ
ferry ᴹ
Fähre ᶠ
traghetto ᴹ

bridge
pont ᴹ
puente ᴹ de mando ᴹ
Kapitänsbrücke ᶠ
ponte ᴹ di comando ᴹ
car deck
pont ᴹ réservé aux automobiles ᶠ
cubierta ᶠ para vehículos ᴹ
Fahrzeugdeck ᴺ
ponte ᴹ per auto ᶠ
folding ramp
rampe ᶠ d'accès ᴹ
puerta ᶠ de guillotina ᶠ
Klapprampe ᶠ
rampa ᶠ pieghevole
porthole
hublot ᴹ
ojo ᴹ de buey ᴹ
Bullauge ᴺ
oblò ᴹ
hull
coque ᶠ
casco ᴹ
Rumpf ᴹ
scafo ᴹ

hydrofoil
hydroptère [M]
hidrodeslizador [M]
Tragflächenboot [N]
aliscafo [M]

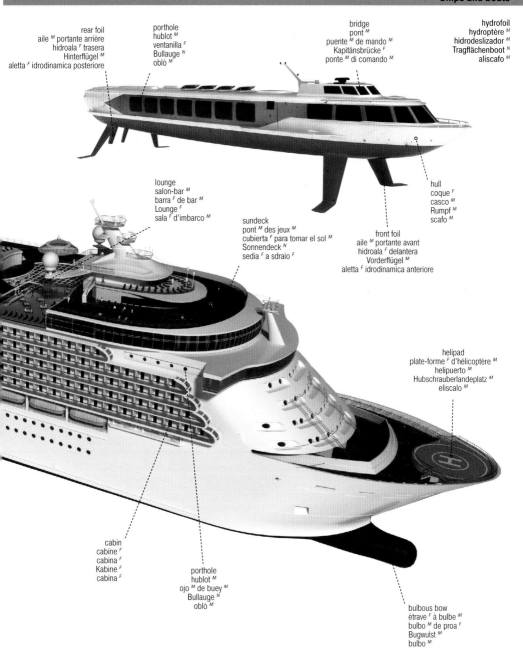

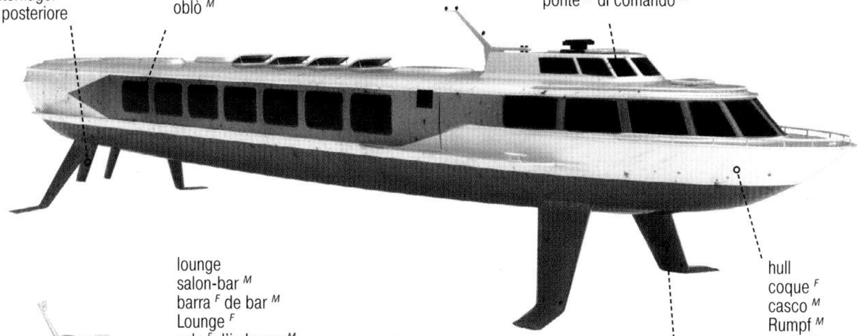
rear foil
aile [M] portante arrière
hidroala [F] trasera
Hinterflügel [M]
aletta [F] idrodinamica posteriore
porthole
hublot [M]
ventanilla [F]
Bullauge [N]
oblò [M]
bridge
pont [M]
puente [M] de mando [M]
Kapitänsbrücke [F]
ponte [M] di comando [M]
hull
coque [F]
casco [M]
Rumpf [M]
scafo [M]
front foil
aile [M] portante avant
hidroala [F] delantera
Vorderflügel [M]
aletta [F] idrodinamica anteriore

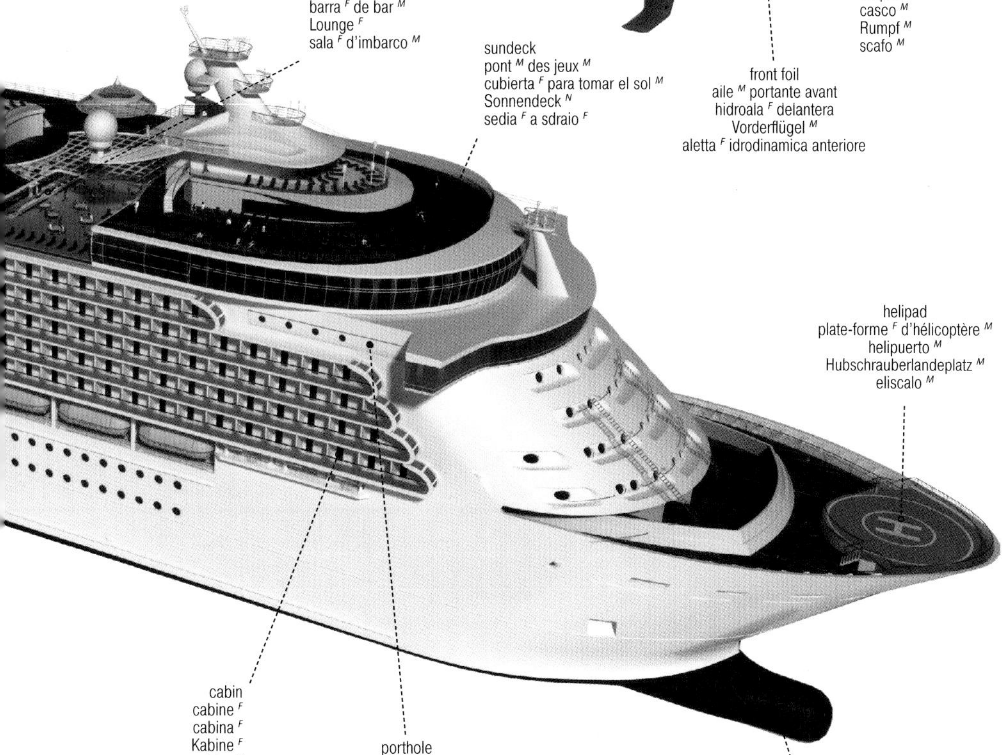
lounge
salon-bar [M]
barra [F] de bar [M]
Lounge [F]
sala [F] d'imbarco [M]
sundeck
pont [M] des jeux [M]
cubierta [F] para tomar el sol [M]
Sonnendeck [N]
sedia [F] a sdraio [F]
helipad
plate-forme [F] d'hélicoptère [M]
helipuerto [M]
Hubschrauberlandeplatz [M]
eliscalo [M]
cabin
cabine [F]
cabina [F]
Kabine [F]
cabina [F]
porthole
hublot [M]
ojo [M] de buey [M]
Bullauge [N]
oblò [M]
bulbous bow
étrave [F] à bulbe [M]
bulbo [M] de proa [F]
Bugwulst [M]
bulbo [M]

Ancillary vessels

Navires ^{M} auxiliaires | Barcos ^{M} auxiliares | Hilfs-, Service- und Arbeitsschiffe ^{N} | Imbarcazioni ^{F} ausiliari

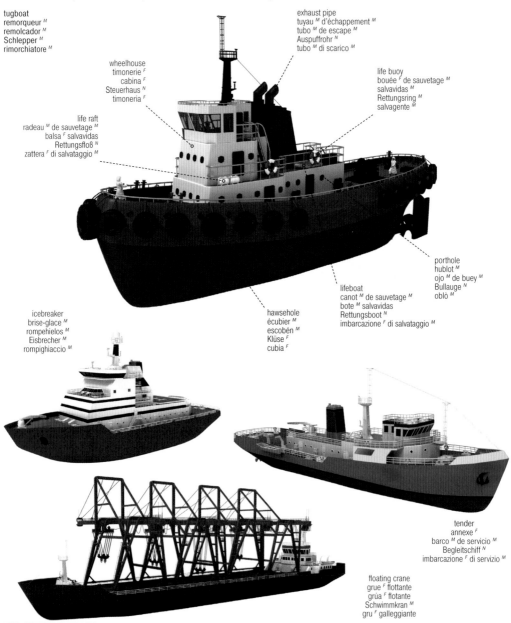

tugboat
remorqueur ^{M}
remolcador ^{M}
Schlepper ^{M}
rimorchiatore ^{M}

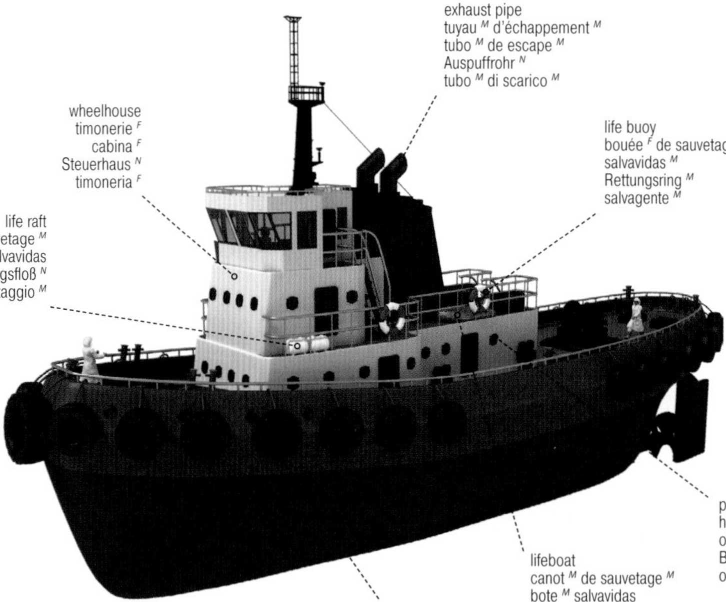
wheelhouse
timonerie ^{F}
cabina ^{F}
Steuerhaus ^{N}
timoneria ^{F}

exhaust pipe
tuyau ^{M} d'échappement ^{M}
tubo ^{M} de escape ^{M}
Auspuffrohr ^{N}
tubo ^{M} di scarico ^{M}

life buoy
bouée ^{F} de sauvetage ^{M}
salvavidas ^{M}
Rettungsring ^{M}
salvagente ^{M}

life raft
radeau ^{M} de sauvetage ^{M}
balsa ^{F} salvavidas
Rettungsfloß ^{N}
zattera ^{F} di salvataggio ^{M}

porthole
hublot ^{M}
ojo ^{M} de buey ^{M}
Bullauge ^{N}
oblò ^{M}

lifeboat
canot ^{M} de sauvetage ^{M}
bote ^{M} salvavidas
Rettungsboot ^{N}
imbarcazione ^{F} di salvataggio ^{M}

hawsehole
écubier ^{M}
escobén ^{M}
Klüse ^{F}
cubia ^{F}

icebreaker
brise-glace ^{M}
rompehielos ^{M}
Eisbrecher ^{M}
rompighiaccio ^{M}

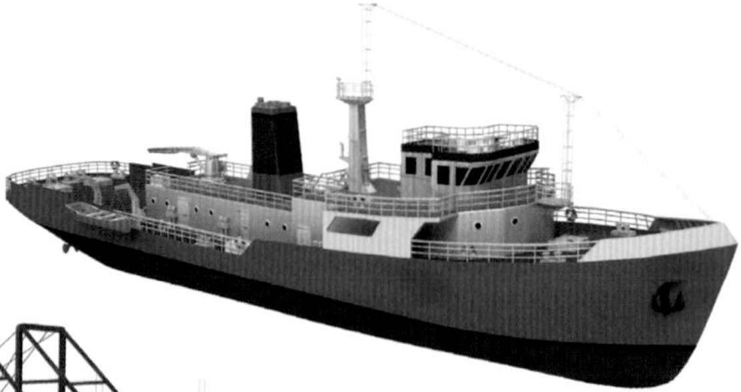

tender
annexe ^{F}
barco ^{M} de servicio ^{M}
Begleitschiff ^{N}
imbarcazione ^{F} di servizio ^{M}

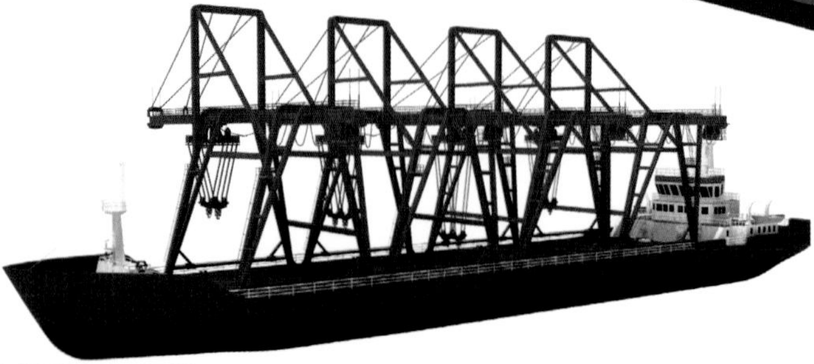

floating crane
grue ^{F} flottante
grúa ^{F} flotante
Schwimmkran ^{M}
gru ^{F} galleggiante

Cargo and fishing vessels

Navires ^{M} cargo et navires ^{M} de pêche ^{F} | Barcos ^{M} cargueros ^{M} y de pesca ^{F} | Fracht- und Fischereischiffe ^{N} | Imbarcazioni ^{F} da carico ^{M} e da pesca ^{F}

container ship
porte-conteneur ^{M}
buque ^{M} de carga ^{F}
Containerschiff ^{N}
nave porta-container ^{F}

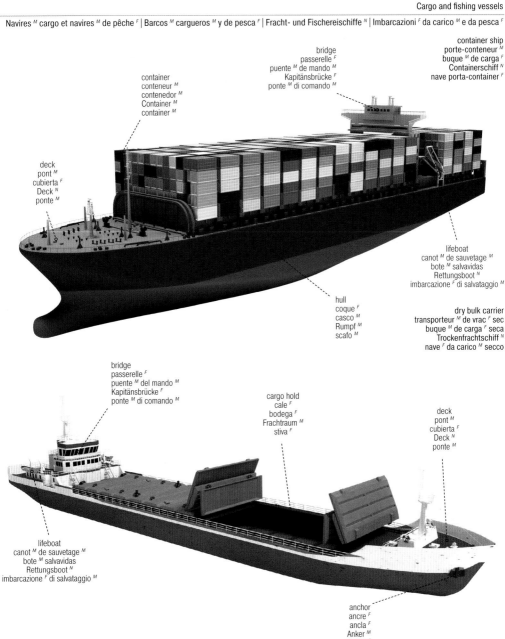

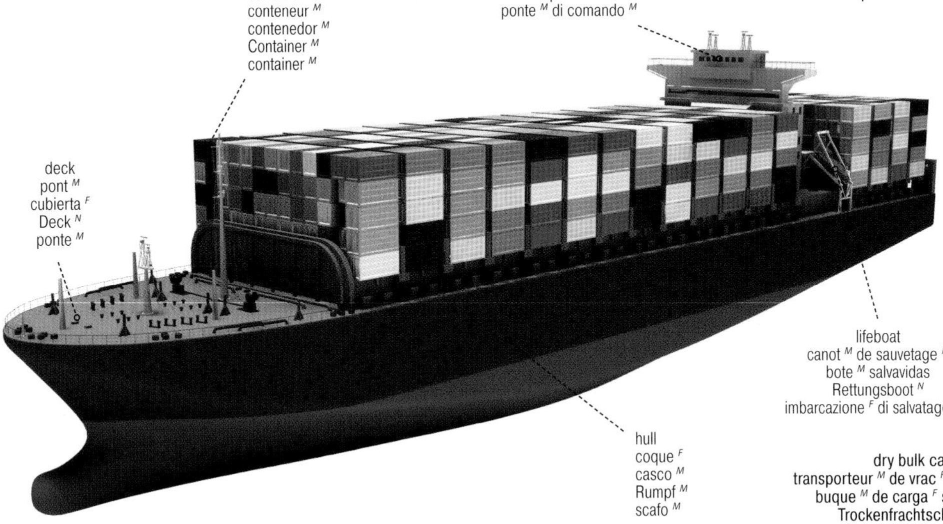
bridge
passerelle F
puente M de mando M
Kapitänsbrücke F
ponte M di comando M
container
conteneur M
contenedor M
Container M
container M
deck
pont M
cubierta F
Deck N
ponte M
lifeboat
canot M de sauvetage M
bote M salvavidas
Rettungsboot N
imbarcazione F di salvataggio M
hull
coque F
casco M
Rumpf M
scafo M

dry bulk carrier
transporteur ^{M} de vrac ^{F} sec
buque ^{M} de carga ^{F} seca
Trockenfrachtschiff ^{N}
nave ^{F} da carico ^{M} secco

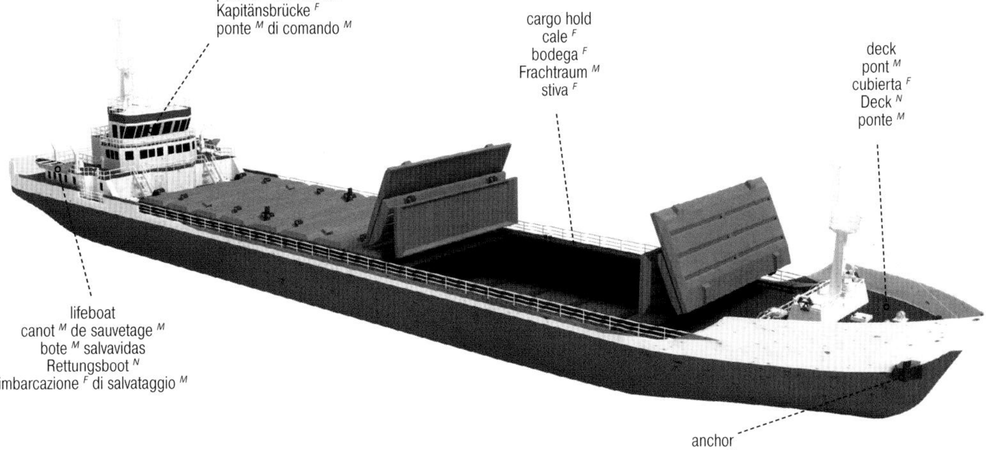
bridge
passerelle F
puente M del mando M
Kapitänsbrücke F
ponte M di comando M
cargo hold
cale F
bodega F
Frachtraum M
stiva F
deck
pont M
cubierta F
Deck N
ponte M
lifeboat
canot M de sauvetage M
bote M salvavidas
Rettungsboot N
imbarcazione F di salvataggio M
anchor
ancre F
ancla F
Anker M
ancora F

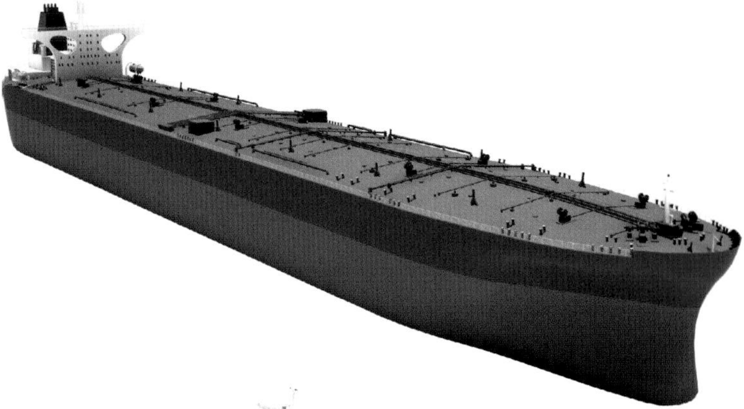

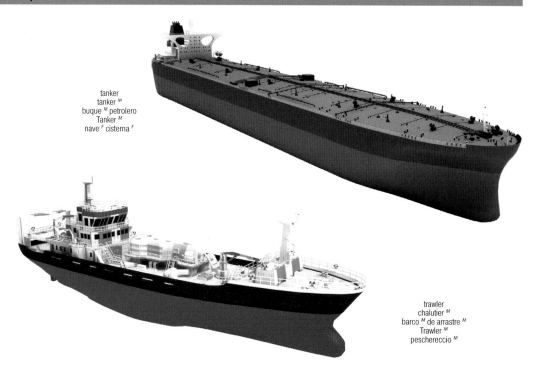

tanker
tanker ^{M}
buque ^{M} petrolero
Tanker ^{M}
nave ^{F} cisterna ^{F}

trawler
chalutier ^{M}
barco ^{M} de arrastre ^{M}
Trawler ^{M}
peschereccio ^{M}

Recreational vessels

Navires ^{M} de plaisance ^{F} | Barcos ^{M} recreativos | Freizeit-Seefahrzeuge ^{N} | Altre imbarcazioni ^{F}

yacht
yacht ^{M}
yate ^{M} a motor ^{M}
Motorjacht ^{F}
yacht ^{M}

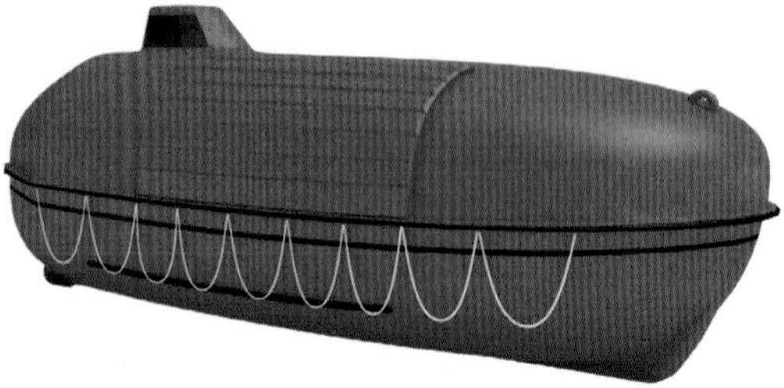

enclosed lifeboat
embarcation ^{F} de sauvetage ^{M} fermée
bote ^{M} salvavidas cerrado
Rettungsboot ^{N}
imbarcazione ^{F} di salvataggio ^{M}

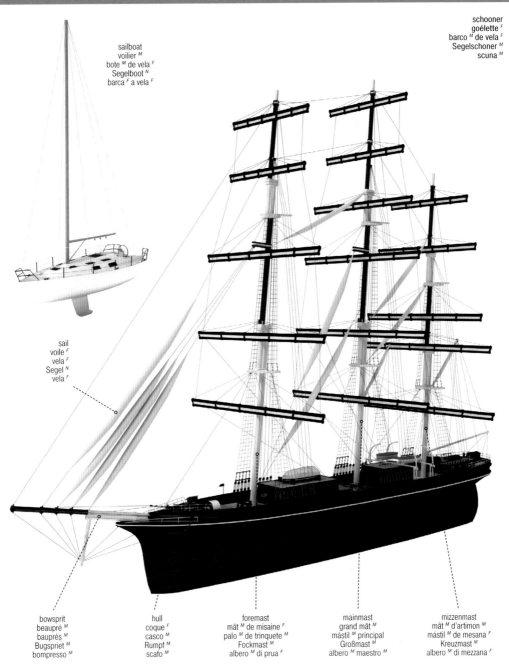

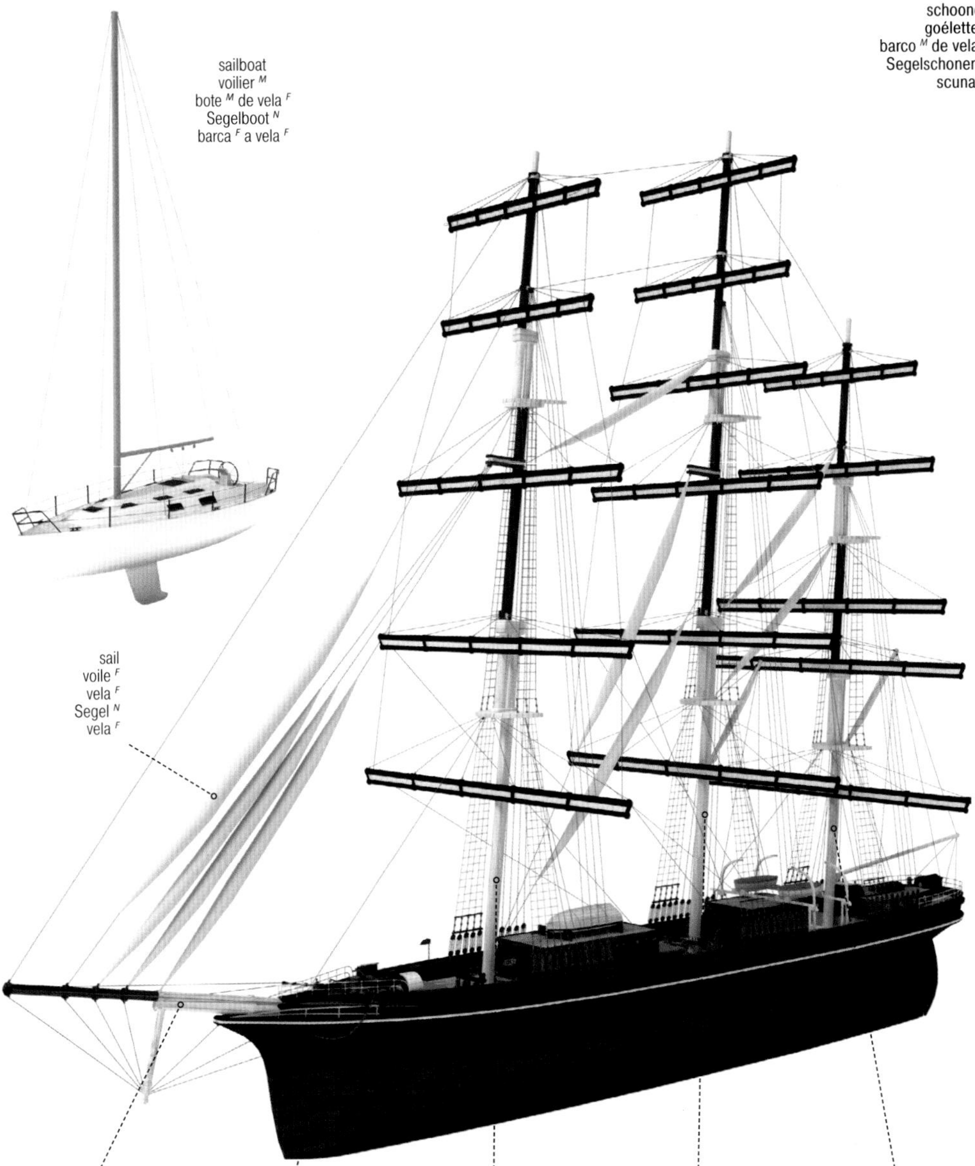
sailboat
voilier M
bote M de vela F
Segelboot N
barca F a vela F
schooner
goélette F
barco M de vela F
Segelschoner M
scuna M
sail
voile F
vela F
Segel N
vela F
bowsprit
beaupré M
bauprés M
Bugspriet M
bompresso M
hull
coque F
casco M
Rumpf M
scafo M
foremast
mât M de misaine F
palo M de trinquete M
Fockmast M
albero M di prua F
mainmast
grand mât M
mástil M principal
Großmast M
albero M maestro M
mizzenmast
mât M d'artimon M
mástil M de mesana F
Kreuzmast M
albero M di mezzana F

personal watercraft: front view
motomarine [F]: vue [F] de face [F]
moto [F] acuática: vista delantera
privates Wasserfahrzeug [F]: Vorderansicht [F]
moto [F] d'acqua [F]: vista [F] anteriore

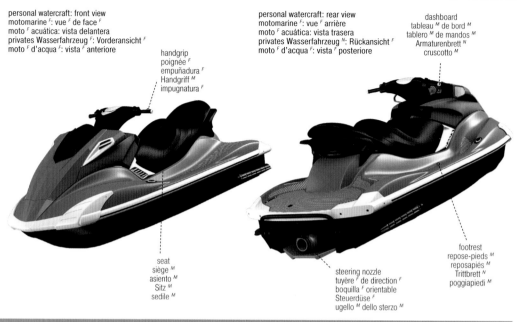

handgrip
poignée [F]
empuñadura [F]
Handgriff [M]
impugnatura [F]
seat
siège [M]
asiento [M]
Sitz [M]
sedile [M]

personal watercraft: rear view
motomarine [F]: vue [F] arrière
moto [F] acuática: vista trasera
privates Wasserfahrzeug [N]: Rückansicht [F]
moto [F] d'acqua [F]: vista [F] posteriore

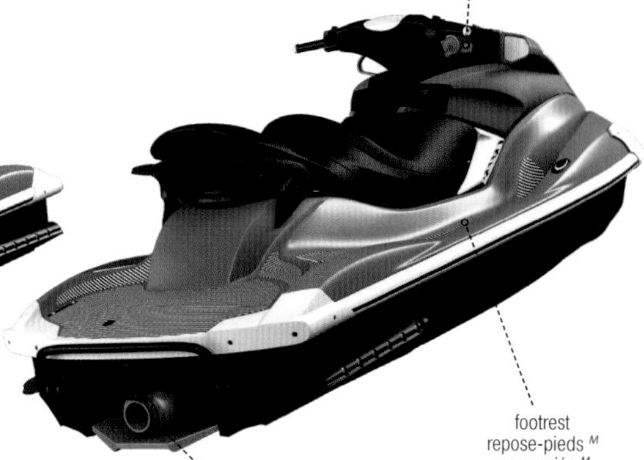
dashboard
tableau [M] de bord [M]
tablero [M] de mandos [M]
Armaturenbrett [N]
cruscotto [M]
footrest
repose-pieds [M]
reposapiés [M]
Trittbrett [N]
poggiapiedi [M]
steering nozzle
tuyère [F] de direction [F]
boquilla [F] orientable
Steuerdüse [F]
ugello [M] dello sterzo [M]

SNOW VEHICLES

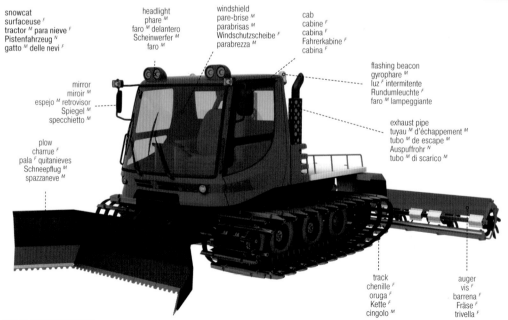

snowcat
surfaceuse [F]
tractor [M] para nieve [F]
Pistenfahrzeug [N]
gatto [M] delle nevi [F]

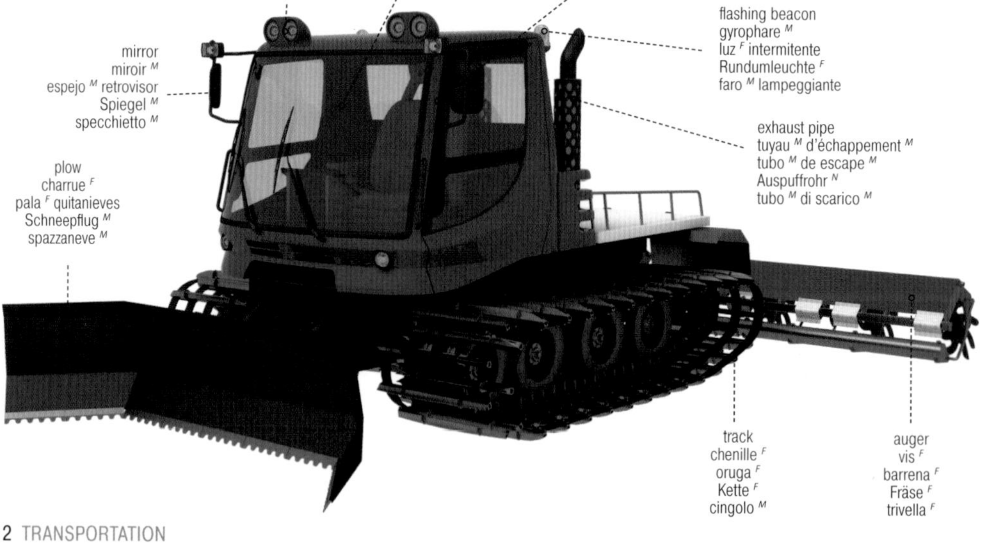
headlight
phare [M]
faro [M] delantero
Scheinwerfer [M]
faro [M]
windshield
pare-brise [M]
parabrisas [M]
Windschutzscheibe [F]
parabrezza [M]
cab
cabine [F]
cabina [F]
Fahrerkabine [F]
cabina [F]
flashing beacon
gyrophare [M]
luz [F] intermitente
Rundumleuchte [F]
faro [M] lampeggiante
mirror
miroir [M]
espejo [M] retrovisor
Spiegel [M]
specchietto [M]
exhaust pipe
tuyau [M] d'échappement [M]
tubo [M] de escape [M]
Auspuffrohr [N]
tubo [M] di scarico [M]
plow
charrue [F]
pala [F] quitanieves
Schneepflug [M]
spazzaneve [M]
track
chenille [F]
oruga [F]
Kette [F]
cingolo [M]
auger
vis [F]
barrena [F]
Fräse [F]
trivella [F]

snowmobile: front view
motoneige [F]: vue [F] de face [F]
motonieve [F]: vista delantera
Schneemobil [N]: Vorderansicht [F]
motoslitta [F]: vista [F] anteriore

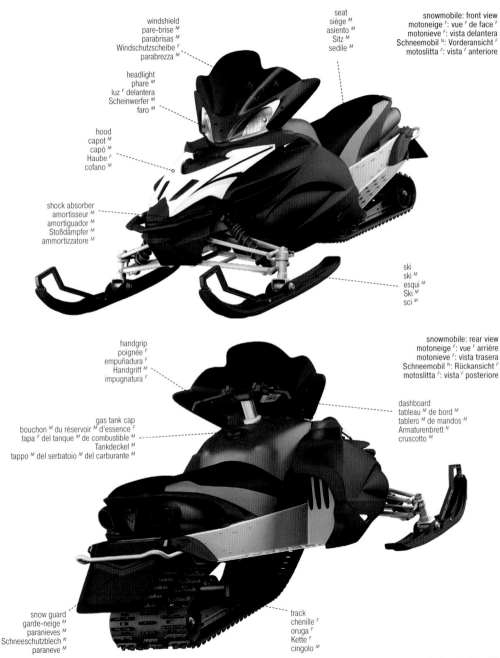

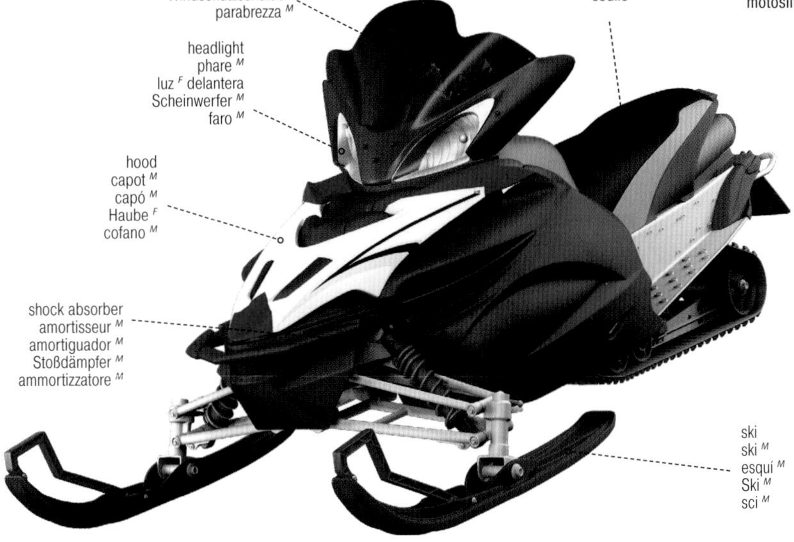
windshield
pare-brise [M]
parabrisas [M]
Windschutzscheibe [F]
parabrezza [M]
seat
siège [M]
asiento [M]
Sitz [M]
sedile [M]
headlight
phare [M]
luz [F] delantera
Scheinwerfer [M]
faro [M]
hood
capot [M]
capó [M]
Haube [F]
cofano [M]
shock absorber
amortisseur [M]
amortiguador [M]
Stoßdämpfer [M]
ammortizzatore [M]
ski
ski [M]
esquí [M]
Ski [M]
sci [M]

snowmobile: rear view
motoneige [F]: vue [F] arrière
motonieve [F]: vista trasera
Schneemobil [N]: Rückansicht [F]
motoslitta [F]: vista [F] posteriore

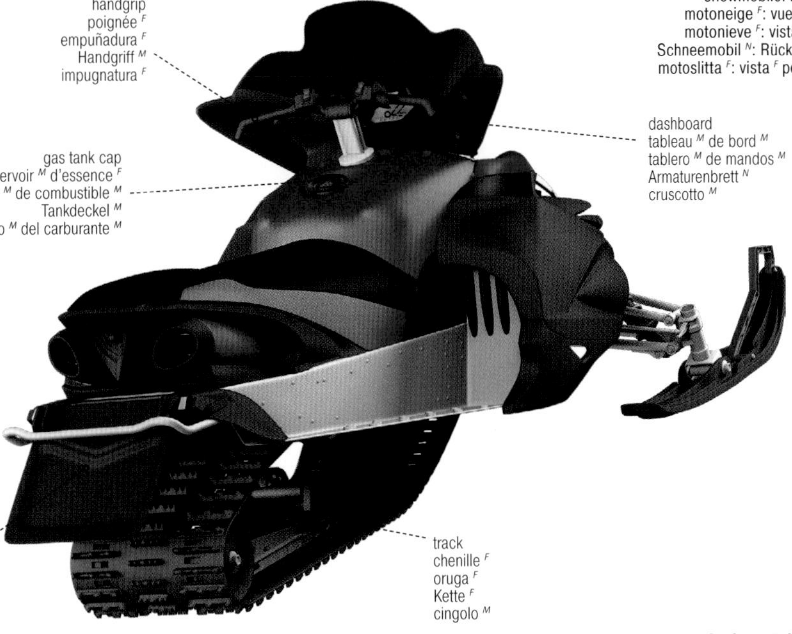
handgrip
poignée [F]
empuñadura [F]
Handgriff [M]
impugnatura [F]
dashboard
tableau [M] de bord [M]
tablero [M] de mandos [M]
Armaturenbrett [N]
cruscotto [M]
gas tank cap
bouchon [M] du réservoir [M] d'essence [F]
tapa [F] del tanque [M] de combustible [M]
Tankdeckel [M]
tappo [M] del serbatoio [M] del carburante [M]
snow guard
garde-neige [M]
paranieves [M]
Schneeschutzblech [N]
paraneve [M]
track
chenille [F]
oruga [F]
Kette [F]
cingolo [M]

cable car
téléphérique [M]
teleférico [M]
Seilbahn [F]
funivia [F]

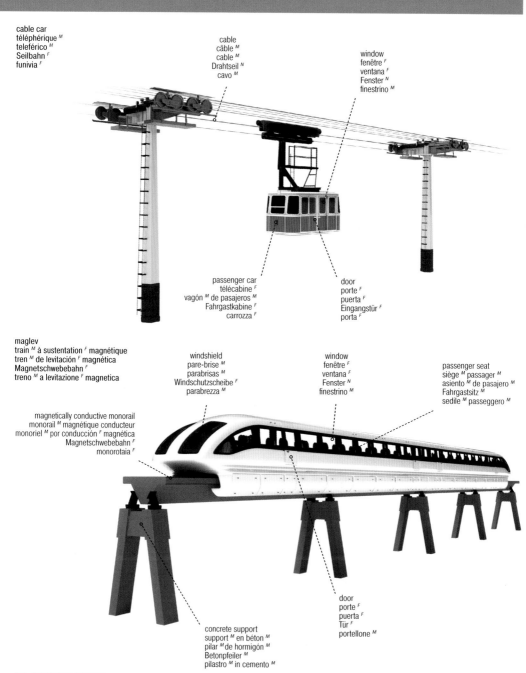

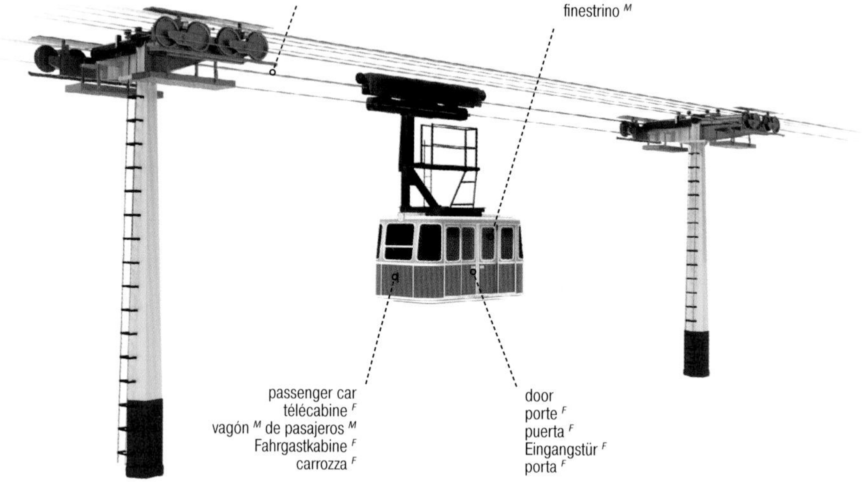
cable
câble [M]
cable [M]
Drahtseil [N]
cavo [M]
window
fenêtre [F]
ventana [F]
Fenster [N]
finestrino [M]
passenger car
télécabine [F]
vagón [M] de pasajeros [M]
Fahrgastkabine [F]
carrozza [F]
door
porte [F]
puerta [F]
Eingangstür [F]
porta [F]

maglev
train [M] à sustentation [F] magnétique
tren [M] de levitación [F] magnética
Magnetschwebebahn [F]
treno [M] a levitazione [F] magnetica

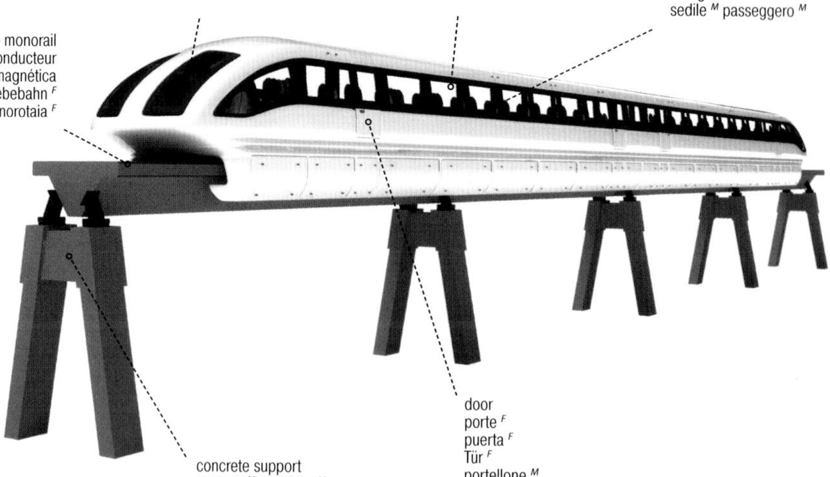
windshield
pare-brise [M]
parabrisas [M]
Windschutzscheibe [F]
parabrezza [M]
window
fenêtre [F]
ventana [F]
Fenster [N]
finestrino [M]
passenger seat
siège [M] passager [M]
asiento [M] de pasajero [M]
Fahrgastsitz [M]
sedile [M] passeggero [M]
magnetically conductive monorail
monorail [M] magnétique conducteur
monoriel [M] por conducción [F] magnética
Magnetschwebebahn [F]
monorotaia [F]
door
porte [F]
puerta [F]
Tür [F]
portellone [M]
concrete support
support [M] en béton [M]
pilar [M] de hormigón [M]
Betonpfeiler [M]
pilastro [M] in cemento [M]

all-terrain crane
grue F tout-terrain M
grúa F todo-terreno M
Geländekran N
gru F

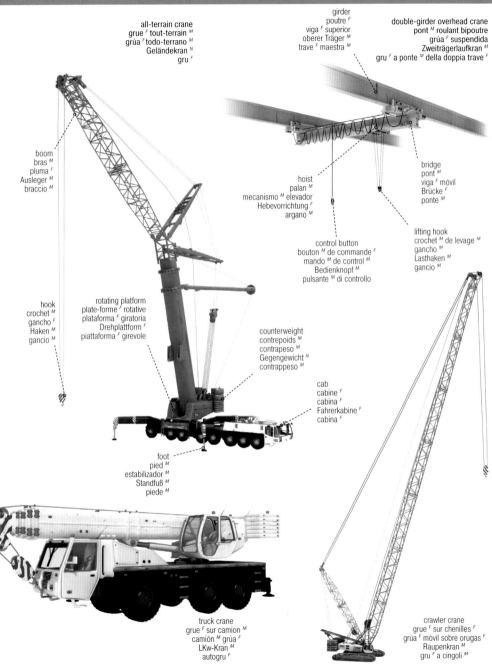

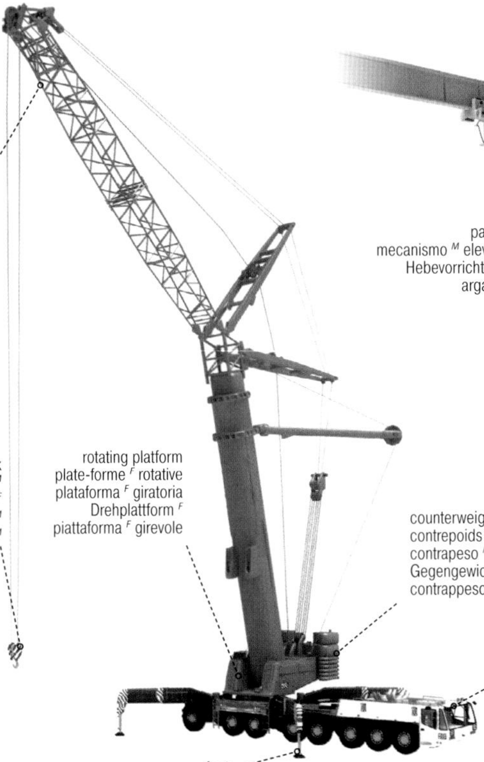
boom
bras M
pluma F
Ausleger M
braccio M
hook
crochet M
gancho F
Haken M
gancio M
rotating platform
plate-forme F rotative
plataforma F giratoria
Drehplattform F
piattaforma F girevole
counterweight
contrepoids M
contrapeso M
Gegengewicht N
contrappeso M
cab
cabine F
cabina F
Fahrerkabine F
cabina F
foot
pied M
estabilizador M
Standfuß M
piede M

double-girder overhead crane
pont M roulant bipoutre
grúa F suspendida
Zweiträgerlaufkran M
gru F a ponte M della doppia trave F

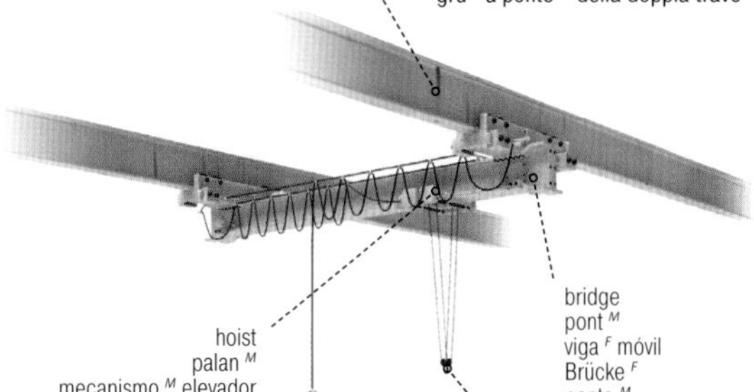
girder
poutre F
viga F superior
oberer Träger M
trave F maestra M
hoist
palan M
mecanismo M elevador
Hebevorrichtung F
argano M
bridge
pont M
viga F móvil
Brücke F
ponte M
control button
bouton M de commande F
mando M de control M
Bedienknopf M
pulsante M di controllo
lifting hook
crochet M de levage M
gancho M
Lasthaken M
gancio M

truck crane
grue F sur camion M
camión M grúa F
LKw-Kran M
autogru F

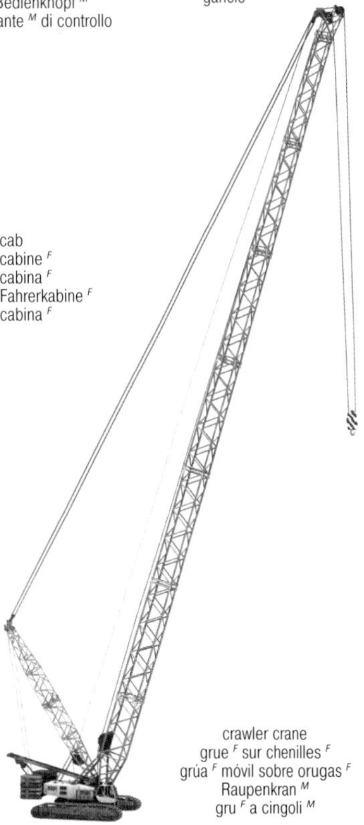

crawler crane
grue F sur chenilles F
grúa F móvil sobre orugas F
Raupenkran M
gru F a cingoli M

harbor gantry crane
grue ^{F} portuaire à portique ^{F}
grúa ^{F} de puerto ^{M}
Hafenbrückenkran ^{M}
gru ^{F} da porto ^{M}

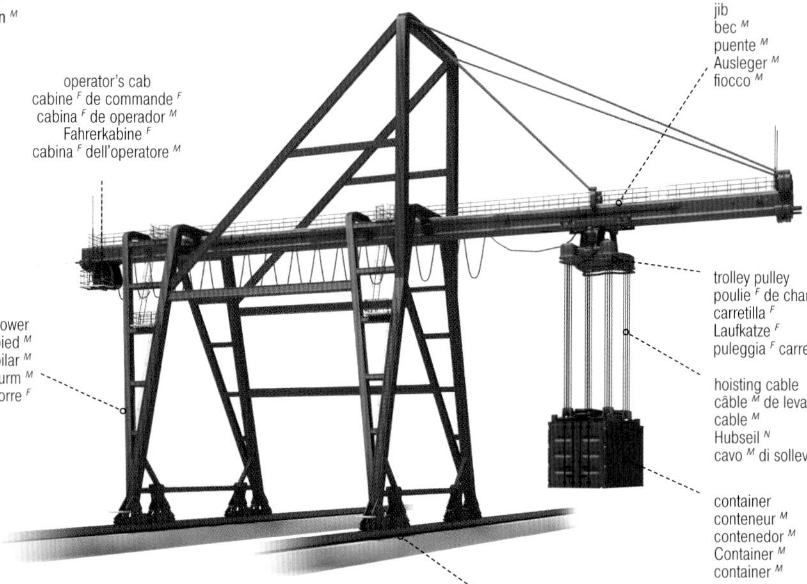

operator's cab
cabine ^{F} de commande ^{F}
cabina ^{F} de operador ^{M}
Fahrerkabine ^{F}
cabina ^{F} dell'operatore ^{M}

jib
bec ^{M}
puente ^{M}
Ausleger ^{M}
fiocco ^{M}

tower
pied ^{M}
pilar ^{M}
Turm ^{M}
torre ^{F}

trolley pulley
poulie ^{F} de chariot ^{M}
carretilla ^{F}
Laufkatze ^{F}
puleggia ^{F} carrello ^{M}

hoisting cable
câble ^{M} de levage ^{M}
cable ^{M}
Hubseil ^{N}
cavo ^{M} di sollevamento

container
conteneur ^{M}
contenedor ^{M}
Container ^{M}
container ^{M}

running track
piste ^{F} de roulement ^{M}
riel ^{M}
Laufschiene ^{F}
rotaia ^{F}

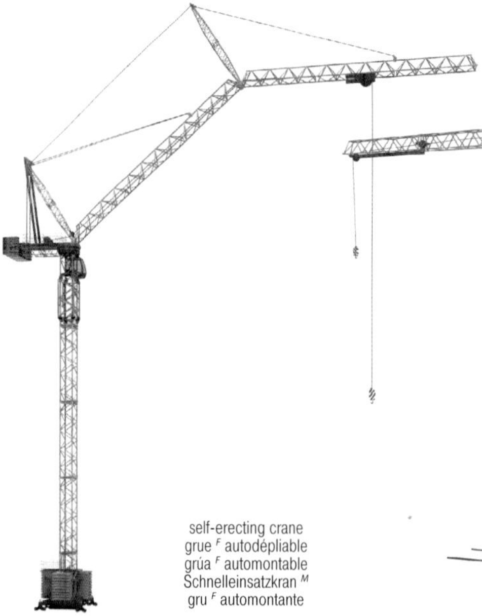

self-erecting crane
grue ^{F} autodépliable
grúa ^{F} automontable
Schnelleinsatzkran ^{M}
gru ^{F} automontante

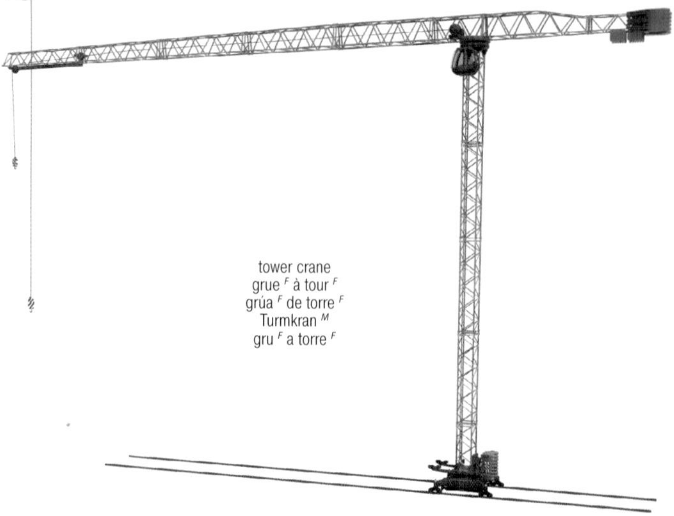

tower crane
grue ^{F} à tour ^{F}
grúa ^{F} de torre ^{F}
Turmkran ^{M}
gru ^{F} a torre ^{F}

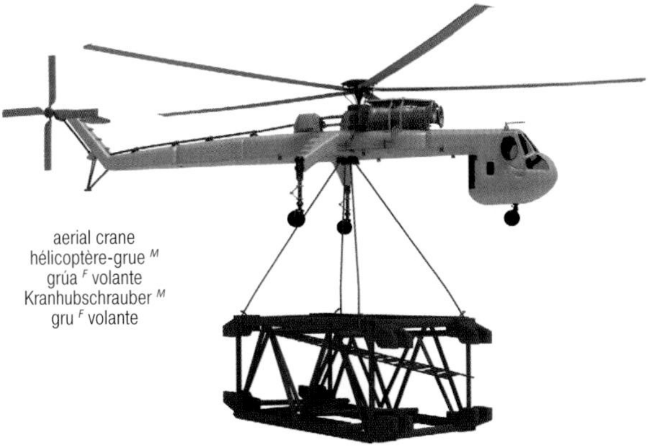

aerial crane
hélicoptère-grue [M]
grúa [F] volante
Kranhubschrauber [M]
gru [F] volante

level luffing crane
grue [F] à portée [F] variable
grúa [F] de estructura [F]
Wippkran [M]
gru [F] a cavalletto [M]

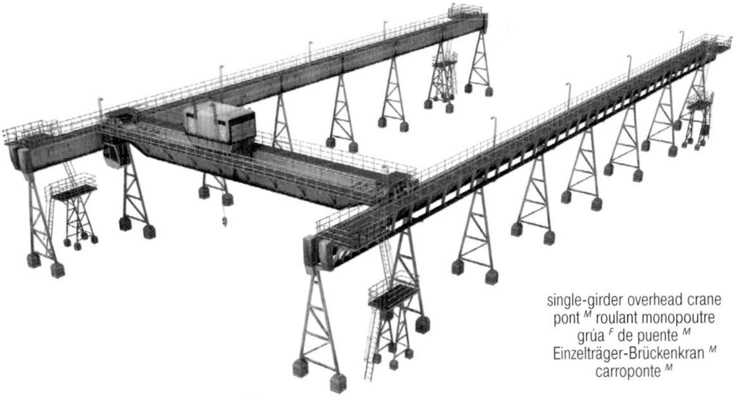

single-girder overhead crane
pont [M] roulant monopoutre
grúa [F] de puente [M]
Einzelträger-Brückenkran [M]
carroponte [M]

gantry crane
grue [F] à portique [M]
grúa [F] pórtico
Portalkran [M]
gru [F] a cavalletto [M]

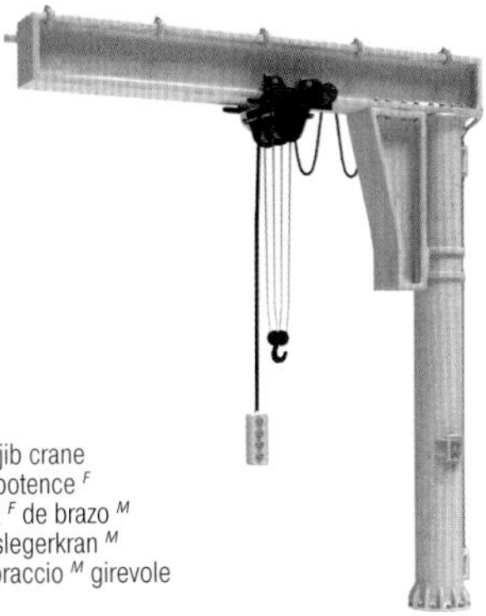

jib crane
potence [F]
grúa [F] de brazo [M]
Auslegerkran [M]
gru [F] a braccio [M] girevole

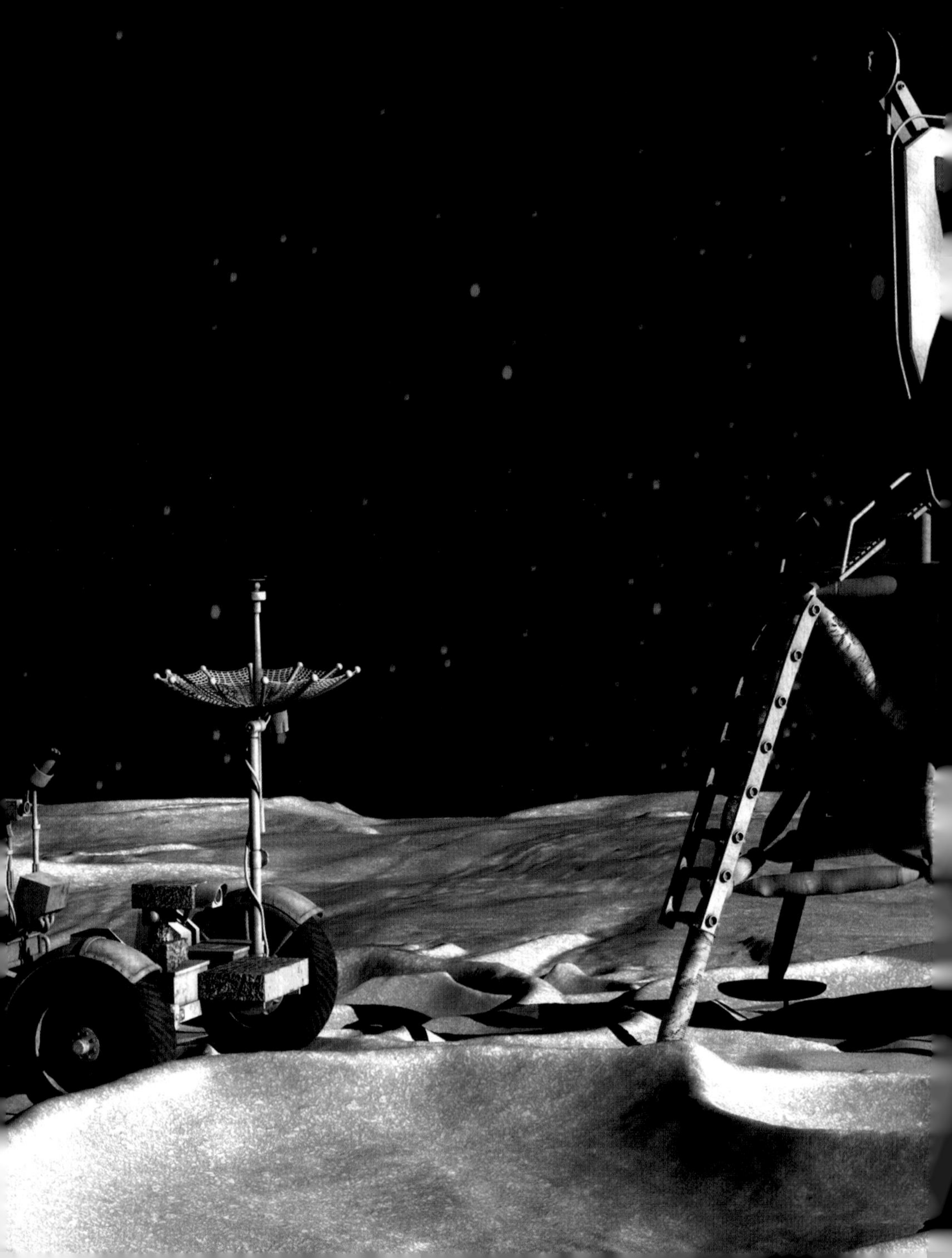

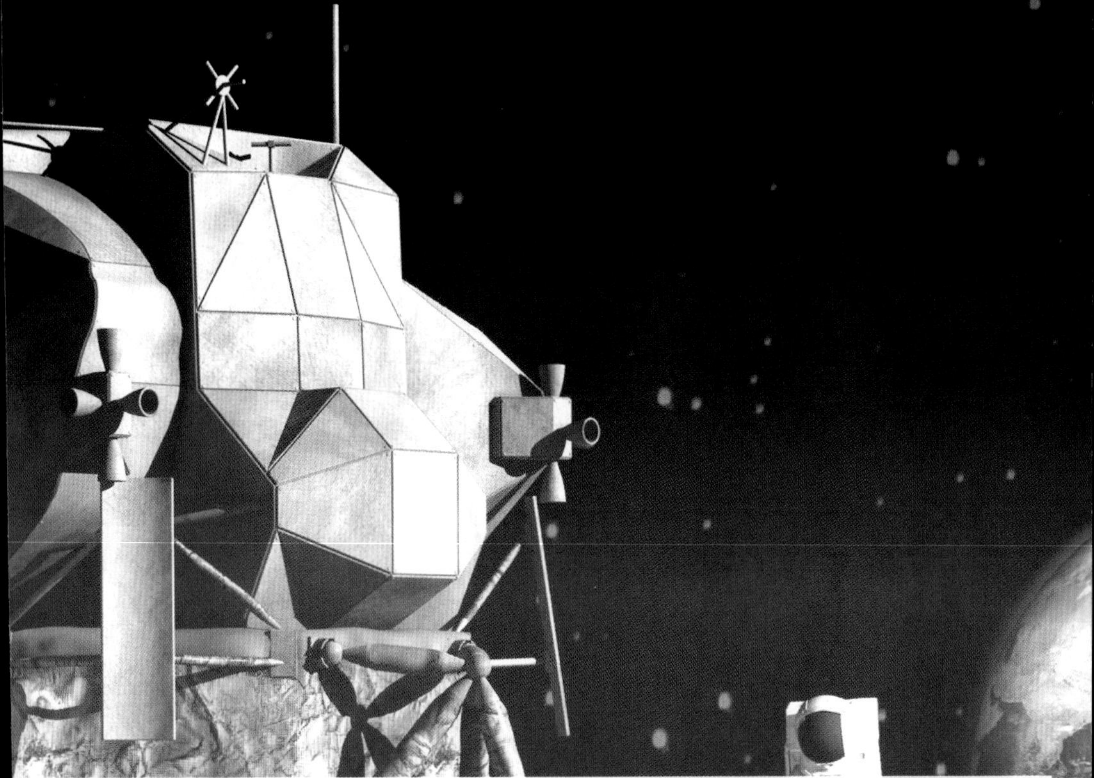

SCIENCE

periodic table
tableau [M] périodique
tabla [F] periódica
Periodensystem [N]
tavola periodica [F]

group
groupe [M]
grupo [M]
Gruppe [F]
gruppo [M]

category
catégorie [F]
categoría [F]
Kategorie [F]
categoria [F]

period
période [F]
periodo [M]
Periode [F]
periodo [M]

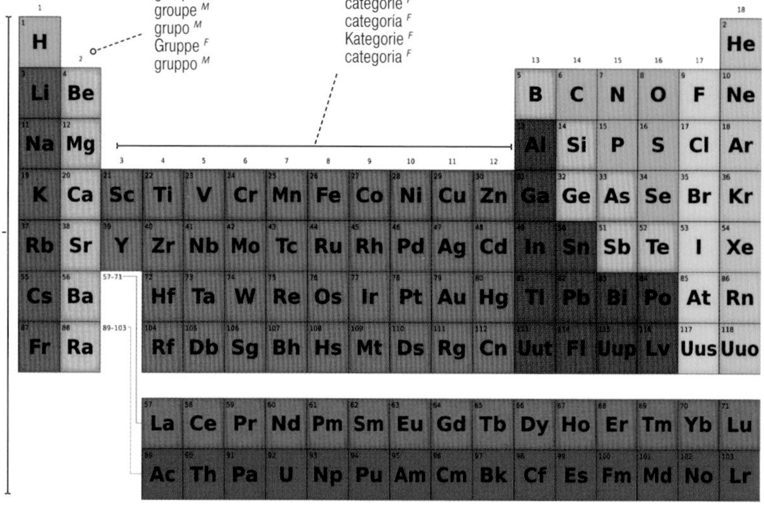
1 2 3 4 5 6 7 8 9 10 11 12 13 14 15 16 17 18
H He
Li Be B C N O F Ne
Na Mg Al Si P S Cl Ar
K Ca Sc Ti V Cr Mn Fe Co Ni Cu Zn Ga Ge As Se Br Kr
Rb Sr Y Zr Nb Mo Tc Ru Rh Pd Ag Cd In Sn Sb Te I Xe
Cs Ba 57-71 Hf Ta W Re Os Ir Pt Au Hg Tl Pb Bi Po At Rn
Fr Ra 89-103 Rf Db Sg Bh Hs Mt Ds Rg Cn Uut Fl Uup Lv Uus Uuo
La Ce Pr Nd Pm Sm Eu Gd Tb Dy Ho Er Tm Yb Lu
Ac Th Pa U Np Pu Am Cm Bk Cf Es Fm Md No Lr

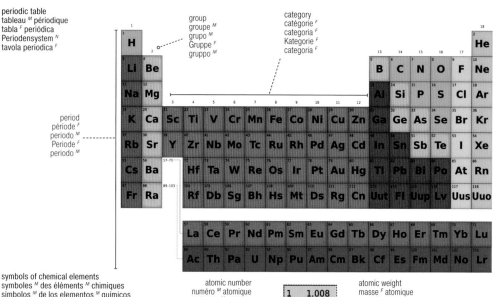

symbols of chemical elements
symboles [M] des éléments [M] chimiques
símbolos [M] de los elementos [M] químicos
Symbole [N] der chemischen Elemente [N]
simboli [M] degli elementi [M] chimici

atomic number
numéro [M] atomique
número [M] atómico
Atomzahl [F]
numero atomico [M]

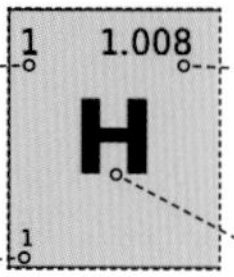
1 1.008
H
1

atomic weight
masse [F] atomique
peso [M] atómico
Atomgewicht [N]
peso atomico [M]

number of electrons
nombre [M] d'électrons [M]
número [M] de electrones [M]
Elektronenzahl [F]
numero [M] di elettroni [M]

symbol
symbole [M]
símbolo [M]
chemisches Symbol [N]
simbolo [M] chimico

Noble gases

Gaz [M] nobles | Gases [M] nobles | Edelgase [N] | Gas [M] nobili

2 He — helium, hélium [M], helio [M], Helium [N], elio [M]

10 Ne — neon, néon [M], neón [M], Neon [N], neon [M]

18 Ar — argon, argon [M], argón [M], Argon [N], argon [M]

36 Kr — krypton, krypton [M], kriptón [M], Krypton [N], krypton [M]

54 Xe — xenon, xénon [M], xenón [M], Xenon [N], xeno [M]

86 Rn — radon, radon [M], radón [M], Radon [N], radon [M]

118 Uuo — ununoctium, ununoctium [M], ununoctio [M], Ununoctium [N], ununoctio [M]

Halogens

Halogènes [M] | Halógenos [M] | Halogene [N] | Alogeni [M]

9 F — fluorine, fluor [M], flúor [M], Fluor [N], fluoro [M]

17 Cl — chlorine, chlore [M], cloro [M], Chlor [N], cloro [M]

35 Br — bromine, brome [M], bromo [M], Brom [N], bromo [M]

53 I — iodine, iode [M], yodo [M], Iod [N], iodio [M]

85 At — astatine, astate [M], ástato [M], Astat [N], astato [M]

117 Uus — ununseptium, ununseptium, ununseptio [M], Ununseptium [N], ununseptio [M]

Transition metals

Métal [M] de transition | Metales [M] de transición [F] | Übergangsmetalle [N] | Metalli [M] di transizione

21 Sc
scandium
scandium [M]
escandio [M]
Scandium [N]
scandio [M]

22 Ti
titanium
titane [M]
titanio [M]
Titanium [N]
titanio [M]

23 V
vanadium
vanadium [M]
vanadio [M]
Vanadium [N]
vanadio [M]

24 Cr
chromium
chrome [M]
cromo [M]
Chrom [N]
cromo [M]

25 Mn
manganese
manganèse [M]
manganeso [M]
Mangan [N]
manganese [M]

26 Fe
iron
fer [M]
hierro [M]
Eisen [N]
ferro [M]

27 Co
cobalt
cobalt [M]
cobalto [M]
Kobalt [N]
cobalto [M]

28 Ni
nickel
nickel [M]
níquel [M]
Nickel [N]
nickel [M]

29 Cu
copper
cuivre [M]
cobre [M]
Kupfer [N]
rame [M]

30 Zn
zinc
zinc [M]
cinc [M]
Zink [N]
zinco [M]

39 Y
yttrium
yttrium [M]
itrio [M]
Yttrium [N]
ittrio [M]

40 Zr
zirconium
zirconium [M]
circonio [M]
Zirconium [N]
zirconio [M]

41 Nb
niobium
niobium [M]
niobio [M]
Niob [N]
niobio [M]

42 Mo
molybdenum
molybdène [M]
molibdeno [M]
Molybdän [N]
molibdeno [M]

43 Tc
technetium
technétium [M]
tecnecio [M]
Technetium [N]
tecnezio [M]

44 Ru
ruthenium
ruthénium [M]
rutenio [M]
Ruthenium [N]
rutenio [M]

45 Rh
rhodium
rhodium [M]
rodio [M]
Rhodium [N]
rodio [M]

46 Pd
palladium
palladium [M]
paladio [M]
Palladium [N]
palladio [M]

47 Ag
silver
argent [M]
plata [F]
Silber [N]
argento [M]

48 Cd
cadmium
cadmium [M]
cadmio [M]
Cadmium [N]
cadmio [M]

72 Hf
hafnium
hafnium [M]
hafnio [M]
Hafnium [N]
afnio [M]

73 Ta
tantalum
tantale [M]
tantalio [M]
Tantal [N]
tantalio [M]

74 W
tungsten
tungstène [M]
tungsteno [M]
Wolfram [N]
tungsteno [M]

75 Re
rhenium
rhénium [M]
renio [M]
Rhenium [N]
renio [M]

76 Os
osmium
osmium [M]
osmio [M]
Osmium [N]
osmio [M]

77 Ir
iridium
iridium [M]
iridio [M]
Iridium [N]
iridio [M]

78 Pt
platinum
platine [M]
platino [M]
Platin [N]
platino [M]

79 Au
gold
or [M]
oro [M]
Gold [N]
oro [M]

80 Hg
mercury
mercure [M]
mercurio [M]
Quecksilber [N]
mercurio [M]

104 Rf
rutherfordium
rutherfordium [M]
rutherfordio [M]
Rutherfordium [N]
rutherfordio [M]

105 Db
dubnium
dubnium [M]
dubnio [M]
Dubnium [N]
dubnio [M]

106 Sg
seaborgium
seaborgium [M]
seaborgio [M]
Seaborgium [N]
seaborgio [M]

107 Bh
bohrium
bohrium [M]
bohrio [M]
Bohrium [N]
bohrio [M]

108 Hs
hassium
hassium [M]
hassio [M]
Hassium [N]
hassio [M]

109 Mt
meitnerium
meitnérium [M]
meitnerio [M]
Meitnerium [N]
meitnerio [M]

110 Ds
darmstadtium
darmstadtium [M]
darmstadio [M]
Darmstadtium [N]
darmstadtio [M]

111 Rg
roentgenium
roentgenium [M]
roentgenio [M]
Röntgenium [N]
roentgenio [M]

112 Cn
copernicium
copernicium [M]
copernicio [M]
Copernicium [N]
copernicio [M]

Alkali metals

Métaux [M] alcalins | Metales [M] alcalinos | Alkalimetalle [N] | Metalli [M] alcalini

3 Li
lithium
lithium [M]
litio [M]
Lithium [N]
litio [M]

11 Na
sodium
sodium [M]
sodio [M]
Natrium [N]
sodio [M]

19 K
potassium
potassium [M]
potasio [M]
Kalium [N]
potassio [M]

37 Rb
rubidium
rubidium [M]
rubidio [M]
Rubidium [N]
rubidio [M]

55 Cs
cesium
césium [M]
cesio [M]
Cäsium [N]
cesio [M]

87 Fr
francium
francium [M]
francio [M]
Francium [N]
francio [M]

Post-transition metals

Métaux [M] pauvres | Metales [M] del bloque [M] P | sonstige Metalle [N] | Metalli [M] di post-transizione [F]

13 Al
aluminum
aluminium [M]
aluminio [M]
Aluminium [N]
alluminio [M]

31 Ga
gallium
gallium [M]
galio [M]
Gallium [N]
gallio [M]

49 In
indium
indium [M]
indio [M]
Indium [N]
indio [M]

50 Sn
tin
étain [M]
estaño [M]
Zinn [N]
stagno [M]

81 Tl
thallium
thallium [M]
talio [M]
Thallium [N]
tallio [M]

82 Pb
lead
plomb [M]
plomo [M]
Blei [N]
piombo [M]

83 Bi
bismuth
bismuth [M]
bismuto [M]
Bismut [N]
bismuto [M]

84 Po
polonium
polonium [M]
polonio [M]
Polonium [N]
polonio [M]

113 Uut
ununtrium
ununtrium [M]
ununtrio [M]
Ununtrium [N]
ununtrio [M]

114 Fl
flerovium
flérovium [M]
flerovio [M]
Flerovium [N]
flerovio [M]

115 Uup
ununpentium
ununpentium [M]
unumpentio [M]
Ununpentium [N]
ununpentio [M]

116 Lv
livermorium
livermorium [M]
livermorio [M]
Livermorium [N]
livermorio [M]

Metalloids

Éléments [M] non métalliques | Metaloide [N] | Metalloide [N] | Metalloidi [M]

5 B
boron
bore [M]
boro [M]
Bor [N]
boro [M]

14 Si
silicon
silicium [M]
silicio [M]
Silicium [N]
silicone [M]

32 Ge
germanium
germanium [M]
germanio [M]
Germanium [N]
germanio [M]

33 As
arsenic
arsenic [M]
arsénico [M]
Arsen [N]
arsenico [M]

51 Sb
antimony
antimoine [M]
antimonio [M]
Antimon [N]
antimonio [M]

52 Te
tellurium
tellure [M]
telurio [M]
Tellur [N]
tellurio [M]

Nonmetals

Non-métaux [M] | No metales [M] | Nichtmetalle [N] | Non metalli [M]

1 H
hydrogen
hydrogène [M]
hidrógeno [M]
Wasserstoff [N]
idrogeno [M]

6 C
carbon
carbone [M]
carbón [M]
Kohlenstoff [N]
carbonio [M]

7 N
nitrogen
azote [M]
nitrógeno [M]
Stickstoff [M]
nitrogeno [M]

8 O
oxygen
oxygène [M]
oxígeno [M]
Sauerstoff [M]
ossigeno [M]

15 P
phosphorus
phosphore [M]
fósforo [M]
Phosphor [N]
fosforo [M]

16 S
sulfur
soufre [M]
azufre [M]
Schwefel [M]
zolfo [M]

34 Se
selenium
sélénium [M]
selenio [M]
Selen [N]
selenio [M]

Lanthanides

Lanthanides [M] | Lantánidos [M] | Lanthanoide [N] | Lantanidi [M]

57 La
lanthanum
lanthane [M]
lantano [M]
Lanthan [N]
lantanio [M]

58 Ce
cerium
cérium [M]
cerio [M]
Cerium [N]
cerio [M]

59 Pr
praseodymium
praséodyme [M]
praseodimio [M]
Praseodym [N]
praseodimio [M]

60 Nd
neodymium
néodyme [M]
neodimio [M]
Neodym [N]
neodimio [M]

61 Pm
promethium
prométhium [M]
prometio [M]
Promethium [N]
promezio [M]

62 Sm
samarium
samarium [M]
samario [M]
Samarium [N]
samario [M]

63 Eu
europium
europium [M]
europio [M]
Europium [N]
europio [M]

64 Gd
gadolinium
gadolinium [M]
gadolinio [M]
Gadolinium [N]
gadolinio [M]

65 Tb
terbium
terbium [M]
terbio [M]
Terbium [N]
terbio [M]

66 Dy
dysprosium
dysprosium [M]
disprosio [M]
Dysprosium [N]
disprosio [M]

67 Ho
holmium
holmium [M]
holmio [M]
Holmium [N]
olmio [M]

68 Er
erbium
erbium [M]
erbio [M]
Erbium [N]
erbio [M]

69 Tm
thulium
thulium [M]
tulio [M]
Thulium [N]
tulio [M]

70 Yb
ytterbium
ytterbium [M]
iterbio [M]
Ytterbium [N]
itterbio [M]

71 Lu
lutetium
lutécium [M]
lutecio [M]
Lutetium [N]
lutezio [M]

Actinides

Actinides [M] | Actínidos [M] | Actinoide [N] | Attinide [F]

89 Ac
actinium
actinium [M]
actinio [M]
Actinium [N]
attinio [M]

90 Th
thorium
thorium [M]
torio [M]
Thorium [N]
torio [M]

91 Pa
protactinium
protactinium [M]
protactinio [M]
Protactinium [N]
protoattinio [M]

92 U
uranium
uranium [M]
uranio [M]
Uran [N]
uranio [M]

93 Np
neptunium
neptunium [M]
neptunio [M]
Neptunium [N]
nettunio [M]

94 Pu
plutonium
plutonium [M]
plutonio [M]
Plutonium [N]
plutonio [M]

95 Am
americium
américium [M]
americio [M]
Americium [N]
americio [M]

96 Cm
curium
curium [M]
curio [M]
Curium [N]
curio [M]

97 Bk
berkelium
berkélium [M]
berkelio [M]
Berkelium [N]
berkelio [M]

98 Cf
californium
californium [M]
californio [M]
Californium [N]
californio [M]

99 Es
einsteinium
einsteinium [M]
einstenio [M]
Einsteinium [N]
einsteinio [M]

100 Fm
fermium
fermium [M]
fermio [M]
Fermium [N]
fermio [M]

101 Md
mendelevium
mendélévium [M]
mendelevio [M]
Mendelevium [N]
mendelevio [M]

102 No
nobelium
nobélium [M]
nobelio [M]
Nobelium [N]
nobelio [M]

103 Lr
lawrencium
lawrencium [M]
laurencio [M]
Lawrencium [N]
laurenzio [M]

Alkaline earth metals

Métaux [M] alcalino-terreux | Metales [M] alcalinotérreos | Erdalkalimetalle [N] | Metalli [M] alcalino terrosi

4 Be
beryllium
béryllium [M]
berilio [M]
Beryllium [N]
berillio [M]

12 Mg
magnesium
magnésium [M]
magnesio [M]
Magnesium [N]
magnesio [M]

20 Ca
calcium
calcium [M]
calcio [M]
Calcium [N]
calcio [M]

38 Sr
strontium
strontium [M]
estroncio [M]
Strontium [N]
stronzio [M]

56 Ba
barium
baryum [M]
bario [M]
Barium [N]
bario [M]

88 Ra
radium
radium [M]
radio [M]
Radium [N]
radio [M]

molecular formula
formule [F] moléculaire
fórmula [F] molecular
Summenformel [F]
formula [F] molecolare

C_3H_8

element symbol
symbole [M] chimique
símbolo [M] químico
Elementsymbol [N]
simbolo [M] dell'elemento [M]

number of atoms
nombre [M] d'atomes [M]
número [M] de átomos [M]
Zahl [F] der Atome [F]
numero [M] di atomi

structural formula
formule [F] développée
fórmula [F] estructural
Strukturformel [F]
formula [F] di struttura [F]

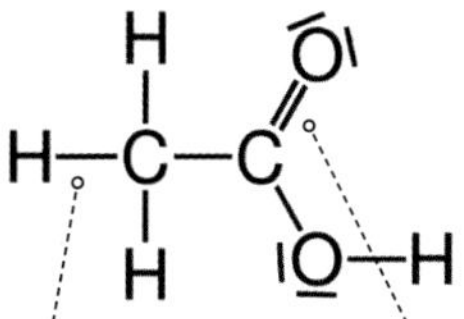

single bond
liaison [F] simple
enlace [M] simple
Einzelbindung [F]
legame [M] singolo

double bond
liaison [F] double
enlace [M] múltiple
Doppelbindung [F]
legame [M] multiplo

Lewis structure
structure [F] de Lewis
estructura [F] de Lewis
Lewis-Formel [F]
struttura [F] di Lewis

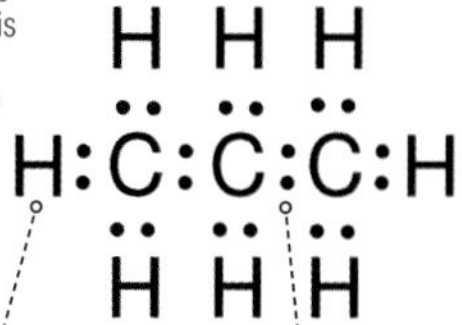

element symbol
symbole [M] chimique
símbolo [M] químico
Elementsymbol [N]
simbolo [M] dell'elemento [M]

valence electron
électron [M] de valence [F]
electrón [M] de valencia [F]
Valenzelektron [N]
elettroni [M] di valenza

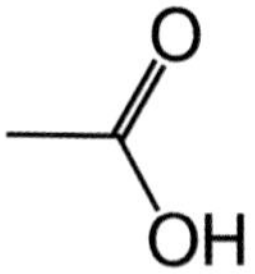

skeletal formula
formule [F] topologique
fórmula [F] esqueletal
Skelettformel [F]
formula [F] scheletrica

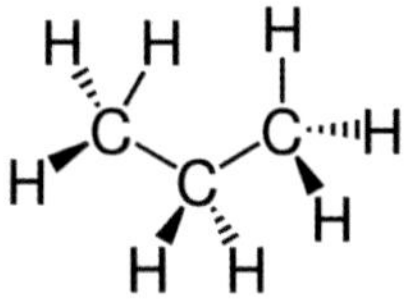

Natta projection
projection [F] de Natta
proyección [F] de Natta
Keilstrichformel [F]
proiezione [F] di Natta

H^+

positively charged ion
ion [M] positif
ión [M] con carga [F] positiva
positiv geladenes Ion [N]
ione [M] caricato positivamente

H^-

negatively charged ion
ion [M] négatif
ión [M] con carga [F] negativa
negativ geladenes Ion [N]
ione [M] caricato negativamente

$\rightleftharpoons$

equilibrium
équilibre [M]
equilibrio [M] químico
Gleichgewicht [N]
equilibrio [M]

$\Rightarrow$

retrosynthetic
rétrosynthétique
retrosíntesis [F]
retrosynthetisch
retrosintetico [M]

$\leftrightarrows$

reaction in both directions
réaction [F] dans les deux directions [F]
reacción [F] reversible
Reaktion [F] in beide Richtungen [F]
reazione [F] in entrambe le direzioni

chemical equation
équation [F] chimique
ecuación [M] química
chemische Formel [F]
equazione [F] chimica

forward reaction
réaction [F] directe
reacción [F] directa
Vorwärtsreaktion [F]
reazione [F] in avanti

$$CH_4 + 2O_2 \rightarrow CO_2 + 2H_2O$$

cholesterol
cholestérol [M]
colesterol [M]
Cholesterin [N]
colesterolo [M]

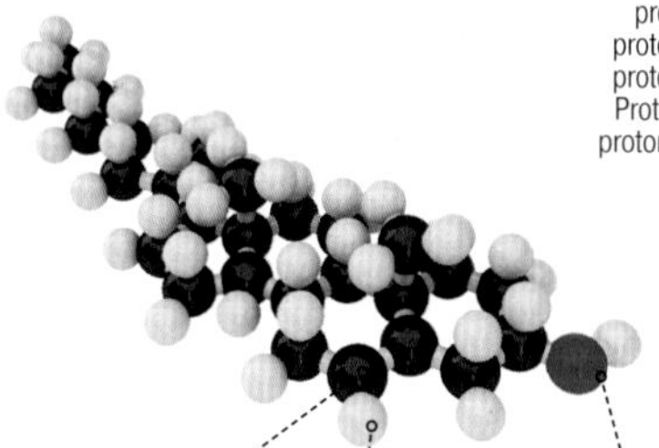

carbon
carbone [M]
carbono [M]
Kohlenstoff [M]
carbonio [M]

hydrogen
hydrogène [M]
hidrógeno [M]
Wasserstoff [M]
idrogeno [M]

oxygen
oxygène [M]
oxígeno [M]
Sauerstoff [M]
ossigeno [M]

atom
atome [M]
átomo [M]
Atom [N]
atomo [M]

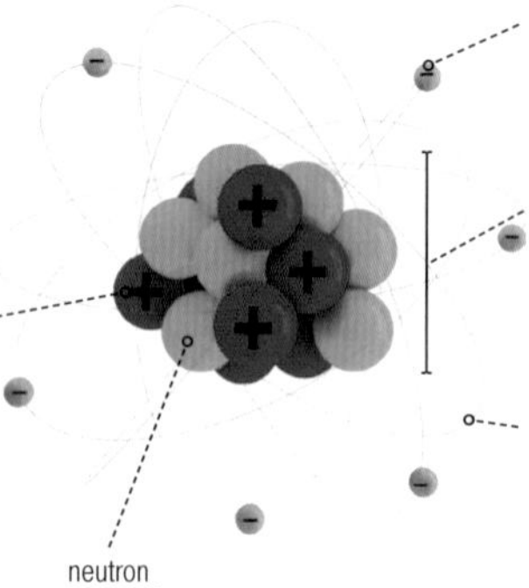

electron
électron [M]
electrón [M]
Elektron [N]
elettrone [M]

nucleus
noyau [M]
núcleo [M]
Kern [M]
nucleo [M]

proton
proton [M]
protón [M]
Proton [N]
protone [M]

orbit
orbite [M]
órbita [F]
Umlaufbahn [F]
orbita [F]

neutron
neutron [M]
neutrón [M]
Neutron [N]
neutrone [M]

nitrogen
azote [M]
nitrógeno [M]
Stickstoff [M]
azoto [M]

carbon dioxide
dioxyde [M] de carbone [M]
dióxido [M] de carbono [M]
Kohlendioxid [N]
biossido [M] di carbonio

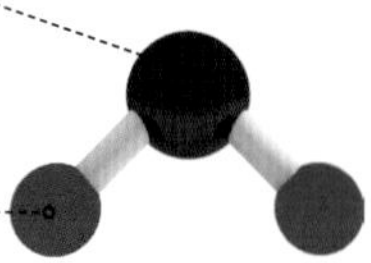

carbon
carbone [M]
carbono [M]
Kohlenstoff [M]
carbonio [M]

oxygen
oxygène [M]
oxígeno [M]
Sauerstoff [M]
ossigeno [M]

Kinematics

Cinématique [F] | Cinemática [F] | Kinematik [F] | Cinematica [F]

v
velocity
vitesse [F]
velocidad [F]
Geschwindigkeit [F]
velocità [F]

a
acceleration
accélération [F]
aceleración [F]
Beschleunigung [F]
accelerazione [F]

g
gravitational acceleration
accélération [F] gravitationnelle
aceleración [F] gravitacional
gravitative Beschleunigung [F]
accelerazione [F] gravitazionale

f
frequency
fréquence [F]
frecuencia [F]
Frequenz [F]
frequenza [F]

n
rotational frequency
fréquence [F] de rotation [F]
revoluciones [M] por minuto [M]
Drehfrequenz [F]
frequenza [F] di rotazione [F]

λ
wavelength
longueur [F] d'onde [F]
longitud [F] de onda [F]
Wellenlänge [F]
lunghezza [F] d'onda [F]

ν
kinematic viscosity
viscosité [F] cinématique
viscosidad [F] cinemática
kinematische Viskosität [F]
viscosità [F] cinematica

I
time
temps [M]
tiempo [M]
Zeit [F]
tempo [M]

T
period duration
durée [F] de la période [F]
periodo [M] de duración [F]
Periodendauer [F]
durata [F] del periodo [M]

ω
angular velocity
vitesse [F] angulaire
velocidad [F] angular
Winkelgeschwindigkeit [F]
velocità [F] angolare

Mechanics

Mécanique [F] | Mecánica [F] | Mechanik [F] | Meccanica [F]

m
mass
masse [F]
masa [F]
Masse [F]
massa [F]

F
force
force [F]
fuerza [F]
Kraft [F]
forza [F]

J
impulse
impulsion [F]
impulso [M]
Impuls [M]
impulso [M]

p
linear momentum
quantité [F] de mouvement [M]
momento [M] lineal
linearer Impuls [M]
momento [M] lineare

I
moment of inertia
moment [M] d'inertie [F]
momento [M] de inercia [F]
Trägheitsmoment [N]
momento [M] di inerzia

M
moment of force
moment [M] d'une force [F]
momento [M] de fuerza [F]
Drehmoment [N]
momento [M] meccanico

L
angular momentum
moment [M] angulaire
momento [M] angular
Drehimpuls [M]
momento [M] angolare

σ
normal tension
tension normale [F]
tensión [F] normal
Normalspannung [F]
tensione [F] normale

τ
shear stress
contrainte [F] de cisaillement [M]
tensión [F] cortante
Scherspannung [F]
sollecitazione [F] di taglio [M]

P
power
puissance [F]
potencia [F]
Leistung [F]
potenza [F]

W
work
travail [M]
trabajo [M]
Energie [F]
energia [F]

ρ
density
masse [F] volumique
densidad [F]
Energiedichte [F]
densità

I
intensity
intensité [F]
intensidad [F]
Intensität [F]
intensità [F]

η
efficiency
rendement [M]
eficiencia [F]
Wirkungsgrad [M]
efficienza [F]

S
entropy
entropie [F]
entropía [F]
Entropie [F]
entropia [F]

F_R
frictional force
force [F] de frottement [M]
fuerza [F] de fricción [F]
Reibung [F]
forza [F] di attrito [M]

γ
specific weight
poids [M] spécifique
peso [M] específico
spezifisches Gewicht [N]
peso [M] specifico

V
specific volume
volume [M] spécifique
volumen [M] específico
spezifisches Volumen [N]
volume [M] specifico

Photometry and optics

Photométrie [F] et optique [F] | Fotometría [F] y óptica [F] | Fotometrie [F] und Optik [F] | Fotometria [F] e ottica [F]

D
diameter
diamètre
diámetro [M]
Brechwert [M]
diametro [M]

I_V
luminous intensity
intensité [F] lumineuse
luminosidad [F]
Lichtstärke [F]
intensità [F] luminosa

Φ_v
luminous flux
flux [M] lumineux
flujo [M] luminoso
Lichtstrom [M]
flusso [M] luminoso

η
luminous efficacy
efficacité [F] lumineuse
eficacia [F] luminosa
Lichtausbeute [F]
efficacia [F] luminosa

L_v
luminance
luminance [F]
luminancia [F]
Leuchtdichte [F]
luminanza [F]

E_v
illuminance
éclairement [M] lumineux
iluminancia [F]
Beleuchtungsstärke [F]
illuminamento [M]

M_v
luminous exitance
exitance [F] lumineuse
emitancia [F] luminosa
spezifische Lichtausstrahlung [F]
emissione [F] luminosa

H_v
luminous exposure
exposition [F] lumineuse
exposición [F] luminosa
Belichtung [F]
esposizione [F] luminosa

f
focal length
distance [F] focale
distancia [F] focal
Brennweite [F]
lunghezza [F] focale

Q_v
luminous energy
énergie [F] lumineuse
energía [F] luminosa
Lichtmenge [F]
energia [F] luminosa

Thermodynamics

Thermodynamique [F] | Termodinámica [F] | Thermodynamik [F] | Termodinamica [F]

λ
thermal conductivity
conductivité [F] thermique
conductividad [F] térmica
Wärmeleitfähigkeit [F]
conducibilità [F] termica

T
absolute temperature
température [F] absolue
temperatura [F] absoluta
absolute Temperatur [F]
temperatura [F] assoluta

ϑ
Celsius temperature
température [F] Celsius
temperatura [F] celsius
Celsius Temperatur [F]
temperatura [F] Celsius

Q
heat
chaleur [F]
calor [M]
Wärme [F]
calore [M]

U
internal energy
énergie [F] interne
energía [F] interna
innere Energie [F]
energia [F] interna

E_{th}
thermal energy
énergie [F] thermique
energía [F] térmica
thermische Energie [F]
energia [F] termica

μ
chemical potential
potentiel [M] chimique
potencial [M] químico
chemisches Potential [N]
potenziale [M] chimico

H
enthalpy
enthalpie [F]
entalpía [F]
Enthalpie [F]
entalpia [F]

Φ_{th}
heat flux
flux [M] de chaleur [F]
flujo [M] de calor [M]
Wärmestrom [M]
flusso [M] termico

S
entropy
entropie [F]
entropía [F]
Entropie [F]
entropia [F]

C_{th}
thermal capacity
capacité [F] thermique
capacidad [F] calorífica
Wärmekapazität [F]
capacità [F] termica

Electricity

Électricité [F] | Electricidad [F] | Elektrizität [F] | Elettricità [F]

Y
admittance
admittance [F]
conductancia [F] falsa
Leitwert [M]
ammettenza [F]

I
electric current
courant [M] électrique
corriente [F] eléctrica
Stromstärke [F]
corrente [F] elettrica

J
electric current density
densité [F] de courant [M] électrique
densidad [F] de transmisión [F] eléctrica
elektrische Stromdichte [F]
densità [F] di corrente [F] elettrica

Q
electric charge
charge [F] électrique
carga [F] eléctrica
elektrische Ladung [F]
carica [F] elettrica

U
electric tension
tension [F]
tensión [F] eléctrica
elektrische Spannung [F]
tensione [F] elettrica

φ
phase shift
déphasage [M]
cambio [M] de fase [F]
Phasenverschiebung [F]
sfasamento [M]

R
resistance
résistance [F]
resistencia [F]
Widerstand [M]
resistenza [F]

X
reactance
réactance [F]
reactancia [F]
Blindwiderstand [M]
reattanza [F]

Z
impedance
impédance [F]
impedancia [F]
Impedanz [F]
impedenza [F]

ρ
specific resistance
résistivité [F]
resistividad [F]
spezifischer Widerstand [M]
resistenza [F] specifica

B
susceptance
susceptance [F]
conductancia [F] ciega
Blindleitwert [M]
suscettanza [F]

F_{L}
Lorentz force
force [F] de Lorentz
fuerza [F] de Lorentz
Lorentzkraft [F]
forza [F] di Lorentz

E
electric field
champ [M] électrique
campo [M] eléctrico
elektrische Feldstärke [N]
campo [M] elettrico

Ψ
water potential
potentiel [M] hydrique
potencial [M] hídrico
Wasserpotential [N]
potenziale [M] idrico

D
electric flux density
induction [F] électrique
densidad [F] de flujo [M] eléctrico
elektrische Flussdichte [F]
densità [F] di flusso [M] elettrico

P
polarization
polarisation [F]
polarización [F]
Polarisation [F]
polarizzazione [F]

α
polarizability
polarisabilité [F]
polarizabilidad [F]
Polarisierbarkeit [F]
polarizzabilità [F]

Magnetism

Magnétisme [M] | Magnetismo [M] | Magnetismus [M] | Magnetismo [M]

P
effective power
puissance [F] effective
potencia [F] efectiva
Effektivleistung [F]
potenza [F] effettiva

B
magnetic flux density
densité [F] de champ [M] magnétique
densidad [F] de flujo [M] magnético
magnetische Flussdichte [F]
densità [F] di flusso [M] magnetico

J
magnetic polarization
polarisation [F] magnétique
polarización [F] magnética
magnetische Polarisation [F]
polarizzazione [F] magnetica

ϵ
permittivity
permittivité [F]
permitividad [F]
Permittivität [F]
permittività [F]

M
magnetization
magnétisation [F]
magnetización [F]
Magnetisierung [F]
magnetizzazione [F]

Φ
magnetic flux
flux [M] magnétique
flujo [M] magnético
magnetischer Fluss [M]
flusso [M] magnetico

C
electric capacity
capacité [F] électrique
capacidad [F] eléctrica
elektrische Kapazität [F]
capacità [F] elettrica

S
elastance
élastance [F]
elastancia [F]
Elastanz [F]
elastanza [F]

L
inductance
inductance [F]
inductancia [F]
Induktivität [F]
induttanza [F]

H
magnetic field strength
intensité [F] du champ [M] magnétique
fuerza [F] de campo [M] magnético
magnetische Feldstärke [F]
intensità [F] del campo [M] magnetico

S
apparent power
puissance [F] apparente
potencia [F] aparente
Scheinleistung [F]
potenza [F] apparente

m
magnetic moment
moment [M] magnétique
momento [M] magnético
magnetisches Moment [N]
momento [M] magnetico

Atomic and molecular quantities

Quantités F d'atomes M et de molécules F | Cantidades F atómicas y moleculares | Atome N und Moleküle N | Masse F atomiche e molecolari

n
amount of substance
quantité F de matière F
cantidad F de sustancia F
Stoffmenge F
quantità F di sostanza

V_m
molar volume
volume M molaire
volumen M molar
molares Volumen N
volume M molare

M
molar mass
masse F molaire
masa F molar
molare Masse F
massa F molare

M_r
relative molar mass
masse F moléculaire relative
masa F molecular relativa
relative Molekülmasse F
massa F molecolare relativa

A_r
relative atomic mass
masse F atomique relative
masa F atómica relativa
relative Atommasse F
massa F atomica relativa

Nuclear physics

Physique F nucléaire | Física F nuclear | Kernphysik F | Fisica F nucleare

σ
effect cross section
section F efficace de l'effet M
sección F eficaz
Wirkungsquerschnitt M
sezione F di effetto M

A
activity
activité F
actividad F
Aktivität F
attività F

τ
mean lifetime
durée F de vie F moyenne
vida F media
Lebensdauer F
vita F media

λ
disintegration constant
constante F de désintégration F
constante F de desintegración F
Zerfallskonstante F
costante F di disintegrazione F

D
absorbed dose
dose F absorbée
dosis F absorbida
Energiedosis F
dose F assorbita

H
equivalent dose
dose F équivalente
dosis F equivalente
Äquivalentdosis F
dose F equivalente

$T_{1/2}$
half-life
période F radioactive
período M de semidesintegración F
Halbwertszeit F
tempo M di dimezzamento M

J
ion dose
dose F ionique
dosis F iónica
Ionendosis F
dosaggio M di ioni M

Radiometry

Radiométrie F | Radiometría F | Radiometrie F | Radiometria F

H
radiant exposure
exposition F énergétique
exposición F radiante
Bestrahlung F
esposizione F radiante

I
radiant intensity
intensité F énergétique
intensidad F radiante
Strahlungsintensität F
intensità F radiante

Φ
radiant flux
flux M radiatif
flujo M radiante
Strahlungsfluss M
flusso M radiante

Q
radiant energy
énergie F rayonnante
energía F radiante
Strahlungsenergie F
energia F radiante

L
radiance
luminance F
radiancia F
Strahldichte F
radianza F

MATHEMATICS
Mathematical symbols

l
length
longueur F
longitud F
Länge F
lunghezza F

b
width
largeur F
anchura F
Breite F
larghezza F

h
height
hauteur F
altura F
Höhe F
altezza F

σ
thickness
épaisseur F
espesor M
Dicke F
spessore M

r
radius
rayon M
radio M
Radius M
raggio M

d
diameter
diamètre M
diámetro M
Durchmesser M
diametro M

s
distance
distance F
longitud F lineal
Abstand M
distanza

A
area
aire F
área F
Fläche F
area F

S
cross-sectional area
superficie F de la section F transversale
área F transversal
Querschnittsfläche F
area F sezione trasversale

V
volume
volume M
volumen M
Volumen N
volume M

Ω
space angle
angle M spatial
ángulo M espacial
Raumwinkel M
angolo M spaziale

+ addition / positive addition [F] / positif suma [F] Addition [F] / positiv addizione [F]	**—** subtraction / negative soustraction [F] / négatif resta [F] Subtraktion [F] sottrazione [F]	**x** multiplication multiplication [F] multiplicación [F] Multiplikation [F] moltiplicazione [F]	**÷** division division [F] división [F] Division [F] divisione [F]	**±** plus or minus signe [M] plus [M] ou moins [M] más o menos Plus-Minus-Zeichen [N] più [M] o meno [M]
= equals signe [M] égal [M] igualdad [F] Gleichheitszeichen [N] uguale	**≠** is not equal to signe [M] de différence [F] inecuación [F] Ungleichung [F] diverso da	**<** is less than plus petit que menor que kleiner als minore di	**>** is greater than plus grand que mayor que größer als maggiore di	**≤** is less than or equal to plus petit ou égal à menor o igual que kleiner als oder gleich wie minore di o uguale a
≥ is greater than or equal to plus grand ou égal à mayor o igual que größer als oder gleich wie maggiore di o uguale a [M]	**√** square root of racine [F] carrée raíz [F] cuadrada Quadratwurzel [F] radice quadrata [F]	**%** percent pourcentage porcentaje [M] Prozent [N] per cento [M]	**Σ** sum somme [F] sumatorio [M] Summe [F] somma [F]	**Π** product produit [M] producto [M] Produkt [N] prodotto [M]
Δ difference différence [F] diferencia [F] Differenz [F] differenza [F]	**∫** integral intégrale [F] integral [F] Integral [N] integrale [M]	**′** derivative dérivée [F] diferencial [M] Ableitung [F] derivata [F]	**°** degree degré [M] grado [M] Grad [N] grado [M]	**∞** infinity à l'infini [M] inifinito [M] Unendlichkeit [F] infinito [M]
∠ acute angle angle [M] aigu ángulo [M] agudo [M] spitzer Winkel [M] angolo [M] acuto	**∟** right angle angle [M] droit ángulo [M] recto rechter Winkel [M] angolo [M] retto	**⊥** is perpendicular to perpendiculaire à perpendicular [F] ist lotrecht mit perpendicolare a	**∥** is parallel to parallèle à paralelo [M] ist parallel zu parallelo a	**⌀** diameter diamètre [M] diámetro [M] Durchmesser [M] diametro [M]
∪ union of two sets union [F] de deux ensembles [M] unión [F] de dos conjuntos [M] Vereinigung [F] von zwei Mengen [F] unione [F] di due insiemi [M]	**∩** intersection of two sets intersection [F] de deux ensembles [M] intersección [F] de dos conjuntos [M] Durchschnitt [M] von zwei Mengen [F] intersezione [F] di due insiemi [M]	**∅** empty set ensemble [M] vide conjunto [M] vacio Leere Menge insieme [M] vuoto	**∈** is an element of appartient à pertanece a Element [N] von appartiene a [M]	**⊂** is included in / is a subset of est compris dans está contenido en ist enthalten in / ist eine Untermenge [F] contenuto in / sottoinsieme di
∀ universal quantification quantification [F] universelle cuantificador [M] universal Allaussage [F] quantificatore [M] universale	**∃** existential quantification quantification [F] existentielle cuantificador [M] existencial Existenzquantifizierung [F] quantificatore [M] esistenziale	**ℕ** natural numbers nombres [M] entiers naturels número [M] natural natürliche Zahl [F] numeri [M]	**ℤ** integers nombres [M] entiers relatifs número [M] entero Ganzzahl [F] numeri [M] interi	**ℚ** rational numbers nombres [M] rationnels número [M] racional rationale Zahl [F] numeri [M] razionali

$\mathbb{A}$
algebraic numbers
nombres [M] algébriques
número [M] algebraico
algebraische Zahlen [F]
numeri [M] algebrici

$\mathbb{R}$
real numbers
nombres [M] réels
número [M] real
reelle Zahlen [F]
numeri [M] reali

$\mathbb{C}$
complex numbers
nombres [M] complexes
número [M] complejo
komplexe Zahlen [F]
numeri [M] complessi

$\mathbb{H}$
quaternions
quaternions [M]
cuaternión [M]
Quaternion [F]
quaternione [M]

π
pi
Pi
pi [M]
Pi [N]
pi [M] greco

$\frac{3}{4}$
simple fraction
fraction [F] ordinaire
fracción [F] ordinaria
gemeiner Bruch [M]
frazione [F] semplice

numerator
numérateur [M]
numerador [M]
Zähler [M]
numeratore [M]

fraction bar
barre [F] de fraction [F]
barra [F] de fracción [F]
Bruchstrich [M]
linea [F] di frazione [F]

denominator
dénominateur [M]
denominador [M]
Nenner [M]
denominatore [M]

e
Euler's number
nombre [M] d'Euler
número [M] de Euler
Euler'sche Zahl [F]
numero [M] di Eulero

φ
golden ratio
nombre [M] d'or [M]
proporción [F] áurea
goldener Schnitt [M]
rapporto [M] aureo

i
imaginary number
nombre [M] imaginaire
número [M] imaginario
imaginäre Zahl [F]
numero [M] immaginario

Roman numerals

I
one
un [M]
uno [M]
eins
uno [M]

II
two
deux [M]
dos [M]
zwei
due [M]

III
three
trois [M]
tres [M]
drei
tre [M]

IV
four
quatre [M]
cuatro [M]
vier
quattro [M]

V
five
cinq [M]
cinco [M]
fünf
cinque [M]

VI
six
six [M]
seis [M]
sechs
sei [M]

VII
seven
sept [M]
siete [M]
sieben
sette [M]

VIII
eight
huit [M]
ocho [M]
acht
otto [M]

IX
nine
neuf [M]
nueve [M]
neun
nove [M]

X
ten
dix [M]
diez [M]
zehn
dieci [M]

XX
twenty
vingt [M]
veinte [M]
zwanzig
venti [M]

XXX
thirty
trente [M]
treinta [M]
dreißig
trenta [M]

XL
forty
quarante [M]
cuarenta [M]
vierzig
quaranta [M]

L
fifty
cinquante [M]
cincuenta [M]
fünfzig
cinquanta [M]

LX
sixty
soixante [M]
sesenta [M]
sechzig
sessanta [M]

XC
ninety
quatre-vingt-dix [M]
noventa [M]
neunzig
novanta [M]

C
one hundred
cent [M]
cien [M]
einhundert
cento [M]

D
five hundred
cinq cents [M]
quinientos [M]
fünfhundert
cinquecento [M]

M
one thousand
mille [M]
mil [M]
eintausend
mille [M]

Circle

Cercle [M] | Círculo [M] | Kreis [M] | Cerchio [M]

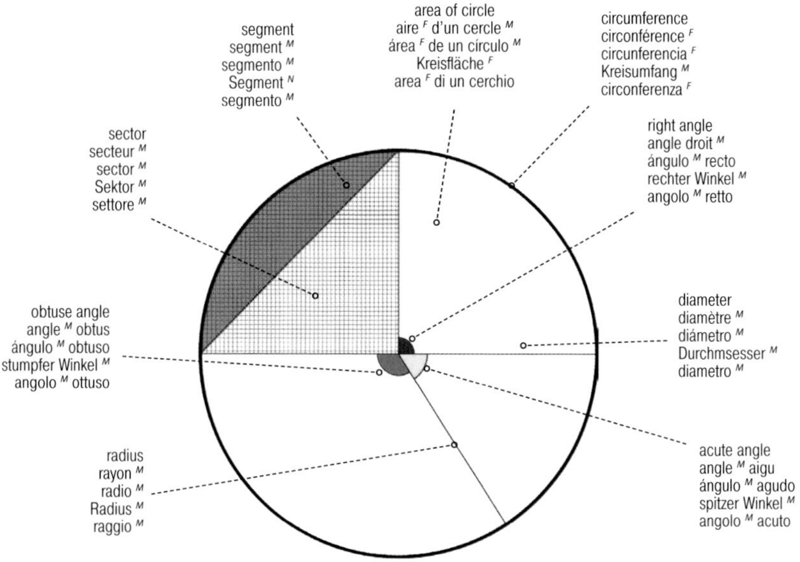
segment
segment [M]
segmento [M]
Segment [N]
segmento [M]
area of circle
aire [F] d'un cercle [M]
área [F] de un círculo [M]
Kreisfläche [F]
area [F] di un cerchio
circumference
circonférence [F]
circunferencia [F]
Kreisumfang [M]
circonferenza [F]
sector
secteur [M]
sector [M]
Sektor [M]
settore [M]
right angle
angle droit [M]
ángulo [M] recto
rechter Winkel [M]
angolo [M] retto
obtuse angle
angle [M] obtus
ángulo [M] obtuso
stumpfer Winkel [M]
angolo [M] ottuso
diameter
diamètre [M]
diámetro [M]
Durchmsesser [M]
diametro [M]
radius
rayon [M]
radio [M]
Radius [M]
raggio [M]
acute angle
angle [M] aigu
ángulo [M] agudo
spitzer Winkel [M]
angolo [M] acuto

Triangles

Triangles [M] | Triángulos [M] | Dreiecke [N] | Triangoli [M]

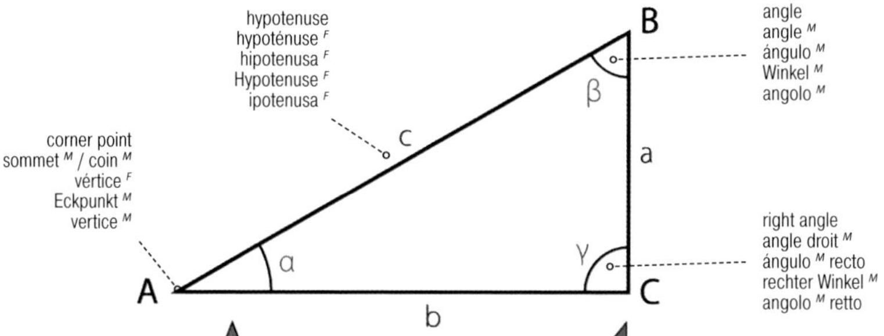
hypotenuse
hypoténuse [F]
hipotenusa [F]
Hypotenuse [F]
ipotenusa [F]
B
angle
angle [M]
ángulo [M]
Winkel [M]
angolo [M]
β
c
a
corner point
sommet [M] / coin [M]
vértice [F]
Eckpunkt [M]
vertice [M]
α
γ
A
C
b
right angle
angle droit [M]
ángulo [M] recto
rechter Winkel [M]
angolo [M] retto

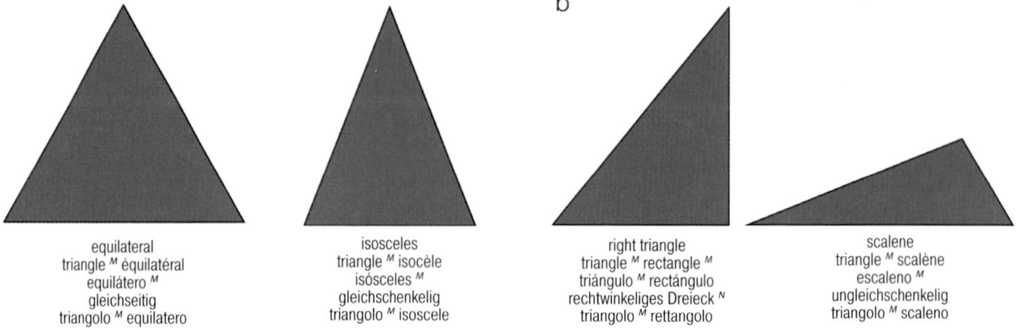
equilateral
triangle [M] équilatéral
equilátero [M]
gleichseitig
triangolo [M] equilatero
isosceles
triangle [M] isocèle
isósceles [M]
gleichschenkelig
triangolo [M] isoscele
right triangle
triangle [M] rectangle [M]
triángulo [M] rectángulo
rechtwinkeliges Dreieck [N]
triangolo [M] rettangolo
scalene
triangle [M] scalène
escaleno [M]
ungleichschenkelig
triangolo [M] scaleno

Polygons

Polygones M | Polígonos M | Polygone N | Poligoni M

square
carré M
cuadrado M
Quadrat N
quadrato M

rectangle
rectangle M
rectángulo M
Rechteck N
rettangolo M

rhombus
rhombe M
rombo M
Rhombus M
rombo M

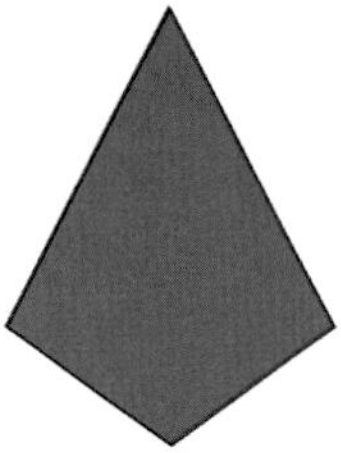

kite
cerf-volant M
deltoide M
Deltoid N
aquilone M

trapezoid
trapèze M
trapezoide M
Trapez N
trapezio M

pentagon
pentagone M
pentágono M
Fünfeck N
pentagono M

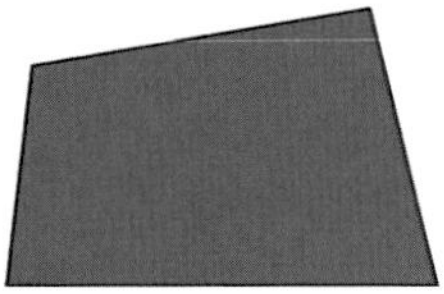

trapezium
trapèze M
trapecio M
Trapez N
quadrilatero M

rhomboid
rhomboïde M
romboide M
Parallelogramm N
parallelogramma M

Diagrams

Diagrammes M | Diagramas M | Diagramme N | Diagrammi M

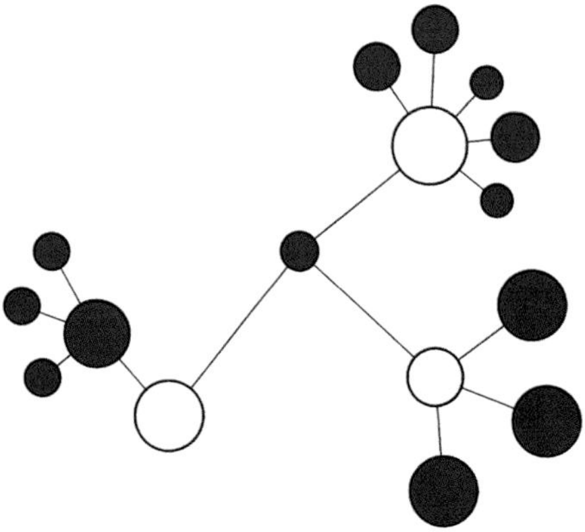

cluster diagram
diagramme M à bulles F
diagrama M de racimo M
Clusterdiagramm N
diagramma M dei cluster M

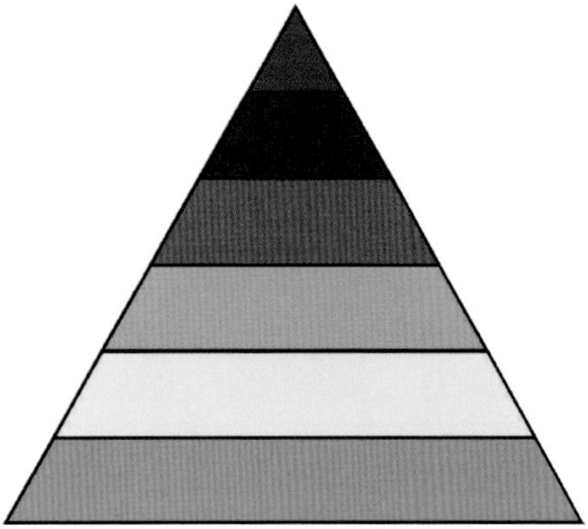

pyramid diagram
diagramme M pyramidal
diagrama M ternario
Pyramidendiagramm N
diagramma M a piramide F

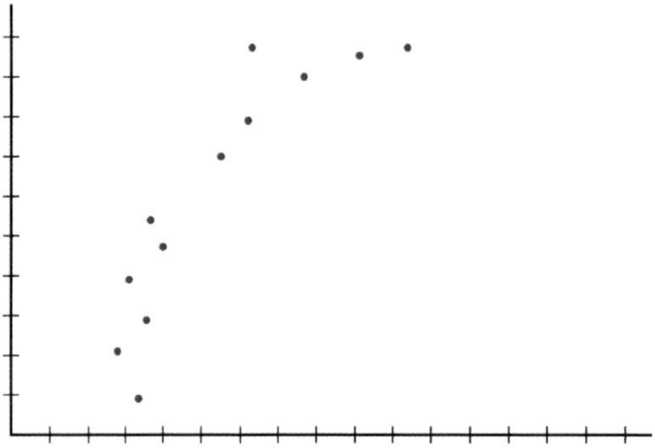

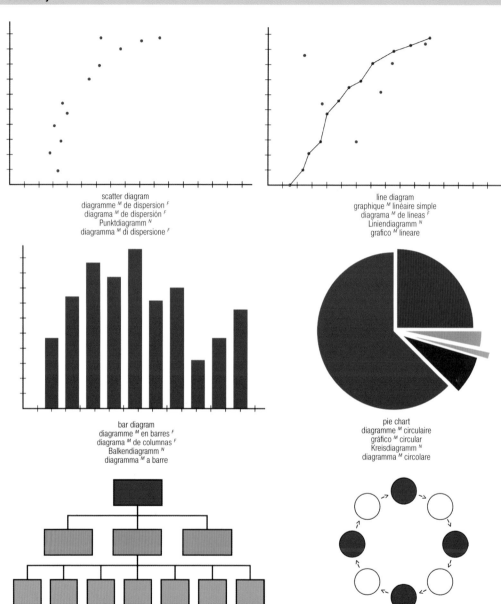

scatter diagram
diagramme [M] de dispersion [F]
diagrama [M] de dispersión [F]
Punktdiagramm [N]
diagramma [M] di dispersione [F]

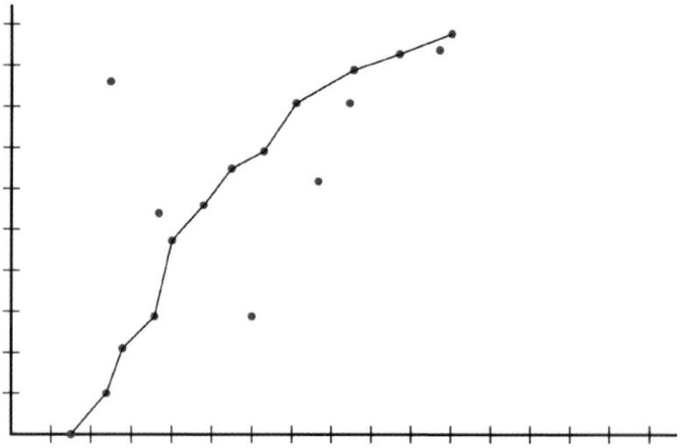

line diagram
graphique [M] linéaire simple
diagrama [M] de líneas [F]
Liniendiagramm [N]
grafico [M] lineare

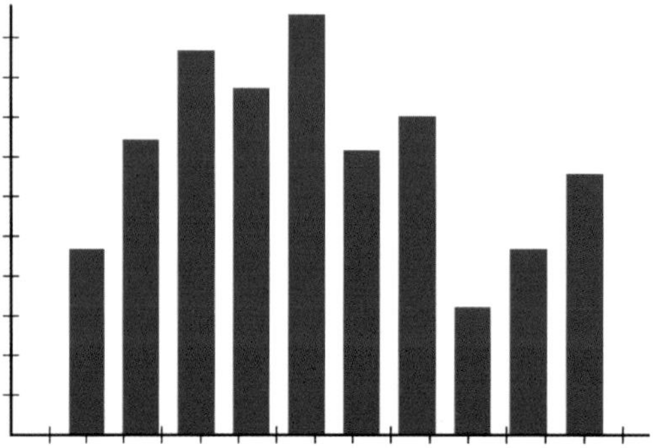

bar diagram
diagramme [M] en barres [F]
diagrama [M] de columnas [F]
Balkendiagramm [N]
diagramma [M] a barre

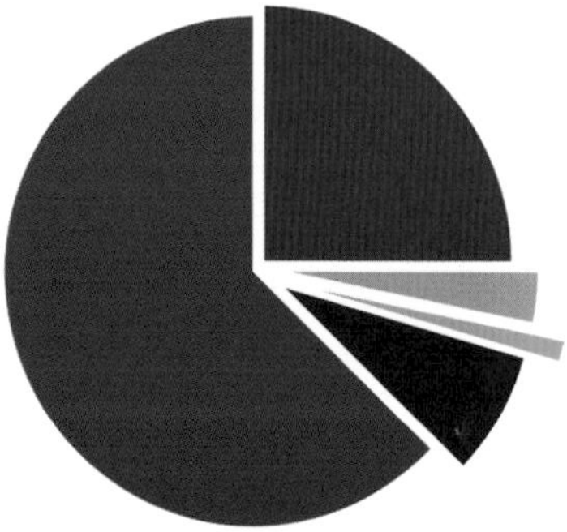

pie chart
diagramme [M] circulaire
gráfico [M] circular
Kreisdiagramm [N]
diagramma [M] circolare

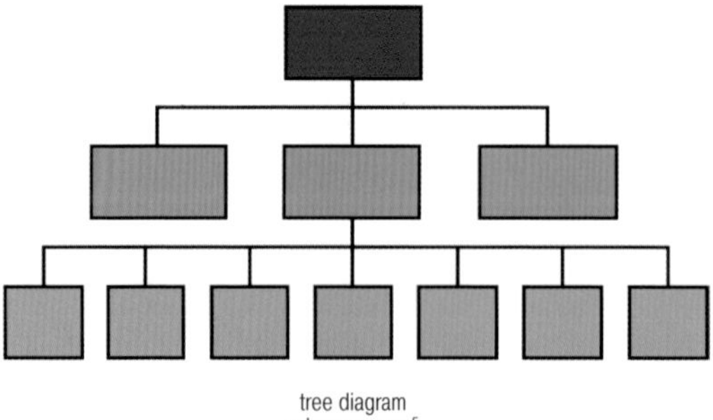

tree diagram
arborescence [F]
diagrama [M] de árbol [M]
Baumdiagramm [N]
diagramma [M] ad albero [M]

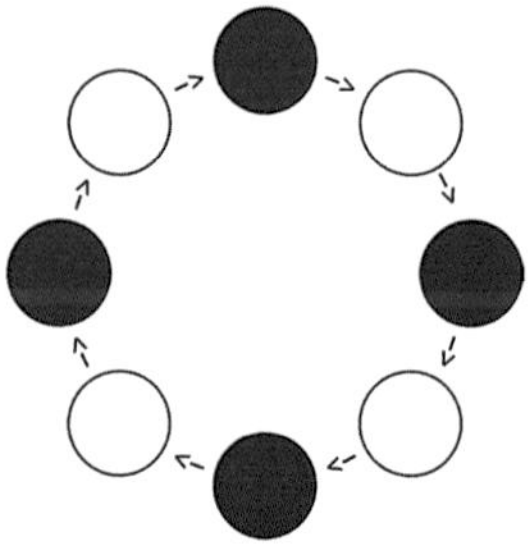

cycle diagram
diagramme [M] cyclique
diagrama [M] de ciclos [M]
Kreislaufdiagramm [N]
diagramma [M] del ciclo [M]

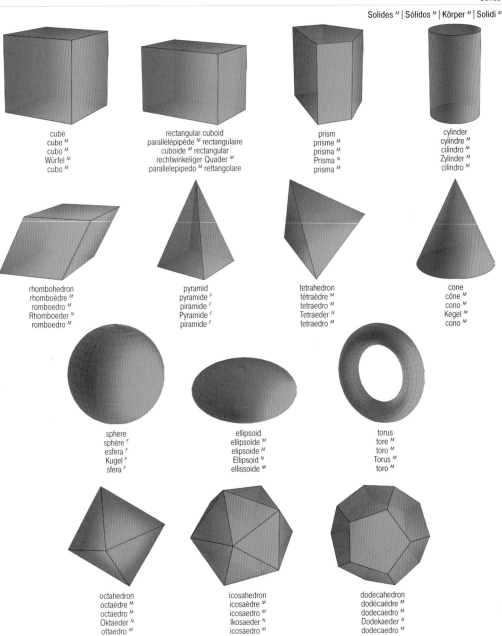

Solides [M] | Sólidos [M] | Körper [M] | Solidi [M]

cube
cube [M]
cubo [M]
Würfel [M]
cubo [M]

rectangular cuboid
parallélépipède [M] rectangulaire
cuboide [M] rectangular
rechtwinkeliger Quader [M]
parallelepipedo [M] rettangolare

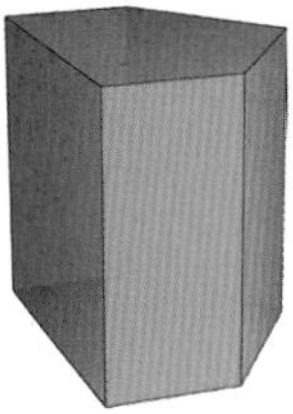

prism
prisme [M]
prisma [M]
Prisma [N]
prisma [M]

cylinder
cylindre [M]
cilindro [M]
Zylinder [M]
cilindro [M]

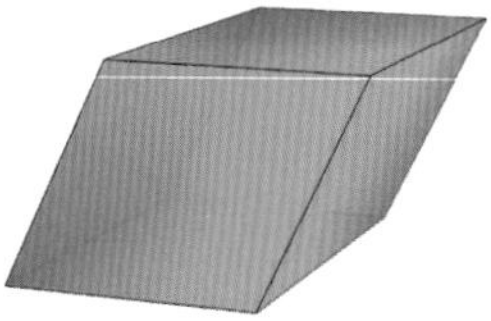

rhombohedron
rhomboèdre [M]
romboedro [M]
Rhomboeder [N]
romboedro [M]

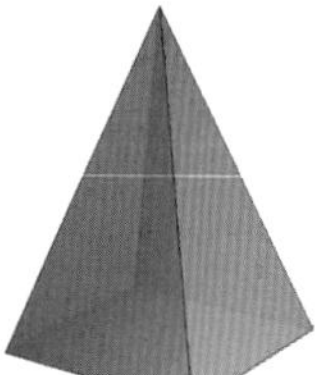

pyramid
pyramide [F]
pirámide [F]
Pyramide [F]
piramide [F]

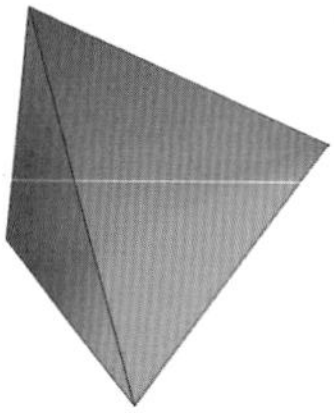

tetrahedron
tétraèdre [M]
tetraedro [M]
Tetraeder [N]
tetraedro [M]

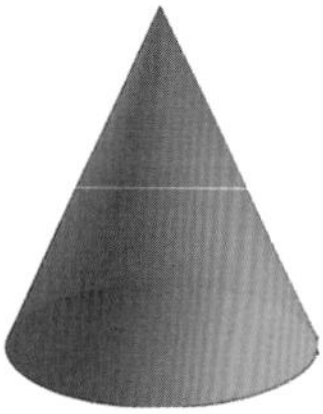

cone
cône [M]
cono [M]
Kegel [M]
cono [M]

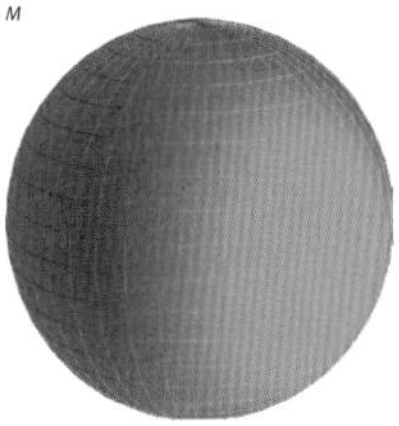

sphere
sphère [F]
esfera [F]
Kugel [F]
sfera [F]

ellipsoid
ellipsoïde [M]
elipsoide [M]
Ellipsoid [N]
ellissoide [M]

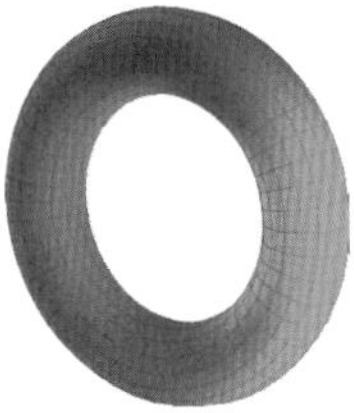

torus
tore [M]
toro [M]
Torus [M]
toro [M]

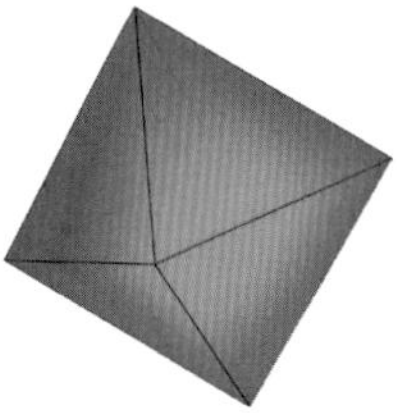

octahedron
octaèdre [M]
octaedro [M]
Oktaeder [N]
ottaedro [M]

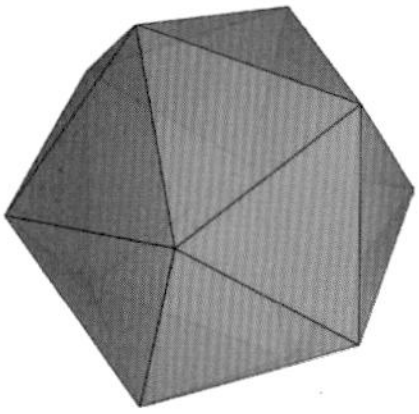

icosahedron
icosaèdre [M]
icosaedro [M]
Ikosaeder [N]
icosaedro [M]

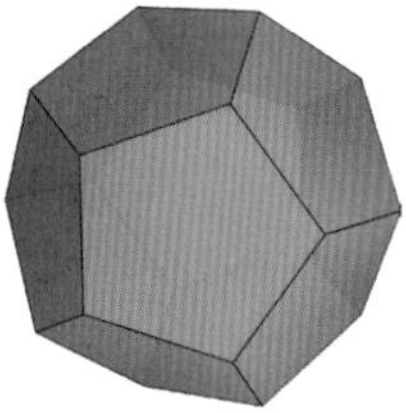

dodecahedron
dodécaèdre [M]
dodecaedro [M]
Dodekaeder [N]
dodecaedro [M]

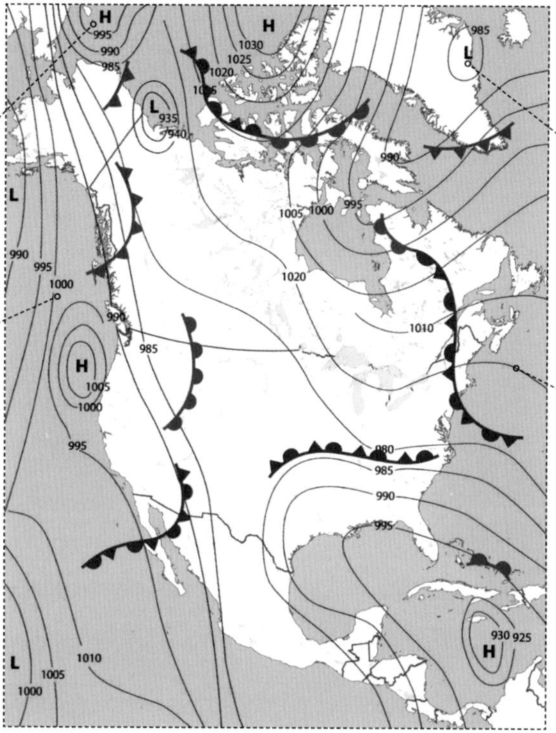

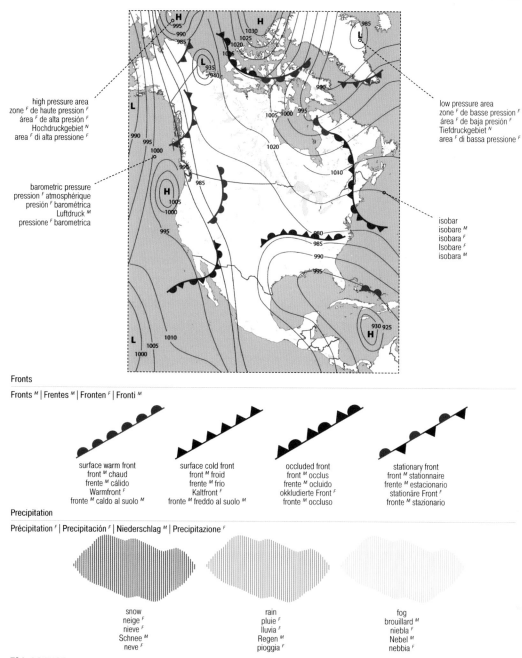

high pressure area
zone F de haute pression F
área F de alta presión F
Hochdruckgebiet N
area F di alta pressione F

barometric pressure
pression F atmosphérique
presión F barométrica
Luftdruck M
pressione F barometrica

low pressure area
zone F de basse pression F
área F de baja presión F
Tiefdruckgebiet N
area F di bassa pressione F

isobar
isobare M
isobara F
Isobare F
isobara M

Fronts

Fronts M | Frentes M | Fronten F | Fronti M

surface warm front
front M chaud
frente M cálido
Warmfront F
fronte M caldo al suolo M

surface cold front
front M froid
frente M frío
Kaltfront F
fronte M freddo al suolo M

occluded front
front M occlus
frente M ocluido
okkludierte Front F
fronte M occluso

stationary front
front M stationnaire
frente M estacionario
stationäre Front F
fronte M stazionario

Precipitation

Précipitation F | Precipitación F | Niederschlag M | Precipitazione F

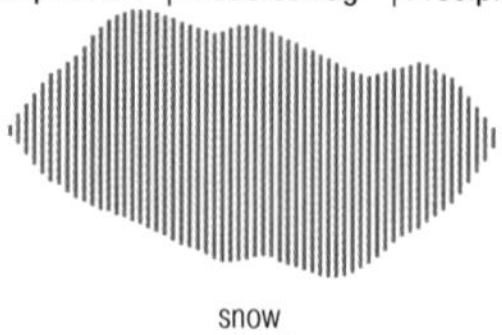

snow
neige F
nieve F
Schnee M
neve F

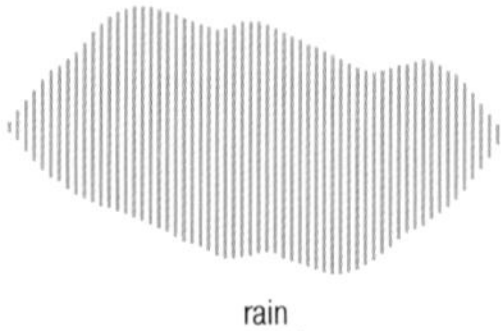

rain
pluie F
lluvia F
Regen M
pioggia F

fog
brouillard M
niebla F
Nebel M
nebbia F

station model
modèle [M] de pointage [M]
modelo [M] de estación [M]
Stationsmodell [N]
modello [M] di stazione [F]

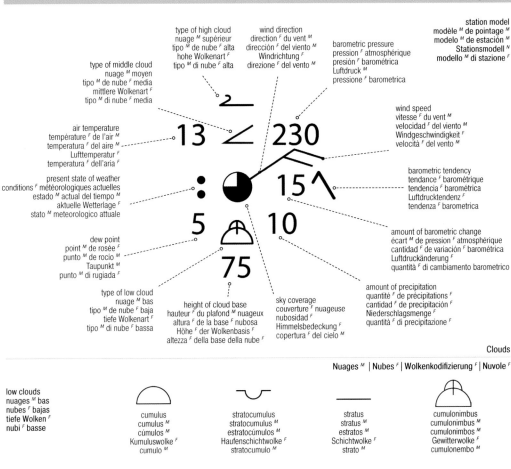

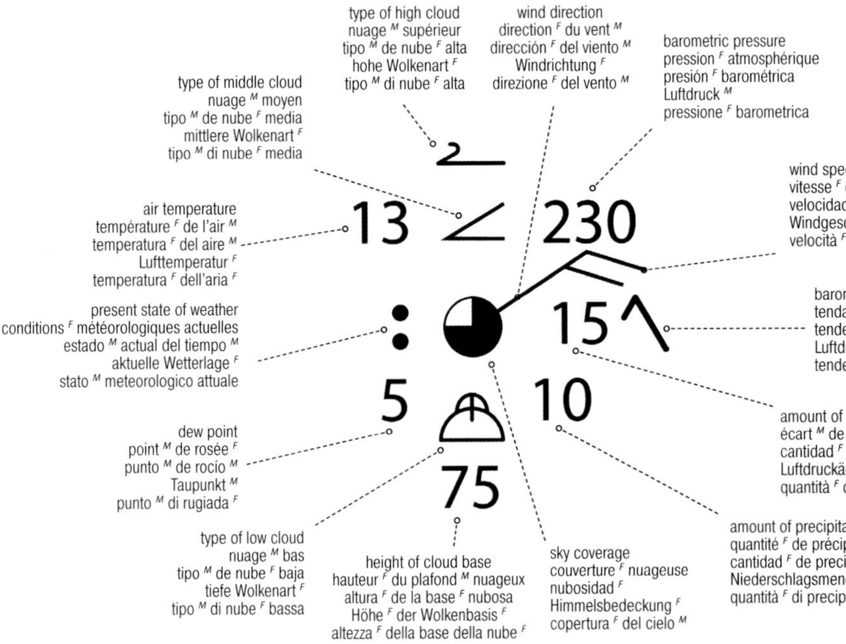
type of high cloud
nuage [M] supérieur
tipo [M] de nube [F] alta
hohe Wolkenart [F]
tipo [M] di nube [F] alta
wind direction
direction [F] du vent [M]
dirección [F] del viento [M]
Windrichtung [F]
direzione [F] del vento [M]
barometric pressure
pression [F] atmosphérique
presión [F] barométrica
Luftdruck [M]
pressione [F] barometrica
type of middle cloud
nuage [M] moyen
tipo [M] de nube [F] media
mittlere Wolkenart [F]
tipo [M] di nube [F] media
wind speed
vitesse [F] du vent [M]
velocidad [F] del viento [M]
Windgeschwindigkeit [F]
velocità [F] del vento [M]
air temperature
température [F] de l'air [M]
temperatura [F] del aire [M]
Lufttemperatur [F]
temperatura [F] dell'aria [F]
13
230
present state of weather
conditions [F] météorologiques actuelles
estado [M] actual del tiempo [M]
aktuelle Wetterlage [F]
stato [M] meteorologico attuale
15
barometric tendency
tendance [F] barométrique
tendencia [F] barométrica
Luftdrucktendenz [F]
tendenza [F] barometrica
5
10
amount of barometric change
écart [M] de pression [F] atmosphérique
cantidad [F] de variación [F] barométrica
Luftdruckänderung [F]
quantità [F] di cambiamento barometrico
dew point
point [M] de rosée [F]
punto [M] de rocío [M]
Taupunkt [M]
punto [M] di rugiada [F]
75
amount of precipitation
quantité [F] de précipitations [F]
cantidad [F] de precipitación [F]
Niederschlagsmenge [F]
quantità [F] di precipitazione [F]
type of low cloud
nuage [M] bas
tipo [M] de nube [F] baja
tiefe Wolkenart [F]
tipo [M] di nube [F] bassa
height of cloud base
hauteur [F] du plafond [M] nuageux
altura [F] de la base [F] nubosa
Höhe [F] der Wolkenbasis [F]
altezza [F] della base della nube [F]
sky coverage
couverture [F] nuageuse
nubosidad [F]
Himmelsbedeckung [F]
copertura [F] del cielo [M]

Clouds

Nuages [M] | Nubes [F] | Wolkenkodifizierung [F] | Nuvole [F]

low clouds
nuages [M] bas
nubes [F] bajas
tiefe Wolken [F]
nubi [F] basse

cumulus
cumulus [M]
cúmulos [M]
Kumuluswolke [F]
cumulo [M]

stratocumulus
stratocumulus [M]
estratocúmulos [M]
Haufenschichtwolke [F]
stratocumulo [M]

stratus
stratus [M]
estratos [M]
Schichtwolke [F]
strato [M]

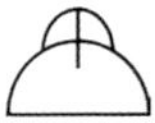

cumulonimbus
cumulonimbus [M]
cumulonimbos [M]
Gewitterwolke [F]
cumulonembo [M]

middle clouds
nuages [M] moyens
nubes [F] medias
mittlere Wolken [F]
nubi [F] medie

altocumulus
altocumulus [M]
altocúmulos [M]
Altokumuluswolke [F]
altocumulo [M]

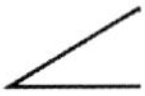

altostratus
altostratus [M]
altoestratos [M]
Altostratuswolke [F]
altrostrato [M]

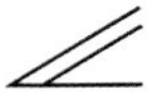

nimbostratus
nimbostratus [M]
nimboestratos [M]
Regenschichtwolke [F]
nimbostrato [M]

high clouds
nuages [M] élevés
nubes [F] altas
höhe Wolken [F]
nubi [F] alte

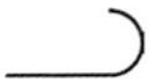

cirrus
cirrus [M]
cirros [M]
Zirruswolke [F]
cirro [M]

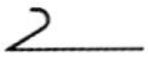

cirrostratus
cirrostratus [M]
cirroestratos [M]
Schleierwolke [F]
cirrostrato [M]

cirrocumulus
cirrocumulus [M]
cirrocúmulos [M]
Cirrocumulus-Wolke [F]
cirrucumulo [M]

Precipitation

Précipitations [F] | Precipitación [F] | Niederschlag [M] | Precipitazione [F]

light intermittent rain
pluie [F] légère intermittente
lluvia [F] leve intermitente
zeitweise leichter Regen [M]
pioggia [F] leggera intermittente

moderate intermittent rain
pluie [F] modérée intermittente
lluvia [F] moderada intermitente
zeitweise mäßiger Regen [M]
pioggia [F] moderata intermittente

heavy intermittent rain
forte pluie [F] intermittente
lluvia [F] fuerte intermitente
zeitweise starker Regen [M]
pioggia [F] forte intermittente

freezing rain
pluie [F] verglaçante
lluvia [F] helada
gefrierender Regen [M]
pioggia [F] gelata

light intermittent drizzle
petite bruine [F] intermittente
llovizna [F] leve intermitente
zeitweise leichter Niesel [M]
piovigginio [M] leggero intermittente

moderate intermittent drizzle
bruine [F] modérée intermittente
llovizna [F] moderada intermitente
zeitweise mäßiger Niesel [M]
piovigginio [M] moderato intermittente

thick intermittent drizzle
forte bruine [F] intermittente
llovizna [F] fuerte intermitente
zeitweise starker Niesel [M]
piovigginio [M] forte intermittente

freezing drizzle
bruine [M] verglaçante
llovizna [F] helada
gefrierendes Nieseln [N]
pioggerella [F] gelata

sleet
giboulée [F]
aguanieve [F]
Schneeregen [M]
nevischio [M]

ice crystals
poudrin [M] de glace [F]
cristales [M] de hielo [M]
Eiskristalle [M]
cristalli [M] di ghiaccio [M]

intermittent light snow
légère chute [F] de neige [F] intermittente
nevada [F] leve intermitente
zeitweise leichter Schneefall [M]
neve [F] leggera intermittente

continuous moderate snow
chute [F] de neige [F] modérée et continue
nevada [F] moderada continua
zeitweise mäßiger Schneefall [M]
neve [F] moderata continua

intermittent heavy snow
forte chute [F] de neige [F] intermittente
nevada [F] fuerte intermitente
zeitweise starker Schneefall [M]
neve [F] forte intermittente

graupel (soft hail)
neige [F] roulée
granizo [M] suave
Graupelschauer [M]
grandine [F] leggera

haze
brume [F] sèche
calima [F]
Dunst [M]
foschia [F]

sandstorm or dust storm
tempête [F] de poussière [F] ou de sable [M]
tormenta [F] de polvo [M] o arena [F]
Staub- [M] oder Sandsturm [M]
tempesta [F] di sabbia [F] o polvere [F]

well-developed dust or sand whirl
tourbillon [M] de sable [M] ou de poussière [F] bien formé
remolino [M] de polvo [M]
gut ausgeprägter Staub- oder Sandwirbel [N]
vortice [M] ben formato di polvere [F] o sabbia [F]

drifting snow, low
poudrerie,[F] basse
ventisca [F] de nieve [F] leve
Schneetreiben,[F] unter Augenhöhe [F]
raffiche [F] di neve,[F] basse

drifting snow, high
poudrerie,[F] élevée
ventisca [F] de nieve [F] intensa
Schneetreiben,[N] über Augenhöhe [F]
raffiche [F] di neve,[F] alte

fog
brouillard [M]
niebla [F]
Nebel [M]
nebbia [F]

lighting visible, no thunder heard
éclairs [M] visibles, pas de tonnerre [M]
relámpago [M] visible, sin sonido [M] de truenos [M]
Wetterleuchten,[N] kein Donner [M] hörbar
fulmine [M] visibile, tuono [M] non udibile

thunderstorm
orage [M]
tormenta [F]
Gewitter,[N] schwach oder moderat, ohne Hagel [N]
temporale [M]

shower of rain and snow, mixed
averse [F] de pluie [F] et de neige,[F] mélangées
chubasco [M] de aguanieve [F]
Regenschauer,[M] gemischt mit Schnee,[M] schwach
precipitazioni [F] di acqua [F] e neve [F] miste

snow shower
averse [F] de neige [F]
nevada [F]
Schneeschauer,[M] schwach
nevicata [F]

rain shower
averse [F] de pluie [F]
chubasco [M]
Regenschauer,[M] schwach
acquazzone [M]

funnel clouds or tornadoes
tubas [M] ou tornades [F]
nubes [F] embudos o tornados [M]
Trichterwolken [F] oder Tornados [M]
nubi [F] a imbuto [M] o tornado [M]

hurricane
ouragan [M]
huracán [M]
Wirbelsturm [M]
uragano [M]

Sky coverage

Partie [F] du ciel [M] couverte | Nubosidad [F] | Himmelsbedeckung [F] | Copertura [F] del cielo [M]

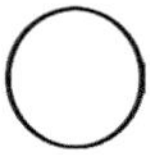

cloudless sky
ciel [M] sans nuage [M]
despejado [M]
wolkenloser Himmel [M]
cielo [M] sereno

clear sky (1/8 sky cover)
ciel [M] clair (1/8 du ciel [M] couvert)
cielo [M] despejado (1/8 cielo [M] cubierto)
sonnig
cielo [M] limpido (1/8 di cielo [M] coperti)

slightly covered sky (2/8 sky cover)
ciel [M] peu nuageux (2/8 du ciel [M] couvert)
levemente nuboso [M] (2/8 cielo [M] cubierto)
heiter
cielo [M] quasi sereno (2/8 di cielo [M] coperti)

cloudy (4/8 sky cover)
ciel [M] nuageux (4/8 du ciel [M] couvert)
medio nuboso [M] (4/8 cielo [M] cubierto)
wolkig
cielo [M] nuvoloso (4/8 di cielo coperti)

5/8 sky cover
5/8 du ciel [M] couvert
5/8 cielo [M] cubierto
bewölkt
5/8 di cielo [M] coperto

overcast sky (8/8 sky cover)
ciel [M] entièrement couvert (8/8 du ciel [M] couvert)
completamente nublado [M] (8/8 cielo [M] cubierto)
bedeckt
cielo [M] coperto (8/8 di cielo coperti)

obscured sky
ciel [M] obscurci
cielo [M] oscurecido
Himmel [M] nicht erkennbar
cielo [M] offuscato

Atmospheric pressure trend

Tendance [F] de la pression [F] atmosphérique | Tendencia [F] de presión [M] atmosférica | Trend [M] des Atmosphärendrucks [M] | Tendenza [F] della pressione [F] atmosferica

rising
en hausse [F]
creciente [M]
steigend
crescente [M]

rising, then falling
en hausse [F] puis en baisse [F]
creciente,[M] después decreciente [M]
steigend, dann fallend
crescente,[M] poi calante [M]

rising, then steady
en hausse [F] puis stationnaire
creciente,[M] después estable [M]
steigend, dann gleichbleibend
crescente,[M] poi stabile [M]

rising or steady, then falling
en hausse ou stationnaire [F] puis en baisse [F]
creciente [M] o estable,[M] después decreciente [M]
steigend oder stabil, dann fallend
crescente [M] o stabile,[M] poi calante [M]

falling or steady, then rising
en baisse [F] ou stationnaire puis en hausse [F]
decreciente [M] o estable,[M] después creciente [M]
fallend oder stabil, dann steigend
calante [F] o stabile,[F] poi crescente [F]

steady
stationnaire
estable [M]
gleichbleibend
stabile [M]

falling
en baisse [F]
decreciente [M]
fallend
calante [F]

falling, then rising
en baisse [F] puis en hausse [F]
decreciente,[M] después creciente [M]
fallend, dann steigend
calante,[F] poi crescente [F]

falling, then steady
en baisse [F] puis stationnaire
decreciente,[M] después estable [M]
fallend, dann gleichbleibend
calante,[F] poi stabile [F]

Wind speed

Vitesse [F] du vent | Velocidad [F] del viento [M] | Windgeschwindigkeit [F] | Velocità [F] del vento [M]

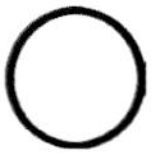

calm
calme [M]
calma [F]
ruhig [N]
calmo [M]

gentle breeze
petite brise [F]
brisa [F] ligera
schwache Brise [F]
vento [M] leggero

moderate breeze
jolie brise [F]
brisa [F] débil
leichte Brise [F]
vento [M] debole

fresh breeze
bonne brise [F]
brisa [F] moderada
frische Brise [F]
vento [M] moderato

near gale
grand frais [M]
viento [M] fuerte
steifer Wind [M]
vento [M] forte

gale
coup [M] de vent [M]
viento [M] tormentoso
stürmischer Wind [M]
vento [M] tempestoso

severe gale
fort coup [M] de vent [M]
tormenta [F]
starke Sturmböen [F]
vento [M] molto burrascoso

storm
tempête [F]
tormenta [F] intensa
Sturm [M]
tempesta [F]

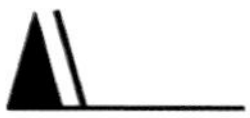

violent storm
violente tempête [F]
tormenta [F] huracanada
orkanartiger Sturm [M]
tempesta [F] violenta

hurricane
ouragan [M]
huracán [M]
Hurrikan [M]
uragano [M]

Color mixing

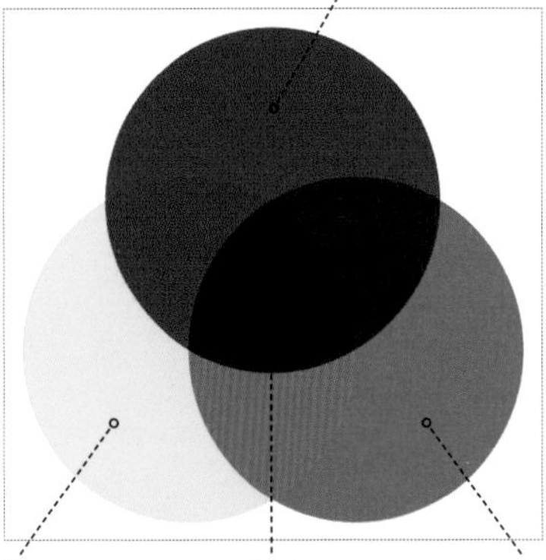
subtractive colors
couleurs [F] soustractives
colores [M] sustractivos
subtraktive Farbsynthese [F]
colore [M] sottrattivo
magenta
magenta [M]
magenta [M]
Magenta [N]
magenta [M]
yellow
jaune [M]
amarillo [M]
Gelb [N]
giallo [M]
black
noir [M]
negro [M]
Schwarz [N]
nero [M]
cyan
cyan [M]
cian [M]
Cyan [N]
ciano [M]

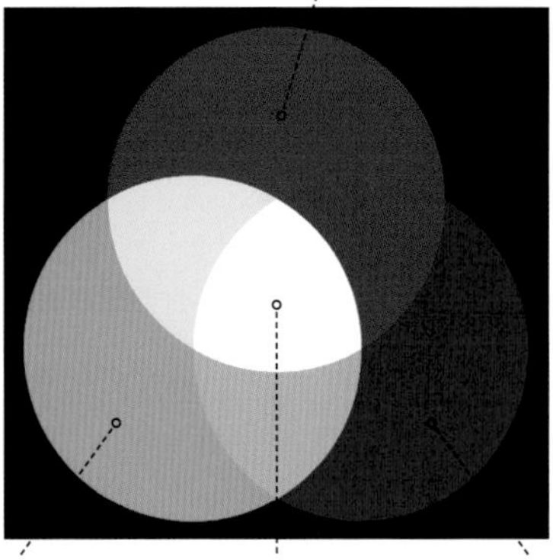
additive colors
couleurs [F] primaires additives
colores [M] aditivos additive
Farbmischung [F]
colore [M] additivo
red
rouge [M]
rojo [M]
Rot [N]
rosso [M]
green
vert [M]
verde [M]
Grün [N]
verde [M]
white
blanc [M]
blanco [M]
Weiß [N]
bianco [M]
blue
bleu [M]
azul [M]
Blau [N]
blu [M]

Color contrasts

contrast of hue
contraste [M] de teintes [F]
contraste [M] del tono [M]
Farbe-an-sich-Kontrast [M]
contrasto [M] di tonalità [F]

simultaneous contrast
contraste [M] simultané
contraste [M] simultáneo
Simultankontrast [M]
contrasto [M] simultaneo

light-dark contrast
contraste [M] clair-foncé
contraste [M] claro/oscuro
hell-dunkel Kontrast [M]
contrasto [M] di chiaro [M] e scuro [M]

saturation contrast
contraste [M] de saturation [F]
contraste [M] de saturación [F]
Sättigungskontrast [M]
contrasto [M] di qualità [F]

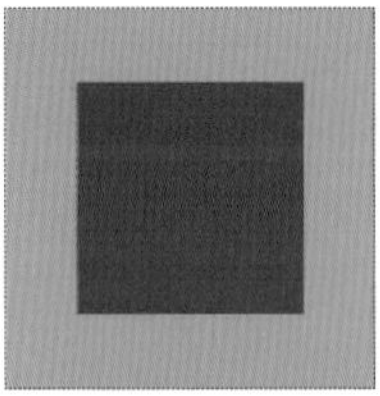

warm-cool contrast
contraste [M] de couleurs [F] chaudes et froides
contraste [M] cálido/frío
warm-kalt Kontrast [M]
contrasto [M] di caldo [M] e freddo [M]

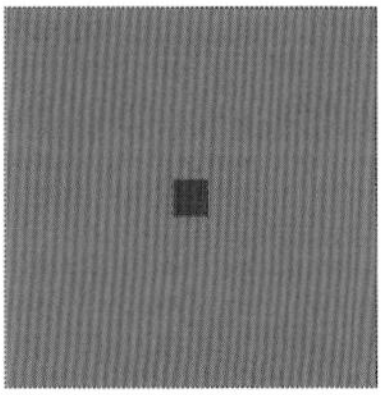

quantity contrast
contraste [M] de quantité [F]
contraste [M] cuantitativo
Quantitätskontrast [M]
contrasto [M] di quantità [F]

complementary contrast
contraste [M] de couleurs [F] complémentaire
contraste [M] complementario
Komplementärkontrast [M]
contrasto [M] dei complementari [M]

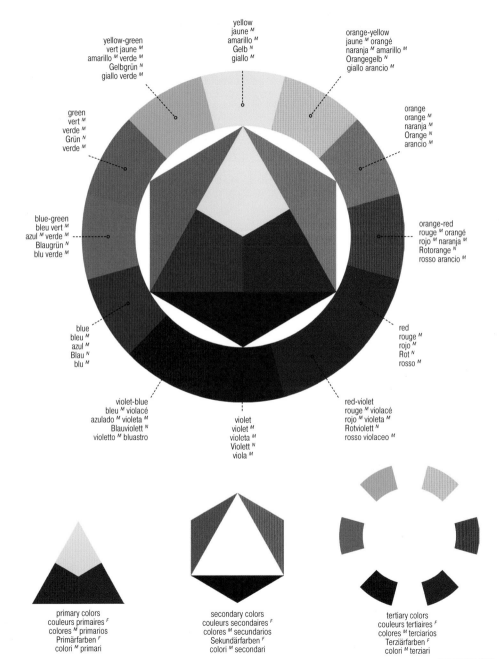

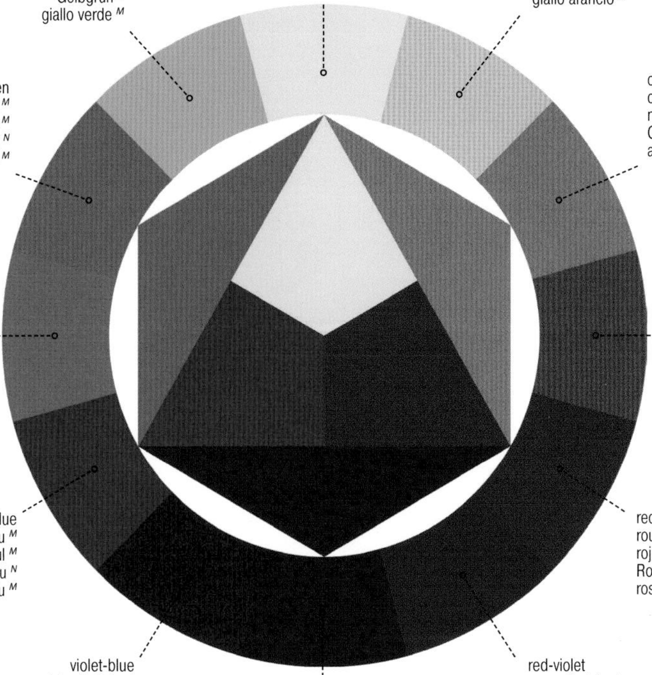
yellow
jaune M
amarillo M
Gelb N
giallo M
orange-yellow
jaune M orangé
naranja M amarillo M
Orangegelb N
giallo arancio M
yellow-green
vert jaune M
amarillo M verde M
Gelbgrün N
giallo verde M
green
vert M
verde M
Grün N
verde M
orange
orange M
naranja M
Orange N
arancio M
blue-green
bleu vert M
azul M verde M
Blaugrün N
blu verde M
orange-red
rouge M orangé
rojo M naranja M
Rotorange N
rosso arancio M
blue
bleu M
azul M
Blau N
blu M
red
rouge M
rojo M
Rot N
rosso M
violet-blue
bleu M violacé
azulado M violeta M
Blauviolett N
violetto M bluastro
violet
violet M
violeta M
Violett N
viola M
red-violet
rouge M violacé
rojo M violeta M
Rotviolett N
rosso violaceo M

primary colors
couleurs primaires F
colores M primarios
Primärfarben F
colori M primari

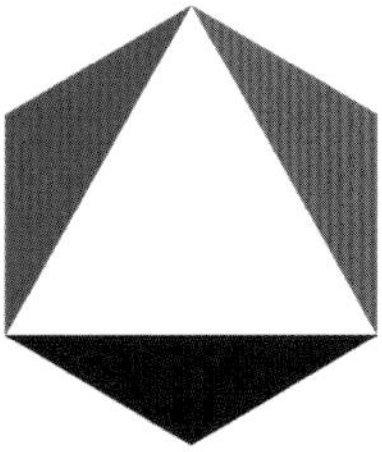

secondary colors
couleurs secondaires F
colores M secundarios
Sekundärfarben F
colori M secondari

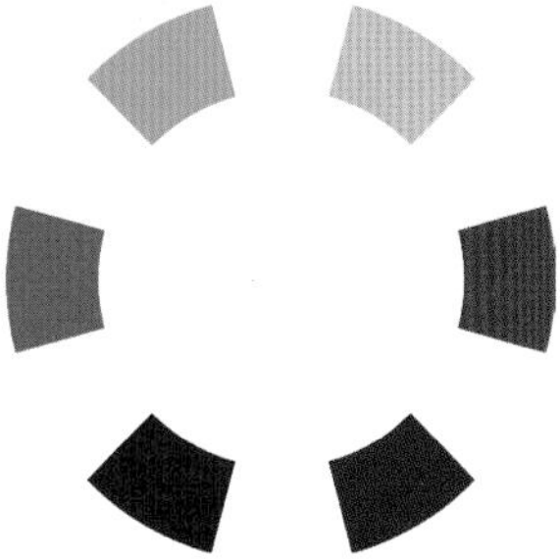

tertiary colors
couleurs tertiaires F
colores M terciarios
Terziärfarben F
colori M terziari

flask on stand
ballon M sur son support M
matraz M con soporte M
Kolben M auf Ständer M
matraccio M su supporto M

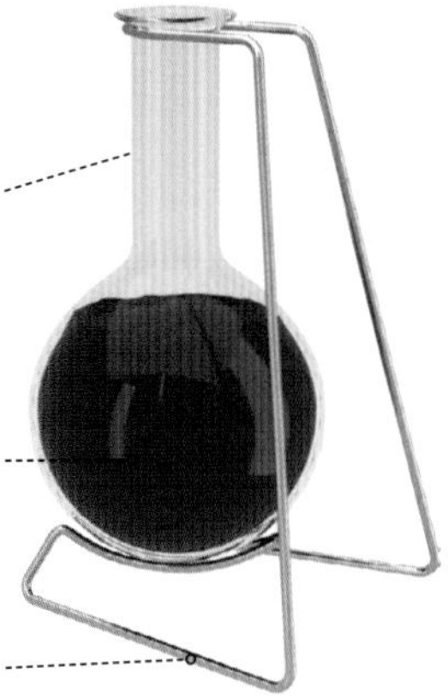

round-bottom flask
ballon M à fond M rond
matraz M
Rundkolben M
matraccio M da laboratorio

liquid
liquide M
líquido M
Flüssigkeit F
liquido M

stand
support M
soporte M
Ständer M
supporto M

flask with glass tubes
flacon M avec tubes M de verre M
matraz M con tubos de vidrio M
Kolben M mit Glasröhrchen N
matraccio M con canne F di vetro M

crucible with cover
creuset M avec couvercle M
crisol M con tapa F
Tiegel M mit Deckel M
crogiolo M con coperchio M

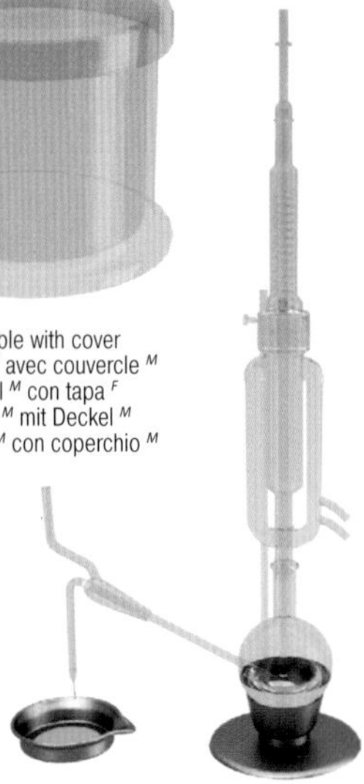

fractional distillation kit
ensemble M de distillation F fractionnée
equipo M de destilación F fraccionada
Set N für die fraktionierte Destillation F
set M per distillazione frazionata

heating mantle
chauffe-ballon M
manta F calefactora
Heizpilz M
mantello M riscaldante

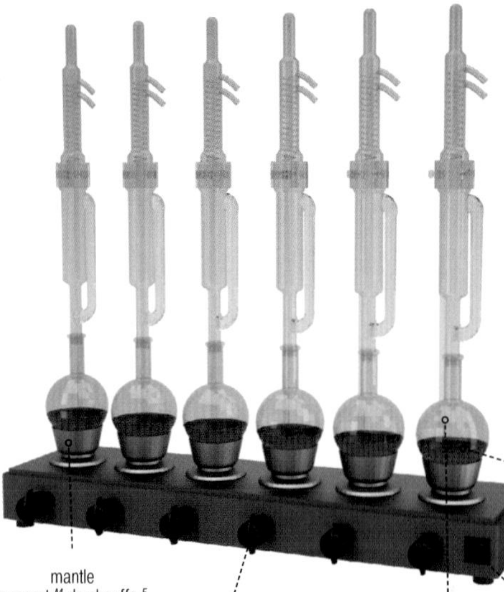

liquid
liquide M
líquido M
Flüssigkeit F
liquido M

mantle
support M de chauffe F
elemento M calorífico
Heizelement N
mantello M riscaldante

heat control knob
bouton M de réglage M de la chaleur F
perilla F de control M de temperatura F
Wärmeregulierungsdrehknopf M
manopola F del controllo M del calore M

laboratory flask
ballon M de laboratoire
matraz M
Laborkolben M
matraccio M da laboratorio

power button
interrupteur M
botón M de encendido M
An-/Ausschalter M
pulsante M di accensione F

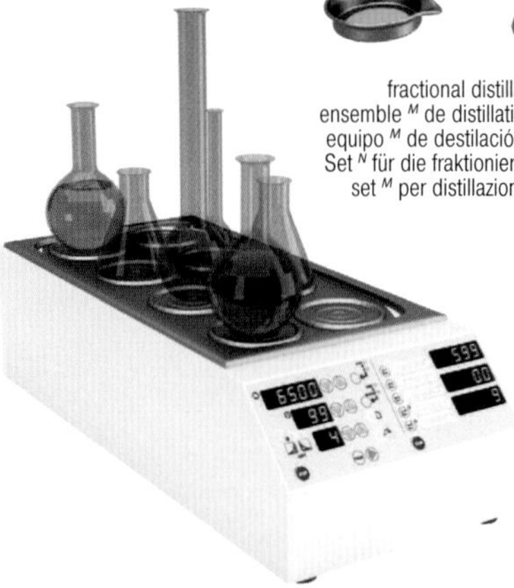

universal heater
chauffe-flacons M universel
calentador M universal
Universal-Erhitzer M
riscaldatore M universale

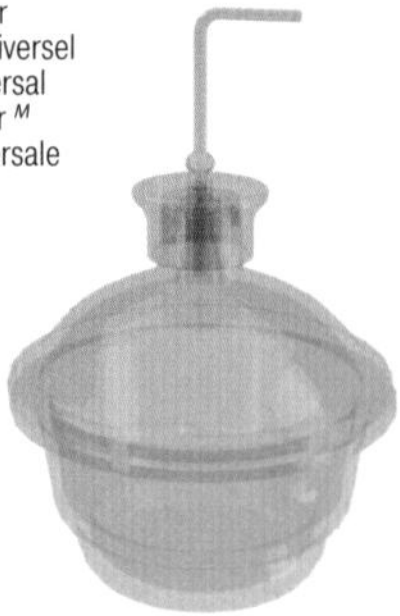

desiccator
dessiccateur M
desecador M
Exsikkator M
essiccatore M

bottle with drying tube
bouteille ^{F} avec tube ^{M} de séchage ^{M}
botella ^{F} con drenadores ^{M}
Flasche ^{F} mit Trocknerröhrchen ^{N}
bottiglia ^{F} con valvola ^{F} essiccante

graduated cylinder
cylindre ^{M} gradué
cilindro ^{M} graduado
Messzylinder ^{M}
cilindro ^{M} graduato

coil condenser
condenseur ^{M} à serpentin
condensador ^{M} de espiral ^{F}
Schlangenkühler ^{M}
condensatore ^{M} a serpentina ^{F}

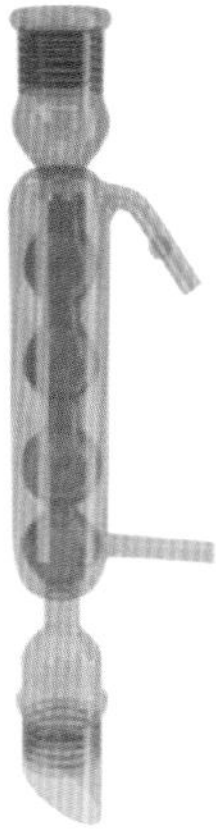

dry ice condenser
condenseur ^{M} à glace ^{F} carbonique
condensador ^{M} de hielo ^{M} seco
Trockeneiskühler ^{M}
condensatore ^{M} a ghiaccio ^{M} secco

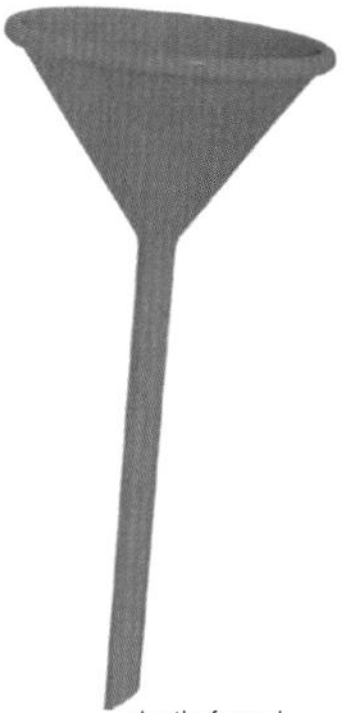

plastic funnel
entonnoir ^{M} en plastique ^{M}
embudo ^{M} de plástico ^{M}
Kunststofftrichter ^{M}
imbuto ^{M} di plastica ^{F}

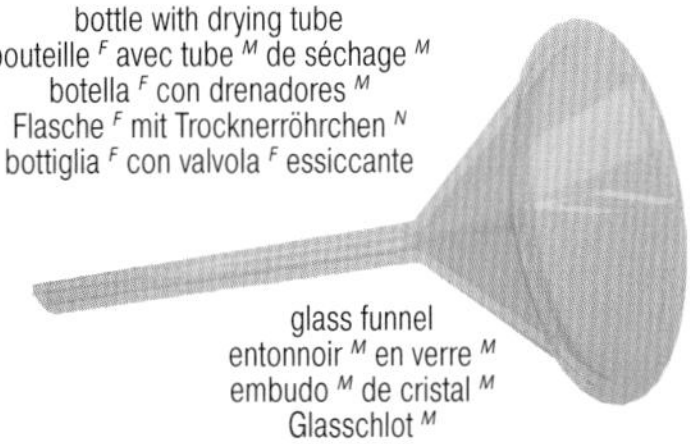

glass funnel
entonnoir ^{M} en verre ^{M}
embudo ^{M} de cristal ^{M}
Glasschlot ^{M}
imbuto ^{M} di vetro ^{M}

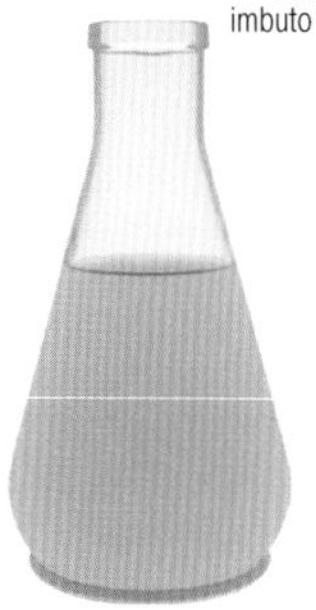

Erlenmeyer flask
vase ^{M} d'Erlenmeyer ^{M}
matraz ^{M} cónico
Erlenmeyerkolben ^{M}
beuta ^{F} Erlenmeyer

beaker with stirring rod
bécher ^{M} avec agitateur ^{M}
vaso ^{M} de precipitado ^{M} con varilla ^{F}
Becher ^{M} mit Rührstäbchen ^{N}
becher ^{M} con bacchetta ^{F} per agitare

bottle with closure
flacon ^{M} avec bouchon ^{M}
frasco ^{M} con tapa ^{F}
Flasche ^{F} mit Verschlussstopfen ^{M}
bottiglia ^{F} con chiusura ^{F}

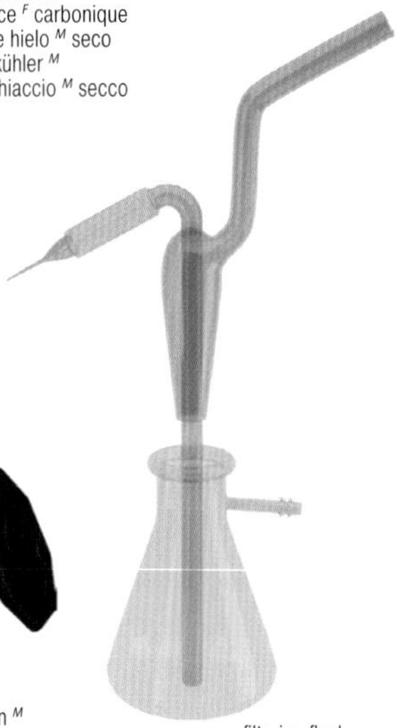

filtering flask
flacon ^{M} de filtration ^{F}
matraz ^{M} de lavado ^{M}
Filterflasche ^{F}
matraccio ^{M} filtrante

glass water bath
bain-marie ^{M} en verre ^{M}
baño ^{M} de agua ^{F} de cristal ^{M}
Glaswasserbad ^{N}
bagnomaria ^{M} di vetro

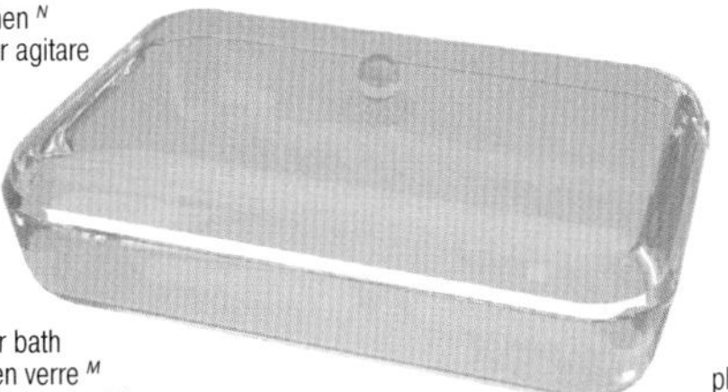

glass tray
plateau ^{M} de verre
bandeja ^{F} de cristal ^{M}
Glasschale ^{F}
vassoio ^{M} di vetro ^{M}

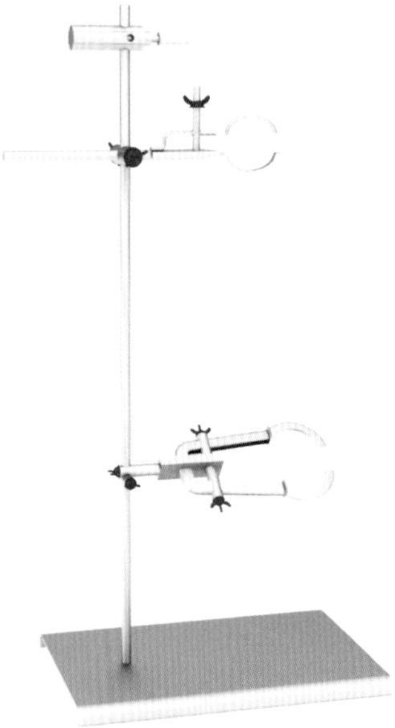

ring stand with clamps
support [M] annulaire avec pinces [F]
base [F] de anillos [M] con abrazaderas [F]
Stativring [M] mit Feststellklemmen [F]
supporto [M] con pinze [F]

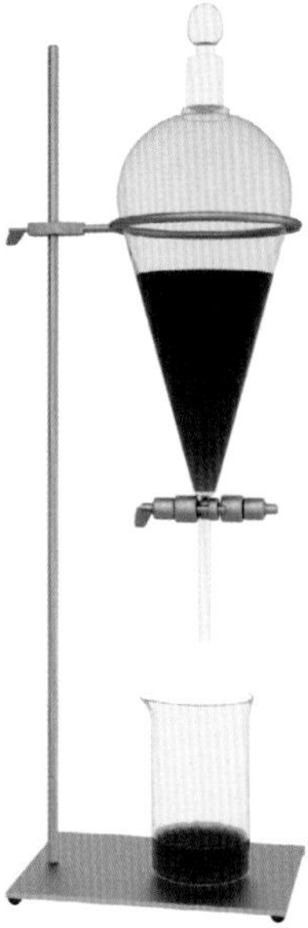

separatory funnel
appareil [M] à décantation [F]
pera [F] de decantación [M]
Scheidetrichter [M]
imbuto [M] separatore

barrel
baril [M] / tonneau [M]
barril [M]
Fass [N]
barile [M]

test tube with stopper
éprouvette [F] avec bouchon [M]
tubo [M] de ensayo [M] con tapón [M]
Reagenzglas [N] mit Stopfen [M]
provetta [F] con tappo

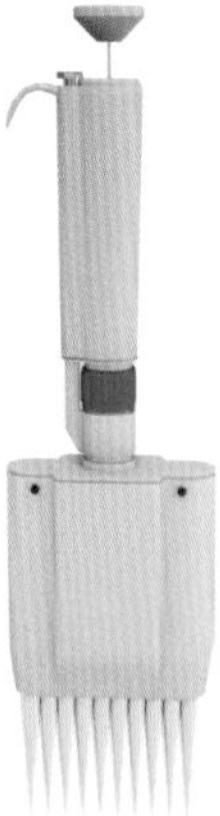

electronic pipette
pipette [F] électronique
pipeta [F] electrónica
elektronische Pipette [F]
pipetta [F] elettronica

filter funnel
entonnoir [M] de filtration [F]
embudo [M] de filtración [F]
Filternutsche [F]
imbuto [M] filtrante

test tube on stand
éprouvette [F] sur support [M]
tubo [M] de ensayo [M] en soporte [M]
Reagenzglas [N] in Halterung [F]
provetta [F] su supporto [M]

beaker with handle
bécher [M] à anse [F]
jarra [F] con asa [F]
Becher [M] mit Griff [M]
becher [M] con manico [M]

wash bottle
flacon-laveur [M]
botella [F] de lavado [M]
Spritzflasche [F]
spruzzetta [F]

beaker
bécher [M]
vaso [M] de precipitado [M]
Becher [M]
becher [M]

Magnetic Mixer
MS 112G
Indifferent
Power

magnetic stirrer
agitateur ᴹ magnétique
agitador ᴹ magnético
Magnetrührer ᴹ
mixer ᴹ magnetico

magnetic stirrer / hotplate
agitateur ᴹ magnétique / plaque ᶠ chauffante
agitador ᴹ magnético
Magnetrührer ᴹ / Wärmeplatte ᶠ
agitatore ᴹ magnetico / piastra ᶠ calda

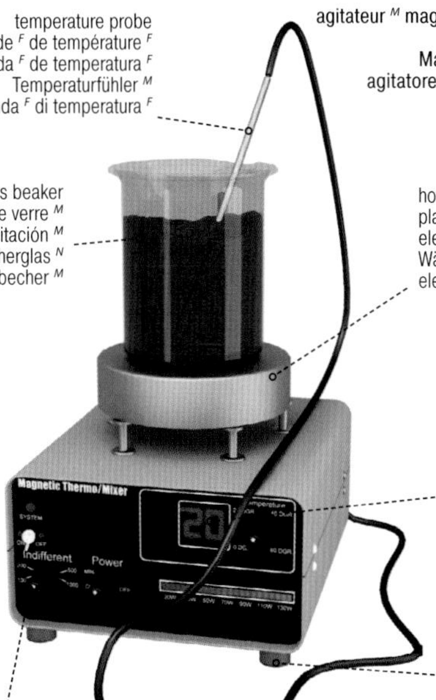
Magnetic Thermo/Mixer
Indifferent
Power

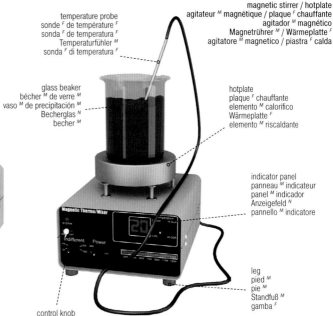

temperature probe
sonde ᶠ de température ᶠ
sonda ᶠ de temperatura ᶠ
Temperaturfühler ᴹ
sonda ᶠ di temperatura ᶠ

glass beaker
bécher ᴹ de verre ᴹ
vaso ᴹ de precipitación ᴹ
Becherglas ᴺ
becher ᴹ

hotplate
plaque ᶠ chauffante
elemento ᴹ calorífico
Wärmeplatte ᶠ
elemento ᴹ riscaldante

indicator panel
panneau ᴹ indicateur
panel ᴹ indicador
Anzeigefeld ᴺ
pannello ᴹ indicatore

leg
pied ᴹ
pie ᴹ
Standfuß ᴹ
gamba ᶠ

control knob
commandes ᶠ
perilla ᶠ de control ᴹ
Drehknopf ᴹ
manopola ᶠ di controllo ᴹ

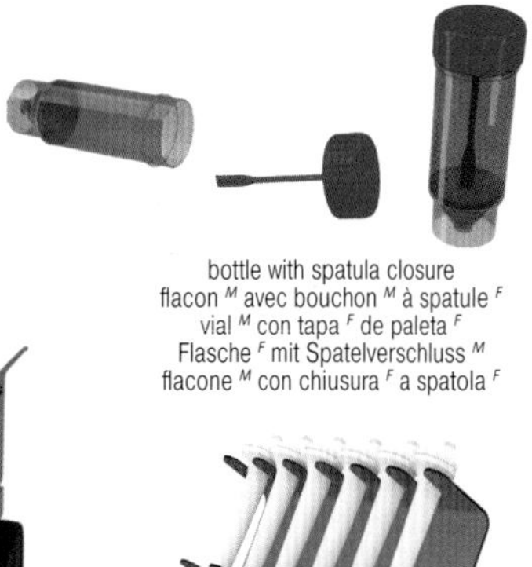

bottle with spatula closure
flacon ᴹ avec bouchon ᴹ à spatule ᶠ
vial ᴹ con tapa ᶠ de paleta ᶠ
Flasche ᶠ mit Spatelverschluss ᴹ
flacone ᴹ con chiusura ᶠ a spatola ᶠ

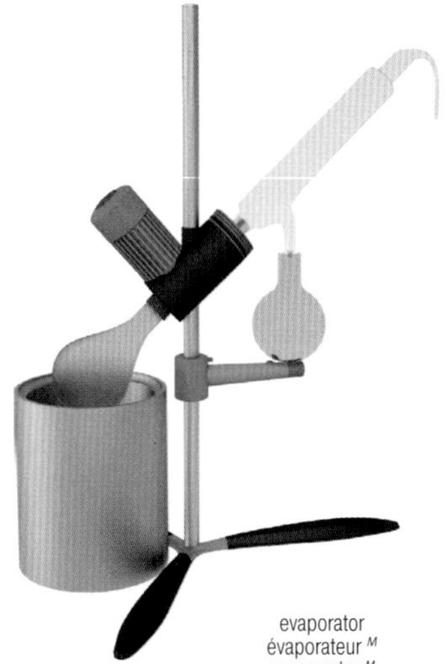

evaporator
évaporateur ᴹ
evaporador ᴹ
Verdunster ᴹ
evaporatore ᴹ

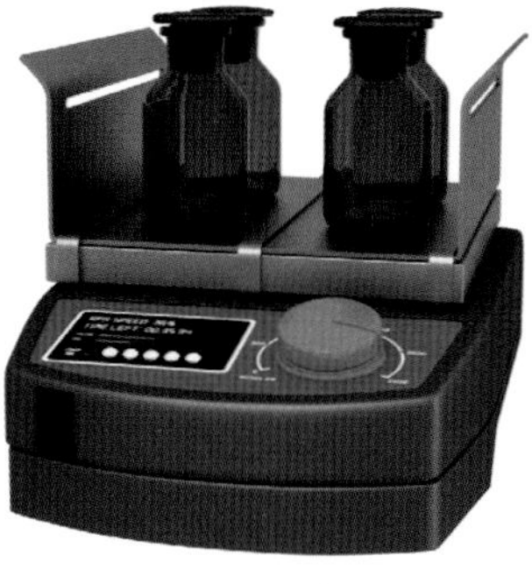

mixing device
dispositif ᴹ mélangeur
dispositivo ᴹ mezclador
Mixer ᴺ
dispositivo ᴹ di miscelazione ᶠ

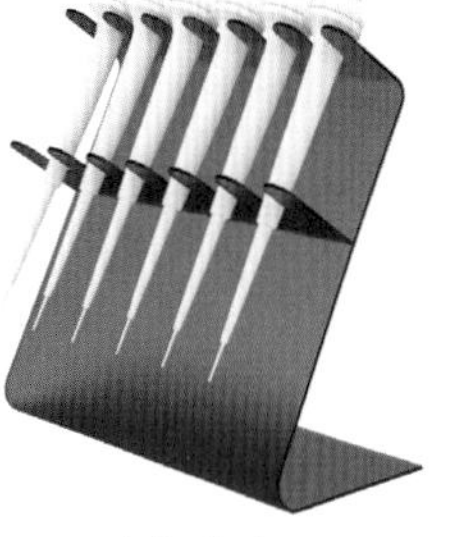

pipette stand
support ᴹ pour pipettes ᶠ
soporte ᴹ para pipetas ᶠ
Pipettenständer ᴹ
supporto ᴹ per pipette ᶠ

fume hood
hotte ^F^ de laboratoire ^F^
campana ^F^ de humos ^M^
Abzugshaube ^F^
cappa ^F^ aspirante

note stand
lutrin ^M^
atril ^M^
Notizenständer ^M^
supporto ^M^ per appunti ^M^

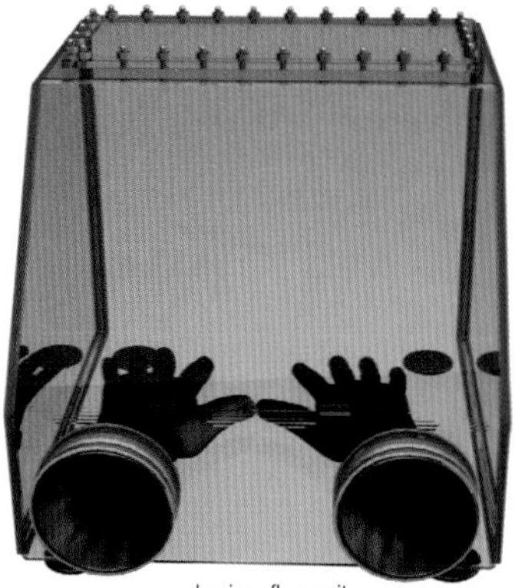

laminar flow unit
unité ^F^ à flux ^M^ laminaire
cabina ^F^ de flujo ^M^ laminar
Sicherheitswerkbank ^F^
unità ^F^ di flusso ^M^ laminare

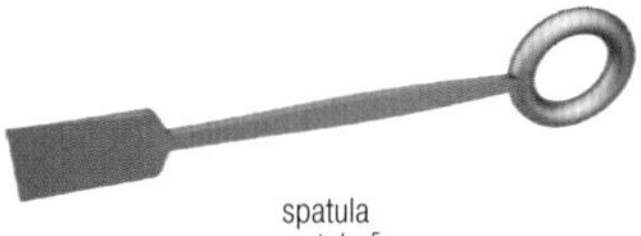

spatula
spatule ^F^
espátula ^F^
Spatel ^F^
spatola ^F^

mobile base cabinet
armoire ^F^ de plancher ^M^ à roulettes ^F^
armario ^M^ móvil
fahrbarer Unterschrank ^M^
armadietto ^M^ a base ^F^ mobile

steam autoclave
autoclave ^M^ à vapeur ^F^
autoclave ^M^ a vapor ^M^
Autoklav ^N^
autoclave ^F^ a vapore ^M^

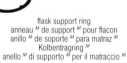

flask support ring
anneau ^M^ de support ^M^ pour flacon
anillo ^M^ de soporte ^M^ para matraz ^M^
Kolbentragring ^M^
anello ^M^ di supporto ^M^ per il matraccio ^M^

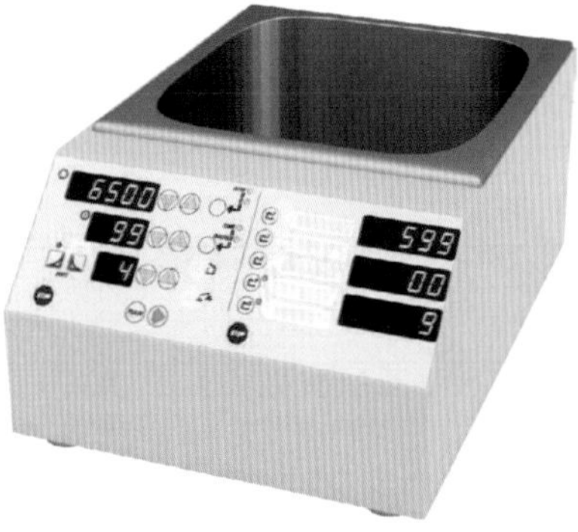
6500
99
4
599
00
9

electric water bath
bain-marie ^M^ électrique
baño ^M^ María ^F^ eléctrico
elektrisches Wasserbad ^N^
bagnomaria ^M^ elettrico

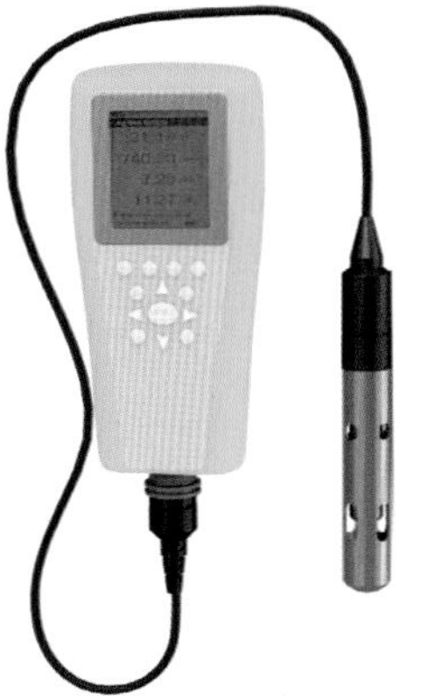

thermometer with probe
thermomètre ^{M} avec sonde ^{F} à fil
termómetro ^{M} con sonda ^{F}
Thermometer ^{N} mit Fühler ^{M}
termometro ^{M} con sonda ^{F}

NOIS CHECKER
65.0

sound meter
sonomètre ^{M}
sonómetro ^{M}
Schallmesser ^{M}
fonometro ^{M}

microscope
microscope ^{M}
microscopio ^{M}
Mikroskop ^{N}
microscopio ^{M}

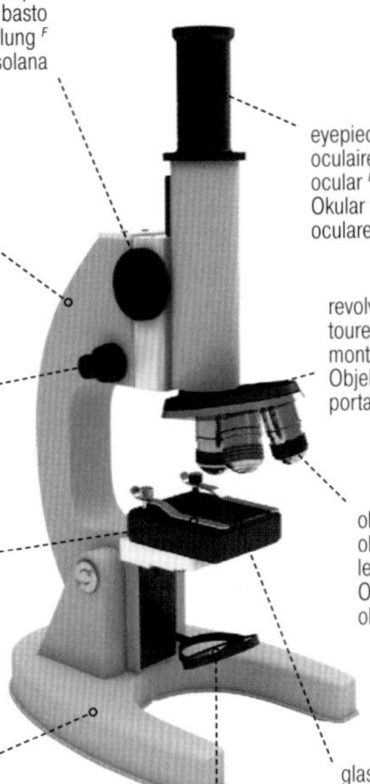

coarse adjustment knob
vis ^{M} macrométrique
perilla ^{F} de ajuste ^{M} basto
Grobeinstellung ^{F}
manopola ^{F} di regolazione ^{F} grossolana

eyepiece
oculaire ^{M}
ocular ^{F}
Okular ^{N}
oculare ^{M}

arm
potence ^{F}
brazo ^{M}
Stativ ^{N}
braccio ^{M}

revolving nosepiece
tourelle ^{F} porte-objectifs ^{M}
montura ^{F} giratoria
Objektivrevolver ^{M}
portaobiettivo ^{M} girevole

fine adjustment knob
vis ^{M} micrométrique
perilla ^{F} de ajuste ^{M} fino
Feineinstellung ^{F}
manopola ^{F} di regolazione ^{F} fine

stage clip
valet ^{M}
enganche ^{M} de plataforma ^{F}
Objekthalter ^{M}
clip ^{F} di fase ^{F}

objective lens
objectif ^{M}
lentes ^{F}
Objektiv ^{N}
obiettivo ^{M}

base
pied ^{M}
base ^{F}
Fuß ^{M}
base ^{F}

glass slide
lame ^{F} porte-objets ^{M}
placa ^{F} de vidrio ^{M}
Glasscheibe ^{F}
vetrino ^{M}

mirror
miroir ^{M}
espejo ^{M}
Spiegel ^{M}
specchio ^{M}

pestle and mortar
pilon ^{M} et mortier ^{M}
mortero ^{M}
Stößel ^{M} und Mörser ^{M}
pestello ^{M} e mortaio ^{M}

magnifying glass
loupe ^{F}
lupa ^{F}
Vergrößerungsglas ^{N}
lente ^{F} d'ingrandimento ^{M}

spray bottle
flacon ^{M} pulvérisateur
atomizador ^{M}
Sprühflasche ^{F}
spruzzatore ^{M}

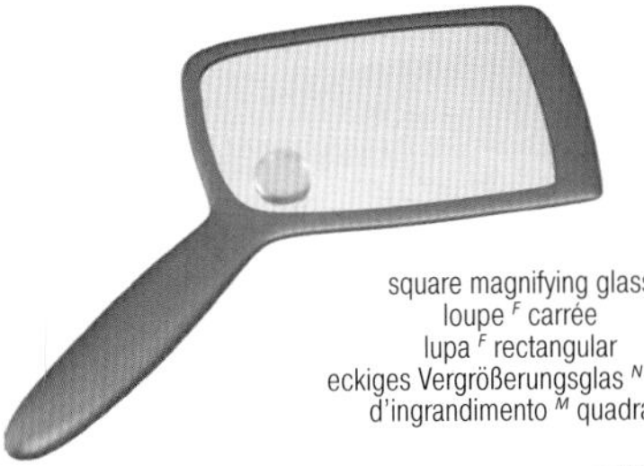

square magnifying glass
loupe ^{F} carrée
lupa ^{F} rectangular
eckiges Vergrößerungsglas ^{N} lente ^{F}
d'ingrandimento ^{M} quadrata

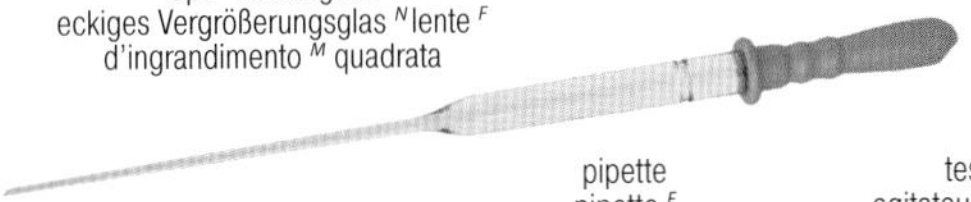

pipette
pipette ^{F}
pipeta ^{F}
Pipette ^{F}
pipetta ^{F}

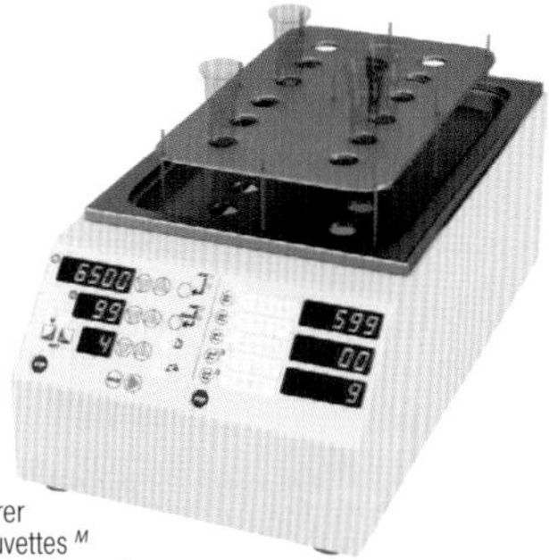

test tube stirrer
agitateur ^{M} d'éprouvettes ^{M}
agitador ^{M} de tubos ^{M} de ensayo ^{M}
Reagenzglas-Rührer ^{M}
agitatore ^{M} per provette ^{F}

rotary evaporator
évaporateur ᴹ rotatif
evaporador ᴹ rotatorio
Rotationsverdampfer ᴹ
evaporatore ᴹ rotante

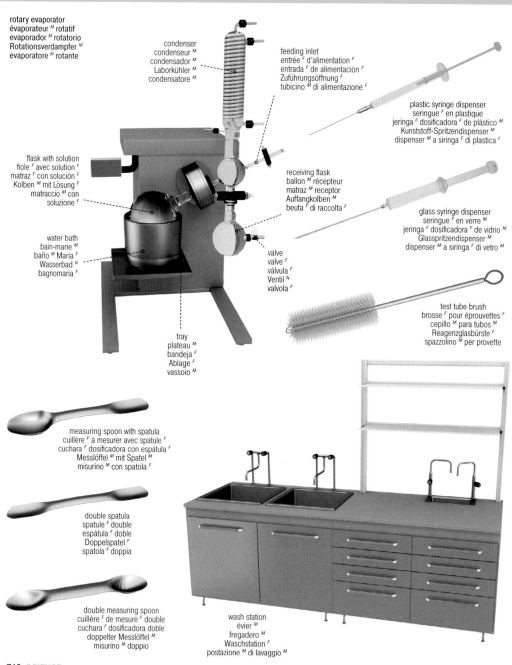

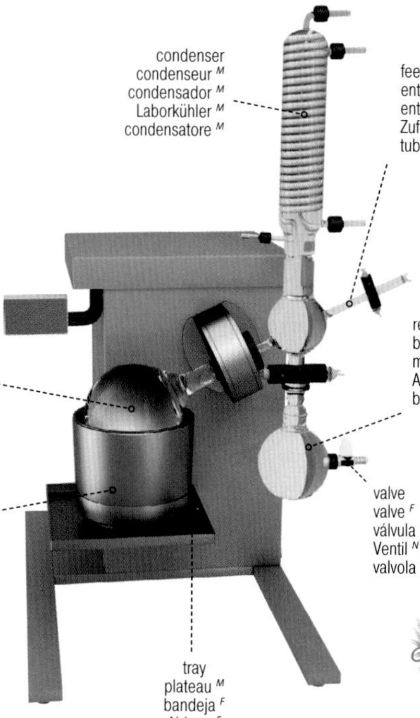
condenser
condenseur ᴹ
condensador ᴹ
Laborkühler ᴹ
condensatore ᴹ
feeding inlet
entrée ᶠ d'alimentation ᶠ
entrada ᶠ de alimentación ᶠ
Zuführungsöffnung ᶠ
tubicino ᴹ di alimentazione ᶠ
flask with solution
fiole ᶠ avec solution ᶠ
matraz ᶠ con solución ᶠ
Kolben ᴹ mit Lösung ᶠ
matraccio ᴹ con soluzione ᶠ
receiving flask
ballon ᴹ récepteur
matraz ᴹ receptor
Auffangkolben ᴹ
beuta ᶠ di raccolta ᶠ
water bath
bain-marie ᴹ
baño ᴹ María ᶠ
Wasserbad ᴺ
bagnomaria ᶠ
valve
valve ᶠ
válvula ᶠ
Ventil ᴺ
valvola ᶠ
tray
plateau ᴹ
bandeja ᶠ
Ablage ᶠ
vassoio ᴹ

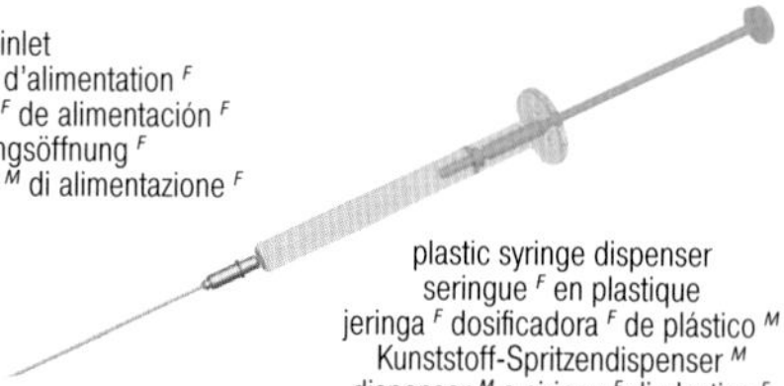

plastic syringe dispenser
seringue ᶠ en plastique
jeringa ᶠ dosificadora ᶠ de plástico ᴹ
Kunststoff-Spritzendispenser ᴹ
dispenser ᴹ a siringa ᶠ di plastica ᶠ

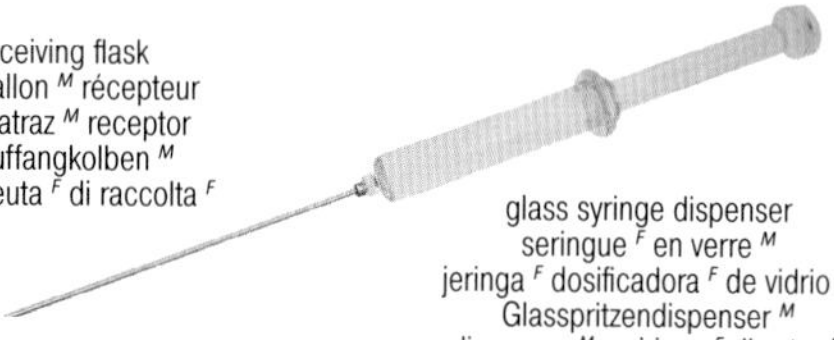

glass syringe dispenser
seringue ᶠ en verre ᴹ
jeringa ᶠ dosificadora ᶠ de vidrio ᴹ
Glasspritzendispenser ᴹ
dispenser ᴹ a siringa ᶠ di vetro ᴹ

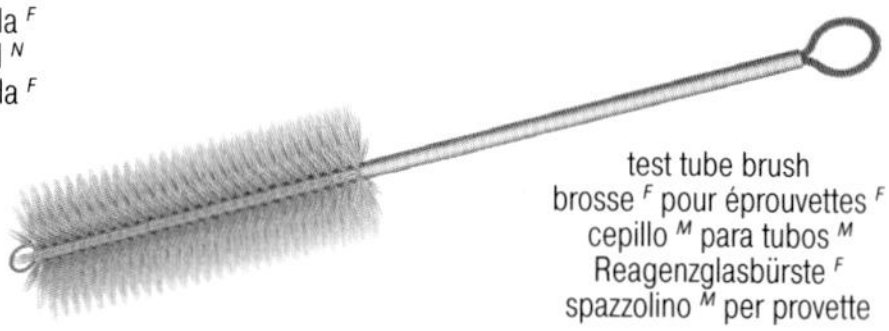

test tube brush
brosse ᶠ pour éprouvettes ᶠ
cepillo ᴹ para tubos ᴹ
Reagenzglasbürste ᶠ
spazzolino ᴹ per provette

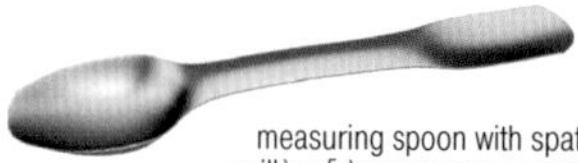

measuring spoon with spatula
cuillère ᶠ à mesurer avec spatule ᶠ
cuchara ᶠ dosificadora con espátula ᶠ
Messlöffel ᴹ mit Spatel ᴹ
misurino ᴹ con spatola ᶠ

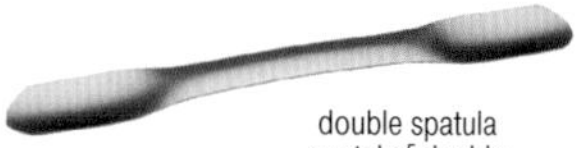

double spatula
spatule ᶠ double
espátula ᶠ doble
Doppelspatel ᶠ
spatola ᶠ doppia

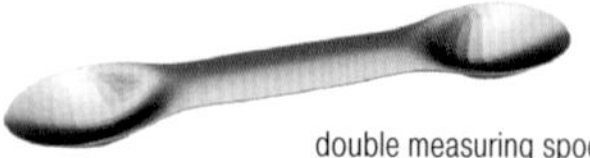

double measuring spoon
cuillère ᶠ de mesure ᶠ double
cuchara ᶠ dosificadora doble
doppelter Messlöffel ᴹ
misurino ᴹ doppio

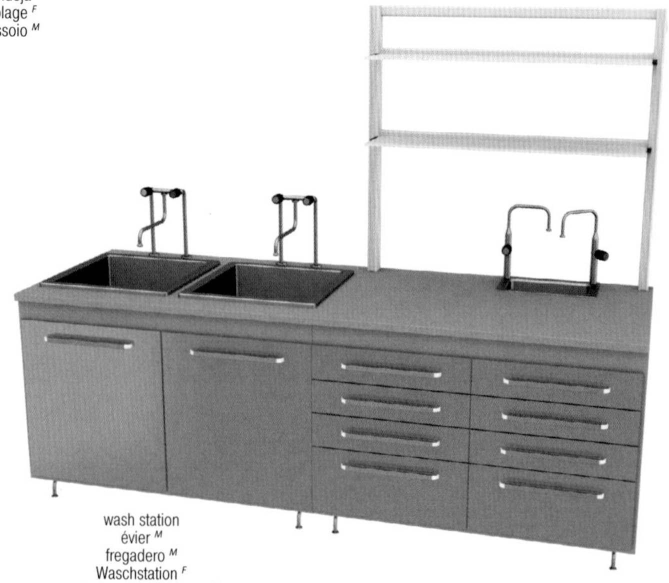

wash station
évier ᴹ
fregadero ᴹ
Waschstation ᶠ
postazione ᴹ di lavaggio ᴹ

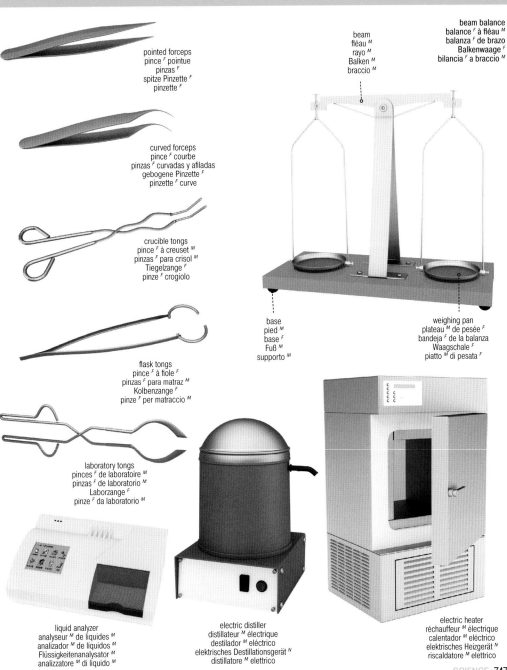

pointed forceps
pince ^{F} pointue
pinzas ^{F}
spitze Pinzette ^{F}
pinzette ^{F}

curved forceps
pince ^{F} courbe
pinzas ^{F} curvadas y afiladas
gebogene Pinzette ^{F}
pinzette ^{F} curve

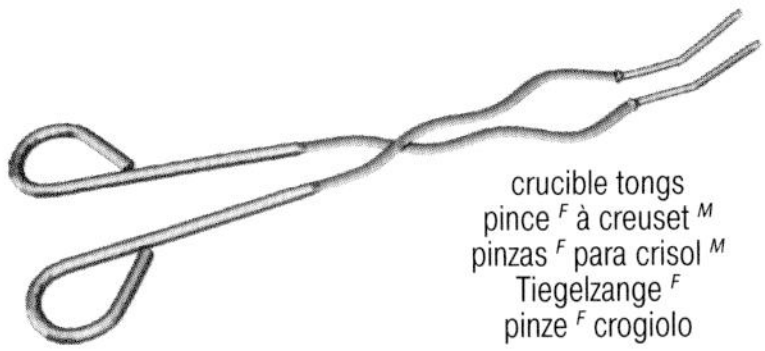

crucible tongs
pince ^{F} à creuset ^{M}
pinzas ^{F} para crisol ^{M}
Tiegelzange ^{F}
pinze ^{F} crogiolo

flask tongs
pince ^{F} à fiole ^{F}
pinzas ^{F} para matraz ^{M}
Kolbenzange ^{F}
pinze ^{F} per matraccio ^{M}

beam balance
balance ^{F} à fléau ^{M}
balanza ^{F} de brazo
Balkenwaage ^{F}
bilancia ^{F} a braccio ^{M}

beam
fléau ^{M}
rayo ^{M}
Balken ^{M}
braccio ^{M}

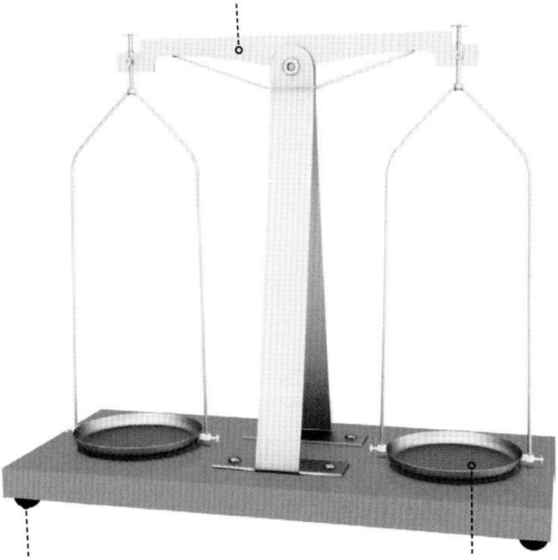

base
pied ^{M}
base ^{F}
Fuß ^{M}
supporto ^{M}

weighing pan
plateau ^{M} de pesée ^{F}
bandeja ^{F} de la balanza
Waagschale ^{F}
piatto ^{M} di pesata ^{F}

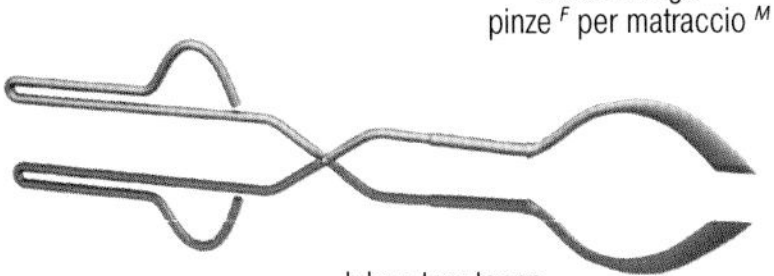

laboratory tongs
pinces ^{F} de laboratoire ^{M}
pinzas ^{F} de laboratorio ^{M}
Laborzange ^{F}
pinze ^{F} da laboratorio ^{M}

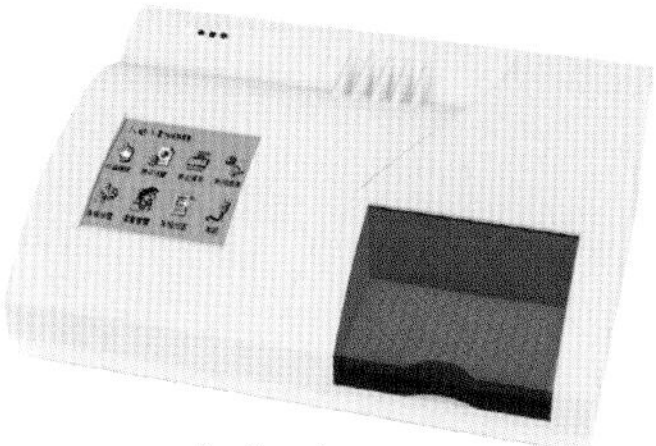

liquid analyzer
analyseur ^{M} de liquides ^{M}
analizador ^{M} de líquidos ^{M}
Flüssigkeitenanalysator ^{M}
analizzatore ^{M} di liquido ^{M}

electric distiller
distillateur ^{M} électrique
destilador ^{M} eléctrico
elektrisches Destillationsgerät ^{N}
distillatore ^{M} elettrico

electric heater
réchauffeur ^{M} électrique
calentador ^{M} eléctrico
elektrisches Heizgerät ^{N}
riscaldatore ^{M} elettrico

glassware dryer
séchoir M à verrerie M
secador M de instrumentos M
Laborglas-Trockner M
essiccatrice F per oggetti M in vetro M

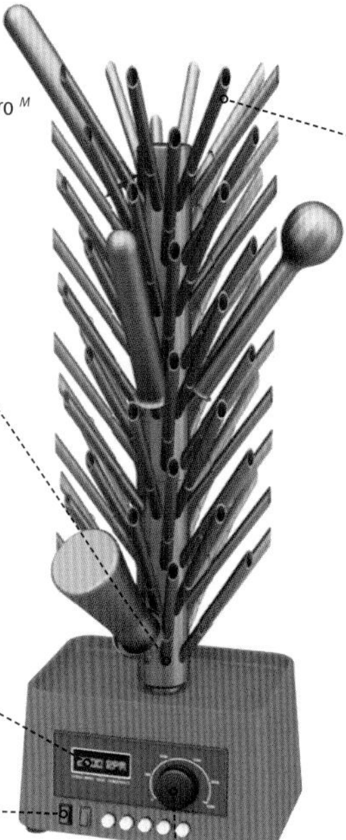

drying peg
goujon M pour plats M
soporte M de secado M
Trocknerstift M
perno M per essiccazione

air channel
canal M d'aération
circuito M de aire M
Luftkanal M
convogliatore M d'aria F

indicator panel
panneau M indicateur
panel M indicador
Anzeigefeld N
pannello M indicatore

power switch
interrupteur M
interruptor M de encendido M
Netzschalter M
interruttore M

control knob
commandes F
perilla F de control M
Drehknopf M
manopola F di controllo

centrifuge
centrifugeuse F
centrifugadora F
Zentrifuge F
centrifuga F

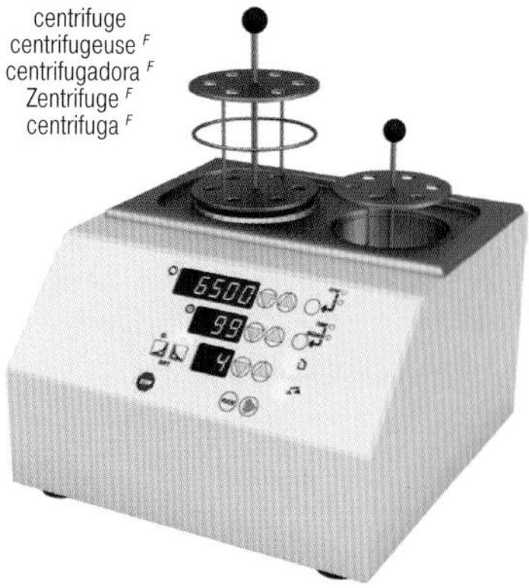

digital microscope
microscope M numérique
microscopio M digital
Digitalmikroskop N
microscopio M digitale

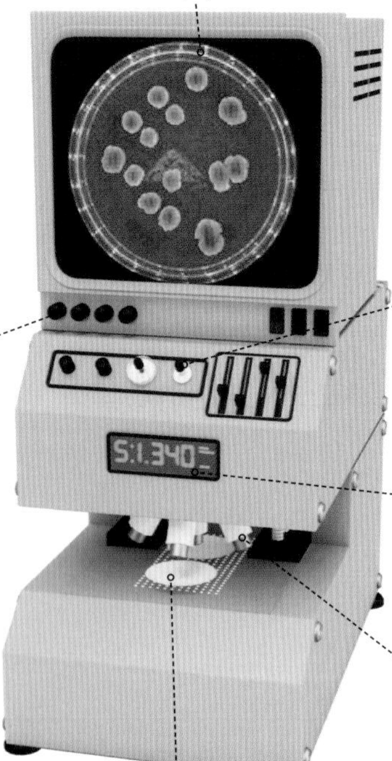

visual display
écran M
pantalla F
Sichtanzeige F
display M

control panel
panneau M de réglages M
panel M de control M
Bedienpult M
pannello M di controllo M

specimen positioning control
bouton M de mise F en position F
de l'échantillon M
controlador M
Proben-Positionierungssteuerung F
controller M di posizione F
del campione M

indicator panel
panneau M indicateur
panel M indicador
Anzeigefeld N
pannello M indicatore

field lens
lentille F de champ M
lente M
Feldlinse F
lente F di campo F

position table
platine F porte-échantillon M
tabla F de posición M
Positionierungstisch M
tavolo M di posizione F

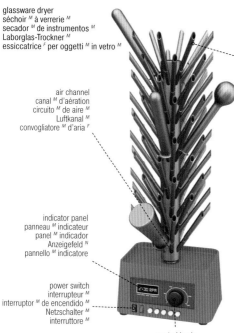

fixed-angle centrifuge
centrifugeuse F à angle M fixe
centrifugadora F de ángulo M fijo
Festwinkel-Zentrifuge F
centrifuga F ad angolo M fisso

features of the Moon
surface ^{F} de la Lune ^{F}
características ^{F} de la luna ^{F}
Mondoberfläche ^{F}
caratteristiche ^{F} della luna ^{F}

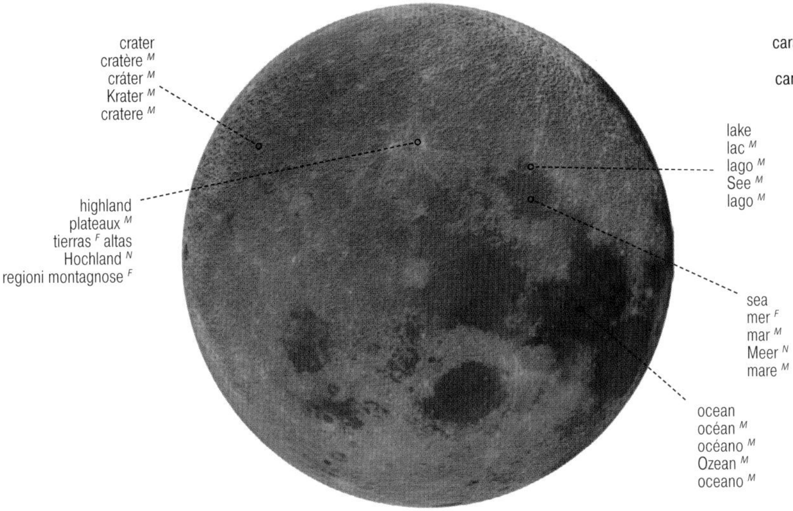
crater
cratère M
cráter M
Krater M
cratere M
highland
plateaux M
tierras F altas
Hochland N
regioni montagnose F
lake
lac M
lago M
See M
lago M
sea
mer F
mar M
Meer N
mare M
ocean
océan M
océano M
Ozean M
oceano M

Phases of the Moon

Phases ^{F} de la Lune ^{F} | Fases ^{F} lunares | Mondphasen ^{F} | Fasi ^{F} lunari

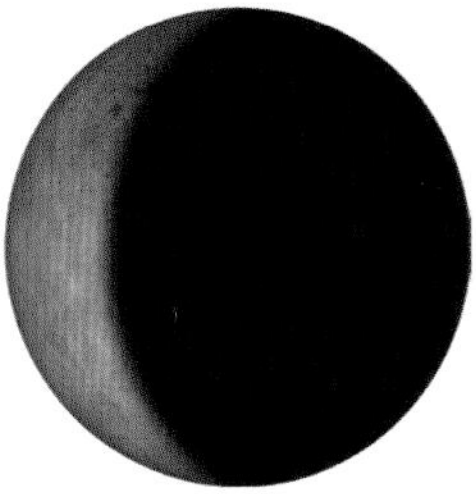

old crescent
dernier croissant ^{M}
luna ^{F} menguante
abnehmend
mezza luna ^{F} calante

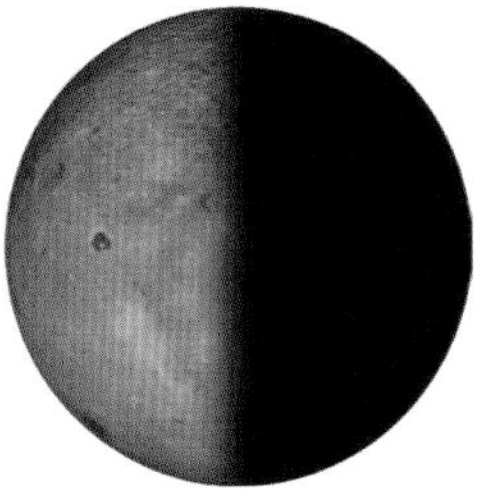

last quarter
dernier quartier ^{M}
cuarto ^{M} menguante
letztes Viertel ^{N}
ultimo quarto ^{M}

waning gibbous
lune ^{F} gibbeuse décroissante
luna ^{F} gibada menguante
abnehmendes Dreiviertel ^{N}
luna ^{F} goobosa calante

full moon
pleine lune ^{F}
luna ^{F} llena
Vollmond ^{M}
luna ^{F} piena

waxing gibbous
lune ^{F} gibbeuse croissante
luna ^{F} gibada creciente
zunehmendes Dreiviertel ^{N}
luna ^{F} gobbosa crescente

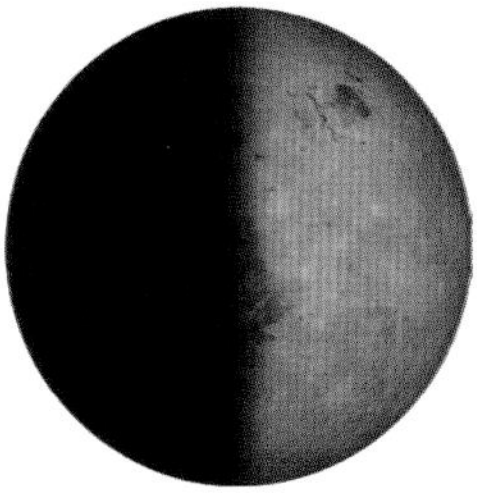

first quarter
premier quartier ^{M}
cuarto ^{M} creciente
erstes Viertel ^{N}
primo quarto ^{M}

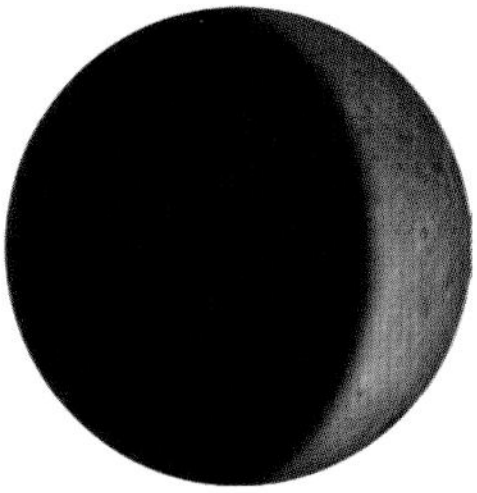

new crescent
nouveau croissant ^{M} de lune ^{F}
luna ^{F} nueva visible
zunehmend
mezza luna ^{F} crescente

new moon
nouvelle lune ^{F}
luna ^{F} nueva
Neumond ^{M}
luna ^{F} nuova

solar system
système [M] solaire
sistema [M] solar
Sonnensystem [N]
sistema [M] solare

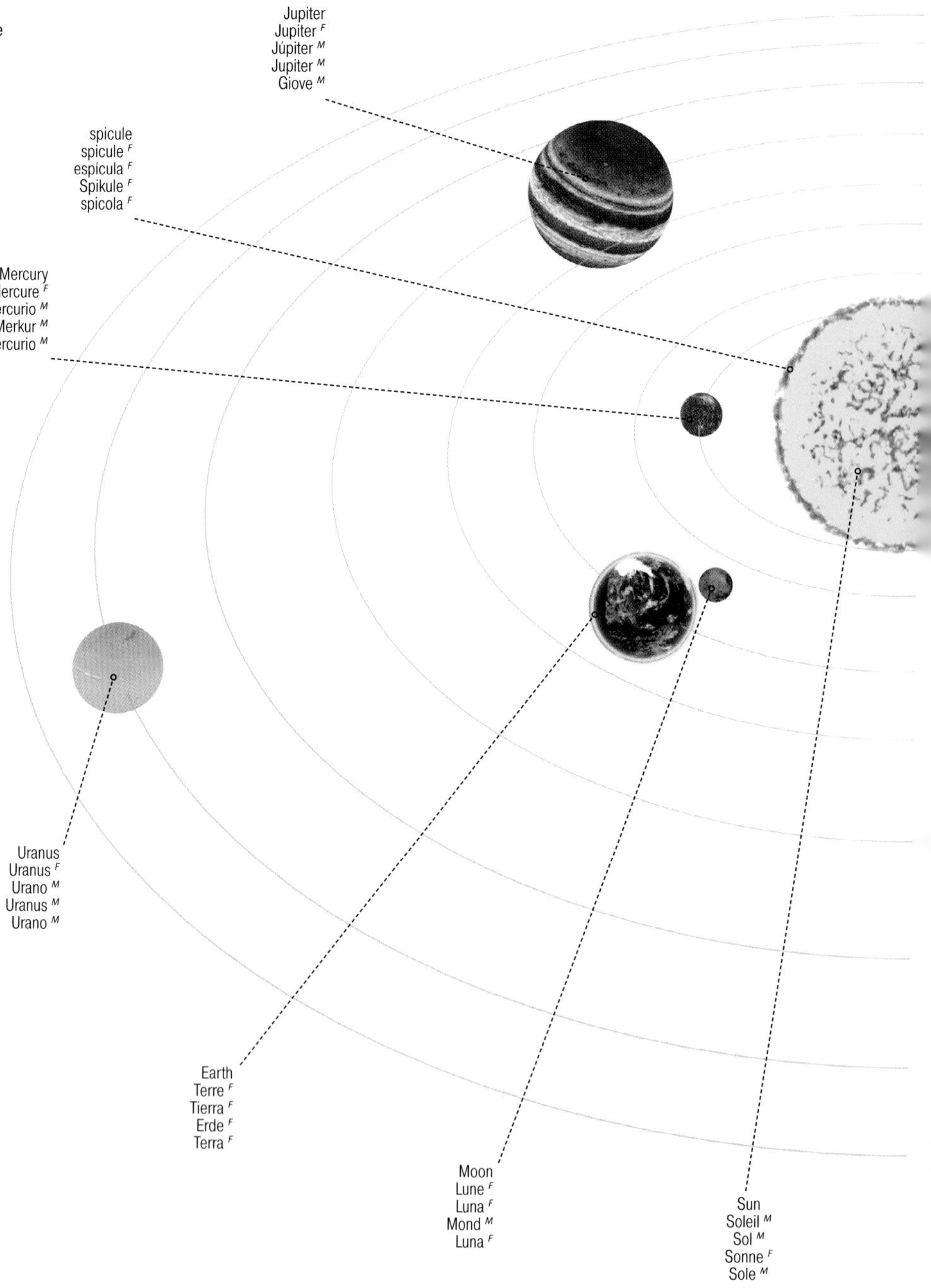
Jupiter
Jupiter [F]
Júpiter [M]
Jupiter [M]
Giove [M]
spicule
spicule [F]
espícula [F]
Spikule [F]
spicola [F]
Mercury
Mercure [F]
Mercurio [M]
Merkur [M]
Mercurio [M]
Uranus
Uranus [F]
Urano [M]
Uranus [M]
Urano [M]
Earth
Terre [F]
Tierra [F]
Erde [F]
Terra [F]
Moon
Lune [F]
Luna [F]
Mond [M]
Luna [F]
Sun
Soleil [M]
Sol [M]
Sonne [F]
Sole [M]

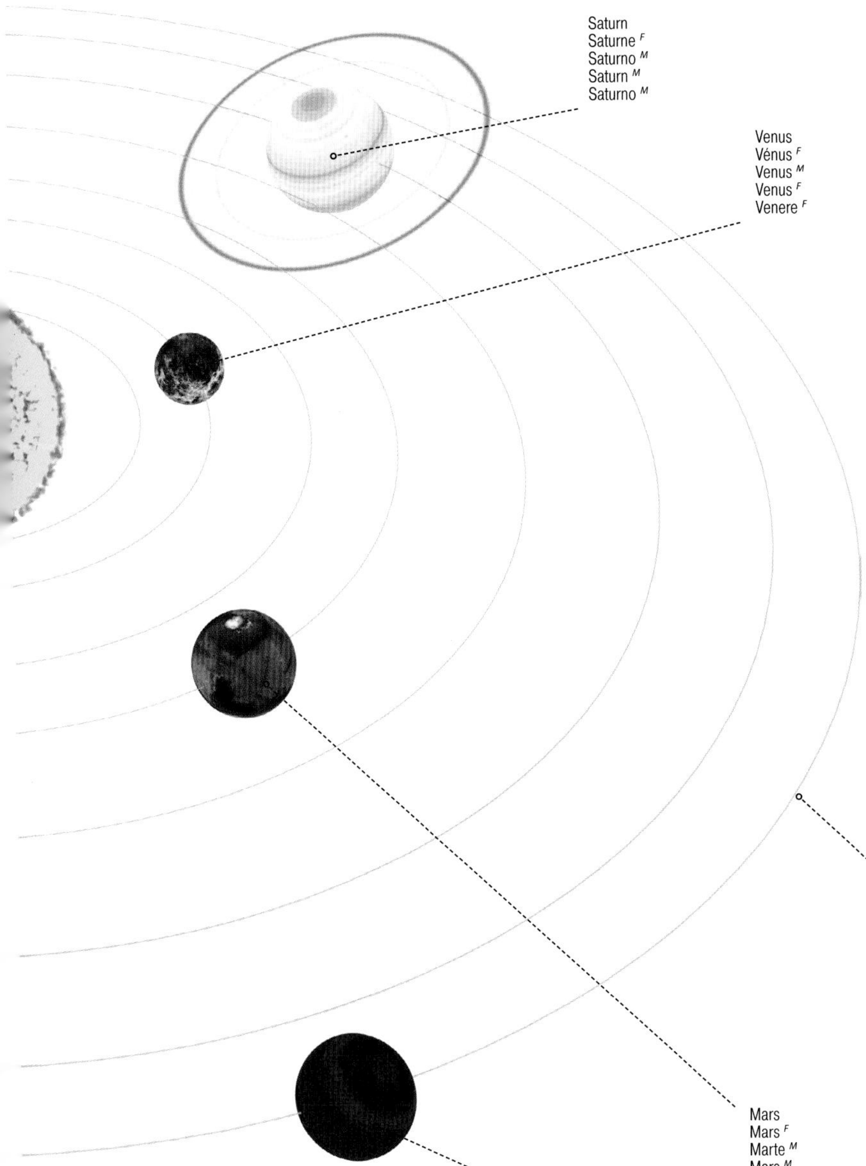
Saturn
Saturne F
Saturno M
Saturn M
Saturno M
Venus
Vénus F
Venus M
Venus F
Venere F
orbit
orbite M
órbita F
Orbit M
orbita F
Mars
Mars F
Marte M
Mars M
Marte M
Neptune
Neptune F
Neptuno M
Neptun M
Nettuno M

seasons of the year
saisons ^F^ de l'année ^F^
estaciones del año ^F^
Jahreszeiten ^F^
stagioni ^F^ dell'anno ^M^

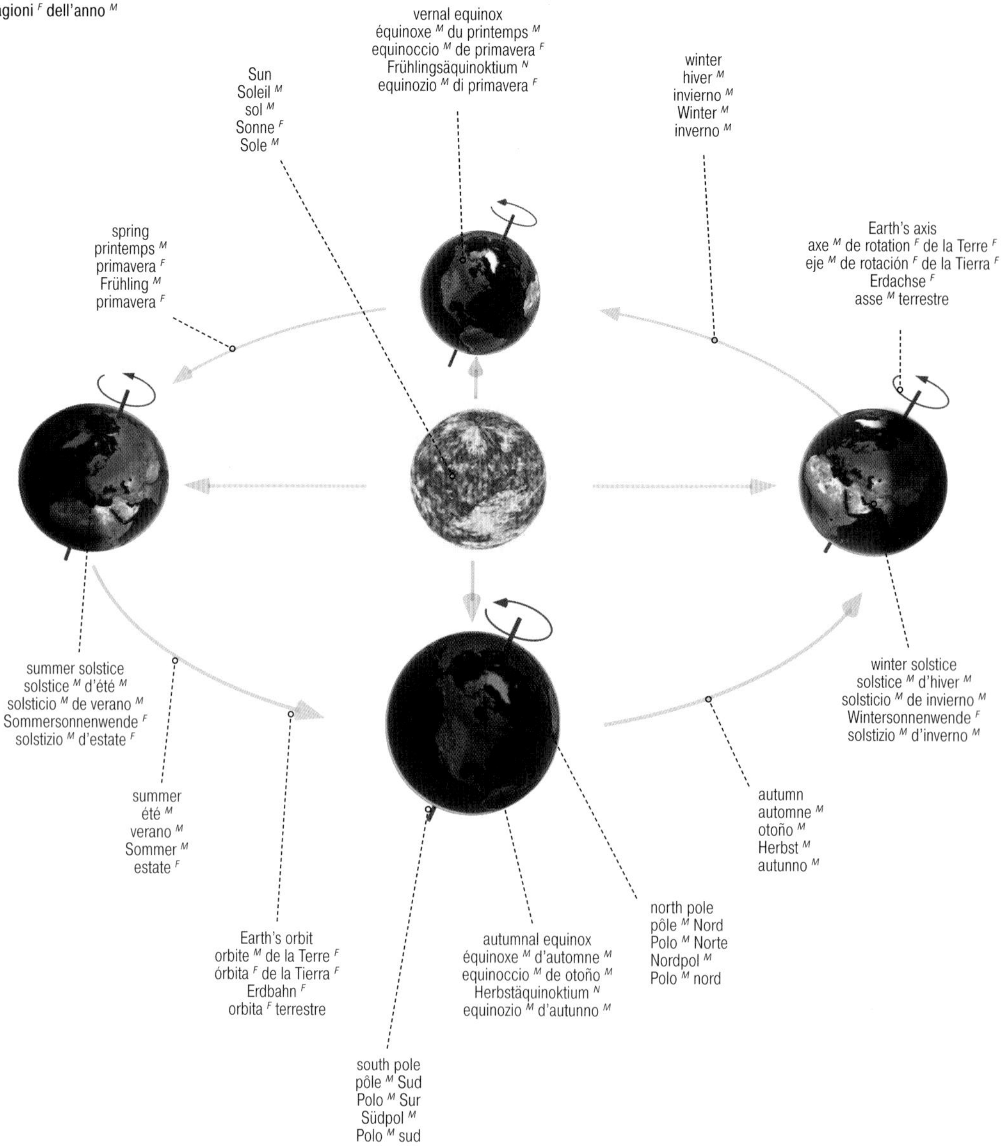
vernal equinox
équinoxe M du printemps M
equinoccio M de primavera F
Frühlingsäquinoktium N
equinozio M di primavera F
Sun
Soleil M
sol M
Sonne F
Sole M
winter
hiver M
invierno M
Winter M
inverno M
spring
printemps M
primavera F
Frühling M
primavera F
Earth's axis
axe M de rotation F de la Terre F
eje M de rotación F de la Tierra F
Erdachse F
asse M terrestre
summer solstice
solstice M d'été M
solsticio M de verano M
Sommersonnenwende F
solstizio M d'estate F
winter solstice
solstice M d'hiver M
solsticio M de invierno M
Wintersonnenwende F
solstizio M d'inverno M
summer
été M
verano M
Sommer M
estate F
autumn
automne M
otoño M
Herbst M
autunno M
Earth's orbit
orbite M de la Terre F
órbita F de la Tierra F
Erdbahn F
orbita F terrestre
autumnal equinox
équinoxe M d'automne M
equinoccio M de otoño M
Herbstäquinoktium N
equinozio M d'autunno M
north pole
pôle M Nord
Polo M Norte
Nordpol M
Polo M nord
south pole
pôle M Sud
Polo M Sur
Südpol M
Polo M sud

structure of the Earth
structure F de la Terre F
estructura F de la Tierra F
Innerer Aufbau M der Erde F
struttura F della Terra

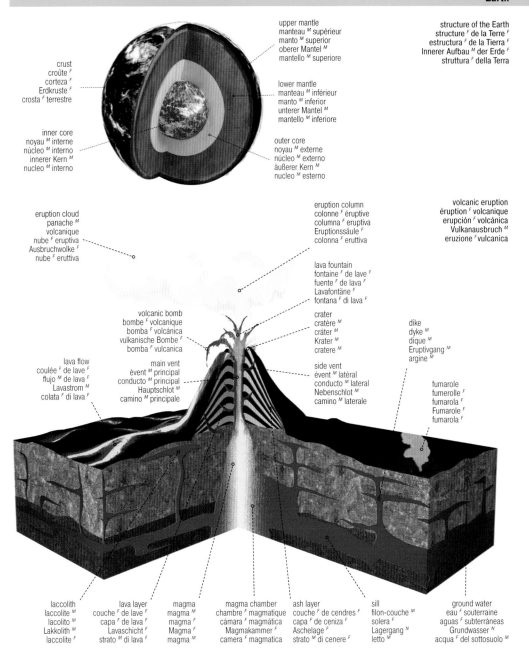

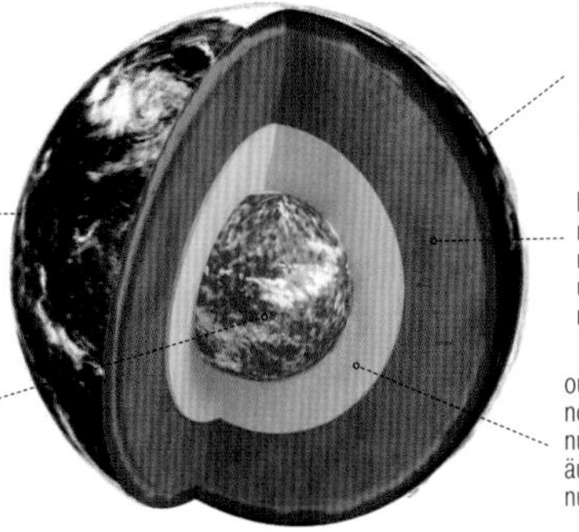
upper mantle
manteau M supérieur
manto M superior
oberer Mantel M
mantello M superiore
crust
croûte F
corteza F
Erdkruste F
crosta F terrestre
lower mantle
manteau M inférieur
manto M inferior
unterer Mantel M
mantello M inferiore
inner core
noyau M interne
núcleo M interno
innerer Kern M
nucleo M interno
outer core
noyau M externe
núcleo M externo
äußerer Kern M
nucleo M esterno

volcanic eruption
éruption F volcanique
erupción F volcánica
Vulkanausbruch M
eruzione F vulcanica

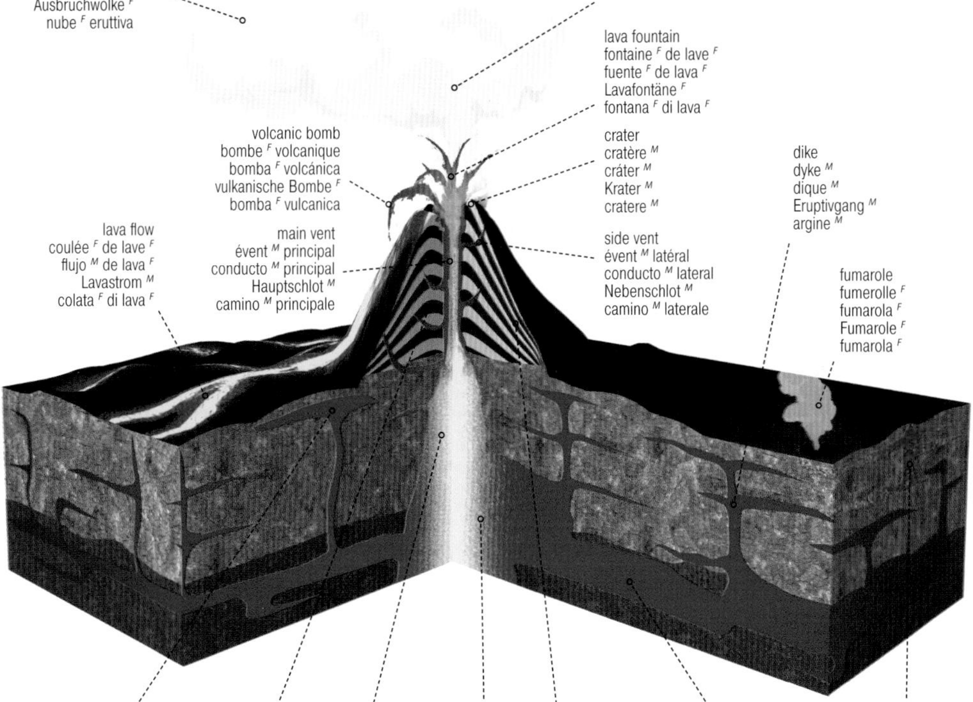
eruption cloud
panache M volcanique
nube F eruptiva
Ausbruchwolke F
nube F eruttiva
eruption column
colonne F éruptive
columna F eruptiva
Eruptionssäule F
colonna F eruttiva
lava fountain
fontaine F de lave F
fuente F de lava F
Lavafontäne F
fontana F di lava F
volcanic bomb
bombe F volcanique
bomba F volcánica
vulkanische Bombe F
bomba F vulcanica
crater
cratère M
cráter M
Krater M
cratere M
dike
dyke M
dique M
Eruptivgang M
argine M
lava flow
coulée F de lave F
flujo M de lava F
Lavastrom M
colata F di lava F
main vent
évent M principal
conducto M principal
Hauptschlot M
camino M principale
side vent
évent M latéral
conducto M lateral
Nebenschlot M
camino M laterale
fumarole
fumerolle F
fumarola F
Fumarole F
fumarola F
laccolith
laccolite M
lacolito M
Lakkolith M
laccolite F
lava layer
couche F de lave F
capa F de lava F
Lavaschicht F
strato M di lava F
magma
magma M
magma F
Magma F
magma M
magma chamber
chambre F magmatique
cámara F magmática
Magmakammer F
camera F magmatica
ash layer
couche F de cendres F
capa F de ceniza F
Aschelage F
strato M di cenere F
sill
filon-couche M
solera F
Lagergang N
letto M
ground water
eau F souterraine
aguas F subterráneas
Grundwasser N
acqua F del sottosuolo M

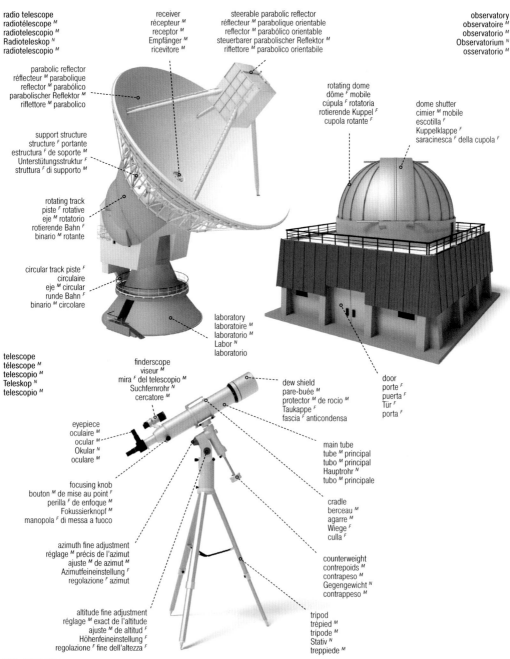

radio telescope
radiotélescope M
radiotelescopio M
Radioteleskop N
radiotelescopio M

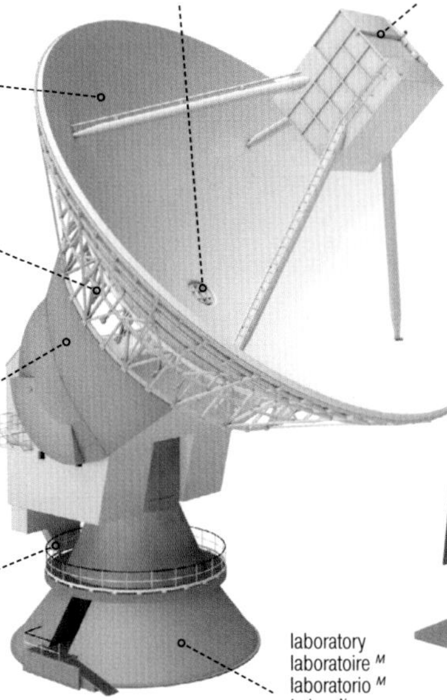

receiver
récepteur M
receptor M
Empfänger M
ricevitore M

steerable parabolic reflector
réflecteur M parabolique orientable
reflector M parabólico orientable
steuerbarer parabolischer Reflektor M
riflettore M parabolico orientabile

parabolic reflector
réflecteur M parabolique
reflector M parabólico
parabolischer Reflektor M
riflettore M parabolico

support structure
structure F portante
estructura F de soporte M
Unterstütungsstruktur F
struttura F di supporto M

rotating track
piste F rotative
eje M rotatorio
rotierende Bahn F
binario M rotante

circular track piste F circulaire
eje M circular
runde Bahn F
binario M circolare

laboratory
laboratoire M
laboratorio M
Labor N
laboratorio

observatory
observatoire M
observatorio M
Observatorium N
osservatorio M

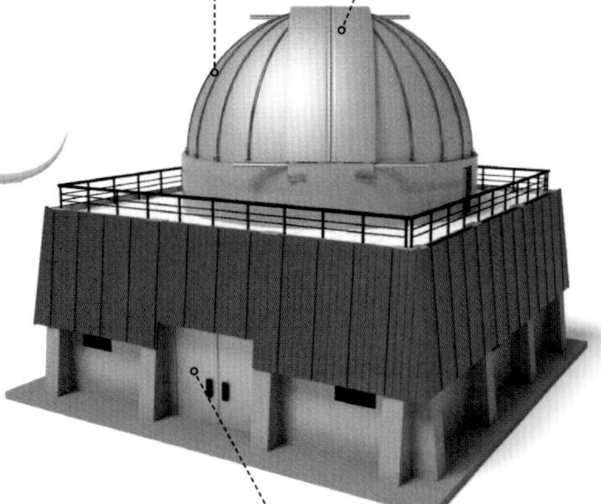

rotating dome
dôme F mobile
cúpula F rotatoria
rotierende Kuppel F
cupola rotante F

dome shutter
cimier M mobile
escotilla F
Kuppelklappe F
saracinesca F della cupola F

door
porte F
puerta F
Tür F
porta F

telescope
télescope M
telescopio M
Teleskop N
telescopio M

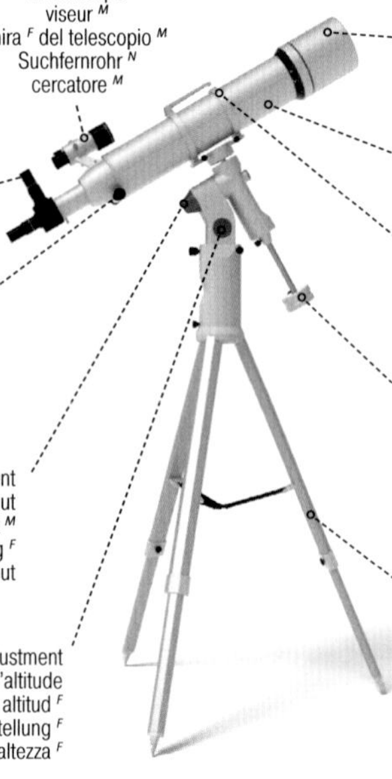

finderscope
viseur M
mira F del telescopio M
Suchfernrohr N
cercatore M

dew shield
pare-buée M
protector M de rocío M
Taukappe F
fascia F anticondensa

eyepiece
oculaire M
ocular M
Okular N
oculare M

main tube
tube M principal
tubo M principal
Hauptrohr N
tubo M principale

focusing knob
bouton M de mise au point F
perilla F de enfoque M
Fokussierknopf M
manopola F di messa a fuoco

cradle
berceau M
agarre M
Wiege F
culla F

azimuth fine adjustment
réglage M précis de l'azimut
ajuste M de azimut M
Azimutfeineinstellung F
regolazione F azimut

counterweight
contrepoids M
contrapeso M
Gegengewicht N
contrappeso M

altitude fine adjustment
réglage M exact de l'altitude
ajuste M de altitud F
Höhenfeineinstellung F
regolazione F fine dell'altezza F

tripod
trépied M
trípode M
Stativ N
treppiede M

International Space Station
Station F spatiale internationale
Estación F espacial internacional
internationale Raumstation F
Stazione F Spaziale Internazionale

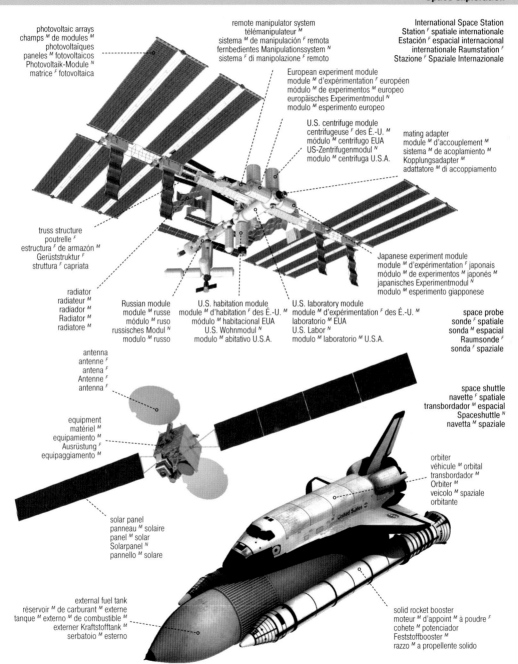

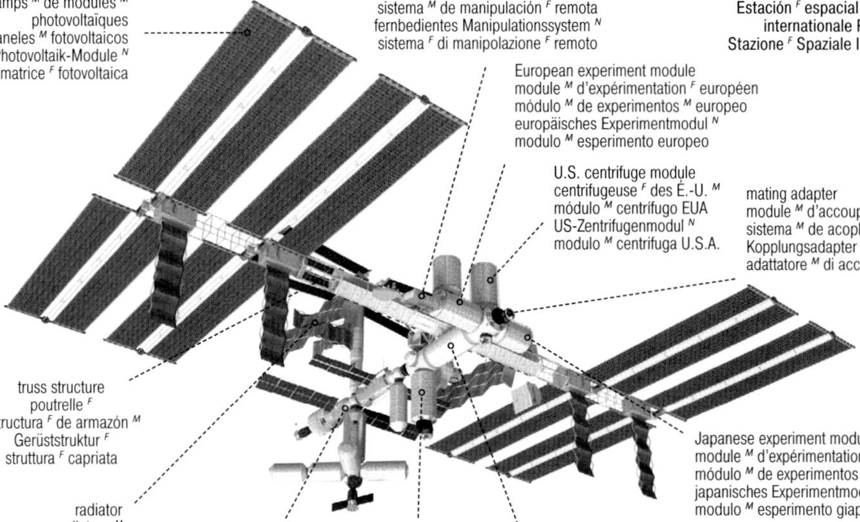
photovoltaic arrays
champs M de modules M photovoltaïques
paneles M fotovoltaicos
Photovoltaik-Module N
matrice F fotovoltaica
remote manipulator system
télémanipulateur M
sistema M de manipulación F remota
fernbedientes Manipulationssystem N
sistema F di manipolazione F remoto
European experiment module
module M d'expérimentation F européen
módulo M de experimentos M europeo
europäisches Experimentmodul N
modulo M esperimento europeo
U.S. centrifuge module
centrifugeuse F des É.-U. M
módulo M centrífugo EUA
US-Zentrifugenmodul N
modulo M centrifuga U.S.A.
mating adapter
module M d'accouplement M
sistema M de acoplamiento M
Kopplungsadapter M
adattatore M di accoppiamento
truss structure
poutrelle F
estructura F de armazón M
Gerüststruktur F
struttura F capriata
Japanese experiment module
module M d'expérimentation F japonais
módulo M de experimentos M japonés M
japanisches Experimentmodul N
modulo M esperimento giapponese
radiator
radiateur M
radiador M
Radiator M
radiatore M
Russian module
module M russe
módulo M ruso
russisches Modul N
modulo M russo
U.S. habitation module
module M d'habitation F des É.-U. M
módulo M habitacional EUA
U.S. Wohnmodul N
modulo M abitativo U.S.A.
U.S. laboratory module
module M d'expérimentation F des É.-U. M
laboratorio M EUA
U.S. Labor N
modulo M laboratorio M U.S.A.

space probe
sonde F spatiale
sonda M espacial
Raumsonde F
sonda F spaziale

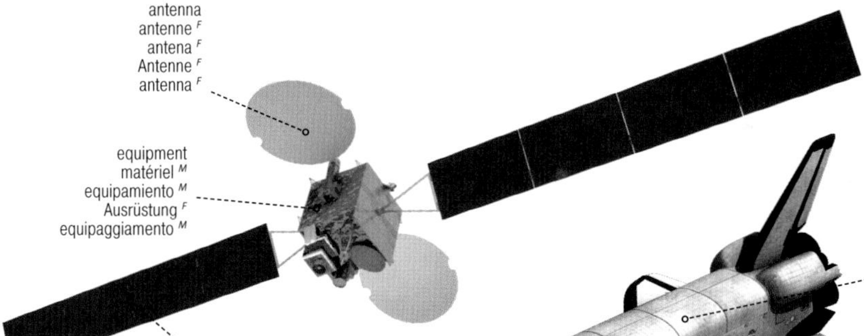
antenna
antenne F
antena F
Antenne F
antenna F
equipment
matériel M
equipamiento M
Ausrüstung F
equipaggiamento M
solar panel
panneau M solaire
panel M solar
Solarpanel N
pannello M solare

space shuttle
navette F spatiale
transbordador M espacial
Spaceshuttle N
navetta M spaziale

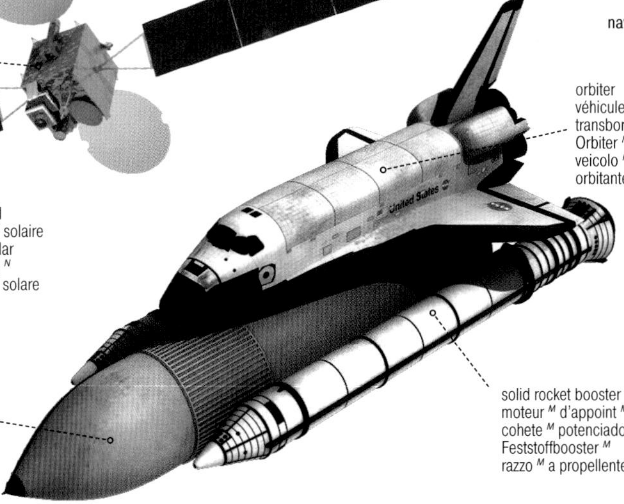
orbiter
véhicule M orbital
transbordador M
Orbiter M
veicolo M spaziale orbitante
United States
external fuel tank
réservoir M de carburant M externe
tanque M externo M de combustible M
externer Kraftstofftank M
serbatoio M esterno
solid rocket booster
moteur M d'appoint M à poudre F
cohete M potenciador
Feststoffbooster M
razzo M a propellente solido

Moon landing
atterrissage ^{M} sur la Lune ^{F}
aterrizaje ^{F} lunar
Mondlandung ^{F}
allunaggio ^{M}

lunar rover
véhicule ^{M} lunaire
vehículo ^{M} de exploración ^{F} lunar
Mondfahrzeug ^{N}
rover ^{M} lunare

landing module
module ^{M} lunaire
módulo ^{M} de aterrizaje
Landemodul ^{N}
modulo ^{M} di atterraggio

Earth
Terre ^{F}
Tierra ^{F}
Erde ^{F}
Terra ^{F}

surface of the Moon
surface ^{F} de la Lune ^{F}
superficie ^{F} lunar
Oberfläche des Mondes ^{F}
superficie ^{F} della luna ^{F}

crater
cratère ^{M}
cráter ^{M}
Krater ^{M}
cratere ^{M}

astronaut
astronaute ^{M}
astronauta ^{M}
Astronaut ^{M}
astronauta ^{M}

space launcher
lanceur ^{M} spatial
lanzadora ^{F} espacial
Trägerrakete ^{F}
vettore ^{M} spaziale

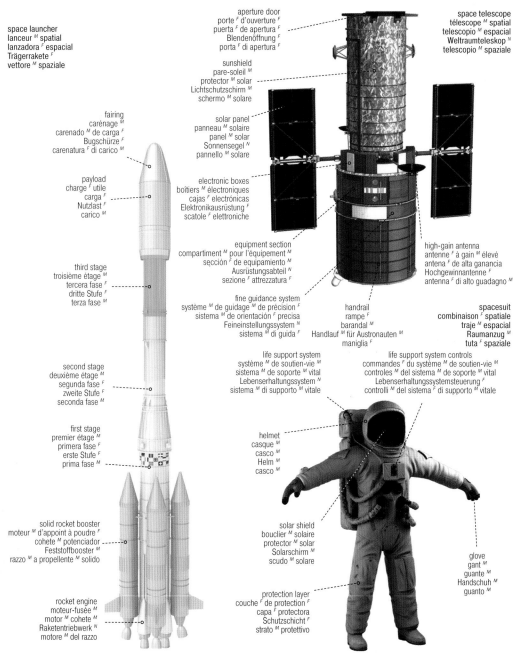

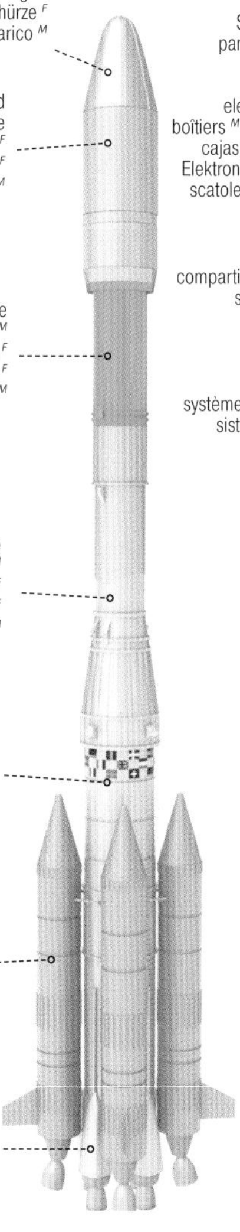
fairing / carénage ^{M} / carenado ^{M} de carga ^{F} / Bugschürze ^{F} / carenatura ^{F} di carico ^{M}
payload / charge ^{F} utile / carga ^{F} / Nutzlast ^{F} / carico ^{M}
third stage / troisième étage ^{M} / tercera fase ^{F} / dritte Stufe ^{F} / terza fase ^{M}
second stage / deuxième étage ^{M} / segunda fase ^{F} / zweite Stufe ^{F} / seconda fase ^{M}
first stage / premier étage ^{M} / primera fase ^{F} / erste Stufe ^{F} / prima fase ^{M}
solid rocket booster / moteur ^{M} d'appoint à poudre ^{F} / cohete ^{M} potenciador / Feststoffbooster ^{M} / razzo ^{M} a propellente ^{M} solido
rocket engine / moteur-fusée ^{M} / motor ^{M} cohete ^{M} / Raketentriebwerk ^{N} / motore ^{M} del razzo

space telescope
télescope ^{M} spatial
telescopio ^{M} espacial
Weltraumteleskop ^{N}
telescopio ^{M} spaziale

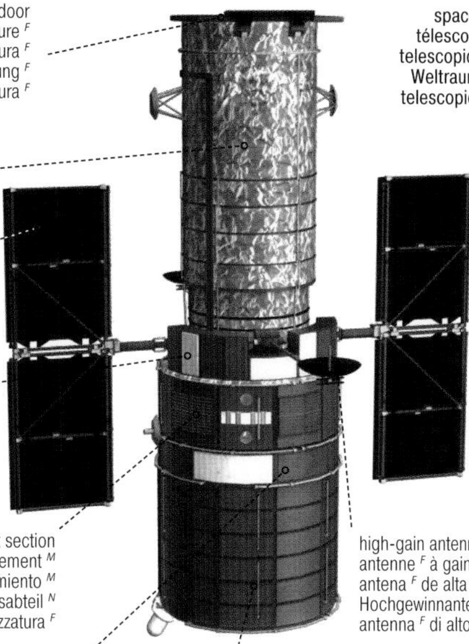
aperture door / porte ^{F} d'ouverture ^{F} / puerta ^{F} de apertura ^{F} / Blendenöffnung ^{F} / porta ^{F} di apertura ^{F}
sunshield / pare-soleil ^{M} / protector ^{M} solar / Lichtschutzschirm ^{M} / schermo ^{M} solare
solar panel / panneau ^{M} solaire / panel ^{M} solar / Sonnensegel ^{N} / pannello ^{M} solare
electronic boxes / boîtiers ^{M} électroniques / cajas ^{F} electrónicas / Elektronikausrüstung ^{F} / scatole ^{F} elettroniche
equipment section / compartiment ^{M} pour l'équipement ^{M} / sección ^{F} de equipamiento ^{M} / Ausrüstungsabteil ^{N} / sezione ^{F} attrezzatura ^{F}
high-gain antenna / antenne ^{F} à gain ^{M} élevé / antena ^{F} de alta ganancia / Hochgewinnantenne ^{F} / antenna ^{F} di alto guadagno ^{M}
fine guidance system / système ^{M} de guidage ^{M} de précision ^{F} / sistema ^{M} de orientación ^{F} precisa / Feineinstellungssystem ^{N} / sistema ^{M} di guida ^{F}
handrail / rampe ^{F} / barandal ^{M} / Handlauf ^{M} für Austronauten ^{M} / maniglia ^{F}

spacesuit
combinaison ^{F} spatiale
traje ^{M} espacial
Raumanzug ^{M}
tuta ^{F} spaziale

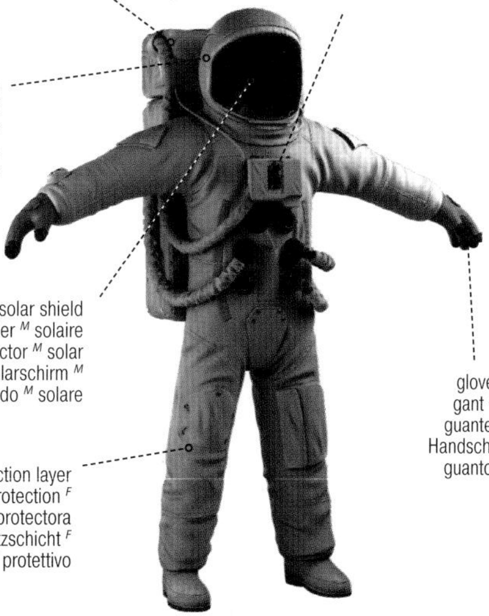
life support system / système ^{M} de soutien-vie ^{M} / sistema ^{M} de soporte ^{M} vital / Lebenserhaltungssystem ^{N} / sistema ^{M} di supporto ^{M} vitale
life support system controls / commandes ^{F} du système ^{M} de soutien-vie ^{M} / controles ^{M} del sistema ^{M} de soporte ^{M} vital / Lebenserhaltungssystemsteuerung ^{F} / controlli ^{M} del sistema ^{F} di supporto ^{M} vitale
helmet / casque ^{M} / casco ^{M} / Helm ^{M} / casco ^{M}
solar shield / bouclier ^{M} solaire / protector ^{M} solar / Solarschirm ^{M} / scudo ^{M} solare
glove / gant ^{M} / guante ^{M} / Handschuh ^{M} / guanto ^{M}
protection layer / couche ^{F} de protection ^{F} / capa ^{F} protectora / Schutzschicht ^{F} / strato ^{M} protettivo

ENERGY AND INDUSTRY

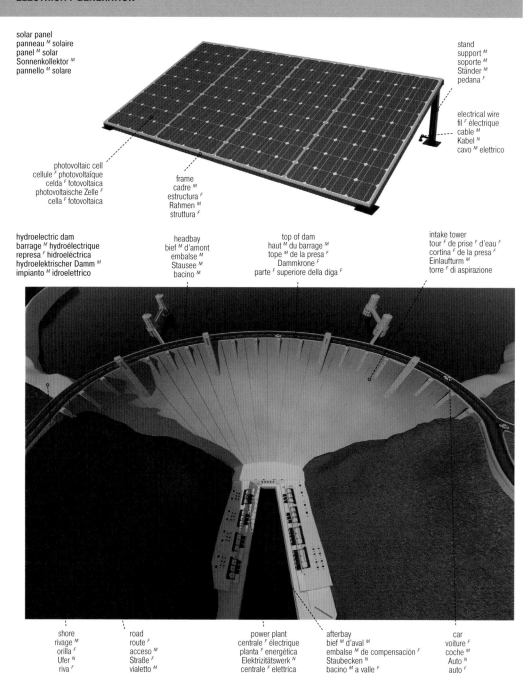

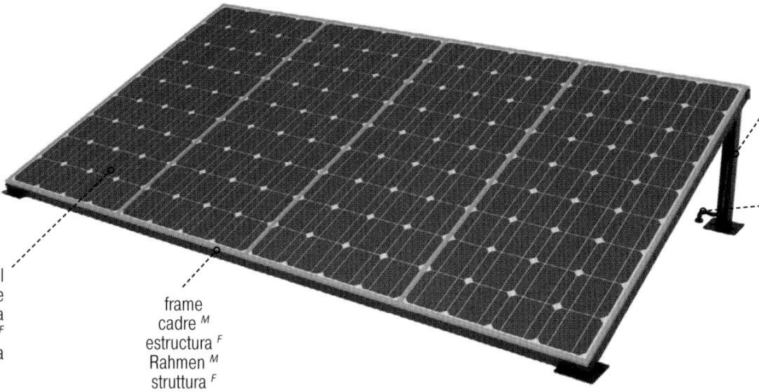
solar panel
panneau M solaire
panel M solar
Sonnenkollektor M
pannello M solare
stand
support M
soporte M
Ständer M
pedana F
electrical wire
fil F électrique
cable M
Kabel N
cavo M elettrico
photovoltaic cell
cellule F photovoltaîque
celda F fotovoltaica
photovoltaische Zelle F
cella F fotovoltaica
frame
cadre M
estructura F
Rahmen M
struttura F

hydroelectric dam
barrage M hydroélectrique
represa F hidroeléctrica
hydroelektrischer Damm M
impianto M idroelettrico
headbay
bief M d'amont
embalse M
Stausee M
bacino M
top of dam
haut M du barrage M
tope M de la presa F
Dammkrone F
parte F superiore della diga F
intake tower
tour F de prise F d'eau F
cortina F de la presa F
Einlaufturm M
torre F di aspirazione
shore
rivage M
orilla F
Ufer N
riva F
road
route F
acceso M
Straße F
vialetto M
power plant
centrale F électrique
planta F energética
Elektrizitätswerk N
centrale F elettrica
afterbay
bief M d'aval M
embalse M de compensación F
Staubecken N
bacino M a valle F
car
voiture F
coche M
Auto N
auto F

transmission tower
pylône M pour transport M de courant M
torre F de transmisión F
Freileitungsmast M
linea F di trasmissione di potenza

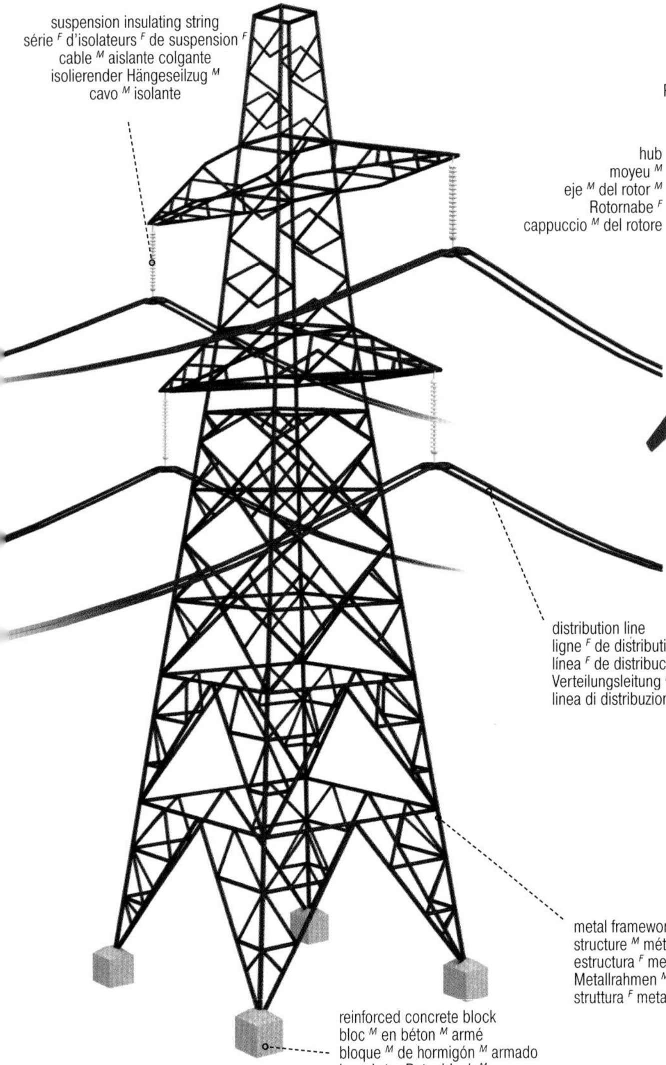
suspension insulating string
série F d'isolateurs F de suspension F
cable M aislante colgante
isolierender Hängeseilzug M
cavo M isolante
distribution line
ligne F de distribution F
línea F de distribución F
Verteilungsleitung F
linea di distribuzione
metal framework
structure M métallique
estructura F metálica
Metallrahmen M
struttura F metallica
reinforced concrete block
bloc M en béton M armé
bloque M de hormigón M armado
bewehrter Betonblock M
blocco M di cemento M armato

wind turbine
éolienne F
turbina F de viento M
Windkraftanlage F
generatore M eolico

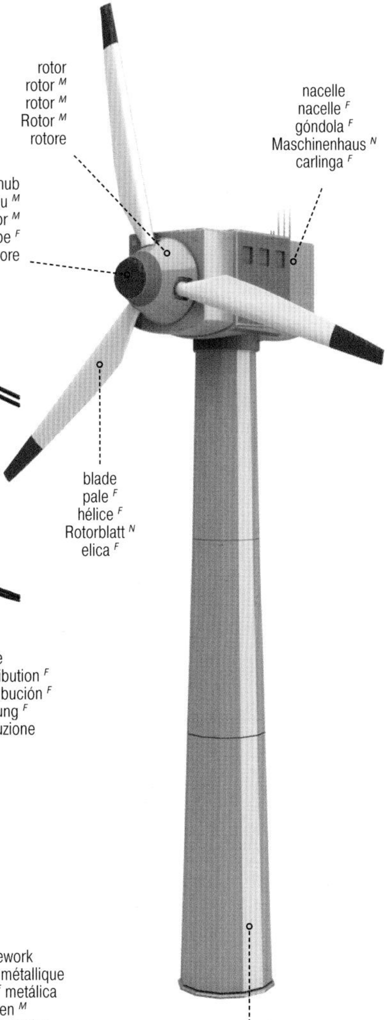
rotor
rotor M
rotor M
Rotor M
rotore
nacelle
nacelle F
góndola F
Maschinenhaus N
carlinga F
hub
moyeu M
eje M del rotor M
Rotornabe F
cappuccio M del rotore
blade
pale F
hélice F
Rotorblatt N
elica F
tower
tour F
torre F
Turm M
torre F

nuclear power plant
centrale ^{F} nucléaire
planta ^{F} de energía ^{F} nuclear
Kernkraftwerk ^{N}
impianto ^{M} per energia ^{F} nucleare

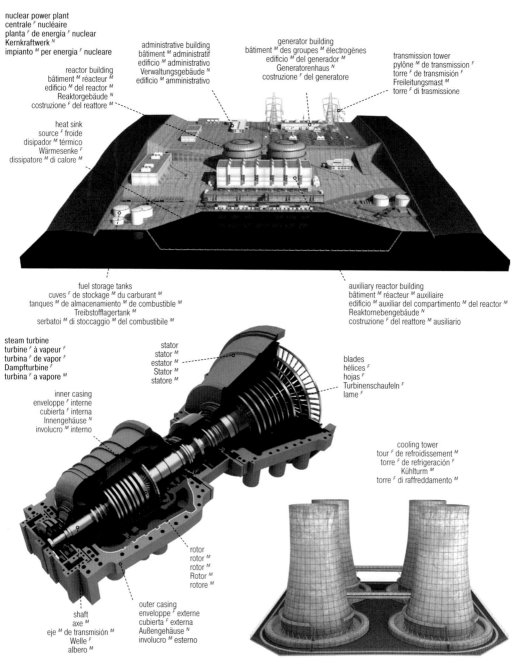

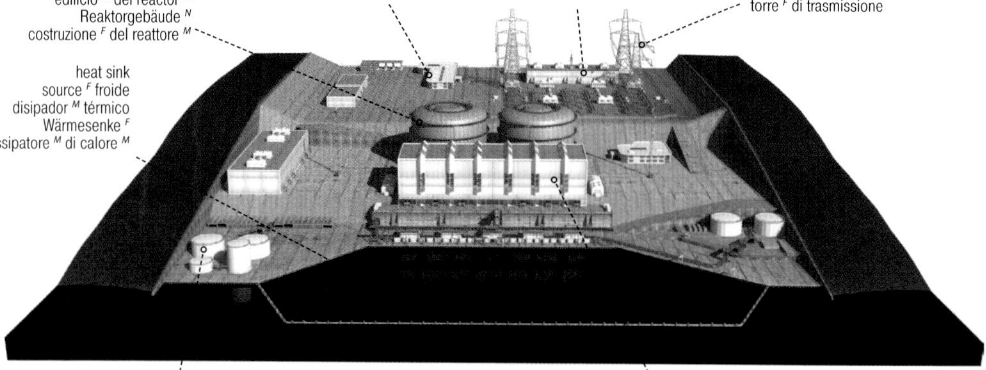
reactor building
bâtiment ^{M} réacteur ^{M}
edificio ^{M} del reactor ^{M}
Reaktorgebäude ^{N}
costruzione ^{F} del reattore ^{M}
administrative building
bâtiment ^{M} administratif
edificio ^{M} administrativo
Verwaltungsgebäude ^{N}
edificio ^{M} amministrativo
generator building
bâtiment ^{M} des groupes ^{M} électrogènes
edificio ^{M} del generador ^{M}
Generatorenhaus ^{N}
costruzione ^{F} del generatore
transmission tower
pylône ^{M} de transmission ^{F}
torre ^{F} de transmisión ^{F}
Freileitungsmast ^{M}
torre ^{F} di trasmissione
heat sink
source ^{F} froide
disipador ^{M} térmico
Wärmesenke ^{F}
dissipatore ^{M} di calore ^{M}
fuel storage tanks
cuves ^{F} de stockage ^{M} du carburant ^{M}
tanques ^{M} de almacenamiento ^{M} de combustible ^{M}
Treibstofflagertank ^{M}
serbatoi ^{M} di stoccaggio ^{M} del combustibile ^{M}
auxiliary reactor building
bâtiment ^{M} réacteur ^{M} auxiliaire
edificio ^{M} auxiliar del compartimento ^{M} del reactor ^{M}
Reaktornebengebäude ^{N}
costruzione ^{F} del reattore ^{M} ausiliario

steam turbine
turbine ^{F} à vapeur ^{F}
turbina ^{F} de vapor ^{F}
Dampfturbine ^{F}
turbina ^{F} a vapore ^{M}

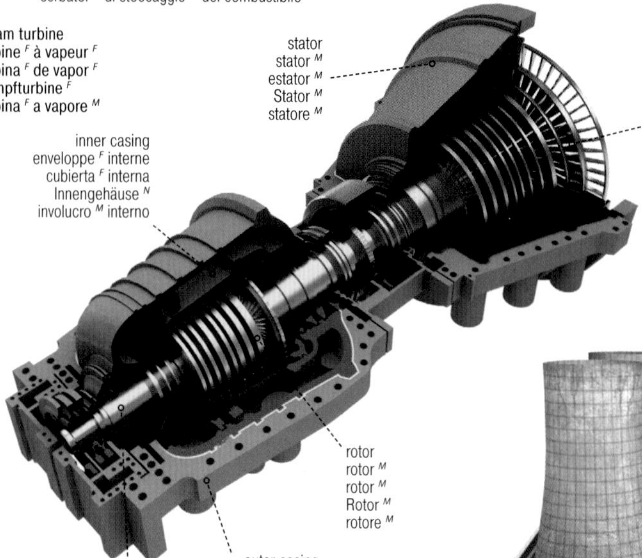
stator
stator ^{M}
estator ^{M}
Stator ^{M}
statore ^{M}
blades
hélices ^{F}
hojas ^{F}
Turbinenschaufeln ^{F}
lame ^{F}
inner casing
enveloppe ^{F} interne
cubierta ^{F} interna
Innengehäuse ^{N}
involucro ^{M} interno
rotor
rotor ^{M}
rotor ^{M}
Rotor ^{M}
rotore ^{M}
shaft
axe ^{M}
eje ^{M} de transmisión ^{M}
Welle ^{F}
albero ^{M}
outer casing
enveloppe ^{F} externe
cubierta ^{F} externa
Außengehäuse ^{N}
involucro ^{M} esterno

cooling tower
tour ^{F} de refroidissement ^{M}
torre ^{F} de refrigeración ^{F}
Kühlturm ^{M}
torre ^{F} di raffreddamento ^{M}

offshore oil platform
plate-forme ^{F} pétrolière en mer ^{F}
plataforma ^{F} petrolera marina
Ölbohrinsel ^{F}
piattaforma ^{F} petrolifera offshore

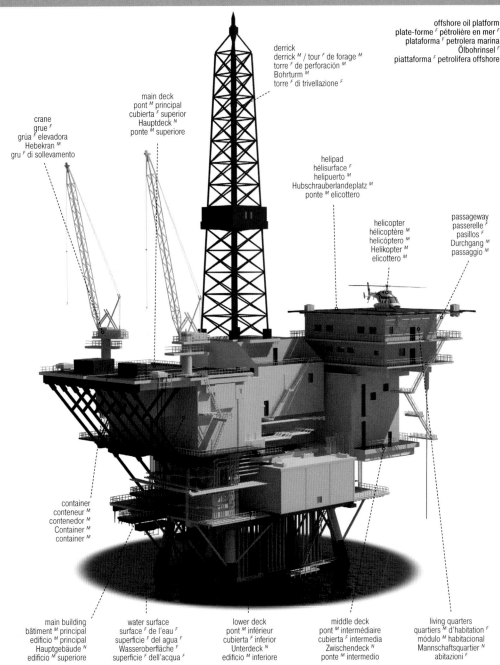

derrick
derrick ^{M} / tour ^{F} de forage ^{M}
torre ^{F} de perforación ^{M}
Bohrturm ^{M}
torre ^{F} di trivellazione ^{F}
main deck
pont ^{M} principal
cubierta ^{F} superior
Hauptdeck ^{N}
ponte ^{M} superiore
crane
grue ^{F}
grúa ^{F} elevadora
Hebekran ^{M}
gru ^{F} di sollevamento
helipad
hélisurface ^{F}
helipuerto ^{M}
Hubschrauberlandeplatz ^{M}
ponte ^{M} elicottero
helicopter
hélicoptère ^{M}
helicóptero ^{M}
Helikopter ^{M}
elicottero ^{M}
passageway
passerelle ^{F}
pasillos ^{F}
Durchgang ^{M}
passaggio ^{M}
container
conteneur ^{M}
contenedor ^{M}
Container ^{M}
container ^{M}
main building
bâtiment ^{M} principal
edificio ^{M} principal
Hauptgebäude ^{N}
edificio ^{M} superiore
water surface
surface ^{F} de l'eau ^{F}
superficie ^{F} del agua ^{F}
Wasseroberfläche ^{F}
superficie ^{F} dell'acqua ^{F}
lower deck
pont ^{M} inférieur
cubierta ^{F} inferior
Unterdeck ^{N}
edificio ^{M} inferiore
middle deck
pont ^{M} intermédiaire
cubierta ^{F} intermedia
Zwischendeck ^{N}
ponte ^{M} intermedio
living quarters
quartiers ^{M} d'habitation ^{F}
módulo ^{M} habitacional
Mannschaftsquartier ^{N}
abitazioni ^{F}

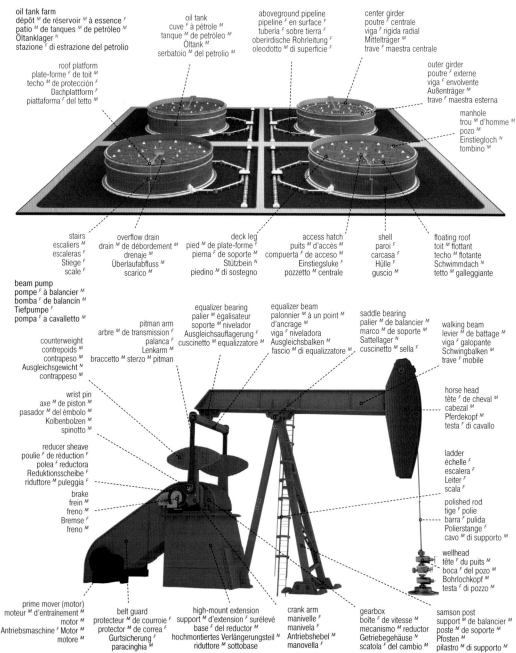

oil tank farm
dépôt [M] de réservoir [M] à essence [F]
patio [M] de tanques [M] de petróleo [M]
Öltanklager [N]
stazione [F] di estrazione del petrolio

oil tank
cuve [F] à pétrole [M]
tanque [M] de petróleo [M]
Öltank [M]
serbatoio [M] del petrolio [M]
aboveground pipeline
pipeline [F] en surface [F]
tubería [F] sobre tierra [F]
oberirdische Rohrleitung [F]
oleodotto [M] di superficie [F]
center girder
poutre [F] centrale
viga [F] rígida radial
Mittelträger [M]
trave [F] maestra centrale
roof platform
plate-forme [F] de toit [M]
techo [M] de protección [F]
Dachplattform [F]
piattaforma [F] del tetto [M]
outer girder
poutre [F] externe
viga [F] envolvente
Außenträger [M]
trave [F] maestra esterna
manhole
trou [M] d'homme [M]
pozo [M]
Einstiegloch [N]
tombino [M]
stairs
escaliers [M]
escaleras [F]
Stiege [F]
scale [F]
overflow drain
drain [M] de débordement [M]
drenaje [M]
Überlaufabfluss [M]
scarico [M]
deck leg
pied [M] de plate-forme [F]
pierna [F] de soporte [M]
Stützbein [N]
piedino [M] di sostegno
access hatch
puits [M] d'accès [M]
compuerta [F] de acceso [M]
Einstiegsluke [F]
pozzetto [M] centrale
shell
paroi [F]
carcasa [F]
Hülle [F]
guscio [M]
floating roof
toit [M] flottant
techo [M] flotante
Schwimmdach [N]
tetto [M] galleggiante

beam pump
pompe [F] à balancier [M]
bomba [F] de balancín [M]
Tiefpumpe [F]
pompa [F] a cavalletto [M]

counterweight
contrepoids [M]
contrapeso [M]
Ausgleichsgewicht [N]
contrappeso [M]
pitman arm
arbre [M] de transmission [F]
palanca [F]
Lenkarm [M]
braccetto [M] sterzo [M] pitman
equalizer bearing
palier [M] égalisateur
soporte [M] nivelador
Ausgleichsauflagerung [F]
cuscinetto [M] equalizzatore [M]
equalizer beam
palonnier [M] à un point [M] d'ancrage [M]
viga [F] niveladora
Ausgleichsbalken [M]
fascio [M] di equalizzatore [M]
saddle bearing
palier [M] de balancier [M]
marco [M] de soporte [M]
Sattellager [N]
cuscinetto [M] sella [F]
walking beam
levier [M] de battage [M]
viga [F] galopante
Schwingbalken [M]
trave [F] mobile
wrist pin
axe [M] de piston [M]
pasador [M] del émbolo [M]
Kolbenbolzen [M]
spinotto [M]
horse head
tête [F] de cheval [M]
cabezal [M]
Pferdekopf [M]
testa [F] di cavallo
reducer sheave
poulie [F] de réduction [F]
polea [F] reductora
Reduktionsscheibe [F]
riduttore [M] puleggia [F]
ladder
échelle [F]
escalera [F]
Leiter [F]
scala [F]
brake
frein [M]
freno [M]
Bremse [F]
freno [M]
polished rod
tige [F] polie
barra [F] pulida
Polierstange [F]
cavo [M] di supporto [M]
wellhead
tête [F] du puits [M]
boca [F] del pozo [M]
Bohrlochkopf [M]
testa [F] di pozzo [M]
prime mover (motor)
moteur [M] d'entraînement [M]
motor [M]
Antriebsmaschine [F] Motor [M]
motore [M]
belt guard
protecteur [M] de courroie [F]
protector [M] de correa [F]
Gurtsicherung [F]
paracinghia [M]
high-mount extension
support [M] d'extension [F] surélevé
base [F] del reductor [M]
hochmontiertes Verlängerungsteil [N]
riduttore [M] sottobase
crank arm
manivelle [F]
manivela [F]
Antriebshebel [M]
manovella [F]
gearbox
boîte [F] de vitesse [M]
mecanismo [M] reductor
Getriebegehäuse [N]
scatola [F] del cambio [M]
samson post
support [M] de balancier [M]
poste [M] de soporte [M]
Pfosten [M]
pilastro [M] di supporto [M]

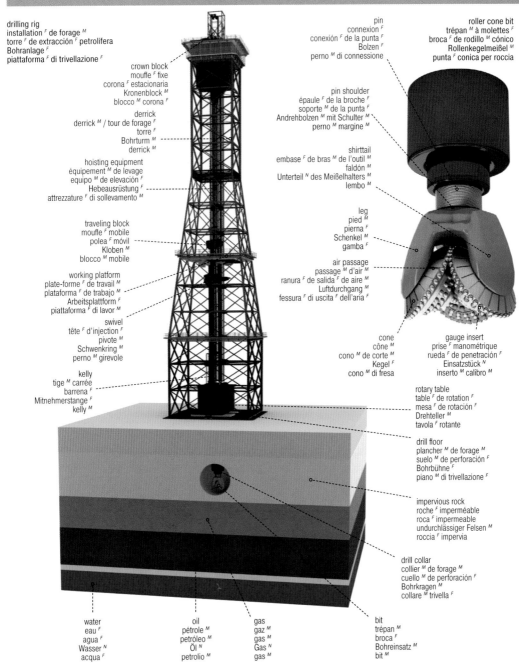

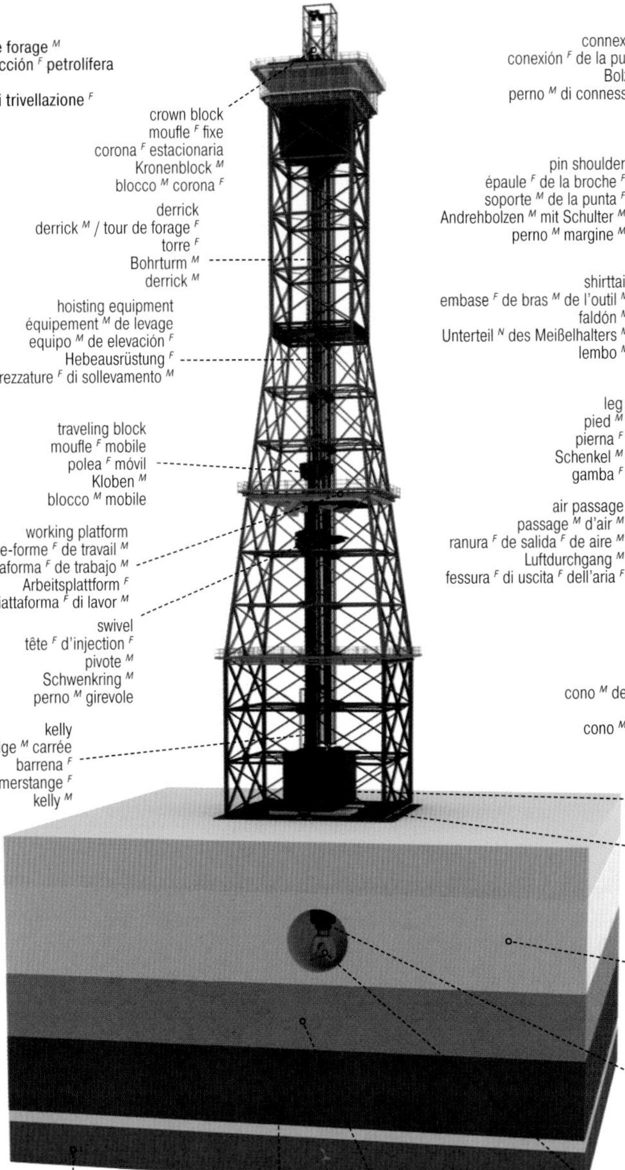
drilling rig
installation [F] de forage [M]
torre [F] de extracción [F] petrolífera
Bohranlage [F]
piattaforma [F] di trivellazione [F]
crown block
moufle [F] fixe
corona [F] estacionaria
Kronenblock [M]
blocco [M] corona [F]
derrick
derrick [M] / tour de forage [F]
torre [F]
Bohrturm [M]
derrick [M]
hoisting equipment
équipement [M] de levage
equipo [M] de elevación [F]
Hebeausrüstung [F]
attrezzature [F] di sollevamento [M]
traveling block
moufle [F] mobile
polea [F] móvil
Kloben [M]
blocco [M] mobile
working platform
plate-forme [F] de travail [M]
plataforma [F] de trabajo [M]
Arbeitsplattform [F]
piattaforma [F] di lavor [M]
swivel
tête [F] d'injection [F]
pivote [M]
Schwenkring [M]
perno [M] girevole
kelly
tige [M] carrée
barrena [F]
Mitnehmerstange [F]
kelly [M]
rotary table
table [F] de rotation [F]
mesa [F] de rotación [F]
Drehteller [M]
tavola [F] rotante
drill floor
plancher [M] de forage [M]
suelo [M] de perforación [F]
Bohrbühne [F]
piano [M] di trivellazione [F]
impervious rock
roche [F] imperméable
roca [F] impermeable
undurchlässiger Felsen [M]
roccia [F] impervia
drill collar
collier [M] de forage [M]
cuello [M] de perforación [F]
Bohrkragen [M]
collare [M] trivella [F]
water
eau [F]
agua [F]
Wasser [N]
acqua [F]
oil
pétrole [M]
petróleo [M]
Öl [N]
petrolio [M]
gas
gaz [M]
gas [M]
Gas [N]
gas [M]
bit
trépan [M]
broca [F]
Bohreinsatz [M]
bit [M]

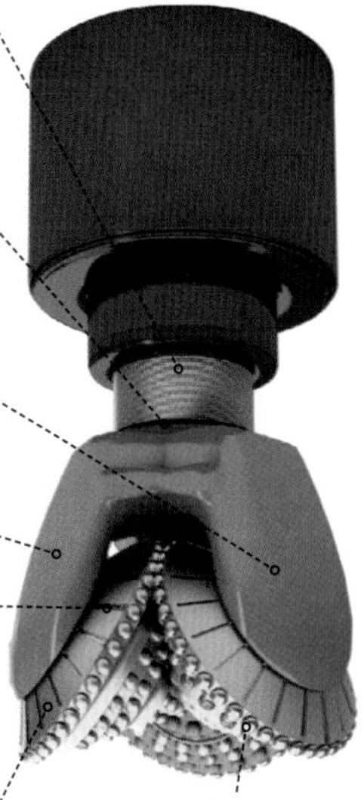
roller cone bit
trépan [M] à molettes [F]
broca [F] de rodillo [M] cónico
Rollenkegelmeißel [M]
punta [F] conica per roccia
pin
connexion [F]
conexión [F] de la punta [F]
Bolzen [F]
perno [M] di connessione
pin shoulder
épaule [F] de la broche [F]
soporte [M] de la punta [F]
Andrehbolzen [M] mit Schulter [M]
perno [M] margine [M]
shirttail
embase [F] de bras [M] de l'outil [M]
faldón [M]
Unterteil [N] des Meißelhalters [M]
lembo [M]
leg
pied [M]
pierna [F]
Schenkel [M]
gamba [F]
air passage
passage [M] d'air [M]
ranura [F] de salida [F] de aire [M]
Luftdurchgang [M]
fessura [F] di uscita [F] dell'aria [F]
cone
cône [M]
cono [M] de corte [M]
Kegel [F]
cono [M] di fresa
gauge insert
prise [F] manométrique
rueda [F] de penetración [F]
Einsatzstück [N]
inserto [M] calibro [M]

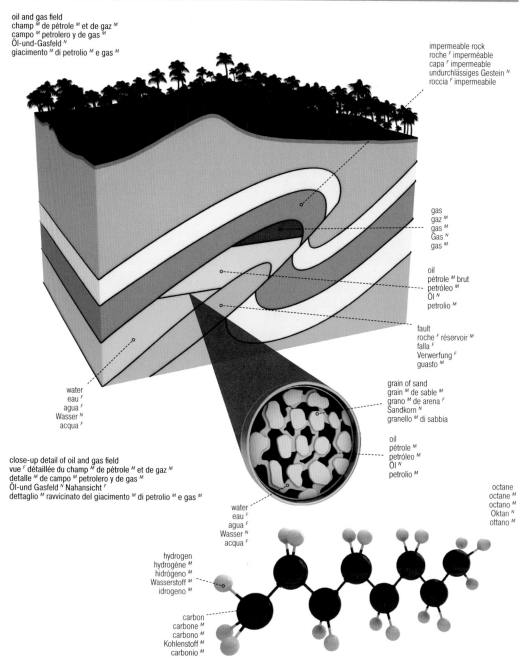

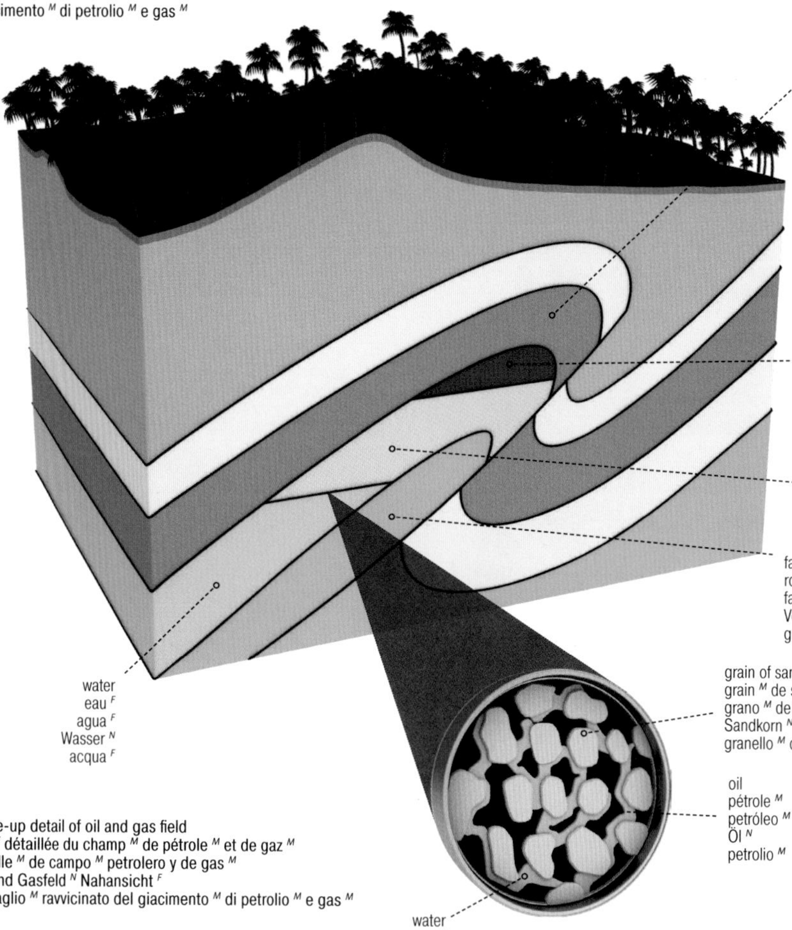
oil and gas field
champ M de pétrole M et de gaz M
campo M petrolero y de gas M
Öl-und-Gasfeld N
giacimento M di petrolio M e gas M
impermeable rock
roche F imperméable
capa F impermeable
undurchlässiges Gestein N
roccia F impermeabile
gas
gaz M
gas M
Gas N
gas M
oil
pétrole M brut
petróleo M
Öl N
petrolio M
fault
roche F réservoir M
falla F
Verwerfung F
guasto M
water
eau F
agua F
Wasser N
acqua F
grain of sand
grain M de sable M
grano M de arena F
Sandkorn N
granello M di sabbia
oil
pétrole M
petróleo M
Öl N
petrolio M
close-up detail of oil and gas field
vue F détaillée du champ M de pétrole M et de gaz M
detalle M de campo M petrolero y de gas M
Öl-und Gasfeld N Nahansicht F
dettaglio M ravvicinato del giacimento M di petrolio M e gas M
water
eau F
agua F
Wasser N
acqua F

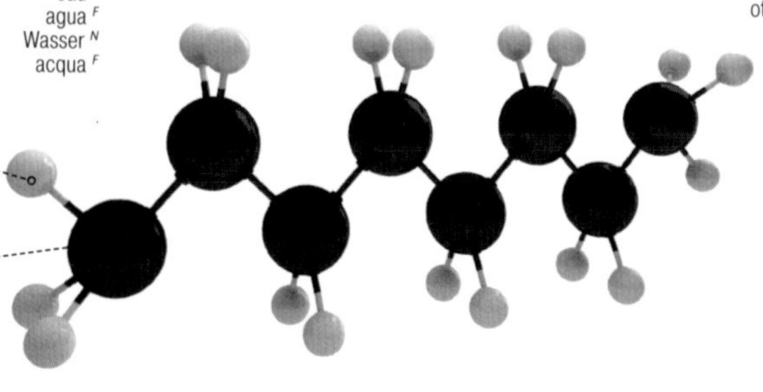
octane
octane M
octano M
Oktan N
ottano M
hydrogen
hydrogène M
hidrógeno M
Wasserstoff M
idrogeno M
carbon
carbone M
carbono M
Kohlenstoff M
carbonio M

offshore oil field
champ [M] pétrolier en mer [F]
campo [M] petrolero costa [F] afuera
Offshore-Ölfeld [N]
giacimento [M] petrolifero offshore

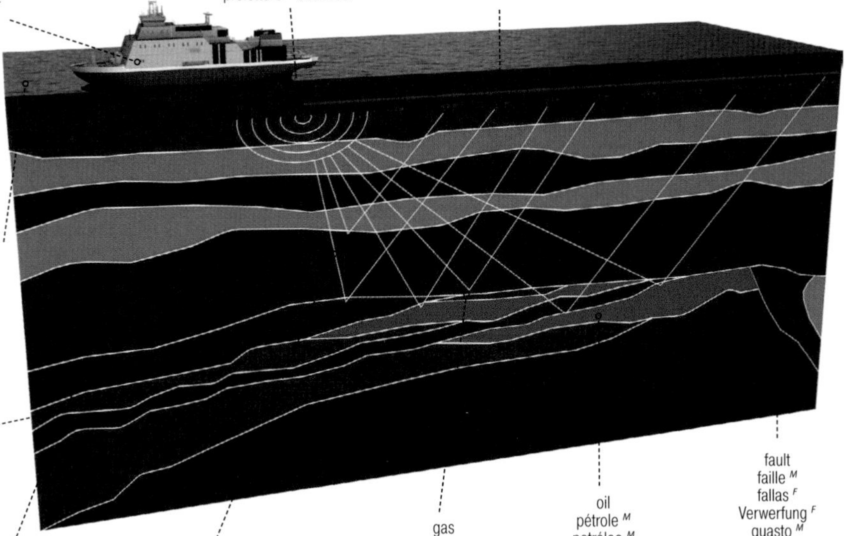

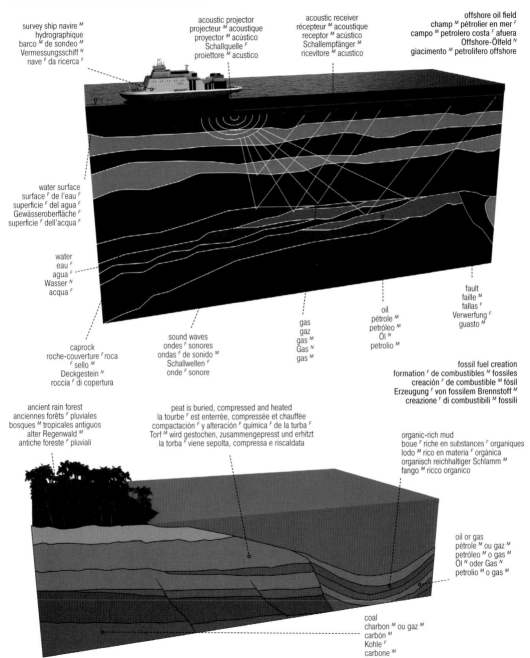

survey ship navire [M] hydrographique
barco [M] de sondeo [M]
Vermessungsschiff [N]
nave [F] da ricerca [F]
acoustic projector
projecteur [M] acoustique
proyector [M] acústico
Schallquelle [F]
proiettore [M] acustico
acoustic receiver
récepteur [M] acoustique
receptor [M] acústico
Schallempfänger [M]
ricevitore [M] acustico
water surface
surface [F] de l'eau [F]
superficie [F] del agua [F]
Gewässeroberfläche [F]
superficie [F] dell'acqua [F]
water
eau [F]
agua [F]
Wasser [N]
acqua [F]
caprock
roche-couverture [F] roca [F] sello [M]
Deckgestein [N]
roccia [F] di copertura
sound waves
ondes [F] sonores
ondas [F] de sonido [M]
Schallwellen [F]
onde [F] sonore
gas
gaz
gas [M]
Gas [N]
gas [M]
oil
pétrole [M]
petróleo [M]
Öl [N]
petrolio [M]
fault
faille [M]
fallas [F]
Verwerfung [F]
guasto [M]

fossil fuel creation
formation [F] de combustibles [M] fossiles
creación [F] de combustible [M] fósil
Erzeugung [F] von fossilem Brennstoff [M]
creazione [F] di combustibili [M] fossili

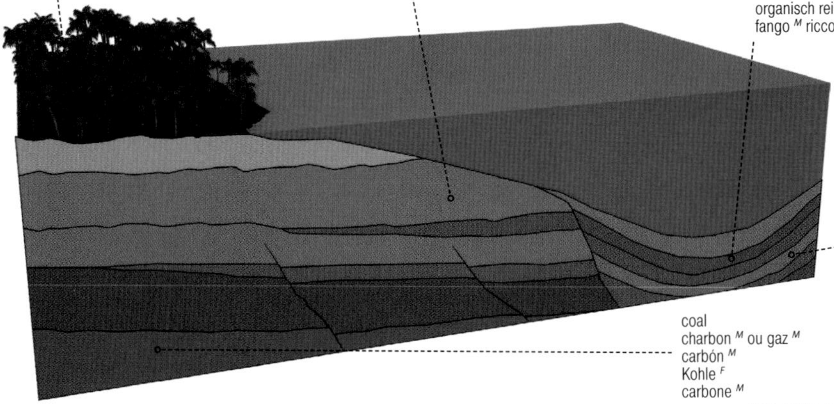

ancient rain forest
anciennes forêts [F] pluviales
bosques [M] tropicales antiguos
alter Regenwald [M]
antiche foreste [F] pluviali
peat is buried, compressed and heated
la tourbe [F] est enterrée, compressée et chauffée
compactación [F] y alteración [F] química [F] de la turba [F]
Torf [M] wird gestochen, zusammengepresst und erhitzt
la torba [F] viene sepolta, compressa e riscaldata
organic-rich mud
boue [F] riche en substances [F] organiques
lodo [M] rico en materia [F] orgánica
organisch reichhaltiger Schlamm [M]
fango [M] ricco organico
oil or gas
pétrole [M] ou gaz [M]
petróleo [M] o gas [M]
Öl [N] oder Gas [N]
petrolio [M] o gas [M]
coal
charbon [M] ou gaz [M]
carbón [M]
Kohle [F]
carbone [M]

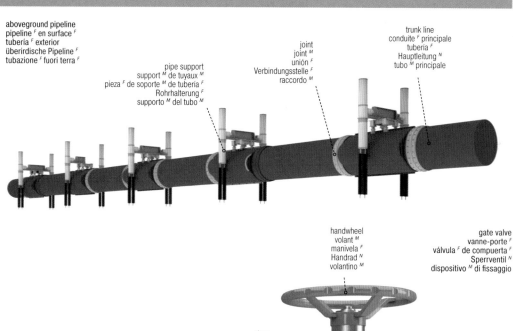

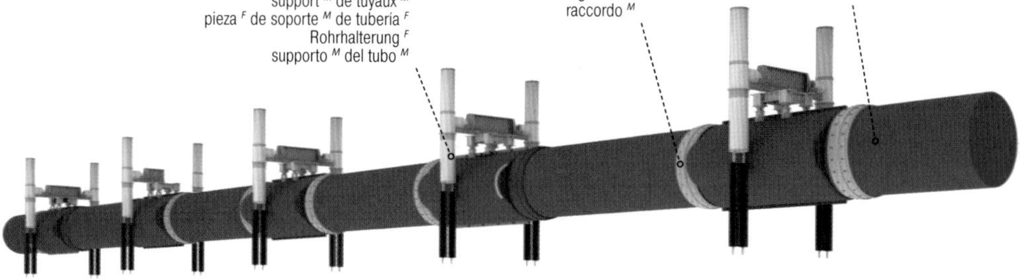
aboveground pipeline
pipeline ^F^ en surface ^F^
tubería ^F^ exterior
überirdische Pipeline ^F^
tubazione ^F^ fuori terra ^F^
pipe support
support ^M^ de tuyaux ^M^
pieza ^F^ de soporte ^M^ de tubería ^F^
Rohrhalterung ^F^
supporto ^M^ del tubo ^M^
joint
joint ^M^
unión ^F^
Verbindungsstelle ^F^
raccordo ^M^
trunk line
conduite ^F^ principale
tubería ^F^
Hauptleitung ^N^
tubo ^M^ principale

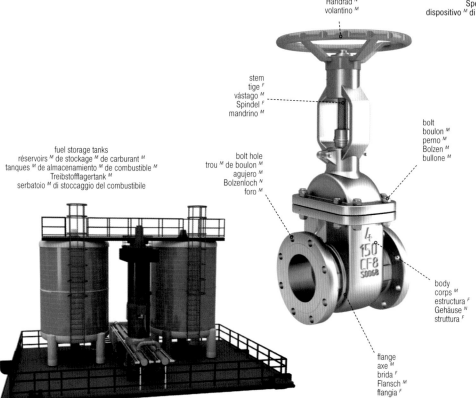

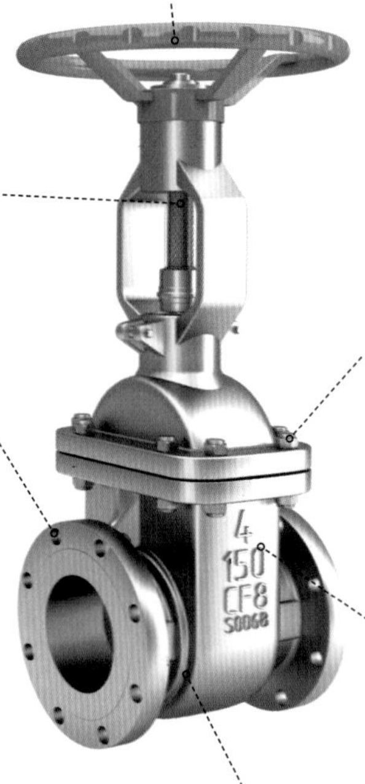
gate valve
vanne-porte ^F^
válvula ^F^ de compuerta ^F^
Sperrventil ^N^
dispositivo ^M^ di fissaggio
handwheel
volant ^M^
manivela ^F^
Handrad ^N^
volantino ^M^
stem
tige ^F^
vástago ^M^
Spindel ^F^
mandrino ^M^
bolt
boulon ^M^
perno ^M^
Bolzen ^M^
bullone ^M^
bolt hole
trou ^M^ de boulon ^M^
agujero ^M^
Bolzenloch ^N^
foro ^M^
4
150
CF8
S0068
body
corps ^M^
estructura ^F^
Gehäuse ^N^
struttura ^F^
flange
axe ^M^
brida ^F^
Flansch ^M^
flangia ^F^

fuel storage tanks
réservoirs ^M^ de stockage ^M^ de carburant ^M^
tanques ^M^ de almacenamiento ^M^ de combustible ^M^
Treibstofflagertank ^M^
serbatoio ^M^ di stoccaggio del combustibile

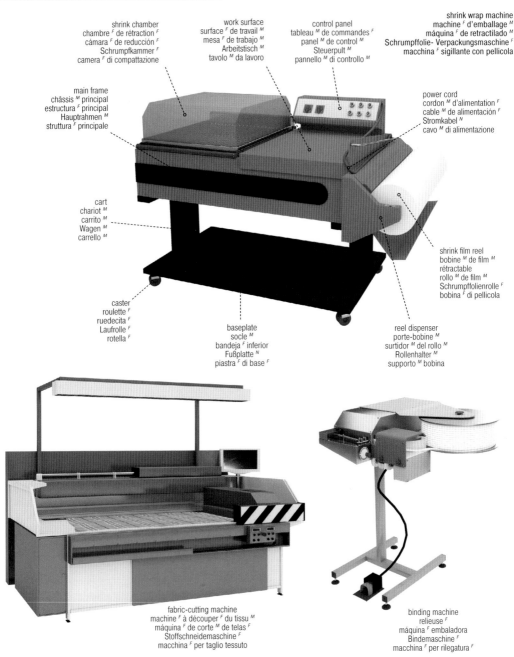

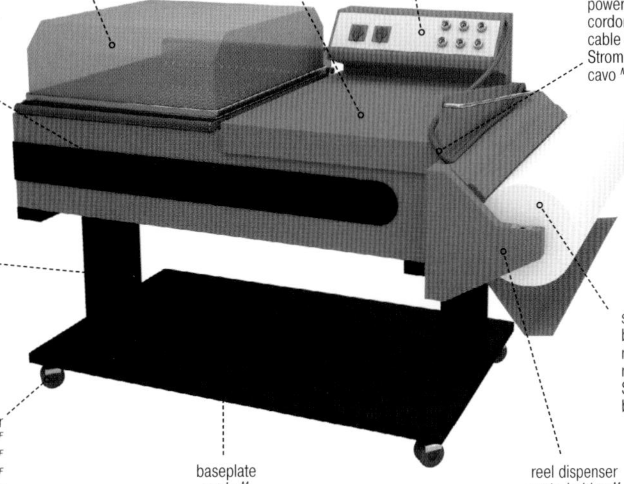
shrink wrap machine
machine F d'emballage M
máquina F de retractilado M
Schrumpffolie- Verpackungsmaschine F
macchina F sigillante con pellicola
shrink chamber
chambre F de rétraction F
cámara F de reducción F
Schrumpfkammer F
camera F di compattazione
work surface
surface F de travail M
mesa F de trabajo M
Arbeitstisch M
tavolo M da lavoro
control panel
tableau M de commandes F
panel M de control M
Steuerpult M
pannello M di controllo M
main frame
châssis M principal
estructura F principal
Hauptrahmen M
struttura F principale
power cord
cordon M d'alimentation F
cable M de alimentación F
Stromkabel N
cavo M di alimentazione
cart
chariot M
carrito M
Wagen M
carrello M
shrink film reel
bobine M de film M rétractable
rollo M de film M
Schrumpffolienrolle F
bobina F di pellicola
caster
roulette F
ruedecita F
Laufrolle F
rotella F
baseplate
socle M
bandeja F inferior
Fußplatte N
piastra F di base F
reel dispenser
porte-bobine M
surtidor M del rollo M
Rollenhalter M
supporto M bobina

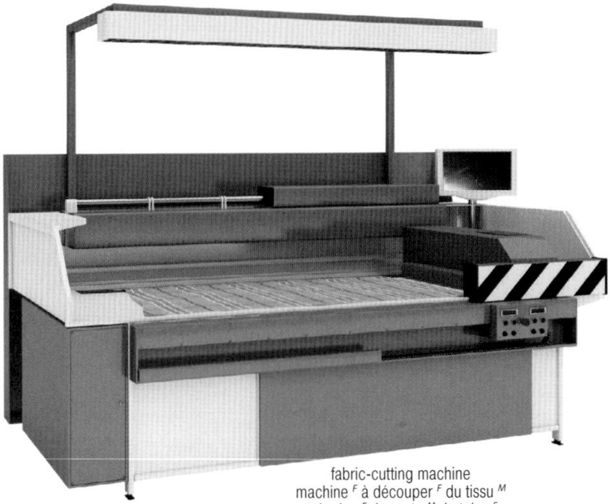

fabric-cutting machine
machine F à découper F du tissu M
máquina F de corte M de telas F
Stoffschneidemaschine F
macchina F per taglio tessuto

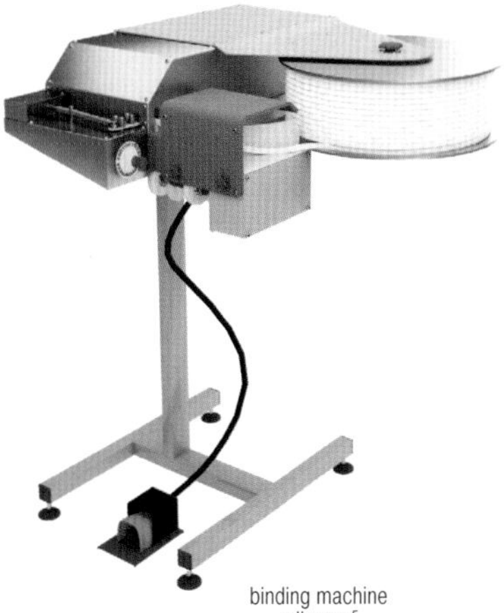

binding machine
relieuse F
máquina F embaladora
Bindemaschine F
macchina F per rilegatura F

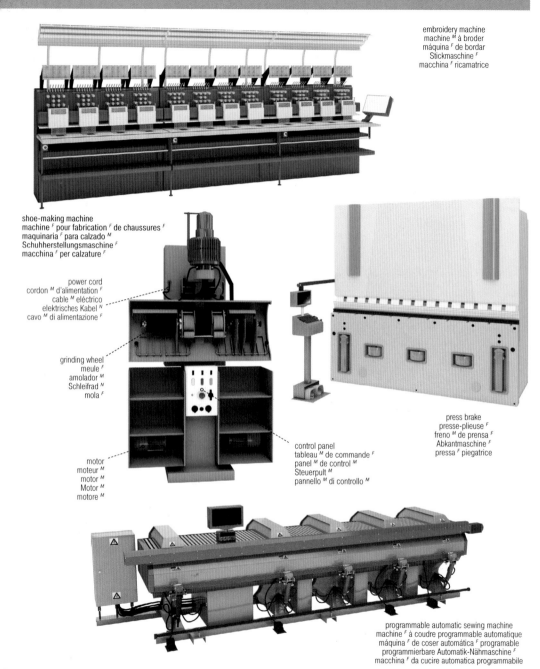

embroidery machine
machine ^{M} à broder
máquina ^{F} de bordar
Stickmaschine ^{F}
macchina ^{F} ricamatrice

shoe-making machine
machine ^{F} pour fabrication ^{F} de chaussures ^{F}
maquinaria ^{F} para calzado ^{M}
Schuhherstellungsmaschine ^{F}
macchina ^{F} per calzature ^{F}

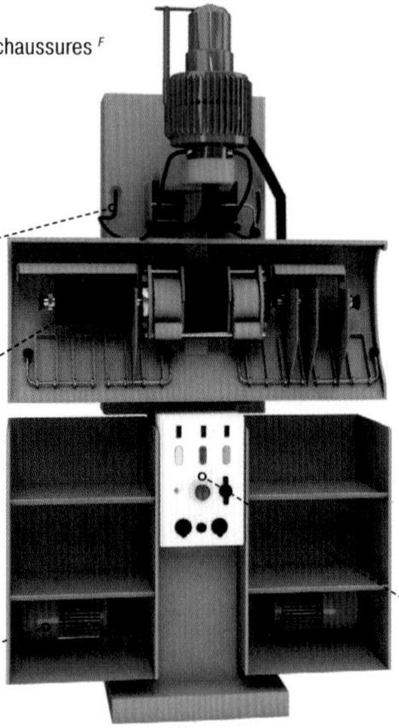
power cord
cordon ^{M} d'alimentation ^{F}
cable ^{M} eléctrico
elektrisches Kabel ^{N}
cavo ^{M} di alimentazione ^{F}
grinding wheel
meule ^{F}
amolador ^{M}
Schleifrad ^{N}
mola ^{F}
motor
moteur ^{M}
motor ^{M}
Motor ^{M}
motore ^{M}
control panel
tableau ^{M} de commande ^{F}
panel ^{M} de control ^{M}
Steuerpult ^{M}
pannello ^{M} di controllo ^{M}

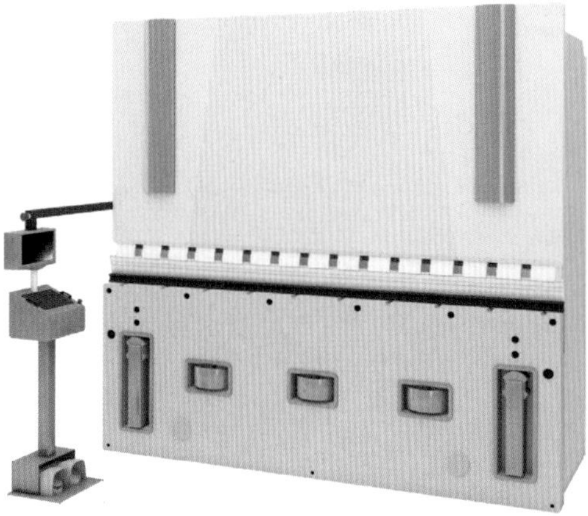

press brake
presse-plieuse ^{F}
freno ^{M} de prensa ^{F}
Abkantmaschine ^{F}
pressa ^{F} piegatrice

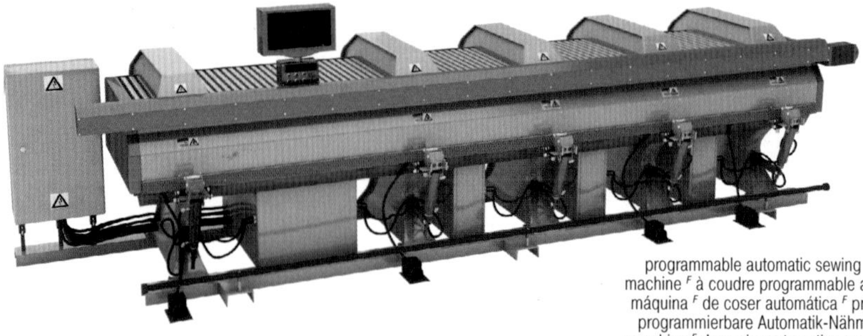

programmable automatic sewing machine
machine ^{F} à coudre programmable automatique
máquina ^{F} de coser automática ^{F} programable
programmierbare Automatik-Nähmaschine ^{F}
macchina ^{F} da cucire automatica programmabile

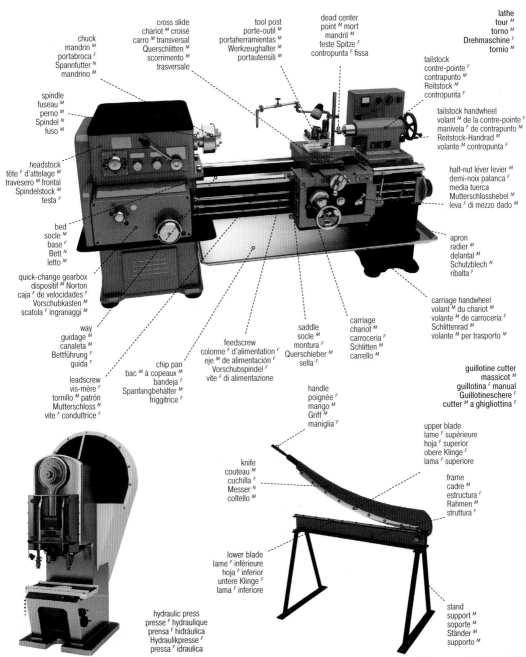

lathe
tour M
torno M
Drehmaschine F
tornio M

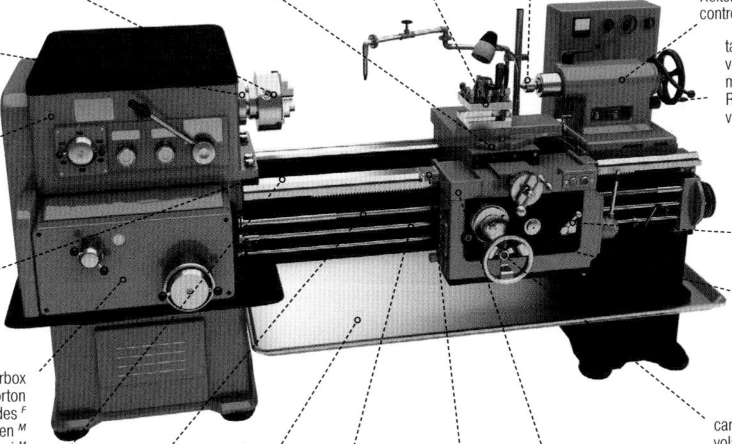
chuck
mandrin M
portabroca F
Spannfutter N
mandrino M
cross slide
chariot M croisé
carro M transversal
Querschlitten M
scorrimento M
trasversale
tool post
porte-outil M
portaherramientas M
Werkzeughalter M
portautensili M
dead center
point M mort
mandril M
feste Spitze F
contropunta F fissa
tailstock
contre-pointe F
contrapunto M
Reitstock M
contropunta F
spindle
fuseau M
perno M
Spindel N
fuso M
tailstock handwheel
volant M de la contre-pointe F
manivela F de contrapunto M
Reitstock-Handrad M
volante M contropunta F
headstock
tête F d'attelage M
travesero M frontal
Spindelstock M
testa F
half-nut lever levier M
demi-noix palanca F
media tuerca
Mutterschlosshebel M
leva F di mezzo dado M
bed
socle M
base F
Bett N
letto M
apron
radier M
delantal M
Schutzblech N
ribalta F
quick-change gearbox
dispositif M Norton
caja F de velocidades F
Vorschubkasten M
scatola F ingranaggi M
carriage handwheel
volant M du chariot M
volante M de carrocería F
Schlittenrad M
volante M per trasporto M
way
guidage M
canaleta M
Bettführung F
guida F
saddle
socle M
montura F
Querschieber M
sella F
carriage
chariot M
carrocería F
Schlitten M
carrello M
feedscrew
colonne F d'alimentation F
eje M de alimentación F
Vorschubspindel F
vite F di alimentazione
chip pan
bac M à copeaux M
bandeja F
Spanfangbehälter M
friggitrice F
leadscrew
vis-mère F
tornillo M patrón
Mutterschloss N
vite F conduttrice F

guillotine cutter
massicot M
guillotina F manual
Guillotineschere F
cutter M a ghigliottina F

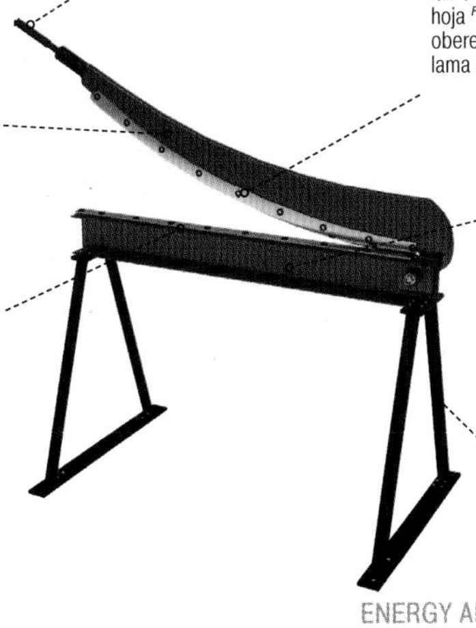
handle
poignée F
mango M
Griff M
maniglia F
upper blade
lame F supérieure
hoja F superior
obere Klinge F
lama F superiore
knife
couteau M
cuchilla F
Messer N
coltello M
frame
cadre M
estructura F
Rahmen M
struttura F
lower blade
lame F inférieure
hoja F inferior
untere Klinge F
lama F inferiore
stand
support M
soporte M
Ständer M
supporto M

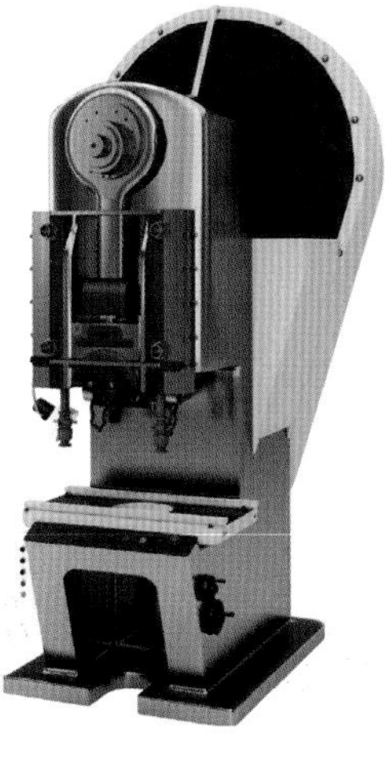

hydraulic press
presse F hydraulique
prensa F hidráulica
Hydraulikpresse F
pressa F idraulica

milling machine
fraiseuse F
máquina F de fresado M
Fräsmaschine F
fresatrice F

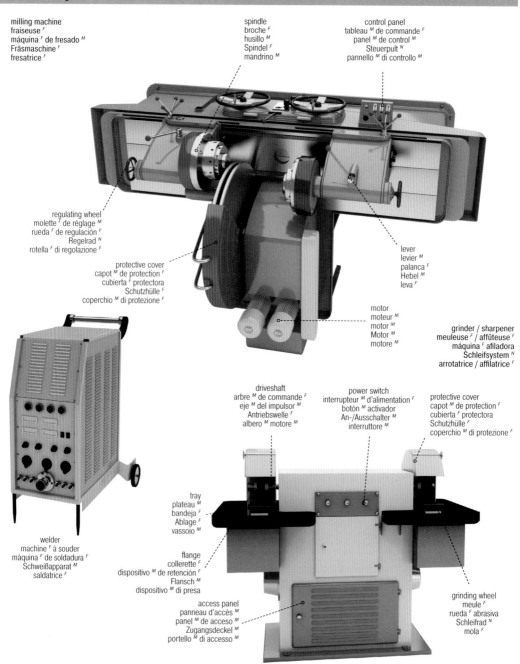

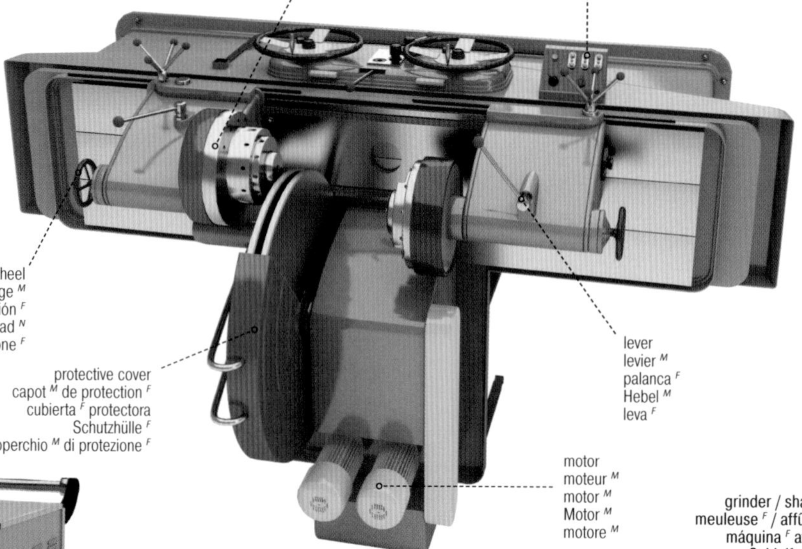

spindle
broche F
husillo M
Spindel F
mandrino M

control panel
tableau M de commande F
panel M de control M
Steuerpult N
pannello M di controllo M

regulating wheel
molette F de réglage M
rueda F de regulación F
Regelrad N
rotella F di regolazione F

lever
levier M
palanca F
Hebel M
leva F

protective cover
capot M de protection F
cubierta F protectora
Schutzhülle F
coperchio M di protezione F

motor
moteur M
motor M
Motor M
motore M

grinder / sharpener
meuleuse F / affûteuse F
máquina F afiladora
Schleifsystem N
arrotatrice / affilatrice F

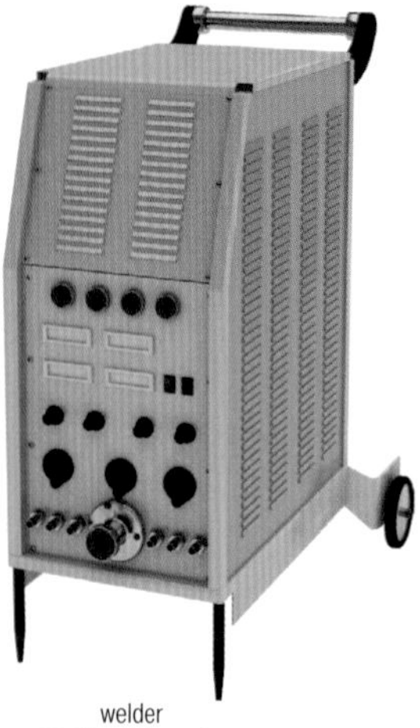

welder
machine F à souder
máquina F de soldadura F
Schweißapparat M
saldatrice F

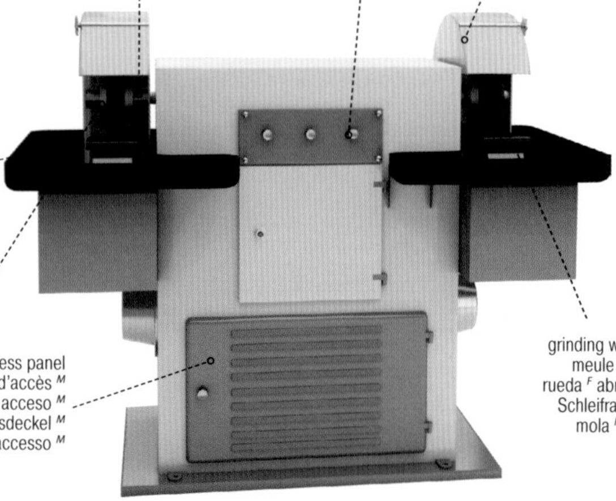

driveshaft
arbre M de commande F
eje M del impulsor M
Antriebswelle F
albero M motore M

power switch
interrupteur M d'alimentation F
botón M activador
An-/Ausschalter M
interruttore M

protective cover
capot M de protection F
cubierta F protectora
Schutzhülle F
coperchio M di protezione F

tray
plateau M
bandeja F
Ablage F
vassoio M

flange
collerette F
dispositivo M de retención F
Flansch M
dispositivo M di presa

grinding wheel
meule F
rueda F abrasiva
Schleifrad N
mola F

access panel
panneau d'accès M
panel M de acceso M
Zugangsdeckel M
portello M di accesso M

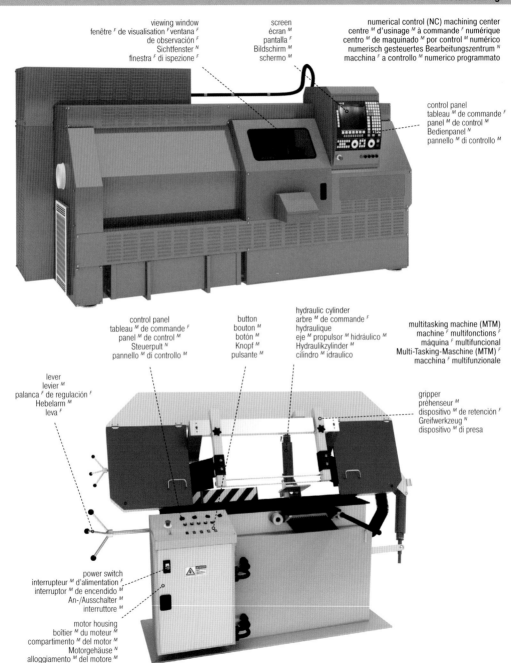

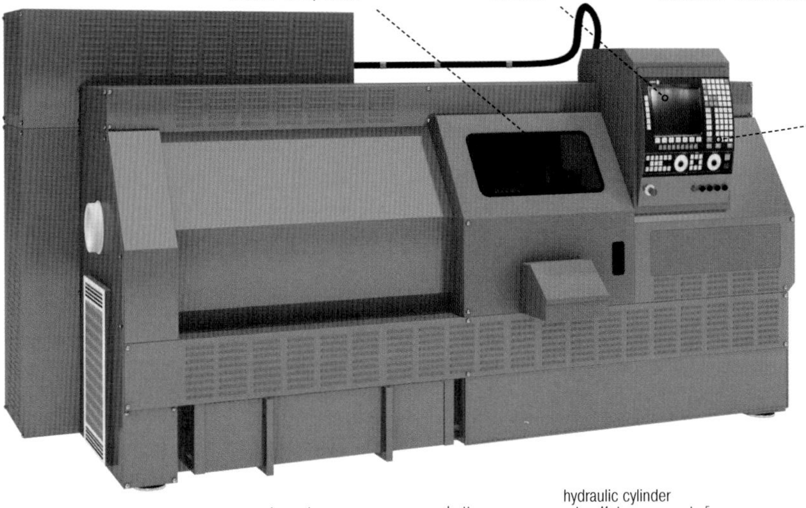
viewing window
fenêtre [F] de visualisation [F] ventana [F] de observación [F]
Sichtfenster [N]
finestra [F] di ispezione [F]
screen
écran [M]
pantalla [F]
Bildschirm [M]
schermo [M]
numerical control (NC) machining center
centre [M] d'usinage [M] à commande [F] numérique
centro [M] de maquinado [M] por control [M] numérico
numerisch gesteuertes Bearbeitungszentrum [N]
macchina [F] a controllo [M] numerico programmato
control panel
tableau [M] de commande [F]
panel [M] de control [M]
Bedienpanel [N]
pannello [M] di controllo [M]

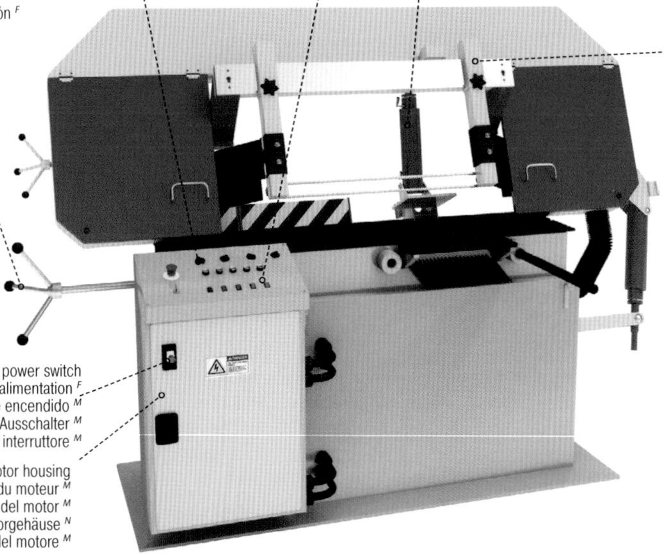
control panel
tableau [M] de commande [F]
panel [M] de control [M]
Steuerpult [N]
pannello [M] di controllo [M]
button
bouton [M]
botón [M]
Knopf [M]
pulsante [M]
hydraulic cylinder
arbre [M] de commande [F] hydraulique
eje [M] propulsor [M] hidráulico [M]
Hydraulikzylinder [M]
cilindro [M] idraulico
multitasking machine (MTM)
machine [F] multifonctions [F]
máquina [F] multifuncional
Multi-Tasking-Maschine (MTM) [F]
macchina [F] multifunzionale
lever
levier [M]
palanca [F] de regulación [F]
Hebelarm [M]
leva [F]
gripper
préhenseur [M]
dispositivo [M] de retención [F]
Greifwerkzeug [N]
dispositivo [M] di presa
power switch
interrupteur [M] d'alimentation [F]
interruptor [M] de encendido [M]
An-/Ausschalter [M]
interruttore [M]
motor housing
boîtier [M] du moteur [M]
compartimento [M] del motor [M]
Motorgehäuse [N]
alloggiamento [M] del motore [M]

cut-off saw
scie [F] à tronçonner
sierra [F] mecánica
Trennsäge [F]
sega [F] troncatrice

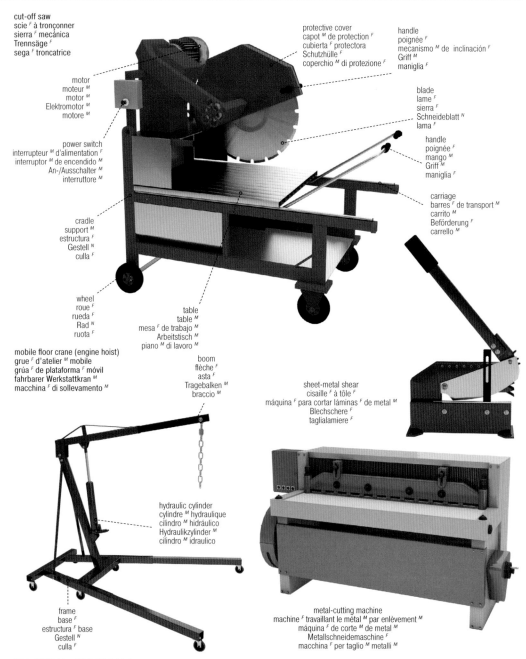

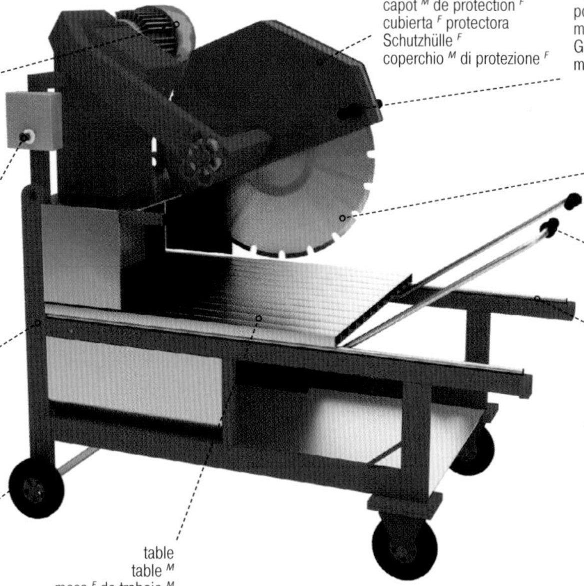
protective cover
capot [M] de protection [F]
cubierta [F] protectora
Schutzhülle [F]
coperchio [M] di protezione [F]
handle
poignée [F]
mecanismo [M] de inclinación [F]
Griff [M]
maniglia [F]
motor
moteur [M]
motor [M]
Elektromotor [M]
motore [M]
blade
lame [F]
sierra [F]
Schneideblatt [N]
lama [F]
power switch
interrupteur [M] d'alimentation [F]
interruptor [M] de encendido [M]
An-/Ausschalter [M]
interruttore [M]
handle
poignée [F]
mango [M]
Griff [M]
maniglia [F]
carriage
barres [F] de transport [M]
carrito [M]
Beförderung [F]
carrello [M]
cradle
support [M]
estructura [F]
Gestell [N]
culla [F]
wheel
roue [F]
rueda [F]
Rad [N]
ruota [F]
table
table [M]
mesa [F] de trabajo [M]
Arbeitstisch [M]
piano [M] di lavoro [M]

sheet-metal shear
cisaille [F] à tôle [F]
máquina [F] para cortar láminas [F] de metal [M]
Blechschere [F]
taglialamiere [F]

mobile floor crane (engine hoist)
grue [F] d'atelier [M] mobile
grúa [F] de plataforma [F] móvil
fahrbarer Werkstattkran [M]
macchina [F] di sollevamento [M]

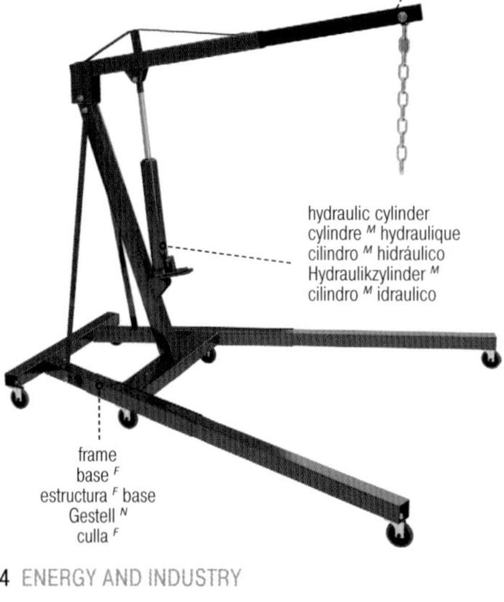
boom
flèche [F]
asta [F]
Tragebalken [M]
braccio [M]
hydraulic cylinder
cylindre [M] hydraulique
cilindro [M] hidráulico
Hydraulikzylinder [M]
cilindro [M] idraulico
frame
base [F]
estructura [F] base
Gestell [N]
culla [F]

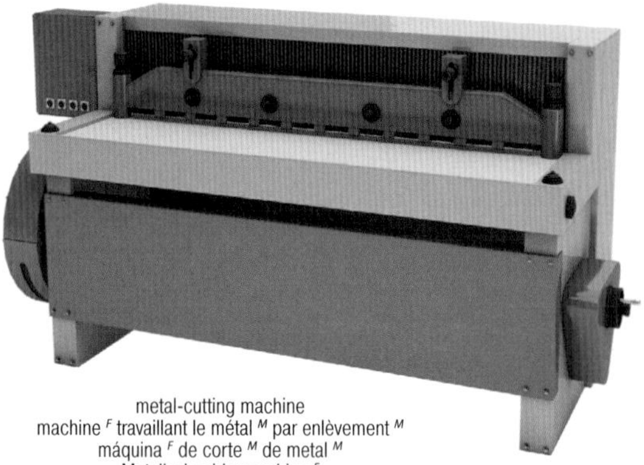

metal-cutting machine
machine [F] travaillant le métal [M] par enlèvement [M]
máquina [F] de corte [M] de metal [M]
Metallschneidemaschine [F]
macchina [F] per taglio [M] metalli [M]

multipurpose mixer
mélangeur ^{M} polyvalent
mezcladora ^{F} polivalente
Mehrzweckmixer ^{M}
miscelatore ^{M} multiuso

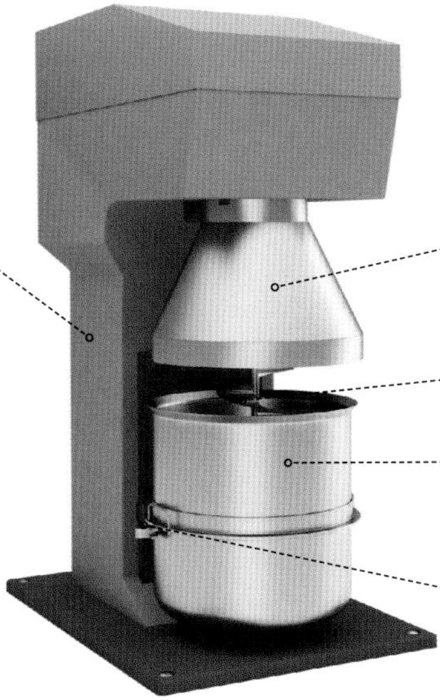

main body
corps du mixeur ^{M}
cuerpo ^{M} del mezclador ^{M}
Hauptteil ^{N}
corpo ^{M} miscelatore

splashguard
pare-éclaboussures ^{M}
salpicadero ^{M}
Spritzschutz ^{M}
paraspruzzi ^{M}

attachment
accessoire ^{M}
accesorio ^{M}
Aufsatz ^{M}
accessorio ^{M}

bowl
bol ^{M}
tazón ^{M}
Schale ^{F}
recipiente ^{M}

bowl support
support ^{M} du bol ^{M}
soporte ^{M} del tazón ^{M}
Schalenauflage ^{F}
supporto ^{M} del recipiente ^{M}

filler
poussoir ^{M} à saucisse ^{F}
dispensador ^{M} de relleno ^{M}
Abfüllmaschine ^{F}
erogatore ^{M} di riempimento

bowl cutter
découpeur ^{M} à cuve ^{F}
máquina ^{F} manipuladora de carne ^{F}
Kutter ^{M}
cutter ^{M} a vasca ^{F} rotante

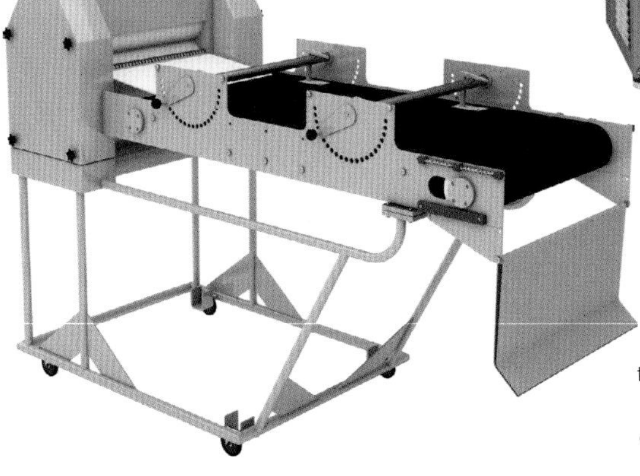

belt conveyor
transporteur ^{M} à courroie ^{F}
banda ^{F} transportadora
Bandförderer ^{M}
convogliatore ^{M} a nastro ^{M}

part of conveyor system
partie F du système F de convoyeur M
parte F de cinta F transportadora
Teil M des Fließbands N
parte F del nastro trasportatore M

alarm
alarme F
señal F de alarma F
Alarmsignal N
allarme M

control panel
tableau M de commandes F
panel M de control M
Steuerpult N
pannello M di controllo M

tunnel
tunnel M
túnel M
Tunnel M
tunnel M

outfeed track
rail M de sortie F
mostrador M de salida F
Auslaufstrecke F
piano M di uscita

tunnel curtain
rideau M du tunnel M
cortinillas F
Tunnelvorhang M
tenda F del tunnel

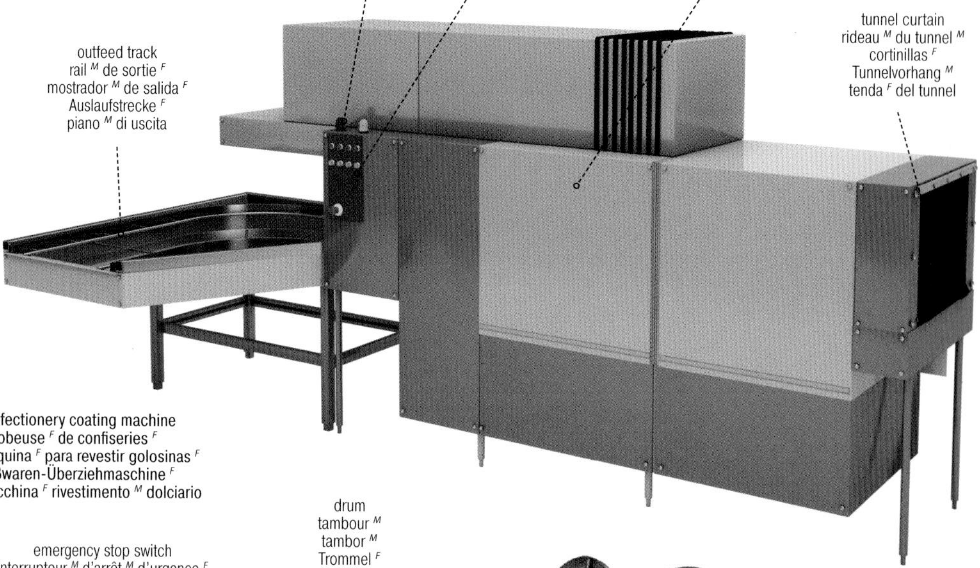

confectionery coating machine
enrobeuse F de confiseries F
máquina F para revestir golosinas F
Süßwaren-Überziehmaschine F
macchina F rivestimento M dolciario

drum
tambour M
tambor M
Trommel F
tamburo M

emergency stop switch
interrupteur M d'arrêt M d'urgence F
interruptor M de parada F de emergencia F
Notausschalter M
interruttore M di arresto M d'emergenza F

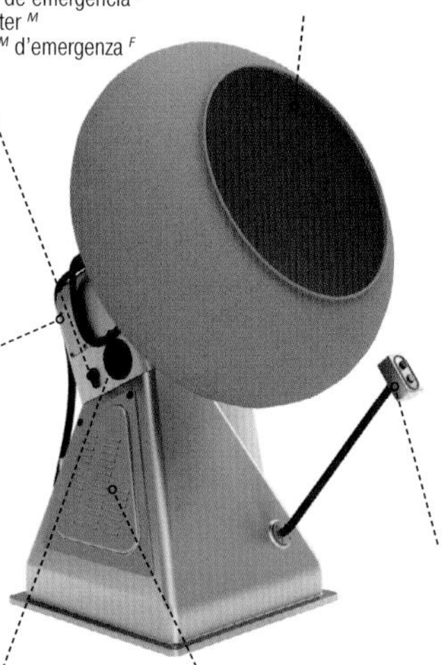

gearbox
boîte F de vitesses F
caja F de engranajes M
Getriebe N
scatola F ingranaggi M

on/off switches
interrupteurs M marche F/arrêt M
interruptores M de encendido/apagado M
Ein-/aus Tasten M
pulsanti M di accensione/spegnimento

drum tilt lock
verrouillage M du tambour par bascule F
bloqueo M de inclinación F del tambor M
Trommelneigungssperre F
blocco M inclinazione F tamburo M

motor compartment
compartiment M moteur M
compartimento M del motor M
Motorraum M
vano M motore

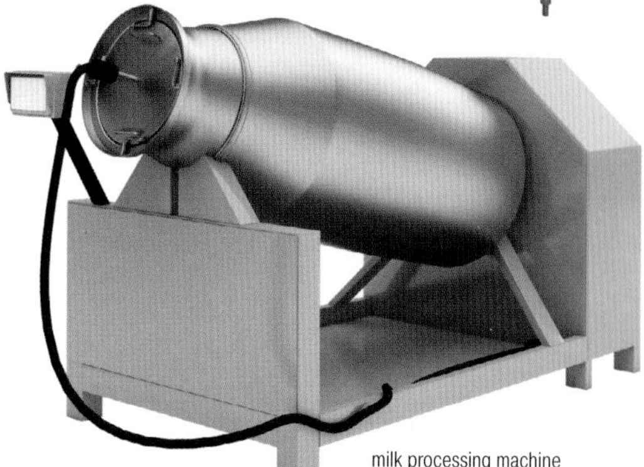

milk processing machine
machine F de traitement M du lait M
máquina F para procesar leche F
Milchverarbeitungsmaschine F
macchina F per trasformazione F del latte M

portioning and forming machine
façonneuse ^{F} et portionneuse ^{F} à pâte
máquina ^{F} moldeadora
Portionierungs- und Formmaschine ^{F}
macchina ^{F} profilatrice e porzionatrice

food slicer
trancheuse ^{F} à aliments ^{M}
rebanadora ^{F} de alimentos ^{M}
Aufschnittmaschine ^{F}
affettatrice ^{F} per alimenti ^{M}

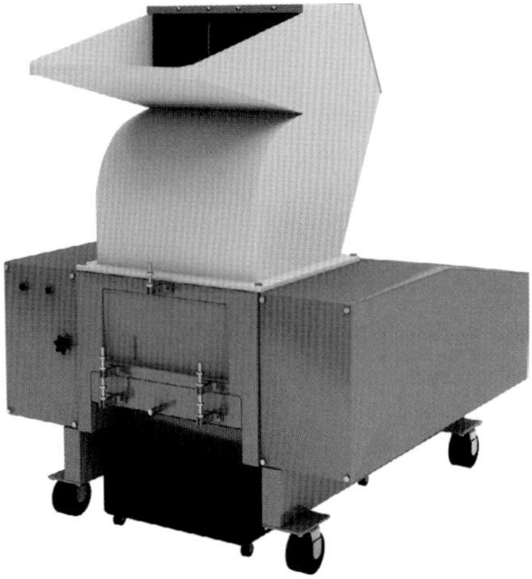

food mill
moulin ^{F}
triturador ^{M} de alimentos ^{M}
Passiermaschine ^{F}
tritatutto ^{M}

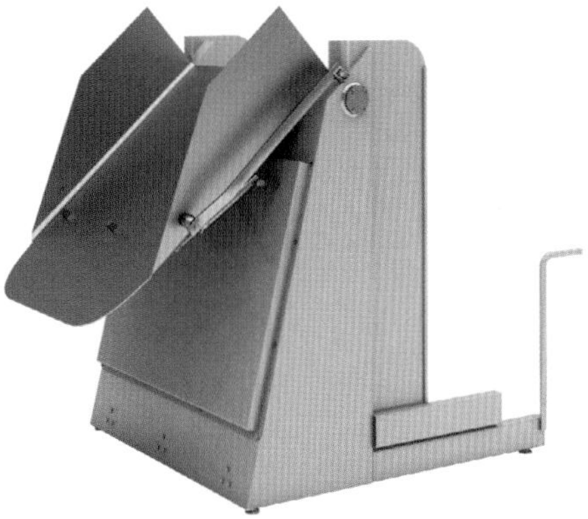

conveyor system feeder
convoyeur ^{M} d'alimentation ^{F}
alimentador ^{M} de banda ^{F} de transporte ^{M}
Futterspender-Fördersystem ^{N}
alimentatore ^{M} del sistema ^{M} trasportatore

face shield
écran [M] facial
protector de cara [M]
Gesichtsschutz [M]
visiera [F]

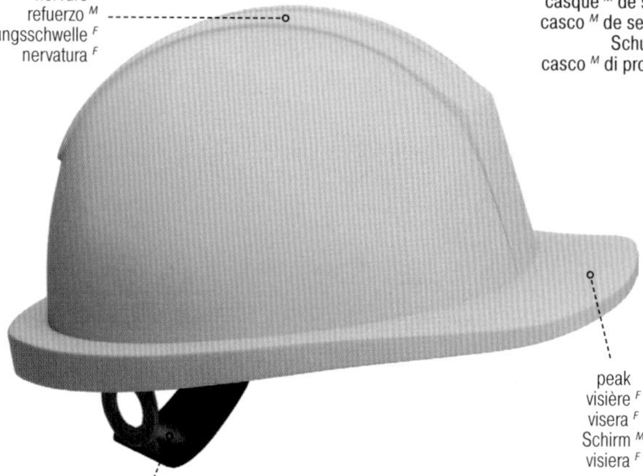
rib
nervure [F]
refuerzo [M]
Verstärkungsschwelle [F]
nervatura [F]
peak
visière [F]
visera [F]
Schirm [M]
visiera [F]
suspension
suspension [F]
cinta [F] para la cabeza [F]
Kopfband [N]
elastici [M] stringitesta

hard hat
casque [M] de sécurité [F]
casco [M] de seguridad [F]
Schutzhelm [M]
casco [M] di protezione [F]

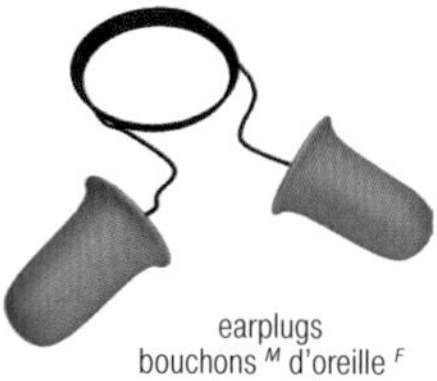

earplugs
bouchons [M] d'oreille [F]
tapones [M]
Ohrstöpsel [M]
tappi [M] per le orecchie [F]

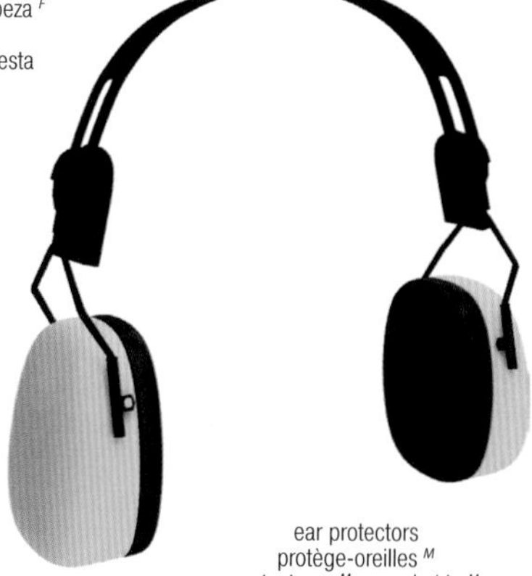

ear protectors
protège-oreilles [M]
protectores [M] para el oído [M]
Ohrenschützer [M]
paraorecchie [M]

safety boots
bottes [F] de sécurité [F] botas [F] de seguridad [F]
Sicherheitsschuh [M]
scarponcini [M] di sicurezza [F]

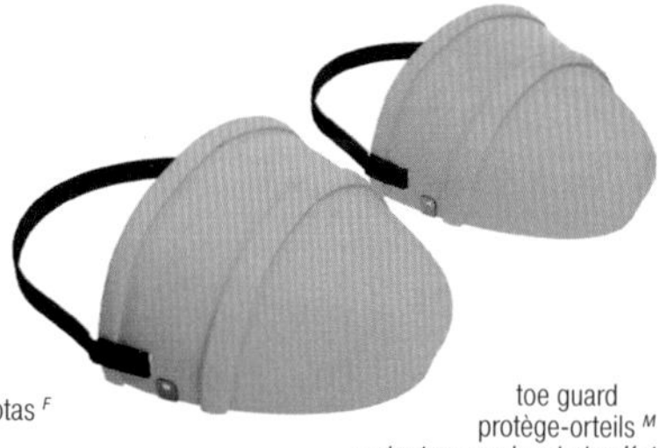

toe guard
protège-orteils [M]
protector para los dedos [M] de los pies [M]
Zehenschützer [M]
puntale [M] di protezione [F]

safety goggles
lunettes [F] de sécurité [F]
gafas [F] de protección [F]
Arbeitsschutzbrille [F]
occhiali [M] di protezione [F] panoramici

dust mask
masque [M] antipoussières [F]
máscara [F] para el polvo [M]
Atemschutzmaske [F]
mascherina [F] antipolvere

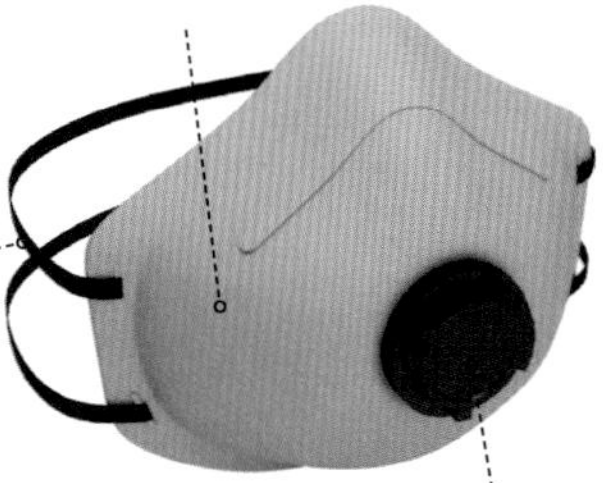

cup
coupelle [F] d'étanchéité [F]
mascarilla [F]
Maskenmembran [N]
calotta [F] filtrante

headband
serre-tête [M]
cinta [F] para la cabeza [F]
Kopfband [N]
elastici [M] stringitesta

exhalation valve
soupape [F] d'expiration [F]
válvula [F] de exhalación [F]
Ausatmungsventil [N]
valvola [F] di espirazione [F]

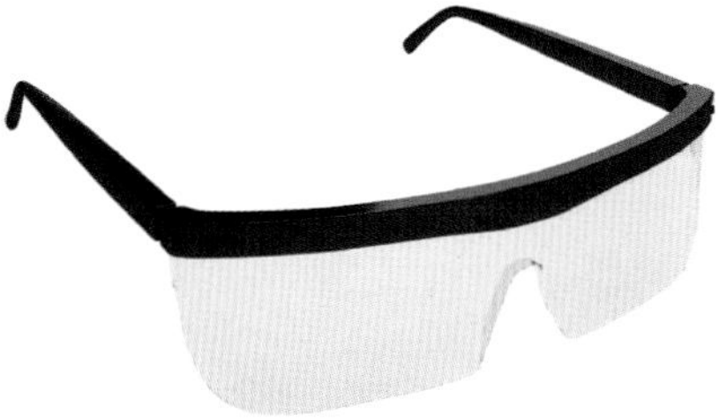

safety glasses
lunettes [F] de sécurité [F]
gafas [F] de seguridad [F]
Schutzbrille [F]
occhiali [M] di sicurezza [F]

half-mask respirator
demi-masque [M] respiratoire
máscara [F] antigás de medio rostro [M]
Atemschutz-Halbmaske [F]
mezza maschera [F] respiratoria

full-face respirator
masque [M] respiratoire complet
máscara [F] antigás de rostro [M] entero
Gasmaske [F]
respiratore [M] integrale

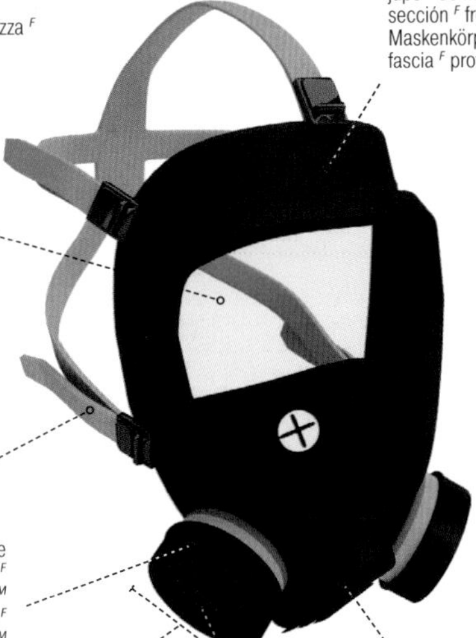

facepiece
jupe [F] de masque [M]
sección [F] frontal
Maskenkörper [M]
fascia [F] protettiva della fronte [F]

visor
oculaire [M]
careta [M]
Sichtscheibe [F]
visore [M]

head harness
serre-tête [M]
correas [F] para la cabeza [F]
Kopfriemen [M]
bordo [M] per la testa [F]

cartridge
cartouche [F]
cartucho [M]
Kartusche [F]
filtro [M]

inhalation valve
soupape [F] d'inspiration [F]
válvula [F] de inhalación [F]
Einatmungsventil [N]
valvola [F] di inspirazione [F]

filter cover
couvre-filtre [M]
tapa [F] del filtro [M]
Filterabdeckung [F]
coprifiltro [M]

exhalation valve
soupape [F] d'expiration [F]
válvula [F] de exhalación [F]
Ausatmungsventil [N]
valvola [F] di espirazione [F]

ENGLISH INDEX

See the detailed table of contents on pages 4–7 and the instructions on pages 8–9 for further assistance in using this dictionary.

A

B

C

D

T

INDEX FRANÇAIS

Veuillez consulter la table des matières détaillée sur les pages 4–7 et les instructions sur les pages 8–9 pour de plus amples informations concernant comment utiliser ce dictionnaire.

A

B

C

D

E

F

Q

R

S

T

U

V

W

X

Y

Z

ÍNDICE ESPAÑOL

Para mayor información sobre cómo usar este diccionario, lea el índice detallado en las páginas 4 a 7, y las instrucciones en las páginas 8 a 9.

A

B

C

P

W

X

Y

Z

DEUTSCHES REGISTER

A

B

F

G

H

I

J

K

L

M

N

O

P

T

U

V

W

X

Y

Z

INDICE DEI NOMI ITALIANI

C

D

E

F

G

H

I

J

K

N

Q

R

S

T

U

V

W

X

Y

Z